AMERICAN WRITERS

AMERICAN WRITERS

A Collection of Literary Biographies

LEONARD UNGER

Editor in Chief

VOLUME III

Archibald MacLeish

to

George Santayana

Charles Scribner's Sons, New York

ISBN 0-684-13673-2 (Vol. I)
ISBN 0-684-13674-0 (Vol. II)
ISBN 0-684-13675-9 (Vol. III)
ISBN 0-684-13676-7 (Vol. IV)

ISBN 0-684-15797-7 (Supp. I)
ISBN 0-684-16482-5 (Supp. II)
ISBN 0-684-17322-0 (Set)

Acknowledgment is gratefully made to those publishers and individuals who have permitted the use of the following materials in copyright.

Introduction
from "Mr. Apollinax," *Collected Poems 1909-1962*, by T. S. Eliot, by permission of Harcourt Brace Jovanovich, Inc. and Faber and Faber Ltd.
from "Sweeney Agonistes," *Collected Poems 1909-1962*, by T. S. Eliot; copyright 1936 Harcourt Brace Jovanovich, Inc.; copyright © 1963, 1964 T. S. Eliot, by permission of Harcourt Brace Jovanovich, Inc. and Faber and Faber Ltd.

"Henry Adams"
from Henry Adams, "Prayer to the Virgin of Chartres," *Letters to a Niece and Prayer to the Virgin of Chartres*, by permission of Houghton Mifflin Company

"James Agee"
from "Draft Lyrics for Candide," *The Collected Poems of James Agee*, ed. Robert Fitzgerald, by permission of Houghton Mifflin Company and Calder and Boyars Ltd.
Part of this essay first appeared, in a different form, in the *Carleton Miscellany* and is used by permission.

"Conrad Aiken"
from *Collected Poems*, copyright 1953 and *Selected Poems*, copyright © 1961, by permission of Oxford University Press

"John Barth"
from John Barth's unpublished lecture "Mystery and

Tragedy: The Two Motions of Ritual Heroism," by permission of Mr. Barth

"John Berryman"
from *Short Poems: The Dispossessed*, copyright 1948 John Berryman; *His Thoughts Made Pockets & the Plane Buckt*, copyright © 1958 John Berryman; *Formal Elegy*, copyright © 1964 John Berryman; *Berryman's Sonnets*, copyright 1952, © 1967 John Berryman; *Homage to Mistress Bradstreet*, copyright © 1956 John Berryman; *His Toy, His Dream, His Rest*, copyright © 1964, 1965, 1966, 1967, 1968 John Berryman, by permission of Farrar, Straus & Giroux and Faber and Faber Ltd.
from "The Lovers" and "The Imaginary Jew," first published in *The Kenyon Review*, by permission of Mrs. Berryman

"Randolph Bourne"
from letters and manuscripts of Randolph Bourne, by permission of Columbia University Libraries

"Van Wyck Brooks"
material drawn from William Wasserstrom, *The Legacy of Van Wyck Brooks*, copyright © 1971, by permission of Southern Illinois University Press

"James Fenimore Cooper"
material drawn from Robert E. Spiller, Introduction to *Cooper: Representative Selections*, copyright 1936, by permission of the American Book Company

"James Gould Cozzens"
from James Gould Cozzens, *Men and Brethren, Ask Me Tomorrow, The Just and the Unjust, Guard of*

AMERICAN WRITERS

Archibald MacLeish

1892-1982

*A*s a poet and man of letters, Archibald MacLeish has illuminated the most serious problems which the twentieth-century literary artist must face, and at the same time has shown how they may be solved. This is not to say that in his work MacLeish himself has completely solved them; but his achievement has been so generally adequate that his poetry seems likely to survive the present antipoetic age and become an inspiration to happier times. The problems are, of course, derived from that famous romantic alienation from the environment almost two centuries ago, a disorder now apparently aggravated out of all cure in an era of mass culture. They consist, on the one hand, in the poet's ethical need to maintain the traditional concern with craftsmanship and, on the other hand, in his equally great desire to communicate with the public— a desire which also is a need. Few successful poets of the present day manage without compromising the one or the other of these endeavors. To sacrifice craftsmanship is to submit to the tyranny of common values, produced by the demotic passion for *equality;* to sacrifice communication, though imaginably in the cause of *quality*, invites, and often with full justice, the charge of snobbishness. In the case of MacLeish, the love of craftsmanship is not snobbish and the sympathy for the contem-porary world is genuine. His poetry has avoided the animosity toward ordinary conditions of modern life which is shown, for example, in some of T. S. Eliot's work. At the same time it—or the best of it—is a poetry of ideas as well as emotions.

MacLeish was born in Glencoe, Illinois, on May 7, 1892. A good private secondary school, Hotchkiss, prepared him for Yale. At the university he was in most ways a thoroughly typical young man of his station (well-to-do middle class) and generation: he has spoken of how much more important it was, to him at Yale, that he played football than that he was enrolled in such and such academic courses. Yet he was elected to Phi Beta Kappa without, presumably, any enormous efforts as a student —a fact suggesting the appropriate commentary. Being graduated in 1915, and already planning to be married, he went to Harvard for the study of law. His marriage, to Ada Hitchcock, took place the following year. In 1917 he enlisted and served with the American army in France, where he attained the rank of captain. His brother Kenneth was killed in the war. MacLeish returned to Harvard and took the law degree in 1919; he stayed there as a teacher of government for a year, but from 1920 to 1923 practiced law in Boston.

He was already a published poet (and at

Yale winner of a prize for poetry), and he continued to write, though without a strong sense of accomplishment. It was nevertheless for the sake of his poetry that he gave up his law office and took his wife and young children to Paris. He hoped, by devoting himself solely to poetry, to be able eventually to make it his vocation and means of support. He lived abroad for nearly six years and there matured as a poet. Those years have been called his expatriate period. Ernest Hemingway, John Dos Passos, F. Scott Fitzgerald, and the already long-uprooted Ezra Pound were among the wandering Americans whom MacLeish knew in Paris. Hemingway, who stayed with the MacLeishes for an extended time, remained one of his closest friends for the next decade. Pound, clearly, was on principle an expatriate; but as applied to himself and the others this term is distasteful to MacLeish, who is certainly correct about it: "expatriate" had better be reserved as a name for those who exiled themselves irrevocably.

MacLeish never had any intention of remaining in Paris for the rest of his life. In 1928 he came back to the United States, a recognized poet at last. Here he was to make his permanent home, although he traveled from time to time, for example to Mexico, where he gathered material for a poem about the expedition of Cortez (*Conquistador*). In the early years of the New Deal he diverted his energies into lucrative journalism, and for the magazine *Fortune* he wrote carefully researched articles on current social problems (see the bibliography following). He composed a stage play in verse, *Panic*, and a series of verse plays for radio—these latter a notable contribution to a new genre already beginning to thrive in Britain but undeveloped in the United States.

Not only his journalistic but also his poetic and especially his dramatic writings in the 1930's manifested the extroverted temperament which equipped MacLeish for the role of "communicator," or public spokesman. This was no new attribute: his poems of the 1920's and earlier could only have come from a man of this type, but in technique they resembled works of introspective writers, symbolists and impressionists, who were very different from MacLeish. In the 1940's he proved perhaps all too well extroverted, in the sense that his public duties left him less time for poetry. As curator of the Nieman journalism collection at Harvard (1938) and as a sympathizer with the Roosevelt administration he became a "target" for presidential appointment to the post of librarian of Congress, in which capacity he served from 1939 to 1944. In 1941–42 he was also director of the Office of Facts and Figures, a wartime information agency of the government; in 1942–43 he worked as assistant director of the Office of War Information, a full-scale propaganda bureau. In 1944–45 he was assistant secretary of state. In 1945 and 1946 he led official American participation in establishing UNESCO and starting its programs. It is clear that MacLeish was not only highly extroverted but also patriotic—something not at all surprising. In World War I he had served with honor. Never truly expatriated, because neither an alienated intellectual nor an aesthete nor a communist, he had lived abroad as a poet in the 1920's when France was less expensive than America and Paris was the capital of the arts. In the 1930's he joined with millions in America who acclaimed Franklin D. Roosevelt first for economic reforms and then for the courage to arm against Hitler. And in the decade that followed, he stood among those who believed that the best hope for future peace lay in international cooperation through the United Nations. If MacLeish can be said to have had a mission as distinguished from a vocation, it has been to integrate the role of poet with that of public man.

Substantially MacLeish's poetic output of the 1940's was limited to the collection *Actfive and Other Poems*. Apart from radio plays, the bulk of his publications in the decade was made up of prose pieces. The best of these, articles dating from the years after Hitler came to power in Germany, appeared in the 1941 volume *A Time to Speak*. In a companion volume of 1943, *A Time to Act*, was published a selection of wartime addresses. The latter are comparatively high-keyed and have now far less interest than the articles, which argued MacLeish's political convictions as these were sharpened in the context of current history. His beliefs, like many other people's in America during those years, underwent two phases: the one of response to the economic ideologies debated generally in the 1930's, the other of response to the Italians' and Germans' strategies of conquest. Since MacLeish has consistently opposed Marxism, and even though he was then a New Dealer with affinities for the native revolutionary tradition as celebrated, for example, by Carl Sandburg, his response in the first phase took a civil-libertarian rather than a socialistic character. It thus was, as in retrospect it appears, irrelevant in fact to the main social issues of the period, when an altered balance of economic power was being brought about between capital and government. His response in the second phase, beginning about the time of the Spanish Civil War, was antifascist and, because libertarian, anti-Marxist still; in 1937 he could use the phrase "common front" in referring to enemies of the fascists, but he rejected the popular-front frenzy and stood ready with a half-Jeffersonian, half-populist definition of American national principles as the United States prepared for war (*The American Cause*, 1941). This time his response was clearly in the spirit of the moment. His wartime and post-war-reconstruction papers, the later ones geared to "peaceful coexistence" as against the cold war, may be found in *Freedom Is the Right to Choose* (1951). He was skeptical of the Truman Doctrine but favored the Marshall Plan.

Withdrawn from government posts, MacLeish enjoyed a long academic career at Harvard as the Boylston professor of rhetoric and oratory from 1949 to 1962, and after a short interval served for four years (1963–67) as Simpson lecturer at Amherst College. His almost twenty years of teaching turned out to be one of the richest periods for his art, especially as a playwright. He has published four more verse plays, one of which, *J.B.*, gained the Pulitzer Prize for drama in 1959 (MacLeish had already won two Pulitzer prizes for poetry —one in 1933 for *Conquistador* and one in 1953 for *Collected Poems 1917–1952*); several volumes of literary criticism and incidental social commentary; and two additional volumes of poems, *Songs for Eve* and *The Wild Old Wicked Man, and Other Poems*.

When MacLeish assembled his *Collected Poems 1917–1952*, he conformed to usual practice in suppressing most of the early work; but as one examines the early poems they are seen to relate, in various and sometimes contradictory ways, to his mature verse. The first volumes, *Songs for a Summer's Day* (1915) and *Tower of Ivory* (1917), display a lively interest in verse forms as such. The former contains sonnets only; but the latter includes, as well, a number of stanzaic exercises and one precocious dramatic piece, "Our Lady of Troy" (which, despite a Swinburnean promise in its title, is akin rhetorically to Jonson's humor plays). The sonnets in *Tower of Ivory* show the inevitable debt to Shakespeare; some of them, the best indeed, could only have derived from the "soldier" sonnets of Rupert Brooke. What is more significant, they imply a taste and probably a need for strict formal boundaries within which to manipulate tone, music, imagery, and argument. A few Keatsian couplets (in "A Library of Law"), examples of ballad measure (notably in "A Sampler"), some regular quatrains (as in "Escape"), a ballade (so entitled), paired sonnets ("Certain Poets"), a Petrarchan sonnet but with two octaves ("Baccalaureate"), and miscellaneous lyrical stanzas fill out this group. The themes are amatory and visionary, mainly in the Aesthetic tradition: there is some superficial paganism, sometimes yoked with Christian symbols, and a great deal of hedonism and a rather Yeatsian preoccupation with an enchanted realm of dream. Antiscientific or at least antipragmatic sentiments, characteristically late-Victorian, come out in the dream poems "Jason" and "Realities." A time-worn motif of mutability, devouring Time, and Death the inexorable recurs abundantly. Yet, even with their intellectual representations, most of these poems seem to achieve more through music than through argument. Often the sound is more *interesting* than the sense. Imagery appears not to be handled deliberately or for the sake of symbolic possibilities, but to be mainly decorative. (At the same time a few emblematic images strike the attention, as in MacLeish's sonnet "The Altar," which uses a metaphysical conceit. Here certain carved garlands, intended as symbols of beauty in general, are discovered to have accidentally shaped the letters spelling a particular woman's name. Various baroque analogues may have influenced the poem.)

In his *Dialogues* with Mark Van Doren (1962; published 1964), MacLeish remarked that when he began writing verse he "took off from Swinburne." That, certainly, was Swinburne as musician only: Swinburne the sensualist was no model in any of MacLeish's early poetry. The decorous "Realities" is as Swinburnean as you please; in fact, it is quite

good, though of low intensity—Swinburne sober. After a few years' fascination with such music, MacLeish reacted against it. It seems that his reaction was a vehement one: his later poetry has, if anything, avoided musicality and has often been downright unmusical. At any rate sense and argument reasserted themselves strongly; an intricate, even devious, rhetoric began to dominate. For a time the sonnet retained his favor, as in the title piece of the volume *The Happy Marriage, and Other Poems* (1924). That long poem (a sort of non-tragical *Modern Love*) is made up partly of sonnets and partly of other regular forms, and the verbal effects produced with these are very skillful. Two sections of "The Happy Marriage" in rhyming couplets (beginning respectively "The humid air precipitates" and "Beside her in the dark the chime") have survived into *Collected Poems*, where they may remind the reader that MacLeish's next important model, after Swinburne, was Eliot. The first of these lyrics was indebted to Eliot in his "Sweeney" period, the second to his "Portrait of a Lady." Both employ symbolistic imagery in a quasi-dramatic context of emotional confrontation—as Eliot's poems had done.

Between 1917 and 1924 MacLeish's style acquired the features of its maturity—conscious symbolism; witty, almost metaphysical strategies of argument; compressed and intense implications—all of these owing much, though quite certainly not everything, to Eliot's example. MacLeish was usually able to resist the Eliot rhythms. His cadences were to have great diversity and to echo many predecessors. His voice, moreover, did not have much in common with the self-conscious orotundity of Eliot's middle period (it had something in common with the Prufrockian tones), and he seldom undertook vocal productions such as dramatic monologues. Indeed, a lasting mark of MacLeish's work has been the weakness of the persona. At times the diction is remote from speech; at other times it may be close to speech but bare of individuality, diffuse, as though spoken by a chorus. For this reason, despite his partial debt to Eliot, MacLeish belongs not only outside of the Browning-Tennyson traditions of monologue but also outside of the American schools which have stemmed from those, the diverse movements represented by E. A. Robinson and Vachel Lindsay, by Frost and the early Pound. Like stream-of-consciousness fiction, which owes a great deal to it, the dramatic monologue indulges introspection in the safety of a disguise. (Perhaps in fiction, as in the poetry of Yeats, freedom rather than safety is in request—the *complexification* rather than the *disengagement* of the writer.) MacLeish's poetry, for the most part, is not introspective, and this is why indeed no persona is wanted. According to its own purposes, its diminution of the persona is a strength: by this means it turns the reader away from the endless labyrinths of subjective illusion and irony, the "echoing vault" of the poetic self, and invites him to contemplate the phenomenal world. It does not vocalize that self: it can and often does fabricate a kind of disembodied speech, or speech whose origin need not be known. It aspires to be, and sometimes becomes, a poetry of spectacle—not always, but especially when, as in the near masterpiece "Einstein" (1926), it is wholly under the control of an intellectual concept. Then the images arrange themselves as objective counterparts of the progress of an idea—Eliot's "objective correlative" intellectualized.

MacLeish in the 1920's increasingly took pains with the formal structure of his poetry. Only through form could the swelling rhetoric be channeled. After the 1924 volume, the sonnet was neglected for a while, but it was not discarded even in *Streets in the Moon* (1926), where free verse of a highly regulated type alternates with blank verse and stanzaic patterns. Blank verse, with a few rhyming lyric passages, was used also for his symbolistic poem *The Pot of Earth* (1925) and his closet drama *Nobodaddy* (1926).

The theme and scope of *Nobodaddy*, referred to by MacLeish as a "poem," are indicated in his preface, which adds that the "emotional experiences" treated there are "not unlike" those dealt with in *The Pot of Earth*, written after it but published before. *Nobodaddy* takes its title from Blake's derisory name for the scriptural God of prohibitions. It adapts the Adam-and-Eve, Cain-and-Abel story to dramatize what MacLeish calls "the condition of self-consciousness in an indifferent universe"; it is a poetic essay, of course, not Biblical commentary. In it, Adam has emerged into humanity, into consciousness of himself as a being distinct from the rest of creation. In this condition he has two choices, a fact which disquiets him and in itself presumably inclines him to the choice he makes. He can either stand in awe of nature ("the Gardener"), accepting the inferiority implicit in obedience to a system he does not understand, or else assert his will to become a god—that is, a rational being superior to nature. Urged by the Voice of his will (metaphorically the Serpent) and by Eve, who does not fear what she has never experienced, natural harshness, Adam eats the forbidden fruit and thus alienates himself by act as well as by will. The consequence is misery: his daring to break the bond of obedience brings down upon his head a flood of superstitious terrors. The Gardener, far from changing into an Avenger, seems to have vanished; but, frantic with guilt, Adam flees the garden, and he and Eve seek the desert. It remains for their sons, Abel and Cain, to complete the drama by, in effect, modernizing the situation. Abel, representative of Adam fallen and burdened with guilt, attempts a mystical reconciliation with the supposed Avenger. Longing to return to the garden, to ignorance and servitude, he invents a relationship with an invented god: religion is born. By blood sacrifice he strives to atone. His brother, Cain, realist and rationalist, and similar to Adam as he was when he heard the Voice of his humanity exhorting him to free himself, asserts human values and the will to power. Abel grovels before the voice of thunder and tries to pull Cain down to his knees in humility. Cain, already godlike in mind, kills him.

It is not clear why Adam is so constituted that he cannot profit from his fall, but because he cannot his son Abel cannot either. It is left for Cain to vindicate reason against superstition; that he has to do so by murder is ironic, to say the least. At any rate none of the four characters comprehends the meaning of these actions. It is for the reader to understand in terms, primarily, of acceptance and rejection. So long as man believed himself to be simply part of nature, he lived in a paradise. Death was there already, the biological cycle had begun, but man had not yet taken it personally—it was still objective. When man became self-conscious, his acceptance of nature changed into resistance, and with its normal machinery of death it seemed a threat to him. Not only was he utterly different from nature, but it was also indifferent to him—though physically he remained within it. He had imagination; nature was all process. The "Gardener" of *Nobodaddy* is merely the principle of life viewed as sympathetic harmony. When this view disappears, and reason replaces it with the stark vision of process, the Gardener gives way to the enemy, the unsympathetic. Physical nature converted into the antagonist of man's will is a desert, a region which will not behave as man desires. The harmony of prelapsarian Eden was that of

man's acquiescent ignorance; the disharmony of the natural world, to fallen man, is that of its uncontrollability. His selfhood defies nature and battles with it but at the last must sink defeated. Abel's attempt to return symbolically to the unfallen state takes the form of a conscious imitation of nature's unconscious cruelty; he grafts human motives upon the indifferent. Abel's sacrifice of a ram is wrong because consciousness cannot atone with unconsciousness. Nature's own profuse bloodletting sets no store by covenants and bargaining; apart from man's imagination such "deals" are meaningless. If human ideals estrange man from nature, and if, nevertheless, with the justice of indifference, nature punishes every act not in harmony with its laws, then man is automatically unhappy.

The idea that human feelings meet nothing like themselves, no sympathetic responses, in nature, and that nature governs the life of the body as if the desires of the mind did not occur, is present in *The Pot of Earth*. But the theme of this poem is the bitterness and pity of those desires so subjected to the Gardener's indifference. Here is the case of the toad beneath the harrow. The poem was published three years after *The Waste Land* of Eliot. The two works are of roughly the same length. They have much similarity, in technique and symbolism alike. In certain notable ways they are dissimilar. *The Waste Land* is a first-person monologue to which are subordinated various genre adaptations. *The Pot of Earth* is mainly a third-person narrative, though with some first-person stream-of-consciousness effects. Stylistically *The Waste Land* is by far the more experimental and radical. Both poems, however, draw upon Sir James Frazer's work *The Golden Bough* for vegetation symbolism which, mythologically and ceremonially, represents the death and resurrection of a fertility god (e.g.,

Adonis) as a type of the seasonal decay and revival of nature. Both also, in applying this symbolism within a modern context of life, emphasize not the victory of life over death, but the reverse of this. On the other hand, they again differ most significantly in what they apply such symbolism to. *The Waste Land,* exploring a gnostic and "spiritualized" sense of death and rebirth, uses a special myth (the Grail legend) concerning an *arrest* of fertility, whose equivalent in the poem is the male protagonist's state of emotional aridity and despair. *The Pot of Earth* applies the vegetation symbolism to its female protagonist's organic functions: the biological cycle takes place in her, as if in a plant springing up, flowering, being fertilized, bearing fruit, and dying. Or, more exactly, the girl or woman herself can be regarded as such a "pot of earth," or Garden of Adonis described by Frazer in the passage which MacLeish prefixed to his poem as a general epigraph. For, like those shallow-rooted plants forced into brief and hectic life under the Syrian sun, only to wither and to be thrown into the sea as symbols of the god bewailed by his sectaries, she leads a transient existence, devoid of any lasting meaning except the biological one. The resurrection of the fertility god means new life for nature, not for the individual. At the conclusion of *The Pot of Earth,* the woman has borne a child and has died; a chestnut tree is in flower; but she rots in the earth. Here the Adonis myth becomes the vehicle for a realization of the inextricability of life and death. MacLeish's second epigraph to the poem (later transferred to Part I) is the "god kissing carrion" passage from *Hamlet;* and Part III is called "The Carrion Spring." In *Hamlet* "carrion" is the prince's coarse designation for Ophelia: evidently the woman in *The Pot of Earth* has a sacrificial role like that to which the Ophelia personage

is doomed in *The Waste Land.* But she has been sacrificed by the indifference of nature, not the brutality of man.

The 1925 text of *The Pot of Earth,* several pages longer than the text printed in *Poems, 1924–1933* (1933) and thereafter, adopts the *Waste Land* technique of making the past and present interpenetrate, so that the modern woman's life cycle is depicted in timeless fusion with that of a primitive world: its incidents are abruptly juxtaposed to details from the Adonis ritual. But the three principal passages in which this effect is created have been omitted from the later printings, leaving the poem free of the startling "intertemporal" counterpoint typical of Eliot, and with a contemporary texture purely. Yet, beneath this, continual allusions to the Adonis ritual remain to suggest a theme of unending recurrence. Perhaps recapitulation, rather than recurrence, is the universalizing motif in *The Pot of Earth* (as, for example, it is in Joyce's *Finnegans Wake*): this woman is eternal woman, and eternal woman typifies reproductive nature, whose dream is her life. She, like the Garden of Adonis in antiquity, blossoms as an emblem, a signature, of some omnipresent and all-involving archetype of cyclical life and death. Her anonymity is as profound as that of Tiresias, the *Waste Land* persona; but whereas he is obscured by Eliot's pretentious legerdemain with literary cross references, she has a constant, though shadowy, identity.

There seems to be a philosophical difference between *The Pot of Earth* and *The Waste Land* in the ways they pose their protagonists against the world. Eliot's poem is very much in a "psychological" tradition; that is, starting from an Idealist's assumption that the individual point of view is of paramount importance because it uniquely focuses knowledge of externals, *The Waste Land* attains form by offering a view from a single point, or through a single narrow peephole. It recalls Bergsonian and stream-of-consciousness fiction. MacLeish's poem seems to start from a Realist's assumption that there is nothing special in point of view as such; that the law of things is common to all. It depicts a *typical* relation of the natural to the human, indeed choosing to examine the fate of someone quite average. Whatever the resemblance of MacLeish's techniques to those of subjectivists and symbolists, his *fond* was otherwise. His poem, like Eliot's, uses Aesthetic and symbolist procedures to assist naturalistic statement, but his is closer to a philosophical naturalism which assumes the total subjection of man to time and chance.

There was much of the eighteenth-century rationalist in the MacLeish of the 1920's and in his political character later; much, also, of the scientific observer of life. He had made an almost complete break with his antiscientific and aesthetical beginnings as a poet. He now accepted the scientists' description of reality—only boggling at its falsification of experience. The external world he confronted was the one described by the astronomers, by the biologists, and above all by the mathematical physicists of his own day. Whereas Eliot and Pound and Yeats were ancients, MacLeish was a modern. One may believe that Einstein's space-time-energy continuum receives, in the work of MacLeish, its most important poetic treatment to date—a treatment not through casual allusion for contemporary color, but through exact intellectual integration with the subject matter of felt life. A thematic carry-over takes place from *The Pot of Earth* to later poems—the conflict between personal hopes and natural law, developed first, perhaps a little less pessimistically, in *Nobodaddy*.

The volume *Streets in the Moon* scrutinizes the state of man the conscious animal in the disheartening universe of curved space and ir-

reversible entropy. In his "Prologue" to this collection, MacLeish salutes a hypothetical "crew of Columbus" who are westward bound but, as in nightmare, toward a "surf that breaks upon Nothing"; and he comments, concerning this apparent fate of the whole human race,

> Oh, I have the sense of infinity—
> But the world, sailors, is round.
> They say there is no end to it.

The paradox of infinite aspirations confined in a world closed and therefore without "end" to aspire beyond is a leading theme of *Streets in the Moon*. The title of the book suggests the double vision: "streets" a symbol of the here and now of consciousness, the "moon" a symbol (defined partly by the counter-romantic use to which Jules Laforgue put it in his poetry) of a myth degraded by science. The volume concludes with the wry humor of "The End of the World," in which a temporal "end" to the circus of life reveals the nothingness above man's head. The poems in between, several of them conspicuously indebted to Laforgue ("Nocturne," "Selene Afterwards," "Hearts' and Flowers' "), to Eliot, or to Pound, and one of them most notably ("Einstein") written in a symbolic manner recalling Mallarmé's "L'Après-midi d'un faune" (but in a rather Miltonic strain!), deal variously with the mystery of existence, with the problem of time (symbolized by the sun, among other things), with death, with love and other relations, and with human character. A few are imagistic; others are elegiac, anecdotal, or narrative and Browningesque. One of the finest poems in this fine collection is the three-part "Signature for Tempo," a meditation on the relativity of time and movement:

Think that this world against the wind of time
Perpetually falls the way a hawk
Falls at the wind's edge but is motionless;

on fourth-dimensional extension:

How shall we bury all
These time-shaped people,
In graves that have no more
Than three dimensions?

(though why not, one could retort, since in fact the graves have the same number of dimensions as the people); and on death as the point in time where all are united:

Whom time goes over wave by wave, do I lie
Drowned in a crumble of surf at the sea's
    edge?—

And wonder now what ancient bones are these
That flake on sifting flake
Out of deep time have shelved this narrow
    ledge
Where the waves break.

"The Too-Late Born," rhetorically very brilliant, is most meaningful in the context of the time poems (its later title, "The Silent Slain," constricts its meaning); it, too, is about the community of the dead. The death of Roland at Roncesvalles has been made archetypal: the "silent slain" could belong to any army, and the fact that "we" survive them is an accident of time—an ironic one, for in due time we shall join them in the universal graveyard of the earth. Themes of mortality are further explored in "No Lamp Has Ever Shown Us Where to Look," "Interrogate the Stones," and "Le Secret humain," in terms of speculations on the "answer" that death is supposed to have in reserve for man, an answer that may simply annihilate the questioner. "Raree Show" asks whether the question is within the mind, but ends with a new question, "Where?" "L'An trentiesme de mon Eage" (its title taken from a line by François Villon which was a favorite of Pound's, and which was used by Eliot in an epigraph and by Pound in "Hugh Selwyn Mauberley") is somewhat in the mood of Eliot's "Gerontion." Through a multiplicity of memories its speaker has arrived at his present place; he then asks, "And by what way shall I go back?" One could answer that there is no need of going back, for "place" is temporal as well as spatial, and what belongs to time contains its past. The poem, having reviewed the past, has already returned to it, through art. But this reply would be satisfactory only to a Bergsonian. In any realistic analysis the question is unanswerable, though MacLeish was to continue asking it in later poems.

One of the most often cited anthology pieces from *Streets in the Moon* is the paradoxical and enigmatic "Ars Poetica." In spite of its Horatian title, which seems to imply simply a verse essay in legislative criticism, a poem about the art of poetry, its true workings are otherwise. It does not frame an address to poets generally, much less to their critics; it is no essay in criticism. Nor yet does it introspectively comment, like Eliot's poem "La Figlia che Piange," on the poet's relation to his own creative process. Perhaps some readers, remembering chiefly the distichs "A poem should be equal to: / Not true" and "A poem should not mean / But be," have interpreted what "Ars Poetica" *says* (that a poem should be like an object beheld in stasis, not like a message or a paradigm) as what it is *for*. If so, they have taken it for a critical essay and have violated its supposed counsel. The central paradox of "Ars Poetica" is that it makes sense only when the reader accepts its sense as a function of form. It then survives as the aesthetic object it approves— with the proviso that the approval must be held as an utterance *in vacuo*, a silence.

A poem should be palpable and mute
As a globed fruit,

. . . .

A poem should be wordless
As the flight of birds.

The real subject of "Ars Poetica" is itself, by a sort of narcissism of the written word as "pure poetry"; this poem exhibits aestheticism circling round, as it were, and returning like the equator upon the round earth. The result contrives a stasis indeed, free or nearly free of time's rotation. The moon of the second part, MacLeish's recurrent symbol of the imaginative world ideally transcending the naturalist's inner and outer landscapes, drifts as poetic subjectivity defying its antithesis, the solar clock. "Ars Poetica," somewhat Yeatsian like various other short poems in the volume, looks also Keatsian: the whole poem speaks with a voice which, like that of the Grecian urn when it equates beauty and truth, belongs to a realm of ideality and is relevant only to that. Such a realm, proper to poetry, conflicts with nature; MacLeish's long poem "Einstein" reviews the naturalistic conception that man, at last, cannot quite escape the prison of his time-bound flesh. That, too, is a Keatsian thought.

"Einstein" in theme recalls *Nobodaddy;* the resemblance proves useful in the unraveling of its complexities. Not only is the subject difficult (like most subjects) unless one already understands it, but also the rhetoric lumbers in obscurity. Nevertheless the poem operates compellingly upon the emotions, and it ought to be one of the best-known philosophical poems of the period. The Einstein of the title is modern intellectual man, scientist, represented microcosmically as a sort of Leopold Bloom, atomic and entire (*ein Stein,* perhaps—a stone, or at least a pebble!), who has inherited the problem and the mission of MacLeish's Cain, the mission of rationality. The Einsteinian universe is rationality triumphant, as indeed it is the triumph of the modern spirit. The poem (a narrative showing the process of "going back,"

by reason, to a condition which seems to repeal Adam's alienation from nature and to reunite his posterity with the primal creator—i.e., in effect deifying man) reveals the way back by recapitulating the way forward, from any infancy to full consciousness. First there is Einstein, man secure in his body-sense and self-contained. Then, his awareness of sense impressions. Then, his mental abstraction of these into a coherent world—

A world in reason which is in himself
And has his own dimensions.

Then, his discovery of his ignorance and impotence in the world's vastness and mystery. Then, his attempt to gain mystical identification with this mystery by sensory and aesthetic contemplation, and most through music,

When he a moment occupies
The hollow of himself and like an air
Pervades all other.

Then (in a passage to which Eliot, who seems to owe several points to this poem, suggests a reply in the closing lines of "Burnt Norton"), his realization that there is no longer a "word" which can translate beauty into thought and thus into himself (the word described as known to the Virgin of Chartres but as now become "three round letters" in a carving was presumably the "AVE" which hailed, in effect, the Incarnation). Then, upon his rejection of mysterious access and Abel's quest, his intellectual formulation of Albert Einstein's theories. And finally, the godlike subduing of nature to himself, so that the physical universe is comprehended in his consciousness, which itself becomes all.

Only one stage remains, and this is denied him. His own flesh cannot melt into his thought: he keeps "Something inviolate. A living something." These phrases return him to the state which was his at the beginning of the poem, where, at minimal definition, the "something inviolate" is the fact "that / His father was an ape." The original Adam, sprung from nature and subject to it, by it condemned to die, persists despite this victory. Those critics are surely wrong who see "Einstein" as antiscientific; rather, the poem, like *Nobodaddy,* affirms the necessary destiny of man to subdue everything to his knowledge—everything but the stubborn, atavistic ape within, which *must* refuse to yield. The anecdotal poem "The Tea Party" says all that need be said about man's sense of his primitivism; "Einstein" says something further, that the animal residuum is man's very life. The tragic fate awaiting this life has already been revealed in *The Pot of Earth.* "Einstein" is not tragic; it is not even precisely critical. It is an intellectual celebration of an intellectual triumph, attended by a voice bidding the *triumphator* remember that he is dust.

MacLeish's tragic sense of the buried life, exposed in the impersonal symbolism of *The Pot of Earth,* is deeply sounded in *The Hamlet of A. MacLeish* (1928). An observation by MacLeish more than a decade later, in his essay "Poetry and the Public World," was made to introduce a kind of renunciation of this poem or at least of the attitudes it expresses: "The Hamlet of Shakespeare was the acceptance of a difficult age and the demonstration of the place, in that age, of poetry. The Hamlet of Laforgue, and after him of Eliot and after him of the contemporary generation, is the rejection of a difficult age and a contemptuous comment upon the hope of poetry to deal with it. . . . [N]ot until contemporary poetry writes the Hamlet of Laforgue and Eliot out of its veins, will poetry occupy, and reduce to the order of recognition, the public-private world in which we live." *The Hamlet of A. MacLeish* is in the tradition of Jules Laforgue's "Hamlet" and of Eliot's Prufrockian and wastelandish poems; and it focuses, certainly, upon

the sufferings of the sensitive man, not upon the problems of the age in its "public" bearings. From the point of view of 1939, after a decade of experiment with "public" themes and at a moment of intense uneasiness about the future of civilization, MacLeish saw his *Hamlet* as too negative, as too much lacking in what the same essay called "acceptance" and "belief." Yet it was probably just as well that he aimed his criticism expressly against Laforgue and Eliot and only lumped his *Hamlet* implicitly with theirs; for really there is a difference in kind between their pessimism and his own in that poem. Quite simply, their pessimism is social, whereas his is cosmic. What Laforgue and Eliot (in his early poetry) found fault with was the special uncongeniality of life for the special personae in their poetry. What MacLeish complains of in his *Hamlet* is the injustice of the universe. Surely a poem which says that life is a fraud is hardly to be criticized for not telling us how to live optimistically.

In "Einstein" there are marginal notes with the double purpose of punctuating the stages of consciousness and locating these in the mind of one individual. In *The Hamlet* such notes have a different purpose: they key the psychological action to Shakespeare's *Hamlet,* from which (being quotations, stage directions, or episode descriptions) they are taken. MacLeish's poems can be thought of as analogous to a transparent overlay which, when superimposed on the map or chart to whose details it is keyed, provides new information or modifies the old. In this case the so-called overlay is fully a map in its own right. It is divided into fourteen sections, corresponding to as many scenes of the Shakespeare play. What it maps with these is the world of consciousness belonging to its protagonist, the modern Hamlet; and this world, like that of the play, shows temporal movement or more properly historical movement, for it is a world common to mankind, whom this Hamlet represents. (As with *The Pot of Earth,* some resemblance to *Finnegans Wake* may be seen.) And if Hamlet is mankind, it would appear that the Ghost is the mysterious father-god of creation, the unknown Nobodaddy, maybe to be known in, or as, Death; Hamlet's mother is the Earth; and the Claudius figure, symbolized in the opening section as both Hyperion (the sun) *and* a satyr, is the tyrant enemy, Time. The characters in this cast do not emerge allegorically, as in a morality play, but symbolistically. That is, as addressed by Hamlet they are persons, but as described and further characterized they become actions, narratives, even landscapes; and the actions take the place of drama. The poem is not dramatic except in that sense in which a speaking voice implies a dramatic situation; nor is that implication a vivid one, Hamlet being mainly a stage-managing consciousness, like Tiresias in *The Waste Land.* The protagonist's mood and temper, conforming to the "nighted color/choler" of Shakespeare's Hamlet, do, however, determine the tone of anguish throughout the poem.

Two of the episodes or symbolic actions of MacLeish's *Hamlet* are particularly bold and memorable. Part III, corresponding to Horatio's description of the Ghost (*Hamlet,* I, ii), is presented in terms of that portion of a Grail romance (the Bleheris version, freely adapted) which contains the adventure of the Chapel Perilous and the adventure of the Grail Castle, including the disclosure of the Grail talismans. The point of this (and of Part IV, answering to the appearance of the Ghost to the prince) is the inscrutability of the death mystery, from whose silence there can be no appeal and into whose secret there can be no initiation—such as the initiation supposed by Jessie L. Weston, in her book *From Ritual to Romance,* to have given rise to the Grail legends. A theme is here restated from *Streets in the Moon.* Part IX,

corresponding to the play within the play, the play of the mousetrap, has a subject recalling St.-J. Perse's "migration" poem *Anabase,* namely the movements of peoples and tribes into new lands, the rise and fall of cultures, the cycle of civilization. And the point of this, in relation to the Shakespearean scene, is that, as the memorial of human aspirations, the whole earth is a blood-stained chronicle of the guilt of nature and Time. These episodes of the poem have the profoundest import because they establish the necessity of the cosmic pessimism which is the mainspring of its tragic movement. They furthermore universalize the rage and grief of the protagonist, inviting all mankind to take part in execrating the conditions of life.

The gloom pervading *The Hamlet of A. MacLeish* is left behind in the next collection, *New Found Land: Fourteen Poems* (1930). Here the over-all tone is one of acceptance— not the unreflecting acceptance urged but resisted in the closing part of the earlier poem, but something urbanely detached. There is a return to the meditativeness of an even earlier period, in poems about memory and time; along with this there is an advance toward a new theme of affirmation, for which a tone of optimism comes into being. Such poems as " 'Not Marble Nor the Gilded Monuments,' " "Return," "Tourist Death," and "You, Andrew Marvell" are retrospective in two senses: they look back to the years and places of MacLeish's sojourn abroad, and they recall his obsessive concern, in those circumstances, with the erosion of life by time. "You, Andrew Marvell" has been anthologized too often, but it is as nearly perfect a poem as MacLeish has ever written. Yet it is only one of a group (Part IV of his *Hamlet* belongs with these) in which he again used the "cinema" technique of passing across the mind's eye a succession of places and faces, each an objective repository of some emotional association for him. The subject of "You, Andrew Marvell" is the poet's past as lodged in the places named, quite as much as it is the poet's present conceived as a moment in the light which is soon to be covered by the darkness inexorably rising in the east. The specific wit in his highly serious "metaphysical" handling of this subject depends not merely on a paradoxical view of diurnal motions (the night rises in the east) but on his present geographical position in relation to the regions reviewed in his mind. Being now presumably in the middle of the American continent, he, at noon, imagines the eastern world slipping into physical night just as, figuratively, it darkens by receding into his personal past.

The new, affirmative theme, though not fully realized in this poem or perhaps anywhere in the collection before the concluding piece, "American Letter," seems to grow out of a personal sense of the east-west imagery. At least "American Letter" defines the line of separation between the past, Europe and Asia, old lands of darkness, and the future, America the "new found land," by declaring that for the American born his life must unfold here: the Old World may enshrine a remembered joy, but the man of the New World is not fulfilled by it. And in "Salute" MacLeish hails the sun, dayspring and midday, as if to assert the preeminence of his symbol of the West. Indeed, he tends now to neglect the moon, which becomes a symbol no longer of that sought realm of myths and dreaming but of a world of stasis, sterility—something praised only in the almost hymnal "Immortal Autumn." His style tends toward greater impersonality as, following Perse, he cultivates dissociated concrete images of immense but vague significance. One very successful instance of this practice occurs in "Epistle to Be Left in the Earth," where its gnomic qualities suit the speaker's list of specific phenomena unreduced to abstract classification.

Conquistador (1932) is a long poem but not an epic, though of epic magnitude in theme, nor yet a chronicle, though based on an account of the Spanish rape of Mexico, *The True History of the Conquest of New Spain*, by Bernál Díaz del Castillo. Its interest derives neither from the portrayal of heroic character nor from adventurous narrative, but from its rendering of discrete episodes as experiences recollected by its narrator. It can hardly be termed panoramic; it is kaleidoscopic, a fantasia of emotions. Though not primarily a narrative at all but a series of tableaux with subjective coloring, it would perhaps remind one of Dante's *Divine Comedy* even if, typographically, its verse did not resemble *terza rima*. Like the *Divine Comedy* it presents a psychological, if not quite a spiritual, quest. This quest, outlined in fifteen books, has the usual temporal and spatial dimensions—temporal into the past buried within the speaker's self, spatial into the Mexican interior and the death of the Aztec culture. The hallmark of the poem, unfortunately, is an unrelieved sense of enormous confusion. In the memory of the speaker, the successive episodes are crowded with detail; and an effect of "nonlinear" construction is heightened by the frequent use of parataxis. That is, the language depends a good deal on coordinated statements, whether or not with conjunctions. That this device was intentional is evident from the special use of the colon as a divider; it is made to separate phrases of all kinds. The elements which are thus compounded stand in any order: logic seems not to be in question, since free association controls largely.

If the influence of St.-J. Perse dominates the larger framework of the poem, affecting the shape of its "grand sweep," still another influence, that of the Ezra Pound of the *Cantos*, often prevails at close quarters. The arbitrary juxtaposition of "significant" details is Poundian. So, too, is one ingredient of MacLeish's subject matter, the use of Book XI of the *Odyssey* in the "Prologue," where Bernál Díaz is given a role like that of the Homeric Tiresias, summoned from the dead along with fellow ghosts to speak to the living. MacLeish drops this mythological device after the "Prologue," in favor of Díaz's book narrative; but the latter may be considered a realistic equivalent to ghostly speech. Though more in key with the Biblical rhapsodies of Perse than with the social grumblings of Pound, *Conquistador* lacks optimism. For one thing it is based on one of the bloodiest and most barbarous exploits in history, one which destroys the empire it conquers and which ends in a retreat. Furthermore it is set forth by a spokesman for the dead and disillusioned, himself aware, in his very book, that death hangs over him. At the last he longs for the impossible resurrection of youthful hope.

O day that brings the earth back bring again

That well-swept town those towers and that
    island. . . .

In general this poem, far from acclaiming the origin of the New World as the harbinger of American civilization, is negative as well as confessional. Díaz, like MacLeish's Hamlet, is a wastelander, and what he longs for is a lost innocence that in fact was never real at all: certainly it did not dwell in the Aztec priestly slaughterhouse or in the hearts of the Spanish butchers either. In the poem it only tantalizes like a gilded dream of El Dorado.

Whatever its defects—and its failures, for if it succeeds it does so as a sequence of vibrant short poems, not as a big poem—*Conquistador* brings MacLeish back definitely to American scenes. *Frescoes for Mr. Rockefeller's City*

(1933) restores the affirmative tone. What is affirmed now is the American dream—the wholesome one—not as an abstraction but in its embodiment by the American land and the pioneer past. The first of the six poems, "Landscape as a Nude," revives an allegorical convention (like *Finnegans Wake*, by the way) to romanticize the land as a voluptuous woman. "Wildwest" and "Burying Ground by the Ties" pay tribute to defeated energies of a past era, to Crazy Horse and to the laborers dead after laying the tracks of the Union Pacific; and at the same time these poems satirize the millionaire railroaders, as does the opening section of the fifth poem, "Empire Builders." The longer, second section of the latter invokes for its contrast the unviolated wilderness explored by Lewis and Clark on their expedition to the Northwest—the description being treated as an "underpainting" beneath a supposed series of panels beautifying the robber barons Harriman, Vanderbilt, Morgan, and Mellon, and for anticlimactic good measure the advertising executive Bruce Barton. The fourth poem, "Oil Painting of the Artist as the Artist," lampoons the anti-American expatriate snob—the T. S. Eliot type, who

. . . thinks of himself as an exile from all this,
As an émigré from his own time into history

(History being an empty house without owners
A practical man may get in by the privy
    stones . . .)

A final poem, "Background with Revolutionaries," makes a point with regard to the controversy (current at the time MacLeish was writing but now almost forgotten) surrounding the Diego Rivera murals for Radio City in New York. Rivera had depicted Lenin among his inspirational figures; Nelson Rockefeller had demurred; and the painting was expunged, to the accompaniment of howls from the Left, amusingly reinforced with the aesthetic plea that art is sacred beyond politics. MacLeish's point in the concluding poem was that Lenin is irrelevant to the spirit of America, which lives in the communion of land with people; a further point, which involves one's reading the fifth poem, optionally, as a coda to the other four, can be that Lenin in his irrelevance is somehow analogous to J. P. Morgan.

There are not only ideological but also functional problems in the *Frescoes*. Ideologically it is dubious whether MacLeish quite conveyed the absurdity of Leninism with his selected profiles of ignorant, neurotic, or simply enthusiastic believers in it; a suggestion emerges from "Background with Revolutionaries" that the fault with these communists may lie in their intellectual pretensions, which do not suit the non-intellectual mystique urged in the poem. And by the same token, earlier in the series, that mystique has been manipulated in order to pillory the railroad magnates, who were not "men of the people" and who ravaged the land for their money-making. Crazy Horse was admirable, apparently, and the virgin wilderness was good and so were the track gangs; but beyond this mystique of the primitive and the peasant the *Frescoes* offered little to a people who owed their power to the railroads and who, in distinction of achievement, had long since outdone the spike-drivers. Obviously the *Frescoes* laud a homegrown radicalism; they reject Leninism as sophisticated (and foreign); but they ignore the complex life of a modern people. Calling themselves frescoes and claiming a pictorial function, they fail to cover, as it were, the wall. They say almost nothing about what Americans do, or why. Given pictorial form, they would pose as great an irrelevance—to Mr. Rockefeller's or anyone's city—as Diego Rivera with his intrusive Lenin.

MacLeish's next volume, *Poems 1924–1933*, not only reprinted the best of his work up to 1933 but also arranged it in nonchronological order. This order could form the subject of a separate study: it seems to indicate many of the relations which MacLeish intended to hold in balance between separate poems. The volume begins with the *Hamlet* and ends with *Conquistador*, the long poems most antithetical to each other as "private" and "public" documents. Scattered through it are previously uncollected pieces; at least six of these rank among the finest of his middle period, namely "The Night Dream," "Broken Promise," "Before March," "Epistle to Léon-Paul Fargue," "Invocation to the Social Muse," and "Lines for an Interment." A sardonic note recalling a few of the poems in *Streets in the Moon* comes up occasionally; of these six, "Invocation to the Social Muse" is the poem most ruled by it. In "Lines for an Interment" a similar note heard before in "Memorial Rain" is intensified into a savage agony. Elsewhere the tone is dispassionate, conveyed through imagery and syntax of a crystal precision reminiscent, almost, of Dryden's noble renderings of Horace and worthy of Landor or Housman at their most painstaking. Of this character are "Before March" and a slighter poem, "Voyage."

Heap we these coppered hulls
With headed poppies
And garlic longed-for by the eager dead . . .

Such effects are concentrated in the poems having great intimacy of theme and voice.

The short volume *Public Speech: Poems* (1936) is strong in social implication, like MacLeish's plays in the same decade; but for part of its length it is different in manner from the usual "public" poetry. It ends with a series of ten poems in various lyric forms, assembled under the general title "The Woman on the Stair"; this, more than anything else in the volume, harks back to an earlier period. One thinks especially of "The Happy Marriage," which also is a series of this type: "The Woman on the Stair," too, is made up of meditative descriptions which chart an emotional relationship. Why should this sequence have been inserted in a book whose very title points to MacLeish's new preoccupation with what poetry can deliver to the public concerning themselves? The answer is that the adjective *public* is not synonymous with *national* or with *political* or with *cultural* in a social scientist's sense; it connotes all that is common, all that touches everyman. Those of MacLeish's poems that treat of the individual in society, or of society in history, do seem public in a more "communal" sense than is possible to a lyric commemoration of love; but this subject, too, can be so treated that its private values become general meanings. Moreover, the first poem in the volume, "Pole Star," celebrates social love, the observance of charity for all, as a guiding principle in an age of misdirections; almost the whole collection is about human bonds of feeling. What *public* meant to MacLeish at this juncture seems to have been dual: in one aspect it came close to our present slack sense of *relevant*; in another it rather implied *impersonal* in something like Eliot's sense, that is, marked by avoidance of self-absorption. In "The Woman on the Stair," personal subject matter becomes archetypal.

"The Woman on the Stair" is really about the psychology of love. The Eros who rules here is the god of maturity; it would be instructive to set beside this another group of lyrics, also a sequence and also a chronicle of love's progress, but focusing on youthful love —Joyce's *Chamber Music*. There the intensities of feeling wear romantic disguises which in turn undergo transformations into fabrics of symbol. Here, viewed alike from the masculine and the feminine sides, are the great intensities—need, selfishness, shame, jealousy, fickleness, boredom—and time's deadly gift,

detachment, all of them functions of a pragmatism that often governs human relations in the mask of the romantic spirit. This sobering vision culminates in the remarkable closing poem, "The Release," a meditation on past time as stasis. What "The Woman on the Stair" projects as a "cinema" sequence, a passional affair involving two people only, becomes in projection a far-reaching commentary on behavior and motivation.

Not only "Pole Star," concerning love, but several other poems at the beginning of *Public Speech* meditate contemporary bearings for traditional wisdom. "Speech to Those Who Say Comrade" defines true as against specious brotherhood. "Speech to the Detractors" rebukes debunkers and petty journalists and acclaims the love of excellence, arguing that a people unwilling to honor its outstanding men is a self-degrading people. "Speech to a Crowd" exhorts men to be self-reliant, not to wait on leadership, not to *be* a crowd. These poems, along with a few in the middle of the volume, may be too inspirational to appeal to readers who are moved by the psychological shrewdness of "The Woman on the Stair." One poem, "The German Girls! The German Girls!" (its title to be understood as a sardonic toast?), takes the form of a quasi-choric exchange and is therefore dramatic in structure though not in form. It damns the militaristic spirit by cataloguing the coarse, brutal, and perverted types that abound among the Nazis. Propaganda though this is, the poem remains fresh because it is dramatic and also because it escapes "pulpit diction."

Two separately published poems on social themes, *Land of the Free—U.S.A.* (1938) and *America Was Promises* (1939), both with topical bearing, relate to diverse areas of concern. The first is hard to judge as poetry because, as published, it was tied to a series of eighty-eight contemporary photographs in order that (according to a note by MacLeish) it might illustrate *them*. The photographs were already collected before the poem was written. The letterpress still makes a poem, but is at some disadvantage in proximity to the pictures. The two arts combine to tell a horrifying before-and-after story of the pioneer settlers in a rich land who, after many generations, have sunk into poverty and squalor through disease, over-crowding, economic exploitation, soil deterio-ration, industrialization, and all the rest. The horror is conveyed mainly by the impact of the photographs as a set, which embraces many contrasts; but the most distressing, i.e., pa-thetic, are far beyond the power of the poem to annotate. The pictures are violent, shock-ing; the poem is "cool," relying on irony. Cer-tainly the contrasts are intrinsic to the two modes: photography is presentational, rumina-tive poetry representational. The style is itself cool, in form a kind of collective monologue; but the pronoun "we" serves also to make the voice impersonal, as if the speaker were radio-broadcasting the report of a disaster. Mac-Leish's use of a "broadcast announcer" voice was frequent in the 1930's. Whether radio was responsible directly (other poets having experi-mented with the same device—Auden, for ex-ample, and Eliot in "Triumphal March"), the fact that MacLeish had written radio plays, in which such a voice was normally essential, suggests that the medium exerted some influ-ence. One problem with having this voice ac-company a photographic series is that, *ex hy-pothesi*, it belongs to a subject confronting hu-man objects seen by the camera, yet it purports to speak in the character of those objects, and this without so much as adopting their dialect.

America Was Promises is indisputably the most eloquent of the "public" poems. It con-trives an absolute alliance between theme and voice; actually the theme helps to flesh the voice so that it surmounts its usual anonymity and acquires the solidity of a persona. Who the persona is is unclear, but what he is is obvi-ous, a prophet but contemporary, a liberator but traditionalist, a revolutionary but sage. The working question asked is "America was prom-ises to whom?"—one answered in several ways, by Jefferson, by John Adams (philosopher of usury for Pound's *Cantos*), by Thomas Paine, and finally in the oracular formula *"The prom-ises are theirs who take them."* The rest of the poem beseeches the vast community of Amer-ica to believe that unless they "take the prom-ises" others will; but there is something incon-clusive about this, for a rhetoric capable of sounding a call to arms seems to have been expended on a plea for faith. References to nations made captive by the Falange, the Ger-mans, or the Japanese might imply something like a war message (the year being 1939); on the other hand, the historical material is of the sort that, unlike MacLeish, a Marxist would have exploited seditiously. In its intellectual ambiguity *America Was Promises* had much in common with the philosophy of the national administration at that period. So seen, of course, the poem is milder than the rhetoric of its conclusion: it is simply urging people to remain loyal to New Deal doctrines at home and American policy abroad. Really it is much better as a poem than as a message: for once, MacLeish's adaptation of St.-J. Perse's geo-graphic evocations seems precisely right.

The long lapse before the appearance of *Actfive and Other Poems* (1948) would itself suffice to set this volume apart. But the double circumstance of the war and MacLeish's pub-lic service, along with the new personal vitality he seems to have experienced at this time, may account for its energies. In spirit this book is fully postwar, and it contains the perceptions of a man who had worked within government and who now had a far more exact idea of the gulf between political dreams and reality. It is the book of his second renaissance. A number of the poems, quite apart from the title piece, are of immense interest technically. They range from "Excavation of Troy," an amusing metaphysical exercise in the slow manipulation of imagery and simile (in the mind of a drowsing girl her lover of many nights gone is like Troy buried under many intervening "layers"), to "What Must," a quick medley of narrative, dialogue, and meditation (telling virtually in a cataract of rhymes the events of a brief love idyl). Several of the poems are ideological: thus "Brave New World," a ballad to Jefferson in his grave (in the tradition of Yeats's "To a Shade") taunts postwar America for its indifference to the plight of nations still unliberated.

The title piece, "Actfive," was the most significant poem by MacLeish since the publication of his *Hamlet*. It does what a major work by a developing poet has to do: it clarifies the meaning of his previous major works in relation to one another, and it subjects to new form the world which his art is trying now to deal with. This poem relates to *The Pot of Earth*, to "Einstein," and to *The Hamlet of A. MacLeish*; and though quite intelligible independently of those, it gains depth and complexity by the relation. The general title, with the ranting manner of Part I, "The Stage All Blood . . ." brings the *Hamlet* to mind; "Actfive" continues, in a manner of speaking, the actions of that nightmarish poem, advancing them beyond the circle of a single protagonist's mind and showing that they involve all men.

Part I proclaims the death of God, of Kingship, and of Man deified—the last murdered by tyrants; and it appeals for one who can become in their stead "the hero in the play," a hero to restore not only peace but Eternity, the principle of very reason. Implicitly both *The Pot of Earth* and, at some distance, *Nobodaddy* are drawn upon here, the one for the indifference of the Absolute, the other for, as well, the hu-

man alienation from it. In turn both are implicitly criticized: they have too palely depicted the stark loathsomeness of the death which proud man has inherited. Part II, "The Masque of Mummers," parades before the reader an absurd train of expressionistic figures, nonheroes yet "each the Hero of the Age"; it is an age whose inhabitants, stripped of privacy and individuality, cling together as in a public amphitheater and witness a charade of social lies—those of the Science Hero, of the Boyo of Industry, of the Revolutionary Hero with the Book, of the Great Man, of the Victim Hero or "pimp of death," of the Visitor or dreamer of millennium, of the State or utopia, of the I or egotist-introspectionist, of the lonely Crowd. Part III, "The Shape of Flesh and Bone," identifies the sought hero at last; it is flesh and bone, unidealized, existential man, instinctive, physical, able to define the meaning of his universe to himself—man the transitory but in spirit indomitable. Archetypes present themselves: "The blinded gunner at the ford," an image borrowed presumably from Hemingway's *For Whom the Bell Tolls*; a profile of Franklin D. Roosevelt, "The responsible man . . . / [who] dies in his chair . . . / The war won, the victory assured"; and other images, of an invalid and a hostage. These exemplify the unposturing, unselfish performance of duty,

Some duty to be beautiful and brave
Owed neither to the world nor to the grave
. . . .
But only to the flesh the bone.

The closing lines reaffirm the unutterable loneliness of man in his universe of death, but, like "Einstein," leave him with his inviolate creaturehood. It is ironic that "Actfive" should so circuitously return to the point insisted upon in "Einstein"; for it steers by the opposite pole, assuming that man's lordly reason, far from having subdued nature to its understanding, has been dethroned utterly. Equally, the animal self here, which can still "endure and love," is all that preserves man from destruction; whereas in "Einstein" it is the only thing that debars him from godhead.

Collected Poems 1917–1952 incorporates a section of "New Poems" which might have made a book by themselves. They protract the *Actfive* renaissance (indeed it has lasted MacLeish into old age). Some half-dozen of them are modern "emblem" poems, being dominated by single images (often elaborated) with connotative value. Blake's "Ah! Sun-flower" is analogous; in MacLeish's "Thunderhead" the physics of lightning symbolizes an aspect of conjugal behavior; in; "Starved Lovers" chrysanthemums symbolize sensuality; in "The Linden Branch" a green bough is metaphorically a musical instrument playing silent music. The newness of this effect consists in the way whole poems are now built round it, as Emily Dickinson's or (using symbol rather than metaphor) Yeats's often are. Yeats, who was to become a major inspiration for MacLeish, must have influenced the style of the end poem of "New Poems," the meditation on metaphor "Hypocrite Auteur," which essentially offers a justification for the effect.

Songs for Eve (1954) really consists of two collections joined together: first the twenty-eight tight, riddling poems (corresponding to the days of the month?) called "Songs for Eve"; then "Twenty-One Poems" of miscellaneous kinds. Despite the general title of the initial set, some of its pieces are for Eve but others are for Adam, the Serpent, the Green Tree, Eve's children, and so on. Perhaps in some sense all indeed are "for" Eve, she being central in the mythic context. Like Yeats's Crazy Jane, Eve is carnal and vicariously creative—in short, Blakean. Through her, Adam is enabled to wake from animality into consciousness; with her, he falls upward "from

earth to God," his soul growing as the awareness within his body, his children succeeding him as rebels and creators destined to rear, in place of the Green Tree of consciousness, the Dry Tree (the Cross) of godlike knowledge. The theme is that of *Nobodaddy* enriched with that of "Einstein." The twenty-eighth poem ends the sequence by lauding "man/ That immortal order can"; and in like manner the last of the "Twenty-One Poems," entitled "Reasons for Music" and dedicated to Wallace Stevens, defines the poet's task as the imposition of form upon the fluid world (a theme of Stevens' own; MacLeish would ordinarily refer to the *discovery* of natural, intrinsic order, except probably in the aesthetic or the moral sphere). The fine keynote poem "The Infinite Reason" paraphrases "Songs for Eve" in effect by speaking of the human mission to read meaning in external reality.

> Our human part is to redeem the god
> Drowned in this time of space, this space
> That time encloses.

Clearly the leading theme of *Songs for Eve*, the whole book, is man's ordering function; the collection is closer to "Einstein" and the other space-time poems of *Streets in the Moon* than are the works in between. Here much is made of the origin of the human soul within space-time, particularly in "Reply to Mr. Wordsworth," where the proposition that the soul "cometh from afar" is refuted by an appeal to Einsteinian physics and—paradoxically—to the felt life of the emotions. The poems "Infiltration of the Universe," "The Wood Dove at Sandy Spring," "The Wave," "Captivity of the Fly," and "The Genius" are emblematic, and they happen also to compose a miniature bestiary. The volume pays tribute impartially to matters of intellect and of feeling; these compressed parables divide between them.

The Wild Old Wicked Man (1968) explores the whole scale of MacLeish's concerns, still optimistically. Old age and youth, time, domesticity, contemporary manners, love, death —these predominate. Introspection is not overworked, but two of the most arresting poems in the volume are "Autobiography," on childhood vision, and "Tyrant of Syracuse," on the subliminal self. In a memorable group of elegies, MacLeish bids farewell to Sandburg, Cummings, Hemingway, and Edwin Muir. The Hemingway poem, only eleven lines long, is one of numerous tributes paid by MacLeish to that onetime friend; it adapts Yeat's concept of "the dreaming back" for a skillful and moving analysis of the unity of the man Hemingway in his life and death. The Muir poem quotes "The Linden Branch," applying to a *green memory* the graceful conceit of the green bough as a musical staff with leaves for notes. Yeats furnished the title of the volume; and the title poem, placed at the end, closes on the theme of

> . . . the old man's triumph, to pursue
> impossibility—and take it, too,

which is a signature for MacLeish's poetry, restating the theme of Adam victorious, fallen upwards into a stasis of art and eternity.

As playwright, MacLeish began with closet drama, with *Nobodaddy* (not to forget the rhetorically lively dramatic poem "Our Lady of Troy" behind that). Though excellent as a trial of philosophical drama, such a work could not have taught him much; thus the strength of his first stage play, *Panic* (1935), is very impressive. For the dialogue, as he explains in a prefatory note, he chose a five-accent line in free (or sprung) rhythm; other passages, those of a choric nature allotted to various supplementary voices, he wrote in three-accent lines. The experiment was contemporary with Eliot's

Murder in the Cathedral; and while MacLeish's verse shows less flexibility than Eliot's there, it is at least as stageworthy. The play is an admirable and curious hybrid. In sum, it is an Aristotelian tragedy with a special catastrophe, the withdrawal of the supporting characters' loyalty (the protagonist, a great man, suddenly ceases to be accepted as that); and this plot is superimposed on a proletarian drama conveyed by expressionistic techniques (anonymous voices of the poor and unemployed in a time of financial crisis). It is the unemployed who make the protagonist's fellow bankers lose confidence in him; and not what he does because of pride, but his vulnerability to the hatred of the mob because of who he is, precipitates the "panic" causing his downfall. The play remains solidly in the classic tradition; for the protagonist, the super-banker McGafferty (the play was first called "J. P. McGafferty"), possesses nobility of spirit and authentic powers of leadership: he really could avert his country's economic collapse if his colleagues would rally round him and pool their resources instead of defaulting. Their refusal to do so might support a "proletarian" interpretation, but in fact the whole botch happens because the proletariat prophesy that it will, when they invade his office and one of their number (a blind "Tiresias") pronounces his doom. "Proletarian" is converted into "psychological." The weakness in *Panic* consists in the unintegrated role of the feminine lead, McGafferty's mistress, Ione, who exercises only a reflector function of emphasizing his arrogance. Her role is crucial theatrically, but in structure the play suffers from it.

In his foreword to *The Fall of the City* (1937), MacLeish discussed the advantages of radio as a medium for verse drama. Looking back a third of a century, one must now regret bitterly the lost opportunities for this genre, which was killed when, in America, radio was killed by television. MacLeish's claims for radio verse were not exaggerated, but the moment was wrong and the remaining time too short. His own early contributions, notably this play and its successor *Air Raid* (1938), have, alas, chiefly a memorial importance. *The Fall of the City*, in which the radio announcer's unique function as described by MacLeish is essential, appears to follow expressionistic models. The Announcer, the Dead Woman, the Messenger, the Orator, as voices bring the most presentational style into the most presentational medium. The poetry has absolute immediacy: since it must express action, it hews to what happens, never deviating into mere lyricism. The techniques are of the simplest: the play employs the unity of (supposed) place, with everything taking place under the Announcer's eyes. *Air Raid* is at once more realistic in terms of radio drama, and more conventional—although less realistic in one sense, for it uses the "newsreel" technique of picking up scenes at which the Announcer is not present. And in this play the poetry ranges away from the main action, as the characters' feelings digress from their imminent danger, so that it has a more various texture. Both plays use a poetry of vivid images and plain colloquialism. In *The Fall of the City* the unit is a line of varying length in sprung rhythm; in *Air Raid* it is a line of five or, less commonly, fewer accents.

When, in the postwar television age, MacLeish returned to radio verse drama tentatively, it was with recognition of its anachronistic status. He called *The Trojan Horse* (1952) a play for broadcasting or for reading without scenery (i.e., like Dylan Thomas' *Under Milk Wood*). It is a one-act piece with one moment of high drama, when Helen realizes that the wooden horse contains those who will destroy her happiness. Otherwise the speeches seem unduly level—a problem in the play for voices, which often thus depends on elocutionary artifice for sharp characterizations. The verse line is of three accents, except in formal speeches, where blank verse occurs. In place of an announcer, there is a brief prologue in which a "modern" voice calls upon an "ancient" voice (Homer) to explain the action; within the play there are a blind man (also Homer) and a girl, whose dialogue serves for choric commentary. This structure foreshadows *J.B.* The effect is of a kind of Chinese-boxes perspective. *This Music Crept by Me upon the Waters* (1953) has been staged as well as broadcast. It is conversational, with no fewer than ten characters filling the one act; they speak a three-accent verse a little like Eliot's in *The Cocktail Party*, but with less straddling from line to line and much tighter rhythm. The people are contemporary, the setting Caribbean, a Paradise island like Prospero's; the theme is the impossibility of a return to innocence and Eden, except for saints or primitives. Others, the romantics, sink into dreams but soon are recalled to reality; still others, the merely idle, are overwhelmed with boredom and drink. The play chides the rich and irresponsible who demand Eden without earning it.

J.B.: A Play in Verse (1958) and *Herakles* (1967) are respectively based on the book of Job and on the Greek hero myth; between them they represent man suffering and acting. J.B. is a King Lear who, divested of all illusions about a benevolent universe, is taught to endure and love, lke the survivors in *Actfive*. Herakles is an Einstein mastering nature, a Cain seeking godhead, confronted finally by the limits of human power and made to see his mere humanity. *J.B.* is constructed as a play within a play, with a remote director-prompter as deity offstage. The God and Satan of the scriptural drama are here impersonated by actor-clowns, Zuss the circus balloon-vendor and Nickles the popcorn-seller, who first stage a play in the deserted circus tent and then become involved in it as chorus for J.B.'s tribulation. J.B. triumphs both over Zuss's humiliation of him and Nickles' temptation to hatred. Learning the truth about his god, he forgives him his injustice. With a love stronger than the unreasoning tyranny of heaven, he justifies that love by beginning to live again when his torment is finished.

Against this eloquent, superbly theatrical play, *Herakles* seems brittle; yet, fantasy though it is, it is founded on a sacred and profound myth. A modern scientist, Professor Hoadley, has received international recognition for his discoveries. Symbolically he is Herakles, his work for human knowledge and power analogous to the hero's labors. His wife corresponds to Herakles' wife, Megara. The analogy extends to the Hoadleys' son, effeminate and hostile, alienated by his father's profession; he represents the sons slaughtered by Herakles in his overweening frenzy after returning from the underwold. If, like Euripides' play (from which MacLeish drew hints), this action begins as a triumph in Act I, it continues as a fantasy of pathos. In Act II Mrs. Hoadley and Megara occupy the stage together, as their two worlds of history and myth interpenetrate and the myth is shown as eternal meaning: Herakles' homecoming and his reunion with the mother of his dead children, at once the repetition and archetype of Professor Hoadley's (the two parts are presumably doubled in production), become symbolic of the mere ruin of life to which the Promethean hero is condemned. He obeys the necessity of fighting evil and harnessing power for man's welfare, but he is destroyed by hatred and the unnatural burden of godhead.

Herakles and *J.B.* show Janus faces of the human struggle to neutralize the blind sentence of death passed upon mankind. Their two scales of poetry, exemplifying MacLeish's maturest talents, correspond to extremes of lyricism and tragic realism in speech.

The prose drama *Scratch* (1971), amplifying Stephen Vincent Benét's 1936 story "The Devil and Daniel Webster," creates a parable with ethical overtones of "Actfive" as well as the Blakean exaltation of Liberty over Law. The story, transformed by MacLeish, achieves a certain mythic dimension, not really because it deals with inveterate problems of American life, though it can indeed symbolize these as MacLeish's "Foreword" contends, but because its hero, Daniel Webster, thinks and acts as if, obedient to a categorical imperative, he embodied the meaning of civilization: he is a type of Prometheus. This strong drama involves a more complex system of implication than *J.B.* Its actual events reduce to a simple linear form. They begin with the leveling of charges against Webster by two accusers, a moral New Englander (Webster's friend Peterson) and the Devil himself (Scratch). They continue with Scratch's attempt to "foreclose" the soul of Jabez Stone, who has bartered it for seven years' good luck. They end with Jabez's legal defense by Webster before a ghostly judge and jury consisting of thirteen dead and damned enemies of American freedom. In the story by Benét, Webster is pure lawyer: he argues successfully on behalf of Jabez that the terrible forfeit must be ruled null and void because the Devil, as a foreign potentate, cannot exercise dominion over a freeborn American citizen. In MacLeish's version, a protagonist more like the historical Webster appears, who has to argue both Jabez's case and *his own*— the latter amounting, in fact, to the whole substance of the drama. The charges against Webster in *Scratch* concern his alleged expedient "sellout" of Liberty to preserve the American Union, through his adoption of the Compromise of 1850; in accepting the Fugitive Slave

Law, he seems a traitor to his fundamental axiom "Liberty and Union, now and forever, one and inseparable." When the jurymen bring in a verdict favorable to Jabez, they do so because touched by Webster's *argumentum ad hominem*, his appeal to their own sense of the "huge injustice" of man's life and death. In particular this appeal holds that every man, even such as the feckless Jabez, owns the Liberty to alleviate his poverty, his suffering, without being accountable to the strictness of the Law. Webster's argument itself is a sufficient reply to his accusers: it demonstrates his devotion to Liberty but does not undermine his resolution as a statesman. Accordingly the jury's verdict (like that of any audience) finds not only for Jabez but also for Webster as, in effect, a co-defendant; and in purely dramatic, theatrical terms the "case" against Webster ends simultaneously with the suit against Jabez Stone. In the forum of history, as Webster sadly acknowledges, the charges against him for accepting the Fugitive Slave Law remain unquashed. MacLeish, too, seems to believe that the historical Webster erred; but in *Scratch*, paradoxically, he arrays against his protagonist only two accusers, the Father of Lies and a New England Abolitionist.

Scratch is a lively drama and a moving one. Yet it had only a brief New York run in 1971. Perhaps, in the years between *J.B.* and *Scratch*, the strong, representative or mythic hero went out of fashion. Perhaps the improvident blasphemer Jabez Stone, if glorified as an antihero, would better have fitted the occasion. Perhaps *Scratch* is both too intellectual and too highly civilized (and patriotic) for the American theatre of the 1970's.

MacLeish from the beginning has held to a course of lonely exploration. His standards are classical and aristocratic. Once his friend Mark Van Doren, presented with an award for "services to poetry," responded with slow and deliberate emphasis that, as for himself, he had tried to serve only the *best* poetry. The remark could have been made by Archibald MacLeish with equally merited pride (the pride which knows the humility exacted by such service) and with equal truth. Part of his devotion has been accorded to craftsmanship. One can praise poets for this, not too much, certainly, but with too much exclusiveness. Often when one has praised it, in Frost or Stevens or Eliot, say, or in Rimbaud, it does not seem sufficient. This century still paddles in the backwash of Aestheticism; but there have been ages, before the subjectivist era, when poetry and the other arts pertained to the things of man—Cicero's *artes quae ad humanitatem pertinent*—and not just to one man's special quirk of vision, to express which he devises exquisite forms. Part of MacLeish's devotion has gone to the human state. Such concern is not poetry, but one is entitled to ask whether, without it, good poetry, let alone the best, can come into being. It must be set down that MacLeish, like the great poets—Yeats, for example—has striven to give form to what pertains not just to himself but to his fellow men.

Selected Bibliography

WORKS OF ARCHIBALD MacLEISH

POETRY

Songs for a Summer's Day (A Sonnet-Cycle). New Haven, Conn.: Yale University Press, 1915.

Tower of Ivory, with a foreword by Lawrence Mason. New Haven, Conn.: Yale University Press, 1917.

The Happy Marriage, and Other Poems. Boston and New York: Houghton Mifflin, 1924.

The Pot of Earth. Boston and New York: Houghton Mifflin, 1925.

Streets in the Moon. Boston and New York: Houghton Mifflin, 1926.

The Hamlet of A. MacLeish. Boston and New York: Houghton Mifflin, 1928.

New Found Land: Fourteen Poems. Boston and New York: Houghton Mifflin, 1930.

Conquistador. Boston and New York: Houghton Mifflin, 1932.

Frescoes for Mr. Rockefeller's City. New York: John Day, 1933.

Poems 1924–1933. Boston and New York: Houghton Mifflin, 1933.

Public Speech: Poems. New York: Farrar and Rinehart, 1936.

Land of the Free—U.S.A. New York: Harcourt, Brace, 1938.

America Was Promises. New York: Duell, Sloan and Pearce, 1939.

Actfive and Other Poems. New York: Random House, 1948.

Collected Poems 1917–1952. Boston: Houghton Mifflin, 1952.

Songs for Eve. Boston: Houghton Mifflin, 1954.

The Wild Old Wicked Man, and Other Poems. Boston: Houghton Mifflin, 1968.

The Human Season: Selected Poems. Boston: Houghton Mifflin, 1972.

PLAYS

Nobodaddy: A Play. Cambridge, Mass.: Dunster House, 1926.

Union Pacific—A Ballet. Produced 1934; published in *The Book of Ballets*, edited by Gerald Goode. New York: Crown, 1939.

Panic: A Play in Verse. Boston and New York: Houghton Mifflin, 1935.

The Fall of the City: A Verse Play for Radio. New York and Toronto: Farrar and Rinehart, 1937.

Air Raid: A Verse Play for Radio. New York: Harcourt, Brace, 1938.

The States Talking. In *The Free Company Presents . . . A Collection of Plays about the Meaning of America*. New York: Dodd, Mead, 1941.

The American Story: Ten Broadcasts. New York: Duell, Sloan and Pearce, 1944.

The Trojan Horse: A Play. Boston: Houghton Mifflin, 1952.

This Music Crept by Me upon the Waters. Cambridge, Mass.: Harvard University Press, 1953.

J.B.: A Play in Verse. Boston: Houghton Mifflin, 1958.

Three Short Plays: The Secret of Freedom, Air Raid, The Fall of the City. New York: Dramatists Play Service, 1961.

Herakles: A Play in Verse. Boston: Houghton Mifflin, 1967.

Scratch. Suggested by Stephen Vincent Benét's short story "The Devil and Daniel Webster." Boston: Houghton Mifflin, 1971.

PROSE

Housing America, by the Editors of *Fortune*. New York: Harcourt, Brace, 1932. (Written by MacLeish.)

Jews in America, by the Editors of *Fortune*. New York: Random House, 1936. (Written by MacLeish.)

Background of War, by the Editors of *Fortune*. New York: Knopf, 1937. (Of the six articles in this collection, all but the third were written by MacLeish.)

The Irresponsibles: A Declaration. New York: Duell, Sloan and Pearce, 1941.

The American Cause. New York: Duell, Sloan and Pearce, 1941.

A Time to Speak: The Selected Prose of Archibald MacLeish. Boston: Houghton Mifflin, 1941.

American Opinion and the War. Cambridge, Mass.: Harvard University Press, 1942.

A Time to Act: Selected Addresses. Boston: Houghton Mifflin, 1943.

Poetry and Opinion; The Pisan Cantos of Ezra Pound: A Dialog on the Role of Poetry. Urbana: University of Illinois Press, 1950.

Freedom Is the Right to Choose: An Inquiry into the Battle for the American Future. Boston: Beacon Press, 1951.

Poetry and Experience. Boston: Houghton Mifflin, 1961.

The Eleanor Roosevelt Story. Boston: Houghton Mifflin, 1965.

A Continuing Journey. Boston: Houghton Mifflin, 1968.

Champion of a Cause: Essays and Addresses on Librarianship, compiled and with an introduction by Eva M. Goldschmidt. Chicago: American Library Association, 1971.

AUTOBIOGRAPHY

The Dialogues of Archibald MacLeish and Mark Van Doren, edited by Warren V. Bush. New York: Dutton, 1964.

BIBLIOGRAPHY

Mizener, Arthur. *A Catalogue of the First Editions of Archibald MacLeish*. New Haven, Conn.: Yale University Press, 1938.

CRITICISM

Falk, Signi Lenea. *Archibald MacLeish*. New York: Twayne, 1965.

—*GROVER SMITH*

Norman Mailer

1923-

WHEN Norman Mailer's *The Naked and the Dead* was published in 1948 it was all but universally acclaimed as a major novel marking the appearance of a new American writer destined for greatness. During the succeeding years, however, though Mailer had some warm defenders, the negative judgments among critics substantially outnumbered the positive as book after book appeared: novels, a play, collections of stories and poems, and gatherings of essays and other fugitive pieces. And yet, unlike most of his generation of novelists —the "war novelists" and the urban Jewish writers—Mailer continued to pursue a course of individualistic development and change which increasingly commanded the attention of peers, critics, and public; if his readers were sometimes baffled and frequently hostile they grew ever more interested. To use a somewhat Maileresque analogy, Mailer somewhat resembled, during his first twenty-five years as a professional writer, an overmatched boxer who, floored in the second round, springs back and sustains the fight far beyond expectations through variety and inventiveness of footwork and temporizing punches.

The match is still not decided. But however it finally comes out, there can be no doubt that the overmatched boxer will at the very least be remembered for his remarkable perform-

ance. Mailer's adversary during the 1950's and 1960's was that plodding but powerful opponent of idiosyncrasy and innovation which Eliot long ago dubbed "the tradition." Mailer had won his first round with a skillful and moving but conventional novel in the realist-naturalist vein. But most of his work since *The Naked and the Dead*, with the exception of a handful of stories from the late forties and early fifties, had been radically innovative in both substance and essential form without satisfying prevailing current conceptions of what constituted serious literary experimentation.

It was Mailer's apparent lack of artistic "seriousness" that troubled his serious critics most. When they were not either ridiculing or dismissing him, their main cry was the lamentation that a major talent was being wasted on trivial material or debased by sloppy craftsmanship. F. Scott Fitzgerald, whose work and career were in many ways similar to Mailer's, was criticized during his lifetime on much the same grounds. But what needed to be stressed in Mailer's case, as in Fitzgerald's, was that he was indeed a serious "experimentalist" writer, though an experimentalist of a different order than his moment in the history of "the tradition" allowed his public easily to recognize, accept, and understand.

James Joyce was the kind of experimentalist who applied innovative techniques to conventionally "realistic" fictional material. He sought out and found new routes to the old novelistic destinations. D. H. Lawrence, on the other hand, was the kind of writer who discovered new destinations—new materials and knowledge, and thus new obligations for fiction. His technical innovations, always less sophisticated, formal, and predominant than Joyce's, were functional consequences and by-products of what can only be called an experimentalist approach to the *subject matter* of fiction. In the course of writing *The Rainbow* and *Women in Love* Lawrence discovered, as he told Edward Garnett, that his subject was no longer "the old stable *ego*" of human character, no longer the "diamond" but, rather, the "carbon" which is the diamond's elemental substance: "There is another *ego*, according to whose action the individual is unrecognisable, and passes through, as it were, allotropic states which it needs a deeper sense than any we've been used to exercise, to discover are states of the same single radically unchanged element. . . . Again I say, don't look for the development of the novel to follow the lines of certain characters: the characters fall into the form of some other rhythmic form, as when one draws a fiddle-bow across a fine tray delicately sanded, the sand takes lines unknown."

These metaphors describing the substantive nature of Lawrence's experimentation with both matter and form after *Sons and Lovers* might as easily apply to Mailer, whose work after *The Naked and the Dead* was similarly concerned with the "allotropy"—the changing "rhythmic form" and "lines unknown"—of the "carbon" of human character under complex stress. And like Lawrence, Mailer seems to have become aware of his new departure only after standing away from the new work in hand to see what he was doing and why he was doing it. While working on *Barbary Shore*, he recalled in an interview, he found his Marxist intellectual convictions continually distracted by compulsive preoccupations with "murder, suicide, orgy, psychosis." "I always felt as if I were not writing the book myself." Other statements by Mailer indicate that much the same creative pathology also ruled the composition of *The Deer Park*, his third novel. The personal stresses and anxieties that underlay the writing of these two novels, and the stories that were spun off from them, found confessional expression in Mailer's fourth book, a compilation of fiction and nonfiction pieces with unifying connective additions called *Advertisements for Myself*, which is the author's intense, immediate, and unabashedly public reappraisal of himself, in 1959, as both artist and human being. Anxiety, compulsion, and hints of psychosis had been the disruptive and only half-conscious creative causes behind *Barbary Shore* and *The Deer Park*. Following the purgation and illumination represented by *Advertisements* they become, in the later novels *An American Dream* and *Why Are We in Vietnam?* and the related volumes of nonfiction, the consciously molded substance of Mailer's hypertrophic images of life in America at mid-century.

A detailed account of this course of change and growth must be left for later. The important fact is that after several more books, plus a string of other accomplishments—including play-producing, movie-making, a fling at architectural design, and a great deal of moral, social, and political punditing, both on paper and on the hoof—the author of *The Naked and the Dead* emerged in the mid-sixties, despite his still uncertain reputation among serious literary people, as decidedly the most active and vivid public figure on the American literary scene.

Like his first published novel and stories, Mailer's early life was at least conventional enough not to foreshadow with any definiteness the panoply of idiosyncrasy that was to come later. Born January 31, 1923, in Long Branch, New Jersey, to Isaac and Fanny Mailer, Norman Mailer was raised and schooled in Brooklyn, graduating from Boys High School in 1939. While at Harvard, where he earned a B.S. degree in aeronautical engineering in 1943, Mailer began writing in earnest, contributing to the *Advocate*, working at his first two (and still unpublished) novels, and winning in 1941 *Story* magazine's annual college fiction contest. In 1944 he married his first wife and was drafted into the army, serving in the Pacific Theater until 1946. During the next year and a half, part of which was spent in Europe, where he was enrolled as a student at the Sorbonne, Mailer wrote *The Naked and the Dead*, which was published with immediate and dramatic success. The public purchased it in such numbers that it held at the top of the best-seller lists for nearly three months. A movie contract was soon in the works; Lillian Hellman was slated to adapt it for the stage; and Sinclair Lewis was moved to dub Mailer "the greatest writer to come out of his generation."

Though Mailer himself once half-dismissed his first novel as a "conventional war novel," and though it was conceived and composed in a manner that Mailer was not to use again in a major work, *The Naked and the Dead* is much more than a "war novel." But in the year of its publication Mailer put on record his view that *The Naked and the Dead*, though cast in the realist mold, is "symbolic," expressive of "death and man's creative urge, fate, man's desire to conquer the elements—all kinds of things you never dream of separating and stating so baldly." And there is no mistaking that the island itself, and the mountain at its center which Sergeant Croft commits himself and his platoon to conquering, acquire an almost Conradian symbolic significance in the eyes of their chief beholders. Here is the soldiers' vision of the setting of their destruction:

"It was a sensual isle, a Biblical land of ruby wines and golden sands and indigo trees. The men stared and stared. The island hovered before them like an Oriental monarch's conception of heaven, and they responded to it with an acute and terrible longing. It was a vision of all the beauty for which they had ever yearned, all the ecstasy they had ever sought. For a few minutes it dissolved the long dreary passage of the mute months in the jungle, without hope, without pride. If they had been alone they might have stretched out their arms to it.

"It could not last. Slowly, inevitably, the beach began to dissolve in the encompassing night. The golden sands grew faint, became gray-green, and darkened. The island sank into the water, and the tide of night washed over the rose and lavender hills. After a little while, there was only the gray-black ocean, the darkened sky, and the evil churning of the gray-white wake. Bits of phosphorescence swirled in the foam. The black dead ocean looked like a mirror of the night; it was cold, implicit with dread and death. The men felt it absorb them in a silent pervasive terror. They turned back to their cots, settled down for the night, and shuddered for a long while in their blankets."

In an interview three years later, just after completing *Barbary Shore*, Mailer made this interesting disclosure about *The Naked and the Dead*: "I don't think of myself as a realist. That terrible word 'naturalism.' It was my literary heritage—the things I learned from Dos Passos and Farrell. I took naturally to it, that's the way one wrote a book. But I really was off on a mystic kick. Actually—a funny thing—the biggest influence on *Naked* was *Moby Dick*. . . . I was sure everyone would know. I had Ahab in it, and I suppose the mountain was Moby Dick. Of course, I also think the book will stand or fall as a realistic novel." This last qualification would also apply, of course, to *Moby Dick*. For Melville saw in the actual hazard and struggle of whaling, as Mailer did in war, the revealed pattern of the grandeur and tragedy of the whole human enterprise. Combat, for Mailer, is the chief means by which the higher laws of life become incarnate in human experience. War is his external subject matter in *The Naked and the Dead*; but his internal theme is the "crisis in human values"—identity, humanity, man, and the nature of their enemies in our time.

With war as the background typification of generalized external crisis, Mailer develops his internal themes by two principal means: first, extensively, through a number of Dos Passos-like diagnostic biographical portraits of a cross section of the fighting men; and second, intensively, through the protracted psychic struggle of mind and personality that takes place between Major General Cummings, the crypto-fascist commanding officer of the invading American forces, and his aide, a questioning liberal named Hearn. Both men have been shaped, though in opposite ways, by reaction against the privileged sterility of their midwestern bourgeois backgrounds. Cummings is the self-created prophet of a new totalitarianism who commands, in the name of his faith in order and authority, the breaking of men's spirits and the destruction of their wills. Hearn, bitter in his discontent, by nature a loner and yet tenderly humane in his half-guilty identification with the men he commands, is the uncertain voice of the liberal ideal of free man. Most of the fighting men are portrayed as already deprived, twisted, or stunted by the disintegrative and totalitarian forces and counterforces at work in their world, the forces whose contention has culminated in the war which now envelops them all. These men are the data of the dialectical contest which is taking place between Cummings and Hearn. That contest, the original of similar recurring patterns of individual contest, including sexual, in most of the rest of Mailer's work, ends in a kind of draw. Hearn and his convictions are wasted when he dies as a casual accident of war on an irrelevant mission. And though the campaign is won, Cummings is in essence defeated because the agency of victory is not his active military intelligence but, rather, a chain of chance accidents beyond his control.

One notices not only that a true hero is lacking from the novel's epiclike action, but that his opposite, a forceful antagonist, is lacking too. And yet a large enveloping energy has gathered, thrust forward, and come through to significant issue. A great spasm of nature, an inevitable motion of history, has superseded the efficacies of individual men in a world that has begun to move across Yeats's threshold of apocalypse where "the best lack all conviction" and "the worst/ are full of passionate intensity."

But at the core of this vast action, his presence stressing the hero's absence, is Sergeant Croft. After the death of Hearn, he leads the platoon on its doomed assault upon the mountain, dominating his men by the sheer intensity of his undefined "hunger" for the mastery of life. A rough prototype of D. J. Jethroe of *Why Are We in Vietnam?*, Croft has been sired by a tough Texas dirt-farmer on a woman conventionally "weak . . . sweet and mild." His father encourages in him a predator's taste for hunting, and he is by nature "mean." Why? "Oh, there are answers. He is that way because of the corruption-of-the-society. He is that way because the devil has claimed him for one of his own. It is because he is a Texan; it is because he has renounced God." The author interprets Croft in an aside as follows: *"He hated weakness and he loved practically nothing.*

There was a crude unformed division in his soul but he was rarely conscious of it." This embryonic "vision" is different from Hearn's superannuated liberalism and Cummings' authoritarian calculus because it is an animal thing—an energy with fierce tendencies but no "form." Croft represents the kinetic life-substance upon which such alternative ideologies as those of Hearn and Cummings must depend for their unforeseeable realizations. In his irrational will and passion, he is the human microcosm of the vast upsurge of inhuman forces in history which express themselves in the ironic irresolutions of the total action of *The Naked and the Dead*.

The Naked and the Dead, then, even if substantially conventional in form and style, is nevertheless one with the rest of Mailer's work in the apocalyptic energies of its vision. Those energies begin to find their requisite new form, and with that a new sort of voice, in the first of Mailer's "experimental" novels, *Barbary Shore*, published in 1951. *Barbary Shore* was the product, as Mailer has written in retrospect, of the author's "intense political preoccupation and a voyage in political affairs which began with the Progressive Party and has ended in the *cul-de-sac* (at least so far as action is concerned) of [his] being an anti-Stalinist Marxist who feels that war is probably inevitable." The omniscient authorial point of view of *The Naked and the Dead* is abandoned in *Barbary Shore* for first-person narrative, which is to continue as the preferred narrative form for Mailer's books thereafter. ("Memory is the seed of narrative, yeah," says D. J. Jethroe, narrator of *Why Are We in Vietnam?*) The book becomes, thus, an adaptation of *Bildungsroman*; its narrative substance is the hero's education for life in our time—or re-education, since he is suffering from amnesia somewhat inexplicitly induced by war and the breakdown of traditional political idealism.

The setting is a Brooklyn rooming house operated by a sexually promiscuous and morally neuter proprietress named, with an irony appropriate to her role as life's presiding norm, Guinevere. In this setting, the case histories of three roomers are presented: an impotent, betrayed, and self-betraying idealist of the old revolutionary left; his demon, a stolid and perverted interrogator for the rightist "totalitarian" establishment; and a mad Cassandra-like girl whose derangement is a consequence and expression of history, and whom, as an exacerbated mirroring of his own distressed psyche, the hero half loves.

The heaviness and inertia of the novel—its garrulous expositions of ideological conflict and the dazed passivity and blankness of Lovett, the hero-narrator, before all he sees and hears—is only a little relieved when at the end he sprints into an inchoate future with a mysterious small object entrusted to his keeping by the failed leftist before his death. The precise nature of the object, which is hotly coveted by the furies of the right, is never specified. But what it means is perfectly clear. It is a symbol or talisman of the sacred idea of man free and whole; and in the moment of the narrator's active commitment to it in the face of the terrible odds and enemies ranged against it, and now against him as well, we are meant to feel that it has taken on the existential power of life itself.

Even this early in his career—after only two novels—it was clear that Mailer's imagination, unique in his generation, was cast in the epic mold. As bard and prophet to an age in which history is at odds with nature or "destiny," he was telling in a fevered voice of the permutations of the heroic imperative in a post-heroic world. His theme was the struggle of life and form against death and chaos. But his subject matter was history. And as he pursued the theme of the ideal through the matter of the actual he made a discovery: in our time the sources and resources of life have shifted, to use the shorthand of Mailer's own symbology, from "God" to "the devil." The vision of life at stalemate in *The Naked and the Dead* and *Barbary Shore* is explained by this discovery, a discovery whose fullness of realization in a changed imaginative vision comes clear in *The Deer Park*, published in 1955.

Desert D'Or, a resort of the rich and powerful modeled on Palm Springs, is the principal setting of *The Deer Park*. It is a denatured interior world of concrete and plastic, of harsh light and blinding shadow, thrown up in defiance of the encircling desert outside. This pattern of division between natural and unnatural that is established in the setting extends also to the characters, in whom desire and will, feeling and thought, the wellsprings of motive and motive's fulfillment in action, have been stricken apart. The natural current of the life-force has somehow been broken. And the inhabitants of this world of trauma and aftermath constitute a gallery of parodies of the human image ranging from the absurd to the piteous to the monstrous. They are, as Mailer wrote in a note to his adaptation of *The Deer Park* for the stage, "in hell."

Sergius O'Shaugnessy, the hero-narrator of *The Deer Park*, is both an orphan and, like Lovett of *Barbary Shore*, a symbolic waif of historical disaster. His surrogate home in the air force and fulfillment in the exercise of the war pilot's impersonal skills of destruction have been snatched from him in a sudden accidental revelation that he is a killer: "I realized that . . . I had been busy setting fire to a dozen people, or two dozen, or had it been a hundred?" In recoil from such horrors of the "real world" he suffers a breakdown, is discharged, and on the winnings from a prodigiously lucky gambling venture, he comes to Desert D'Or, retreat of the gods of the "imag-

inary world," to rest, drift, gaze, and spend. A blank slate to be written on, an empty vessel to be filled, and—his vision of the burned flesh of his victims having rendered him sexually impotent—a low flame needing fuel, Sergius O'Shaugnessy is the framing consciousness of an ample world crowded with people exhibiting versions of his own predicament. Among the most important of these are Charles Francis Eitel, a gifted and formerly powerful Hollywood director, and Marion Faye, dope pusher, impresario of call girls, and connoisseur of the moral nuances of sadism. Both of these men become friends of O'Shaugnessy and objects of his studious moral attention.

Eitel has had a golden age, a brief heroic period in the thirties when as a true artist he made courageous movies on contemporary social themes, and when as a man of integrity he put his life on the line in behalf of the fated struggle for democracy in Spain. In reflexive response to the corruption of integrity which has overtaken his art as he has risen to power in Hollywood, Eitel rebuffs a congressional investigating committee seeking from him incriminating political testimony against his colleagues. In consequence, the industry blackballs him; and his loss of power and identity in the "imaginary" world is measured in personal terms by his loss of potency as both artist and lover. This sequential pattern of aspiration, action, corruption, moral illumination, renunciation, exile, and impotence precisely parallels the pattern of Sergius' life. Eitel is the distillate of the best values of the past by which Sergius has been fathered and orphaned, and for Sergius, consequently, the question of Eitel's destiny—the question of his potential for rebirth and self-renewal—has crucial moral significance.

Eitel stumbles upon a "second chance" in the form of Elena Esposito, and he muffs it.

Another man's castoff, she is soiled, tawdry, and simple. She is a poor dancer and a worse actress, and her manners are absurd. And yet she has the dignity and courage, and finally the beauty, of a being wholly natural. Eitel's affair with her becomes the nourishing ground of a new life for him. His sexual potency is restored, and with it his creative potency as he begins to work on a script which he imagines will be the redemption of his integrity as artist and man. But this new access of life fills him with fear; it is the stirring in him of the heroic imperative, with its attendant commitments to solitary batle, lonely journeyings in the unknown, and the risks of failure and defeat. The doors of Hollywood begin to open again, and the thrones and dominations of the "imaginary" world solicit his return: all he must do is confess and recant before the committee, and he may pass back through those doors. Half because of fear, half because of old habit, Eitel takes the easy way of surrender, shunning the hazardous alternatives (as Elena, significantly, does not) represented by those dark angels of life and truth, Don Beda, high priest of satyrism and orgy, and Marion Faye, the hipster prophet of criminal idealism. His harvest is the life-in-death of security through compromise, the corruption of his script and his talent, and eventual marriage to a broken and exhausted Elena, which is possible now that they are no longer "wedded" in a sacramental sense.

Elena is a noble figure—defeated, but honorably so, in her fated but heroic contest with time and what Hardy calls "crass casualty." Eitel's enemies have been lesser ones—history and social circumstance—and his defeat is pitiful rather than noble, because he has "sold out." But he has at least the saving grace of his ironic intelligence, which enables him to understand, when she proudly refuses his first offer of marriage, the principle of Elena's nobility: "the essence of spirit . . . was to choose the thing which did not better one's position but made it more perilous." Later on, when she has no more resources of refusal and he nourishes upon her defeat by "sacrificing" himself in marrying her, he understands his own corresponding cowardice: "there was that law of life so cruel and so just which demanded that one must grow or else pay more for remaining the same."

Eitel is Mailer's version of the traditional hero in his last historical incarnation. Vision, passion, and courage have dwindled in Eitel to intelligence, compassion, and guilt—the "cement" of the world, as Marion Faye contemptuously labels the last two, which binds men, enfeebles them, and turns them into spiritual "slobs." Eitel's very strengths are weaknesses, his virtues are faults, in a world where the apocalyptic beasts of anxiety and dread are raging in prisons of compromise and falsehood. And as the novel draws to its close and Eitel begins to fade into the penumbra of Sergius O'Shaugnessy's memorializing imagination, we are aware that the passing of the man is also the passing of the values he represented. Flanked by comic Lulu Meyers, a movie sex goddess who on impulse marries for "love" rather than career, and by tragic Marion Faye, whose anarch's code of black moral reason leads him behind prison bars, the now enlightened Sergius is the chief chalice-bearer of new human values. He becomes a bullfighter, stud, and teacher of both arts. And he begins to write, his books presumably fired by the existential perils and ecstasies of combat and sexuality. Though the novel ends on a cheerful note of metaphysical exhilaration, Sergius, both as a character and as an archetype of new styles of human value, is vague and inchoate as well as faintly absurd. Sergius has survived all sorts of traumas and temptations and come through to freedom, but he is not very much more fully realized as an exemplar of new values in action than was his predecessor, Lovett. He has come to terms with the world that has wounded him, and like the good Emersonian "fatalists" that all such Mailer heroes are, he affirms it as his destined inheritance from nature and history. But neither he nor his author has yet found the requisite life-style, the new heroic mold through which to turn understanding and affirmation into creative, perhaps redemptive action.

Life threatened in our time by the forces of death is Mailer's subject everywhere. When as a realist, as in *The Naked and the Dead*, life is stalemated and defeated by the forces of death. In the next two novels the intensities of anxiety and dread underlying Mailer's subject matter begin to dominate the rational, circumjacent forms of the realist, distorting them in the direction of the expressionistic and the surreal. And with this modification of form comes a coordinate modification of the heroes in whom the issue of the life-death struggle is finally centered. The narrator-hero of *Barbary Shore*, for whom the action encompassed by his consciousness is an elaborately instructive morality play, in the end escapes paralysis and spiritual death. The similarly educated narrator-hero of *The Deer Park* not only escapes but, as he bids fond farewell to the memories of the defeated and destroyed, discerns in the very chemistry of the disease and decomposition all around him the flicker and spur of new possibilities for life. "Think of Sex as Time," says "God" in a final dialogue with Sergius, "and Time as the connection of new circuits."

Barbary Shore and *The Deer Park*, both of them fictional investigations of the operative laws of death and endings, are novels that end with beginnings. Mailer's next novel, *An American Dream*, published in 1965, is in every way an extension and intensification of the manner and substance of its two predecessors.

It begins, significantly, with an ending: the hero saves himself from spiritual death by committing a murder that restores him to life, action, growth. Seen in relation to *An American Dream*, the two preceding novels have the look of a single imaginative action of a precursory nature: a complex psycho-dramatic "sloughing-off," to use Lawrence's terms in *Studies in Classic American Literature*, of the "old consciousness" of an outworn idealistic humanism in preparation for a "new consciousness" requisite for survival and significant life in a psychotic world bordering on apocalypse and yearning toward death. The experiential educations of Mikey Lovett and Sergius O'Shaugnessy in *Barbary Shore* and *The Deer Park* are preparations of this "new consciousness" for active engagement with the world. Steve Rojack and D. J. Jethroe—respectively heroes of *An American Dream* and *Why Are We in Vietnam?*—are the beneficiaries of this process. Rojack, in a moment of freeing impulse, murders his rich, preternaturally domineering, death-threatening wife, Deborah, a "bitch-goddess" of American power and the summation of the death-force of historical fate. The charge of this self-galvanizing destruction of his immediate enemy propels him into action, turning fear, fatigue, and despair into a redemptive energy of desperation. With a courage nourished on the ultimate dread, the dread of death, he runs a varied course of triumphs—besting the sexual enmity of a cold nymphomaniac, the hunting wile of the police, the competition of a Negro stud of legendary sexual prowess, and an engulfing sea of guilt and self-doubt summoned by Deborah's father, Barney Kelly. He even finds love along the way, with a tender, used, and charming cabaret singer named Cherry. A composite of American realities like Deborah, she is Deborah's opposite and complement, a plucky victim of the forces of which Deborah is the emblematic goddess and proprietress. At the end Rojack is still running—his roles and costumes of war hero, congressman, professor, television personality, and husband of a socialite left far behind—now toward the darker and simpler challenges of the jungles of Guatemala and Yucatán.

In *Why Are We in Vietnam?* (1967), D. J. Jethroe has already reached his Guatemala and Yucatán. High on pot, the prose of the Marquis de Sade and William Burroughs, and the cheerfully psychotic inspiration that he may be the voice of a "Harlem spade" imprisoned in the body of the son of a white Dallas tycoon, he tells the story of how he got that way. It is an initiation story (new style) as *An American Dream* was a new-style story of sacrifice and redemption. The initiation, product of a hunting "safari" to Alaska with his father, Rusty, D.J.'s best friend, Tex, and assorted guides and associates, has two phases, both of them involving radical divestments and ultimate tests of courage. In the first phase, D.J. breaks spiritually with his father when, out of habits of competitive vanity and self-justification, his father claims the grizzly bear that D.J. has mortally wounded, violating not only the father-son bond as reinforced by the hunt (stalking their dangerous quarry D.J. sees himself and his father as "war buddies") but also the sacred blood bound between killer and prey. Thinks D.J., "Final end of love of one son for one father." The second phase of the initiation, fruit of the alienation and frustration sown by the first, is the twenty-four-hour northward foray of D.J. and Tex, alone and without guns or instruments, into the wild heart of the Brooks Range. In an ecstasy of fear and trembling they witness a pageant of savageries—wolf, eagle, bear, caribou, and moose, the figments of natural life locked in struggle with death—culminating in a cosmic eruption of the Northern Lights that is so mag-

nificent and intense as to bring them to the border of orgy and fratricide: "they were twins, never to be as lovers again, but killer brothers, armed by something, prince of darkness, lord of light, they did not know." They make a bond in an exchange of blood, "the deep beast whispering, Fulfill my will, go forth and kill." At the end, D.J., now eighteen, looks beyond the Brooks Range of his initiatory "Guatemala and Yucatán" toward his mature destiny: "Hot damn, Vietnam."

D.J. is the voice of the anxieties and compulsions that have accumulated beneath the patterns of America's history and exploded at last in the manifest violence and chaos of its present. In the electric North, which is the voltaic pile of a continent's repressed, distorted, and perverted life-energies, he has faced Demogorgon, and he comes back metamorphosed, a rudely American voice of bardic ecstasy and prophecy. Completing the journey of transformation only begun by Lovett and Sergius O'Shaugnessy, D.J. and Steve Rojack have successfully tracked the power of life, thieved by a conspiracy of history with nature from its traditional home in the light, to its new home in darkness. In accomplishing this, they become exemplars of that "new consciousness" requisite to continuing life's ancient battle against death in a psychotic world bordering on apocalyptic crisis.

Richard Poirier, identifying Mailer with Eliot's vision, sees him as similarly spurred by the "de-creative" aspects of creation. But if this is true, Mailer is even more closely related to Lawrence, who in the voice of Rupert Birkin of *Women in Love* discerned among the "marsh-flowers" of "destructive creation" certain blossoms that while they were spawned by the all-enveloping historical process of "universal dissolution" were not "*fleurs du mal*," but, rather, "roses, warm and flamy." Lawrence himself was one of these exotic exceptions.

And so is Mailer. If the roots of both writers necessarily nourish upon the food of darkness, the blossoms produced are bright with the warm colors of life, and grow toward the light. In Lawrence the blossom is the "man who has come through," the separate natural self released through the death of the conventional social self into a living and changing "star-equilibrium" with the otherness of nature and woman. In Mailer it is all this and a bit more: history, impelled by the American dream turned to nightmare, is a third constituent of the otherness, and the reborn self becomes an "existential hero."

Advertisements for Myself (1959) and *The Presidential Papers* (1963) are large and various but nevertheless unified collections of pieces, mostly nonfiction, written during the dozen years following Mailer's tentative effort and partial failure to achieve a new form in *Barbary Shore*. As books principally about their author, *Advertisements for Myself* and *The Presidential Papers* taken together have the shape, like *Barbary Shore* and *The Deer Park*, of a single action, the complex and difficult action of "sloughing off" the "old consciousness." "The existential hero," first coming to full life in *An American Dream* and *Why Are We in Vietnam?*, is Mailer's realization of this new style of consciousness. And *Advertisements for Myself* and *The Presidential Papers* are the record of its gestation in the mind of its creator, and of the large and small deaths prerequisite to its coming to birth.

Mailer uses his own "personality," he tells us, as the "armature" of *Advertisements*—an image aptly descriptive of both its form and its impact. The reciprocal emotions of dread and determination whirl at the center of the book, as its author frankly appraises, at mid-career, his qualified victories and larger defeats during more than a decade of trying to live up to his potentials and ambitions as a man and writer. The pieces collected in *Advertisements*—stories, essays, and poems; polemics, meditations, and interviews; fragments of plays-in-progress and novels-to-be—are the measure of the worth of the life being lived, the substance of the tale being told. It is a tale, like Fitzgerald's in the *Crack-Up* essays, of early success, subsequent failure and demoralization, and the reflexive counterthrust of self-regeneration and re-creation. *The Naked and the Dead*, which catapulted him to sudden and youthful fame, had, as he tells us in *Advertisements*, been "easy to write." But nothing would be so easy again, for this success was the beginning of his "existentialism," which was "forced upon [him]," as he says, by his finding himself "prominent and empty," a "personage," at twenty-five. He must justify the prominence and fill the emptiness. With such heroic models before him as the life-style of Hemingway and the *oeuvre* of Malraux, he thrusts experimentally into new territory with *Barbary Shore*, "the first of the existentialist novels in America." The hostility and ridicule with which it is greeted in 1951 knock him down. Deflated, ill, and anxious, he turns to writing "respectable" short stories in the earlier manner and jaunty socio-political polemics for such magazines as *Partisan Review* and *Dissent* (of which he also becomes an editor). All this is a sort of distraction and temporizing in the face of the big comeback, the planned colossal counterpunch which might dazzle the world with a starfall and revelations: a projected eight-volume novel of cosmic proportions whose framing consciousness, a minor man and an artist *manqué* named Sam Slovoda, has an alter ego dream-hero named Sergius O'Shaugnessy. The great work hovering in the wings refuses to emerge. But two related fragments appear, both of them again in the new manner: the story "The Man Who Loved Yoga," which is to be the great work's prologue, and a protracted but relevant detour from the main route, a novel called *The Deer Park*.

The story of the vicissitudes accompanying *The Deer Park*'s publication and reception, most of it recounted in *Advertisements*, could itself be the stuff of a novel. The bad reception of *Barbary Shore* in 1951 and Mailer's divorce in 1952 are elements of a continuing pattern of gathering personal distress which characterize the years of *The Deer Park*'s composition. These distresses reach a penultimate crisis when *The Deer Park*, already in page proof, is suddenly held up by its publisher: Stanley Rinehart finds in it something unacceptably obscene. Just recently Mailer has accepted the challenge of writing an essay called "The Homosexual Villain" at the invitation of the magazine *One*, an undertaking which has blown up a "log jam of accumulated timidities and restraints" in him. Partially as a consequence, he refuses to make the change in *The Deer Park* for Rinehart, and the deal is off. The next ten weeks, at the end of which *The Deer Park* will be accepted by Putnam after refusal by several other houses, is a time of crisis for Mailer. He has undergone another death—the death of certain illusions about himself as "a figure in the landscape," and about the "honor" of publishers and writers in the American present—and feels himself becoming a "psychic outlaw."

Drawing his powers now from forays into the worlds of jazz, Harlem, and marijuana, he sees that the style of *The Deer Park* is wrong for the narrator he wants to create—it is too poetic, in the vein of Fitzgerald's Nick Carraway. He begins to rewrite from page proof, thirsting for the kind of self-redemptive success which would change the world a little, and at the same time dreading the possibility of a bad reception and low sales. The revised *The Deer Park*, once published, is only a "middling success." And Mailer measures the quality of its success not only by sales and reviews but also by the glimpses of possibility that have begun to emerge for the harried author with his last-minute impetus to rewrite it. Though tentative and incomplete, the accomplished changes adumbrate a new hero: the tender, wounded, and detached observer of the earlier version has begun to turn into a Sergius O'Shaugnessy who is not only "good" but also "ambitious"; a Sergius who, instead of virtuously spurning Hollywood's offer to film his life, might have taken the bait in a spirit of adventure and run it to some perilous triumph. The published book, its author laments, is but a hint of what might have been: the masterpiece in Mailer's generation equivalent to *The Sun Also Rises* in Hemingway's. As a "middling success," *The Deer Park* represents to its author his gross failure to bid on "the biggest hand" he had ever held, and a discovery that after all he hadn't the magic to "hasten the time of apocalypse."

But even so, this fumble, this failure, is no dead end. Like the emptiness of his success with *The Naked and the Dead*, and the fullness of his failure with *Barbary Shore*, it is a threshold to possibility. He has a vision, now, of what he must try to be and do as a writer, and of how considerable are the odds ranged against him. And like Sergius, who takes up bullfighting at the end of *The Deer Park*, he moves directly into the arena of the world's action as a matador of existential polemics—a rebel general of "Hip"—in the pages of *The Village Voice*, which he helped found in 1955. Though a fresh excursion into novel-writing is delayed by these side trips into journalism, *The Village Voice* pieces are important as snapshots of the "new" Mailer soon fully to emerge as exemplar and spokesman of the needed "new consciousness." His first important effort in the new mode is the essay *The*

White Negro, written in 1957 and first published, by City Lights, in 1958 (it was reprinted in *Advertisements*).

A speculative psycho-cultural essay on the modern predicament, *The White Negro* is a paradigm of the vision, the ideas, the motifs and symbols that will shape all of Mailer's future work in whatever form. The Hipster refuses to capitulate to the repressive denaturing, dehumanizing death-force of a "totalitarian" society. But because he is active—unlike the bourgeois "beat" who withdraws and passively sublimates in the surrogate quasi-life of song, flowers, meditation, hallucinogens, and "love"—he is confronted by the immediate dangers of physical violence and death. Like the black he is an *un*citizen (hence the label "white Negro") and danger is the medium of his life. Pleasure is his end; energy, courage, and wile are his means. The dynamic poise of his life-style implies the constitution, in microcosm, of a whole culture: decorums of manners, dress, language; an ethic; an aesthetic; even, finally, a metaphysic and a theology. The philosophy of the Hip, Mailer reflects, is the formed insight of a "radical humanist" "brooding" on the energizing phenomenon of the black revolution in contemporary America.

The Hipster is, of course, only one of many possible realizations of the "new consciousness" of which Mailer is the prophet. He is but one version of the idea of the existential hero, whose incarnation not only *may* but *must* be limitless and unpredictable. For the existential hero is the Dostoevskian underground man come aboveground into the Tolstoian mainstream of history. It is not known what he will be there, only that he will *do*—his being a function of his acting, rather than the other way around. He is a Sisyphus released from the stone of his dogged abstract commitment, a Hemingway galvanized into new life by the very terrors that threaten paralysis and death.

Evading the fateful impasse between heroic "intactness" and human "completeness" that destroyed Fitzgerald's Dick Diver, he is a vital synthesis of the polar values of self-control and spontaneity represented in *The Deer Park* by Marion Faye, the black puritan of moral scruple, and Don Beda, the rosy orgiast of the senses. Extensively educated in anguish, division, and impotence, Sergius O'Shaugnessy has just touched the regenerative power of that synthesis when the book of his salvation closes. The same efflorescence in his creator, which achieves full bloom in *The Presidential Papers*, seems to have been nourished by a similar curriculum, as recounted in *Advertisements*, of prior defeats and despairs. *Advertisements*, in contrast to its successor, *The Presidential Papers*, is a book in the mode of elegy, recording in lyric regret and anger the difficulty passing of romantic idealism and the death of youth's illusions. But *Advertisements* also has elegy's *dramatic* mode, being shaped as a total action embodying patterns of divestment and purgation which yield up at last a clear prospect of fresh possibilities: "Tomorrow to fresh woods, and pastures new." *The White Negro*, which Mailer tells us was written in the depths of "fear that I was no longer a writer," turns out to be the bright and central song of a "man who has come through." It is after all, he sees, one of his "best things." In it, and in the pair of stories in the "existential" mode, "The Time of Her Time" and "Advertisements for Myself on the Way Out," published at the close of *Advertisements*, can be found, as he says, "the real end of this muted autobiography of the near-beat adventurer who was myself."

The end of a life, whether well or badly lived, Mailer writes in *Advertisements*, is "seed." The "seed" of the agonies survived by the hero of *Advertisements* is *The Presidential Papers*, in which the author steps forth, recreated as public man and existentialist prophet, to address America and its leaders on the exigent realities of the age.

The "armature" of this book is not the author's personality in crisis, but, rather, an *idea* —the idea of "existential politics": "Existential politics is simple. It has a basic argument: if there is a strong ineradicable strain in human nature, one must not try to suppress it or anomaly, cancer and plague will follow. Instead one must find an art into which it can grow." In *The Presidential Papers* the pattern of personal crisis and salvation of self traced in *Advertisements* has been transmuted, by the chemistry of analogy so characteristic of Mailer's imagination, into the public terms of politics and history. But though the drama is now public rather than private, Mailer's self is no less central to the action. In the preface to *The Presidential Papers* he defines his role: to infuse John F. Kennedy, whose glamour and magnetism give him the potential of an "existential hero" in the arena of politics, with the requisite "existential" political consciousness. Mailer's commitment here is to steal back, for the languishing forces of "God," some of the energies of life which have passed over to the forces of darkness. But because history has moved so far on the downward path of de-creation, he must do it as a kind of undercover agent: he must perforce speak as a "devil." His first success as a metaphysical Robin Hood is his brilliant *Esquire* piece on Kennedy's nomination by the 1960 Democratic convention, which was written, despite his candidate's moribund "liberal" program, for the purpose of getting this rare man, so blessed "with a face," elected. (For it was Mailer's belief that this essay, a product of his "Faustian" pact with "Mephisto," was the generative cause of Kennedy's small plurality over Nixon in the election.) The rest of *The Presidential Papers* is a contemporaneous critique (with the blood, sweat, and tears of immediate response staining the pages) of "the Kennedy years," that ambiguous and perhaps despair-making historical return on its author's original existential wager.

Of all the fine pieces following, perhaps the most memorable is the essay on the Patterson-Liston fight, subtitled "Death." This essay is many things: It is a skillful piece of evocative journalism about an actual event; a symbolist's reading of the forces at war in the submerged psyche of America; a strange, oblique prophecy, through a poet's analysis of the attrition and inevitable doom of the spirit of American liberal idealism, of Kennedy's assassination. It is also a gaily profound exploration of the absurdity, and perhaps the peril, awaiting the writer as performing tragic-comedian whose ambition is to ride at the same time both bright Pegasus and the dark horses of wrath. But if the end—or "seed"—of life is life itself, then that effort must be made in spite of all hazard: "To believe the impossible may be won," Mailer writes elsewhere in *The Presidential Papers*, "creates a strength from which the impossible may be attacked." And in our time, though the memory of "God" and the light may shape ultimate heroic purpose, the hero draws nourishment for his "humanism" (a favorite recurring word of Mailer's) from the devil's realm, venturing ever more deeply —as Mailer does in the barbarous poems and scatological dialogues collected in *Cannibals and Christians*—into the territories of darkness.

Cannibals and Christians, published in 1966, is not so good a book as its two omnibus predecessors, though it has its bright spots, such as the piece on Goldwater's nomination and the temptation it wakens in its author to ride this newest bandwagon of the devil. The drama of self-discovery and re-creation, which gave unity to the brilliance and variety of *Advertisements* and *Papers*, is slowed and muffled in *Cannibals* by the didactic accents of the guru who gazes upon a vision that is cooling toward dogma and repetition. But it is perhaps understandable that the imaginative breakthrough represented by *An American Dream* should be followed by a somewhat studious contemplation of the truths revealed, for something more than half of the stuff of *Cannibals* was written shortly after *Dream*. Mailer himself seems to be aware of the condition. Written in a time of "plague" and under a lurid cloud of apocalyptic expectations, the collection is concerned with themes, he says, more appropriate to a novel. He feels again the impulse to "go back to that long novel," announced several years back but still unwritten. *Cannibals*, he reflects, may be the last such collection for a while. Af course, it was not the last.

After *Cannibals*, in addition to publishing *Why Are We in Vietnam?* Mailer produced off Broadway his dramatization of *The Deer Park*, a crisply successful play in which a much clearer and more effective Sergius O'Shaughnessy was purchased at the expense of the novel's richly internal realization of Eitel and Elena. He also directed, produced, and starred in three full-length "existential" films of his own conceiving. The requisite honors began, belatedly, to come his way: in 1967 he was elected to the National Institute of Arts and Letters. And in October of the same year, this author of twelve books, father of six children, and veteran of four wives—"heroines all," he once gallantly affirmed—proved his continued interest in the public life of his time by getting himself arrested, jailed, and fined for an act of civil disobedience in the great Washington demonstrations against the war in Vietnam.

The immediate result of this experience was *The Armies of the Night*, published in the spring of 1968, a kind of autobiographical novel with a protagonist called "Mailer" who is at once an absurd citizen of "technology-land" in crisis and a bard of the bright dream that lies behind the thickening miasmas of the betrayed and perishing republic. It is unquestionably one of Mailer's best books—passionate, humorous, acutely intelligent, and, as always, eloquent in its empathy with the drift of history. It has new riches in it, too, of a more incidental kind, such as a gallery of sharply intimate verbal cartoons, highlighted with the reflected pigments of Mailer's own uniquely anxious self-image, of such primary men of the 1960's as Robert Lowell, Dwight Macdonald, and Paul Goodman. But most striking of all are its undercurrents of a softer emotion, a new tenderness for life that lets the author muse warmly along the way on his troubled love for his wife, his children, his mythic America. There is even a touch of nostalgic religious craving in it, a small recurring thirst for "Christ." But though the texture of feeling is more varied, the old Mailer, familiarly gravid with the epic furies and ambitions of a diminutive Brooklyn Achilles, still prevails, as the following excerpt reveals:

"Mailer, looking back, thought bitter words he would not say: 'You, Lowell, beloved poet of many, what do you know of the dirt and the dark deliveries of the necessary? What do you know of dignity hard-achieved, and dignity lost through innocence, and dignity lost by sacrifice for a cause one cannot name? What do you know about getting fat against your will, and turning into a clown of an arriviste baron when you would rather be an eagle or a count, or rarest of all, some natural aristocrat from these damned democratic states? No, the only subject we share, you and I, is that species of perception which shows that if we are not very loyal to our unendurable and most exigent nner light, then some day we may burn. How dare you condemn me! . . . How dare you scorn the explosive I employ?' "

Lowell falls backward at this moment in the

narrative, a noble Hector going bump on his head, as if toppled by the lightning bolt of his adversary's thought. Though *The Armies of the Night* is tempered with new softnesses and warmths, such passages would deter one from concluding too easily that Mailer might have been getting ready to write his hymn of reconciliation—his *Tempest* or "Lapis Lazuli," his *Billy Budd* or *Old Man and the Sea*.

Good as *The Armies of the Night* is, and prolific in a variety of media as Mailer has been since its publication, the great opus so long ago announced remains unachieved. Were such varied and frequent detours from the high road of novel-writing threatening, at this prime of his creative life, the ultimate dissipation of Mailer's talent as a major writer? This already familiar question was raised yet again by an interviewer in *Playboy* for January 1968. Mailer answered that the pattern of his career was dictated by his instinctive feeling that "the best way to grow was not to write one novel after another but to move from activity to activity, a notion that began with Renaissance man." He did not mention the example of Milton, but he might as well have. Then, coming down off the high horse of the moment's rhetoric, he added genially, "It's not my idea, after all."

He was, of course, right both about himself and about "the tradition." With the romantic movent the imaginative writer became alienated from public life. Next, under the neoclassical reactive pressure of modernist formalism, he became in a sense alienated even from his work—which was not to be an utterance but an object, a product of the "impersonal" operations of imagination. With this background in view, it is clear that Mailer's uniqueness as a mid-century writer lay in his conscious cultivation, in the manner of Yeats, of a dynamic interrelation between his art and his life-style. Intensely himself, he was never-

theless the writer reborn in the dimension of public man. Engorged with the inclusive themes of his age and his nation, his work has been nevertheless deeply personal. "I've been working on one book most of my life," he told the *Playboy* interviewer. "Probably since I started with *Barbary Shore*, certainly with and since *The Deer Park*, I've been working on one book." As he tells us in the introduction to *Cannibals and Christians*, he is, like Lawrence, Henry Miller, and Hemingway, writing "one continuing book . . . of [his] life and the vision of [his] existence." He might also have mentioned Fitzgerald, whom he resembles in this respect as well as in many others, including his sense of the integral relation between the moral health of the artist and the quality of his art conceived as "style." "A really good style," said Mailer in his *Paris Review* interview of 1964, as if in echo of a dozen similar testimonies by Fitzgerald, "comes only when a man has become as good as he can be. Style is character."

As late as the early sixties, fairly literate people—often critics and teachers—were still saying that though Mailer certainly had a novelist's gift he "couldn't write." He was in their minds a kind of James Jones who, with no appropriate arsenal of sophistication, had gone adventuring into frontier territories of the imagination and was never heard of again. "I can't read him any more," they would say; and it was at least evident that these people who made themselves responsible for keeping up with Bellow and Malamud, Styron and Barth—current writers favored with recognition by the critical establishment—*weren't* reading him, whether or not they *couldn't* read him. To them he was at once nuttier than D. H. Lawrence, dumber than Sinclair Lewis, artistically more unselective than Thomas Wolfe, these faults clumsily wrapped in a style as undistinguished as Dreiser's. Because they weren't reading him it wasn't possible to argue with any hope of success that his "beliefs" were the poetical vehicles of a metaphysician's speculative insights; that he was the only important novelist on the American scene who was also an authentic and sophisticated intellectual; that if he was temperamentally the inclusive artist, he was also deftly capable of the lean and compact virtuoso performance; and that as a "stylist" his brilliancy was matched by his variety and range. An example from *The Armies of the Night*:

"There was an aesthetic economy to symbolic gestures—you must not repeat yourself. Arrested once, TV land would accept him (conceivably) as a man willing to stand up for his ideas; get busted twice on the same day, and they would view him as a freak-out panting for arrest. (Mailer's habit of living—no matter how unsuccessfully—with his image, was so ingrained by now, that like a dutiful spouse he was forever consulting his better half.)"

The preceding is Mailer as incisive stylist, cutting an idea down to the gem of epigram at its center. Following is Mailer as progenitive stylist, pushing out from the central root-and-trunk idea a branch-bud-and-leaf exfoliation of confirmatory images:

"It is the wisdom of a man who senses death within him and gambles that he can cure it by risking his life. It is the therapy of the instinct, and who is so wise as to call it irrational? Before he went into the Navy, Kennedy had been ailing. Washed out of Freshman year at Princeton by a prolonged trough of yellow jaundice, sick for a year at Harvard, weak already in the back from an injury at football, his trials suggest the self-hatred of a man whose resentment and ambition are too large for his body. Not everyone can discharge their furies on an analyst's couch, for some angers can be relaxed only by winning power, some rages are sufficiently monumental to demand that one try to become a hero or else fall back into that death which is already within the cells. But if one succeeds, the energy aroused can be exceptional. . . . One thinks of that three-mile swim with the belt in his mouth and McMahon holding it behind him. There are pestilences which sit in the mouth and rot the teeth—in those five hours how much of the psyche must have been remade, for to give vent to the bite in one's jaws and yet use that rage to save a life: it is not so very many men who have the apocalptic sense that heroism is the First Doctor. . . . With such a man in office the myth of the nation would again be engaged. . . ."

Mailer's style is a style of eddying gusts and pointed audible silences textured on a background of the musing, ruminating, wondering human voice. Voice is the medium of his style, wit and amplification its chief instruments of artistic control. Through dynamic interplay of the reciprocal rhetorics of incision and proliferation, Mailer's style intends, through rhetorical implosion and explosion of the facts and patterns of common life, to force a new vision upon the reader, to disclose to him the submerged realities of his experience—to transform him, galvanize him, free him to become the vehicle of apocalypse. It is predictable that an imagination so metaphysically ambitious as Mailer's should generate fictions which, though open-ended and loosely shaped, contain a dense internal unity of interlocking analogies, and that that unity should be mirrored in a prose coordinately dense with analogizing metaphor.

Mailer's style of imagination is a *forcing* style: it exerts *force* upon reality; it seeks to *force* reality into the matrix of an idiosyncratic vision. This *urgency* is the key to Mailer's most prominent strengths: the relentless energy of desperation which makes *An American Dream* a single breathless action, and gathers the many moods and modes of *Advertisements* into a sharply unified portrait of the artist as a young man fighting the demons of crack-up; the monumentality of certain of his chief theme-bearing characters—John F. Kennedy and Herman Teppis, Sonny Liston and Deborah Kelly Rojack—who remain in the memory as vivid larger-than-life creatures of myth; and the fluency everywhere, from the close, sharp lash of the goading scatologist to the barreltoned magniloquence of the bard.

But these strengths are shadowed by related weaknesses: a flatness, stockness, vagueness in characterization often, when the fictionist in the author inevitably capitulates to the didact; a tendency to flatulence and clotted heaviness of expression that threaten to choke the naturally vigorous life of the prose; and an occasional self-permissive garrulousness that can, also, turn into tedium. One becomes bored, then finally deafened, by the sado-masochistic acid-head behop and chowder mannerisms of D. J. Jethroe's nonstop answer to the question Why Are We in Vietnam?, though there are "good things" in this work, and tightened up it might have made a memorable short story or novella. Sergius O'Shaugnessy is unfortunately vague, and Marion Faye is flat; their central moral significance in *The Deer Park* is diminished to abstraction and formula by their failure to be as human as the roundly conceived moral cripples surrounding them in the populous world of Desert D'Or. (Collie Munshin is a pretty bloom of humanity by comparison.) And the ingenious dialogues on the metaphysics of death and excrement in *The Presidential Papers* and *Cannibals and Christians* are, when all is said and done, overextended and boring. And boring is, of course, one of the most undesirable things you can be in the Mailer canon of humane values. These qualities represent a temptation perhaps innate to Mailer's kind of sensibility. In *The Armies of the Night*, for example, he is attracted by the

idea of "a short novel about a young American leading a double life in college as a secret policeman." Such a novel might be somewhat less vulnerable to prefabricated literary patterning than *Vietnam* (father-son tensions, heterosexual-homosexual tensions, man-beast tensions, all framed in a "significant" Texas-Alaska polar symbology); but even so it would threaten to become an "idea for a novel novel," something quite "made up" and possibly *forced*.

Toward the end of *The Armies of the Night*, Mailer writes of his feelings upon his release from jail after the demonstrations in Washington: "yes, in this resumption of the open air after twenty-four hours, no more, there was a sweet clean edge to the core of the substance of things—*a monumentally abstract remark which may be saved by the concrete observation* that the air was good in his lungs . . . [italics added]." The bard, perhaps wearied by labor too large and prolonged, has mauled a small bright human fact with the dull brutality of abstraction; and "Mailer," throwing off the robes of office, rebukes his alter ego for this crime against nature.

Mailer once wrote a story called "The Paper House," one of his conventionally "realistic" stories of the early 1950's that he did not take very seriously a decade later. The story is all about how reality takes its vengeance upon the criminal abstractionist. The setting is Japan. An arrogant, boorish, and selfish G.I. named Hayes is unsparingly loved by Yuriko, a geisha uncommonly endowed with dignity as well as tenderness. By night he nourishes upon her love. By day he is the thorough cynic: "crap" is what he calls the unhappy story of her family's misfortunes, her indenturing to training and service, and her final and staunch pride in earning the status of "first-class geisha." Crap: she is a common whore. He subconsciously wants to marry her, the natural concomitant in him of her unqualified love. But instead he drunkenly jeers at her: she is a common whore, and he will return to the States without her. When she responds by claiming him with increased vigor he strikes and strips her, brutally humiliating her before her peers and their clients. Later, when he meekly returns, she is as warm with him as ever, but sad and a bit withdrawn. What does this mean? She must go on a journey very soon, somewhat before his own departure for the States. Where? he persists. Why? What sort of journey? Finally he learns: because she, a first-class geisha, has been publicly dishonored by her lover, she will commit hari-kari. Crap! he cries in irritable disdain. He will speak no more of it. A whore is a whore! But through the days that follow, her familiar tender attentions are touched with silent grief. Though he does not deign to speak of her threat, inside he aches with dread. And on the appointed day he cannot hold himself back from going to her. He finds her dressed in white, "without ornament, and without makeup," pleased that he has come after all to say "Bye-bye." As she turns to go to her self-appointed justice, he catches her by the arm, crying, "You got to stop this. It's crap." "Crap-crap," says Yuriko in answer, giggling. And hidden all around, the other geishas echo, "Crap-crap." Hayes retreats, and the girls follow him, a massed march of laughing, bright-kimoned angels of derision jeering the conquered bully through the town to the chorused tune of "Crap-crap, Crap-crap."

A memorably fine story in its own right (Mailer acknowledges indebtedness to Vance Bourjaily for the anecdote on which it is based), it is also a model of Mailer's vision of marriage (in the soul-dimension Hayes and Yuriko are already "married') as the ultimate battleground of the laws of strife that govern love and sexuality, and in turn all of life. Alternatively turned on its side, upended, and inverted, "The Paper House" becomes a paradigm of the love-as-soulmaking-or-soulbreaking-combat themes of *The Deer Park*, "The Time of Her Time," and *An American Dream*. But it can also be read as a paradigm of the larger operations of a yet more ultimate law. In sharp contrast to his tender and humane buddy who narrates the story, Hayes is terrified of empathy. His is the naturally totalitarian temperament, bellowing, pounding, *forcing* reality to the shape of his belief. But Yuriko, whose unreasoning love frightens him into his worst brutality, *is* reality. The dignity of her otherness will not bend; she will not, finally, be forced. Her suavely just humiliation of her lover is so satisfying because it is a *natural* justice, a perfect illustration of the penalties which in the natural scheme of things are levied against unrepentant abstractions who sin, through violence or neglect, against the actual.

This formula may provide one explanation of why it is that some people "can't read" Mailer and why even those who can and do read him find themselves at times, especially when reading his fiction, fatigued, irritated, hankering after something which the apocalyptic apparatus of his imagination quite purposely extracts and draws off from his material so that no dilution will threaten the strong potion of his doctrine. Perhaps it is thanks to the just and beneficent workings of Yuriko's law that Mailer cannot finally succeed in this effort. Perhaps this explains why his best work, the work that moves as well as amazes, is his most "impure"—as in *The Deer Park*, where the mere presence of Charles Francis Eitel and Elena Esposito mocks, with the awesome poignant reality of their flawed selves and failed love, the unreality of Sergius O'Shaugnessy and Marion Faye, those stiff and faceless standard-bearers of the author's abstract redemptive "truth."

While Mailer has steadfastly refused to be

apologetic about his journalism, he has equally steadfastly identified his highest goals as a writer with some major achievement as a novelist. In *The Armies of the Night* he shows himself quite openly if good-humoredly annoyed by Robert Lowell's insistent praises of him as our greatest "journalist" at the same time he envies Lowell's quiet authority in the role of "poet." It is a fact, I think, that the large and responsive audience Mailer had won at the close of the sixties would tend to agree, no doubt to the writer's chagrin, that his "best" work has been in nonfiction. In putting forth my own concurrence I would want to make clear that while I view *Barbary Shore* and *Why Are We in Vietnam?* as inferior achievements (they are "abstract" in my sense of the word: they busy themselves making points rather than peopling a world; and the mannerisms of their prose, portentous in one case, ranting in the other, are inadequate compensation for this impoverishment) they nevertheless have interest and deserve respect in the total picture of Mailer's career as honorable attempts at experiment and innovation.

Granting the solid excellence—its truth of substance and feeling, as well as its art—of *The Naked and the Dead*, and the daring virtuosity of *An American Dream*, only *The Deer Park* remains in the running for honors as a "great" novel. Its depth and breadth of imaginative engagement with our time, its acute and inclusive sensing of our palsied and anxious life in mid-century America, through deft selection of setting and symbol and deft portraiture of a dozen varied secondary characters that are real as well as symptomatic, make it impressive. But as we move toward the core of this book— the affair between Elena and Eitel—surely we move from the impressive into the field of force of something like "greatness." Eitel, the hero-gentleman demeaned by history, is a complex character of almost tangible reality; he has all

the fullness of being that Fitzgerald could not finally give to Dick Diver. Elena, the soiled broad and dumb waif of petty disasters, is rich with an inner gift of instinctive warmth and natural dignity worthy of Cleopatra; she is one of the few great woman characters in American fiction after James. The delicate, tender persistence of Mailer's articulation of the life of their affair, its growth, flowering, deterioration, and crippled resolution, is rare and magnificent. It is the *real* "armature" of the book, despite Mailer's efforts to give that power to his prophets of new consciousness, Marion Faye and Sergius O'Shaugnessy. Because Sergius, like Lovett in *Barbary Shore*, seems neither intelligent nor sensitive nor good enough, nor even *visible* enough, to attract the friendship and confidence of a man like Eitel, we do not believe in him. But we cannot quite console ourselves by saying, with Lawrence, "Never trust the author, trust the tale," because we are distracted and fatigued as we read by the badgering of Mailer's forcing style of imagination—and the book's armature slows, finally, and falters. *The Deer Park*, one can say (Mailer's exactly opposite account of its shortcomings notwithstanding), was a potentially great novel flawed by an authorial excess of misled good intentions. It is perhaps yet another validation of Yuriko's law that what remains persistently alive in one's memory of *The Deer Park* is Eitel and Elena, and the real world, intimate and at large, of which they were the vital center.

In the middle 1950's Mailer professed a credo that would still seem to hold for him in the 1970's: "I suppose that the virtue I should like most to achieve as a writer is to be genuinely disturbing. . . . It is, I believe, the highest function a writer may serve, to see life (no matter by what means or form or experiment) as others do not see it, or only partially see it, and therefore open for the reader that literary experience which comes uniquely from the novel—the sense of having one's experience enlarged, one's perceptions deepened, and one's illusions about oneself rendered even more untenable. For me, this is the highest function of art, precisely that it is disturbing, that it does not let man rest, and therefore forces him so far as art may force anything to enlarge the horizons of his life." It is clear that most of his work to date has been done in the light of this statement of principle, and it seems probable that it will continue to be, if only because it is the kind of principle that any serious novelist of whatever artistic or philosophic persuasion would be likely to subscribe to with dedication. But it could be argued that in his fiction, at least, Mailer has yet to write a book worthy of the strictest interpretation of his principle. If he eventually completes the multivolume quasi-epic of neo-Joycean structure and Burroughs-*cum*-Tolstoian substance that he once promised, it probably will not be the novel, any more than his others have been, that fulfills the high aims of this credo. If he is to write a truly "great" novel, it will be the product of some new, subtler, and perhaps unimaginably humbler synthesis of the gifts for which he has now come to be appreciated. Perhaps he will learn something from his readers' obstinate tendency to prefer his nonfiction, where, with no sacrifice of his skills and all benefit to the power of his vision, he is mired in reality, hobbled to the facts of time, place, self, as to an indispensable spouse of flesh and blood who continually saves him from his other self that yearns toward wasteful flirtations with *Spiritus Mundi*. In any case, he will have to come to know truly, if in his own way, the "Thou" to which the "I" of Martin Buber's world is inexorably wedded, and he will have to find his own style of that "negative capability" which Keats identified as the root of true imagination.

Perhaps Mailer would dismiss such cavils as typical of the solemnly moribund mentality of official literary criticism. And yet he might be reminded that the newly respectful interest in his works, represented even by such exceptions as these, is the natural harvest, sought or not, of his maverick persistence in his calling—and for Mailer writing has always been, literally, a "calling"—despite the years of criticism's ignorant undervaluation of him. He has finally forced criticism, which once dismissed him as a sensationalist barbarian egomaniac who couldn't write, to eat its own words, salted and spiced with the true savor of his actual achievements. Criticism has been made to confess at last that Mailer is a symbolist and mythmaker, the alchemy of his imagination being capable of turning excrement, madness, and perversion into lambent revelations of the condition of man and God; that he is a true intellectual—acute, sophisticated, and dead serious in his probing criticisms of the life of his time; that he is an extraordinary prose stylist in the big-voiced American tradition of Melville and Faulkner, and that he is fortunately endowed, as most apocalyptics are not, with the easing human graces of wit and humor. Even such a book as *Advertisements for Myself*, which at the time of its publication so outraged and embarrassed the critics with its naked revelations of its author's wounds and vanities, has now come to seem, in the manner of Fitzgerald's *Crack-Up* essays, a nobly original undertaking of self-definition, moving in content and daring in execution. *Advertisements* represented the invention, furthermore, of a new form (let's call it, to borrow a contemporaneous term that has been misapplied elsewhere, the "nonfiction novel"), a form that has since served him especially well in *The Presidential Papers* and *The Armies of the Night*, and will no doubt continue to do so.

Mailer became what he now is, a leading writer of his time, by reacting with aggressive creativity to what he was not in the middle 1950's—a *recognized* leading writer. He took the fact of his situation and ran it imaginatively to a transforming myth. He literally created himself in the imaginations of his contemporaries, winning a domain where, before, he had been all but denied standing room. And the work that generated the myth and brought it to its fullness of life, from *Advertisements for Myself* to *The Armies of the Night*, was both masterly and unique.

But what came after, the magazine pieces and the books assembled from them, didn't seem the same. Mailer as imaginative master of the fact now seemed the fact's appendage. Where he had once ruled, and thrillingly, he now served, engagingly. A forthcoming championship boxing match, a space exploration, a national election—one knew that Mailer would interest himself in such events, and that soon one would be reading his published prose about his interesting himself in them. One had begun to know what to expect from Mailer because Mailer had succeded in just the way he did succeed.

A partial exception to this rule, perhaps, was *The Prisoner of Sex* (1971), Mailer's counterattack against the attack of a new generation of women's rights intellectuals upon male "chauvinism," including Mailer's own neo-Lawrencean brand of phallic mysticism. But the exception lay in the disappointment, this time, in finding one's expectations confirmed. The ideology of women's liberation was something politically new and vital in modern life, and Mailer's response to it was not "existential." It was only charming, shrewd, and stylish, an extension of cocktail-party dialectics and effective public showmanship. Mailer's response to the women ("the ladies") indicated that he did not understand that they were serious, and that this was not to be just another copy move in the sex game.

New books came forth from Norman Mailer in cheap disposable form (*St. George and the Godfather*, 1972, Mailer's account of the Nixon and McGovern candidacies for the presidency, was published only in a paper-cover edition), while large retrospective tomes (*The Long Patrol*, "twenty-five years of writing from the work of Norman Mailer," 1971) were issued in hard cover and at very high prices. An interpreter of symbols might see in this phenomenon a suggestion that Mailer's growth became arrested when he achieved "success," and that any following books were to be stuck on the achieved central monument as mere confirmatory fillips. This is, of course, a disagreeable interpretation for readers of Mailer who think of him as a uniquely gifted American writer of major stature. It might even be disagreeable for readers who just continue to enjoy his books without necessarily "thinking."

I hope that a reader of these words in some more or less distant future will be able to recall to himself that Mailer's next great period began, once the elections of 1972 were out of the way and the anguish of the Vietnam war was laid to rest, when Mr. Mailer, despite his own predilections and the monetary blandishments of publishers, decided *not* to write a book on the second Fraser-Ali championship fight.

Selected Bibliography

WORKS OF NORMAN MAILER

NOVELS AND COLLECTIONS OF SHORT STORIES
The Naked and the Dead. New York: Holt, Rinehart and Winston, 1948.
Barbary Shore. New York: Holt, Rinehart and Winston, 1951.

The Deer Park. New York: Putnam, 1955; Dial Press, 1967.

An American Dream. New York: Dial Press, 1965.

The Short Fiction of Norman Mailer. New York: Dell (paperback), 1967.

Why Are We in Vietnam? New York: Putnam, 1967.

The Executioner's Song. Boston: Little, Brown, 1979.

Ancient Evenings. Boston: Little, Brown, 1983.

Tough Guys Don't Dance. New York: Random House, 1984.

PROSE

Advertisements for Myself. New York: Putnam, 1959.

The Presidential Papers. New York: Putnam, 1963.

Cannibals and Christians. New York: Dial Press, 1966.

The Armies of the Night. New York: New American Library, 1968.

The Bullfight, a Photographic Narrative with Text by Norman Mailer. New York: CBS Legacy Collection Book, distributed by Macmillan, 1967.

The Idol and the Octopus: Political Writings by Norman Mailer on the Johnson and Kennedy Administrations. New York: Dell, 1968.

Miami and the Siege of Chicago: An Informal History of the Republican and Democratic Conventions of 1968. New York: World, 1968.

Of a Fire on the Moon. Boston: Little, Brown, 1970.

The Prisoner of Sex. Boston: Little, Brown, 1971.

Maidstone, a Mystery. New York: Signet (paperback), 1971.

The Long Patrol, twenty-five years of writing by Norman Mailer, edited by Robert F. Lucid. New York: World, 1971.

Existential Errands. Boston: Little, Brown, 1972.

St. George and the Godfather. New York: Signet (paperback), 1972.

Marilyn [Monroe], a biography. New York: Grosset & Dunlop, 1973.

The Fight. Boston: Little, Brown, 1975.

Some Honorable Men: Political Conventions. 1960-1972. Boston: Little, Brown, 1976. (A collection of earlier writings.)

Genius and Lust. New York: Grove Press, 1976.

A Transit to Narcissus: A Facsimile of the Original Typescript. New York: Fertig, 1978.

Of a Small & Modest Malignancy, Wicked & Bristling with Dots. Limited ed. Northridge, Calif.: Lord John Press, 1980.

Black Messiah, Mailer, Norman et al. Ellensburg, Wash.: Vagabond Press, 1981. (Anthology in tribute to Henry Miller.)

Of Women and Their Elegance. Stamford, Conn.: Pinnacle Books, 1981.

Pieces. Boston: Little, Brown, 1982. (Essays.)

Pontifications. Boston: Little, Brown, 1982. (Interviews.)

PLAY

The Deer Park. New York: Dial Press, 1967.

POEMS

Deaths for the Ladies, and Other Disasters. New York: Putnam, 1962.

CRITICAL AND BIOGRAPHICAL STUDIES

Aldridge, John W. Time to Murder and Create. New York: McKay, 1966.

———. "From Vietnam to Obscenity," Harper's, 236:91–97 (February, 1968). In Lucid, pp. 180–192.

Alter, Robert. "The Real and Imaginary Worlds of Norman Mailer," Midstream, 15:24–35 (January, 1969).

Baldwin, James. "The Black Looks at the White Boy," Esquire, 55:102–06 (May 1961). In Lucid, pp. 218–37; in Braudy, pp. 66–81.

Bersani, Leo. "Interpretation of Dreams," Partisan Review, 32:603–08. In Lucid, 171–79; in Braudy, pp. 120–26.

Blotner, Joseph. The Political Novel in America. Austin and London: University of Texas Press, 1966.

Braudy, Leo, ed. Norman Mailer, a Collection of Critical Essays. Englewood Cliffs, N.J.: Prentice-Hall, 1972.

Breit, Harvey. The Writer Observed. Cleveland and New York: World, 1956.

Brown, C. H. "Rise of New Journalism," *Current*, 141:31–38 (June 1972).

Burgess, Anthony. "The Postwar American Novel: A View from the Periphery," *American-German Review*, 35:150–56 (Winter 1965–66).

Carroll, Paul. "An Interview with Norman Mailer," *Playboy*, 15:69–84 (January 1968). In Lucid, pp. 259–95.

Corrington, J. W. "An American Dream," *Chicago Review*, 18:58–66 (Summer 1965).

Cowan, Michael. "The Americanness of Norman Mailer," in *Norman Mailer, a Collection of Critical Essays*, edited by Leo Braudy. Englewood Cliffs, N.J.: Prentice-Hall, 1972. Pp. 143–57.

Dienstfrey, Harris. "Norman Mailer," in *On Contemporary Literature*, edited by Richard Kostelanetz. New York: Avon, 1964.

Eisinger, Chester E. *Fiction of the Fifties*. Chicago: University of Chicago Press, 1963.

Elliott, George P. "Destroyers, Defilers, and Confusers of Men," *Atlantic Monthly*, 222:74–80 (December 1968).

Flaherty, Joe. *Managing Mailer*. New York: Coward-McCann, 1970.

Foster, Richard. "Mailer and the Fitzgerald Tradition," *Novel*, 1:219–30 (Spring 1968). In Braudy, pp. 127–42.

Glicksberg, Charles I. "Norman Mailer: The Angry Young Novelist in America," *Wisconsin Studies in Contemporary Literature*, 1:25–34 (Winter 1960).

Gordon, Andrew. "*The Naked and the Dead:* The Triumph of Impotence," *Literature and Psychology*, 19:3–13 (1969).

Green, Martin. "Amis and Mailer: The Faustian Contract," *Month*, 3:45–48, 52 (February 1971).

Greer, Germaine. "My Mailer Problem," *Esquire*, 76:90–93, 214, 216 (September 1971).

Harper, Howard M., Jr. *Desperate Faith*. Chapel Hill: University of North Carolina Press, 1967.

Hassan, Ihab. "The Novel of Outrage: A Minority Voice in Postwar American Fiction," *American-German Review*, 34:239–53 (Spring 1965).

Hoffman, Frederick J. "Norman Mailer and the Heart of the Ego: Some Observations on Recent American Literature," *Wisconsin Studies in Contemporary Literature*, 1:5–12 (Fall 1960).

Kaufmann, Donald L. *Norman Mailer: The Countdown*. Carbondale: Southern Illinois University Press, 1969.

Kazin, Alfred. *Contemporaries*. Boston: Little, Brown, 1962. "How Good Is Norman Mailer?" in Lucid, pp. 89–94.

Leeds, Barry H. *The Structured Vision of Norman Mailer*. New York: New York University Press, 1969.

Lodge, David. "The Novelist at the Crossroads," *Critical Quarterly*, 11:105–32 (Summer 1969).

Lucid, Robert F., ed. *Norman Mailer: The Man and His Work*. Boston: Little, Brown, 1971.

Ludwig, Jack. *Recent American Novelists*. Minneapolis: University of Minnesota Press, 1962.

Macdonald, Dwight. "Massachusetts vs. Mailer," in Lucid, pp. 203–17.

Marcus, Steven. "An Interview with Norman Mailer," *The Paris Review*, 8:28–58 (Winter–Spring 1964). In Braudy, pp. 21–41.

Manso, Peter, ed. *Running against the Machine: The Mailer-Breslin Campaign*. Garden City, N.Y.: Doubleday, 1969.

Martien, Norman. "Norman Mailer at Graduate School: One Man's Effort," *New American Review* (September 1967). In Lucid, pp. 245–55.

Millet, Kate. *Sexual Politics*. Garden City, N.Y.: Doubleday, 1970.

Millgate, Michael. *American Social Fiction: James to Cozzens*. Edinburgh and London: Oliver and Boyd, 1964.

Newman, Paul B. "Mailer: The Jew as Existentialist," *North American Review*, 2:48–55 (July 1965).

"Norman Mailer: An Interview," in *Writers at Work: The Paris Review Interviews* (third series), with introduction by Alfred Kazin. New York: Viking Press, 1967.

Peter, John. "The Self-Effacement of the Novelist," *Malahat Review*, 8:119–28 (October 1968).

Podhoretz, Norman. "Norman Mailer: The Embattled Vision," *Partisan Review*, 26:371–91 (Summer 1959). In Lucid, pp. 60–85.

Poirier, Richard. "T. S. Eliot and the Literature of Waste," *New Republic*, 156:19–25 (May

20, 1967).

Schrader, George A. "Norman Mailer and the Despair of Defiance," *Yale Review*, 51:267–80 (Winter 1962). In Braudy, pp. 82–95.

Schulz, Max F. "Mailer's Divine Comedy," *Contemporary Literature*, 9:36–57 (Winter 1968).

Sheed, Wilfrid. "Genius or Nothing: A View of Norman Mailer," *Encounter*, 36:66–71 (June 1971).

Sokoloff, B. A. *A Comprehensive Bibliography of Norman Mailer*. Limited ed. Darby, Pa.: Darby Books, 1970.

Solotaroff, Robert. "Down Mailer's Way," *Chicago Review*, 19:11–25 (June 1967).

Tanner, Tony. "The American Novelist as Entropologist," *London Magazine*, 10:5–18 (October 1970).

———. "On the Parapet: A Study of the Novels of Norman Mailer," *Critical Quarterly*, 12:153–76 (Summer 1970).

Toback, James. "Norman Mailer Today," *Commentary*, 44:68–76 (October 1967).

Trilling, Diana. "The Radical Moralism of Norman Mailer," in *The Creative Present*, edited by Nona Balakian and Charles Simmons. Garden City, N.Y.: Doubleday, 1963. In Lucid, pp. 108–136; in Braudy, pp. 42–65.

Volpe, Edmund L. "James Jones—Norman Mailer," in *Contemporary American Novelists*, edited by Harry T. Moore. Carbondale: Southern Illinois University Press, 1964.

Wagenheim, Allen J. "Square's Progress: *An American Dream*," *Critique*, 10:45–68 (Winter 1968).

Waldmeir, Joseph J. "Only an Occasional Rutabaga: American Fiction since 1945," *Modern Fiction Studies*, 15:467–81 (1969–70).

Weber, Brom. "A Fear of Dying: Norman Mailer's *An American Dream*," *Hollins Critic*, 2:1–6 (1965).

Willingham, Calder. "The Way It Isn't Done," *Esquire*, 60:306–08. In Lucid, pp. 238–44.

Witt, Grace. "The Bad Man as Hipster: Norman Mailer's Use of Frontier Metaphor," *Western American Literature*, 4:203–71 (Fall 1969).

Wood, Margery. "Norman Mailer and Nathalie Sarraute: A Comparison of Existentialist Novels," *Minnesota Review*, 6:67–72 (Spring 1966).

—*RICHARD FOSTER*

John P. Marquand

1893-1960

JOHN PHILLIPS MARQUAND was for almost forty years a highly remunerated writer of short stories and serials for the mass-circulation magazines. But, although much of his career was spent as a dependable producer of a kind of fiction which the protagonist of *Wickford Point* called "that half-world of the imagination governed by editorial fact," he began in 1937 publishing distinguished novels of manners, in which he gave firm, skillful, accurate, and ironic representations of the upper-class and upper-middle-class social world. In 1949 he declared, "I would like, before I'm through, to have a series of novels which would give a picture of a segment of America during the past fifty years." In his nine novels of manners he succeeded to a degree that makes him an important—although often neglected—figure in twentieth-century American fiction.

When he published *The Late George Apley,* after fifteen years as a "front cover name" for the *Saturday Evening Post,* he was greeted with critical enthusiasm, treated as a redeemed penitent, and expected to cry "Mea culpa" and sin no more. Yet, while he certainly grew restive under its conventions, Marquand never developed a contempt for popular fiction. So he continued to write it, although at a decreased rate, to the distress of some of his critics and the silence of a growing number of

those who had taken him seriously in the late 1930's. The last three of his works published before his death were *Life at Happy Knoll,* a collection of amusing and lightly satiric stories about a country club, originally published in *Sports Illustrated*; *Stopover: Tokyo,* the last (and best) of his novels of international intrigue featuring Mr. Moto; and *Women and Thomas Harrow,* one of the best and most serious of his major novels.

Jim Calder, the writer of commercial fiction in *Wickford Point,* says, "We . . . took a pride in our product, not the wild free pride of an artist, but the solid pride of a craftsman." And, he says, "This escapist literature for a hopeless but always hopeful people possessed a quality of artisanship that demanded high technique." This artisanship Marquand could employ in the writing of popular fiction with the unabashed intention merely to entertain; and he could also use it to give his serious fiction a silky smoothness and clarity that made it attractive to a mass audience. But it rendered his serious work suspect to critics whose predilections are toward work whose difficulty is on the surface—in its use of language, of image, and of symbol—rather than in the complexities of human relationships and the ambiguities of social problems.

Marquand was not an extensive or dedicated

experimenter with the art of fiction, but a practitioner of the novel of social realism as it had been developed in the nineteenth century. He tried to represent man in his social milieu and to reveal man's character through his conduct and the choices he made in his society, rather than through the exploration of the inner self. He brought to the portrayal of his middle-aged protagonists the artistic ideals of Trollope, Howells, and Henry James, and the objective of making a satiric picture of reality which he learned from Sinclair Lewis, whose work he admired greatly. Like these masters of his, he declared, "I can only write of what I know and have seen."

What he knew best when he began his career as a serious novelist was the Boston of the patrician classes, the New England of the upper middle classes, and the New York of commercial fiction and advertising. For him the most significant figure of his world seemed to be what he once called "the badgered American male—and that includes me—fighting for a little happiness and always being crushed by the problems of his environment." He was convinced that this frail and often unthinking reed was not unique to the environment in which Marquand knew him best. In 1949 in an introduction to the Modern Library edition of *The Late George Apley*, he wrote, "The mental approach of . . . Apley . . . [is] observable in every civilization, and one which must exist whenever society assumes a stable pattern."

Yet, as he was keenly aware, America was a civilization in which society maintains no stable patterns. The American novelist who would test his characters against a static social order or fixed conventions must ultimately despair of his native land as a subject for his art, as Cooper, Hawthorne, and James had done. The impact which democracy makes on manners converts the novelist from being a

tester of character by established standards to a portrayer of character under the persistent impact of change. The social novelist's subject becomes mutability rather than order, and his testing cruxes occurs when change rather than stasis puts stress on the moral values of his characters. "Social mobility," a term which he borrowed from the social anthropologists, thus becomes a recurrent condition, even in Boston, in Marquand's novels. The problems of caste, class, and social movement he knew intimately, and found fascinating.

In his serious novels, Marquand drew extensive, accurate, convincing, and often uncomplimentary pictures of the world he knew best, writing of it with an ease that masked the penetration of the study which he was making. In his polished and patrician way, he defined the ambitions, the intentions, and above all the frustrations of the average moderately successful middle-aged citizen with an acuteness that made many of his readers meet his characters with a shock of self-recognition.

Although he was probably impatient with the young existentialists as he clearly was with those who prate in Freudian terms of "free social guilt," his major novels define a moral and spiritual emptiness, a sense of loneliness and quiet despair, that is not far removed from Kafka and Sartre. The fact that his people, when they face the emptiness of their lives, take less spectacular courses than do the standard existential heroes—that they respond with a private school's "stiff upper lip" and sense of duty and dignity—should not blind us to the fact that Marquand's characters, like Hemingway's waiter, find themselves at last alone in a "clean, well-lighted place," muttering their traditional Puritan prayers to some great *nada*, whose answers are to be read in the stifling grasp of a social environment. Yet this pessimism is usually masked behind a gently ironic tone, and these characters are handled with the wry detachment of the novelist of manners and not, except in a few cases, in tragic terms or with bitterness.

Marquand's total career is remarkably like that of the protagonists of his novels, and the totality of his work, both early and late, has a unity of thrust and impact that few people have recognized—perhaps because most of those who regard the novels after *The Late George Apley* as works of art have never looked carefully at the so-called hack work which preceded them. In fact, the shadowy outline of subject, method, and manner for the later novels is at least faintly discernible in even the earliest of Marquand's works.

John Phillips Marquand was born on November 10, 1893, in Wilmington, Delaware, where his father was working as a civil engineer for the American Bridge Company. But his New England roots stretched far back into the history of America. He was on the maternal side a direct descendant of Governors Thomas and Joseph Dudley of the Massachusetts Bay Colony, a grandnephew of Margaret Fuller, and a close relation of the Hales. The Marquands were of Norman-French descent, having migrated from the island of Guernsey to New England in 1732 and settled in Newburyport, thirty-two miles north of Boston. There they were privateers, ship builders and owners, and sea captains; for long generations before John's birth the male Marquands had been sons of Harvard, including his father, Philip, who was graduated in 1889.

The early years of John's childhood were passed in some affluence. His father became a successful broker in New York City, where he bought a town house in the East 30's, was listed in the New York Social Register, and later moved to a sumptuous home with two servants and a footman at Rye. This affluence

was short-lived, however, for the Panic of 1907 completely wiped out Philip Marquand's holdings. He returned to his profession, accepted an engineering job on the Panama Canal, and took his wife with him. John, then fourteen, was sent to the Marquands' ancestral home at Curzon's Mill, Kent's Island, on the Artichoke River, four miles west of Newburyport. There he lived with two aunts and a great-aunt, all maiden ladies, kinspeople of the Hales and friends of John Greenleaf Whittier, who, according to rumor, often rowed across the Merrimack River from Amesbury to visit them and, perhaps, to pay quiet court to John's great-aunt, Mary Curzon. Everything in his background and tradition indicated that he would attend Groton, Exeter, St. Mark's, or some other illustrious private school, but there was nothing in the family coffers to make it possible.

Thus the impoverished inheritor of a distinguished social and intellectual tradition attended the public high school in Newburyport and experienced "downward mobility." He applied for the scholarship which the Newburyport Harvard Club gave, but his application was rejected. He then secured a scholarship awarded by a fund established to finance at Harvard students committed to the study of scientific subjects. There he made none of the clubs, despised the chemistry which he was pledged to study, and won what modicum of fame was to be his through work on the *Lampoon*. In his sketch of himself for the twenty-fifth anniversary of his class he wrote: "Harvard is a subject which I still face with mixed emotions. I brought away from it a number of frustrations and illusions which have handicapped me throughout most of my life." Thus he resembled those many protagonists of his whose fathers are failures—however charming —and who suffer the snubs of a public school boy among private school graduates. And it was also little wonder that much of his early historical fiction looked back with longing nostalgia to those days of New England's past when his ancestors dominated Newburyport and stretched out through their trading ships to touch the remote corners of the great world.

But if Harvard gave him little chemistry and less comfort, it did introduce him to the delights of books and writing. Upon graduation he was hired by the *Boston Evening Transcript*, that bible in newsprint for the Brahmin Boston of the time. He began as a reporter at fifteen dollars a week; he was transferred to the twice-weekly magazine section, and, at the end of a year, he was raised to twenty-five dollars a week. However, about this time Battery A of the Massachusetts National Guard, which he had joined while he was at Harvard, was mobilized and sent to the Mexican border. In July 1916, he became a private in a military unit made up largely of Boston socially elite and was sent to El Paso, Texas, where he manicured the horses and kept the stables clean.

In April 1917, Marquand went to the Officers' Training Camp at Plattsburg, New York, where he worked hard and headed the first lieutenants' list when his class completed its training in August. He arrived in France as an officer of the Fourth Division, Artillery Brigade Headquarters. He fought well as a combat soldier with the 77th Regiment Field Artillery at the Vesle River, at Saint-Mihiel, and in the Argonne. He was under shellfire many times and survived two gas attacks.

He sailed from Brest on November 2, 1918, to join a new division in America as its captain, but when the ship arrived in the New York harbor the Armistice had been signed, and Marquand was demobilized. He was impressed, he later said, with the changes that had occurred. "America, when I had left it, had been an orderly place, and now it was seething with all sorts of restive discontent. . . . It all

adds up now in my memory to maladjustment and discomfort, disbelief in old tradition and suspicion of the present and the future." These experiences were to form one of his major subject matters, and the painful sense of change was to remain hauntingly with him.

He got a job on the magazine section of the *New York Tribune*, but he soon moved, with the humorist Robert Benchley's aid, to the J. Walter Thompson Advertising Agency, where he worked as copywriter on advertising campaigns for Blue Buckle Overalls, O'Sullivan's Rubber Heels, and Lifebuoy soap. Although he sensed, he later said, that "There began to be a new type of hero in this postwar world . . . the business man," he himself disliked this new man's world very much.

When he had saved four hundred dollars, he resigned and went to the Marquand place at Curzon's Mill to write a novel, *The Unspeakable Gentleman*, a tale of Newburyport in the year 1805. His narrator, Henry Shelton, was a man looking back upon an experience of his youth; Shelton's father was "the unspeakable gentleman," a charming and deadly rascal, engaged in a complex French royalist plot and accompanied by a beautiful and mysterious French lady. The plot is made up of extravagant derring-do, and its characters are given to striking preposterous poses. Yet *The Unspeakable Gentleman* bears a significant relationship to much of Marquand's later writing: it is concerned with the New England past; its narrator-protagonist is by birth a member of the ruling class who has been brought to lowly and humiliating station by the actions of his father; and it demonstrates Marquand's concern with the past viewed from the vantage point of a later time. For example, its fifth chapter begins, "Even today, as I pen these lines, the picture comes back with the same intensity, but little mellowed or softened with the years." In 1940, Marquand said, "I meant every word of it when I did the work. It was in every way the best I could do at the time—and that goes for everything I've done since."

The *Ladies' Home Journal* paid $2000 for the novel and published it as a serial in 1921; Scribners issued it as a book in 1922, and it sold 6000 copies; his career as a professional writer was launched with what appeared to be spectacular success. In 1921 he had sold a short story to the *Saturday Evening Post*; now he began selling more of them and showed sufficient promise to be unsuccessfully solicited by Ray Long, the editor of *Cosmopolitan*, to become one of his "regulars."

Also in 1921, flushed with the sale of *The Unspeakable Gentleman*, he had made a trip to Europe, the first of a great many journeys to far places, which by the end of his life had taken him—for pleasure, for material for stories, or from military necessity—to most of the familiar spots and many of the forgotten corners of the earth. In 1949 he could say, "I have seen the Assam Valley, Bushire in Persia, the Gobi Desert, the Sahara Desert, the Andes, Iceland, Ascension Island, Lake Chad, the Amazon, the Nile, the Ganges, the Coliseum and the Taj Mahal." He was several times in China—Peking he thought the most interesting city in the world—and in Japan, Manchukuo, Egypt, Arabia, Central Africa, and the Amazon Valley. Despite the fact that, as he often expressed it, "always his steps were turning home," Marquand was a restless man; he felt the call of far places, and his delight in other social and cultural patterns was strong. He was particularly impressed with the Chinese concept of *fêng-shui*, which he thought of as "the balance of things." It was the statement of a Chinese soothsayer that he needed a mustache for *fêng-shui* that led him to grow a small one which he wore for the remainder of his life.

On this first of many journeys, he became engaged in Rome to Christina Sedgwick, whom he had met a year before in New Hampshire, and to whom he was married on September 8, 1922, in Stockbridge, Massachusetts. She belonged to one of the most important New England families and was the niece of Ellery Sedgwick, who, as editor of the *Atlantic Monthly*, was the literary arbiter of Boston. This marriage brought him, he said, "face to face with the capitalist system." The couple settled in Boston in an old house on Beacon Hill; Marquand joined the Tavern and Somerset clubs, purchased a share in the Athenaeum Library, hired a maid-of-all-work, bought a car, and, upon the arrival of the first of their two children, employed a nurse. In 1949 he ruefully observed, "And ever since then I've been over a barrel."

The financial basis on which the lives of these "Proper Bostonians" rested came from Marquand's successful application of his talent and his growing technical skill to the production of fiction for the mass-circulation magazines. In the first decade of his career, between 1921 and 1931, he published five serials and fifty-nine short stories in the *Saturday Evening Post*, the *Ladies' Home Journal,* and *Collier's.* Three of the serials became books, a fourth one was combined with three short stories and published in the book *Four of a Kind* (1923). The *Post* was paying from $500 to $3000 apiece for his short stories and from $30,000 to $40,000 each for his serials. Although he was having to write for a living, clearly the living it brought was quite good, for the Marquands were able to live in a style well known to John's ancestors but quite beyond the means of his branch of the family after 1907. But the Boston acquaintances of the Marquands had little knowledge of his literary efforts and no respect for them. His wife wanted him to try a different vein; she would have preferred that he write for her Uncle Ellery Sedgwick in the

Atlantic—a luxury which he felt that he could not afford. "She didn't realize that my Uncle Ellery would have given me a nice silver inkwell, or a hundred dollars, and that wouldn't pay the bills," he said several decades later, when he was in a position to afford being—and, indeed, was—an *Atlantic* contributor.

In commenting on these ten years in which he learned his craft, Marquand wrote in 1954: ". . . the development of literary skills and techniques, I think, rests mainly upon personal experience. . . . Most [writers] have faced a discipline of having a list of periodicals, popular and otherwise, reject their earlier efforts. Others, in a higher income bracket, have been able to indulge in the luxury of destroying their less mature creations at the moment of production. Personally I have not been so fortunate as to have fallen into either of these categories." Hence, he learned his trade by working assiduously at it. Commercial writing demanded fine craftsmanship, even though it was expended on shallow formulas.

Most readers think of this period of Marquand's career as being given over to mystery stories and Mr. Moto's international intrigues; but these actually came later. The short stories of this period dealt with the New England past, with the Danser family and with the March family (both early forms of the Brills of Wickford Point), with prep schools and colleges, with romances of the business world and with gallant young officers in the war. O. Henry and Kipling are to be seen dimly behind them. The short novel *Only a Few of Us Left*, collected in *Four of a Kind*, is about Jimmy Lee, a sporting gentleman of the highest social order, who is to reappear with only slight modifications as Minot Roberts in *So Little Time*.

The Black Cargo (a serial published as a book in 1925) returns to the history of Newburyport. Charles Jervaile, the narrator, is looking backward to his youth. His ineffectual father had been dispossessed, and Charles was engaged in a struggle to regain the place that was rightfully his. Much of the book, loaded with a nostalgic romanticism, takes place on Yankee trading ships in the Pacific. At this time, Marquand had a strong desire to escape into the past. "I wanted to be lost in it. . . . I was . . . in love with candlelight and old ships," he said.

Fourteen stories published in the *Post* in 1929 and 1930 trace the rise and slow decay of the Swales, who built and ruled Haven's End (a fictional counterpart of Newburyport), and the gradual economic growth of the lowly Scarlets, keepers of taverns and makers of shoes, who come to own Haven's End without gaining an attendant social position. Ten of these tales, ranging from the seventeenth to the twentieth century, Marquand revised and published as the book *Haven's End* (1933), which shows his growing concern with the process of social change. An early result of his interest in the New England past was a biography, *Lord Timothy Dexter of Newburyport, Mass.* (1925), a record in mannered style and with arch scholarship of a notorious New England eccentric. He revised this book extensively, particularly in tone and attitude, in the posthumously published work *Timothy Dexter Revisited* (1960), in which he shifts his concern from biographical data, whimsy, and pedantic accuracy to an attempt to understand the environment that made Dexter what he was. The revised book is an illuminating personal testament to Marquand's love of Newburyport and the New England past.

Warning Hill (a serial, published as a book in 1930) deals with the very recent past in New England, told through Tommy Michael's recollections of events during his young manhood in Michael's Harbor. Tommy's father was a fascinating and charming failure. Tommy, himself of the upper middle class, reaches, from his own ambiguous social situation, both downward toward the lower-class Streets and upward toward the upper-class Jelletts who live on Warning Hill and are the social rulers of Michael's Harbor. Tommy falls in love with Marianne Jellett, only to find that, although he amuses her, she views him as "a village boy." Tommy wins success as a golfer, goes on to Harvard, where he is accepted by the "right" people, becomes an army officer, and finally achieves self-definition through his own rejection of the Jelletts. Many of the situations well known to Marquand's later readers are to be found in this novel, as are attitudes and techniques that are usually associated with the post-*Apley* period. At one place in the story, Marquand observes, "He was standing in that sunny place with his whole life in the balance, though of course he did not know. Does any one ever know until it is too late?" And another character says to Tommy, ". . . we're on the fringe of things, and we're the saddest people in the world, brought up to something that we've never had, and wishing for all sorts of things." The distance in attitude, tone, and meaning is not great between Michael's Harbor and the Clyde of *Point of No Return;* and Tommy Michael faces a situation very similar to that of Willis Wayde with the Harcourts.

By 1931, Marquand says, he was being made "restless' by the popular magazine short story. "I was violently anxious to prove that this form of writing could be popular and at the same time exhibit more serious elements." He was beginning to be concerned, he wrote, "with methods of connecting past and present in order to give reality to romance." How much of this new resolve was the result of his experiences with the stories which became *Haven's End,* how much was the result of the success —at least in a technical sense—of *Warning Hill,* and how much was connected with a personal "revolt," which occurred about this time, we cannot say, and perhaps he could not either. Of the "revolt," he declared: "I was disillusioned about a great many things, a great many people—about much that I'd had full faith in. . . . I had left my wife. There was much that had happened."

That he succeeded in the early thirties in making his "formula" stories carry what he believed to be a heavier weight of significance is shown in his 1954 selection from his short works, *Thirty Years.* In it he reprints only one story written before 1930—"Good Morning, Major" (1926), a war story which Edward J. O'Brien included in his 1939 collection of *Fifty Best American Short Stories.* On the other hand, he selected for *Thirty Years* four stories originally published in 1930, 1931, and 1932: "Rainbows," "Golden Lads," "High Tide," and "Fourth Down." A fifth story from this period, "Deep Water," was reprinted in the 1932 *O. Henry Memorial Award Prize Stories.*

During the period between 1931 and 1934, he was also seeking new subject matter, as one can see who examines the series that appeared in the *Post* dealing with a young officer in J. E. B. Stuart's Confederate cavalry. In 1934–35 he went to the Orient looking for new material. The first fruits of the search are to be seen in *Ming Yellow* (a serial, published as a book in 1935). An adventure story laid in Peking and portions of North China, *Ming Yellow* is a combination of local color and the novel of manners. Marquand was fascinated by the way in which "form permeated every phase of personal conduct and governed every situation," and by the very complex set of standards by which the Chinese lived. Despite its indifferently managed plot *Ming Yellow* points toward the serious novelist of manners which Marquand was becoming.

Before he left for his Oriental tour in late 1934, Marquand had begun to work on *The*

Late George Apley, because, as he has said, "this was the first time in a hectic period of child-rearing and bills that I could afford to write something that might not be readily salable." In March 1935, when he was in Peking, China, Mrs. Christina Marquand obtained a divorce in Pittsfield, Massachusetts. In Peking in the same year, he met Adelaide Hooker and her mother, who were on a Garden Clubs of America tour. Adelaide was rich and related by marriage to the Rockefellers. After Marquand returned to the United States in 1936 they became engaged, and they were married in 1937.

In the meantime Marquand's Oriental tour began paying off. In 1935 the *Saturday Evening Post* serialized *No Hero*, a story of adventures in Japan and Shanghai when K. C. Jones, ex-naval flyer, becomes entangled with a Japanese intelligence agent named Mr. Moto. Mr. Moto was to be a popular figure, the center of intelligence activities in five additional serials which became books as *No Hero* did. It was followed the next year by *Thank You, Mr. Moto*, a tale of the intrigues which can sweep through Peking. *Think Fast, Mr. Moto* (1937), in which a young New Englander, Wilson Hitchings, finds himself involved with Mr. Moto in Honolulu, was the third of the famed series. A fourth Moto serial, *Mr. Moto Is So Sorry*, appeared in 1938. It is a tale of two Americans, Sylvia Dillaway and Calvin Gates, caught in international intrigue between the Japanese and the Russians in Mongolia. The fifth book in the series, *Last Laugh, Mr. Moto*, appeared in 1942.

Among Mr. Moto's major accomplishments may have been the freeing of his creator to work on a different kind of book. For the Mr. Moto serials were enormously successful and became the basis for a popular series of motion pictures in which Peter Lorre portrayed the Japanese secret agent. In Mr. Moto

Marquand had found a fictional character that seemed to lend himself to extensive and highly remunerative elaboration, and a plot situation that utilized his knowledge of far places—although Mr. Moto is Japanese, the actual settings of each of these spy tales is a different segment of the Orient. Marquand involves in the Moto stories a variety of American characters—the protagonists change for each story—while Mr. Moto remains his smiling self, as incredible as his name, which Marquand learned was impossible as a Japanese name long after he and Peter Lorre had made it a well-established reality in what Marquand called the "half-world of the imagination." (In the final Moto story, he apologizes repeatedly for the impossibility of the name.) It is a mistake to call Mr. Moto a detective or to call Marquand a writer of detective stories or even of mysteries in the traditional sense. These books are spy thrillers of a very high order, but they lack the tight construction of the detective story.

The final Mr. Moto story, *Stopover: Tokyo* (1957), has a situation as impressively cynical as those in the "realistic" and pseudo-tragic tales of espionage and betrayal that were to become popular in the 1960's and 1970's, and its qualities of characterization and style are superior. Only W. Somerset Maugham, Graham Greene, and perhaps Eric Ambler handled the spy thriller with more sophisticated grace and toughness of mind than Marquand at his best.

The Late George Apley, which had been started in 1934 and left half-finished until 1935, was completed in 1936, when portions of it appeared as self-contained episodes in the *Saturday Evening Post*, and was published as a book in 1937. The extent to which Mr. Moto financed his creator's rebellion against the inhibitions of the commercial writer and the restrictions of the Boston environment can be seen by examining Marquand's publications in the *Post* in 1936. In February and March *Thank You, Mr. Moto* appeared and in September and October *Think Fast, Mr. Moto;* in addition five short stories were published during the year, as well as episodes from *Apley* in November and December. Never again was Marquand to publish as much in a single year. The success of *The Late George Apley,* which won the Pulitzer Prize in 1938, gave his career a new direction, a seriousness that it had not had before, and—ironically—a financial success greater than he had dreamed of in the days when he was writing commercial fiction exclusively. *Apley,* conceived, Marquand said, as "a savage attack on the old water side of Beacon Street" and presented as a parody of the "collected letters" with commentary, was the first of three satiric studies of Boston which Marquand was to write.

After the publication of *Apley* he continued, on a diminished scale, his writing of adventure serials: in 1937 he published in the *Post* the serial *3-3-8,* and in 1938, the serial version of *Mr. Moto Is So Sorry* appeared in the *Post* and *Castle Sinister* was serialized in *Collier's.* Much of *Wickford Point* was serialized in a modified form in the *Post* in early 1939; it appeared in book form as his second major novel late in that year. An adventure serial, *Don't Ask Questions,* also appeared in 1939. An English edition of this story was published in 1941, but it was not republished in America. The third of his major novels, *H. M. Pulham, Esquire,* was published in February 1941, after portions of it had been serialized in *McCall's.*

These three novels form a kind of triptych, defining in three sharply contrasting panels Marquand's view of Boston. *The Late George Apley* is a portrait of old Boston and its tradition, which had flowered in Concord in the mid-nineteenth century. In *Wickford Point* Marquand turned his satiric attention to a decaying family loosely bound to the Transcendentalists and themselves the possessors of a very minor nature poet in the family tree. *H. M. Pulham, Esquire* is a self-portrait of a contemporary Bostonian, a post-World War I businessman, whose ineffectual revolt against his class fails and who now believes himself to have a happier and better life than, as the reader knows, he actually does have. Taken together these three panels constitute a complex and varied definition of an attitude which dominates one segment of America and which probably is, as Mr. Marquand insisted, not unique to Boston but is to be found wherever society begins to allow the past to establish firm controls over the present.

These three novels completed what John P. Marquand had to say of Boston and its society. However, their success with the critics and in the marketplace and the successful presentation of two of them as motion pictures and one as a play established Marquand in the public view as the novelist of Boston. He was in the ironic position of having moved from the production of "popular magazine fiction" to the writing of distinguished novels only to find himself still stereotyped in his readers' minds: now as a producer of New England satiric regionalism. He was intensely aware of this tagging; he said, "Self-consciously and often with hopeful determination I have moved my characters to Hollywood, Washington, New York, and Paris, and also to New York suburbs and Palm Beach." Perhaps he moved them when the moves were not demanded or wise, but, in any case, he was not again to be primarily the portrayer of the New England Brahmin and his sterile code.

During the early forties Marquand's own experience was undergoing sufficient change to justify his shifting locales and professions in his portrayal of the segments of American society which he knew with any intimacy. In

1941 and 1942 he was in Hollywood working on dialogue for the motion picture version of *H. M. Pulham, Esquire*; these experiences formed the basis for his picture of the vulgarly opulent movie world in *So Little Time* (1943). His reaction to the Japanese attack on Pearl Harbor was strong, and the accelerating rate of change in his world, now faced with a second international war, was frightening to him. An obvious temporary casualty was his Japanese secret agent, whose penultimate appearance in *Last Laugh, Mr. Moto* showed him active in causes less our own than his earlier adventures had been. Marquand, in 1942 in a *Collier's* serial, *It's Loaded, Mr. Bauer* (published as a book in England but not in America), shifted to wartime espionage adventures in South America, but the change in locale proved unfortunate. He obviously felt an emotional affinity to the fixed social and cultural traditions of the Orient and had little sympathy for South American culture.

In 1944 Marquand became a special consultant to the secretary of war. He spent much of 1944 and 1945 in Washington in this role, and these experiences underlie the Washington sequences of *B. F.'s Daughter* (1946). In 1945 he became a war correspondent, attached to the navy in the Pacific. The result of this effort was a series of articles in major magazines, some excellent short stories about navy brass, and a short novel *Repent in Haste* (1945), which, although serialized in so prestigious a magazine as *Harper's,* is a very minor work, little better than the short novels which he wrote in the 1920's and 1930's, despite its serious effort to portray a new generation at war. In 1944 Marquand became a member of the editorial board of the Book-of-the-Month Club, a $20,000 a year position which he thoroughly enjoyed and which he held until his death. In 1943 and 1944 he collaborated with George S. Kaufman on a dramatic version of *The Late George Apley,* which was produced with great success in 1946.

Neither of Marquand's two novels dealing with wartime America, *So Little Time* and *B. F.'s Daughter,* is completely successful, perhaps because Marquand was writing of experiences too recent for him to have achieved the necessary detachment and perhaps, also, because he was attempting some very limited experiments with new fictional techniques. But both books are serious attempts to deal with the frighteningly fast changes that war makes. In the New England satires, the enemy appeared to be a caste-conscious society failing to respond to change. In *So Little Time* and *B. F.'s Daughter* not society but time itself is the great villain, social change is time's inevitable manifestation, and war is an accelerating device which destroys too rapidly the structure and tradition of society.

In 1949 Marquand published *Point of No Return,* usually considered to be, along with *Apley,* one of his two best works. It is the story of Charles Gray, a native of Clyde, Massachusetts, where he had been a "Spruce Street boy" in a world in which the "Johnson Street people" were the social rulers. He goes to the public high school rather than a private school and attends Dartmouth College instead of Harvard, and these stigmas of inferiority haunt him throughout his life. At the time of the forward action of the story, he is one of two middle-aged men being considered for promotion to a vacant vice-presidency in the conservative Stuyvesant Bank (apparently modeled after the Fifth Avenue Bank of New York City). He is sent on a mission to his native town, which seems to be modeled directly on Newburyport. There, in the flood of memories, he relives his childhood and youth, when his father had been a charming ne'er-do-well and Charles had almost, but not quite, married Jessiva Lovell, of the upper upper class, although he was himself plainly only lower upper class. The broad outlines of Charles Gray's situation and character Marquand had experienced himself and had been sketching in his fiction for a long time; Gray is, *mutatis mutandis*, the hero of *The Unspeakable Gentleman* and of *The Black Cargo* and a close relative of Tommy Michael of *Warning Hill.*

This novel is unique in the thoroughness with which Marquand functions as a sociological analyst. For his interest is now centered not so much in Charles's personal dilemma as in the world that has made him, in the pattern of social gradation and of change in Newburyport and in New York. In his analysis of the social forces of Clyde, Massachusetts, Marquand produces a significant commentary on one segment of American society. "Marquand's insights into the nuances of the social hierarchy of Newburyport, in *Point of No Return*, form," Max Lerner asserts in *America as a Civilization,* "a necessary supplement to the picture that [W. Lloyd] Warner gives of the structure of the same town." (Marquand was familiar with the work of social-anthropologist Warner which resulted in a massive, five-volume study of Newburyport. A one-volume abridgment, *Yankee City,* is now available, and it makes an illuminating commentary on Marquand's method in *Point of No Return.*)

The popularity of *Point of No Return* was immense, and, although the literary critics gave it relatively short shrift, the reviewers and social historians saw it as a major social document. Probably no other American novelist since Sinclair Lewis has examined the class structure of a small American city with the accuracy and illuminating insight that Marquand employed in this novel.

After *Point of No Return,* he was to produce three major novels. Although his earlier work clearly adumbrates these books, each of them represented a significant variation from its predecessors. Each was a study of success—its costs, its joys and its deprivations—whereas the earlier novels had been essentially portraits of defeat. And each of the last three novels varied significantly from its predecessor in technique.

Melville Goodwin, USA (1951) is an ironic picture of the professional soldier and of the quality of the "opinion molders" who make him a kind of demigod. The professional soldier, his courage, and his code were persistent themes throughout Marquand's whole career. He once said, "I have seen more generals in my lifetime than I may have wished, and they always have fascinated me as social specimens." The novel is told by Sidney Skelton, a nationally famous radio commentator, who represents unconsciously much that is sentimentally mindless in contemporary American life. The two—Skelton and Goodwin—test each other in a richly complex satire. Misunderstood by most of the critics, who saw the book as an affirmation, *Melville Goodwin, USA* has the most skillfully ironic use of an unreliable narrator that Marquand ever attempted.

In 1950 and 1952 Marquand published the only two short stories which he was truly proud of—"Sun, Sea, and Sand" and "King of the Sea." Both are satiric pictures of the idle rich in the Mulligatawny Club in the Bahamas. They were, he said, "the end result of many rather groping experiments in short fiction." He felt that he had "solved the problem of writing a story that the readers of a popular magazine might enjoy and yet a story that a few critics might take seriously." They were greeted with what Marquand in typical humorous overstatement called "restrained enthusiasm."

In 1953 Marquand suffered a heart attack, which may have led to the 1954 volume *Thirty*

Years, a collection of short stories, sketches, articles, and addresses drawn from his total career and introduced by illuminating headnotes. It is to this volume and to his several recorded interviews that the critic must turn for Marquand's theory of fiction, as well as for easily accessible examples of his short stories—a form which he highly respected and in which he believed few Americans had succeeded. (He considered Hemingway the finest of American practitioners of the genre.)

In a thoughtful discussion of the novel in *Thirty Years,* Marquand embraces the realistic tradition. "A novel," he says, "is great and good in direct proportion to the illusion it gives of life and a sense of living. It is great in direct proportion to the degree it enfolds the reader and permits him to walk in imagination with the people of an artificial but very real world, sharing their joys and sorrows, understanding their perplexities." When he lists his choices for true greatness they are Balzac, Tolstoi, Dostoevski, Fielding, and Smollett.

If *Thirty Years* was a heart patient's backward glance o'er travel'd roads, its author still had much to write, both in the popular vein, where something of the Mulligatawny Club was to be present in the gentler comedy of *Life at Happy Knoll* (1957) and where Mr. Moto was to have his finest adventure in *Stopover: Tokyo* (1957), and in serious fiction.

In 1955 he published *Sincerely, Willis Wayde,* a devastating picture of the big business promoter and the Marquand book that is most nearly in the mode of Sinclair Lewis. In *Willis Wayde* Marquand for the only time in a serious novel avoids extensive use of the flashback, and centers his attention directly on his satiric butt, Willis Wayde. The result is a harsh and unsympathetic picture of a lower-middle-class boy who succeeds, through unremitting effort, in becoming what his father calls "a son

of a bitch." This most pitiless of Marquand's books echoes situations which he had earlier treated with sympathy. For Wayde alone of his protagonists Marquand has contempt.

In 1958, he divorced Adelaide Hooker Marquand, and it was in a spirit of bitter reaction against women that he wrote his last novel, *Women and Thomas Harrow* (1958). (In an interview in 1959 he said, "It is a reflection on the American male of the twentieth century that only his secretary is good to him. Not his wife. The American wife in the upper brackets is aggressive, arrogant, domineering. . . . She is invariably difficult.") This story about the three unsuccessful marriages of a very talented and successful playwright is a kind of ironic *The Tempest* to Marquand's career. Upon its publication he declared it to be his last novel, and the book has a twilight sense of putting away the players and closing the box in the mood of an embittered Prospero. When Tom Harrow looks back over the skillful and successful use he has made of his great dramatic powers, it is with a sense of nothingness that makes the book finally very dark indeed.

During the last decade of his life, Marquand was enjoying the fruits of success. If his stock was low with his critics, it was high with his large body of readers who poured over $10,000,000 into his bank account (much of it going for taxes, of course). He was living and working in his restored family home on Kent's Island, had an apartment in the most fashionable part of New York City, spent a lot of time in Bermuda and the Bahamas, and enjoyed the golf courses of Pinehurst, North Carolina. But if his "successful" heroes are to be taken as in any sense a reflection of their maker's feelings, Marquand's own version of the Horatio Alger story, like that of several of his heroes, found him "risen from the ranks" only to discover in the upper echelons a discontent and an emptiness that had made the game hardly worth the candle. Still, even if this attitude was, as he believed, typical of the beleaguered American male, his own experience of it was transmuted and rendered of value through the success with which he converted it into both accurate social pictures and disturbing studies of spiritual dryness.

It is hard not to hope—and, indeed, not to believe—that he was aware of this by no means small achievement before he died peacefully in his sleep in his home on Kent's Island on July 16, 1960.

Thomas Harrow had what Marquand called "the ambivalent curse of being able to be a part of things, and yet to stand away from them untouched." This quality of "double vision" Marquand himself possessed to a remarkable degree. As even a brief sketch of his life shows, his protagonists not only move about in a social world which Marquand knew intimately; they also have fundamental relationships to that world which parallel their creator's. This "ambivalent curse" enabled Marquand to employ his dry wit and astringent irony on his world and on many of his own experiences, both understanding and being amused by himself, his society, and his regular acquaintances. He once told an interviewer, "I am always critical of myself. . . . Unfortunately, by nature and by—if it may be called so—by artistic temperament, I am not bitter. If I use satire, I try to use it kindly."

In dealing with experience, Marquand was anxious to record what he called "the extraordinary panorama of society, the changes in life since the horse and wagon days." Yet in portraying that panorama, he turned, as many writers of the social novel have, to the novel of character. In *Timothy Dexter Revisited,* written at the very close of his career, he said: "I have learned something I should have learned long ago—that few individuals are important in themselves. The environment that produced and tolerated Dexter is far more interesting than the man." But it is the man, revealed through the impact of that environment upon him, that is the central interest of Marquand's serious novels.

One of the obvious clues to the centrality of character in his work is the looseness and, it sometimes seems, the nonexistence of plot. Even his early adventure stories and his Mr. Moto tales have relaxed construction, and his major novels so far concentrate on character rather than event that they may seem to the casual reader to be formless, flowing with the narrator's whim. An excellent example of this quality can be shown by comparing the dramatic version of *The Late George Apley,* on which George S. Kaufman collaborated with Marquand, with the novel itself. In the stage version a unified—and virtually new—plot had to be supplied in order to give dramatic statement to the attitude of the Boston Brahmin that was the intention of the novel.

Leo Gurko has called the similarity of Marquand's basic situations and central characters a "high-level formula." In one sense he is correct. Marquand in 1959 told an interviewer from *Cosmopolitan,* ". . . what interests me personally in fiction is to take my central character, not in his youth or early manhood, but when he is nearly through, when he is faced with an important decision in his life. I then prefer to have him go back to his early past." The result is that seven of his nine novels of manners deal not with plots in any conventional sense but with crucial situations—what Marquand calls taking "a man facing the crisis of his life" and "show[ing] how he got there"—with the protagonist looking backward in memory to his formative years. The exceptions to this backward movement as the controlling structural pattern are in *The Late George*

Apley, where an "official" biographer is writing about a deceased friend, and *Sincerely, Willis Wayde,* where the sequence of events is presented in a straightforward fashion, from childhood onward. In *Willis Wayde,* despite this chronological sequence of events, the actions are viewed from an undefined vantage point in the present. This vantage point that establishes a relationship between past and present for the chief actions through their presentation by backward looks was a hallmark of Marquand's fiction from *The Unspeakable Gentleman* onward. It is very effective in pointing up the contrast between past and present, whether it is used to create the romantic nostalgia of his historical fiction, best seen in *Haven's End,* or to explore the methods by which the actions and the environments of the past make and control the present. In *Timothy Dexter Revisited,* which emphasized the magnitude of the social changes that occurred in Marquand's lifetime, he says, "There is no use weeping over things that are gone. They can never be retrieved in their ancient combinations." These nine novels attempt, not to re-create that past, but to picture that part of it which survives in the memories and impressions of the present.

Marquand in these books is writing of people and professions that he knew; his protagonists come from a world in which Marquand had lived; and they face—with inadequate spiritual defenses but with the self-conscious will to play their roles in a manner that gives attention to how things are done and shows a reasonable sense of decorum—problems of character and conscience that he believed to be common to his world. These similarities of structure, class, and theme have blinded those who have casually examined Marquand's work to the substantial technical achievements which in different ways mark his several books. His irritation that, as he says, "I am called by most critics meaningless and repetitive," is justified,

for despite common elements that run through much of his work, neither charge can be substantiated in the fullest sense, if his work is viewed as the representation of a society and its various types through a variety of technical devices and fundamental methods.

The basic method of *The Late George Apley* is that of parody, an aping of the diction and attitudes of editors of what Marquand called the "collected letters of V.I.P.s in Boston (and elsewhere) throughout which were scattered numerous biographical interpolations prepared by an often unduly sympathetic editor." Horatio Willing, vain, pedantic, and smug Boston "man of letters," is editing the correspondence of George Apley, a very proper Boston Brahmin. What he is doing differs from other "official" records of its sort only in the fact that Apley's son John has insisted on the inclusion of matter usually excised. Willing's attempts to explain these events in Apley's life and certain of Apley's attitudes join with his own pedantry and pompous diction and his long, imprecise sentences to make Willing himself the chief target of Marquand's satire, and thus to create for him a role as a satiric overstatement of his society, a comic caricature—a role that is present in each of Marquand's novels. Style, it has been said, is the man; but in *The Late George Apley* it becomes a device for social criticism. The use of Willing to tell the story of Apley results in a double view of the Brahmin type and in a double portraiture that gives depth to the study; Willing is an object of satiric caricature and Apley is a more likable person caught in the same inexorable social traps as Willing is.

A comparison with Sinclair Lewis' *Babbitt* may be helpful. Both Babbitt and Apley are the products of their social worlds, however different the worlds themselves may be. Both attempt revolt and from time to time challenge their worlds. Both are fundamentally good men, and both are made into something that neither wants to be by quiet and almost continuous but invisible pressure. The authors of both books were men with unusually keen ears for the jargon of trades, professions, and social classes. It is even true—although perhaps not important—that both Lewis and Marquand were successful popular writers before they turned their hands to unkindly picturing of their contemporaries. But these similarities serve also to illuminate a fundamental difference. In *Babbitt* the voice we hear is that of Sinclair Lewis, and it is often raised in strident and unmistakable condemnation. In *Apley* Marquand never speaks, and the voice we hear is that of the narrator Willing. Lewis is not in any way a butt of his own invective, where Willing is at the center of Marquand's target. Hence we watch Babbitt from afar and feel that he is remarkably like our neighbors. But we can watch Apley more appreciatively than we can watch his narrator, and thus we can see him as in some ways like ourselves.

Marquand on one occasion spoke of this addition of parody to the epistolary form as "possibly a new addition," but it probably owes some substantial debt to W. Somerset Maugham's *Cakes and Ale*, and certainly a part of its basic impulse derives from George Santayana's *The Last Puritan,* which he called "A Memoir in the Form of a Novel," whereas Marquand subtitled *Apley* "A Novel in the Form of a Memoir."

Although the time sequences had been handled loosely in *Apley,* Marquand's next novel, *Wickford Point,* represented an apparently even looser use of time, but one which, on closer examination, is very artful. The story is presented through the reminiscences of Jim Calder, a writer of popular magazine fiction, as a series of events in the brief forward motion of the story trigger his recollections of the past, within which most of the significant action is

to be found. Once more, the narrator is a lesser character than some of the people in the narrative, but Jim Calder is a more admirable person than Willing, and, indeed, has frequently been viewed as at least a semiautobiographical portrait. Edward Weeks, Sedgwick's successor as editor of the *Atlantic* and the publisher of some of Marquand's later short pieces, felt that Marquand's personal voice and views were more clearly discernible in *Wickford Point* than in any other of his novels. And certainly Jim Calder is used to say some quite uncomplimentary things about the world of commercial fiction. But Calder lacks the courage and the will to break away from a commercial writer's role and to attempt in his own right to create a truer picture of the world he knows. That important role he allows to fall to the pretentious and ludicrous middle-western Harvard professor, Allen Southby, who visits Wickford Point in order to learn enough about it to enable him to write a "serious" novel about New England life. If Calder is in part an autobiographical figure, it is the reflector of an attitude which Marquand had experienced in the days of his popular adventure-story writing. And at the center of the story is Bella Brill, who is, as Calder suggests, a Thackerayesque woman, reminiscent of Becky Sharp or Beatrix Esmond. Jim, who has always been her confidant and to a certain extent her captive; Joe Stowe, her former husband, whom she desires to remarry because he is a success; Howard Berg, whom she plots to marry for his money—all function to reveal her in her shallowness, selfishness, and genteel depravity. The result is a detailed, convincing, very urbane and polite study of frivolous bitchery.

Jim's diction and sentence structure are those of the professional writer, and, although ostensibly relaxed, they have a directness, a clarity, and an accuracy that Willing's had lacked. Willing writes such crabbedly pedantic sentences as this one which is a part of a description of a wedding: "It is the writer's belief that nearly any man must look back to this important period in his life with somewhat mingled emotions, in that the new social contacts and this new and beautiful relationship cannot but cause a certain amount of mental confusion." In contrast Jim Calder writes of Bella Brill: "Bella's violet eyes were half-closed, but her lips were just a trifle grim. Her expression made me wonder if she had ever loved at all. She had certainly talked enough about it. I wondered if she had been secretly in love with her father, her brothers or her mother. Certainly she had never given any visible sign of such undeveloped weakness." Each book is, in a sense, a stylistic tour de force. But the publication of *H. M. Pulham, Esquire* revealed what many had not fully understood— that Marquand had a finely discriminating ear for American speech, a sensitivity to the significance of word choice and sentence structure that probably has not been surpassed in American writing since Mark Twain. Willing's narrative might have been a parody of a literary form, requiring sensitivity to the printed page; Calder's might have been Marquand's own voice. But Pulham's first-person narrative is a triumph of stylistic exactness. The language and attitudes of a Boston investment counsel are perfectly caught and are used successfully to portray Harry Pulham, as he reveals himself through contemplation about the writing of his "class life" for the twenty-fifth reunion of his Harvard class.

This ability to capture the very accent of American upper-middle-class and upper-class speech, to employ its jargon with authenticity, and to know the precise degree of exaggeration to use in order to point out its absurdity and pretension, Marquand was to use with increasing effectiveness. In *So Little Time,* he moves to the world of the theater, with Jeffrey Wilson,

successful play-doctor who dreams of writing his own great play, while the clocks, accelerated by the outbreak of war, rush inexorably on. Marquand uses Jeff Wilson as a viewpoint character, writing of him in the third person, but employing Wilson's thought formulated in Wilson's style as his medium. A comparison of the style of these four books should silence all critics who accuse Marquand of self-imitation except those who are tone-deaf.

In *B. F.'s Daughter* Marquand attempts to use two viewpoint characters: Polly Fulton Brett is the principal one and Bob Tasmin is the secondary one. While he does an excellent job of creating a significantly different voice for each, the novel does not quite come off, chiefly because Polly's tone of voice seems slightly out of key. In *Point of No Return* he uses once more the viewpoint pattern of *So Little Time,* employing a third-person presentation of Charles Gray's reminiscences couched in the language of a middle-aged conservative New York banker.

In certain respects *Melville Goodwin, USA* is Marquand's greatest triumph of style. It is told in the first person by Sidney Skelton, a fairly typical mass-communications and "entertainment world" figure. But much that Skelton relays comes to him from the reminiscences of General Goodwin, as he is being interviewed by a writer from a magazine that is doing a "cover story" on him, and from conversations with the General's wife. Skelton plays a role rather like that of Horatio Willing in *The Late George Apley,* in that his language and his attitudes define him as shallow, confused, and lacking in fundamental integrity. That he develops a great admiration for General Goodwin and expresses it with vigor and at length, was taken by many critics as indicative of Marquand's appreciation of the military, whereas it is in fact a satiric attack on mass-communication journalism that makes a demigod of a man of the limited mind of Melville Goodwin. That a very complex criticism of value systems both in the military and in the world of "opinion molders" is being made has escaped the attention of many of his readers, with the result that the novel which is, in a technical sense at least, his most complex and skillful, has lacked an appreciative audience. Certainly Marquand never carried his concern with point of view and style to greater lengths or employed it more effectively. Many readers who should have known better read *Goodwin* the same way that they would have read *Apley* if they had taken Willing as an admired spokesman for the author.

Sincerely, Willis Wayde, by contrast, is Marquand's simplest book in terms of point of view. It is a third-person narrative focused sharply on Wayde and moving forward in chronological sequence. A similar simplicity appears in *Women and Thomas Harrow*, where the third-person viewpoint reports the thoughts of Tom Harrow, but where the structure is that of the brief crucial forward movement of plot, within which the narrator recalls the pertinent parts of the past. Tom Harrow was probably speaking for his creator when he said: "I want to hear the talk. . . . There are different kinds of talk. . . . I want to get it classified. . . . Some people say one thing; others with the same thoughts express them differently. Stockbrokers talk alike and bankers in a slightly different way. I like to listen for the difference."

There is basically little that is new in Marquand's fictional methods. They are those of the realist, employing an unreliable narrator who tells the story through retrospection and in the language and attitudes of the profession, class, and locale from which he comes. But the skill with which Marquand employed this method is quite unusual, and the subtlety with which he uses it for satiric portraits should

never be underestimated. Command of the tools of the trade does not make a novelist great— that is a function of many factors, including the things upon which the tools are used—but such command does make a novelist a fine craftsman, and that Marquand certainly was. His clarity, sureness of touch, firmness of structure, and wit are all of a high order.

Since he centered his attention in these books on character shaped by environment and on the tension between self and society which defines the value systems of people and the context of social structures, the test of Marquand's ultimate importance in the American novel must rest with the people he created and the problems he gave them. No other American novelist since Sinclair Lewis has had a sense of the significant social detail that is as great as Marquand's. John O'Hara sees more than Marquand but has difficulty selecting. Louis Auchincloss is certainly approaching a comparable mastery of the world of high society in New York, but so far his considerable talents and his perceptive eye have been tied to areas much narrower than Marquand's finally proved to be.

Marquand's major theme is the defeat of the self by society, and he intends this theme to have a broader basis than might appear if we think of it as the defeat of the self by a special society at a special time. One of the illuminating things about his Boston trilogy is that he covers a very broad span of years. The powerful thing that is Boston society slowly embraces the young whenever you find them, and its iron claw may express itself in various ways at different times but never painlessly.

When we look beyond the remarkable virtuosity of Marquand's narrative point of view to the central characters whose portraits he draws, we find him less a satirist than we had expected. The world he describes with all its foibles and fools is one in which he is finally comfortable if not contented. His protagonists are pleasant to meet, with few exceptions admirable to do business with, and delightful golfing companions. If they are surrounded in large measure by fools and pour out their efforts fruitlessly on unfertile soil, their lot seems to him little different from that of most "American males." If they seek but never find "the ideal woman" they partake, he feels, of the common experiences of our world.

The crucial event in most of these novels occurs at a point where the opportunity for personal choice has already passed. It does not change the character's position in the world but, rather, confirms it. Titles like *So Little Time* and *Point of No Return* underscore this position. The standard Marquand hero in the past once faced the forks in Frost's yellow wood and took the road most traveled by. At that moment of choice each of them had tried to rebel without success. And now in his backward searchings each is seeking to understand the point in time when his choice of roads became irrevocable.

George Apley's rebellion centered around Mary Monahan, an Irish girl whom he loved. The family applied the standard therapy of a trip abroad and it worked in the standard way. Her reappearance to rescue him from public humiliation long after he has accepted the pattern of his world and is imposing it on his son is melodrama, finally unworthy of the seriousness of the author of the book. Jim Calder's rebellion is against the claims—emotional and familial—of Wickford Point and he would like to rebel also against the shallow commercial fiction which he writes but he recognizes, he says, that "a serious novel is a very great gamble for one who must live by writing." It is a gamble that he lacks the courage and will to make. Freedom from Wickford Point is to be found with the New York girl, Pat Leighton, but only the most superficial reader will feel that his marriage to her, which constitutes the novel's apparently happy ending, can bring him the happiness which a larger rebellion—against the world of popular fiction—would have brought.

Harry Pulham, following the war, cuts the family cord for a time and tries his fortunes in New York where he works for an advertising agency and falls in love with Marvin Myles, but he returns home at last to become an investment counsel, marry the family-approved Kay Motford, and settle down to a life without ecstasy or delight but with reasonable contentment. Jeffrey Wilson rebels against his wife, the way he earns his living as a play-doctor, and the exigencies of time. But his affair with Marianna Miller, an actress, and his attempt to write a great play both fail, and he settles down with admirable, stoic courage to the mixture as before. Charles Gray marries the right girl, makes the right steps, and finally sees that the vice-presidency of the bank, for which he had been struggling, is an undesirable trap but one which he cannot avoid, since he has passed "the point of no return." Both Sidney Skelton and General Melville Goodwin are discontented with their worlds, and the General tries to have an affair with Dottie Peale and leave his wife, but the military service habits are too strong and he goes back to his wife and his troops, while Skelton rises even higher in his morally precarious world.

In *Sincerely, Willis Wayde* Marquand produced his least typical book. Willis Wayde is a lower-middle-class boy befriended by the Harcourts, an old New England family of mill owners. But Willis belongs to a new, amoral, and totally selfish business world, one in which the "management team" and the organization man are at home and in control. The ethical problems which the Harcourts had taken seriously are in no sense issues for Willis or his world. Willis is, as Marquand once remarked, "quite a stinker," and in telling his story Marquand writes in bitterness and anger. In this novel, he revives situations from *Warning Hill* and *Haven's End,* but he uses them with a deepening and darkening anger. In *B. F.'s Daughter* he had portrayed Burton Fulton, a self-made businessman as he was seen by his daughter, Bob Tasmin, an aristocrat who liked him and loved Polly, and Tom Brett, the liberal New Deal bureaucrat whom Polly married. But B. F. had been a belated "robber baron," a man of great ability, great independence, and great integrity. Critics comparing B. F. and Willis Wayde have often accused Marquand of changing his mind about business, when, in fact, he is portraying two different generations. To contrast Burton Fulton and Willis Wayde is to see a shocking decay of integrity in the business world.

Shortly after the publication of *Women and Thomas Harrow,* two years before his death, Marquand said, "I have decided that I am out of the tempo of the times. Unless I go mad, I'm not going to write another novel. . . . I think when any novelist reaches the point in his career where he is out of the argot of his times, then he should stop." In this novel about a fabulously successful writer, he says much about literary success, much about writing to fit the moment's need and to make money. Thomas Harrow finds himself at last convinced that "the only true reality in the world existed there [in books]—the reality of appeal of mind to mind." When he moves from this world of the imagination to that of his daily life, he sees himself and his wife "clasped together by a hideous loneliness."

In this valedictory to the novel by Marquand, Thomas Harrow is a strangely moving figure, a man of fundamental integrity, now a little out of touch with his times and desiring to do the "right thing." He attempts suicide by wrecking his car on a guard rail at a cliff that overlooks the sea. Having failed, he figuratively picks up his burden again and drives on home to accept once more the pattern of his responsibility, however joyless. He concludes in the last sentence of the novel, "In the end, no matter how many were in the car, you always drove alone."

Within these nine novels Marquand had portrayed what he once said "interested [him] most in the phenomena of human nature—the individual caught in a pattern of social change, usually tragically." This individual he examined as Boston Brahmin, as popular writer, as Boston investment counsel, as play-doctor, as "robber baron," as conservative banker, as professional soldier, as "organization man," and as successful playwright. These men in Boston, New York, Hollywood, and Washington were caught in a rapidly changing world, marked by two great wars and a social and moral transformation. The sureties were gone, whether we judge them to be social orders, moral commitments, or religious sanctions. Tom Harrow stops by the old First Congregational Church to be greeted by the Reverend Mr. Godfrey, who preaches sermons on "How Happy Are You Inside?" and who assures Harrow that they're "both in show business." Harrow is offended and recalls the pastor who had married him and his first wife in that church, but seems not to see that the outcome of that marriage actually underscores the death of the religion under whose authority it was performed.

But if Marquand's protagonists ultimately find themselves strangers and afraid in a world of vast change, they still lack tragic proportions, because they are too easily betrayed. For example, at the end of *H. M. Pulham, Esquire,*

Harry writes a conclusion to his class "life" in which he portrays himself as happy and successful—a conclusion which is seriously undercut by our knowledge that he is a cuckold. His assertion at the end of the novel also seems to mark how much he really misunderstands his world: "I can not share with my classmates the discouragement and pessimism which has been engendered by the New Deal. It seems to me only a phase and that matters will be better soon in business and in national life. I do not believe either Mr. Roosevelt or Germany can hold out much longer and I confidently look forward to seeing a sensible Republican in the White House." The time of that remark was 1940.

Edith Wharton once said that a "frivolous society can acquire dramatic significance only through what its frivolity destroys." Marquand seems to be saying that a staid and backward-looking society can best be portrayed by what it stifles in able, good, but weak men. Thus these various protagonists become finally, not tragic figures, but standards for measuring their society. This is comedy rather than tragedy because the men and their goals lack tragic magnitude, because, deserving what they get, it becomes satirically appropriate that they should get it—and that their own recognition scenes should be wry rather than wrathful.

A great deal of the delight in reading Marquand comes from the many satiric pictures of the minor characters. The tweedy Harvard professor Allen Southby, in *Wickford Point*; the perennial old grad Bo-jo Brown, in *H. M. Pulham, Esquire*; the bureaucrat Tom Brett in *B. F.'s Daughter*; Walter Newcombe, the ignorant and pompous foreign correspondent of *So Little Time*. The list could be multiplied many times. In these minor characters a world is created with great success, its very tone and quality caught in the amber of precise language. In portraits of these people Marquand's comic powers are shown and his novels become witty representations of ourselves viewed in the steel glass of the satirist.

Furthermore, Marquand is a social historian of considerable magnitude. He has caught the language, the cadence, the attitudes, and the absurdities of upper-middle-class America. In *So Little Time*, for example, is a remarkably accurate and complete picture of a state of mind common in America in the early forties, yet the novel is so tied to the immediate emotional pressures of its time and to precise historical events that it is his most dated book. The new breed of businessmen and the new business world are imprisoned in *Sincerely, Willis Wayde*; the temper of decayed intellectualism and excessive pride in the New England remnants of transcendentalism is defined in *Wickford Point*. Country life for the very wealthy has seldom been portrayed in its ridiculous aspects more thoroughly than through Fred and Beckie, in *So Little Time*, where life is very, very rural, and very, very simple, and the hay in the barn (used as a playroom) has been fireproofed. One of the most truly memorable of Marquand's satiric sketches is that of the social-anthropologist Malcolm Bryant, who is using techniques learned from the study of primitive cultures to examine the social structure, caste, and class distinctions (upper-upper, middle-upper, lower-upper, upper-middle, middle-middle, lower-middle, upper-lower, middle-lower, lower-lower) of Clyde in *Point of No Return*. And among the best realized of these small and totally convincing portraits done in acid is that of Walter Price, in *Women and Thomas Harrow*, who keeps endlessly constructing noble pasts for himself and who is not above declaring that he helped Shaw with *Major Barbara* and referring to F. Scott Fitzgerald as "Fitzy."

Actually it is difficult to think of a foible of Marquand's world which he has not shown.

He might have been writing of himself when he said in *Women and Thomas Harrow*, "His interest in people and places never lagged, and his instinct for caricature was as good as his memory for names and places," and added, "It was his persistent curiosity that had given his work vitality." These interests united to a remarkably accurate ear and great craftsmanship made Marquand a valuble recorder of "his segment of the world."

He confessed once that he had never been able to write poetry or to keep rhythm in his head. And the element of poetry is missing in his work; never does he try to use this world to suggest a more ideal reality, and he does not try "To see a world in a grain of sand And a heaven in a wild flower." His work is not designed to lift the spirit or to translate the immediate into the eternal; and he valued in other writers these same realistic qualities which he practiced. The Melville revival he recognized, but he did not share the enthusiasm of its symbol-seeking critics. Sinclair Lewis, at his best, he regarded as perhaps the major twentieth-century novelist; and he was even willing to talk with some appreciation of Booth Tarkington, although he doubted that Faulkner belonged in the company of his favorites as John Dos Passos did. In many respects he was more like Anthony Trollope than any other novelist, although he also shared many attitudes, subjects, and methods with John Galsworthy.

His subject was the actual society which he knew, and he valued it for itself, not as symbol or metaphor for transcendent truths or abstract ideals. If its manners sometimes bordered on the ridiculous, he pointed a self-conscious and mocking finger, and, while laughing, like the Thackeray of *Vanity Fair*, seemed to use the first-person plural pronoun when he thought of society, however carefully he eschewed it in writing. The puppet-master was himself always a part of the show.

There lingered over his world the sense of change, and all the wry amusement at the absurdities which that change produced could not completely mask Marquand's sense that his was an unhappy generation. Even in a late thriller like *Stopover: Tokyo* he stated his feeling that "The world was unhappy." Jack Rhyce, the protagonist, knows that "He and his generation were children of discontent." Rhyce's analysis of this discontent seems strange for a spy thriller but it states Marquand's position very clearly—more plainly, in fact, than he states it in novels of more serious import and subtler method: "All his generation had been born and nurtured in an age of discontent, but he was not able to explain the reason for it, unless that a system or a way of life was approaching dissolution. Logically there were less reasons for unhappiness today in any part of the world than there had been fifty years before. The cleavage between wealth and poverty had been greater then, and the voice of social conscience had only been a whisper. Communication and industrial advance had been negligible compared with the present, and so had public health and expectancy of life; yet back in that harder day the world had been much happier. There had been security then in that everyone knew what to expect. There had been strength and order, which perhaps were the attributes that mankind most desired." But he knew, too, that the past had had its problems, frustrations, and defeats. The mood that overshadows his Vanity Fair, like that of Thackeray's, is "Ah! *Vanitas Vanitatum!* Which of us is happy in this world? Which of us has his desire? or, having it, is satisfied?"

Maxwell Geismar once said, "Mr. Marquand knows all the little answers. He avoids the larger questions." The statement, although true in a sense, is more witty than wise. Denied the soaring reaches of transcendental thought or poetic elevation, he dealt with the little answers in large part because the people of whom he wrote were people who asked little questions of life, except in those confused moments when they merely raised frightened cries. Gertrude Stein, just before she died, asked, "What is the answer?" Receiving no reply, she laughed and said, "In that case, what is the question?" Marquand's people really never face the nature of their existence, even in dying. Perhaps the harshest thing that can be said about them is that they don't know what the larger questions truly are and, unlike Miss Stein, never ask. In *Women and Thomas Harrow*, Marquand says, ". . . most of mankind (excepting always those who were helped by psychoanalysts . . .) never knew where they were going until they got there; and when you were there, you could never find a backward turn."

The life, world, and times of these people who are so obsessed with the material trivia of their daily deeds, the stifling formulas of their caste and class, the busyness of making money, and the confused personal diplomacy which their marriages demand are indeed unflattering but very amusing pictures of ourselves. Mark Schorer said of Sinclair Lewis, ". . . he gave us a vigorous, perhaps a unique thrust into the imagination of ourselves." Perhaps an equivalent claim can be made for Marquand. He examined the social condition of our lives with irony and grace, and his "badgered American male" captures in his recurrent problems and poses, not only how we behave, but also how hollow our lives often are at the core. He speaks both to our social historical sense and to the unslaked spiritual thirst which our aridity creates. To our age, at least, he speaks with ease and skill, with irony and wit, but above all with the authority of unsentimental knowledge.

Selected Bibliography

WORKS OF JOHN P. MARQUAND

The Unspeakable Gentleman. New York: Scribners, 1922.

Four of a Kind. New York: Scribners, 1923. (Three short stories and the short novel *Only a Few of Us Left.*)

The Black Cargo. New York: Scribners, 1925.

Lord Timothy Dexter of Newburyport, Mass. New York: Minton, Balch, 1925. (Biography.)

Warning Hill. Boston: Little, Brown, 1930.

Haven's End. Boston: Little, Brown, 1933. (Loosely connected collection of ten short stories.)

Ming Yellow. Boston: Little, Brown, 1935.

No Hero. Boston: Little, Brown, 1935. (The first Mr. Moto book.)

Thank You, Mr. Moto. Boston: Little, Brown, 1936.

Think Fast, Mr. Moto. Boston: Little, Brown, 1937.

The Late George Apley. Boston: Little, Brown, 1937.

Mr. Moto Is So Sorry. Boston: Little, Brown, 1938.

Wickford Point. Boston: Little, Brown, 1939.

Don't Ask Questions. London: Robert Hale, [1941].

H. M. Pulham, Esquire. Boston: Little, Brown, 1941.

Last Laugh, Mr. Moto. Boston: Little, Brown, 1942.

So Little Time. Boston: Little, Brown, 1943.

It's Loaded, Mr. Bauer. London: Robert Hale, [1943].

Repent in Haste. Boston: Little, Brown, 1945. (Short novel.)

The Late George Apley. A Play (with George S.

Kaufman). New York: Dramatists Play Service, 1946.

B. F.'s Daughter. Boston: Little, Brown, 1946.

Point of No Return. Boston: Little, Brown, 1949.

Melville Goodwin, USA. Boston: Little, Brown, 1951.

Thirty Years. Boston: Little, Brown, 1954. (Collection, with commentary, of short stories, sketches, travel accounts, and lectures.)

Sincerely, Willis Wayde. Boston: Little, Brown, 1955.

Life at Happy Knoll. Boston: Little, Brown, 1957. (Collection of twelve related short stories.)

Stopover: Tokyo. Boston: Little, Brown, 1957.

Women and Thomas Harrow. Boston: Little, Brown, 1958.

Timothy Dexter Revisited. Boston: Little, Brown, 1960. (Extensive revision, with much personal commentary, of *Lord Timothy Dexter.*)

BIBLIOGRAPHIES

White, William. "John P. Marquand: A Preliminary Checklist," *Bulletin of Bibliography,* 19:268–71 (September–December 1949).

———. "Marquandiana," *Bulletin of Bibliography,* 20:3–12 (January–April 1950).

———. "John P. Marquand since 1950," *Bulletin of Bibliography,* 21:230–34 (May–August 1956).

———. "More Marquandiana, 1956–1969," *Serif,* 6:33–36 (No. 2, 1969).

CRITICAL AND BIOGRAPHICAL STUDIES

Auchincloss, Louis. *Reflections of a Jacobite.* Boston: Houghton, Mifflin, 1961. Pp. 139–48.

Beach, Joseph Warren. *American Fiction, 1920–1940.* New York: Macmillan, 1941. Pp. 253–72.

Boynton, Percy H. *America in Contemporary Fiction.* Chicago: University of Chicago Press, 1940. Pp. 48–52.

Brady, Charles A. "John Phillips Marquand: Martini-Age Victorian," in *Fifty Years of the American Novel: A Christian Appraisal,* edited by Harold C. Gardiner, S.J. New York: Scribners, 1952. Pp. 107–34.

Breit, Harvey. "An Interview with J. P. Marquand," *New York Times Book Review,* April 24, 1949, p. 35.

Brickell, Herschel. "Miss Glasgow and Mr. Marquand," *Virginia Quarterly Review,* 17:405–17 (Summer 1941).

Butterfield, Roger. "John P. Marquand: America's Famous Novelist of Manners," *Life,* 17:64–73 (July 31, 1944).

De Voto, Bernard. *The World of Fiction.* Boston: Houghton, Mifflin, 1950. Pp. 272–82.

Eisinger, Chester E. *Fiction of the Forties.* Chicago: University of Chicago Press, 1963. Pp. 289–94.

Geismar, Maxwell. *American Moderns: From Rebellion to Conformity.* New York: Hill and Wang, 1959. Pp. 156–64.

Glick, Nathan. "Marquand's Vanishing American Aristocracy: Good Manners and the Good Life," *Commentary,* 9:435–41 (May 1950).

Gray, James. *On Second Thought.* Minneapolis: University of Minnesota Press, 1946. Pp. 87–93.

Greene, George. "A Tunnel from Persepolis: The Legacy of John Marquand," *Queens Quarterly,* 73:345–56 (Autumn 1966).

Gross, John J. *John P. Marquand.* New York: Twayne, 1963.

———. "The Late John P. Marquand: An Essay in Biography," *English Record,* 19:2–12 (No. 2, 1968).

Gurko, Leo. "The High-Level Formula of J. P. Marquand," *American Scholar,* 21:443–53 (October 1952).

Hamburger, Philip. *J. P. Marquand, Esquire.* Boston: Houghton, Mifflin, 1952.

Hicks, Granville. "Marquand of Newburyport," *Harper's,* 200:105–08 (April 1950).

Houghton, Frederick, and Richard Whitman. "J. P. Marquand Speaking," *Cosmopolitan,* 147:46–50 (August 1959). (An interview.)

Kazin, Alfred. *Contemporaries.* Boston: Little, Brown, 1962. Pp. 122–30.

Marquand, John P. "Apley, Wickford Point, and Pulham: My Early Struggles," *Atlantic,* 198:71–74 (September 1956).

———. "Hearsay History of Curzon's Mill," *Atlantic,* 200:84–91 (November 1957).

Millgate, Michael. *American Social Fiction: James*

to *Cozzens*. New York: Barnes and Noble, 1964. Pp. 182–85.

Roberts, Kenneth. "Memories of John P. Marquand," *Saturday Review*, 39:14–15 (September 15, 1956).

"Spruce Street Boy," *Time,* 53:104–113 (March 7, 1949).

Tuttleton, James W. *The American Novel of Manners*. Chapel Hill: University of North Carolina Press, 1972.

Van Gelder, Robert. "An Interview with a Best-Selling Author: John P. Marquand," *Cosmopolitan*, 122:18, 150–52 (March 1947).

————. *Writers and Writing*. New York: Scribners, 1946. Pp. 38–41. (An April 1940 interview with Marquand.)

Wagenknecht, Edward. *Cavalcade of the American Novel*. New York: Holt, 1952. Pp. 438–43.

Weeks, Edward. "John P. Marquand," *Atlantic*, 206:74–76 (October 1960).

—C. HUGH HOLMAN

Herman Melville

1819-1891

HERMAN MELVILLE was born in 1819, died in 1891, and has been adopted by the twentieth century as a writer peculiarly its own. Heir to the great tradition of romantic literature, he wrote realistically of life at sea and became a popular storyteller who responded to the cultural conflicts of the mid-nineteenth century with such shrewd and passionate ambivalence that his own age eventually found him incomprehensible and left his writings for a later generation to interpret in almost as many ways as there are readers. From the outbreak of the American Civil War until the end of World War I he was an almost completely forgotten writer. Now he is one of his country's most widely read, frequently discussed, and greatly admired authors.

The familiar image of Melville today is that of all his surviving portraits—bearded, formal, and reserved, as though he were holding himself aloof from a world of getting and spending and wasted powers. It is easy to imagine him as the author of the book which puzzles and challenges his latest critic. It is less easy to imagine him as the boy who went to sea in order to escape the boredom of rural schoolteaching, who signed himself up for a whaling voyage on Christmas Day because he could not get a respectable job as a legal scrivener, who deserted his ship to live among cannibals, and

who was to date his intellectual development from his twenty-fifth year and write *Moby Dick* at the age of thirty-one. There is a mystery about the man as well as about his works which teases and excites the imagination.

For a century, until recent scholarly investigations, the actual events of his life were so obscure that readers of his autobiographical romances were unable to tell whether specific statements were fact or fiction. He was born to adversity on August 1, 1819, in New York City, where his father was a well-to-do importer whose business was severely damaged by the scarcity of foreign exchange during America's first postwar depression. After eleven years of struggle, Allan Melville moved his family (by then consisting of his wife, Maria Gansevoort Melville, and their eight children, of whom Herman was the third child and the second of four boys) to Albany, where Herman attended the Academy for two short years of formal education before his father's death forced him to find employment in a bank. Less than two more years of schooling, before he reached the age of eighteen, prepared him for the simple duties of elementary schoolteaching and the literary career he was to follow—although, like Benjamin Franklin before him, he engaged in a considerable amount of self-education by joining a young men's literary and debating society and contributing to the local newspaper in the village of Lansingburgh, to which his widowed mother had moved.

In the summer of 1839 the attraction which the sea held for both the Melville and the Gansevoort members of his family induced him to make a trial voyage to Liverpool as a merchant sailor, and during the following summer he tried his inland fortune by traveling west to the lead mines around Galena, Illinois, where an uncle had settled. Another severe financial depression, however, had preceded as well as driven him westward, and he was forced to return to New York and shave his whiskers in order to look like a Christian (as his older brother put it) while vainly attempting to impose his abominable handwriting upon some lawyer in need of a clerk. Something like the desperation he was later to attribute to Ishmael, the narrator of *Moby Dick*—a damp, drizzly November of the soul—caused him to join a whaling voyage to the South Pacific, for a whaler in those days was the last refuge for criminals and castaways. But Melville was free and adventurous—a sturdy, energetic young man of five feet nine and a half whose blue eyes could twinkle with humor beneath his father's high brow and waving brown hair. Desperate though he may have been in committing himself to an undefined voyage of three years or more, he was still interested in adventure when he sailed out of New Bedford on the new ship *Acushnet* on Sunday, January 3, 1841.

His voyage took him to Rio, around Cape Horn, up the coast of South America to the Galápagos Islands, and for cruises along the Line before Melville and a friend found conditions intolerable and deserted in the Marquesas on July 9, 1842. By mistake they took refuge in the valley of the Typees, who were notorious as a tribe of cannibals, and Melville remained in captivity for a month before being rescued by an Australian whaler, the *Lucy Ann*. An ailing captain, drunken mate, and mutinous crew made conditions worse on the *Lucy Ann* than they had been on the *Acushnet;* and when the vessel put into Papeete, on September 20, Melville refused further duty. He was placed under shore arrest and brought to trial but allowed to escape after his ship sailed on October 15. With one of his shipmates he then went to the neighboring island of Moorea, or Eimeo, where the two men remained as wandering beachcombers until November 3 when the master of the *Charles and Henry*, out of Nantucket, hired Melville as a harpooner for the run to the next port. After an uneventful voyage he was discharged in Lahaina, in the Hawaiian Islands, on May 2, 1843, and made his way to Honolulu, where he decided to settle down as a clerk in a drygoods store for at least a year. The promise of a quick voyage home, however, persuaded him to sign on board the U.S. frigate *United States* on August 17. But it was not until early October of the following year that the ship reached Boston and Melville was discharged and allowed to rejoin his family in Lansingburgh, where they welcomed him with relief and listened with enthusiasm to the stories of his adventures.

Out of these stories grew his first book, *Typee: A Peep at Polynesian Life,* to give it its American title—which might have some relationship to the spirit in which it was composed. For Melville seems already to have been the good storyteller who was later to astound Mrs. Nathaniel Hawthorne with his vividness, and his sisters and their friends were good listeners. They thrilled to his dangers and could be easily teased by ambiguous references to South Sea maidens who were as charming as any from Lansingburgh or Boston but whose impulses (as everybody knew) were considerably less inhibited. Furthermore, the Typees were widely known as man-eaters, and although Melville had never known a human being to pass their lips he was not averse to taking advantage of their reputation for the sake of suspense. From the very beginning Melville played a game with his audience as he strung out his stories to book length with picturesque descriptions, details from memory, and other details gathered from reference books.

The game was continued, in another way and by force of circumstances, when his older brother, appointed to a diplomatic post in London, took the manuscript with him to England and submitted it to John Murray, whose imprint could be expected to guarantee the success of an American edition. Murray was willing to accept it for his Home and Colonial Library (which was advertised to consist of books as exciting as fiction, but all true) if he and his readers could be assured of its authenticity. Gansevoort Melville gave his personal assurance that his younger brother was not "a practised writer," as Murray suspected, but a genuine sailor, and Herman undertook to provide three new chapters and additional revisions and details which enabled the book to be published as a sober two-volume *Narrative of a Four Months' Residence among the Natives of a Valley of the Marquesas Islands* on February 27 and April 1, 1846. In the interim, on March 17, it was published in New York under its more lively American title. It was an immediate success in both countries, and Melville was so assured of the fact in advance that he began working at once on its sequel.

He had learned something from his publishers, and *Omoo,* the sequel, was a more carefully calculated narrative. It was less teasing than *Typee,* more straightforward and convincing as a narrative of real experience, more coherent in its tone of humorous realism; and its characters, especially the narrator's companion Dr. Long Ghost, seemed drawn for a popular comic illustrator. Yet in substance it was the same sort of book *Typee* had been—a combination of memory, imagination, and research in which the author used the same device of extending each week of his real adventures into a month in order to be plausible about what might have happened to him. Because its factual background has been better established by scholars, *Omoo* in fact gives a better indication than *Typee* of the nature of young Melville's literary imagination. All he wrote was focused upon the actuality of experience, but he wrote less about what had happened to him than about what he might have experienced had he participated more fully in the events he knew about. Both books were products of that area of consciousness where memory and imagination blend and are controlled only by the desire to tell a good but convincing tale.

In the meantime, before *Omoo* was completed in December 1846 and published in the following spring, Melville was being attacked from two sides—quietly for his romance, and vociferously for his realism. John Murray continued to be suspicious of *Typee* and kept insisting upon documentary proof of its veracity. So Melville was triumphant when his fellow deserter from the *Acushnet,* Richard Tobias Greene, appeared and offered to authenticate the narrative up to the time of his earlier escape from the Typees. "The Story of Toby" was added to subsequent editions of the book and also published by Murray as a separate pamphlet. The other objection was met by suppressing certain of the realistic details in later editions. Melville had been quite candid in his criticisms of the behavior of missionaries and the social effects of their activities in the South Seas and had commented with a sailor's matter-of-factness upon the customary behavior of native females on visiting ships. The storm raised against him, in the United States, as a "traducer of missions" led to the publication of a second, expurgated, edition of his book by his American publisher, Wiley and Putnam, and his transfer to the Harpers for the publication of *Omoo* and his later novels.

His next book and first actual novel, however, was to be a problem. He had based *Typee* upon his experiences in the Marquesas and *Omoo* upon those in Tahiti, and although he had deliberately excluded any account of the whale fishery from these books he had no pattern, at the moment, for using the material which was later to go into *Moby Dick*. He was telling, with great success, a continued story of adventure while exploiting the novelty of the South Seas (which had not before been treated in fiction), and he had no more adventures of the same sort to recount. His voyage on the *Charles and Henry* had been uneventful and unprovocative. He would have to invent a series of incidents which, for the first time, would be entirely unrelated to any core of personal experience. He may have been doubtful of his ability to do so, for before he went back to his writing he rallied his friends and visited Washington in an attempt to get a job in the Treasury Department. When the attempt failed, he took up his pen again with more forced energy than persuasiveness.

The impulse behind Melville's energy at this time was matrimonial. He had been courting Elizabeth Shaw, daughter of the chief justice of Massachusetts and one of his sisters' friends who had listened to him tell the tales of *Typee,* and he wanted to settle in a larger place than Lansingburgh. He had been spending an increasing amount of time in New York City, becoming acquainted with the complexities of the publishing world and finding congenial associates in the literary circle gathered around the scholarly editor, Evert Duyckinck. In turn, Duyckinck found him a promising contributor of comic articles to *Yankee Doodle* and serious reviews to the new *Literary World*. Removal to the city made sense for a man who was being compelled to become a professional writer. Accordingly, after his marriage on August 4, 1847, he borrowed money to buy a house large enough for his whole family—his wife and his mother, his four unmarried sisters, his younger brother Allan and his bride, and his youngest brother, Thomas, who at the age of seventeen had already been two years away from home on a whaler. There, at Number 103 Fourth Avenue, he settled down in late September to throw himself with enthusiasm into the world of literature and begin working again on the manuscript of his third book.

The new book, eventually called *Mardi,* was to be neither a popular nor an artistic success, but its composition provides an extraordinary illustration of the growth of an artist's mind. The basic reason for its failure is structural, because it represents an unresolved conflict between Melville's conscious effort to find a unifying narrative corresponding to the picaresque sort he had been using and his unconscious compulsion to relate his writing to his own experiences, which were now predominantly literary and intellectual. For the unschooled author began reading widely and avidly during this period, and his writing reflected his reading—Dante and Rabelais, Spenser and other Elizabethans, Robert Burton and Sir Thomas Browne, La Motte-Fouqué and other German romancers, Coleridge and the English romantics, and philosophers from Seneca to David Hartley. The early chapters in which he attempted to invent adventures like those in *Typee* and *Omoo* soon gave way to a more romantic but still adventurous interlude and this in turn to a sort of satiric travelogue in which a group of type characters discoursed, according to type, on the world around them as it was portrayed with increasingly purposeful symbolism in the form of a South Sea archipelago called Mardi. The narrator's original companion (corresponding to Toby and Long Ghost) was abandoned entirely after the romantic interlude, when the author departed completely from the pattern of his earlier books, but a certain connection was kept between the interlude and the travelogue by making the beautiful maiden introduced in the first the object of a quest in the second.

Incoherent though all this seems and is, there was a certain imaginative focal point for it within Melville's immediate experience. Books had become more exciting to him than cannibals and whales, and he was actually recording, while trying to do something else, his adventures among books. The quest reflected La Motte-Fouqué's quest in *Undine* and in *Sintram and His Companions,* Spenser's Red Crosse Knight's quest for Holinesse, and the Rabelaisian quest for the Oracle of the Bottle. His use of allegory came from these writers, especially Spenser, and others—including the compilers of popular books on the meaning of flowers. His eccentricities of manner and style were often those of Burton's *Anatomy of Melancholy* and of Sir Thomas Browne. And one of the companions on the quest was specifically created to express his new philosophical interests. The result, inevitably, was chaos, but the apparent chaos was the turbulent effect of a vigorous mind exploring a new world which it was to conquer and control.

The tendency toward control, in fact, is evident in *Mardi* itself. For as the book progressed Melville's mind became more critical and speculative than it had been in the first half of the narrative. He had made his quest an allegorical search for happiness in which the hero was led forward by pure desire and driven from behind by the threat of danger from the consequences of a past action. And he had evidently decided from the beginning that happiness was not to be found in the sensuous temptations of any-

thing like Spenser's Bower of Bliss. But at some point in his writing the quest quit being a casual narrative device holding together his random thoughts and opinions and acquired, instead, an intellectual seriousness. Religion especially interested him as a potential source of happiness, but not the institutionalized religion which he examined and rejected in the book as he had already rejected it in his actual observations on missionaries in the South Seas. Yet he allowed his philosophical companion to take refuge in the allegorical island of Serenia, where the dictates of reason and of Christian charity were one; and eventually his historian and poet were also directed there, while his representative ruler renounced all thought of happiness and returned to his turbulent country. But the hero and narrator, Taji, was more romantic: his was an endless quest as he pursued his intangible goal, followed by the specters of his past, "over an endless sea."

This was the book as Melville thought he had completed it on the eve of the French Revolution in the spring of 1848. But the intellectual development revealed in it was not yet complete. For when news of the events in Europe reached him, Melville's imagination was stirred, as it had never been before, by the signs of immediate social change, and he increased the size of his book one-sixth by the insertion of some twenty-three chapters of political allegory. These referred to the revolutions in France (Franko) and other parts of Europe (Porpheero), to the Chartist movement and the international and fiscal policies of England (Dominora), to the problems created by slavery and by geographical expansion in the United States (Vivenza), and to various other matters ranging from the potato famine in Ireland to conditions in India. They reveal an extraordinary perceptiveness, in depth, to the long-range significance of contemporary events; and perhaps the most interesting of these chapters, from this point of view, are those in which he anticipated the social consequences attendant on the closing of the American frontier and on the California gold rush, which had not yet occurred at the time he wrote. The young man who had so recently moved to the city and entered the larger world of the mind had acquired an unusual amount of knowledge, understanding, and vision in a remarkably short time.

Melville had also acquired something else while writing *Mardi* which he did not recognize or appreciate. He knew before the book was published in March 1849 (by Bentley, in London, for Murray had refused it) that it would be a failure, and financial necessity compelled him to return at once to his old successful vein—the autobiographical romance. The richest of its novelties, his South Sea adventures, had been exhausted, except for the whaling materials, but he still had the events of his trip to Liverpool, which he worked into *Redburn: His First Voyage* and completed by the end of June. He always spoke of it as a book he despised and may actually have done so. He knew that so many men had written of their youthful experiences before the mast that the subject was hackneyed, and he knew, too, that he could not afford to put into this book the sort of intellectual and literary excitement which had damned *Mardi* as a commercial venture. But he did not know that the emotions he felt while writing could be projected into the past or into a fiction in a way that would give his words a vitality he himself did not associate with the intentional context of meaning.

With *Redburn* Melville became a novelist—so persuasively so, in fact, that many later readers have had difficulty accepting the evidence that he himself was some four years older than his hero when he first went to sea and that the most memorable parts of the book are pure fiction. It is true that most of the char-

acters in the novel were Melville's actual companions, some under their real names, on his first voyage. But Jackson, the most memorable of them because of his strange hold over the crew and his dramatic death, was alive at the end of a trip which included no casualties of any sort. Melville himself was by no means the timid, undersized innocent who serves as the narrator, nor did the ship carry immigrants or the plague on its return voyage. Yet the personality of the narrator and the circumstantial accounts of the outbreak of a virulent disease in a crowded steerage seem to reflect an emotional involvement which makes the book more convincing than either *Typee* or *Omoo*.

The probability is that Melville was more deeply involved in *Redburn* than in his earlier books but that it was the involvement of the moment, not of the past through memory. Wellingborough Redburn may have been not at all like Herman Melville but he could very easily be an older brother's affectionate representation of Thomas Melville, who had gone to sea at the age of fifteen, who had recently returned and left again on a voyage to China, and who was so much on Herman's mind that *Redburn* was dedicated to him. And if Melville's own return from Liverpool had not been on a plague ship crowded with immigrants, he was nevertheless writing the latter part of his book while the blue cholera was creating panic in New York after having been brought there by an immigrant ship the preceding December. The unregulated conditions on board such ships were notorious, and Melville knew the slums from which their passengers came. A man whose imagination and emotions could be deeply stirred by contemporary events (as Melville's had been when he wrote the political chapters of *Mardi*) may readily have undertaken, out of a sort of indignant humanitarianism, to make the public realize that it was suffering from its own indifference to the welfare of the less fortunate. "For the whole world is the patrimony of the whole world," he wrote with reference to the agitated question of whether "multitudes of foreign poor should be landed on our American shores"; "there is no telling who does not own a stone in the Great Wall of China." *Redburn* is a convincing book because the emotions which controlled it were genuine, profound, and pervasive enough to affect its style: the writing in the first part reflects the simplicity of his involvement in a boy's point of view, whereas that of the last half has the detachment of an observer who realizes the significance of what he is writing about.

But Melville had no time, at the moment, to realize the significance of his literary achievement. He was heavily in debt and turned at once to a book based on his naval experience, writing *White Jacket* at the rate of nearly three thousand words a day during July and August while reading proofs on *Redburn*. Once again he used real people, drawn out of his memory, as characters, but most of the events of the voyage around Cape Horn were fictitious. He borrowed freely from various sources the numerous comic incidents which were sprinkled through it, but what he called its "man-of-warish" style was a holdover from the indignant humanitarianism of *Redburn*. Some of his indignation was undoubtedly a reflection of his past resentment against arbitrary restraints and cruelties of naval life, and his brutal ship's surgeon, though perhaps real enough, belonged to a literary tradition that went back to Smollett. But the abolition of flogging was being agitated at the time he wrote, and the pervasive theme of his emphasis upon it as an unnecessarily cruel but all-too-usual punishment was in the interest of reform. Both in *White Jacket* and in *Redburn* he exhibited the naturalistic impulse to portray vividly the evils of society in the hope that legislative action would be taken against them.

Yet *White Jacket* was a deeper book than its predecessor had been. Its subtitle labeled it "The World in a Man-of-War" and its concluding chapter drew an elaborate analogy between the frigate and the earth, sailing through space with clean decks and dark storerooms of secrets beneath the "lie" of its surface. For Melville had found the microcosm of his man-of-war, despite its friendly companionship of the foretop and its occasional comedy, a cruel world of arbitrary power and discipline, motiveless malice, ruthlessness, and brutality. Above all, it was a world of constraint, in which men had to swing their hammocks without "spreaders," turn on signal when they were allowed to sleep on the crowded deck, and go sleepless because precedent and convention required the storing of gear in the daytime. It was a world of absolute command from above and of mystery and subterranean darkness below. Perhaps Melville felt the constraint to an unusual degree while writing, for he had sacrificed his customary summer vacation to the book and was working through the August heat in a city so panic-stricken from the cholera that people were afraid to go outdoors or eat their customary food. Physically as well as financially, the world was pressing in upon him, and he must have felt it. At any rate, there was an incipient violence in the emotion underlying *White Jacket* which suggested that at any moment its author might break loose.

Whatever the constraint Melville may have felt during the summer was relieved in October 1849, when he decided to go abroad in an effort to get better terms for *White Jacket* than he had been able to get, by correspondence with his English publisher, for *Redburn*. He also planned to collect material for a historical novel based upon the real life of an American Revolutionary patriot who had been captured by the British and had lived for forty years in

England as an exile. But the trip was to have unexpected consequences. For one thing, it renewed his sea memories. The captain of his ship gave him a private stateroom with a porthole through which he could gaze at the ocean, and he was also allowed the freedom of the rigging so that he could recapture all the old emotions of being at the masthead. For another, it proved to be an exciting intellectual experience. Two of his fellow passengers, George J. Adler and Frank Taylor, were young men of philosophical inclinations with whom he could discuss the subject which had so interested him in the concluding chapter of *White Jacket*—"Fixed Fate, Free-will, Foreknowledge absolute." Their interest in German Transcendentalism appealed to the man who had become acquainted with Emerson, for the first time, only eight months before and had been surprised to find in him deep thoughts rather than "myths and oracular gibberish." He was to talk to them, on every occasion he could make, even after the voyage was over and he was in London and Paris.

By the time Melville returned home, on February 1, 1850, he seems to have laid aside his plan for the historical novel. At any rate, by May 1 he had seen *White Jacket* through the press and was able to write Richard Henry Dana, Jr., that he was "half way" in a book which he referred to as "the 'whaling voyage.'" And on June 27 he promised the completed volume to his English publisher "in the later part of the coming autumn" and described it specifically but with some exaggeration as "a romance of adventure, founded upon certain wild legends in the Southern Sperm Whale Fisheries and illustrated by the author's own personal experience, of two years and more, as a harpooner." In the middle of July he was ready for a vacation and left for Pittsfield, Massachusetts, where Evert Duyckinck visited him in early August and wrote that "Melville

has a new book mostly done—a romantic, fanciful and literal and most enjoyable presentment of the Whale Fishery—something quite new."

These early references to the book which was to become *Moby Dick* are of unusual interest because they introduce the most teasing question which arises in any effort to follow the development of Melville's creative imagination: How did it happen that he was to spend a year of agonized composition upon a "mostly done" manuscript and transform it from a romance with autobiographical overtones into the powerfully dramatic novel it became? He seems to have had no intention, when he went on his vacation, of doing more than filling out his narrative with realistic details gathered from books of reference he had collected for that purpose. But once again the emotions of immediate experience were to project themselves into his fiction, transform it, and give it—this time—not only the vitality of his own life but the tensions of the century in which he lived.

The trigger action for his explosion into greatness was that of a single day, August 5, 1850, during his vacation when one of his neighbors arranged an expedition and dinner party for all the literary celebrities of the region—the New Englanders who summered in the Berkshires and Melville and the New York guests he had invited up for a visit. The expedition was to the top of Monument Mountain, where Melville, Nathaniel Hawthorne, and Oliver Wendell Holmes were made gay by the elevation and champagne and brought back to sobriety by the New York critic Cornelius Mathews, who insisted upon making the occasion literary by reading William Cullen Bryant's solemn poem about the Indian lovers who had leaped to their death from the projecting ledge on which Melville had been performing sailor's antics. Holmes's satiric impulses were aroused, and the result was a literary quarrel which continued throughout the "well moistened" dinner party later. It focused upon the theory of the influence of climate upon genius and the question whether America would produce a literature as elevated as its mountains and as spacious as its plains. The New Englanders (as Holmes's Phi Beta Kappa poem *Astraea* of a few days later was to show) were skeptical of the New Yorkers' enthusiasm.

Melville's part in the argument seems to have been more mischievous than serious, but he was impressed by it and even more impressed by his first meeting with Hawthorne. His aunt had given him a copy of *Mosses from an Old Manse* at the beginning of his vacation, but he had not yet read it. Now, having met the author, he read it with the extraordinary enthusiasm he expressed in the belated review he wrote for the *Literary World* before his New York friends went home. Hawthorne proved the greatness of American literature, he contended, under the anonymous signature of "A Virginian spending July in Vermont"; but it was a greatness of heart and mind, observable in Hawthorne's willingness to present the "blackness" of truth—the same dark "background against which Shakespeare plays his grandest conceits" and which "appeals to that Calvinistic sense of Innate Depravity and Original Sin, from whose visitations, in some shape or other, no deeply thinking mind is always and wholly free." In Hawthorne and his *Mosses* Melville found an attitude of mind which courageously reflected all his doubts concerning the transcendental idealism and optimism that had interested him during his recent voyage and had affected his reading since.

The impression made by Hawthorne was so great that Melville cultivated his acquaintance assiduously during the following months and eventually dedicated *Moby Dick* to him. Yet he did not become a wholehearted convert to his new friend's "black" skepticism. He was

himself a man of greater vitality, more of a man of action, than Hawthorne; and although the two shared an interest in the Gothic romance, Hawthorne's interest was in the Gothic atmosphere whereas Melville's was in the romantic hero—the Byronic wandering outlaw of his own dark mind. Furthermore, Melville had borrowed *Sartor Resartus* at the time he finished collecting his whaling library for the revision of his book, and he found in Carlyle's transcendentalized version of the romantic hero a character who was as "deep-diving" as Emerson but who had proved himself susceptible to Hawthorne's pessimism and capable of defying it. In one of his stories in the *Mosses,* "Earth's Holocaust," Hawthorne had set forth allegorically his belief that evil could not be destroyed because it was constantly being recreated by "the all-engendering heart of man." Melville was inclined to agree. But the best "strong positive illustration" Melville found of the "blackness in Hawthorne" was in the story of "Young Goodman Brown" and his allegorical but unanswered cry for "Faith." In Carlyle's book Melville found a hero who could live in such a spiritual state of "starless, Tartarean black" that he could hear the Devil say "thou art fatherless, outcast, and the Universe is mine" but who still had the courage and the energy to say "*I am not thine, but Free, and forever hate thee!*" Whether he was as sensible as Young Goodman Brown (who went into a lethargy when he was made to suspect, either by a dream or by a real experience, that the world was the Devil's) might be questionable. But he was more heroic and, to Melville's mind, more admirable.

Melville's literary interests, in short, reveal the tensions that existed in his mind at the time he began what otherwise might have been the routine job of revising his manuscript. They were vital tensions, not only in terms of his own sensitivity but in their profound effect upon Western civilization during the nineteenth century—tensions set up by the conflict between the will to believe and the need to be shown, between transcendentalism and empiricism in philosophy, between religion and science, between faith and skepticism. These were not tensions to be resolved, as so many of Melville's contemporaries tried to resolve them, for no satisfactory resolution has yet proved possible. Melville, at his deepest and most complex creative level, made no attempt to resolve the conflict. Instead, he dramatized it. And it may be that the ambiguity and ambivalence inherent in the dramatic Shakespearean qualities of *Moby Dick* are responsible for the fact that it has a greater appeal to the puzzled and questioning twentieth century than do the writings of Melville's contemporaries who were more explicitly concerned with the same tensions.

In any event, Shakespeare was an important element in the literary and intellectual ferment which went into the making of *Moby Dick*. Melville had become excited about him at the time he discovered transcendentalism, in February 1849, when he wrote Evert Duyckinck that "if another Messiah ever comes twill be in Shakspeare's person." And he kept looking, in his review of the *Mosses*, if not for another Messiah at least for another Shakespeare— perhaps "this day being born on the banks of the Ohio." Hawthorne had "approached" him, for a nineteenth-century Shakespeare would not be an Elizabethan dramatist but a part of his "times" with "correspondent coloring." There is no doubt but that Melville was excited by the company and the literary debate of August 5, 1850, and it may have been that this excitement was intensified by a feeling of challenge. Within a few days he was to denounce the "absolute and unconditional adoration of Shakespeare" and his "unapproachability" as one of "our Anglo-Saxon superstitions." Might not he himself be another man "to carry

republican progressiveness into Literature as well as into Life" by writing a novel that had the quality of Shakespearean tragedy?

However this might be, his novel began to change from a story of the whale fishery to a story of "the Whale." Captain Ahab (named for a man who had "done evil in the sight of the Lord") remained the protagonist in his narrative, but his antagonist was neither the worthy mate Starbuck nor any member of his exotic crew. It was the great white whale with a humped back and hieroglyphics on his brow, known throughout the fishery as Moby Dick and notorious for the viciousness with which he had turned upon the men who had hunted and attempted to destroy him. Ahab himself had been his victim on a previous voyage when the whale had sheared off his leg and started a train of cause and effect that resulted in his further mutilation by its splintered substitute. And Ahab, a queer "grand, ungodly, god-like man," had embarked on a voyage of revenge which would follow the paths of the migrating leviathan throughout the vast Pacific until he and the whole ship's crew were destroyed and the narrator alone was left to tell the tale. In order to make the voyage plausible Melville had to draw upon the whole body of available whaling lore in extraordinary detail. He also had to make his captain, from the narrator's point of view, mad.

But the power of the book does not come from the realistic fantasy of the voyage or from the obsessed madness of the traditional Gothic or romantic protagonist who is half hero and half villain. On the contrary, it comes from the fact that Ahab is one of the few characters in literature genuinely "formed for noble tragedies." Like Lear, he is a noble individual whose only flaw is a single mistake in judgment. And like Hamlet, at least as Coleridge interpreted him, his mistake is that of a disordered judgment—that of a man with a "craving after the indefinite" who "looks upon external things as hieroglyphics" and whose mind, with its "everlasting broodings," is "unseated from its healthy relation" and "constantly occupied with the world within, and abstracted from the world without—giving substance to shadows, and throwing a mist over all commonplace actualities." For to Ahab "all visible objects" were "but as pasteboard masks" from behind which "some unknown but still reasoning thing puts forth the mouldings of its features." To him the white whale was the emblem of "outrageous strength, with inscrutable malice sinewing it"; and it was "that inscrutable thing" which he hated, and he was determined to "wreak that hate upon him."

Whether Ahab's attitude should be interpreted in psychological or philosophical terms is an important question with respect to Melville's biography. The narrator, Ishmael, uses psychological terms in his accounts of the phases Ahab goes through while "deliriously transferring" his idea of evil to the whale as an object which would visibly personify it and make it practically assailable. Ahab himself, of course, sounds like Carlyle's hero asserting his individual freedom and defying the Devil's claim to the universe. The weight of the evidence, derived from the book and from letters written at the same time, appears to favor a rather close identification of the author's point of view with that of the narrator. Melville's conscious fable in *Moby Dick* seems to lead to the conclusion that a belief in the emblematic nature of the universe is a form of madness. His rational judgment apparently concurred with that of Hawthorne: the white whale was a natural beast, and the evil in him was a product of the "all-engendering heart" or mind of Ahab. But, for the moment, Melville's personal philosophy is not relevant to an interpretation of *Moby Dick* as a work of literature. "Dramatically regarded," as he himself put it, "all men tragically great are made so through a certain morbidness." The important point is that Ahab's "morbidness," whether a sane conviction or a mad obsession, was the tragic flaw in his character which directed his heroic behavior toward destruction.

Yet if one goes beyond superficial interpretation into an attempt to explain the strange power of *Moby Dick*, Melville's personal beliefs do become important and his chapter on "The Whiteness of the Whale" becomes particularly relevant. For here he collects evidence for the existence of a sort of knowledge which is more intuitive than the rational empiricism used by Ishmael to explain "crazy Ahab" in the immediately preceding chapter. The inference to be drawn is that Melville was not wholly convinced of the validity of the fable his rational mind constructed in order to provide himself with a plot of the sort he found and admired in Hawthorne. The conflict between transcendentalism and empiricism was not something which he merely observed and then dramatized. It was something that he experienced and felt deeply within himself. Ahab, who sometimes doubted whether there was anything beyond the "wall" of the emblematic material universe, was only slightly more mad than the storyteller who condemned him but sometimes doubted whether the material world of experience provided the ultimate form of knowledge. Melville could easily imagine within himself the rage to believe, the madness, he attributed to his hero as a "tragic flaw."

In fact, if one explores the creative level which lies beneath an artist's identification with the intellectual and emotional conflicts of his age, there is abundant evidence of a deeply rooted desire in Melville to be as heroically mad as Ahab. Such evidence is to be found in his imagery. The image of the fatherless outcast had been a controlling one in his earlier books. He had been the deserter in *Typee*, the runaway in *Omoo*, the escaped captive in *Mardi*, the orphan in *Redburn*, and the poor sailor denied a charitable daub of paint in *White Jacket*. And in *Moby Dick* he was Ishmael, the homeless wanderer. The image, of course, was that of his own life from the time he left school at his father's death until he married, bought a house, and established himself in New York. But in *White Jacket*, as we have seen, a new and conflicting image began to emerge and become dominant—that of constraint and subterranean mystery, with emotional overtones of incipient violence. The loss of his wandering bachelor's freedom, his crowded household, his serious financial problems, and the peculiar cooped-up desperation of his writing *Redburn* and *White Jacket* during the plague may have all contributed to its emergence. But its origin probably was in something deeper—in the feeling of growth, so vividly expressed in a letter to Hawthorne in June 1851, which made him believe that what he was most moved to write was banned and that all his books were "botches." He felt himself one of those "deep men" who had something "eating in them" and frustrating them. It was time for him to deny his fatherless, outcast state and assert his freedom, like Carlyle's hero, with his "whole Me." Looking at all the things that hemmed him in, he might well suspect that "there's naught beyond" but still cry with Ahab "How can the prisoner reach outside except by thrusting through the wall?"

The imagery of constraint, frustration, and the obscure mystery of frustration is so pervasive in *Moby Dick* that one is almost compelled to believe that the secret of its vitality lies somewhere in Melville's own heroic attempt, by using all the resources of language and invention he could command, to thrust through the wall of frustrations he could not fully understand. "I have a sort of sea-feeling," he had written Evert Duyckinck in December

1850, when the ground was covered with snow. "My room seems a ship's cabin; and at nights when I wake up and hear the wind shrieking, I almost fancy there is too much sail on the house, and I had better go on the roof and rig in the chimney." And at the end of the following June, when the book was half through the press, he wrote Hawthorne of his disgust "with the heat and dust of the babylonish brick-kiln of New York" and his return to the country "to feel the grass—and end the book reclining on it." It was only natural, perhaps, that he should have also written Hawthorne that the book was baptized (like Ahab's harpoon) in the name of the Devil, for there was a great deal of Ahab's passion in Melville while he wrote.

Moby Dick was completed shortly before its author's thirty-second birthday and published in London on October 18, 1851, and in New York about four weeks later. Hawthorne understood the fable, and his understanding gave Melville, for a moment, "a sense of unspeakable security" and an awareness of more pervasive allegorical implications than he had intended. But the book was not a success. Although the reviews were better, the sales were no greater than those of *Mardi*. Once again Melville had to face the fact that if he poured his whole self into a book it was almost certainly doomed to commercial failure.

While he was writing *Moby Dick* Melville's way of life was drastically changed. He had bought a house, Arrowhead, and a hundred and fifty acres of ground in the Berkshires, and he had set himself up as a farmer. There his second son was born during the autumn of 1851, and there, during the winter, he contemplated his next literary project. Hawthorne's appreciation of *Moby Dick* in November had stirred his ambition: "Leviathan is not the biggest fish," he had written; "—I have heard of Krakens." But by January 1852 he apparently faced the fact that he would make very little money from the sort of books he wanted to write and decided that, if dollars damned him, he would go ahead and be damned. He would try to do something that would be popular. And so he wrote Mrs. Hawthorne (who had surprised him by liking the whaling story) that he would not again send her "a bowl of salt water" but "a rural bowl of milk." He offered the new book to his English publisher, Richard Bentley, soon afterward; and when Bentley cited his losses on the earlier books as an argument in favor of a contract for half-profits instead of a substantial advance, Melville suggested that he "let bygones be bygones" and publish the new work under an assumed name such as "Guy Winthrop." For it was "very much more calculated for popularity than anything you have yet published of mine—being a regular romance, with a mysterious plot to it, and stirring passions at work, and withal, representing a new and elevated aspect of American life."

By this time, April 16, 1852, the rapidly written book was completed and in type at his American publisher's, and it is difficult to understand how its author could have written about it in such terms. For this "rural bowl of milk" was *Pierre; or, The Ambiguities*, surely the most perverse of Melville's novels in its unrestrained imagination, about which Bentley worried, and its offensiveness to the "many sensitive readers" with whom he was concerned. It was probably planned as a sort of satiric variation on the *Moby Dick* fable in a situation and setting which would have a greater appeal to feminine readers. Its hero, Pierre Glendinning, was a sophomoric version of Captain Ahab who also had his vision of the absolute and acted accordingly. But Pierre's intuition was of good rather than evil—of an absolute morality superior to that of the every-day world which surrounded even his idyllic existence with an affectionate widowed mother on a large country estate. It led him, when he became convinced that a strange dark girl in the vicinity was his illegitimate half sister, to pretend marriage with her in order that she might have the Glendinning name without disturbing his mother's devotion to his father's memory. And it also led him to disinheritance, to a fantastic existence in New York City as a writer among a group of Transcendental Apostles, and to a tragic end which was more melodramatic than that of Captain Ahab.

Melville may have persuaded himself while trying (in vain) to sell the book to Bentley that he had managed to combine genial satire with the mysterious plot and passions of the Gothic romances which had so interested him during the early stages of writing *Moby Dick*. But if he did he was ignoring the fact that the major—and, from a commercial point of view, the most damning—ambiguity in *Pierre* reflected his compulsive desire to resolve the emotional and intellectual conflict which had made *Moby Dick* so effectively dramatic. Did Pierre Glendinning deserve any sympathy at all for his immature behavior while pursuing some ideal of absolute morality? Was there any validity in the sort of evidence for intuitive knowledge that Melville had assembled the year before for his chapter on "The Whiteness of the Whale"? Or was a person who believed in the transcendental absolute simply fooling himself? By presenting Ahab dramatically as an obsessed madman, he had made the answer to such questions as these a matter of opinion rather than one for investigation; and he had expressed his own rational opinion in the fable of the book. But the questions continued to haunt him.

For Pierre was not mad. He was very young and very foolish but in no sense neurotic, obsessed, or crazy. And Melville could not resist the impulse to explore the psychology of his behavior, following "the endless, winding way" (as he put it) of "the flowing river in the cave of man" wherever it might lead in a manner that would not be permitted in a "mere novel." He did it with an honesty and a subtlety which resulted in the first genuine psychological novel in American literature. But the way led him to the ruinous theme of incest. At the beginning he had made the dark Isabel beautiful in order to keep Pierre from seeming too perfect and immaculate: his hero would have been less ready to "champion the right," Melville observed, had he not been invited to do so by beauty rather than ugliness. His intention had been to make her beauty one of those "mere contingent things" of which Pierre would be unaware while it served the artistic purpose of keeping the "heavenly fire" of his enthusiasm within a plausible vessel of human "clay." But Melville's years at sea and in strange lands had given him a greater understanding of human frailty than of Victorian proprieties, and he allowed the "contingent" attraction of Isabel to develop beyond the limits of discretion before the book reached its melodramatic conclusion. Once more he had gone too far in putting too much serious thought into a book designed for popular consumption.

He had also gone beyond simple indiscretion. For *Pierre* shows signs of strains and tensions quite different from those in *Moby Dick*. It contains less ambivalence and more indications of conflicting purpose. The superficial romanticism of its idyllic episodes and mysterious plot was calculated to make it a popular novel, but the serious probing into psychological depths represented the kind of speculation that had been widely condemned in *Mardi* and *Moby Dick*. The amused detachment with which Pierre was treated as a "sophomore" probably represented an effort to achieve the

"genialities" Melville admired in Hawthorne, but the amusement sometimes became sardonic. He drew upon his own early background to a considerable extent for the details of Pierre's, but as he approached the present a touch of bitterness crept in. His picture of Pierre at his writing plank was a comic portrayal, in Carlylese, of a desperate attempt to write the great American novel; but it was based so much upon the grim conditions under which he himself had been writing during the past three years that the comedy had to be forced and exaggerated in order to avoid the risk of self-pity. The serious elements in the book are many and varied, but they all serve to create the total effect of an author who was attempting the light touch with an uncontrollably heavy hand.

More than ever, perhaps, Melville was feeling the spiritual claustrophobia which had become evident in the summer of 1848. The image of the vault is frequent in *Pierre*, and the statue of Laocoön appears, near the middle of the book, in a niche off the stairs leading to Mrs. Glendinning's chamber. One of the most memorable incidents in the story is the section in which Pierre, in a dream, identifies himself with Enceladus, imprisoned in the earth with only the stumps of his once audacious arms, striving in vain to assault the heavens. Melville's comment on this section indicates clearly that Pierre could and did use his knowledge of old fables to elucidate his own dreams and that he found this one "most repulsively fateful and foreboding" only because he failed to wrest from it its ultimate meaning: "Whoso storms the sky gives best proof he came from thither! But whatso crawls contented in the moat before that crystal fort, shows it was born within that slime, and there forever will abide." Pierre never learned to strike the "stubborn rock" of fable "and force even aridity itself to quench his painful thirst" for self-knowledge. But Melville did. And what he learned, while writing *Pierre*, helps explain the mystery of some of his writings which were to come later.

Commercially as well as artistically *Pierre* was Melville's greatest failure. The reviewers were unanimous in condemning it, and fewer than three hundred copies were to be sold during the entire year following its publication. The wise old judge who was his father-in-law became worried as soon as he read the book. He knew that Melville was a popular writer only when he wrote about ships and sailors, and so he persuaded the young man to go with him on a trip to Nantucket, where he was holding court in early July 1852. He planned to have Herman meet some of the people connected with whaling in New Bedford and Nantucket and then have a refreshing vacation at Martha's Vineyard and the Elizabeth Islands. Melville was willing to go and also to keep his eyes open for fresh literary material.

But what he found was not what Judge Shaw probably hoped for. No suggestion of adventure—either of escape or of bold defiance—came his way and fired his imagination. Instead of being impressed by the daring seafaring men of Nantucket he was impressed by the patient women of the island who waited, so often in vain, for their husbands' return from distant lands and seas. The story he brought back with him, well documented, was that of a certain Agatha Robertson whose husband had deserted her for seventeen years and then returned and deserted her again with no reproach from Agatha. The whole story and the incidents connected with it, he felt, were "instinct with significance"; but he hesitated about writing it and tried in vain to get Hawthorne to do so before he decided, with the beginning of his winter writing season in December 1852, to undertake it himself. There is no evidence that Melville ever wrote or even

made a fair beginning of the Agatha story, but his interest in it and his unproductive winter are both significant in view of his preoccupation with the theme of patience when he did begin to write again.

During this period of nonproductivity his family decided that writing was bad for him and that he should apply to the new Democratic President, Hawthorne's friend and classmate, Franklin Pierce, for a diplomatic post abroad. They enlisted the help of so many friends and made such a case for the desirability of a change in occupation for him that they created a lasting impression of a nervous breakdown from "too much excitement of the imagination." But they failed to get him an appointment and failed to divert him from the profession of writing. On the contrary, Melville decided, during that winter, to turn more professional than he had ever been before. He agreed to become a contributor to the new *Putnam's Monthly Magazine* at five dollars a page (the highest price paid any of its contributors), and *Putnam's* introduced him to its readers in the issue of February 1853 as the first of "Our Young Authors." His first contribution, which, however, did not appear until November and December, was "Bartleby, the Scrivener; A Story of Wall-Street," not only the first of his short stories but one of the most interesting and revealing of all the documents in the history of Melville's imaginative life.

In the first place, "Bartleby" is a classic but unusual fable of patience—unusual because it tells of a patience which has within itself the tensions of both acceptance and defiance. Its hero is not active, like Captain Ahab or even Pierre. He is completely passive. But he is as defiant as either. He makes no attempt to storm the sky, but he does not crawl in the slime. He would simply "prefer not to" crawl or to conform to any of the expectations of him.

His force of character is great but entirely negative. Furthermore, there seems to be little question but that this was a fable deliberately created by Melville in a search for self-knowledge. For the patience of Bartleby was much closer to that of his own temperament than was anything he could find in the story of Agatha or the women of Nantucket. Various real incidents may have contributed to the substance of the fable, but the powerful center of its invention seems to have been a soul-searching speculation about "what might have been." Suppose Melville had obtained and accepted a job as a lawyer's clerk instead of defiantly going to sea and writing such defiant books as *Mardi*, *Moby Dick*, and *Pierre*. What might his fate have been? Melville looked in his heart and wrote that it would be pretty much the same as Pierre's—death in the Tombs.

"Bartleby" is a story extraordinarily rich in its suggestiveness, but, next to its soul-searching quality, its most interesting characteristic is its conscious use of a dominant image—as though Melville, like Pierre, had been directed by his most haunting dreams to a fable that was capable of revealing his condition. The wall that Ahab saw in Moby Dick is everywhere in this "Story of Wall-Street." Bartleby faces it in his employer's office and in the exercise yard of the Tombs, and he dies quietly at its base. Pierre's dream of Enceladus was of a no more profound symbol of confinement. It was a symbol that had crept gradually into Melville's writings, probably without his awareness, but this time he used it as consciously as he might have done had he been attempting to exorcise it. He did not succeed. But as he continued to write short stories he continued to be conscious of his own feeling of frustration, to seek its possible cause, and to use his search as a device for giving meaning to the fables he created.

One such story was the otherwise trivial "Cock-a-Doodle-Doo!" published in *Harper's Monthly Magazine* for December, in which he explained the behavior of a character similar to Bartleby in terms of pride. But he had more ambitious plans for the winter and did not continue this kind of analysis. Despite the failure of *Pierre* the Harpers were eager for another novel from him, and on December 7, 1853, they gave him an advance of $300 for a work on "Tortoises or Tortoise-Hunting" which he hoped to complete in January. He knew the Galápagos Islands well enough, from experience and through reading, to provide the background; but unfortunately he had no story, and the best he could find was that of a Chola woman who was left alone on desolate Norfolk Isle when her husband and brother died in a fishing accident. Her experience should have appealed to whatever had haunted him in the Agatha story, but he could make nothing of it. "She but showed us her soul's lid, and the strange ciphers thereon engraved," he said, "all within, with pride's timidity, was withheld." He seems to have turned to Spenser and other poets for suggestions and inspiration for an allegorical narrative of patience, but when the Harpers' publishing house burned, shortly after he received his advance, and he thought their book-publishing activities would be suspended, he lost his incentive for proceeding with a difficult job. He turned his material into a series of ten sketches and sold them to *Putnam's* for serial publication, as "The Encantadas," in the spring. The whole affair was unfortunate because the Harpers were offended and Melville lost the encouragement and support of his publishers when his creative energies were at their lowest ebb.

The little additional writing Melville managed before the spring planting season touched upon the theme of frustration in economic terms. It consisted of two pairs of contrasting sketches, "The Two Temples" and "Poor Man's Pudding and Rich Man's Crumbs," and the first was particularly effective in the use it made of the imprisonment image when the poor man who was excluded from the congregation of a wealthy church became locked in the bell tower. It was rejected by *Putnam's*, however, on the grounds that it might disturb the magazine's "church readers"; and if Melville had any deep or serious impulse to find further social and economic symbols for the "wall" around him he repressed it. Instead, he turned in the late spring to the historical novel he had planned in 1849. *Israel Potter; His Fifty Years of Exile* was published serially in *Putnam's* and in book form (by Putnam rather than the Harpers) in the spring of 1855. Actually, he had little personal reason to get wrought up over the world's economic distinctions. He was making a living from his farm, his bank balance was increasing, and, although he satirized the mercenary spirit of Benjamin Franklin in *Israel Potter* and the cruel salesmanship of "The Lightning Rod Man," he presented the readers of *Harper's* for July 1854 with "The Happy Failure"—a man who had worked on an invention for as long as Melville himself had worked at writing and found kindness in his heart only when his device failed.

Yet Melville did not seriously consider himself a failure, as a writer or in any other way, and during the following winter he undertook one of the most ambitious and impressive of all his literary projects. It was to be the story of a South American slave ship, bound from Valparaiso to Callao, on which the slaves revolted, killed the owner, and forced the captain to promise to take them to Africa. Based upon a real story told by a New England ship's captain, Amasa Delano, it was focused on Captain Delano's gradual realization of the situation when the South American vessel appealed to him for help. It was one Melville

could handle by developing its "significances" as he had developed those in *Moby Dick,* and it quite evidently appealed strongly to his imagination. Here was all he needed to enable him to project his deepest feelings out of himself and into the characters of a fiction—the Spanish captain, Don Benito Cereno, surrounded by an ominous crowd of blacks whose leader played the role of a devoted servant but was always prepared to cut his master's throat; and the New England captain who was aware that there was something beyond the wall of his perception and to whom the mystery could be unveiled in a dramatic climax. Here were the ships and the sea that Melville knew so well, the material for the plausibly grotesque symbolism he loved, and a number of technical legal documents he could expound upon. It did not have the dramatic possibilities of *Moby Dick*, but it had the potentialities of a great novel in the Gothic tradition, historically true in fact and so close to Melville's own experience in setting that he could let his imagination control it without the risk of implausible fantasy.

He proposed the book to *Putnam's* in March 1855, but the magazine had just acquired a new publisher whose new reader advised him to "decline any novel from Melville which is not extremely good." And the advice was apparently taken, at the worst of all possible times. For Melville was still estranged from the Harpers, and he had just experienced what his wife called "his first attack of severe rheumatism in his back—so that he was helpless." He also must have been deeply discouraged because in April he sent to the magazine the portion of the book he had written, complete with legal documents but without explanation. The reader complained of the "great pity that he did not work it up as a connected tale instead of putting the dreary documents at the end" but advised its acceptance on the ground that it was Melville's "best style of subject" although he continued to fret that he "does everything too hurriedly now." After many delays it was published as a long short story, "Benito Cereno," and only a careful comparison of Melville's version of the "dreary documents at the end" with their originals gives a clue to the full substance of the novel Melville might have written had either he or his publishers possessed greater confidence in his energy and talents.

But he continued to write, and his writings show that he continued to search his own consciousness for fables of frustration. Marriage was one explanation he seems to have considered in "The Paradise of Bachelors and the Tartarus of Maids" in *Harper's* for April—although the allegory of gestation he introduced into the second part suggests that Elizabeth's pregnancy (with their second daughter, and fourth and last child) was more in his mind than marriage itself. "The Bell Tower" in the August *Putnam's*, however, was more serious, because it seems to have been closely connected in his mind with "Benito Cereno" and because it seems to be an introspective consideration of his own literary career. More flamboyant in style than any of his other stories, it was a parable of an overambitious architect who was destroyed by a flaw in his own work; and, for once, Melville made his meaning plain: "So the creator was killed by the creature. So the bell was too heavy for the tower. So the bell's main weakness was where man's blood had flawed it. And so pride went before the fall."

From the point of view of popular success, his own work had been weakest when he put his human "blood" in it, and his pride was going rapidly before the crippling illness from which he suffered all summer. "I and My Chimney" (which was accepted by *Putnam's* in September but not published until the following March) is almost certainly a humorous account of the physical examination of his injured back rather than of his mental condition as some traditions have maintained. And it is this preoccupation with physical frustration which helps explain the peculiarities of *The Confidence Man*—the last piece of prose fiction he was to publish during his lifetime—which he wrote during the winter of 1855–56. The book is a double-bitted satire, attacking gullibility in its first part and cynicism in its last, and its imagery reflects and perhaps explains its attitude and tone. The parts first composed (including the story of China Aster interpolated in the latter part) are bitter, and they are also pervaded by the imagery of illness, disability, and twisted bones. The last part, written after Melville had begun to recover, has more of the tone of Shakespearean comedy with its hero in motley, an Autolycus playing the role of Touchstone. Melville in fact had returned to Shakespeare and had found in him, as the introductory sketch for the collection of *Piazza Tales* (published before *The Confidence Man* was completed) indicates, a means of relief and escape from bitterness. But the dramatic intensity which Shakespeare had inspired in *Moby Dick* was gone.

Melville, at the age of thirty-seven, seemed worn out. He had sold the productive half of his farm in the spring of 1856, and his family was worried about his health. Judge Shaw agreed to finance a trip to Europe and the Holy Land, and Melville left on October 11 for Scotland, England (where he saw Hawthorne), and the Mediterranean; he returned on May 20, 1857, with restored energy and the full notebook that his father-in-law doubtless hoped for. But he was not to return to writing. The firm of Dix and Edwards, which had been the most recent of his publishers, had been dissolved; and although he was invited to contribute to the new *Atlantic Monthly* he was persuaded that lecturing would be more profitable. Accordingly, for three years, he traveled the lecture circuit, going as far south as Tennessee and as far west as Chicago and Wisconsin, talking about "Roman Statuary," "The South Seas," and "Traveling—Its Pleasures and Pains." But he was not successful on the platform, and soon after the beginning of his third season he gave it up and decided to make a trip around the world on a sailing ship captained by his younger brother Tom.

He had amused himself by writing verses before he left, and he left behind a volume of poems for Elizabeth to publish if she could. Neither the volume nor the trip, however, materialized. The ship was indefinitely delayed in San Francisco, and Melville was homesick enough to hurry home by steamer. After the outbreak of the Civil War he tried in vain for a commission in the navy and eventually managed to sell the rest of his Pittsfield property and move to New York City, where he continued to write verses about the progress of the war. By the end of the hostilities, he had almost enough to make a volume, and he filled it out and published, through the Harpers in 1866, *Battle-Pieces and Aspects of the War* with a prose supplement advocating peaceful reconciliation with the South. Although there was no question about his firm Union sympathies, the poems and the supplement were sufficiently detached from the strong political feelings of the day to make him properly eligible, during a period of reform, for appointment to a position he had been seeking for some years—that of deputy inspector in the New York Custom House. He received it in the early winter of 1866 and held it for nearly twenty years.

During these years Melville continued to be quietly but unprofessionally interested in writing. Poetry seemed to be the best means he

found for occupying his mind, and the quantity of it increased as he filled the numerous quarter sheets he could conveniently carry around in his coat pocket. In 1870 he began buying books again (a sure symptom, in him, of literary activity) and in 1875 his secret could no longer be kept: "pray do not mention to any one that he is writing poetry," Elizabeth wrote her mother after revealing it; "—you know how such things spread and he would be very angry if he knew I had spoken of it." Yet within the confidence of the family his uncle Peter Gansevoort heard the report and generously offered to subsidize the publication of Melville's most ambitious work—a narrative poem of about 18,000 lines called *Clarel: A Poem and Pilgrimage in the Holy Land.*

Clarel was supposed to be a philosophical poem, based on Melville's own pilgrimage of nineteen years before, dealing with a young man's search for religious faith. But its imaginative design is that of a novel. The plot centers on a wandering pilgrimage undertaken by Clarel and a group of companions while he is waiting for his sweetheart, Ruth, to pass through a period of mourning for the death of her father. The time is between the symbolic dates of Epiphany and Ash Wednesday, and the climax occurs when Clarel returns to Jerusalem and finds that Ruth, too, has died and that such wisdom and faith as he has acquired must be subject to the test of deep and bitter emotion. And within this framework of design Melville placed the most extraordinary and interesting group of characters he had ever created: the mysterious hunchbacked Roman, Celio; Nathan, the Puritan Zionist from Illinois; the American recluse, Vine, who resembled Hawthorne; Nehemiah, the gentle, saintly version of Captain Ahab who had learned to accept the universe; the misanthropic Swede, Mortmain; Ungar, the embittered Confederate, with American Indian blood; the smoothly armored Anglican priest, Derwent; the eager believer, Rolfe, who is more bronzed in body than in mind and may have been an ironic partial portrait of Melville himself; and a score or more of others representing many nationalities and beliefs. Melville's interest in people and his knowledge of mankind had obviously increased enormously since he had quit writing fiction.

More significantly, though, he had become less interested in absolute truth and the means of attaining it than he had been in his youth. The conflict which had created the dramatic tension in *Moby Dick* had, in the course of a quarter century, become for him almost conventionally symbolized in the controversy between religion and science; and, although he used this at length in his poem, it no longer seriously bothered him. The psychological interests which had emerged in *Pierre* had become stronger and more diverse. He was more interested in the kinds of people who could hold such a variety of beliefs with such great ranges of intensity. Human beings would always find symbols for their emotions of faith and despair, he decided, and inspiration, observation, and introspection were simply different means of obtaining emotional satisfaction instead of being conflicting ways to "truth."

In the light of this change in the direction of Melville's imaginative development it seems a pity that he did not write his poetry early and his novels late in life. For *Clarel*, fascinating though it is in many respects, is not a great or even a good poem. The major characters are entirely too discursive, and their discourse is often hard to follow in the jingling octosyllabics in which most of it is composed. It was less designed for popularity, in fact, than any other of Melville's works; and when it appeared, in two volumes, on June 3, 1876, it was almost completely ignored.

Yet a return to print had a stimulating effect on Melville, and although he was almost a completely forgotten author he spent a good deal of time during the last years of his life gathering his literary resources. He had poems from his last years in the Berkshires, poems from his trip abroad that he called "Fruit of Travel Long Ago," and other poems called "Sea Pieces" that he had written from time to time. He was also experimenting and was to continue to experiment with prose sketches of picturesque individuals and appropriate poems to go with them. Near the end of his life he was to publish two small volumes of verse in limited editions of twenty-five copies for his friends (*John Marr and Other Sailors* in 1888, and *Timoleon* in 1891) and was to collect and organize for publication at least two more. The best of the poems are those that preserve or seem to preserve the fresh emotions of some special occasion or the retrospective pieces (such as "After the Pleasure Party," among the longer ones) of a man who continued to be puzzled by the many mysteries of life but had become content to make the best of his own. Yet his final burst of creative energy and one of the finest works of his imagination was not in the form of poetry but in the prose fiction he had completely neglected for over a generation.

Billy Budd, Sailor differs from Melville's earlier novels because it was a mature and successfully controlled outgrowth of the inquisitiveness about human behavior which made *Clarel* so remarkable. It developed out of one of his experiments in combining prose and verse, such as the one he published as "John Marr"—an introductory sketch of a remarkably handsome young sailor who was condemned to be hanged as the ringleader of an incipient mutiny and who expressed his last sentiments in a ballad composed on the eve of the execution. But Billy, as he crept into Melville's imagination with all the physical signs of noble birth, seems to have been difficult to sketch. He appears to have first been imagined as guilty and then as innocent of the charge, and the conception of innocence was the germ from which the story grew. Why should an innocent man be hanged? The best inference to be drawn from the surviving working manuscript is that Melville's first impulse was to answer that he was a victim of another man's wickedness. He had personally known, if the record of *White Jacket* can be trusted, a ship's master-at-arms with an evil sadistic genius beneath a bland exterior, and he was acutely aware of the power for evil that a malicious person in such a position might possess. Out of his memory and still-indignant awareness, he created the character of John Claggart, who was to accuse the innocent Billy of a crime and be killed by a spontaneous blow from the speechless sailor. And for this, under the Articles of War, Billy had to be hanged.

Yet Melville had learned that the world was far too complex to be pictured in black and white. Evil and goodness might exist side by side, as he made clear in the almost allegorical exaggeration of these qualities in Claggart and Billy, but reality was in between. Billy had not struck "through the mask" of anything (as Ahab had tried to do) by hitting Claggart. Justice was not absolute, as Pierre had believed, but man-made. Billy had to be hanged not as a matter of course but by decision of court-martial. And Melville also had within his experience a court-martial such as Billy would have had to endure: his cousin, Guert Gansevoort, had presided over such a one under the direction of Captain Alexander Mackenzie of the brig *Somers* in 1842 and had hanged the son of the secretary of war on a similar charge. The affair had created a scandal which was being revived

at the time Melville was working on the *Billy Budd* manuscript, and it was still a family mystery that Guert should have been almost broken by his action while insisting that it "was *approved* of God." Here was a mystery that appealed to the mature Melville more than the mystery of Iago.

So, as his manuscript went through its various later stages of painful revision, he created the character of Captain Vere, master of H.M.S. *Indomitable* (or *Bellipotent*, as he finally decided to call it) during the Napoleonic wars, who resembled both Guert Gansevoort and Captain Mackenzie and was a wise and good man who loved Billy as a son but forced a reluctant court to condemn him to death. He talked privately with Billy to such effect that Billy died with the words "God bless Captain Vere" on his lips. But the captain was not blessed. He was haunted. He himself died murmuring the words—though not in accents of remorse—"Billy Budd, Billy Budd."

Billy Budd has almost as many meanings to as many readers as *Moby Dick*, and perhaps for the same reasons. It has the hidden ambivalence of any work of art which grows by accretion rather than by design, the ambiguity that is found in any intelligent and honest attempt to solve a profound problem of human behavior, and the power which an author only manages to get into a book when he succeeds in capturing in his own person the major tensions of his age. For the problem that bothered Melville in *Billy Budd* was not the problem of knowledge that had worried him in his youth. It was the problem of man. Is he a social being, responsible to the welfare of the society to which he belongs? Or is he an independent moral individual, responsible to his private awareness of guilt and innocence? This was the dilemma Captain Vere faced when, in Melville's fiction, the preservation of discipline in the British fleet was absolutely requisite to the preservation of England's freedom. Melville's solution was to make him behave as a social being but pay a penalty by suffering the private agonies of his private conscience.

The problem, however, was not a fictitious one. When Melville finished the last revision of his manuscript, on April 19, five months before his death in 1891, society had become far more complex than it had been when he dealt with the validity of individual awareness in *Moby Dick* forty years before. *Billy Budd* was not to be published until 1924, many years after its author's death. But the problem with which it dealt has not lessened with the passing years. Man's relationship to his private self and to the society in which he dwells is still the greatest source of tension of modern times. And one of Herman Melville's strong claims to greatness is that his imaginative development kept abreast of the times—despite neglect and adversity and more than one failure, the acuteness and depth of his sensitivity never failed.

His strongest claim, however, may be based upon an imagination which reached ahead of its times and provided for posterity a unique literary mirror in which it could examine itself. *Moby Dick* is like no other novel of the nineteenth century. Part drama and part personal narrative, it permits a hero to have the stage and compel that willing suspension of disbelief which is the essence of dramatic art. But, when belief becomes too great a strain, it permits escape through the person of a narrator who is sometimes a detached observer, skeptical commentator, or active participant in the action and sometimes an amusing, scholarly, and reminiscent author. Most twentieth-century intellectuals are part Ahab and part Ishmael—using symbols to master an overwhelming naturalistic universe while suspecting that the effort might be neurotic—and to them the form and rhetoric of *Moby Dick* has a powerful appeal. Melville's sensitivity to man's suspicion of his private self is the source of his greatest fascination to modern minds.

Selected Bibliography

WORKS OF HERMAN MELVILLE

COLLECTED EDITIONS

The Works of Herman Melville, 12 volumes (London: Constable, 1922–23), with 4 supplementary volumes of poetry and posthumous prose (1924), is the most complete edition of Melville yet issued.

Complete Works (Chicago and New York: Hendricks House) is in two editions, a trade edition with editorial notes and a subscribers' edition with additional textual notes. It includes *Collected Poems*, edited by H. P. Vincent (1947); *Piazza Tales*, edited by E. S. Oliver (1948); *Pierre*, edited by H. A. Murray (1949); *Moby Dick*, edited by L. S. Mansfield and H. P. Vincent (1952); *The Confidence Man*, edited by Elizabeth Foster (1954); *Clarel*, edited by W. E. Bezanson (1960); *Omoo*, edited by Harrison Hayford (1970).

The Northwestern-Newberry Edition of *The Writings of Herman Melville*, edited by Harrison Hayford, Hershel Parker, and G. Thomas Tanselle, 15 volumes (Evanston, Ill.: Northwestern University Press, 1967–   ), will provide a critical text for Melville's complete works together with a complete textual history and a historical note on the composition and publication of each volume. *Typee* (1968), *Omoo* (1968), *Redburn* (1969), *Mardi* (1970), *White Jacket* (1970), *Pierre* (1971) have been completed. Each volume is also issued in an inexpensive paperback edition.

ORIGINAL AMERICAN EDITIONS

Typee: A Peep at Polynesian Life. New York: Wiley and Putnam, 1846.

Omoo. New York: Harper, 1847.

Mardi and a Voyage Thither. New York: Harper, 1849.

Redburn: His First Voyage. New York: Harper, 1849.

White Jacket; or, The World in a Man-of-War. New York: Harper, 1850.

Moby Dick; or, The Whale. New York: Harper, 1851.

Pierre; or, The Ambiguities. New York: Harper, 1852.

Israel Potter; His Fifty Years of Exile. New York: Putnam, 1855.

Piazza Tales. New York: Putnam, 1856.

The Confidence Man, His Masquerade. New York: Dix, Edwards, 1857.

Battle-Pieces and Aspects of the War. New York: Harper, 1866.

Clarel: A Poem and Pilgrimage in the Holy Land. New York: Putnam, 1876.

John Marr and Other Sailors. New York: De Vinne, 1888.

Timoleon. New York: Caxton, 1891.

The Apple Tree Table and Other Sketches. Princeton, N.J.: Princeton University Press, 1922.

Shorter Novels of Herman Melville. New York: Liveright, 1928. (Includes *Billy Budd*, first published in London by Constable in 1924.)

CURRENT EDITIONS OF SPECIAL INTEREST

Billy Budd, Sailor. The Phoenix Edition (Chicago: University of Chicago Press, 1962) is the Hayford-Sealts text. Most others are reprints of either the Weaver or the Freeman texts.

Moby Dick. The Modern Library Giant Edition (New York: Random House, 1944) contains the Rockwell Kent illustrations; the Bobbs-Merrill Edition (Indianapolis, 1946) contains technical illustrations and also explanatory notes; the Oxford Edition (New York, 1967) includes excellent photographs and drawings; the Norton Critical Edition (New York, 1967) provides the most comprehensive collection of critical and other supplementary material and the best text currently available.

The Confidence Man. New York: Norton Critical Edition, 1971.

Typee. The Signet Classics Edition (New York: New American Library, 1965) records the substantive differences between the first English and the first American editions and the bowdlerizations made in the American Revised Edition.

The Complete Short Stories of Herman Melville. New York: Random House, 1949. The best edition of the shorter pieces.

Selected Poems. New York: Doubleday Anchor, 1964.

Selected Poems of Herman Melville. New York: Random House, 1970.

JOURNALS, CORRESPONDENCE, AND MANUSCRIPTS

"Journal of Melville's Voyage in a Clipper Ship," *New England Quarterly*, 2:120–39 (January 1929).

Journal of a Visit to London and the Continent by Herman Melville, edited by Eleanor M. Metcalf. Cambridge, Mass.: Harvard University Press, 1948.

Melville's Journal of a Visit to Europe and the Levant, October 11, 1856–May 6, 1857, edited by Howard C. Horsford. Princeton, N.J.: Princeton University Press, 1955.

Family Correspondence of Herman Melville, 1830–1904, edited by V. H. Paltsits. New York: New York Public Library, 1929.

The Letters of Herman Melville, edited by Merrell R. Davis and William H. Gilman. New Haven, Conn.: Yale University Press, 1960.

Billy Budd, Sailor (An Inside Narrative), edited by Harrison Hayford and Merton M. Sealts, Jr. Chicago: University of Chicago Press, 1962. (A careful edition of Melville's working manuscript which provides both a reading text and a genetic text with introduction and notes.)

CRITICAL AND BIOGRAPHICAL STUDIES

Anderson, C. R. *Melville in the South Seas.* New York: Columbia University Press, 1939.

Arvin, Newton. *Herman Melville.* New York: William Sloane Associates, 1950.

Berthoff, Warner. *The Example of Melville.* Princeton, N.J.: Princeton University Press, 1962.

Bowen, Merlin. *The Long Encounter: Self and Experience in the Writings of Herman Melville.* Chicago: University of Chicago Press, 1960.

Brodtkorb, Paul, Jr. *Ishmael's White World: A Phenomenological Reading of Moby Dick.* New Haven, Conn.: Yale University Press, 1965.

Chase, Richard. *Herman Melville.* New York: Macmillan, 1949.

Davis, M. R. *Melville's Mardi: A Chartless Voyage.* New Haven, Conn.: Yale University Press, 1952.

Dryden, Edgar A. *Melville's Thematics of Form.* Baltimore, Md.: Johns Hopkins Press, 1968.

Gilman, W. H. *Melville's Early Life and Redburn.* New York: New York University Press, 1951.

Howard, Leon. *Herman Melville: A Biography.* Berkeley and Los Angeles: University of California Press, 1951.

James, C. L. R. *Mariners, Renegades, and Castaways.* New York: James, 1953.

Leyda, Jay. *The Melville Log: A Documentary Life of Herman Melville, 1819–1891.* 2 vols. New York: Harcourt, Brace, 1951. (Reprinted, with supplementary entries, New York: Gordian Press, 1969.)

Mason, Ronald. *The Spirit above the Dust: A Study of Herman Melville.* London: John Lehmann, 1951.

Metcalf, Eleanor M. *Herman Melville: Cycle and Epicycle.* Cambridge, Mass.: Harvard University Press, 1953.

Mumford, Lewis. *Herman Melville.* New York: Harcourt, Brace, 1929.

Olson, Charles. *Call Me Ishmael.* New York: Reynal and Hitchcock, 1947.

Sedgwick, W. E. *Herman Melville: The Tragedy of Mind.* Cambridge, Mass.: Harvard University Press, 1944.

Simon, Jean. *Herman Melville, marin, métaphysicien et poète.* Paris: Boivin, 1939.

Stern, M. R. *The Fine Hammered Steel of Herman Melville.* Urbana: University of Illinois Press, 1957.

Stone, Geoffrey. *Melville.* New York: Sheed and Ward, 1949.

Thorp, Willard. *Herman Melville.* New York: American Book, 1938.

Weaver, R. M. *Herman Melville, Mariner and Mystic.* New York: Doran, 1921.

SPECIAL TOPICS

Bernstein, John. *Pacificism and Rebellion in the Writings of Herman Melville.* The Hague: Mouton, 1964.

Braswell, William. *Melville's Religious Thought.* Durham, N.C.: Duke University Press, 1943.

Finkelstein, Dorothee. *Melville's Orienda.* New Haven, Conn.: Yale University Press, 1961.

Franklin, H. Bruce. *The Wake of the Gods: Melville's Mythology.* Stanford, Calif.: Stanford University Press, 1963.

Hetherington, H. W. *Melville's Reviewers, British and American, 1846–1891.* Chapel Hill: University of North Carolina Press, 1961.

Hillway, Tyrus, ed. *Moby Dick Centennial Essays.* Dallas, Texas: Southern Methodist University Press, 1953.

Parker, Hershel, ed. *The Recognition of Herman Melville.* Ann Arbor: University of Michigan Press, 1967.

————. *Moby-Dick as Doubloon.* New York: Norton, 1970.

Pommer, H. E. *Milton and Melville.* Pittsburgh: University of Pittsburgh Press, 1955.

Pops, Martin Leonard. *The Melville Archetype.* Kent, Ohio: Kent State University Press, 1970.

Rosenberry, E. H. *Melville and the Comic Spirit.* Cambridge, Mass.: Harvard University Press, 1955.

Sealts, M. M., Jr. *Melville as Lecturer.* Cambridge, Mass.: Harvard University Press, 1957.

————. *Melville's Reading: A Check-List of Books Owned and Borrowed.* Madison: University of Wisconsin Press, 1966.

Sundermann, K. H. *Herman Melvilles Gedankengut.* Berlin, 1937.

Thompson, Lawrance. *Melville's Quarrel with God.* Princeton, N.J.: Princeton University Press, 1952.

Vincent, H. P. *The Trying Out of Moby Dick.* Boston: Houghton Mifflin, 1949.

————. ed. *Bartleby the Scrivener* (Melville Annual, 1965: A Symposium). Kent, Ohio: Kent State University Press, 1966.

————. *Melville and Hawthorne in the Berkshires* (Melville Annual, 1966). Kent, Ohio: Kent State University Press, 1968.

Wright, Nathalia. *Melville's Use of the Bible.* Durham, N.C.: Duke University Press, 1949.

—LEON HOWARD

H. L. Mencken

1880-1956

*H*ENRY LOUIS MENCKEN died in his sleep of a coronary occlusion on Sunday, January 29, 1956, in the row house on Hollins Street in Baltimore where he had lived most of his life. At midday on Tuesday a few people met at the neighborhood undertaker's just down the street. his brothers, August and Charles, and his sister Gertrude; Hamilton Owens, the chief editor of the Baltimore Sunpapers at that time; Alfred Knopf, his publisher; James Cain, the confectioner of hard-boiled fiction; the musician Louis Cheslock, most faithful of friends; and some others—fewer than a dozen in all. Hamilton Owens had been invited by August Mencken to preside. He rose, said briefly that they came together, as Henry had wanted, a few old friends to see him off, then sat down. The undertaker's men in their black suits took the body away, to the crematory, followed only by brothers August and Charlie. The company sat about uneasily for a few minutes and then scattered into the winter day.

The funeral of an unbeliever is more somber than most, since the usual remarks about a life everlasting are out of bounds. This one must have set some sort of record for bleakness, for in a way it was redundant. Mencken had been leading a ghostly life, "ready for the angels," since the day eight years before when he was knocked out by a cerebral thrombosis that af-

fected his speech and partly paralyzed him. He recovered fully though slowly from the paralysis but was left cruelly handicapped in other ways, robbed of the ability to read and write, unable to remember the names even of his friends. Seen on one of his rare public appearances he appeared no different at first. He had been restored to what, following an earlier illness, he had called his "former loveliness": the dumpy figure that he liked to call matronly, the ruddy face, the scowl, the laugh, the popping blue eyes. But this was a deception. The croak of his voice was the same, but the words that issued were those of a stranger. The shell was intact, but the essence had been shattered; and the grim jest of it was that Mencken knew this deep inside as well as anyone else and yet was helpless to do anything about it.

But though he had to endure that long winter of wordlessness, it was surely not true that his career had been cut short. His daily newspaper work embraced better than half a century. The first and the last things he wrote for publication were printed in newspapers, and it must be remembered that Mencken thought of himself as a newspaperman before anything else. The flood of his critical writing, in the old *Smart Set* magazine mainly (the best of it re-published in his *Prefaces* and *Prejudices*), swept away the deadening literary standards, and the deadly standard-bearers, of our early twentieth century and cleared the way for a tremendous flowering of new writing. As a slashing and wonderfully comic critic of American life and institutions, he attained for a time a stature and influence such as no other American writer has ever known. Though he disclaimed scholarly pretensions, his *The American Language* systematically explored for the first time our native tongue as it must be distinguished from British English and provided a solid basis for American linguistics. As a political commentator he carried immense authority for a time—though this waned with the coming of that upheaval called the New Deal and was gone entirely by the time he had ceased writing. He wrote a formal treatise on political theory, religion, and ethics. He tried his hand at verse and the drama. And the autobiographical sketches brought together in his *Days* books re-create the life of an American city, Baltimore, at the turn of the century with such gusto and uproarious humor and unabashed sentiment that their claim to immortality is secure. All this—and his letters, too. Mencken the writer was cut down cruelly, but not cut short.

Mencken was third-generation Baltimore German. Baltimore was one of the chief ports of entry for the big German immigration of the mid-nineteenth century—the Forty-Eighters. Most of them moved on to make their main impression on the land and life of the Midwest. But many found Baltimore congenial, with its already well-established German community, and went no farther. Mencken's grandfather Burkhardt was one of these. Stiff-necked, immensely proud of the Mencken family's long roll of learned men, diligent and thrifty, he prospered in the tobacco business and founded a numerous family. His eldest son, August, held likewise to the tobacco business,

prospered, and married Anna Abhau, daughter of another German Forty-Eighter.

It was into this conventional west Baltimore German family where values were certitudes, love and discipline were dispensed with a lavish and impartial hand, and security was never in question that Henry Louis Mencken was born on September 12, 1880. Insofar as any childhood can be easy, his was. "We were lucky," he wrote many years later of this childhood, "to have been born so soon." And he looked back at his childhood and indeed at the life it had prepared the way for without any regrets at all: "If I had my life to live over again I don't think I'd change it in any particular of the slightest consequence. I'd choose the same parents, the same birthplace, the same education (with maybe a few improvements here, chiefly in the direction of foreign languages), the same trade, the same jobs, the same income, the same politics, the same metaphysic, the same wife, the same friends, and (even though it may sound like a mere effort to shock humanity), the same relatives to the last known degree of consanguinity, including those in-law." It may not be far from the truth to say that he took the lonesome integrity of his mind and spirit from tough old Burkhardt, from his father, August, a talent for gaiety in company, and from his mother certain qualities that rarely show in his writing, especially his unexpected gentleness, his instant sympathy for the troubled, and his devotion to family life and routine.

His education moved ahead in the Baltimore German way, which is to say with the solidest kind of family backing. At the age of six he was handed over to Professor Friedrich Knapp and his thoroughly Teutonic Institute, a no-nonsense place, and did well in most subjects. In due course he was translated to a public high school, the Polytechnic Institute, where the main emphasis was then and still is on science and technology. This change was made by his father in the mistaken belief that little Harry had an aptitude for such matters. Though in his own words little Harry "had no more mechanical skill than a cow" he was tempted for a time by the mysteries of chemistry and photography and he was graduated— he was not quite sixteen—at the head of his class, even winning the competition for a gold medal in electricity. So much for science and his formal education.

His education in letters was a parallel and separate thing. The Mencken family was not particularly bookish, but there were books around, and the magazines of the time, and his introduction to the delights of the printed word came when he was seven by way of *Chatterbox*, the hard-cover annual which started generations of young English gentlemen on their way to literacy. He absorbed it so thoroughly, Englishness and all, that in middle life he confessed to knowing "more about Henry VIII and Lincoln Cathedral than I know about Millard Fillmore or the Mormon Temple at Salt Lake City." Young Henry dutifully did all the things the boys of his neighborhood were expected to do—he was a member in good standing of the neighborhood gang, he frequented the firehouse. But such occupations had to compete with "a new realm of being and a new and powerful enchantment" and before very many years had lost the battle. The "powerful suction of beautiful letters" had caught him and he never again escaped. He tackled Grimm's fairy tales—not much to his taste. He began to explore the contents of the old glass-front secretary that stands to this day in the Hollins Street middle sitting room with most of the same books still in it, a miscellany of things pretty much beyond his ken, hence all the more intriguing. And then he came upon *Huckleberry Finn*, "probably the most stupendous event of my whole life." The story of this encounter is set down in his sketch "Larval Stage of a Bookworm." By the age of nine he had his card for the neighborhood branch library and had begun "an almost daily harrying of the virgins at the delivery desk." He was caught for fair: "I began to inhabit a world that was two-thirds letterpress and only one-third trees, fields, streets and people. I acquired round shoulders, spindly shanks, and a despondent view of humanity. I read everything that I could find in English, taking in some of it but boggling most of it. . . . to this day [at 60] I am still what might be called a reader, and have a high regard for authors."

A second stupendous and decisive event is confessed in another of his sketches, "In the Footsteps of Gutenberg." It was the gift from his father, not long after his discovery of the magic of Mark Twain, of a toy printing press, a Dorman No. 10 Self-Inker costing $7.50, together with a font of No. 214 type costing $1.10. Mark Twain had made him a consumer of letters; this made him a producer. It put "the smell of printer's ink up my nose at the tender age of eight, and it has been swirling through my sinuses ever since." Other Christmas presents came along, to divert him momentarily— the set of water colors, the camera, the microscope, the galvanic battery, the set of carpenter's tools. But "it was the printing-press that left its marks, not only upon my hands, face and clothing, but also on my psyche. They are still there, though more than fifty years have come and gone."

His father, sensible man, saw Harry as logical heir to the tobacco business and had small patience with the notion of a career in writing or publishing. Henry was required to learn the rudiments of the business, including the way to roll a cigar. This was the cause of some friction between father and son, but there was never the slightest doubt in Henry's mind that the tobacco business was not for him, and, to cut the story short: "When, on my father's death, as I was eighteen, I was free at last to choose my trade in the world, I chose newspaper work without any hesitation whatever, and, save when the scent of a passing garbage-cart has revived my chemical libido, I have never regretted my choice. More than once I have slipped out of daily journalism to dally in its meretricious suburbs, but I have always returned repentant and relieved, like a blackamoor coming back in Autumn to a warm and sociable jail."

And so it was, four days after his father's death in 1899, that he presented himself at the office of one of Baltimore's several newspapers, the *Herald*, and was turned down. But his persistence earned him free-lance assignments, then a staff job. He soon demonstrated his ability and moved swiftly through every job in the office: police reporter, drama critic, Sunday editor, city editor, and by 1906 at the age of twenty-five actually the editor of the paper— only to see the *Herald* fail for reasons with which he had nothing to do, and to find himself out of a job.

It was then that he joined the *Sun* (locally the Sunpaper), a newspaper believed by the local gentry to be the one true source of wisdom and current intelligence, which remained his journalistic home to the end of his career. He did venture away from time to time for reasons that were various, but always returned "repentant and relieved." His connection with that paper (and its evening sister) turned into something unique in American journalism. The *Sun* provided the real launching pad for his career as a national figure and in turn gained immeasurably from the relationship.

From the beginning, however, he did not limit his writing to daily journalism, prodigious

though his output for the *Herald* was. He began experimenting with verse, and selling it. He was a "stringer," providing features for out-of-town papers. He became a fabricator of short stories for most of the popular magazines of the day—formula fiction loaded with blood and thunder, done by the yard and showing small trace of the style we think of as Mencken's. He was available for hack jobs—even doing a prospectus for Loudon Park Cemetery, where, fittingly, his gravestone now stands. He didn't stop reading, either. He was sopping up the new writers who had things to say and said them well, such men as Shaw and Conrad; and always Mark Twain; and others such as Huxley and Nietzsche and Spencer and James Huneker and William Graham Sumner, the author of *Folkways*. They fixed his philosophical bearings once and for all (though these had been pretty well set already), and on them he honed his ideas and his style.

The hack period began to recede, and in 1905 he published his "first real book," as he called it, *George Bernard Shaw: His Plays* (he preferred not to count a little book of rather dreadful verse that too much fuss was later made about simply because copies were rare: the poetic muse kept clear of him always). This essay offered the first intimations of the Mencken style and his formidable critical capacity, immature though they were. It was no great success though it was well reviewed, but for him it broke the ice: he was a published critic. Mencken recalled, in his *Newspaper Days,* his enchantment on the arrival of its proofs. His editor at that time, an understanding man named Meekins, insisted that he take the day off to read them. "So I locked myself in as he commanded, and had a shining day indeed, and can still remember its unparalleled glow after all these years."

Three years later he published his *Philos-*

ophy of Friedrich Nietzsche, a better book and still very much worth the reading. William Manchester, in *Disturber of the Peace,* best of the several Mencken biographies and studies, says, "The subject . . . was Mencken's Nietzsche, not Nietzsche's Nietzsche. There is a difference." It is probably a better guide to Mencken than to Nietzsche, to the extraordinary toughness and stiffness of his mind beneath its lively movement at the surface. He alluded to this quality himself from time to time. In a letter to the writer Jim Tully in 1940 he said: "I never listen to debates. They are dreadful things indeed. The plain truth is that I am not a fair man, and don't want to hear both sides. On all known subjects, ranging from aviation to xylophone-playing, I have fixed and invariable ideas. They have not changed since I was four or five years." And I remember a casual remark he made to me at about the time of that letter, when his thinking was going so strongly against the national grain. Speaking of another newspaper editor he said: "John is a reasonable man. Try it on him. A good argument will always fetch him, but not me." He was not boasting. Neither was he confessing. He was stating a fact.

There was another and important branching out early in his association with the *Sun.* Mencken's duties as an editorial writer were not arduous and they used up only a portion of his energy. A chance encounter with Theodore Dreiser, then a magazine editor, led him to another chance encounter with George Jean Nathan; and out of that all-day meeting of two men as unlike as two could be, yet so surprisingly alike in their disgust with contemporary life and letters, there came a partnership that lasted better than two decades. The inspiration of the partnership was a magazine of dubious reputation, the *Smart Set,* which was about to undergo one of its rejuvenations, or reincarnations. Mencken had been invited to do a

monthly full-length piece for it on books, Nathan to do dramatic criticism. The result was something like a volcanic eruption. The shallow standards and appalling inanity of most American writing and the theater of the early years of this century were the targets of both. With high spirits, total confidence in their own judgments, and a torrent of brilliant invective, they laid about them, bashing heads, pulling down idols, puncturing inflated pomposity, infuriating the sources of conventional wisdom, sweeping away the rubbish that then passed for literature and drama. Prodigious labor was required, and it was a bravura performance. Mencken's stint was a monthly article of about five thousand words, and his anthologist Huntington Cairns, adding it all up, found that from November 1908 to the end of December 1923 he performed it one hundred and eighty-two successive months for a total of better than 900,000 words. The preparatory reading involved in this may be imagined. Mencken was equal to it because he was one of those reading prodigies who can gulp down books a page at a time missing nothing of consequence.

As contributors the two dominated the magazine, which was by no means an appropriate medium for such intellectual high jinks but better than none. In due time (1914) the magazine became theirs as joint editors. As editors they wrote much of it themselves under a fragrant bouquet of pseudonyms. Betty Adler, the Mencken bibliographer, has tracked down and confirmed 23 pseudonyms and lists 13 more as probabilities; the chances are there were others, used interchangeably or jointly by the two. But they also searched out new talent, so buttressing their criticism with evidence of what they did like. Sweeping out the rubbish was not enough. They wanted non-rubbish to replace it, and this they set about discovering— a labor at which Mencken proved remarkably adept. Once he got on the scent of a promising writer he was unshakable—he cajoled, browbeat, sent gifts, fed ideas. There is a large risk of error in this hunting out of new writers, but he was equally skillful at ditching whatever failed to make the grade.

The *Smart Set* was a tour de force, a gale of fresh air across the campuses, a serial spoof, bellwether of a new generation, an object of delighted devotion.

Mencken and Nathan worked out a modus for editing which reduced red tape to zero. Nathan held down the New York office with the help of a secretary of monumental impassivity, a Miss Golde. Mencken did his reading, writing, and scouting for talent, and carried on his enormous correspondence, from his quarters on the third floor of the family home in Hollins Street, periodically taking the train to New York for a day which he and Nathan divided between merrymaking and the planning of the next issue.

But I get ahead of the story. Not long after Mencken's emergence through the *Smart Set* as a national critic of letters, things began to happen to the *Sun* in Baltimore. The *Sun* of that day was a staid institution much impressed with its rectitude and infallibility, one of the four pillars of Baltimore life, along with the Washington Monument, the Shot Tower, and Federal Hill, and just about as exciting. A whim of complacency and accumulated inhibitions, it began to go downhill even as a commercial enterprise, and it was sold to a group of wealthy Baltimore citizens headed by an aggressive publisher, formerly a competitor, who was resolved to pump some life back into it. The decision was made to spawn an evening sister, and to Mencken fell the task of providing this new *Evening Sun* with a personality and point of view, mainly by way of its editorial page. This he set about doing; and so (1911) his column, "The Free Lance," came

into being. He was given a free hand, and took every advantage of this and of the title. The column swiftly became the sort of thing that no one of consequence in Baltimore dared not to read; and the subjects were whatever came into his head. Baltimore had seen nothing like it before. He was into everything: the mucky world of municipal politics, local forms of beastliness and gentility, particularly when combined in the same person, new trends in writing, the deplorable condition of the sewage and water systems as reflected in the local typhoid death rate, the barbarous condition of the national culture—everything. The predominant qualities Mencken endowed the *Evening Sun* with were impertinence, riotous good humor, a high degree of literacy—with the back of the hand for every form of sham and a strenuously libertarian bias.

Mencken's output, not confined to the column by any means, was large. But thanks to the compulsive orderliness of his mind he worked with extraordinary economy. Pieces done for the *Smart Set* were reworked for the "Free Lance" column; "Free Lance" material found its way rearranged and expanded into the magazine; and much of all this eventually wound up in his books: the *Prejudices, The American Language, Notes on Democracy,* and so on. Mencken was never the man to waste a good thing on a single audience.

So things went for Mencken in the years before World War I, exuberantly, as he juggled two careers: those of a literary critic of rapidly growing stature and of a newspaper columnist knowing no bounds except those of libel and common prudence. There was no time for larger works, though these had begun to gestate in his mind; and the only thing that appeared between hard covers was his priceless little drama without words. *The Artist, A Drama without Words* (1915), which was later reprinted in his *A Book of Burlesques* (1916).

But as the war approached, he found himself under growing constraint in both careers. He was, to put the matter shortly, pro-German. As he explained his position toward the end of the war to a correspondent, the medical historian Fielding Garrison, "The fact is that my 'loyalty' to Germany, as a state or a nation, is absolutely nil. I haven't a single living relative there; I haven't even a friend there. . . . But I believe I was right when I argued that unfairness to [the Germans] was discreditable and dangerous to this country, and I am glad I did it." Other things—pride of ancestry, his bourgeois German upbringing, his philosophical underpinnings, his contempt for the quality and the personalities of American politics—contributed to his attitude. And being Mencken he said his say—loudly, bluntly, mockingly. At the *Smart Set* this was felt in the countinghouse, and as a critic he began to find himself vulnerable to *ad hominem* attacks, many of them shockingly irrelevant and abusive, from those who had smarted under his criticisms. At the Sunpapers the cleavage between his views and the ardently Wilsonian management of the papers grew so broad as to be intolerable. In 1915 his "Free Lance" column came to an end abruptly; and except for a comic opera episode as a war correspondent for the *Sun* in Germany, which ended with American entry into the war, his contributions to the paper dwindled to little and then nothing. In the literary world the counterattacks on him increased ominously with the war fever. His *A Book of Prefaces* (1917), consisting of a series of critical studies, was viciously reviewed by, among others, Stuart Sherman. Sherman was then the leading academic critic, and his far from academic attack amounted to this: the opinions of the man Mencken on prose fiction are beneath contempt because he is no patriot. Then, too, there was a misunderstanding with his new publisher, Alfred Knopf (soon happily

resolved; they were destined to have an enduring friendship). Certain other journalistic enterprises worked out unsatisfactorily, as did an interim arrangement with another publisher, his friend Philip Goodman, and the *Smart Set* found itself compelled to trim its sails.

The war years were years of misery for Mencken, carrying the brand of pro-Germanism though his loyalty as a citizen was never in real doubt. He was left with no means but his private correspondence for venting his opinions. He solved the problem—that is to say, the problem of one who must write but is constrained on all sides—by plunging into his linguistic project, *The American Language,* which had been simmering gently for a long time. The conclusion of this landmark work was being written, appropriately, as the war ended. It was a critical and popular triumph when published a year later, in 1919. The impression it made on the new college generation especially, by its style, its humor, and its lightly worn scholarship, was tremendous. That same year saw also the publication of the first volume in the series of *Prejudices,* consisting of reprints from the *Smart Set,* the *Evening Sun,* and some other sources. Each new *Prejudices* volume was awaited avidly by the new Menckenites, and the series ran to six before the curtain was rung down on it in 1927. And in 1919, too, Mencken resumed his formal connection with the Sunpapers, this time as editorial adviser to the publisher, and as a weekly contributor to the editorial page of the *Evening Sun.* He was also available for special assignment. (His reporting of the Scopes antievolutionary trial in Dayton, Tennessee, yielded some of his finest descriptive writing, including his famous account of the hysterical goings-on at a back country revival meeting; yet for some reason it was never brought together in a book.)

The *Smart Set* had somehow managed to

struggle through the war years. How rough the going had been is exposed in a letter Mencken wrote to Dreiser in 1920 explaining its modest rates for contributions: "If it hadn't been for the fact that each of us has a small independent income, we'd have been down and out a dozen times. All this for your private eye. . . . I go into it simply to purge your mind of any notion that you may harbor that we are Shylocks." It now emerged basically intact, and was clearly what the new generation wanted.

In brief, the Mencken Period had begun. He offered what the times needed: a clearinghouse for the cynicism and discontents of the postwar years and a lash for their excesses wielded with alternating scorn and high good humor. The work he did in bringing out and supporting the new writers (Sinclair Lewis and Fitzgerald typically) and continuing his championing of Dreiser and Conrad and a score of others was carried on with the greatest gusto. At last he could really take literature out of the hands of the decorous and the genteel and make it something meaningful (he could not have done this had the talent not been waiting in the wings ready for a persuasive impresario). And yet even as he reached the peak of his influence as a critic of letters he began to move out of this role and into criticism of the American mores. This was not a new role for him, of course, but it now got far more emphasis: the truth is that imaginative writing was beginning to bore him. His work for the *Evening Sun* reflected this—it ran more and more to political and social commentary. His *Prejudices* books reflected this, too, the first of these being devoted almost entirely to writers and writing—what he called beautiful letters and the bozart—and the last containing hardly anything relating to current writing. The change in his interests was reflected also in the *Smart Set*, where increasingly he tacked away

from literature and toward life, in spite of Nathan's persistence in the old course.

The two were in fact growing apart. In a revealing letter to literary journalist Burton Rascoe, Mencken described the bases and also hinted at the limitations of their long collaboration: "Our point of contact is our complete revulsion from American sentimentality. . . . We work together amicably because we are both lonely, and need some support. . . . we come together on several essentials, e.g. our common disinclination to know authors or to belong to literary coteries, our lack of national feeling, and (perhaps most important) our similar attitudes toward money, religion, women, etc." But Nathan, the complete aesthete, absorbed as always in the theater, was cold to that "show"—the excesses and absurdities of the jazz age—which so dazzled and delighted Mencken as a theme for writing.

This is really what ended that long partnership. Though Mencken had no conscious intention of neglecting the arts he wanted the emphasis placed on American life—to him, the American comedy. In addition Nathan was fairly oblivious to the shoddy trappings of the *Smart Set*, but they had begun to bother Mencken. He hankered for a "swell" review, to be Brahmin in its typographical dress if not in its contents. Knopf stood ready to back such a review, and indeed had proposed it and offered to finance it; and so, after a sufficiency of preliminary planning and wrangling, the *American Mercury* got its name, the *Smart Set* was published for the last time in December 1923, and in January 1924 the new critical review appeared in its Garamond typeface and ultra-dignified green cover. The Mencken orbit was moving toward its apogee, and the reception of the *Mercury* far exceeded the expectations of the three principals, in circulation and in acclaim. Its first issues promptly became collectors' items. The impassive Miss Golde had somehow been mislaid and was succeeded by the efficient and self-effacing Edith Lustgarten in the New York office and the equally efficient and self-effacing Rosalind Lohrfinck (known simply as Lohrfinck though Mencken professed to be dimly aware that she had a private life and even a husband) at the Baltimore end of things. Otherwise the manner of operation was not greatly different from *Smart Set* days, though quarters were moved into the Knopf office and there was a need for more of those trips to New York.

And yet the crack in the collaboration was widening, and becoming evident even to bystanders. In a long letter to Nathan, written before the *Mercury* was many months old, Mencken, who was uneasy about the course of things, brought the matter into the open: "Its chances are not unlike those which confronted the Atlantic in the years directly after the Civil War: it has an opportunity to seize leadership of the genuinely civilized minority of Americans. . . . Our interests are too far apart. . . ." It was a plea to thresh out their differences if that were still possible, subconsciously a bid for dominance. Nathan, seeing the course of things, accepted it with good nature. After fewer than a dozen issues he abandoned his co-editorship, though he kept on as a contributor; and before the decade was over he and Mencken had parted completely—not in anger but as intellectual and emotional strangers. Mencken carried on alone, with an assistant (Charles Angoff, who proved in the end to be no friend and whose *H. L. Mencken, a Portrait from Memory,* put out in the year of Mencken's death, was a bitter and distressing performance).

The Mencken wave swept on, with the *Mercury* riding its crest; and there was hardly a page of this but showed the hand of the editor.

He was at once the most ingratiating and the most exacting of editors. Contributions were responded to with unprecedented speed, and the blow of every rejection was softened by one of Mencken's inimitable notes. Rascoe once wrote: "I have yet to meet a man under thirty-five with articulate ideas who has not a sheaf of those lively, hearty notes whereby Mencken conveys a maximum of good cheer and boisterous comment within a minimum of space." Acceptance for publication brought immediate payment, and (quite unprecedented in the experience of free-lance writers) a conveyance of copyright was forthcoming immediately after publication. This act of generosity cost nothing, yet earned enormous dividends in the good will of a whole generation of young writers struggling for recognition. He was ever attentive to the legitimate interests of his contributors, yet determined always to have his way. An article with a clumsy opening, a feeble conclusion? Out with them! In with new ones from his own typewriter, but always there was advance warning along with a plea for acquiescence when he was dealing with a style-conscious writer. He was marvelous at finding the one-article man—the jailbird or the cab-driver with a story to tell. He constantly tapped the well of working newspapermen, but found it shallower than one might think; of his early newspaper colleagues he once wrote: "At least half the members of the staff had literary ambitions of some sort or another, but not one of them ever got anywhere as a writer in the years following." He ransacked the campuses and the ranks of campus journalists for youngsters of promise, and gave many of them their start.

Mencken himself did but one book from the ground up, so to speak, during this period, which was the latter half of the twenties. That was not a success: his *Notes on Democracy* (1926). Even that one was mainly a rewriting job based on previously published material. It was done in such time as he could spare from his furious magazine editing, his continuing daily journalism, and responses to the calls now being made on him increasingly in his role as a unique national figure, certainly the most hated, and also perhaps the most admired, American of his time. These calls were of many sorts, but mainly from academe. Here is one described in a letter to Philip Goodman: "I am lecturing at Goucher College tonight: an annual affair. The audience consists of 250 virgins. I begin on the subject of national literature, but at 8.35 modulate gracefully into the Old Subject in F sharp minor. I always advise them to marry early, as, after all, the most sanitary and economically secure way of life for a Christian girl." But of course he refused dozens for every one he accepted.

The magazine itself began to show evidence of strain, of stridency. Mencken's commentaries on books continued, and at length, but there was a forced quality in much of this now, and they tended to turn into lectures on his special brand of sociology. His waning interest in literature as literature began to show in the magazine's fiction, too: having given a whole generation of new writers the stage and the audience they needed, he had slipped out of the audience, or at least was on the way to the exit. In his preoccupation with manners and morals, he actually began to miss new writing talent, worse, to misjudge it: Hemingway, for example, and Faulkner, and Thomas Wolfe. The frantic twenties were beginning to burn themselves out, and so apparently was the chief barker of this gaudiest of side shows, though by ordinary standards the magazine continued to prosper throughout the decade.

In 1929, Mencken completed the second of his trilogy treating formally of politics, religion, and morals: his *Treatise on the Gods* (1930). As Cairns remarks, he had plowed new

land when he wrote *The American Language*, which was in every sense an original work, in subject as well as treatment. Religion was another matter, a preoccupation of powerful minds since the dawn of human consciousness, the most thoroughly worked field of all: small room here for originality. What he could do, and did, was to restate the materialist-rationalist position as so thoroughly developed in the nineteenth century by Huxley and others, but in contemporary terms, bringing to bear the abundant new material of psychology and the study of human institutions. He saw the religious motive as a prudent form of hedging against the terrors of the unknown, and organized religion as an elaborate tool for bamboozling and manipulating the credulous masses, a tool of government really. There was not a trace of the mystic in him, and while acknowledging the genuineness of the mystical experience, he looked upon it as one of the puzzles not yet worked out by scientific means. He came by his antireligious position quite naturally, first through his grandfather Burkhardt, then through his father, then by degrees through his reading. The constant prevalence of what he felt to be a delusion had absorbed him from adolescence on. Writing of the place of religion in his family, he commented many years later to A. G. Keller, a Yale anthropologist and disciple of William Graham Sumner, "My mother went to church now and then, but her doctrinal ideas seem to have been very vague, for I never heard her mention them. I think she went simply as a sort of social gesture. My father accompanied her no more than two or three times in my recollection, and even then he went under protest. Religion was simply not a living subject in the house." Anathema to the conventionally religious, his *Treatise on the Gods* is nevertheless a storehouse of learning and curious information; and it has ample helpings of the characteristic

Mencken audacity and wit. It received a far better reception than his *Notes on Democracy,* as
possibly it deserved to, and it sold well. It was
his last substantial success for some time, and
its appearance coincided with a sharp break in
what had seemed the unbreakable pattern of
his private life, the tender episode of his
middle-aged courtship and marriage.

In spite of the public impression to the contrary, Mencken's personal life followed a rigorous and austere routine. At the center of it
was the family house in Hollins Street presided
over with quiet authority by his mother, Anna.
The loss of her in 1925 had affected him far
more than he could have anticipated, in the
small ways that so quickly add up to a big way,
and his correspondence is full of references to
her death. To Jim Tully he wrote, for example:
"You ask if I feel lonely here. My belief is that
all authors are essentially lonely men. Every
one of them has to do his work in a room
alone, and he inevitably gets very tired of himself. My mother's death in December, 1925,
left me at a loss. My sister is keeping house but
the place seems empty. It is hard to reorganize
one's life after 45."

It is too pat to say that he turned to Sara
Haardt on the rebound. Yet without doubt his
mother's death was contributory to his growing
attachment to Sara and his need for the qualities she had to give. He had met her at one of
those annual lectures to the Goucher College
virgins. She taught there—a young lady from
the deep South, a minor but fastidious novelist
and short story writer with a faint aura of the
anachronistic about her, reserved and physically frail. Their marriage in 1930 took all
but a few of their closest friends by surprise,
and was greeted with ironic delight by editorial
writers from coast to coast. That the author of
In Defense of Women and chief railer at the
institution of holy matrimony should himself
succumb, and be married by a parson at that!

Mencken took the public ribbing in good part,
and so did Sara, though somewhat nervously,
as they settled down to the sedate idyll which
both knew, or had reason to suspect, could not
last long. It was broken frequently by her ill-
nesses, and it ended with her death five years
later—a cruel blow to Mencken however much
he had anticipated and prepared for it. He told
Hamilton Owens shortly after her death that
the doctors had given her only three years at
the time of their marriage. "Actually she lived
five, so that I had two more years of happiness
than I had any right to expect." It had been
a precious, bittersweet thing, and life in the
apartment which they had established on Baltimore's handsome Mount Vernon Place, and
where Sara had indulged her bent for the Victorian style, had lost its meaning. In due
course he returned "completely dashed and
dismayed" to the house in Hollins Street to
take up life again with his brother August, his
shadow from then to the end.

In the meantime other troubles of a
worldly and professional kind had been piling
up on him. As the times had embraced him
following World War I, so now with the crash
and the onset of the Great Depression they
were ready to reject him. A nation dazed and
hurt by the collapse of its financial and industrial structure, by farmers dispossessed and city
people caught overnight with no means of subsistence, by soup lines and apple sellers, and a
steady shower of overextended brokers leaping
out of Wall Sreet windows, ceased to enjoy
being described as a gaudy human comedy.
That kind of talk, and writing, might be tolerable and even entertaining in a going concern.
To a people on the ropes, it seemed suddenly
petty and irrelevant. It was a time of shocked
and bitter reaction, and among the victims of
this was Mencken's unchanging and unchange-
able devotion to individuality, self-reliance,
and limited government. To his readers he

ceased abruptly to be a champion of the individual and herald of freedom and became an arch-reactionary—this without changing his position one iota. His newspaper polemics seemed suddenly and oddly out of date; he lost the faith and credit of the new generation of college students (that was perhaps the worst blow save Sara's death); the circulation of the *Mercury* began to slide. One does not write easily in the face of a situation like that; and Mencken's writing showed it. The familiar refrains turned stale, the variations were no longer amusing.

One blow came after another. The decision to abandon the *Mercury* was taken in 1933 and was actually welcomed by him (it lived on for a while under another editor, then passed from hand to hand, always downward). The third of his trilogy on politics, religion, and morals, the *Treatise on Right and Wrong* (1934), got a critical mauling and had a poor sale—a far poorer sale than the same book would have had, certainly, ten years before, for it is highly readable still.

The Depression moved into what he considered the fantastic excesses of the Roosevelt New Deal. He had voted for Roosevelt while confessing privately that he thought him "a weak sister," but quickly changed his mind. So far as he was concerned, the Rooseveltian devaluation of the dollar was on a par with the coin clipping of an earlier day, which is to say a form of refined thievery, and Roosevelt's manner of doing it, which involved pulling the rug out from under his own delegation to the London Economic Conference, the behavior of a cad. Cynical as Mencken was about the courts in general and the caliber of the men who manned them, Roosevelt's scheme for packing the Supreme Court and so ensuring the color of constitutionality for whatever he might do shocked him beyond measure. The mixture of soft-voiced paternalism and polit-

ical ruthlessness so finely blended in the character of Roosevelt II (as he called him) grated on his nerves like the jangle of an out-of-tune piano. "I begin to believe seriously," he wrote to the publisher B. W. Huebsch, "that the Second Coming may be at hand. Roosevelt's parodies of the Sermon on the Mount become more and more realistic. The heavens may open at any moment. Keep your suitcase packed."

As he responded in typical vein to the course of events it became clearer day by day—and to none more clearly than Mencken himself—that he was no longer being listened to. His day as reigning critic of manners and politics was over. In journalism he continued to take special assignments for the Sunpapers but he abandoned his famous *Evening Sun* Monday articles early in 1938. War was brewing again across the Atlantic, and with his Washingtonian belief in no foreign entanglements he was bitterly against American involvement; but he saw it coming. Wishfully, he played down Hitler as a clown who could not long hold the stage. To George S. Schuyler, the Negro journalist, he wrote in 1939: "Roosevelt is hot to horn into the European mess, and his wizards believe that if he can scare the country sufficiently, it will be possible to reelect him [for a third term] next year. I am inclined to agree that this is sound political dope." He dreaded the recurrence of war fever with its intolerance, its vindictiveness, its restraints on free expression, and at the beginning of World War II he gave up writing regularly for the *Sun* though he remained as editorial adviser. Every superior journalist has feelers: Mencken's told him it was time to shut up, at least so far as public affairs were concerned.

With that durable good sense that governed him through the downs as well as the ups of his career, he had in the meantime turned to other things. One of the defenses he fell back on was the labor without end that he made for himself in American linguistics. On returning to Hollins Street and at the bottom of his loneliness following the death of Sara, he plunged into the work of rewriting, enlarging, and in many ways, reshaping *The American Language* for its fourth edition. This was published in 1936. The reception of it proved that whatever may have happened to his standing as a publicist, in this other field it was secure. Supplement I and Supplement II, massive works and complete in themselves, came along in due course (1945 and 1948).

More surprising was the way he opened an entirely new lode. Those who knew Mencken well knew how false was the impression of his personality that his no-quarter polemical writing gave. That was his battle dress. To be sure it was not exactly a mask, since he loved the give and take of public controversy. But it did conceal a much more complicated personality through which ran a broad stream of sentiment and warm humanity. His love affair and marriage with Sara had exposed this briefly to an astonished public. Now, disarmed as a con troversialist, he yielded to it in his writing. He turned to the recollection of his childhood in the Baltimore of another day, that childhood for which he had no regrets, in a series of sketches written for the *New Yorker* magazine. They were by turns rollicking, mordant, warmhearted, and nostalgic; and they were greeted with surprise and delight. These were brought together in his book called *Happy Days*, published in 1940. In its preface he conceded that "the record of an event is no doubt often bedizened and adulterated by my response to it," but insisted on the essential truth of the sketches as both autobiography and social history. As props to memory he had consulted his father's old accounts, miraculously intact, and other "contemporary inscriptions."

There followed in 1941 a second volume, *Newspaper Days*. This second group of autobiographical sketches, covering his first years of newspaper life in Baltimore, he described as "mainly true, but with occasional stretchers," and he commended them to the understanding sort of reader who, in Charles Lamb's phrase, felt no call to take "everything perversely in the absolute and literal sense." Absolutely and literally true they certainly were not, as for example his deathless story of "A Girl from Red Lion, P.A." They were better than that: they caught and preserved the smells and flavor and temper of an era. The success of these two volumes inspired a project for a full autobiography to be done on a scale of one book per decade; but he thought better of it: his good sense told him that the mood could not be sustained into the years of his combative maturity. He did one more book of reminiscences, *Heathen Days* (1943), which made pleasant enough reading and did well but lacked the perfect autumnal quality of its predecessors, and called quits on this enterprise.

Mencken was coming to the end of his days as a writer. There was his book of quotations, fruit of a lifetime of clipping and marking and note-saving, and a very different thing from Bartlett's. It was published in 1940 as *A New Dictionary of Quotations*. His *Christmas Story*, a brief bit of mellow buffoonery on a sardonic theme, was published in 1946. In 1948 he returned to the Sunpapers after much urging, and reluctantly, to cover the presidential conventions of that year, including the rump convention of the Wallace Progressive party, which proved to be an extravaganza made to order for his talents. The rigors of the campaign itself were no longer for him, but that fall he did contribute a few more things to the paper from home base. His last piece of newspaper writing was published on November 9 of that year, a few days after the election. It was on a subject unrelated to the election, and I will return to it a bit further on, for it was an appropriate epitaph to a man who had spent much of his life battling for the rights of the individual.

Two weeks later he was taken by the thrombosis that ended his career with such terrible finality. One last book had occupied him toward the end of his writing years: a book of aphorisms and short statements culled from his notes. The manuscript, completed and ready for the printer, was found some years later and was published as *Minority Report: H. L. Mencken's Notebooks* following his death in 1956.

It is in character that the last four sentences of Mencken's final book (that same posthumous *Minority Report*) have to do with his style as a writer: "The imbeciles who have printed acres of comment on my books have seldom noticed the chief character of my style. It is that I write with almost scientific precision— that my meaning is never obscure. The ignorant have often complained that my vocabulary is beyond them, but that is simply because my ideas cover a wider range than theirs do. Once they have consulted the dictionary they always know exactly what I intend to say. I am as far as any writer can get from the muffled sonorities of, say, John Dewey."

It is true enough that there was never anything muffled or fuzzy (though there was plenty of sonority) about what Mencken wrote. His meaning was always transparently clear. But the passage is worth looking at closely because it illustrates how much more than that there was to the Mencken style, which is loaded with artifice. Scientific precision? On the face of it, this example is loaded with imprecisions. The word "imbeciles," for example. A great deal that had been written about Mencken's books was silly, certainly. But the men who had written about Mencken, silly though they might be, were certainly not imbeciles by any available definition of that word. Nor had

they written "acres" on the subject—another flagrant inexactitude. Nor did the ignorant often complain about his vocabulary, because the ignorant did not often read him. When they did, it was not his vocabulary that bothered them. As to the elements of his vocabulary that might be complained of, resort to the dictionary was no help because they were either words of his own invention—"booboisie," "bozart"—or old words deftly provided with new meanings and bent to his special uses. His vocabulary was most definitely not beyond his readers: the complaints were from readers who understood only too well what he was saying and were responding precisely as he intended them to respond. The complaints were the flutterings of hit birds.

To write with scientific precision is to take mathematics for a model, avoiding all emotive overtones, rejecting anything that might color a plain statement of fact or interfere with the unfolding of a rational argument—to reject the art of rhetoric, in other words. But Mencken was a supreme rhetorician. Far from being scientific, his use of words was aesthetic. He used them as an artist uses color and a musician the arrangement of notes in clusters—to play upon the senses and emotions of his readers, to make them laugh, sigh, weep, go along with him, grind their teeth in fury, and to put across his point whether it was intrinsically worth making or just a piece of wayward mischief. That paragraph on style, with its deceptive bluntness, clarity, and simplicity, illustrates pretty well how much more complicated it is than he would ever admit.

For the origins of his style one can go straight back to his discovery of *Huckleberry Finn* in his ninth year, which he described as "probably the most stupendous event of my life." It was indeed. He devoured everything he could find by Mark Twain, whose manner of writing was without question the chief influence on his own. Twenty-five years later he wrote (in the *Smart Set*): "I believe that 'Huckleberry Finn' is one of the great masterpieces of the world, that it is the full equal of 'Don Quixote' and 'Robinson Crusoe.' . . . I believe that it will be read by human beings of all ages, not as a solemn duty but for the honest love of it, and over and over again. . . . I believe that Mark Twain had a clearer vision of life, that he came nearer to its elementals and was less deceived by its false appearances, than any other American who has ever presumed to manufacture generalizations. . . . I believe that, admitting all his defects, he wrote better English, in the sense of clearer, straighter, saner English, than either Irving or Hawthorne. . . . I believe that he was the true father of our national literature, the first genuinely American artist of the blood royal. . . . He was one of the great artists of all time. He was the full equivalent of Cervantes and Molière, Swift and Defoe. He was and is the one authentic giant of our national literature."

From Mark Twain he learned many things, never to forget them, including these: that sentiment is nothing to be ashamed of though sentimentality is, that the way to meet human venality is to meet it head on, that compassion and a sense of humility need never be concealed, and that, in Mark Twain's words, "the secret source of Humor . . . is not joy but sorrow. There is no humor in heaven." From Mark Twain came the qualities that make Mencken the American humorist second only to Mark Twain himself. Alistair Cooke considers that Mencken has been overrated as a thinker and "underrated as a humorist with a deadly sensible eye on the behavior of the human animal." Mark Twain gave him that eye, or at least inspired him to use his own, and much of his apparatus as a writer.

There were other sources, all going back to his childhood and youth, for he was quick to discover that there are ways, and ways, of writing. Thomas Huxley fascinated him not only for what he had to teach but also for his utter clarity, and he mentioned Huxley many years later as "the greatest of all masters of orderly exposition. He taught me the importance of giving to every argument a simple structure." In his view Huxley's prose "was the best produced by an Englishman in the Nineteenth Century."

At several places in his writing, Mencken points to the old *New York Sun*, "especially its editorial page," as an influence on his style, an influence both good and bad—"good because it taught me that good sense was at the bottom of all good writing, but bad because it . . . made me overestimate the value of smart phrases." There is a touch of irony in this, considering how Mencken lambasted editorial writers throughout his life: it turns out that his animus was against the third-raters, not against the competent ones.

He sucked up much from Nietzsche and Shaw and Macaulay, though he never failed to take a poke at Macaulay later on for his pretentiousness. Cooke summarizes their contributions almost too patly: "Nietzsche suggested the outlandish metaphors, Macaulay the feigned omniscience . . . Shaw taught him most." Both Shaw and Mencken, as he writes, "are superior popular educators who kick up a terrific dust on the intellectual middle plateau between the philistine and the first-rate scholar. What makes both of them more memorable than many of their betters is their style." But Mencken never had Shaw's malice and he wholly lacked "the shrill spinster note that in the end wearies all but the most dedicated of Shaw's disciples."

Shaw was, as we know, the subject of Mencken's first book. Mencken admitted that "there was a good deal of empty ornament" in that book, as in his early *Smart Set* work which came along shortly after, but that "afterward I began to tone down, and by the time I was thirty I had developed a style that was clear and alive. I can detect no diminution of its aliveness as I grow older." In this latter remark (from *Minority Report*) he is unduly modest. Of all his writing, the most flexible, subtle, and responsive to his demands was the autumn-blooming style of his autobiographical sketches.

Of stylistic characteristics peculiar to him, there were many. I mention four.

One of these was his belief that the function of criticism—coming ahead even of the discovery of the true and the beautiful—was to be interesting. He never forgot the man on the receiving end: the reader. Always before him as he wrote was the vision of a reader who might fall into a doze with a book, one of his, in his lap; or of the newspaper reader who might pause for a moment over what he had written, yawn, and move on to the next column.

Corollary to this was the care he took to be always on the offensive. He had discovered early that what the public likes is a fight. His first purpose being to catch and hold the interest of the reader, he always charged. This made for difficulties if in all honesty he was compelled to bestow praise. But he had a way around that, too. "When I have to praise a writer, I always do it by attacking his enemies."

Another was his constant resort to the *reductio ad absurdum*, which as James Farrell says he often handled not only cleverly but even brilliantly. The object was to make his victim a butt of ridicule. Here he was most plainly Mark Twain's disciple, who saw laughter as the one really effective weapon of an honest man in an imperfect and on the whole inattentive world. Other weapons might, with time and diligence, make some impression on humbug, but as Mark Twain said, "only laughter can blow it to rags and atoms at a blast."

The fourth was the care with which he placed his readers, those he wanted to persuade, on his side in any argument. He wrote, as he never tired of assuring his readers, for "the nobility and gentry," for "the truly civilized minority." Anyone taking the trouble to read him could therefore consider himself complimented. By inference his readers could never possibly be identified with the bores, shams, and Neanderthals whom he delighted to take apart, or share in the slightest their meanness of spirit, their stupidity, their ignorance, and their wrongheadedness. Before going into battle, Mencken always saw to it that the cheering section—his reader—was in good heart and ready to back him. He was a master at this sort of rhetorical sleight of hand.

In discussing "the Mencken philosophy," let us begin by acknowledging that Mencken was not a philosopher. Cairns calls him a positivist, and though the word is probably the right one if Mencken must be given a philosophical label, it seems curiously formal and inappropriate for one of such commonsensical cast of mind. And the tag "skeptic" used in its philosophical sense is even less appropriate. The philosophical skeptic has an open mind, he is a doubter, but he stands ready to be convinced by rational argument—if he can't break down the argument. Philosophical skepticism is apt to be the refuge of timorous but clever men since philosophical arguments can be quite easily destroyed, by the cheap and easy device of questioning the major premise if by no other, and the skeptic is thus spared on high philosophical grounds the inconvenience and vulnerability involved in taking a position on anything. Mencken was abundantly skeptical of the motives of men, especially when they purported to be lofty, and of the postures assumed by public figures. But he was no skeptic: he had a set of convictions as unshakable as

Gibraltar. He knew his own mind, and as I have suggested he was not prepared to allow anyone to change it.

The point is that he was simply not interested in first causes or fine-spun theories of knowledge: metaphysics bored him; more, it enraged him, since efforts to prove the unprovable by word-defining and logic-chopping (which is the self-assigned task of metaphysicians) struck him as being the vainest of all parlor games. His view is put with utmost starkness in a famous letter to Burton Rascoe: "My notion is that all the larger human problems are insoluble, and that life is quite meaningless—a spectacle without purpose or moral. I detest all efforts to read a moral into it." But his disgust with philosophy's efforts to account for the universe and its contents, including man, did not, as I say, leave him a skeptic. He believed (and this is where the word "positivism" comes in) in the tangible, the measurable, the verifiable. He described himself once as "a materialist of the materialists," and put it another way in a letter in which he wrote of his "congenital dislike of Plato" and his preference for feet-on-the-ground Aristotle. What science could discover and verify, that he believed; and it must be admitted that during the past several hundred years science has taken a lot of territory away from philosophy.

This gave him all the base he needed for his work as what he called a "critic of ideas." It was the shooting box from which he blasted away at organized religion. It provided him with his political position, which was at once antidemocratic and passionately libertarian. It was from this point of view that he saw human beings and the whole rickety structure of human institutions.

Pushing aside formal philosophy, then, Mencken started with the proposition (certainly verifiable) that the human organism despite its manifold wonders is a badly botched job. ("God nodded," he once exploded in the midst of the hay fever season, "when he designed my nose.") From that he moved on to the proposition (also verifiable) that all men are not created equal. Equal they may be, or should be, before the law, and equally entitled to opportunity; but demonstrably they are not equal in their native physical and intellectual endowment. The natural incompetence and gullibility of the masses he held to be a matter of simple fact, confirmed every day and everywhere, and the existence in much smaller numbers of superior men a matter equally beyond dispute.

And from this, though he had nothing better to offer ("I am interested in pathology, not therapeutics"), came his criticism of democratic theory and practice. The mass of men, buffeted by forces beyond their strength and understanding, do not yearn for freedom but for security. They turn automatically to the man who promises this. They are the natural prey of demagogues always ready to exploit them for their own purposes, and no system is better adapted to demagoguery than popular democracy. Democracy always and inevitably tends toward mobocracy.

But nothing could be more mistaken than to assume from this that Mencken would have preferred any totalitarian form. He detested Hitler and Mussolini and every other kind of demagogue either hard or soft. His concern was simply that under popular democracy, in which decisions are so often motivated by appeals to envy and promises of something for nothing, the victims are the superior man, the creative man, the self-respecting man—"the only sort of man who is really worth hell room, to wit, the man who practices some useful trade in a competent manner, makes a decent living at it, pays his own way, and asks only to be let alone. He is now a pariah in all so-called civilized countries." Mencken's bill of particulars against democracy boiled down to his simple belief that democracy, given its head, dislikes and hamstrings the producer and the creator.

Though he never put it that way, Mencken was in fact a strict constitutionalist. Given a constitution beyond the reach of easy amendment, that is to say a set of rules that did really restrain the mob and its masters, that put limitations on government and made them stick, kept speech free, and provided equal justice, the superior man probably had as good a chance as under any other conceivable system. But where is the constitution that is invulnerable to the mob when it has really been inflamed? His own experience as a critic of national policy in two world wars left him with small faith in the protections of the United States Constitution or any other. It is interesting that Mencken's political ideas are taken far more seriously in Europe today, among those familiar with them, than they are in his native land. Europeans have more, and more bitter, memories of curdled democracy than Americans do.

A study of Mencken's political ideas necessarily begins with his *Notes on Democracy*. But this is marred by a certain stridency and an overindulgence in bathos and paradox. His ideas somehow come out better in his topical writings on political issues and personalities. Most of the best of these things are brought together in *On Politics: A Carnival of Buncombe*, edited by Malcolm Moos, and in *Prejudices: A Selection*, edited by James T. Farrell. They amplify the comments on his philosophy which are offered above.

Mencken's ingrained habit of calling things and people by their right names, and his clear-eyed refusal to confuse what is what with what ought or ought not to be, led people into false inferences about his likes and prejudices. What he disliked above all was pretense. "As I say,

all my work hangs together. Whether it appears to be burlesque, or serious criticism, or mere casual controversy, it is always directed against one thing: unwarranted pretension." Thus he referred to Jews as matter-of-factly as he referred to Methodists, jested about Jewish traits that to him seemed comic, criticized specifically Jewish activities that he thought harmful. This to L. M. Birkhead, a Unitarian pastor, is illustrative: "I believe there is another difficulty in the anti-Semitic question. After all, a man who believes sincerely that the Jews are a menace to the United States ought to be allowed to say so. The fact that he is wrong has got nothing whatsoever to do with it. The right to free speech involves inevitably the right to talk nonsense. I am much disturbed by the effort of the New York Jews to put down criticism. It seems to me that they are only driving it underground, and so making it more violent." This was Mencken talking free speech, not anti-Semitism. He cared nothing for racial or social stigmata and looked past them to the man. A small expression of this is that one of the two well-known paintings of him was done by a Jew, the other by a Negro.

And so it was with his jocosities about "the colored brethren" which reflected the mores of his time and the culture of the Negro community in Baltimore then and throughout the country generally. He didn't pretend not to notice differences. And yet the very last thing he wrote, the article in the *Evening Sun* of November 9, 1948, which I have already mentioned, was an angry protest against the conviction of a mixed group of seven who had challenged Baltimore's segregation ordinances by staging what he called "an interracial tennis combat" on the courts of a public park. "Is such a prohibition . . ." he asked, "supported by anything to be found in common sense and common decency? . . . My answer . . . is a loud and unequivocal No. A free citizen in a free state, it seems to me, has an inalienable right to play with whomsoever he will, so long as he does not disturb the general peace. If any other citizen, offended by the spectacle, makes a pother, then that other citizen, and not the man exercising his inalienable right, should be put down by the police."

No sturdier defender of civil liberties has ever lived, and it was in character that he should have ended his writing, as a newspaperman grinding the grist of the news, with a simple statement supporting them.

The public Mencken, as I hope I have made clear, was different in many ways from the private Mencken. To the public generally, and especially after the press took to quoting him on anything and everything in the late twenties and early thirties, he was a roistering fellow who had an acid tongue and a club in his hand and was given to every sort of excess. He went along with this cheerfully, and even encouraged it. Why not? It gave him an instant audience, one running into the millions, for anything he might want to say. Others might coat their pills with sugar: he used a tart and astringent coating and found the public equally ready to swallow it. His role as the arch enemy of Prohibition gave him a supplementary reputation as a fearful boozer.

His manner in company somewhat fortified that larger, vaguer reputation. In a gathering that was large and mixed he could be subdued and even ill at ease, but among men whom he found congenial he was a marvelous companion—exuberant, boisterous, often ribald. I recall his daily visits to the Sunpapers back in the days when I was a green young editorial writer. His loud greeting was at once gay and gruff. He would disappear into one sanctum or another, that of the editor or the publisher, and from behind the door would issue muffled roars of laughter. It wasn't the response to a

monologue, quite. He dominated, but he knew the difference between conversation and a one-man show. He enjoyed practical jokes, and often gave them a sharp edge—as for instance that fake institution known as "The Loyal Legion of American Mothers," which was "dedicated to avoiding foreign entanglements and keeping American womanhood pure." Much mischief was done under that and other equally grotesque letterheads.

But all this exuberance and much of his enormous correspondence were the compensations of a lonely man, a loneliness implicit in his work. In his *Minority Report* there is this: "I know a great many more people than most men, and in wider and more diverse circles, yet my life is essentially one of isolation, and so is that of every other man. We not only have to die alone; we also, save for a few close associates, have to live alone." And the bleakness of his view of the nature of things only fortified the loneliness and pessimism. "The natural state of a reflective man," he wrote in another context, "is one of pessimism."

His private life, save for some exceptions to be noted, was orderly and austere. After breakfast his day began with an hour or two of dictation to Lohrfinck, his secretary. When she had gone, he worked until noon on his notes and files and some writing; following luncheon he put on his public manner for his daily visit to the Sunpapers, with arrival punctually at two o'clock. By mid-afternoon he was in Hollins Street again to work on his papers until about five. Then a book, or the better part of one, perhaps a brief nap, the return of Lohrfinck with a load of letters to sign and seal, and a short walk to the mailbox before his supper (his concession to exercise); after supper, which was finished before eight, came his main bout of writing for the day, which normally stretched on to about ten o'clock, in his third floor quarters; then downstairs to unwind, usually with his brother August, or out to Schellhase's, a *gemütlich* little restaurant, for a couple of glasses of beer with an old friend or two; and then home to bed not long after eleven o'clock, to read until he fell asleep.

There was not much room in such a routine for roistering. His weekly letdown came on Saturday nights with an odd assortment of cronies who made up the Saturday Night Club. They met in the early days above Al Hildebrand's fiddle shop, to grind out music together, Mencken at the piano with a heavy hand. Later they had a second-floor room at Schellhase's; and after the music there was beer and merriment. Music was Mencken's avocation, his companion and pleasure throughout his life: "I'd rather have written any symphony of Brahms' than any play of Ibsen's. I'd rather have written the first movement of Beethoven's Erotica than the Song of Solomon. . . . In music a man can let himself go. In words he always remains a bit stiff and unconvincing." His musician friend Louis Cheslock, possibly a prejudiced witness, always insisted that "in the same sense that Beethoven was aware of the language of sound, Mencken was aware of the sound of language."

His other recreation, growing out of his hypochondriacal temperament, was hospital visiting. Ill-health, to him, was the great human curse and calamity; and that sympathy for human suffering, that compassion for the lot of man in general which he kept so well concealed from his larger public, got its release out of visits to the sick. He was a familiar figure in the halls of Johns Hopkins Hospital and of all the other local pesthouses, as he liked to call them.

He traveled occasionally, but the preparations had a way of turning into crises, and the chief effect of such holidays was to make him long for the familiar ambience of Baltimore and the routine of home.

As for his reputation as a formidable boozer, it was without basis. As a youngster on the police beat (he tells in one of his sketches), he learned the lesson from a tough old fire department surgeon whom he came to know and admire that alcohol is not a stimulant but a depressant: "His words . . . continue to lurk in my mind, to this day. In consequence . . . I employ it of an evening, not to hooch up my faculties but to let them down after work. Not in years have I ever written anything with so much as a glass of beer in my system. My compositions, I gather, sometimes seem boozy to the nobility and gentry, but they are actually done as soberly as those of William Dean Howells." He was always, from adolescence onward, a "cagey" drinker—the first to raise his glass, but the last to empty it. He had no real taste for spirits and was forever finding excuses to avoid them.

A man always strict with himself, a disciplined man who severely rationed his pleasures, this was Mencken. To James Farrell he once said this: "Farrell, if you want to develop further as a writer, there are three things to stay away from. Booze . . . women . . . and politics." If he said that to one young writer, he said it to a hundred; and he followed his own prescription.

Mencken's output was prodigious. The Adler bibliography runs to 349 pages, and even this formidable listing excludes his letters. Guy Forgue, in the preface to his admirably edited selection of these letters, estimates that those deposited in public libraries and private collections must run to around 15,000. It is an estimate very much on the low side. Some years ago I discussed the output of Mencken's letters with his brother August and mentioned 50,000 as a not unlikely number. August had lately made an estimate—not by trying to count, but by weight—of the number of letters addressed to Mencken in connection with a single work, *The American Language*, and came up with the figure of 65,000. Although this was an estimate of letters received, it also meant 65,000 replies, because Mencken's red-letter rule was to answer all letters and on the day of their receipt. What the total output of all kinds must have been, long ones and short ones, others amounting to essays, is anyone's guess. And the odd thing is that every one of these, no matter how perfunctory, was relieved by a phrase, a suggestion, a sharp comment, a touch of grotesquerie that made it hard to throw away. As for his longer letters, when he rolled up his sleeves and really went to work, some are Mencken at his best, as critic of life and letters and as self-revelation. Forgue's collection, of letters to writers mostly, is in fact one of Mencken's most absorbing books.

Mencken has been spared, fortunately, the deadly Collected Edition which abandons discrimination for comprehensiveness and which serves as a tombstone for so many writers whose work, in part, might otherwise live. As a newspaperman he wrote most of the time for the moment; but as Alistair Cooke quite properly insists, there is a great deal of life, maybe immortality, in a fair bit of that stuff. The thing to do is to let time winnow it. The process is well begun in the several selections of his *Prejudices* and newspaper political pieces by Cooke, Farrell, and Moos and in Cheslock's gathering of his pieces on music. A much fuller anthology by Huntington Cairns, called *H. L. Mencken: The American Scene*, ranges all across his work and with sound judgment. Certain storehouses of Mencken material, notably the Mencken room in the Enoch Pratt Free Library of Baltimore and the New York Public Library collection, offer ripe pickings for the future.

Of his formal treatises—his *Notes on Democracy, A Treatise on the Gods*, and *A Treatise on Right and Wrong*—what is likely to be the verdict? He obviously put great store by them as a distillation of his views on the three abiding human preoccupations, with politics (or the art of living together without too much trouble) and with religion and morals (together, the art of living with oneself). But neither as a corpus nor individually can they really be called successful. The first, as suggested already, is badly organized, undisciplined, and shrill despite many a penetrating and cathartic paragraph. It overstates. It leaves the reader, shall we say, not quite persuaded. Its leading ideas are set forth better anyway in his posthumous *Minority Report*, a book which will continue to appeal to readers with a taste for the aphoristic form, and in his journalism, where they are illuminated by concrete issues and people. As for *A Treatise on the Gods* and *A Treatise on Right and Wrong*, both smell too strongly of the lamp, which is to say that they seem somehow concocted. The reading that went into them was extraordinarily wide. They contain much curious information. But Mencken's concern to make them *interesting*, to "fetch" the reader, seems inappropriate to what at bottom were intended as sober and deadly serious treatises. One is left with the conviction, again, that his leading ideas were better put by the thinkers from whom he absorbed them, that he added relatively little of his own beyond the form of the statement, that in any case they are far better stated in his topical writing, and that he is not at his best in the sustained development of ideas. Mencken was simply not a systematist.

The one exception to that generalization is his great *The American Language*. And it is not hard to see why. Here Mencken the stylist, Mencken the word-juggler, is at work investigating the raw materials of his own great talent and constant preoccupation. He is studying his native tongue, his own means of communication—its origin, its evolution, the springs that feed it, its marvelous suppleness and fluidity. The theme needed systematic exploration, for it had never been given this before; and it took a man sensitive to every nuance of speech and writing to do it. Mencken was that man; and his fascination as well as his supreme capacity for the task shows through as it does nowhere in the three efforts at systematization mentioned above.

Yet *The American Language* comes up against another fate. It deals with a living and changing thing. Even in the course of its four editions (the first in 1919 and the fourth in 1936), the growth and change of the language required many modifications, including modifications of the central thesis. The American language, having grown away from British English, the two had begun to coalesce again through a reverse process: the modification of British English along American lines by extensive borrowings. McDavid's one-volume abridgment (1963) required much more than abridgment: it required extensive updating. The original *American Language* will live as a period piece, a monumental work of scholarship fixing the language as of its time, like a still shot from a film, and full of wit and wisdom. But the title shows signs of developing a life of its own, like Bartlett, Webster, Roget, and even Fanny Farmer.

If we leave out this singular case, the surest candidates for immortality seem to be his *Happy Days* and *Newspaper Days*, redolent of a life that is gone yet no more to be forgotten than the Wild West, and done in a style ripened and purged of excess, a style that as Cooke says is "flexible, fancy-free, ribald, and always beautifully lucid; a native product unlike any other style in the language." Those books and the best of his "transient" work: they are the essential Mencken. They are what he gave to our literature which time is least likely to tarnish or erode.

Selected Bibliography

WORKS OF H. L. MENCKEN

George Bernard Shaw: His Plays. Boston: Luce, 1905.

The Philosophy of Friedrich Nietzsche. Boston: Luce, 1908.

A Book of Burlesques. New York: Lane, 1916; revised edition, New York: Knopf, 1920.

A Book of Prefaces. New York: Knopf, 1917.

In Defense of Women. New York: Goodman, 1918; revised edition, with new introduction, New York: Knopf, 1922.

The American Language. New York: Knopf, 1919; second edition, revised and enlarged, 1921; third edition, revised and enlarged, 1923; fourth edition, enlarged and rewritten, 1936.

Prejudices: First Series. New York: Knopf, 1919.

Prejudices: Second Series. New York: Knopf, 1920.

Prejudices: Third Series. New York: Knopf, 1922.

Prejudices: Fourth Series. New York: Knopf, 1924.

Notes on Democracy. New York: Knopf, 1926.

Prejudices: Fifth Series. New York: Knopf, 1926.

Prejudices: Sixth Series. New York: Knopf, 1927.

Treatise on the Gods. New York and London: Knopf, 1930.

Making a President: A Footnote to the Saga of Democracy. New York: Knopf, 1932.

Treatise on Right and Wrong. New York: Knopf, 1934.

Happy Days, 1880–1892. New York: Knopf, 1940.

Newspaper Days, 1899–1906. New York: Knopf, 1941.

Heathen Days, 1890–1936. New York: Knopf, 1943.

The American Language: Supplement One. New York: Knopf, 1945.

Christmas Story, illustrated by Bill Crawford. New York: Knopf, 1946.

The American Language: Supplement Two. New York: Knopf, 1948.

Minority Report: H. L. Mencken's Notebooks. New York: Knopf, 1956.

SELECTED EDITIONS OF WORKS AND LETTERS

The American Language, abridged with annotations and new material by Raven I. McDavid, Jr. New York: Knopf, 1963.

A Bathtub Hoax and Other Blasts and Bravos from the Chicago Tribune, edited by Robert McHugh. New York: Knopf, 1958.

A Mencken Chrestomathy, edited and annotated by the author. New York: Knopf, 1949.

H. L. Mencken: The American Scene, a Reader, selected and edited with an introduction and commentary by Huntington Cairns. New York: Knopf, 1965.

H. L. Mencken on Music, selected by Louis Cheslock. New York: Knopf, 1961.

Letters of H. L. Mencken, selected and annotated by Guy J. Forgue, with a personal note by Hamilton Owens. New York: Knopf, 1961.

BIBLIOGRAPHIES

Adler, Betty, with the assistance of Jane Wilhelm. *H. L. M.: The Mencken Bibliography.* Baltimore, Md.: Johns Hopkins Press for Enoch Pratt Free Library, 1961. (Lists, so far as can be ascertained, Mencken's shorter works, newspaper and magazine contributions, and miscellaneous writings, as well as his books; also lists critical studies of Mencken and his work, including many brief studies, published and unpublished.)

Frey, Carroll. *A Bibliography of the Writings of H. L. Mencken,* with a foreword by H. L. Mencken. Philadelphia: Centaur Bookshop, 1924.

Porter, Bernard H. *H. L. Mencken, a Bibliography.* Pasadena, Calif: Geddes Press, 1957.

Swan, Bradford F. *Making a Mencken Collection.* New Haven, Conn: Yale University Gazette, 1950.

CRITICAL AND
BIOGRAPHICAL STUDIES

Adler, Betty, ed. *Menckenianna, a Quarterly Review.* Baltimore, Md.: Enoch Pratt Free Library, 1961–. (A serial miscellany of reminiscences, papers, reprinted items, etc., plus a bibliographical checklist.)

Angoff, Charles. *H. L. Mencken, a Portrait from Memory.* New York: Yoseloff, 1956.

Boyd, Ernest Augustus. *H. L. Mencken.* New York: McBride, 1925.

DeCasseres, Benjamin. *Mencken and Shaw, the Anatomy of America's Voltaire and England's Other John Bull.* New York: Silas Newton, 1930.

Goldberg, Isaac. *H. L. Mencken.* Girard, Kansas: Haldeman-Julius, 1920.

——. *The Man Mencken, a Biographical and Critical Survey.* New York: Simon, 1925.

H. L. Mencken, a reprint of three articles: "Fanfare," by Burton Rascoe; "The American Critic," by Vincent O'Sullivan; "Bibliography," by F. C. Henderson. New York: Knopf, 1920.

Kemler, Edgar, *The Irreverent Mr. Mencken.* Boston: Little, Brown, 1950.

Manchester, William. *Disturber of the Peace: The Life of H. L. Mencken,* with an introduction by Gerald W. Johnson. New York: Harper, 1951.

Wagner, Philip M. "Mencken Remembered," *American Scholar,* 32:256–74 (Spring 1963).

——PHILIP WAGNER

Edna St. Vincent Millay

1892-1950

MANY years after the death of Edna St. Vincent Millay a friend continued to cherish a memory of the young poet as she had seen her once, flashing up Macdougal Street in Greenwich Village, laughing as she ran, her long hair flying about her shoulders, a young man on her heels earnestly enacting the comedy of pursuit.

The image is pleasing and it is not deceptive as a reflection of the special grace that characterized both the temperament and the literary gift of an artist with a high sense of drama. One recalls inevitably a line by Keats as Edna Millay herself so often did. One sees figures of the classic tradition like many that pervade her own work. There she and her companion are, "forever panting and forever young."

There is the further significance to the recollection that it exactly satisfies the impression left on many of her readers by the poet who presented herself, in an early revelation, as one who was disposed to burn her candle at both ends and to bathe her tantalizingly smiling face in its "lovely light." For the two decades of her ever-rising popularity—the twenties and thirties of the century—she seemed to personify the spirit of the time: its exuberance, its defiance of convention, its determination to discover and to declare a sharply defined identity.

But to remember her only as the nymph of Greenwich Village, exulting playfully in freedom, would be to turn away from nearly all that was of genuine importance to the experience which she put herself to exquisite pain to communicate. Seen whole she emerges out of myth not as a gay figure but as a tragic one; not as a precocious perennial schoolgirl but as an artist born mature and burdened with a scrupulous sense of responsibility toward her gift; not as a changeling child of mysticism but as a creature whose essential desire was to find identity with the balanced order of nature; not as a woman merely but as a creator who inevitably contained within her persona masculine as well as feminine attributes.

The theme of all her poetry is the search for the integrity of the individual spirit. The campaign to conquer and control this realm of experience is conducted always in terms of positive and rigorous conflict—the duel with death, the duel with love, the duel of mind pitted against heart, the duel with "The spiteful and the stingy and the rude" who would steal away possession of beauty.

It is not too fanciful to say that she was born old while she remained forever young, and her personal history explains the fortunate anomaly. Rockland, Maine, was her native place (she was born there on February 22,

1892) and she lived her childhood in a succession of towns in the same state. The parents were separated, and, though Edna Millay communicated freely and amicably with her father, it was to her mother that she gave a devotion earned by the quite extraordinary aptitude for guidance that Cora Millay showed in relationship to her three daughters. Trained to be a singer, the mother took time from her duties as breadwinner, serving as a district nurse, to coach town orchestras and to write out scores for their members. She found time also to teach her daughter Edna to write poetry at the age of four and to play the piano at the age of seven.

Despite the meagerness of the bread-and-butter resources of Cora Millay's matriarchal society its advantages to a buoyant young mentality were many. Opportunities for self-instruction abounded. The daughters contrived theatrical entertainments, produced a body of "instant" folklore, and presented to their world an attractive picture of close-knit solidarity among proto-bohemians exactly of the later Greenwich Village type. Mrs. Millay, removing a cigarette from her lips to utter mild acerbities at the expense of mediocre ideals and concessive attitudes, educated her daughters in independence of outlook.

Though she had been awakened early to interests of the arts and of the mind, Edna Millay had no opportunity to go to college until she was in her twenties. She was able to receive formal instruction belatedly with the help of a chance acquaintance who, recognizing unusual quality in a shy girl who had already written the poem "Renascence," found the money to send her, first, to a speed-up indoctrination course at Barnard and, then, to Vassar. She showed herself to be a superior student; acted with spirit, conviction, and talent in many student plays; and, managing to let love of learning triumph over a distaste for regimentation, rounded out a highly creditable undergraduate career at twenty-five. She wrote the baccalaureate hymn for her class and revealed herself as anything but a schoolgirl versifier by opening it with these lines:

Thou great offended God of love and kindness,
  We have denied, we have forgotten Thee!
With deafer sense endow, enlighten us with
    blindness,
  Who, having ears and eyes, nor hear nor see.

Greenwich Village had become quite recently the febrile state of mind so well known to social historians, and Edna Millay, immediately upon her arrival in it, became a conspicuous representative of its temper. Habits of industry combined with inborn discipline enabled her to work simultaneously on three levels of productivity. She wrote poems which were published in magazines of prestige as well as in the popular ones of the period. She played central roles in productions of the Provincetown Players, some of her own authorship. Under the pseudonym Nancy Boyd she turned out satiric stories and prose sketches which were valued by several editors, among them Frank Crowninshield of *Vanity Fair*. In the Village atmosphere Edna Millay prospered as few American poets had managed up to that time to do. The printed volumes of her poetry went into the hands of an unprecedentedly large following and her popularity was further increased by her appearances in public recitals of her work and by readings over a nationwide hook-up on radio.

As symbolic figure—the "free woman" of the age—Edna Millay could not have eluded close examination of her personal history. This was an interest which the candor of her love poems seemed uninhibitedly to endorse and, as she once made wry confession in a moment of frivolity, she never had "in the presence of clergymen denied these loves." The history of her friendships was intense, filled with *Sturm und Drang*. She seems to have surprised many of her admirers quite out of the usual routine of responses—made up as these often are of inverse vanity and zeal for conquest—into an almost awed awareness of herself as a person, of her glowing particularity. It was perhaps the special grace of her integrity which made her physical attractiveness seem to be even greater in sum than itemized descriptions of eyes, hair, throat, figure added up to. She had gaiety to give but without provocativeness, candor but with no abandonment to license, love in large measure but held within the confines of a somehow austere decorum.

These considerations are relevant to an examination of her work. The same quiet reverence for vitality under discipline is the distinguishing quality of her poetry. At its best it is characterized by a kind of orderly surrender to ecstasy.

She married at last. Eugen Boissevain was an exuberant man of Dutch ancestry who had been a successful man of affairs. He gave up his business as importer when he assumed responsibility for the care of this woman of high talent who became in her early middle years an invalid with physical crises aggravated in crucial instances by what she herself described as "very handsome . . . all but life-size" nervous breakdowns. After two years of marriage filled with gaiety and work the poet and her genial protector retired to a place with which their lives were to be identified for nearly a quarter of a century—Steepletop, near Austerlitz, New York. Their way of life retracted into a simpler pattern partly because of Edna Millay's uncertain health, partly because money difficulties began to press upon them bluntly forbidding bohemian extravagances. But both at the New York farmhouse and on an island retreat off the coast of Maine friends were received warmly and the severely enforced routine of work was interrupted by the pleasures to which Edna Millay continued to be devoted throughout her days—swimming, bird-watching, gardening, and music-making.

In these settings the poet labored to discipline her gift with the conscientiousness she had always required of herself. But she saw her popularity and her reputation wane. The tragedy of a decline in critical favor was sharpened by the severity of the judgments which she herself made on some of her later products. When she felt that she had written bad poetry she suffered on a level of intensity quite similar to that which she had enjoyed as ecstasy in her happiest and most creative moments.

Eugen Boissevain died suddenly in the fall of 1949 after an operation for a lung condition. A period of haunted loneliness followed for Edna Millay but it lasted only a little more than a year. On a morning in October of 1950 she was found dead on the stairs of Steepletop. Characteristically she had been going to bed with a work of poetry in her hands—the proof pages of Rolfe Humphries' translation of the *Aeneid*.

It is often said of the major figures of the arts that each seems to create a universe all his own and to measure its vast dimensions with untransferable techniques. In the realm of painting this is true of Michelangelo just as, in literature, it is true of Dante and Milton. All three confront us with an overwhelming awareness of Heaven, Earth, and Hell revealed in explicit images and dramatized in a tumult of events. It is true also that Shakespeare created whole societies and civilizations of men and women having such amplitude and luster, such imperious and conflicting passions, that he had to create also a new world to hold them.

No such gigantic stature can be claimed for a poet like Edna Millay. Her theme was too personal, too intimate to herself to fill out the dimensions of a supernatural realm of imagination. Indeed it might be said that her unique effort was to perform the miracle of creation in reverse. A universe already made pressed its weight on the sensibility, the aptitude for awareness, of one individual: "Infinity/Came down and settled over me. . . ."

The poet's need is to apprehend the "radiant identity" of life and to embrace it ardently. "World, world, I cannot get thee close enough." This reunion with nature—universal nature—is immediately important to one person, alone and aided only by his own integrity. The search is for the self; the struggle is to be reborn out of chaos to "a sense of glad awakening."

The journey in search of wholeness for the individual, an adventure which has obsessed the minds of the philosophers of the past and the psychiatrists of the present, cannot be left safely to further exploration by the computers of the future. It continues, therefore, to be of no trivial interest as it is presented in the poems of Edna St. Vincent Millay.

It should not be taken as an indication of a failure to grow that Edna Millay produced when she was only nineteen years old one of the most characteristic, most memorable, and most moving of her poems. The intuitions of artists do not reach them on any schedule of merely logical development. All the wisdom they ever attain may be at their command in the beginning. Later statements of it seem to serve chiefly to corroborate or to enrich, out of a diversity of experience that may be tragic without being fatal to faith, the items of the credo as it was first presented. In "Renascence" Edna Millay announced the theme to which four more decades of her life were to be spent in the most intense kind of concentration. "The

soul can split the sky in two,/And let the face of God shine through." This confrontation with the divine can be dared and endured because man is one with the divine.

Edna Millay presented the inner life of the spirit always as a conflict of powerful forces. The will to live and the will to die are elementally at war in "Renascence." Consciousness of the world's misery is so desperately immediate to the poet's imagination that

> For my omniscience paid I toll
> In infinite remorse of soul.
> All sin was of my sinning, all
> Atoning mine, and mine the gall
> Of all regret. . . .

There can be no escape from so formidable a burden of awareness but into the grave. But it is no passive rejection that the spirit experiences. The weight of infinity must be flung off with a gigantic effort.

> And as it went my tortured soul
> Burst forth and fled in such a gust
> That all about me swirled the dust.

The peace of death is achieved and the vulnerable spirit hears from above its hiding place the rain's "friendly sound." The impulse toward surrender *itself* has roused the counter impulse toward a participation more passionate than ever before in the values of human existence. In another convulsion of nature, dramatizing the imperious contradictions of the spirit, the grave is washed away.

> Ah! Up then from the ground sprang I
> And hailed the earth with such a cry
> As is not heard save from a man
> Who has been dead, and lives again.
> About the trees my arms I wound;
> Like one gone mad I hugged the ground. . . .

The meaning of this battle of the wills is clear.

The anguish of existence must be endured as the tribute owed to its beauty.

> The world stands out on either side
> No wider than the heart is wide;
> Above the earth is stretched the sky,—
> No higher than the soul is high.

This is the identity between man's nature and the nature of the universe which need only be recognized for the release of incalculable benefits. But an enormous struggle must be waged within the self to establish man's loyalty to the values of life.

An account of the running battle between life and death claimed first place among the poet's preoccupations through her writing career. The effectiveness of the report is heightened by an awareness, sometimes bitter and sometimes merely rueful, that now one side commands ascendancy over will and now the other. In a poem ironically called "Spring" the desperate reproach is offered: "Beauty is not enough." Death is everywhere; with furtive cunning, its forces invade life itself.

But the mood passes. The characteristic one reasserts itself in "The Poet and His Book." Now the plea is for life even after death, the immortality of an imperishable achievement, however small. The poet will live in his book if only the "stranger" can be persuaded to "turn the tattered pages."

Sometimes, as in "Moriturus," the ambivalent attitude begs for an unreasonable indulgence: to have "Two things in one;/ The peace of the grave,/ And the light of the sun . . ." But the fantastic notion of a reconciliation between life and death fades in a moment. Militant life asserts its claims more positively than ever before. Death is stripped of the majesty in which fear has slavishly dressed him. He is discovered to be nothing: "He is less/ Than Echo answering/ 'Nothingness!'" The will to live mounts through many crisp and angry stanzas.

The poet allows raillery to creep into her declaration of war. She speaks like a housewife who has quite enough of irrelevant harassments as she declares that she will hold death off by "bolting" her door "with a bolt and a cable:/ I shall block my door/ With a bureau and a table. . . ." But she means every savage and decisive word as death is finally warned that

> With his hand on my mouth
> He shall drag me forth,
> Shrieking to the south
> And clutching at the north.

It is indicative of a striking consistency of outlook even in the midst of the poet's conflicts that in this prophetic vision of what her doomed battle with death will be she reaffirms vigorously her sense of identity with the universe. The world is still no wider than the heart is wide. She shrieks for help to the south as if it were her close ally and clutches at the north, feeling it to be a possession that is being unjustly torn from her.

As she grew older the tone of her quarrel with death tended to become more subdued. In "Dirge without Music" the inevitability of the loss of the valued people of her life is grudgingly accepted. But the wasteful pattern of existence is nonetheless rebuked with a kind of womanly primness:

> Down, down, down into the darkness of the grave
> Gently they go, the beautiful, the tender, the kind;
> Quietly they go, the intelligent, the witty, the brave.
> I know. But I do not approve. And I am not resigned.

This understatement is more moving than a harangue by a bitter fatalist could be. Tucked neatly away into the reticence of the judgment is the suggestion that, as one who is closely identified with nature, the poet could have managed things better if her human insight had been allowed to prevail. Such variations of tone in her report on the duel of life against death lend the best and most original of her personal qualities to the development of an old, familiar theme. The parallel may be suggested that, just as a mother must have faith in her child lacking any evidence to justify it, so the believer in life must show a similar courageous unreasonableness. Edna Millay is perhaps at her best when she casts her vote of No Confidence in death.

During the 1930's and the 1940's history with its stubborn, mindless reiteration of the chants of war deposited its grievous weight on Edna Millay's imagination. Inevitably the theme of life against death found its most tragic variation as she seized bitterly on the drama of life becoming actually the ally of death. She endured the sufferings of the time not merely as any sensitive noncombatant must but rather as one who, having been conscious always of the crucial character of the conflict between creative and destructive forces, felt deeply involved in what might well prove to be a final defeat for humankind.

But in the poems of this period her protest against death is put forward no less vigorously than before simply because the ecstasy of rebirth has become far less easy to evoke. In "Apostrophe to Man (on reflecting that the world is ready to go to war again)" a formidable denunciation is hurled at the world's whole company of men and women: "Detestable race, continue to expunge yourself, die out./ Breed faster, crowd, encroach, sing hymns, build bombing airplanes. . . ." Indignation at the will to die bursts out not merely from the scattered pronouncements of such staccato verse; it is present also in the most elegantly polished of the sonnets, mixing pity with despair in equally bitter parts. The sequence to which she gives the over-all title "Epitaph for the Race of Man" presents her misgiving at its most bleak. A vision is summoned up of the planet about to grow cold after the final suicide of humankind. "Man and his engines be no longer here."

High on his naked rock the mountain sheep
Will stand alone against the final sky,
Drinking a wind of danger new and deep,
Staring on Vega with a piercing eye,
And gather up his slender hooves and leap
From crag to crag down Chaos, and so go by.

But the militant mind is not truly ready even now for any such tight-lipped acceptance. The belief in rebirth is too powerful to crumple under the worst of threats. New visions and new hopes break through. The poet sees man waking in terror in the night to find the almost but not quite final disaster hurtling down upon his house: "a pitchy lake of scalding stone." Suddenly her faith in his cunning and his resolution is roused again.

Where did he weep? Where did he sit him
    down
And sorrow, with his head between his knees?
Where said the Race of Man, "Here let me
    drown"?
"Here let me die of hunger"?—"let me freeze"?
By nightfall he has built another town:
This boiling pot, this clearing in the trees.

So, engulfed in global madness, the poet's belief in the will to live cannot be driven from an unyielding intelligence. She has indeed rejected the witty young woman's notion that "a bureau and a table" will be enough to bar the intrusion of defeatist sentiment. She might be addressing the early, overconfident self when she suggests that a maturity born of experience is needed to "broaden the sensitive/ Fastidious pale perception . . ." No emotion, however inevitable or however blameless, may assume control over the regenerative will. "I must not die of pity; I must live." Nor is it enough simply to stay alive; ecstasy must be reclaimed. The poet will "pour away despair/ And rinse the cup, eat happiness like bread."

Triumphantly something quite like the tone of "Renascence" declares itself anew.

Thou famished grave, I will not fill thee yet,
Roar though thou dost, I am too happy here;
Gnaw thine own sides, fast on; I have no fear
Of thy dark project, but my heart is set
On living—I have heroes to beget
Before I die. . . .

So many of Edna Millay's pages are devoted to critical moments of the love duel that it has been possible, even for reasonably well informed readers, to be aware only of her confidences about "what arms have lain/ Under my head till morning." To their loss they have ignored her equal preoccupation with other themes. Still it is true that some of her most searching observations about the human condition are concerned with the approach to ecstasy through the identification of man with woman. It would, however, be to deceive oneself to approach these poems as if they were exercises in eroticism. Despite the many sidelong references to the physical relationship, the enclosing interest is that of human love as a total experience of the psyche involving, on the positive side, intellectual communication and sympathy of taste and, on the negative side, the endless warfare of two egos that cannot effect a complete surrender into oneness.

The limp endorsement of correct and appropriate sentiments which has made up so much of love poetry, particularly that written by women, is conspicuous for its total absence from these ardent but anxious confrontations of man and woman. It is significant of Edna Millay's approach to the psychological crisis of love versus hate—and to the even more de-

structive tragicomedy of love slackening away into indifference by the influences of time, change, and disillusion—that she does not speak of these matters simply as a woman. Often in her highly dramatic representations of the love duel she assumes the man's role and she plays it with no nervous air of indulging in a masquerade. She is concerned with the mind as the retort in which all the chemical reactions of love take place and, because her own intelligence partook of both masculine and feminine characteristics, the poems convey the impression that the exactitude of science, in control of the impulses of intuition, has been brought to bear to reveal much that those changes involve in a man's temperament as well as in a woman's.

Again, as in her account of the conflict of the will to live and the will to die, the love duel is presented with high drama as one that is destined to go on and on indecisively because the adversaries are only too well matched in aggressiveness and submissiveness, in strength and weakness, in sympathy and treachery.

The ecstatic instant, captured with a delicate but firm precision in many of the love poems, found what is perhaps its best expression in Sonnet I of *Fatal Interview*. The sight of human love is set before us through the eyes of a god. Hermes, airborne by his winged sandals, skims over "a pearled and roseate plain beneath." Then, unintelligibly at first, he feels the intervention between himself and his goal of a force from earth. The immeasurable distance between divine sense and human sense obscures the meaning of the encounter, but at last the god becomes aware of a concentration of passion more intimate, more pure, than any a god has ever known. His response is one of rueful jealousy. He asks himself how it can be that man, the creature "built of salt and lime" whose "borrowed breath" must presently send him "labouring to a doom I may not feel," has found, nonetheless, an incomparable blessing to alleviate, even to justify, the pain of his journey to a "dusty end." Hermes feels "the proud eyes of bliss" turned upon him. He is almost tempted to reject his divine condition that he may identify himself with creatures so to be envied. "Up, up, my feathers!—ere I lay you by/ To journey barefoot with a mortal joy."

The reverential gaiety of this mood, which finds room for humor in the midst of the contemplation of bliss, characterizes much of Edna Millay's love poetry. Its popularity may be accounted for by the intoxicating quality that brings the immediacy of a highly personal emotion to the poetic statement. The merit that gives the work permanence is the fastidiousness of the style in which the spontaneity is captured.

In her younger days Edna Millay sometimes allowed her exuberant vitality to escape into verses the levity of which made her famous, perhaps to the injury of her reputation as a serious poet. There are, for example, the eminently quotable lines of "Thursday."

And if I loved you Wednesday,
　　Well, what is that to you?
I do not love you Thursday—
　　So much is true.

And why you come complaining
　　Is more than I can see.
I loved you Wednesday,—yes—but what
　　Is that to me?

These flourishes of audacity do not touch at all closely on the center of her understanding of the love duel. There she held a formidable awareness of the power of change which is not in the least like the vague consciousness of impermanence in which so many poetic spirits have fluttered wih languid futility. Swinburne "sighs" that "no love endures." The fact that

it was a badly tarnished stereotype of emotion when he uttered it has not dissuaded romantics from echoing it ever since. Edna Millay used the sharpest tools of her intelligence to hew out for herself a unique place among poets by undertaking to discover *why* no love endures. What she says is that the loophole in commitment offers the necessary escape route by which the self saves its integrity. There can be no such thing as total surrender except with degradation or with, what is worse, dishonesty. In love the giving must be generous and free, but there must be withholding, too, if the self is to remain whole. In Sonnet XLVII of *Fatal Interview* the point is made:

Well, I have lost you; and I lost you fairly
In my own way, and with my full consent.
If I had loved you less or played you slyly
I might have held you for a summer more,
But at the cost of words I value highly. . . .

It is understood in advance that the reward of this conscientiousness will be to know the full bitterness of the loss, for "Time does not bring relief; you all have lied/ Who told me Time would ease me of my pain."

The immediacy of experience is communicated in images that are piercingly personal. Very often the suggestions of the figurative language are so unexpected that they seem to spring out of an immediate passion which catches deliberately and desperately at punishing words. Love has been "stung to death by gnats." "My kisses now are sand against your mouth,/ Teeth in your palm and pennies on your eyes." Only out of the whirlwind of an unstudied grief could a voice speak with just this accent.

It is because she was bold enough to examine the problem of the psychological distance between man and woman—one that cannot be breached and should not be violated—that Edna Millay may be said to have made an original contribution to the literature of the love duel.

In the sonnet called "Bluebeard" she assumes the voice of a man speaking to an importunate woman.

This door you might not open, and you did;
So enter now, and see for what slight thing
You are betrayed. . . . Here is no treasure
    hid. . . .

Yet the private consciousness is valuable, even in its meagerness, precisely because it is private.

Look yet again:
An empty room, cobwebbed and comfortless.
Yet this alone out of my life I kept
Unto myself, lest any know me quite. . . .

To violate this sanctuary is to destroy love.

And you did so profane me when you crept
Unto the threshold of this room tonight
That I must never more behold your face.
This now is yours. I seek another place.

The tragedy of rejection has its counterpart in the tragedy of acceptance. The poem called "On the Wide Heath" in effect tells the Bluebeard story again with the temper of the actor presented exactly in reverse. Against a bleak background a man on foot makes his way toward home at nightfall. He knows what sort of scene awaits him. He will enter there "The kitchen of a loud shrew" to find besides his wife "a wordless poaching son and a daughter/ With a disdainful smile . . ." Then with the deftness and economy of means that she had learned in the theater the poet springs her appalling surprise. The man is willing to go

Home to the worn reproach, the disagreeing
    The shelter, the stale air; content to be
Pecked at, confined, encroached upon,—it be-
        ing
    Too lonely, to be free.

Again it is the ability to capture in colloquial language and in one brief thunderclap of drama the essence of a tragic psychological struggle that lends to Edna Millay's long discussion of the love duel its effects of variety and flexibility.

The tone of melancholy misgiving in the face of the emotional crisis is pervasive in these studies. But the warming, the nourishing, the half-maternal aspects of the experience of love are not neglected. In Sonnet LI of *Fatal Interview* Edna Millay echoes a sentiment to which Shakespeare gave a masculine accent. Her feminine version seems no less eloquent, no less moving.

If in the years to come you should recall
When faint at heart or fallen on hungry days,
Or full of griefs and little if at all
From them distracted by delights or praise;
When failing powers or good opinion lost
Have bowed your neck, should you recall to
    mind
How of all men I honoured you the most,
Holding you noblest among mortal-kind:
Might not my love—although the curving blade
From whose wide mowing none may hope to
    hide,
Me long ago below the frosts had laid—
Restore you somewhat to your former pride?
Indeed I think this memory, even then,
Must raise you high among the run of men.

It is characteristic of Edna Millay's temper —not merely its prevailing but its almost uninterrupted mood—that she enters upon the search for beauty as if this, too, were a struggle. In the poem called "Assault" she blurts out the half-welcoming, half-fearful exclamation: "I am waylaid by Beauty." There is no coyness in this air of alarm. To the acutely alerted sensibilities of eyes and ears beauty reveals many aspects and sounds in different voices. She hears it in the croaking of a frog quite as clearly as in the song of a skylark, and each declaration of its presence is something to be appraised with scrupulous attention. She speaks sometimes of "savage beauty." Even when the impact on her senses is not violent it is still an experience to be received warily—on guard. Beauty in the guise of April is challenged with the suggestion that it comes with crafty intent like a seducer. "You can no longer quiet me with the redness/ Of little leaves opening stickily. / I know what I know."

This is to say that the mind has its right to evaluate beauty. It should not yield in limp acceptance as if faced by something of divine origin and therefore, like a god of Greek mythology, not to be denied its will. What Edna Millay persuades a reader that she does indeed know is that beauty must be endured as well as enjoyed. To surrender to beauty without resistance would be to lose an exhilarating aspect of the experience. It must be participated in, but the terms of one's compact with beauty must be understood to be one-sided. "Beauty makes no pledges." In return for the awe that the observer feels in its presence nothing is promised other than awareness itself. Beauty manifests itself in the glow of a bird's wing and in the rotting limb of a tree; it exists in monumental forms and in minute ones. But in the ardent search for its benefits, great or small, the disciple must never forget that his devotion must be to an influence that continues serenely to be godlike, aloof, and impersonal. "Beauty never slumbers/All is in her name."

That she is not entirely consistent in developing her religion of beauty need not be found disturbing. She is no more given to shifts of interpretation than mystics must ever be. Beauty may be aloof and impersonal but it is also an element in the process of rebirth, the faith in which the poet takes her deepest comfort. It even becomes in certain poems the food on which she feeds. Her figures of speech suggest again and again that, as a woman, she felt an almost organic closeness to the working of gestation. A conscientious expectant mother, she will search for beauty even "where beauty never stood . . ./ Having a growing heart to feed."

Part of the nourishment that she receives from awareness of beauty is provided by what is for her the immediate actuality of sensuous experience. Better than any imagining is the presence in the eye of a satisfying scene or the reverberation in the ear of lovely sound.

Not, to me, less lavish—though my dreams
    have been splendid—
Than dreams, have been the hours of the actual
    day:
Never, awakening, did I awake to say:
"Nothing could be like that," when a dream
    was ended.
Colours, in dream; ecstasy, in dream extended
Beyond the edge of sleep—these, in their way,
Approach, come even closer, yet pause, yet
    stay. . . .

The experiences of the actual, which she goes on to enumerate as containers of ecstasy, include those offered by "Music, and painting, poetry, love, and grief." Then at the close of the sonnet her pantheistic faith in the oneness and the continuity of nature reasserts itself. Real and reassuring to her are the harmony of opposites, the unity that may be resolved out of contradictions, and the inevitability of rebirth following decay. Beauty can be endured because the poet has been able to convince herself in the end that "the budding and the falling leaf" are "one, and wonderful,—not to be torn/Apart."

In "Moriturus" the young artist warned the world with humorous defiance that she would "take it hard" when death threatened her. It was precisely because she continued throughout her life to take it hard, when she was confronted by confusing manifestations of beauty, that she was able to communicate so great a sense of vitality to each phase of the adventure. She was always an actor in the drama: a militant defender of beauty against its defilers. And she was resolutely faithful to the integrity of her own perceptions. She never attempts to encompass more of a sense of the wonder of the natural world than her own eyes can see. What moves her is the recollection of a familiar scene, fixed in memory by some small detail of local color. Significance is imparted to the image by a subtle infusion of the poet's emotion as she remembers this glimpse of the seacoast or that corner of a city street: "Eager vines/ Go up the rocks and wait"; "These wet rocks where the tide has been,/ Barnacled white and weeded brown"; "Yellow leaves along the gutters/ In the blue and bitter fall." Armed with awareness, the one who is "waylaid" by beauty may find exultation in the simplest of experiences. Edna Millay did indeed seem to write all her poems to give permanence to a moment of ecstasy.

It was not merely in encounters with nature that she felt herself to be encompassed by beauty and deeply involved in a struggle to receive its blessing. She wrestled with the angel in the realm of art and also in that of pure intellectual effort. Two of the most memorable of her sonnets dramatize these vigorous exercises of the spirit.

The words "On Hearing a Symphony of Beethoven" may suggest that the poet has, for once, been reduced to a mood of passive receptivity, willing to receive beauty ready-made and placative. But that was never Edna Millay's temper. Even as listener she was participant in a struggle to earn the benefit of an experience. In this poem she seizes upon music as another instrument for finding out the truth that is implicit in beauty. Not too much—though something—may be made of the fact that Edna Millay, her mother's daughter, knew many musical scores in as much detail as does even the most conscientious of orchestra conductors. But it was not from the circumstances of being well instructed that her responsiveness sprang. In her seat at a concert she was able to become a collaborator in the creative undertaking because creativity was ever the spontaneous impules of mind and senses working together.

So, in the sonnet, Beethoven's achievement becomes hers by right of possession. She does not hold that right with vague gratification. She grapples with it, prepared to do battle for it. "Sweet sounds, oh, beautiful music do not cease!/ Reject me not into the world again." The meaning of what she hears is something broader and deeper than any discipline in the technique of musical composition could make intelligible. Here again is the message of rebirth, another statement of the inextinguishable virtue of vigorous creative effort. The truth implicit in this beauty is vital and vivifying. "Mankind made plausible, his purpose plain." The poet's supercharged awareness drives several ways at once toward comprehension. A pantheistic vision of the oneness of all life—suffering, decaying yet surviving—suggests the line "The tranquil blossom on the tortured stem." Tranquillity and torture: they, also, are "one, and wonderful,—not to be torn/ Apart." Not in nature, not in the music of Beethoven, not in the responsive intelligence of Edna St. Vincent Millay.

It is of inescapable significance that in a poem which on the surface seems merely to explore the most pallid of academic interests, "music appreciation," there should be so many words which describe a militant stance, an attitude of defensive wariness in the face of an adversary: "Reject me not," "scatter [my towers]," "my rampart." If the sonnet seems to have an untarnished originality of temper, after many years of familiarity with it, that must be because Edna Millay dares to suggest that the enemies of "man's purpose" are not merely the formidable ones who scatter destruction in the form of bombs. There are other enemies whom she identifies as "The spiteful and the stingy and the rude," who devastate the landscape of the spirit with showers of tawdry and mediocre values. In defense of the purposes of life it is necessary to be ready to do battle on all fronts against not merely the great incalculable forces of "Doom," which must inevitably espy our towers in the end, but also against those who undermine our ramparts with the erosive agents of meanness and vulgarity.

The other sonnet describes an even more original adventure in search of beauty. A surprising and highly specialized sort of sensibility is involved in this exercise. Edna Millay was in fact a highly skilled amateur in the science of mathematics and she might well have just put away some self assigned task in the field when she wrote "Euclid Alone Has Looked on Beauty Bare." But it is not really a celebration of the aesthetics of geometry that is contained in this poem. The enclosing mood is that of reverence for the intelligence of man. This creature, whom she has often described as deserving only pity for his weakness or scorn for his perversity, is capable, in moments when his essential genius has just been born anew, of seizing upon knowledge in a dazzling flash of lucidity. With little to guide him but his self-instructed technique of divination he dares to explore the very depths of abstract thought: "O blinding hour, O holy, terrible day,/ When first the shaft into his vision shone/ Of light anatomized!" The unique drama of this foray into a realm of learning—one that not merely was uncharted but had not previously even been

imagined to exist—needs no underscoring. In her deft summation of the significance of the experience, as its effects ray out and touch all men everywhere, Edna Millay contents herself with one personal comment:

> Euclid alone
> Has looked on Beauty bare. Fortunate they
> Who, though once only and then but far away,
> Have heard her massive sandal set on stone.

Sober gratitude for the privilege of perceiving beauty has, in this sonnet, its most characteristic expression. But there is another implication to be read between the lines touching on the central theme of the poet's long debate with man. What is tragic for her is the irony that a being with the audacity to claim for himself such awesome attributes of mind should often allow his nature to be degraded by negative attributes of pettiness. She is appalled to see his grandeur dissipated—as she might have said, using words that she applied to the loss of love—"in little ways."

From first to last, through every phase of her development, Edna Millay continued to be intensely herself and no other. Whether her theme was death, love, beauty, or the refreshing impulse of the will to live she spoke always with an accent that was unique to her. Of language she made a homespun garment to clothe her passions and her faith.

That she was able to create effects of striking originality is discovered to be only the more remarkable when a characteristic poem is examined closely and its thought is found to wear "something old" and "something borrowed" from the left-over wardrobe of tradition. Edna Millay was a product as much of the nineteenth century as of the twentieth. The influence of tradition moved her a little backward in time. A too great reverence for her early instruction—not only at her mother's knee but also at Keats's—probably accounts for all the "O's" and "Ah's," the "would I were's," the "hast's," the "art's," the "wert's," the "Tis's." It must account also for the inversions of normal word order which sometimes impede the plunge of her hardihood in thought.

Even in more important matters of vocabulary, imagery, and symbolism her impulse toward expression was governed by convention. Despite her interest in science she felt its discipline to be alien to her always personal style of utterance. She did not find in its language a new source of imaginative power such as Auden has exploited. Despite her obsession in the late years with the crisis of war, such a reference as one to "Man and his engines" reveals an uninvolved attitude toward the special concerns of the machine age. The hoe, as symbol, was an instrument of which she was intensely hand-conscious but the airplane's power seemed not to have for her the figurative significance that it had for Randall Jarrell. Despite the fact that she grew up in the shadow of Freud and must have participated in endless talk about the ego and the id in the loft-studios of Greenwich Village, she was not prompted to follow the leads of psychology and psychiatry down into the caves of memory as were Jeffers and Warren. The familiar image, drawn from the treasury of metaphor upon which Shakespeare also depended for imaginative resource, seems never to have dismayed her. She was not inhibited by fear of intelligibility; she was not tempted to prod the imagination with tortured similes. For her, death still swung his scythe and the poems in which he does so with the old familiar ruthlessness betray no nervous apprehension that the instrument may have become rusty or blunted with the use of ages.

Because she absorbed tradition deeply into herself she seems able to revitalize its language with the warmth of her own temper. Her words become fertile from the nourishment which, as woman, she communicated to them as if by an umbilical link.

Simplicity, spontaneity, the seeming absence of calculation combine to produce her best effects. An apron that has fallen from a clothesline and lain all winter in a snowdrift until it has become stiff with frost may still be restored, soft and pliable, to appropriate purposes of housewifely solicitude and care. This, as a symbol of restoration, is one that could have come into the mind only of an observer who trusted her own intuitions. Associations of idea between enormous plight and commonplace remedy never fail to stimulate this alert and resourceful imagination. Edna Millay blocks death's way "with a bureau and a table," convinced of her own rightness in seizing upon this urgent, though rudimentary, tactic of defense. If the overtone of humor is lost upon the literal ear that matters comparatively little. What she conveys with a surprising freshness is the thought that, in the enormously important struggle to survive, any immediate and awful crisis must be faced with the means ready to hand.

Often she speaks in the voice of a woman engaged in a familiar chore of the common round. But the task becomes symbolic of the urgent need to keep the forces of life alive in threatening circumstances. A housewife lighting a fire on her hearth must ". . . thrust her breath against the stubborn coal,/ Bringing to bear upon its hilt the whole/ Of her still body."

Sometimes the accent of a man is heard as he considers the ultimate defeat of all his hopes, as tiller of the land, under the encompassing blight of war. The blessing of rebirth has been canceled and he sees the vast emergency shrunk, in all the irreversible trend of devastation, to the dimensions of one of his own fields. Once more the graphic representation is small but complete.

> No toil
> Of rake or hoe, no lime, no phosphate, no
>   rotation of crops, no irrigation of the land,
> Will coax the limp and flattened grain to stand
> On that bad day. . . .

More often than with either definitely declared voice she speaks as a detached observer of natural sights and sounds. These souvenirs of experience are shared with a reader in language that seems entirely casual; it has been borrowed for the moment from more studied performers in the realm of poetry simply to convey a passing impression. A stream separated into two parts by stones attracts a wanderer's attention. An impression of "The soft, antiphonal speech of the doubled brook" must be recorded simply because it is something charming to remember. More typical of the poet's method is the device of catching a symbolic significance, some warning of the threat against survival, in an image that seems to be, all at once, spontaneous, startling, and inescapably true.

"The Buck in the Snow" brings together the assets of surprising imagery, symbolic overtone, and touching comment. The observer has watched the deer and his mate in the orchard on a winter day.

> I saw them suddenly go,
> Tails up, with long leaps lovely and slow,
> Over the stone-wall into the wood of hemlocks
>   bowed with snow.

Later she comes on the buck, shot and left to die. "Now lies he here, his wild blood scalding the snow." Life and death, together; heat and cold, inseparable. And the observer imagines the plight of the mate.

> a mile away by now, it may be,
> Under the heavy hemlocks that as the moments
>   pass
> Shift their loads a little, letting fall a feather of
>   snow—
> Life, looking out attentive through the eyes of
>   the doe.

In no poem is there a better example of Edna Millay's gift for blending the archaic with the colloquial than in the "Ballad of the Harp-Weaver." The literary form is borrowed from the past but the purpose of the poem is to protest against the social evils of Edna St. Vincent Millay's own time. A kind of utilitarian fantasy such as only she could have imagined suggests to a poverty-stricken woman that she can weave from the strings of her harp "the clothes of a king's son." The treatment of this delicate material is successful because the poet uses only the commonplaces of everyday speech to evoke a mood of touching benevolence. In the Monday morning language, associated with the simplest kind of domesticity, she persuades even the least pliable reader to be glad that fragile whim has transcended reality. For example, the mother addresses her child:

> "Little skinny shoulder-blades
>   Sticking through your clothes!
> And where you'll get a jacket from
>   God above knows.

> "It's lucky for me, lad,
>   Your daddy's in the ground
> And can't see the way I let
>   His son go around!"

It is not unlikely that in this experiment— the exact like of which she never again attempted—Edna Millay paid tribute to her mother. To a sensitive and loyal daughter it must have seemed to be almost literally a fact that Cora Millay wove out of music a warm security for her children. What is of chief interest, however, is that in this instance Edna Millay herself wove out of a combination of literary tradition, family tradition, sentiment, and memory an experience as simple and universal as any to be found in the extensive literature of balladry.

An important element in the highly personal tone of all her poetry is the wit that flashes through not merely the exercises in light vein but her most serious reflections as well. The epigram was for her an entirely spontaneous form of expression and its unexpected sparkle of insight often illuminates even the darkest moments of the sonnets.

In the early poems wit is used often with deliberately audacious intent. It mocks at prudery, at self-deception, at all the false sentiments of the *unco guid.* Typical is the much-quoted poem about the "little Sorrow/ Born of a little Sin." The nymph of Greenwich Village trying to be penitent finds "a room all damp with gloom/ And shut us all within." The tone of raillery foretells the end. The "little Sorrow would not weep," the "little Sin would go to sleep."

> So up I got in anger,
>   And took a book I had,
> And put a ribbon on my hair
>   To please a passing lad,
> And, "One thing there's no getting by—
> I've been a wicked girl," said I;
> "But if I can't be sorry, why,
>   I might as well be glad!"

From the standpoint of a sympathetic reader another thing "there's no getting by" is that this poem has serious flaws. The second line of the last stanza is clumsily thrust in to occupy space and to provide a rhyme. The third and fourth owe more to the tradition of Housman (and his small standing army of "light-foot lads") than Edna Millay who wished only to cultivate her own voice should have been willing to pay. But the epigram of the final two lines justifies the effort. Seldom has virtue, in lugubrious false face, been dismissed from the scene with such enviable and persuasive high spirit.

Edna Millay's wit was never petty. She was generous toward all her adversaries except mediocrity, war, and death. And in fashioning an epigram she revealed her most fastidious respect both for truth and for elegance. In the later poems her wit is so unobtrusive, so modest, that it might be missed entirely by a reader hoping to find a showy attribute identified by a capital letter. But it is always subtly present, embedded in a theme, as is the wit of Henry James. The tight-packed phrase, the unexpected revelation of how opposites of impulse may be found to blend, the sudden illumination of an ambiguity—these are the veins of wisdom through which wit runs in the sonnets. In the one numbered XL in *Collected Sonnets* the subject is once more the love duel. Here a struggle is enacted between heart and mind, between imprecisely defined loyalties and the subtly destructive impulses of treachery. Fiction and drama have often dealt at length with such crises; Edna Millay compresses the conflict between loving-obsessively and still-not-loving-enough into fourteen lines. The epigrammatic couplet at the end reveals the subtle quality of the dilemma. A woman reminds herself that she will continue to consume her life in preoccupation with one face "Till all the world, and I, and surely you,/ Will know I love you, whether or not I do."

Edna Millay's wit is not always bittersweet. It can be galling and acidulous. In the sonnet "To Jesus on His Birthday," the poet rejects hypocrisy once more, this time with uncompromising severity. She is appalled, as she sits at a Christmas service, by the magisterial cynicism with which a "humble gospel" is betrayed to please "the proud." Her anger is too great to be disciplined and she snatches hastily for words into the vocabulary of scorn. "Up goes the man of God before the crowd;/ With voice of honey and with eyes of steel . . ." But the shopworn metaphors—voice of honey, eyes of steel—betray only a momentary loss of control. Speaking once more in her own unaffected voice the poet utters an epigram of devastating effectiveness: "The stone the angel rolled away with tears/ Is back upon your mouth these thousand years."

A close examination of the work of any artist is certain to reveal flaws. The very urgency of the desire to communicate must tempt any poet sometimes to override obstacles recklessly. With Edna Millay the individual line seldom limps though it may now and again betray an obvious determination to be vigorous. There is little sense of strain in the use of rhyme and, even in the early poems when her effects threaten to become self-conscious, she avoids the temptation to indulge in the verbal acrobatics of clever versifiers as even Byron does. What troubles her appraisers most of all is the willingness to snatch up old trophies of metaphor and set them up among her own inspirations as if she were unaware of the difference of freshness between them.

But in the end vigor and spontaneity prevail in technique as they do in passion. The singing quality of the lyrics, of the free forms of verse and of the formal sonnets, too, is consistently clear and true. A reader gratefully accepts—as she herself does—the intoxicating stimulation of the air she breathes.

Throughout her life Edna Millay's chief concern was to canalize creative energy into the production of poems that bespoke her innermost awarenesses. In her last years this concentration became so intense that almost all other interests were severely excluded. Yet in earlier phases she was responsive to challenges of many kinds. The world which she felt to be "No wider than the heart is wide" pressed in upon her and made various demands of that heart. Never the sort of artist whose blood becomes frozen in the veins at the touch of an outside influence, she showed herself to be flexible, adaptable, and—sometimes to her disadvantage—willing to take on the coloration of political, social, and moral crises of immediate moments.

She wrote prose, as she wrote poetry, with an at once witty and intensely sober regard for her own values. The personal letters glow— sometimes they seem feverishly to glitter—with the élan that sustained her, however precariously, through the crucial moments of her experience. Her preface to the volume of Baudelaire translations reveals a critical intelligence of distinction. Only the adroit satiric sketches written under the pseudonym Nancy Boyd depart from her preoccupation with poetry. These exercises, too, display a kind of coloratura virtuosity. They draw freely on her gift of wit and have importance as lucid in direct reflections of her attitudes: her unwavering honesty, her distate for pretense, sentimentality, and concessiveness.

More sympathetic to her essential interests were her experiments in the theater prompted, at first, by loyalty to the innovative purposes of the Provincetown Players. These and later productions for other sponsors all took the form of poetry. As actress *manquée*, Edna Millay understood the various involvements of the drama and faced the most difficult problems that it has to offer with characteristic conscientiousness and flexibility.

Aria da Capo is her most successful expression in dramatic form. This statement of her indignation at man's will to die is stripped down to the essentials of parable; its power is that of a surprise attack on the sensibilities. Using the figures of the traditional theater—Pierrot, Columbine, and a group of shepherds—she puts into the mouths of these unalarming folk colloquial utterances which reveal the tragedy of her conviction that war—always and everywhere—flares ironically out of a blend of lethargy and meanness.

Two young men tending their flocks relieve their boredom by playing at the game of building a wall between their fields. It is woven out of colored crepe paper and becomes a symbol as solidly effective for theatrical purposes as the material and the human motive involved are flimsy. Immediately the existence of a divisive influence creates hostility. In a succession of minute episodes jealousy develops out of whim and baseness out of jealousy until, in the end, the two contrive to kill each other. In the rehearsal for a play which encloses the parable, Pierrot and Columbine represent the society which, with slack disregard for human good, frivolously ignores the disaster. The man bespeaks the mind turned cynical by awareness of evil; the girl, mere mindlessness. Pierrot says: ". . . You see, I am always wanting/A little more than what I have—or else/A little less. . . ." In the simple complexity of the treatment these themes are allowed to declare their momentous significance. The drama is directly on target and its very brevity increases the effectiveness of impact.

A late experiment with verse drama, *Conversation at Midnight*, reached the stage almost a quarter of a century after it was published and more than a decade after the poet's death. In effect the author of "The Poet and His Book" echoed the early plea "Do not let me die." The tenacious intelligence showed its familiar variability and vitality in a New York production which found faithful adherents. Another performance by a Los Angeles group gave the work not merely a *succès d'estime* but an extended run.

Yet *Conversation at Midnight* remains pseudo-drama, lacking a concentrated drive toward effective vicarious experience. Edna Millay herself considered it to be "an interesting book" but "not really a play." The original manuscript, lost in a fire, had to be reproduced out of memory after the first creative urgency had lost its force. The result is, as she wrote, "jerky and patchy," an often awkward parade of attitudes forced into the form of stage dialogue but lacking the genuine fervor of conflict.

The faults of the work are inherent in the original concept. This requires a group of men, met for a session of late-night drinking and ratiocination, to use the occasion for a kind of war game in which they fire rounds of ammunition over each other's heads, hitting only distant, theoretical targets. Each guest represents a point of view, aesthetic, social, or moral; each in turn has his say, in a piece of stylized elocution, about capitalism, Communism, commercialism, Nazism, and, of course, love in a world that is out of sorts with spontaneity. All is spoken in earnest; much of the talk is witty and stimulating; some of it inevitably seems trivial in its cloudy references to situations in the lives of the characters which there has been neither time nor occasion really to evoke. Nothing resembling dramatic tension can rise out of these arguments which never intermingle, never affect each other, never in the end manage to clarify idea.

A different kind of problem is presented by *The King's Henchman*. Commissioned by the Metropolitan Opera Association of New York to provide a libretto for a score by Deems Taylor, Edna Millay worked with her usual intensity of conscientiousness to serve the tradition of music to which she was devoted. Her narrative, drawn from sources of legend similar to those which have prompted the many retellings of the Tristram and Iseult story, found dedicated admirers among those who heard the dozen and more performances of the opera given at the Metropolitan itself or the performances of the traveling company which presented it to a wide American audience. The austere dignity of *The King's Henchman*, it must be observed, rebukes for their banal and vulgar triviality the passions of many of the most conspicuous figures of operatic tradition, including those of *Madama Butterfly, La Traviata,* and *The Girl of the Golden West.* The experiment added a significant page to the history of opera in America.

And yet the technique of music drama remained foreign to Edna Millay's direct, candid, personal style of communication. The conventions of the medium dimmed with artificial grandeur the flashes of intuition which illuminate her more characteristic considerations of the love duel. She herself made uncompromisingly severe judgment upon the work. In a letter to her publisher, reconsidering her work in the theater, she tells of trying to rework a spoken drama out of *The King's Henchman.* But the result, she wrote, was "hopelessly contaminated. It smells of libretto." This she thought a pity because, as she went on to say, "some of my very best poetry is to be found in *The King's Henchman,*—to be found, that is, by a reader tough enough to struggle through acres of ostentatious and pedantic drivel in order to get to it."

Under a blast of criticism so withering an impersonal appraiser of the work rights himself in defensive attitude. There are lines in the libretto which, heard only once, remain in the mind forever as final definitions of certain experiences of love and grief. Some of these are sung by the henchman, Æthelwold. He is the

eternal "man's man" who has occupied himself with battles in defense of his king's interest and never found time for love. Then, in Ælfrida he finds the inescapable woman. Though she is intended for the king as his bride her presence at his side brings Æthelwold himself to an extremity of need. He cries out:

Ah, thy sweet look,
Thine arrowy, sweet, sweet look!
'Tis sunk to the feather in my heart.

At the end of the opera he kills himself in desperate shame over his treachery. King Eadgar sings the obituary of the hero and his words bring something quite startlingly new to a theme as old as written literature: the intrinsic value of the human spirit at its best.

Not all of us here,
Nor all of England weeping,
Should weep his worth,
That was so young and blithe and bold,
Whom the thorn of a rose hath slain.

Wherefore let us hoard our tears for
a little sorrow,
And weep not Æthelwold at all.

The plays, made to order under special circumstances, constitute only part of the burden that Edna Millay put dutifully upon her gift. There were crises of social life which gave gross affront to the most fundamental of her convictions and she could not withhold her protests. These took poetic form but—as she later knew to her chagrin—she was able at such times only to rear up the framework of a poem, gaunt and horrifying. To the lines with which she clothed the structure she could communicate her impotent rage but not the essence of compassion which she wished to memorialize.

There was, for example, her involvement in

the Sacco and Vanzetti case. This *cause célèbre* enlisted the minds and the passions of many liberals who were convinced that a cruel miscarriage of justice threatened traditional liberties. Two political rebels, accused of armed robbery and murder, were tried and retried in the courts of Massachusetts but always, as their defenders insisted, under the shadow of hatred for their theoretical beliefs. Not men but their ideology was actually on trial and— again in the opinion of the protestants— revenge was the unmasked motive in which American society, through some of its officers, was permitting itself to indulge. Edna Millay was a participant in mass meetings held to call public attention to the crisis. She was eloquent also in a personal interview with the governor of Massachusetts and in a letter urging him "to exert the clemency which your high office affords."

When Sacco and Vanzetti were finally ordered to be executed, Edna Millay wrote the poem "Justice Denied in Massachusetts," a desperate and bitter threnody.

Let us abandon then our gardens and go home
And sit in the sitting-room.
Shall the larkspur blossom or the corn grow
    under this cloud?
Sour to the fruitful seed
Is the cold earth under this cloud,
Fostering quack and weed, we have marched
    upon but cannot conquer;
We have bent the blades of our hoes against
    the stalks of them.

The unwilling, half-stifled protest that a reader makes in his turn against these utterances springs from the impression that a just and honest sentiment is being overdramatized. Is the abject surrender to despair really congenial to the poet's spirit or does this lamentation have to be brought under the charge of being tainted by hysteria? The conviction is clearly genuine but the excess of passion with which it is expressed still seems dubious. The literary crisis is not ameliorated when the poet yields her mind to the most cliché of imaginings: "We shall die in darkness, and be buried in the rain."

It is right for a poet to be a participant in the affairs of everyday living. With her special talent for doing precisely this, Edna Millay could not withhold her word. The respect must be paid her of considering anything she wrote as a work of art. Viewed in that light it becomes evident that poems written for occasions come forth misshapen at their birth by the influence of propaganda. In work that was truly her own even her bitterest protests against the will to destroy were informed by a still abiding faith; such poems reveal her militant spirit at its most staunch. The weakness of "Justice Denied in Massachusetts" must be attributed to the fact that it was not nourished by an inner will but fed on the inadequate substitute of propaganda.

The most conspicuous of the poems that Edna Millay regretted having written is *The Murder of Lidice*. The occasion that prompted it was one of such monstrous horror that any excess of passion in response to its tragedy must be condoned in advance. The leveling of a Czechoslovakian town and the mass martyrdom of all its men, women, and children— Hitler's revenge for the killing of one of his most sinister lieutenants—offers a theme for lamentation too big to be encompassed in words. Edna Millay might have reminded herself that it is well to save one's tears for a little sorrow. Lidice could, indeed, not be wept at all.

Judgment against its quality as literature may be left to her. As she once wrote: "It has some good lines, but not many, and not very good. This piece should be allowed to die along with the war which provoked it."

It must be added that the occasions which,

as she would have said, pressed in on her did, in the end, evoke true poetic expression. The theme of war recurs again and again in the later poems. The sonnets are full of references to its shadow on the earth. Each of these, matured by contemplation and refined by discipline, is moving; each informs the mood with the pathos of remembering all the opportunities that, in his heedlessness and haste, the "shining animal, man," has managed to throw away. She has only to speak again in her own voice to have all of her eloquence and her freedom from pretense restored. In the last of the sonnets the questions so long debated between mind and heart are resolved at last into a compassionate grief which can be endured even if heart and mind—and Edna Millay, too—still do "not approve," still are "not resigned."

The longest distraction from her personal preoccupations which Edna Millay was led into came from the temptation to experiment with translation. All her life she read Latin poetry for nourishment to mind and to technical facility; for her own pleasure she frequently translated poems from French and Spanish into English. A protracted period of effort in this field began when George Dillon suggested that she examine, in the form of a preface to a proposed volume, his translations of Baudelaire's *Les Fleurs du Mal*. In preparing to do so she was trapped inadvertently, as she has reported, into translating first a single line of one poem, then the whole poem, and finally many more. In the end George Dillon received her gratefully as fellow translator and, in their book, the initials of each identifies the maker of the contribution.

As translator Edna Millay was conscientious and sympathetic. She felt the much-misrepresented spirit of Baudelaire to have been "tortured and idealistic." His impulse was "to conquer ugliness by making beauty of it." She wished neither to purify him of what have been regarded as his perversities nor to tamper with his technique in the use of verse forms. She hoped to "scratch the iron palate of the modern reader" and gave him a stout, stimulating taste of the true Baudelaire. What must be made clear is that the mind of the poet was given its special turn by an ironic distaste for hypocrisy. What he defiantly calls his "flowers of evil" are, in truth, nothing so obviously poisonous and malign. They are really—as Edna Millay says in her preface, unable to resist the temptation to turn criticism into poetry—"flowers of doubt . . . flowers of grief . . . flowers forced on the sterile bough of the mind's unblossomy decay."

She was determined to clothe Baudelaire's verse forms in English leaving the original anatomy intact. Accordingly she edged her way patiently toward "the unbridgeable gulf between two minds" and at last found a rapport. She studied the psychological differences between two cultures in their predilection for one meter over another. She acquainted herself with disparities between two languages in resources of vocabulary. She took account of unlikenesses of emphasis resulting from such matters as the greater intensity of vowels in French. Her treatments of the poems of Baudelaire reproduce his forms as nearly as is possible. But they achieve much more than that. One feels that ideas and passion, conveyed by Edna Millay, could have originated in no other intelligence than that of Baudelaire.

Though her approach was as respectful—totally respectful—as only that of a fellow artist can be, she found herself renewed, as poet, by association with a compatible spirit. (She, too, was tortured and idealistic.) Inevitably she brought something of her own into these re-creations. Baudelaire's garden of the flowers of evil blooms under a foreign sky; it regains life in a new soil. The climate of Edna Millay's intelligence tends to heighten the color of images and to develop in them greater detail of design. What is formal in Baudelaire's language—stylized and formulary—is set aside sometimes in favor of effects more casual and —in English, certainly—more evocative of receivable emotion. In the poem called "Les Sept Vieillards" a literal translation of one line would be "These seven hideous monsters had the air of being eternal." Edna Millay renders it, putting the reference to monsters into an earlier line: "Somehow I knew they were eternal,—I could tell."

In her preface to the book of poems, presented in both French and English, Edna Millay speaks of her treatments as "adaptations" rather than as translations. They may be included in the small body of literature which, in effect, makes new land to fill in the unbridgeable between two minds. This is what Robert Lowell has done brilliantly in what he prefers to call his "imitations" of the poems of many other poets. Without doing violence to original intent—even when literal translation seems to be impossible—these two artists of adaptation manage to absorb the influence of one man's spirit, extend that influence across time, and draw it into sympathetic association with the values of an essentially different culture.

Edna St. Vincent Millay has been praised extravagantly as the greatest woman poet since Sappho. She has also been dismissed with lofty forbearance as a renegade from the contemporary movement in poetry and sometimes been treated almost as a traitor because she never broke defiantly with the past. But both eulogy and denigration seem to hang upon her figure like whimsical investitures. Neither costume suits the occasion when her enduring presence rises up before us to bespeak a mind that has not lost its vigor. Her talent shrugs off these

irrelevances—still staunch, still self-reliant, and still self-fulfilled. What we hear is a voice urging upon us the will to survive, uttering its sentiments with the grace and gravity of an intense and highly personal awareness. The fervor has not been dissipated from her words nor has the lucidity faded from her patterning of them into idea and conviction. In its most ardent moments the performance shows the same familiar spontaneity, disciplined into elegance without loss of power. It should be enough to call this talent unique among those that have appeared in our time. Rejecting comparison and eluding classification, an artist who has spoken so clearly and so persuasively seems tacitly to remind us that there is really no acute need to try to grade achievement according to an established formula or to consider austerely, precisely, what place may be accorded to her in the hierarchy of genius.

But acceptance of this gift as a natural phenomenon need not preclude the effort to discover its significance as a manifestation of the creative impulse in America. That she was peculiarly a product of our native way of life critics and the general public alike recognized when she first appeared. In the nymph of Greenwich Village phase she appeared to be the very embodiment of a characteristic and widespread spirit, roused by the circumstances of the time. As she grew older her temper was affected by other circumstances just as the temper of the country and the century was affected by new crises and new obligations. The tragic quality of the human experience became, for Edna St. Vincent Millay, ever more and more evident. It should not be suggested that the miseries of war, of depression, and again of war chastened her, mellowed her, or performed any of the improving operations which disaster is often said to perform on the docile. Her fundamental outlook did not change; she would seem to have been born with her special insights clear before her eyes. But her temperament was enriched and her intelligence was spurred to an ever more alert display of will by the pressure of many threats. Without any loss of wit, the early frivolity dropped away leaving her nature fully revealed as champion, even at a moment when calamities multiplied, of faith in "the shining animal's" ability to be reborn.

So, in the end, she was more surely the embodiment of the American outlook than she had been in the beginning. Indeed she enclosed the ethos of these United States in the twentieth century within the variety of her temperament. Even the contradictions and unresolved conflicts that tormented her were the same ones that have confused our culture. The granite of New England was in her and so was the flexibility of bohemia. She was American in her recklessness and in her reserves; in her mixture of audacity and decorous formality; in her devotion to learning and in her determination to put it to creative use; in her impulse toward rebellion, corrected and controlled by her respect for tradition; in her will to carry the battle to the enemy even when she knew the adversary to be the invincible one, death. The blend in her intelligence of traits derived from many sources of American vitality conveys the striking impression that she contained within herself important aspects of our native genius, alerted to a fine intensity of insight.

It is this absorbing—and, surely, durable—interest that claims for her a permanent place in the history of American poetry. She belongs to an impressive company of artists who came to maturity and found their voices during the second quarter of this century. Many of these have undertaken to explore the darkest caves of the secret mind of man and they have developed new poetic forms in which to record their experiences. Among them the figure of Edna St. Vincent Millay is conspicuous because she stands alone and in a blaze of light.

It is impossible not to understand what she has to say, impossible not to be moved by the simple, direct, eloquent statements of her convictions. The world, which she had held no closer at the beginning of her life than she did at the end, gave her as much of pain as it did pleasure. Love, beauty, and life itself had all to be endured as well as enjoyed. But the human experience had meaning for her. The round of the seasons still kept to its pledge of rebirth and renewal. From that faith she drew the strength to impart dignity and beauty—as she said of Baudelaire's achievement—to even the most cruel phases of the adventure of our time.

Selected Bibliography

WORKS OF EDNA ST. VINCENT MILLAY

POETRY

Renascence and Other Poems. New York: Harper, 1917.

A Few Figs from Thistles. New York: Harper, 1920.

Second April. New York: Harper, 1921.

The Harp-Weaver and Other Poems. New York: Harper, 1923.

The Buck in the Snow. New York: Harper, 1928.

Poems Selected for Young People. New York: Harper, 1929.

Fatal Interview. New York: Harper, 1931.

Wine from These Grapes. New York: Harper, 1934.

Huntsman, What Quarry? New York: Harper, 1939.

Make Bright the Arrows. New York: Harper, 1940.

Invocation to the Muses. New York: Harper, 1941.

Collected Sonnets. New York: Harper, 1941.

Collected Lyrics. New York: Harper, 1943.

Poem and Prayer for an Invading Army. New York: Harper, 1944.
Mine the Harvest. New York: Harper, 1954.
Collected Poems. New York: Harper, 1956.

PLAYS

Aria da Capo. New York: Harper, 1920.
The Lamp and the Bell. New York: Harper, 1921.
Two Slatterns and a King. New York: Harper, 1921.
The King's Henchman. New York: Harper, 1927.
The Princess Marries the Page. New York: Harper, 1932.
Conversation at Midnight. New York: Harper, 1937.
The Murder of Lidice. New York: Harper, 1942.

TRANSLATION

Flowers of Evil, from *Les Fleurs du Mal,* by Charles Baudelaire. New York: Harper, 1936. (with George Dillon).

PROSE

Distressing Dialogues (Pseudonym, Nancy Boyd.) New York: Harper, 1924.
Letters of Edna St. Vincent Millay, edited by Allan Ross Macdougall. New York: Harper, 1952.

BIBLIOGRAPHY

Yost, Karl. *A Bibliography of the Works of Edna St. Vincent Millay.* New York: Harper, 1937.

(See this volume for a listing of critical and biographical studies through 1936.)

CRITICAL AND BIOGRAPHICAL STUDIES

Bogan, Louise. *Achievement in American Poetry, 1900–1950.* Chicago: Henry Regnery, 1951.
Davidson, Edward. "Edna St. Vincent Millay," *English Journal,* 16:671–82 (1927).
Gregory, Horace, and Marya Zaturenska. *A History of American Poetry, 1900–1940.* New York: Harcourt, Brace, 1946.
Humphries, Rolfe. "Edna St. Vincent Millay, 1892–1950," *Nation,* 171:704 (December 30, 1950).
Ransom, John Crowe. "The Poet as Woman," in *The World's Body.* New York: Scribners, 1938.
Sheean, Vincent. *The Indigo Bunting.* New York: Harper, 1951.
Taggard, Genevieve. "A Woman's Anatomy of Love," *New York Herald Tribune Books,* April 19, 1931, p. 3.
Tate, Allen. "Miss Millay's Sonnets," *New Republic,* 66:335–36 (May 6, 1931).
Van Doren, Carl. *Three Worlds.* New York: Harper, 1936.
Wilson, Edmund. "Epilogue, 1952: Edna St. Vincent Millay," in *The Shores of Light.* New York: Farrar, Straus and Young, 1952.

——JAMES GRAY

Arthur Miller

1915-

SOME playwrights have complained that the drama is one of the more naïve forms of art, and many, many playwrights have complained that dramatic criticism is one of the most naïve forms of criticism. Probably a prime example of that critical naïveté is the centuries-old and apparently fruitless battle about the nature of tragedy. In our time that battle has hovered around the cliché that tragedy cannot be written in the modern world. Modern man, so the argument goes, has shrieveled in stature; his society has somehow lessened the significance of his soul in contrast to Athenian or Elizabethan society, which apparently did not make moral dwarfs of Athenians or Elizabethans. In this view, modern man is equated with Elmer Rice's Mr. Zero or one of Rossum's Universal Robots. Naturally, the events which happen to such ciphers can scarcely have the intensity of meaning of those events which happened to Oedipus and Lear.

Most of the interesting modern playwrights have fortunately paid very little attention to this view and have quietly gone about their business of creating a large and significant repertory of plays. Despite sporadic attempts, impelled mainly by the critics, to return to traditional forms, most of the interesting modern playwrights have plowed new fields. Endeavoring to create a drama equal in intensity to tragedy, they have either turned away from tradition entirely or utilized it in some fresh fashion. Mythology in modern dress, symbolism, expressionism, that neo-expressionism called vaguely the Theater of the Absurd, and that absurd theater called vaguely the poetic drama have all had their champions. Certain pre-eminently brilliant dramatists, such as Strindberg and Shaw, could create the tragic effect by other types of plot and in a much less traditional manner than that discovered by Aristotle in the dramas of Sophocles. However, the triumphs of Strindberg and Shaw did not invalidate Aristotle's perception; they merely emphasized that there are two tragic traditions in the Western world—the austere and the experimental.

Perhaps the austere tradition may be most easily traced by the plot structure that Aristotle discovered in *Oedipus Rex*. Certainly, considering structure alone, one may easily see that Euripides, Shakespeare, O'Casey, and Tennessee Williams belong to one tradition, and Sophocles, Racine, Ibsen, and Arthur Miller to another. Yet the plays of Miller have more than a merely structural similarity to those of Sophocles and Racine and Ibsen. Like the plays of those earlier men, Miller's also vitally embody the austere tragic spirit. That embodiment, in a time which is overwhelmingly eclectic and experimental, gives the real meaning and the real importance to the work of Arthur Miller.

Arthur Miller was born on October 17, 1915, in the Harlem section of Manhattan. His father was a prosperous manufacturer, and his mother, herself the daughter of a manufacturer, had been a teacher in the public school that Miller attended in Harlem. Miller was such a poor student that, although his teachers looked him up in their records after he had become a notable playwright, none of them could actually remember him. He failed many subjects, including algebra three times. He was more interested in sports than in school, and later remarked, "Until the age of seventeen I can safely say that I never read a book weightier than *Tom Swift*, and *Rover Boys*, and only verged on literature with some of Dickens."

The family fortunes having been lost in the crash of 1929, Miller went to work after high school in an automobile parts warehouse on Tenth Avenue in Manhattan. During this time he picked up a copy of *The Brothers Karamazov* under the impression that it was a detective story and read it on the subway to and from work. The book made such an impact upon him that he determined to be a writer, and for two and a half years he saved thirteen dollars a week from his fifteen-dollar salary in order to finance a year in college. Finally, after some eloquent letter writing on his part, he was admitted to the University of Michigan as a journalism student. He managed to maintain himself in college by a small salary as night editor of the *Michigan Daily*, by aid from the National Youth Administration, and by an occasional prize won by his writing. In college he began to write plays and twice won Michigan's Avery Hopwood Award. One of these prize plays, *The Grass Still Grows*, also won

the Theatre Guild National Award of $1250 in 1938.

Miller received his B.A. in 1938, and returned to New York to work with the Federal Theatre Project in its last months. For the project he wrote a comedy, but plans for its production were abandoned when Congress did not appropriate funds to continue the theater. Out of a job, Miller turned to writing for radio as well as to working in the Brooklyn Navy Yard and in a box factory. In 1940 he married Mary Grace Slattery, whom he had met in college, and they subsequently had two children.

Miller did not relish writing for radio. The medium had too many taboos and restrictions, and its scripts had to be short and almost banally simple. As he remarked to a *New York Times* interviewer in 1947, "I despise radio. Every emotion in a radio script has to have a tag. It's like playing a scene in a dark closet."

Although radio in the 1940's was a wasteland as vast as the television of today, Miller found in it more freedom than did many other writers. He did not have to grind out unvarying and unending segments of *Portia Faces Life* or *Fibber McGee and Molly*, for much of his work was done for *The Cavalcade of America* and *The Columbia Workshop*, two series which offered some opportunity for variety and originality. Actually, his many scripts must have served as a kind of artistic discipline, for he became skillful enough to pound out a completed half-hour script in eight hours.

A few of Miller's radio scripts have been published. Their intrinsic merit is not enormous, but they show a freshness fairly rare for radio, and they help to refute the notion of Miller as a totally humorless conscience of his race. "The Pussycat and the Expert Plumber Who Was a Man" is a light, Saroyanesque fantasy about a talking cat who blackmails some influential politicians into letting him run for governor. Two of the speeches suggest the central preoccupations of Miller's mature work. At one point Tom the cat remarks, ". . . the one thing a man fears most next to death is the loss of his good name. Man is evil in his own eyes, my friends, worthless, and the only way he can find respect for himself is by getting other people to say he's a nice fellow." This concern is precisely what bedevils John Proctor at the end of *The Crucible* and Eddie Carbone at the end of *A View from the Bridge*. This premise—that the most valid and fertile subject for the drama is the attempt to show man struggling to be at one with society —is basic to probably all of Miller's work.

Miller has frequently discussed this theory. For instance, in his essay "On Socal Plays," prefacing the 1955 edition of *A View from the Bridge*, he wrote that this social concern was the primary one of the Greek tragic writers and that the attempts of modern dramatists to show man striving for his individuality could end only in meaningless case histories. He wrote: "The social drama, as I see it, is the main stream and the antisocial drama a bypass. I can no longer take with ultimate seriousness a drama of individual psychology written for its own sake, however full it may be of insight and precise observation. Time is moving; there is a world to make, a civilization to create that will move toward the only goal the humanistic, democratic mind can ever accept with honor. It is a world in which the human being can live as a naturally political, naturally private, naturally engaged person, a world in which once again a true tragic victory may be scored." Without such a social basis, the drama, he thought, would turn to its "true opposite, the antisocial and ultimately antidramatic drama." This was written in the mid-1950's before some of those plays of Tennessee

Williams which seem most truly the dramatic extension of one man's individual psychology, and before the great flux of antisocial dramas which have been lumped together under the description Theater of the Absurd.

This preoccupation is interesting to find in Miller as far back as 1941, but his solution to the problem then was considerably simpler than what he could later accept. In "The Pussycat and the Expert Plumber Who Was a Man," Tom is exposed by an expert plumber named Sam and explains his exposure by remarking, "a cat will do anything, the worst things, to fill his stomach, but a man . . . a man will actually prefer to stay poor because of an ideal. That's why I could never be president; because some men are not like cats. Because some men, some useful men, like expert plumbers, are so proud of their usefulness that they don't need the respect of their neighbours and so they aren't afraid to speak the truth." In his mature plays up to *The Misfits*, Miller postulated that men do need the respect of their neighbors. It is this need that makes John Proctor retract his lie and Eddie Carbone insist upon his.

Another of Miller's radio scripts, "Grandpa and the Statue," has less merit than "The Pussycat," but the theme that man needs society is more evident. Grandpa Monaghan refuses to contribute money for the pedestal for the Statue of Liberty, and the story shows how he learns that his decision was wrong. He finds that he needs society and must be an integral part of it, and the statue comes to symbolize for him all that he inarticulately feels.

A third radio play, "William Ireland's Confession," is a droll historical script about the author of some notable Shakespearean forgeries. Its psychology is simplified for radio, but it is not a bad script. This radio play, and a patriotic one about the wartime merchant marine, "The Story of Gus," are worth noticing because of their fluently shifting scenes. The freedom in a radio script to shift scenes simply and easily may well have had some bearing on much of Miller's later work, such as *Death of a Salesman*, *A View from the Bridge*, and *After the Fall*. Despite the realistic manner of *The Man Who Had All the Luck*, *All My Sons*, and *The Crucible*, Miller has never regarded realism as an end in itself, but only as a tool to be mastered.

The radio plays may have had another influence on the development of Miller's mature technique. Two of these plays are stories told by a narrator and one of them concludes with a scene in Heaven. In his mature plays, Miller has been absorbed by the problems that Ibsenian realism did not quite satisfactorily solve. These are the problems of how to range more broadly through time and of how to probe more deeply into the mind than the front-parlor drama allows. Without wishing to curtail the objectivity of realism, he has wanted to combine with it some of the subjective strength to be found in various nonrealistic manners like that of the dream play or expressionism. As he wrote in "On Social Plays," the struggle taking place in the drama today is "a struggle at one and the same time to write of private persons privately and yet lift up their means of expression to a poetic—that is, a social—level." His most effective way so far of solving this problem is by the technique of the narrator, which he first used in these early radio plays.

Having made something of a reputation by his radio work, Miller was hired in 1944 by Lester Cowan, a movie producer, to visit army camps and gather material for *The Story of GI Joe*, a film to be based more or less on Ernie Pyle's newspaper columns. He spent a couple of months at army camps, observing various types of training, and talking with officers and men. What came out of the experience was his book of reportage, *Situation Normal*. The book is still worth reading, although not so much for its rather superficial reporting as for a pervasive idealism which Miller would probably now consider naïve. Actually, the book sheds more light on Miller the writer than on the war and the army.

His producer had commissioned him to find out what the war and the army were really like, so that this film would be an honest one that avoided the usual cinema clichés. To this purpose, Miller added another, for "you cannot," he wrote, "make a true picture of this war until you make up your mind as to what this war is about." Actually, the book makes clear that Miller had already decided what the war was about and that he was really attempting to discover his conclusions in the men he talked to. His attempts to draw generalizations from the soldiers about the nature of fascism and democracy came to nothing, however, and even in his discussions with Ernie Pyle he did not find this broad concern with the reasons for the war. He wrote: "It is terrible to me that everything is so personal; I mean that never in any of these calculations about the soldier can I honestly bring in the socio-political context of this war. I can't seem to find men who betray a social responsibility as a reason for doing or not doing anything. Maybe it was always so. Maybe that's why Tom Paine got drunk all the time." He was too honest a reporter to describe what he did not see, but he was also too committed a thinker to relinquish his preconceptions. "I can't give up the idea that political and economic beliefs have something to do with how these men react to this training and to the idea of fighting." Perhaps, he thought, the soldiers did have the beliefs for which he was searching, even though "in a totally unsuspected guise, in different forms than writers usually conceive them . . . through some osmotic absorption."

To oversimplify Miller's view somewhat, he regarded the war as a struggle between the principles of democratic equality and fascistic tyranny, and his book shows him determined to discover this same view in men for whom it was a purely academic and even an irrelevant point. His book makes quite clear that this view, even though he did not find it in the soldiers, is still going to be the focal point of the film which is jelling in his mind. In other words, Miller is attempting in this first book exactly what he would attempt again and again in his mature plays—to give to individual man, from the workings of society, his reason for existence, his personal significance, and his morality. Here his quest seems quixotic, for, although there were broad, underlying political and economic reasons for the war, those reasons had little connection with the individual soldier. In *Situation Normal* Miller is rationalizing, almost creating the connection. In his subsequent work up to *The Misfits*, he continued to search for connections. To an extent with *The Misfits* and almost totally with *After the Fall*, Miller seems to have given up the search, so actually one might read his career to date as a growing disillusionment with social idealism.

Miller had his first professional production of a play when *The Man Who Had All the Luck* appeared on Broadway on November 23, 1944, and lasted for four performances. The play gives the impression of being almost a student exercise. To paraphrase Willy Loman, it seems contrived, but not well contrived. The crucial situation at the end of the last act is strong, but artificial, a theatrically constructed situation rather than a real and inevitable one. Indeed, the drama throughout is a kind of poorly made well-made play that progresses through a series of climaxes to the greatest climax. Nevertheless, it is more loosely structured than an Ibsen play. It is spread over four

years rather than a few days, and the entire story is dramatized rather than merely the events immediately preceding the climax. The characters are clearly drawn, but some are purely illustrative and are dropped when their purpose is served, rather than being meaningfully interwoven throughout the story. All of the characters seem fugitives from a regional folk drama, and this tendency is especially noticeable in the first act. Perhaps the point might be made clear just by listing some of their names—J. B. Feller, Amos Beeves, Hester Falk, Dan Dibble.

The strength of the play is its emphasis upon moral responsibility, and that same emphasis would be the strength of Miller's mature work. The main character, David Frieber, or David Beeves as he was called in the produced version, feels guilty for having been successful without real merit or effort. He feels destined to pay for his good luck by the stillbirth of his child. If his child's death makes up for his unmerited good luck, he can then, he feels, sink all of his efforts into raising mink and can succeed for once by his own abilities. When the child is born perfectly healthy, David becomes obsessed by his need for success until his wife forces him to let the mink die, although the death of the animals will wipe away most of their prosperity.

Several themes touched vaguely upon in this play become the clearly enunciated ones of *All My Sons* and *Death of a Salesman*—the themes, for instance, of money and morality and of individual responsibility. Here, however, individual responsibility is not really connected to man's social responsibility. The play is set in no really believable background, but is a kind of disengaged moral fable about a particular individual. To the mature playwright, that fact would seem a major fault.

In writing the play, Miller had tried, he remarked, "to grasp wonder, I had tried to make it on the stage, by writing wonder. But wonder had betrayed me and the only other course I had was the one I took—to seek cause and effect, hard actions, facts, the geometry of relationships, and to hold back any tendency to express an idea in itself unless it was literally forced out of a character's mouth; in other words, to let wonder rise up like a mist, a gas, a vapor from the gradual and remorseless crush of factual and psychological conflict."

To solve this problem, Miller returned to *The Brothers Karamazov*, and found "that if one reads its most colorful, breathtaking, wonderful pages, one finds the thickest concentration of hard facts." He also decided that "the precise collision of inner themes" must occur "during, not before or after, the high dramatic scenes," and that the climax must be held back and back until the themes were properly clear. In other words, he came closer to the austere Ibsenian tragedy whose chief components were a meticulously drawn, real society, a tightly constructed cumulative structure, and an overwhelming insistence on significant theme.

The other pertinent point about the play is that Miller learned from it that his themes must be ones which deeply, personally involved him. Puzzling over the faults of the play, he found that ". . . two of the characters, who had been friends in the previous drafts, were logically brothers and had the same father. Had I known then what I know now I could have saved myself a lot of trouble. The play was impossible to fix because the overt story was only tangential to the secret drama its author was quite unconsciously trying to write. But in writing of the father-son relationship and of the son's search for his relatedness there was a fullness of feeling I had never known before; a crescendo was struck with a force I could almost touch. The crux of *All My Sons*, which would not be written until nearly three years later, was formed; and the roots of *Death of a Salesman* were sprouted." With this discovery Miller found himself. In his best-known plays, as in perhaps the best dramas of the Western world, the larger society is reflected by the little society of the family. That little society, that microcosm, Miller knew intimately and documented revealingly.

Although Miller is primarily a playwright, he has written a novel and several short stories. His novel *Focus*, published in 1945, was generally well received and sold about 90,000 copies in its hard-cover edition. The specific subject of the book is anti-Semitism, but its more general concern is that irrational hatred directed toward practically any racial minority.

The story charts the social education of Lawrence Newman, an easygoing Gentile with a vague, casual prejudice against Jews. When a new pair of glasses makes him appear Jewish, he is demoted from his job. Affronted, Newman resigns, but is unable to get his particular kind of job elsewhere because other people now also take him for a Jew. When his neighbors form a Christian Front to run a small Jewish merchant out of the neighborhood, Newman is apathetic about joining, and his actions make the others so suspicious that he is also taken by them as a Jew. Newman himself recognizes no kinship with Mr. Finkelstein the merchant and advises him for his own safety to leave the neighborhood. Newman refuses to leave because he regards his own case as different. No matter what the Christian Front thinks, he is really a Gentile. It is not until he is set upon by a group of toughs and with Finkelstein fights them off with baseball bats that he realizes his actual kinship. When he reports the attack, he allows the police to consider him a Jew, thus admitting to himself not so much Jewishness as something broader, the brotherhood of man.

The theme is strongly stated, and the book

remains engrossing despite its quite fuzzily drawn background. A more damaging fault is the unconvincing change in Newman. It is quite conceivable that, under the pressure of the story's events, a man would change from apathy to involvement. But Newman in the beginning of the story is pictured as a flabby, middle-aged Prufrock; in the middle he for no convincing reason attracts and marries a beautiful woman; by the end he is almost a hero of popular melodrama, athletically repelling assailants with his baseball bat.

In the smaller matters of Newman's changing character, Miller is more successful—for instance, when Newman, conscious of appearing Jewish, represses his usual gestures, refuses to count his change, and overtips the waitress. In the difficult larger task of showing how a man's character changes when his face changes, Miller is less convincing. The fault does not detract from the force of the book's point, but it does from its value as a work of art. It is a book of the moment, no worse than Laura Z. Hobson's *Gentleman's Agreement*, but no better either.

Miller's first really accomplished work was the play *All My Sons*, which was produced on January 29, 1947, and had a Broadway run of 328 performances. The play established Miller as a dramatist of much promise and was given the Drama Critics Circle Award as the best American play of the season. That award was something of an overestimation, for the same season saw the first production of O'Neill's masterly *The Iceman Cometh*. Nevertheless, *All My Sons* is a strong, traditional well-made play whose technique insists upon comparison with the realistic plays of Ibsen. Like them, *All My Sons* begins almost immediately before the climax of its story. Most of the story has occurred before the curtain rises and is revealed by exposition subtly interwoven with the current action. Actually, this structure

was not unique with Miller or Ibsen or even Racine. One may find precisely the same structure in *Oedipus Rex*; in Sophocles' play, as in Miller's, the revelation of a criminal whose crime has occurred years earlier is the crux of the present action. However, in Miller's play the Oedipus character is split in two—one half being the father and criminal and the other half the son and detective.

This structure is difficult to handle, for the playwright must explain rather than dramatize most of the action, and the great bulk of exposition always threatens to dissipate the dramatic impact of the play. There are probably three chief ways to combat this threat: by the evocative beauty of the dialogue, by irony, and by an adroit blending of current action with explanation of past action. In his *Oedipus Rex*, Sophocles superbly managed all three ways. In his social plays, Ibsen lacked poetry, but his permeating irony largely compensated for the realistic flatness of his style, and he did blend his past and present action with incomparable adroitness. In *All My Sons*, Miller handles his plot consummately, but he notably lacks both the poetry and the irony. Nevertheless, structure alone can carry a play very far, and Miller's play, because of its structure, remains absorbing theater.

It is the story of Joe Keller, a small manufacturer, who during the war allowed some faulty engine blocks to be shipped to the air force. When a number of planes crashed, Keller and his partner were brought to trial. Keller was finally released and his partner blamed, although Keller himself was really responsible. The theme, then, is one of morality and money, and the action centers around the attempt of Keller's son Chris to find the truth and to fix the responsibility, and of Keller to avoid his responsibility. The point of his guilt is only brought home to him after a letter is produced proving that his other son Larry had also considered his father guilty and had died in combat as a kind of expiation. Then Joe recognizes that the other pilots who died were "all my sons" and in expiation he kills himself.

This action does not at first dominate the play. It is brought to a head by the current action, a false plot which seems at the beginning to be the story's major substance. Chris has asked his brother's fiancée home because he intends to marry her. However, Chris's mother refuses to believe that Larry really died in battle, and much of the play's first two acts is an attempt to convince her, so that Chris and Ann may marry.

As in *Oedipus Rex* or *Ghosts*, the real plot emerges from the present action like a ghost from the past. It comes to dominate that action and to be the center of the play. This plot from the past, even in the beginning of the play, is constantly intruded; we are constantly reminded of Joe's trial and Larry's death. Such a technique may seem at first to slow the pace, until we see that it is revealing the real action. When such a parallel plot is well handled, there is a suspenseful tension as the relationship between past and present becomes ever clearer.

Like Ibsen's social plays, Miller's play is economical. All of his characters, even the minor ones, have an integral relation to the theme. No characters are introduced merely to illustrate or to facilitate the mechanics of the plot. Such economy emphasizes the play's closeness to traditional austere tragedy. This is a family tragedy; the father is a man of some importance who falls from power to ignominy. The lives of his entire family are blighted by his crime. Such a description might just as well apply to the royal family of Thebes or to the Alving family of Norway.

There is even in the play a hint of fate inexorably guiding the destinies of the characters. It is the ghost from the past, the dead son, whose words precipitate the tragic climax. In one of the minor characters who is preparing a horoscope of the dead son, the play even has a prophet. That last fact suggests the distance between the austere stylized tragedy of Sophocles and Racine and the austere realistic tragedy of Ibsen and Miller. Ibsen had attempted to inject the supernatural into some of his realistic dramas—such as, for instance, the white horses in *Rosmersholm*. Perhaps his intention was to compensate for a lack of grandeur and tragic import which might derive from realistic dialogue and a middle-class setting. Ibsen, was not, however, entirely successful in bringing a sense of fate into the front parlor, and turned away in his last plays from the illusion of total realism. Miller's intrusion of the supernatural is even more apologetically introduced than Ibsen's white horses. Most of the characters discount the horoscope, and the audience takes Miller's prophet as a mildly comic relief in a basically serious play. Consequently, Miller loses even the small effect that Ibsen gained, and his play seems smaller.

The smallness is particularly evident in the play's conclusion. Toward the end of the last act, Miller increases the intensity of the action to an extent that seems overwrought and frenetic when compared to the ambling and realistic tone of the earlier part. There is in the theater, unless the play is done excellently, some incongruity, as if the ending of an Elizabethan blood tragedy had been attached to a play by Terence Rattigan.

Nevertheless, despite its lack of irony, of really composed dialogue, and of characters who live outside of a theater, *All My Sons* is a real accomplishment. Its characters, if somewhat flat, do not have the dishonest flatness of many stage characters. Its theme seems likely to remain deeply pertinent for American society, and it is a model of structural craftsmanship. Probably its excellences of theme and structure will keep it fresh for as long as those excellences kept green the plays of John Galsworthy. That is certainly a limited immortality, but scarcely a contemptible one.

The promise of *All My Sons* was more than fulfilled when *Death of a Salesman* was produced on Broadway on February 10, 1949, and ran for 742 performances. It was excitingly staged by Elia Kazan and given memorable performances by Mildred Dunnock, Arthur Kennedy, and the excellent Lee J. Cobb as Willy Loman. To many viewers the play seemed the most meaningful and moving statement made about American life upon the stage in a great many years, and it is still generally considered Miller's masterpiece. The play was awarded the Pulitzer Prize for drama, and solidified its author's reputation as a leading American dramatist and one of the country's significant writers.

Willy Loman, the salesman of the title, is like Joe Keller a typical embodiment of the modern business morality, but he is also a more universal figure. One feels that Joe Keller's individual story points up a valid flaw in the American dream, but that Willy's story is larger than one man's. Like even the great tragic figures of Sophocles and Shakespeare, Miller's Willy is both an individual and a broadly relevant type.

It is difficult to say what makes a character attain this rare meaningfulness. Perhaps Willy's universal quality stems, paradoxically, from his well-developed individuality. Certainly his broad meaningfulness partly stems from the compassion with which he is presented. With all of his faults—his weakness, his density, his petty irritations and self-delusions—this compassion yet remains dominant in the mind of the audience. Perceptive people probably consider that their own characters are similar compounds of weakness, delusion, and folly, but each man recognizes in himself, beneath his weight of self-criticism, an alleviating

quality, a basic humanity. Whatever he has done, he at least meant well. This fact does not atone for his faults, but it is the extenuating circumstance that finally liberates Orestes and Hamlet and, in the Christian story, the sons of Adam. Miller has touched here a central chord in his view of Willy, and, except for *A Memory of Two Mondays,* he has not been interested in touching it again. That fact probably explains why *Death of a Salesman* has moved audiences more deeply than Miller's other work. All of his plays are condemnations of human nature, but *Death of a Salesman* condemns with pity and sorrow.

More generally considered, Willy is the modern man who has accepted wholeheartedly the twentieth-century version of the American dream, and who then reacts like the psychologist's rat when it discovers that the door to its particular dream has been inexplicably shut. Willy has swallowed the modern version of the Horatio Alger myth, that unrealistic notion that if you are a clean-living and diligent bank clerk you will marry the boss's daughter and become chairman of the board. Whatever its flaws, this male Cinderella story had some admirable qualities. It approved of honesty, industry, and thrift, and so it was not quite the view that you would get something for nothing. Its modern version has become debased, and is dangerously close to the view that you will get something for nothing. Willy has applied himself; he has been diligent and thrifty; he has extolled the businessman's virtues; he has tried to be "well-liked." For this he should have been rewarded, but no reward comes, and Willy is numbly baffled by the failure of the American dream.

Willy's story points up how the Alger story and, presumably, the national morality have become tarnished. To the Alger hero, there was no discrepancy between his ideals and his life. In Willy's time, there is a double standard, and he is not entirely aware of it. While preaching to his sons clean living, friendliness, sportsmanship, and honesty, his life denies these qualities. He has a mistress on the road, his friendliness does not really sell merchandise, and it dimly occurs to him that people don't really consider it even friendliness. His son Biff, the star athlete in high school, does not finally win out over Bernard the greasy grind, and Willy's values do not lead to success and happiness. A basic tolerance for dishonesty permeates his actions, and this dishonesty is reflected in the lives of his sons.

Nevertheless, in their broadest sense, Willy's hopes and goals were pure, and pity and sorrow arise for his agony when he does not attain them. Like Oedipus, Willy Loman made the wrong choice. He hitched his wagon to the wrong star. We can feel pity and sorrow for his mistake rather than contempt, for, after all, he was searching for a star.

The language of the play is much better than that of *All My Sons*. It contains some of the tragicomic irony that Ibsen used so effectively in his social plays. For instance, Willy remarks: "Oh, I'll knock 'em dead next week. I'll go to Hartford. I'm very well liked in Hartford. You know, the trouble is, Linda, people don't seem to take to me." Or:

WILLY: Chevrolet, Linda, is the greatest car ever built. . . .

LINDA: . . . you owe Frank for the carburetor.

WILLY: I'm not going to pay that man! That goddam Chevrolet, they ought to prohibit the manufacture of that car!

Such touches are not as pervasive as in Ibsen, but there are enough to suggest a fuller, more anguished, more pathetic, and more contradictory humanity than Miller had presented in *All My Sons*.

Another ironic device contributing to the fullness of Willy's character is the exaggerated speech which the audience but not the speaker realizes is too farfetched to come true. Each of the Lomans has such speeches, but the most and the finest are Willy's. For instance: "You and Hap and I, and I'll show you all the towns. America is full of beautiful towns and fine, upstanding people. And they know me, boys, they know me up and down New England. The finest people. And when I bring you fellas up, there'll be open sesame for all of us, 'cause one thing, boys: I have friends. I can park my car in any street in New England, and the cops protect it like their own."

The play is a notable technical achievement, for in it Miller broke out of the realistic confinements of time and space and psychology. At one time he called the play *Inside His Mind*, and much of the play is seen through Willy's eyes. The viewpoint is not quite constant, and it is a little difficult to tell from what viewpoint some of the scenes should be seen. However, as there should be no confusion in production about the point of any of the scenes, the question of who technically is the narrator is somewhat academic.

In theme and technique, the play accomplishes exactly what Miller wanted. It is not confined to Ibsen's front parlor or to the few hours preceding the climax, nor do we have to interpret what a person feels merely from what he says. The play beautifully balances the interior of a man's mind with a full evocation of his world. By his own standards, Miller had succeeded, and his standards in this instance coincided with everyone else's.

Miller's adaptation of Ibsen's *An Enemy of the People* was produced on Broadway on December 28, 1950, but, despite a cast headed by Fredric March, Florence Eldridge, and Morris Carnovsky, it lasted only 36 performances. Although not an eloquent play, Miller's version is fluent and streamlined. The stiff and old-fashioned flavor of the Archer translation is far from Miller's mid-century Americanese, which strikes the ear as both colloquial and easy. Many of Ibsen's long expositions and tirades are drastically reduced, so that the adaptation is only about two-thirds the length of the original. Ibsen had a tendency to lengthen, sometimes almost interminably, the action following the climax, and Miller's abridgment of the last act makes the play more emphatic to modern ears than Ibsen's leisurely recapitulation of each dramatic point. The other main abridgment is in the meeting scene, which Miller may have pared down too much. His cutting swiftens and heightens the action, but probably loses some of the rhetorical force of Ibsen's long speeches.

Miller made three other notable changes. He made the play from a five-act one into a three-act and five-scene one. He made the curtains more theatrically effective, and, although he has opposed theatrical effect for its own sake, Miller does not despise it when it rises honestly out of the action. Finally, Ibsen tended to write set scenes in the French style, each scene existing in its separate compartment and a set of new characters being introduced for each succeeding scene. Miller runs many of these scenes into each other and eliminates or smooths over the transitions between them. Such tinkering could not be entirely successful without violently wrenching Ibsen's structure, but Miller does reduce the—to modern taste—tight artificiality which Ibsen inherited from the well-made play.

More interesting than Miller's innovations in Ibsen's script is his choice of this particular play and the light that his choice throws upon his own work. Reading Ibsen was for Miller almost as crucial as reading Dostoevski. Of course, Ibsen's obvious influence, particularly if one thinks of *All My Sons* or *The Crucible*, was for a firmly wrought form and structure. Miller has spoken almost in the same breath of the "enthralling dramatic experience of reading Ibsen" and of his dissatisfaction with formless "slapped together" plays like Michael V. Gazzo's *A Hatful of Rain*. Nevertheless, for Miller as well as for Shaw, technique was not the ultimate lesson to be learned from Ibsen. Ibsen's real strength and importance to Miller is ". . . his insistence, his utter conviction, that he is going to say what he has to say, and that the audience, by God, is going to listen. . . . Every Ibsen play begins with the unwritten words: 'Now listen here!' And these words have shown me a path through the wall of 'entertainment,' a path that leads beyond the formulas and dried-up precepts, the pretense and fraud, of the business of the stage. Whatever else Ibsen has to teach, this is his first and greatest contribution." In other words, "Attention must be paid," and a serious play achieves its drama primarily from its content rather than from its emotional effects. This point, that a play must be a significant statement, is Ibsen's chief legacy to the modern playwright and the chief reason why Arthur Miller is one of the sons of Henrik.

The reason for Miller's adapting this particular play, which is not one of Ibsen's great achievements, throws much light on Miller's own preoccupations. He remarked in his preface to the play that its theme was "the central theme of our social life today. Simply, it is the question of whether the democratic guarantees protecting political minorities ought to be set aside in time of crisis. More personally, it is the question of whether one's vision of the truth ought to be a source of guilt at a time when the mass of men condemn it as a dangerous and devilish lie." This same view impelled the writing of *The Crucible* and this same problem Miller himself had to face six years later when he was called to appear before the House Committee on Un-American Activities. This plays suggests the answer that, when the times are out of joint, the individual must to himself be true. Stockmann, as Miller puts it, "clings to the truth and suffers the social consequences. At rock bottom, then, the play is concerned with the inviolability of objective truth. Or, put more dynamically, that those who attempt to warp the truth for ulterior purposes must inevitably become warped and corrupted themselves."

This conclusion about the corruption of society is a distinct change from the premise of *Situation Normal* and *All My Sons,* which suggested that society is the giver of morality and that man succeeds or fails by his ability to find a home in that society. It is a conclusion which apparently Miller sought to avoid and which he accepted only after much struggle. In the 1940's his view was one of a simple social idealism, and the issues were clear-cut. As Quentin remarks in *After the Fall:* ". . . the world [was] so wonderfully threatened by injustices I was born to correct! How fine! Remember? When there were good people and bad people? And how easy it was to tell! The worst son of a bitch, if he loved Jews and Negroes and hated Hitler—he was a buddy. Like some kind of paradise compared to this." However, Miller was too perceptive a man not to be moved by the nature of his society, and it seemed to him that that society was growing more and more malevolent. Consequently, we find a confusion in his writing; we find succeeding works contradicting the previous ones. *Situation Normal* applauded society, but *Focus* condemned it. *All My Sons* applauded society, but *Death of a Salesman* and *The Crucible* condemned it. *A View from the Bridge* applauded society, but *A Memory of Two Mondays* condemned it. In other words, much of Miller's work does not derive from inalterable conviction, but from a conflict of two opposed convictions.

That conflict appears clearly in his adaptation of Ibsen. In Ibsen's crucial fourth scene, Dr. Stockmann is pushed to defend a biological aristocracy of superior men, like the Superman of Nietzsche. This concept is an almost inevitable conclusion of the fierce condemnation of society that grows out of the play's action, but it is not a point that the perplexed Miller was yet willing to admit. He therefore eliminated this speech from the play. Much of Miller's work up to *The Misfits* is centered around this conflict between the ideal and the real. Some of his plays expressed one view, some the other, but he was being increasingly pushed in one direction, and by *The Misfits* he had made his mind up.

Miller is a slow, painstaking, and deliberate writer who sometimes composes thousands of pages to get a hundred that are right. Consequently, his next original play, *The Crucible,* did not appear until January 22, 1953. It was generally thought a sound work but a lesser one than *Death of a Salesman.* In its original run it achieved only 197 performances, but its off-Broadway revival several years later played well over 500. Its merits were at first overshadowed by the notoriety of its most obvious theme. The subject of the play, the Salem witch trials of 1692, was distractingly applicable to what has been called the witch hunts of the 1950's. Now, when the most impassioned fervor of Communist hunting has abated, the play may probably be judged on its own merits, unobscured by newspaper headlines.

The Crucible is a strong play, and its conclusion has much of the force of tragedy. It has not the permeating compassion of *Death of a Salesman,* but there is more dramatic power to John Proctor's death than there was to Willy's. It is a harder-hitting play, and its impact stems from Proctor's death being really a triumph. You cannot pity a man who triumphs. Willy Loman's death was a failure, and his suicide only a gesture of defeat. Him you can pity.

The Crucible is really a more dramatic play than *Death of a Salesman*. The earlier play attempted to construct a plot about Willy's losing his job, and Biff's attempting to gain one, but these strands of plot were only a frame on which to hang the exposition of a man's whole life. The plots of *Death of a Salesman* are not the center of the play, but in *The Crucible* the action is the play's very basis, its consuming center. One watches *Death of a Salesman* to discover what a man is like, but one watches *The Crucible* to discover what a man does. *Death of a Salesman* is a tour de force that succeeds despite its slim action because its real center is the accumulation of enough significant detail to suggest a man. In the life of John Proctor, one single action is decisive, dominating, and totally pertinent, and this action, this moment of decision and commitment, is that climax toward which every incident in the play tends. *Death of a Salesman* is not traditionally dramatic, at least in the Aristotelian sense that the center of a drama is an action. *The Crucible* is so dramatic, and the centrality of its plot explains its greater strength.

That strength is also explained by the clarity with which the theme of *The Crucible* emerges from its plot. The theme of *Death of a Salesman* does not emerge so much from its story as from its illustration and exposition. For that reason it is necessary for Linda and Charley in their laments to explain the meaning of Willy's life, and actually Linda is still explaining what the play means in the last scene. *The Crucible* requires no such exposition, for the play's meaning has been acutely dramatized. The exposition in *Death of a Salesman* is dramatic only in the way that the keening in *Riders to the Sea* is dramatic. It is a lyrical evocation of emotion rather than a dramatic one.

The Crucible is more traditionally dramatic in one other way. The theme of a play is made more intense by the hero's either making a discovery of past folly (Oedipus, Lear) or being presented with an agonizing dilemma (Orestes, Hamlet). Proctor's story has elements of both situations. His past folly, which he has been trying unsuccessfully to live down, is his seduction of Abigail Williams, and this fault eventually destroys him when Abigail turns against him and accuses him of witchcraft. The center of the play, however, is his dilemma about commitment. This dilemma is stated in each act in somewhat different terms. In Act I, Proctor washes his hands of the town's problem and refuses to be involved in the absurd charges of witchcraft being made by a small group of frightened, hysterical girls. In Act II, he is pushed into involvement when Abigail denounces his wife, Elizabeth, as a witch. In Act III, he attempts legally to rescue the accused, but by resorting to law also attempts to avoid being involved himself. Finally, at the end of the act, he can only achieve justice by involvement, and so he accuses Abigail and becomes himself one of the accused. Proctor's identification with the accused is not yet total. He drags his feet as did Lawrence Newman. He suffers with them for months in prison, but in the final moment before his execution he signs a confession of witchcraft. His reason is that he is really different from them. He cries: "I cannot mount the gibbet like a saint. It is a fraud. I am not that man. My honesty is broke, Elizabeth; I am no good man. Nothing's spoiled by giving them this lie that were not rotten long before." Proctor is still striving for a compromise, but Miller will allow him none. Proctor signs the confession to save his life, but the judges demand that the confession be made public, and he finds that he cannot live in society uncommitted. He must be either totally and publicly against the accused or totally and publicly with them. There is no middle ground of private commitment and public neutrality. This is Proctor's final dilemma as it was Lawrence Newman's and Joe Keller's, and Miller will not, at this point in his career, allow the individual to escape from his social obligation into his private life.

Two points connect this situation with the tradition of austere tragedy. First, an individual is pushed to definition, forced to irreclaimable and self-destructive action. That self-destruction is, paradoxically, an affirmation of morality, for it asserts that belief is more important than life. Second, the individual discovers his need to choose, and his agony comes from his awareness. Reason, said Milton, is but choosing, and Proctor's aware choice is the choice of a reasoning man. That last point indicates the distance between Proctor's tragedy and Willy Loman's. Willy's is a kind of passive, uncomprehending, mute, brute suffering. Whatever peace Willy attains by his death is the peace of oblivion, but whatever peace Proctor attains is the peace of knowledge. Willy's is a pathetic tragedy, Proctor's an austere one. Willy's story arouses pity; Proctor's, suffering. Willy's death is a lament for the destruction of value; Proctor's, a paean to its creation. And finally, Willy's is the story of man's failure, and Proctor's is the story of man's triumph.

Technically the play is not as interesting as *Death of a Salesman* or as tightly structured as *All My Sons*. Its structure is, however, appropriate for the retelling of the witch hunt story and for the revelation to Proctor of the need for commitment. Its language is not as lyrically evocative as that of *Death of a Salesman*, but it does not need to be. In *Death of a Salesman* language had to be a substitute for plot; here it can be unobtrusively subservient. Actually the dialogue of the play is a considerable accomplishment. It suggests the flavor of seventeenth-century speech without becoming distractingly archaic and without sacrificing simplicity, strength, or suppleness.

Death of a Salesman may always be considered a better play than *The Crucible* for two reasons. First, there were no distracting headlines to hurt the initial impact of the earlier play, and the American theater is so commercially and journalistically oriented that even a later success can rarely erase the first impression. Second, and even more important, the emotions evoked by the pathetic tragedy are closer to the surface than those aroused by the austere one. Hamlet is a fuller and more intelligent view of humanity than is Cyrano, and Proctor is a more informed one than Willy, but they will never arouse as many tears. The fault is not in the playwright but in the naïveté of his form, and the naïveté of his form is dictated by the naïveté of his audience—in other words, by human nature.

Two and a half years later, on September 29, 1955, Miller had produced on Broadway two one-act plays, *A Memory of Two Mondays* and *A View from the Bridge*. The production was not entirely happy, and the plays closed after a moderate run of 149 performances. Later Miller revised and expanded *A View from the Bridge* into two acts, and its subsequent London production achieved considerable success.

On the plays' first production, most of the critics paid little or no attention to *A Memory of Two Mondays*. However, one of the most astute critics, the canny Irishman Frank O'Connor, thought it the better play, and Miller himself remarked in the introduction to his *Collected Plays* that "Nothing in this book was written with greater love, and for myself I love nothing printed here better than this play."

One of the clichés about Miller is that he has no humor. There is really a great deal of humor in his work, and in no place is it more theatrically effective than in this superb little tragicomedy. Miller himself calls the play "a pathetic comedy," and it would be hairsplitting to quarrel with his definition. There is more of pathos than of tragedy in the play, and one of its main effects is the pity evoked for the people who stay on in the automobile parts warehouse after Bert leaves to go to college.

Even so, the play has some effects stronger than pathos. The old, hardy, ribald Gus, impelled to carouse all weekend because of twenty-two years of accumulated monotony from the warehouse, yet obsessed with guilt for having been carousing when his wife was dying, awakens an emotion stronger than pity. He first lugs two Ford automobile fenders around all weekend. Then he draws all of his money from the bank and goes on a last great spree, buys a suit of clothes, rents three taxis simultaneously, drinks, calls all of his friends long-distance, and finally dies in one of his taxis. Automobiles were the cross of Gus's life, but he did die with some heroic bravado. Gus's life just as fully squashes him as Willy Loman's did to him, but he is more than a low man or a new man or a GI Joe killer. He has also his load of guilt, but he has a vigor about him, an indomitability.

This play is a considerable achievement. Tragicomedy requires that the stories of a number of people be told. It requires that not merely one mood, but various conflicting ones be evoked. It usually requires irony and it often uses lyricism and song. These qualities are all present in Miller's play, and it is remarkable that he was able to pack so much in so effectively. In a way it is like trying to pack *The Plough and the Stars* into one act and succeeding. This is a moving, technically adroit, and beautiful job, one of the rare instances of a one-act tragicomedy.

Miller's descent from the austere tragic writers is nowhere more evident than in the first version of *A View from the Bridge*. That play seems an attempt to utilize the austere technique of Sophocles in a modern setting, just as

Maxwell Anderson's *Winterset* was an attempt to do the same thing with the manner of Shakespeare. Miller's first version uses the sparest outline of the traditional tragic plot, a typical tragic situation, and a chorus, and it is written in what might be tolerantly called free verse. Its traditional austerity is discussed by Miller in his essay "On Social Plays," where he remarks: "*A View from the Bridge* is in one act because . . . these *qualities* of the events themselves, their texture, seemed to me more psychologically telling than a conventional investigation in width which would necessarily relax that clear, clean line of his catastrophe." The story is about Eddie Carbone, a longshoreman in Brooklyn, who has raised his niece Catherine from a child. Now that she is older, he is reluctant to let her go. Eddie and his wife, Beatrice, take in two Italian relatives, Marco and Rodolpho, who have entered the country illegally to find work. When Catherine and Rodolpho fall in love, Eddie becomes desperate in his attempts to hold on to the girl's affections, and he finally turns the men in to the immigration officials. Denounced to the neighborhood by Marco, Eddie denies his guilt, and when the two men fight Eddie is killed.

The play is strongly effective on the stage, yet, except in the broadest sense as a story of a man driven by a secret passion, it probably has a lesser relevance than do the stories of Joe Keller or Willy Loman. Like Willy, Eddie does not fully understand or at least admit the force that is destroying him, and like John Proctor, Eddie is ultimately concerned with saving his name. At the climactic moments of both *The Crucible* and *A View from the Bridge,* the protagonist is destroyed by his need to secure a place in society. In all of Miller's plays up to this time, morality is established by the society. In *Death of a Salesman* and *The Crucible* the morality is false; in *All My Sons* and *A View from the Bridge* it is valid. Up to this last play, Miller still saw the establishment of a social morality as the way out of the impasse of studies of individual disintegration which formed, he thought, the subjects of the bulk of serious drama and fiction in modern times. However, there are two social moralities in this play—the valid one which proves Eddie morally wrong for denouncing the illegal immigrants and which is held by the people, and the legal morality which no one believes in. The recognition of two social moralities is really a step away from the view of *All My Sons*, as well as another indication that Miller's work so far was in the nature of an interim report from a mind still irresolute.

A View from the Bridge, like *The Crucible*, has seemed a cold play, and actually Miller's only warm plays have been *Death of a Salesman* and *A Memory of Two Mondays*. Here, Miller's impatience with realism led him to draw a sparer protagonist than he had before, but the real coldness stems not from the relative lack of detail about Eddie, but from the artist's detachment from him. Miller has frequently gone on record as being opposed to plays which aim for easy theatrical effect rather than for significant point. His point is clearly made in *A View from the Bridge*, but the many touches of pervasive sympathy that made Willy Loman and Gus humanly relevant are missing. As Miller wrote in his introduction to the revised version of the play: "It seemed to me then that the theater was retreating into an area of psycho-sexual romanticism, and this at the very moment when great events both at home and abroad cried out for recognition and analytic inspection. In a word, I was tired of mere sympathy in the theater. The spectacle of still another misunderstood victim left me impatient. The tender emotions, I felt, were being overworked. I wanted to write in a way that would call up the faculties of knowing as well as feeling." The revision of the play made

Eddie theatrically somewhat fuller, but, as Miller remarked, "Eddie is still not a man to weep over; the play does not attempt to swamp an audience in tears." Whether an audience will allow such a play to succeed on its own grounds is still debatable. Racine and Ibsen succeeded, but in our own time the two authors who have most brilliantly striven to widen the intellectual content of a play, Bernard Shaw and Bertolt Brecht, have notably failed. Audiences frequently laugh at Shaw's jokes and forget or ignore what the jokes were about, and audiences at Brecht's *Mother Courage* insist on reading pathos into a place where the author wanted point.

In the theater, Miller's revision is not quite a total success. Eddie becomes fuller and Beatrice is drawn more into the action, but the theatrical quality of the earlier version is toned down. The lyric speeches of the lawyer Mr. Alfieri, who acts as a kind of chorus, are made shorter, more prosaic, and less theatrical. The climactic scene is toned down, and the fight between Marco and Eddie is shorter and less dramatic. When Eddie is stabbed he does not crawl across the stage and grasp Catherine's leg before he dies; rather, he dies in Beatrice's arms. This reconciliation with his wife perhaps normalizes Eddie more, but it also lessens his stature.

The impulse behind the play is commendable testimony to Miller's attempt to write meaningfully rather than to accept easy emotional effects and oversimple theatrical issues. Whether he can dispense with the easy emotional effect and force an austere and intellectual drama upon the modern stage is highly debatable. Foremost among the earlier American dramatists who wanted to make the drama a forum for intelligent discussion is Elmer Rice. Nevertheless in an introduction to two of his most intelligent and least successful plays, Rice held that a full and significant statement in a play was a contradiction and an impossibility, and that the drama demands that point be simplified and reduced to the usual theatrical tales of love and murder. Whether this view is ultimately true will not depend upon the Ibsens, Shaws, Rices, Brechts, and Millers of the modern drama who have tried to refute it, but upon the growth to maturity of the audience.

There followed a long hiatus in Miller's work for the stage that may be traced in part to his personal life and in part to his politics. Several of his plays had been attacked by organizations of the far right for their alleged Communist leanings (the same plays had run into trouble in Russia because of their alleged capitalist leanings), but his trouble with his own government really began when the State Department in 1954 refused him a passport "as a person believed to be supporting the Communist movement." His name was blackened somewhat more in 1955 when he was preparing a film scenario about the work of the New York Youth Board with juvenile delinquents. The American Legion and the Catholic War Veterans so strenuously objected to Miller on the basis of his alleged Communist sympathies that the film was ultimately dropped.

On June 21, 1956, Miller appeared before the House Committee on Un-American Activities and talked freely about his support of various Communist Front groups in the 1940's, and of how he had attended some Communist-sponsored meetings of writers. All questions about himself he answered fully and frankly, but he refused to answer two questions requiring him to name people whom he had seen at the meetings. For his refusal to name names, he was cited for contempt of Congress, fined $500, and given a suspended sentence of thirty days in jail, but he was also given a passport valid for six months.

The case was widely covered in the press because of Miller's eminence as a writer and also because of a turn his personal life had taken. His marriage had been deteriorating for several years, and in 1956 he divorced his wife and married Marilyn Monroe, the film actress. At the time, it seemed rather as if Albert Einstein had married Gypsy Rose Lee, for Miller was considered, as most playwrights are not, an intellectual, and Miss Monroe seemed the apotheosis of the dumb blonde.

To judge by what clearly are portraits of her in the short story "Please Don't Kill Anything" and in *After the Fall*, as well as by many overt remarks, Miller saw in Miss Monroe a rare example of innocence in the modern world, and the growing disillusionment of his own thought certainly prompted him to grasp at innocence. His troubles with the government were ultimately settled and the contempt citation was reversed, but his marriage kept him in the limelight. During these years he wrote much but published little, and his marriage began to absorb ever more of his time. According to Maurice Zolotow, Miss Monroe's biographer, whose testimony is supported by some comments in *After the Fall*, she drew him more and more into her own career.

The main accomplishment of these years was the film *The Misfits,* which began as a short story, became a novel and then a film script, and was finally published as a kind of novelized film script. The film, which was in some ways a vehicle for Marilyn Monroe, was not enthusiastically received, even though it was directed by John Huston and had also in its cast Eli Wallach, Montgomery Clift, and Clark Gable. It was a good film, honestly observed and craftily put together, but despite the presence of Marilyn Monroe it was not a conventionally glamorous film and did not abound in the naïve theatricalities which the cinema demands. Many of the best-regarded films—even

The Birth of a Nation, Greed, Stagecoach, Citizen Kane, Casablanca—will hardly stand up under a second viewing which thoughtfully regards their content and is not swept away by their excitement. *The Misfits* has less of such conventional excitement than many films, but would probably grow in meaning rather than diminish on a second viewing.

The story concerns three cowboys in the modern West who drift aimlessly through life, muttering in the teeth of the modern world, "it's better than wages." The central part of the story is a mustang hunt carried on by airplane and truck. The mustang herd is now almost as small as the few men who hunt them, and the reason for the hunt is the ignoble one of selling the animals for dog food. What was once "a good thing to do . . . a man's work," has somehow gone wrong. As the oldest cowboy, Gay, explains it to the girl Roslyn: "We start out doin' something, meaning no harm, something that's naturally in us to do. And somewhere down the line it gets changed around into something bad. Like dancin' in a night club. You started out just wanting to dance, didn't you? And little by little it turns out that people ain't interested in how good you dance, they're gawkin' at you with something altogether different in their minds. And they turn it sour, don't they? . . . This . . . this is how I dance, Roslyn. And if they made somethin' else out of it, well . . . I can't run the world any more than you could. I hunt these horses to keep myself free. That's all."

In other words, Miller was talking about the destruction of innocence, and this film was his strongest indictment so far of both society and the family. The society is tawdry and valueless, and the family itself has disintegrated. Guido's wife has died, Perce has run away from home, Gay's children avoid him, and Roslyn's marriage has broken up. An effective symbol of this disintegration is the half-finished house which Guido started and then abandoned. This house in the desert is the closest that Miller had yet come to portraying a wasteland world in which things fall apart and the center cannot hold. The only true relationships are those casually formed between wandering misfits who still snatch what brief joys they can in a world in which they are ever more anachronistic.

But, although this was Miller's grimmest statement so far, he does not in the film entirely face up to the implications of his indictment. His characters are, as they must be for a movie, quite simple, almost childlike. Also a resolution comes too easily. In some indefinable way by freeing the mustangs they had caught, they become absolved of the sin of the world, and they all, with the possible exception of Guido, recapture a kind of innocence. Perce returns home to his family, and Gay and Roslyn have each other. As the picture closes, they are talking about a home, raising a family, and making a new start.

The film is finally neither meaningful enough nor dramatic enough because its point needs to be explored more thoroughly than Miller can do in a film. He is just not able to use enough words, and his ending seems therefore not much more than the traditional Hollywood ending of the banal clinch and the ride off into the sunset. To make it work, this theme needs more depth, more meaning poured into it. That meaning Miller would try to include in his next play, *After the Fall*, when his indictment would be not only of society and of the family but also of the individual. The real trouble with *The Misfits* is that it is a movie, and the real difference in theme between it and Miller's later play is that there are still in the movie a few individuals who can attain honor and innocence.

In 1960, Miller and Miss Monroe found life together intolerable, and they divorced. In

1962, he married Ingeborg Morath, a photographer for Reuters, and completed a new play, *After the Fall*, which was the initial presentation of the Lincoln Center Repertory Company. The play was so obviously based on Miller's life that its true merits were at first difficult to see. The journalistic critics were generally impressed while the critics attached to little reviews tended to attack it with a curious vehemence. Although the more literary of the reviewers dissented, most observers felt that the play was brilliantly staged by Kazan and enacted by an accomplished cast, which was headed by Jason Robards, Jr., and had Barbara Loden in the role that approximated the character of the recently dead Marilyn Monroe.

After the Fall is very possibly a masterpiece, but its excellence may not clearly emerge until the false glamour of its autobiographical elements has dimmed with time and also until critics cease to compare it with some more conventional play—even if that play is *Death of a Salesman* itself. Miller's increasing dislike of superficially aroused emotion on the stage has in this play increased his emphasis upon the theme, and an inevitable consequence is the diminution of emotional appeal. The same phenomenon can be seen in Shaw, whose plays have also been criticized as being all head and no heart. One might question whether this is a mature criticism and, indeed, whether the conventional drama is a particularly mature art. There may well be, as *After the Fall* and much of Shaw's own work seem to suggest, a deeper layer of emotion, more pertinent and more integrally connected to self-knowledge.

At any rate, *After the Fall* is Miller's most intellectually probing play, and Quentin is a central character too complicated to be summed up by simple reactions of love and pity. The play tells what happens to a man after the loss of intellectual innocence, after his Fall. Simple views of morality have failed

Quentin, and he has lost his innocence not only as an individual but as a member of the family and a member of society as well. As an individual he has seen the wreckage of two marriages. He has seen the failure of love both in his own family and among his friends, both in his own country and in the world. Almost every person in this play betrays love. In Quentin's words, "I loved them all, all! And gave them willingly to failure and to death that I might live, as they gave me and gave each other, with a word, a look, a truth, a lie—and all in love!" Each person in the play seems to so sacrifice others for his own survival that love is made a travesty. As Quentin viciously puts it when dissecting Maggie's thoughts: "And I am full of hatred, I, Maggie, the sweet lover of all life—I hate the world! . . . Hate women, hate men, hate all who will not grovel at my feet proclaiming my limitless love for ever and ever!"

This picture of the individual scrambling to his own survival over the corpses of love is shown again and again in the play: in Quentin's two marriages, in his grateful relief when his friend Lou dies and he can avoid involvement in Lou's problems, in his deserting his father to go to college, in his mother's betrayal of him as a boy, in her betrayal of his bankrupt father, in the decision of Quentin's friend Mickey to betray his friends to the House investigating committee—in instance after instance, the individual betrays love to save himself. All of Quentin's three women accuse him of self-absorption, and the accusation is a true one, but it is also true for every other character in the play, save perhaps Holga, whom Quentin is thinking of marrying at the end of the play. Even Quentin's second marriage, which is analogous to Gay and Roslyn's love in *The Misfits*, is shown to be merely a delusion that innocence can be recaptured. It cannot, and Maggie and Quentin turn on each other, and in a ghastly scene he refuses to help her save her own life.

The failure of love in a broad social sense is symbolized by the Nazi concentration camp and by the guilt that Quentin feels for it. Miller makes what happened in the concentration camp a macrocosm of what the individual does to others. When Quentin asks Holga, "Do you ever feel when you come here . . . some vague . . . complicity?" she answers, "Quentin . . . no one they didn't kill can be innocent again." Further, Mickey's decision to name names before the House committee is both a comment upon the moral failure of a society which asks the individual such a question and an example of a futile attempt to recapture a lost innocence. That innocence is, however, forever gone.

In light of this triple condemnation of society, the family, and the individual, it is apparent that Miller feels the inadequacy of the view of his earlier work. If this condemnation were the entire theme of *After the Fall*, the play would be one of the blackest of our time. However, Holga, who goes with Quentin to see *The Magic Flute*, is the character who brings a kind of hope—a bleak hope, to be sure, but the only kind that would not seem a shoddy theatrical trick after the fable of this play:

HOLGA: I had the same dream each night— that I had a child; and even in the dream I saw that the child was my life; and it was an idiot. And I wept, and a hundred times I ran away, but each time I came back it had the same dreadful face. Until I thought, if I could kiss it, whatever in it was my own, perhaps I could rest. And I bent to its broken face, and it was horrible . . . but I kissed it.

QUENTIN: Does it still come back?

HOLGA: At times. But it somehow has the virtue now . . . of being mine. I think one must finally take one's life in one's arms, Quentin.

You must, as Quentin screams to Maggie, "see your own hatred, and live!" The damned and blasted and fallen man does not live "in some garden of wax fruit and painted trees, that lie of Eden, but after, after the Fall, after many, many deaths. . . . And the wish to kill is never killed, but with some gift of courage one may look into its face when it appears, and with a stroke of love—as to an idiot in the house— forgive it; again and again . . . forever?"

This is a remarkable statement from a battered man, and Quentin's grasping at this scrap of tattered certainty is far, far from the young Communist sympathizer of the 1940's holding aloft his white and unsullied banner, or from the starry-eyed author of patriotic simplicities in *Situation Normal*, or from the simple affirmations and condemnations of *The Man Who Had All the Luck*, *All My Sons*, or even *Death of a Salesman*. It is a statement to file away with other hard-won, hard-boiled verities like Stephen Dedalus' courage to be wrong or Faulkner's "They will endure." It is not precisely a *Reader's Digest* kind of sentiment, but it is probably one of the few mature remarks ever made in an American play.

Technically the play is a brilliant accomplishment. In it Miller solves his perennial problem of how to retain sufficient real psychology and a full feel of the real world and at the same time to attain a free flow of time and to probe more deeply into a man's mind than conventional realism allows. This play manages all of these matters without falling into the pitfalls of extreme expressionism or of the Theater of the Absurd. The play is told to an invisible narrator who might be, as Miller remarks, Quentin's analyst or God, but who really is Quentin himself. The play is an examination of conscience, and it takes place— to use the title which Miller discarded for *Death of a Salesman*—Inside His Mind.

By suggesting the way a man thinks, Miller

is able to probe in detail and in depth Quentin's life. The play unfolds not by logical progression, but seemingly at random. Quentin shies away from certain thoughts, proceeds by association, doubles back upon his own thoughts, and yet there is no feeling of random repetition, but of an ever-increasing significance. One device holding the play together is the irony of stray thoughts that flit momentarily across Quentin's mind. For instance, a frequent apparition is the figure of Louise, Quentin's first wife, playing solitaire, and this figure appears as a swift accusation of Quentin's self-absorption in scenes with, for instance, Maggie, the second wife. Other figures —Holga, his mother, his young admirer Felice —also appear instantaneously, and their mere appearance makes what they stand for in Quentin's life comment ironically upon a different situation. Strindberg in his dream plays also probed fascinatingly into man's mind but less logically and probably too chaotically for the simple necessities of the drama. Inheriting Ibsen's feel for structure and for point, Miller arranges the Strindbergian situation into a kind of order. Probably the only other American who has so ambitiously attempted the same thing is O'Neill in that baffling and brilliant chaos of a play, *The Great God Brown*.

Despite the charge of coldness and despite Quentin's considerably lacking the stature of Hamlet, to whom he has been compared, there is much fine characterization in the play. Maggie is the best character that Miller has drawn or attempted to draw since Willy Loman, and the other characters are not stinted, for even some minor parts are theatrically meaty roles. In sum, *After the Fall* did not ultimately solve all of Miller's technical problems, and it did not, of course, ultimately answer the problems that have bedeviled him and his world. In the play, he even condemned that world in terms blacker than he had ever used before,

but he also seemed to discover that the questions worth asking are more complex than he earlier knew.

On December 3, 1964, in its second season, the Lincoln Center Theater presented another play of Miller's, *Incident at Vichy*. Set in a "place of detention" in Occupied France in 1942, the play traces the agonies of a group of prisoners who have just been arrested. In form the play is a piece of adroit but quite straightforward realism. In theme it is basically a simpler restatement of the theme of *After the Fall*: all men are guilty because all men are human. Had the play appeared before *After the Fall*, it would have seemed more impressive. Coming afterward, it marked—despite its strength and honesty—no advance for Miller as either a theatrical technician or a thinker.

The unusual quickness with which Miller composed the play does suggest that he needs his own stage to spur him into activity. Unfortunately, the widespread dissatisfaction with the Lincoln Center Theater's first two seasons caused Miller (along with the group's artistic directors) to sever connections with the company.

The Millers now live on a farm in Connecticut, and they have had one child. In 1965, Miller was elected president of P.E.N., the international writers' society, and served two terms. In 1967, he issued a collection of short stories, *I Don't Need You Any More*. This was a workmanlike and sometimes moving collection, made up of the fugitive pieces he had over the years published in various magazines. In 1969, he collaborated with his wife on a short book called *In Russia*, which contained a long, fascinating essay by him and a portfolio of excellent photographs by her.

His most recently produced play, at this writing, is *The Price*. This four-character play opened in New York on February 7, 1968, was successfully produced in London, and the television production in the United States won Emmy awards for two of its actors, George C. Scott and the late David Burns.

The play is not as ambitious as *After the Fall*, which was both a personal and a social statement. As *Incident at Vichy* was primarily a social statement, *The Price* is primarily a personal statement. It is a more compelling play than *Incident at Vichy*, but it is not as well integrated. Of its four characters, the wife is, as are most of Miller's women, the most palely drawn and the least integral. The center of the play is the clash of the two brothers over their attitudes to their dead father. The protagonist is the policeman who has given up his prospects in order to support his father, and who has paid the price for this familial devotion in discontent and the consciousness of his own wasted life. What the policeman, who is ironically named Victor, has won for his sacrifice is, however, a hollow prize. His physician brother, Walter, points out that the father neither needed nor wanted the sacrifice, that Victor was really aware of this and used his sacrifice as an excuse for himself. On the other hand, Walter, who was more perceptive and more superficially callous, has won little himself. His nominal success has brought with it a nervous breakdown, the dissolution of his marriage, and a pathetic assertion of the value of his present life.

The central thread of the play comes to no resolution and to no statement. What we are given is an increasing revelation of two characters who seem to represent facets of Miller himself. Certainly Quentin of *After the Fall* also contained a good deal of Miller, but that play connected Quentin with his society. In Victor and Walter Franz, we have mainly personal revelation, and it smacks of self-indulgence. Further, we have seen it all before. The two brothers and their imperfect father have bedeviled Miller since *The Man Who Had All the Luck*, and we have seen them in both *All My Sons* and *Death of a Salesman*. One gets, then, the feeling of a kind of personal exorcism, rather than of the public statement one finally demands of a play.

What is exciting about *The Price* is its consummate comedy. The last half of the first act is given over to the development of the character of the old Jewish furniture dealer, Gregory Solomon, who is one of Miller's finest characters. Solomon is droll, canny, sad, uncertain of himself because of his age, and finally indomitable. When he comes into the play, it rises triumphantly. Miller has been taken so seriously that his flair for comedy has been little noted. There was, however, a great deal of comedy in *Death of a Salesman*, and *A Memory of Two Mondays* is a tragicomic tour de force. Gregory Solomon should have been the center of *The Price*, for he throws the play as hopelessly askew as did Falstaff the *Henry IV* plays. If Miller develops this facet of his talent, he may add a startling dimension to a distinguished career.

Dramatic criticism proceeds largely by cliché. The original cliché about Miller after the success of *All My Sons, Death of a Salesman,* and *The Crucible* was that he was a playwright of intense seriousness who attempted to evolve a modern equivalent of tragedy from a preoccupation with social issues. Since *After the Fall*, that cliché has become somewhat pejoratively modified. Now Miller's discussion of social issues is often thought to be a naïve reflection of the left-wing thought of twenty-five years ago. Tom Driver typically reflected this view in his remark, "The plays will survive, I think, as a challenge to a certain kind of acting, as the achievement of a man of the theater, and not as literary works or expressions of social ideas."

This attitude, to my mind, reflects the intellectual's traditional misunderstanding of the drama, and relegates what is theater to something more trivial than what is literature. Miller is, of course, a man of the theater, but the literature of the theater is not something that can be extracted from the total notion of theater. A good play may sometimes be studied as literature, just as a Cadillac may sometimes be used as a chicken coop. A play is something akin to literature, touching it, and occasionally comparable to it, but having no more integral basis for comparison than ham does to eggs.

About Miller, we can be sure of at least this much: he is one of the five or six incontestably fine writers for the theater that America has produced. His position in the drama of America and, indeed, in the drama of the twentieth century, is both secure and high.

Selected Bibliography

WORKS OF ARTHUR MILLER

PLAYS AND BOOKS

"The Pussycat and the Expert Plumber Who Was a Man," in *100 Non-Royalty Radio Plays,* compiled by William Kozlenko. New York: Greenberg, 1941.

"William Ireland's Confession," in *100 Non-Royalty Radio Plays,* compiled by William Kozlenko. New York: Greenberg, 1941.

The Man Who Had All the Luck, in *Cross-Section, 1944,* edited by Edwin Seaver. New York: L. B. Fischer, 1944.

Situation Normal. New York: Reynal and Hitchcock, 1944.

Focus. New York: Reynal and Hitchcock, 1945.

"Grandpa and the Statue," in *Radio Drama in Action,* edited by Erik Barnouw. New York: Farrar and Rinehart, 1945.

"That They May Win," in *The Best One-Act Plays of 1944,* edited by Margaret Mayorga. New York: Dodd, Mead, 1945.

"The Story of Gus," in *Radio's Best Plays,* edited by Joseph Liss. New York: Greenberg, 1947.

All My Sons. New York: Reynal and Hitchcock, 1947.

Death of a Salesman. New York: Viking Press, 1949.

An Enemy of the People. New York: Viking Press, 1951. (Adaptation of Ibsen's play, with a preface).

The Crucible. New York: Viking Press, 1953. (This play was printed with an additional scene in *Theatre Arts,* October 1953.)

A View from the Bridge. New York: Viking Press, 1955. (Contains also *A Memory of Two Mondays* and the important preface "On Social Plays." The revised version in two acts was first printed in *Collected Plays* and later, with a new introduction, was reprinted alone [New York: Viking Press, 1960].)

Collected Plays. New York: Viking Press, 1957. (Contains *All My Sons, Death of a Salesman, The Crucible, A View from the Bridge* in its revised version, *A Memory of Two Mondays,* and an important fifty-page introduction.)

The Misfits. New York: Viking Press, 1961.

After the Fall. New York: Viking Press, 1964.

Incident at Vichy. New York: Viking Press, 1965.

I Don't Need You Any More. New York: Viking Press, 1967.

The Price. New York: Viking Press, 1968.

In Russia (with Inge Morath). New York: Viking Press, 1969.

ARTICLES AND STORIES

"It Takes a Thief," *Collier's,* 119:23 75–76 (February 8, 1947). (Story.)

"Subsidized Theatre," *New York Times,* June 22, 1947, sec. 2, p. 1.

"Tragedy and the Common Man," *New York Times,* February 27, 1949, sec. 2, pp. 1 and 3. Reprinted in *Theatre Arts,* 35:48–50 March 1951.

"Arthur Miller on 'The Nature of Tragedy,'" *New York Herald Tribune,* March 27, 1949, sec. 5 pp. 1–2.

"The 'Salesman' Has a Birthday," *New York Times,* February 5, 1950, sec. 2, pp. 1 and 3.

"Monte Sant' Angelo," *Harper's,* 202:39–47 (March 1951). (Story.)

"Many Writers: Few Plays," *New York Times,* August 10, 1952, sec. 2, p. 1.

"Journey to 'The Crucible,'" *New York Times,* February 8, 1953, sec. 2, p. 3.

"University of Michigan," *Holiday,* 14:41, 68–71, 128–32, 136–37, 140–43 (December 1953).

"A Modest Proposal for Pacification of the Public Temper," *Nation,* 179:5–8 (July 3, 1954).

"The American Theater," *Holiday,* 17:90–98, 101–02, 104 (January 1955).

"A Boy Grew in Brooklyn," *Holiday,* 17:54–55, 117, 119–20, 122–24 (March 1955).

"Picking a Cast," *New York Times,* August 21, 1955, sec. 2, p. 1.

Untitled comment, *World Theatre,* 4:40–41 (Autumn 1955).

"The Family in Modern Drama," *Atlantic,* 197:35–41 (April 1956).

"Concerning the Boom," in *International Theatre Annual,* No. 1, edited by Harold Hobson. London: John Calder, 1956. Pp. 85–88.

"Global Dramatist," *New York Times,* July 21, 1957, sec. 2, p. 1.

"The Writer's Position in America," *Coastlines,* 2:38–40 (Autumn 1957).

"The Misfits," *Esquire,* 48:158–66 (October 1957). (Story.)

"Brewed in 'The Crucible,'" *New York Times,* March 9, 1958, sec. 2, p. 3.

"The Shadows of the Gods," *Harper's,* 217:35–43 (August 1958).

"Bridge to a Savage World," *Esquire,* 50:185–90 (October 1958).

"My Wife Marilyn," *Life,* 45:146–47 (December 22, 1958).

"I Don't Need You Any More," *Esquire,* 52:270–309 (December 1959). (Story.)

"Please Don't Kill Anything," in *The Noble Savage,* No. 1. Cleveland and New York: World, 1960. Pp. 126–31. Also printed in *Redbook,* 117:48–49 (October 1961). (Story.)

"The Playwright and the Atomic World," *Tulane Drama Review,* 5:3–20 (June 1961).

"The Prophecy," *Esquire,* 56:140–41, 268–87 (December 1961). (Story.)

"Glimpse of a Jockey," in *The Noble Savage,* No. 5. Cleveland and New York: World, 1962. Pp. 138–40. (Story.)

"The Bored and the Violent," *Harper's,* 125:50–56 (November 1962).

"On Recognition," *Michigan Quarterly Review,* 2:213–20 (Autumn 1963).

"Lincoln Repertory Theatre—Challenge and Hope," *New York Times,* January 19, 1964, sec. 2, pp. 1 and 3.

"With Respect for Her Agony—But with Love," *Life,* 56:66 (February 7, 1964).

"Our Guilt for the World's Evil," *New York Times Magazine,* January 3, 1965, pp. 10–11, 48.

"The Role of P.E.N." *Saturday Review,* 49:16–17 (June 4, 1966).

"It Could Happen Here—And Did," *New York Times,* April 30, 1967, sec. 2, p. 17.

"Arthur Miller Talks," *Michigan Quarterly Review,* 6:153–84 (Summer 1967).

"Notes and Comment," *New Yorker,* 43:19 (January 13, 1968).

"New Insurgency," *Nation,* 206:717 (June 3, 1968).

"Writers in Prison," *Encounter,* 30:60–61 (June 1968).

"Battle of Chicago: from the Delegate's Side," *New York Times Magazine,* September 15, 1968, pp. 29–31.

"Kidnapped," *Saturday Evening Post,* 240:40–42 (January 25, 1969).

"Broadway from O'Neill to Now," *New York Times,* December 21, 1969, pp. 1 and 7.

"Bangkok Prince," *Harper's,* 241:32–33 (July 1970).

"War between Young and Old," *McCall's,* 97:32 (July 1970).

"Fame," *Yale Literary Magazine,* 140:32–40 (March 1971).

BIBLIOGRAPHIES

Eissenstat, Martha Turnquist. "Arthur Miller: A Bibliography," *Modern Drama,* 5:93–106 (May 1962.)

Hayashi, Tetsumaro. *Arthur Miller Criticism: 1930–1967.* Metuchen, N.J.: Scarecrow Press, 1969. (Often incorrect and unreliable).

CRITICAL AND BIOGRAPHICAL STUDIES

In addition to the articles and books listed below, the reviews of the New York drama critics might also be consulted.

Allsop, Kenneth. "A Conversation with Arthur Miller," *Encounter*, 8:58–60 (July 1959).

Brandon, Henry. "The State of the Theatre: A Conversation with Arthur Miller," *Harper's*, 221:63–69 (November 1960). Also printed in Brandon's *As We Are*. New York: Doubleday, 1961.

Carlisle, Olga, and Rose Styron. "The Art of the Theatre II: Arthur Miller, an Interview," *Paris Review*, 10:61–98 (Summer 1966).

Corrigan, Robert W., comp. *Arthur Miller: A Collection of Critical Essays*. Englewood Cliffs, N.J.: Prentice-Hall, 1969.

Evans, Richard I. *Psychology and Arthur Miller*. New York: Dutton, 1969.

Feron, James. "Miller in London to See 'Crucible,'" *New York Times*, January 24, 1965, p. 82.

Gassner, John. *The Theatre in Our Times*. New York: Crown, 1954. Pp. 342–48, 364–73.

Gelb, Barbara. "Question: 'Am I My Brother's Keeper?'" *New York Times*, November 29, 1964, sec. 2, pp. 1 and 3.

Gelb, Philip. "Morality and Modern Drama," *Educational Theatre Journal*, 10:190–202 (October 1958).

Goode, James. *The Story of the Misfits*. Indianapolis, Ind.: Bobbs-Merrill, 1963.

Greenfeld, J. "Writing Plays Is Absolutely Senseless, Arthur Miller Says, but I Love It," *New York Times Magazine*, February 13, 1972, pp. 16–17.

Griffin, John and Alice. "Arthur Miller Discusses *The Crucible*," *Theatre Arts*, 37:33–34 (October 1953).

Gruen, Joseph. "Portrait of the Playright at Fifty," *New York*, October 24, 1965, pp. 12–13.

Hascom, Leslie. "'After the Fall': Arthur Miller's Return," *Newsweek*, 63:49–52 (February 3, 1964).

Hayman, Ronald. *Arthur Miller*. London: Heinemann Educational, 1970.

Huftel, Sheila. *Arthur Miller: The Burning Glass*. New York: Citadel Press, 1965.

Martin, R. A. "Arthur Miller and the Meaning of Tragedy," *Modern Drama*, 13:34–39 (May 1970).

McCarthy, Mary. "Naming Names: The Arthur Miller Case," *Encounter*, 8:23–25 (May 1957).

Morley, Sheridan. "Miller on Miller," *Theatre World*, 41:4, 8 (March 1965).

Moss, Leonard. *Arthur Miller*. New York: Twayne, 1967.

Murray, Edward. *Arthur Miller, Dramatist*. New York: F. Unger, 1967.

Nelson, Benjamin. *Arthur Miller, Portrait of a Playwright*. New York: McKay, 1970.

Popkin, Henry. "Arthur Miller: The Strange Encounter," *Sewanee Review*, 68:34–60 (Winter 1960).

Samachson, Dorothy and Joseph. *Let's Meet the Theatre*. New York: Abelard-Schuman, 1954. Pp. 15–20.

Schumach, Murray. "Arthur Miller Grew Up in Brooklyn," *New York Times*, February 6, 1949, sec. 2, pp. 1 and 3.

Seager, Allan. "The Creative Agony of Arthur Miller," *Esquire*, 52:123–26 (October 1959).

Tynan, Kenneth. "American Blues: The Plays of Arthur Miller and Tennessee Williams," *Encounter*, 2:13–19 (May 1954). (Reprinted in Tynan's *Curtains*. New York: Atheneum, 1961. Pp. 257–66.)

United States House of Representatives, Committee on Un-American Activities, Investigation of the Unauthorized Use of United States Passports, Part 4, June 21, 1956. Washington, D.C.: United States Government Printing Office, November, 1956.

Welland, Dennis. *Arthur Miller*. New York: Grove Press, 1961.

Williams, Raymond. "The Realism of Arthur Miller," *Critical Quarterly*, 1:140–49 (Summer 1959).

Wolfert, Ira. "Arthur Miller, Playwright in Search of His Identity," *New York Herald Tribune*, January 25, 1953, sec. 4, p. 3.

————*ROBERT HOGAN*

Henry Miller
1891-1980

HENRY MILLER is likely to outlast a great many writers who at the moment seem more important. Fifty years from now, a hundred years from now, he will remain a significant figure of our time. The future will remember him for a variety of reasons, not all of them literary. For Henry Hiller is not only a writer, he is a phenomenon. His life, his creed, his motives, and his work are all of interest to an enormous public. He is venerated by an extraordinary number of people at home and abroad, not all of them cranks by any means. His name is news and is bound to become history. He epitomizes a movement, a trend, perhaps a revolution in mores. To many he represents a cause. For such reasons his work and reputation are as difficult to appraise now as were those of Rousseau and Byron in their day. Like them he should probably be viewed first as a public figure, and only then as a writer.

Most conspicuously, Henry Miller is the man who broke the barriers on what is loosely called pornography, whose books won test cases and made certain words printable in English-speaking countries. *Tropic of Cancer*, first published overtly in this country in 1961, soon became the subject of more widespread litigation than any other literary work in history and eventually required a Supreme Court decision. The controversy stirred up by *Ulysses* and *Lady Chatterley's Lover* was mild by comparison—though in England the trial of Lady Chatterley had already established precedent and Miller's works have consequently appeared there without challenge.

The publication of *Tropic of Cancer* in America created a furor, with some sixty lawsuits waged in different states. It was also an enormous success, with 1,500,000 copies sold within a year, and another 1,000,000 the following year. Thus almost thirty years after he had written the book Henry Miller became a best seller in his native land, and after many years of poverty a rich man. *Tropic of Cancer* was followed by *Tropic of Capricorn* in 1962, and *Black Spring* in 1963. Then in 1965, all the other banned books appeared at once: *The World of Sex*, *Quiet Days in Clichy*, and the three volumes of *The Rosy Crucifixion—Sexus, Plexus*, and *Nexus*. These books had previously been published in France and had occasionally appeared in America in small editions sold illicitly, usually by dealers in erotica.

The publication of Miller's books would make an interesting study in itself. There have been hundreds of editions and translations all over the world, a good share of them pirated. The history of his authorized publications might be briefly summed up in the names of a few publishers: Jack Kahane of the Obelisk Press in Paris, who specialized in pornography for the tourist trade, published Miller's first five books; James Laughlin of New Directions, champion of experimental writing, introduced Miller to American readers; Bern Porter, who ran a private press in the forties, was one of the many who printed fugitive Milleriana; Maurice Girodias of Olympia Press, son and successor of Jack Kahane, was prosecuted and sentenced by the French government for publishing, among other works, *Sexus*; and most recently, Barney Rosset of Grove Press has forced acceptance of the banned books in the United States. All have taken up Miller as a cause and professed the highest motives in publishing his works; all have taken risks in doing so, but only Girodias has suffered seriously. Laughlin has probably been the most disinterested, Rosset certainly the most successful in establishing Miller in the marketplace. The industry of private publishers like Bern Porter has produced a great variety of miscellaneous ephemera, pamphlets for the most part drawn from Miller's books, which have become collector's items and which have complicated the bibliographer's task.

During the years when he was struggling for recognition Miller became a legendary character, a kind of folk hero, the Paul Bunyan of literature, larger than life as exile, bohemian, and rebel, the great champion of freedom of expression and other lost causes. He appealed to highbrows and lowbrows alike, although in the early years his admirers were not always able to obtain his works. He gained a good deal of sympathy in 1943 when the *New Republic* published his open letters begging for food, clothing, or cash and offering watercolors in exchange. This campaign was so successful— in spreading his reputation at least—that later when the GI's in France began buying up copies of his *Tropics* at a great rate and his

financial problems were solved, his name remained a byword for the plight of the creative artist in America.

When he settled in Big Sur, on an isolated stretch of the California coast, the place became famous. His legend grew, and strange stories circulated about the Henry Miller "cult," most of them sensational and false. Pilgrims came to visit Miller from all parts of the country and abroad, so many that eventually he had to leave. It is characteristic of America and this day of public images that Miller should still be identified as the monkish Sage of Big Sur, while the place, once a colony for poor writers and artists, should be transformed into a fashionable resort. It is surely more significant that his example has had a profound effect on many writers and artists the world over, among whom he is venerated as a free spirit. And the lengthened shadow of the man is most apparent in the fact that he is the original hippie and Zen saint—in this as in so many other ways thirty years ahead of his followers.

Miller has also played a conspicuous public role as outsider, rebel, and iconoclast. He is in fact a genuine anarchist, a confirmed enemy of society, constitutionally opposed to any system. Miller's position has a long tradition in America. His anarchy derives from the individualism of his heroes, Emerson, Thoreau, and Whitman, the latter in Miller's opinion "the greatest man America ever produced." Similarly his anti-Americanism, though cultivated abroad, is of the home-grown variety, and in latter years, without abating his vehement criticism of America, he has gone so far as to confess that he is 100 per cent American. At first his iconoclasm appears to be a product of the thirties; doubtless he will be remembered by historians as a voice out of the Great Depression, a writer of protest. But though his early works are wonderfully expressive of that era, the depression atmosphere has nothing to do with the thirties. Henry Miller had been living in the depression all his life; the depression mentality is to be found throughout his work, and in his autobiographical narratives can be traced back to his childhood. He was always a bottom dog in spirit, always an outsider, always—to use one of his favorite words—a bedbug.

Perhaps the best way to view him is as a writer of satire. If we can accept John Dos Passos' definition, "A satirist is a man whose flesh creeps so at the ugly and the savage and the incongruous aspects of society that he has to express them as brutally and nakedly as possible to get relief." Much of Dos Passos' essay on "Satire as a Way of Seeing," though written for George Grosz's drawings, applies with remarkable aptness to Miller's writings. "He seeks to put his grisly obsession into expressive form the way a bacteriologist seeks to isolate a virus. . . . Instead of letting you be the superior bystander laughing in an Olympian way at somebody absurd, [he] makes you identify yourself with the sordid and pitiful object. His satire hurts." If Miller is indeed a satirist, then he belongs to a very special breed. He has the satirist's usual irreverence, but none of his indignation. Though appalled at the world around him and despairing of its future, he is not depressed but elated by the spectacle. He has been profoundly affected by Spengler, yet is full of high spirits. He dances with glee as the world goes to pieces. His pessimism is that of the satirist, but his comic despair is *sui generis.*

Whether or not Miller can be regarded as a satirist, there can be no doubt about what he is against. He is radically anti-bourgeois, anti-white-Nordic-Protestant, and, as already noted, anti-American. He is utterly opposed to the bourgeois ethic of work and wealth. To him

Christianity is bankrupt, the American dream a nightmare. What he hates most in America is the utilitarian cult of progress, efficiency, and the machine, all of which he sees as dehumanizing, soul-destroying forces. He is anti-Utopian because he does not believe in economic or political solutions. He is anti-civilization, to such a point that "civilization" is a dirty word in his vocabulary. "Civilization is drugs, alcohol, engines of war, prostitution, machines and machine slaves, low wages, bad food, bad taste, prisons, reformatories, lunatic asylums, divorce, perversion, brutal sports, suicides, infanticide, cinema, quackery, demagogy, strikes, lockouts, revolutions, putsches, colonization, electric chairs, guillotines, sabotage, floods, famine, disease, gangsters, money barons, horse racing, fashion shows, poodle dogs, chow dogs, Siamese cats, condoms, pessaries, syphilis, gonorrhea, insanity, neuroses, etc., etc." This definition makes him sound more like a prophet of doom than a merry-andrew, but it is precisely such a collection of horrors that will touch off his gaiety.

Although Miller is anything but a coherent thinker, his attitudes are all of a piece. They recur throughout his work, consistent from start to finish. In his attitudes he is a close successor to D. H. Lawrence; his experiences have led him to Lawrence's conclusions. He shares Lawrence's vision of humanity being ground apart by the machine; his response closely resembles that of Lawrence, Dionysian, anti-intellectual, instinctive; he turns to the same life-giving sources, art, religion, and sex. To use a favorite term of contemporary criticism, both are prophetic, apocalyptic writers. Here the resemblance ends. Temperamentally the two are altogether different, as different as tragedy and comedy. Where Lawrence is inclined to play the messiah, Miller prefers to play the clown.

Art, religion, and sex. Miller is easily recognized as an apostle of art and sex, but the religious element may be harder to detect in his work. By conventional standards he is immoral, profane, and blasphemous. He is not pious, virtuous, solemn, puritanical, dogmatic, or orthodox—he has none of the attributes that Americans usually associate with religion, and he clearly has no use for them. Yet Miller regards himself as a religious man, frequently mentions God in his work, and readily alludes to such religious figures as Gautama, Jesus, and, his favorite, Lao-tse. What he means by God and religion is often hard to determine, because he is so completely eclectic in his views. Often in his early works, God means simply the divine afflatus or self-fulfillment. And religion, especially in his later works, can include anything that might loosely be labeled mysticism or metaphysics. Miller has always been attracted to all kinds of exotic and esoteric systems, such as astrology, theosophy, and occultism. In rejecting organized Christianity, he did not close his mind to religion, but, rather, opened it to all manner of unconventional para-religious beliefs, preferably Oriental in origin. And in religion as in everything else he remains a hedonist, an anarchist, and a humorist; this combination makes it particularly difficult for more conventional minds to accept Miller as a religious person.

Sex is of course the most controversial element in his work; it assumes many forms and serves many purposes. Sometimes it is purely gratuitous, mere bawdy storytelling, but at other times it is symbolic. At its most meaningful sex serves as the most powerful weapon against the system he is attacking. It is the life-force, the only force that can rescue man from the machine. Here again Miller resembles Lawrence; but he does not go on with Lawrence to develop a mystique of sex. With him sex is usually casual, carnal, anarchic, and indiscriminate. In writing about it, he is crude, blunt, explicit. Worse still, he uses the everyday words that he learned in the streets as a boy.

These words are still explosive in print. It is probably Miller's language more than anything else that aroused the censors, and still makes it exceedingly difficult to debate the pornography-obscenity issue dispassionately. There is also a problem of definition, and in the law courts a question of the writer's intent. Miller cheerfully admits that he is an obscene writer, but claims not to be a pornographer. He bases his distinction largely on candor: obscenity to him is direct, while pornography is suggestive. Pornography might be described simply as aphrodisiac, obscenity as disgusting. Pornography is romantic, making sex appear more alluring than it actually is; while obscenity, to the contrary, makes sex repulsive or ridiculous. By now no one challenges Miller's motives much; certainly he did not write about sex to make money—he is not a pornographer in that sense. In time the whole issue is likely to appear ludicrous, a quaint episode in a changing cultural pattern. After all, pornography has flourished mainly in a few puritanical countries during the last two hundred years or less; elsewhere and at other times, sex has almost invariably been regarded as comical. Already there are signs that the English-speaking peoples are growing less squeamish about reading the dozen or so words that make up the obscene vocabulary. If so, Henry Miller has been largely responsible for their acceptance in print.

As might be expected, Miller is as iconoclastic on the subject of literature as on any other subject. He constantly argues that what he is writing is not literature, for "literary," like "civilization," is a nasty word in his vocabulary. What he objects to chiefly in literature is "the insufferable, the obsessional lucidity of the mind" in such writers as Proust, Joyce, Pound, and Eliot, the "mortuary odor" of form and tradition. To these analytical writers he opposes Rimbaud, Dostoevski, and D. H. Lawrence. Literature should be written entirely from the subconscious, not from the head. It should flow spontaneously, it should not be concerned with form. "The terrible emphasis today upon plot, action, character, analysis, etc.—all this false emphasis which characterizes the literature and drama of our day—simply reveals the lack of these elements in our life." Such statements show what he had in mind when he wrote his own books: he would re-create life as he lived it.

For all his anti-literary protest, Miller has plenty of literary ancestors. His very intransigence belongs to a venerable tradition, that of the literary underworld. As a literary outlaw, he is the descendant of such writers as Petronius, Villon, Rabelais, Balzac, Restif de la Bretonne, and Lautréamont, all the rogues and picaros and *poètes maudits*, as well as the ancestors previously mentioned. By now he is well on the way to becoming an ancestor himself, with numerous descendants. Though inadequately recognized, his influence is perhaps the most pervasive in American writing today. Such dissimilar writers as Burroughs and Kerouac, Mailer and Brautigan, are in their different ways indebted to Miller, and the Beats have hailed him as a precursor. To a remarkable degree, the present generation of American writers has inherited his traits: egocentric and confessional; shocking, violent, obscene; rambling, incoherent, formless; antisocial, anarchic, solipsistic; "mystical"; hallucinatory, nightmarish, ecstatic, apocalyptic.

The explanation for Miller's extreme individualism can be found in his biography: briefly, he is a self-made man. Self-educated, formed by his experiences, slow to mature and self-taught as a writer, he struggled for years before he broke through with *Tropic of Cancer*, by which time his opinions were fully formed. Self-made in the Emersonian sense, he was as intransigent as Thoreau, the American he most resembles, once due allowance is made for the differences in character and setting: Miller is neither disciplined nor ascetic, and the streets of megalopolis were his Harvard and Walden. An account of his first forty years shows that he constantly rebelled against the standards of his society, formed his own, and lived by them as much as possible. During much of his life he has lived marginally. In a country where work is synonymous with virtue, he has seldom held a steady job and has preferred the hand-to-mouth existence of a beggar or bum. He has knocked about a good deal, working at one time or other as "dish-washer, bus boy, newsie, messenger boy, grave-digger, bill sticker, book salesman, bell hop, bartender, liquor salesman, typist, adding machine operator, librarian, statistician, charity worker, mechanic, insurance collector, garbage collector, usher, secretary to an evangelist, dock hand, street car conductor, gymnasium instructor, milk driver, ticket chopper, etc." Thoreau too worked at odd jobs.

Miller's employment record is taken from the "Autobiographical Note" written in 1939 for *The Cosmological Eye*, the book which introduced him to American readers. That note and the Chronology appended to *The Henry Miller Reader* twenty years later provide the best objective account of Miller's life. Subjective accounts appear all through his writings, but the facts are often romanticized, warped, and otherwise colored for the particular effect he seeks. The "Autobiographical Note" is not only brief and factual; it also provides a sort of *apologia pro vita sua* that helps one to understand the motives behind Miller's life and writings. "My grandfathers came to

America to escape military service. . . . From five to ten were the most important years of my life; I lived in the street and acquired the typical American gangster spirit. . . . The Spanish-American war, which broke out when I was seven, was a big event in my young life; I enjoyed the mob spirit which broke loose and which permitted me to understand at an early age the violence and lawlessness which is so characteristic of America. . . . I had no desire to earn a living, no sense of economy, and no respect for my elders or for laws or institutions. I defied my parents and those about me almost from the time I was able to talk."

Miller's work is full of his boyhood memories of Brooklyn and his later experiences in New York City. Born in the Yorkville section of New York on December 26, 1891, he grew up in Brooklyn, went to school there, and to this day retains much of his Brooklyn accent. As a young man he often crossed Brooklyn Bridge to Manhattan, where his father had a tailor shop. Until 1930 New York was his home. "I am a city man through and through; I hate nature, just as I hate the 'classics.' " Of his early years Miller has written most lyrically in two sections of *Black Spring*, "The Fourteenth Ward" and "The Tailor Shop." The world he depicts is not the "American" New York of Whitman or Edith Wharton, but the immigrant melting pot with its teeming neighborhoods, all redolent of the old country. In this polyglot world Miller learned to speak German before English and grew up with the sound of Yiddish and Polish in his ears. As a boy he ran wild in the streets, while his father moved in a comfortable masculine atmosphere of bars and good eating, with the easy comradeship of actors, salesmen, and other sporting types. In his prime Henry's father appears to have been gregarious, easygoing, and bibulous; later Henry nostalgically envied his father's way of life. Henry's mother, who was

rigidly conventional, seems to have inspired the rebel in him; he never had a kind word to say of her. There was a streak of insanity in the family, amusingly represented in Tante Melia, pathetically in Henry's sister.

The best insight into his family background is provided in "Reunion in Brooklyn," written when Miller returned home after ten years abroad and regarded his family with a cold eye. A marvel of restraint, it nevertheless compels sympathy and horror, as Miller is forced to witness the helplessness of his grotesquely dying father domineered by a compulsive, niggardly wife. The result is a merciless portrayal of American family life with all its monstrous middle-class virtues. The son himself plays his part in this parable of the middle-aged prodigal and feels twinges of bourgeois remorse. Like many artists in America, Miller had to combat not only public opinion but also his own sense of shame, ingrained despite his better judgment, at having failed to earn money. In *Black Spring* Miller writes, "In the past every member of our family did something with his hands. I'm the first idle son of a bitch with a glib tongue and a bad heart." But elsewhere he says there were poets and musicians among his German ancestors.

His formal education ended after high school. He enrolled at City College of New York but, unable to stand the academic routine, only stayed for about two months. Then for a period of ten years or more, he worked at a great variety of jobs, never for any length of time, and drifted across the country and back. During this time he also trained strenuously, both in athletics and music. He writes of velocity exercises at the piano and training for the Olympics—figuratively perhaps, but his furious energy suggests a creative drive frenetically seeking expression. He continued his education on his own, reading, attending lectures, talking with famous or unknown persons. His autobiographical notes are full of momentous encounters, such as: "Met Emma Goldman in San Diego: turning point in life." Or "Met with Robert Hamilton Challacombe of the Theosophical Society, Point Loma, California. Decisive event. Led to meeting with Benjamin Fay Mills, ex-evangelist." But chiefly he read. Voraciously and indiscriminately he absorbed works on a wide range of subjects. And he read with the autodidact's sense of discovery, oblivious to received opinion. The result, recorded in *The Books in My Life*, proves a rather erratic liberal education, with emphasis on Oriental mysticism and adventure fiction. Here Belloc and Madame Blavatsky rub elbows with Nietzsche and Spengler. The last two probably affected his thinking more than any other writers. His first serious effort at writing was an essay on Nietzsche's *Antichrist*. He wrote it on the job, in his father's tailor shop, according to one account, or when he was working for a mail-order house, according to another; in the latter version he was caught by the boss and fired forthwith. Whichever is true, he was obviously more interested in Nietzsche than in business.

In 1920, already a married man and a father, he settled down to a steady job for almost five years. In the best American tradition he began at the bottom, but after a few months' apprenticeship he was at the top, as employment manager of Western Union in New York City. Incredibly enough, he was just the man for that position. The whole story demonstrates Miller's extraordinary ability to charm people with words. With a mixture of brashness and persuasion that any salesman would envy, he demanded an interview with the president of the company, and was promptly hired for a highly responsible position, though he had to serve as a messenger first to get acquainted with the system. So the story goes in *Tropic of Capricorn*, and there is no reason to doubt

it. The man who hired Miller must have sized up his particular gifts, his quick perception, his ability to manage people, his essential toughness. It was a heartbreaking job. Every day he had to interview, hire, and fire messengers, sometimes by the hundreds—a total, he claims, of 100,000 in five years. All forms of human life passed by him every day, mostly the desperate and derelict. They educated him in anguish and cynicism; they made him hardboiled and compassionate. Hence the attitude that pervades his work. If he had any illusions about the system before, he lost them all now. The experience opened his eyes forever. "It was a slaughterhouse, so help me God. The thing was senseless from the bottom up. A waste of men, material and effort. A hideous farce against a backdrop of sweat and misery. . . . The whole system was so rotten, so inhuman, so lousy, so hopelessly corrupt and complicated, that it would have taken a genius to put any sense or order into it, to say nothing of human kindness or consideration." Not only *Tropic of Capricorn* but all of Miller's books are informed by this view.

One day the vice-president of Western Union suggested to Miller that someone should write a book about the messengers. What he had in mind was a Horatio Alger story, but the idea that seized Miller was altogether different. Suddenly he saw the opportunity to vent his fury against the company and the American dream. "I was determined to wipe Horatio Alger out of the North American consciousness." In 1922, he sat down and wrote his first book during a three-week vacation. "Clipped Wings" was the story of twelve Western Union messengers. The manuscript has disappeared, but some idea of its contents can be gathered from *Tropic of Capricorn*, where Miller briefly recapitulates five case histories. The characters are out of Dostoevski, gentle souls, insulted and injured, who run amok or suffer violence;

the stories are full of bitterness and horror, ending in murder or suicide, usually both. Miller confesses that the book was a hopeless failure because he knew nothing about writing and could not cope with such overwhelming material. But it gave him the urge to go on writing.

In 1924 he quit Western Union, resolved never to take another job and determined to become a writer. As a matter of fact he worked again at many jobs, for it took him ten years to get published and he was often hungry. During this time he wrote three novels that have remained in manuscript, "Moloch," "Crazy Cock," and "This Gentile World," in addition to many shorter works. Emulating Whitman he peddled his prose-poems from door to door. By this time he had divorced his first wife and married the femme fatale of his autobiographical works. A taxi dancer with intellectual aspirations, she encouraged him to write and supported him financially. She also deployed her charms in selling his prose-poems, sometimes signed with her name. In 1928 she found the money which permitted them to spend a year in Europe. That trip opened up a new world for Miller. He had been oriented toward European culture as a young man by Emma Goldman, and more recently by his boyhood friend Emil Schnellock, a painter who had spent several years abroad. But he was still a provincial, Europe was still a romantic dream, and he went there as a tourist—in the same frame of mind as most Americans traveling in Europe in the twenties. Two years later he returned there to live. His wife was to join him and did in fact make several brief visits to Paris, but their separation ended in divorce, and for the next fifteen years Miller led the bachelor existence recorded in *Tropic of Cancer* and other books. Miller's autobiographical accounts are full of decisive moments, but unquestionably his return to Paris in 1930

marked the turning point in his life. Only there and then was he able to complete the metamorphosis that would make him a writer. He stayed there until 1939 and might never have left if the war had not forced him to return to America.

It is hard to imagine Miller without Paris. French culture suited him as no other would have done; it liberated him and permeated him, satisfying his psychic and artistic needs. In Paris he wrote his best books and found a publisher willing to take them. Oddly enough, he settled there by chance, or as he would have it, Paris was in his horoscope; he had intended to go to Madrid but ran out of money and never got any farther than Paris. But Paris promptly became his city and his way of life. During his first two years there he lived from hand to mouth, but starving in Paris was incomparably better than starving in New York and provided him with a wealth of new material. He lived largely by his charm. With his faculty for making friends and his great conversational gifts, he soon found fourteen people willing to feed him a meal a week in exchange for his company. Generous himself to a point of prodigality, he never hesitated to accept the generosity of others. After two years, he moved into an apartment with Alfred Perlès, a writer and kindred sprit. For two and a half years they lived together in the ugly proletarian district of Clichy, and they continued the greatest of friends until 1938, when Perlès migrated to London. These were the happiest and most productive years of Miller's life.

In his writings Miller has no doubt exaggerated his sufferings. The real misery was not being published. Yet he could not give up; the demon within him demanded expression. He had brought his latest manuscript with him to Paris, but there again met discouragement. Finally in desperation he decided to write as he pleased—not for the publishers but for himself. Since no one would publish what he wrote anyway, he was free to write in his own fashion. Up to this point his writing had been "literary," that is, derivative. Now he found his own voice. In the fall of his second year in Paris he began to write *Tropic of Cancer*. It was not published until 1934, but Miller was a writer at last.

Miller writes in two main genres. His work is about evenly divided between narrative and expository modes. He is best known for his narrative works, such as the early *Tropics*. Critics have usually treated these books as novels, because Miller's method is that of fiction, but he has always insisted that he is writing autobiography or "autobiographical romances." They might best be described as confessions and the method as picaresque. They are confessions in Rousseau's sense of the word, introspective, autobiographical monologues; like Rousseau, Miller is usually trying to argue a thesis from his personal experience.

The expository writings are harder to classify. They would usually be defined as essays, but they assume a variety of forms: letters, criticism, travel, portraiture, anecdote, reminiscence, opinion. The personal essay admits plenty of latitude, which Miller has taken, incorporating a good deal of narrative technique. The essays represent Miller in his shorter flights and most commonly serve as a vehicle for his ideas, or, rather, opinions. Most of them were originally written for periodicals and later collected for publication in book form. Miller himself has no use for literary genres—or literary criticism for that matter. To him all of his work expresses a man.

The richest period of Miller's writing career is also the most varied. This is the period he spent in Paris and its immediate aftermath. In a volcanic creative outburst, he produced stories, articles, books, at the rate of a volume a year. During this decade he wrote the three picaresque narratives generally regarded as his best and most characteristic works, *Tropic of Cancer*, *Black Spring*, and *Tropic of Capricorn*. He also wrote two books in epistolary form, *Aller Retour New York* and *Hamlet*, the latter in collaboration with Michael Fraenkel. At the same time he worked on a study of D. H. Lawrence; edited a zany little magazine; published books by his friends; wrote several stray pamphlets and enough articles and stories to fill two miscellanies, *Max and the White Phagocytes* and *The Wisdom of the Heart*. Upon his return to New York in 1940 he wrote a manifesto, *The World of Sex*; the two narratives that constitute *Quite Days in Clichy*; and an account of his visit to Greece in 1939, *The Colossus of Maroussi*.

Of all his books *Tropic of Cancer* (1934) gave him the most trouble. Although the manuscript was promptly accepted by the Obelisk Press, its publication was deferred for more than two years. Meanwhile Miller rewrote it three times. Neither his struggle nor the publisher's delay is surprising. Miller had to learn how to write all over again, and Jack Kahane had to calculate the risk of publishing a violently obscene book. He took a copy of the manuscript around to various colleagues in the publishing world to sound out his chances. They were impressed by the book, but felt that it could never be published, even in France, where few people read English and censorship was virtually nonexistent. The book was probably improved by the delay, which kept Miller revising and gave him plenty of opportunity to practice his new mode of expression.

Tropic of Cancer is an account of the adventures and encounters of an American in Paris. Written in the first person and the present tense, it conveys a strong sense of the speaking voice and the continuing moment.

The narrator is named Henry Miller, and the technique is basically interior monologue, reporting successive states of mind and sensation as they occur, with all the fragmentary nature of the true stream of consciousness: a hodge-podge of incidents, memories, hallucinations, sights, ruminations, conversations, nightmares. There are frequent interruptions and shifts, back and forth in time, or altogether out of time into dream and fantasy. The disorder is intentional. Miller wanted "to get off the gold standard of literature," to write as he spoke, and to revise nothing that he had written. Behind his bewildering technique there is some organization, however; the structure is roughly chronological, with distinct episodes succeeding each other and following the calendar from autumn to summer. The book is also divided into chapters, unnumbered and untitled, but each with a theme. Then there is the overriding theme of "cancer and delirium." These organizing principles are not readily apparent; the first impression created by the book is one of chaos, with the first chapter the most chaotic. In fact the uninitiated reader is likely to miss the underlying themes altogether, for what is far more striking at first is Miller's intention to record "all that which is omitted in books." The reaction of many readers is shock; others are unimpressed by Miller's attempt to shock; still others are bored. But those who can accept the obscenity calmly may begin to find meaning behind it.

"The world is a cancer eating itself away." If the whole system is cancerous, even radical surgery is futile. Miller finds cancer in all the vital parts, in religion and art as well as politics and war. The whole modern world is an obscenity, compared to which his obscenity is wholesome. Miller offers no hope, no cure; he is not a reformer. He merely presents a picture of the world as he sees it, full of depravity, disease, filth. Through squalid scenes and characters he presents a repulsive view of humanity. Yet, far from being disgusted himself, he is delighted with squalor; he wallows in the lower depths. His response to cancer and delirium is obscenity and comedy.

The two central chapters, the crudest and funniest in the book, offer perhaps the best examples. One presents Miller's impressions of India through three despicable creatures: his employer (a truly Petronian touch of self-irony!), Mr. Nonentity, with his pearls and his prayers and withered arm clearly representing the wealth of the Indies, its religious mumbo jumbo and its impotence; Kepi, the parasite, lecher, and pimp; and the disciple of Gandhi, forgetting his holy mission in dissipation, and committing a faux pas that outrages the gentility of a brothel. Miller exhibits no veneration for the mystical, mysterious Orient here. On the contrary, he shows all that is venal, contemptible, sordid—and ludicrous. Yet from these three clowns he intuits three marvelous perceptions: a Keatsian vision of India's god-like temple sculptures rising out of this frail flesh; a profound awareness of India's staggering problems and despair at their (American) solution—plumbing, machinery, and efficiency; and finally, in a reverie proceeding from Gandhi to Gautama and Jesus, a devastating recognition of man's dunghill existence. He reaches the rockbottom of disillusionment here, but is emancipated in the process: ". . . suddenly, inspired by the absolute hopelessness of everything, I felt relieved . . . nothing had been destroyed except my illusions. I myself was intact. . . . henceforth I would live as an animal, a beast of prey, a rover, a plunderer. . . . Physically I am alive. Morally I am free."

The next chapter offers a key to much of the sex and obscenity in Miller's writing. By far the longest chapter in *Tropic of Cancer*, it deals with a number of subjects, centered around the amours of Van Norden and Carl, two of Henry Miller's friends. Van Norden is obsessed with sex. It is he and not the author who overuses the four-letter words in his monotonous monologues. Henry Miller as usual is the amused listener and spectator. With a detachment that is downright scientific he watches Van Norden engage in sex with a pitiful hungry prostitute, a mechanical act without meaning: "It's like watching one of those crazy machines which throw the newspaper out, millions and billions and trillions of them with their meaningless headlines. The machine seems more sensible, crazy as it is, and more fascinating to watch, than the human beings and the events which produced it. . . . As long as that spark of passion is missing there is no human significance in the performance." The newspaper is another important symbol in this chapter, bringing together the horrors and inanities of the modern world, but the central conjunction is money and sex. Carl's affair with a rich woman complements Van Norden's bout with the prostitute; the roles are reversed, with Carl selling his services. Miller is sometimes sentimental about prostitutes, but not here. To give oneself for money is not only meaningless but debasing. Miller values passion and despises money. The chapter ends with a rhapsody on the paintings of Matisse, which make human flesh eternally beautiful. Only in the world of art does man escape from money and machinery.

Black Spring, published in 1936, two years after *Tropic of Cancer*, deals with many of the same themes, but in a different mood. "I am Chancre, the crab, which moves sideways and backwards and forwards at will. I move in strange tropics," Miller announces, explaining the connection between this and the earlier book. And the black spring of the title is another metaphor of the world's blight. But he is less fierce now, less hungry, more euphoric. There is less sex and obscenity, less action and

violence. Instead of taking place only in the immediate present, the narrative moves in time and place, from Paris to memories of Brooklyn and New York and on to other planes, to reverie and fantasia. There is more delirium than cancer now, more dream, hallucination, and schizophrenia, as Miller explores different modes and levels of perception. The subject of *Black Spring* is really the imagination in all its forms, especially the creative imagination.

Each of its ten self-contained sections is an exercise in a different medium of art or the imagination, or in several media. "The Angel Is My Watermark!" for instance investigates literary inspiration, the vision of the mad, and watercolor technique. It begins with Miller possessed by "the dictation" that goes on in his head, beyond his control. He can only write down what is being dictated to him until finally it ceases, leaving him exhausted. He then turns to a fascinating book on art and insanity, which prompts him to do a watercolor. The rest of the piece explains how a watercolor happens, through a process as fortuitous as his writing. "When you're an *instinctive* watercolorist everything happens according to God's will."

Another selection ("Into the Night Life . . .") is the scenario of a nightmare. Vividly pictorial, it is like a surrealist film, full of irrational sequences, screaming terrors, Freudian guilt and logic. Like any good nightmare it is experienced: one is there, being pursued, unable to run, locked in, frantically trying to find a way out. The world tilts and the scene shifts constantly in this "Coney Island of the mind," where memories are jumbled together with Gothic visions in a world of crazy symbols that make sense.

Miller has written a great deal about the creative process elsewhere, but never so effectively. *Black Spring* demonstrates the creative imagination at work on all levels. "In ordinary waking life," Miller explains in his surrealistic vocabulary, "the author suffers from normal vision but in the frontispiece he renders himself myopic in order to grasp the immediacy of the dream plasm. By means of the dream technique he peels off the outer layers of his geologic mortality and comes to grips with his true mantic self, a non-stratified area of semi-liquid character. Only the amorphous side of his nature now possesses validity. By submerging the visible I he dives below the threshold of his schizophrenic habit patterns. He swims joyously, ad lib., in the amniotic fluid, one with his amoebic self." Miller believes that writing should be as spontaneous and unconscious as possible. Hence his own writing is full of free association and improvisation. There are passages of automatic writing—cadenzas, he sometimes calls them—when the dictation possesses him. Miller at the typewriter is like a centaur; he becomes one with the machine, and works in furious bursts. The result is a succession of discontinuous virtuoso passages that show where he sat down to write and where he left off.

Stylistically *Black Spring* is a dazzling book, the work of a rampant imagination intoxicated with words. Miller is a poet of reckless abandon, his language exuberant and prodigal, often used for sound rather than meaning. Fond of jargon and parody, he readily spins off into nonsense and jabberwocky. "Jabberwhorl Cronstadt," a verbal caricature of a friend, parodies his multisyllabic pontification and turns it into nonsense. During the course of his conversation, Jabberwhorl grows progressively drunk, and the language reels: " '. . . the great vertiginous vertebration . . . the zoospores and the leucocytes . . . the wamroths and the holenlindens. . . . every one's a poem. The jellyfish is a poem too—the finest kind of poem. You poke him here, you poke him there, he slithers and slathers, he's dithy and clabber-

ous, he has a colon and intestines, he's vermiform and ubisquishous.' "

As that final pun indicates, Jabberwhorl's jellyfish is descended from James Joyce as well as Lewis Carroll. "Jabberwhorl Cronstadt," indeed the whole of *Black Spring*, is full of Joycean passages. Like the great parodist Miller writes not in one style, but in many. Not only is each section of *Black Spring* written in a different style, but individual sections are written in a chameleon style that borrows its constantly changing colors from a dozen sources. Besides Joyce the authors he most frequently resembles are Proust and Whitman. Like the *Tropics*, *Black Spring* is Proustian in its view of coexistent time and place stimulated by memory and the senses; Miller's writing is evocative and nostalgic. His affinity to Whitman is more fundamental, for Whitman contributes to his stance as well as his style. "For me the book is the man," Miller declares, "and my book is the man I am, the confused man, the negligent man, the reckless man, the lusty, obscene, boisterous, thoughtful, scrupulous, lying, diabolically truthful man that I am." Miller's rhetoric is like Whitman's, with long rhythmic lines pulsing along through present participles. His description of the Seine could be scanned as Whitmanesque verse.

. . . this still jet rushing on from out of a million
    billion roots,
this still mirror bearing the clouds along and
    stifling the past,
rushing on and on and on while between the
        mirror
    and the clouds moving transversally
I, a complete corporate entity,
a universe bringing countless centuries to a
    conclusion,
I and this that passes beneath me
and this that floats above me
and all that surges through me . . .

Like Whitman too, Miller is fond of catalogues. *Black Spring* is full of them. One catalogue of American names runs on for two full pages, recapitulating the American scene from American Can to the Banks of the Wabash.

Tropic of Capricorn (1939), the third of Miller's personal narratives, is more strictly autobiographical. Whereas *Tropic of Cancer* portrayed the author-narrator living in the eternal creative present, *Tropic of Capricorn* goes back to the years before he had discovered himself as a writer. In trying to explain how and why he became a writer he reviews more than thirty years of his past experience. He succeeds mainly in conveying his sense of alienation from American life. Capricorn, the sign of the zodiac, symbolizes his destiny and complements the rich symbolism of cancer. For cancer is not only the symbol of disease and corruption, it is also the zodiacal sign of the poet and the versatile, maneuverable crab. "Opposite Cancer in the zodiac (extremes of the Equinox—turning points) is Capricorn," Miller wrote in a letter to Anaïs Nin at the time he was finishing his second *Tropic*, "the house in which I am born, which is religious and represents renaissance in death. Cancer also means for me the disease of civilization, the extreme point of realization along the wrong path—hence the necessity to change one's course and begin all over again." Hence too the dominant theme of resurrection which runs all through the work, in many images of suffering, death, and revival as well as more explicit allusion. Miller is most explicit when he examines his horoscope. Born too late, on December 26 instead of the day before, he was nevertheless "born with a crucifiion complex . . . born a fanatic." He has experienced crucifixion and resurrection in several forms: he has gone "beyond the sense of desperation and futility," beyond tragedy and survived, but transformed; he has gone "through too great love" and been

born again; and though he does not say so explicitly in *Tropic of Capricorn*, it was in his thirty-third year that he quit Western Union in order to be reborn a writer. Such experiences have carried him beyond human suffering to the point of detachment and gaiety. He is a man who has been to the bottom and risen again, purged of his feelings. But his literary model is not so much Dante's *Purgatorio*, which he cites, as *Lazarillo de Tormes*. The character he presents is that of the solitary, self-reliant rogue, at odds with society, improvising his life from day to day, accepting windfalls or hard knocks as they come. The narrative alternates between good luck and bad; the windfalls are usually sexual, the misfortunes his sufferings as an alienated individual. Since his luck is often good, it is hard to take his sufferings too seriously.

The first part of the book is devoted to Miller's experiences with the Cosmodemonic Telegraph Company. The subject gives him such momentum that the writing comes pouring out in a continuous torrential rush for the first fifty pages or so. After that the pace slows down somewhat to a continuous drift from one episode to another. After another fifty pages it has become more ebb and flow, without any discernible direction, carrying the flotsam and jetsam of the past. The monologue is like that of a garrulous old man with his mind out of focus, reminiscing endlessly, running on and on from one anecdote to another and another, interrupting himself, leaving parts unfinished, groping for some significance that was once there. But there are also some brilliant passages, like the long opening section and the famous Rabelaisian idyll in the middle. The critics who praise *Tropic of Capricorn* most highly remember its brilliance and forget the logorrhea.

During his years in Paris Miller wrote, in addition to his more famous narratives, enough expository prose to fill five volumes. His second book to be published, *Aller Retour New York* (1935), is set down in the form of a letter to his friend Alfred Perlès. It is a kind of travel book, begun in New York, where Miller had gone for a visit, continued aboard a Dutch ship, and completed in Paris. The epistolary form allows him ample freedom for description and comment: a picaresque tour of New York City during Prohibition, criticism of the American scene, ridicule of the stolid Dutch, relief upon his return to Paris.

Miller had always been a great letter writer, but this was his longest letter to date. It was soon dwarfed by his correspondence with Michael Fraenkel, begun in 1935, continued for three years, and eventually published as *Hamlet* (1939–43). Fraenkel, who appears in *Tropic of Cancer* as Boris, was a great talker who loved to engage Miller in endless philosophical discussions. They hit upon the scheme of writing out their ideas in letters to each other until they had written a book of exactly one thousand pages. Since they could argue on any topic, they arbitrarily agreed on a badly written work by a celebrity and settled on *Hamlet* in preference to *The Merry Widow*. Perlès, who was supposed to contribute, soon dropped out, unable to keep up the pace. But Miller and Fraenkel were inexhaustible. The correspondence is more like a conversation, or, rather, a debate, with long-winded alternating speeches. Miller's final letter runs to one hundred pages. Shakespeare's *Hamlet*, which was only a pretext, is soon forgotten, as the correspondence rambles in all directions. What gives it drama, as both must have realized, is the conflict between mind and spirit in the two characters: the systematic, cerebral, pessimistic philosopher and the mercurial, visceral, ebullient clown. Miller found the letter a congenial form, a written monologue, running on about the weather, ideas, books, recent experiences,

all loosely linked by the amusing personality of the writer.

In addition to his books of the thirties, Miller wrote a number of miscellaneous pieces, usually for little magazines. A representative sampling is to be found in his first collection, *Max and the White Phagocytes* (1938). Some of the material is familiar from his other books: a denunciation of American life reminiscent of *Aller Retour New York* and four letters from *Hamlet*. There are two narratives written in the vein of *Tropic of Cancer* and *Black Spring*: "Via Dieppe-Newhaven," an amusing account of an abortive trip to England, where Miller was locked up as a suspicious character, and "Max," a character sketch of a Jewish refugee in Paris who is so low on the human scale that he begs from Miller. Written in 1935, "Max" is one of Miller's most perceptive works, a sardonic comment on the Christian treatment of Jews that is prophetic of impending horrors. What Max really begs for is sympathy, understanding, and recognition as a fellow human being. Miller, in an extraordinary mixture of compassion and ruthlessness, dramatizes his own mixed feelings about this grotesque incarnation of all human suffering. Max is at once comical and tragic, ludicrous, pathetic, and contemptible. But *Max and the White Phagocytes* is composed mainly of essays on art, literature, and the films. These present Miller in a new guise, as a critic.

As might be expected, his criticism reflects a good deal on his own work. In an essay on the painter Hans Reichel, "The Cosmological Eye," he admires the mystic perception akin to madness that produces visionary paintings. In "The Eye of Paris" he praises the photography of Brassaï in terms that call to mind his own ways of seeing Paris; most appropriately, Brassaï's wonderful photographs of Paris night life, showing the prostitutes with their doll-like painted faces, were later used to illustrate *Quiet Days in Clichy*. In describing Anaïs Nin's diary, Miller shows how close his own confessions are to that form; his "Scenario," as a prefatory note explains, was inspired by one of her surrealist fantasies. In an essay on the art of the film, especially as practiced by Luis Buñuel, he appreciates a veiw of the world that is his own, both in its values and violence; the nightmare section of *Black Spring*—"Into the Night Life . . ."—resembles nothing so much as a film by Buñuel.

Miller makes an excellent critic of the visual arts. He has the years of appreciation, the understanding of the media, the taste, and the ability to express his vision that make a successful art critic. He is less successful as a literary critic. The two major literary essays in *Max and the White Phagocytes*, both provocative, nevertheless reveal certain limitations. "The Universe of Death" is part of a study of D. H. Lawrence that Miller struggled with for years, but never succeeded in finishing. He has explained that he was too close to Lawrence to see him objectively; the essay reveals other difficulties as well. What was supposed to be the last chapter of a book on Lawrence proves to be an attack on Proust and Joyce. In cursing them Miller seems to forget how close he is to them as a writer; much of his criticism reads like a rabid attack on the filth, stench, and corruption of Henry Miller. Of course Miller feels a far greater affinity for Lawrence; he too believes that writing should come from the solar plexus and not from the head. But the solar plexus is not the best portion of the anatomy for producing literary essays.

"An Open Letter to Surrealists Everywhere," though full of illuminating remarks, first shows up failings that are to characterize much of Miller's later writings: the tendency to harangue, the inability to sustain an argument, the facile generalization, and the free association of opinions. Basically Miller's trouble as

an essayist stems from the fact that he is a man not of ideas but of attitudes. There is nothing wrong with this until he makes the mistake of choosing the wrong medium, using intellectual machinery to convey emotion. Generally he succeeds when he uses the essay for impressionistic description and appreciation, but not when he uses it to exhort or denounce.

Miller has produced four more miscellanies, if we count *The Cosmological Eye* (1939). His first book to be published in the United States, it reprints all but one of the selections from *Max and the White Phagocytes*, three sections of *Black Spring*, and three new pieces. The other three volumes are similar gatherings from various sources, including excerpts from works in progress or works never finished, such as his study of D. H. Lawrence. *The Wisdom of the Heart* (1941) is the best source for his reflections on philosophy and its expression in art, philosophy in a broad sense, embracing psychology and mysticism; the book includes two essays on Balzac, whose illuminism appealed profoundly to Miller. *Sunday after the War* (1944) is noteworthy for its three selections from *Sexus*, then unpublished, and for "Reunion in Brooklyn," that harrowing portrayal of his family, based on his observations after ten years' absence. *Stand Still Like the Hummingbird* (1962) sweeps together a very uneven collection of essays, mostly on literary subjects.

In 1939, after the publication of *Tropic of Capricorn*, Miller decided to take a prolonged vacation. For years his good friend Lawrence Durrell had been inviting him to come to Greece. Miller had resisted the temptation, reluctant.to break his working routine so long as *Tropic of Capricorn* was unfinished, but now he was free. After more than nine years in Paris he wanted to get away for a time and take a new perspective. He had worked hard during those years, he had completed his major projects, and he was ready for a complete change of scene and tempo. With a great sense of freedom and lightness he turned toward the Mediterranean world. A holiday spirit pervades Miller's account of his six months in Greece, *The Colossus of Maroussi* (1941). But his elation is somewhat sobered by the outbreak of war, which eventually forced him to return to America. The book was written in New York during the year following his visit to Greece. The mood of Greece was still upon him, and only intensified by his loathing of America and his feeling of being cut off.

The *Colossus of Maroussi* is one of Miller's finest books. The visit to Greece had been a high moment in his life, deeply affecting him in a number of ways. His account is much more than a travel book, though it is that too, dramatically conveying the spirit of place through the observer's personal intuitions. To Miller Greece was a holy land that aroused all his religious awe. On its bare rock men and gods had struggled and worshiped and left a record that could still be read. Miller's experience of the sacred places of Greece is deliberately unhistorical; what he wanted was not archaeology or history but a feeling of kinship with the men of the past. Significantly he began his trip to Greece by visiting the oldest region in France, the Dordogne Valley, whose caves bore testimony of the aesthetic and religious impulses of Cro-Magnon man. Disheartened by his own time, Miller preferred to take a millennial view of the human race.

Greece not only stirred antediluvial memories, it opened up several new worlds. It was both ancient and modern, with its pastoral landscape and Athens a blaze of electric lights. It was also an earthly Paradise. Always a city dweller, Miller had never before lived among the elements. In Greece the warm sea purged and rejuvenated him; Greece was a land of sun and sky and dazzling light; at night the astrologic world of the stars and planets was close

at hand. But it was the Greeks themselves who most appealed to him. With their spontaneous warmth and their love of talk, they offered the kind of male comradeship he had been looking for all his life. The book is a record of great friendships and casual encounters with ordinary folk, with whom he communicated quite effectively by pantomime. The greatest character of all is his friend Katsimbalis, the colossus of the title, a man who grew larger than life when he talked, who poured enormous dramatic energies into his monologues. "I like the monologue even more than the duet, when it is good," Miller remarks. "It's like watching a man write a book expressly for you: he writes it, reads it aloud, acts it, revises it, savours it, enjoys it, enjoys your enjoyment of it, and then tears it up and throws it to the winds." Occasionally, inspired by Katsimbalis, Miller also performs. In fact, Katsimbalis is simply an alter ego, a man of similar talents, a manic, mythomanic, megalomanic character made in his own image.

Greece also brings out the Romantic enthusiast in Miller. He is in favor of all that is natural, free, and instinctive, unspoiled by civilization. He likes haggling and takes delight in being cheated by transparently wily Greeks. He prefers the slums at its base to the Acropolis itself, the murderer to the corporation executive, shabby old hotels to modern comforts. His antipathies are just as explicit as his sympathies, and his cantankerous crotchets just as Romantic: "I don't like jails, churches, fortresses, palaces, libraries, museums, nor public statues to the dead." In Greece he turns his back on France with its rational, controlled, ordered way of life; in fact he renounces all of Western civilization. And he is most intolerant of the Americanized Greeks he meets everywhere he goes, who appreciate the worst of American materialism and nothing of their own culture. Underlying many of his attitudes is the war, the final proof that the modern world is dehumanized and death-driven.

The same attitudes pervade another travel book, *The Air-Conditioned Nightmare* (1945). When Miller returned from his ten years in Europe he decided to tour the United States and record his impressions as he went. He spent a year zigzagging across the country and back. His account of the journey is as erratic as his route. It would hardly serve as a guide to the United States, but it provides a good index to Miller's opinions. Chiefly he is appalled by his native land. The country is magnificent, but the people are dead, all but the Negroes, Indians, and an occasional nonconformist. The American way of life has created a spiritual and cultural wasteland, with its obsession for objects and money, its modern conveniences, advertising, radio programs, movies, comic strips, battleships, bombs, vitamins, canned foods. "Why is it that in America the great works of art are all Nature's doing? There were the skyscrapers, to be sure, and the dams and bridges and the concrete highways. All utilitarian. Nowhere in America was there anything comparable to the cathedrals of Europe, the temples of Asia and Egypt—enduring monuments created out of faith and love and passion. No exaltation, no fervor, no zeal—except to increase business, facilitate transportation, enlarge the domain of ruthless exploitation."

For all its anathemas, *The Air-Conditioned Nightmare* is a thoroughly American book. Miller rages *because* he is truly American, because he believes in the national ideal with a fundamentalist fervor. The book is very American in flavor. Miller is in love with American names, adept at catching the American idiom, and most in sympathy with the American characters he singles out: cranks and dreamers, shrewd homespun individualists, or just plain folks. The very notion of a transcontinental odyssey is in the best native tradition, with unexpected adventures and excursions off the beaten track a part of the pattern. Miller is a burlesque pioneer, a helplessly inept mechanic at the mercy of glib repairmen and his secondhand Buick; "Automotive Passacaglia" recounts his vicissitudes with that temperamental machine. Poor eyesight makes his journey as hazardous as that of the early settlers, and he captures some of the westering drive in crossing the endless miles of hot, barren landscape—only to find in southern California everything he loathes. His report of that exhausting drive, "From Grand Canyon to Burbank," is immediately followed by an account of his first evening upon arrival, "Soirée in Hollywood," a satire on besotted, aggressive, wealthy Americanism. The shift in tempo, tone, and setting could not be more striking. Taken together, the two recapitulate the western course of empire from the pioneering journey to the corruption of the Promised Land.

Originally Miller planned to write two volumes of *The Air-Conditioned Nightmare*, but like many of his projects, this one had a way of changing as it went along. The second volume, *Remember to Remember* (1947), is a sequel only in the sense that it presents the same man airing similar opinions. Both volumes are miscellaneous collections of sketches. The second is built around persons rather than places, for Miller's travels had ended in 1944, when he settled in Big Sur. Here again, as in the earlier volume, he makes a point of discovering unsung genius and prefers to believe that the genuine artist is always unrecognized. The book is prefaced by a long political sermon on the state of the post-atomic world and contains another three times as long which repeats many of the same views. Henry Miller on war and peace sometimes sounds like Henry

David Thoreau, but often lacks the common sense and is often shrill. The best parts of the book are his reminiscences of France in the title essay; "Astrological Fricassee," another Hollywood party where the conversation brilliantly carries the satire; and "The Staff of Life," a humorous essay on the tasteless, colorless, odorless, soulless white bread that sums up what is wrong with the United States.

Apart from his book on Greece and his two books on America, during the forties Miller devoted himself mostly to his confessions. In 1940 he wrote two short books containing some autobiographical elements, *The World of Sex* and *Quiet Days in Clichy*. In 1941–42 he began work on his long, slightly fictionalized autobiography, *The Rosy Crucifixion*, writing the part that was published as *Sexus* in 1949; he revised *Sexus* several times as he moved from New York to Los Angeles to Big Sur. In 1947 he began writing the second part, *Plexus*. Again there was a considerable delay before publication; *Plexus* first appeared in French in 1952. The third part, *Nexus*, was written some ten years later, only appearing in 1960; at that time it was labeled "Volume I," and Miller still planned to write a second volume. All of these books are more or less obscene and could not be published openly in this country at the time they were written. *The World of Sex* was published in a limited edition in 1940 by Ben Abramson of the Argus Book Shop in Chicago; the others did not appear in American editions until 1965.

Quiet Days in Clichy, as the title suggests, narrates personal experiences of the early thirties when Miller was living in Clichy with his friend Perlès. The material is like that in *Tropic of Cancer*, but the book seems to have been written by a different man. It is good storytelling and realistic reporting, but it has none of the vehemence that made the earlier

book a cry of passionate protest, and none of the "ecstasy," none of the heightened subjective vision that informed the earlier writing. The explanation may lie in the fact that the manuscript disappeared from sight for fifteen years and Miller rewrote it for publication in 1956. In the thirties his writing was always elated, euphoric, airborne; in the fifties, his prose became more pedestrian.

The World of Sex was also rewritten. In 1957, when Olympia Press decided to publish it in Paris, Miller revised the text extensively. The second version adds nothing to the first, and often takes the bite out of incisive passages with fussy alterations. By 1957, Miller was a different man; he had assumed his Big Sur mantle and was addressing an audience. In 1940, he was merely trying to clarify some of his ideas and did not care if no one listened. *The World of Sex* is his *biographia literaria*, a key statement that defines the role of sex in his writings and in his life. Written at midpoint in his career as a kind of postscript to *Tropic of Capricorn*, it serves to explain his purpose in that book and to introduce the other autobiographical volumes that are to follow.

Sexus, *Plexus*, and *Nexus*, taken together, are simply an enormously expanded *Tropic of Capricorn*. All these books deal with Miller's life during the twenties when he was trying to discover himself. This is the central story that he has been trying to tell ever since 1932, when he started writing *Tropic of Capricorn*, the story of his "rosy crucifixion," when he died as an ordinary mortal and was resurrected as a writer. Originally he thought he could explain the miracle in one volume. It took him five or six years to finish *Tropic of Capricorn*, only to discover that the mystery had eluded him. The events he narrated were in some mysterious way deeply significant to him, yet he had not succeeded in explaining the significance even to himself. In the Coda he admits that he has lost the way: "I wander aimlessly, trying to gain a solid, unshakable foothold whence I can command a view of my life, but behind me there lies only a welter of crisscrossed tracks, a groping, confused, encircling, the spasmodic gambit of the chicken whose head has just been lopped off." This statement applies even more to the subsequent volumes. The three parts of *The Rosy Crucifixion* cover the same ground much more exhaustively, yet the point seems to recede farther and farther all the time. The mystery is intertwined somehow with the great love of his life, which coincided with his metamorphosis. Mona or Mara, as she is called, seems to embody the mystery. *Tropic of Capricorn* was dedicated "To Her," though she did not figure much in that book. She is the principal character of the later volumes, but still she remains something of an enigma, mysterious in her origins, elusive and devious in her ways. Somewhat hysterical, apparently a pathological liar, perhaps a Lesbian, she nevertheless continues to fascinate Miller and represents for him the eternal inscrutable feminine. Whatever her character, Mona played a crucial role in Miller's self-realization. She prevailed upon him to quit his job and practically forced him to write. She was also determined that he go to Europe, and, as Miller tells the story in *Nexus*, found a patron who paid her for Miller's writing. The trilogy spans the period between 1923, when he first met her in a dance hall, and 1928, when they were about to sail for Europe.

Miller's method is rather like psychoanalysis. He seems to be putting down everything he can remember about the period, in hopes that some meaning will ultimately emerge from the mass. He claims to be writing according to a plan that was "dictated" to him in 1927, and he hopes to isolate the crucial moments of his life, but the writing gives the impression of having been put down at random, as it occurred to him in reminiscence, and never edited. A great deal of space is given to his early friends, his experiences and conversations with them, largely pointless except that they feel he is destined to become a writer. To him the most significant acquaintances are Russian Jews, who bring to life the world of his idol, Dostoevski, and who exude a rich and ancient culture. Miller wants to become a Jew, wants to escape the respectable, bourgeois, Gentile America of his birth.

As might be expected, the three volumes of the trilogy differ considerably. *Sexus* is the most obscene of all Miller's works, and the sexual episodes, which alternate regularly with neutral passages, often seem gratuitous. The other two volumes contain hardly any obscenity. *Sexus* is also the most disorganized, with constant digressions, reminiscences, and other excursions interrupting the main thread. In *Plexus* and *Nexus* the narrative becomes more factual and straightforward, and as a result offer a clearer explanation of Miller's emergence from his past. The writing also grows progressively easier and more natural. Only *Nexus* deals much with Miller's efforts to write. His chief concern in *Sexus* is fornication, and in *Plexus*, surprisingly, is making money. The whole trilogy reports some unlikely ventures, with Miller running a speakeasy, selling encyclopedias, hitchhiking to Florida to get in on the real estate boom, grave-digging, even psychoanalyzing a psychoanalyst friend. The first two volumes, though redeemed by occasional virtuoso passages, are far too long. Miller as always is good at evoking scenes, the more squalid the better. The most vivid passages in *Sexus* are a description of the East Side ghetto and another of a church in Naples. *Plexus* retails some wonderful dreams and several good stories. But there is a great deal of weary plodding between such passages. *The Rosy*

Crucifixion is four times as long as *Tropic of Capricorn*, with little of the humor, ferocity, or pyrotechnics.

During his years at Big Sur Miller's writing deteriorated, often becoming what he had revolted against in the thirties, "literary" in the bad sense, inflated with subjunctives, rhetorical questions, and exclamations. He lapsed into a fatal facility, writing more and more about less and less, quoting clichés as though they were choice aphorisms. Success did him no good. As his fame increased, all kinds of people came to Big Sur on pilgrimage to visit the Sage, and many more wrote fervent letters. "Henry has as many fans as a movie star," Alfred Perlès noted in *My Friend, Henry Miller*, finished at Big Sur. As he became a famous personage, Miller made the mistake of taking himself too seriously. His later essays are solemn and pontifical, as he addresses the faithful.

The Books in My Life (1952) is embarrassingly egocentric. Written at the request of his friend Lawrence Clark Powell, the librarian who supplied him with books, it is not the interesting record of an autodidact's education it could have been, but a laundry list. Miller considers everything that happens to him momentous, not only in the past but even in the future. In addition to an appendix listing the hundred books that influenced him most there is one listing the books he still intends to read. In short, he has lost his sense of humor and his sense of balance. There is too much Rider Haggard here, not enough Lao-tse. The book is mainly about the late-nineteenth-century romances he read as a boy and does not come to grips with the writers who influenced him as a man. Of course he has every reason to include his boyhood reading, but as he rereads that Victorian prose, he falls under its spell and lapses into the same stilted, pseudo-archaic language which no man ever spoke, the same melodramatic and platitudinous sentiments.

"Ah, there's the miracle! Whoso has the power to affect us more and more deeply each time we read him is indeed a master, no matter what his name, rank or status be." Written immediately after *Plexus*, *The Books in My Life* betrays what is wrong with *The Rosy Crucifixion*: Miller's model is Rider Haggard's *She*.

Miller's book about Rimbaud tells more about that writer's effect on him, though Rimbaud was not a formative influence like Dostoevski or Whitman. Miller became absorbed in Rimbaud long after he was an established writer himself. In 1943 he undertook to render *A Season in Hell* into a comparable American idiom, but he finally gave up the attempt and wrote instead two long essays on Rimbaud. These first appeared in the New Directions anthologies of 1946 and 1949 and were eventually published as a book, *The Time of the Assassins* (1956). Despite its subtitle, this is not really a study of Rimbaud, but a collection of rambling reflections on his life and character, in which Miller finds astonishing parallels to his own. Though rather megalomaniacal, the book does show a relation between the two—not in their destinies, as Miller likes to imagine, but in their Romantic agonizing. The book also shows Miller's affinity for other anguished spirits of the late nineteenth century and places him squarely in the late Romantic tradition. The Coda tells more in a few pages than all the discursive ruminations of *The Books in My Life*.

Big Sur and the Oranges of Hieronymus Bosch (1957) presents Miller's meditations from his own particular Walden. The idyllic setting of Big Sur quite naturally brought to mind Thoreau, the American frontier, and Utopian communities. But by the time he wrote about it, Miller's life there was anything but serene. Shortly after moving to Big Sur, he had married for the third time, but this marriage had broken up and his wife had left him with two small children to look after. In 1953 he married for the fourth time and was relieved of some of his child-rearing duties. But every year brought more admirers to Big Sur. Harried by visitors, correspondence, and household chores, he could scarcely find time to write. As a result his writing is more distracted than ever. "Where was I?" he keeps asking himself, trying to pick up the thread of an essay. Quite rightly he calls the main body of the book "A Potpourri." He ranges here from amusing storytelling to long-winded preaching, demonstrating once again that he is best as a storyteller, worst when philosophizing. The best section of the book is the self-contained narrative that was published separately the previous year as *A Devil in Paradise*. It tells the story of his acquaintance with Conrad Moricand, an astrologer Miller had known in Paris and made the mistake of inviting to Big Sur, only to be imposed on outrageously.

Miller's life in Big Sur finally became too complicated, and in 1960 he left. In a sense he came back down to earth, but he has written little since. For a year he traveled about Europe, lionized by writers and publishers. Then he retired to southern California, where he has found a relatively peaceful life and devoted himself to an art he has always loved, painting watercolors. He has often said in his later years that when he had finished his life's work, *The Rosy Crucifixion*, he would turn to nonsense and slapstick; and at the age of seventy he finished his first play, *Just Wild about Harry* (1963), a mixture of vaudeville, melodrama, and musical comedy, filled with popular songs from his entire lifetime. Apart from this, all of his writing published in recent years belongs to the past. Several selections of his work have appeared, of which by far the most comprehensive is *The Henry Miller Reader*, edited by Lawrence Durrell with Miller's running com-

mentary. Several volumes of letters have been published, the most noteworthy being his lively correspondence with Durrell from 1935 to 1959 and his letters to Anaïs Nin, which tell much about his most creative years, from 1931 to 1946.

For a time, with the publication of his banned books, Miller was more notorious than ever. But since the sexual emancipation of the 1960's he has come to be regarded as a pioneer rather than a pornographer.

Gradually a calmer view of his work is emerging, not only in the public mind but among literary historians. His final place has yet to be determined, but he is being generally recognized as one of the important writers of his time, one of the most expressive of the thirties, and certainly the best surrealist writer America has produced. And while it is hard to imagine that the *Tropics* will ever be taught in the schools, several of his books should occupy a lasting place in American literature.

Selected Bibliography

The bibliography of Henry Miller is somewhat confused by expatriate publication, amateur enterprises, and other unusual circumstances. Two of his books were first published in translation. Some works appeared independently and were later incorporated into others; for example, *A Devil in Paradise* (1956) became part of *Big Sur and the Oranges of Hieronymus Bosch* (1957). A number of essays were first published in pamphlet form and later collected in miscellanies, such as *Money and How It Gets That Way* (1938), anthologized many years later in *Stand Still Like the Hummingbird* (1962). Some pamphlets reprint excerpts from already published works; some are merely advertising brochures. To clarify the record, the list below gives only the first edition in English and only pamphlets containing material which does not appear elsewhere.

WORKS OF HENRY MILLER

Tropic of Cancer. Paris: Obelisk Press, 1934.

What Are You Going to Do about Alf? Paris: Printed at author's expense, 1935.

Aller Retour New York. Paris: Obelisk Press, 1935.

Black Spring. Paris: Obelisk Press, 1936.

Max and the White Phagocytes. Paris: Obelisk Press, 1938.

Tropic of Capricorn. Paris: Obelisk Press, 1939.

Hamlet (with Michael Fraenkel). Vol. I, Santurce, Puerto Rico: Carrefour, 1939. Vol. II, New York: Carrefour, 1941. Vol. I complete, New York: Carrefour, 1943.

The Cosmological Eye. New York: New Directions, 1939.

The World of Sex. [Chicago: Ben Abramson, Argus Book Shop, 1940.]

The Colossus of Maroussi. San Francisco: Colt Press, 1941.

The Wisdom of the Heart. New York: New Directions, 1941.

Sunday after the War. New York: New Directions, 1944.

Semblance of a Devoted Past. Berkeley, Calif.: Bern Porter, 1944.

The Plight of the Creative Artist in the United States of America. Houlton, Me.: Bern Porter, 1944.

Echolalia. Berkeley, Calif.: Bern Porter, 1945.

Henry Miller Miscellanea. San Mateo, Calif.: Bern Porter, 1945.

Why Abstract? (with Hilaire Hiller and William Saroyan). New York: New Directions, 1945.

The Air-Conditioned Nightmare. New York: New Directions, 1945.

Maurizius Forever. San Francisco: Colt Press, 1946.

Remember to Remember. New York: New Directions, 1947.

The Smile at the Foot of the Ladder. New York: Duell, Sloan and Pearce, 1948.

Sexus (Book One of *The Rosy Crucifixion*). Paris: Obelisk Press, 1949.

The Waters Reglitterized. San Jose, Calif.: John Kidis, 1950.

The Books in My Life. New York: New Directions, 1952.

Plexus (Book Two of *The Rosy Crucifixion*). Paris: Olympia Press, 1953.

Quiet Days in Clichy. Paris: Olympia Press, 1956.

The Time of the Assassins: A Study of Rimbaud. New York: New Directions, 1956.

Big Sur and the Oranges of Hieronymus Bosch. New York: New Directions, 1957.

The Red Notebook. Highlands, N.C.: Jonathan Williams, 1958.

Reunion in Barcelona. Northwood, England: Scorpion Press, 1959.

Nexus (Book Three of *The Rosy Crusifixion*). Paris: Obelisk Press, 1960.

To Paint Is to Love Again. Alhambra, Calif.: Cambria Books, 1960.

Watercolors, Drawings, and His Essay "The Angel Is My Watermark." New York: Abrams, 1962.

Stand Still Like the Hummingbird. New York: New Directions, 1962.

Just Wild about Harry. New York: New Directions, 1963.

Greece (with drawings by Anne Poor). New York: Viking Press, 1964.

WRITINGS EDITED BY OTHERS

Nights of Love and Laughter, with an introduction by Kenneth Rexroth. New York: Signet, 1955.

The Intimate Henry Miller, with an introduction by Lawrence Clark Powell. New York: Signet, 1959.

The Henry Miller Reader, edited by Lawrence Durrell. New York: New Directions, 1959.

Lawrence Durrell and Henry Miller: A Private Correspondence, edited by George Wickes. New York: Dutton, 1963.

Henry Miller on Writing, edited by Thomas H. Moore. New York: New Directions, 1964.

Henry Miller, Letters to Anaïs Nin, edited by Gunther Stuhlmann. New York: Putnam, 1965.

Writer and Critic: A Correspondence with Henry Miller, edited by William A. Gordon. Baton Rouge: Louisiana State University Press, 1968.

Collector's Quest: The Correspondence of Henry Miller and J. Rives Childs, 1947–1965, edited by Richard Clement Wood. Charlottesville: University Press of Virginia, 1968.

BIBLIOGRAPHIES

Moore, Thomas H. *Bibliography of Henry Miller*. Minneapolis: Henry Miller Literary Society, 1961.

Renken, Maxine. *A Bibliography of Henry Miller, 1945–1961*. Denver: Alan Swallow, 1962.

Riley, Esta Lou. *Henry Miller, an Informal Bibliography, 1924–1960*. Hays, Kansas: Fort Hays Kansas State College, 1961.

CRITICAL AND
BIOGRAPHICAL STUDIES

Baxter, Annette. *Henry Miller, Expatriate*. Pittsburgh: University of Pittsburgh Press, 1961.

Durrell, Lawrence, and Alfred Perlès. *Art and Outrage*. London: Putnam, 1959.

Gordon, William A. *The Mind and Art of Henry Miller*. Baton Rouge: Louisiana State University Press, 1967.

Hassan, Ihab. *The Literature of Silence: Henry Miller and Samuel Beckett*. New York: Knopf, 1968.

Hutchison, E. R. *Tropic of Cancer on Trial: A Case History of Censorship*. New York: Grove Press, 1968.

Mailer, Norman. *The Prisoner of Sex*. Boston: Little, Brown, 1971.

Millett, Kate. *Sexual Politics*. Garden City, N.Y.: Doubleday, 1970.

Nelson, Jane A. *Form and Image in the Fiction of Henry Miller*. Detroit: Wayne State University Press, 1970.

Nin, Anaïs. *The Diary of Anaïs Nin, 1931–1934*, edited by Gunther Stuhlmann. New York: Swallow Press and Harcourt, Brace & World 1966.

————. *The Diary of Anaïs Nin, 1934–1939*, edited by Gunther Stuhlmann. New York: Swallow Press and Harcourt, Brace & World, 1967.

Perlès, Alfred. *My Friend, Henry Miller*. London: Neville Spearman, 1955.

Rembar, Charles. *The End of Obscenity: The Trials of Lady Chatterley, Tropic of Cancer, and Fanny Hill*. New York: Random House, 1968.

Wickes, George. *Americans in Paris*. New York: Paris Review Editions (Doubleday), 1969.

————, ed. *Henry Miller and the Critics*. Carbondale, Ill.: Southern Illinois University Press, 1963.

Widmer, Kingsley. *Henry Miller*. New York: Twayne, 1963.

Writers at Work: The Paris Review Interviews, Second Series. New York: Viking Press, 1963.

—————*GEORGE WICKES*

Marianne Moore

1887-1972

WE KNOW this poet by her voice, by her "astonishing invention in a single mode," by her delicate, taxing technique; we know her for the "relentless accuracy" of her eye.

This is Marianne Moore, ironist, moralist, fantasist.

She was born in 1887 in St. Louis, Missouri, and has written of herself that she is a Presbyterian and was brought up in the home of her grandfather, the Reverend John R. Warner, who was for twenty-seven years the pastor of Kirkwood Presbyterian Church in St. Louis, that her brother was a chaplain in the navy for forty and more years, and that the books to which she has had access have been, on the whole, serious.

Of her father, John Milton Moore, she has told us little. It is known that he left his family when his daughter was an infant. To her mother, Mary Warner Moore, she paid significant tribute in a postscript to the *Selected Poems*: "In my immediate family there is one 'who thinks in a particular way'; and I should like to add that where there is an effect of thought or pith in these pages, the thinking and often the actual phrases are hers."

In 1894 the family moved to Carlisle, Pennsylvania. It was at Metzger Institute in that town that she was educated and at Bryn Mawr, from which she graduated in 1909. The next year she studied at the Carlisle Commercial College and from 1911 to 1915 was in charge of the commercial department of the United States Indian School at Carlisle. If it remains a curiosity that she taught such subjects as typing and bookkeeping to young Indians it is less surprising, in view of her late pronounced interest in baseball and her early flair for tennis playing, that she coached the boys in field sports. In 1911 she spent a summer in England and France, where, in Paris, she went to every museum but two. In 1918 she moved to New York, living on St. Luke's Place, teaching first at a private school. From 1921 to 1925 she was an assistant at the Hudson Park branch of the New York Public Library. Some critics have made something of this (part-time) library work, suggesting that her years of easy accessibility to so many card catalogues and pamphlets gave her the clue to her unique method of happening on a poem. But 'from Miss Moore's account she was more engaged in reviewing "silent-movie fiction" than in working behind the stacks with well-wormed collections of odd learning, and it would seem that her bent for collecting rare data and, taking "a wing here" and "a leg there," fitting something of them into poems was sufficiently native to her without the experience at the neighborhood library.

Her verse first appeared in *The Egoist,* an English periodical, in *Poetry,* and in Alfred Kreymborg's *Others* in 1915, and later she began to attend those small gatherings held at Kreymborg's apartment in Greenwich Village for such young experimenting poets as Wallace Stevens and William Carlos Williams. Although H.D. had been her classmate at Bryn Mawr, neither knew of the other's "interest in writing"; but in 1921 it was H.D. and Bryher (Winifred Ellerman, then Mrs. Robert McAlmon) who published through the Egoist Press, without the author's knowledge, *Poems,* a collection of twenty-four that had appeared in English and American magazines.

Ezra Pound had already spoken of her work and Mina Loy's as a kind of "dance of the intelligence" (*logopoeia*) and possessed of an "arid clarity" (*Little Review,* 1918), and in 1923 when a pamphlet of her poems, *Marriage,* was published in the United States and in England, T. S. Eliot wrote: "I can only think of five contemporary poets—English, Irish, French and German—whose works excite me as much [as] or more than Miss Moore's."

By 1920 she was beginning to publish in the *Dial,* and in 1925 she received its award for "distinguished service to American letters" for *Observations,* her first book to be published in this country. In the same year she became acting editor of the *Dial* and remained with it until 1929 when it expired. *Selected Poems* appeared in 1935 with an introduction by Eliot, famous for its pronunciamento: "My conviction, for what it is worth, has remained unchanged for the last fourteen years: that Miss Moore's poems form part of the small body of durable poetry written in our time."

Miss Moore has been brilliantly served from the beginning by the most astute of critics and the most perceptive of poets. If Pound and Eliot took up her cause, a poet-critic like Yvor Winters furthered it, and it remains for R. P. Blackmur and Morton Dauwen Zabel to have compounded penetrating estimates of her work. Of a later generation, Randall Jarrell, Lloyd Frankenberg, and Vivienne Koch have been brilliant and dedicated. She has not suffered from neglect or misunderstanding, and though her work went against the main current and tradition of (English) poetry, she was not scouted for it. Can we say that she was fortunate in being with *Zeitgeist* rather than against it, or out of it? She has been compared with Emily Dickinson more than once and is it a proof of "progress" or was it a mere lucky accident that she was not penalized for her magnificent originality as Emily was?

In the fifties Miss Moore received from officialdom the recognition that poets, critics, and readers had given her for many years, her *Collected Poems* (1951) receiving the Bollingen and Pulitzer prizes and the National Book Award. In 1954 that long labor, her translation of the *Fables* of La Fontaine, appeared and in 1955 *Predilections,* a collection of her reviews and essays. She became a member of the National Institute of Arts and Letters in 1947 and of the American Academy in 1955.

"But we prove, we do not explain our birth," she wrote in "The Monkey Puzzle," and if this does not apply as sharply to life itself nevertheless let the poems lead the way.

Like William Carlos Williams she wanted, when young, to be a painter. But then she also thought of studying medicine and found the biology courses exhilarating. "Precision, economy of statement, logic employed to ends that are disinterested, drawing and identifying, liberate—at least have some bearing on—the imagination, it seems to me," she has said in an interview with Donald Hall in the *Paris Review.* We think we can see the bearing it has had. Might we not attribute to her what she did to Henry James: "a rapture of observation"? For who has held up to inspection more "skeined stained veined variety"? But this fascination with every shade and tone of the "minute particulars" was only one element of many in *Observations*.

Of *Observations* (1924) one might say: it is first and last a voice. The voice of sparkling talk and sometimes very lofty talk, glittering with authority. It has dismissed poetic diction, indeed is rigorous in its exclusion of the traditional or the romantic sensuous word, phrase, and implication. It works in a new area of language and meanings because it has new insights to bring to subjects not before then quite approximated by poetry. It is experimental and/or revolutionary because it is excluding the magical, the lyrical, the incantatory, and the musical; nature and the seasons, the moon, old Floridas of the imagination, the street scene and the fire sale. Bringing a new diction to another kind of "subject matter," it employed the cadences of prose in a rhythm based on speech. But whose speech? If at moments one might think of Congreve, at others of Henry James, it is essentially her uniquely mother-English own, running with a rapid, finely nerved energy. Held tautly to the line articulation, when so finely intermeshed, is meant, like a dance, to last just so long and not a second longer.

There are highly visual poems such as "The Fish," "A Grave"; there are epigrammatic poems out to discriminate, not describe; there is "Roses Only," a model of ambiguity, where a virtue is made of writing on two subjects as if they were one and of saying one thing while meaning another. But this is true of many poems.

The contours of these poems are sharp and fine-edged—Blake's "hard and wiry lines of rectitude"—like many of the objects described: "the pierced iron shadows of the cedars," "sculptured scimitars." Her liking for the "strict proportions" of the hard and definite equals her care for symmetries of pattern and such mathematical niceties as in "The Fish," where the number of syllables per line in each stanza is 1/3/8/1/6/9 and where the portioning out of syllables works for a fine pointing up by sound, sight, and meaning. That is, the word weights are so balanced and nicely adjusted that (typographically aiding, too, the deaf) the force has to fall where it does on the telling when not the killing word—i.e., the word that drives all the point of the poem home to the heart. We hear it in

> the chasm side is
> dead.

Sound also tends to the crisp and quick, energetic consonants rather than lolling alliterations: "Bundles of lances all alike, partly hid by emeralds from Persia," or "Greece with its goat and its gourds."

With a concern to narrow limits, to reduce the means of expression to what is indispensable, she understands, like certain painters, the necessity of not going beyond the line. Thus the firmness of the contours, the self-containment of the poem, which often goes by a crooked mile to its usually ringing, often epigrammatic close.

If many of the essential characteristics of her style meet the little laws laid down by the Imagists—the absence of introspective self, the concentration upon the object-subject, conciseness, a rhythm "which corresponds exactly to the emotion or shade of emotion"—can we say that Imagism was her distant parent? There are the early brief "To a Chameleon," "An Egyptian Pulled Glass Bottle in the Shape of a Fish," "A Talisman." Like most Imagist poems they are static, concentrated on rendering the one instant of the object as clearly and firmly as possible. But "A Talisman" (1912), selected by Eliot as being the only poem to suggest a slight influence of H.D. rhymes and is formally developed, unlike most Imagist poems, and is conventional beside "To a Chameleon," which is already more free and idiosyncratic and already (1916) taking the syllable as the measure rather than the foot, indicating that if she had learned from the Imagists how to approach the object with an intense scrutiny she had learned almost as soon how to take over a method for strictly her own purposes.

And if *precision* had become the watchword of the Imagists—T. E. Hulme, first Imagist and "father" of them all, is said to have introduced the word to modern literary criticism in his essay "Romanticism and Classicism" and it it known that Pound as early as 1912 was calling for poetry to be as precise as prose—these poems had it, and not only of the "minute discriminations" (Blake) but of the very articulation of movement.

Precision in this case also goes with wit and certain moral and intellectual convictions. Hers is no poetry of emotional conflict or discord or disillusionment. If in "Bowls" we have an implicit-explicit criticism of the blind worship of the present and in other poems satiric rejections of popular prejudices ("The vestibule to experience is not to/be exalted into epic grandeur"), there is little notice, head-on, of the disorders of the present. The open social scene was not her province. We do not have the flavors of the age in terms of rancid butter or oyster shells. (Her objectified world is in this sense interior.) Two lines in "New York" might sound a theme: "one must stand outside and laugh/since to go in is to be lost." If these lines suggest that laughter can be a weapon of self-preservation, do they not also suggest a recognition of differences about which nothing can be done? It is essential not to go in and be lost.

But in the decade of *The Waste Land* she partakes of no cynical or despairing view. From the first her highly defined world seems based on a clear-cut recognition of ethical values she considers still extant though many would have it proved that such values have been vitally assailed if not destroyed. It might be said that this poet, devoted to the paradox, strikes one as a figure of paradox too: with her clear moral and intellectual convictions not just exactly of the times, but with her forged weapons of technique the pure exemplar of the modernist. But what is a satirist (when she is) who doesn't have strong moral convictions? One is tempted to add that in her case morality seems a facet of sensibility.

One could remark also of her philosophic calm, that strong sense of being in touch with the *adagia,* with a resolute sense of wisdom about life, that it is what has been remarked of the Chinese, "a necessary armor to protect the excessive susceptibility to emotion."

Thus *Observations* brought to verse a new subject matter and to the line a new rhythm, the rhythm of prose in all its succinctness, by this latter completing the circle Flaubert had begun in 1855 when he wrote (in a letter) that he wished to bring the rhythms of poetry to prose. If this book has been equaled by her later books it has never been surpassed and exists a twentieth-century monument like *Harmonium, A Draft of XXX Cantos,* and *The Waste Land.*

Like Williams and Cummings she suspected the comma (Apollinaire was the first to do so) and thought it "wholesome" not to capitalize the beginning of lines, disliked the connective (but so did Emily Dickinson) in the interests of intensity. "Titles are chaff," she said in an early poem and circumvented the plague of having to title poems by making the first line serve as title. To such an instance of inventiveness can be added others: notes—listed at the back of each book—and, in the case of *Observations,* even an index appended!

If the notes can't be considered as what's left over of what couldn't be put into the poem, neither can they be considered as necessary for the deeper understanding of the poem. They frequently give us delightful information on, say, the price of unicorn horns, but primarily they serve as a reading list, giving us the authors of those phrases that as specimens of wit have been rescued for us. In this way Miss Moore is a kind of curator of verities and "briefs, abstracts and chronicles" of past literatures. "Acknowledgments seem only honest," said Miss Moore.

This inlaying of quotations with the black hooks that so nicely help to set a brilliance apart has been compared with the collage technique of Braque, Picasso, and Kurt Schwitters. Miss Moore first introduced it in 1915. And her innovation has since become a part of literary tradition.

Her approach to rhyme was also radical. In about half of the poems in *Observations* she avoids it altogether. In "The Fish," "Black Earth," "To Statecraft Embalmed," to name a few, the pattern is formal and the rhyme scheme elaborate. It is rarely insistent, however. Most of the time the rhyme endings are all but submarine in effect because the meaning of the line runs on to the next line and no pause is wanted by the reader, or are so light in sound and echoed so faintly—"Ming" and "something"—that they're almost not heard. (It might be noted that Hopkins wanted his verses to be recited as running on without pause, the rhymes occurring in their midst like a phonetic accident —which is what Miss Moore wanted and got.)

Also wanting a distribution of emphasis more light and even, as in French, she took the syllable as the measure rather than the foot, working always for the effect of unstressed or only faint and lightly stressed rhythms. This was, more or less, an extension of the prose effect. (In three poems puns are suggested on

"feet" and we know that in 1918 Miss Moore wrote an article on the unaccented syllable in *The Egoist*. She also wrote in *The Oxford Anthology of American Literature*, Volume II: "Regarding the stanza as a unit, rather than the line, I sometimes divide a word at the end of a line, relying on a general straightforwardness of treatment to counteract the mannered effect."

Almost from the beginning she proceeds by an express method of her own dialectic. The absurd will rest side by side with the exotic, the commonplace by the exquisite. "There is no progress without contrairies," said Blake and many of her poems seem to have their source in this dictum. They seem to move by the pull of contrasts and by that tension set up. The incongruities and the discrepancies, the contradictions and oppositions—these are what she harnesses and keeps either in tandem or under one yoke.

Juxtaposition of incongruities is of the essence. But not in the ways of other modernists. She is not working with a sensuous language for violently mysterious effects, or juxtaposing words for the sake of shocks of collision. Rather, her language is strictly tempered and clear, almost classical in its moderation and lack of rhetorical splurge. Verb is firmly connected to noun, there is no straining of language within the sentence unit for a tremor of associations setting up strange trains of disrelations. But she did put these clear lines together in such a way that the firm orderly thought or epigramlike description is set next to another in a manner not to have been foreseen. The surprise, the shock, exists in between the spaces that have been leaped over by a swift imagination. Transitions thus seem more like transpositions, a strange flowering of truth upon fact.

If the drama of many a poem lies in the strife of its particulars, we have the same acting against and reacting in the pull of the learned or scientific word against the idiomatic or concrete word: "the elephants with their fog-colored skin/and strictly practical appendages," for example, where "fog-colored" works against the mockery of the abstract words applied to the simple trunk. And words like "occipital" and "phenomena" or such phrases as "cycloid inclusiveness," "fractional magnificence," "hairy carnivora," and "staple ingredients" frequently serve ironic purposes. Then there is the august decorum of "he superintended the demolition of his image in the water by the wind," and "the pulse of its once vivid sovereignty," whose magnificence of phrasing has something of the strange beauty of that poet of the sentence, Sir Thomas Browne. This Latinate-laconic imperious elegance is to be found less in later books. But formal balances and syntactical parallelisms persist. "He is swifter than a horse; he has a foot hard/as a hoof; the leopard/is not more suspicious" (reminding us of Habakkuk) or "the/king gave his name to them and he was named/for them."

In "Injudicious Gardening" (the title itself a small joke) it's as if this poet mocks herself, turning against the musical inflections of the first stanza with the slightly freezing abstractness of the second:

If yellow betokens infidelity,
    I am an infidel
        I could not bear a yellow rose ill will
        Because books said that yellow boded ill,
    White promised well;

However, your particular possession—
    The sense of privacy
        In what you did—deflects from your
            estate
        Offending eyes, and will not tolerate
    Effrontery.

The colder movement of the Latinate words drawn up to their full height and marched out

to rebuke is felt in "Roses Only." Its effect of hectoring hauteur is dependent in part on the formal propriety of its diction and an elaborate sentence structure in which clause succeeds clause with all but martial progress to achieve the permanent brilliance of

> Guarding the
> infinitesimal pieces of your mind, compelling
>   audience to
> the remark that is better to be forgotten than to
>   be remembered too violently,
> your thorns are the best part of you.

Both early and late Miss Moore has been a curator of that sacred cow, the statistic. In "Virginia Britannia" the hedge-sparrow "wakes up seven minutes sooner than the lark"; Lapland reindeer in "Rigorists" "run eleven miles in fifty minutes." But it is only in "New York" that the use of a business barbarism—"estimated in raw meat and berries, we could feed the universe"—crisply points up the grand uselessness of such an estimate. In this mimicking of the language of business and other clichés she escapes being flat by being so succinctly sharp. To say it another way, she was one of the first of the poets to take rather intractable antipoetic material, the business phrase, the statistic, the cliché, and by her arrangement of it in relation to other phrases, bend it to her own purposes—i.e., the poetry of the unpoetic. An example is her use of the banking phrase in "Roses Only": "You do not seem to realize that beauty is a liability rather than/an asset." The competency of that has entered the tone of many a poet.

"Marriage," that exercise in paradox, that divertimento of speculation on the "interesting impossibility," is a particularly striking example of the swift transition and the alternating between contraries. William Carlos Williams called it "an anthology of transits." One could also call it a tour de force of digressions, a masterpiece of sudden departures. Plying between homage paid to and mockery made of "This institution,/perhaps one should say enterprise," we see that if it is the public nature of it that arouses deft skepticism it is its private significance that is given such tribute as "This fire-gilt steel/alive with goldenness." But since marriage is both eminently private and public, she can be but in the position of taking away with one hand what she gives with the other. To the subject of love itself—not specifically amorous love but " 'the illusion of a fire/effectual to extinguish fire' " which makes marriage seem " 'a very trivial object indeed' "—she brings nothing less than splendor in two passages, in one of which she puts Adam and Eve into an Eden that has all the quaintness of a primitive woodcut. "Plagued by the nightingale . . . dazzled by the apple." But nothing in this poem stands still. It is premised on the necessity of swiftness and we are no sooner in Eden than out of it, in some drawing room with the "shed snakeskin of politeness," just as we are never far from such sharp turnings of the tables as " 'For love/that will gaze an eagle blind . . . from forty-five to seventy/is the best age.' " Its method of progression is not only fleet but abrupt, connectives being dropped or leaped over. Darts are released at women's prejudices against men and men's against women; there are submerged hints of feminist argument at work but these too are tossed off. Guarded, covering up its tracks almost as soon at is makes them, it is a kind of masked dance on the excruciating point of how to be free though in bondage, and at the close we learn that "liberty and union" are perhaps possible only for those with a "simplicity of temper"—if the summary is more important than the *aperçus* dropped along the way.

Does it seem to go by fits and starts? But how many overlappings there are along the way. What matters is the sequence of airy notions, what matters is that the wit not be grounded by the heaviness that usually goes with too much expansion. What matters is the impact which the successive words make on us. "Marriage" is a rapidly moving train that once you are on it carries you from glittering landing stage to stage, none of which you are really allowed to get off at, or stay solemnly with. In grasping for analogies, one thinks of Chinese painting which stretches out the viewpoint along the entire panorama so that mountains and waterfalls all appear to be moving toward us, although if such paintings avoid leading the eye into a single depth, this scarcely applies to the poem's action. Word playing on brilliant surfaces, it alludes as much to depths behind depths. One is tempted to quote Henry James: "To be explicit was to betray divinations."

In "The Past Is the Present" she has not only fallen upon her form early, she is also defining for us, although she is speaking about Hebrew poetry, what it is that she is doing and going to be doing. Or so, at least, we can interpret it in view of all the poems that followed. Moreover she announces early (the poem was first printed in *Others* in 1915) one of her touchstones. And this is no less than the Bible. (We see by the notes in *Observations* how many phrases from George Adam Smith's *The Expositor's Bible*, Richard Baxter's *The Saints' Everlasting Rest*, A. R. Gordon's *The Poets of the Old Testament*, how many phrases too from ministers' sermons, are inlaid into poems. Is it incidental or not that in a foreword to the *Marianne Moore Reader*, 1961, she should write: "My favorite poem? asked not too aggressively—perhaps recalling that Henry James could not name his 'favorite letter of the alphabet or wave of the sea.' The Book of Job, I have sometimes thought. . . .") If we remember that early period when the Imagists had already set verse free and damned rhyme, we can think of this poem as being the last word in an intense argument held in some book-lined room:

If eternal action is effete
   and rhyme is outmoded,
      I shall revert to you
   Habakkuk, as on a recent occasion I was
        goaded
        into doing by XY, who was speaking
          of unrhymed verse.
This man said—I think that I repeat
   his identical words:
      'Hebrew poetry is
  prose with a sort of heightened conscious-
        ness.' Ecstasy affords
      the occasion and expediency deter-
        mines the form.

If external action (plot—in literature? resolution—in life) is effete and *if* rhyme is outmoded (assumptions of the unseen argufier made to seem both absurd and pretentious), if the new broom of the present wants to sweep half the past away, she will revert to Habakkuk. Nothing later than that minor prophet of the Bible, and nothing more fashionable. Is the goading XY the same "this man" who delivers the energizing definition of Hebrew poetry that can and will be applied to her own work? "Prose with a sort of heightened consciousness"? The Reverend Edwin H. Kellogg is credited in the notes with "Hebrew poetry is prose" but to this has been added the very important "with a sort of heightened consciousness." The heightening of consciousness is all and an answer in the argument. There is verse and verse. Bad free verse is simply prose without that heightening. Moreover she herself is using rhyme in this poem, unlike old Habakkuk. And in the last line she kicks away from the contradictions inherent in the situation to hand us with abrupt decisiveness the keys to the secret of the creative instant. "Ecstasy affords

the occasion and expediency determines the form." "Expediency" is the shock word here following so close on "ecstasy." You might say that it disinfects a word so much distrusted in this century. (Much later, in "The Hero," we have: "looking/upon a fellow creature's error with the feelings of a mother—a/woman or a cat" where "cat" takes the curse off "mother," let alone "woman.") Nevertheless, ecstasy it is. One does what one can with the lightening flash. How to seize it except by the most expedient method at hand? Form, it would seem, is determined by the raptus. "Spirit creates form" ("Roses Only"). Is form to be equated with the shell that the mollusk makes, his being's expediency too, the artist's form as organic to himself as the shell is to the snail? Miss Moore has defined it for us: "I feel that the form is the outward equivalent of a determining inner conviction, and that the rhythm is the person."

The force and fire of Biblical language is also a subject of "Novices" but before we arrive at it an artillery of wit is brought to bear on a kind of overrefined and underfed modern literary mind "confusing the issue," "blind to the right word, deaf to satire." The poem glitters with so much summed-up intensity that its energy feels like—is it Irish? fury? A fury of byplay, at least. "Acquiring at thirty what at sixty they will be trying to forget . . . they write the sort of thing that would in their judgment interest a lady; / curious to know if we do not adore each letter of the alphabet that goes to make a word of it." The raillery continues: "according to the Act of Congress, the sworn statement of the treasurer and all the rest of it," which is surely calculated to reduce the opponent to a recognition of his own asininity. Other sidewise allusions, metaphorical extensions such as in the lines beginning "Dracontine cockatrices" and those on the "lucid movements of the royal yacht," contribute to the argument more elaborately, the latter lines preparing for the tremendous onslaught of the powerful and dazzling conclusion. And certainly the finical quibblings, the "willowy wit" of those, one suspects, all-too-precious novices, who are bored incidentally by "the stuffy remarks of the Hebrews," get what they deserve as the "unforced passion of the Hebrew language" is hurled at them. What begins in witty ire ends in a grandeur not far from the Miltonic sublime as two authorities meet—the sea and Biblical language.

> Obscured by 'fathomless suggestions of colour',
> by incessantly panting lines of green, white with concussion,
> in this drama of water against rocks—this 'ocean of hurrying consonants'
> with its 'great livid stains like long slabs of green marble',
> its 'flashing lances of perpendicular lightning' and 'molten fires swallowed up',
> 'with foam on its barriers',
> 'crashing itself out in one long hiss of spray'.

The action of language is developed in terms of the action of the waters, and all in a blaze of glory and claps upon claps of energy. The method is to rush you into splendor and leave you with dazzle. "People's Surroundings" ends with such a triumphant progress, "The Monkeys" in a burst almost as breathtaking.

> —strict with tension, malignant
> in its power over us and deeper
> than the sea when it proffers flattery in exchange for hemp,
> rye, flax, horses, platinum, timber, and fur.

This roll call of nouns in the last line is a choice example of Moorish sound at its finest and it is an effort to remember that they are but shipper's items transmuted into splendor.

The unexpected contiguity of flax with horses and timber, so hard a substance, with rich fur—thus this poem that begins with the drolleries of the zoo moves into high comedy when a cat makes a speech worthy of any autocrat defending the art of the few against the Dunciad many. His astringent remarks on those protesting that they can't understand the new and difficult in art (Brancusi, Picasso?—this poem was first published in 1917) has a further refinement of irony, for the cat scorns these objects of his wit for suspecting art to be just what it really is: "strict with tension, malignant in its power over us and deeper than the sea. . . ."

"The Labours of Hercules" undergoes a similar mutation, commencing with the absurd and by a series of progressions closing on the note of a moral rhetoric which is to have an echo later in "In Distrust of Merits" and " 'Keeping Their World Large.' " Formally it is a series of propositions couched in the infinitive, "To popularize the mule," etc., and with the same kind of symmetrical nicety closes with another kind of grammatical repetition:

> 'that the Negro is not brutal,
> that the Jew is not greedy,
> that the Oriental is not immoral,
> that the German is not a Hun.'

Shifting after its humorous opening to the literary-critical note, "to teach the bard with too elastic a selectiveness/that one detects creative power by its capacity to conquer one's detachment," it arrives after two extensions or witty divagations at

> to prove to the high priests of caste
> that snobbishness is a stupidity,
> the best side out, of age-old toadyism,
> kissing the feet of the man above,
> kicking the face of the man below

which in its directness of putting the quality of

bootlicking under the most searching light has an effect of almost shockingly savage insight. Beginning with humor, ending with the moral imperative, this poem has, like "The Monkeys" and "Novices," its pattern of progress until, the reversal achieved, we are in another field of thought.

"Those Various Scalpels" not so much progresses as changes key, if one may revert to the musical analogy, and in the phrase "rustling in the storm/of conventional opinion" drives with ruthless swiftness to the heart of the matter: all this wrought artfulness of appearance, this Renaissance-jewel-encrusted and farthingaled semblance of the utmost of aristocratic vanity—for what? Nothing more than *conventional opinion*? We are prepared and not prepared for this swift reversal by the ringing insistence of the repetitions "your hair," "your eyes," "your raised hand" which, for all the tribute that so much intent attention implies, warn us by their pain-suggesting images of "eyes, flowers of ice/and/snow sown by tearing winds on the cordage of disabled ships" and "your cheeks, those rosettes/of blood on the stone floors of French châteaux" with their hint of shadowy plots and sudden assassinations. That this epitome of sterile cruelty whose arrows are lances (nicely hid by jewels), whose weapons are surgical instruments, that this idol of a frigid self-involvement whose beauty can give nothing but pain, is rebuked with a brilliance surpassing the brilliances that described her is a spectacular achievement.

> But
> why dissect destiny with instruments which
> are more highly specialized than the tissues
> of destiny itself?

Otherwise one sees in this poem how the visual is tempered by the abstract, how repetition of phrasal structure is employed for an imposing rhetorical effect, how the symmetrical stanzas (two of nine lines and three of eight lines) have in each stanza a one-syllable first line, a last line of four, three, or two syllables, a third line usually of twelve or fourteen syllables, and how the whole effect of shape, of repetition, emphasizes the formal splendor of the phrasing. The effect makes for a sense of volume, of receding planes and sudden perspectives as in architecture, or in baroque music.

Miss Moore created a new form (to fit her manner) primarily by means of a new rhythm, a new way of organizing details and the insights that spring from them. But there is no critical terminology for this new form and one has to fall back on old ways of classifying. Call "A Grave" a soliloquy if you like, and "New York" too. Or call "Roses Only," that lecture to a flower who is also, it would seem, a woman, a kind of version of the moral essay. Call "People's Surroundings," that study of the kind of places people make for themselves, and "Sea Unicorns and Land Unicorns," that fanciful treatise on the power of the mind to make immoderate legends and to reason almost anything into existence—call them both descriptive essays. But the terms "moral essay" and "descriptive essay" are grab-bag terms and don't really apply. The culmination, in any case, of this kind of free-ranging discursive structure for which there is no term is to be found in "An Octopus," that stupendous aggregate of minerals, animals, weathers, while "Sea Unicorns and Land Unicorns" anticipates the more circuitous organization of Miss Moore's later work. In the latter, her manner with the marvel, the fantastical, is to be methodical, as if giving us information in part. This treatment of the fabulous as if it were quite as probable as the so-called fact wonderfully emphasizes its rare lusters. The poem rises and falls, alternating between passages like " 'cobwebs, and knotts, and mulberries' " and "Britannia's sea unicorn with its rebellious child." In a differing fashion for purposes of humor and for the subtle sake of contrast there will be amidst the rare knowledges and textures the opposing note of " 'in politics, in trade, law sport, religion' "—a broad sober worldly tone which counteracts the elegant quaintness and faery richness of " 'myrtle rods, and shafts of bay.' " And this dynamics of some high pitch of verbal excitement frequently succeeded by a calm or ironic or dryly prosaic passage is to be found in many poems.

(This poem is also an instance of the way she makes a new unity out of parts of old learnings and culled phrases. In later work, from "The Jerboa" to "Elephants," one sees even more complex examples of this drawing upon all kinds of sources to create a new imaginative reality. In "The Plumet Basilisk" Miss Moore weds the legendary, the naturalistic, and history with a scarcely restrained sumptuousness to present to us the half-miraculous attributes of a very real creature. Chinese legends relate him to the great dragons of the East; myths of "the chieftain with gold body" and the jade, the amethysts, and the pearls of half an Incan empire are gathered in to gild his little gorgeousness. A love of the marvelous is combined with factual notations (obtained from the *Illustrated London News* and other sources) to re-create a beast whose very being seems to be one more proof of Nature's pure fantasy. Has zoology truly such instances? Yes. And in "Nine Nectarines" there is the haunting bit of knowledge on the "red-cheeked peach" that according to ancient Chinese thought "cannot aid the dead,/but eaten in time prevents death." Declared in passing, that knowledge is there to give us the tang, the taste of incredible theory.)

"People's Surroundings" is notably a shuttling between the opposites, a play on that favorite eighteenth-century device, the antithesis,

as it tacks here and there, creating rich effects that it contradicts a few lines later, pitting splendors against absurdities, the utilitarian against the artful, movement being one of its powers. Stylistically the poem alternates between the crisp speech rhythms setting forth the plain or efficient and two grand flights, the one beginning with Bluebeard's tower and the closing section, which is a very Whitman catalogue, if you will (one line beautifully echoes him: "in magnificent places, clean and decent"), a very cavalry charge, a pure poetry of namings:

captains of armies, cooks, carpenters,
cutlers, gamesters, surgeons and armourers,
lapidaries, silkmen, glovers, fiddlers and ballad-
    singers . . .

The rich appreciation of the ridiculous in this poem, from the "vast indestructible necropolis" of office furniture to "the municipal bat-roost of mosquito warfare," crops up again in "England" in the greatly gay originality of "plain American which cats and dogs can read!"

And when there is not the satirical that crisps the line, there is its easier twin, humor. If the irony preserves (like amber), the humor sweetens. In later work humor becomes allied with fantasy. In *Observations* it frequently seems a kind of irrepressible outburst—from the fir trees, "austere specimens of our American royal families," to "the spiked hand/that has an affection for one/and proves it to the bone" (though the first is a joke and the latter a pun).

At one or not with this sense of humor is the apt harnessing of the likely with the unlikely, even the "antipoetic." Thus the "industrious" waterfall, the not lulling but plaguing nightingale, young bird voices compared to the intermittent "squeak/of broken carriage-springs," this latter a refreshing accuracy that produces in the reader that nervous response which to some extent resembles what is provoked by the experience itself. Not only has an unhackneyed equivalent been found, but a new association has widened the field of reference, modified it too. For it is the squeak of *carriage-springs*, the something slightly antiquated.

And isn't humor that relishes the incongruity and notices the irrelevancy a facet of candor and honesty, and a part of a desire to see the whole and not to exclude the just incidentally thorny or what cannot be classified, the contradictory? Surely in league with it seems the appreciation for "naturalness" whether it is that of the hippopotamus or Peter the cat or the "mere childish attempt . . . to make a pup/ eat his meat from the plate."

This taste for the spontaneous, the "beautiful element of unreason," "a tireless wolf," "a wild horse taking a roll," might be contrasted to the connoisseur's zest for "the hair-seal Persian sheen," old Waterford glass, or for what, when it is rare, could not be more rare, when it is jeweled, the most jeweled, when it is blue, a dragonfly blue. The larger, looser, bolder touch—"The tug . . . dipping and pushing, the bell striking as it comes," and "when the wind is from the east,/the smell is of apples, of hay"—is about as strong an element in her work as these curio-collector notations are.

In nine poems Miss Moore is both poet and critic, writing incidentally about literature in general or poetry in particular. Was she also telling her readers just what it was that she herself had set out to do? Jean-Paul Sartre has said that there is no new technique without a metaphysic. And because her approach to the poem was so radically different, did she have her interests in setting forth as plainly as a subtle mind might her own intentions? One might make a case for this in looking at the celebrated "Poetry" with its shocker of a first

line: "I, too, dislike it: there are things that are important beyond all this fiddle." It is an early poem (1919). It is also a difficult poem. Seemingly straightforward, it is oblique when you look into it and complex in terms of what's left out as well as what's put in. And with its iconoclastic and reformist frankness it is upsetting a good many applecarts.

The tone of the opening is cutting. "Reading it, however, with a perfect contempt for it." Why should poetry have to be read with a perfect contempt? And whose poetry? All poetry? Then it turns out that it is not all poetry that is being talked about, that it is possibly just the poetry of her contemporaries—or even not all her contemporaries. It is the poetry of "half poets" and when she dislikes their "fiddle" it is when it is "so derivative as to become unintelligible." What, then, is being argued for? The opposite of the derivative—the original, the honest, the "genuine." A new touchstone is being set up. This touchstone is not the old and famous *beautiful and true*. It is the *genuine*. There is more to be said about the *genuine*. "Hands that can grasp, eyes/that can dilate, hair that can rise,/if it must, these things"—signs of the emotional animal—"are important not because a/high-sounding interpretation can be put upon them but because they are/useful." The *genuine* is, then, the *useful*, the functional. But since there are a great many uses of the word "useful" and we are most acquainted with it in its dreariest, most utilitarian sense, the word has a double edge. *Useful*. Isn't the poet just possibly taunting the aesthetes by choosing a word with such hateful, factual, hard edges? A word that can also be called an epitome of understatement— as if to say the sky is *useful*, or rain, the sun, or for that matter poetry. There is another challenging section. We learn of what is more important than "all this fiddle." It is "the bat/

holding on upside down . . . elephants pushing, a wild horse taking a roll . . . the base/ball fan, the statistician . . . and 'business documents and/school-books.' "

A prodigious activity somehow gets set up between these assorted items and by their selection Miss Moore tells us as exactly as analogy can do "what is important." Not only the star, the rose, the sea, but matters and subjects not already made acceptable by literary tradition. "One must make a distinction/ however: when dragged into prominence by half poets, the result is not poetry."

A fresh subject matter is not enough. In order to make it seem true poets must be "literalists of the imagination." A poet must imagine so exactly and astutely that, in the words of Morton Dauwen Zabel, he can "see the visible at the focus of intelligence where sight and concept coincide and where it becomes transformed into the pure and total realism of ideas."

Furthermore, without the "imaginary gardens (with real toads in them)," which is a symbol for the aesthetic order, the arrangement of these "phenomena" in a modifying structure and texture, the wolf or the whatnot, will only seem "dragged in." It will not have been assimilated, it will acquire no new reality, and it will have lost its original own. There will be no poem, in short. Only a half poem.

(Miss Moore's heightening of the phrase of William Butler Yeats on Blake—"He was a too literal realist of the imagination"—is famous. By portmanteau effect she rendered a daring new meaning. Like many of her finest phrases it combines opposites as compactly as possible. Such paradoxes are her elixirs.)

When this poem appeared in the second edition (1925) of *Observations* it was quite another animal, for it was stripped from its original thirty lines (in *Poems*) to thirteen lines,

stripped, too, of its complexities. The bat, etc., are still there, but they are "pleasing" rather than "important," and the main emphasis is upon clarity.

> but when they have been fashioned
> into that which is unknowable,
> we are not entertained.
> It may be said for all of us
> that we do not admire what we cannot
>   understand:
> enigmas are not poetry.

In *Selected Poems* it returns to the original version save for the omission of three phrases, and has not been altered since.

If Miss Moore was making a strong stand for intelligibility and clarity in this version of "Poetry" she criticizes the "unknowable" in other poems. "In the Days of Prismatic Colour" there are the lines

> complexity is not a crime but carry
>   it to the point of murki-
>   ness and nothing is plain

and a variation in "Picking and Choosing":

>   Words are constructive
> when they are true; the opaque allusion—
>   the simulated flight
> upward—accomplishes nothing.

"When I Buy Pictures" concludes:

It comes to this: of whatever sort it is,
it must be 'lit with piercing glances into the
    life of things';
it must acknowledge the spiritual forces which
    have made it.

In other poems there are other critical dicta as triumphantly perceptive.

In his introduction to the *Selected Poems* T. S. Eliot classified the poetry of Marianne Moore as descriptive rather than lyrical or dramatic. But to what new uses description is put! And is such a poem as "New York" simply descriptive? Is it not a turning and unfurling upon a given point: the commercial statistic that New York (in 1921) was the center of the wholesale fur trade? A bizarre enough "fact" in view of all else that the city was the center of—from which the poem leaps straight off into "starred with tepees of ermine and peopled with foxes,/the long guard-hairs waving two inches beyond the body of the pelt." This latter line of a strange half-humorous beauty, a detail (of furrier's knowledge) within a detail, is complemented by an even more rarefied detail on deerskins and these two by the aside, later on, that quotes the follied vanity of a Gonzaga duchess: " 'if the fur is not finer than such as one sees others wear,/one would rather be without it.' "

If these extensions of texture (in more ways than one) act as brief rests or pauses, the poem otherwise moves swiftly in a continuousness of visual action which allows for no intrusion of what would thin out its density. Thus by no other transition than the phrase "It is a far cry" we are with " 'the queen full of jewels' " and "the beau with the muff" and the contrasting of two pasts with some only implied hint that English palefaces bought furs from redskins at that fur-trading center, the conjunction of the Monongahela and the Allegheny. For this is not the vital point: the vital point is that "scholastic philosophy of the wilderness/ to combat which one must stand outside and laugh/since to go in is to be lost." If the subjective depth of this sets up many questioning echoes, we have at least one answer. "It is not the dime-novel exterior,/Niagara Falls, the calico horses and the war-canoe." It is not even "the plunder." It is, in Henry James's phrase, " 'accessibility to experience.' " *Accessibility to experience*—a prescription for

the artist! The poem juggles with the past, the present, Europe, America, outlandish and wonderful Indian names until the grand light of James's phrase gives one answer too to staying outside. *Accessibility* suggests that one may go inside, even be lost, agreeably.

Of these specificities which are not cloyed by generalizations, one remembers that "to explain is to deform." In this poem of as much wit as description, passage must be rapid. Another poet might have lingered with the beauties of deerskins and wilting eagle's-down, in which case the point of the wit might have been dulled. And if we are with the furs one moment and the " 'queen full of jewels' " the next, it is up to us to consider the impact of the contrast between two pasts, both of which are our heritage.

Of the maintenance of such tension Miss Moore has this to say in an essay called "Feeling and Precision," first published in the *Sewanee Review* in 1944: ". . . expanded explanation tends to spoil the lion's leap—an awkwardness which is surely brought home to one in conversation. . . . Yet the lion's leap would be mitigated almost to harmlessness if the lion were clawless, so precision is both *impact* and exactitude, as with surgery; and also in music, the conductor's signal . . . which 'begins far back of the beat, so that you don't see when the down beat comes. To have started such a long distance ahead makes it possible to be exact. Whereas you can't be exact by being restrained.' "

One is exact just because one is so aware of so many shades of meaning or of "ivory white, snow white, oyster white and six others." And in the same way that the conductor's beat must begin far back of the downbeat, the poem acquires its power by virtue of the distance it has to travel before the poet's perceptions can encompass the range of his feeling.

Again, "The Monkey Puzzle" encloses its theme so thickly in arresting particulars that it is tempting to be adrift with them, charmed by the strange freshness, simply content with the outraying allusions to the Foo dog and Flaubert's Carthage. Its subject is, however, a rare pine tree, "a complicated starkness," a "this [that] is beauty" growing in a fastness and like Gray's desert flower, unseen, unknown, "in which society's not knowing is colossal,/the lion's ferocious chrysanthemum head seeming kind by comparison." The force of this astounding comparison (and the oxymoron that makes the lion a little less fearful but far more beautiful) serves only to intensify the plight of this rare tree that "knows" (trees have prescience, cats talk like artists, elephants philosophize, and jaybirds don't know Greek) " 'it is better to be lonely than unhappy.' " Its isolation as profound as any early American genius's, what can it do but endure its own singularity in its own irreparable solitude? This is to bring perhaps too much to the surface what is implied and embodied in a visual intricacy not unlike the tree's own thicket.

This concreteness can sometimes make a poem seem almost unpossessable on first reading because the meanings are so realized in the specificities themselves. These lines from "The Jerboa" might serve to illustrate: "Those who tended flower/beds and stables were like the king's cane in the/form of a hand." It is for the sake of compression and the desire not to obstruct the movement of the poem that the king's attitude toward the poor is personified. But the sting of the observation may not come at once: that the king depends on the poor as he would on a cane, that they are simply commodities to him, to be useful, as a cane is. The visual strangeness of a cane "in the form of a hand" may so divert the reader that he forgets to consider its significance. Sometimes too

the argument of a poem may be submerged, only to emerge openly, at certain moments. The poem moves in its maze of associations, the disconnected connections magnetized in a manner we cannot see on first acquaintance. And always Miss Moore states but doesn't "explain." Or lines may be of such an epigrammatic rigor that the very parts seem like wholes, or poems within poems. This alone (from "Snakes, Mongooses"), "one is compelled to look at it as at the shadows of the alps/imprisoning in their folds like flies in amber, the rhythms of the skating rink," is but one example of those perceptions compact as definitions, brimming with the energy of having pinned it down and gotten it right. Charles Lamb has spoken of the obscurity of too much meaning. Intense clarity can also blind, like the sun at noon.

But as to all this and as to those poems where the clarity of the image and the density of allusion make for that fascinating combination of what is both lucid and ambiguous at the same time, Miss Moore has, as usual, the last word: "A few unexplained difficult things —they seem to be the life-blood of variety."

As for that magnitude of particularities, "An Octopus," though it does not necessarily divert "one from what was originally one's object" (to quote from "England"), it does delay one along the way as description becomes a kind of plot and its own drama. All is in action, from the old glacier itself that "hovers forward 'spider fashion/on its arms' " to its fir trees with "their dark energy of life," its animals, seen in some characteristic behavior and on the move, even its stationary flowers active in their complications of colors and designs.

In its serial construction there is a regular recurrence of outriding phrases that allow for sidelights, tangential glances sometimes pert in tone such as the line on the icy glacier itself, "made of glass that will bend—a much needed invention," or lines that permit us to consider the sheer deadness of Park Portfolio language when it is legal or such purely "poetic" extensions (of the ponies with glass eyes) as "brought up on frosty grass and flowers/and rapid draughts of ice-water." Not to forget the mountain guide in his "two pairs of trousers" reminding us of Thoreau's Irishman who wore three. The aside, the brief digression, the Jamesian parenthesis might be called a part of the Moore method and are to be found in many poems. They serve, as they do in "An Octopus," to make for a kind of brio of the irrelevantly relevant and for the effect that R. P. Blackmur phrased so acutely: "husky with unexhausted detail . . . containing inexhaustibly the inexplicable."

In the last section, about the Greeks, which also gives another character to the glacier,

Relentless accuracy is the nature of this
    octopus
with its capacity for fact

(as if it were a terribilita of an artist), one sees how the tempo at which one must read is dictated. The passage begins slightly after "The Greeks liked smoothness"

ascribing what we clumsily call happiness,
to 'an accident or a quality,
a spiritual substance, or the soul itself,
an act, a disposition, or a habit,
or a habit infused, to which the soul has been
    persuaded,
or something distinct from a habit, a power—'
such power as Adam had and we are still
    devoid of.

As if Experience were correcting Theory, this kind of Schoolman's ethereal speculation in finely defining phrase upon phrase, one qualifying the other and all kept in musical suspension, is given this forceful, brusque stop, a stop even to our hopes.

In "Camellia Sabina" there is the same kind of rapid moving out onto a single hard flashing line after the airy humors and mercurial play of the "upland country mouse," that "Prince of Tails," dashing around the "*concours hippique*" of the grape-arbor "in a flurry/of eels, scallops, serpents/and other shadows . . . The wine-cellar? No/It accomplishes nothing and makes the/soul heavy"—the abruptness of this and the swift change of rhythm severely preparing us for the renunciatory "The gleaning is more than the vintage."

From the *Selected Poems* (1935) on we see more "inscape," hear more music, meet more fantasy and far more animals. Stanzaic structure is more elaborate together with a new complexity of detail, the line is more musically nuanced, with more verbal interplay and more sub-patterns of internal rhymings and end rhymings. The ironist and the satirist has been succeeded by the fantasist-humorist, and the hard-driving electrical speed of the free-verse line (as exemplified by the ruthless, relentless progression of a poem like "A Grave") by more light and subtle rhythms. Seven of the eight new poems of *Selected Poems* are seven new departures. One is not like the other. In each a new version of a form is explored. In "The Frigate Pelican" one can fancy that form is in part imitative, so deftly are the rhythms of flight suggested by certain lines and by wordplays; there is a gliding from one stanza to another, like the feints of bird-winging. The thickly woven texture of "The Plumet Basilisk," that essay on dragonhood, is so closely qualified that it suggests the very density of tropical vegetation. Of later poems "Virginia Britannia" (*What Are Years*, 1941) takes description to a new height. As one of her many place poems, it is of flowers, birds, and history so interwoven that its long lines seem to move like feelers, reaching out and advancing on all sides at once, the theme of colonizing arrogance (as symbolized by the strangler figs) growing out of the very elements of the scene and at one with it. In these instances detail is given a new kind of day and with it, necessarily, a slowing of tempo, or delayings and detainings by Hopkinsesque word clusters. Such word clusters do what Hulme in 1915 or so asked the new poetry to do ("to make you continuously see a physical thing, to prevent you from gliding through an abstract process") and aid in compacting multiple parts swiftly for the sake of impact.

The high interest in design and pattern, first seen in "The Fish" (1918), is carried on in "Nine Nectarines," in which precision of sight —even a subdividing of it—is heard in the intricately echoing fineness of sound. And "The Jerboa" with its neatness and firmness achieves an especial kind of visual and aural beauty by virtue of its flexibly confining pattern, the six-line stanza with a rhyme scheme that exerts the nicest control over the faint chimings. Working with highly selected clarities of dapple dog-cats and small eagles, it evolves (in the first section) into a kind of tale-telling, a rigorously simplified recounting of the habits and tastes of a people forgotten save by historians and encyclopods. They are "violently remembered" in this poem:

> Lords and ladies put goose-grease
> paint in round bone boxes with pivoting
> lid incised with the duck-wing

> or reverted duck-
> head

The acuteness of the visual achievement might be exemplified with the power of

> the wild ostrich herd
> with hard feet and bird

necks rearing back in the
dust like a serpent preparing to strike,

and delicacy of sound by "They looked on as theirs/impallas and onigers."

The concern to strike for the resonances of color that we see in the "coachwheel yellow" of "Critics and Connoisseurs"—which gives us at least two sensations at once, the pleasure of the coachwheel and the shade of its color—is to be found in "duck-egg greens, and egg-plant blues" (note the nice balancing of consonants) or "calla or petunia/white." Instead of a metaphor we are given a further qualification. Such precisions both intensify the experience and keep it under close control as the measurements and temperatures of what's seen are exactly taken. Her "pride, like the enchanter's,/is in care, not madness." With the lines

> in the stiff-leafed tree's blue-
> pink dregs-of-wine pyramids
> of mathematic
> circularity

she circumvents the near-impossibility of translating so exotically natural an impression by pinning down, first of all, the mixture of hue and likening it to something definite but unexpected—yes, and not wine but dregs-of-wine —and next by comparing its form to the at first concrete *pyramids* and then abstract *circularity*. But the eye that can see "boats/at sea progress white and rigid as if in a groove" has long since found the secret way of getting at the truth of the pure first shock of visual impression. Is it a "science of the eye" or the free daring of imagination that brings opposites together that had never met before?

Held up to inspection with the same bold fidelity are her animals, who, if they are frequently parts of a web of allusions that ally them to more philosophies than they could dream of, are always known first and last to us by their beautiful *thisness* of claws, dapples, quills, delineated with the vital accuracy of a Bewick, the English engraver who cared just as much for the originality of the particulars. We see them not only in their fine suits of fur and feather, we see them also in the fitness and niceness of those "skills" by which they earn their living, defend themselves, and keep up their populations. We see them as craftsmen and we see them as artists too. The frigate pelican hides (as "impassioned Handel") "in the height and in the majestic/ display of his art," the jerboa's leaps "should be set/to the flageolet," the "wasp-nest flaws" on the paper nautilus are compared to "the lines in the mane of a Parthenon horse." And sometimes they are compared to works of art or artists. The pangolin, "Leonardo's indubitable son" (in the *What Are Years* version), is "compact like the furled/fringed frill/on the hat brim of Gargallo's hollow iron head of a/ matador."

Gide in *Travels in the Congo* wrote of his rare tamed antelope: "I must study Dindiki's ethics and aesthetics, his peculiar manner of moving and defending and protecting himself. Every animal has succeeded in finding out his own particular manner, outside of which there seems to be no salvation for him." It is the beast's particular manner that Marianne Moore has found. The style of the poet—style, "that specialisation of sensibility"—has met the "style" of the animal. Her celebrated objectivity exemplifies that detachment that the West Wind symbolizes in "Half Deity." If it is his delighted disinterest that spurs the butterfly into really becoming a half deity, that same detachment in the artist permits the object, the beast, to be seen for itself, brought into existence or a second existence. Cézanne said: "The landscape is reflected in me and I am its consciousness." When the plumet basilisk is in danger and all his forces leap into play, when he is that "nervous naked sword on little feet," when he has the black eyes of a "molested bird" "with look of whetted fierceness/in what is merely/breathing and recoiling from the hand," we can only feel that the poet has entered into the blood and breath of the beast, transmitting its very reality into our hands, and that observation has become a passion.

Thus her "studies" are always dramas. Each animal poem begins at the point of an action. It's night and the pangolin is setting forth or the frigate pelican has just robbed another bird of its fish, all in midair. We have no stuffed animals. She does not, as Audubon did, paint her birds when they're dead. But she is no "externalist." "The power of the visible/ is the invisible." Thus the jerboa of the "Chippendale" claws, described as if some Supreme Cabinetmaker had thought him up, is no "conqueror"; he is "freeborn," "has happiness" in the abundance of all that he needs which is almost nothing, not even water, and becomes the occasion for a secret discussion on the powers of a being to live in an energy of delight, in spontaneous accord with his portion of the universe. And in "The Pangolin" three refrains of Shakespearean munificence and hymnlike sobriety work against the descriptive weave. As in "The Frigate Pelican" there is the sudden outbreak of the personal voice—*"Festina lente. Be gay/civilly? How so?"*—in the midst of this improvisation on a bird's flight, so this personal-impersonal refrain is set against the pangolin's "exhausting trips" until at the close, our cousinship with this " 'Fearful yet to be feared' "animal so insinuatingly established (as it was in "Peter," who is "one of those who do not regard/the published fact as a surrender"), we see ourselves and him in a universal context.

The prey of fear, he, always
curtailed, extinguished, thwarted by the
dusk,
work partly done,
says to the alternating blaze,
'Again the sun!
anew each day; and new and new and
new,
that comes into and steadies my soul.'

Danger is three-fourths of an animal's life and its every element; these poems don't let us forget it. For the plumet basilisk it is only nightfall that protects him from men who can kill him. The ostrich has circumvented extinction by his solicitude for his young; the butterfly is pursued by a child, the young birds by a cat; the devilfish must zealously guard her eggs. What thorns of a rose are "proof" against "the predatory hand"? "All are/naked, none is safe." And if "Hercules, bitten/by a crab loyal to the hydra,/was hindered to succeed," there are those who "have lived and lived on every kind of shortage," not unlike the jerboa.

We come into the themes of armor and unarmedness and self-protectiveness, to humility "His shield," to the pangolin again, the "frictionless creep of a thing/made graceful by adversities, con/versities," to the not aggressive, tentative snail whose "contractility" of horns "is a virtue as modesty is a virtue." In "The Fish" the "defant edifice" with "marks of abuse" upon it "has proved that it can live/on what can not revive/its youth. The sea grows old in it." And one can add "resistance with bent head, like foxtail/millet's" and "tough-grained animals as have . . . earned that fruit of their ability to endure blows," or "that which it is impossible to force, it is impossible to hinder" (as true of poetry as of this vital vegetable, the carrot, of "Radical") and see how many times difficulty, deprivation, "society's

not knowing," struggle (even for a strawberry) are themes implied in the early work, more openly stated in the later. In "The Monkey Puzzle" the solitude of singularity is accepted, to be endured, but in "Sojourn in a Whale" it is suggested that the impossible, the constricting condition can be circumvented by the power of the being to "rise on itself" as water does "when obstacles happened to bar/the path" (which is one answer to the complacency of the proverb "Water seeks its own level").

As the themes of the scarred but defiant and enduring interact with the theme of the wild animal's precarious existence, so the themes of bondage and freedom interact with these. "What Are Years?"—that exultant psalm—is built upon the paradox that only in the acceptance of limitations can one be released from them (as the caged bird, "grown taller as he sings, steels/his form straight up" and in "his mighty singing/says, satisfaction is a lowly/thing, how pure a thing is joy"). This Christian paradox is not abandoned. In "His Shield" freedom is defined as "the power of relinquishing/what one would keep"; in "Spenser's Ireland" a reversal: "you're not free/until you've been made captive by/supreme belief." The devilfish's "intensively/watched eggs coming from/the shell free it when they are freed" suggests not only the gestation of a work but much else. The poem frees the poet when he has expressed it and delivered it. The devilfish who possesses her eggs is as much possessed by them; so the jailor by the jailed. The freedom of the one is the freedom of the other. In "The Jerboa" the people "who liked little things" but had slaves, kept "power over the poor," and even put baboons to work for them are in bondage compared with the jerboa, both indubitably himself, a happy animal, and emblem of the spirit; they are in bondage to their materialities, their petty customs, rituals, superstitions. The jerboa with nothing but immaterial abundance is free.

So is the elephant of "Melancthon" (formerly "Black Earth"), that earliest of heroes (1918), who has richly accepted the rough conditions of existence, who has survived earthquakes and lightning. He does what he does which pleases no one but himself, his spiritual poise is not in pride (though he is too confident to be humble) but in that kind of seeing and hearing which the senses only have when the soul is master. He trumpets: "My ears are sensitized to more than the sound of/the wind." He is the hardy master of the ("patina of") circumstance like any Chinese sage. Lesser heroes are the cat of "Silence" and "Peter" himself, both eminently self-reliant and honorably what they are, with no apologies.

Other heroes are the student of "The Student" who can "hold by himself" and the hero of "The Hero," who is a kind of hero-in-reverse, without the heroics. Of touchy nerves, he doesn't like "suffering and not/saying so." He can also be vexing or, like "Pilgrim having to go slow/to find his roll; tired but hopeful." He is certainly the opposite of the tragic hero or the standard nerveless hero. But, jumpy like the pangolin, he is not empty: he knows "the rock crystal thing to see—the startling El Greco/brimming with inner light—that covets nothing that it has let go."

A facet of the hero is the "decorous frock-coated Negro" "with a/sense of human dignity/and reverence for mystery, standing like the shadow/of the willow." The willow, most pliant of trees and fragile of bough. Heroism, like any good thing, is precariously maintained. (It is also "exhausting.") The seemingly random course of this poem rather beautifully fits the exposition of a hero full of inner hesitations, and if it could be said that this poem is a poem about a person who has found his spiritual rock to abide by, it could also be said of "The Steeple-Jack" that it presents us with a vision of the place where this rock might be. Certainly this poem remains one of Miss Moore's most charmed ones. That "Dürer would have seen a reason for living/in a town like this, with eight stranded whales/to look at; with the sweet sea air coming into your house/on a fine day" is already more than enough to establish the tone from which nothing thereafter, not one accent, departs, the tone of a state of what seems to amount to purest felicity. As well, it expresses so fine an appreciation for the irregular, the not self-conscious, the moderate, modest, and free, the slightly crooked, the not-correct but vital, that it remains a triumph of the unexpected, of things caught in their essential dress, their *quidditas*. Nowhere does Miss Moore's zest for the idiosyncratic and genius for selecting the exactly right and irresistible detail shine forth more warmly, from "the whirlwind fife-and drum of the storm" to the action that keeps danger and hope in tension when the steeplejack lets down his rope "as a spider spins a thread." There is in this local setting endeared the gusto of a very idiomatic, very home-grown paradise, the only paradise that some of us can believe in, the one that's found, when it is found, on earth, when "there is nothing that ambition can buy or take away."

And in another mode "A Carriage from Sweden" creates out of the view of a "museum-piece . . . country cart/that inner happiness made art" some platonic ideal of "stalwartness, skill," and fey grace. The musical "Spenser's Ireland" creates all the wayward elusiveness of an enchanter's place. Remarkable for its "flax for damask" passage, its "guillemot/so neat and the hen/of the heath," it is the presence of the unsaid far underneath the said that produces at least a half of this delicate combination of magic and ruefulness.

Returning to the subject of the hero, are there not-heroes? Very few. Even her animals are "good," as Randall Jarrell has pointed out. But in "The Hero" there is a "sightseeing hobo," a fool of shameless questions. Very little time is spent on her, no more than is spent on that group of people in "The Icosasphere" who are "avid for someone's fortune." "Through lack of integration"—could understatement be more excessive?—"three were slain and ten committed perjury,/six died, two killed themselves, and"—studied anticlimax—"two paid fines for risks they'd run." For why flay a dead horse? "Heroes need not write an ordinall of attributes to enumer/ate/what they hate." If presidents punish "sin-driven senators by not thinking about them," Miss Moore, it might be inferred, prefers too to ignore certain obvious forms of tawdry or berserk behavior. However that may be, this Websterian plot of misconduct (lacking only incest) is mentioned only in passing and is simply one element in a poem that sets up very dryly relationships between the "rare efficiency" of birds' nests made in "parabolic concentric curves" and the icosasphere that an engineer, lacking the instinct of the birds, had to take infinite pains to learn how to make, and the still living enigma of how the Egyptians ever got their obelisks up. That the birds' nests put mortal "lack of integration" to shame, and the obelisks Mr. J. O. Jackson's icosasphere, it is left up to the reader to "make out."

Interacting veins between early work and later work are evident not only in themes but also in certain imagery. The elephant, for example, has two whole poems to himself, but his trunk turns up in at least four other poems. The sea appears both early and late, and so does water imagery. In "The Fish" there is the vividness of all that scuttling under water life of volatile flux and flow (and the mysterious correspondence of the "crow-blue" mussel shell "opening and shutting itself like/an/injured fan" with the hatchet-scarred cliff). There is

"A Grave," that masterpiece that calls the sea "a collector, quick to return a rapacious look" haunted by the beauty of the metaphor that wins life from death:

men lower nets, unconscious of the fact that
    they are desecrating a grave,
and row quickly away—the blades of the oars
moving together like the feet of waterspiders
    as if there were no such thing as death.

In "An Egyptian Pulled Glass Bottle in the Shape of a Fish" there is "a wave held up for us to see/In its essential perpendicularity" while water in "The Steeple-Jack" is "etched with waves as formal as the scales/on a fish." In "Dock Rats" there is the "steam yacht, lying/like a new made arrow on the/stream" and the sea's "horse strength." Not to forget the concluding lines on the grandeur of the waters in "Novices."

In "Marriage" the image of " 'the heart rising/in its estate of peace/as a boat rises/with the rising of the water' " suggests not only the image of waters in "Sojourn in a Whale" but also the central image in "What Are Years?" of the one who "in his imprisonment rises/upon himself as/the sea in a chasm, struggling to be/free."

The birds of "A Grave" that "swim through the air at top speed" remind one of the seagulls in "The Steeple-Jack" "flying back and forth over the town clock" and the beautiful merry-go-round study of the frigate pelican's flight. In "In the Days of Prismatic Colour" we might associate the cliff of "The Fish" with what survives, what is organic to existence, the very bedrock of things as it is celebrated in the lines

       Truth is no Apollo
Belvedere, no formal thing. The wave may go
    over it if it likes.
Know that it will be there when it says,
    'I shall be there when the wave has gone by.'

But though certain themes and imagery appear and reappear, there is a continuous unfolding, a deepening and widening of range, a constant experimenting with new modes or new aspects of a form. "Half Deity," notable for its symmetrical beauty, is a little model of dramatic development, the West Wind acting as a *deus ex machina* to allow for the butterfly's full emergence, full achievement of his transfiguration. ("Bird-Witted" is another, less formally elaborated.) "In Distrust of Merits," written during World War II, achieves, with its powerful rhythmic impulsion, its refrain, "They're fighting, fighting, fighting," majestic scope and harrowing depth. But it is particularly by the veracity of the poet's own directly subjective voice questioning, self-questioning, holding dialogue with itself, that the poem achieves its moral power. "They're fighting that I/may yet recover from the disease, My/Self; some have it lightly; some will die. 'Man/wolf to man' and we devour/ourselves." It is in such ways that Miss Moore's "morals" become a way of seeing the eternal. Again the theme of heroic acceptance that is also withstanding, that may become transcendence, is exemplified in the lines " 'When a man is prey to anger,/he is moved by outside things; when he holds/his ground in patience patience/patience, that is action or/beauty.' " (And "Beauty is everlasting/and dust is for a time" the poem concludes.) We see again her democratic hero's aristocratic self-sufficiency based upon his endeavor of self-knowledge, the aesthetic of his ethics. Indeed, Miss Moore's awareness of the incessant conflict that the "firebrand that is life" is grounded in gives her poetry that gusto of what she has called "helpless" sincerity.

It is an aside to point out that at least two of her animals, the impalla and the tuatera, will soon become extinct unless they are put on a list of animals-to-be-preserved-in-zoos, though it is an aside pertinent to other rareties always in danger of becoming extinct. Against such general pervasive threat her various later poems, "Efforts of Affection," "Voracities and Verities," "By Disposition of Angels," yield us searching insights to "steady the soul," ending on "Bach-cheerful" tonic chords of affirmation. One all but hears the lofty resoluteness of Lutheran hymns.

But how awkward it is to paraphrase. It goes against the tight grain of these poems to expiate upon their themes, for they are never as openly stated as this kind of generalizing might lead some innocent reader to suppose. Rather, insights always seem pulled from out the very heart of the particulars.

> What is there
> like fortitude! What sap
> went through that little thread
> to make the cherry red!

This comes in "Nevertheless" as if it had been a secret wrenched forth just at that moment when happening upon the trials of a plant she discovered how in its élan vital it had persisted. And thus her moral insights seem "proved on the pulse" to use Keats's phrase; they taste of the savor of conflict, they are the secret truths fought for and not the hawked wise-saws, the maxims of the copybooks.

Marianne Moore is, as she said of William Carlos Williams, "indomitably American," whether she is with sweet reasonableness correcting its critics (in "England") or joking upon "the original American menagerie of styles" (in "An Octopus"), although the earlier debate between past and present, Europe and America, is far less noticeable in her later work. Like Emily Dickinson she is irresistibly original. With Thoreau she dislikes the showy ("I don't like diamonds"), which includes gardenia scent and the overemphatic, all of which is at one with her capacity to make us feel the finest shadings.

By the patience and passion of her "eye" she has proved that the stripes of the tulip *can be counted*; her greater glasses, one might say, have revealed to us how much had not been seen until she saw. By her excitable "detecting" (a numinous word for her) she has given us a new world of marvelous specifics or a new-old world of what had been seen before but seen without feeling. This is to say it had not been seen at all.

A few words may be in order regarding the *Complete Poems* which appeared in 1967 on Miss Moore's eightieth birthday. As a kind of preface the terse warning "Omissions are not accidents" prepared the reader for the reduction of "Poetry" to three lines from twenty-nine (the original version is printed in the Notes) and for small but never insignificant excisions in twelve of the poems that first appeared in *Observations*. Poems are also excluded, notably "Melancthon," that had survived up until this volume. "Roses Only," long ago rejected, and three other poems from *Observations* remain outside the pale. Likewise rejected from the canon are "Walking-Sticks and Paper-Weights and Water Marks," "Half Deity," and "See in the Midst of Fair Leaves" from *What Are Years*. But if some poems are retired, others are returned. "The Student," from *What Are Years*, left out of the *Collected Poems* is now back in the *Complete Poems*. An early poem, "To a Chameleon," which appeared in *Poems* under another title, and "A Jellyfish" from *Observations* were included in *O to Be a Dragon* and both are in the *Complete Poems*. "Sun" from *Observations* appeared in *Tell Me, Tell Me* and is also in the *Complete Poems*. "To a Prize Bird" from *Observations* reappears again in the *Complete Poems* after having been absent from the *Selected* and *Collected Poems*. "I May, I Might, I Must," an early poem that

did not even appear in *Poems,* appears both in *O to Be a Dragon* and the *Complete Poems*. All the later poems from the volumes after the *Collected Poems* are included without omissions, plus four poems hitherto uncollected and nine selections from *The Fables of La Fontaine.*

There are other revisings to be noted: the restructuring of "Nine Nectarines" and "Camellia Sabina" for the sake of turning an internal rhyme into an end rhyme and the removal of stanzas from "The Frigate Pelican" and "The Buffalo" (although periods kindly tell us of their absence) and of phrases from "The Plumet Basilisk." However, "The Steeple-Jack," which was severely cut when it appeared in the *Collected Poems,* is now restored, save for a few alterations, to its original state as we knew it in the *Selected Poems.*

It might also be noted that the later poems undergo a change. For all of their "gaiety in finished form," their elaborate lightness and quickness, they tend on the whole to work more on the surfaces, to be open at the loss of that previously intricate relationship between the surface and the depths. Some are rather public, like the two poems about baseball that are a tour de force of specificities for the initiated but less than that for the uninitiated; "Rescue with Yul Brynner" and "Carnegie Hall: Rescued," also public are more mannered than vital. Do Mr. Eisenhower's tiringly earnest phrases in "Blessed Is the Man" serve the good that the antipoetic has done in other poems? Or "the drip-dry fruit/of research second to none" in "Saint Nicholas"? But there is the rich and humorous robustness of "Tom Fool at Jamaica" with its

> Senational. He
> does not
> bet on his animated
> valentines

and the tact with which nostalgia is avoided in

the evocation of that childish charm of "An Old Amusement Park," implication being all, for where it was is now La Guardia Airport. "No Better Than a 'Withered Daffodil' " and "The Sycamore" work in a new measure of music, the latter with its small blunt shock:

> We don't like flowers that do
> not wilt; they must die, and nine
> she-camel hairs aid memory

and its last lines:

> retiringly formal
> as if to say: "And there was I
> like a field-mouse at Versailles."

And if Miss Moore does not explore new veins, or mine the former as deeply, her major poems to which many of these later ones are minor will remain as a part of our heritage and the achievement of the language. "Freckled integrity," Tom Fool's "left white hand foot— an unconformity; though judging by results, a kind of cottontail to give him confidence," independence, resolution: these are some of the qualities that forge the armor of what becomes no longer armor but "patience/protecting the soul as clothing the body/from cold, so that 'great wrongs/were powerless to vex.' " In our sort of age Miss Moore's "mirror-of-steel un-insistence," her faculty for digesting the "hard yron" of appearance, as Wallace Stevens said, triumphantly speaks for man forever caught on the horns of his own dilemma but man resisting by grace of his understanding, by grace through his works of the vision of the underlying order of the universe.

*　　*　　*

Marianne Moore died at the age of eighty-four on February 5, 1972.

Selected Bibliography

WORKS OF MARIANNE MOORE

POETRY

Poems. London: Egoist Press, 1921.
Marriage. New York: Manikin, Number Three, Monroe Wheeler, 1923.
Observations. New York: Dial Press, 1924.
Selected Poems with an introduction by T. S. Eliot. New York: Macmillan; London: Faber and Faber, 1935.
The Pangolin and Other Verse. London: Brendin Publishing Company, 1936.
What Are Years. New York: Macmillan, 1941.
Nevertheless. New York: Macmillan, 1944.
A Face. Cummington, Mass.: Cummington Press, 1949.
Collected Poems. New York: Macmillan; London: Faber and Faber, 1951.
The Fables of La Fontaine. New York: Viking Press, 1954. (Published as *Selected Fables of La Fontaine.* London: Faber and Faber, 1955.) (Translation.)
Like a Bulwark. New York: Viking Press, 1956.
O to Be a Dragon. New York: Viking Press, 1959.
Complete Poems. New York: Viking Press, 1967.

PROSE

Predilections. New York: Viking Press, 1955; London: Faber and Faber, 1956. (Essays.)
The Ford correspondence. *New Yorker,* 33:140–46 (April 13, 1957). (Reprinted by Pierpont Morgan Library, New York, 1958.)
Puss in Boots, The Sleeping Beauty, and Cinderella, by Charles Perrault, adapted by Marianne Moore. New York: Macmillan, 1963.

READER

A Marianne Moore Reader. New York: Viking Press, 1961.

BIBLIOGRAPHY

Sheehy, Eugene P., and Kenneth A. Lohf. *The Achievement of Marianne Moore: A Bibliography, 1907–1957.* New York: New York Public Library, 1958.

Tate, Allen. *Sixty American Poets, 1896–1944.* Washington, D.C.: Library of Congress, 1954.

CRITICAL AND BIOGRAPHICAL STUDIES

Auden, W. H. "Marianne Moore," in *The Dyer's Hand and Other Essays.* New York: Random House, 1962.

Blackmur, R. P. "The Method of Marianne Moore," in *Language as Gesture.* New York: Harcourt, Brace, 1952.

Bogan, Louise. *Selected Criticism: Prose and Poetry.* New York: Noonday Press, 1955. Pp. 252–57.

Burke, Kenneth. "Motives and Motifs in the Poetry of Marianne Moore." *Accent,* 2:157–69 (Spring 1942).

————. "Likings of an Observationist," *Poetry,* 87:239–47 (January 1956).

Doolittle, Hilda (H.D.). "Marianne Moore," *Egoist,* 3 (No. 8):118–19 (August 1916).

Eliot, T. S. A review of *Marriage* and *Poems, Dial,* 75:594–97 (December 1923).

Engel, Bernard F. *Marianne Moore.* New York: Twayne, 1964.

Frankenberg, Lloyd. "The Imaginary Garden," in *Pleasure Dome.* Boston: Houghton Mifflin, 1949. Pp. 119–50.

Gregory, Horace, and Marya Zaturenska. "Marianne Moore: The Genius of *The Dial,*" in *The History of American Poetry, 1900–1940.* New York: Harcourt, Brace, 1946. Pp. 317–25.

Hall, Donald. Interview, *Paris Review,* 7:41–66 (Winter 1961).

Hoffman, Frederick J. *The Twenties: American Writings in the Postwar Decade.* New York: Viking Press, 1955. Pp. 176–79, 260–61, and *passim.*

Jarrell, Randall. *Poetry and the Age.* New York: Knopf, 1953.

Kenner, Hugh. "Supreme in Her Abnormality," *Poetry,* 84:356–63 (September 1954).

————. "Meditation and Enactment," *Poetry,* 102:109–15 (May 1963).

Marianne Moore Issue, *Quarterly Review of Literature,* 4 (No. 2):121–223 (1948), edited by José Garcia Villa. (Contains essays by Elizabeth Bishop, Louise Bogan, Cleanth Brooks, George Dillon, Wallace Fowlie, Lloyd Frankenberg, Vivienne Koch, John Crowe Ransom, Wallace Stevens, John L. Sweeney, William Carlos Williams, T. C. Wilson.)

Nitchie, George W. *Marianne Moore.* New York: Columbia University Press, 1969.

Pound, Ezra. "Marianne Moore and Mira Loy," *Little Review,* 4:57–58 (March 1918). (Reprinted in *The Little Review Anthology,* edited by Margaret Anderson. New York: Hermitage House, 1953. Pp. 188–89.)

Sargeant, Winthrop. "Humility, Concentration and Gusto," *New Yorker,* 32:38–75 (February 16, 1957).

Tomlinson, Charles, comp. *Marianne Moore: A Collection of Critical Essays.* Englewood Cliffs, N.J.: Prentice-Hall, 1970.

Weatherhead, Kingsley A. *The Edge of the Image: Marianne Moore, William Carlos Williams, and Other Poets.* Seattle: University of Washington Press, 1967.

Williams, William Carlos. "Marianne Moore," *Dial,* 78:393–401 (May 1925).

Winters, Yvor. "Holiday and Day of Wrath," *Poetry,* 26:39–44 (April 1925).

————. *In Defense of Reason.* New York: Swallow Press and W. Morrow, 1947.

Zabel, Morton Dauwen. "A Literalist of the Imagination," *Poetry,* 47:326–36 (March 1936).

——JEAN GARRIGUE

Wright Morris

1910-

WRIGHT MORRIS has been the most consistently original of American novelists for more than a quarter of a century which has borne witness to his originality by refusing to keep his novels in print. Faulkner once occupied the same position, though not for so long a time; and Morris' longer stay may have been his own fault, as Leslie Fiedler once remarked, because he would never join a gang. Perhaps he could not because he had anticipated and discounted too many of them. He discovered early that life, from any rational point of view, was absurd but took the discovery as a matter of fact rather than as a revelation of philosophical truth. He developed a sympathy for common humanity and an eye and ear for its peculiarities without becoming an alienated or angry young man. He realized that the American archetype of the self-sufficient hero was inappropriate to the modern world and simply avoided the traditional character instead of preserving the cliché with an "anti-hero" or some other man of straw. He lit out for the Territory, in the words of Huck Finn, ahead of the rest and made it, in his own play on the words, a territory in time rather than in space. Because of this he may prove to be not only the most original but also the most important American novelist of the mid-century.

But for that reason, too, he is difficult to represent, justly, in any succinct account of his work. The charm that he exercises over his occasional readers is that of wit, humor, and vividness in his presentation of ordinary people who somehow become extraordinary under his touch; and his consistent followers are fascinated by the extraordinary range and depth of his human understanding. A great variety of midwestern, eastern, far western, and southern Americans appear in his novels, and so do French, Germans, Austrians, Italians, Greeks, and Mexicans of all sorts—all of them believably and amusingly human. No other American novelist has approached him in the rich variety of his raw materials and in the ability to keep them raw enough to seem real while they are being handled with an art as sophisticated as that of Henry James. The range of Morris' work cannot be separated from its texture; and any figure in the carpet must be sought beneath the realistic depth and comic surface of the nap.

Although Morris writes from experiences with which he is deeply concerned, the figure is not autobiographical. The chief facts of his life are quickly told: He was born in Central City, Nebraska, on January 6, 1910, and lived with his father in various small Nebraska towns and in Omaha before moving to Chicago in 1924. He entered Pomona College in 1930, after several months on the Texas ranch of his uncle Dwight Osborn. Withdrawing from college in 1933, he spent a year in France, Germany, Austria, and Italy, and then settled in California and began writing. During the summers of 1938 and 1939 he lived in Wellfleet, Massachusetts, where he developed the interest in photography that he cultivated and turned to professional use on a long tour of the United States in 1940–41 and on two later trips to his native Nebraska. He lived in Pennsylvania from 1944 until 1954, when he began spending much of his time abroad—especially in Mexico, Venice, and Greece—and in California. Since 1963 he has been teaching at San Francisco State College and living in Mill Valley. Many incidents that appear in Morris' books—some with annoying repetition—are obviously loosely related to one or another of these periods in his life. But his usable experiences have been of the sort that he could reshape freely in his imagination or else they have been like Wordsworthian "spots of time" which nourished his mind and created inward agitations. And the serious autobiographical element in his work comes from his constant concern, while writing, with the relationship between the identifiable past and the unknown future and with the part the artist plays in clarifying it.

The first two of his novels were exploratory in their attempt to discover a point of view which would enable him to handle material in which he was emotionally involved with a detachment that would control any impulse he might have to base art on emotion. *My Uncle Dudley* (1942) was perhaps more fully drawn from personal experience than any novel he was to write later. Its cast of characters consisted of eight men, a boy, and a secondhand Marmon automobile; and its plot was a comic odyssey of misadventure from the lotus land of southern California, through the mountains of Arizona, and across the plains to the flooded banks of the Mississippi. The trip was one Morris had made with his father in the spring of 1927, but the most important single episode in the book (an arbitrary arrest and a bad night in a Mississippi jail) was based upon an experience only a few months old and still fresh in the author's mind at the time the book was written. The passengers and the jail episode were both skillfully used to bring out the character of Uncle Dudley, whose ridiculous pear-shaped figure and successful operations as a confidence man did not prevent him from living up to his proverbial and even mythological name—he was every boy's "Uncle Dudley" to whom he could tell anything and expect understanding, sympathy, and wisdom in return. He was also a wily and audacious Ulysses, and his final gesture of audacity—in a completely invented scene—fulfills the somewhat obscure fictional promise of the earlier incidents and gives meaning to the book.

The theme of audacity, often highly eccentric, was to become an important one in Morris' novels. Quite early, here, Dudley had described himself as a "horseless knight" who had once thought he was meant to "ride up front and holler and point at the promised land." But now, disillusioned by the realization that there was no one dream good for all the people, he found that he had acquired more armor than a man should need but had found no horse to mount. Later, in the Mississippi jail, he discovered a man who professed to be "a dam good horse"—Furman, recognized by the inmates as the best man in the jail, who was regularly put there for spitting in a cop's eye and who unconsciously parodied Tom Paine by insisting that his place had "come to be wherever such basterds is." Furman had spat on every officer except the sadistic Cupid; and when Uncle Dudley was released on the roadside, ill and exhausted by his experiences, he somehow found the spirit to mount Furman's hobby: chewing his cigar into brown juice, he laughed as gaily as he had ever laughed and spat Cupid squarely in the eye. He was dragged back into the police car and to whatever sadistic punishment awaited him, and the narrator's last view was of the car swinging into town with his Uncle Dudley's arm out gallantly signaling the turn.

The audacity of Uncle Dudley's performance, however, is more significant in the light of Morris' later uses of the theme than it might have appeared to be in this first novel. Of more immediate importance was Morris' effort to solve the technical problem of achieving sufficient detachment from his material to avoid being dominated by it. He did so by using an adolescent narrator known only as the Kid— one of the many kid storytellers who appear to have composed a substantial portion of American literature. But Morris' adolescent was not a persona (as were the comparable narrators in Mark Twain, Sherwood Anderson, Hemingway, and Faulkner) whose verbal limitations enabled the author to escape conventionality or triteness in the communication of emotion. He was a sound-camera which recorded no emotion at all. He enabled the author to appear completely detached from the experiences recorded in the book—to appear in the role of T. S. Eliot's artist as a catalytic agent or in the role of Hughes Mearns's haunting "man who wasn't there."

Yet Morris was unable to accept Eliot's fantasy of the artist as "a bit of finely filiated platinum," and the reality of the artist's existence, both as a human being and as a catalytic agent, became the subject of his next book. *The Man Who Was There* (1945) was concerned with a character who makes his presence felt through his absence: he is "there" not as a person but as a personality as well as a catalytic agent whose brief associations with the characters in the novel expand their notions of their own experience. Agee Ward has gone to war and been reported missing in action, and the novel deals with his actual past and the present he has achieved in the minds of those who knew him—such remarkable characters as Grandmother Herkimer and Private Reagan in the first section and the Spavics, Mrs. Krickbaum, Gussie Newcomb, and Mr. Bloom in the third. The Agee Ward remembered in the first section was a younger version of the Kid, that in the last was an incipient Uncle Dudley. He had gone to war, according to Mrs. Krickbaum, because of his concern for "the human predicament": he "didn't like it, but he was in it" and "Bad as it is, he said, we had to keep it *hu*-man!" In effect, he did, and made it comic as well. Morris left no doubt of his belief that a man—portrayed as an artist in this instance—could be "there" in the sense that he was a cause which had a humanizing effect upon a future of which he was not and could not be aware.

This belief and the characters used to reveal it were to prove prophetic of a long line of development in Morris' fiction. Another line was foreshadowed in the middle section, which he called "The Three Agee Wards" and in which he anticipated the photo-text technique and the substance of his next two books. The first Agee Ward was presented through the medium of "The Album," which contained descriptions of real and imaginary family photographs (some of them to be reproduced later in *The Home Place*) and of drawings and correspondence of the sort Morris himself might have sent a friend during his travels in Europe. The second was introduced in "The Ward Line," which was factually based on Morris' return to Nebraska in the days of the Dust

Bowl and the discovery of his father's surviving relatives. And the third was identified by the village barber, who recognized "The Osborn Look" and knew that he was "there," in the person of his mother, thirty years before. Time was almost an illusion before the barber's sense of human continuity. And so was space. "Where you're goin' is where you're from," he said; and with these casual words he attributed to man that transient and ephemeral position in time and space which was to haunt Morris' imagination for the next twenty years.

His next three books were primarily concerned with the problem of man's identity in time and space, and for them he developed a medium which made artistic use of the stability of vision and the suggestiveness of words. His earlier use of the Kid as a sound-camera had the disadvantage of keeping the lens and the microphone together; and the device of the Album in *The Man Who Was There*, while separating the two, obscured the distinction by requiring a verbal representation of the picture. His new medium was a combination of photographs with a text to which they bore a suggestive rather than illustrative relationship.

His first experiment with the method, in *The Inhabitants* (1946), was much too ambitious because it was an attempt at the admittedly impossible—to show "what it is to be an American." It was impossible because Morris shared (and repeated) Uncle Dudley's conviction that "there's no one thing to cover the people, no one sky . . . no one dream." But he could seek out "the inhabitants," from New England to California, and let the photographs show the houses people grew up in (either to keep or to leave) and let the people themselves talk or think aloud in the complementary prose text. The houses and the people were both "inhabitants." For Morris, while photographing an architectural quality of the sort that Thoreau said grew "from within outward, out of the necessities and character of the indweller," insisted that each man was himself "inhabited" by what he had grown up in. And he made use of this idea in his photographs when he subtly suggested a continuity in the "uncoverable" American experience by tracing the survival of New England architectural decoration through the porches of the Midwest and Colorado mining towns until it culminated in a desolate and windowless adobe house with a classic Yankee door lintel.

Although *The Inhabitants* attempted too much (especially for a volume of only slightly more than a hundred pages) it anticipated several books to come, particularly *The Home Place* (1948), in which Morris undertook an intensely personal exploration of the early background that "inhabited" him and, through him, so many of his books. More conventional than *The Inhabitants*, it modified the purely suggestive or poetic relationship between text and photographs and was something that might be considered an extra-illustrated novel. But the photographs are primary and the story obviously designed for a less sophisticated understanding than *The Inhabitants* demanded. In it the character who had once been Agee Ward was transformed into Clyde Muncy (though still an Osborn on his mother's side), a writer with a wife and two children who were refugees from the housing shortage in New York and were returning to the Muncy home place near Lone Tree, Nebraska, with some hope of finding a place to live in. While they were visiting the aging Uncle Harry and Aunt Clara the convenient death of Uncle Ed made available the house across the road. It had been promised to Cousin Ivy, who would farm Uncle Harry's eighty acres; but their need superseded Ivy's, and they would have had the place if the wife,

Peggy, had not discovered what Morris observed in *The Inhabitants*: "I've never been in anything so crowded, so full of something, as the rooms of a vacant house." They move on instead.

The story of *The Home Place* is contrived but the "spots of time" captured in the narrative make this book crucial to an understanding of all Morris' Nebraska novels and several of the others. Here is the explanation of the problem Agee Ward has with the difference between kinesthetic and pictorial memory: the pump, which seemed so far away when he was a small boy carrying water, was as close to the house as he saw it in his mind's eye. Here in pictures are the objects which so many of Morris' characters share as childhood memories: the Model T Ford, the corncob stove, the rusty tractor, the solitary egg, the outdoor privy, and the old wooden grain elevator in which two small boys might hide and peek out to see the world end. Everything was old and worn out. The drought and dust storms of the thirties had killed the trees, weathered the buildings, and withered the people. One can easily see, looking through *The Home Place*, why Morris had difficulty in distinguishing between nostalgia and nausea in his attitude toward Nebraska. When he returned and photographed these early scenes and artifacts, he found it a place to be from rather than to be in, but not a place to forget. The people who had not gone away had endured hardships that made men. Their memories were long, and such returned natives as Agee Ward and Clyde Muncy found themselves more real as memories than they were as persons.

In *The World in the Attic* (1949)—a sequel to *The Home Place*, though published without photographs—the Muncy family has moved on from Lone Tree to the town of Junction, where Clyde's mother's family had lived and where his father had been the station agent for the Chicago, Burlington, and Quincy railroad. Stopping for a bite to eat and to see Clyde's old school friend Bud Hibbard, they spend the night and Clyde opens a door into a Nebraska which has something in common with Faulkner's Mississippi. It is the world of Bud's grandmother, "Aunt Angie," who inhabits the kitchen and basement of the big house built by her son Clinton for his bride, imported from the deep South and known to the children of Clyde's generation as "Miss Caddy." Upon Clinton's death, Aunt Angie had sealed her domain and settled down in a tough determination to outlive her daughter-in-law, who had retired into the even more private world of her upstairs bedroom (the "attic" of the title). She does, though no one is sure that her wandering mind is aware of it until she makes her grotesque appearance, through the long-sealed door, at the funeral.

The Home Place marked the climax of Morris' search for identity through the discovery of the past which "inhabited" him and gave him the individual character he was always to maintain. He accepted his destiny as a midwestern novelist as completely as Faulkner accepted his as a southern one. As a writer he kept going to where he was from. But the Midwest to which he had returned at the end of the Dust Bowl era was a static world in the attic which he refused to abide in. If the West had declined instead of advancing with the twentieth century, he would explore the East —though not without nostalgia for the masculine world of his childhood. But he took with him, in his imagination, several characters from *The World in the Attic*: one husband with his conviction that he was married to "the finest creature on God's green earth," another with his tendency to withdraw into his own affairs and accept his home as his wife's domain, and a strong-minded eccentric old grandmother. What would happen to them in the eastern Eden which had not been devastated by dust and decay?

The first two novels of Morris' new exploration— *Man and Boy* (1951) and *The Works of Love* (1952)—were closely intertwined in conception and in composition. In the rather slight *Man and Boy* the story deals with the events of a single day before the end of World War II. The Boy has died heroically, and the navy is to name a destroyer in his honor. Mother rises to the occasion in her own inimitable way while her husband, Warren, merely goes along as the man who hides from her whims when he can, yields to them when he must, and remembers the Boy as a youngster to whom he had given an air rifle which caused the bird-loving Mother to abolish Christmas forevermore and the Boy to assert himself as a hunter and perhaps inevitably seek his final escape by death in action.

The book was suggested by a real occurrence and by Morris' amused but fascinated view of the eccentricities of a real managing female, but it developed imaginatively out of his effort to understand the control such a woman could have over the fallen race of man. "Mother"—Mrs. Violet Ames Ormsby—was not only the central character but also the heroine of the book, who could ride roughshod over United States Navy protocol as readily as she could over the weak-willed Mr. Ormsby or the Boy, Virgil, who was "there" in such different ways to his two parents. Rather curiously Morris attributed her discovery of the value of aggressiveness to an incident which was a part of his own experience and which he was to develop more fully in a short story, "The Rites of Spring"—a visit to an Uncle Dwight's ranch in Texas, where she responded aggressively (as the narrator of the later piece did not) to the threat of a little boy who frightened her by his wild behavior with a piece of broken glass. He

also drew upon his own experiences when he hinted at a background for Mr. Ormsby similar to that of the boy who was already beginning to evolve in *The Works of Love*. But the crucial character in Morris' search for an understanding of the spiritual Amazon was Private Lipido, a small soldier in a big helmet who joined the party to protect Mr. Ormsby from Mother, assaulted her dignity from behind, and was so overcome by his failure that by the end of the ceremony he was more attentive to her than Mr. Ormsby was. Mother did not owe her position to the weak "Momism" Philip Wylie was attributing to the American male at about the same time: there was strength of character and a basic dignity beneath her comic eccentricities.

The comedy of *Man and Boy* is almost perfectly balanced by the pathos of *The Works of Love*, in which the central character, Will Brady, is the sort of man from whom Mr. Ormsby might have inherited his capacity for acceptance. Like Mr. Ormsby's father, he was a big egg man from the Midwest; and, though temporarily successful in business, he was helpless in his unbearable connections with women who were too insensitive to appreciate his humble and inarticulate works of love. There were four of them: the prostitute who laughed at his proposal of marriage, the prostitute who ran away and sent him another man's child to adopt, the hotel owner's widow who slept tightly wrapped in a sheet, and finally the cigar-counter girl—nearer in age to his adopted son —who ran away with a "Hawayan" and reappeared as an alcoholic streetwalker. There was also the boy whom he loved as Willy Brady, Jr., and tried pathetically to understand by reading *Tom Sawyer* and *Penrod*. Will's works of love, for these and others, consisted of a sensitive kindly benevolence; and when he had abandoned his business and his suburban house in Omaha and drifted alone to

Chicago, he got the sort of job he had symbolically earned—that of a department store Santa Claus—and a death he invited almost as he had always invited disappointment.

Will Brady's story is one of the most moving that Morris has ever told, because it is the story of a man who had a dream of unpretentious goodness which could not be fulfilled—or, as Uncle Dudley might have put it, the story of a man who had a gentle horse but was too gentle to ride it. The book is reminiscent of Sherwood Anderson and is partially dedicated to his memory as a "pioneer in the works of love." But Morris is closer to the Anderson who created the "grotesques" of *Winesburg, Ohio* and the earlier novels than to the Anderson who believed that a man who abandoned material success could find a better life: Will Brady could offer goodness, but he could find no one to accept it for what it was. The works of love were all on one side.

Morris worked longer on *The Works of Love* than on any of his earlier novels, beginning it nearly six years before he published the redaction of a much longer manuscript, and the book is rich in memories of his own adolescence and filled with allusions to the artifacts, spots of time, and individuals who appear in his other early works. It gives the impression of being an intensely personal novel with a fictitious plot created out of private feelings. A certain reserve seems particularly evident in his treatment of the women who play so important a part in Will Brady's one-sided life. All of them are self-centered, all are willing to exploit Will in their various ways, all are incapable of such peripheral works of love as understanding and tolerance, and all are somewhat unreal. Morris was able to present in sharp but not unappreciative caricature an aggressively callous type of female but not the merely insensitive kind, and in his next and perhaps best novel of this period he returned to a new version of Violet Ormsby and gave her a husband with more personality than he had allowed Mr. Ormsby and more force of character than he had attributed to Will Brady.

The Deep Sleep (1953) may, in fact, become a classic study of American family life. Judge Howard Porter has just died when the story opens, but he is very much a "man who was there" in the memory of Parsons (the hired man who knows more about the family than its members know about themselves) and in the mind of Paul Webb, the son-in-law who recalls the man he knew as a public figure and discovered as a private individual on the day before his funeral. The Judge had been a person of power and influence in the state, and Parsons had known him as a man to be deeply respected while Webb knew of the high regard for him among his associates in Philadelphia. But he had never been known at all by his mother (the eccentric "Grandmother," whose prototype had appeared as "Aunt Angie" in *The World in the Attic* and as Violet Ames's mother in *Man and Boy*) and was rarely "there" as a human being to his wife—only twice, within the testimony of the novel: once in Italy, five years after their wedding, when their marriage "sort of came to a point" and the first of his two children was conceived; and again at the end of a long day of preparations for the funeral, when she admitted to her daughter Katherine, "I'm going to miss your father." Katherine's own position in the novel is ambiguous. As a young girl she had decided to lead her own life instead of withdrawing into herself (as her brother, like Virgil Ormsby, did before he too was killed in the war), and as the wife of the artist Webb she had escaped into another world, which enabled her to feel sorry for her parents' bondage to the petty routine of home life. But Morris allowed her to behave at times like her mother's daughter —as though he suspected that every woman is an Eve, born of man's deep sleep, and a potential instrument of his destruction.

The discoveries Paul Webb makes during the long day, however, cast a new light on the marital relationship of the Porters. The Judge had told Parsons that "Around the house . . . I leave it up to the Missus," but Webb uncovers evidence of the Judge's many small evasions of his wife's compulsion to keep everything under control. He learns of the shallow ford in the river where the Judge parked his car and pretended to be on an island, the basement toilet where he sat in darkness and knew that for twenty years a bottle of whiskey had been on hand in case of need, and the attic where he smoked cigars and kept the expensive Swiss watch he had bought to celebrate the high point of his marriage and had been required to put in "a safe place" after temporarily losing it on a bird-watching expedition. He had left all the responsibilities of the house to Parsons (who was in some respects closer to Mrs. Porter than he was), yet he was not, in any spiritual sense, withdrawn from his wife. He felt as surely as Parsons did that she was "a remarkable woman," and, dying, he insisted that her empty bed be drawn within reach of his hand because he didn't like to be alone. He cried out against his mother, but he cleaved to his wife even though she drove him to petty concealments which destroyed his dignity.

There is a certain mythological unity in these three novels of the early fifties: *Man and Boy* is a comic prelude to a drama of the fall of man. Showing man in his fallen state, it is appropriately staged in a bourgeois setting far removed from the Great Plains where man was dominant and woman merely endured. *The Works of Love* is a representation of the fall, which is synchronized with Will Brady's migration eastward and toward greater material prosperity until he was forced to give it up. And *The Deep Sleep* is Morris' attempt to justify the fall in the Miltonic sense of asserting that whatever passes for Providence in twentieth-century metaphysics is free from guilt. For there is no God in Morris' imaginative universe—and no Satan, in the form either of a serpent or of a social system. Man falls, like Milton's angels, "self-tempted, self-depraved"; but he falls from the "single imperfection" Milton attributed to Man—a "deficience" within himself which was "the cause of his desire/ By conversation with his like to help/Or solace his defects." Or, to put the explanation into terms closer to those Morris himself used, man needs challenge and love while woman wants security; and if he meets his challenge well enough to fall into the deep sleep of security, out of it will come the woman, bone of his bones and flesh of his flesh, who will tempt him to destruction through his works of love.

Within this imaginative pattern *The Huge Season* (1954), though a novel quite different in kind, may be seen as closely related to the others through Morris' continued concern with the mystery of Paradise lost. It is different in kind because most of its raw material is related to Morris' college days rather than to his earlier background or to his observations of the inhabitants of the "wild station wagon country" of the Pennsylvania Main Line and also because it is the first of his stories to be told from the single viewpoint of a fully characterized persona. The persona is Peter Foley, professor of classics in a small Pennsylvania college, whose memory operates on two distinct levels: One is that of his conscious attempt to recapture for a book the circumstances of a strange "captivity" he had experienced during his first two years in a small California college when he shared a dormitory suite with several young men, all of whom were iron filings in the field of a magnet provided by Charles Lawrence—a tennis player. The other is that of the free associations created by the events of a single day spent in New York after one of his suitemates, Jesse Proctor, had testified before the Senate Committee on Un-American Activities. They run together, at the end, when Foley realizes that the captivity has been lifelong and that he has at last escaped.

The Huge Season is a haunting book because it deals with a form of human bondage more subtle than that portrayed in the trilogy on the fall of man. Yet the theme is the same, with much larger implications. Lawrence's determination to be a great tennis player, despite the handicap of one bad arm to begin with, represents the same irrational compulsiveness that is displayed by Mrs. Ormsby in her determination to live by platitudes and Mrs. Porter's obsession with keeping things in order even to the extent of hanging out used paper towels to dry. His more sensitive suitemates—Foley, Proctor, and to a lesser extent Lundgren—can only follow him and protect him where he is vulnerable. Lawrence was a man on a horse, as Uncle Dudley would have put it, but it was the compulsiveness of his horsemanship rather than the direction of his leadership which captivated the others against their wills.

The composition of *The Huge Season* appears to have been a turning point in Morris' literary development. The first of his novels to be focused upon a character (Lawrence) who was entirely a product of his imagination, it was also the first to end on a note—underplayed though it was—of assured freedom. A possible clue to the imaginative and emotional change reflected in it may be found in an odd and seemingly irrelevant passage halfway through the book. Foley's cat had brought home an apparently dead chipmunk, deposited it bottom side up on a flagstone, and given it a few casual cuffs. Then "the chipmunk sprang up like [a] spring-wind toy and began to dance

. . . his little tail like a banner, hopping back and forth on the cool flagstone." The incident reoccurred day after day during the summer while the chipmunk got fat and Foley began to read Darwin and "spend nights brooding on a creative evolution of his own. Founded on what? Well, founded on audacity. The unpredictable behavior that lit up the darkness with something new. . . . Perhaps, Foley thought, Mother Nature was originating again. . . . Maybe she had come to feel, quite a bit like Foley, that she had played her cards wrong in the first place and that the time had come to put a few trial irons into the fire. . . . If what Nature had in mind was survival, Man had ceased to be at the heart of Nature and had gone off on a suicidal impulse of his own. And Foley's chipmunk, among others, had got wind of it."

Foley, later, during his day in New York, was to think of himself as "having come from no more than the glint in the eye of a chipmunk with nothing on its mind but a sublime audacity," and Morris himself was to continue to play with this fancy. He conceived of *The Field of Vision* (1956) in terms of the spectator's reaction to a bullfight in which the ring served as talisman attracting the "durable fragments of a man's life" and forcing him "to come to imaginative terms with them." Of his seven principal characters, he used five for his major purpose: McKee (a small-town Babbitt or older and more prosperous Bud Hibbard, who had just enough imagination to be held in captivity by a flamboyant boyhood friend), Lois (his wife, not as eccentric as Mrs. Ormsby or Mrs. Porter but as "stiffly laced into her corset of character"), Scanlon (Lois' father, the eighty-seven-year-old hermit of Lone Tree, an ex-plainsman who had seen the century turn but had failed to turn with it and was now only "the mummified effigy of the real thing"),

Gordon Boyd (the boyhood friend, "the man who was there," who had been a sort of Lawrence in his youth but was now a professional hero, long unemployed, who could not even be a successful failure), and Dr. Lehmann (a Brooklynized German psychiatrist, who was almost as odd as the few patients who stayed with him). Two other characters were actively in the consciousness of the others, though Morris did not directly reveal their own: Gordon, McKee's eight-year-old grandson, an "infant Davy Crockett" who bore Boyd's name; and Paula Kahler, Lehmann's apparently simple-minded housekeeper and patient.

In exploring the durable fragments of the lives of his five characters, Morris achieved a range and depth that is to be found in none of his earlier novels. Scanlon, too blind to see where he was but aroused by the cry of "*agua*" when the matador's cape needed wetting down, returned completely to the past and a vivid recollection of the wagon train that lost most of its members from thirst as they crossed the Death Valley. Lois, who fainted and had to leave when a boy was almost gored, saw mostly Boyd and remembered the sexual awakening he had aroused with a kiss and she had suppressed by marrying McKee. McKee, who tried to see the fights but looked after Lois as a matter of course, remembered Boyd and his unsuccessful attempt to walk on water, his own youthful failure in courage, and the strange influence Boyd continued to exercise upon him. And Boyd, who saw more of the fights than the others, remembered Ty Cobb's pocket which as a boy he had torn off the pants of the great ballplayer and throughout his years of seedy decay had kept as a private talisman—a conjure-rag of dreams—and his only permanent possession.

All represented some aspect of fallen man —regression and withdrawal, repression, ser-

vitude, and failure—brilliantly presented in terms which kept the human condition human. The two characters who appeared to have fallen furthest from the human condition, however, represented something else. The half-clown and half-charlatan, Lehmann, could see the fights and also Paula at his side, quietly knitting and unaware of what was going on. He remembered her history. Born Paul, and gentle almost to saintliness in the opinion of the director of a Chicago YMCA, his patient had been discovered as a chambermaid in a Brooklynn hotel where she had strangled an amorous bellhop in an elevator and lapsed into complete placidity. By an act of imagination— "with nothing on its mind but a sublime audacity"—an individual had re-created itself, and Dr. Lehmann's mind had been audacious enough to come to imaginative terms with that fact. So, as with the chipmunk in *The Huge Season*: "In Leopold Lehmann the inscrutable impulse was reaching for the light. As it was in Paula Kahler. As it was in the species with the bubble at the top. But the thrust, even in reaching for the light, must come from behind. . . . In reaching for more light man would have to risk such light as he had. It was why he needed help. It was why he had emerged as man. It was according to his nature that he was obliged to exceed himself." The oddest of characters in Morris' field of vision represented the best odds he could see in favor of human evolution.

This evolution was not Darwinian. It was a modern version of the "reconciliation of science and poetry" which Joseph Le Conte had taught young Frank Norris two generations before and which has perhaps been best brought up to date by Loren Eiseley after he had spent days, with Morris, watching a real cat and a real chipmunk put on the performance described in *The Huge Season*. In writing of *The*

Field of Vision Morris referred to the "unchanging drives" of the imagination (the less audacious Le Conte had called it "Divine energy" and Eiseley had called it "the human heart") and said that the book had grown from his belief that the "imaginative act is man himself." His later books were to be based upon this belief too—at least in the sense that their invention was affected by the change this belief made in Morris' aims as an artist. Henceforth he was to be concerned with coming to imaginative terms with the past less than with those forces which might affect the future.

Yet it was a reassertion of his belief in evolution that kept *Love among the Cannibals* (1957) in the mainstream of his literary development; otherwise it might well have slipped into that backwash of talent usually reflected in the Hollywood novel. The most rapidly conceived, written, and published of all his novels, *Love among the Cannibals* deals with the two middle-aged members of a second-rate song-writing team, Macgregor and Horter, who pick up a couple of girls and take them to Acapulco for a week of productive work. One is a southern "chick"—Macgregor's Million Dollar Baby, who becomes his dime-store bride—and the other is a classic example of the primitive female, Eva by name but to Horter simply "the Greek," who believes that the mind is of the body and who makes Horter share her conviction until he loses her to an aging professor of marine biology, Dr. Leggett. The story is of people who live on each other to the accompaniment of a restless theme song asking "What next?" and it is, in some respects, a zany version of Morris' earlier meditations on the fall of man with an emphasis on sex rather than housekeeping. And throughout the story is the visual symbol of their car—a fireman-red convertible with green leather upholstery and a built-in record player—which is symbolically stripped to its chassis in the way

Macgregor and Horter are stripped by their experience, to the "essentials" of the immediate present. *Love among the Cannibals* is the only Morris novel in which the past is apparently judged so inessential that it is completely missing.

Yet Horter's emotion is more profound than any that could surge under the influence of a cardboard moon. Sexual, it is quite different from the casual sexuality which even to Macgregor (a true Hollywood caricature) is less important than the hackneyed sentimentality he considers "the real thing." Horter identified it for what it was while he watched the beginning of Professor Leggett's fall. As Leggett was stuttering with enthusiasm over the "primeval ooze of life" he had fished from the bottom of the sea, Horter observed "that the professor's passion, however platonic in its intentions, had undergone a transformation in the magnetic field of the Greek. His passive ooze had picked up her charge . . . and one fine moment, placing his hand on hers, he would feel the spark. *My child*—he would say, and undergo a shattering development. The sea-green fermenting ooze would not be in his bottle, but in his blood." Horter knew. He saw her as something always "in the process of becoming something else," and whatever he may have contributed to what she called her "development" it was evident, by the end of the book, that she had contributed to his.

It was probably appropriate at this time that Morris should have paused in his career and taken stock of his own aims as a novelist within the mainstream of the American novel. He did so in *The Territory Ahead* (1958), a book of criticism explicitly concerned with the uses and abuses of the past in the light of the immediate present—his obsessed fictional preoccupation. In it he reveals his intense admiration for the perceptive genius and expert craftsmanship of Henry James ("the artist who apprehended much of life without the crippling effects of having lived it") and for the indispensable vitality of D. H. Lawrence's belief that "if life itself could be lived to the full art would grow out of it." Morris reconciled such incongruous admirations through his belief that "If man is nature self-conscious . . . art is his expanding consciousness, and the creative act, in the deepest sense, is his expanding universe." But his own problem was one of the artist who "might well ask how, in such a spinning world as ours, he is to know that he stands in the *present*." "There are no pat answers," he replied, "but there are clues. Since he must live and have his being in a world of clichés, he will know this new world by their absence. He will know it by the fact that he has not been there before. The true territory ahead is what he must imagine for himself. He will recognize it by its strangeness, the lonely pilgrimage through which he attained it, and through the window of his fiction he will breathe the air of his brave new world."

When Morris returned to the Nebraska scene in *Ceremony in Lone Tree* (1960), he actually did present a new world, which had evolved in his earlier books but was now entirely re-created, peopled, and given substance by his imagination. The town of Lone Tree, hardly more than a symbolic name in his earlier novels, was given definite character as a ghost town whose principal inhabitant was Tom Scanlon, a hermit who lived in the past and occupied the abandoned hotel where he had raised the three daughters who were returning with their families for the ceremony of celebrating his ninetieth birthday. Five of the characters from *The Field of Vision* were there: Scanlon himself, Lois (now his oldest rather than his youngest daughter), her husband McKee, their grandson Gordon (now apparently younger than he had been in the

earlier book), and Boyd, whom McKee had invited in an ill-advised moment. The family was filled out by Maxine, Scanlon's second daughter, with her husband, Bud Momeyer, and their daughter Etoile, who had her Aunt Lois' beauty but none of her inhibitions. The Momeyers brought with them, though not in person, an awareness of Bud's nephew Lee Roy, who had recently used his car to run down and kill two taunting schoolmates and had shared headlines with another boy from the same town who had run wild and killed ten people in an effort to "be somebody." The third daughter, Edna Ewing, was also there with her husband, the caricature of an Oklahoma colonel, and a ten-thousand-dollar bull pup; and so were two other McKees: young Gordon's older brother, the handsome, horsey, and inarticulate Calvin, and his outspoken mother, Eileen. Boyd had picked up en route and brought along for the shock a pathetically young divorcée whom he calls "Daughter" and whose stereotyped swearing gives Etoile a new vocabulary. The same freight that brought them brought a stranger to the group (but not to Morris' readers), Willy Brady, Jr., who had grown up to become an ineffectual writer of Westerns under his middle name, Jennings.

Most of the action is comic. The women struggle, in their characteristic ways, with the problems of eating and sleeping under conditions little better than those of camping. Etoile and Calvin "elope" while returning from a neighboring town with a team of mules which they hope will arouse their grandfather out of his half-century of lethargy and take him back to his frontier days. Bud, who has never really grown up, innocently stalks and kills the expensive pup with his bow and arrows. McKee observes Boyd, a still grandiloquent but no longer pathetic failure who seems to have lost even Ty Cobb's pocket—the last relic of his dreams. Lois accidentally fires a revolver from her bedroom window, and that, with the noise of the mules, rouses Scanlon to the memory of his Death Valley adventure: he dies with the old query "That you, Samuels?" on his lips and the expectation of meeting Miss Samantha, his bride. There is no tragedy in Scanlon's death —which, in fact, could be described as a sort of posthumous performance—or in his departure from Lone Tree when a final masterly scene of thoughtless confusion makes plausible the symbolic removal of his remains in the Conestoga wagon in which he was born.

However comic the action and most of the characters in *Ceremony in Lone Tree* might be, the book is loaded with both overtones and undertones of violence. The overtones appear in the formal introduction of Lee Roy into "the roundup" of characters, in the frequent references to the random murderer, and in the constant pretense of shooting by young Gordon. The undertones are introduced by the experience of Boyd, who drives from Mexico to Lone Tree by way of Nevada, where an atomic test is scheduled and a tourist camp owner writes after his name on the register "Wake before bomb." No bomb was set off, but the suggestion of an explosion hanging fire pervades the events at Lone Tree. It occurs in the consciousness of all the characters to whom the reader is directly exposed: in the nervous tension of Lois and Maxine, in Boyd's desperate efforts to "clown it up," in McKee's memories and awareness, in Etoile's adolescent sexuality and Calvin's frightened responses, and even in Jennings' haunting recollections of men who played Santa Claus. Morris relieves it by comedy when he has the gentle Bud, playing Indian, kill the bull pup (perhaps the only animal, in any of Morris' novels, which is not sympathetically portrayed) and lets the Ewings get so excited that they rush off to the insurance company with its body instead of taking

Scanlon's to the undertaker. There is more tension in *Ceremony in Lone Tree* than in any of the preceding novels: Morris had shucked his Nebraska characters out of the husks of his previous fiction and brought them to renewed life in his imagination.

He did much the same for his post-Nebraska characters in *What a Way to Go* (1962). Its central figure, Arnold Soby, is the same sort of innocuous small-college professor as Foley in *The Huge Season*; and, as in the earlier novel, he is the only character toward whom the author is in any way omniscient. It contains in the person of Miss Winifred Throop the domineering female of the Pennsylvania novels, this time in the role in which Morris had discovered her in real life—that of headmistress of a fashionable girl's school, though here retired, out of her native habitat, and considerably less sure of herself. It also includes a host of the grotesques Morris likes to observe and mimic: Miss Kollwitz, and avid peeler of fruit, who was a teacher of modern languages and Miss Throop's companion and protector; Mr. Lipari, pickling himself in brandy while he crossed the Atlantic for an audience with the Pope; Signor Condotti-Pignata, who wanted to be another Botticelli but had either too much or too little imagination to succeed; Dr. Hodler, the pompous Swiss-German professor of classics; the dwarfish and impish Austrian Herr Perkheimer, who was going to rescue Greece from generations of photographic ash by shooting new scenes with unloaded cameras; a flock of German *Wandervogel,* led by the efficient Fraulein Kretschmar and the giant Herr Holzapfel with a baby face and the mind of an arrested adolescent; and a score or more of incidental characters, all vividly captured in caricature. Finally there is the equivalent of "the Greek" in *Love among the Cannibals* —a real one in Professor Soby's memory of his short marriage to a young bride, and a potential one in the person of the seventeen-year-old Cynthia, Miss Throop's niece and the Galatea of every man's Pygmalion. Awkwardly outgrowing her clothes, devoted to Popsicles, with bands on her teeth, Cynthia was nevertheless Primavera to Signor Pignata, Nausicaa to Professor Hodler, Fräulein Liebfraumilch to Perkheimer, and a terror to Herr Holzapfel. To Soby she was, in one respect, a familiar experience of his life as a college professor and, in another, a crucial challenge to his literary imagination.

For Soby—sane, safe, considerate Soby—had depths beyond the depths revealed by Peter Foley. His strange captivity was to Thomas Mann's *Death in Venice* because his young Greek bride had enabled him to understand the bacchanal of Aschenbach's dream and to recognize a profound wisdom beneath the morbid symbols of German romanticism. He hoped to express it in his own way in a book on "the wisdom of the body" but had no conscious notion of what such wisdom was. It was not sexual violence, which he had experienced, but something as imaginative in its way as was Aschenbach's infatuation with Tadzio. Perhaps it was of the spinal cord ("That living root that connected the brain of man with his primeval tail") or of the eye itself, which had "a small brain of its own . . . a tiny bud of the brain . . . attached to the back of it" where "the visible world was made visible." Soby, like Foley, had apparently read Darwin, who had said (in a sentence Morris used as an epigraph for the book), "I remember well the time when the thought of the eye made me cold all over." But Soby was not a scientist devoted to impersonal rationality. He was a humanist who suspected that "the wisdom of the body counselled the brain what to feel and think," that it might be "the source of fiction, as well

as what were known as facts." Cynthia stimulated it. Soby did not lust for her. On the contrary, she reminded him "of the Virgin's silver beauty/ All fish below the thighs." When he looked at her, he saw something "out of this world"—"far out"—and was drawn to her more mysteriously than Aschenbach had been drawn to Tadzio. He made her—or she made herself—his bride.

Although it is one of the most richly and exaggeratedly comic of all Morris' books, *What a Way to Go* treats seriously the problem of reality. Cynthia Pomeroy was a carefully calculated representation of the type of character toward which he had been groping with Agee Ward and Charles Lawrence. Easy enough to sketch in caricature, she was impossible to paint or to direct in the pageant of Nausicaa receiving Ulysses because she was in the unstable process of change (as Soby so clearly realized) and such stability as she possessed existed in the eyes of the beholder who tried to fit her into the pattern of whatever dream he most cherished. But she could not be frozen in a cliché or become a bee in amber. The only thing that one could be sure of was that she was alive. She represented the primitive force which produced a drive toward the unknown. Reality was to be found, fleetingly, somewhere along the way. Soby realized this and, with the wisdom of the body, clutched at it. But what he caught we are never told. For *What a Way to Go* raised a question which could be answered negatively but not, in any permanent sense, positively. One of Cynthia's realities might have been captured in Signor Pignata's painting had he ever been able to settle upon the way to paint her. It could not have been captured in a photograph of the Nausicaa pageant Dr. Hodler tried to stage. She was a stimulus to the creative eye rather than an artifact for the eye of the camera, and her reality was to be found in her effect. Like the characters in *Ceremony in Lone Tree*, who are more fully realized than those of *The Home Place*, she has more reality in the novel than she could ever have in most people's lives.

In *Ceremony in Lone Tree* and *What a Way to Go*, Morris apparently found his creative inspiration in the attempt to do for himself what he had attempted to have his characters do in *The Field of Vision*—to gather up the durable fragments of his experience and come to imaginative terms with them. The first novel was an imaginative reconstruction of his actual and creative association with Nebraska; the second, with those of his more recent experiences in the East and in Europe. But he had other business with his personal past which he had to settle before he could exorcise it from the dominant and almost obsessive position it had held for two decades in his imagination. This was with the period from early 1930 through the middle of 1934, which included the months he had spent on his uncle's ranch in the Texas Panhandle, his college years, and his *Wanderjahr* in Europe. He came to grips with it in *Cause for Wonder* (1963).

He did it through the mind of Warren Howe, a middle-aged writer who thirty years before had passed four months in strange captivity (as Morris himself had) to an ancient castle and its mad owner in the Austrian Alps. Howe received an invitation to the madman's funeral and in seeking a companion for the trip brought this period of Morris' life to a focus upon the most haunting part of it. He first sought out his Texas uncle, Fremont Osborn, in a chapter which provides the context for many of the "spots of time" scattered through Morris' other novels; and then approached a former college friend, Charles Horney, in another chapter which may explain why Morris took off for Europe instead of taking a degree.

Finally he persuaded Sol Spiegel, a Santa Monica junk dealer and his former companion on a bicycle trip through Italy, to accompany him on what was to prove another strange adventure.

Although the book is divided into two sections, the first called "Time Present" and the second "Time Past," it actually presents a continuous narrative; and the time division refers to the focal point of Howe's awareness, calling attention to Morris' use of a movie-camera technique which enables him to zoom in on something distant in time in a way that was impossible with the still-camera technique of *The Home Place* or the use of narrative juxtaposition in *The Huge Season*. In the continuity of the story Howe and Spiegel arrive at Schloss Riva to find the Meister, Monsieur Etienne Dulac, very much alive and the finest human symbol of "sublime audacity" in any of Morris' novels. He had himself been responsible for sending out the invitations and had succeeded in rounding up two other people from Howe's past, Wolfgang Prutscher and Katherine Brownell, for the fantastic events of twenty-four hours during which "George" (the Till Eulenspiegel of the castle roofs) scatters white paint as he had once scattered snow and the seventy-five-year-old crippled Meister slides down a mountainside and dies peacefully in bed—the last and possibly planned eccentricity of a long career devoted to giving other people cause for wonder.

The events of the twenty-four hours, however, are less real to Howe than those evoked from the past, some of them a part of Morris' own experience and some of them his imaginings of what the Meister might have done had he maintained his characteristic audacity through World War II. The reality in the book is of a sort that could be better appreciated by Arnold Soby than by any but its most sensitive readers: something to be found, fleetingly, somewhere along the way of eternal change as the past is being transformed into the future. Dulac was more real than Scanlon because he had more to pass on—an audacity which would continue to lead a life of its own—and a recipient better conceived for that purpose than Gordon McKee had been. The recipient was Katherine's grandson Brian, a child prodigy shaped like Uncle Dudley; and the greatest cause for Howe's wonder during the whole fantastic day was the relationship between him and the old man. As Dulac placed his hand on Brian's head "Howe sensed the flow of an alternating current. The past into the present, the present into the past. . . . From the old, the charge was now being passed to the new. *What charge? That was what one never knew.* The new, unused heads, like empty deep-freeze cartons, would not give up their meaning—if it could be said they had one—until thawed. The present would prove to be whatever proved unexpendable. Good or bad. If it existed it had proved itself. . . . As a pallbearer, the boy carried the future, or nothing at all."

Cause for Wonder is the most difficult of Morris' books because it is (with the possible exception of *The Works of Love*) the most private and because it required the most complex technique to come to imaginative terms with the durable experiences on which it was based—so durable, in fact, that the published book represented his fifth attempt to deal with them over a period of twenty-six years. More completely concerned with the author's individual past than either of the other two novels of the early sixties, it also brought him closer to a concern for the future; and, in doing so, it marked the culmination of another major stage in his literary development. The two which were to follow were to be free from the signs of struggle with his own past which had

marked his work for two decades. Better than any of his other novels, they were to show where he stood in the uncertain and insecure present.

One Day (1965) not only marks the release of Morris' field of vision from those spots of time which attracted it toward his own past but displays as well the full development of a fictional technique which enabled him to bring into almost perfect balance the two qualities which distinguish him among modern American novelists: the extraordinary range of knowledge and sympathetic understanding he can apply to the representation of human beings in the infinite variety of their comic humors, and the seriousness and honesty of his search for meaning and hope in a world that so many of his contemporaries have been content to present as absurd.

The technique he uses is that of achieving intensity by means of the classical unities of time and place. In several of his earlier novels he had confined the action to the events of a single day, and in most of these he had kept it close enough to a single place to allow his characters to move from scene to scene plausibly within his time pattern. In all of them, however, he had increased the range of his story by using such devices as the interpolated manuscript (in *The Huge Season*) and individually labeled points of view which allowed him to present not only the awareness but (as in *The Field of Vision*) the memories of his various characters. In *One Day*, however, he observed the unities with a more-than-classic strictness by keeping the action between predawn and midnight in the small northern California town of Escondido and consistently focusing it upon the animal pound in the town's center; and he achieved a greater unity of effect by telling his story (and the stories of his individual characters) from the consistent point of view of an omniscient novelist. The day was November 22, 1963, but Morris avoided any journalistic exploitation of President Kennedy's assassination. He presented it as a day of "such unspeakable human folly" as to raise the question whether mankind should follow the pattern of its own civilization or take Whitman's advice to "turn and live with animals" because they bring better "tokens"—however mysterious in their origin—of man's self.

The pattern of questionable civilization is set by Evelina Cartwright, who dominates the town with her loud voice and hearty manner, her tourist gift shop, her high-class animal pound, and her strange collection of protégés: Luigi Boni, the Venetian barber and her pet artist; the Yucatanian dogcatcher, Ignacio Chavez; the hard-of-hearing superintendent of the pound, Wendell Horlick, with his frustrated wife and grasping son Irving; and the astrologist and fortuneteller, Adele Skopje, who is hardly conscious of anything in the present. Its promise of the future is to be found in the person of Evelina's childlike daughter Alec, who has been a freedom rider in the deep South and has brought home her illegitimate mulatto child and secretly deposited it in the pound as a gesture of protest. She innocently believed this would shake the world until she became disillusioned by the ability of her mother and everybody else to take the gesture in full stride—just as most of them could take the assassination of the President.

The question of turning away from the pattern of civilization is raised in the mind of the local veterinarian, Harold Cowie, because he is worried about the modern necessity for "giving up" in order to survive: "Cowie had given up people, Alec had given up her child, numberless lovers had given up love, and increasing numbers had given up their conscious lives. A non-conscious life they still lived, and

the future looked bright for non-conscious dying. But to be fully conscious was to be fully exposed. . . . As a matter of survival one gave it up. At one and the same moment this was an act of salvation and an act of destruction."

In giving up, one might give up to many things; and it was in giving himself up to an American archetype that the President's assassin, by implication in Cowie's mind, became a member of the Escondido community. He was, in his way, like Evelina and Alec: "In representing nothing bigger than himself, Lee Oswald represented more than enough. He did in Texas. He did in all of America. A free man, he testified to the horrible burden of freedom: how connect with some*thing*? How relate to some*one*? It was no accident that he singled out the man who represented the maximum of human connections, and displaced this man, this symbol of connections, with himself. Lee Oswald had merely deprived another man of what, in his opinion, he had been deprived: the right to the pursuit and possession of happiness. As an American it was not necessary for him to speak for others: his life and happiness depended on his speaking for himself. His life, and as it so often happened, another man's death."

Alec had been right in her desperate cry: "I did it. We all did it." For, Morris had continued through Cowie's chain of thought, "This senseless crime not only made history: it made American sense. In each American ear the word from Dallas would acquire its own troubled burden of meaning, and its own intolerable burden of meaninglessness. What word was it? How well Cowie knew it. *Impotence*. The assurance that nothing said, nothing written or cabled, nothing accepted or rejected, nothing suffered or felt, nothing now up before Congress or still in the blue prints, nothing dug out of the past or prescribed for the future, would restore to a man his belief in his power to affect the course of human events. He might exert it, but believe in it he did not."

This was all the wisdom of the mind that could be brought to bear on the tragedy. The wisdom of the body had nothing to offer. Conchita, the wife of Chavez, and Dora, the wife of Luigi, possessed it and were able to grieve passionately during the day and sleep peacefully through the night; but their husbands lay awake with thoughts of death or frustration. The thoughts of the sleepless American women were, like those of Alec, "of no moment." Cowie's sleepless thoughts, however, were. Though impotence in its extremity could make a man "murderously potent," most people could not act but, like Alec, merely protest; and his nightmare was of "what might happen anywhere under the sign of impotence": of some "day without end" when "impotence and protest would lie down in darkness, like lovers, and issue from that union would turn up in Dallas, in Escondido, and in towns yet to be heard from. . . . Where such lovers lay down, such issue would turn up. In one voice they would cry for Havoc, in another for Help. Whoever told it this would prove to be a story as strange, or stranger than that of Lee Oswald, common as the air that bathed the globe, inscrutable as death. An American story. No matter who told it, that's what it would be."

Such a novel as this would be profoundly pessimistic were it not filled with Morris' fascination with life. He may not have approved of Escondido and its more aggressive inhabitants, but he appreciated it in all its details and prized them in all their peculiarities: the managing Evelina and the frustrated Miriam Horlick, Adele Skopje, the movie-type sheriff, the friendly owner of the liquor store, and Cowie, with whom he shared a few remaining specks of time. He obviously delighted in his oddball characters, the Chavez and Boni families, and

the people who came into the novel through their and Alec's and Cowie's memories; and he took a sardonic delight in the portrayal of the broad-bottomed Irving, who was bound to succeed in Escondido, and of "Protest" Jackson, who was equally bound to succeed in the mass-media coverage of freedom riders. He also made the animals fascinating: Evelina's neurotic and Cowie's antisocial cat, and especially the hound Larkspur, who fell in love with Wendell Horlick in Pennsylvania and crossed the continent with him, sitting erect in a rumble seat, wearing motorcycle goggles and a hat with ribbons under her chin, and perhaps audaciously enjoying life as a girl until she got to Escondido and went to pieces when she discovered what it was really like to escape a dog's life.

The imaginative richness and vitality of *One Day* is much more powerful than its intellectual despair, and it was an expression of Morris' faith as a novelist: he must be true to the present in which he lives, even though the implications of that present may be tragically inscrutable to the intellect. But so long as the creative imagination exists and finds substance to feed its energy something will come out of it. One might like to play with the fancy that nature should make a new beginning with a chipmunk, a cat, or a dog, but he knows that man has the head start. Man's capacity for tenderness (to which Eiseley attributed human survival) as well as the infinite variety of his oddities is unmatched in the animal world, and if he can come to imaginative terms with his eccentricities he may find in them the necessary compensation for his follies. The effort to do this has been the emerging figure in the carpet of Wright Morris' fiction.

It seems obvious from *One Day* that Morris could imagine no possible shock to the rational mind that might disturb the normal tenor of existence in a small town where people have withdrawn into live oddity or deadendedness, giving up consciousness, as he put it, in the interest of survival. But what of the irrational force of life itself? Morris has not yet been willing to speculate upon what it might lead to in the future, but he has always been willing, joyously if somewhat sardonically, to affirm and demonstrate its existence. Nowhere has he or anyone else done so more entertainingly than in the most perfect of his short novels, *In Orbit* (1967).

The setting is the small Indiana town of Pickett, and the irrational forces which strike it in another single day are represented by an American teen-age high school dropout and an erratic type of cyclone known as a "twister." Jubal Gainer is on his way to be inducted into the army when he suddenly finds that his world is too much with him and takes off on a stolen motorcycle, runs out of gas, and creates havoc in the town. He attempts to rape the feeble-minded "Miss Holly" Stohrmeyer (who thinks, from his helmet, that she has been visited by a spaceman) and stirs her guardian, Sanford Avery, and the local newspaper editor, Curt Hodler, in an unexpected way by his act. He pushes a bag of cherries over the head of odd little Professor Haffner and sends him to the hospital. He rewards Oscar Kashperl's talent for divining the unknown by stabbing him. He politely rescues Charlotte Hatfield when she catches her shoe in a grating and rebuffs her efforts at further acquaintance yet watches from the darkness as she dances while the cyclone rips the roof off the house. And at the end, he rides away with her shoes in his helmet. The cyclone, with all its death and destruction, will probably fade into the memory of other storms long before Jubal Gainer ceases to be remembered as another man who was there.

But the relative effect of these two natural forces is irrelevant. Morris is no longer concerned with the past but the present. And the present is in Jubal rather than in the people he leaves behind. He rides away, low in the saddle, "like a diver who has gone too deep and too long without air." Before him lies "the sunrise on the windows of the Muncie Draft Board" and perhaps the plains of China: "There is no place to hide. But perhaps the important detail escapes you. He is in motion. Now you see him, now you don't. If you pin him down in time he is lost in space. Somewhere between where he is from and where he is going he wheels in an unpredictable orbit. He is as free, and as captive, as the wind in his face . . . the rain-scoured light gleams on his helmet, like a saucer in orbit, where the supernatural is just naturally a part of his life."

Although Morris was writing about a particular character—a juvenile delinquent who looked like a spaceman and acted like a bull in a china shop, violent but not vicious—he could have found no better words to express his conception of the role of the artist in modern life. There should be no place (as he had made clear in his comments on T. S. Eliot in *The Territory Ahead*) for him to hide. He should be in motion, wheeling in an unpredictable orbit somewhere between where he is from and where he is going, something mysterious and inexplicable, perhaps, but just naturally a part of life. That he himself should have been able to play that role for more than a quarter of a century is his most remarkable achievement.

The conception of the artist which Morris has formed and followed, however, has created an obstacle to his reception by the public. His refusal to accept the traditional form of the novel which focuses attention upon the adventures of a central character (a hero or heroine of one sort or another) has bewildered the professionally rapid readers who have found his book as perplexing as they found those of the early Faulkner. On the other hand, the newer variety of critics have been put off by his Jamesian insistence upon the artist's role as the man who was there as a creative, affective intelligence which refuses either to be pinned down or evaded. It is the artist, Morris insists, whose vision counts. It is he, rather than the reader, who should be in orbit.

An awareness of his detachment from the successful exploiters of mass media is evident in his recent troubled book of criticism, *A Bill of Rites, a Bill of Wrongs, a Bill of Goods* (1968). More concerned with the social than the literary scene and filled with "laughter at what ceases to amuse," it contains a chapter on "Reflections on the Death of the Reader" which meditates upon the professional reviewer whose function is to make reading unnecessary, the machine-trained reader who can go through an "average" novel in an hour, and the "overtrained, symbol-haunted reader" who can take no pleasure in the elusiveness of a living thing but must pin it to a board in order to categorize it. "A different level of consciousness," Morris says, "seems to be engaged in the student who is studying *The Sound and the Fury*, and the reader, however naïve, who settles down with nothing but the book." The reader whose passing he mourns is the one willing to settle down with nothing but a receptive mind and a book: "Until a dialogue exists between the writer and this reader, on terms established by the author, a book is powerless to speak, or persuade, or do more than level a tipping table."

Can such a dialogue exist in the modern world of mass media, instant communication, pop art, and audience participation? Has the world become nothing more than "A Museum of Happenings"? This is the question which troubles him, especially as it is raised by the existence of artists who do not believe in art, by "the writer's misgiving, in theory and practice, of the ultimate truth of imagination," and by the creative critic who turns every work of art into "the raw material for endless series of appropriations." *A Bill of Rites* is an angry book by a man who has devoted his life to the claims of the imagination and has had his claims pre-empted by psychedelic dropouts or disallowed by such superficial doubletalk as "the media is the message."

But it is a book which faces the practical dilemma of the serious imaginative writer in the present. Should he give up, in the interest of survival, his sense of his own uniqueness and address himself to "creative" readers who have learned to make raw material out of art? Or should he insist upon the artist's peculiar power to transform the raw material of reality into something that Keats had called "the truth of Imagination"? Morris revealed his own position when he commented on "a student of the modern novel" who had recently asked him— "off the cuff and man to man"—if he didn't think the trapped fly in one of his books was "a symbolic cliché": "The Midwest setting of this novel," he said, "simply buzzed with trapped flies, and so did the book. They were flies when they came to my mind and they were still flies when I put them on the page. . . . That they might also prove to be symbols was not my proper business. When the writing is good everything is symbolic, but symbolic writing is seldom good. Symbol hunting is the fashionable safari for the vacationing writer and reader—a way of killing time."

Such a statement may be extreme, but it represents the stand of a responsible novelist against the "liquidation" of art by "an endless series" of critical or even schoolboyish "appropriations." The responsibility of the novelist which Morris asserts is that of accepting the real world and bringing it into a field of vision which will give it meaning. The meaning will be imaginative and suggestive rather than rational and reductive. If the suggestion is powerful enough it will stir the imagination of the reader, induce him to share the author's vision, and to that extent become symbolic. But the controlling power will be the mind of the writer, not that of the reader. The artist may be in the category of a neurotic chipmunk, a placid transvestite, a host at his own funeral, or a dog who thinks she is human; but without the sublime audacity of his creative imagination the world will degenerate into a museum of happenings in which the past is unknown and the future nonexistent.

For Morris this seems unlikely to occur. He has continued over an extraordinary length of time in new attempts to know the past and assert the future. *God's Country and My People* (1968) is another representation in photographs of the weather-beaten, time-haunted Nebraska (with bits of Chicago) from which he came, accompanied by a text based upon associated memories. The photographs are more varied than those in his earlier composite books, and the text is more clearly autobiographical in its references to his own people. His grandfather who first crossed the broad Missouri to settle on the plains, his parents, the village barber who remembered everything and everybody, and numerous relatives are all there in an actuality which casts some light on his fiction; but he has also included among them characters from *The Field of Vision* and *Ceremony in Lone Tree*, conjured up from some of real and imaginary fragments he had dragged into his own exile and reassembled into something of value that was not a part of his tangible memories. In this book the line between memory and imagination has been abolished: his biological ancestors and his brain children alike have become inhabitants of the territory behind with which he must come to terms before moving into that which is ahead.

This new concern for his imaginative past may have been partially responsible for his decision to publish, in 1972, the novel *War Games* which he had written in 1951–52 but had withheld from publication because its characters had potentialities not yet fully realized. In any event, it reveals the more lurid background originally conceived for Paula Kahler (here Paul Kopfman or "Mrs. Tabori") of *The Field of Vision* and the commonplace origin of Dr. Lehmann as a man of understanding in the person of Colonel Roger Foss. Told with some of the suspense and within some of the limitations of a detective novel, the story shows how much Morris was to be affected by the evolutionary ideas developed in *The Huge Season* and how the eccentricities he attributed to such characters as the colonel's wife, Hyman Kopfman, and the bellhop Tabori could be used to make real such people of greater value as Lois and young Gordon McKee and old Tom Scanlon.

In the meantime Morris had turned again to the mystery of the future in another short novel which avoided explicit speculations of any kind. On the surface *Fire Sermon* (1971) is a simple story following a familiar pattern. The focal character is a ten-year-old boy, Kermit, whose only relatives are an eighty-two-year-old great-uncle, Uncle Floyd, with whom he lives in a trailer in California and an older Aunt Viola in Nebraska. The news of Aunt Viola's death starts the boy and the uncle on a crazy cross-country trip during which they acquire the company of two hippie hitchhikers, Stanley and Joy, who represent everything that is anathema to the uncle but who also represent (as Uncle Floyd suddenly realizes) the younger generation to which the boy belongs. When they reach Aunt Viola's home they find it stuffed with all the relics of the family's past; and when it is accidentally destroyed by fire, the uncle takes off into the night in his ancient car and leaves the younger generation to itself.

Stanley is indifferent to the boy's loss, but Joy is sympathetic and tries to explain. "Fire transforms," she pronounces. "Fire purifies," she says to the boy in the last sentence, giving him "her warm, friendly smile."

An allegory suggested by the title seems equally simple. The fire (from an overturned lamp) had been started by passion, the uncle's passionate indignation against the casual sexual passion of the hippie couple, against which Buddha's Fire Sermon had been preached; and it certainly purifies the boy of all physical connection with his past. But things are not quite what they seem on the surface. The Fire Sermon is more like Eliot's than Buddha's, although it is a young boy rather than an old man who is the blind observer "throbbing between two lives"—that of his eccentric uncle and equally eccentric aunt, and that of the tribal eccentricity of the insensitive Stanley and the smiling, vacuous Joy. Furthermore, he is unlike the other small boys in Morris' novels in that he is in a state of almost complete innocence, wise enough to know that he has been abandoned by the old generation but too innocent to be taken in by the new: when Joy raises her arms skyward and puts on her Buddhistic act of acceptance, he thinks her long "OOOOOooooo MMMMM mmmmmmmmmm" must be "an animal call of some kind, at least for birds."

In *Fire Sermon* the eccentric characters Morris handles so well are all contributors to a carefully directed museum of happenings in which the promise of the future is taken from them and placed in the hands of a very normal little boy who, at the moment, can only grasp an old ox shoe as a token of the luck he knows he is going to need. But the transfer is made with such skill and restraint that it is a convincingly understated demonstration of imaginative faith. The result is a novel which will haunt some readers as a crucial drama of the times in which they have somehow failed to play a part.

In continuing to meet the responsibilities he has set for himself as a novelist, Morris has worked and reworked the raw material of his actual and imaginary experiences into a fictional reality which has a life—and a potentiality for future existence—of it own. And in doing so he has, in the words of one of his most recent and perspective critics, made "the novel seem brand new again." The newness is genuine. Morris must be taken on his own terms or not at all. But the terms have been more thoughtfully developed and established in practice for a longer time than those of any other American novelist writing today. What he asks his readers to take is an artist's effort to reconcile the truth of fact with the truth of imagination and "make it new." His own unique medium is the high seriousness of brilliant comedy in which the absurd is laid bare without bitterness and perhaps with as much faith in the past and hope for the future as a sensitive and well-informed intellectual in modern America can manage.

Selected Bibliography

WORKS OF WRIGHT MORRIS

BOOKS (FIRST AMERICAN, PAPERBACK, AND FOREIGN EDITIONS)

My Uncle Dudley. New York: Harcourt, Brace, 1942. Westport, Conn.: Greenwood Press, 1970.

The Man Who Was There. New York: Scribners, 1945.

The Inhabitants. New York: Scribners, 1946. (Photographs and text.)

The Home Place. New York: Scribners, 1948. (Photographs and text.) Lincoln: University of Nebraska Press (Bison), 1969.

The World in the Attic. New York: Scribners, 1949. Lincoln: University of Nebraska Press (Bison), 1971.

Man and Boy. New York: Knopf, 1951. London: Gollancz, 1952. *Il padre dell'eroe.* Turin, Einaudi, 1954.

The Works of Love. New York: Knopf, 1952. Lincoln: University of Nebraska Press (Bison), 1972.

The Deep Sleep. New York: Scribners, 1953. London: Eyre and Spottiswoode, 1954. *Die Gläserne Insel.* Stuttgart: Goverts, 1957. Frankfurt: Fischer Bücherei, 1960. Augsburg: Bibliothek Suhrkamp, 1967. *Un sonno profondo.* Milan: Arnoldo Mondadori Editore, 1961.

The Huge Season. New York: Viking Press, 1954. New York: Pyramid Press, 1969. London: Secker and Warburg, 1955. *Die Masslose Zeit.* Stuttgart: Goverts, 1958.

The Field of Vision. New York: Harcourt, Brace, 1956. New York: New American Library (Signet), 1957. London: Weidenfeld and Nicolson, 1957.

Love among the Cannibals. New York: Harcourt, Brace, 1957. New York: New American Library (Signet). 1958. London: Weidenfeld and Nicolson, 1958. *Amore tra i cannibali.* Milan: Feltrinelli, 1958, 1961; Garzanti, 1966. *Liebe unter Kannibalen.* Stuttgart: Goverts, 1959. Frankfurt: Fischer Bücherei, 1962. *O amor entre canibais.* Rio de Janeiro: Casa Editoa Vecchi, n.d.

The Territory Ahead. New York: Harcourt, Brace, 1958. New York: Atheneum, paperback, 1963. (Essays.)

Ceremony in Lone Tree, New York: Atheneum, 1960. New York: New American Library (Signet), 1962. London: Weidenfeld and Nicolson, 1961. *Unterwegs nach Lone Tree.* Munich: Piper Verlag, 1962. *La Dernière Fête.* Paris: Gallimard, 1964. *Ceremonia en Lone Tree.* Buenos Aires: Plaza and Janes, 1967.

What a Way to Go. New York: Atheneum, 1962. *Miss Nausikaa.* Munich: Piper Verlag, 1964.

The Mississippi Reader. Garden City, N.Y.: Doubleday (Anchor), 1962. (An anthology, edited by Morris.)

Cause for Wonder. New York: Atheneum, 1963.

One Day. New York: Atheneum, 1965.

In Orbit. New York: New American Library, 1967; Signet edition, 1968.

A Bill of Rites, a Bill of Wrongs, a Bill of Goods. New York: New American Library, 1968. (Essays.)

God's Country and My People. New York: Harper and Row, 1968. (Photographs and text.)

Wright Morris: A Reader, edited by Granville Hicks. New York: Harper and Row, 1970. (Contains *The Works of Love, The Field of Vision,* "The Ram in the Thicket," "The Safe Place," and selections from other works.)

Green Grass, Blue Sky, White House. Los Angeles: Black Sparrow Press, 1970. (Three short stories: the title story, "Since When Do They Charge Admission," and "Drrdla.") Cloth and paper.

Fire Sermon. New York: Harper and Row, 1971.

War Games. Los Angeles: Black Sparrow Press, 1972. Cloth and paper.

Love Affair: A Venetian Journal. New York: Harper and Row, 1972. (Photographs and text.)

SHORT STORIES

"Ram in the Thicket," *Harper's Bazaar,* 82:133, 182–94 (May 1948). (Reprinted in the *National Book Award Reader.* New York: Popular Library, 1966. Also reprinted in *Contemporary American Short Stories,* edited by D. and S. Angus. New York: Fawcett, 1967.)

"Where's Justice?" in *Cross Section, 1948,* edited by Edwin Seaver. New York: Simon and Schuster, 1948. Pp. 221–30.

"A Man of Caliber," *Kenyon Review,* 11:101–07 (Winter 1949).

"The Lover," *Harper's Bazaar,* 83:118, 175–80 (May 1949).

"The Sound Tape," *Harper's Bazaar,* 85:125, 175–77 (May 1951).

"The Character of the Lover," *American Mercury,* 73:43–49 (August 1951).

"The Rites of Spring," in *New World Writing,* No. 1. New York: New American Library, 1952. Pp. 140–45.

"The Safe Place," *Kenyon Review,* 16:597–600 (Autumn 1954).

"The Word from Space—A Story," *Atlantic Monthly,* 201:38–42 (April 1958). (Reprinted in *Magazine of Science Fiction,* 15:111–18 [September 1958].)

"The Cat in the Picture . . ." *Esquire,* 49:90–94 (May 1958).

"Wake before Bomb," *Esquire,* 2:311–15 (December 1959).

"Lover, Is That You?" *Esquire,* 65:70, 132–36 (March 1966).

"Since When Do They Charge Admission," *Harper's Magazine* (May 1969).

"Drrdla," *Esquire* (August 1969).

"Green Grass, Blue Sky, White House," *New Yorker* (October 25, 1969).

"Magic," *Southern Review* (January 1970).

"How I Met Joseph Mulligan, Jr.," *Harper's Magazine* (January 1970).

"A Fight between a White Boy and a Black Boy in the Dusk of a Fall Afternoon in Omaha, Nebraska," *New Yorker* (June 6, 1970).

"Fiona," *Esquire* (July 1970).

"Here is Einbaum," *New Yorker* (June 26, 1971).

"In Another Country," *Atlantic Monthly* (May 1972).

"Trick or Treat," *Quarterly Review* (Fall 1972).

"Babe Ruth's Pocket," *The Ford Times* (September 1972).

"Notes from a Venetian Journal," *The American Scholar* (Autumn 1972).

ESSAYS

"The New Criticism," *American Scholar,* 20:359 (Summer 1951).

"The Violent Land—Faulkner and Expressionism," *Magazine of Art,* 45:99–103 (March 1952).

"How Come You Settled Down Here?" *Vogue,* 119:117–19 (April 1952).

"Norman Rockwell's America," *Atlantic Monthly,* 200:133–38 (December 1957).

"The Territory Ahead," in *The Living Novel: A Symposium,* edited by Granville Hicks. New York: Macmillan, 1957. Pp. 120–56.

"Our Endless Plains," *Holiday,* 24:68–69, 138–43 (July 1958).

"Henry James's *The American Scene,*" *Texas Quarterly,* 1:27–42 (Summer–Autumn 1958).

"The Cars in My Life," *Holiday,* 24.43–53 (December 1958).

"The Ability to Function: A Reappraisal of Fitz-

gerald and Hemingway," in *New World Writing,* No. 13. New York: New American Library, 1958. Pp. 34–51.

"Mexican Journey," *Holiday,* 26:50–63 (November 1959).

"Nature before Darwin," *Esquire,* 52:64–70 (November 1959).

"Lawrence and the Immediate Present," in *A D. H. Lawrence Miscellany,* edited by Harry T. Moore. Carbondale, Ill.: Southern Illinois Press, 1959. Pp. 7–12. (Reprinted from *The Territory Ahead.*)

"The Open Road," *Esquire,* 53:98–99 (June 1960).

"Made in U.S.A.," *American Scholar,* 29:483–94 (Autumn 1960).

"One Law for the Lion," *Partisan Review,* 28: 541–51 (May–June 1961).

"Conversations in a Small Town," *Holiday,* 30:98, 100, 103, 107, 108 (November 1961).

"Shooting the Works," *Partisan Review,* 4:578–86 (Fall 1962)

"The Function of Nostalgia," in *F. Scott Fitzgerald. A Collection of Critical Essays,* edited by Arthur Mizener. Englewood Cliffs, N.J.: Prentice-Hall, 1963. Pp. 25–31.

"Death of the Reader," *Nation,* 198:53–54 (January 13, 1964).

Foreword to Mark Twain's *Pudd'nhead Wilson.* New York: New American Library (Signet), 1964.

Afterword to R. H. Dana's *Two Years before the Mast.* New York: New American Library (Signet), 1964.

"Letter to a Young Critic," *Massachusetts Review,* 6 (No. 1):93–100 (Autumn–Winter 1964–65).

Introduction to Sherwood Anderson's *Windy McPherson's Son.* Chicago: University of Chicago Press, 1965.

"The Lunatic, the Lover, and the Poet," *Kenyon Review,* 27:727–37 (Autumn 1965).

"The Origin of a Species, 1942-1957," *Massachusetts Review,* 7 (No. 1):121–35 (Winter 1966).

"How Things Are," in *Arts and the Public,* edited by James E. Miller and Paul D. Herring. Chicago: University of Chicago Press, 1967. Pp. 33–52; see also pp. 230–53 *passim.*

"Introduction: A Cause for Thanks," in *Themes and Directions in American Literature,* edited by R. B. Browne and D. Pizer. Lafayette, Ind.: Purdue University Press, 1969.

Comments by Morris on his own writings are in: *Write and Rewrite*, edited by J. Kuehl. New York: Meredith Press, 1967 (also published by Appleton-Century-Crofts as *Creative Writing and Rewriting*). *Afterwords: Novelists on their Novels*, edited by T. McCormack. New York: Harper and Row, 1969. *Writers as Teachers, Teachers as Writers*, edited by J. Baumbach. New York, Holt, Rinehart and Winston, 1970.

PHOTOGRAPHS AND PHOTO-TEXTS

"The Inhabitants," in *New Directions in Prose and Poetry, 1940*, edited by James Laughlin. Norfolk, Conn.: New Directions, 1940. Pp. 145–80.

"White House," *Twice a Year*, 5–6:116 (Fall–Winter 1940 and Spring–Summer 1941, double issue).

"The Inhabitants," *Direction*, 3:12–13 (November 1940).

"Landscape with Figures," in *New Directions in Prose and Poetry, 1941*, edited by James Laughlin. Norfolk, Conn.: New Directions, 1941. Pp. 253–77.

"The Inhabitants," *Photography* (London), July–August 1947, pp. 26–29.

"The Inhabitants," in *Spearhead: An Anthology*. Norfolk, Conn.: New Directions, 1947, Pp. 191–201.

"The American Scene," *New York Times Magazine*, July 4, 1948, pp. 14–15.

"An Author Remembers His Home Place in Nebraska," *Life*, 25:8–10 (July 26, 1948).

"Home Town Revisited," *New York Times Magazine*, April 24, 1949, pp. 24–25.

"Guest of Honour—No. 12—Wright Morris (U.S.A.)," *Photography* (London), July 1949, pp. 14–15.

"The World in the Attic," *Photography* (London), September 1949, pp. 17–26.

"Summer Encore," *New York Times Magazine*, November 13, 1949, pp. 26–27.

"Built with More Than Hands," *New York Times Magazine*, December 25, 1949, pp. 12–13.

"The Home: Echoes from Empty Houses," in *The Nation's Heritage*, Vol. 1, No. 3 (1949), no pagination (24 photographs).

U.S. Camera Annual, 1949, edited by Tom Maloney. New York: U.S. Camera Corp., 1949. P. 30.

"Out of Shoes Come New Feet," *New York Times Magazine*, June 11, 1950, pp. 20–21.

"Privacy as a Subject for Photography," *Magazine of Art*, 44:51–55 (February 1951).

BIO-BIBLIOGRAPHICAL MATERIAL

The basic checklist of Morris' publications from 1942 to 1961 is by Stanton J. Linden and David Madden in *Critique*, 4 (No. 3):77–87 (Winter 1961–62). It also lists reviews of his books, sources of biographical information and critical comments. This has been supplemented and brought up to 1963 by Madden in his full-length critical study, *Wright Morris*, pp. 177–84, which omits the reviews but provides valuable annotations for all Morris' shorter pieces and for the secondary material. This "Selected Bibliography" only adds recent titles and does not supersede the two on which it is based. Additional bio-bibliographical information may be found throughout *The Territory Ahead* and the essays listed above. The dust jacket for *The Field of Vision* provides a valuable comment on that book by the author, and "Comments by Wright Morris" are included in Granville Hicks's excellent review of *Ceremony in Lone Tree* in *Saturday Review*, 43:11 (July 9, 1960).

Bleufarb, Sam. "Point of View: An Interview with Wright Morris," *Accent*, 19:34–46 (Winter 1959).

Breit, Harvey. "Talk with Wright Morris," *New York Times Book Review*, June 10, 1951, p. 19.

Busch, Arthur J. "Fellowships for Photography," *Popular Photography*, 2:22–23, 82 (October 1942).

Hutchins, John K. "On an Author," *New York Herald Tribune Book Review*, June 3, 1951, p. 2.

Kuehl, John, ed. *Write and Rewrite*, New York: Meredith Press, 1967. (Published in paperback as *Creative Writing and Rewriting*. New York: Appleton-Century-Crofts, 1967.) Pp. 98–129.

Kunitz, Stanley J., ed. "Wright Morris," *Twentieth Century Authors*, First Supplement. New York: H. W. Wilson, 1955. Pp. 691–92.

"Main Line Author of the Month," *Main Line,* June 1951, pp. 24, 41–42.

Warfel, Harry R. *American Novelists of Today.* New York: American Book, 1951. p. 312.

"Wright Morris in Oberlin," *Plum Creek Review* (Oberlin College, Ohio), Spring 1965 (Interview.)

CRITICAL STUDIES

Aldridge, John W. "Wright Morris's Reputation" in *The Devil in the Fire.* New York: Harper's Magazine Press, 1972.

Allen, Walter. *The Modern Novel in Britain and the United States.* New York: Dutton, 1964. Pp. 315–17.

Baumbach, Jonathan. "Wake before Bomb: *Ceremony in Lone Tree," Critique,* 4:56–71 (Winter 1961–62). See also *The Landscape of Nightmare.* New York: New York University Press, 1965. Pp. 152–69.

Booth, Wayne C. "The Two Worlds in the Fiction of Wright Morris," *Sewanee Review,* 65:375–99 (Summer 1957).

———. "The Shaping of Prophecy: Craft and Idea in the Novels of Wright Morris," *American Scholar,* 31:608–26 (Autumn 1962).

Carpenter, Frederic. "Wright Morris and the Territory Ahead," *College English,* 21:147–56 (December 1959).

Coles, Robert. "The Manners, the Manners" (on *God's Country and My People)* in "Books," *New Yorker,* October 18, 1959.

Dommergues, Pierre. *Les Ecrivains américains d'aujourd'hui.* Paris: Presses Universitaires de France, 1965.

———. *Les USA.* Paris: Editions Bernard Grasset, 1967.

Eisinger, Chester E. *Fiction of the Forties.* Chicago: University of Chicago Press, 1963. Pp. 328–41.

Fiedler, Leslie. *Love and Death in the American Novel.* New York: Criterion Books, 1960. Pp. 323–24, 471–72.

Garrett, George P. "Morris the Magician: A Look at *In Orbit," Hollins Critic* (Hollins College, Virginia), Vol. 4, No. 3 (June 1967).

Hassan, Ihab. *Radical Innocence: Studies in the Contemporary American Novel.* Princeton, N.J.: Princeton University Press, 1961; New York Harper and Row, 1966. Pp. 6, 78, 101.

Hunt, John W., Jr. "The Journey Back: The Early Novels of Wright Morris," *Critique,* 5:41–60 (Spring–Summer 1962).

Klein, Marcus. *After Alienation.* Cleveland and New York: World, 1964. Pp. 196–246.

Madden, David. "The Hero and the Witness in Wright Morris' Field of Vision," *Prairie Schooner,* 34:263–78 (Fall 1960).

———. "The Great Plains in the Novels of Wright Morris," *Critique,* 4:5–23 (Winter 1961–62).

———. *Wright Morris.* New York: Twayne, 1964.

Trachtenberg, Alan. "The Craft of Vision," *Critique,* 4:41–55 (Winter 1961–62).

Waterman, Arthur E. "The Novels of Wright Morris: An Escape from Nostalgia," *Critique,* 4:24–40 (Winter 1961–62).

LEON HOWARD

Vladimir Nabokov

1899-1977

SINCE Proust we have accepted the view that memory is an art, maybe the sole art to have survived God's death, and that nostalgia may encapsulate a metaphysic. Until V. V. Nabokov came to America in 1940 we Americans had no great modern artist in nostalgia of our own, although F. Scott Fitzgerald strikes the authentic note when he imagines Nick Carraway observing Gatsby waiting for the green light in the closing paragraphs of *The Great Gatsby*. Gatsby mistakes the past for the future —the characteristic error of nostalgists—when he anticipates a reunion with Daisy, that shopworn Louisville Lolita, which "was already behind him, somewhere back in that vast obscurity beyond the city, where the dark fields of the republic rolled on under the night." And Fitzgerald's power of evocation in this instance arises from the fact, tragic for his entire career, that he too is a nostalgist, "borne back ceaselessly into the past," victim of a disposition and attitude he rarely was able to command for the servicing of his art.

"Nostalgist" is a graceless term. In *Pale Fire* Nabokov coins the expression "preterist: one who collects cold nests" for the artist who commands the past qua past, never confusing it with present and future although his created characters may do so, and drawing from this beguiling imaginative realm rich material for an art of memory which illuminates the whole range of time through which the artist has lived. Considering William Faulkner's obsession with lapsed time in his Yoknapatawpha County sequence we might think that he before Nabokov is the great American artist of preterism. Yet in Faulkner time is spatialized, into an echoing corridor where characters like Quentin Compson and Rosa Coldfield run furiously, doing battle with ghosts from Civil War times and earlier; or it is frozen into a hallucinatory instant when ghostly men-at-arms relive at close of day their moment of glorious risk under the rapt eye of a defeated eccentric like the Reverend Gail Hightower.

Preterist art, by contrast, works in a cooler, more classical fashion. Both Proust and Nabokov establish clear boundaries between past and present, provide elaborate and meticulously drafted maps for their realms of recollection, and carefully choose the grounds, or privileged moments, at which past and present will be allowed, briefly and dangerously, to meet and commingle. The goal of these artists is something more important than self-discovery or the discovery of cultural and regional identity. It is the discovery and definition of human consciousness, conceived as the master key to the riddle of reality, conceived also as providing limited, transitory glimpses of the realms of essence.

Neither Proust nor Nabokov permits this essentially metaphysical quest to sterilize his fictional art. Both remain great tragicomic novelists in close touch with the actualities of man in contemporary society and with central issues of modern history. Thirst for the eternal never alienates their loyalty to the human condition although it may constitute the deepest source of their great originality and power as stylists and fabulists. In the following pages I shall try to indicate the range, charm, and contemporary relevance of Nabokov's prose artistry without, I hope, ever quite losing sight of his cunning, wholly devoted pursuit of certain overwhelming questions which the publicists of the death of God once thought, mistakenly, to have put to death as well.

Nabokov was born in 1899 into a rich, accomplished, and socially enlightened St. Petersburg family which had given admirals, scholars, and statesmen to the Russian nation over many generations. He enjoyed a privileged and secure boyhood, dividing his time between the beautiful Nabokov country estate called Vyra and a town house ample and elegant enough to accommodate under the Soviets a foreign diplomatic mission and later a school of architecture. He attended an excellent and progressive school in the city and spent his holidays at the country estate, where he became an expert tennis player and amateur lepidopterist, and on the French Riviera, to which the Nabokovs were accustomed to travel annually by train to enjoy sea bathing and the sedate life in luxurious hotels led by the high European bourgeoisie of that vanished time. This Edenic phase was abruptly terminated when Vladimir's father, who had been a lead-

ing member of the Russian Constituent Assembly, took his family south to Yalta to avoid the Red armies of the Bolshevik Revolution and, upon the collapse of White military resistance in the Crimea, fled with them into exile in Western Europe.

Between 1919 and 1922 Vladimir, who had learned English thoroughly from governesses and tutors while a small child, studied modern languages and literature at Trinity College, Cambridge. After graduating with first-class honors he rejoined his family in Berlin and set about launching a career as an émigré poet, critic, and novelist. In 1922 his beloved and admired father fell victim to a pair of Russian right-monarchist gunmen while chairing a political meeting and Vladimir, the oldest son, became head of a family for which the condition of exile from its native country was destined to be permanent.

Throughout the 1920's and 1930's, writing in Russian under the pen name V. Sirin and residing first in Berlin and then in Paris, Nabokov produced a brilliant series of poems, stories, and novels which established him as unquestionably the most gifted Russian writer-in-exile of his generation. At the same time, his attitude toward the endless political intrigues, fantasies of imminent Romanov restoration, religious manias, and literary cabals of the Russian émigré circles centering on Berlin, Prague, and Paris remained detached, ironic, and independent. He suffered with his fellow Russians the inconvenience and indignity of the Nansen passport, issued by the League of Nations to stateless persons, and financial problems at times forced him into such temporary extraliterary expedients as coaching tennis, teaching language, and composing chess problems for magazines. But there was no extended period during the difficult first two decades of his career when he was deflected from his main task—the creation of a major literary oeuvre in Russian, culminating in *Dar* or *The Gift* (1938), a masterpiece of wit, poetic fantasy, and stylistic games which remains, in my opinion, one of his three finest novels, as well as one of the great books of twentieth-century literature in any language.

In 1940 when Nabokov departed for America, accompanied by his wife, Véra, and young son Dmitri, a new twenty-year phase of his career opened. Begun in the distress and obscurity of a second exile during wartime, it was to turn, but not fully until after 1955 and the publication of *Lolita*, into an extraordinary, and perhaps peculiarly American, success story. As early as 1939, while still in France, he had begun to write in English, no doubt in wary anticipation of an impending move to England or America as Hitler's troops were massing to overrun Western Europe as far as the Atlantic. He settled first in the Boston area, taught Russian literature at Wellesley while simultaneously conducting scientific research in lepidopterology at the Harvard Entomological Museum, and brought out his first full-length literary work in English, the beguiling and melancholy *The Real Life of Sebastian Knight*, in 1941.

Over approximately the next decade and a half there occurred the amazing transformation of this middle-aged, twice-exiled European artist, scientist, and scholar into the great American author whom the world acknowledges today. His stories and verses and the chapters of his memoir about his Russian and European years appearing in the *New Yorker* during the late 1940's and early 1950's, which showed a constantly expanding command of English written style and its American vernacular adjuncts, established him with an American audience. At Cornell, where he taught Russian literature for some ten years after leaving Boston, he was able to pursue the nostalgic

yet profound studies in Pushkin which culminated in his monumental four-volume translation of *Eugene Onegin* with commentaries (1964). Cornell also exposed him to the pleasures, pangs, pomps, and bizarreries of American academic life, an experience he would put richly to use in writing the comic and touching prose sketches that make up *Pnin* (1957) and the third of his three greatest books, *Pale Fire* (1962). Even the long American academic vacations made a signal contribution, for it was during summers away from Cornell, while traveling extensively through North America on butterfly-hunting expeditions, that he became familiar with the ambience of highways and byways, the subculture of motels, filling stations, frazzled eateries, and bypassed, desperate resorts which contribute so sinister and pitiful a flavor to the imaginative environment of *Lolita*.

Publication of *Lolita*, the second of his triumvirate of masterpieces, in 1955, marks the full emergence of the butterfly from the chrysalis, the point at which Nabokov was able to come at long last into full control of his artistic destiny. The book's financial success permitted him to resign his Cornell post, and a much-enhanced interest in all aspects of Nabokov's work throughout the English-speaking world has led over the past decade to the publication in excellent English translations (most of them by his son Dmitri) of nearly all the novels and novellas he had brought out in Russian during the twenties and thirties. This important project, which is still under way, has won a magical second life for the work of Nabokov's pre-American career while simplifying the task of evaluating his total achievement in fiction and confirming his position in the forefront of modern writers.

Since 1960 Nabokov has lived abroad once again, in Montreux, Switzerland. He remains an American citizen, revisits the United States frequently, and continues to affirm an affectionate attachment to this country in recent published interviews. Although he turned seventy in 1969 and was honored by a Festschrift to which a wide international array of critics, scholars, and creative writers contributed, he is still in full career as a writer himself. In 1967 he brought out his own Russian translation of *Lolita* and 1969 saw publication of *Ada; or Ardor*, a quarter-million-word "family chronicle" novel in English, conceived in a rather baroque stylistic vein and containing some spectacular erotic episodes along with an elaborate plot, a stunningly original setting, and a lengthy terminal essay on the nature of time. Not now, and it is to be hoped, not for many years to come, can a critical commentator pretend to say the last word about this, as it were, amphibious Russian and American creative personality.

Speak, Memory (1951, revised edition 1966), called *Conclusive Evidence* in the British edition and *Drugiye Berega* (Other Shores) in a less well known and partly variant Russian version, is both an autobiography covering Nabokov's first forty-one years and a carefully shaped work of art devoted to the muse of memory, "Mnemosyne." For our purposes it provides a bridge between its author's lived experience and his re-creation of that experience in writing; and, not surprisingly, because it is a creative work of first rank, it reveals themes, conceptions, and images which one finds in various combinations and enlargements in his fiction proper.

It begins, rather like the famous first chapter of Dickens' *Great Expectations*, with an account of the infant child's awakening to consciousness. Awareness of self is born simultaneously with an awareness of an imprisonment in time, a time stranded between two eternities of darkness, all-past and all-future, a time defined as "walls . . . separating me and my bruised fists from the free world of timelessness," a prison that "is spherical and without exits." Rebellion against this tragic state of affairs is also born with consciousness of it and seeks in consciousness itself—in the heightening of consciousness we call imagination—a way out. There is no way out "short of suicide." This is surely one master idea in all of Nabokov's work. Yet through consciousness, through reflection on the riddling and cryptic appearances of the world, both outer and inner, in which the prisoner finds himself immured, he begins to discover or invent patterns, themes, repetitions, which hint at or gesture toward a possibility of transcendence into "the free world of timelessness" from which he has been banished through the catastrophic accident of biologic birth. And art, supremely, is the reflection of consciousness through which these discoveries become possible.

If the world is made of cryptic and riddling appearances, what can the prisoner discover, even through the agency of imagination, that amounts to more than deception piled on deception, *trompe l'oeil* painting on a prison wall? In chapter one of *Speak, Memory* Nabokov tells of General Kuropatkin, a visitor to the St. Petersburg house who amused the five-year-old Vladimir by arranging matches on the divan, first horizontally to form the sea in calm weather and then zigzag to form a stormy sea. The matches were scattered when the General, interrupted by an aide, rushed off to take command of—and to lose!—Russia's war in the Far East against Japan. Fifteen years later, when Nabokov's father was fleeing to southern Russia, he encountered on a bridge a gray-bearded peasant who asked him for a light. It was General Kuropatkin in disguise.

Here Nabokov remarks, "What pleases me is the evolution of the match theme," and we shall not take his point at all if we take the story altogether unseriously. The difference between the General, mocked by riddling destiny in the matter of matches, and Nabokov, reflecting upon a "repetitional theme," is considerable. Both the writer and the General are prisoners of contingency but the latter abides in dungeon darkness while the former has found a light by which he can see and reflect upon where and what he is. Thus, at the beginning of *Drugiye Berega*, Nabokov can speak of his autobiographical aim, which is "to describe the past with utmost precision and to discover in it extraordinary outlines: namely, the development and repetition of hidden themes in the midst of one's overt destiny"; and, near the beginning of *Speak, Memory*, he can mention "the anonymous roller that pressed upon my life a certain intricate watermark whose unique design becomes visible when the lamp of art is made to shine through life's foolscap." The artist is at least free to spy out and to pursue, in the light of art, patterns removed from the domain of the absurd and meaningless by virtue of the mere fact that they *are*, visibly, of a certain shape and design: "the following of such thematic designs through one's life should be . . . the true purpose of autobiography."

Nevertheless, the basic theme is imprisonment, and Nabokov's novels are full of characters like Humbert Humbert whose frenzied pursuit of a certain "thematic design" called nymphets serves only to confirm his squalid, pitiful, and pathological enslavement. If liberation into timelessness is a real goal then all this activity of hunting down and following up, this spying and descrying in the light of consciousness and conscious art, falls far short of a real attained freedom. On Nabokov's own terms, is not the distinction between the artist-autobiographer and the unfortunate General simply the difference between a prisoner who takes exercise by creeping along the walls of his cell, holding aloft a guttering candle or feeble battery flashlight, and one who stays still in darkness waiting for death? They are both serving a life sentence and who therefore is to say that the less active one has made the worse adjustment?

This conclusion ignores a second great resource of the artist and autobiographer blessed with the power of imaginative reflection—his gift for making images. Toward the end of *Speak, Memory* Nabokov gaily describes the impact of the writings of the youthful and brilliant V. Sirin on Russian readers raised "on the sturdy straightforwardness of Russian realism." These readers, who were not in on the secret that Sirin and Nabokov are the same person, "were impressed by the mirror-like angles of his clear but weirdly misleading sentences and by the fact that the real life of his books flowed in his figures of speech, which one critic has compared to 'windows giving upon a contiguous world . . . a rolling corollary, the shadow of a train of thought.' "

The anonymous critic, who is certainly Nabokov himself in still another playful disguise, points up with the first of his comparisons the transcendent function of aesthetic images in Nabokov's work. Images are openings. Made out of words and from the materials of contingent experience, they paradoxically and magically create apertures in the walls of imprisoning time, transparencies which let in light from the free world of timelessness. Nabokov says of his own early works that the best "are those in which he condemns his people to the solitary confinement of their own souls." Actually, it is a cruelly true remark about all of his best works. But there is a way out, or at least a way of seeing out, for those who have sufficient imagination to fashion or discover an opening into timelessness. A number of Nabokov's "people," early and late, are driven to madness and death through their devotion to false images. Yet these failures, which must be seen finally as failures of imagination, of the image-making function in a generic sense, are never meant to suggest that the pursuit of transcendence through imagination should be abandoned as a hopeless project. If, for Nabokov, man is in prison, and if even the true images that he may descry or invent through artful intensities of consciousness tend, as they do in Yeats's great meditation on image making, "Among School Children," to break the heart by mocking man's contingency, the images still remain the only clue to the only thing worth attending to—the nature of the reality that lies outside the prison wall. The search for windows remains fundamental to Nabokov's powerfully imagistic art: there are really no alternatives, except a collapse of consciousness or the physical act of suicide.

Speak, Memory itself sumptuously and cunningly triumphs over lapsed time and uses the master image of apertures to do so. At the beginning the author sees "the awakening of consciousness as a series of spaced flashes, with the intervals between them gradually diminishing until bright blocks of perception are formed, affording memory a slippery hold." By the third chapter these perceptual blocks have stopped dancing and the author can refer, more straightforwardly, to "the act of vividly recalling a patch of the past." By now the method of the book, which is to deal in separate chapters with a single block, patch, image, or frame of recalled experience, has become clear. But method and content fuse as he recalls crucial early experiences and scenes involving windows and introduces the bright patches constituted by stained glass and butterfly specimens into the account of his growing up on the family estate. The train windows of the St. Petersburg-to-Paris Express dominate in the seventh chapter, and the vertiginous experience of glimpsing bright flashes of landscape outside the rushing train reinforces the original account of infant consciousness as a series of spaced flashes. Nabokov begins Chapter Eight by remarking casually that he is going to show a few "slides" and within the chapter manages to put together the account of an actual Magic-Lantern Projection evening arranged by his tutor with a recollection of his discovery of the beauty of glass slides seen in work with the microscope. The latter were "translucent miniatures, pocket wonderlands, neat little worlds of hushed luminous hues" where, while contemplating this particular form of bright patch, he found a "delicate meeting place between imagination and knowledge."

In the context of memory this delicate meeting place is what the whole book is exploring; and the possibility of such exploration depends on the imagery of bright patches framed in an aperture. Even the boldly colored comic strips brought to him from America by his uncle—characteristically he is more interested in the pointillist technique of their reproduction than in the story they tell—become part of the pattern; as does "one last little garden" he walked in with his wife and son at St. Nazaire, just before going on board ship to sail to America —a garden with "a geometrical design which no doubt I could easily fill in with the colors of plausible flowers."

What is most fascinating about the memory-art of *Speak, Memory* is that things long dead and vanished in the past come fully to life precisely by being placed within a series of frames, by being "reduced" or "fixed" in a pattern, by being subdued to imagery and artifice. If memory speaks it speaks visually, beckoning through a window, and we are left in the face of this happy mystery to reflect that the charmed life possessed by objects, persons, and places that time has consumed owes nothing to the prison house of temporality and everything to the art by which they have been evoked out of the "contiguous world" that Nabokov has opened the windows of his figures and images upon.

Collectors—of butterflies and cold nests—are often solitary men. But *Speak, Memory*, established upon the intuition of man's ineluctable solitude, terminates, through a happy inconsistency, in communion. Its last chapter, addressed to Nabokov's own wife and recollecting the birth and infancy of Dmitri, celebrates nothing less than a happy marriage. This marriage is the single gift out of the past which needs no re-creation in art. Nabokov says, "I must know where I stand, where you and my son stand"; and where he stands, in the now of affectionate concern to which the book returns from its exploration of the past, is upon "mortal love." All or nearly all of Nabokov's books are dedicated to his wife, Véra, whose name in Russian is also the word for faith, belief, religion, and trust. Let us turn now to his novels proper to see what happens to his intuition of man's imprisonment in consciousness and time, his theme of transcendence through image making, and his faith in mortal marital love as he creates over a period of more than forty years a body of work in fiction which is like no other writer's anywhere in our part of the twentieth century.

There are now available in English eight Nabokov novels originally composed in Russian and six composed in English. Before giving extended consideration to four of these books—my choices reflect factors of personal taste, a sense of where the inner dialectic of Nabokov's artistic vision is most significantly at work, and a keen sense of the space limits of the essay form—I have a particular point to make about all his novels that can best be clarified through briefer discussion of a fairly large number of them.

The point is this: Nabokov's novels are never direct imitations of life. Invariably, they are imitations of life. A Nabokov novel does not begin with or issue from a selection of experience with concomitant selection of a governing point of view. Rather, it issues from the deliberate selection of a formal narrative type or structure, occasionally from selection of nonfictional narrative forms such as the biography, and, just once, from selection of the non-narrative form of scholarly commentary and emendation. Nabokov is a spirited and learned parodist of prose forms accumulated through the evolution of literary history in the West, yet his impulses to parody are not pedantic or frivolous; nor do they constitute acts of aggression against either literary history or literary art. Rather, he has a sophisticated and true awareness of how forms of literary art and organization are forms of consciousness *au fond*, of how a given type of narrative frames a definite perspective on experience. One kind of narrative, to change the metaphor, fences out—in terms of characterization, angle of narration, the representation of place or of societal data, the ordering of events, the tone and pace of narration, and so forth—one entire set of human possibilities while fencing in some other set. To put this oversimply, a gothic romance will usually eschew a hard, dry narrative tone, while a novel cast in the form of a confession will not employ the viewpoint of omniscience. A crime novel will usually be more logically ordered with respect to plot than a metaphysical fantasy emphasizing enigmatic aspects of reality. A *Bildungsroman* will stress the accumulating experience and viewpoint of one central character over that of other characters, and a ghost story, unless it is merely a debunking of the supernatural, will use supernatural material as though apparitions are real.

Nabokov uses all the types I have mentioned and others as well with full awareness of what each ordinarily can and cannot be made to do.

Precisely because he is so aware he often introduces twists and drastic modifications, even sometimes breeds type with type, working somewhat on the analogy of the gifted laboratory experimenter who moves out from the known to the unknown by viewing the materials of his experiment from unexpected angles and combining them in new ways. It is a highly conscious process. Nabokov has nothing but contempt for the concept of simple sincerity in art, which he equates with a fatuous willingness to pour old spoiled wine into leaky bottles. He is, for example, one of the great originators in contemporary letters of that fictional hybrid called black comedy. Black comedy in his hands is just such a product of scrupulously supervised crossbreeding as no artistic practice or critical method founded upon moralistic notions of the sincere in art could have created or predicted.

King, Queen, Knave (1928), second earliest of his novels to receive English translation, conforms to the fictional type that centers on a young man of humble provincial origins who seeks social and commercial advancement in the city, only to become corrupted there and lapse back into a deeper obscurity. An obvious exemplar, to which Nabokov obliquely refers in a foreword written for the English translation of 1968, is Dreiser's *An American Tragedy*; but Nabokov's detached, deliberately diagrammatic treatment of his central characters—Dreyer, a Berlin department store owner, Martha, his unfaithful and treacherous wife, and knavish Franz, his dull, gullible, and ultimately treacherous nephew—reduces the central intrigue, a scheme to murder Dreyer that is attempted and bungled by the wife and nephew, to a kind of puppet show acted out by mannequin-like creatures whose relationships and conflicts can be fully specified by the cipher language of a game of cards: K (unwittingly) against QKn with a mysterious trump card of

accident introduced at the last moment to give the game to K. *King, Queen, Knave*, by taking the nature out of Dreiserian (and Flaubertian) naturalism, exposes the bare bones of naturalistic contrivance. It also exposes the emptiness and sterility of an "advanced" German bourgeois milieu where people live lives of blank desperation in houses designed, decorated, and furnished according to the rational, geometric canons of the Bauhaus and the Dutch *De Stijl* movements.

The Eye (1930) is a novella belonging to the category of ghost story. An unhappy, self-obsessed young Russian named Smurov shoots himself because he is unlucky in love, is uncertain of his true nature, and imagines himself despised by various Russian expatriates frequenting a certain lodging house in Berlin. He then returns as a ghostly spy and wanders through the minds of the people who had spurned him in life, taking note of the several wholly distinct and incompatible versions of his own identity which different minds go on entertaining. At the end it appears that he is not dead after all, nor is the original mystery about the nature of "the true Smurov" cleared up to either his or the reader's satisfaction. This abiding mystery is a lively and illuminating way of pointing to the problems of identity created by the stance of extreme self-consciousness. *The Eye* is, at once, a comic investigation of late adolescent self-concern, the portrait of a shy, autistic, and endearing young man who ought to take up writing as a strategy for self-encounter, a fable about the vocation of the imagining and remarking artist and the price he pays in isolation and self-effacement for his special kind of awareness, and, finally, perhaps an early self-portrait of the artist who wrote it.

The Defense (also 1930) is the first of several novels which invent extraordinary variations on the imaginary biography. When Nabokov has this type in hand his central character is always remarkable and usually a genius. Moreover, the author nearly always chooses to emphasize the deep solitude and the inevitable estrangement from other people that represent the price exacted by destiny for the gift of high imaginative or intellectual powers. Most of Nabokov's central characters are unrepentant individualists; his geniuses are merely the extreme limit of the general case.

Luzhin, the Russian-born hero of *The Defense*, is a forlorn, inarticulate, and physically graceless chess genius, a sort of *idiot savant* of the international tournament circuit. After a wretched boyhood and a lonely adult career it becomes his fate to fall in love (with a good woman who loves him in return) when it is too late, when his mind has been taken over by a paranoid affliction which resolves the issues, projects, and challenges of his daily life into a series of chess moves based upon an unwinnable defensive strategy. What Nabokov calls "chess effects" are worked into the narrative throughout, reaching a climax in the last scene—one of the great tours de force in all of Nabokov's fiction. Here Luzhin, the king at check in his own apartment, the rooms and corridors of which appear to him under the aspect of the game he is forced to play and cannot win, tries to break out of the entrapment by bursting through the frosted white square of the bathroom window. But he falls to his death into a chasm of "dark and pale squares" which show him "exactly what kind of eternity was obligingly and inexorably spread out before him."

Nabokov's preface to the English translation of *The Defense*, published in 1964, appears to hint that Luzhin's losing moves are based on an actual historic match, the "Immortal Game" played between L. Kieseritzky and A. Anderssen during a London tournament of masters in 1851. Although in *Speak, Memory* he characterizes his hobby of composing chess problems as a "beautiful, complex and sterile art" there is nothing bloodless about the "combinational" artistry of *The Defense*, and Luzhin himself, in his gentleness, profound introversion, and total incapacity for coping with the "real world," remains one of Nabokov's most touching and lovingly drawn characterizations. For Nabokov the chessboard appears as "a system of stresses and abysses," possessed of the same three-dimensional qualities and fatal choices as life itself. By the same token, life in Nabokov's novels can sometimes appear, as it certainly does in *The Defense*, to be a three-dimensional chess game the issue of which is clouded by a terrible, teasing question: are men the players at the board or are they merely the pawns and other pieces of the game? And if the latter, who controls the play?

John Shade, the "preterist" poet in *Pale Fire*, opts for the second theory and finds solace in the notion that the life he does not control becomes endurable through his contemplative appreciation of its intricate "web of sense":

> Yes! It sufficed that I in life could find
> Some kind of link-and-bobolink, some
>   kind
> Of correlated pattern in the game,
> Plexed artistry, and something of the same
> Pleasure in it as they who played it found.

But it is doubtful that Shade could respond with unqualified appreciation to the sequence of "topsyturvical coincidence" that led to his own violent death, and there are Nabokov novels which address the clouded issue of human fate and freedom with anything but equanimity. Two of these are perhaps best treated in close proximity because they are both novels about "actual" imprisonment and oppression at the hands—under the heel, rather—of political state power.

Invitation to a Beheading (1938) follows the fictional type of metaphysical fantasy with political overtones that we are familiar with from the works of Franz Kafka. One can believe Nabokov's disclaimer of any knowledge of Kafka at the time of its composition around 1934, and still remain free to surmise that the book does respond imaginatively to certain grotesque and awful features of modern totalitarianism that Kafka's fiction had prophetically anticipated. The hero, Cincinnatus C., is sequestered in a solitary cell within a castle fortress and awaits execution by beheading. His crime, called "gnostical turpitude" in the bill of indictment against him, is to have remained an individual, thinking his own thoughts and reflecting on the world in his own way. He has no ally within the prison, unless it is Emmie, the jailer's child, who appears mysteriously within his cell, shows him enigmatic stick drawings which appear to diagram an escape route, and leads him, as if in a cruelly deceptive dream, through a maze of corridors that return him finally to his own cell. He is tricked at every turn: the other "prisoner" who tunnels through his cell wall turns out to be his executioner; his unfaithful wife sides with his tormentors; even the window high on one wall through which he longs to look out upon the "Tamara Gardens," a paradisal place where "we used to roam and hide" in childhood, is a painted fake complete with a clockwork spider spinning a synthetic web.

What is demanded of Cincinnatus before his beheading is something even worse than his confession to crimes he has not committed. It is complete, self-degrading cooperation in his own undoing. The regime, farcical in its inefficiency and the downright clownishness of its officials, maintains itself on a single obscene and inhuman principle, that of collaboration. In securing Cincinnatus' conviction, the defense attorney has collaborated with the prosecutor and the judge with both. At the ultimate reach of infamy the prisoner is expected to waltz with the jailer, compliment the prison governor on the excellence of the prison accommodation, admire the axeman for his expertise, and post to his decapitation as if honored by an Invitation to the Dance. Declining the invitation, Cincinnatus resists quietly to the end. Yet it is just this bizarre feature of the wholly corrupt prison world of *Invitation* that evokes direct parallels with the actual history of modern totalitarian states. Whether we think of the ritualistic public confessions of the Moscow treason trials in the 1930's or of the Nazi death camps in the 1940's, where prisoners were encouraged to compete for the privilege of dying last by helping the guards to torture and kill their fellow prisoners, we are contemplating the same perversion of the collaborative principle.

Despite these historical parallels, *Invitation to a Beheading* is scarcely a work of fictional realism. The temporal setting is future—almost no—time; the fortress and the adjacent town, with its winding streets, public fountain and statues, the Tamara Gardens and the woodland beyond, seem to belong to the vaguely medieval world of Central European folklore rather than to the world we know. By contrast, *Bend Sinister* (1947), characterized by Nabokov as having "stylistic links" to *Invitation*, comes much closer to the type of the overtly political novel. In 1947 the small nations of Eastern Europe were bending left under pressure from the U.S.S.R. *Bend Sinister*, for all its qualities of fantasy and its many passages which hint that the oppressions suffered by its main characters reflect universal conditions, depicts a turning away from individual freedoms toward an imposed collectivism that closely resembles what was happening in such countries as Poland, Bulgaria, Hungary, Rumania, and Czechoslovakia during the immediate postwar period.

Bend Sinister, written in English, is perhaps

Nabokov's only morbid book. Its hero, Adam Krug, a distinguished philosopher and university professor in a nameless country whose inhabitants speak a Slavic language of sorts, sees his beloved wife succumb to illness within the first few pages. Better for Krug to have died with her in view of what is to come. The country has been taken over by a revolutionary clique preaching perfect equality but employing totalitarian methods of terror and under the control of a dictator called Paduk—the Toad. Paduk, who is an old schoolfellow of Krug's, the sadistic bully of the play yard, and whose name is a virtual anagram of the Russian *upadok*, signifying decay, decline, degeneration, wants Krug broken into conformity so that less prominent citizens of the country will not be inspired by Krug's notorious individualism to go on thinking thoughts of their own.

The means taken to break him are awful and yet perfectly familiar to anyone who has read the newspapers during the past three or four decades. Krug is summoned to a blandishing and threatening interview with the Toad himself, "clothed from carbuncle to bunion in field gray," his eyes those "of a fish in a neglected aquarium." When the tactic is unsuccessful, the state apparatus of terror takes over. Krug is driven from the university and subjected to harassment and spying by the police. His only son, David, upon whom Krug lavishes the affection of a grief-stricken widower as well as a doting father, is stolen from him, tortured, and then murdered. Finally, Krug is put into solitary confinement after having been shown on film the particulars of his son's fate.

Both *Invitation to a Beheading* and *Bend Sinister*, to the extent that they are concerned with politics and society, reflect a bottomless pessimism about politics and the social process in our time. While reading these books one keeps remembering that their author was driven into exile and saw his father killed because of "politics" and that the absolute individualism of Nabokov's world view tends to deny him the consolation of belief that any agency, operating in or beyond history, will eventually redeem the sufferings inflicted on innocent and decent people by savage and incompetent ideologues and power brokers in this century. Both books end with spectacular Nabokovian *coups de théâtre* the significance of which remains perfectly equivocal. At the moment of his beheading, Cincinnatus finds that he is on his feet and walking freely through collapsing and disintegrating bits of stage scenery, "in that direction where, to judge by the voices, stood beings akin to him." And at the moment when Krug, in prison, is about to awaken to the "hideous misfortune" of his lot, Nabokov tells us *in propria persona* that "I felt a pang of pity for Adam and slid towards him along an inclined beam of pale light—causing instantaneous madness, but at least saving him from the senseless agony of his logical fate." In each case, especially in the second, the author plays God, arriving from beyond the prisoning "form" (logical and teleological) of the story to help the helpless character. But there is nothing in Nabokov's sense of the human plight as a whole to which these acts of compassionate intervention provide an analogy. There is no God of compassion or redemption in the universe at large who will do for "Adam" what the author Nabokov does for his characters by means of a merely ironic, and in some sense despairing, trick of fiction.

After thus illustrating my point about the way Nabokov employs, modifies, and reanimates various narrative structures or types—the way in which his books are artful imitations of imitations—I want now to consider in more depth the several books in the Nabokov canon of fiction to which one finds oneself returning frequently; the books which express most hauntingly and richly his deepest sense of life; which in particular represent the core of permanence in his work, or, rather, the permanent addition he has made to the house of fiction in our time.

I have in mind four novels—two from the 1930's originally written in Russian, two from the 1950's and 1960's originally written in English—which arrange themselves across the language barrier and the time gap as two related pairings. The first pair consists of *Kamera Obskura* (1933)—titled *Camera Obscura* in its first translated version (London, 1936) but retitled *Laughter in the Dark* in its revised American translation of 1938, which I am following here—and *Lolita* (1955). These are intimately related as melodramas of audacious metaphysical crime centering upon the theme of the "nymphet." The second pair consists of *Dar* (1938; 1952), translated as *The Gift* in 1963, and *Pale Fire* (1962). The first is a book about a young poet which uses the framing devices of imaginary biography and the *Künstlerroman* to explore the themes of poetic art, Russian literary culture, and young love. The second is a book about an old poet which uses the devices of scholarly commentary, imaginary autobiography, and poetry itself to explore the themes of poetic art, of the irredeemability of time past, and of human solitude in counterpoise with wedded love.

Laughter in the Dark and *Lolita* differ tremendously in nearly all respects, not least in the degree of self-awareness of their chief characters, the suggestively named Albinus and the self-designated "Humbert Humbert." Yet Albinus and Humbert stand closer together in a crucially important respect than any other two characters in Nabokov. Both are possessed by a thirst for the infinite, suffer from the metaphysical obsession traditionally named the "de-sire and pursuit of the whole." Further, both have received a true intuition that the route to the infinite is through attachment to an adorable image or eidolon, yet both blunder, perversely and fatally, by haplessly confounding the image with its illusory reflection or echo in the flesh of a child-woman. The consequence is that they fall, into an enslavement entailing their torture and mockery by demonic men, artists themselves, who as film makers are in the business of degrading images, who as nemeses raised by the obsessions of their victims have (and delight in) the task of punishing Albinus and Humbert for their idolatrous passions.

Literally, "camera obscura" means "dark chamber." More comprehensively, a camera obscura is any dark chamber including photographic cameras, darkened cinema palaces, a prison cell, and, for Nabokov, the cranial cell behind the eyes wherein imprisoned consciousness languishes, with a lens or opening through which an image may be projected in "natural" colors onto a receptive surface. Nabokov's choice of the camera obscura as a guiding metaphor in his account of Albinus' dismal fate becomes perfectly logical and appropriate, given his powerfully visual imagination, his notion of images as windows and apertures, his notion of man as a prisoner languishing within walls of time and contingency, and his conviction that imagination is the faculty of consciousness which attempts to spy beyond the prison walls through image making. Albinus, an art dealer and connoisseur, sins through the eyes, by entering a darkened motion picture house and glimpsing there something deeply illicit and corrupt which he mistakes for a vision of human felicity. He is led on and on into deeper and darker mistaking until he receives the appropriate punishment for his misuse of the faculty of vision. Physically blinded, morally degraded, mocked, confined, and at last murdered by his vicious young mistress, he is the object of that awful laughter in the dark made mention of in the American translation's title.

Laughter in the Dark makes darkly ironic play with the "optical" themes of art connoisseurship, painting and caricature, film making, life modeling, and film stardom in conjunction with a melodramatic plot recalling the famous German film *Die Blaue Engel* to suggest that, whereas true art is a way of seeing truly in darkness, attachment to false images leads only to a deeper benightedness and closer confinement.

Albinus, a prosperous Berlin art dealer possessed of a genuine "passion for art" and a bourgeois German "happy family" reaches that familiar critical point in early middle age when a man of his type may fall prey to a malaise of uneasiness and dissatisfaction whose causes are half spiritual and half sexual. He thinks of launching new art projects and dreams of amatory adventures with pretty young girls that would restore to his life a dimension of erotic intensity missing from his marriage. The new art project takes shape from an idle habit he has fallen into of "having this or that Old Master sign landscapes and faces which he, Albinus, came across in real life: it turned his existence into a fine picture gallery—delightful fakes, all of them." He is interested in the new popular art of the movies and conceives the clever, possibly profitable scheme of producing cartoons which will animate a famous painting by one of the Dutch Old Masters like Brueghel and give the figures in the static picture a continuing life through an entire episode. At the beginning it would be something simple, "a stained window coming to life," yet to begin at all he needs a collaborator combining knowledge of art with skill as an animated cartoonist. Unfortunately, the man for the job,

one Axel Rex, a gifted graphic artist and caricaturist, is away in America drawing newspaper cartoons.

Albinus writes to Rex, who warms to the scheme and asks for large advances of money to undertake the work. Meanwhile Albinus wanders one day into a movie house called the Argus and sees in the dark the outline of his fate: "the melting outline of a cheek which looked as though it were painted by a great artist against a rich dark background." The possessor of the cheek, an usherette named Margot Peters, who is about seventeen and looks even younger, responds to Albinus' tentative advances. He begins an affair with her that soon becomes wretchedly obsessive for him and that scandalizes his family and friends and leads to the breakup of his marriage.

To this point, we can say that Albinus has indeed confused the passions appropriate to art and to life and is punished for it. But the book to this point has barely begun and the aftermath has little relevance to this merely cautionary moral. In becoming involved with Margot and with Rex, Albinus has crossed an invisible line into an absolutely sinister world organized as a conspiracy against him, a world of complete deception where the animate images of art and pseudo-art are manipulated by a master craftsman in the art of evildoing. To begin with, Margot, the tough, amoral, mindless slum child, turns out to be entirely a creature of the camera-obscura world. She has been first an artist's model posing for life classes in an art school, next the model and mistress of Axel Rex before his American sojourn, and her career as usherette is intended to be merely a stopover on the way to becoming a screen star. In the end she indeed becomes as a motion picture actress that "silver ghost of romance"—impalpable, depthless, talentless, soulless, the net product of advertising, publicity, and opportunistic manipulation

—and, ironically enough, the human creature redefined as sheer artful image that Albinus had gone seeking when he began to frequent movie houses and sign real faces with the signatures of Old Masters.

It is a shattering coincidence that Margot should have been connected with Axel even before Albinus met her, although it is no surprise that she joins forces with him to manipulate and then destroy Albinus after Axel's return. Nabokov invariably uses such coincidences, plays with such loaded dice, in order to draw the reader away from his "realistic" expectations and to introduce him to a world where fate has little to do with character and functions like a conspiracy whose ultimate aim, as in the delusional systems of paranoiacs, is never actually made clear. Axel is a real artist of considerable talent who has made a career of faking pictures and drawing vicious caricatures, and who believes "that everything . . . in the domain of art . . . was only a more or less clever trick." He is a real confidence man too, with the practical aim of separating Albinus from his money. But his taste for the confidence game goes far beyond the practical. He sees himself as a "stage manager" who can be counted on to arrange the "roaring comedy" of Albinus' miseries and the kind of manager he "had in view was an elusive, double, triple, self-reflecting magic Proteus of a phantom, the shadow of many-colored glass balls flying in a curve, the ghost of a juggler on a shimmering curtain."

Here the stage manager melts into the performer, with Margot also on stage (or screen) to assist the clever magician or evil Magus in his show. Throughout the book Margot has the particular assignment, after leading Albinus on, of closing him in. She is always shutting doors on him and eventually seals him into permanent blindness as the result of an auto accident for which she is actually responsible.

The phantom role comes to full flower for Axel when Albinus, after he has been blinded, takes a house in Switzerland and lives there alone—he imagines—with his adored Margot. In fact Axel is also in the house, a silent presence, going naked and making love to Margot under Albinus' very nose. He likes to watch Margot make faces of "comic" disgust when Albinus, thinking they are alone, embraces the girl tenderly. He will touch the blind man gently with the tips of his bare toes and dissolves in silent laughter when Albinus assumes that it is Margot's caressing touch. And he will sit close to him for hours until the blind man, sensing a presence near him, reaches out, whereupon Axel gleefully moves back out of reach. At this time Albinus is a man in ruins with most of his money gone; so the impulse to mischief which continues to drive Axel and Margot really does constitute a "motiveless malignity." It is a "comic" performance by devils playing "disinterestedly," i.e., for love of their "art," to an audience of one who cannot see.

Eventually Albinus learns what has been going on from his decent brother-in-law, Paul. He takes refuge in Paul's Berlin house and on a certain day manages to entrap Margot in the drawing room of the old family apartment, which she is busily looting of the art objects he had collected during his career as a connoisseur. He is armed and tries to sense where she is so that he can kill her. Their grim struggle, conducted behind closed doors and for him wholly in darkness, results in his own death when Margot grabs the revolver and shoots him. The final paragraphs, written as directions for a film or stage scene, stress that the door of the drawing room is now open and "the door leading from the hall to the landing is wide open, too." As we have seen with *Invitation to a Beheading*, physical death is the opening into freedom for the doomed, betrayed prisoner, although neither book can follow the released man through that opening.

Much of *Laughter in the Dark* is composed in Nabokov's sprightliest and most playful vein. But to complain of the author's apparent callousness to the sufferings of his central character is to miss the important point. Albinus' "passion for art," which betrays him into a realm of sexual and social pathology, really does contain "immortal longings" with which the author has complete sympathy. But the author understands, as Albinus does not, that the beguiling images and forms beckoning in the murk of human reality are for seeing and not for possessing—an insight available to the true artist though not to the connoisseur with his checkbook and collections. "Albinus' specialty had been his passion for art; his most brilliant discovery had been Margot. But now . . . it was as though she had returned to the darkness of the little cinema from which he had once withdrawn her." On his way into the Argus Cinema, Albinus had noticed a poster showing "a man looking up at a window framing a child in a nightshirt." This representation, which will reappear as an imagistic theme in *Lolita*, scrupulously balances an idea of aspiration toward something purely beautiful with the pathology of voyeurism and sexual perversion. It is also a warning which Albinus cannot read or heed because he is so mad for form that he will not distinguish between form and its replica or model: "Now, the vision of the promised kiss filled him with such ecstasy that it seemed hardly possible it could be still further intensified. And yet beyond it, down a vista of mirrors, there was still to be reached the dim white form of her body, that very form which art students had sketched so conscientiously and so badly."

Lolita's unique appropriation of the American landscape, its comic and sinister play with American social institutions and roles and their deep-lying anomie, the wit and beauty of its endlessly inventive narrative style, coming in the midst of a bad decade for American fiction, fell upon our literary scene like a small hurricane ("Hurricane Lolita"!). Fifteen years later criticism was just beginning to take the measure of the book. When the critical history of the American novel in the 1960's and 1970's is written, *Lolita*'s presence and influence in that history will be major and central. *Lolita* killed fictional naturalism, already moribund, with one merciful blow. More important, it nerved a new generation of writers to meet the drastic and fantastic realities of American life with a countering imaginative fierceness and boldness. Our most interesting recent writers, from Barth to Burroughs from Thomas Berger to Thomas Pynchon, owe more to Nabokov, to the Nabokov of *Lolita* especially, than to any other contemporary figure, American or foreign.

In terms of Nabokov's own work *Lolita* has a similar centrality and prominence. In it he comes to find accommodation with the nymphet theme, which had been echoing and re-echoing in his work for decades, and links the theme lucidly to the master themes of nostalgia (or preterism) and of imagination which form the principal coordinates of his entire created world. Unlike Albinus, who never understands what he is doing, Humbert Humbert, conducting his own defense—"O ladies and gentlemen of the jury"—and, as critics often fail to note, his own prosecution, comes to know fully what he has done and is responsible for. He is in all of Nabokov's fiction the supremely conscious individualist, the wholly confident manipulator of the bewildering variety of his roles, and in this confidence reflects Nabokov's own masterly grasp of his most complex creation in character.

Nabokov has remarked of Humbert that although he went straight and properly to hell after the guards found him dead of a coronary in his cell, where he awaited trial for the slaying of Quilty, the man who had taken Lolita from him, Humbert may be allowed the privilege of returning to earth for one day each year. On that day one might expect him to haunt the environs of the little mining town in the American West, mentioned in the book's concluding pages, "that lay at my feet, in a fold of the valley," from which rose "the melody of children at play." Here it was that the bestial and enchanted hunter of nymphets rejoined the human race when he at last "knew that the hopelessly poignant thing was not Lolita's absence from my side, but the absence of her voice from that concord." And if we are inclined to suspect his sentiments here there is another late episode which indicates the same belated conversion. Lolita has written him after years of silence and absence to say she is married, pregnant, and in need of money. He finds her in a shack in "Coalmont," eight hundred miles from New York City, bigbellied, worn out at seventeen, and he wants to steal her away again or kill her if she will not come. But then he realizes that he loves her *as she is*, not merely as the echo or memory "of the nymphet I had rolled myself upon with such cries in the past. . . . Thank God it was not that echo alone that I worshiped." The "echo" of course points to the "eidolon" he had pursued lifelong, spying into "jewel-bright" windows and depraving little girls because the print of sexual characteristics was still so faintly impressed upon their childish bodies that he could pretend when savaging them that he was cleaving to a pure form and recapturing the lost Edenic time he had spent in childhood with "Annabel Lee." Lolita is spectacularly and maturely pregnant, no longer the "Idolores" of his original quest. He earns his overnight pass from hell by loving her and leaving her—several thousand dollars richer—going

off to hunt down and kill the "rival devil," Quilty, whose taste for sexual frolics with children, as with dwarfs, is an ordinary piece of psychopathy lacking transcendental overtones.

But even at Coalmont Humbert does not relinquish his habit of imaginary role playing. He casts the scene as Don José's final confrontation with Carmen ("*Changeons de vie, ma Carmen*," etc.) and says goodbye to his "American sweet immortal dead love," who has just made him understand for the first time that "the past was the past," under the aspect of a fat tenor from grand opera. One of the joys of *Lolita* is Humbert's role playing. Just as the book as a whole encapsulates and parodies every literary confession of a great sinner from St. Augustine to Sade, Rousseau, and Stavrogin, so do Humbert's roles introduce a rich variety of imaginative frames and thematic aspects through which the book's action may be viewed.

To touch very lightly on this matter, consider the following. When Lolita is Bee or Beatrice, Humbert is Dante and the evoked mode is an inversion of "divine comedy" (hellish comedy?). When she is "Dolores Disparu," Humbert is Proust's Marcel lamenting the vanished Albertine and the mode is Proustian speculation about the enigmas of time and memory. When she is Vee (Virginia Clem), Humbert is Edgar Allan Poe and the frame is artist's biography in the era of "romantic agony." When she merges with "Annabel" Humbert is the child narrator of Poe's famous poem. And when Humbert, fleeing the mysterious Aztec red convertible with Lolita through the American night, murmurs "*lente, lente, currite noctis equi*," Humbert is Faustus, Lolita is both Helen and Gretchen, and the mode, if not the mood, is that of Marlowe's tragic morality play. Also there are Humbert's less literary roles, each played to the hilt: the spy and voyeur ("Humbert Humbert—two eyes burning in the dark"), the European gentleman with a "past," the family friend, the husband and mature lover, the "stepfather" concerned to guard his little charge safely through the toils of teendom, the private investigator, the madman, the devil slayer ("guilty of killing Quilty"), and, finally and throughout, the pleader-prosecutor at heaven's bar—"O winged gentlemen!"

Nabokov's own cryptic key to *Lolita* was given in a 1956 "Postscript" to the first American edition. There he said the idea came to him in Paris in 1938, during an attack of neuralgia and after reading a "pointless" newspaper story about a scientist who attempted to teach an ape to draw. The ape did produce a drawing, but it was only of the bars of its cage. Humbert, that greatly talented ape, attempts a break-out, an act of transcendence, through his mad and cruel pursuit of the eidolon, incarnate in little Dolores Haze, Lolita, but he merely succeeds in confirming his confinement in matter, in the grossly sensual self, in vice and in time. One can add to this very little, except perhaps—since *Lolita* is already an assured American classic—a suggestion of how the book reverberates through our specifically American historic culture.

The core element of Humbert's sexual perversity, arch-romanticism, and derangement is an attitude toward time which may remind us of other eccentric or deranged heroes of American fiction. Humbert is fixated on the past— on his childhood love affair with "Annabel Lee"—and his pursuit, seduction, and enslavement of Dolores Haze are an attempt to reinstate in the present and preserve into the future what was irretrievably lost in the past. The expensiveness of indulgence in this illusion is very great: it costs no less than the wrecking of a child's life, as Humbert finally admits after abandoning his corrupt rationalizations concerning the natural depravity and sexual precocity of American little girls. Humbert and his

time problem are summed up on the final page of *The Great Gatsby*, from which I quoted at the onset of this essay, and in a number of other classic American texts.

But how can this vile European stand in for an archetypal American? There is really no problem. America, as a "brand new, mad new dream world where everything [is] permissible," is Europe's dream of itself according to the romantic error that past time is retrievable. Emerson, Whitman, and Hart Crane might have approved Humbert's thought, if not his exact words and their appalling application. We are all Europeans when we dream that dangerous, beguiling, ever-so-American dream.

These speculations can be pushed a bit further under the general rubric of fate, freedom, and America. *Lolita*, because it is heavy with fate, would seem to present a situation in which the margin of freedom which interests us in fictional characters, particularly in the characters appearing in modern books, has diminished virtually to nothing. For instance, Humbert is obsessed, Lolita is enslaved, Charlotte Haze is totally duped, and a character like Quilty is the slave of his sinister vices. Add in fate as the "synchronizing phantom" arranging happenstance and coincidence upon wholly mysterious principles and freedom disappears altogether from the book. From another angle, there is freedom in *Lolita* of a rather awful sort. Humbert is free, unencumbered with compunction before his "conversion." Through most of the book he has the freedom of his viciousness, as does Quilty. Humbert's actions take place at a point in history when traditional sanctions have lapsed or at least loosened, and there would be very little consensus of judgment against his deeds from the "enlightened" sector of the community, apart from agreement that he is psychologically "disturbed." This in effect forgives and forgets by understanding or claiming to.

Dolores Haze also is free in a sense, in that the nature of contemporary American "suburban" culture ties her to nothing, asks nothing of her, presents her with nothing. What is she? A junior consumer, of comic books and bubble gum, a "starlet" with a thirst for cheap films and Coke. There is a great vacancy in and around her, a voidness and loneliness only partly created by Humbert's machinations. This vacancy is cultural in the first instance, American.

For Europe, as first de Tocqueville and then D. H. Lawrence have expounded, America has figured as the place beyond cabined and confined traditions and sanctions. It had been the place where time itself might be redeemed, where the dream of a new Eden, of a second life, could be realized. Naturally, there has been a dark, pathological side to this. America has been the place indubitably attractive to great mischief makers, psychopaths, men on the run, unclubable and violent persons, con men. Humbert lives on the dark side of the American freedom I am describing. There is some truth in the statement that what drove Humbert to America was his vice and the hope of satisfying it in the land of opportunity. And there is also some truth in the idea that the history of Lolita, who died in childbed in a town of the "remotest Northwest" on her way to Alaska, the last American frontier, expresses the final decadence of that European myth which we call the American Dream.

Nabokov has called *The Gift* "the best, the most nostalgic of my Russian novels." It is also, even in the excellent English translation of 1963, the least accessible of Nabokov's major works to the general English-speaking reader. As a *Künstlerroman* celebrating the life of literature and the literary life, it tells the story of a young Russian émigré poet and critic named Fyodor Godunov-Cherdyntsev discovering his artistic powers and finding love as

well over a three-year period in Berlin during the mid-1920's. But *The Gift* is also a complex, playful, and creative work of literary criticism oriented toward the pre-Soviet Russian cultural tradition and aimed as a sidelong polemic against certain dubious values obtaining among literary and cultural pundits of the Russian émigré community in Western Europe. Lacking close knowledge of the literally dozens of minor and major Russian writers the book alludes to, and of the many issues and personalities from the expatriate cultural scene at which the book takes a fling, the reader may well feel he should acquire, along with a mastery of Russian literature, history, and the language, that ideal insomnia which Joyce recommended to the ideal reader of *Finnegans Wake.*

Nevertheless, the main focus of Nabokov's revaluation of tradition is quite clear. Centering his attack on the liberal and progressive critic and novelist N. G. Chernyshevski, he tasks the progressive wing of nineteenth-century Russian culture, and by implication the liberal wing of the émigré community, with a confusion of values whereby "enlightened" writers of small talent have been overpraised at the expense of better writers possessing unacceptable social and political views. For Nabokov and for Fyodor, the great tradition begins in Pushkin and is passed down through a select few poets and prose writers whose social views, radical or conservative, are of no bearing whatsoever. It is a tradition and dialogue of artists constituting the supreme gift the Russian literary genius and language have to offer, a gift which Fyodor aspires to receive, through an utmost effort of critical understanding, to share in to the limit of his developing artistic powers, and to pass on uncompromised whether or not he ever has the good fortune to return to a Russia in which a poet like himself can once again carry on serious work.

The Gift is arranged in five big chapters and

each chapter advances Fyodor's personal history while simultaneously undertaking assessments and recapitulations of Russian art. In the early chapters Fyodor works at his own poetry, finds ways of supporting himself in a city whose people and their civic ways interest him not in the slightest, meets and begins courting a delightful and sensitive Russian girl named Zina Mertz whose vulgar stepfather is Fyodor's landlord. A mysterious poet-critic named Koncheyev appears and disappears at intervals. In rapid, allusive dialogue Fyodor and this imaginary alter ego, with whom Fyodor is always in essential agreement about artistic values, work out their aesthetic credo and dismiss from contention all those mystics, progressives, and poetasters who, in their arrogantly youthful view, appear as excrescences on the brilliant surface of Russian literature. Chapter Two, which might be called the book of the father, shows Fyodor absorbed in biographical and critical studies of his poetic master, Pushkin, while also collecting information about the career of his fleshly father, a great naturalist-scientist who had disappeared at the time of the Bolshevik Revolution on his way back from one of his long expeditions in Central Asia. Fyodor's largely fictional reconstructions of these journeys, written under the stylistic influence of Pushkin and filled with exotic yet scientifically exact descriptions of the plants, butterflies, and landscapes encountered en route, form one of Nabokov's most marvelous achievements in prose.

In Chapter Three Fyodor explores deeper into questions of the creative process in poetry, works out the important connections between the art of Pushkin and what is worth cherishing in later Russian verse, and begins research and writing for a "critical" biography of Chernyshevski. Chapter Four is in its entirety a very funny yet mainly accurate and learned short biography of Chernyshevski. It intro-duces an imaginary authority named Strannolyubski (Strangelove?) who reports that during Chernyshevski's Siberian exile "once an eagle appeared in his yard. . . . It had come to peck at his liver but did not recognize Prometheus in him." Nabokov's (and Fyodor's) purpose is to expose Chernyshevski as the false Prometheus of Russian tradition, a savant whose sincere good intentions and abundant sufferings in the cause of righteousness cannot excuse the dullness, dogmatism, and anti-aesthetic bias of his judgments and influence.

Chapter Four, which might be called the book of the false father, forms the polemical climax of *The Gift*. If one aim of the work has been to locate and consolidate the great tradition of Russian writing the corollary aim has been to expose an anti-tradition incarnate in social critics of the Chernyshevskian school whom Nabokov insists on seeing not only as the promulgators of a sound tradition of reformism and social concern but also as responsible for their own and others' bad writing, for a misappropriation of the Russian Hegelian tradition leading to dogmatic Marxist-Leninism, and, finally, for the worst excesses of Soviet philistinism in the cultural sphere.

Chapter Four gave great offense to critics and progressives of the émigré world, so much so that it was not printed as part of the book until 1952. Chapter Five, anticipating this reaction, presents excerpts from imaginary book reviews of Chapter Four. Nabokov faithfully renders the style and bias of numerous literary pundits, including several who write from a politically reactionary or fanatically religious point of view. But the best review, a sympathetic one, is contributed by "Koncheyev," who reappears just when he is needed to aid the beleaguered and beset Fyodor in his "heretical" undertakings: "[Koncheyev] began by drawing a picture of flight during an invasion or an earthquake, when the escapers carry away with them everything that they can lay hands on, someone being sure to burden himself with a large, framed portrait of some long-forgotten relatives. 'Just such a portrait,' wrote Koncheyev, 'is for the Russian intelligentsia the image of Chernyshevski, which was spontaneously but accidentally carried away abroad by the émigrés, together with other, more useful things. . . . Somebody suddenly confiscated the portrait.' "

At the end of *The Gift* Fyodor has grown the wings of a true poet, has drawn a luminous portrait of Russian literary art as he understands it, is happily and reciprocally in love with Zina, who is ready to go anywhere with him. Writing to his mother in Paris he remarks that while it is sheer sentimentality to expect to return to Russia, he can live more easily outside of his native country than some because he has taken away "the keys to her"—of language, art, and memory—and because someday "I shall live there in my books." *The Gift*, which is Nabokov's happiest book, is also his "goodbye to all that," the work in which he frees himself from his Russian past, narrowly and nostalgically considered, by earning a free entry into the vital dialogue of Russian art over the centuries. Both a summing up and a new starting point, it perhaps freed him also for the successful appropriation of a new language and culture when the European war drove him to American shores in 1940.

Like early Shakespearean comedy—for instance, *Love's Labour's Lost*—*The Gift,* which is full of buried rhyming poetry and contains stanzas from *Eugene Onegin* written out as prose, takes delight in the processes of its own artifice. *Pale Fire*, on the other hand, is the work in which the devices cultivated lifelong by a great artist, the game he has been playing, the long dream of his imagination, are transmuted into something like the total dream and artifice of eternity. The 999-line poem in the novel, "neo-Popean" in technique and in its metaphysical arguments from design, and Wordsworthian in its autobiographical cast, is also Nabokov's "Sailing to Byzantium," while *Pale Fire* as a whole is a work like *The Tempest* in which the artist simply hands over his tools to the supreme artificer or artificers who control the ultimate dazzling game.

We can, I believe, brush aside the comic irony whereby John Francis Shade's fine poem is delivered into the hands of the bungling pedant and paranoid "editor," Kinbote, first because the poem, with its tail in its mouth, first line fused with last line, survives serene and intact, composing a magical, fiery circle which Kinbote, for all his incompetent "readings," unwarranted "emendations," and occasional outright forgings of "canceled lines," cannot violate; and second because, as Shade the poet knows, the work of imagination is unceasing, is owned by no one, and may even surface in the psychotic fantasy of a madman or in the egotistic inventions of an incompetent scholar. There are two great imaginative inventions tangled together in *Pale Fire*. One is Shade's autobiographical poem and the other is Kinbote's sad, funny, "true" autobiographical novel about the exiled King of Zembla, Charles the Beloved, which he composes through the devices of commentary and index. At a point in infinity, in the "involute abode" of uncreated fire and unfiltered light, at a point beyond entanglement and deception, the two "poems" are indeed identical, to each other and with all work of the imagination wrought at a sufficient intensity of longing for true, unimpeded vision.

That is of course from an ideal point of view. In "actuality," in the corporeal and phenomenal world, poems and other works of art are at best images and reminiscences of essence, working at the remove of reflected and diminished luminescence. Shade, with his subtle understanding of being as both utter mystery and perfect design, with all his unearthly poetic genius and his earthbound devotion to a beloved wife and a dead daughter, to strong drink and the rank comedy of faculty intrigue at Wordsmith U., comprehends fully that man's nature and human art can only fitfully reflect a perfection that lies elsewhere; which is why he qualifies the noun of his poem's title with the adjective "pale." And Kinbote, who professes religious orthodoxy and likes to argue the position against Shade's mystical agnosticism over the chessboard, reaches the same conclusion in different terms when he speaks of "God's Presence—a faint phosphorescence at first, a pale light in the dimness of bodily life, and a dazzling radiance after it."

One may see Shade's and Kinbote's relation as that of genius and its parasite or even that of Prospero to Caliban, but this ignores their mysterious rapport, the conspiratorial way that each of these lonely and eccentric figures serves and supports the other's deepest aspiration. Kinbote, who is in "fact" one V. Botkin, an American scholar of Russian descent recently dicharged from a mental hospital, reinvents himself twice, as Charles Kinbote and as Charles the Beloved, thereby effecting a bizarre escape from "a personality consisting mainly of the shadows of its own prison bars." This illegal and mendacious procedure earns him the suspicious contempt of the dragonish faculty wife, Mrs. Hurley. But she is silenced when Shade speaks authoritatively and approvingly of "a person who deliberately peels off a drab and unhappy past and replaces it with a brilliant invention." As an artist he understands the sources, in human failure and heartbreak, of art's most brilliant contrivances and draws his friend in under the protection of that understanding. When Shade is dead and Kinbote first reads "Pale Fire" he is shocked to discover that the poem is not in fact the work called

"Solus Rex," about the King of Zembla, which he had imagined Shade to be writing at his dictation. But then he rereads it: "I liked it better when expecting less. And what was that? What was that dim distant music, those vestiges of color in the air? Here and there I discovered in it and especially, especially in the invaluable variants" (Kinbote's own forgeries) "echoes and spangles of my mind, a long ripplewake of my glory." Even if the poem is not quite the *romaunt* of Zembla the Fair, it will do almost as well, especially now that he has the poem in his keeping: "My commentary to this poem, now in the hands of my readers, represents an attempt to sort out those echoes and wavelets of fire, and pale phosphorescent hints, and all the many subliminal debts to me."

"*My* commentary . . . *my* readers . . . debts to *me*." Our pleasure in this delicious satire on scholarly arrogance and bias is intense but should not cause us to miss the point that Shade's *opus posthumous*, from the standpoint of Shade's own playful artist's temperament, has passed into the hands of its ideal editor, a fellow artist. In short, there is a sense, only half absurd, in which Kinbote's is a great scholarly commentary. For what other editor has ever been present from the beginning, present throughout, and in at the kill during the making of a great poem? The highest goal of scholarship, which is to recapture the life out of which the masterpiece emerged, to capture the life of the poem as well, is served, however lefthandedly, by Kinbote's scandalously unprofessional commentary on "Pale Fire."

But Kinbote's most important service to John Shade is to conduct him to his death "from a bullet meant for another." It would be tedious to demonstrate that Shade would not have died had he never befriended Kinbote and, in particular, had he not gone strolling from his own house to Kinbote's to partake of the doubtful pleasures of a dinner consisting of "a knackle of walnuts, a couple of large to-matoes, and a bunch of bananas" washed down with Imperial Tokay wine. What is much more interesting is that Kinbote, abetted no doubt by the "synchronizing phantom" of fate we have noticed in other Nabokov works, delivers Shade to a death the elderly poet is fully and hungrily prepared for.

The poem, "Pale Fire," is a tender recapitulation of Shade's attachments to and entanglements with the things of this world. It is full of affection for Sybil, the faithful wife, and agonized feeling for the ugly daughter whose suicide was the single tragic event of the couple's long, contented life together. And it takes delight in the sheer play of all phenomena as these reveal themselves to the poet's five senses or are recalled in their perfected "preterite" form through the artistry of memory. But the poet, from the very first couplet ("I was the shadow of the waxwing slain/ By the false azure in the windowpane"), casts his poem as a retrospection from the realm of death and joins himself with eager curiosity to the limitless mystery surrounding the little life his poem looks back upon. Each canto comes to center on a death experience—the momentary swoons ("a sudden sunburst in my head/ And then black night") he had known in childhood, the lonely dying of his daughter, his wonderfully cranky researches into death at the Institute of Preparation for the Hereafter—until the fourth canto, which is broken off before the second line of the concluding couplet of the whole poem falls into place.

It is broken off at the 999th line—"Trundling an empty barrow up the lane"—because Kinbote interrupts him with his importunate dinner suggestion. They walk across the yards to Kinbote's house. The assassin fires from the porch, Shade falls, and the poem completes itself: "I was the shadow of the waxwing slain." The poet vanishes into eternity by way of van-ishing into his poem. We, and Kinbote, are left with a thousand lines (999 plus 1) making a perspective on a vanishing point of light and life receding into darkness. Perhaps this darkness, could one but view it along with Shade from the other side of life and death, would disclose itself as the very heart of light.

From a technical standpoint *Pale Fire* as novel triumphs over the most recalcitrant and inappropriate materials for fiction—a poem cum editorial notes and an index. Also, its striking subversion of the ordinary unitary conception of a fictional character—I am thinking of the schizoid editor's triple identity and the consequently shifting identities of such personages as Emerald-Izumrudov and Gradus, alias Jack Grey, alias d'Argus, etc., who pursue and harass him—makes good an old claim of Nabokov's that character to the artist in fiction is a "compositional resource" like any other, to be dissolved and reconstituted as freely and repeatedly as his themes require. But *Pale Fire* is something much more winning than a mere technical triumph. More than any other of his novels it shows a humane and tender sympathy for its imprisoned characters and seems to promise a final fulfillment of their immortal longings—if not now, sometime; if not here, then elsewhere.

Selected Bibliography

WORKS OF VLADIMIR NABOKOV

NOVELS AND COLLECTED SHORT STORIES

Mary (*Mashen'ka*). Berlin: "Slovo," 1926. English translation, New York: McGraw-Hill, 1970.

King, Queen, Knave (*Korol', Dama, Valet*). Berlin: "Slovo," 1928. English translation, New York: McGraw-Hill, 1968.

The Defense (Zashchita Luzhina). Berlin: "Slovo," 1930. English translation, New York: Putnam, 1964.

The Eye (Soglyadatay). Paris: Contemporary Annals, No. 44, 1930. English translation, New York: Phaedra, 1965.

Glory (Podvig). Paris: Contemporary Annals, Nos. 45–48, 1932. English translation, New York: McGraw-Hill, 1971.

Camera Obscura (Kamera Obskura). Paris: Contemporary Annals, Nos. 49–52, 1932–33. English translation, London: John Long, 1936; American edition with author's alterations and retitled *Laughter in the Dark*, Indianapolis: Bobbs-Merrill, 1938.

Despair (Otchayanie). Berlin: Petropolis, 1936. English translation, New York: Putnam, 1966.

Invitation to a Beheading (Priglashenie na Kazn'). Paris: Dom Knigi, 1938. English translation, New York: Putnam, 1959.

The Gift (Dar). Paris: Contemporary Annals, Nos. 63–67, 1937–38 (without the fourth chapter). New York: Chekhov Publishing House, 1952 (complete). English translation, New York: Putnam, 1963.

The Real Life of Sebastian Knight. Norfolk, Conn.: New Directions, 1941.

Bend Sinister. New York: Henry Holt, 1947.

Lolita. Paris: Olympia Press, 1955. Russian translation, New York: Phaedra, 1967.

Pnin. New York: Doubleday, 1957.

Nabokov's Dozen. New York: Doubleday, 1958. (Thirteen short stories.)

Pale Fire. New York: Putnam, 1962.

Nabokov's Quartet. New York: Phaedra, 1966. (Four long short stories.)

Ada, or Ardor: A Family Chronicle. New York: McGraw-Hill, 1969.

MEMOIRS

Conclusive Evidence. London: Victor Gollancz, 1951; New York: Harper, 1951. Subsequently retitled in American reprintings *Speak, Memory*. Revised and expanded edition under latter title, New York: Putnam, 1966.

Drugiye Berega [Other Shores]. New York: Chekhov Publishing House, 1954.

VERSES

Poems. New York: Doubleday, 1959.

Poems and Problems. New York: McGraw-Hill, 1970.

TRANSLATIONS

Three Russian Poets: Translations of Pushkin, Lermontov and Tiutchev. Norfolk, Conn.: New Directions, 1944.

The Song of Igor's Campaign. New York: Random House, 1960.

Eugene Onegin, by Aleksandr Pushkin. 4 vols. New York: Pantheon, 1964.

CRITICISM

Nikolai Gogol. Norfolk, Conn.: New Directions, 1944.

BIBLIOGRAPHIES

Field, Andrew. "In Place of a Bibliography" and "Concluding Remarks," in *Nabokov: His Life in Art*. Boston: Little, Brown, 1967. Pp. 352–83.

Zimmer, Dieter E. *Vladimir Nabokov: Bibliographie des Gesamtwerks*. Hamburg: Rowohlt, 1963.

CRITICAL AND BIOGRAPHICAL STUDIES

Appel, Alfred, and Charles Newman, eds. *Nabokov: Criticism, Reminiscences, Translations and Tributes*. Evanston, Ill.: Northwestern University Press, 1970.

Dembo, L. S., ed. *Nabokov the Man and His Works: Studies*. Madison: University of Wisconsin Press, 1967.

Dupee, F. W. "The Coming of Nabokov," in *"The King of the Cats" and Other Remarks on Writers and Writing*. New York: Farrar, Straus and Giroux, 1965. Pp. 117–41.

Field, Andrew. *Nabokov: His Life in Art*. Boston: Little, Brown, 1967.

Proffer, Karl. *Keys to Lolita*. Bloomington: Indiana University Press, 1968.

Smith, Peter Duval. "Vladimir Nabokov on His Life and Work," *Listener*, 68:856–58 (November 22, 1962). (Text of broadcast interview.)

Stegner, Page. *Escape into Aesthetics: The Art of Vladimir Nabokov*. New York: Dial, 1966.

—*JULIAN MOYNAHAN*

Howard Nemerov

1920-

THERE is an instructive passage in *Journal of the Fictive Life* in which Howard Nemerov speaks of the sources of poetic power: "I conceive this responsibility of [lyric] poetry to be to great primary human drama, which poets tend to lose sight of because of their privilege of taking close-ups of single moments on the rim of the wheel of the human story. The poet will improve his art who acknowledges the necessity of always returning to that source; he will fail who always writes another poem instead. Hence it has seemed to me that I must attempt to bring together the opposed elements of my character represented by poetry and fiction."

These "opposed elements" in Howard Nemerov's character are reflected in his life and work: in the tensions between his romantic and realistic visions, his belief and unbelief, his heart and mind; and in his alternating production of poetry and prose. It is somehow typical that this humanitarian who writes of war as madness ("Redeployment") enlisted in the Royal Canadian Air Force when he graduated from Harvard in 1941. It is also typical that this "Jewish Puritan of the middle class" who "Grins at the consolations of religion as at a child's/ Frightened pretensions" is a deeply religious poet who, in his central poems (e.g., "Runes") looks into "the dark marrow and the

splintery grain" and sees "nothing that was not wood, nothing/ That was not God."

Journal of the Fictive Life documents, by analyzing his own dreams, the deeply divided personality already evident to readers of his poetry and fiction. Despite his growing "success," financial, familial, critical, and popular, Nemerov's dreams are "spectacularly pessimistic" (which he typically calls a "rude awakening"). My theme here is that this inner division, under the constant pressure of Nemerov's poetic discipline and intelligence, accounts for the power of this writer who has become, more than any other contemporary poet, the spokesman for the existential, science-oriented (or science-displaced), liberal mind of the twentieth century.

The quality that sets Nemerov's writings apart from other modern writers is its consistent intelligence, a breadth of wit in the eighteenth-century sense of the word, expanded to cover a very modern awareness of contemporary man's alienation and fragmentation. One of the primary divisions of Nemerov's mind is apparent in his ability to remind his readers of both Pope and Dostoevski at the same time, a split symbolized by poems like "The Salt Garden," where man is alternately proud of his "good house" and "garden green,/ . . . Turnip and bean and violet/ In a decent order set," and torn by a desire to abandon civilized life for "the wild waters" where "his salt dream lies."

Nemerov's own upbringing was an extremely civilized one, a privileged one, and this, coupled with his awareness of the miseries of this world, undoubtedly led to guilt feelings or at least a cynicism at life's capriciousness (he writes in the *Journal*, "I want the world to think me a nice fellow, while I know I am not").

He was born on March 1, 1920, in New York City, and this city dominated the imagery of his poems until he moved to Vermont in 1948. His wealthy and culture-minded parents sent him to the exclusive Fieldston School, where the young Nemerov was an outstanding student and a good athlete. Graduating in 1937, he then went to Harvard, receiving his A.B. just in time for World War II. Like many other modern poets (Jarrell, Ciardi, Dickey), he was romantically attracted to the air force, with the romance gradually turning to horror at the war's realities. Nemerov served first as a flying officer with the RAF Coastal Command, attacking German shipping over the North Sea, and then in 1944 switched to the Eighth United States Army Air Force, based in Lincolnshire. He married an English girl, to whom he's rather unfashionably still married, and in 1945 was discharged as a first lieutenant.

After the war, Nemerov and his wife lived in New York City for a year, during which he wrote *The Image and the Law*. Running short of money, in 1946 he accepted a position as instructor of English at Hamilton College, Clinton, New York; in 1948 he joined the faculty at Bennington College, with which he was associated until 1966, when he moved to Brandeis University in Massachusetts. The Nemerovs have three sons, David, Alexander, and Jeremy, the period just before Alexander's

birth being the subject of Nemerov's "meditations" in *Journal of the Fictive Life*.

In 1958–59 he was a visiting lecturer in English at the University of Minnesota, and in 1962–63 was writer-in-residence at Hollins College in Virginia. He also served as consultant in poetry at the Library of Congress in 1963–64, succeeding Louis Untermeyer and preceding his friend Reed Whittemore, with whom he worked for several years on the delightful and irreverent magazine *Furioso* (predecessor of today's *Carleton Miscellany*). In 1969–70 he was writer-in-residence at Washington University, in Missouri.

As he notes in the *Journal*, his writing has slowly been attracting a widening audience. In 1966 he delivered the Joseph Warren Beach Lecture at the University of Minnesota to an appreciative standing-room-only crowd (the lecture has been published in the *American Scholar*, summer 1967). He has received numerous awards, including a Guggenheim in 1968 and the Frank O'Hara Memorial Prize in 1971. In 1965 he was made a member of the National Institute of Arts and Letters, and in 1966 a fellow of the American Academy of Arts and Sciences.

Howard Nemerov, who never went to graduate school, finds teaching "a fairly agreeable way of making a dollar": it "makes possible a more or less quiet life." When asked to name the best contemporary American poet, he replied, "For me to do so would be not only immodest, but very possibly inaccurate as well." But in the opinion of a growing number of readers and critics, Nemerov is a major American writer, and certainly one of the best poets writing today. Versatile and prolific, he has published to date three novels (*The Melodramatists*; *Federigo, or, The Power of Love*; *The Homecoming Game*), two collections of short stories (*A Commodity of Dreams*; *Stories,*

Fables & Other Diversions), two verse plays (*Cain, Endor*), eleven books of poetry (*The Image and the Law, Guide to the Ruins, The Salt Garden, Mirrors & Windows, New & Selected Poems, The Next Room of the Dream, The Blue Swallows, A Sequence of Seven With a Drawing by Ron Slaughter, Winter Lightning, The Painter Dreaming in the Scholar's House, Gnomes and Occasions*), two collections of essays and criticism (*Poetry and Fiction: Essays*; *Reflexions on Poetry and Poetics*), and the unclassifiable literary-psychoanalytical *Journal of the Fictive Life*. He also edited and introduced Longfellow's poems in the Laurel Poetry Series and is the editor of *Poets on Poetry* and *Poetry and Criticism*.

The twentieth century, perhaps every century, has been often derided as an unpoetic age, especially the second half of it: where is the successor to Frost, Eliot, Williams, Auden, Yeats? The fact is that there are plenty of successors, that excellent poetry is being written by many modern poets, and that no doubt a few of them will withstand "windy time/ and the worm," and emerge as that strange and amorphous creature, the Major Poet. Of the "war generation" poets, Nemerov and Lowell are the two who have held up best, and the development of Nemerov is the most striking.

The sixty-seven poems contained in *The Blue Swallows* (1967), published exactly twenty years after Nemerov's first book, represent not so much a culmination of his efforts as another step along a clearly defined technical evolution, and another elucidation (another series of examples) of what might be called a philosophy of minimal affirmation. Like his gulls and swallows, Nemerov circles around and around the things of this world, finding them insubstantial, frightening, illusory, beautiful, and strange. Nowhere is his divided view

of man as both hopeless and indomitable better expressed than in the conclusion of "Beyond the Pleasure Principle":

There, toward the end, when the left-handed
  wish
Is satisfied as it is given up, when the hero
Endures his cancer and more obstinately than
  ever
Grins at the consolations of religion as at a
  child's
Frightened pretensions, and when his great
  courage
Becomes a wish to die, there appears, so
  obscurely,
Pathetically, out of the wounded torment and
  the play,
A something primitive and appealing, and still
  dangerous,
That crawls on bleeding hands and knees over
  the floor
Toward him, and whispers as if to confess:
  again, again.

In *The Blue Swallows* the polarities of Nemerov's thought are typically symbolized by physics and theology ("This, That & the Other"), reality and imagination ("The Companions"), pain and significance ("Creation of Anguish"). He has come a long way from his first slim volume, *The Image and the Law* (1947), but there is continuity as well as development.

The title of his first book refers to the two ways man has of looking at things, realistically through the eye (image) and imaginatively through the mind (law), and what Nemerov looks at is, in a word, death. Poem after poem revolves around his war-given realization of the casual, callous, accidental, and inevitable fact of death.

You watch the night for images of death,
Which sleep in camera prints upon the eye.

Fires go out, and power fails, and breath
Goes coldly out: dawn is a time to die.

and

> You try to fix your mind upon his death,
> Which seemed it might, somehow, be
>   relevant
> To something you once thought, or did, or
>   might
> Imagine yourself thinking, doing. When?

Along with death, war and the city are Nemerov's main subjects, often in the same poem (e.g., "The Frozen City"). Two other major aspects of this early work should be mentioned because they carry over to his later poetry: religion and wit. Poetry and religion both attempt to carve meaning out of chaos—poetry by form, religion by faith. But Nemerov's poetry is often *specifically* religious, by vocabulary, by reference, by subject. Saints and angels abound in his poetry; references to Christ, God, St. Augustine, Aquinas, and the like are also frequent. It is clear that the Old Testament, especially, is influential (as in his later plays, *Cain* and *Endor*). A representative poem in *The Image and the Law* is "Lot's Wife," in which Nemerov uses the woman as a symbol for a world in tears, trapped between lust and faith, unwilling and unable to commit itself fully to either.

> I have become a gate
> To the ruined city, dry,
> Indestructible by fire.
> A pillar of salt, a white
> Salt boundary stone
> On the edge of destruction.
>
> A hard lesson to learn,
> A swift punishment; and many
> Now seek to escape
> But look back, or to escape

> By looking back: and they
> Too become monuments.
>
> Remember me, Lot's wife,
> Standing at the furthest
> Commark of lust's county.
> Unwilling to enjoy,
> Unable to escape, I make
> Salt the rain of the world.

The satirical turn of Nemerov's mind which dominates his novels is also evident in his poetry. His wit ranges from "Rump-Trumpet, the Critic/ . . . Who would have to rise above himself/ In order to talk through his hat," to the more subtle debunking in "History of a Literary Movement." Nemerov has said "the serious and the funny are one"; the same dark viewpoint underlies both his "witty" and his "serious" poems, and often these elements are fused (e.g., "The Truth of the Matter"). This is as true of *The Blue Swallows* as of *The Image and the Law*. These poems, with their ironic detachment, are not "cold" poems, but their voice "is that of a man thinking," as Nemerov has said about Wallace Stevens.

In *The Image and the Law* and *Guide to the Ruins* (1950) Nemerov is "writing the war out of his system," as they say; he is also, more important, writing Eliot, Yeats, and Stevens out of his system.

ELIOT   Descending and moving closer
        I saw the sad patience of
        The people awaiting death
        (They crossed their bony legs,
        Their eyes stared, hostile and
        Bright as broken glass).

YEATS   But I, except in bed,
        Wore hair-cloth next the skin,
        And nursed more than my child
        That grudge against my side.
        Now, spirit & flesh assoil'd,

I lace my pride in,
Crying out odd and even
Alas! that ever I did sin,
It is full merry in heaven.

STEVENS   What, Amicus, constitutes mastery?
The perdurable fire of a style?

The early poems in general have an abstract, literary quality, an esoteric vocabulary, many allusions. One marked tendency in Nemerov's technical development has been a growing directness, not toward the "country" simplicity of Robert Frost but toward the simplicity of a highly educated man trying to convey the substance of his meditations clearly. Compare, for example, these two descriptions of October, the first early, the second late (1962):

A) An old desperation of the flesh.
Mortification and revivification
Of the spirit. There are those
Who work outdoors, and others
Who pull down blinds against the sun.

B) Now I can see certain simplicities
In the darkening rust and tarnish of the time,
And say over the certain simplicities,
The running water and the standing stone,
The yellow haze of the willow and the black
Smoke of the elm, the silver, silent light
Where suddenly, readying toward nightfall,
The sumac's candelabrum darkly flames.

In both poems the subject is the same, October being used as a metaphor for death, but the qualities Nemerov has gained are evident: a greater subtlety of rhythm, more visual imagery, a feeling of control that communicates itself as part of the "message."

Guide to the Ruins, however, represents a considerable advance in Nemerov's growth as a poet, leading directly toward *The Salt Garden*, where he reaches his poetic maturity. Such poems as "The Lives of Gulls and Children," "Elegy of Last Resort," and "Fables of the Moscow Subway" indicate that Nemerov has found his most characteristic voice: a quiet intelligent voice brooding lyrically on the strange beauty and tragic loneliness of life.

But they knew the Atlantic kind he was,
And for this moment saw him swaying
In the grey dark above the cold sea miles,
Wingtips ticking the spray of the slow waves,
Leaning on the unhavening air the dangerous
Sustaining of his own breastbone; they knew
The indifference of time dragging him down.
And when after silence they turned away,
"No one has ever been here before,"
They cried, "no one, no one, no one."
Their mournful word went out, no one,
Along the shore, now that they turned for home
Bearing the lonely pride of those who die,
And paced by the sweet shrieking of the quick.

Guide to the Ruins is filled with a great variety of styles: epigrams, fragments, ballads, lyrics, fables, sonnets, elegies, madrigals, even a carol. Its greatest advance over *The Image and the Law* is a lessening of the Audenesque flatness of the first book: a line like "Swinging over the wash and rush of the sea" is an almost onomatopoeic example of the marriage of rhythm and image which marks Nemerov's later poetry—for example, these lines from *The Blue Swallows*:

See now, the ships depart through the dark
   harbor
And past the breakwater rocks where the first
White-riding wave hits at the hull and washes
   on.
Rhythm of voyages, going out and coming
   back,
Beat of the sea, procession of times and seasons,
Command of variables, calculus of fluxions
Cuius Nomen est Oriens . . .

Guide to the Ruins, though much broader in scope than *The Image and the Law*, is still very much concerned with war. The "ruins" (also "runes") are the ruins of civilization after World War II, and the war is not really over, as seen in such poems as "Redeployment," "A Fable of the War," "The Bacterial War," and "To a Friend." Nemerov's double vision, his sense of being trapped between art-faith and science-reality is much in evidence, as in the raging lines "And when the Germans bled the babies white/ Where was the *skepsis* of the sculptor's art/ The question is of science not to doubt/ The point of faith is that you sweat it out." Nemerov's religion, like Dostoevski's, is not one of easy acceptance; it involves constant doubting and agony of spirit. The doubting is, paradoxically, a positive value in Nemerov's poetry: it prevents him from preaching. His religious position, to judge from his writing, is that of a nonpracticing Jew engaged in a continual dialogue with Christianity, searching for its meaning, testing its relevance in the modern world. Unlike Bernard Malamud, his former colleague at Bennington, Nemerov does not write very often specifically about "Jewishness" (though in a letter he has said, "I was frightened by the Old Testament when a child, and have never got over it"). In the *Journal* he notes that at Harvard he was almost converted to Catholicism on "foolish" aesthetic grounds, but he has always drawn back to affirm his essential Jewishness. Perhaps his clearest statement on this theme is in "Debate with the Rabbi"; in the first three stanzas the Rabbi chides the protagonist for losing his religion. Then the poem concludes:

Stubborn and stiff-necked man! the Rabbi cried.
   The pain you give me, said I.
Instead of bowing down, said he,
   You go on in your obstinacy.
   We Jews are that way, I replied.

The union in several poems of religion and war marks a development in Nemerov's pessimism that will become more noticeable in later writings: the celebration of life despite the horror of the surroundings, perhaps *because* of the horror: "I stretch myself on joy as on the rack,/ And bear the hunch of glory on my back." The book as a whole is undoubtedly too much under the influence of the later Yeats, but a certain Yeatsian toughness of spirit has stayed with Nemerov as he forged his own style. His use of gulls, for example, inevitably reminds one of Yeats's swans (or Stevens' pigeons, Keats's nightingales): they symbolize the grace and rather arrogant pride of nature, the "Atlantic" beauty which holds heaven and earth together. These birds appear in many of the best of Nemerov's later poems ("The Gulls," "The Salt Garden," "The Town Dump"), but even this early, in individual poems like "The Lives of Gulls and Children," he has mastered the Yeats influence and speaks in his own manner.

There is, in the lines "They would have reached out hands to him/ To comfort him in that human kind/ They just were learning," a slight hint of another influence, later to become stronger: the quiet conversational tone of Robert Frost (Frost would have written "They were just learning"). Nemerov is one of the few poets to learn something from Frost, to assimilate the Frostian narrative technique, as seen in Nemerov's story poem "The Pond" (from *The Salt Garden* and appended to *Journal of the Fictive Life*).

Guide to the Ruins was sensibly criticized as lacking "a center of gravity or of force, the sense of a strong controlling sensibility." It is in *The Salt Garden* (1955) that Nemerov first unifies his talent. "The Goose Fish," "The Scales of the Eyes," "The Sanctuary," "The Quarry," "I Only Am Escaped Alone to Tell Thee," "The Salt Garden," "The Pond," "Deep

Woods" are just a few which have already become much anthologized. This book, praised by virtually all critics, had the misfortune to run up against *The Collected Poems of Wallace Stevens*, which swept the literary awards of 1955.

The Salt Garden is unified by Nemerov's growing interest in nature. The typical adjective describing nature is "brutal," and the link between brutal nature and "decent" bumbling man is found in the liquids, ocean and blood, which fuse into man's "salt dream," the submerged and subconscious call of the wild. The title poem, for example, begins with the speaker admiring his "good house," and the garden and lawn "In a decent order set"; he is proud that he has reclaimed the land from what was once "the ocean floor." But the "salt wind," the memory of "the ocean's wrinkled green"—unlike his smooth green garden—and finally "the great gull," which contemptuously surveys the speaker's "poor province," humble him, as he imagines the "wild sea lanes he wandered by/ And the wild waters where he slept/ Still as a candle in the crypt." Written in short-lined unevenly rhymed verse, this poem encompasses the main theme of the book: man's divided nature. A clear and "easy" poem of rational man rationally musing on his estate, "The Salt Garden" has as its counterpart the long and "difficult" "The Scales of the Eyes," which is a nighttime fantasy, a Freudian dream sequence, on the same subject. One can detect in "Scales" the influence of Theodore Roethke's poetry (e.g., the surreal "The Shape of the Fire"), which, as Nemerov himself has noted, is also partly "a result of the Freudian discoveries"—as are many of Nemerov's analyses in *Journal of the Fictive Life*. This series of eighteen short "dream songs" (like Berryman's later ones) traces a man's inward journey from despair (winter) to hope (spring). It presents a stream-of-consciousness nightmare vision of

New York as graveyard ("Dead men in their stone towns") and offers a general vision of modern civilization as inferno ("From Coney Island to Phlegethon/ Is no great way by ferris wheel").

"The Scales of the Eyes" (a title with Joycean possibilities) not only holds together as a sequence, but also many of the individual sections are effective lyrics by themselves, eerie scenes of some dreamland out of an Arthur Davies painting.

> The low sky was mute and white
> And the sun a white hole in the sky
> That morning when it came on to snow;
> The hushed flakes fell all day.
>
> The hills were hidden in a white air
> And every bearing went away,
> Landmarks being but white and white
> For anyone going anywhere.
>
> All lines were lost, a noon bell
> I heard sunk in a sullen pool
> Miles off. And yet this patient snow,
> When later I walked out in it,
>
> Had lodged itself in tips of grass
> And made its mantle bridging so
> It lay upon the air and not the earth
> So light it hardly bent a blade.

The poem which strikes one most strongly at first is "I Only Am Escaped Alone to Tell Thee," a tour de force describing the underlying agony of a superficially prosperous nineteenth-century woman. Nemerov takes the reader by degrees from a description of the lady to the "black flukes of agony." First he compares the mirror, "the long inaccurate glass," to "troubled water," and the "immense" shadow to a "giant crab." Having established the sea and giant motif, Nemerov goes on to describe her "strict" corsets and the "huge arrangements of her hair" as "no rig for dallying," and finishes with a simile comparing the lady to "a great ship," not unlike Milton's description of Delilah in *Samson Agonistes*. Then Nemerov pushes the metaphor to the furthest step, and his packed conclusion refers back to the corsets, the sea, the mirror, and the light referred to earlier:

> I know
> We need not draw this figure out.
> But all that whalebone came from whales.
> And all the whales lived in the sea,
> In calm beneath the troubled glass,
> Until the needle drew their blood.
>
> I see her standing in the hall,
> Where the mirror's lashed to blood and foam,
> And the black flukes of agony
> Beat at the air till the light blows out.

In *The Salt Garden*, Nemerov's fascination with the workings of the human mind first becomes clear (his poetry is filled with images of reflections, mirrors, cameras, dreams in dreams, etc.), a fascination that is still stronger in the *Journal* and *The Blue Swallows*; also, Nemerov has clearly been influenced by Owen Barfield's ideas on perception in Barfield's *Poetic Diction: A Study in Meaning* (for the second edition of which Nemerov wrote an introduction). In the *Journal* Nemerov states: "I hate intelligence, and have nothing else." Poem after poem fastens on man's mind, its loneliness, its limitations, its appeal: the joys of meditation which turn in on themselves and make nothing happen. One of the central poems on this subject in *The Salt Garden* is "The Sanctuary," written in a blank verse whose meditative rhythms and intelligent voice mark it as Nemerov's own:

> Over a ground of slate and light gravel,
> Clear water, so shallow that one can see
> The numerous springs moving their mouths of
>   sand;

And the dark trout are clearly to be seen,
Swimming this water which is color of air
So that the fish appear suspended nowhere and
In nothing. With a delicate bend and reflex
Of their tails the trout slowly glide
From the shadowy side into the light, so clear,
And back again into the shadows; slow
And so definite, like thoughts emerging
Into a clear place in the mind, then going back,
Exchanging shape for shade. Now and again
One fish slides into the center of the pool
And hangs between the surface and the slate
For several minutes without moving, like
A silence in a dream; and when I stand
At such a time, observing this, my life
Seems to have been suddenly moved a great
Distance away on every side, as though
The quietest thought of all stood in the pale
Watery light alone, and was no more
My own than the speckled trout I stare upon
All but unseeing. Even at such times
The mind goes on transposing and revising
The elements of its long allegory
In which the anagoge is always death;
And while this vision blurs with empty tears,
I visit, in the cold pool of the skull,
A sanctuary where the slender trout
Feed on my drowned eyes. . . . Until this trout
Pokes through the fabric of the surface to
Snap up a fly. As if a man's own eyes
Raised welts upon the mirror whence they
    stared,
I find this world again in focus, and
This fish, a shadow dammed in artifice,
Swims to the furthest shadows out of sight
Though not, in time's ruining stream, out of
    mind.

The anagoge is always death: but it is not war-death that Nemerov now addresses, but death as part of nature, "time's ruining stream." Meditations all lead to the reality of death, the unreality of life, culminating in several poems in

The Blue Swallows, like "In the Black Museum," which ends "Or as two mirrors vacuum-locked together/ Exclude, along with all the world,/ A light to see it by. Reflect on that."

The concluding poem of *The Salt Garden* is "Deep Woods," in which Nemerov expresses his feeling about the hugeness and permanence of nature as against small impermanent man. Walking through these deep New England woods is like a "dream of being lost"—a dream Nemerov frequently has. Like Frost, Nemerov is a realist, and does not romanticize nature (which does not, after all, need it).

Line, leaf, and light; darkness invades our day;
No meaning in it, but indifference
Which does not flatter with profundity.
Nor is it drama. Even the giant oak,
Stricken a hundred years ago or yesterday,
Has not found room to fall as heroes should. . . .

Insisting on the reality, Nemerov goes through the list of enchanted forests, the "Black Forest where the wizard lived," the Chinese forest "with bridge, pagoda, fog," the forests "invented by Watteau or Fragonard," and, in modern times, by Disney. But the real "deep woods" is so primitive, so virginal, so untouched by man that it is like the Garden of Eden before the Fall:

                    Most probably
Nothing will happen. Even the Fall of Man
Is waiting, here, for someone to grow apples;
And the snake, speckled as sunlight on the rock
In the deep woods, still sleeps with a whole
    head
And has not begun to grow a manly smile.

Mirrors & Windows (1958) continues with the elements already noted, plus a new one: Nemerov's quiet confidence in himself as a poet, a feeling that he can control internal despair with external craftsmanship. A great

many of these poems (e.g., "Holding the Mirror Up to Nature," "Painting a Mountain Stream," "Writing," "To Lu Chi") are about Nemerov writing poetry, a subject continued in later books: "Maestria" in *New & Selected Poems*; "Vermeer" and "Lion & Honeycomb" in *The Next Room of the Dream*; "The May Day Dancing," "Projection," and "Style" in *The Blue Swallows*. The trend toward nature begun in *The Salt Garden* continues in *Mirrors & Windows*, the difference being that in the later book he is consciously aware that he is a *poet* looking at nature, trying to capture it in his poems: "Study this rhythm, not this thing/ The brush's tip streams from the wrist/ of a living man, a dying man./ The running water is the wrist." The claims made for art—as for everything else—are minimal; he never claims for poetry powers not to be found in it. On the contrary, he is typically deprecating about his "modest art" which makes him—like Keats's poet—"appear a trifle colorless." Nemerov's honesty leads him to admit that even art is not permanent.

Miraculous. It is as though the world
were a great writing. Having said so much,
let us allow there is more to the world
than writing; continental faults are not
bare convoluted fissures in the brain.
Not only must the skaters soon go home;
also the hard inscription of their skates
is scored across the open water, which long
remembers nothing, neither wind nor wake.

Art and beauty (e.g., the birds in "The Town Dump") are what make life bearable, but nothing makes life understandable, nothing makes death meaningful. In *Mirrors & Windows* Nemerov's philosophy of minimal affirmation can be clearly seen.

"A Day on the Big Branch" is a good example of Nemerov's attitude, which might be called realistic romanticism. That is, the poems seem to be composed by a romantic sensibility which is at the same time too analytical and too honest to see things other than as they really are. In "A Day on the Big Branch" a group of, one would guess, college teachers have had an all-night poker party and, "still half drunk," they drive "to a stream in the high hills" with a vaguely formed "purgatorial idea," "the old standard appeal to the wilderness." And the wilderness *is* beautiful, "a paradise/ for ruined poker players, win or lose," and they lie back on the rocks waiting for something to happen. "The silence . . . / grew pregnant; but nothing else did." Nemerov's rocks are "hard as rocks." Nevertheless, something is learned, something "concerning patience/ and enduring what had to be endured . . . / weathering in whatever weather." The men talk of the war and of life, and the majestic beauty of nature forces them into "poetry and truth," which may be the same thing:

> so that at last one said, "I shall play cards
> until the day I die," and another said,
> "in bourbon whiskey are all the vitamins
> and minerals needed to sustain man's life,"
> and still another, "I shall live on smoke
> until my spirit has been cured of flesh."

Then the men climb downstream again, noting how the stream ("time's ruining stream") during a recent flood had smashed three bridges "practically back to nature," drive home, and resume their card game. Written in Nemerov's flexible and disciplined blank verse, "A Day on the Big Branch" is a mature achievement: one senses that Nemerov's irony (rocks as "hard as rocks") has been subdued to greater uses than in his earlier poetry.

The poems in this book are life-reflecting mirrors, and windows through which we see with the poet's "infinitely penetrant" eye. Consequently, the poems are extremely visual, and especially concerned with the movement of light: ". . . within the ledges/ the water, fast and still, pouring its yellow light,/ and green . . . falling in a foam/ of crystal to a calm where the waterlight/ dappled the ledges as they leaned/ against the sun." The last poem of the book, "Holding the Mirror Up to Nature," is typical, and sums up Nemerov's dark view of the universe. His use of mirrors reminds one of Hart Crane's lines which Nemerov used as an epigraph to *Federigo*: "As silent as a mirror is believed/ Realities plunge in silence by. . . ." The object of poetry is to catch as in a mirror the beauty and terror in life, not to make life prettier, not to make it easier for us, not even to help us understand it. Poetry can, if it is truthful, show us some aspect of real life by stopping it in a frame (the poet's discipline) and one can simply say, "How beautiful. How terrible." "Holding the Mirror" concludes:

> I know
> a truth that cannot be told, although
> I try to tell you, "We are alone,
> we know nothing, nothing, we shall die
> frightened in our freedom, the one
> who survives will change his name
> to evade the vengeance for love. . . ."
> Meanwhile the clouds go on clowning
> over our heads in the floodlight of
> a moon who is known to be Artemis
> and Cynthia but sails away anyhow
> beyond the serious poets with their
> crazy ladies and cloudy histories,
> their heroes in whose idiot dreams
> the buzzard circles like a clock.

Mirrors & Windows is the work of a confident poet. M. L. Rosenthal, in his review, said that in "a good poet a fine mind is one of God's greatest blessings." Sense and sensibility are abundant in this book, and it should have made clear to the critics that Nemerov is not the "cold" writer he has often been accused of being. (His writing is more endangered by sentiment than cerebration.) Perhaps under the not-very-softening influence of nature, his feelings—always present—are more in evidence in these poems permeated by a humanitarian and stoic outlook.

New & Selected Poems (1960) contains fifty-eight poems, only fifteen of them new. Actually, the best part of this book is Section II, which includes thirty-five poems from *The Salt Garden* and *Mirrors & Windows*, a sustained performance hard to match anywhere. The new note in *New & Selected Poems*, suitable for the maturing poet, is an even more overriding concern with his "deare times waste." Time and the loss of innocence, of friends, of hope, are the themes of the new poems. "I cried because life is hopeless and beautiful," he writes, and the beauty teaches him to "endure and grow." Nemerov's pessimism, dark as ever, is nevertheless not an empty nihilism: he affirms "the stillness in moving things" while attacking the emptiness of modern life.

The central poem here is "Runes," Nemerov's longest poem, symmetrically consisting of fifteen-line stanzas. Like "The Scales of the Eyes," "Runes" is a sort of dream fantasy, but it is more tightly organized, the fifteen stanzas being meditations clustered around the images of water and seed, "where time to come has tensed/ Itself." (In Engle and Langland's *Poet's Choice*, 1962, Nemerov chooses "Runes" as his favorite among his own poems.) The run-on blank verse lines consistently match rhythm and content: a "liquid sense trembles in his lines."

The basic theme of "Runes" (ruins) is mutability, and the dominant tone is religious, sometimes pantheistically Wordsworthian or transcendentally Emersonian. By watching water, "Water of dirt, water of death, dark water," the poet tries to find the secret of the universe, of life. Water is a "many-veined bloodstream," an "echoing pulse," "a mirror

of/ The taste of human blood." Sometimes lyrically, sometimes satirically, Nemerov turns his theme over and over in the many-prismed glass of his verse. Typical of his impeccable style is stanza XII:

Consider how the seed lost by a bird
Will harbor in its branches most remote
Descendants of the bird; while everywhere
And unobserved, the soft green stalks and tubes
Of water are hardening into wood, whose hide,
Gnarled, knotted, flowing, and its hidden grain,
Remember how the water is streaming still.
Now does the seed asleep, as in a dream
Where time is compacted under pressures of
Another order, crack open like stone
From whose division pours a stream, between
The raindrop and the sea, running in one
Direction, down, and gathering in its course
That bitter salt which spices us the food
We sweat for, and the blood and tears we shed.

The water streaming in the seed streams through our world, our bodies, holding everything together in its always-changing permanence. The subtle rhythms support the imagery in a fusion of form and content; run-ons, alliteration, repetition, all playing important roles in the structure. The "s" sound in "soft green stalks and tubes," the "d" sound in "hardening into wood, whose hide,/ Gnarled, knotted" reinforce the meaning; the rhythm, stopped by "whose hide,/ Gnarled, knotted," flows forward again with "flowing, and its hidden grain." The end of the first sentence holds the paradox of permanent impermanence in the ambiguous "streaming still." The onomatopoeic "crack" splits the second sentence, whose alliteration and longer phrases ("gathering in its course/ That bitter salt which spices us the food/ We sweat for") underline the stanza's conclusion.

Satirically, still working with water, Nemerov speaks of our "dehydrated time"; one perhaps thinks of Eliot's *Waste Land*, but this is clearly Nemerov, not Eliot; he has by this time mastered his influences. Some of his satire is tough indeed: "The plastic and cosmetic arts/ Unbreakably record the last word and/ The least word, till sometimes even the Muse,/ In her transparent raincoat, resembles a condom." How to act in this kind of world, *which* sailor —the Homeric or the Dantean Ulysses—to emulate? Watching the water, symbol of eternal regeneration, Nemerov prepares us for death, "the pit where zero's eye is closed"; the secret, found in "small freshets/ Leaping and limping down the tilted field/ In April's light," is—to keep the secret "hidden from yourself." Working, like the metaphysical poets, with paradox, Nemerov implies that to prepare for life one should study nature, at the same time keeping the secret (nature is death) hidden from oneself.

Perhaps because of certain satirical poems (e.g., "Life Cycle of Common Man," "Boom!"), some critics wondered that Nemerov could be, as one put it, "strangely light-hearted about the whole enterprise" (the harshness of life); surely this is a mistaken reading of Nemerov. There is sometimes the tough gaiety of Yeats and sometimes the serene acceptance of Wordsworth, but Nemerov is never really light-hearted. The typical tone is one of quiet anquish (often based on personal experience, such as his father's death).

> Only he died
> that day. "Unlucky boy," my father said,
> who then was dying himself without a word
> to anyone, the crab's claw tightening
> inside the bowel that year to the next
> in a dead silence. I do not know if things
> that happen can be said to come to pass,
> or only happen, but when I remember
> my father's house, I imagine sometimes
> a dry, ruined spinster at my rainy window
> trying to tally on dumb fingers a world's

incredible damage—nothing can stand it!—and watching the red shirt patched against the sky, so far and small in the webbed hand of the elm.

> Nothing can stand it, nothing will yield: there
> is no lightheartedness here.

"Mrs. Mandrill" (another Joycean title) is Nemerov's equivalent of Wallace Stevens' "Sunday Morning," where the dying Mrs. Mandrill muses on God, death, and nature (of which she is about to become a part). Some of the lines are memorable for their surreal power: "I was a little thing, before my face/ broke like a cheese"; "hearing this creature cry/ before her wet heart spills and goes to seed." Nature is really "unintelligible" to man, though we can learn from it by analogy (in "The Companions" in *The Blue Swallows* he says, "That's but interpretation, the deep folly of man/ To think that things can squeak at him more than things can"). But when we die we become a part of nature and the natural process—"they mean me now," thinks Mrs. Mandrill. One thinks of Thomas Wolfe's "And the strange and buried man will come again, in flower and leaf the strange and buried man will come again. . . ."

One last poem in *New & Selected Poems* that should be mentioned is "Maestria," because it leads directly to Nemerov's two best poems on "poetics"—"Vermeer" and "Lion & Honeycomb" in *The Next Room of the Dream.* In "Maestria" Nemerov points out that it is not the *meaning* of a poem that is important: "you need not agree with its views/About money or the meaning of numbers" (e.g., Pound, Dante). It would no doubt "be better to be always right," but a good poem outstrips the errors and "mortality of its maker,/ Who has the skill of his art, and a trembling hand."

> There remains
> A singular lucidity and sweetness, a way
> Of relating the light and the shade,

The light spilling from fountains, the shade
Shaken among the leaves.

In his introduction to Barfield's *Poetic Diction*, Nemerov writes: "But when the poet is older, if he has continued to write, it is at least probable that he will reach a point, either a stopping point or a turning point, at which he finds it necessary to inquire into the sense of what he has been doing, and now the question of poetic diction becomes for him supremely important, nothing less than the question of primary perception, of imagination itself, of how thought ever emerged (if it did) out of a world of things. There is some evidence that poets reaching this point—I think for example of Yeats, Valéry, Stevens—may feel acutely their want of formal philosophical training, so that they either abandon poetry and turn to study for a time, or else direct their poetry itself toward this study."

There is some evidence that Nemerov himself has reached this point in *The Next Room of the Dream* (1962): "The time came/He had to ask himself, what did he want?/ What did he want when he began/ That idiot fiddling with the sound of things." The subject matter of this book indicates his decision to stay close to "great primary human drama." Besides the two one-act verse plays, *Cain* (1959) and *Endor* (1961)—more successful as verse than as drama—poem after poem shows Nemerov's humanitarianism, notably "The Iron Characters," where he pities (more precisely: Nemerov *presents*; *we* pity) important men, governors, executives, who have broken under their responsibilities; but he concludes, pushing sympathy to its furthest limit, "Let the orphan, the pauper, the thief, the derelict drunk/And all those of no fixed address, shed tears of rejoicing/ For the broken minds of the strong, the torn flesh of the just." It is, Nemerov implies, common helplessness that unites us.

In *Next Room of the Dream* the poems continue to simplify, emphasizing natural description and precise observation. In "Human Things," describing the effects of a sunset on a barn: "even/ Nail holes look deep enough to swallow/ Whatever light has left to give." Describing goldfish, he writes "The bearded goldfish move about the bowl/ Waving disheveled rags of elegant fin/ Languidly in the light."

The poem which best summarizes the general philosophy of the book is one called "Nothing Will Yield." Art smashes on the rocks of reality:

Nothing will yield. The pretty poems are dead,
And the mad poets in their periwigs,
Bemused upon a frontispiece before
The ruined Temple of Art, and supervised
By the Goddess of Reason leaning from a cloud,
In reality died insane. Alas, for the grave
And gaudy forms! Lord Hi and Lady Ho,
Those brazen effigies upon a plinth
Of pink granite, seem immutable,
But seem.

And yet there is still beauty, though beauty is always sad: "Lachrymae Christi is/A beautiful sound, a Neapolitan wine,/ The Tears of Christ. And yet nothing will yield." In spite of this, poets will always speak their "holy language," in the teeth of despair. Nemerov concludes: "It takes great courage to go on the stage."

Seemingly effortlessly, Nemerov writes in blank verse, quatrains, triplets, sonnets, and a great variety of complex rhyme schemes; one senses immediately a poet with complete control of the tools of his trade, a poet for whom discipline means inspiration rather than restriction. Consistently simple, clear, direct, he time and again cuts open our experience to the anguished bone. In "Somewhere," Nemerov speaks of all the tragic events happening *ex-*

actly now: "A girl this evening regrets her surrender with tears," errant schoolboys, vicious fathers, gluttons waiting to vomit, unfaithful wives.

The stones of the city have been here for
        centuries,
The tides have been washing backwards and
        forwards
In sunlight, in starlight, since before the
        beginning.
Down in the swamp a red fox runs quietly,
        quietly
Under the owl's observation, those yellow eyes
That eat through the darkness. Hear the shrew
        cry!

The rocking rhythm of "In sunlight, in starlight," the repetition of "quietly, quietly," are precise meaningful technical devices, and the poem ends with the nice irony of people listening to stories somewhere, stories of lust and violence, enraptured by "the sweet seductions/ Punishable by death, with the song's word: long ago."

"Vermeer" expresses Nemerov's view on the relation between nature and poetry: "Taking what is, and seeing it as it is,/ Pretending to no heroic stances or gestures,/ Keeping it simple; being in love with light/And the marvelous things that light is able to do,/ How beautiful!" The job of the poet is to present these things to the audience "and make it stick." Like Wilbur's "Juggler" ("who has won for once over the world's weight"), Nemerov's artist can make people "for one moment happy/ In the great reckoning of those little rooms/ Where the weight of life has been lifted and made light." But the capstone of *The Next Room of the Dream* is "Lion & Honeycomb," the closest thing to Nemerov's *ars poetica*, which begins "He didn't want to do it with skill,/ He'd had enough of skill," and concludes:

So there he was, this forty-year-old teen-ager
Dreaming preposterous mergers and divisions
Of vowels like water, consonants like rock
(While everybody kept discussing values
And the need for values), for words that would
Enter the silence and be there as a light.
So much coffee and so many cigarettes
Gone down the drain, gone up in smoke,
Just for the sake of getting something right
Once in a while, something that could stand
On its own flat feet to keep out windy time
And the worm, seomething that might simply
        be,
Not as the monument in the smoky rain
Grimly endures, but that would be
Only a moment's inviolable presence,
The moment before disaster, before the storm,
In its peculiar silence, an integer
Fixed in the middle of the fall of things,
Perfected and casual as to a child's eye
Soap bubbles are, and skipping stones.

"Out of the eater came forth meat, and out of the strong came forth sweetness." Nemerov in this poem presents Samson's riddle as a parable of poetry. Poetry is the honey in the carcass of a lion; the poet manufactures this honey from the decaying grandeur surrounding him. In "Lion & Honeycomb" Nemerov both defines and exemplifies what he is trying to do. The rhythms of the poem are "Perfected and casual": note, for example, the placement of "Grimly," the balance of "So . . . so/Gone . . . gone." Unpretentious and simple, like "Soap bubbles" and "skipping stones," this poem shows Nemerov to be at a peak in his poetic powers.

But while *The Next Room of the Dream* seems to record a crisis and resolution in Nemerov's poetry, *Journal of the Fictive Life* (1965), records an unresolved crisis in Nemerov's fiction: an inability to complete another novel. This might be a good place to look back at Nemerov's novels, and see their relation to his poetry. Nemerov's fiction is in some danger of slipping undeservedly into oblivion: his novels and short stories are out of print, despite a generally good critical reception on their first appearance. One reason for this neglect is that his stories are uncompromising in their intellectual and moral implications, and unromantic in their presentation. In fact, one of his major themes is the disaster incurred when romantic people ("melodramatists") clash with reality. Reality, to Nemerov, is infinitely complex; the simplest act (speeding in a car, taking a bath) can, to a subtle mind, have enormous and far-reaching consequences. These books do not duck these complexities, and thus, despite much high humor, would have to be lucky to capture the popular imagination.

Like his poems, they are basically pessimistic. The condition of man is not an enviable one: we act foolishly and understand imperfectly. Nemerov's dark viewpoint, which in his poetry is redeemed by beauty (e.g., the wild birds in "The Town Dump"), in his fiction is redeemed by humor. There is in Nemerov much of the attitude of the "Absurd" playwrights: life may be meaningless, but at least we can laugh at it, and with laughter comes acceptance. Wallace Stevens wrote that poetry makes our completely inexplicable lives acceptable; humor has this function in Nemerov's novels. It involves looking at life honestly and not giving in to the modish despair Nemerov satirizes in his poem "To the Bleeding Hearts Association of American Novelists." For example, the death of Susan Boyne in *The Melodramatists* is tragic and unexpected, and yet ludicrous; it has a lot in common with the death of Jerry in Albee's *Zoo Story*. Both are semi-suicides which take the action out of the realm of dialectic: death, at least, is real. Unsentimental, without illusions, Nemerov's comic viewpoint presents man as hopelessly inept and at the same time unquenchably enduring.

There has been some development in Nemerov's prose, though not so striking as in his poetry, but even in his first novel his salient qualities are apparent: humor, intellectual precision, fantasy, and a smooth, "classical" prose style. *The Melodramatists* (1949) is a wild first novel. Stylistically it is an odd but appealing mixture: a Trollope bitten by a Heller, perhaps, or vice versa, combining a slow, old-fashioned elegance of prose with comic, almost surrealistic events. It switches from Socratic dialogue to drunken orgy, from dialectic to destruction, without missing a beat. The action takes place among an old Boston "Brahmin" family, and the tone is consistently satirical. Though compared by reviewers to Waugh and Huxley, Nemerov seems stylistically closer to more leisurely writers—Trollope, as mentioned above, or Henry James, in his elegance of phrasing and (like his poetry) precision of observation:

"When her mother wept, as she did now, all the jewels on her fingers and at her throat winked in sparkling connivance as at a joke which, they seemed to say, you too might appreciate, were you as detached as a stone—cold as this sapphire, hard and cutting as this diamond. Mrs. Boyne's tears fell heedlessly where they might, into her coffee, over the bright little spoons and dessert knives, stained the damask cloth. . . ."

A perhaps more profitable comparison can be made with a novelist greatly admired by Nemerov: Thomas Mann (Nemerov has two essays on Mann in *Poetry and Fiction: Essays*). If there is any real similarity between *The Melodramatists* and another novel, it would be with

Mann's *Magic Mountain*. Just as Herren Settembrini and Naphta tirelessly engage in a religious, philosophical, and scientific debate for the soul of Hans Castorp, so in *The Melodramatists* Dr. Einman and Father Meretruce debate for the souls of Susan and Claire, debates which are never resolved, but which culminate in disaster.

The action in *The Melodramatists* proceeds from sanity to madness, in several ways. The thin line between madness and sanity is one of Nemerov's chief themes—it shows up in *Federigo, The Homecoming Game*, and in several of his short stories ("A Secret Society," "The Web of Life"), as well as in poems like "The Iron Characters" and "The Rope's End." The plot here, as in most of his fiction, is a bizarre and often grotesque vehicle for his satire. The two main targets are psychiatry, in the person of Dr. Einman, and religion, in the persons of Father Meretruce and the Hungarian nuns. The religion Meretruce represents is a false one, and, indeed, religion as a panacea for society's ills turns out very badly in this book. The only real religious experience in it is incurred by Claire and described as a spiritual rape; and even prayer is described repulsively:

"The Hungarian nuns were praying at an almost breathless speed. They were knelt down near to and facing a wall to which they addressed a continuous muttering. They rocked slightly back and forth, and swayed a little from side to side; the flow of their words was interrupted only occasionally for a brief instant in which one of them would gulp back from the corners of her mouth an excess of saliva, or swiftly wipe her lips at the wrist of her garment."

It is no wonder Claire eventually loses her faith.

The major theme in *The Melodramatists* is the inability of these characters to cope with reality. The only character who is *not* a romanticist is Mother Fosker, and this grotesque old madam caters to the romanticism of society in general by basing her "entertainments" on illusion—the illusion of love, of pursuit, of youth, of gaiety. And time after time Nemerov digresses in his learned and amusing way on the nature of romanticism:

"It is easy to imagine the other worlds that might be. One, for example, of a delicious lubricity, indiscriminate and always pleasant copulation *à la Thélème*, and every nymphomaniac there remains sixteen for always and always but is an intelligent conversationalist, charmed by poetry and good music, who can repeat to you word for word the entire *Book of the Courtier*. There on Urbino's windy hill, where blows Castiglione's wise and sexual beard, the sun varies in color from a bloody incandescence in the morning to a dusk of lavender, heliotrope, pale rose, and a few ruins by Piranesi delicately accent the small cumulus clouds artistically piled at one corner of a sky which is not too large."

There are weaknesses in the book. It is longer than it need be—the part played by Roger, though often amusing, seems unnecessary. Some of the discussions seem too long; some scenes are a little like a bad play; some of the humor strains too hard to be clever ("we know where our breed is bettered"). But in general *The Melodramatists* is a highly successful first novel, a book by an erudite and witty young man who presents his criticism of society without writing the usual disguised autobiography. The Boyne mansion stands at the end of the book as an apt symbol of society: science and religion (Einman and Meretruce) are prisoners upstairs, while lust and lechery reign below. But, as in the final stanza of many of his poems, in the final passage of the book all is not hopeless. In a "minimal affirmation," Claire reacts to this debacle not by breaking down, but by turning to music:

"Claire got up, and, without looking at Hogan or John or the priest, went to the harpsichord. She sat down and began to play, inattentively at first but presently with more care, a little piece in fugue. The instrument was out of tune and not only that, but broken glass tinkled on some of the strings, but it seemed not to matter. The morning light seemed to clear the room as the voices in a minor key steadily moved to and from one another, showing an inexorable confidence in their not quite harmonious world."

The house (the world) is a catastrophe, but it endures, and begins again.

Nemerov's second novel, *Federigo, or, The Power of Love* (1954), is, among other things, a sex farce, a sort of rococo updating of a story from, perhaps, Boccaccio's *Decameron*. While Nemerov is not coy, and will use on occasion the suitable four-letter words, his handling of sexual scenes is basically psychological, not detailed or graphic. Concentrating on *style*, on good writing, rather than on titillation or easy shock, Nemerov bypasses contemporary vogues to write a novel that is consistently in good taste (in this way, and others, often reminding one of Vladimir Nabokov). *Federigo* is Nemerov's best novel, a tour de force whose intricate plot unravels with the inevitable logic of Chaucer's "Miller's Tale"; crammed with wit and wisdom, it begins with a lovely sentence: "Young men in our country are brought up to believe that they have a destiny, a guiding idea shaped like a star; most of them pass their lives in unawareness that this destiny is gradually becoming the sum of everything that has happened to them, and need not have been represented by a star in the first place, being perhaps more like the false beacon set up by smugglers to direct a vessel toward a convenient disaster. Disaster, *dés*, from, *astre*, a star."

The plot, really an elaborate joke, is the line on which Nemerov hangs his criticism of society and his psychological insights into existential man. But he compounds the "unreality" of this novel by introducing an element of high fantasy, an element very prominent in his short stories (e.g., "Yore," "The Sorcerer's Eye"). Fantasy in *Federigo* centers around the character of Federigo himself. Actually, there are three Federigos: the invented Federigo (the one used by Julian and Marius in their letters); the real Federigo (Federigo Schwartz, a shadowy figure who looks like Julian and whom Elaine has met); and the apparition Federigo, who appears throughout the book to Julian, walking through walls, recalling scenes of Julian's childhood, predicting the future, disappearing and appearing at will. This Federigo, literarily speaking, has much in common with the devils which appear in Mann's *Doctor Faustus* and Dostoevski's *The Brothers Karamazov*: he is a taunting intellectual sort of fellow, and Julian is never quite clear whether he actually sees him or just imagines him. One reason *Federigo* is successful is that it seems to mirror the "opposed elements" already noted in Nemerov's poetry.

Federigo is used by Nemerov to develop Julian's character, and consequently we understand more about Julian than we did about any of the characters in *The Melodramatists*. Federigo is indeed the devil, but he is also Julian's second self—the devil in every man which is usually suppressed. Through Federigo we know the worst of Julian Ghent: a hint of homosexuality, a yearning for the death of his wife, an emptiness of spirit. "To make me leave you alone," says Federigo, "you must be other than you are." When Julian, at the end, discovers he is not cut out to be unfaithful, Federigo disappears.

The problem Federigo causes Julian is the problem of sanity. If Federigo "is the Devil," Julian thinks, then "I am insane." But Nemerov's point is that it is not Julian who is insane, but life in general: "But Julian considered that all these fine ladies and gentlemen gathered here, listening to the fine talk, kept in their hearts the secret of lust, that their inmost thoughts were concentrated on sex, that madness thinly veiled possessed them all, the madness which all the forces of society seemed designed at once to· provoke and restrain but never to allay."

Julian (Jay) Ghent is—like Fitzgerald's Jay Gatsby—a romanticist who bangs hard against reality, though, this being a comedy, he survives. The power of love (the ironic subtitle) is really not very powerful in a world where people are not sure whom they love, or in what way. Julian tries to become a great lover, and fails except by mistake with his wife. The animals in the zoo seem to Julian to be neater and more dignified than humans; and toward the end of the book when Marius and Elaine walk along the shore the huge head of a dead fish grins up at them (the same fish as in Nemerov's most anthologized poem, "The Goose Fish"). Human love, Nemerov realizes, has "pitched his mansion in/ The place of excrement"; more than that, there are no lights in this mansion and one needs luck to stumble into someone's arms.

Federigo is as smoothly written as *The Melodramatists*, but sharper, more epigrammatic: "The future is in the lap of the gods, and they are standing up to see what is going to happen." It is not only the epigrams, however, which strike the reader of Nemerov's prose. His sentences have a fine balance, an almost Baconian resonance, marked by impeccable grammar and a rising and falling rhythm:

"Julian and Sylvia Ghent are still together, without being altogether certain why; though it is true that there was born to them a child, whose creation could have been dated to that night. This child was a boy, whom they named Peter." This balance is often achieved by rhythmically matched clauses and phrases, frequently joined by the semicolon: "They had, she believed, a modern marriage; this was, however, the expression people typically used. . . ." The colon, too, is frequently used by Nemerov to set up parallel lists and descriptions:

"The furniture too rebuked them, entering into the spirit of the silence: the clean-lined, slender legs of the low, modern tables, the alert appearance of the couch with its square corners and straight back, the inquisitive curve of a lamp which bent its bell-head heavily from a corner; all these smart impersonal objects, as coldly reasonable here as they had been in the shops whence they came, all at once achieved the identity of unhappiness: if we thought you would be like this, they seemed to say, we would not have come here."

To sum up (as Nemerov typically says in his critical reviews), *Federigo* can be best explained in the words of Marius when Sylvia tells him about the letters. "How very funny," he says. "Yet how very serious, too." Of course, the same could be said about *The Blue Swallows* or *The Next Room of the Dream*.

The Homecoming Game (1957), a humorous takeoff on a sort of Rover Boy plot, is his last and least ambitious novel, its enthusiastic reception at least partly caused by Nemerov's growing reputation. Ironically, this book made Nemerov the most money, being turned into a vapid Broadway comedy by Lindsay and Crouse, and a ridiculous Hollywood movie starring Jane Fonda. "All one winter and spring," writes Nemerov in *Journal of the Fictive Life*, "my shoulder ached from carting those checks to the bank." This "capriciousness in the relation between work and pay" is one of the reasons he has not written another novel: "how easy it would be to become a writer who worked for the money."

The Homecoming Game is set at a small old eastern coeducational college (physically reminding one of Hamilton); Charles Osman, the protagonist, is a history teacher who has just flunked the star quarterback. Nemorov turns this cliché into a tremendously complicated situation, a moral and philosophical tangle almost impossible to unravel. The second half of *The Homecoming Game* redeems what begins as a weak performance. Even Nemerov's style falters a bit in the beginning, occasionally approaching uncomfortably close to the old "Tom Swifties," as on pages 30–31:

"Charles laughed rather hopelessly. . . ."

" 'Yes,' she said earnestly. . . ."

" 'You speak delightfully of "us," ' Charles said glumly. . . ."

" 'Where in all this is Blent?' Charles asked angrily. . . ."

Also, the improbability of the given situation, before Nemerov ingeniously works it out, tends to keep the reader uninvolved. One can accept a student athlete being offered a bribe—that happens all the time—and one can gleefully accept wild events such as the student falling into the pep-rally bonfire and getting burned to death: a macabre symbol of a pagan ritual; but it is harder to accept the student council threatening the professor, the quarterback and the professor being in love with the beautiful daughter of trustee Herman Sayre, the quarterback being from the home town of Senator Stamp, Stamp and Sayre both being such primitive types, the president being such a servile and contemptible coward: these touches in toto do not succeed the way *Federigo* succeeds.

Nemerov uses football as a multivalent symbol of society, life, and death. Charles, like

Nemerov, has a metaphysical turn of mind (also like Julian Ghent in *Federigo*, who compares at great length his bathroom to a church); football, to Charles, is like society because it consists of "orderly violence," reminding him of all the products of civilization, from war to cities to symphonies. It is like death because it ends so abruptly; it seems so real, and then is gone. It is like life because of its ebb and flow, and because it is, somehow, deceptive:

"Football is unreal, if you care to say so; but as you grow older many things become unreal, and football stands out somehow as an image. And there under the shadow of the stone, empty stadium, after the captains and the kings depart, after all the others too depart, in that last lonely and cold air, you may, if you care for games, experience something of what is meant by vanished glory. Symbolical—perhaps. But it is commonly allowed that you may more easily call the things of this world symbolical than say what they are symbolical of."

In no other book has football, that national phenomenon, been so subtly analyzed as in *The Homecoming Game*. Despite a lack of memorable characters, the madness that grips the students (which, Nemerov points out, has disturbing similarities to the madness of Nazi Germany), the ridiculous but real tension on the campus, the pressures on faculty members who have star athletes in their classes, the power plays of alumni and trustees, and even the beauty of the actual game itself (and even when the beautiful game is beautifully fixed), are all unforgettably presented in this novel.

Nemerov's three novels, plus his book of short stories (*A Commodity of Dreams*, 1959, *Stories, Fables and Other Diversions*, 1971), are remarkable in their consistency of superior writing. Too intellectual, perhaps, for real popularity, they nevertheless should not be out of print. One charge that has been made against all of them (similar to one made against his poetry) is that Nemerov treats his characters coldly. The real problem is that readers do not know how to take Nemerov: Is he being funny, or what? Is he kidding us?

The point is that Nemerov, like the "Absurd" playwrights, is humorous and serious at the same time. One should not confuse seriousness with solemnity; Nemerov is never solemn but is always, even at his funniest, serious. When Julian and Sylvia sit up in bed and recognize each other, this is funny; but it also underlines Nemerov's thesis: we think we know what we are doing, but we do not; we think we are in control of the situation, but we are not. "Reality," observes Mr. le Mesurier in "Yore," "is always improbable," and man's understanding of reality is always incomplete and distorted. Because Nemerov's major prose mode is satire and comedy (while his major poetic mode is lyric), this "coldness" is necessary; if a figure is to be comic, he must be fallible and weak (Falstaff, Pangloss, Don Quixote, Humbert Humbert). Because Nemerov looks on fate as inexorable, enigmatic, and accidental, and sees man as a victim of this fate, his writing must be either tragic or comic; it cannot be heroic or sentimental. Basically speaking, Nemerov's prose is comic; Nemerov's poetry is tragic: both come from the same fatalistic philosophy, representing the two ways that the "opposed elements" of his character show their responsibility to the human drama.

In *Journal of the Fictive Life* Nemerov attempts to fuse these elements by plunging into confession and self-analysis written in a cross between poetry and prose. Proceeding by epigram ("The novel is marriage. Poetry is infidelity") and association, Nemerov analyzes his inability to write a fourth novel by analyzing his dreams, his relationship with his parents and wife, his taboos and prejudices, in a Dostoevskian manner:

"As though to say: Yes, I am a loathsome fellow, but beautifully composed!

"And all through these so intimate, so personal, observations runs the thought that I shall one day publish them, in a gesture of confessional defiance or proud self-contempt. For I am trying to tell the truth, and it is a trouble to me."

Anyone interested in the link between the subconscious mind and creativity will find riches in this book. There is much also that helps one understand particular poems, parts of the novels, and various influences such as Nabokov and Empson. The most surprising aspect of the book, however, is its sexual frankness, an area in which Nemerov has previously been reticent.

Journal of the Fictive Life is the record of a disturbed man who turns the rather awesome battery of his intelligence inward on his own mind, seeking the source of his disturbance. But the source is, simply, his humanness; here also is the source of reconciliation, as the *Journal* ends with the birth of Nemerov's son and a hopeful pointing toward the "magical poetry" of Shakespeare's Last Plays.

Nemerov's next work, *The Blue Swallows* (1967), is a worthy successor. It has the variety, wit, and technical skill we have come to expect; it is also full of wisdom and gentleness.

> . . . even the water
> Flowing away beneath those birds
> Will fail to reflect their flying forms,
> And the eyes that see become as stones
> Whence never tears shall fall again.
>
> O swallows, swallows, poems are not
> The point. Finding again the world,
> That is the point, where loveliness
> Adorns intelligible things
> Because the mind's eye lit the sun.

Without basically changing his dark philosophy, or losing his satirical edge, Nemerov has progressed steadily in his poetry to a broader, more tolerant view, less bitter and more sad. While the themes and images are often specifically contemporary (Auschwitz, burning monks, a Negro cemetery, cybernetics), Nemerov is mainly concerned with finding timeless metaphors for the human condition, "relation's spindrift web." In poem after poem we are likened (without his saying so explicitly) to cherries picked off trees, snowflakes falling in black water, lobsters waiting in a tank, days falling to darkness, planted rows dwindling to wilderness, fields becoming shadows. These poems are used more or less contrapuntally with tremendously effective satire on the Great Society ("Money," "On the Platform," "To the Governor & Legislature of Massachusetts"). A typical example (not best, but chosen for brevity) is "Keeping Informed in D.C.":

Each morning when I break my buttered toast
Across the columns of the *Morning Post*,
I am astounded by the ways in which
Mankind has managed once again to bitch
Things up to a degree that yesterday
Had looked impossible. Not far away
From dreams of mine, I read this dream of
    theirs,
And think: It's true, we *are* the bankrupt heirs
Of all the ages, history *is* the bunk.
If you do not believe in all this junk,
If you're not glad things are not as they are,
    You can wipe your arse on the *Evening Star*.

Nature, still treated unromantically, permeates these poems; in "The Companions," which is a sort of modern "Immortality Ode," Nemerov describes the pull toward nature that, for example, Frost writes about in "Directive." Nemerov refuses to see "messages" there, and yet "there came those voices up out of the ground/And got into my head, until articulate sound/ Might speak them to themselves." A

fascination with light, "Firelight in sunlight, silver pale," still plays over his pages, and indeed each of these poems can be thought of as a "small flame" like that which concludes the book's final poem:

So warm, so clear at the line of corded velvet
The marvelous flesh, its faster rise and fall,
Sigh in the throat, the mouth fallen open,
The knees fallen open, the heavy flag of the
    skirt
Urgently gathered together, quick, so quick,
Black lacquer, bronze, blue velvet, gleam
Of pewter in a tarnishing light, the book
Of the body lying open at the last leaf,
Where the spirit and the bride say, Come,
As from deep mirrors on the hinted wall
Beyond these shadows, a small flame sprouts.

One reason why Nemerov speaks effectively to this age is that his poetry attempts to come to terms with science: not just psychology, as in the *Journal*, but "hard" science. Light years and nebulae, the speed of light, electrodes, a heterodyne hum, physicists and particles are typical subjects for him. His general position seems to be that science is "true," but never quite accounts for our lives (though it tries): science lacks "blood" and "mystery"; it misses the essential.

For "nothing in the universe can travel at the
    speed
Of light," they say, forgetful of the shadow's
    speed.

While Nemerov's typical form is still the loose blank-verse line, in *The Blue Shadows* he uses more short-lined poems, trimeter and dimeter, than in his earlier work, keeping with his trend toward simplicity. In this form, too, his rhythms are varied and subtle, as in the first stanza of "Celestial Globe":

    This is the world
    Without the world.

I hold it in my hand
A hollow sphere
Of childlike blue
With magnitude of stars.
There in its utter dark
The singing planets go,
And the sun, great source,
Is blazing forth his fires
Over the many-oceaned
And river-shining earth
Whereon I stand
Balancing this ball
Upon my hand.

The Blue Swallows is the work of a poet who is a master of his craft; rhythm, image, sound fuse in poem after poem. And the poetry speaks to us, as poems should. There is no certainty, much agony, our minds bow down "Among the shadows/ Of shadowy things,/ Itself a shadow/ Less sure than they." Nemerov's general intelligence and craftsmanship perhaps seem old-fashioned today, when blood-and-guts, a confessional softness, and a sort of sloppiness are thought to be more "honest" or "spontaneous"; he is perhaps closer in this to, say, Pope, who is also out of favor (nevertheless the eighteenth century is called the Age of Pope). And underneath the darkness, fragmented and dying, Nemerov continually strikes the existential spark, as in the conclusion of his poem describing an oil slick polluting a stream:

The curve and glitter of it as it goes
The maze of its pursuit, reflect the water
In agony under the alien, brilliant skin
It struggles to throw off and finally does
Throw off, on its frivolous purgatorial fall
Down to the sea and away, dancing and
    singing
Perpetual intercession for this filth—
Leaping and dancing and singing, forgiving
    everything.

Selected Bibliography

WORKS OF HOWARD NEMEROV

POETRY
The Image and the Law. New York: Henry Holt, 1947.
Guide to the Ruins. New York: Random House, 1950.
The Salt Garden. Boston: Little, Brown, 1955.
Small Moment. Los Angeles: Ward Ritchie, 1957. (Broadside.)
Mirrors & Windows: Poems. Chicago: University of Chicago Press, 1958.
New & Selected Poems. Chicago: University of Chicago Press, 1960.
Endor. New York: Abingdon, 1961.
The Next Room of the Dream. Chicago: University of Chicago Press, 1962.
The Blue Swallows. Chicago: University of Chicago Press, 1967.
A Sequence of Seven with a Drawing by Ron Slaughter. Detroit: Tinker Press, 1967.
Winter Lightning. London: Rapp and Whiting, 1968.
The Painter Dreaming in the Scholar's House. New York: Phoenix Book Shop, 1968.
Gnomes and Occasions. Chicago: University of Chicago Press, 1972.

FICTION
The Melodramatists. New York: Random House, 1949.
Federigo, or, The Power of Love. Boston: Little, Brown, 1954.
The Homecoming Game. New York: Simon and Schuster, 1957.
A Commodity of Dreams & Other Stories. New York: Simon and Schuster, 1959.
Stories, Fables and Other Diversions. Brookline, Mass.: David R. Godine, 1971.

OTHER PROSE
Poetry and Fiction: Essays. New Brunswick, N.J.: Rutgers University Press, 1963.
Journal of the Fictive Life. New Brunswick, N.J.: Rutgers University Press, 1965.

Reflexions on Poetry and Poetics. New Brunswick, N.J.: Rutgers University Press, 1972.

EDITED VOLUMES
Longfellow. New York: Dell, 1959.
Poets on Poetry. New York: Basic Books, 1965.
Poetry and Criticism. Cambridge, Mass.: Adams House and Lowell House Printers, 1965.

CRITICAL STUDIES AND REVIEWS

Arrowsmith, William. "Recent Verse," *Hudson Review*, 1:98–105 (Spring 1948).

Bartholomay, Julia. *The Shield of Perseus.* Gainesville: University of Florida Press, 1972.

Berryman, John. "Waiting for the End Boys," *Partisan Review*, 15:254–67 (February 1948).

Bogan, Louise. "Verse," *New Yorker*, 37:129–31 (April 1, 1961).

Boyle, Kay. "Saluting Kings and Presidents," *Nation*, 214:184–87 (February 7, 1972).

Burke, Kenneth. "Comments on 18 Poems by Howard Nemerov," *Kenyon Review*, 60:117–31 (Winter 1952).

Carruth, Hayden. "The Errors of Excellence," *Nation*, 192:63–64 (January 21, 1961).

Ciardi, John. "Dry and Bitter Dust," *Saturday Review*, 44:66 (February 11, 1961).

Daiches, David. "Some Recent Poetry," *Yale Review*, 40:352–57 (Winter 1951).

Dickey, James. *Babel to Byzantium.* New York: Farrar, Straus and Giroux, 1968. Pp. 35–41.

Duncan, Bowie, ed. *The Critical Reception of Howard Nemerov.* Metuchen, N.J.: Scarecrow Press, 1971.

Eberhart, Richard. "Five Poets," *Kenyon Review*, 14:168–76 (Winter 1952).

Elliott, George P. "Fiction Chronicle," *Hudson Review*, 10:288–95 (Summer 1957).

Fitts, Dudley. "Poetry Chronicle," *Partisan Review,* 22:542–48 (Fall 1955).

Flint, R. W. "Poetry," *New York Review of Books,* 1:26–27 (Special Issue 1963).

Foster, Richard. "Neither Noble nor Savage, but Nice," *Minnesota Review*, 1:109–13 (Fall 1960).

Gerstenberger, Donna. "An Interview with Howard Nemerov," *Trace*, 35:22–25 (January–February 1960).

Harvey, Robert D. "A Prophet Armed: An Introduction to the Poetry of Howard Nemerov," in *Poets in Progress*, edited by E. B. Hungerford. Evanston, Ill.: Northwestern University Press, 1962. Pp. 116–33.

Howe, Irving. "A Cultivated Mind Willing to Bend to the Work at Hand," *New York Times Book Review*, March 29, 1964, p. 5.

Jarrell, Randall. "Recent Poetry," *Yale Review*, 45:122–32 (September 1955).

Jerome, Judson. "For Summer, a Wave of New Verse," *Saturday Review*, 46:30–32 (July 6, 1963).

Johnson, W. R. "Review," *Carleton Miscellany*, 4:120–24 (Spring 1963).

Kizer, Carolyn. "The Middle of the Journey," *Poetry*, 92:178–81 (December 1958).

Knock, Stanley F., Jr. "Renewal of Illusion," *Christian Century*, 80:84–85 (March 20, 1963).

Kunitz, Stanley. "Many Exertions, Some Excellencies," *New York Times Book Review*, July 21, 1963, p. 4.

Mizener, Arthur. "Spring Fiction," *Kenyon Review*, 19:484–93 (Summer 1957).

Rosenthal, M. L. " 'False Wentletrap! Avaunt,' " *Nation*, 187:27–28 (August 16, 1958).

———. "Something That Might Simply Be," *Reporter*, 29:54–58 (September 12, 1963).

Waggoner, Hyatt H. *American Poets.* Boston: Houghton Mifflin, 1968. Pp. 610–14.

Whittemore, Reed. "Observation of an Alien," *New Republic,* 138:27–28 (June 23, 1958).

Wright, James. "Some Recent Poetry," *Sewanee Review*, 66:657–68 (October–December 1958).

—PETER MEINKE

Reinhold Niebuhr

1892-1971

MAN has always been his most vexing problem. How shall he think of himself?" These are the opening lines of the Gifford Lectures which Reinhold Niebuhr delivered at the University of Edinburgh in the spring and autumn of 1939, and they identify the theme that unified all his thought and writing, even as early as the 1920's, when he first appeared on the national scene as the young pastor of a Detroit congregation of the Evangelical Synod who was projecting a critique of both religion and modern culture more radical than anything that had yet emerged from liberal Protestantism. What is the proper estimate of man? This was Niebuhr's fundamental question. As he said in his Gifford Lectures, "The obvious fact is that man is a child of nature, subject to its vicissitudes, compelled by its necessities, driven by its impulses, and confined within the brevity of the years which nature permits its varied organic forms allowing them some, but not too much, latitude. The other less obvious fact is that man is a spirit who stands outside of nature, life, himself, his reason and the world." He stands, in other words, at a point of juncture between nature and spirit: he is subject to all the brutal contingencies of nature and history; and yet, in the incalculable reaches of his freedom, he has the capacity to stand outside the forces of nature and to sub-

due them to his purposes. And not only does man's radical freedom permit him to transcend the necessities of nature and every concretion of historical circumstance: he can also transcend himself, making himself the object of his own knowledge, of his own judgment and for-giveness—and deception. When the full human truth is collapsed into some simplistic formula that overstresses either man's uniqueness and dignity or his affinity with the world of nature and his misery, then the consequence, inevi-tably, is some fatuity which is irrelevant to the real complexity of things. This was the funda-mental insight at the core of Reinhold Nie-buhr's entire thought, and it provided the con-trolling principle of the theological work and the brilliant forays into social and political criticism that made him a figure of command-ing importance in American intellectual life from the late 1920's until the time of his death in 1971.

In an autobiographical essay published in 1956, Niebuhr spoke of the central interest of his life as having been "the defense and justi-fication of the Christian faith in a secular age, particularly among what Schleiermacher called Christianity's 'intellectual despisers.' " And this was indeed the principal focus of his career. But, unlike Schleiermacher at the beginning of the nineteenth century, Niebuhr did not approach the characteristic intellectual expressions of his age from the premise that *anima humana naturaliter Christiana*; and thus he did not understand his task to be one of identifying what is already proximately Christian in the major secular philosophies of the modern period with which the Christian faith finds itself in contention: the field of "apologetics" did not, in other words, in its traditional form, provide the basic emphasis of his thought and writing. Like his distinguished European colleagues in theology, Emil Brunner and Karl Barth, he held as his deepest conviction that the Christian estimate of man is truer and profounder than any of its secular alternatives, whether classical or modern; and his chief concern, therefore, was to accomplish such a transvaluation of modern secularity as might disarm his contemporaries into a fresh apprehension of the cogency and relevance to their condition of the analysis of the human quandary implicit in Biblical faith.

But Niebuhr also wanted to keep a lively awareness of "the falsehoods and corruptions which may use a final truth as their instrument in actual history." The genuinely prophetic cast of his mind always kept him alert to the necessity of bringing "the judgment of Christ to bear as rigorously on the household of faith as on the secular and the pagan world, even as the prophets of Israel were as severe in mediating the divine judgment upon Israel as upon Babylon." In this connection, he was particularly critical of two recurrent temptations in the history of the Church—the one to establish as an absolute some special *status quo* in the social or economic order (in the name of the eternal verities of faith); and the other to take up an obscurantist attitude toward the intellectual disciplines of culture.

Indeed, it was his stringently iconoclastic stance—vis-à-vis at once Schleiermacher's "cultured despisers of religion" and his "religious despisers of culture"—that conditioned Niebuhr toward a way of doing theology that was essentially polemical. And it was this penchant for polemic that kept him from producing the kind of serenely architectonic system of theology that was possible for a Protestant thinker like Paul Tillich or such a Catholic theologian as Lionel Thornton. The whole texture and drive of his thought were "dialogical"; for him, Christianity wins the deepest kind of self-knowledge only as it risks the rough-and-tumble of radical encounter with its chief competitors. And, in his own work, he never had any great predilection for the stricter forms of systematic theology.

It is just his tendency to conceive the work of Christian theology in polemical terms that makes it exceedingly difficult for his interpreters to specify the genre that most accurately describes the rich and enormous body of his published work. Was he primarily a specialist in the application of theological perspectives to the issues of social ethics? Is he properly viewed in the terms in which he was regarded by men like Walter Lipmann and Hans Morgenthau and George Kennan and by many secular intellectuals, as one whose principal role was that of practical strategist and theoretical interpreter of politics? Or do others, such as Arthur Schlesinger, Jr., and Charles Frankel and Will Herberg, reach a better vantage point in more spaciously conceiving his role as that of philosopher of history? These are undoubtedly all views that are arguable and that are indeed partially validated by the leadership that Niebuhr gave to such organizations as the Congress for Cultural Freedom, the Americans for Democratic Action, the Liberal party in New York State; by the profound impact of his political thinking on the State Department's Policy Planning Staff in the 1940's; by the volumes of social and political criticism that he contributed to such organs of the national intelligence as the *Atlantic Monthly*, *Harper's*, the *Yale Review*, the *Sewanee Review*, the *Virginia Quarterly Review*, the *Partisan Review*, the *American Scholar*, the *Nation*, the *New Republic*, the *New Leader*, and the *Reporter*; by his editorship of the fortnightly paper *Christianity and Crisis*; and by many of his books—notably *Moral Man and Immoral Society* (1932), *Christianity and Power Politics* (1940), *The Nature and Destiny of Man* (the two volumes of his Gifford Lectures, published in 1941 and 1943), *The Children of Light and the Children of Darkness* (1944), *Faith and History* (1949), *The Irony of American History* (1952), *Christian Realism and Political Problems* (1953), and *The Structure of Nations and Empires* (1959).

But, delving beneath all the rich multiplicity of theme that his thought presents, the interpreter of Niebuhr has finally to reckon with that in his work which gives body and substance to everything else, and this is the analysis of the fundamental constitution of man's *humanum*—of the mysterious heights and depths of *human being*—that forms his whole sense of reality. He stands in that great line of Christian thinkers—stretching from Augustine to Pascal and from Kierkegaard to Berdyaev—whose principal preoccupation is with anthropology, with the doctrine of man. And his eminence in American cultural life is in large part a consequence of the brilliance and passion with which he rendered the intricate tableau of man's historical existence. It is he, indeed, more than anyone else who (in the period of his lifetime) reinstated for the intellectual community in the United States a sense of the peculiar kind of toughness and grandeur that are possible for the Christian vision. And there is perhaps no other American thinker of the recent past (excepting Paul Tillich, as a German *émigré*) whose work is so capable of competing for our attention with great European systematicians like Jaspers and Heidegger or with those—such as Faulkner and Camus and Sartre and Auden—who have expressed the most vital poetic vision of our period.

Though Niebuhr's thought moves most deeply within the dimension of theological anthropology, it was always hammered out in the process of his responding to whatever presented itself as problematic in the social and political environment of his time. In this connection, one feels that the first great formative experience of his life occurred during the years in Detroit (1915–28) when, as a young parson, the blighting effect upon human life of modern industrialism, as it was manifest in the vast automobile manufactory of Henry Ford, began to focalize for him the crisis of the person in an advanced technocratic civilization. After his birth in Wright City, Missouri, in the summer of 1892, as the third son and fourth child of the Reverend Gustav Niebuhr and his wife, Lydia, his boyhood was spent first in St. Charles, Missouri, and then in Lincoln, Illinois, the places where his father had the major part of his career as a pastor of the Evangelical Synod (a small Lutheran denomination which merged with a Calvinist communion in 1934 to form the Evangelical and Reformed Church—this in turn merging with the Congregationalists in 1956 to form the United Church of Christ). And then, after four years at Elmhurst College (in Elmhurst, Illinois) and three at Eden Theological Seminary in Missouri, he had two years in the Divinity School of Yale University, which awarded him the M.A. degree in the spring of 1915. So, in taking up his work that autumn as the minister of the Bethel Evangelical Church in Detroit, he was having his first encounter with life in a large industrial metropolis. And here it was, in Detroit—in the years following World War I, when the motorcar industry was in the flush of its first great boom—that Niebuhr, as he confronted the Ford system, began to discover the real costs, in the worker's dehumanization, of this delightful new machine with which the world had fallen in love. The Ford administration was, to be sure, loudly trumpeting their magnanimity in having instituted a five-day week and in paying a minimum wage of five dollars a day. But they said nothing of the nervous tensions that were exacted of their workers through the cunning innovations of their efficiency experts; nor did they acknowledge the long annual periods of unemployment for which no compensation was provided out of the company's reserves of a quarter of a billion dollars. As Niebuhr later remarked, "Ford was celebrated throughout the world as a great humanitarian and undoubtedly regarded himself as one." But he himself, as a working parson in Detroit, knew young men so broken by their labor in the automobile foundries that they had to spend the better part of their weekends in bed. And he had directly observed the appalling conditions of work in the factories. After visiting one of them he recorded his impressions in his diary (*Leaves from the Notebook of a Tamed Cynic*, 1929): "The heat was terrific. The men seemed weary. Here manual labor is a drudgery and toil is slavery. The men cannot possibly find any satisfaction in their work. They simply work to make a living. Their sweat and their dull pain are part of the price paid for the fine cars we all run. . . . We all want the things which the factory produces and none of us is sensitive enough to care how much in human values the efficiency of the modern factory costs."

On Niebuhr's reckoning, the claims of the Ford people to produce a cheap car of good quality were to be granted; but, increasingly in the 1920's, he came to feel that the production of this little tin lizzie entailed a rape of human personality so brutal as to make a mockery of the moral pretensions of the Ford establishment. It is not therefore surprising that his first book, *Does Civilization Need Religion?* (1927), was a direct consequence of the reflections on the predicament of the person in a technocratic society that were induced by his Detroit experience. It is pervasively imbued with alarm at the threat of depersonalization that is posed by the fundamental structures of life in an industrial civilization. The question raised in the title of the book is answered affirmatively because "the social imagination which religion, at its best, develops upon the basis of its high evaluation of personality" makes for a profound "reverence for human personality." It was a time, he felt, when the main task of social reconstruction needed to involve resistance against the tendency of a technocratic culture to make men mere functions of economic process—and in such a time, he argued, the reverence for man that is fostered by the religious imagination must be acknowledged as indispensable.

But Niebuhr was already beginning to question the relevance to the modern situation of the particular forms of the religious imagination represented by liberal Protestantism. Its social idealism—as expressed in the tradition of men like Washington Gladden, Francis Peabody, Lyman Abbott, Shailer Mathews, and Walter Rauschenbusch—had, to be sure, voiced an authentic protest against much of the moral crudity of laissez-faire capitalism, but its overreadiness to identify the shape of its own meliorism with the Kingdom of God betrayed a "psychology of defeat" and a pathetic abrogation of the distinctive office of religion in the cultural order. For "a religion which is perfectly at home in the world has no counsel for it which the world could not gain by an easier method." When, for the sake of impressing the world with its "mundane interests," religion so secularizes itself as to become merely "a kind of harmless adornment of the moral life," then it is nothing more than a dispensable excrescence. Already in the late 1920's Niebuhr had begun to feel that something like this kind of failure had resulted from that whole impulse in liberal Protestantism that had found its characteristic expression in the Social Gospel movement. This was a style of Christian thought that prided itself on "its bright and happy worldliness," and, in permitting its commitment to any kind of transcendent religious position to be dissipated in eagerness to transform "the natural and social environment of personality," it was by way of degenerating into merely another kind of "culture-religion" and of losing its capacity for genuinely radical criticism. "Whenever religion feels completely at home in the world," said Niebuhr, "it is the salt which has lost its savor." Yet, though his book of 1927 anticipated his later and more stringent critique of theological liberalism, it was itself, fundamentally, an expression of the ethos of the liberal movement in American Protestantism—most notably perhaps in the persistence with which it took "religion" (or something called "high religion") as its main premise, Christianity being implicitly regarded as merely one expression of the *homo religiosus*.

A year after the appearance of this first book Niebuhr resigned his Detroit pastorate and went to New York City to join the faculty of Union Theological Seminary, where he was to remain until his retirement in 1960. But his removal from a parochial ministry to an academic post was in no way accompanied by any withdrawal from the arena of social action and political debate; indeed, if there was any shift in this phase of his life, it was toward a deepening of involvement. In 1929 he was serving with Paul Douglas (then a professor at the University of Chicago, and later to become a member of the United States Senate) and John Dewey on the Executive Committee of the League for Independent Political Action; he was still active in the Fellowship of Reconciliation, the leading pacifist organization on the American scene; and in 1930 he was founding the Fellowship of Socialist Christians and running for Congress as the candidate of the Socialist party in the Morningside Heights community of New York City. And, despite all these and other activities in public life, his restless pen was fast becoming one of the most prolific in American intellectual life.

Throughout the early years in New York Niebuhr was steadily moving toward a more radical political orientation and a more conservative theological position. These were of course years—the early 1930's—of economic stoppages and social breakdown: everywhere, despite the nation's enormous productive capacity, there was grinding poverty. And the wintry bleakness that had settled down not only on the American scene but on the larger part of the Western world brought to men the sense of being somehow utterly unprotected before the irrational hazards of life in a technological culture. It was indeed a time that found its aptest description in Yeats's lines in "The Second Coming":

Things fall apart; the centre cannot hold;
Mere anarchy is loosed upon the world,
The blood-dimmed tide is loosed, and
    everywhere
The ceremony of innocence is drowned;
The best lack all conviction, while the worst
Are full of passionate intensity.

As Niebuhr contemplated the shambles, he became deeply convinced that modern liberalism, whether in its secular or in its religious version, could not be expected to provide any relevant guidance for social and political reconstruction. The secular tradition of Locke and Jefferson and Stuart Mill and John Dewey appeared to him to be very largely the ideological expression of the characteristic utopianism of bourgeois mentality, with its faith that "the egoism of individuals is being progressively checked by the development of rationality . . . and that nothing but the continuance of this process is necessary to establish social harmony. . . ." In accordance with such a faith, social injustice is believed to have its main roots in ignorance—which must itself gradually yield before the extension of enlightenment through education and before the power of moral suasion. But to suppose that justice is guaranteed by the characters of individuals rather than social systems and, in the ordering of society, to pin one's faith on the extension of scientific intelligence is to be blinded to the living actualities of politics. For, wherever there is injustice in society, there is some significant disproportion of power, and whichever group it is that constitutes the agency of exploitation can be dislodged only when power is raised against it. By the early 1930's Niebuhr had become convinced that no realistic recognition of this fact could be expected from secular idealists whose mild Pelagianism was for him most perfectly instanced in the social philosophy of John Dewey.

Nor could he find Protestant liberalism to be any less bankrupt; in fact, by now he had come to regard it as involving little more than a re-interpretation of the Christian faith in accordance with the system of secular values descending from the Enlightenment. In its identification of the Kingdom of God with that ideal society which secular idealists expected to develop through an evolutionary process, in its belief that man's natural egoism was being progressively checked through "the growth of a religiously inspired goodwill," in its simple confidence in the possibility of politically incarnating the absolute imperatives of the Gos-

pel, in its radiant optimism about the moral plasticity of human nature, in its incorrigible habit of supposing that "if only" men would take the Sermon on the Mount seriously then all human tensions would become easily manageable—in all this Niebuhr discerned what he took to be proof of the spiritual dependence of Christian liberals on the secular piety of bourgeois idealism. So, in the face of the social debris of 1930, he found the Social Gospel, with its naïve preachments about the "service motive," to be as incompetent and irrelevant as secular rationalism.

It was out of this profound exasperation with "the liberal culture of modernity" that his famous book of 1932 was written, *Moral Man and Immoral Society*. And its explosive effect in American theological circles has been unequaled by the impact of any other single book of the last half-century. As the English theologian Alan Richardson recalls, it seemed, "especially to those of the older generation, to be the outpouring of a cynical and perverse spirit, very far removed from the benevolent and sanguine serenity which was held to be the hallmark of a truly Christian mind." Indeed, it seemed to many of his Christian readers that, far from laying the ground for any kind of theological reconstruction, Niebuhr was destroying the very possibility of a Christian philosophy, for, as Professor Richardson says, "their dearest assumptions concerning man's perfectibility, his kinship with the divine, his natural goodness, were [being] . . . demolished with ruthless iconoclasm." But Niebuhr felt that Christianity could not be relevantly related to the malaise of modern society until it achieved an understanding of the problem of power more sophisticated than that of either secular or religious moralism. And it was toward such a sober realism that his book was poised.

To those who proposed education and scientific intelligence as the sufficient solvent of social disorder—and chiefly to John Dewey—Niebuhr wanted to say that "while it is possible for intelligence to increase the range of benevolent impulse . . . there are definite limits in the capacity of ordinary mortals . . . to grant to others what they claim for themselves." Men simply are not as careful of the interests of their fellows as they are of their own. And the inability of reason, however highly developed, to overcome this natural sluggishness of the moral imagination makes nonsense, he declared, of the whole theory of the "cultural lag" for which the social science of the period had such a great fondness—the notion that the achievement of social and political harmony waits only upon the development of "experimental procedures" in the common life commensurate with the experimentalism of the physical sciences. No, said Niebuhr, the natural egoism of social collectives is such that a tolerable justice can be achieved only by guaranteeing to each group enough power to counterbalance that of other groups by which it might be exploited. In short, his contention was that the ordering of society is a matter of *politics*, not of pedagogy.

And against the moralism of liberal Christianity, Niebuhr asserted that the ethic of *agape* represents "a final and absolute possibility which is, in some respects, equally distant from all political programs because all of them involve elements of coercion and resistance which are foreign to a commonwealth of pure brotherhood and love." The relevant norm, in other words, for political decision and social policy is not love but justice, not the uncoerced self-oblation of the Kingdom of God but the kind of mutuality that envisages a decent balance between the claims and counterclaims of the contending factions which constitute a dynamic society. To attempt to derive proximate social and political judgments from the ab-solute ethic of the Sermon on the Mount is merely to indulge in a sentimental perfectionism that obscures the concrete possibilities of social reformation—which never move beyond an uneasy armistice between the demands of love and the demands of competing power blocs.

The problem, then, to which *Moral Man and Immoral Society* addressed itself was the problem of power. Its most basic contention was that, though to some extent "it may be possible . . . to establish just relations between individuals . . . purely by moral and rational suasion and accommodation," in "inter-group relations this is practically an impossibility. The relations between groups must therefore always be predominantly political rather than ethical, that is, they will be determined by the proportion of power which each group possesses at least as much as by any rational and moral appraisal of the comparative needs and claims of each group." Instead of sentimental dreaming about the "beloved community" of Protestant liberal idealism, the course of responsibility, then, requires strict attention to the most judicious ways in which force may be deployed toward the end of securing a just distribution of power within the commonalty.

It was precisely his growing sense of the impossibility ever of discarding the tactics of force in the relations between nations and social classes that increasingly led Niebuhr in the early 1930's to doubt the cogency of pacifism. His book of 1932 makes it clear that, by this time, he had reached the point of having virtually to abandon his earlier commitment to the pacifist position. For, instead of making their witness simply as a way of disavowing the moral ambiguity inherent in all the more tentative norms of relative justice, American pacifists were in the habit of claiming the gospel of nonviolence (Christ-*cum*-Gandhi) to be a viable alternative at the level of *political* strategy. And though in 1932 Niebuhr was still somewhat uncertain about the possibility of validating international war, it had become apparent to him, at least in terms of the class struggle, that the more conventional forms of pacifism were but another indication of the political incompetence of Christian liberalism, of its penchant for the purity of ideals and its distaste for the practical requirements of social strategy in a morally ambiguous world. The trouble with pacifists, he had come to feel (as he was to say a few years later to the Canadian Richard Roberts), was that they supposed they could live in history without sinning; their moral fastidiousness was too great to permit them to pit self-interest against self-interest as a way of achieving justice; and, in thus abdicating from the messiness of politics, they were in effect preparing to submit "to any demands, however unjust, and . . . to any claims, however inordinate." Men like the missionaries Kirby Page and E. Stanley Jones and the editor of the *Christian Century*, Charles Clayton Morrison, were calling this the "way of Jesus" or the "way of the Cross," but, for Reinhold Niebuhr, it was simply a way of contracting out of history.

In *Reflections on the End of an Era*, the book which appeared two years after *Moral Man and Immoral Society*, Niebuhr continued to argue the importance of developing a political theory which would be radical "not only in the realistic nature of its analysis but in its willingness to challenge the injustices of a given social system by setting power against power until a more balanced equilibrium of power is achieved." At this stage in his development, his reaction against the optimistic moralism of liberal Christianity was leading him toward Marxism, for here at least was a system into which there was built some sense of the recalcitrances of history, of the duplicitousness of which man is capable, and some

realistic understanding of the dynamics of power in human affairs. The Marxist analysis of "the logic" of modern history struck him as essentially sound: he liked its apocalyptic melodramatism, its imagination of judgment and disaster, which more closely approximated, he felt, the spirit of Hebrew prophecy than liberalism, either secular or religious; and he, too, had begun to feel that capitalism was doomed.

Though Niebuhr on occasion chose to refer to himself in the early 1930's as a "Christian Marxist," it would in fact be erroneous to regard Marxism as having had any greater importance for him than as a kind of armory that furnished additional resources of rhetoric for the critique of liberalism. His impatience with what he took to be the bumbling of the New Deal in the first eight years of the Roosevelt administration did, to be sure, confirm his misgivings during this period about the capacity of capitalism to effect any deep reform of itself—so that, in this way, he was open to Marxist pessimism about bourgeois society. It is also true that it was not until the end of the decade that the issues of foreign policy led him to see the dangerous irrelevance of the Socialist party's isolationism; it was only then that Roosevelt's crafty expedience began to represent for him, instead of mere lack of principle, precisely the kind of realistic exercise of power that he had always regarded as the hallmark of political sagacity. Many years elapsed, in other words, before Niebuhr came round to acknowledging that the kind of mixed economy and pragmatic political program that had been elaborated under the New Deal may have been "a better answer to the problems of justice in a technical age than its critics of either right or left had assumed."

But, for all of the captiousness with which he evaluated public policy in the first two terms of the Roosevelt administration, he was never in any sense a doctrinaire Marxist. Arthur

Schlesinger, Jr., has brilliantly reviewed this aspect of Niebuhr's thought, reminding us of the anxiety he was expressing throughout the decade about the tendency of Communist Messianism to breed a reckless fanaticism and, through the socialization of economic power, to create an inordinate political tyranny. The Moscow trials of 1938 and the Hitler-Stalin pact of '39 were, of course, for him, as for many others, an unambiguous disclosure of the corruption at the very center of the Communist movement. And, thereafter, the virulence of the Communist movement was nowhere more trenchantly exposed than in his voluminous political and theological writings.

So it is not incorrect to say that Niebuhr never had any serious illusions about Marxism. Yet its rhetoric and certain of its insights (its organic view of society, its theory of class conflict and social ideology, its definition of the problem of social injustice in terms of economic inequality) did for a time sharpen his polemic against liberalism, particularly at the point of its illusions about the possibility of simply translating ethical ideals into political actuality. It is this phase of his thought that is perhaps most apparent in *Reflections on the End of an Era.*

But, then, the very ruthlessness of Niebuhr's deflation of moralism as a style of social and political thought made it necessary that he should himself eventually attempt to restate in a constructive way the relation of ethics to politics. This was the task that he began to undertake in his book of 1935, *An Interpretation of Christian Ethics*—and particularly in the famous chapter of that book that is called "The Relevance of an Impossible Ethical Ideal." Here it was that Niebuhr's campaign against the "free-floating imperatives"—the phrase is Donald Meyer's—of Social Gospel idealism began to issue in a recovery of the doctrine of original sin, and his analysis of

social and political reality thus moved into the more fundamental dimension of theological anthropology. Indeed, it would not be oversimplifying his development to say that by the mid-1930's he had truly become for the first time a theologian, his thought being now fecundated by the more emphatically distinctive insights of the Christian faith.

The essential question that is tackled in *An Interpretation of Christian Ethics* is how one moves from the ethic of *agape*, with its radical perfectionism, to viable norms of ethical discrimination in the historical order. Niebuhr's contention was that the bankruptcy of both conventional orthodoxy and liberal Christianity is nowhere more in evidence than in the extent to which this problem, from both perspectives, ceases to be a real problem. For orthodoxy, in prematurely identifying the radical imperatives of faith with the myths of a prescientific age and with "canonical moral codes" of the past, abdicates from any genuine effort to make its heritage relevant to contemporary experience. Liberalism, on the other hand, in its anxiety "to prove . . . that it does not share the anachronistic ethics or believe the incredible myths of orthodox religion," has so completely adjusted what is radical in the Christian faith to "the characteristic credos and prejudices of modernity" that all the tension between "the transcendent impossibilities of the Christian ethic of love" and the immanent possibilities of the historical process has disappeared.

Niebuhr wanted very much to insist that the normative element in Christian ethical thought is radically perfectionist and transcendent. For the *agape* of the Cross, in its sacrificial heedlessness and universalism, represents a degree of moral rigorism that surpasses any simple historical possibility: it makes no concessions even to the most "natural" self-regarding impulses and distances itself from every form of self-assertion, even from "the necessary prudent defenses of the self, required because of the egoism of others." The ethic of *agape* is, in short, an utterly unprudential rigorism which is impossible of fulfillment by the natural man in the immediate situations of historical existence.

Yet, as Niebuhr consistently maintained after the appearance of his book of 1935, *agape* is the only adequate final norm of human life, because no other does full justice to the dimension of depth in which the human spirit is set. It does not, to be sure, "deal at all with the immediate moral problem of every human life—the problem of arranging some kind of armistice between various contending factions and forces. It has nothing to say about the relativities of politics and economics, nor about the necessary balances of power which exist and must exist in even the most intimate social relationships." But, then, it is the nature of man, through his radical freedom, perpetually to transcend all the cohesions that make up his communal life: he is not bound by any of them. He is, of course, "imbedded in the passing flux" of nature and history and is "the prisoner of the partial perspectives of a limited time and place." But the fact that, through reason and memory and imagination, he can surmount himself and his world indeterminately means that his life cannot find its true ground in any of the proximate norms that emerge out of historical experience, and that he is therefore driven by the inner dynamism of his nature toward a transcendent norm.

This was for Niebuhr the mark of the unique dignity of man, that, though mortal and "imbedded in the flux of finitude," he stands, by reason of his radical freedom, under ideal possibilities. But it is precisely his situation on this frontier between the temporal and the eternal, between the realm of nature and the realm of spirit, that makes possible at once everything that is noble and everything that is ignoble in the human drama. Man is always trying to "translate his finite existence into a more permanent and absolute form of existence. Ideally men seek to subject their arbitrary and contingent existence under the dominion of absolute reality. But practically they always mix the finite with the eternal and claim for themselves, their nation, their culture, or their class the center of existence. This is the root of all imperialism in man and explains why the restricted predatory impulses of the animal world are transmuted into the boundless imperial ambitions of human life." Thus it is that "devotion to every transcendent value is corrupted by the effort to insert the interests of the self into that value. The organizing center of life and history must transcend life and history, since everything which appears in time and history is too partial and incomplete to be its center. But man is destined, both by the imperfection of his knowledge and by his desire to overcome his finiteness, to make absolute claims for his partial and finite values. He tries, in short, to make himself God." And this is the root and the nature of sin.

The seat of the trouble, in other words, is not finitude itself, but finitude pretending to be something more than finite. *An Interpretation of Christian Ethics* suggests that it is just its illumination of this profound pathos of human spirituality that constitutes the genus of the classical Christian doctrine of "original sin." Niebuhr had little patience, however, with the tendency of traditional orthodoxy to so historicize the myth of the Fall as to convert the doctrine of "original sin" into a doctrine of "inherited corruption." "If original sin is an inherited corruption, its inheritance destroys the freedom and therefore the responsibility which is basic to the conception of sin. The orthodox doctrine is therefore self-destructive." And sin is "original" only in the sense of its being pervasively and perennially characteristic of human existence.

Now this incorrigible tendency of the human creature always to claim more for himself than he ought to claim, always to mingle idealizing pretensions with his most ideal aspirations, and to accentuate "his natural will-to-live into an imperial will-to-power by the very protest which his yearning for the eternal tempts him to make against his finiteness"— this deep crookedness and duplicity of the human heart is not something that can be broken by simple rational suasion or by moralistic exhortations to "follow in His steps." The self-emptying love that is incarnate in the New Testament picture of Jesus as the Christ does, indeed, surpass the limit of man's moral possibilities, and to confront it is to be reduced to despair. But it is precisely out of such despair that there arises "the godly sorrow which worketh repentance." And it is just here, Niebuhr suggested, that we may discern "the relevance of an impossible ethical ideal": the law of love is, to be sure, an impossibility: yet it cannot be "relegated simply to the world of transcendence," for always "it offers immediate possibilities of a higher good in every given situation," and it is for this reason that it proves itself to be the true pinnacle of the moral imagination. A perfectionist ethic presents us, in other words, with a final norm that transcends the range of possible achievement; but, though it is never fully realized in either intention or action, it makes possible the kind of searching criticism of both intention and action that provides the impetus for the highest moral creativity.

So to conceive the relation of the sacrificial heedlessness of *agape* to the various modes of calculated mutuality that make up the realm of proximate norms and achievement is not, however, wholly to dispel the suspicion that Niebuhr's ethical thought arouses, that it does in some degree involve a very abstract kind of Kantian formalism. Though he made frequent use of such general principles of morality as equality and justice and freedom, he never proposed any systematic definition of precisely how it is that such "middle axioms" bring the "possibilities of a higher good" disclosed by the absolute norm of *agape* into immediate relation to the concrete issues of moral perplexity. He tended to see the ethical situation as one in which an absolute norm always makes possible a critical perspective on whatever systems of reciprocity men devise for the conduct of life. But never did he manage fully to rescue from the realm of the problematical the precise nature of the assistance that the unprudential rigorism of a perfectionist ethic offers men living in a world in which it is perilous ever to forswear prudence. It does, to be sure, offer a vision of higher "possibilities," but this hardly provides a workable canon of ethical discrimination.

The whole shape and direction of his argument in the book of 1935 (which was originally presented as the Rauschenbusch Memorial Lectures in the Colgate-Rochester Divinity School) made it clear that Niebuhr's social and political analysis and his debate with "the liberal culture of modernity" were gradually deepening down into a fundamental restatement of Christian theology. In its theological richness, it was his book of 1937, *Beyond Tragedy*, that made this maturing process unmistakably manifest, for here it began to be evident that his tutelage under the Fathers and the Reformers—and particularly under Augustine—was making for a brilliant recovery of the great themes of classical Christianity.

Beyond Tragedy—like the moving book that appeared in 1946, *Discerning the Signs of the Times*—is a collection of "sermonic essays" which grew out of sermons that had been preached in college and university chapels. Both books put us in mind of what a pity it is that so few of Niebuhr's sermons reached the printed page—and these in a form representing such a systematization of the original deliverances that they have very nearly ceased to be examples of the sermon as a genre of rhetoric and have become theological essays. For he was one of the great Christian preachers of the modern period, his only peer on the American scene perhaps having been the Presbyterian George Buttrick (sometime dean of the Chapel of Harvard University). But his immense popularity in the great churches and university chapels of the land was never won by way of reliance, even in the slightest degree, on the vague hyperbole and tawdry homiletical devices of the conventional sorcerer of the pulpit. Those who faced his lucid and mercurial brilliance from the pew will surely agree that their deepest impression was that of an enormously shrewd and worldly intelligence whose overriding interest centered in the special kind of illumination that is cast by the Christian faith on the major perplexities of modern man. The general impression (as T. S. Eliot said of Pascal) was of a man "highly passionate and ardent, but passionate only through a powerful and regulated intellect"—who was speaking "to those who doubt[ed], but who [had] the mind to conceive, and the sensibility to feel, the disorder, the futility, the meaninglessness, the mystery of life and suffering, and who [could] only find peace through a satisfaction of the whole being."

The basic analysis of the human situation in *Beyond Tragedy* moves very much along the same line that is taken in *An Interpretation of Christian Ethics*: "Man is mortal. That is his fate. Man pretends not to be mortal. That is his sin. Man is a creature of time and place, whose perspectives and insights are invariably conditioned by his immediate circumstances. But

man is not merely the prisoner of time and place. . . . He is not content to be merely American man, or Chinese man, or bourgeois man, or man of the twentieth century. He wants to be man. . . . His memory spans the ages in order that he may transcend his age. His restless mind seeks to comprehend the meaning of all cultures so that he may not be caught within the limitations of his own." Without all this "man could not come to his full estate. But it is also inevitable that these towers should be Towers of Babel, that they should pretend to reach higher than their real height; and should claim a finality which they cannot possess." In the ever wider and wider spheres of reality which he is capable of envisaging, man "knows that he ought to act so as to assume only his rightful place in the harmony of the whole. But his actual action is always informed by the ambition to make himself the centre of the whole." Thus it is that "guilt and creativity are inextricably interwoven" in human existence. Yet "Christianity does not regard the inevitability of guilt in all human creativity as inherent in the nature of human life. Sin emerges, indeed, out of freedom and is possible only because man is free; but it is done in freedom, and therefore man . . . bears responsibility for it," rather than creation or existence as such. The testimony that creation as such is essentially good is, in short, a basic affirmation of the Christian faith, for its trust is in "a good God who created a good world, though the world is not now good."

But the fact that that which contaminates the world with the poisons of sin arises out of man's freedom means that the hope of the fulfillment of life must be a hope that envisages a fulfillment beyond the possibilities of historical existence. "The possibilities of the fulfilment of this life transcend our experience not because the soul is immortal and the body is mortal but because this human life, soul and body, is both immersed in flux and above it, and because it involves itself in sin in this unique position from which there is no escape by its own powers. The fulfilment of life beyond the possibilities of this existence is a justified hope, because of our human situation, that is, because a life which knows the flux in which it stands cannot be completely a part of that flux. On the other hand this hope is not one which fulfils itself by man's own powers." God, therefore, "must complete what remains incomplete in human existence."

Yet "the Kingdom of God must still enter the world by way of the crucifixion." Though love is the law of life, "when it enters the world of relative justice and balanced egotism it is destroyed in it. The suffering servant dies on the cross." The paradox at the heart of the Christian faith arises out of the assertion that, nevertheless, in this apparently tragic fact we may discern man's deliverance from his woe. For He who dies upon the Cross, though He is God incarnate, also represents the essential nature of man, the "second Adam," as St. Paul says; and the crucifixion of the second Adam by the first Adam, in proving that human nature has deviated from its own inner law, proves also that sin is not an essential part of human nature as such. It does, to be sure, prove that "sin is so much a part of existence that sinlessness cannot maintain itself in it." But it also establishes that "sin is not a necessary and inherent characteristic of life. Evil is not a part of God, nor yet a part of essential man. This Saviour is a revelation of the goodness of God and the essential goodness of man, *i.e.,* the second Adam. He is indeed defeated in history but in that very defeat proves that he cannot be ultimately defeated. That is, he reveals that it is God's nature to swallow up evil in Himself and destroy it. Life in its deepest essence is not only good but capable of destroying the evil which has been produced in it.

Life is thus not at war with itself. Its energy is not in conflict with its order. Hence the Saviour truly says: 'Weep not for me.' "

Now what in part makes this book of 1937 so notable a milestone in the development of Niebuhr's thought and in twentieth-century theology is the radicalism with which it carries forward the proposal that had been made in *An Interpretation of Christian Ethics* regarding the necessity of interpreting Christian dogma in "mythical" terms. In the earlier book he had expressed his impatience with the tendency of traditional orthodoxy to so literalize the mythical element in religious discourse as to annul what is truly dialectical in the Christian apprehension of time and eternity. The real genius of myth as a mode of thought is, as he argued there, that "it points to the timeless in time, to the ideal in the actual, but does not lift the temporal to the category of the eternal (as pantheism does), nor deny the significant glimpses of the eternal and the ideal in the temporal (as dualism does)." But traditional orthodoxy, in developing the Biblical view of reality into a rigid supernaturalist scheme of two discrete levels of being, simply achieves an obscurantist petrifaction of apprehensions whose dynamic and dialectical character ought to be preserved. So an ancillary theme in the argument of *Beyond Tragedy* concerns "the necessary and perennially valid contribution of myth to the biblical world view."

We are, for example, says Niebuhr, "deceivers yet true, when we say that God created the world," for this is not to account for the origin of the world in some particular and datable moment of cosmic history; but in no other way can the mythical imagination of religious faith express its sense of the transcendent majesty of God and of the utter dependence upon Him of everything that exists. "We are deceivers, yet true, when we say that man fell into evil," for the Garden of Eden is to be found on no one's map, and the Fall is locatable on no historical calendar; but, though the myth of the Fall designates no single historical occurrence, it does in a way speak profoundly of that which is presupposed in every human action. "We are deceivers, yet true, when we affirm that God became man to redeem the world from sin. The idea of eternity entering time is intellectually absurd." Nevertheless, when Christianity speaks of God's Word having been made flesh, it is asserting that "God's word is relevant to human life"; it is declaring "that an event in history can be of such a character as to reveal the character of history itself; that without such a revelation the character of history cannot be known." And so, too, are we "deceivers, yet true, when we insist that the Christ who died on the cross will come again in power and glory, that he will judge the quick and the dead and will establish his Kingdom"; but in this way Christianity speaks of its belief that the human enterprise will not end tragically, and it declares that "the ground of our hope lies not in human capacity but in divine power and mercy. . . ."

This, then, is the reading of the Christian faith that Niebuhr offered in *Beyond Tragedy.* And by the late 1930's it was becoming apparent not only on the American scene but also in British and European circles that here was a gifted new presence in modern theology who had already found the authority of his own brilliant and commanding voice. At the great conference in Oxford in 1937, where the world leadership of the rapidly burgeoning ecumenical movement in non-Roman Christianity was gathered in an impressive convocation, he was a striking figure. The greeting that was uttered by William Temple (then Archbishop of York, later of Canterbury) on this occasion of their first meeting—"At last I've met the troubler of my peace"—doubtless expressed what was being felt by many of Christendom's most dis-

tinguished theologians. The word was fast getting round that Reinhold Niebuhr, along with Karl Barth and Emil Brunner and Paul Tillich, was one of the most formidable strategists of "Neo-Orthodoxy"—though the term "Neo-Orthodoxy" was one with which he himself was not happy, and this piece of journalistic jargon was later to be rejected by many others, as a clumsy counter that in many ways distorted the actual situation in the theology of the period.

It came as no great surprise to Niebuhr's colleagues in the theological community when he was invited to the University of Edinburgh as the Gifford lecturer for the spring and autumn of 1939, an old and famous post whose only previous American incumbents had been William James, Josiah Royce, William Ernest Hocking, and John Dewey. It was in the following year that his volume *Christianity and Power Politics* appeared, a book made notable in part by the powerful critique of Christian pacifism that it presented, as the clouds of war began to hover ominously over the international horizon. But this work was quickly overshadowed by the Gifford Lectures on *The Nature and Destiny of Man*, the first volume of which, when it was published in 1941, brought the general recognition that this was Niebuhr's masterpiece.

The design of this central achievement of his career is so grandly conceived, and, in its execution, is architecturally so intricate that it is impossible to produce any simple compression of the argument that gathers up and does justice to its innumerable themes. Nor is it possible in a brief essay to convey any vivid impression of that special richness of texture in the Gifford Lectures which is a result of the author's seeming to carry in his head the whole of Western intellectual tradition and to have a constantly simultaneous vision of all its myriad strands. In so curtailed an exposition as this must be, one must simply take the risk of settling upon the particular angle that affords the best view of the entire structure and, having done this, proceed then to indicate something of what is entailed in this perspective on the whole. When such rigorous concision is imposed, it would seem that the Gifford Lectures will be most fruitfully regarded as involving one of the profoundest and most original essays of the modern period in the phenomenology of selfhood. The two volumes of *The Nature and Destiny of Man* have, of course, many other dimensions: they present many startlingly fresh and acute interpretations of various phases of theological and philosophic tradition, and of movements in general intellectual and cultural history (Hellenism, Renaissance humanism, Romanticism, Marxism, etc.); and Niebuhr's own constructive theological position is extended toward a formal theory of history, a systematic Christology, and a remarkably brilliant restatement of the eschatological motifs in the Christian faith. But the decisive fulcrum is the inquiry into the nature of selfhood.

The guiding premise of Niebuhr's anthropology is grounded in a vision of human existence as composed, in its most essential character, of ambiguity. Man is, on the one hand, a creature of nature who is "unable to choose anything beyond the bounds set by the creation in which he stands": he needs air to breathe and space in which to abide; he cannot survive without the nourishment of warmth and food; yet, however abundant may be that nourishment, his life is but of short duration—and, as Pascal says, he is "engulfed in the infinite immensity of spaces . . . which know [him] not." But, though frail and subject to the contingencies of nature and history, he stands above "the structures and coherences of the world," being able to order them and reorder them toward ends of his own choosing. And not only can he make the structures of nature and history the

object of his own thought and the instruments of his creativity; he can also make himself the object of his thought, and even the self which thus surmounts itself—and this on into indeterminate degrees of self-transcendence.

Man was, for Niebuhr, "both free and bound, both limited and limitless." It was the necessity of recognizing this essentially ambiguous character of the human situation that provided him with the basic requirement of adequacy in terms of which he evaluated the various accounts of man's estate that are furnished by the history of culture. He found the trouble with most of the great alternatives to the Christian faith—whether in classical rationalism or Renaissance humanism, in modern naturalism or in idealistic and romanticist philosophies—to lie in their tendency to collapse this fundamental antinomousness of human existence into some formula which either overstresses man's "dignity" and understresses his "wretchedness" or overstresses his limitation and fails sufficiently to appreciate his radical freedom. But the genius of what he called "Biblical faith" did for him become most apparent precisely in the kind of dialectic that it maintains between its doctrine of man as creature and its doctrine of man as *imago Dei*. The contention that he argued, with great learning and rhetorical power, in book after book—but most persuasively, perhaps, in *The Nature and Destiny of Man*—was that "the Christian view of man is [most] sharply distinguished from all alternative views" just in the clarity with which it perceives that man belongs to *both* realms, to the realm of nature *and* to the realm of spirit.

It is, in Niebuhr's view, precisely this duality of emphasis that permits Christianity to give so profound an account of the origin and nature of sin. Its alertness to the human position as a point of juncture between nature and spirit gives it an especially acute perspective on the psychological environment in which sin becomes possible. This environing *possibility* of sin—which is "the inevitable concomitant of the paradox of freedom and finiteness in which man is involved"—Niebuhr defined as anxiety. For it is this—namely, anxiousness—which is the psychological consequence of man's being "both free and bound, both limited and limitless." And it is the analysis of anxiety in its relation to freedom and sin—with its subtle echoes, occasionally, of the similar analysis conducted in Kierkegaard's *The Concept of Dread*—that constitutes one of the most brilliantly original contributions in the first volume of the Gifford Lectures.

"Man is anxious not only because his life is limited and dependent and yet not so limited that he does not know of his limitations. He is also anxious because he does not know the limits of his possibilities. He can do nothing and regard it perfectly done, because higher possibilities are revealed in each achievement. All human actions stand under seemingly limitless possibilities. There are, of course, limits but it is difficult to gauge them from any immediate perspective. There is therefore no limit of achievement in any sphere of activity in which human history can rest with equanimity." The human condition is like that of "the sailor, climbing the mast (to use a simile), with the abyss of the waves beneath him and the 'crow's nest' above him. He is anxious about both the end toward which he strives and the abyss of nothingness into which he may fall." It is this suspension betwixt finiteness and freedom that gives rise to that sense of vertigo that induces man's profoundest dispeace. Anxiety is not itself sin; it is only the precondition of sin and the "source of temptation," to make oneself the basis of one's security or to escape from the anguish of freedom by immersing oneself in some natural vitality. But though anxiety, once conceived, tends to

bring forth pride and sensuality, it does not, as the precondition of sin, make sin logically necessary: sin is committed in freedom and "can therefore not be attributed to a defect in [man's] essence. It can only be understood as a self-contradiction, made possible by the fact of his freedom but not following necessarily from it." That, says Niebuhr, is "the doctrine of original sin, stripped of literalistic illusions"— that, though sin does not necessarily follow from our human nature as such, it is nevertheless so pervasive in every moment of human existence that it seems, therefore, in Kierkegaard's phrase, to "posit itself."

But, now, though human life, even in its most saintly expressions, nowhere seems to be uninfected by sin, the historical drama is by no means an affair of sheer moral anarchy. It is the Christian faith that in Christ the true meaning of history has been disclosed, that in the *agape* of the Cross the final norm of man's life has been revealed. Which means—since this norm, though disclosed, remains unfulfilled— that the actuality of man's historical existence is set within an "interim" between the First and the Second Coming of Christ; and it is to the exposition of the doctrine of history as interim that the second volume of the Gifford Lectures is very largely devoted. Here, in the interim, "sin is overcome in principle but not in fact," and thus love has "to live in history as suffering love because the power of sin makes a simple triumph of love impossible." History is not without meaning, but it presents no decisive fulfillments of its own meaning, for every realization of good is stained by the improbities of sin. Thus the New Testament hope of the *parousia,* of the suffering Messiah's coming again with "power and great glory," though it requires "demythologization," yet "embodies the very genius of the Christian idea of the historical. On the one hand it implies that eternity will fulfill and not annul the richness and variety which the temporal process has elaborated. On the other it implies that the condition of finiteness and freedom, which lies at the basis of historical existence, is a problem for which there is no solution by any human power." In short, the Christian faith reaches its ultimate pinnacle in the belief that "only the infinite pity of God is equal to the infinite pathos of human life": this is the robust confidence that lies at the heart of Niebuhr's entire thought. So one feels that the old Scotswoman had laid hold of the crux of things when, after listening to his lectures at the University of Edinburgh, she told him: "I dinna understand a word ye said, but somehow I ken ye were making God great."

The numerous books that Niebuhr produced after the appearance of the two volumes of *The Nature and Destiny of Man* all represent special applications of the structure of thought that, in its main outlines, was completed by the Gifford Lectures. In 1944 his lectures on the West Foundation at Stanford University were published under the title *The Children of Light and the Children of Darkness*, and the best concise statement of Niebuhr's stratagem here is given in the book's subtitle—"A Vindication of Democracy and a Critique of Its Traditional Defence." His central thesis in this work finds perhaps its aptest summation in the famous sentence in his preface which says: "Man's capacity for justice makes democracy possible; but man's inclination to injustice makes democracy necessary." The book is in part poised against those who, in underestimating— whether in the secular terms, say, of Hobbes or in the religious terms of Luther—man's capacity for justice, invariably tend toward some form of political absolutism. But its fiercer polemic is reserved for "the children of light," for the sentimentality of the conventional liberal democrats who "are usually fool-

ish" because their "too consistent optimism in regard to man's ability and inclination to grant justice to his fellows obscures the perils of chaos which perennially confront every society, including a free society. . . . When this optimism is not qualified to accord with the real and complex facts of human nature and history, there is always a danger that sentimentality will give way to despair and that a too consistent optimism will alternate with a too consistent pessimism." And the unillusioned profundity with which the fortunes and misfortunes of post-Enlightenment democratic ideology are analyzed puts one in mind of the similar analysis that Camus was to undertake a few years later in *L'Homme révolté*.

The book on democracy also looks forward to the book of 1952, *The Irony of American History*, in which Niebuhr undertook a closer specification of the predicament of democratic society in terms of the American experience. Here, again, it is "the children of light" who are dealt with most critically. For theirs, he suggests, is the legacy that makes it most difficult today for America to address itself with sobriety to the troubled scene of international politics; that is to say, both New England Puritanism on the one hand and Jeffersonian-Virginian Deism on the other have bequeathed us a spiritual heritage that induces a sense of America as God's new "Israel," as a "separated" people through whom mankind makes a new beginning. But the conviction of innocence that is thereby wrought so deeply into the nation's sense of its identity ill equips it for the exercise of power in its present position of supremacy in the world community. And the American situation is rendered particularly ironical by the fact that what we face in our chief foe (Russian communism) is very largely an intensification of many of our most characteristic values and illusions—our materialism, our preoccupation with technics, our "innocence" and self-righteousness, and our supposition that we are the masters of historical destiny. Indeed, the refutation of our forefathers' hopes that is offered by the reality of our present situation makes irony, in Niebuhr's view, the definitive category for the interpretation of American history; and we are saved, he suggests, only by the triumph of practice over dogma, only by "the ironic triumph of the wisdom of common sense over the foolishness of [our] wise men."

After the close of World War II, the rapid and terrifying intensification of Cold War politics, under the threatening specter of the big mushroom, increasingly prompted Niebuhr to explore the relevance of an eschatological faith in a period of frustration and disappointment, when "the moral and spiritual resources to achieve a just and stable society in global terms are not yet available." And, in the volume of "sermonic essays" called *Discerning the Signs of the Times*, which appeared in 1946, he undertook to speak of the special kind of sanity which may be the fruit of such a faith in this late, bad time.

It is, he said, an "age between the ages," when " 'one age is dead and the other is powerless to be born.' The age of absolute national sovereignty is over; but the age of international order under political instruments, powerful enough to regulate the relations of nations and to compose their competing desires, is not yet born." We are therefore a people who must learn how to live with the problem of frustration. And, in a time when contemporary history offers us nothing but "calculated risks" and disappointed hopes, we must also learn "to do our duty without allowing it to be defined by either our hopes or our fears." For "we do not know how soon and to what degree mankind will succeed in establishing a tolerable world order. Very possibly we will hover for some centuries between success and failure, in

such a way that optimists and pessimists will be able to assess our achievements, or lack of them, with an equal degree of plausibility. In such a situation it is important to be more concerned with our duties than with the prospect of success in fulfilling them." But when we make the meaning of our life dependent wholly upon what we hope to accomplish tomorrow or the day after tomorrow, and when that achievement fails to be the perfect fulfillment of our highest hopes, our last state is apt to be worse than the first, the confusion of cynicism and despair having succeeded the confusion of optimism and illusion.

So, amidst the hell of global insecurity in which we live today, we shall perform our duties with the greater steadiness if we have something of the faith expressed by St. Paul when he declared: "Whether we live, we live unto the Lord; and whether we die, we die unto the Lord: whether we live therefore, or die, we are the Lord's." It is in "this final nonchalance about life and death, which includes some sense of serenity about the life and death of civilizations, that we shall find the strength for doing what we ought to do, though we know not what the day or the hour may bring forth." In a period "when our hopes so far exceed our grasp that we can not count on historic fulfillments to give completion to our life," the radicalism of an eschatological faith "may beguile a few from their immediate tasks." But those who are sober will find their steps fixed and established by the knowledge that "if in this life only we have hope in Christ, we are of all men most miserable." Such a peace as this "will offend both rationalists and moralists till the end of history. . . . But it alone does justice to the infinite complexities and contradictions of human existence. Within this peace all of life's creative urges may be expressed and enlarged. There is therefore no simple calm in it. It is as tumultuous as the ocean, and yet as serene as the ocean's depths, which bear the tumults and storms of the surface." And it is the only peace that will permit us to steer a steady course through the uncharted waters of life, in the difficult period to which history has committed us.

Discerning the Signs of the Times was followed, in 1949, by *Faith and History*, which more rigorously systematized many of the themes in the Gifford Lectures into a formal philosophy of history. And, thereafter, most of Niebuhr's writing—*The Irony of American History* (1952); *Christian Realism and Political Problems* (1953); *Pious and Secular America* (1958); *The Structure of Nations and Empires* (1959); *Man's Nature and His Communities* (1965)—was concerned with the issues of politics, either in the dimension of history or formal theory or of concrete public policy. One feels that the hazards of life in the late years of the century increasingly brought him to something like the position expressed by Lionel Trilling in *The Liberal Imagination*, that our present "fate, for better or worse, is political." So he wanted, increasingly, to force into the definition of politics so rich and complicated a conception of humanity as might enable our politics to be not merely a politics of survival but also a politics for the redemption and renewal of human life.

In one significant book of this period, however, he resumed and further developed that aspect of his thought which I have spoken of as entailing a phenomenology of selfhood. Though *The Self and the Dramas of History* (1955) may bring to focus issues on which it was natural for Niebuhr to be meditating during his long and desperate illness in the early 1950's, his having been able to produce so intricately reasoned and brilliant a book after a series of small strokes provides an interesting measure, in human terms, of the man's resilience and genius. This work, in defining human

selfhood in terms of man's capacity for "dialogue," reveals how deeply he was influenced by the Jewish existentialist, Martin Buber; in a manner recalling Buber's classic *I and Thou*, he, too, regards the life of man as a fundamentally "dialogic life," since human being is, for him, always being-in-relationship. But, whereas Buber sometimes appeared to view the form of the I-Thou relation as essentially monadical, Niebuhr insisted on the large degree to which the I-Thou reality is influenced by "the dramas of history"; and it was from this perspective that he analyzed the three dimensions of the dialogue in which man is constantly engaged—with himself, with his neighbors, and with God. "Man is primarily a historical creature," says Niebuhr—which means, in his view, that the self is at once determined by the necessities of nature and is yet able "to transcend not only the processes of nature but the operations of its own reason, and to stand, as it were, above the structures and coherences of the world." The self is not only patient of natural process: it is also free enough of it to create culture, though it "is not simply a creator of this new dimension, for it is also a creature of the web of events, in the creation of which it participates." Human existence is, in other words, "a compound of freedom and necessity"—which is to say that each aspect of man's "dialogic life" is historical. And the central contention of Niebuhr's book of 1955 is that the *historical* character of dialogic life is more truly and profoundly described by the poetic-dramatic categories of Biblical personalism than by classical rationalism (with its concern to submit the self to structures of ontology) or philosophic idealism (which, as in Hegel, absorbs the rough angularity of the existing self into universal mind) or romanticism (which ascribes to the realm of the organic "what is clearly a compound of nature and spirit") or modern psychology (whether in its behavioristic or Freudian versions).

Now, with the full stretch of Niebuhr's thought in view, the significance of his role in American intellectual life asks, finally, for some definition. And though his career may still be so much a part of the immediacy of the contemporary scene as to make remote the possibility of an adequately measured assessment, at least it can be said (as Arthur Schlesinger, Jr., has remarked) that here was a thinker of enormous power who succeeded in restating the great themes of Christian theology "with such irresistible relevance to contemporary experience that even those who have no decisive faith in the supernatural find their own reading of experience and history given new and significant dimensions." He is perhaps the one American ever to have established his claim on that modern theological pantheon which includes such Europeans as Friedrich Schleiermacher and Albrecht Ritschl and Sören Kierkegaard and in which such distinguished figures of the recent past as Paul Tillich and Rudolf Bultmann and Karl Barth will also ultimately find their place. And—excepting possibly Kierkegaard (whose posthumous reputation is a development of our own period) and Paul Tillich, whose influence has been widely felt—there is no other Christian theologian of the modern period whose work has exerted so profound an impact upon secular intellectual life. This is perhaps most immediately measurable in the field of political thought, where, as Hans Morgenthau says, he was our "greatest living political philosopher, perhaps the only creative political philosopher [in American thought] since Calhoun." This is a judgment which Professor Morgenthau and many others are prepared to make not merely because of the immense volume of brilliant analysis of the concrete issues of modern poli-

tics that Niebuhr produced over more than forty years. In this vein, of course, his work was powerfully influential in the thinking of many of the ablest journalists and theoreticians and architects of public policy in this country. But his eminence in the realm of political thought, as Professor Morgenthau rightly suggests, is more centrally a result of the kind of awareness that he—more than any other American thinker of his time—promoted of the essentially "tragic character of the political act."

Niebuhr was occasionally charged by his colleagues in the theological community with being too much inclined, in his political thinking, toward a kind of rough-and-ready pragmatism insufficiently controlled by moral and theological principle—or by what they sometimes heavily denominated as "vision." But he knew that, though that balancing of claims and counterclaims by which justice is achieved can never provide the absolute norm of a social ethic, there is—short of disavowing our historical responsibilities—no escaping our involvement in these morally ambiguous pressures. He also knew that, however much "vision" may accord a certain slender dignity to our politics, the dynamism of history is such that the consequences of political action have a way of outrunning both the intent that prompted the act and any capacity that might have been mustered to foresee those consequences—so that, for the responsible man, there is no deliverance from the rough-and-ready expedience of pragmatic realism. In his strong sense of what he liked to call the "indeterminate possibilities" of history, he does indeed put us in mind of William James and his vision of the universe as open and dynamic; and, in his commitment, at the level of political methodology, to a radically empiricist experimentalism, he was, for all of the antagonism that he expressed in his earlier years, not far removed from John Dewey. So, in terms of American cultural tradition, in his profound concern to invest Christianity with relevance for the social and political order, he is to be seen as an heir of the Social Gospel, despite his early rejection of its tendency to identify Christianity with the religion of progress; and, despite the polemical way in which he frequently faced many of its chief representatives in American philosophy, he is also to be seen as an heir of pragmatism.

Though he gave short shrift to the people who were being called in the early 1950's "the new conservatives," their fondness for quoting Edmund Burke did not blind him to the wisdom in Burke's view of politics as the art of the possible. Nor did he ever forget that, however many new possibilities for the realization of good each new development in history may bring, it also brings new hazards corresponding to these new possibilities—so that (as he said in the second volume of *The Nature and Destiny of Man*) "the new level of historic achievement offers us no emancipation from contradictions and ambiguities to which all life in history is subject." History, in other words, "is not its own redeemer. The 'long run' of it is no more redemptive in the ultimate sense than the 'short run.'" And thus it is that the choices which we make are never choices which have any chance of achieving a final settlement of the human problem: the peace of the *civitas terrena* is always an uneasy peace, and, as a consequence, in one of its dimensions, politics is, in its very nature, something essentially tragic.

But then, of course, to define Niebuhr's importance in secular intellectual life as having consisted in part in his reinstatement of a sense of what is tragic in political existence, is to be reminded that here is indeed the basic emphasis not only of his political thought but of

his total account of what André Malraux has taught us to speak of as *la condition humaine.* For, radical as his commitment was to the Christian faith, he never lost his fidelity to what Unamuno called "the tragic sense of life." It is doubtless in this aspect of his vision that the literary community has found its most congenial access to his work. Here, the extent and depth of his influence—though widely observed—are more difficult to measure than in the field of social and political thought. His presence as a shaping force in American literary life is something that is more often conveyed in the nuances of stress and intonation than in the form of documented reference. The late F. O. Matthiessen, for example, in his European journal of 1947, *From the Heart of Europe* (published in 1948), acknowledging Niebuhr's great influence on himself, gives a clear hint of what lay behind his own powerful critique of "the nineteenth-century belief in every man as his own Messiah" in *American Renaissance.* Or, again, one suspects that the kind of stringently critical assessment of modern liberalism that Lionel Trilling has conducted in much of his writing owes something, in part, to the current of ideas that were seminally present in Reinhold Niebuhr. And his influence can be felt not only in contemporary criticism but also in the realm of our creative literature as well—as, for example, in the trenchant reassessment of Jeffersonian liberalism, in Robert Penn Warren's *Brother to Dragons* (with its likeness, in basic ideas, to *The Children of Light and the Children of Darkness*), or in Frederick Buechner's equally trenchant reassessment of a later, Stevensonian liberalism in his fine novel of 1958, *The Return of Ansel Gibbs* (written after Buechner had had a period of study under Niebuhr at Union Seminary).

That, outside theological circles, Niebuhr's

wider influence on the American cultural scene should today be felt to have been that of an eloquent spokesman for "the tragic sense of life" does, however, put us in mind of what may be the chief inadequacy in his work as a Christian theologian. And this is related to our earlier observation of what seems regularly to have been his inability, finally, to overcome the disjunction in his ethical thinking between the *agape* of Christ and the various forms of mutuality in human relations that are the aim of all concrete ethical decision in the historical order. The sacrificial love of Christ, is, in Niebuhr's view, a love which transcends all considerations of reciprocity and is therefore "beyond history," since historical existence is, perennially, a matter of adjusting the claims and counterclaims which men bring to one another in all the relations of life. Now, to be sure, this absolute norm furnishes a vantage point from which complacency about any particular system of mutuality can be criticized. But he never succeeded in making clear precisely how it is that the *agape* of Christ which is "beyond history" affords a way of concretely taking account of all the quandaries which men face in attempting to build systems of reciprocity that are just and humane. The fundamental issue here is, of course, one which concerns the way in which the order of grace becomes effectually operative in history. But it is just at this point—where the logic of his task as a Christian theologian required him to indicate what is involved in the whole drama of redemption—that Niebuhr was least satisfactory. He had a genius for setting forth the kind of critical pressure that the Christian doctrine of man exerts on many of the characteristic forms of modern thought. But, as one of his critics, Paul Lehmann, has suggested, "the Cross, which is apprehended and interpreted as the *basis* of a new wisdom and power, is not ade-

quately apprehended and interpreted as *operative* wisdom and power." Which is to say that there is no systematic specification of how it is, in the perspective of Christian faith, that God actually renews and transforms human life. And this vagueness which characterizes his rendering of the doctrine of redemption is of a piece with his failure to develop systematically the doctrines of the Holy Spirit and of the Church (which Christianity has classically regarded as that extension of the Incarnation whereby God continues the atoning work that was begun in Christ).

But, though Niebuhr's rendering of the great themes of the Christian faith was in certain respects unfinished and incomplete, he did, nevertheless, clarify with a singular power the continuing vitality of Reformation Christianity and the possibilities for cogent interpretation of modern experience that are still resident in its basic message. Perhaps no other native American thinker of this century has invested a Christian position with such relevance to the political and general intellectual situation of his time; and, as a consequence, his career is among the most eminent in that forum of thought which has given to the nation its most creative engagements.

Selected Bibliography

For the period up to 1954, the definitive checklist of Dr. Niebuhr's writings is to be found in *Reinhold Niebuhr's Works: A Bibliography*, by D. B. Robertson (Berea, Ky.: Berea College Press, 1954). Professor Robertson's bibliography is particularly valuable as a guide to the hundreds of articles that Niebuhr contributed to American journals in the years after he published his first pieces in the *Atlantic Monthly* in 1916.

WORKS OF REINHOLD NIEBUHR

Does Civilization Need Religion?—A Study in the Social Resources and Limitations of Religion in Modern Life. New York: Macmillan, 1927.

Leaves from the Notebook of a Tamed Cynic. Chicago: Willett, Clark and Colby, 1929.

The Contribution of Religion to Social Work. New York: Columbia University Press, 1932.

Moral Man and Immoral Society: A Study in Ethics and Politics. New York: Scribners, 1932.

Reflections on the End of an Era. New York: Scribners, 1934.

An Interpretation of Christian Ethics. New York: Harper, 1935.

Beyond Tragedy: Essays on the Christian Interpretation of History. New York: Scribners, 1937.

Christianity and Power Politics. New York: Scribners, 1940.

The Nature and Destiny of Man: A Christian Interpretation. Vol. I, *Human Nature*. New York: Scribners, 1941. Vol. II *Human Destiny*. New York: Scribners, 1943. (Since 1949, Scribners has been making available a one-volume edition of these Gifford Lectures.)

The Children of Light and the Children of Darkness: A Vindication of Democracy and a Critique of Its Traditional Defence. New York: Scribners, 1944.

Discerning the Signs of the Times: Sermons for Today and Tomorrow. New York: Scribners, 1946.

Faith and History: A Comparison of Christian and Modern Views of History. New York, Scribners, 1949.

The Irony of American History. New York: Scribners, 1952.

Christian Realism and Political Problems. New York: Scribners, 1953.

The Self and the Dramas of History. New York: Scribners, 1955.

Love and Justice, edited by D. B. Robertson. Philadelphia: Westminster Press, 1957.

The Godly and the Ungodly: Essays on the Religious and Secular Dimensions of Modern Life. London: Faber and Faber, 1958.

Pious and Secular America. New York: Scribners, 1958.

Essays in Applied Christianity, edited by D. B. Robertson. New York: Meridian Books (World), 1959.

The Structure of Nations and Empires: A Study of the Recurring Patterns and Problems of the Political Order in Relation to the Unique Problems of the Nuclear Age. New York: Scribners, 1959.

Reinhold Niebuhr on Politics, edited by Harry R. Davis and Robert C. Good. New York: Scribners, 1960.

A Nation So Conceived: Reflections on the History of America from Its Early Visions to Its Present Power (with Alan Heimert). New York: Scribners, 1963.

Man's Nature and His Communities. New York: Scribners, 1965.

Faith and Politics: A Commentary on Religious, Social, and Political Thought in a Technological Age, edited by Ronald H. Stone. New York: Braziller, 1968.

The Democratic Experience: Past and Prospects (with Paul E. Sigmund). New York: Praeger, 1969.

CRITICAL AND BIOGRAPHICAL STUDIES

Allen, E. L. *A Guide to the Thought of Reinhold Niebuhr*. London Hodder and Stoughton, n.d.

Bingham, June. *Courage to Change: An Introduction to the Life and Thought of Reinhold Niebuhr*. New York: Scribners, 1961.

Carnell, Edward J. *The Theology of Reinhold Niebuhr*. Grand Rapids, Mich.: W. B. Eerdmans, 1951.

Davies, D. R. *Reinhold Niebuhr: Prophet from America*. London: James Clarke, 1945.

Fackre, Gabriel J. *The Promise of Reinhold Niebuhr*. Philadelphia: Lippincott, 1970.

Hammar, George. *Christian Realism in Contemporary American Theology: A Study of Reinhold Niebuhr, W. M. Horton, and H. P. Van Dusen*. Uppsala, Sweden: A.-B. Lundequistska Bokhandeln, 1940.

Harland, Gordon. *The Thought of Reinhold Nie-*

buhr. New York: Oxford University Press, 1960.

Hofmann, Hans. *The Theology of Reinhold Niebuhr*, translated by Louise Pettibone Smith. New York: Scribners, 1956.

Kegley, Charles W., and Robert W. Bretall, eds. *Reinhold Niebuhr: His Religious, Social, and Political Thought*. Vol. II of *The Library of Living Theology*. New York: Macmillan, 1956. (Includes essays by Emil Brunner, Paul Tillich, John C. Bennett, Paul Ramsey, Arthur Schlesinger, Jr., Kenneth Thompson, Richard Kroner, Daniel D. Williams, Alan Richardson, William John Wolf, Paul Lehmann, and others.)

Landon, Harold R., ed. *Reinhold Niebuhr: A Prophetic Voice in Our Time*. "Essays in Tribute" by Paul Tillich, John C. Bennett, and Hans J. Morgenthau. Greenwich, Conn.: Seabury Press, 1962.

Meyer, Donald B. *The Protestant Search for Political Realism, 1919–1941*. Berkeley and Los Angeles: University of California Press, 1960. See especially Chapters XIII and XIV.

Stone, Ronald H. *Reinhold Niebuhr: Prophet to Politicians*. Nashville and New York: Abingdon Press, 1972.

Thelen, Mary Frances. *Man as Sinner in Contemporary American Realistic Theology*. New York: King's Crown Press, 1946.

Vignaux, Georgette P. *La théologie de l'histoire chez Reinhold Niebuhr*. Neuchâtel: Delachaux & Niestlé, 1957.

—*NATHAN A. SCOTT, JR.*

Frank Norris

1870-1902

FRANK NORRIS' name is much better known today than anything he ever wrote. The manuals of American literature bestow measured praise on *McTeague* (1899) and *The Octopus* (1901), note that *The Pit* (1903) was a relative failure, and mention the posthumous *Vandover and the Brute* (1914). They go on to report that Norris introduced French naturalism into American fiction, discovered the talent of Theodore Dreiser, and influenced legislation designed to curb the railroad monopolies.

A more complete account would have to include a long, pseudo-romantic narrative in verse called *Yvernelle: A Legend of Feudal France* (published in 1892 while Norris was an undergraduate), a sheaf of short stories, enough literary criticism to fill a volume, and three more novels: *Moran of the Lady Letty* (1898), *A Man's Woman* (1899), and *Blix* (1899). No more can be said for *Moran* than that it is as entertaining as many of Jack London's stories, and no more implausible; even less can be said for *A Man's Woman*; but the total achievement is considerable for a writer who died at thirty-two. He did not exert the general influence on American letters of a Howells, and his work has attracted no circle of admirers like Stephen Crane's, but in spite of certain lurid flaws his best writing remains immensely effective.

The circumstances of his life had much to do with the eventual nature of his writing, and even explain some of the variations in its quality. His father, Benjamin, a self-made Chicago businessman, was gifted at making money; his mother, Gertrude, had at one point flirted with a stage career, and had cultural tastes that made the money welcome. From his birth, in Chicago in 1870, Norris had what were known as the "advantages." When the family pulled up roots and moved to San Francisco, in 1884, Benjamin Norris went into real estate and did even better. But San Francisco was not to be enough for the children of Gertrude: in 1887, after vicissitudes that included the death of a brother, and a brief and unsuccessful stay in London, young Norris found himself studying art at the celebrated Académie Julien, in Paris. He was barely seventeen.

How much of the lush Paris of those years Frank Norris saw is problematical. For a year his family was also in the city; then they returned to the States and for a few months young Frank was alone—until his practical father, discovering that his son was writing tales of medieval knights instead of working at his art classes, summoned him home. The son obediently matriculated at the University of California.

He seems to have learned little about French

literature during his stay in Paris. Instead, he had been intensely caught up by a sort of romantic medievalism: the lore of chivalry, armory, and the antique hardware of the Musée de Cluny. The writing that had displeased his father had been sketches concocted for his younger brother. Nothing shows that he read, say, Zola, let alone any representative of the then flourishing French Symbolists. But at least he must have learned to read French.

At the University of California he assumed the role of a *boulevardier,* but not so thoroughly as to separate him from the somewhat strenuous undergraduate life of the Berkeley of that time. He joined a fraternity, and sometimes took part in the hazings and rushes he would later defend as proper training for muscular and blond young Anglo-Saxons. It appears that a chronic estrangement from the most elementary mathematics prevented his taking a degree, but he did, during his college years, pick up the ideas about human evolution, more Spencerian than Darwinian, that are reflected in his novels.

Meanwhile his parents had divorced, so that Norris was relieved of all pressure from his father to take up a business career. He went east, entered Harvard as a special student, and came under the benign influence of Lewis E. Gates. The Harvard English Department was ambivalently disposed toward the teaching of "creative" writing. Some members, Gates among them, obviously believed that the subject could be taught. Others followed Irving Babbitt (whose appointment was actually in French) in declaring that teaching men how to say things before they had anything to say was so much poppycock.

Norris was grateful for Gates's encouragement, and doubtless also for the incentive to work regularly. He had already begun to write: his stories had appeared in the undergraduate magazine at Berkeley, and he had had a con-

tribution or so in the San Francisco *Wave.* More important, he had been working on the opening chapters of *McTeague.* Gates, who was familiar with Continental literature, was in a position to see what he was trying to do. Clearly the stay in Paris was belatedly having an effect: Norris had been reading Zola. *McTeague* showed the influence, as did *Vandover and the Brute,* which Norris began work on in Cambridge. Although he would finish neither during the year in Cambridge, he appears to have kept both novels going at once.

Norris was taken far more by Emile Zola's individual example than by French naturalism as a whole. Although he later professed enthusiastic admiration for Flaubert, the naturalistic current that originates in the latter's *Education sentimentale,* and is transmitted by the Goncourt brothers to writers like Joris-Karl Huysmans, apparently left him untouched. Doubtless he was temperamentally unable to accept Flaubert's principle that the essence of most lives is their sheer monotony. All Norris' own novels are so full of action that one can hardly imagine his grasping the notion that monotony can be the matter of fiction. He had no perception of the great truth, so clear to all the naturalists, including Zola, that both monotony and horror are mitigated by the presence of a style.

Americans rarely perceive the stylist in Zola, and Norris was no exception. The creator of the Rougon-Macquart series spent hours listening to the speech of working people, learning their special vocabularies and the unique language of each trade. Hence the rare quality of the *discours indirect libre,* or "reported speech," in which he makes his characters think. Norris, on the other hand, merely makes his characters sound ignorant, without catching the flavor and quality of what they say that would do so much to admit the reader to their lives.

He was more aware of the theoretical background of Zola's naturalism, but can hardly be said to have been impressed by it. Positivistic determinism, and the influence of heredity and environment, play only a small role in *McTeague* and a yet smaller one in *Vandover*. Norris does remember, in *McTeague*, to attribute his hero's regression to a strain of alcoholism in the family, but there is not even this to explain the decline of Vandover, whose trouble would be described by any puritanical moralist as a weakness of character.

There are grounds for wondering whether Norris ever really understood the nature of French naturalism at all. Naturalism, he argues in one of his later critical pieces, is the opposite of realism. The latter, he says, is occupied with the everyday behavior we encounter in our usual lives, whereas naturalism is concerned with the unusual and extraordinary, with life on a social level unfamiliar to us, or with happenings unlikely to occur in life as we know it. The formulation sounds strangely like Hawthorne's famous distinction between romance and novel, but Norris is thinking here of Zola: he cites as an example the incident in *La Débâcle* where a soldier discovers that he has bayoneted his old and dear comrade in arms. Norris simply mistakes Zola's idiosyncratic penchant toward melodrama for the characterizing trait of naturalism as a whole.

Yet if Norris had not read Zola, *McTeague*, *Vandover*, and, later, *The Octopus* would surely not be the novels they are. If the manuals are stretching a point in making him the prime importer of naturalism into America, it is still entirely true that he is the link between our local naturalism and one of the great exponents of the French variety.

In college he had been exposed to a peculiarly American version of the theory of evolution. Starting from the brute beast, man has risen to the level where he now is, civilized, capable of intellection, possessing what may be thought of as a soul. There is reason to hope that he will continue to evolve, always upward, toward new heights. But this applies to man in the mass. In each individual there is something of the primordial beast, latent but still alive, and if anything goes wrong evolution may easily reverse its direction and the civilized being regress toward the original, brutal condition of the race. This is what happens to McTeague and Vandover.

The theory is alien to Zola's determinism; its optimism—man is headed for a greater good, while at the same time evil in individuals is explained and justified—is more intense than any that Zola or his contemporaries ever achieved. But at the same time it lends itself to the adoption of Zola's favorite literary techniques.

Minute scholarship has revealed numerous incidents and scenes in Norris' novels that are suggestive of Zola, and more particularly of *La Terre* and *La Bête humaine*, which were the novels Norris particularly preferred. But Norris' debt is greater than the total of reminiscences and borrowings. The shape of his best novels, taken as wholes, suggests that Zola's practice was never far from his mind.

The plot of *McTeague* conforms to the traditional naturalist pattern. All the needed data are given at the start, and the main action —except the ending—flows out of the data; no fact is withheld to allow the story to take an unexpected twist, and the facts given mean what they purport to mean.

McTeague would be an ordinary working man except that he has learned dentistry by watching an itinerant charlatan. He sets up his "parlors" in San Francisco, falls in love with one of his patients, and shortly marries her, but in getting Trina he makes an enemy of another suitor, Marcus Schouler. The latter reports him for practicing without a license and the state shuts his office. The loss of his livelihood sets off a decline; he takes to drink; a streak of sadism comes to the fore; he tortures his wife to make her tell him where she keeps the $5000 she has won in a lottery. She refuses, having herself become a victim of the avarice that has always been her great weakness. Finally McTeague kills her, takes the money, and returns as a fugitive to the mining country in the Sierras where he started life.

Nothing in all this seems unlikely; the story was in fact suggested by newspaper accounts of a particularly squalid murder in a poor section of San Francisco. Less likely are the two prominent subplots. In one of these, a man who has married a crazy Mexican girl for the totally imaginary gold plate she keeps saying she has inherited finally slits her throat in a fit of lust for gold. And all the while an elderly couple who live in the same lodging house as the McTeagues and the other pair indulge in a somewhat mawkish, evening-of-life romance. But these are minor, and detract less from the main story than from Norris' reputation for good taste—unless, indeed, the old-age idyll is in the novel as a propitiatory sop to the bad taste of the novelist's contemporaries. The main line of the story, in any case, is up to the naturalist standard of plausibility.

The characters of *McTeague* are working people and the life Norris paints is that of the working class. Like Zola he has documented his work by direct observation; his book is not only a "novel of San Francisco" but more specifically one about life on Polk Street. He knows his Polk Street well enough to give the effect of telling the truth about what one of his successors in naturalism, James T. Farrell, calls "the exact content of life in given circumstances." The story moves in and out of the eating joints, bars, and houses, among a mixed population of poor wage-earners, some of whom are underprivileged immigrants like the girl McTeague marries.

Such a world encourages violence. Two messy murders, sundry beatings, a case of mayhem, McTeague's torturing of Trina, and the fight in the desert that ends in the death of both McTeague and Marcus, combine to make *McTeague* a much more violent book than many produced by Norris' French model. And in contrast with his American contemporaries, Norris is quite willing to show his reader physical damage. There had been violence, and to spare, in earlier American writing, including *The Red Badge of Courage*; but whereas a writer like Crane tends to deflect his reader's eye from the effects of violence—the most we know of Jim Conklin's mortal wound, for example, is that it looks as if he had been chewed by wolves—Norris resolutely shows us what has happened.

Sex, on the other hand, he treats with a reticence that Zola would hardly have understood. In one episode McTeague kisses Trina "grossly" on the mouth while she is anesthetized in his dental chair; later in the book, Trina spreads her hoard of gold pieces on her bed and lies down naked on the coins; but having made clear that his characters are moved by powerful, and sometimes perverse, sexual drives, Norris is content to let the matter rest. This was doubtless as much as the American public would have permitted. The changes in taste that have intervened in the last seventy years should not be allowed to obscure the fact that even this incomplete explicitness, like indeed his finding the materials of a story in the life of the working class, was new and bold.

In making *McTeague* a case history, also, Norris was not necessarily following his French masters. Even though Zola and the Goncourts exploited this pattern repeatedly, it is also implicit in the notions of evolution he picked up in college: something goes wrong in the individual's life, the beast within emerges, and regression is inevitable. Norris did not need Zola to tell him this, and it may even be that encountering an already familiar idea when he turned his undergraduate attention on French naturalism merely deepened an existing commitment.

Nothing, of course, inhibited his following Zola closely in the use of symbols. The outsized replica of a tooth McTeague hangs outside his parlors plays the same role as the still in *L'Assommoir*, the coal-pit tower in *Germinal*, or the locomotive in *La Bête humaine*: it sums up and interprets his life. He has wanted the tooth obsessively, and is completely content once he has gotten it; having to give it up again represents the total shock of his catastrophe, whereas the gilt that covers it symbolizes the consuming greed for money that grows on all the principals as the story moves toward the end.

By and large, Norris was right in inscribing his wife's copy of one of his novels "from the boy Zola." By itself, *McTeague* would justify the quip. Yet if there is much of Zola in this story there is even more of Norris. Between the son of the real-estate magnate and the poor mine-boy who turns dentist the social gap is wide. However interested Norris may be in such characters, they are not his kind of people. He is incapable of the sympathy that so often allowed the socialist Zola to see life as it looked to his characters; and the benign detachment of the Goncourts, explicable only by their unthinking, perhaps totally unconscious acceptance of European class distinctions, is unavailable. In America all men are created equal, but all men are not equally admissible to membership in a fraternity on the Berkeley campus. His preference for white and Protestant, Anglo-Saxon characters, almost blatant in his later novels, is already in evidence; his treatment of the ways and speech of Trina Sieppe's German immigrant family sounds at times like condescending parody.

Yet at the same time, a number of the changes Norris made in his manuscript before publication seem intended to increase his reader's liking for McTeague. Particularly in the last few chapters, when the murderous brute has become a pitiable, hunted creature, our sympathy is intended to reach out to him. And he is never mean or treacherous. Norris does not excuse his weaknesses by a sentimental appeal to overpowering environmental circumstances, but he does not condemn him, either. The trouble is that the part of the story where we are most expected to feel sympathy is also by far the one hardest to believe. The attempt fails, in large part because *McTeague* is the work of an inexperienced and still clumsy writer.

The clumsiness and inexperience show up even in passages of undeniable power. In the following, the dentist and his friends have been out on a picnic, and what began as a friendly wrestling match between McTeague and his one-time crony, Marcus, has suddenly turned into a real fight, with Marcus biting through his opponent's ear.

"Then followed a terrible scene. The brute that in McTeague lay so close to the surface leaped instantly to life, monstrous, not to be resisted. He sprang to his feet with a shrill and meaningless clamor, totally unlike the ordinary bass of his speaking tones. It was the hideous yelling of a hurt beast, the squealing of a wounded elephant. He framed no words; in the rush of high-pitched sound that issued from his wide-open mouth there was nothing articulate. It was something no longer human; it was rather an echo from the jungle.

"Sluggish enough and slow to anger on ordinary occasions, McTeague when finally aroused became another man. His rage was a kind of obsession, an evil mania, the drunkenness of passion, the exalted and perverted fury of the Berserker, blind and deaf, a thing insensate.

"As he rose he caught Marcus's wrist in both his hands. He did not strike, he did not know what he was doing. His only idea was to batter the life out of the man before him, to crush and annihilate him upon the instant. Gripping his enemy in his enormous hands, hard and knotted, and covered with a stiff fell of yellow hair—the hands of the old-time car-boy—he swung him wide, as a hammer-thrower swings his hammer. Marcus's feet flipped from the ground, he spun through the air about McTeague as helpless as a bundle of clothes. All at once there was a sharp snap, almost like the report of a small pistol. Then Marcus rolled over and over upon the ground as McTeague released his grip; his arm, the one the dentist had seized, bending suddenly, as though a third joint had formed between wrist and elbow. The arm was broken."

The young novelist's inexorable repetitiousness is part of a consciously adopted technique. From the beginning the motifs of physical size, blond or yellow hair, huge hands, strength, and subhuman stupidity have been constantly present. The passage merely expands the subject of his overwhelming animality. This insistence, rather than the occasional remarks about a theoretical determinism scattered through the early chapters, is what prepares us for McTeague's eventual reversion to the brute.

To other, more sophisticated techniques, Norris is almost aggressively indifferent. He is not in the least interested in "showing" as opposed to "telling." His immense willingness to comment on the action, to explain the cause of everything that happens—as when he tells us what the man's voice sounded like—is more pronounced here than it will be in the later novels, although he will never rid himself of it entirely. The same is true of his use of a third-person, omniscient point of view, giving himself a clear view into the mind of any character he likes and thus putting himself in the perilous position of reporting the motivations of conduct that the reader might better be trusted to deduce from behavior.

It has probably required little more than this to undermine Norris' reputation among twentieth-century critics. The enormous weight of preference for the novel according to Henry James, with its severe restriction of point of view to the "central moral consciousness," has put older and simpler procedures in a poor light. Everything in the complaints of adverse judges like Lionel Trilling and the late Joseph Warren Beach in their dismissals of the novels of Dreiser is equally applicable to Norris. The particular impact of *McTeague* cannot be accounted for by Jamesian calculus, nor will it be admitted by critics who do not concede the occasional aesthetic effectiveness of massive accumulations of detail.

McTeague opens with a typical Sunday afternoon in the life of the hero—his dinner, his pitcher of steam beer, his nap in his own dental chair. Then comes a turn-back to his youth in the mines and to his time with the charlatan who taught him his trade. Next there is a minute description of his physique, and another of his office, including a first mention of the symbolic gilded tooth. Only after this does the novel move outside for a description of life in Polk Street. Finally, McTeague spots his chum and future nemesis, Marcus, and the first episode, the taking of a dog to a veterinary hospital, ensues. The reader has, so to speak, been given a detailed view of the habitat and the habits of the animal McTeague, and been prepared to watch the animal perform.

Such procedures may properly be called Zolaesque, since Zola used them, but they are not necessarily naturalistic in every case. Norris learned much from Zola that Zola had learned from his own predecessors. It is a naturalist strategy to give the reader all the necessary data, as *McTeague* does, at the beginning and then let the ensuing action flow out of these data, withholding nothing that could allow the story to take an unexpected twist, and making the data mean exactly what they purport to mean. But the device of showing the animal in his minutely described habitat was standard literary technique; Zola doubtless learned it from Balzac. Consequently it is fair to say that *McTeague* is a naturalistic novel, but in the sense that Zola's are naturalistic: an excellent example of nineteenth-century realism, but with special emphasis on the biological and the deterministic. Through Zola, Norris got the instruments for attempting a slice of American life, seen steadily and whole. Historically, the fact that it was offered to a public, whose pabulum consisted of romances like *When Knighthood Was in Flower* and the output of F. Marion Crawford, imparts an additional significance.

Vandover and the Brute must be judged with greater caution. The manuscript came to light well after Norris' death. Norris may have been unwilling to publish it, or, more likely, may have been unable to find a publisher. His brother Charles revised the manuscript, although qualified opinion today holds that the latter probably did not supply the ending, as was once thought to be the case. What Norris' own feelings about the book, as we know it, would have been is a matter for speculation, at best.

Yet Norris' hero, this time, is remarkably like the author, and whereas the things that befall McTeague could not conceivably happen to people of the novelist's own kind, what happens to Vandover certainly could do so. This novel attempts a study of a representative of the San Francisco middle class, and for his

naturalistic documentation Norris appears to have turned to his own autobiography.

Young Vandover returns to San Francisco with a Harvard education of sorts and the intention of developing his talent in painting. Somehow he never gets started, and the tendency to frivol away his time grows on him. He becomes more and more devoted to "vice" and "bestial pleasures," and at length seduces a girl who offers little resistance but who commits suicide when she finds herself pregnant. This event sets off a chain reaction: Vandover loses the "nice" girl he has never quite got round to marrying; Vandover's father dies; the dead girl's family brings a suit; the distraught Vandover allows himself to be cheated out of his property by an old friend of Harvard days; he gambles away what little is left, and finally his sanity wavers and collapses; he becomes a case of lycanthropy.

Lycanthropy is a mental condition in which a man thinks that he is a wolf, and behaves like one. The state is relatively rare, although well enough known to have appealed to the imaginations of certain French romantics like the poet Pétrus Borel. Few of Norris' readers can ever have seen a case, and doubtless some learn of the disease by reading his story. But the lycanthropic state, as Vandover experiences it, sounds hideous, and we cannot help wondering just what depths of vice, debauchery, and bestial pleasure brought it on.

Vandover's essays in sin seem, on the whole, rather mild and even timid. One can imagine the memory of them making a tenderly nurtured individual somewhat neurotic and guilt-ridden, but hardly anything worse. We must, of course, allow for the inhibitions imposed by the taste of the moment. The record shows, for instance, that Norris' publisher, Doubleday, wanted him to rewrite the passage in *McTeague* where "Little Owgooste," forced to sit too long while his family watches a variety show, wets his pants. If current notions of delicacy made this humble incident unpalatable to cultivated taste, what chance would there have been of describing explicitly any sort of riot among the fleshpots?

Norris' difficulty was that he was trying to follow a French model in a climate where it was impossible to do so. Zola, like the Goncourts, had been devoted to case histories of the more picturesque sort, and Norris' choice of lycanthropy is surely worthy of the master. But although Zola may have put off some readers by creating, for example, a character whose major accomplishment was the loudness of his farting, he clearly did not alienate the reading public at large, or dismay his publisher. And the direct picturing of monumental debauches in novels like *Nana* being permitted, the decline and fall of characters like Nana herself is fully motivated; the reader is not left casting about for the reason. This fact measures the distance then separating Paris from New York.

But why should Norris himself not have seen the disproportion between sin and retribution? One can only propose a plausible hypothesis. Vandover's trajectory is remarkably like the young novelist's own: origins in San Francisco; sojourn in the more sophisticated East; return—imminent in Norris' case when he was starting *Vandover*—to California with the intention of living a life that by local standards was abnormal. Whereas Vandover will paint, Norris intends to write, and neither will involve himself in ordinary ways of earning a living. If, when he got home, Norris should be unable to settle down and justify his mother's faith in his talent, then what disaster might not lie ahead? If *Vandover and the Brute* is read as transposed fantasy of this sort, the issue of plausibility does not arise.

Such a reading, on the other hand, is an invitation to the amateur psychoanalyst. What was the effect on Norris of being brought up by this strong-willed woman whose commitment to the life of the spirit—even though it took the genteel form of organizing Browning Clubs—was real enough so that she would let him live a writer's financially precarious life? And would not an explicitly documented career in sin reveal a knowledge that might desecrate the relationship of mother and son? Such questions have their special interest, even their fascination. But answering them would be an exercise in pure speculation.

Norris' biographer, Franklin Walker, was persuaded that beneath his superficial sophistication, Norris had a strong streak of puritanism in him, that within the morally noncommittal naturalist there lurked a hidden but severely disapproving moralist. This is not impossible. And the preference Norris shows in his less serious fictions for clean-minded, two-fisted, asexual but vigorous heroes tends to support the view. He was, after all, the contemporary of the founders of Boy Scouting and of the hit-the-line-hard ethics of the first Roosevelt. *Vandover* has moments when it sounds like *Stover at Yale*.

One of the most alert of Norris' interpreters, Donald Pizer, proposes an even simpler solution: lycanthropy is a possible stage on the way to paralytic insanity related to paresis. Pizer may be right. Paresis results from the presence of spirochetes in the bloodstream. Assuming that Norris knew of this fact, he may have been trying to say, as plainly as the prevalent taboo on mentioning syphilis would let him, that his hero's escapades had left him the victim of venereal disease. But if this was what the novelist intended, all literary difficulties are not automatically removed. If Norris is saying subtly that his man is syphilitic, it must also be admitted that such subtlety is anything but characteristic. In fact, it would be hard to catch Norris being so subtle anywhere else in his collected works. And even if this instance is the exception that proves the rule, so far as the technique of fiction is concerned, it leaves Norris still in the predicament of having obscured the pivotal motivation of Vandover's story. Easiest of all the explanations to accept would be precisely that Norris did not publish the book—except for some isolated chapters—because he felt that the problem had not been solved.

Vandover is thus a flawed book; it is not an uninteresting one and has a charm unexpected in naturalist fiction. The opening descriptions of life at Harvard are worthy forerunners of classics, some of them forgotten, like George Weller's *Not to Eat; Not for Love*. And there are period pieces, picturing the gay blades of the nineties, that stand by themselves. If Vandover's downfall could only have been made more convincing this novel might not have been dwarfed, as it is, by *McTeague*.

Norris was not so persuaded, it must appear, as we are today that in *McTeague* and *Vandover* he had found his natural manner. He went through a brief period when he abandoned his first, instinctive ways in an effort to please the genteel. But eventually, late in 1899 —thus after *Moran of the Lady Letty, A Man's Woman,* and *Blix*—he returned to "straight naturalism with all the guts." The expression is one he used in a letter to his friend Isaac Marcosson to tell him about his "Epic of the Wheat," of which the first volume would be *The Octopus*.

The example of Zola shows up as plainly in *The Octopus* as it does in *McTeague* or *Vandover*, but in a different way. The earlier novels had each focused on one character and the vicissitudes he passes through when his congenital weakness becomes dominant. In this respect, they suggest the relatively unad-

venturous Zola of novels like, say, *Son Excellence Eugène Rougon*. The Wheat trilogy, on the other hand, recalls the Zola of the great social frescoes like *Germinal* and the sprawling poems of fecundity like *La Terre* and *La Faute de l'Abbé Mouret*—the militant enemy of social abuses who combined his crusading prose with a deeply neo-pagan poetry in praise of elemental life.

Norris had planned a cyclical work, with three stories less closely interrelated than those in the Rougon-Macquart series, but treating closely related subjects. *The Octopus* describes the raising of the grain; *The Pit* continues with the buying and selling of it; and the third volume was to have been devoted to its distribution overseas. Norris died (in 1902) before he could start the third. We have only *The Octopus* and *The Pit*; and by common consent the former is greatly the better of the two, because Norris' knowledge of the machinery of business was too small, or else his feeling for business as an epic force was not intense enough. *The Octopus* may also be a better job than *McTeague*, because of its superiority in design and in articulation, but this is not generally conceded. And yet, for a number of years, *The Pit* consistently outsold these other novels and presumably had more readers. This may be for no more obscure reason than that *The Pit* has a tycoon for a hero.

In the center of *The Octopus*, like the mine in *Germinal*, is the railroad, pushing out its tracks like tentacles across California and squeezing to death everything it touches. The story is based upon an actual incident in the history of the Southern Pacific, and denounces an abuse that really existed, a system of preferential freight rates designed to extract every penny the traffic would bear.

Yet although Norris met people like Ida M. Tarbell during his months in New York, he hardly qualifies as a dedicated muckraker. He is not against Big Business on principle, and he seems even to have admired the successful business figures of his time. His disposition is more reminiscent of American Populism: when respectable, middle-class people like himself are suddenly required to wrestle with a colossus, his sympathies are on their side.

The country people in *The Octopus* have been farming land leased from the railroad, with the option eventually to buy, and have made a profit up to the time when the railroad first raises rates and then calls in the options; the price charged for the land, out of all proportion to its value at the time the farmers originally took over, is based on the value of the property after it has been improved by the farmers themselves, at their own expense. The wheat ranchers finally revolt, meet the posse sent to evict them in a pitched battle along an irrigation ditch. Those who are not killed are ruined.

The other major force in the story, along with the soulless and inhuman corporation, is the wheat itself. In a way, the heroine is the fecund American earth. Norris' long descriptions of the sowing, germination, cultivation, and harvest are without parallel in American literature; one has to go to Tolstoi for anything to rival them. Not even the bad agricultural methods of the ranchers—whom Norris does not defend for having taken too much from the earth too rapidly and without putting enough back—can exhaust this natural wealth. And in a sense the real crime of the railroad is to have frustrated nature by making it impossible for men to go on feeding other men with the wheat. By its neo-pagan adoration of nature as force, no less than by its broad canvases, the size of its landscapes and of the events that take place in them, *The Octopus* is a very Zolaesque book.

That this has not been fully recognized simply attests that criticism has been more attentive to Zola's theoretical utterances than to his practice, and is relatively unaware of how much more Zola owed to the causal theories of Hippolyte Taine than the debt he acknowledged. Zola's pronouncements sound as if the whole key to his notion of the "experimental" novel was Taine's introduction to his *History of English Literature*, in which Taine posits a narrowly biological basis for his determinism. It happens that this introduction was meant to catch the attention of a general reading public, at the cost of being relatively sensational in the statement of Taine's beliefs, and is peppered with such dicta as "Vice and virtue are chemical products, like sulphuric acid and sugar." In a letter written somewhat later in life, Taine remarked that he wished to God he had never written some of these capsule formulations.

Earlier than the introduction, he had written a much less flamboyant and sensational statement of his theory in a book called *Les Philosophes classiques*. Here he outlines a system of causality in which the essential notion is one of impersonal forces underlying the working of nature. Although his illustrations are biological, as they are in the introduction, it is clear that forces of another kind—for example, social or economic—are not logically excluded. With respect to this fundamental perception, the famous formula of heredity, environment, and historical moment that Taine propounds in the introduction constitutes a grouping into categories of certain impersonal forces. Later in Taine's career, especially after 1870, he tends to emphasize forces that are social or even political. In Zola's novels, though not in his theoretical declarations, fascination with impersonal force is recognizable everywhere.

Seen in this perspective, the central subject of *The Octopus* is one that Zola would not have disowned. Mere men are powerless to change the course either of the growth of wheat or of the economic operations of the railroad. Both are impersonal, and both obey their own internal laws. (Hence the argument of one of the railroad officials that a corporation operates according to laws that cannot be changed, or their effect mitigated, by the members.)

But an impersonal force in itself is difficult to deal with in a work of literature. It must be concretized, either in a representative character or in a transparent symbol. One cannot well hate or love a legal entity, but one can discharge all kinds of emotion upon the figure of S. Behrman, the crass and repulsive agent of the carrier who also personifies the evil within it. And one can be frightened and revolted by an octopus.

The locomotive that nearly hits the young poet, Presley, in the opening chapter, is less a machine than a symbol of malevolent power.

"He had only time to jump back upon the embankment when, with a quivering of all the earth, a locomotive, single, unattached, shot by him with a roar, filling the air with the reek of hot oil, vomiting smoke and sparks; its enormous eye, Cyclopean, red, throwing a glare far in advance, shooting by in a sudden crash of confused thunder; filling the night with the terrific clamour of its iron hoofs. . . .

"Then, faint and prolonged, across the levels of the ranch, he heard the engine whistling for Bonneville. Again and again, at rapid intervals in its flying course, it whistled for road crossings, for sharp curves, for trestles; ominous notes, hoarse, bellowing, ringing with the accents of menace and defiance; and abruptly Presley saw again, in his imagination, the galloping monster, the terror of steel and steam, with its single eye, Cyclopean, red, shooting from horizon to horizon; but saw it now as the symbol of a vast power, huge, terrible, flinging the echo of its thunder over all the reaches of the valley, leaving blood and destruction in its path; the leviathan, with tentacles of steel clutching into the soil, the soulless Force, the iron-hearted Power, the monster, the Colossus, the Octopus."

This passage could be used to show that Norris was not an accomplished stylist. The metaphors, in particular, will not survive even the friendliest scrutiny: the leviathan does not have tentacles, and the octopus, who does have them, does not use them for clutching the soil; the whistles of steam locomotives did not bellow. This frightening Thing undergoes too many metamorphoses in a brief space just so that we will be frightened by it. But it is less important that he should be denounced for straining after effect than that he should have felt the straining necessary. The symbol must be established, by all the resources of rhetoric he can muster. This is the elevated style of a period that found its models in the emphatic improvisations of political and pulpit eloquence, but it is nonetheless an elevated style. Norris is calling upon it to confer importance upon a symbol which will give us something we can really hate.

By a similar process, S. Behrman, the agent, is made similarly useful. There is no causal connection between Behrman's job and his insensitiveness, his grotesque taste in dress, his crude manners. He could serve the company as well if he were blessed by the opposite qualities. But the reader can detest this man, with his varnished straw hat and his vest covered with embroidered horseshoes, and through him the organization he serves. There is supposed to be poetic justice in the accident at the end of the story, when Behrman is killed by the wheat. He personifies a force, and must be killed by a force. His presence, like the recurring symbol of the locomotive, connects the principal line of the story with the tradition of naturalism.

Just as in *McTeague*, however, Norris' naturalism is not unrelieved. Interwoven with the main action are a number of subplots that cannot by any stretch be called naturalist.

Presley has come to the wheat-growing San Joaquin Valley to write a long poem about the land and its Spanish past. Before the year is out he gives up the project in favor of a poem about the here and now, and the realities of life in the Valley; it attacks the trusts. His role in the novel is to provide the point of view of an educated and refined sensibility. Norris does not use him, as Henry James would have done, as the consciousness through whom all the action is refracted. We see the events from his angle only upon occasion. But his sensitive responses to them allow Norris to avoid some of the commentary he might otherwise have felt impelled to insert, and at the same time the story of what happens to his poem forms an implicit commentary on the conflict between the major forces in contention.

Presley's friend Vanamee, the sheep-herding mystic, has little connection with the principal thread of the novel except that his sheep are the ones run down by the locomotive in the first chapter. He prefers solitude and stays aloof from the concerns of the ranchers. Years before, his one true love had been brutally raped by some unknown, and then died after childbirth. By some extrasensory means that is never explained beyond calling it a concentration of mental energy, he believes that he can bring her back. Vanamee, rather than the Mexican parish priest who is included only for local color, appears to represent the spiritual in a situation where the other characters are overwhelmingly preoccupied with the material: for the farmers, engrossed in their struggle for life, a devotion like his would be unthinkable.

For us, on the other hand, the event it pro-duces is unbelievable. Feeling that his dead fiancée is drawing nearer, Vanamee takes to waiting for her in a mission garden, and finally she does indeed come, over the new wheat—in the person of the now-grown child, who looks exactly like her. The reader is expected to believe that this girl has lived in this country neighborhood since her birth without Vanamee's having heard the least rumor of it.

In another subplot, the rancher Annixter, a crabbed health-faddist with marked misogynistic leanings, is attracted to the young and wholesome Hilma Tree, the dairymaid. When she rejects the chance to become his mistress, Annixter discovers that the strange stirrings within him must be love. He proposes marriage and is accepted; they spend their honeymoon in San Francisco, and by the time when, after their return, Annixter is killed in the battle by the irrigation ditch, we have been persuaded that love of a fine woman has made him a better man. The touch of Dickensian sentimentality is less obtrusive than the idyll of the old couple in *McTeague*, probably because Annixter is one of the harried ranchers and thus plays another role in the story besides that of hero in a love affair.

A fourth subplot involves one Dyke, an engineer who loses his job with the railway, then finds himself forced off his farm, tries to meet his desperate need for money by robbing a train, kills a trainman, and is finally hunted down as a fugitive. All Dyke has ever wanted is to give his little daughter a decent education in a seminary for young ladies.

Thus while in its main lines *The Octopus* has much of the typical naturalist novel, much else in it does not conform to the naturalist pattern. From episode to episode the railroad wins and the farmers lose; force crashes against force with the inevitable outcome. Courts, legislature, posses combine to crush the hopeless individuals. And when all is finished we are shown examples of the wrecked lives of the dispersed farmers. But this in itself does not account for the subplots to which Norris has clearly given much attention.

After *The Octopus*, *The Pit* is a disappointment. Norris did not know Chicago as he knew the land and people of California, and what he knew about trading in wheat futures was not enough to fill a book. The second installment of his epic accordingly shrinks to the dimensions of a domestic love story.

The hero, Curtis Jadwin, has made one fortune in real estate and appears about to make another in wheat. He marries a genteelly cultivated girl from New England and installs her in a luxurious mansion near the Lake. They move in a society that justifies Henry James's complaint that America is socially too poor and thin to support a novel. Laura Jadwin's efforts to refine her husband do not succeed, and his success at the Exchange enflames his gambling instinct. While he is busy trying to corner the world's supply, she is very tempted to run off with a former suitor, the effete aesthete Corthell. Jadwin is ruined when his corner breaks. The marriage barely survives.

Norris revives his usual devices. The book is built around the familiar recurrent symbol— in this case the metaphor of the Wheat Pit as a gigantic whirlpool—shored up by his most ambitious prose. He invokes the economic law of supply and demand, and the natural law that when men are hungry more food will be planted, to play the roles of impersonal forces. Although *The Pit* is not so complex and heavily populated as *The Octopus*, he is still working in broad, panoramic frescoes. There is even a hint of Jadwin's decline under adversity, but its course is arrested by the presence of a good woman.

For once a Norris novel has a fully realized, if not completely winning, heroine. One suspects the brunette and slight Laura Jadwin is a composite of his mother, Gertrude Norris, and Jeannette Black Norris, his wife. She is, in any case, no mere love-object of a muscularly masculine hero, but is treated as interesting in her own right: a very considerable share of the novel is given over to her story, from Massachusetts to Chicago and from girlhood through marriage to neglect, temptation, and final reconciliation. Unfortunately, Norris also makes her self-centered and occasionally downright selfish. But despite her shallowness she is real and, in Norris' world, new.

Jadwin, on the other hand, is a close relative of McTeague. A tycoon born on the farm, one of the generation whose wealth did not inhibit their liking to sit out on the "front stoop" on warm spring evenings, he has the powerful muscles, awkwardness, and ineradicable lack of polish of the working man. With him is contrasted Corthell, who represents "art" while Jadwin represents "life"; there is no doubting Norris' preference for the energetic and still primitive philistine over the pallid man of refinement.

For Norris is faithful to the clichés of his age. A man who gets to the top of the pile does so by virtue of superior qualities of energy and strength. Social Darwinism here supports the Protestant ethic. Society is not inherently bad, but it encourages frivolity and the cultivation of the less virile qualities of character. Cities are interesting but corrupt, while strength of character comes from contact with the land and the elements.

Norris' critical essays, perfunctory and sketchy as many of them are, reveal a hard core of anti-intellectualism, with the characteristically American contradiction that consists of respect for and, simultaneously, suspicion of education. They contain no seriously articulated notion of the purpose and value of the literary activity to which he has nonetheless committed his own life, but declare repeatedly that "life" is better than "art." Jadwin is the kind of hero he could, and did, admire.

This is why Jadwin is not a very convincing Titan. If this fundamentally simple and uningenious man could corner the world's wheat, it is hard to see why any reasonably shrewd though not especially intelligent character, given enough money, could not do the same thing—and why, indeed, it is not done with distressing regularity.

There is no escaping it: *The Pit* reveals Norris' great weakness. An inadequate understanding of human character is intimately related to the defect in his style that vitiates even the central metaphor of his book. The image of the great whirlpool strikes us as vastly overwritten simply because Jadwin's accomplishment is not so great as Norris thinks. Jadwin, himself, is not big enough and words alone will not make him so. It would not be unjust to say of his performance in *The Pit* what Lionel Trilling says of Dreiser in all his novels: he does not write well because he thinks poorly.

Hence a survey of his contribution to American naturalism must conclude that it is indeed right to call him a naturalist but that calling him one does not account fully for the whole nature of his talent. There is another, nonnaturalist side to him even in his best work. When one turns to the rest, what this side was becomes unmistakable. Most of Norris' critics have dutifully noted the strain of melodrama that persistently turns up in his stories, but usually to minimize it as perhaps regrettable but not particularly important. Yet it is a constant factor in his successes (except *Vandover*) and his failures (except, perhaps, *Blix*).

Norris had gone home from Harvard, in the summer of 1895, with two unfinished novels and no immediate intention of going on with his writing. Before the year ended he was in South Africa reporting for one of the San Francisco papers on the unrest that preceded the Boer War. He was present at the fiasco of Jameson's raid, saw such excitement as there was to see, was under fire at least once, and caught a fever that put an end to any thought of further African adventure.

There followed two years of sporadic writing and journalism in San Francisco. He resumed writing for the San Francisco *Wave*, turning out sketches, essays, and some of the short stories that were posthumously collected in *The Third Circle* (1909). With renewed health came a certain tendency toward dissipation—of a rather mild sort, from all appearances—and the renewed discovery that writing can be hard work. During 1897 he seems to have gone through a period of marked depression.

But in 1896 he had met Jeannette Black, and the progress of the courtship coincided with a return of creative energy. Early in 1898 Norris was writing an adventure story for publication by installments in the *Wave*. This was *Moran of the Lady Letty*. In New York, S. S. McClure had been reading Norris' incidental writings in the *Wave*, and, with the first installments of *Moran* in print, invited Norris to come to New York and take a job. McClure had joined forces with Frank Doubleday, in the house of Doubleday, McClure, and Company, by the time Norris got there.

This was how Norris came to be the editorial reader who drew the firm's attention to the manuscript of Dreiser's *Sister Carrie*. Meanwhile Doubleday and McClure published *Moran of the Lady Letty* in 1898 and *McTeague*, at last completed, in 1899. *Moran* went largely unreviewed, and *McTeague*, though praised by Howells, stirred considerable protest—there were cries of "stamp out this race of Norrises"—without raising the kind of scandal that sells books in quantity. Even

Howells had suggested that Norris might do well in future to avoid the extreme realism for which we read *McTeague* today. Doubtless convinced that Howells was right, Norris went to work on *A Man's Woman*, a novel incapable of shocking any taste at all other than the purely literary. His letters show that he found the book disastrously hard to write and was perfectly aware of not having brought it off. He published it, even so, in newspaper installments during 1899 and in book form in 1900.

His one other excursion outside naturalism was *Blix*, a transposition into fiction of his romance with Jeannette Black. The hero, Condy Rivers, is a young writer who falls in love with a well-bred girl—he nicknames her "Blix" —who has little patience with the frivolity of contemporary San Francisco society. Condy has most of the amiable characteristics of a young college graduate, including a tendency to fool away time and money gambling at his club. Blix learns poker and beats him consistently, until he finally gives up the pastime. Being autobiographical well beyond the degree reached in *Vandover*, this love story adds an interesting sidelight on the latter novel: the suggestion is strong, in *Blix*, that Norris entertained private worries about going to the dogs. In the novel, as in real life, he does not do so: Blix eventually leaves for the East and Condy receives a providential invitation from an eastern publisher that will enable him to follow her.

Some critics, including the late Lar Åhnebrink, have found this novel "charming." Its accounts of the couple's walks along the edge of the Pacific, and one of a fishing expedition to an inland lake, are in fact informed by a kind of heartwarming felicity. But more significant for the present purpose are the chapters in which, on their walks, the couple fall in with the keeper of a life-saving station who has knocked about the world extensively and has a fund of stories to tell. These Condy drinks in, to store against the day when he will need them for his books. This is "material" and also contact, albeit at second hand, with "life." Condy's cultivation of this parasitical relationship suggests the importance for Norris of his own conversations with one Captain Joseph Hodgson of the Fort Point Coast Guard station.

Books of action and adventure were selling well, but Paris, Berkeley, and Harvard had prepared Norris poorly for such enterprises. However convinced he was that "life is better than literature," in this sense he had not lived. He was entirely willing to be a romancer as well as a novelist, but the competition was stiff: Stevenson, Richard Harding Davis, Kipling, and Joseph Conrad had all gone places and done things.

So had Norris, briefly. Like so many others he had been an accredited correspondent in the Spanish-American War and had seen some of the fighting, but, like his trip to South Africa, this expedition seems to have given him little to use in his fiction. Condy's attachment to "Captain Jack" suggests strongly that he felt a kind of poverty of invention in himself. Did Norris entertain the same feeling? His willingness to work with secondhand materials, like the delight he took, according to one of his letters, in the writing of *Moran*, excites suspicions of his seriousness. Was he a writer with "something to say" that gave him trouble in the saying, or was he merely a rather talented young man who wanted terribly to be a writer?

Alternative answers may be proposed. His early commitment to naturalism may have been only experimental. Or it may be that he was short of money, wanted to marry, and loved Jeannette Black more than he did any special literary mode. What is certain is that *Moran of the Lady Letty*, and even more so *A Man's Woman*, attest the fallibility of a method that capitalizes upon vicarious experience.

Moran has the distinction of being one of the best yarns about salt water and derring-do ever written by an author who knew nothing firsthand about either. Even while his novel was coming out in installments, Norris was hearing from knowledgeable friends about his howlers in nautical terminology and procedures. He seems to have listened unperturbed and was perhaps right in doing so: reviewers of his finished book were much more critical of the superabundance of unnecessary incident than of bloopers about the art of navigation. But his ignorance of his subject was not, of course, unrelated to the proliferation of episodes.

Of these there is surely God's plenty. Ross Wilbur, a San Franciscan, Yale graduate, and dedicated ladies' man, happens into a dockside saloon to while away the time between a tea and a debutante party, drinks a Mickey Finn, is dropped through a trapdoor, and finds himself shanghaied aboard a disreputable schooner manned by a Chinese crew and commanded by a white thug. They drop down the coast looking for anything they can scavenge or salvage, and meet the derelict *Lady Letty*. Aboard the drifting hulk is one living soul, a somewhat post-adolescent Norse goddess, big, blonde, beautiful, and profane, but absolutely unfamiliar with men. An accident leaves her and Wilbur to command the schooner and its Chinese crew through a series of wild adventures. These include a night battle on the shore, against the crew of a marauding Chinese junk, for the possession of a piece of ambergris. Excited by the fighting until she does not know who is her enemy, the girl Moran throws her-

self upon Wilbur in berserk rage. He subdues her by physical force—and as he holds her helpless Moran learns to love the man who has mastered her.

When, after other and no more credible adventures, they bring their ship back to California, Wilbur has become another man. He has killed an opponent in armed combat. His muscles are hard. And at the same time he has been regenerated by the primitive maiden, and the once effete Yale man is now thoroughly out of patience with the social whirl, to which he cannot think of returning. Similarly, Moran has been changed by her contact with a cultured and civilized man into a charmingly feminine, though incompletely tamed, young woman.

At this point Norris played with the idea of sending them on another voyage, this time around Cape Horn to join the filibusterers drawn to Cuba by the approach of war. This he renounced, however, in favor of having Moran murdered by a skulking Chinese crewman she and Wilbur had protected from the vengeance of an enemy tong. The choice had the obvious merit of ending the yarn and getting an inconveniently antisocial heroine off Norris', and his hero's, hands.

Moran easily sustains a first reading, though most readers would require a special incentive to undertake a second: the strain of suspending disbelief is simply too great.

A Man's Woman is no less demanding, and offers even less in the way of reward. The story involves an Arctic explorer who comes home from an expedition to the northern wastes, where most of his companions died, to claim the love of a rich woman who has turned her back on an empty social life, founded a nurses' home, and herself become a nurse. Later he forces her to abandon nursing his closest friend—a survivor of the expedition—just as the latter is at the crisis of typhoid, because he objects to her endangering herself. The friend dies, but the couple marry—and after some months the hero renounces his bliss to depart on a new expedition to the North Pole.

The heroine, Lloyd Searight, is another Moran in physique and pale Nordic beauty, but has wealth, education, and unmitigated idealism in addition. Ward Bennett, the explorer, is a McTeague in a Brooks Brothers suit: he even has the same jutting jaw and somewhat Neanderthal brow. Well-born, educated, intelligent, but at the same time full of uncontrolled brute energy, he is devoted to getting exactly what he wants—the love of a woman, one last exhausted effort from companions dying on an ice floe, or the assent of his fiancée to desert a man who will perish without her aid. In the Arctic he proves himself capable of any extreme—and is no less so when he returns to civilization. When Lloyd's horse threatens to run away with her, for example, he kills the beast with one blow of his geologist's hammer.

The book presents the reader with more psychological improbabilities than he can easily tolerate. Would any man, in the name of love, insist on leaving his friend to die wretchedly for lack of nursing? Would a woman of Lloyd's alleged intelligence and pride have accepted being forced into such a situation? Would any woman with a minimum of self-respect have fallen in love with this educated gorilla in the first place? The difficulty of belief was already great in *Moran*; here it is insuperable.

The important truth about *A Man's Woman* is not so much that this novel is melodramatic, as that the melodrama taken as such is of low quality. *Moran of the Lady Letty*, even more shamelessly devoted to a world divided without nuance into bad people and good people, inattentive to proportions between cause and effect, subordinating motive to action, caring little if anything about probability, and depending heavily on the reader's overlooking its defects in his eagerness to learn what happens next, is far less offensive. Norris has poor Moran murdered in cold blood simply to be rid of her. Wilbur has left her aboard the schooner moored just offshore while he does an errand in San Francisco; the one Chinese remaining with them attacks her with his knife; love has civilized her to the point where she cannot use her strength to resist; the murderer leaves her body aboard, slips the cables so that the schooner will be wrenched free at any strain, and swims ashore; the captain of the lifeboat station finds her dead and brings the news to Wilbur just as the *Lady Letty* breaks away; Wilbur can only helplessly watch his schooner standing out to sea bearing the body of his beloved into the sunset. We do not greatly object, possibly because we know that Norris, himself, did not take the book very seriously and had a huge good time writing it.

But the final chapters of *McTeague* are not just an expedient for breaking off a yarn; from the sketches submitted as "themes" in Lewis E. Gates's writing class, it is clear that they were in the original plan. His delay in finishing the book is evidence that he was not entirely sure of their fitting with the rest.

He makes poor McTeague take flight back into the Sierras, looking for safety in the scenes of his boyhood, lets him find gold he will never be able to spend, endows him with a special sixth sense that infallibly warns of danger. As the posse approaches, McTeague takes flight again down the Panamint Range and into the desert. His implacable enemy, Schouler, insists on following him alone, after the posse, which he has now joined, turns back. The chase continues through the desert, which Norris widens beyond its geographical dimensions for the purpose, until the inexorable pursurer catches up. They fight; and McTeague kills Schouler—but only after the latter, in one last surge of strength, shackles himself to McTeague with handcuffs for which there is no key. They are miles from the nearest water.

Few, even among Norris' enthusiastic admirers, argue that this abrupt change in modes of fiction enhances *McTeague.* Nevertheless, the common judgment is that the turn to a flight-and-pursuit pattern does not impair the quality of the earlier part of the novel. They are perhaps right, but the same plea cannot be made in favor of *The Octopus,* because this whole novel is structured on the principle of melodrama, and one's final judgment depends on how well one feels the melodrama succeeds.

The essence of melodrama is violent contrast, and *The Octopus* is built of violently contrasting scenes. The slaughter of Vanamee's sheep, in the opening chapter, follows the scene of quiet conversation in which the sheepherder reveals so much of himself to Presley. The arrival of the bad news that the railroad has called in its options comes directly after the pages about the merriment of the whole ranching community at Annixter's barn dance. The sequence on Annixter's honeymoon with Hilma in San Francisco is sandwiched between accounts of how Dyke has been starved off his own land, and of how he robs the train—which happens to be the express that is bringing the couple back to the ranch. The episode of the great jack-rabbit drive and its attendant slaughter ends with the word that a posse is coming, and the ranchers hurry home to be slaughtered themselves.

There is thus no change in method toward the close of the book, when Norris adopts a technique of alternating fragments of pieces of dissociated but contrasting action. In the penultimate chapter, after disposing of various minor characters—Minna Hooven, for example, is driven to prostitution—Norris picks up, first, a dinner party at the home of one of the officials of the railroad, and, second, the wanderings of old Mrs. Hooven and six-year-old Hilda, penniless and looking for a place to sleep. The night is cold, and the woman and child are desperate; the dinner, at which Presley is surprised to find himself a guest, is elaborate and succulent. The camera switches back and forth between the dinner and the waifs in increasingly rapid rhythm, with each shot briefer than the one preceding. Finally we see the couple sink down under a bush. We return to the dinner:

"Just before the ladies left the table, young Lambert raised his glass of Madeira. Turning toward the wife of the Railroad King he said:

" 'My best compliments for a delightful dinner.' "

Then back to the bench:

"The doctor, who had been bending over Mrs. Hooven, rose.

" 'It's no use,' he said; 'she has been dead some time—exhaustion from starvation.' "

These last pages are not only immensely effective in themselves but also entirely appropriate in the structure of the novel: they accelerate the rhythm that the reader has felt from the beginning. The rapid and incessant reversals of fortune are rushed to a kind of climax. The technique is the one that would be adopted, a decade or so later, for the wordless narrations of the early movies. To describe it one is almost forced to fall back upon the vocabulary of the cinema.

The final chapter moves in a much slower tempo. The hated S. Behrman has come to watch the lading of a ship that will carry some of the railroad's surplus wheat to the starving

Orient. The operation is automatic. No one else is about. By itself the golden stream pours out of a hopper and falls into the hold. Behrman loses his balance, lands in the hold with the flood pouring in upon him. He struggles against it, tries to find a ladder, screams. The wheat mounts inexorably. His struggles weaken. At the end of the sequence one sclerotic hand sticks out above the rising surface of the grain. Then the hand, too, disappears beneath the flowing gold.

This ending is almost obligatory. The logic of *The Octopus* requires this last, crowning contrast, emphasized by the slowness of the pace and the fadeout at the end. It returns us to the conflict of the great, elemental forces: the railroad has won its battle on the purely human plane; nothing can be done for victims; but in the titanic struggle in which they have been pawns the scapegoat representing the force of the corporation is overwhelmed by the force of the wheat, which is the force of nature itself.

And at the same time, Behrman's end satisfies another compelling need. The villain must not be allowed to prosper from his misdeeds. That everyone else should suffer without his being punished would violate the fundamental law of melodrama. Also, as befits melodrama, the punishment has to be ironic; it is right that Behrman should die under the weight of the wealth he has helped accumulate.

The reader has been prepared for this crowning irony from very early on. The principle underlying the contrasts of events that determines the structure is basically an ironic one. We learn very soon that whenever anything seems to be going well for any of the characters he is merely being deluded and that new misfortune will shortly come upon him. We know what the character does not—that no matter what he does to avoid it, trouble will come.

Of course, there is nothing inherently melodramatic in such irony in itself. It frequently appears in the most respected tragedy—for example, the *Oedipus*. But in tragedy it is an aspect of the human condition and its presence is inevitable, whereas in melodrama it is present because someone has stacked the cards.

At his best, Norris is not greatly worried about credibility, and coincidence is endemic, not only in *Moran* and *A Man's Woman* but in the novels he took more seriously as well. McTeague's carrying his poor canary in its gilded cage through weather that would have killed a gamecock, Norris' extending the boundaries of the desert so that McTeague can get too far away from water, like Vanamee's not knowing—for all his supersensory powers—that the lost fiancée's daughter has been right there in the neighborhood, appear not to have disturbed him, and are unlikely to disturb a present-day reader. And one finds no disabling defect at the beginning of *The Octopus* when, to introduce his dramatis personae and finish rapidly with the exposition, he arranges for young Presley to meet practically every important character in the book, and hear all the local news, in the course of one afternoon's bicycle ride down the valley. But elsewhere he rigs the game precisely for the sake of irony. Bad news, we have noticed, always arrives *after* moments of joy or jollity. And of all the trains poor Dyke could have chosen to rob, he must fall on none other than the one carrying the Annixters home from their honeymoon. In such instances the relationship between cause and effect is, to say the least, incoherent.

Once the first excitement of reading has worn off, one wonders even if the death of S. Behrman was not contrived, also. The holds of ships are normally equipped with ladders. Behrman is not so stunned by his fall that he is unable to flounder about. Yet he does not flounder along the bulkhead, where the wheat would be less deep and where, even if blinded by dust, he would know that he could find a ladder by groping with his hands. Did Behrman truly die an ironic death, or was he, like Moran, simply murdered by his author?

Seen in the light of his most successful novel —which after all we must take *The Octopus* to be—Norris emerges as an instinctive melodramatist working with naturalist materials. The formula may be extended to describe the author of *McTeague*, and, in some degree, of *Vandover* and *The Pit*. It accounts for the nature of his successes and at the same time for his characteristic awkwardness in dealing with such problems as the elementary one created by the fact that a novelist is supposed to deal with live men and women.

In especial, women. Apart from the heroine of *Blix* (which, as an idyll, belongs to a special critical category) and Laura Jadwin in *The Pit*, his women are either kept in auxiliary roles, like Trina and the other feminine figures in *McTeague*, and presented in terms of one or two simple character traits, or else handled with extraordinary gingerliness. The reader would be at a loss to say, for example, what the "fast" Ida Wade, whom Vandover seduces, actually looks like. She is hardly more than an object for the momentary attention of Vandover. And Moran, although described much more completely, impresses much less as a human female than as a wish fulfillment.

Moran's long hair, statuesque body—she stands six feet, with broad hips and deep breasts—and blond complexion may have been meant to make her look like a seagoing Brünnhilde, and his point is clear; but in her ignorance, innocence, and sexual unawareness she seems even more a statue come to life— the Galatea of a timid erotic fantasy. As a story, *Moran of the Lady Letty* needs little more than she provides, however; complexity

of character, or depth, would make her presence inconvenient for the hurried romancer.

Hilma Tree, in *The Octopus*, has a much more important literary function: she is the young woman for whom Annixter, one of the central figures in the book, makes over his life. She is another tall, blond, and opulent woman, and more amply described than any other woman in the book. But Norris simply refuses to let the reader look at her. The dominant adjectives in the descriptions— "sane," "honest," "strong," "alert," "joyous," "robust," "vigorous," "vibrant," "exuberant"— indicate only Annixter's responses to her. Doubtless the reader is expected to respond in the same way, but his impression is more likely to be that Annixter, still eccentric, has gone off the deep end for a country wench who washes her face and knows how to milk a cow. Of Lloyd Searight, the heroine of *A Man's Woman*, there is little more to say.

But while what the critics commonly report about Norris' women is undeniable, reports on his men are easily overdone. It is true that several of his heroes run to a type: evolution has produced, if we judge by them, nothing finer than the blond, strong, somewhat prognathous, perhaps a bit dumb but never inactive Anglo-Saxon. In comparison, other races are inferior; white supremacy is axiomatic. Orientals are treacherous by nature; other foreigners can hardly be taken seriously and at times are simply comic. McTeague is a brute, but occupies a place on the evolutionary ladder on which Ross Wilbur occupies a higher rung; the latter needs only to have the social veneer worn away, and the muscular primitive beneath brought out, by a few months of buccaneering. Ward Bennett is, in Norris' eyes, the complete "man's man." Beside men like these, intellectuals and persons of advanced aesthetic taste show up badly. Even emotional sensibility seems a bit suspect: Norris is all admiration when Bennett leaves old companions to die disabled on the Arctic ice, and shows no indignation when Jadwin shrugs off the thousands who will have no bread because he has forced up the price of wheat.

Yet, especially in his later novels, a very considerable number of male characters do not conform to pattern. Aside from Jadwin himself, most of the men in *The Pit* have little of the Nordic superman about them; in *The Octopus* there are none. Annixter is a man of action when need arises, and shoots it out with the drunken cowboy Delaney when the latter tries to break up the barn dance, but as a group, he, the Derricks, and their friends are ordinary citizens. Toward the end of his life Norris may have been coming around to the idea that the common American man can be something of a hero.

Critics have been at pains to show that Norris meant to reveal, discreetly, the sexuality of his characters in such incidents as McTeague's kissing the anesthetized Trina. They are quick to concede, however, that the attempts are very discreet indeed, that at most the novelist intended only to implant the idea of sexuality in the reader's mind and leave the rest to his imagination. But, on the whole, this is not convincing. Norris shies away not only from sex, but also from most aspects of private, domestic life. One remembers only one pregnancy in his novels, that of poor Ida in *Vandover*—of course a bad thing that brings its own punishment. Among Laura Jadwin's complaints, which after several years of married life are not few, there is no mention of her being childless. One is left with the uncomfortable conclusion that these women were not real enough to have children.

In any event, the population of Norris' world is too unvaried, and perhaps his understanding of life itself was not deep enough, to permit writing the kind of social and psychological novels that Henry James has taught us to prefer. Possibly because his understanding of life itself was also melodramatic, so that he saw men and women only in melodramatic relationships, he did not feel the need. Something of the sort seems to have been his great limitation. It was only when he could bring the techniques of melodrama to deal with a subject adapted to and tolerant of the limitation that he wrote enduring work.

He had planned another "epic," which would have retold the story of Gettysburg, with one volume for each of the three days. For the ultimate judgment of his talent, it is a pity that he did not live to write it. That he was thinking of a subject that, by its nature, did not involve women suggests at least faintly that he had discovered where his bent lay. He might have suffered from the inevitable comparison with Stephen Crane, but even this would have been revealing.

Today, his novels reveal their weaknesses more strikingly than their strengths. Henry James has reformed our notion of the novel. Psychoanalysis has changed our understanding of human personality. An intervening generation of stylists and technicians—Hemingway, Wolfe, Fitzgerald, Faulkner—has given us a new respect for the word, and perhaps also a new suspicion of the word used carelessly. We have come to expect that a novel will offer us the spectacle of "ethics in action," and at the same time the vectors of stress in our ideas of social and personal morality point in totally different directions. Even the country Norris was writing about has changed beyond recognition. It follows that we cannot appreciate Norris' achievement unless by a vigorous, and sympathetic, effort of the historical imagination.

His better books insisted, by their example, that literature was a serious matter—in a time which, to judge by its recorded preferences, had not granted this point. His blend of naturalism and melodrama was, as Dreiser's career also testifies, as much as the country could take before the great expansion of tolerance in taste that came, not without resistance in many quarters, after 1918. We think today that it opened the way not only for Dreiser but for all the novelists who, without professing the naturalist faith, have needed the freedom in choice and treatment of subject that the naturalists were the first to claim.

In France and elsewhere, naturalism aimed to produce a kind of shock effect: the exposure of the animal behavior of the human animal was not expected to be accepted with tranquillity. Naturalism was working with a new dimension of humanity, and offering a new explanation of certain puzzling aspects of human behavior. Not that Norris was, by nature, animated by a desire to shock people. But the testimony of contemporary critics of *McTeague* is convincing: their genteel rejection of the novel is evidence that it did, in fact, shock. The shock had to be achieved, and its first effect dulled, before the American novel could move into the wide field it occupies today. We can measure its potential for shock by the fact that even now, in spite of our habit-induced dullness, Norris' picture of life as actually lived in a given time and place has retained some power to shock.

Meanwhile what V. L. Parrington called critical realism aimed, more or less consciouslessly, at exposing imperfections and abuses in society and in the political structure, often by making the reader identify himself with the victims. To the extent that *The Octopus* still arouses our sympathies for the wheat ranchers, even though the depredations of the railroads have long since become an academic matter, we have to call this novel a success.

And further, in spite of his penchant for melodrama, Norris' better novels played their part in substituting flesh and blood people for the myth-figures—the Sheriffs, Rangers, Cowboys, and such—in the literature of the American West. If we honor writers like Stephen Crane for their part in this achievement, we can hardly deny Norris the credit he, too, deserves.

Selected Bibliography

WORKS OF FRANK NORRIS

Yvernelle. Philadelphia: Lippincott, 1892.

Moran of the Lady Letty. New York: Doubleday and McClure, 1898.

McTeague. New York: Doubleday and McClure, 1899.

Blix. New York: Doubleday and McClure, 1899.

A Man's Woman. New York: Doubleday and McClure, 1900. (Serialized in 1899.)

The Octopus. New York: Doubleday, Page, 1901.

The Pit. New York: Doubleday, Page, 1903.

The Responsibilities of the Novelist and Other Literary Essays. New York: Doubleday, Page, 1903.

Vandover and the Brute. Garden City, N.Y.: Doubleday, Page, 1914.

Complete Edition of Frank Norris. Garden City, N.Y.: Doubleday, Doran, 1928. (Contains the works listed above, and in addition reprints Norris' short stories, Vol. IV, and journalistic writings, Vol X.)

The Letters of Frank Norris, edited by Franklin D. Walker. San Francisco: Book Club of California, 1956.

The Literary Criticism of Frank Norris, edited by Donald Pizer. Austin: University of Texas Press, 1964. (Collects, with illuminating commentary, all Norris' important criticism.)

A Novelist in the Making, edited by James D. Hart. Cambridge, Mass.: Harvard University Press, 1970. (A collection of Norris' student themes with annotated texts of *Blix* and *Vandover and the Brute,* and an indispensable introduction.)

BIBLIOGRAPHY

Lohf, Kenneth A., and Eugene P. Sheehy, comp. *Frank Norris: A Bibliography.* Los Gatos, Calif.: Talisman Press, 1959.

CRITICAL AND
BIOGRAPHICAL STUDIES

Åhnebrink, Lars. *The Beginnings of Naturalism in American Fiction.* Cambridge, Mass.: Harvard University Press, 1950.

Biencourt, Marius. *Une Influence du naturalisme français en Amérique: Frank Norris.* Paris: Giard, 1933.

Cargill, Oscar. *Intellectual America: Ideas on the March.* New York: Macmillan, 1941. Pp. 89–107.

Chase, Richard. *The American Novel and Its Tradition.* Garden City, N.Y.: Doubleday, 1957. Pp. 185–204.

Collins, Carvel. Introduction to *McTeague.* New York: Holt, Rinehart and Winston reprint, 1950.

Cooperman, Stanley. "Frank Norris and the Werewolf of Guilt," *Modern Language Quarterly,* 20:252–58 (September 1959).

Folsom, James K. "Social Darwinism or Social Protest? The 'Philosophy' of *The Octopus,*" *Modern Fiction Studies,* 8:393–400 (Winter 1962–63).

Geismar, Maxwell. *Rebels and Ancestors.* Boston: Houghton Mifflin, 1953. Pp. 3–66.

Hicks, Granville. *The Great Tradition.* New York: Macmillan, 1933. Pp. 168–75.

Howells, William Dean. "Frank Norris," *North American Review,* 175:769–78 (December 1902).

Kazin, Alfred. *On Native Grounds.* New York: Reynal and Hitchcock, 1942. Pp. 97–102.

Lynn, Kenneth S. Introduction to *The Octopus.* Boston: Houghton Mifflin (Riverside Editions reprint), 1958.

Marchand, Ernest. *Frank Norris, a Study.* Stanford, Cal.: Stanford University Press, 1942.

Millgate, Michael. *American Social Fiction: James to Cozzens.* New York: Barnes and Noble, 1964. Pp. 38–53.

Pizer, Donald. *The Novels of Frank Norris.* Bloomington: Indiana University Press, 1966.

Taylor, Walter F. *The Economic Novel in America.* Chapel Hill: University of North Carolina Press, 1942. Pp. 282–306.

Walcutt, Charles C. *American Literary Naturalism, a Divided Stream.* Minneapolis: University of Minnesota Press, 1956. Pp. 114–56.

Walker, Franklin D. *Frank Norris: A Biography.* Garden City, N.Y.: Doubleday, Doran, 1932.

—W. M. FROHOCK

Flannery O'Connor

1925-1964

ARY FLANNERY O'CONNOR was born in
Savannah, Georgia, on March 25, 1925. She
was the only child of Regina L. Cline and Edward F. O'Connor, Jr. Both families were
Roman Catholic. The Clines were a prominent
family in the state, Regina Cline's father having been mayor of Milledgeville for many
years.

Mary Flannery grew up as rather a solitary
child until she attended parochial school. She
loved pet fowl all her life. When she was five,
an aunt gave her, as a curiosity, a bantam
chicken that walked backwards, and it was this
that led to her first national celebrity. The
Pathé News people filmed little Mary O'Connor with her trained chicken, and showed the
film around the country.

In 1938 Edward O'Connor was discovered
to have disseminated lupus, an incurable
disease in which the body forms antibodies to
its own tissues. The O'Connors moved to Milledgeville, to the Cline house in the center of
town. At Peabody High School, Mary Flannery
was lively as well as studious. She wrote and
illustrated books, and in her senior year she
listed her hobby in the yearbook as "Collecting
rejection slips." Among other pets she had a
quail named Amelia Earhart and a tame
goose; she rode horseback and made Masonite
jewelry. In 1941 Edward O'Connor died. Mary

Flannery graduated from high school the next
year, and enrolled in the Women's College of
Georgia (then the Georgia State College for
Women) in Milledgeville.

At college Mary Flannery majored in English and social science; she was art editor of
the newspaper, editor of the literary quarterly,
and feature editor of the yearbook. She wrote
fiction for the literary quarterly, *The Corin-
thian*, but she thought of herself primarily as
a cartoonist. In her senior year she submitted
cartoons to the *New Yorker*, which encouraged
her but never bought any.

She was graduated with an A.B. in 1945.
One of her English teachers had submitted
some of her stories to the Writers' Workshop
of the University of Iowa, and she was
awarded a Rinehart Fellowship at the Workshop. She now came to think of herself primarily as a fiction writer. In Iowa City she
worked hard at writing, and continued to send
out stories. The first one that sold appeared in
Accent in 1946. In June of 1947 she received
the degree of Master of Fine Arts in Literature.
She stayed on at the university for another
year, then went to Yaddo, where she began
her first novel, *Wise Blood*, and later moved
to an apartment hotel in New York. Four
chapters of *Wise Blood* were published in
Mademoiselle, Sewanee Review, and *Partisan*

Review in 1948 and 1949. In New York, she became friendly with two other literary Roman Catholics, Robert and Sally Fitzgerald. When they bought a house in Ridgefield, Connecticut, in the summer of 1949, she moved out with them as their boarder, all the while continuing to work on *Wise Blood*.

Late in 1950 Flannery O'Connor became very sick; in Atlanta her ailment was diagnosed as disseminated lupus. She was pulled through with blood transfusions, and the disease was arrested with injections of a cortisone derivative, ACTH, then in the experimental stage. When Miss O'Connor was released from the hospital in the summer of 1951, she was too weak to climb stairs, so she and her mother moved to Andalusia, a dairy farm a few miles outside Milledgeville. There Mrs. O'Connor managed the farm, and Miss O'Connor, when her health improved in the fall, went back to writing, in a ground-floor room.

Wise Blood had been accepted for publication by Harcourt, Brace while Miss O'Connor was in the hospital, and it was published in 1952, to a chorus of praise and misunderstanding by some reviewers, outrage and misunderstanding by others. The daily routine at Andalusia became fixed. Flannery wrote in the mornings, then her mother drove them into Milledgeville to have the excellent lunch at the Sanford House. In the afternoons and evenings, if there were no visitors, she watched the fowl on the farm, read, or painted. The massive doses of ACTH weakened her bones; eventually her hip bones would not bear her weight. She used a cane at first, then from 1955 on she got around on aluminum crutches with arm supports.

Milledgeville liked Flannery O'Connor and was proud of her, but tended not to read her work and to be shocked and dismayed by what it did read. At least at first, many of the towns-people resented her fiction as a mockery of the Baptist and Methodist faiths. If she wanted to make fun of religion, a number of them felt, she should write about her own religion and make fun of *it*.

She kept up an extensive correspondence with a great many people, some of whom she never met. Any crank could write her and get a reply. A few of her letters have been published since her death, and they show her to have been an eloquent if often whimsical correspondent. In the same anti-intellectual spirit in which she sent Uncle Remus postcards to friends, she slipped readily into a folksy idiom: "I have done forgot," "them interleckchuls," and such.

Although Miss O'Connor disliked travel, and her crutches made it difficult to get around, she accepted all the lecture invitations that she could, even if they paid little or nothing. She always read her lectures word for word, and it is clear, now that several of them have been published, that they were very carefully composed, that they say exactly what she meant to say in exactly the words in which she meant to say it.

The special quality of her verbal humor, always delivered deadpan, is hard to describe. Perhaps it was Irish, but if so it was the corrosive Irish wit of Stephen Dedalus and his father, not the bejabers of stage Paddy. She took a sardonic pleasure in being photographed, grim and unsmiling, against the unpainted and dilapidated house of their Negro tenant farmers, and she remarked of the resulting photograph: "Looks like Sherman's just gone through." Of the Uncle Remus Museum in nearby Eatonton, the birthplace of Joel Chandler Harris, she said, "It's the only air-conditioned slave cabin in the United States." Of her trip to Lourdes: "I had the best-looking crutches in Europe." One year she gave her mother a jackass for Mother's Day, explaining it as "For the mother who has everything." She once told an interviewer that she always read "A Good Man Is Hard to Find" to college audiences because it was the only story of hers that she could read aloud "without busting out laughing."

A fair share of honors and awards came Flannery O'Connor's way during her lifetime. She received a Kenyon Review Fellowship in Fiction in 1953, and a renewal of it in 1954; a grant from the National Institute of Arts and Letters in 1957, and a grant from the Ford Foundation in 1959. Her stories won the O. Henry first prizes in 1957, 1963, and 1964. In 1962 she received an honorary Litt.D. from St. Mary's College, Notre Dame, and in 1963 a similar degree from Smith.

Early in 1964, while she was at work on an untitled third novel (a collection of stories, *A Good Man Is Hard to Find*, appeared in 1955; a second novel, *The Violent Bear It Away*, in 1960), Flannery O'Connor had to have an abdominal tumor removed. It proved benign, but the lupus became reactivated and her kidneys were affected. Miss O'Connor knew she was dying. She hoped only to finish enough stories for a book. By a marvel of the will, she did. She died early on August 3, 1964. *Everything That Rises Must Converge* appeared posthumously in 1965.

Shortly after the publication of *The Violent Bear It Away*, Flannery O'Connor wrote to Sister Mariella Gable, O.S.B., "I can wait fifty years, a hundred years, for it to be understood." Her reputation, here and abroad, was growing in the last years of her life, and greatly increased since her death. *Wise Blood* was published in France (because of the dialect a feat of translation by Maurice Coindreau) and was received as an important Existentialist novel. So far, the growing acclaim has not been accompanied by any comparable understanding of her meanings and purposes. It is toward that end that the following pages modestly aspire.

Flannery O'Connor's first novel, *Wise Blood* (1952), is a tragicomic account of the making of an anchorite in our unlikely time. The young protagonist, Hazel Motes, called "Haze" (a haze in the eyes, a mote in the eyes, a beam in the eyes?), loses his faith while in the army, and becomes an apostle of negativism. He goes from his native Eastrod (the rood in the East?), Tennessee, to a city called "Taulkinham" that is obviously Atlanta, to preach the "church of truth without Jesus Christ Crucified." He wears a preacher's bright blue suit and a preacher's fierce black hat, but the only sign he gives of his power is a mysterious "Take your hand off me" to a policeman and a truckdriver (the *Noli me tangere* of the risen Christ in John's Gospel). As a result of Haze's refusal to go along with a religion-faker who calls himself Onnie Jay Holy (and is actually named Hoover Shoats), a man is hired to dress up as Haze and replace him, and Haze eventually murders the False Prophet, his *Doppelgänger*.

Another sort of antagonist is a boy named Enoch Emery, who works as a guard at the city park, and has his own religious mystery: in fixed ritual stages he must daily have a sacramental milkshake and make suggestive remarks to the waitress, then visit the zoo animals and make obscene comments on their appearance, finally go to the museum and pay his devotions to a mummy. These are Enoch's Stations of the Cross, as we note from the pun I have italicized: "We got to *cross* this road and go down this hill. We got to go on foot," Enoch tells Haze, but he does not know why. Eventually Enoch steals the mummy, which he thinks of as "the new jesus," and presents it to Haze, who smashes it. Enoch also reads the comics "every evening like an office." Eventually he finds his religious fulfillment dressed in a stolen gorilla costume, but it is as the apostle of the mummified "new jesus" that he functions in Haze's pilgrim's progress.

There is still another false prophet, a fake blind man named Asa Hawks who pretends to have blinded himself with lime to justify his belief in Redemption. Haze puts Hawks in the role of Elijah in his new faith, and expects "a secret welcome" from him. What he gets instead is Hawks's homely little fifteen-year-old daughter, Sabbath Lily, who moves into Haze's bed, becomes the Madonna of the new jesus (she cradles the mummy in her arms, and addresses Haze as its "daddy"), and eventually turns into a monster of sexual voracity and heartlessness. She calmly watches as Haze improves on her father by *really* blinding himself with lime, then she as calmly deserts him.

The other important character in the novel, far more than a property or a symbol, is a high old rat-colored Essex automobile that Haze buys after he moves out of the room of a whore named Leora Watts. The Essex is Haze's religious mystery: It is Woman (the salesman asks him "would you like to get under and look up it?"), Ordination (Haze preaches No Jesus from its hood, as his grandfather had preached Jesus from the hood of his car in Haze's childhood), and Redemption ("Nobody with a good car needs to be justified," Haze tells Sabbath Lily, in the book's most wonderful line). Haze kills the False Prophet by running over him with the Essex, which then leaves, in a kind of Calvary sweat, "little bead-chains of water and oil and gas on the road"; when a policeman gets the Essex off the road by the simple expedient of pushing it over an embankment, Haze is left with no place to go but an inner Calvary of blindness, asceticism, and sacrificial death at the hands of the police.

The techniques for unifying this garish and diverse material include a heavy reliance on symbolism. The principal symbol that unifies (along with the mummy and the Essex) is the "wise blood" of the title. Enoch knows things "by his blood," because "He had wise blood like his daddy." He protests to Haze: "You think you got wiser blood than anybody else." Of course Haze *thinks* he has wise blood—the blood of the natural body that is his only reality—and he preaches "the church that the blood of Jesus don't foul with redemption"; but Haze, in the author's view, really *has* wise blood: the blood of his grandfather, the inherited vocation, that preaches *through him* Christ's Blood, shed to redeem.

Haze's "church of truth without Jesus Christ Crucified" is not only a body of doctrine, it is an important symbol. Here are some of its more striking tenets: "I don't say he wasn't crucified but I say it wasn't for you"; "Jesus is a trick on niggers"; "There was no Fall because there was nothing to fall from and no Redemption because there was no Fall and no Judgment because there wasn't the first two. Nothing matters but that Jesus was a liar"; "I believe in a new kind of jesus . . . one that can't waste his blood redeeming people with it, because he's all man and ain't got any God in him"; "I preach the Church Without Christ, the church peaceful and satisfied!" This is wonderfully funny, and a sharp mockery of secular rationalism, but on another level it is desperately in earnest, an indictment of the smug and secular Church today. This is made clear by a sly joke in a conversation between Haze and his landlady about his Church Without Christ: " 'Protestant?' she asked suspiciously, 'or something foreign?' He said no mam, it was Protestant."

Two principal strands of covert symbolism affirm what Haze denies. One is the oaths the characters use unconsciously. "Good Jesus," Enoch says. "My Jesus," Haze mutters, or "Sweet Jesus Christ Crucified." Sabbath Lily's explanation of why she is abandoning Haze gives us the book's deepest meaning in a brilliant pun: "She said she hadn't counted on no honest-to-Jesus blind man." The other is the rock-strewn landscape. When he was ten, Haze's guilt at seeing a naked woman in a tent show and picturing his mother in her place had led him to punish himself by walking with "stones and small rocks" in his shoes. Out driving the Essex, he sees a boulder on which is painted a call to repentance and "Jesus Saves." Later we are told: "Hazel Motes's face might have been cut out of the side of a rock" in his indifference to Enoch, and he ends the scene by throwing a rock at Enoch. Haze's duffel bag contains a Bible "that had sat like a rock in the bottom of the bag for the last few years." Blinded and chastising his flesh at the end, he lines his shoes with "gravel and broken glass and pieces of small stone." Eventually we recognize these stones, rocks, and boulders: they are tokens of the Rock, Peter's Church.

As this covert symbolism suggests, the development of the action is elaborately foreshadowed. One such motif is the general denial of Haze's denial of his vocation (from the negation of the negation, a wisdom). Hawks says "I can hear the urge for Jesus in his voice" and tells him "Some preacher has left his mark on you"; and Sabbath Lily tells Haze retrospectively, "I seen you wouldn't never have no fun or let anybody else because you didn't want nothing but Jesus!"

Haze's self-blinding is even more elaborately foreshadowed in the imagery, starting with the name "Hazel Motes," which opens the novel. Hazel dismisses Hawks as "a blind fool," and

rhetorically asks the first audience to which he preaches: "Don't I have eyes in my head? Am I a blind man?" Enoch sees the reflection of Haze's eyes in the glass of the mummy case as "like two clean bullet holes." Sabbath Lily tells her father why she likes Haze's eyes: "They don't look like they see what he's looking at but they keep on looking." When Haze drives out into the country with Sabbath Lily, the sky has "only one cloud in it, a large blinding white one with curls and a beard" (perhaps a little too patly God the Father). Haze tells Sabbath that his Essex is so superior because "It was built by people with their eyes open that knew where they were at," and by way of comment, the First Person of God turns into the Third, the Holy Ghost: "The blinding white cloud had turned into a bird with long thin wings and was disappearing in the opposite direction."

After Haze blinds himself, his landlady thinks: "Why had he destroyed his eyes and saved himself unless he had some plan, unless he saw something that he couldn't get without being blind to everything else?" At the end of the book, the landlady recognizes that she needs Haze: "If she was going to be blind when she was dead, who better to guide her than a blind man? Who better to lead the blind than the blind, who knew what it was like?" When she next sees him, he has been clubbed to death by the police. The landlady looks into his eyes "and the deep burned eye sockets seemed to lead into the dark tunnel where he had disappeared." As she stares, with her eyes shut, she sees him "moving farther and farther away, farther and farther into the darkness until he was the pin point of light" (this pinpoint of light had earlier been identified as the star over Bethlehem). Haze has been advancing "backwards to Bethlehem," in her words, and he has finally arrived there.

The organization of *Wise Blood* is thus a tight network of imagery, symbolism, and foreshadowing. The plot of the novel is much less tight, since the whole episode of Enoch and the gorilla suit is unrelated to Haze, and Enoch simply falls out of the book dressed as a gorilla. The language similarly shows that Miss O'Connor had not reached the stage of full control of her material. Some of it represents the perfect plain style of her later triumphs, but some of the tropes are so garish or elaborate as to be distracting, and thus ineffective. At one point, for example, Haze's face looks "like one of those closet doors in gangster pictures where someone is tied to a chair behind it with a towel in his mouth."

Perhaps the most remarkable thing about *Wise Blood*, in comparison with the later fiction, is its pervasive sexuality. Enoch prays to Jesus to help him escape from the woman who adopted him, and Jesus' answer to the prayer is the use of sex as aggression: "I went in her room without my pants on and pulled the sheet off her and giver a heart attact." The zoo animals that Enoch has to observe as a station of his cross represent sex as shameful: "If I had a ass like that," Enoch says prudishly of an ape, "I'd sit on it. I wouldn't be exposing it to all these people come to this park." One of the events that lead Haze to seduce Sabbath Lily involves sex as ludicrous: Leora Watts gets up one night while he is asleep and cuts "the top of his hat out in an obscene shape." Haze's sexual attachments in the novel are deeply perverse: a corrupt mother, a corrupt child, and an old Essex.

Wise Blood has been much misunderstood. If anything, the confusion was deepened in 1957, when the author printed her first public statement of her intentions, the essay "The Fiction Writer and His Country" in Granville Hick's symposium *The Living Novel*. In it Miss O'Connor writes: "For I am no disbeliever in spiritual purpose and no vague believer. I see from the standpoint of Christian orthodoxy. This means that for me the meaning of life is centered in our Redemption by Christ and that what I see in the world I see in its relation to that." Her intentions were more specifically clarified in the author's note to the second edition of *Wise Blood* in 1962, in which she describes the work as "a comic novel about a Christian *malgré lui*, and as such, very serious."

The problem is that the novel's Christian themes are put paradoxically, even negatively, the way Haze progresses to Bethlehem. One is Original Sin. In the army, Haze wants to lose his faith because he wants to escape from the knowledge of his fallen nature, "to be converted to nothing instead of to evil." He tells Hawks, "If I was in sin I was in it before I ever commited any," and he tells a waitress, "If Jesus existed, I wouldn't be clean." Another important theme is Affirmation by Blasphemy. Haze tells his sidewalk audience, "The only way to the truth is through blasphemy," and he reaffirms this doctrine against Onnie Jay Holy's principle, "If you want to get anywheres in religion, you got to keep it sweet." Haze later tells a boy at a filling station that "he had only a few days ago believed in blasphemy as the way to salvation, but that you couldn't even believe in that because then you were believing in something to blaspheme."

A third Christian theme of *Wise Blood* is Vocation. The landlady thinks of Haze, after he is blind, "He might as well be one of them monks . . . he might as well be in a monkery." Haze throws away his leftover money each month; he puts rocks in his shoes, and when the landlady asks him why, he says, "To pay," but he does not tell her what he is paying *for*, and it seems unlikely that he knows. When she discovers that he wears barbed wire around his chest, she tells him, "People have quit doing it." "They ain't quit doing it as long as I'm doing it," Haze answers. It is clear that he has founded a private monastic order, ascetic and penitential, and that the truth he formerly preached negatively he now witnesses to mutely, and will be martyred for. With no institution to channel its violence, in Miss O'Connor's view, his call can only destroy him.

Of the ten stories of *A Good Man Is Hard to Find* (1955), the three best, in my opinion, are "The Artificial Nigger," "Good Country People," and "The Displaced Person." "The Artificial Nigger" was Miss O'Connor's own favorite, and it makes impressive claims to be considered her best story. It tells of two backwoods Georgians, an old man named Mr. Head and his grandson Nelson, who go to the terrifying city for Nelson's first visit. The action of the story is their estrangement and reconciliation, but it is a readjustment as profound as that of the Conroys of Joyce's "The Dead." Nelson has never seen a Negro before, and the preliminary events of the story are encounters with real Negroes—first a huge Negro man on the train, wearing a yellow satin tie with a ruby stickpin, then an enormous Negro woman they meet on the street, whom Nelson inexplicably wants to hold him and mother him.

The dramatic crisis in the story is Nelson's running into an elderly white woman on the street, knocking her down and scattering her groceries. Mr. Head panics and re-enacts Peter's denial: " 'This is not my boy,' he said, 'I never seen him before.' " Nelson's subsequent hatred and contempt, and Mr. Head's guilt and shame, are wonderfully funny and moving, profoundly true and beautiful. Their reconciliation comes when they see, decorating a lawn, a shabby plaster statue of a Negro eating a watermelon. In the same voice, each exclaims: "An artificial nigger!" This communion transforms them magically, and they ex-change identities: "Mr. Head looked like an ancient child and Nelson like a miniature old man." The artificial Negro is God's grace: "They could both feel it dissolving their differences like an action of mercy." Mr. Head has a moment of true repentance and charity, he and the boy are united in love, and the story is over.

The protagonist of "Good Country People" is the author's cruelest self-caricature: Joy Hopewell, hulking, thirty-two, a learned Doctor of Philosophy. She has an artificial leg as a result of a hunting accident, she has changed her name legally from Joy to Hulga, she wears a yellow sweat shirt with a picture of a cowboy on a horse, and she is an atheist. When a simple-seeming country boy appears selling Bibles, she sets out to seduce him, and she appears for their date (in a perfect touch) wearing Vapex on the collar of her shirt, "since she did not own any perfume."

The Bible salesman appears to be another Hazel Motes, wearing the same bright blue suit and wide-brimmed hat, and protesting "I'm just a country boy." He turns out to be the False Prophet instead: when they are alone in the barn loft he reveals that his hollow Bible contains a flask of whiskey, a pack of pornographic playing cards, and a package of condoms. "You ain't so smart," he tells Joy-Hulga as he disappears down the loft trapdoor with her artificial leg, "I been believing in nothing ever since I was born!" It is the exposure of a fake Christian, but more significantly it is the exposure of a fake atheist, her intellectual pride and superiority revealed to be only ignorance and gullibility. Unfortunately, the story does not end where it should, with the symbolic defloration of the theft of the leg and the Bible salesman's reproof, but goes on for two paragraphs of superfluous irony.

"The Displaced Person" is the longest and most ambitious story in the book. In it a Polish

Catholic refugee, Mr. Guizac, comes to work for Protestant Mrs. McIntyre, a widow who runs a dairy farm. He is the displaced person, but in the course of the complex tragic action, Mr. Shortley, the native hired man, becomes a displaced person when Mrs. McIntyre fires him, Mrs. Shortley becomes a displaced person when she dies of a stroke as they depart, Mr. Guizac becomes further displaced when the rehired Mr. Shortley carelessly allows a tractor to run over his spine, and Mrs. McIntyre herself becomes a displaced person at the end, collapsed, bedridden, and alone.

None of these melodramatic events, however, is the significant action of the story. The central figure in the story is a peacock, who enters in the first sentence, following Mrs. Shortley up the road, and exits in the last, when the priest feeds him bread crumbs on his weekly visit to instruct the bedridden Mrs. McIntyre in the doctrines of his Church. The peacock is a traditional symbol of Christ's divinity and the Resurrection. In the story he functions as a kind of spiritual test: Mrs. Shortley never notices him; Mrs. McIntyre sees him only as "another mouth to feed"; her husband the late Judge had kept peacocks because "they made him feel rich"; the priest is overwhelmed by the peacock's beauty, and says of the spread tail, "Christ will come like that!"

As the peacock symbolizes Christ's divine nature, so the displaced person symbolizes His human nature. In the story's key conversation, Mrs. McIntyre says, in reference to Mr. Guizac, "He didn't have to come in the first place," and the absent-minded old priest, mistaking her reference, answers, "He came to redeem us." Later, annoyed with all the religious talk, Mrs. McIntyre says indignantly to the priest, "As far as I'm concerned, Christ was just another D. P." But Mr. Guizac does more than embody Christ as he is displaced, suffers, and is slain. "That man is my salvation," Mrs.

McIntyre had said earlier, in praise of Mr. Guizac's hard work, and the remark has Miss O'Connor's usual double meaning. "I am not responsible for the world's misery," Mrs. McIntyre tells Mr. Guizac later. But his death, in which they are all equally guilty, is redemptive for her insofar as it abases her pride and prepares her to accept the burden of the world's misery.

The other stories in the book are less impressive. The title story, "A Good Man Is Hard to Find," is a melodrama about a family casually wiped out by an escaped criminal called the Misfit, and in spots it is cruelly funny. "The River" is about a young boy who finds a symbolic baptism in drowning. Like *Wise Blood*, it relies heavily on the ironic use of profanity: "Well then for Christ's sake fix him," Harry's father says to the woman taking care of him, who does just that; "Healed of what for Christ's sake?" Harry's mother asks, unaware that the question contains its answer. The story is a little too pat, however, and the empty secular life of the parents is an unconvincing travesty. "The Life You Save May Be Your Own" is a slice of Tobacco Road, redeemed by Mr. Shiftlet's automobilolatry (the car represents an ideal marriage to him, as to Hazel Motes, and his destination is significantly "Mobile") and by a superb comic ending.

"A Stroke of Good Fortune" is the one markedly unsuccessful story in the book, a leaden tract against complacency and contraception. "A Temple of the Holy Ghost" is a portrait of the artist as a sardonic twelve-year-old girl, a Roman Catholic among rustics who identify Latin hymns as "Jew singing." "A Circle in the Fire" does not quite bring off its terror, but it has one moment of magnificent empathy, when the young girl sees the naked boys bathing in the woods, and thinks, not of how they look, but of how they *see*: "The trees must have looked like green waterfalls through his wet glasses." It is just this empathy that is lacking at the end, when she looks at her mother's face and sees it "as if it might have belonged to anybody, a Negro or a European or to Powell himself." Mrs. Cope has become a displaced person like Mrs. McIntyre, but she is never seen from inside as the boy Powell is. The remaining story, "A Late Encounter with the Enemy," is sharply satiric, of the deviled corsages of Hollywood as of the South's Confederacy cult, but it rises to distinction only in the incongruous final tableau: the old general's corpse sitting in the Coca-Cola line.

Her second novel, *The Violent Bear It Away* (1960), is Miss O'Connor's masterpiece. It tells the terrible initiation of a reluctant prophet. The adolescent protagonist is Francis Marion Tarwater (his name is as richly symbolic as Hazel Motes's: Francis Marion is the "old swamp fox" of the Revolutionary War, tarwater is a discredited folk cure-all). He is recognizable by the author's usual sign of election, Jesus' *Noli me tangere*, early in the book. When the old Negro, Buford Munson, finds young Tarwater drunk and his great-uncle dead, Buford says, "He was deep in Jesus' misery," and young Tarwater replies, "Nigger . . . take your hand off me." The great-uncle, Mason Tarwater, was a mad prophet who made his living distilling bootleg whiskey, and kept "worthless black game bantams" as the old Judge kept worthless peacocks. The secular antagonist, George F. Rayber (raper?), young Tarwater's uncle and old Tarwater's nephew, is an ambiguous figure. He is Satanic, taking on, "like the devil," any look that suited him, but he is a *monk* of Satan, controlling the family curse of violence and madness in his blood ("he was the stuff of which fanatics and madmen are made") by "a rigid ascetic discipline," by rationality and good works. His

mad barefoot pursuit of young Tarwater through the streets of the town is a penitential pilgrimage; more than Tarwarter, Rayber looks "like a fanatical country preacher," and young Tarwater tells him perceptively (my italics): "It's *you* the seed fell in."

Rayber's idiot son, Bishop, is less a character than a sacrament: young Tarwater has been commanded by his great-uncle to begin his ministry by baptizing Bishop, and when he has the opportunity he compulsively baptizes and drowns him. The novel's other important character is Satan. He first appears as a skeptical voice in young Tarwater's drunken head, then as a vision of a friendly stranger in a panama hat; he returns as a voice to direct the drowning of Bishop; he appears in the flesh at the end of the novel to drug and rape young Tarwater in the final stage of his initiation into deranged prophecy.

The Violent, like *Wise Blood*, is tightly unified by symbolism. The principal unifying symbol is burning. Evils "come from the Lord and burn the prophet clean," old Tarwater had told the boy; "even the mercy of the Lord burns." Young Tarwater imagines his return to the city after he receives his prophetic call, when "he would return with fire in his eyes." Old Tarwater once wrote a warning to Rayber: "THE PROPHET I RAISE UP OUT OF THIS BOY WILL BURN YOUR EYES CLEAN." After the old man's death, Tarwater burns their shack, intending to cremate the corpse in defiance of old Tarwater's fervent wish to be buried to await the Resurrection. On his way to the city, young Tarwater takes the glow of its lights to be the fire he set (a foreshadowing of his eventual return as a prophet). His eyes appear to Rayber to be "singed with guilt." (They foreshadow his madness, as Haze's eyes foreshadow his blindness.) A girl evangelist challenges Rayber as a damned soul and says, "The Word of God is a burning Word to burn you clean!" Young Tarwater burns himself clean in a secular sense after the rape by firing the woods where it occurred, but he has been burned clean in his great-uncle's sense, too: his "scorched eyes" now look "as if, touched with a coal like the lips of the prophet, they would never be used for ordinary sights again." He then sets fire to his own woods, sees the fire he has set as the expected sign over his great-uncle's grave, "the burning bush," and hears God's command: "GO WARN THE CHILDREN OF GOD OF THE TERRIBLE SPEED OF MERCY." He sets his "singed eyes," in the book's last sentence, "toward the dark city, where the children of God lay sleeping." He is finally a prophet, and a madman.

A second important symbol, balancing judgment with mercy, is spiritual feeding. When old Tarwater got into his coffin to try it on for size, the boy saw "nothing showing but his stomach which rose over the top like overleavened bread." The bread symbolized by the old man's belly is "the bread of life," Jesus, and young Tarwater decides that he is "not hungry for the bread of life." But when Rayber, in pursuing him through the city, sees him staring obsessively at a loaf of bread in a bakery window, Rayber thinks characteristically, "If he had eaten his dinner, he wouldn't be hungry." Young Tarwater tells a truckdriver who gives him a lift that he is hungry for real food; "I ain't hungry for the bread of life." Later he drinks the stranger's drugged liquor and remarks: "It's better than the Bread of Life!" Standing over his great-uncle's grave at the end, he has a vision of Mason Tarwater on the banks of the Lake of Galilee, eating the multiplied loaves and fishes, and he is "aware at last of the object of his hunger, aware that it was the same as the old man's and that nothing on earth would fill him." (As the old man's belly is the bread, his eyes are the fishes: "silver protruding eyes that looked like two fish straining to get out of a net of red threads"; "mad fish-colored eyes.")

The other important symbol in *The Violent Bear It Away* is Bishop, the holy idiot. Bishop's habitual toy is a trashbasket with a rock in it. He is able to make peanut butter sandwiches "though sometimes he put the bread inside." At one point Rayber realizes that young Tarwater is looking at Bishop but seeing "only a spot of light." These are all symbols we have noted before: Peter's Rock, the living Bread, the Star of Bethlehem. The woman who runs the resort where the murderous baptism occurs makes Bishop's sacramental nature explicit. When Tarwater drives Bishop away for touching him, she reproves Tarwater, "Mind how you talk to one of them there," and glares at him fiercely, "as if he had profaned the holy."

The structure of foreshadowing is more economical than that of *Wise Blood* and no less effective. Old Tarwater had warned his grand-nephew of the special dangers incurred by prophets: " 'You are the kind of boy,' the old man said, 'that the devil is always going to be offering to assist, to give you a smoke or a drink or a ride, and to ask you your bidnis. You had better mind how you take up with strangers.' " A salesman predicts of Tarwater, "He won't come to no good end." Rayber takes Tarwater back to Tennessee because "He saw no way of curing him except perhaps through some shock." Everything unfolds as prophesied: the devil gives Tarwater a ride, the shock cures, the cure is a no good end, at least in the world's eyes. Unlike that of *Wise Blood*, the narrative structure of *The Violent* is perfectly shaped; there are no loose ends like Enoch Emery. Here is *The Violent*'s magnificent first sentence: "Francis Marion Tarwater's uncle had been dead for only half a day when the boy got too drunk to finish digging his grave and a Negro named Buford Munson, who had come to get a jug filled, had to finish it and drag the body from the breakfast table where it was still sitting and bury it in a decent and Christian way, with the sign of its Saviour at the head of the grave and enough dirt on top to keep the dogs from digging it up." The novel unfolds the motifs of the opening sentence inexorably, from this first drunkenness to the final drugged drunkenness and transformation. Even the sodomic rape, not much appreciated by the reviewers, is right and inevitable: it is at once the ultimate violation of the untouchable anointed of the Lord, a naturalistic explanation for the shaman's spirit possession, and a shocking and effective metaphor for seizure by divine purpose. (Yeats makes a similar use of rape in "Leda and the Swan.")

The book's language is sparse and functional. Old Tarwater's instructions for his burial read like the best Twain ("Get two boards and set them down the steps and start me rolling and dig where I stop and don't let me roll over into it until it's deep enough"). The tropes, however imaginative, are for the most part economical and functional; for example, "The words were as silent as seeds opening one at a time in his blood." Even a few far-fetched ones, such as Rayber's eyes looking "like something human trapped in a switch box," seem to justify themselves.

Finally there is the problem of the book's meaning. The chief clue is the title epigraph, Matthew 11:12, printed in very large type across the double title page: "From the days of John the Baptist until now, the kingdom of heaven suffereth violence, and the violent bear it away." This has been widely misinterpreted. The Authorized Version translates the last clause "and the violent take it by force," and the New English Bible reads "and violent men are seizing it." Its clear meaning is that the violent are enemies of the kingdom, capturing it from the righteous, as a sign of the imminent coming

of the Messiah, the Christ. In this sense the Tarwaters are mad fanatics carrying away the kingdom from its lukewarm heirs, and Rayber is an equally mad fanatic preaching secular salvation. Rayber sees himself "divided in two—a violent and a rational self." Violence and madness are the curse in the family's blood, but Rayber succeeds in controlling them. The effect of the novel's events on young Tarwater is to extirpate the rational self instead, to burn away all reason and leave him entirely violent and mad.

It is in this extreme sense that young Tarwater is an allegory of the Church, which must lose the world to save it. Where *Wise Blood* is about Vocation along with several other mysteries, *The Violent* is wholly and centrally about Vocation and the prophet's necessary stage of resistance to Vocation (from Moses' pleading his speech defect to Jonah's taking flight). When old Tarwater said that if he died without baptizing Bishop, the baptism of Bishop would be "the first mission the Lord sends you," "the boy doubted very much that his first mission would be to baptize a dim-witted child." When his great-uncle tells of their freedom, young Tarwater feels "a slow warm rising resentment that this freedom had to be connected with Jesus and that Jesus had to be the Lord."

The analogy with Bible prophets is made again and again: "The old man compared their situation to that of Elijah and Elisha"; persecuted by Rayber, the old man is simultaneously "Jonah, Ezekiel, Daniel, he was at that moment all of them—the swallowed, the lowered, the enclosed"; arriving at Rayber's house, young Tarwater is similarly transformed: "His whole body felt hollow as if he had been lifted like Habakkuk by the hair of his head, borne swiftly through the night and set down in the place of his mission." When young Tarwater realizes his mission regarding Bishop, "He did not look into the eyes of any fiery beast or see a burning bush. He only knew, with a certainty sunk in despair, that he was expected to baptize the child he saw and begin the life his great-uncle had prepared him for."

In the book's boldest image, repeated after the drowning of Bishop, young Tarwater pictures himself "trudging into the distance in the bleeding stinking mad shadow of Jesus." He tirelessly insists to Rayber, of his great-uncle, "He ain't had no effect on me." The stranger's voice assures young Tarwater that he has not been called or received a sign, that all he feels are sensations, whereas Jonah's three days in the belly of the fish, "That was a sign; it wasn't no sensation." "The Lord speaks to prophets personally," the stranger adds, "and He's never spoke to you." But slowly, relentlessly, through denial and burning, murder and rape, Tarwater hears his call and responds, and in his madness he will preach the truth. Man is both vessel and instrument of divine purpose, and divine purpose is not answerable to human reason.

In *Everything That Rises Must Converge* (1965), the finest of the stories, to my taste, and the one least like anything Miss O'Connor (or anyone else) has done before, is "Parker's Back," the last story she wrote before her death. It tells of a young man named O. E. Parker whose only distinction is a passion for having himself elaborately tattooed. In what he believes is an accommodation to his wife's Fundamentalist piety, Parker has a Byzantine mosaic of a staring Christ reproduced on his back. He is then literally *christophoros*, Christ-bearing, "witnessing for Jesus" on his hide. Under this coloration Parker is transformed and reborn, resuming the Old Testament prophet names, Obadiah Elihue, that he has always concealed behind his initials, and suffering a Punch and Judy martyr-

dom as he passively allows his wife to punish his "idolatry" by beating him with a broom until "large welts had formed on the face of the tattooed Christ." The story is simultaneously uproarious and deeply moving, and the metaphor of tattooing—bloody, painful, indelible; garish, out of fashion, ludicrous—for the burden of Redemption is uncanny and perfect, a truly metaphysical conceit.

A long and ambitious story, "The Lame Shall Enter First," is impressive in a more familiar fashion. It is another look at the trio of Rayber, Bishop, and young Tarwater (in fact, according to Robert Fitzgerald's introduction to *Everything That Rises*, it uses material cut from *The Violent*). Superficially, the story is pathetic sociology: a well-meaning but unimaginative widower, Sheppard, neglects his son Norton, mainly because an older boy, Rufus Johnson, clubfooted and criminal, seems much more in need of help; the consequence is Norton's suicide. On a more perceptive level, Rufus is not a poor deprived cripple, but evil, demonic, a type of Satan; and Sheppard learns the reality of these entities to his cost. (This is Fitzgerald's reading in the introduction, encouraged by the statement in the story that finally Sheppard "saw the clear-eyed Devil, the sounder of hearts, leering at him from the eyes of Johnson.") But this is Sheppard's interpretation, not the author's. Miss O'Connor's own reading, I believe, is consistent with her radical Christian dualism and far more challenging: not Rufus but *Sheppard* is the type of Satan, taking over God's prerogatives in His assumed absence; and Rufus is the true prophetic voice of Judgment, saying of Sheppard "He thinks he's Jesus Christ!" and challenging him, "Satan has you in his power." (This is the reading of Sister Rose Alice, in "Flannery O'Connor: Poet to the Outcast," in which she paraphrases the story's action as "The repulsive good defeats the urbane evil.")

The third triumph in the book is "The Enduring Chill," a devastatingly funny, if ultimately serious, story of a pretentious young man whose dramatic coming home to die turns out bady. The story mows down its targets with general ruthlessness: the Church is wickedly satirized in a scatterbrained and irascible old priest, blind in one eye and deaf in one ear; such secular "experience of communion" as racial integration comes off no better. The symbols are masterly. When Asbury, the romantic invalid, turns his head away in irritation from his mother's talk about the dairy herd, he confronts "a small, wall-eyed Guernsey . . . watching him steadily as if she sensed some bond between them." When he gets up to his room, there is a water stain on the ceiling that looks like "a fierce bird with spread wing," with "an icicle crosswise in his beak." In the comic ending, the bond between Asbury and the wall-eyed Guernsey is the discovery, by the local doctor Asbury despises, that his supposedly fatal disease is only undulant fever, caught from drinking unpasteurized milk; in the apocalyptic ending that follows the comedy, the fierce bird on the ceiling is discovered to be the Holy Ghost, "emblazoned in ice instead of fire," and, implacably, that terribly swift mercy descends upon him.

The other stories are less impressive or are flawed in some fashion. The title story, "Everything That Rises Must Converge," has a fine ending, Julian's "entry into the world of guilt and sorrow" when his mother has a stroke occasioned by a Negro woman who rose and converged with her. It is beautifully foreshadowed from the story's first sentence, but the characters, a travesty segregationist mother and a travesty integrationist son, are not adequate to the finely structured action. "Greenleaf" takes another look at the widow running a dairy farm. Here she is Mrs. May, " good Christian woman with a large respect for religion, though she did not, of course, believe any of it was true." Her punishment is undergoing a rather Freudian Dionysiac mystery in which a scrub bull, "like some patient god come down to woo her," gores her to death "like a wild tormented lover." Unfortunately, the two worlds of Bacchic ecstasy and regional satire in the story coexist uneasily. "A View of the Woods" is a perfect comic story about a conflict between a grandfather and a nine-year-old grandmother just like him, up to its natural ending after the first paragraph on page 80; then it falls into the unnecessary multiple death of Jacobean drama. The melodramatic "The Comforts of Home" travesties Miss O'Connor's familiar triad of parent-child-intruder, and is the one story in the book that seems to me a mistake from the beginning. "Revelation" is a marvelously funny apocalypse for the Laodiceans that goes on too long. "Judgement Day" is a reworking, shortly before Miss O'Connor's death, of an old story first written at Iowa in 1946, and is thus the only story in the book set outside Georgia. It is a magical and compelling account of the death and symbolic resurrection of an old Georgia man in New York City, made resonant by the author's sense of her own imminent death; only the Negro characters in it (perhaps part of the early material) fail to ring true.

In all her writing, Flannery O'Connor has certain preoccupations that seem almost obsessional. A few simple images recur so strikingly that every reader notices them: the flaming suns, the mutilated eyes, the "Jesus-seeing" hats, the colorful shirts. These images may be obsessive with the author, but they are used organically in the fiction. The sun in "A Circle in the Fire" is a symbol and specific foreshadowing of the boys' incendiary threat: "It was swollen and flame-colored and hung in a net of ragged cloud as if it might burn through any second and fall into the woods." The sunset in "Greenleaf" is another "swollen red ball," but as Mrs. May watches, "it began to narrow and pale until it looked like a bullet." It is narrow and pale to resemble the moon, since the bull first appeared to woo Mrs. May "silvered in the moonlight"; it looks like a bullet because the bull will soon come like a streak to penetrate her body, bull-bullet indeed.

A few recurrent symbols are more complex than these. One is the young preacher in bright blue suit and stern black hat. His principal embodiments are Hazel Motes and the False Prophet in *Wise Blood*, and the Bible salesman in "Good Country People," but we see traces of him everywhere: the bright blue suit on the preacher who introduces the girl evangelist who tells Rayber that he is a damned soul in *The Violent*; the stern black hat on the old man in "Judgement Day." These are not simply a uniform, but emblems: the blue suit glares with raw Fundamentalist fervor, the black hat represents what the old man's daughter dismisses as "a lot of hardshell Baptist hooey." The False Prophet dresses like Haze to steal his mission, but as a consequence of the transformation he dies an exemplary Christian death, confessing his sins and calling out "Jesus help me"; the Bible salesman disguises himself to cheat the gullible, but instead he is instrumental in bringing Joy-Hulga to the beginnings of humility in humiliation.

The peacock is another complex symbol. It is central in "The Displaced Person," but it appears in many places: the innocent deaf girl in "The Life You Save May Be Your Own" has "eyes as blue as a peacock's neck," and learns to say only one word, "bird"; Joy-Hulga is "as sensitive about the artificial leg as a peacock about his tail"; the little girl in *The Violent* preaches "Silver and gold and peacock tails, a thousand suns in a peacock's tail," and

Rayber thinks of her as "one of those birds blinded to make it sing more sweetly." As the peacock was a personal image of the Second Coming for the old priest and of wealth for the old Judge in "The Displaced Person," so it seems to have been a personal image of freedom and beauty (that is of *art*) for Miss O'Connor. In an article, "Living with a Peacock," in *Holiday*, Miss O'Connor wrote: "My frenzy said: I want so many of them that every time I go out the door I'll run into one." Of this abundance, which in another aspect is God's grace, the deaf girl has only the useless beauty, Joy-Hulga only the vulnerability.

Another complex symbol can only be called, in acknowledgment of Miss O'Connor's debt, Georgia Snopesism. It is principally embodied in two families, the Shortleys in "The Displaced Person" and the Greenleafs in "Greenleaf," but there is much more than a touch of it in the Pritchards in "A Circle in the Fire" and the Freemans who are the "good country people" of the story of that title. These families of tenant farmers usually include a man who is stupid, incompetent, and malevolent; a wife with "a special fondness for the details of secret infections, hidden deformities, assaults upon children"; and two or more mindless and voracious children. More than any other figures in Miss O'Connor's work, these Snopes families are social, even class, symbols (as are their Mississippi counterparts in Faulkner). They represent the southern poor white class seen as intrinsically vicious. In the stories, they murder Mr. Guizac and let the bull gore Mrs. May; in our newspapers, they have other victims.

As this suggests, not only do images and symbols recur, but fixed groupings of people recur, and certain figures in these fixed groups are consistently travestied. Fitzgerald's introduction to *Everything That Rises* refers to what he calls the "family resemblance" shown by many of the characters in the stories and novels, but this is less a matter of recurrent figures than of recurrent relationships. One is the duo of practical mother and dreamy child on a dairy farm. In "A Circle in the Fire" they are a "very small and trim" woman and a "pale fat girl of twelve"; in "Good Country People" they are a mother who "had no bad qualities of her own but she was able to use other people's in such a constructive way that she never felt the lack," and Joy-Hulga; and so on. This mother and daughter are complementary in a curious fashion: each is caricatured as seen by the other, the resourceful widow as smug and empty, the arty child as useless and affected. In the later stories of *Everything That Rises*, this pairing is varied. Mrs. May in "Greenleaf" has two sons, of whom only the younger is an intellectual, although the older manages to be equally unsatisfactory: he sells insurance, but it is "the kind that only Negroes buy." Mrs. Fox in "The Enduring Chill" similarly has two children, who between them compose the familiar character: Asbury has the artistic pretensions, his sister Mary George the scathing tongue. This last splitting is repeated in the fragment of the unfinished novel published in *Esquire* as "Why Do the Heathens Rage?"

A relationship that does not involve mutual travesty is one between a boy and his mother's brother or father. The first of these is Haze and his grandfather, the circuit preacher. In "The Artificial Nigger" this pair becomes Mr. Head and his daughter's son Nelson; in *The Violent* we get the complexity of young Tarwater and his mother's brother Rayber, Rayber and *his* mother's brother old Tarwater, with the two Tarwaters in the duplicated magical relation of mother's brother of a mother's brother to sister's son of a sister's son. In "A View of the Woods," the pairing becomes mother's father and *girl*. In "The Lame Shall Enter First," Rufus Johnson lives with his crazy grandfather (presumably his mother's father), until the old man goes off "with a remnant to the hills," to prepare against the destruction of the world by fiery flood. The point of this relationship is that the grandfather or uncle is the true father, and the grandson or nephew (however he resists it) is the true heir. This replacement of the father as authority by the mother's brother or father would be natural enough in the writing of an author whose father died in her childhood, but before settling for an autobiographical cause here we should notice that the mother's brother rather than the father as family authority is an important feature of primitive matriliny, and thus of much of our most resonant myth and legend.

The third set of characters is the trio of parent, child, and wolf cub, first exemplified by Rayber, Bishop, and young Tarwater in *The Violent*. We see it again in "The Lame Shall Enter First," with Sheppard, Norton, and Rufus Johnson, and less satisfactorily in "The Comforts of Home," with Thomas' mother, Thomas, and Star, the nymphomaniac girl the mother brings home. Travesty consistently accompanies this grouping, too, but here parent and child do not judge each other, but are both judged harshly by the outsider. Through Tarwater's eyes, we see Rayber as a blind fool and Bishop as a worthless idiot; through Rufus' eyes we see Sheppard as a blasphemous dogooder and Norton as a spiritless nonentity. This is not so neat in "The Comforts of Home," since "Star Drake" is too preposterous a character to judge anyone; essentially, there we see the absurd gullibility of Thomas' mother's absolute faith in human goodness through his eyes, and we similarly reject Thomas' absolute lack of charity as evidenced by his behavior.

Half a dozen important themes run through all Miss O'Connor's work. One is a profound equation of the mysteries of sex and religion. When young Hazel Motes sees the naked woman at the carnival, his mother tells him "Jesus died to redeem you" as she switches him, and the two guilty mysteries merge inextricably in his mind. As the title of "A Temple of the Holy Ghost" (a Christian metaphor for the body) makes clear, the story is centrally concerned with this equation. The twelve-year-old girl protagonist is initiated into sexual mystery by her older cousins, who tell her of the hermaphrodite they saw at the carnival; at the same time she imagines herself a Christian martyr in a Roman arena; when the sun goes down "like an elevated Host drenched in blood" to end the story, it is the blood of menstruation and childbirth as well as of martyrdom and Christ's Passion. The neatest of these sex-religion equations is Mrs. McIntyre's reaction, in "The Displaced Person," to the priest's own equation of Christ and the peacock's tail: "Mrs. McIntyre's face assumed a set puritanical expression and she reddened. Christ in the conversation embarrassed her the way sex had her mother."

Another recurrent theme is change of identity, transformation, death-and-rebirth. Parker in "Parker's Back" is transformed by the tattoo, but most often in the fiction transformation occurs by renaming. Harry Ashfield becomes Bevel, who counts, in "The River"; Joy chooses a way of life by becoming Hulga in "Good Country People"; Hoover Shoats transforms himself into Onnie Jay Holy to run a fake religious radio program called "Soulsease"; Rayber tries to remake young Tarwater by calling him "Frankie"; even Parker needs a baptismal name change from O. E. to Obadiah Elihue to be fully transformed.

A theme of great power in the work is what might be called the perverse mother. When Leora Watts first goes to bed with Hazel Motes, she tickles his chin "in a motherly way," calls him "son," and calls herself "Momma." The mummy in the novel is not only a mock Christ child but a pun on "mommy," as a Freudian would guess from its place as the ultimate revelation of Enoch's Mystery cult. (This guess is supported in "Everything That Rises Must Converge" by Julian's picture of his mother, "shrunken to the dwarf-like proportions of her mortal nature, sitting like a mummy.") Here are Joy-Hulga and the Bible salesman seducing each other in the barn loft: "His breath was clear and sweet like a child's and the kisses were sticky like a child's. He mumbled about loving her and about knowing when he first seen her that he loved her, but the mumbling was like the sleepy fretting of a child being put to sleep by his mother." Norton in "The Lame Shall Enter First" finds his dead mother in the sky through a telescope, but the only mother he finds in reality is death by hanging. Parker's mother "would not pay for any tattoo except her name on a heart, which he had put on, grumbling." Tarwater's mother, like Rayber's, was a whore, or so both Tarwaters are pleased to affirm.

Miss O'Connor's principal theme is what Walter Allen in *Esprit* excellently calls "a world of the God-intoxicated," pointing out that Rayber in his denial is as much intoxicated by God as are the Tarwaters. Miss O'Connor's male characters are God-intoxicated in a variety of ways. Those who have found their calling as preachers articulate the author's radical dualism. The preacher in "The River" challenges: "Believe Jesus or the devil! . . . Testify to one or the other!" Old Tarwater (and, we assume, Haze's grandfather) similarly rejects everything not Christ as anti-Christ. We see a youthful version of this figure in Rufus Johnson. Rejecting salvation from Sheppard, Rufus hisses: "Nobody can save me but Jesus." "If I do repent, I'll be a preacher," he says. "If you're going to do it, it's no sense in doing it half way." Sheppard sees him as "a small black figure on the threshold of some dark apocalypse." Rufus may continue to choose the devil, as Haze tried to do, or he may yet accept the call, as young Tarwater eventually does. The mark of election, the *Noli me tangere*, is on all three, but they are free to choose whether to preach the Word or, like Parker, mutely to witness it on their flesh.

One way that intoxication with God expresses itself, in short, is Satanism. The Misfit in "A Good Man Is Hard to Find" is a ruthless killer because "Jesus thown everything off balance." The Misfit preaches the same radical Christian dualism from a different pulpit: "If He did what He said, then it's nothing for you to do but throw away everything and follow Him, and if He didn't, then it's nothing for you to do but enjoy the few minutes you got left the best way you can—by killing somebody or burning down his house or doing some other meanness to him. No pleasure but meanness." The Misfit has chosen the second alternative, but he admits at the end of the story, after wiping out the harmless family, "It's no real pleasure in life." Rufus lies and steals, he tells Sheppard, because "Satan . . . has me in his power," and in the course of the story he succeeds in converting Norton to Satanism (and thus to suicide), since, as Sheppard recognizes (in the story's central irony) but cannot understand, "The boy would rather be in hell than nowhere."

Another form God-intoxication paradoxically takes is Rationalism. The first of these antagonists in Miss O'Connor's work is the enigmatic figure of Mr. Paradise in "The River," who comes to the healings to mock and to display his unhealed cancerous ear, but who always comes. He is a curious ritual figure, the ceremonial scoffer, the Bishop of Misrule, and his shepherd's crook as mock-pastor is the giant peppermint stick with which he tries to save Harry from his death. Rayber is a fuller treatment of the same figure. He, too,

is a mock-pastor (he named his son "Bishop"), and when old Tarwater baptized young Tarwater as a baby, Rayber then blasphemously baptized him a second time on the buttocks. Rayber has a catcher-in-the-rye "vision of himself moving like an avenging angel through the world, gathering up all the children that the Lord, not Herod, had slain," its Eden "some enclosed garden . . . where he would gather all the exploited children of the world and let the sunshine flood their minds." Rayber turns off the girl evangelist's indictment by turning off his hearing aid, but in his case we know, thanks to analyses by young Tarwater and by the author, that he is not deaf to Christianity but so responsive to it that all his positions are counter-positions. Rayber's views caricature enlightened secular humanism by being stated as the negatives of Christian dogma, thus: "The great dignity of man," he tells young Tarwater, "is his ability to say: I am born once and no more."

If the male characters are all God-intoxicated, the female characters in Flannery O'Connor's fiction are mainly self-intoxicated. Smugness and self-satisfaction, often represented by women, is another important theme. Here is Mrs. Cope in "A Circle in the Fire" talking to Mrs. Pritchard: " 'Every day I say a prayer of thanksgiving,' Mrs. Cope said. 'Think of all we have. Lord,' she said and sighed, 'we have everything.' " The hoodlum boys who bring her to judgment state the truth she has forgotten: "Man, Gawd owns them woods and her too." Mrs. Cope, reciting all they have to be thankful for, "a litany of her blessings," becomes the monstrous comic figure of Mrs. Turpin in "Revelation." When she proclaims in the doctor's waiting room, "Thank you, Jesus, for making everything the way it is!" the Wellesley girl springs at her throat with a howl, throws a fit on the floor, and cries a revelation out of it, "Go back to hell where you came from, you old wart hog." This is a symbolic equivalent to the boys' judgment of Mrs. Cope, as the vision in which Mrs. Turpin sees the good Christians like herself in a hellfire in which "even their virtues were being burned away" is a symbolic equivalent to the boys' firing Mrs. Cope's woods.

In Flannery O'Connor's moral universe, in short, Hazel Motes may have backed himself into heaven, but fat Mrs. Turpin seems destined for hell. This dualism relates to another theme, the transvaluation of values in which progress in the world is retrogression in the spirit. When Mr. Shiftlet in "The Life You Save May Be Your Own" tells the old woman, "the monks of old slept in their coffins!" she replies, "They wasn't as advanced as we are." This is Miss O'Connor's standard joke. Old Tarwater speaks for the author when he tells the boy of Rayber's intention to give him "every advantage," and adds, "You have me to thank for saving you from those advantages."

It is thus necessary to imitate the monks of old, to deny the world, and Naysaying is another of Flannery O'Connor's major themes. "Flying is the greatest engineering achievement of man," Rayber says, and young Tarwater answers him, "I wouldn't give you nothing for no airplane. A buzzard can fly." Similarly, Mary Fortune denies that anyone has ever whipped her or ever could, although her grandfather has just seen her whipped; "I don't need no new shoe," Rufus Johnson insists to Sheppard, with his clubfoot barely covered by the old torn shoe. These lying denials are a higher truth, the truth of the spirit that contradicts the weakness of the flesh.

Flannery O'Connor's meanings are not only Christian, they are Christian mainly in the mystic and ascetic tradition of St. John of the Cross ("Hence the soul cannot be possessed of the divine union, until it has divested itself of the love of created beings"), rather than in the humanitarian tradition expressed in I John 4:20 ("If a man say, I love God, and hateth his brother, he is a liar").

Miss O'Connor is said to have been pleased when the London *Times* identified her as a "theological" writer. As a fiction-writing theologian, she seems the most radical Christian dualist since Dostoevski. There are two of everything in her work, one Christ and one anti-Christ. There are two wafers, and since Rayber rejects Christ, "he felt the taste of his own childhood pain laid again on his tongue like a bitter wafer." There are two baptisms, the one old Tarwater gives and the one Rayber gives. There are two rivers in "The River," one "the rich red river of Jesus' Blood," the other the mundane river in which Mr. Paradise appears "like some ancient water monster." There are two fires in "A Circle in the Fire," one the fiery furnace in which the prophets dance, "in the circle the angel had cleared for them," the other set in the woods by the boys. The same two fires appear at the end of *The Violent*, when Tarwater raises himself from the ground, and "the burning bush had disappeared. A line of fire ate languidly at the treeline." There are two Hazes in *Wise Blood*, one a false prophet, and two young Tarwaters in *The Violent*, one of whom dissociates himself from the other as mad.

Miss O'Connor's subject is Vocation only in this radical dualist or tragic sense, that the way to sanctity is through the greatest sinfulness. She reported with pride to a friend that a young nun showed her full comprehension of *The Violent* when she said that she understood Tarwater perfectly: "He was struggling with his vocation. I've been through that—I know just how he felt and you did, too." The relationship between the two realms of experience, the young nun's spiritual struggle and Tarwater's criminal actions and passions, is analogical: murdering an idiot becomes a proper metaphor for Christian baptism, firing a woods a proper metaphor for Christian confirmation. In a time of desperate unbelief, in Miss O'Connor's view, the Christian sacraments must be understood to be equally desperate, and the language of desperation is violence and crime.

Two more thematic consequences of Flannery O'Connor's radical Christian dualism remain to be noticed. One is the False Christ. Hazel Motes says: "What do I need with Jesus? I got Leora Watts." When he leaves Mrs. Watts, the old Essex becomes his substitute Jesus. The car Mr. Shiftlet acquires by marrying and deserting the deaf girl is similarly a substitute Christ; when he finally gets it running "He had an expression of serious modesty on his face as if he had just raised the dead." Mr. Shiftlet explains his philosophy to the old woman: "The body, lady, is like a house: it don't go anywhere; but the spirit, lady, is like a automobile: always on the move." Thomas in "The Comforts of Home" and Sheppard in "The Lame Shall Enter First" do not have false Christs, they *are* false Christs.

The remaining Christian theme is best put by St. Paul in I Corinthians 1:25, "Because the foolishness of God is wiser than men," and 3:19, "For the wisdom of this world is foolishness with God." The way to wisdom is through folly as the way to sanctity is through sin. Old Tarwater, taken to the insane asylum in a straitjacket for his wild prophesying, is God's Fool, and young Tarwater's vision of following "the bleeding stinking mad shadow of Jesus" hinges on the same paradox: Jesus' way is mad only by "the wisdom of this world."

Protestant Fundamentalism is thus Miss O'Connor's metaphor, in literary terms, for

Roman Catholic truth (in theological terms, this reflects ecumenicism). Why did she see through a glass darkly, rather than face to face? There are many answers, and no certain answer. One answer that she gave to interviewers, that Protestant Fundamentalism was the milieu in which she grew up, is not really satisfactory. True, there are not many Catholics in rural Georgia, but then there are not many (or any) Hazes or Tarwaters either. Miss O'Connor gave a deeper answer in an interview with Granville Hicks: "I'm not interested in the sects as sects; I'm concerned with the religious individual, the backwoods prophet. Old Tarwater is the hero of *The Violent Bear It Away,* and I'm right behind him 100 per cent."

In a letter to Sister Mariella Gable, O.S.B., quoted in the memorial issue of *Esprit,* she wrote: "People make a judgment of fanaticism by what they are themselves. To a lot of Protestants I know, monks and nuns are fanatics, none greater. And to a lot of monks and nuns I know, my Protestant prophets are fanatics. For my part, I think the only difference between them is that if you are a Catholic and have this intensity of belief you join the convent and are heard no more; whereas if you are a Protestant and have it, there is no convent for you to join and you go about the world getting into all sorts of trouble and drawing the wrath of people who don't believe anything much at all down on your head. This is one reason why I can write about Protestant believers better than Catholic believers—because they express their belief in diverse kinds of dramatic action which is obvious enough for me to catch."

Whatever caused Miss O'Connor to choose Protestant Fundamentalism as her metaphor for Catholic vision, it was a brilliant choice. It gave her imagery that is naturally dramatistic, as she says, and, as she does not say, it freed her from the constraints of good taste—the young nun who identified her struggles with Tarwater's could not, as the protagonist of a novel, be made to undergo experiences comparable to his. The gains enormously outweigh the losses. If Flannery O'Connor, by choosing a tent revivalist subject matter, could not write such a portrait of serene saintliness as J. F. Powers' "Lions, Harts, and Leaping Does," in exchange she was spared the necessity of writing Powers' pious fables about the rectory cat. In any case, neither was in accord with her gifts or her temperament.

As a Catholic born and brought up in Georgia, Miss O'Connor always insisted not only on her right to the imagery of southern Protestantism, but on its peculiar fitness for her as a Catholic. In a letter, she wrote: "Now the South is a good place for a Catholic literature in my sense for a number of reasons. 1) In the South belief can still be made believable and in relation to a large part of the society. We're not the Bible Belt for nothing. 2) The Bible being generally known and revered in the section, gives the novelist that broad mythical base to refer to that he needs to extend his meaning in depth. 3) The South has a sacramental view of life. . . . 4) The aspect of Protestantism that is most prominent (at least to the Catholic) in the South is that of man dealing with God directly, not through the mediation of the church, and this is great for the Catholic novelist like myself who wants to get close to his character and watch him wrestle with the Lord."

Flannery O'Connor was a loyal Georgian and a loyal southerner, in her fashion. She was not only a southerner but a white southern lady. In one aspect this was an ironic stance. She told friends that she had not read *Lolita* because "White Southern ladies can't read such

books," a remark she must often have heard about her own work. But it does not seem to have been an ironic stance in regard to the race question, on which Miss O'Connor maintained a consistent public silence. There are, however, curious symbolic statements in her work. "Her fiction does not reflect the social issues, particularly the racial problems, which beset the South during her lifetime," says John J. Clarke in *Esprit*. I think that it does, and more powerfully and truly than that of anyone else, but the expression is always implicit, covert, cryptic. As her mad prophets are metaphoric for Roman Catholic truth, so in a sense all the fierce violence in her work is metaphoric for violence done the Negro. This is most clear in *Wise Blood*, when ten-year-old Haze is trying to figure out what dirty mystery is going on in the carnival tent. We follow the sequence of his thoughts from "It's some men in a privy," to "maybe it's a man and a woman in a privy," to his sudden question to the barker: "Is it a nigger? . . . Are they doing something to a nigger?" (I would exchange many high-minded tracts on the Question for the insight in that progression.)

The Negroes in the stories are seen externally, as a conventional white southern lady would see them, with no access to their concealed sensibility, but occasionally one of them will say something (there are several such remarks in "The Displaced Person") that shows how much the author knows about that sensibility. Negroes in the fiction sometimes carry profound spiritual meaning, as in "The Artificial Nigger" or in the figure of Buford Munson in *The Violent*. In several stories, and in the fragment of the unfinished novel, Negroes are images of fraternity. In the deepest sense, Harry in "The River," who goes to his death because he wants to *count*, or Norton in "The Lame Shall Enter First," who hangs himself because he wants to be *some*where, are symbols for Negro aspirations and frustrations; they are symbolic Negroes or "artificial niggers," in fact, and the author knew it.

Which brings us to the question of integration. Mr. Guizac, the displaced person, is a full integrationist out of desperation: he is trying to marry his sixteen-year-old Polish cousin to the Negro Sulk, to get her out of the refugee camps. It is this project, which Mrs. McIntyre characteristically describes as a match between a "poor innocent child" and a "half-witted thieving black stinking nigger," that leads to his fall from Mrs. McIntyre's favor and thus to his fate. Mr. Guizac's integrationist slogan is minimal: "She no care black. . . . She in camp three year." Insofar as he embodies Christ the Displaced Person, however, his implicit integrationist slogan is maximal: God died to redeem all mankind.

Integrationism is savagely travestied as sentimental and fatuous in Julian in "Everything That Rises Must Converge" and Asbury in "The Enduring Chill," but the opposing view is just as savagely travestied in their mothers. "They should rise, yes, but on their own side of the fence," Julian's mother says, and the title, as well as her stroke, is the rejoinder.

We understand the nature of Miss O'Connor's opposition to integration when we see Asbury think of smoking with the Negroes who work for his mother as "one of those moments of communion when the difference between black and white is absorbed into nothing." In Miss O'Connor's radical Christian dualism, this is a secular and thus a false communion, and integration in general is a secular and thus a false salvation. Whereas her friend Father Merton finds integration so deeply inherent in the Christian concept of Incarnation that he regards any trace of racism in a Roman Catholic as automatically self-excommunicat-

ing, Miss O'Connor insists with Dostoevski that the only equality is to be found in the spiritual dignity of man, in the mystic communion of the Sacraments.

It is not easy to place Flannery O'Connor in a literary tradition. The writer to whom she is most indebted stylistically, Mark Twain, is never mentioned in discussions of her work, nor did she ever identify him as an influence, so far as I know. Yet if *The Violent Bear It Away* has any single progenitor, it is *Adventures of Huckleberry Finn*. Miss O'Connor's mature writing has very little to do with Faulkner or any of what is called "southern" literature. The writer who most influenced her, at least in her first books, is Nathanael West. *Wise Blood* is clearly modeled on *Miss Lonelyhearts* (as no reviewer noticed at the time), and contains many specific reminiscences of it. Hazel Motes has a nose "like a shrike's bill"; after he goes to bed with Leora Watts, Haze feels "like something washed ashore on her"; Sabbath Lily's correspondence with a newspaper advice-columnist is purest West; and all the rocks in *Wise Blood* recall the rock Miss Lonelyhearts first contains in his gut and then becomes, the rock on which the new Peter will found the new Church. The European writer Flannery O'Connor most profoundly resembles (in method, not in scale) is Dostoevski. Like him she created a deeply understood Enemy out of her own liberal and enlightened dreams. "Ivan Karamazov cannot believe," she wrote in her introduction to *A Memoir of Mary Ann*, "as long as one child is in torment" —no more can Rayber or Sheppard, she might have added.

It is surely too early to evaluate Flannery O'Connor's work or place it in our literature, but some beginnings can be attempted. Two points must be made immediately. The first is that despite the prevailing opinion, she was primarily a novelist, not a short-story writer, and consequently her novels are better and more important than even the best of her stories. The second is that any discussion of her theology can only be preliminary to, not a substitute for, aesthetic analysis and evaluation.

The strengths of Flannery O'Connor's writing are those qualities in it that have been most disliked and attacked: the apocalyptic violence, the grotesque vision, the vulgarity. "Her novels suffer, I believe, from an excessive violence of conception," Warren Coffey wrote in *Esprit*, contrasting them with her stories. But it is precisely this violence in the novels—these murders and burnings, blindings and rapes—that is the heart of their imaginative power, as is murder in Dostoevski's novels. It is the violence of desperate Christianity, of the desperate and verbally inarticulate South, of a nation no longer quiet about its desperation. William Esty wrote scornfully, in *Commonweal*, of Flannery O'Connor's "cult of the Gratuitous Grotesque." Her fiction is grotesque, certainly, but never gratuitously so. For example, in the opening scene of "The Lame Shall Enter First," Norton eats a piece of chocolate cake spread with peanut butter and ketchup; when his father gets him upset, he vomits it all up in "a limp sweet batter." This is not only grotesque but thoroughly repulsive, and no less repulsive to the author, but it is entirely functional and necessary in the story: it perfectly symbolizes the indigestible mess of Sheppard's "enlightened" views, which Norton will similarly be unable to keep down. Flannery O'Connor herself answered the charge definitively in an unpublished lecture: "I have found that any fiction that comes out of the South is going to be considered grotesque by the Northern critic, unless it is grotesque, in which case it is going to be considered realistic." Nor is this merely a matter of the northern critic. All

art, to the extent that it is new and serious, is shocking and disturbing, and one way of dismissing those truths that get through to us is as "grotesque."

We must not ignore the weaknesses of Flannery O'Connor's fiction. Her stories came to rely too often and too mechanically on death to end them. The deaths are ruinous to "A View of the Woods," and unnecessary in other stories. Her best stories—"The Artificial Nigger," "Good Country People," "Parker's Back" —neither end in death nor need to. One reason for her melodramatic endings seems to be theological. "I'm a born Catholic and death has always been brother to my imagination," Miss O'Connor told an interviewer in *Jubilee*, "I can't imagine a story that doesn't properly end in it or in its foreshadowings." It was one of her rare confusions of theology with aesthetics.

These endings result from a misjudgment in craft, as do those occasions—in "Good Country People" and "A View of the Woods" —in which she runs on past a story's natural finish. Other than these, the only fault in her fiction is a tendency to travesty. Caricature is a legitimate resource of art, and a magnificently effective one in her hands, but her caricature sometimes fell into over-caricature and lost its truth, so that we cannot believe in the existence of certain of her secular intellectuals or Negroes. If they are not people, they cannot function as symbols, since, as she says in the lecture on the grotesque, "It is the nature of fiction not to be good for much else unless it is good in itself."

Flannery O'Connor's fiction is a powerful example of what Kenneth Burke calls "symbolic action," functioning for the author as well as for the reader. The root meaning of "caricature" is "overload," and in this sense Miss O'Connor created characters and their dramatic oppositions by separating, exaggerat-

FLANNERY O'CONNOR / 359

ing, and polarizing elements in herself. The Tarwaters and Rayber are the Yang and Yin of the author, each made extreme, in just the fashion that Stephen and Bloom are, or Ahab and Ishmael. These opposites held in tension externalize an inner war, but they do so dramatically and they progress to a dramatic resolution, in the process exorcising ambivalence and resolving doubt. "I have written a wicked book," Melville wrote to Hawthorne when he had finished *Moby Dick*, "and feel spotless as the lamb." As Dostoevski could find all that was most detestable, Stavrogin and Smerdyakov, deep inside himself, so Miss O'Connor could find inside herself Hazel Motes, the blind fanatic, and Joy-Hulga, the spiteful atheist. And in finding them, in incarnating them in art, she rid herself of them. The stories are full of bitter hate *in order that* the author may be friendly and loving; the novels scream doubt and denial *in order that* the author may be devout and serene.

As this symbolic action transforms the author, so it transforms the reader. We undergo these terrible events, as horror-filled as Greek tragedy, to be purged and sweetened, even kept devout (in our different devotions). Few of Flannery O'Connor's readers, few even of her Roman Catholic readers, can share her desperate and radical Christian dualism, as she was fully aware. But it constituted a natural dramatism for fiction, as did Dostoevski's religion, and a fiction in no sense parochial. As a writer she had the additional advantage, as West did, of multiple alienation from the dominant assumptions of our culture: he was an outsider as a Jew, and doubly an outsider as a Jew alienated from other Jews; she was comparably an outsider as a woman, a southerner, and a Roman Catholic in the South. This is not to say that her views, or her alienation, produced the fiction; many have held more radical views, and been far more alienated,

while producing nothing. Her gifts produced the fiction, but her situation gave them opportunities, and enabled her to exercise her intelligence, imagination, and craft most effectively. Her early death may have deprived the world of unforeseeable marvels, but she left us, in *The Violent Bear It Away*, parts of *Wise Blood*, and the best stories, marvels enough.

Selected Bibliography

WORKS OF FLANNERY O'CONNOR

FICTION

Wise Blood. New York: Harcourt, Brace, 1952.

A Good Man Is Hard to Find. New York: Harcourt, Brace, 1955.

The Violent Bear It Away. New York: Farrar, Straus and Cudahy, 1960.

Everything That Rises Must Converge. New York: Farrar, Straus and Giroux, 1965. (With an introduction by Robert Fitzgerald.)

The Complete Stories. New York: Farrar, Straus and Giroux, 1971.

NON-FICTION

"The Fiction Writer and His Country," in *The Living Novel*, edited by Granville Hicks. New York: Macmillan, 1957. Pp. 157–64.

"The Church and the Fiction Writer," *America*, 96:733–35 (March 30, 1957).

"Living with a Peacock," *Holiday*, 30:52 (September 1961).

Introduction to *A Memoir of Mary Ann*. New York: Farrar, Straus and Cudahy, 1961, 1962.

Note on *The Phenomenon of Man*, by Pierre Teilhard de Chardin, *American Scholar*, 30:618 (Fall 1961).

"The Regional Writer," *Esprit*, 7:31–35 (Winter 1963).

"Why Do the Heathens Rage?" *Esquire*, 60:60–61 (July 1963).

"The Role of the Catholic Novelist," *Greyfriar*, 7:5–12 (1964).

BIBLIOGRAPHY

Brittain, Joan. "Flannery O'Connor: A Bibliography," *Bulletin of Bibliography*, 25 (1967): 98–100, 123–124.

CRITICAL AND
BIOGRAPHICAL STUDIES

Baumbach, Jonathan. "The Acid of God's Grace: *Wise Blood* by Flannery O'Connor," in *The Landscape of Nightmare*. New York: New York University Press, 1965. Pp. 87–100.

Critique, Vol. 2, No. 2 (Fall 1958). (An issue jointly devoted to Flannery O'Connor and J. F. Powers, with a bibliography and articles on the former by Caroline Gordon, Sister M. Bernetta Quinn, O.S.F., Louis D. Rubin, Jr., and George F. Wedge.)

Esprit, Vol. 8, No. 1 (Winter 1964). (A memorial issue.)

Farnham, James F. "The Grotesque in Flannery O'Connor," *America*, 105:277–81 (May 13, 1961).

Ferris, Sumner J. "The Outside and the Inside: Flannery O'Connor's *The Violent Bear It Away*," *Critique*, 3:11–19 (Winter–Spring 1960).

Fitzgerald, Robert. "The Countryside and the True Country," *Sewanee Review*, 70:380–94 (Summer 1962).

Friedman, M. J. "Flannery O'Connor: Another Legend in Southern Fiction," in *Recent American Fiction: Some Critical Views*, edited by Joseph J. Waldmeir. Boston: Houghton Mifflin, 1963. Pp. 231–45.

————, and Lewis Lawson, eds. *The Added Dimension: The Art and Mind of Flannery O'Connor*. New York: Fordham University Press, 1966.

Gable, Sister Mariella, O.S.B. "Ecumenic Core in Flannery O'Connor's Fiction," *American Benedictine Review*, 15:127–43 (June 1964).

Gossett, Louise Y. "The Test by Fire: Flannery O'Connor," in *Violence in Recent Southern Fiction*. Durham, N.C.: Duke University Press, 1965. Pp. 75–97.

Hart, Jane. "Strange Earth: The Stories of Flannery O'Connor," *Georgia Review*, 12:215–22 (Summer 1958).

Hawkes, John. "Flannery O'Connor's Devil," *Sewanee Review*. 70:395–407 (Summer 1962).

Hendin, Josephine. *The World of Flannery O'Connor*. Bloomington: Indiana University Press, 1970.

Hicks, Granville. "A Writer at Home with Her Heritage," *Saturday Review*, 45:22–23 (May 12, 1962).

————. "A Cold, Hard Look at Humankind," *Saturday Review*, 48:23–24 (May 29, 1965).

Hyman, Stanley Edgar. "Flannery O'Connor's Tattooed Christ," *New Leader*, 48:9–10 (May 10, 1965).

Joselyn, Sister M., O.S.B. "Thematic Centers in 'The Displaced Person,'" *Studies in Short Fiction*, 1:85–92 (Winter 1964).

Malin, Irving. *New American Gothic*. Carbondale: Southern Illinois University Press, 1962. *Passim*.

Martin, Carter W. *The True Country: Themes in the Fiction of Flannery O'Connor*. Nashville, Tenn.: Vanderbilt University Press, 1969.

Meaders, Margaret Inman. "Flannery O'Connor: 'Literary Witch,'" *Colorado Quarterly*, 10:377–86 (Spring 1962).

[Meyers], Sister Bertrande, D.C. "Four Stories of Flannery O'Connor," *Thought*, 37:410–26 (Autumn 1962).

Rose Alice, Sister, S.S.J. "Flannery O'Connor: Poet to the Outcast," *Renascence*, 16:126–32 (Spring 1964).

Solotaroff, Theodore. "You *Can* Go Home Again," *Book Week*, 2:1, 13 (May 30, 1965).

Spivey, Ted R. "Flannery O'Connor's View of God and Man," *Studies in Short Fiction*, 1:200–6 (Spring 1964).

Stelzmann, Rainulf A. "Shock and Orthodoxy: An Interpretation of Flannery O'Connor's Novels and Short Stories," *Xavier University Studies*, 2:1 (March 1963).

Stern, Richard. "Flannery O'Connor: A Remembrance and Some Letters," *Shenandoah*, 16:5–10 (Winter 1965).

Tate, Mary Barbara. "Flannery O'Connor: A Reminiscence," *Columns*, 2:1 (Fall 1964).

—STANLEY EDGAR HYMAN

John O'Hara

1905-1970

AN AUTHOR whose books have sold over fifteen million copies and whose popularity has maintained itself firmly since 1934, who has won the National Book Award, and who nevertheless is savagely treated most of the time by most of the critics presents an unusual challenge to the student who undertakes to survey his whole career. The problem is compounded by the fact that, whereas, in my opinion, O'Hara is an extraordinarily good and important writer of short stories and an inferior novelist, his reputation and financial success depend upon his novels.

O'Hara was born in Pottsville, Pennsylvania, in 1905, the eldest of eight children of a successful doctor. The family was prosperous, Irish, and Roman Catholic. Regardless of the prosperity, the latter two elements seem to have put John O'Hara at a deep psychological disadvantage in conservative, Anglo-Saxon, Protestant eastern Pennsylvania. His privileged youth carried him to the point of admission to Yale University, at the age of twenty—and then his father died and the security vanished. Instead of going to Yale, O'Hara worked as a reporter on various Pennsylvania newspapers, went to New York in 1927, and for a year ran through various writing and secretarial positions until, in the spring of 1928, he began to publish stories in the *New Yorker*.

He married Helen Pettit in 1931, was divorced in 1933, and became suddenly famous with the publication of *Appointment in Samarra* in 1934. The success took him to Hollywood, where he worked as a film writer and reviser until the mid-1940's. During this period he moved back and forth between Hollywood and New York and continued to write novels and short stories. His second novel, *Butterfield 8*, came in 1935 along with *The Doctor's Son and Other Stories*. He married socially prominent Belle Wylie in 1937, published a third novel, *Hope of Heaven*, in 1938, and in the same year began to publish the famous "Pal Joey" stories in the *New Yorker*.

The musical *Pal Joey* by Rodgers and Hart, based on these stories, was a great success in 1940; and the stories were collected in book form that same year. During World War II O'Hara served as a correspondent with the Third Fleet in the Pacific. Two further volumes of short stories, *Pipe Night* (1945) and *Hellbox* (1947; the last until *Assembly*, 1961), were followed by a big novel, *A Rage to Live*, in 1949. *The Farmers Hotel* appeared in 1951, *Sweet and Sour* in 1954, and a major novel, *Ten North Frederick*, in 1955. A revival of *Pal Joey* won the Drama Critics' Award in 1952, and *Ten North Frederick* was given the National Book Award for fiction for 1955.

This period of triumphs was accompanied by deep personal troubles. O'Hara almost died of hemorrhaging stomach ulcers in 1953, and his wife died of heart disease at the age of thirty-nine, in 1954. His third marriage, to Katharine Bryan, came in 1955. He then published a flow of successful novels and volumes of short stories. *From the Terrace* (1958) was his largest and most successful novel. Others are *A Family Party* (1956), *Ourselves to Know* (1960), *Sermons and Soda Water* (1960), *The Big Laugh* (1962), *Elizabeth Appleton* (1963), *The Lockwood Concern* (1965), and *The Instrument* (1967).

The subjects of this considerable output are (1) eastern Pennsylvania, (2) actors and movie people in New York and Hollywood, and (3) a Philadelphia–New York–Washington triangle of business, war, and society. O'Hara's special virtues are an eye for significant detail and an ear that catches not only all the rhythm and style of dialogue but also its nuances of tone. He can bring to life in two or three sentences any character from the crudest illiterate up through the vast lower middle class of semiliterates and on to intellectuals and socialites. At the same time his dialogue can reveal the rise and fall of temper, the ploys of one-upmanship, the abrasions of marriage, the pomposities of rich gangsters, and the simplicities of the well-bred. These virtues come to play supremely in the short story, where with just these skills O'Hara has given us glimpses of modern life as subtle and controlled as anything by such masters of the genre as Chekhov or Katherine Mansfield. This is a high accomplishment; the American short story may well be our best literary achievement in prose— and O'Hara stands close to our top.

The weakness of O'Hara's novels is related to the excellence of his short stories: America lacks the manners to sustain what Aristotle called a "significant action of some magnitude"

—not that there is no cultural tradition or social context of manners, values, and customs; but that our writers have generally not been willing to assume a position of acceptance within and create from its values an action that dramatizes its typical problems. The serious American writer more generally rejects the standard American values of business and status—without which the relations among individuals, already more intricately various and slippery than they might be if our manners were more uniform, become difficult to manage in the sustained action of a full novel. Here is where the short story can explore and illuminate endless varieties of situations in which individuals struggle for understanding, mastery, trust, or love. O'Hara has written well over 350 short stories, and in this impressive gathering he has hardly repeated himself. He has brilliantly explored the manners of America on many levels.

More than with most of our outstanding novelists, in fact, O'Hara's subject is that of the novel of manners, but a number of qualities in his novels limit his achievement in the genre. First, the range of conduct that O'Hara records is enormous. All degrees of violence, scoundrelism, selfishness, cruelty, pride, ruthlessness, and decency appear. Second, such conduct is boldly unpredictable. The most faithful wife will suddenly cuckold her husband, or turn from loving him to despising or hating him. The confirmed bachelor will marry a young girl. The gangster will act honorably. The unusual reaction is more likely than not. Third, O'Hara records all such conduct with the detachment of a photographer. He does not establish a moral frame of reference, and hence there is no pattern of rewards or punishments, no ideal scale, whether moral, philosophical, or religious; some people get away with murder while others suffer for the smallest errors or none at all. Some violate the basic decencies with impunity; others are done in for a lapse of manners. O'Hara *seems* to admire style, candor, and integrity in character, but he does not reward these qualities in action. Fourth, O'Hara does not *dramatize* a substantial *action* in which various life patterns are enacted, with developed problems and conflicts resolved by crucial decisions leading to serious consequences. Instead, he surrounds his dramatic action with great tracts of historical exposition and discussion, plus tireless descriptions of How It Was in style, fashion, travel, politics, saloons, rackets, houses, servants, clubs, food, horses, automobiles, and so on. Fifth, his tone is often so cold, sardonic, hostile, or contemptuous as to reduce his people to absurd or malignant monsters. Sixth, he is, paradoxically, so involved with the rich in his stories that he loses sight of the large patterns in which they move. He shows the nuances of power, of one-upmanship, and of arrogance among them without showing the general social frame that defines their significance. Rather, he is himself present talking to them with insightful questions or demonstrating that he knows what makes them tick better than anybody, including themselves, so that his own display of insight reduces their freedom and subordinates their problems— problems already reduced by the confinement of O'Hara's preoccupation with sex, power, and status. The qualities listed here, nevertheless, constitute a special and remarkable contribution to modern American literature.

Many of O'Hara's stories could be described as exempla of anger and aspiration—or as pictures of the conflicts generated by the friction between personal irritability and status hopes. There are some people who are born with status, and then there are others who are aware of it, who think about it a good deal and reach out for it, but who never quite, down in the depths of their own hearts, make it.

There are so many variations played on the theme that it is not easy to isolate the factor that makes the aspirant unsure and uncomfortable. It may be two or three generations back in his forebears; it may be some youthful error that continues to gnaw at his self-image; it may be simply that his wife has a little more status than he. Whatever it is, it figures prominently in the hero's consciousness.

It is tempting to seek some pattern, some development, in O'Hara's use of this theme, but doing so brings one directly into the complicating factor of O'Hara's own relation to the problem. The point can be illustrated with a parallel circumstance in the life and work of Ernest Hemingway. Hemingway's early problem was fear, a nerve-shattered terror brought about by wounds in World War I. The terror apparently came clothed in a shame of what he felt as cowardice; and he set to work writing about his horrors in order to exorcise them. And step by step Hemingway did master his fears. For this conquest he paid a price. He became identified with violence—boxing, hunting, bullfighting, war—to the point where it sometimes seemed that he could not age gracefully but must keep on breaking bones and having sprains and concussions until death set him free. He achieved various degrees of objectivity while dealing with or circling round his theme. Hemingway worked his way from such a fear of cowardice that he only hinted at violence to the point where he could anatomize courage and fear in *For Whom the Bell Tolls*, and on to the later books where he could treat them from a higher level entirely, almost free of the early anguish.

O'Hara's theme of social status moves in and out of autobiographical focus in the same way. In *Appointment in Samarra* the hero has status but destroys himself by not living up to it. There is a *very* great deal of discussion in the novel about who belongs and who does not, what clubs count, what prep schools, what colleges, and how people make the grade in Gibbsville. The laborer, the mobster, the well-born hero, all think about status and how they relate to it. Almost three decades later, in *Sermons and Soda Water*, a character from *Samarra* reappears. He is Jim Malloy, who is clearly a persona of O'Hara. Having come up from the wrong side of the tracks in Gibbsville, he is now a rich and famous writer, a celebrity in his home town, where he moves occasionally among the elect, terribly at ease in Zion, going to the Club, the big dances, the most established family circles. He is now higher than Gibbsville and can generously condescend to the old town. A few years later in *Elizabeth Appleton*, O'Hara brings a very well born and well bred lady to a small college town and shows how she constitutes a different order of creature, with her own laws and morals; yet he shows her serious limitation, too. By the time of *The Lockwood Concern*, he has mastered the problem so completely that he can write a novel avowedly about the upstart's search for status, showing how a family tries through three generations to found a feudal domain in which it will be the baronial family —but fails because the effort destroys the meager spirit of the chief aspirant. He lacks the heart to become a true baron.

Like Hemingway, O'Hara has paid a price for his victory. He has sacrificed his story line, again and again, to his extended expositions of Who Has the Upper Hand. His issues seem gradually to have faded, to have lost their vitality, so that the novels have the authenticity of detail but lack the problems that make for strong plots. They relax into gossipy reportage, into scenes of edgy friction and violence between friends or lovers, and into the painstaking chronicle of bygone works and days.

The Instrument explores the same depths of sex and status where a soulless hero "fulfills" his stark drives in incidents that would not seem to make a self. The hero this time is a playwright who eats up other creatures and disgorges them in his art, yet he will compel the reader's interest and almost complete identification. Critical reviews of this book have compressed the thesis of the present essay into witty sentences: The people, writes Charles Poore in the *New York Times*, "are modernity's resident worldlings. . . . They are jetters from the boondocks; their ambition is to be affluent and in. What they do apes more styles than it sets. . . . At the bosky end of a New York–Vermont axis trust Lucas to find gentry. The Atterburys give him a cramming course in good-gracious living and the art of the cultivated put-down. . . . the money-musky cadenza on the vulgarity of talking about money." Josh Greenfeld, also in the *Times*, speaks of ". . . the vaunted O'Hara skills . . . arched eyebrows snobbery . . . the fine O'Hara eye . . . the celebrated O'Hara ear. . . . There is also the coy O'Hara evasion . . . the shallow O'Hara depth-analysis."

The bad-tempered quarrel in which one or both parties evince a stubborn nastiness is the keynote of the O'Hara action. Stubbornness is close to the heart of it. The quarrelers seem eager to establish an impossible line and then refuse to budge an inch from it. There is never any persuasion, any compromise, any reconciliation. They would rather take umbrage than second thought. They would rather give a blow than an inch. They will not think anything less than the worst of each other. The wounds of *amour propre* never heal. When the continuation of the action demands a working reconciliation, it has the quality of two steel rods bending a millimeter or two toward each other.

For one who has read a good deal of O'Hara, the prevalence of bad temper comes to be related to the instant insight, because both suggest his anger at an unmanageable world—an anger that is satisfied by dreams of power and the vicarious exercise of it. Rather than reason and explain, one reacts to a slight with a blow or an insult. From impotence and insecurity (buried in the unconscious, surely) one adopts the pose of a seer who can divine exactly what makes people tick, in a flash of pure understanding. The narrator in *Ourselves to Know*, who is a thinly veiled persona of O'Hara, at one point creates by sheer vision a whole sequence of events that nobody living could know. He suddenly knows that Parson Betz raped Zilph Millhouser fifty years ago and later committed suicide from shame. He has to know to fill these details into his story, but more important he *chooses* to know as a demonstration of psychic power. Versions of this sense of phenomenal insight pervade the whole corpus of O'Hara's work, a basic strategy of his art being the creation and exercise of power. These qualities also animate a large area of contemporary society, into which O'Hara has *felt* perhaps more deeply than any other important writer.

The lifelong concern with status springs from the same set of attitudes. The writer knows just how everybody relates to everybody else. He has privileged communications from the highest, whom he sees in their most unguarded moments and whom he evaluates from a position that is insightfully superior to theirs. They are willing to tell him things that they did not know about themselves until he asked them the perfect question; and even as they articulate these interesting discoveries one must feel that the author knew the answers before he phrased his inquiries. Every gleam of insight reveals the author's grasp of the great social world. He can love a jewel like Polly Williamson at first glance and take two novellas to show us how she was more won-

derful than he could have known—but he did know at first glance. At the same time he can anatomize her aristocrat husband for the stupid arrogant bully he is.

The pen is the mightiest sword, which is another way of saying that the author's voice resounding in these works rings with assumed power, insight, judgment. It is the voice of a superaristocratic seer, a person superior in experience, in knowledge, in tolerance, and in all the details of social punctilio. It is also, unfortunately, a voice which gives off overtones of resentment, insecurity, and pride whenever it speaks.

Appointment in Samarra is a story of *hubris* in a modern setting. Whom the gods will destroy, they first make mad, said the Greeks, expressing their sense of the headstrong, blind infatuation that drives some people on a course of action that can only lead to their destruction. This story takes place in 1930, after the stock market crash of 1929 but before people realized what the Great Depression was going to mean. It is laid in Gibbsville, Pennsylvania, a town of 24,000 inhabitants in the eastern Pennsylvania anthracite region, which is to become the spiritual focus of a great many of O'Hara's stories. I say focus rather than site, because the influence of Gibbsville is felt in many stories that are laid in surrounding towns.

The *hubris* of the protagonist, Julian English, derives in an ambiguous way from the prime condition in all of O'Hara's work—social status. Julian comes from an established Gibbsville family. He is in with the in crowd. His father is a doctor, his mother a lady. There is money in the family on both sides. Julian has always had great success with the ladies, and when he took the step he married one of the very best girls in town. Caroline Walker English is a beauty with character and charm.

Julian's problems are people and alcohol. People—are they for him or against him? Do they respect him properly? Do they trust him? Can he trust them? Again and again a scene will turn upon such feelings. It is a continuous game of one-upmanship—who makes the slipperiest allusions, who needles without being caught out, and who understands best what makes for status in the community. Everybody is dependent on a complexity of values: Jews are out. Catholics are powerful because they stick together, but they cannot have top status. Poles are aggressive and successful, but they are excluded from the highest circles. Money counts tremendously, but not absolutely. Service in World War I is important. Julian didn't have to go, because he was not old enough, but he could have lied about his age and got in. He will never be quite up to those who served. Then there is Ed Carney, the bootlegger and mobster who flourishes in Gibbsville because the prosperous people do a good deal of drinking. His power stimulates social ambitions, and we see him beginning to move up. He likes Julian English because the latter has always treated him like a human being, and he regards him with some real awe, as a "gentleman."

Julian is a Cadillac dealer; he belongs to the right clubs; he has a wife whom everybody praises. But he is a heavy drinker and irascible. It is no secret that heavy drinkers go up and down from high spirits to deep gloom. Of course, O'Hara is not writing a case study of a drinker. On the contrary, drink seems to be a condition of life for people in Julian English's class. It's just that he drinks more than others and plunges into deeper glooms. One night at a big dance at the Lantenengo (the name rings through most of O'Hara's stories) Country Club, Julian is sitting at a table with an upstart named Harry Reilly, from whom he

has borrowed twenty thousand dollars. Julian resents Harry because he is an upstart, because he owes him money, and because Harry has a "crush" on his wife, Caroline. So, some time after three o'clock in the morning, through a rich haze of drink, and for no immediate reason, he throws his highball in Harry's face—throws it so hard that the ice cube gives Harry a black eye.

Mortally humiliated, Harry will surely seek revenge. He is the only one with a lot of ready money, and Julian's "friends" will not stand by him because, as Caroline reminds her husband, " 'practically every single one of your best friends, with one or two exceptions, all owe Harry Reilly money.' " What follows is more senseless than tragically inevitable—yet tragedy today can in a minor key be made of *hubris* and circumstance, just as it was in Greek times. Julian has some of the nobility and splendor (the climbers all regard him with a certain awe) that mark the tragic hero. He is too sure of himself to take care, and so he arrogantly contributes to the coil of events that gathers rapidly around him. Dancing late at a roadside place, the next night, he goes out to his car with the mistress of Ed Carney, who sings at the place, for a half-hour of lovemaking. That afternoon Caroline had promised to go out in the car with him, at the intermission of the dance, and start a baby, if he didn't get drunk. But he did get drunk and irascible, partly because Harry Reilly had refused to see him that afternoon when he called to apologize, but largely because One Thing Leads to Another whether in Thebes or Gibbsville. The next afternoon, consumed with guilt and remorse, he gets into a bottle- and fist-fight at the Gibbsville Club, where he learns that one of his oldest friends has always hated him. Caroline cancels their big party for that evening and goes home to her mother. That night Julian gets very drunk and commits suicide by letting his motor run in the garage. When Harry Reilly learns of the suicide, he says, " 'He was a real gentleman. I wonder what in God's name would make him do a thing like that?' "

Between the incidents, which occupy perhaps a quarter of the book, there are episodes that fill in the life around Gibbsville by going up and down the social scale as well as back and forth in history to establish personal relations, memories, triumphs, and defeats. A substantial number of episodes detail the life of Caroline, showing how a fine girl drifts along, narrowly missing two marriages that might have been good, falling in love with Julian when she was twenty-seven, and now trying to make the best of what she has come into. Everywhere the driving forces are money, status, and sex, with the latter getting a sort of detailed attention that marked O'Hara as a voice of new freedom. High indeed in the appeal of this book was the candid immediacy of its realism. The details of business, finance, society, and crime are as accurately and minutely presented as the inflections of speech in dialogue, and they convey a sense of people drifting through a haze of convention, boredom, and despair. In this haze the people are depressed and bad tempered, quick to take offense, unsure of their loves and hates, able to damage themselves irretrievably by a gesture or a whim of desire. Nobody seems to be quite centered inside his skin, sure of where he is and who he is. The conventional things they do in Gibbsville do not satisfy their yearnings for Reality, whatever it is. Life is not only passing but also blurring and shifting around them. They drift through sports, business, sex, conversation, drink, but they are able to upset the easy ride with an uncontrollable outburst of rage. This is, perhaps, another way of saying that the manners do not suffice: the forms which presumably embody their spirits do not fulfill them. These brilliant penetrations of the American spirit are O'Hara's particular achievement.

If Gibbsville and *Samarra* mark the base of the O'Hara triangle, his first volume of short stories starts us at the bottom of one side, which is his theater and cinema complex. *Pal Joey* is a special and famous example of sardonic reportage. It consists of a series of letters from "a glittering, two-bit, night-club heel" to a pal who is also in the entertainment business and is coddled and flattered because he is clearly doing better than Joey. The letter writer sings in cheap joints, charms the ladies as best he can, and trusts no man or woman. They are all prey in the moral jungle he inhabits, and they are not always easy prey: Joey has to scramble to stay even.

The first letter sets the tone and style: "Well I heard about this spot through a little mouse I got to know up in Michigan. She told me about this spot as it is her home town altho spending her vacation every year in Michigan. I was to a party one nite (private) and they finely got me to sing a few numbers for them and the mouse couldn't take her eyes off me. She sat over in one corner of the room not paying any attention to the dope she was with until finely it got so even he noticed it and began making cracks but loud. I burned but went on singing and playing but he got too loud and I had to stop in the middle of a number and I said right at him if he didnt like it why didnt he try himself."

The mouse gets him this night-club spot in Ohio. He is soon on the radio and entertaining at private parties. He buys a fine car and charms the daughter of a bank president, meanwhile giving the mouse the cold shoulder. But Joey is a careless predator. He tells his pal too much, and his pal goes somewhat hastily after the mouse, who has left Ohio for New York, and she writes "this annonamous letter" to the banker's daughter that brings Joey's romance—and his job—to a disastrous conclusion.

Next he is in Chicago at a new spot, scrounging for money and exploiting girls, working for mobsters and getting into trouble because his cynical activities produce resentments. Joey is as mean as men come. Recounting his exploits, he is never apologetic, scarcely indignant at the outrages he elicits from stronger predators. He is unusual in that the reader does not generate an ounce of sympathy for him. Among the dogs where he lives, he is the coldest, warmed only by a naïve enthusiasm that makes him interesting if not lovable.

Pipe Night is another collection of stories and sketches that display the familiar characteristics bordering on reportage, glimpses of all sorts of American people caught with their blinds down and their frailties glaring. Thirty-one sketches in a small volume concentrate on showing literally just *how* people talk, try to communicate, and usually fail because they do not have the language or the manners and knowledge of manners that would enable them to think below the surface of the clichés among which they live. They are epiphanies of the moral and cultural underworld that prevails in our time. Brittle tableaux of empty people. Voices perfectly heard and reproduced, echoing emptinesses. Here there are no rich, yearning, inarticulate inner selves striving to communicate, but, rather, the jangling, brassy notes of cheap instruments that have never been tuned toward gentleness or understanding.

The range and accuracy of O'Hara's observation compensate richly for the bleak deprivations of spirit upon which his eye consistently lights. Their qualities can be felt if we review several of them. "Walter T. Carriman" is a verbose, fatuous "tribute" by a friend, whose prose style is represented by the following sentence: "Not having been surrounded in his childhood by great riches, which have been known to disappear overnight, leaving their possessors with memories to dwell upon to the boredom of less comfortably placed friends of later years, Walter, on the other hand, was not raised in poverty and squalor, the details of which can, in their recital save in the hands of a Dickens or an equally great artist, prove equally boresome." The peaks of eulogizing rhetoric are regularly separated by valleys (if not crevasses) of qualification. Walter was fond of sports in the required American fashion until the high-school "training rules proved irksome to a lad of Walter's spirit and he dropped the sport in freshman year. (The truth is that Walter took his first cigarette at the age of fourteen and from then on was a rather heavy smoker.)" The resonating pomposities carry Walter from theater usher to classified-ad taker ("a post requiring infinite patience, a good ear, a cheery speaking voice, and a legible hand, the last, by the way, an accomplishment of Walter's which I seem to have overlooked in my 'roundup' of the man's numerous good points") to food checker to freight clerk, after which "Walter next returned to the transportation field, serving briefly as a conductor on the street railways of Asbury Park . . ."; thence to night clerk in a hotel and so on to obesity and an early death by heart failure. The banality of the life glows in the falsity of the tribute, and the two combine to convey a sense of barrenness that would be hard to exceed.

Until we move on to the following sketches. "Now We Know" is the brief exchange between a bus driver and a girl who gets on his bus first, at the end of the line, every morning. He makes jokes like not opening the door till she bangs on it, conversations follow, and presently he declares his love along with the news that he has asked for a transfer to another line.

He has a wife and children that he cannot leave, but he can think of nothing but the new girl. So now they know. The moment of anguished confession escapes from the life sealed in the quiet desperation of routine. "Free" tells of a lady from Pasadena arriving at her hotel in New York for an annual three-day shopping spree. With plenty of money, her family left behind but safe, she takes a hot bath and plans her day with a daydream: she will exchange warm looks with a handsome man in the street, and then she will pass on without encouraging him further. She'd like to, but she will not, although she is "free." In "Can You Carry Me" a vulgar motion-picture actress abuses the editor of a magazine that has published an unfriendly article. Over drinks, she tells him that she is suing his magazine for a million dollars —until they get pretty drunk and go to bed together.

"A Purchase of Some Golf Clubs" gets its interest from what is unsaid. A girl sits in a bar drinking; a mechanic off duty talks to her, discovers that she is trying to sell an elegant set of golf clubs, with a leather bag, for twenty-five dollars. She has to have the money to retain a lawyer because her husband is in jail for hitting a man with his car while drunk. So the fellow takes the clubs, although he never plays golf, and the girl says she wishes he didn't drink so much. All this amounts to is the briefest encounter between people from (apparently) very different ways of life. The boy in "Too Young" is a high-school sophomore, infatuated with a college girl at the beach club, who discovers that she is having an affair with a motorcycle cop. He thought her sublimely untouchable; she was using the cop, cynically, to satisfy her physical needs. In "Summer's Day" the ubiquitous theme of status cuts across the pathos of age. A very old couple—but he is wearing the hatband of a Yale club—accept the homage of a rising Irishman who did not make any club at Yale. In the bathhouse the old man overhears teen-agers talking about what a pitiful old pair he and his wife are, hears the Irishman smack one of them briskly for his bad manners, and wonders how he will ever again be able to face the Irishman or his wife, "But then of course he realized that there was really nothing to face, really nothing." In "Radio" a couple trade abuse and insults over one Harry, who owes money to the husband and has had an affair with the wife. One gathers that this Harry so impressed the husband that he was putty in Harry's hands, and now the husband strikes his wife some hard blows in the face and tells her that she is "stuck" with him for good. The cruel, stupid dialogue seems unsurpassably authentic. In "Nothing Missing" a fellow fresh from a year in prison stops in a small-town gift and book shop, talks to the apprehensive girl in charge, stares at her—and stares (not having seen a girl for a year)—then leaves dispiritedly. Again, no communication.

A couple of hard, smart guys from Hollywood make fun of "The King of the Desert," a dude rancher, needling and subtly mocking, until one of them gets careless and says to the other, " 'What'd I tell you? A bit of a jerk' "— and lands on the floor, out cold, from the rancher's punch. Significantly, it is status again —the rancher's admission that he feels a bit superior because he comes from *Mayflower* stock—that precipitates the explosion. A tavern owner running "A Respectable Place" makes the mistake of letting the Patrolmen's Benevolent Fund pay the damage when a drunken cop shoots up his bar. He makes no complaint, just lets them take care of the damage; but the cops harass him with contrived summonses, and he soon has to close his place. In another story Laura meets by chance the man she loved passionately and planned to run away with ten years ago. She was "On

Time," but he did not appear, and so she went back to her husband. Now she learns from him that he was hit by a taxi and broke a leg on that critical day. Relief from her humiliation flows over her like balm. To set the score straight, however, she tells him that, after all, she had changed her mind and did not come to their meeting place. In "Graven Image" a gentleman named Browning meets an Under Secretary, who is clearly not a gentleman, for dinner in a Washington hotel. Browning, an old-line conservative, wants a job in the war machine from his successful friend. They define their status-gap when the Under Secretary notices that Browning, wearing a wristwatch, does not show his Porcellian emblem on a chain, and the latter tells Joe that if he had made the exclusive club at Harvard he might not have had the resentful drive that had carried him to the top. Mollified, the Under Secretary promises the job; Browning is so pleased that he orders a celebrative drink—and then makes his fatal error in a passage that must be quoted. Notice how Browning reveals the arrogance of class, the arrogance that cannot feel what it is like to be on the outside looking hungrily in, the arrogance that is, finally, unforgivable. Browning says:

" 'But as to you, Joe, you're the best. I drink to you.' The two men drank, the Under Secretary sipping at his, Browning taking half of his. Browning looked at the drink in his hand. 'You know, I was a little afraid. That other stuff, the club stuff.'

" 'Yes,' said the Under Secretary.

" 'I don't know why fellows like you—you never would have made it in a thousand years, but'—then, without looking up, he knew everything had collapsed—'but I've said exactly the wrong thing, haven't I?'

" 'That's right, Browning,' said the Under Secretary. 'You've said exactly the wrong thing. I've got to be going.' "

The reversal in this story is very neat: one's sympathy must be with the gentleman Browning at first, for the Under Secretary demonstrates an uncouth arrogance of power as well as bad manners; but Browning is destroyed at the end by a deeper and blinder arrogance.

The catalogue of exhibits continues with a drunken movie star, a middle-aged stockbroker unaccountably in love with a charming teenager, a civilian having an affair with a navy wife and suffering in a mixture of passion, subterfuge, and disloyalty, and a dozen more. Always the ear is perfect, the setting quickly and deftly established, the marks of conflicting status delineated. A night-club girl talking to a sailor says, " 'Also I was with a unit we entertained for the sailors a couple places.' " He explains somewhat illiterately that he is getting training in diesels and saving his money. She thinks he is a hick, but she would like to be considered as a person by him. He thinks she is an "actress" with vast experience—and ends by calling her "hustler" when she rebuffs him. Thus two on approximately the same level cannot penetrate their own stereotypes. Their misadventure is balanced by a hilarious conversation in which a punchy fighter tries to bribe an ethical editor to buy some stories about the ring.

O'Hara has made his own little genre in these sketches. It's a world of snobs and misfits where the elements of culture and status do not cohere into any approach to the good life. The people are crude, or trapped, or hateful, or greedy, or arrogant. They are edgy and suspicious, feeling their ways among the shadows of ignorance, fear, and mistrust. Swagger, cruelty, wealth, success do not finally enable them to escape from the prison of self.

From the Gibbsville base and the theater-world side, we move to the other side: New York–Philadelphia–Washington business and society, which completes the triangle of

O'Hara subjects. Of course the three areas overlap, in the person of their narrator.

Sermons and Soda Water is composed of three novellas related by one Jim Malloy, the writer who has been the O'Hara persona since *Appointment in Samarra*. Malloy had not made the social grade in Gibbsville, being Catholic and new there. But now he has risen so high that he hardly thinks about old Gibbsville. He has rubbed elbows with movie stars and shared pillows with Long Island socialites from old, old families. These stories are presented as insightful (if condescending) anecdotes on How It Is by one who knows all the postures of American status. One look and Malloy can tell how much class is present. Classy people cannot be known by their conduct—for they are capable of everything—unless it is viewed by an expert. He places them accurately whether they do anything or not. The rich and well-born are freer than their simpler compatriots; they suffer extremes of privilege and frustration; their class is to be known by nuances of speech and attitude that are not always visible to the common reader; if they have a quality in common that Malloy seems to admire, perhaps it is guts—or a certain aplomb in coming to terms with what happens to them.

These novellas are distinguished by an unusual manner and tone. The narrator tells them as the events appeared to *him*, so that in effect each story is an incident of autobiography. There are the characters, and then there is the way they appeared or related to Malloy. He sees them at intervals and is brought up-to-date on events. He can record his conversations with them, or he can tell us how they seemed to him or how he felt about them after a time. So he lives among them not as a character but as an autobiographical representative of the author. The effect is unusual and interesting; it is as if the reader were privileged to spend a long night with O'Hara in his study while he chatted easily and discursively about his recollections, assuming that his friendly companion was more interested in the storyteller than in the people he told about—although of course the story was fascinating because of the intimate and casual manner in which it was told.

"The Girl on the Baggage Truck" (the first novella) is about Charlotte Sears, a movie actress who almost makes a tremendous marriage—but the man kills himself and disfigures her in an automobile accident. Ironically, it transpires that he was a crook about to be indicted, and she was just passing her prime as an actress. The story takes Jim Malloy into Long Island society, but not until he has talked about Charlotte's enormous Hollywood contract, got into bed with her, and divined that her lover is a phony. Out among the blooded millionaires, Jim is so "in" that he can discuss matters of status with friends there who would never dream of speaking on such topics to *hoi polloi*. For example, he's talking with Charley Ellis, heir to millions, about the millionaires at a party. Junior Williamson, Charley explains, is one of the royalty, " 'and the others are the nobility, the peerage.' " There are no commoners. Can one get in? asks Malloy. " 'What if I married Polly Williamson?' " She is Junior's wife, and both have enormous fortunes. " 'Well, you wouldn't marry her unless you were in love with her and she was in love with you, and we'd know that. You'd get credit for marrying her in spite of her dough and not because of it. But you could never look at another woman, not even flirt a little. You couldn't start spending her money on yourself. You'd have to get something to do that her money wouldn't help you with. *And* if Polly had an affair with another guy, you'd take the rap. . . .' " Presently Malloy goes over to Polly Williamson, whom he has scarcely met, and says, " 'I have to tell you this. It may be the wrong time, Mrs. Williamson, and it may not last, and I know I'll never see you again. But I love you, and whenever I think of you I'll love you.' " She replies, " 'I know, I know. Thank you for saying it. It was dear of you.' "

This exchange is the heart of the story. Malloy knows *real* class when he sees it. And real class responds to his tribute as only it can. Charley says, " 'Oh, that was a damn nice thing to do, to make her feel love again. The existence of it, the urgency of it, and the niceness.' " On the heels of this triumph, bad temper characteristically flares up; Jim tells the crook he is a crook.

The second novella, "Imagine Kissing Pete," is about a spirited girl with class who marries an oaf. The marriage goes bad for three reasons, any one of which could make a story. First, there is the fact that Bobbie married Pete not only on the rebound but also to spite the fellow who jilted her. Second, there is the Depression, and Pete loses his job and sits around glum and drinking. Third, Pete, who was a prudish virgin, goes wild at the discovery of sex and chases wives so outrageously that he and Bobbie are excluded from their former social life. The data outrun the needs of the story, but again the real transaction here is between the reader and Jim Malloy, whose relaxed reportage is at the focus of attention. There is time for Jim to dig around in Gibbsville gossip and expose the depravities of Prohibition, time for a remarkable display of the abrasions among and within married couples of the younger set, time for a fight after a Country Club dance. Bobbie and Pete, who reappear after some time, go far down till they hit bottom and start back up. Bobbie, from Lantenengo Street, becomes the (respectable) belle of a tavern near the factories. But somehow they weather the storm, rediscover some affection, and raise a child who graduates from Princeton with the top prizes. The whole story seems obscurely to hint that class will win out, but it does not say so. Perhaps the happy ending is pure luck. O'Hara does not try to suggest a meaning in his account of how it was. The most reliable inferences that we can make have to do with people's immediate reactions to situations.

"We're Friends Again" (the third novella) moves back to the Long Island people of "The Girl on the Baggage Truck." Jim has a long evening with a pair of socialites, after which he drops (rather drunk) into bed with a Broadway actress (also rather drunk, but an old friend). In the morning they worry about whether they were noticed by the columnists. How can the "beautiful young actress" and the "sensational young novelist" fail to have been noticed at the "21" and "El Morocco"? They can't—but this prelude serves to float us into the social world where Jim Malloy can relate to the richest of them. This is Polly Williamson, so splendid and beautiful and classy that he loved her at first glance two novellas back. Now she is his fan, reads his novels, and even shows up in Boston to see his play because she fears that it may not make it to Broadway. She is the ultimate American woman; he is her culture hero. The point of the story is that this Polly Williamson, heiress to millions, is married to a bone-crushing woman-chasing multimillionaire who resembles no one so much as Tom Buchanan of *The Great Gatsby*. She seems to be a nobly suffering, utterly proper aristocrat; but it transpires that for years she has been having an affair with a quiet Boston aristocrat, which almost nobody suspected, and she marries him later. And so again we find that we just don't know what goes on under the surface, although it is almost sure to be more sex than we suspect. Malloy is delighted to discover that Polly's "real" marriage is with the quiet Bostonian. "It is always a pleasure to discover that someone you like and have underestimated on the side of simplicity turns out to be intricate and therefore worthy of your original interest," he says. The bulk of the story is *discussion*, in the Shavian sense—information about how it was that comes out after the fact as people chat over lunch or a drink. It is very interesting. The simplicity of the prose, the bits of information about millionaires, society, the War Office, and sex may make up for the fact that the people are not deeply known. Yet their conversations are absorbing. On the last page of the third novella, Jim Malloy discovers that his old and very good friend Charley Ellis was deeply in love with his wife, who told nasty tales about Polly and her Boston man and was an America-Firster. Jim concludes, "I realized that until then I had not known him at all. It was not a discovery to cause me dismay. What did he know about me? What, really, can any of us know about any of us, and why must we make such a thing of loneliness when it is the final condition of us all?" The special quality of O'Hara is that he can be so interesting in describing the glittering surface of How It Was with respect to status, money, drinking, and sex.

There are gross lapses of taste in these tales, where the axes of realism, sex, and status cross. It's all right for Jim Malloy to explain that Nancy Preswell, who is going to marry Charley Ellis, is a bitch, but one may doubt the taste of his telling the actress with whom he spent the previous night that he can take her out for a snack after her play and still—if she refuses to go to bed with him again—pick up a girl at one of the night clubs. The ploy succeeds, and Julie re-embarks on their affair for some months. It goes on until one day they have a half-hearted discussion about whether they should marry. She decides against it because they are both very bad Catholics, but still

Catholics, and a marriage between them would have to be permanent. She has had a couple of abortions, she says, but if she becomes pregnant by Jim she will tell him and hope he will marry her. But it isn't really love, and a paragraph later she drops into his apartment for her things, because the man she had been planning to marry when Jim showed up again has come back. So they go to bed for a last turn, the details of which are vivid but not significant except to show that conventional ideas about how people feel and relate do not correspond to what takes place in the jungle they inhabit. Love and sex don't often go together. Women love one man but desire another and marry a third because he is rich. Or they marry one and immediately discover the need for an affair. Human relations are almost never *right*, and it is plain that nobody knows where he stands. People are drained of the capacity for love or belief or idealism—even though they have very strong opinions on many subjects and will, over the second drink, fight anybody over them. The disillusion lends no tone of bitterness or despair to the stories. The facts are recited with detachment, candor, and gusto. And the aristocrats continually surprise us by being more brave, intelligent, honorable, intricate, faithful, and idealistic than anybody supposed. It is a puzzling world, and nobody has caught its gleam and movement so well as O'Hara.

The Big Laugh, back on the sour side of O'Hara's triangle of subjects, anatomizes stage, screen, and Hollywood. The hero, Hubert Ward, O'Hara explains, is a bad man—a really bad man. He lies, cheats, and steals, attracts women with cryptic comments, superficial good manners, and Brooks Brothers shirts. A flashback shows how he got that way, with a suicide father, a drunken mother (of good family), and no proper discipline. The story especially abounds in Hollywood information and instant insights. Hubert's first movie producer sees that men and women will dislike him but that the women who go to see him in evil minor roles will not tolerate having him killed or degraded at the end—all this in a flash. The wise directors and producers (the action is in the 1920's) foresee the great stock market crash of 1929 (as such people typically do in O'Hara novels), but they do not take any steps to protect themselves. There is a good deal of condensed, vivid conversation about How It Was in Hollywood then among the most important people. There are devastating disclosures of relations (mostly sexual) and mores (also mostly sexual). There are frequent brutal exchanges that follow—or produce—the instant insights. It's all packed in so tight that it makes interesting reading even though it does not go below the surface.

Hubert Ward soon makes good Hollywood money, lives devoid of loyalty or affection for anybody, and frets in boredom and bad temper against his life. He is ready to make some outrageous mistake, exactly the way Julian English threw his drink in the face of Harry Reilly in *Samarra*, and set up his own downfall. And he does. He goes to bed with the wife of a big producer, Charley Simmons, who is his good friend—and gets himself kicked right out of the world. Here is a good example of how O'Hara keeps his reader at a disadvantage. Mildred Simmons is half of her very successful husband's brains. She knows and understands everybody. She is entirely faithful although every man in the society tries to make love to her. Charley Simmons loves Mildred and is correspondingly faithful. With all her brains, experience, and insight, however, she believes that Charley is having an affair with another woman. So she makes love with Hubert (after years of chaste but confidential friendship with him) right in her own house

during a party, quarrels with Charley, and tells him what she has done—and the roof falls in on Hubert. Thus the same people who are incredibly smart, wise, practical, and experienced all of a sudden make the most violent and incredible mistakes. Much happens but one does not understand why. Nor does this end it. Charley gets drunk, falls from the second story, and kills himself before anybody knows he has cashiered Hubert. This sequence is glibly misinterpreted later by one of the smartest men in the business, talking to Hubert. He explains that Mildred Simmons in fact killed Charley. " 'He couldn't face the fact that he was as much of a son of a bitch as you or me. . . . He was dead as soon as Mildred told him about you. . . . Because she didn't *have* to tell him, the bitch. But when she told him, he knew she was doing it to ruin him.' " Just about everything is wrong here, but it comes straight from a horse's mouth in a typical scene of insights that the reader cannot evaluate any more than he can know why the speaker thinks what he does.

The intricacies of mysterious insights and unpredictable reversals of character lead to an explanation of the title of the book: "Paradox! . . . the big laugh is Hollywood, everything about it. And everywhere you went there was a big laugh, like Hubert Ward suddenly becoming respectable. But the *big* laugh, he said, was going to be when they found out that you were more respectable as a bum than as . . . a hypocrite." This looks like thought but is only rhetoric parading as thought, yet it catches the spirit of aggressive phoniness that O'Hara has made the hallmark of Hollywood.

So Hubert is off the hook and swimming with the big fish again without having missed a stroke. He is also continually presented having long fascinating conversations with important people; the reader cannot fail to be attracted to him. Like the author, he engages us by his candor, no matter how amoral the tone or how brutal the revelations.

Just at the point where boredom and fretfulness threaten to destroy him, Hubert makes a superb marriage to a girl of brains, beauty, character, family, and money, who truly loves him. He becomes respectable, very rich, and famous well before he is thirty, and he works hard to fulfill his new image.

But further abysses of unfathomed motivation soon open before us. Nina, the gracious, cultivated, warm lady, who married Hubert for love and somewhat against her conventional better judgment, actually "had knowingly married a rogue . . . and [now] she discovered and rediscovered that the domesticated rogue was boring her." On this gossamer thread of improbable motivation—which contradicts everything we know about her—she becomes critical, Hubert becomes resentful and testy; and nasty insults soon pass between them and generate unforgivable acts. A strong love simply evaporates, leaving no residue of loyalty, affection, or mutual respect on either side. It is this result that is the most improbable: they have a son, they are rich and respected, they have made a dignified way of life together, and most of all Nina is a woman of breeding and character—and it all disappears in smoke after one flash of bad feeling.

Hubert stays rich and successful, wandering now from woman to woman, and that is the end of the "novel." The paradoxes of O'Hara were never more striking: the vivid dialogue, which makes every scene real, renders conduct that is inexplicable and contrary to all expectations, although we "see" it happening as clearly as if we were present. In this society, it is difficult to see how Hubert Ward is more evil than anyone else. Women who are said to be rather good people initiate the adulteries

for which Hubert is condemned. Nina, the blooded socialite, marries him for the wrong reasons and turns against him when she becomes bored. O'Hara's women can fall to any depth. The one he professes to admire most in this book is absolutely, unreservedly promiscuous. He admires her because she is honest about it. His women are generally lustier, hardier, more deceitful, more self-sufficient, and more selfish than his men.

The Big Laugh is thus composed of meretricious paradoxes in situation, character, and motivation. If we see it as a culmination of O'Hara's development to this point, we may conclude that the fate which presided over *Samarra* has become deified or satanic Absurd.

Elizabeth Appleton might seem to qualify as a novel of manners in the traditional sense. Perhaps any novel that has status as its subject would so qualify, especially if it is standard social status involving conflicts among levels of manners and wealth. Elizabeth is a tennis-playing Long Island society girl, with a finishing school education and a fortune. She is beautiful and elegant and shy. John Appleton comes on the scene as a summer tutor of a neighboring boy. He is an athlete, too, and he plays tennis with Elizabeth all summer and finally proposes. When he meets her parents, he is able to win her father but the super-snobbish mother can only be held at bay by the knowledge that this young scholar who is going back to teach history in a small Pennsylvania college is the fourth generation of Harvard men in his family.

John is from one of the first families of Spring Valley, Pennsylvania, but he is in fact a stuffy type. He's a popular lecturer who fancies himself somewhat more intellectual than he is. Elizabeth subdues her social tendencies, dresses simply, conceals her fortune, and in every way subordinates herself to the task of being a good wife for the rising professor. There is a setting here for any sort of penetration of manners that the author chooses to pursue. O'Hara proceeds with broad strokes. The raging hatred between Elizabeth's parents is revealed; the mother's dominance comes into head-on conflict with John when Elizabeth is having her first baby—and John stands his ground and wins. The life of the small college is explored—its fraternities, its wealthy trustees, its struggles for power, its possessive benefactors. We see how Spring Valley is divided between the college circle and the rich "Hill" crowd, wealthy alumni who are now sending their children to eastern prep schools and Ivy League colleges and no longer see their old college as the exclusive sanctuary it once was.

The action proper appears to begin when John, aged forty and a full professor, gets so carried away by his New Dealish liberalism that he delivers a lecture to his history class in which he seems to imply that one of the richest local benefactors of the college was an unscrupulous robber baron. The rich man has his supporters. Academic freedom is important, but the best people in town believe that John Appleton was mistaken and irresponsible. This blunder of unsophisticated liberalism (which we might venture to guess that O'Hara sees as fatheaded academic pretentiousness) carries us deeper into the heart of the town and opens up long discussions of status. John *was* wrong, it appears, and he needs help to get himself off the hook. Elizabeth has been resenting her subordination, the dull faculty people, the lack of gaiety in their lives. John lays it on the line: " 'We could join the country club and hear just the opposite,' " he says, referring to the liberal talk that bores her. " 'To my untutored ear they're [i.e., the country-club people] just as boring as my friends are to you.' " And she lets him have it between the eyes with

" 'You know perfectly well I voted for Roosevelt, even if my heart wasn't in it. And if it comes down to that, my mother and father *know* the Roosevelts and none of these friends of yours do. My uncle was in the same class *and* the same club as Mr. Roosevelt at Harvard, long before any of your friends ever heard of him.' " Thus a typical O'Hara couple can fly at each other's throats as suppressed grievances and bad feeling boil up. With friends, lovers, couples, business associates, parent and child the same rages overflow suddenly and disastrously.

Following her party, Elizabeth begins an affair with Porter Ditson, an eccentric individualist who lives without working, being from the second or third wealthiest family in town. Passionately in love, they can find time only for sex together and there is none for the sustained communication that people in love need. Elizabeth apparently does not need it. She wants her sexual satisfaction and gets it. They must, however, manage time for relaxed discussions of snobbery that contribute to their mutual esteem. Porter says, " 'I've lived here all my life, and I see people like Mary's father every day. But I'd never go to his house, and he'd never think of asking me.' " She acknowledges that the highest society in town looks up to her, and with queenly complaisance she allows the local leader to help with their secret meetings. When the war intervenes, John Appleton takes a naval commission, and Elizabeth and Porter have three years of more or less secure sex between 1942 and 1945. The development and consummation of their relation is presented in detail, not as a moral problem but as a sensual experience. Elizabeth's scruples are easily disposed of, and Porter has none.

As the end of the war nears, Elizabeth terminates the affair—for no apparent reason except that she has decided it is time to end it. He loves her and wants to marry her; she loves him in her way; but it's time for a change. They discuss, and Porter explains that whereas she can separate her sex from her marriage and renounce him because finally marriage is more important to her, he has loved her steadily and painfully all the time and still wants to marry her. Rather than be merely an occasional incident in her life, he declares that he will never see her again. He could not bear to have only a part of the woman. Elizabeth is revealed as at once very sensual and rather limited. She is incapable of the depth of relation that Porter wants, incapable because she is not intelligent enough. And as Porter sums it up, " 'Sexy as you are, passionate and exciting and abandoned like today, the sex you get with John is really as much as you need.' " She can want the more exciting sex that she has with Porter, whom she loves, but she does not love him enough to *have* to have him. That is her limit. The break with Porter turns a corner for her: "Elizabeth Appleton became more explicitly a recognizable American type; the wife who frankly and equally participates in her husband's career while making it plain that she wants no other career of her own."

John Appleton has been an ambiguous character. He is small-town, self-righteous, narrowly intellectual—or perhaps Elizabeth finds him a bit boring because of her own limitations. Back at the college, he thrives as the new dean of men, but little errors in his past, some accidental, some too small to be described here, add up to justify the opposition he has aroused and keep him from being made president. At the end, when the students are protesting because John has not been made president, he pacifies them, declares his fidelity to the college, and winds up the story with a good O'Hara-esque outburst in which he pol-

ishes the double-dealing old president off with a rich flood of abuse: " 'Why you lying son of a bitch . . . yellow-belly . . . You're chicken, fellow.' "

Elizabeth regrets what she has done to Porter, resents her life a little, finds John lacking in both guts and intellect, and confesses that she has stayed by her marriage for a variety of reasons that add up to inertia: habit, children, disapproval of divorce combine to balance her slight will to break loose into a better life. The characterization of Elizabeth is brilliantly original.

The great bulk of the book consists of reportage on college politics and local status, not organized into a substantial action but described somewhat at random to give a feeling of a partly seen complex of people and institutions among which the Appletons live. The action is pinched, abandoned, diverted, and then its thin thread released from time to time to let Elizabeth make a decision. Her problems, John's problems, and Porter's problems (not to mention those of at least four other people who enjoy the focus of interest in various chapters) do not sustain the book through anything approaching its total movement. As a novel of manners, *Elizabeth Appleton* shows our social fabric to be so loosely woven that people do not feel it. There are so many levels of wealth, education, status, and morality in the book that these elements do not cohere into a substantial social reality. O'Hara dips into the variousness here and there, somewhat at random, to draw out interesting scenes for his immediate purpose, while a larger purpose or picture does not exist.

The Lockwood Concern is a major work that reveals so many facets of O'Hara's mature talent, so rich an exposure of his preoccupations, and so profound a look into his view of the human heart that it repays careful scrutiny. It is the four-generation saga of a family that aspires to wealth, position, and so much as they understand of culture. If their master thrust is toward status, their master bias is secretiveness, which in turn flowers in heartlessness. With their eyes on advantage and their lips sealed against imprudent disclosures, they cannot open themselves to another person. Starved of love, they become treacherous, libidinous, haughty, cruel, and indifferent.

The word "Concern" in the title means a financial dynasty, or the conception of such a dynasty. Ironically, it is taken from the Quaker idea of a moral or religious preoccupation. The Lockwoods are dedicated to spreading their holdings into domains, elevating their families into dynasties, and entrenching their powers so that nothing can dislodge them. The long view is sustained by the ineffable dream of status, as if the perspectives of property or wealth were glittering causeways across which strode the giant figures of the family clothed in the embroidered velvets of ultimate prestige.

The dynastic vision of time provides the angle by which O'Hara sees the parts of his story and arranges them. There are four generations of Lockwoods: Moses was born in 1811 and came to Swedish Haven, Pennsylvania, in 1833, under dubious auspices. He killed a man the night of his arrival and another some years later, and the unresolved question of his guilt hangs over the family thereafter. Moses has a son named Abraham and two mad daughters who constitute another dark corner in the family's past as well as a key to the men's treatment of their women. Abraham, born about 1840, joins his father in banking and transportation and starts the massive accumulation of property. He has two sons, George and Penrose, born in 1873 and 1877, who carry the operation into the twentieth century and figure centrally in the story. George is the protagonist. It is he who

expects to bring the Concern to fruition; and it is he whose two children, George and Ernestine, fail to sustain the dynastic pattern for which they were intended.

The broad lines of the action reflect business plans, sexual adventures and misadventures, and problems of status. These are presented in essays, dramatic incidents, and lengthy discourses, the latter either by characters or by the author. The incidents are not unlike O'Hara's short stories. They show How It Was at the occasion, but they do not make the larger pattern of the story. Any sort of incident, crisis, or person can be thrust into the chronicle at any moment—and is.

The larger pattern encompasses much more than can be rendered either dramatically or through particular personal problems—and so it reveals much less of people's developing lives. That is, the broad chronicle sweep, covering generations and vast social growths, soon takes most of the crucial issues out of the characters' hands, because they are not seen as an individual's problems. Society happens: towns grow, businesses expand, clubs and institutions carry on their control of status, and exclusive schools function. The characters *appear* from time to time among these institutional movements, but they do not seem generally to *make* them. We see samples of a business lunch, a discussion of status, an assignation. These show the way life is, but they are not crucial or essential stages in an integrated action, and thus they do not particularize the characters involved, as decisions respecting key issues in their lives would do. It is as if we watched a city for a time through a wide lens, and then zoomed down to focus on a small group of people sitting at a table drinking and talking, and then zoomed back to the distant big view. No matter how clearly and interestingly we heard those people at the table, we should not feel that their discussion was *causing* the great stir and flow of the city's life. All these considerations must be kept in mind as we look at what happens in the story; they are the *how* of its happening, the key to O'Hara's form.

The novel begins in 1926 with a description of the magnificent wall that is going up around George's property—that is, around thirty acres of it, which are part of a two-hundred-acre farm bought from some old settlers. As the wall is being completed, all signs of the old settlers' ownership are cleared away; then a magnificent house is built inside the wall, with George there every day keeping track of the work. Only when it is done does his wife, Geraldine, return from New York and see it. We shall return to this symbolic wall and house. Here it begins to work when, on the night of the day that the mansion is completed, a boy is impaled and killed on the spikes that march around its top. The boy was up in a tree, trying to spy inside. George immediately goes to New York to escape the inquest and its notoriety; but he tells Geraldine that he came just to tell her personally that the house was finished. She says, " 'Well, that's sweet, but I don't believe it. You do unexpected things, but you're not sentimental.' "

In disclosing character, O'Hara often relies on surprise, or what I call the instant insight, rather than using the considered choices that reveal a character in a significant action. Surprise comes when a character reacts unforeseeably. It is often made plausible by O'Hara's remarkable ear for language. In his dramatic scenes the voices of the characters resonate with the banalities of life, and we cannot doubt their reality. If we are surprised by their conduct, we are not therefore incredulous; rather, we suspect that they act from pent-up emotions or a habitual violence more than from conscious choice.

There is in this device a certain amount of one-upmanship on O'Hara's part. He is showing that he knows people better than his reader. He is on safe ground, having made them; but use of the device has other implications. It replaces the revelation of character-in-conflict-and-choice. Because O'Hara typically devotes a major portion of a novel to long expository historical and social analyses, giving a full account, for example, of social tensions in Gibbsville or a discussion of the financial activities by which a previous generation accumulated its wealth, there is not time for a continuous action. Instead, we have these little concentrated intrusions of short-story-like scenes. Typically, a character will be introduced in such a scene. Then he will be seen incidentally or from a considerable distance for several chapters; and then he will reappear under the microscope of another concentrated dramatic encounter, and we learn startling new facts about him from the reactions of others.

In *The Lockwood Concern* this procedure is standard. George sends Geraldine to Brooks Brothers to buy him some shirts, so that he can phone Swedish Haven about the boy killed on his wall. When she returns, she says that the salesman would gladly have sent the shirts to the hotel. George explains that over the telephone he would have had to answer questions about half the people in Lantenengo County, and she replies, " '*That's* why you made me go. I was wondering. But you always have a reason for things. I've learned that.' " That evening at dinner with friends Geraldine remarks that she isn't "in" on George's plans while they are being formed. Because she had been impatient with him in the afternoon, perhaps, George takes deep offense at this remark, and afterwards in a few sentences launches what turns out to be a permanent estrangement.

From this incident, we go back to 1921 and see George's son Bing expelled from Princeton for cheating and reviled so brutally by his father that he leaves for California, thus dealing an irreparable blow to the Concern. Then there is a giant step backward, to Moses Lockwood, founder of the Swedish Haven dynasty, who dies with a fortune of $200,000 in bank stock and property. His son Abraham joins good clubs at the University of Pennsylvania, gains some distinction as an officer assigned to the War Department in Washington, and makes social and financial strides by convincing rich Philadelphia friends that his ties are in New York, where the big money and the high society flourish. Building his empire, grooming his son George at a fashionable private school, Abraham nevertheless finds that he cannot get into the exclusive Philadelphia club, and he is gently told that he should not expect it for George, though perhaps his grandson will make it if the fortune holds up. Status requires family and money—and "family" means several stable generations, no matter how uncultivated.

The structure is apparent by now. At page 181 (of 432) we have gone back to the roots and we have made our way to third-generation George at prep school. Henceforth the story is chronological, taking us through George's college days at Princeton, replete with status tensions and sex. He breaks his first engagement, with "Dutchy" Eulalie Fenstermacher, but he is permitted honorable scruples about the breach, and the reader at this point identifies with him. The sentiment stumbles into banality when George confides to his college friend O'Byrne (another O'Hara persona) that his grandfather killed two men and that he's not "true gentry." O'Byrne remarks that that " 'explains a few things . . . certain hesitancies,' " and tells George, " 'I noticed you're not always as sure of yourself as you ought to be. Most of the time, yes. But not always. . . . Your son will be an aristocrat. Then you ought to have him marry an Italian or a Spaniard be-

fore the inbreeding starts.' " By now the reader is likely to have these reactions: that everybody here thinks about status more than most people do; that a wealthy Princeton undergraduate who had come from an exclusive prep school would probably not worry about what his grandfather did; that the author here as always is revealing his own high competence on questions of status.

Going now into Book II, we find that the story has returned to the time of the first page. George learns from a very aristocratic fund-raiser from the very aristocratic prep school that his son Bing has in about five years since he left home moved into oil riches in California. When the man departs, we witness one of O'Hara's close-ups. Geraldine, who has been missing for almost three hundred pages, comes in and engages in a long bitter conversation with George. Bored and angry with her, George goes to New York to make love with the secretary, Marian Strademyer, whom his brother Penrose loves almost to distraction. After George leaves her apartment, Penrose comes up in a jealous rage—apparently because she has not answered the telephone—and kills her and himself. George carries on as if he were not responsible or even involved. Son Bing comes home for the funeral. George now hates him and his California success and brutally abuses him; in return, he gets a dose of caustic dislike. That night, after the funeral, Bing makes love to his dead uncle's wife, while George peeks and listens from his study. The ambiguities of this "bad blood" are disturbing: it's his own blood, but it justifies his having driven Bing from the house for cheating at Princeton.

As we move into the essential action, the treatment becomes briefer rather than fuller. Whereas Book I filled 280 pages, Book II has filled only 70, and Book III, where the real action comes, will fill 65. Book III introduces

George's daughter, Ernestine, who has scarcely been mentioned before. She comes home from Europe, reluctantly, and during the first evening there are instant insights and profound disclosures as she and George converse. George realizes that he has never loved anyone until the present happy moment when he is talking to his daughter *without calculation*. She makes him "feel needed" because she is "miserably unhappy." Thus she "takes him out of himself"! After this calculated definition of love, other disclosures follow fast. Ernestine confesses that she always felt " 'that the Lockwoods . . . were never quite respectable.' " Now, this is a hundred-year perspective that a girl of Ernestine's advantages would hardly achieve, particularly if she has not thought much about it before, even though the author has to make her say that she has. In her generation her father owns the town, has been to the most exclusive prep school plus Princeton, dresses in the very best style. The notion of not quite having made it socially haunts O'Hara and comes out in almost every book—here most improbably.

Now Ernestine opens up to her father about her extraordinarily depraved life abroad, and George straightway makes plans for her to marry Preston Hibbard, a scion of Boston millions. Managed meetings lead to love, all right, but Hibbard reveals a homosexual background, while Ernestine confesses that she has been desexed by an operation for venereal disease. They nevertheless marry because George wills it and George has seldom failed to have his way.

When he learns that Bing, in California, has been involved in corrupt deals and is headed for catastrophe, George sighs with relief because his savage treatment of Bing has been justified. The bad blood was there from the beginning, not to be controlled in any way. The great panoramic *fated* movement of society, mentioned earlier, is directly involved here: characters discuss and analyze; George offers his instant insights into the way people are; but there seldom is any moral, ethical, or philosophical vision of happenings. No meaning is attributed to them, for they are merely *seen*. George's conduct could be traced to pique caused by Geraldine's coldness, Bing's rejection, a millionaire's condescension, or his first wife's insight into his adultery. Pique, annoyance—covering a moral void in a hollow man. George moves like a zombie—rigid, inscrutable, grim, arrogant. Pique now takes him to a prostitute who is so obliging that he decides to set her up in style as his permanent mistress. After all, kings have kept mistresses, and he can afford one, too. He returns to Swedish Haven in a frenzy of pride and determination. There, after reviewing his family's career and concluding that he comes from a superior breed, he falls down the secret stairway that descends from his study closet—and dies, not hoist by his own petard but tumbling into his own hidden well of vanity and secretiveness.

The notions of secrecy and pride are developed in an elaborate system of symbolism centering around the great house that George builds. A house is a universal sign of man's desire for privacy and security, but George Lockwood's house is special. Only when the surrounding iron-spiked wall is up and its heavy gates are in place do the workmen come to build the house inside. When the house is finished and the last workman gone, George directs a group of Italian craftsmen from New York, who are already on the premises doing special interior woodwork, to install a hidden stairway from the second floor to the basement, accessible through secret panels controlled by concealed springs. And only then does Geraldine return from New York to set about furnishing and decorating.

The stairway, which represents George's master bias of prideful secrecy, figures three times in the narrative. Once he uses it to discover his son Bing making love to Penrose's widow on the night of his funeral. Once on impulse he reveals it to the young man who is just what George wants to be: the rich and well-born Preston Hibbard. For the third incident, George comes secretly home, with thoughts of the prostitute who will be his mistress. Defying Geraldine, he shows how his inability to love has reduced him to the most mechanical of relations. In the climax of cold, will-ridden secrecy, he enters his secret stairway—for no important reason—and falls to his death. But he lies dying long enough to realize the nightmare of his separateness.

Published in 1965, *The Lockwood Concern* might seem to break the clear line of development that we have traced in O'Hara's approach to status, for *Sermons and Soda Water* of 1960 has risen to a peak of complacency from which the grubbing aspirations of the Lockwoods represent a long falling-off. The explanation must be that this book which deals so exclusively with status is saying that it is a barren pursuit, that George is rendered sterile, secretive, and unloving because he has fixed his eyes upon a cold dead star whose baleful influence blights the spirit. What is by no means clear in this presumed message (for O'Hara nowhere interprets his recital of How It Was) is whether the quest for status blights the Lockwoods or the crafty secrecy of the Lockwoods blights their quest for status. If theory would lead us to the former interpretation, the tone of the book would seem more pervasively to resonate with the latter effect. Where every page abounds with details about status, where O'Hara never fails to tell us whether George took the Packard, the Lincoln, or the Pierce-Arrow, we can hardly fail to conclude that

this is reality, this is the substance of the author's world.

O'Hara's special characteristic surely is the violent, bitter, abrasive quality of human relations in his books. Drunk, aimless, socially insecure, morally adrift, his people are equally violent and unexpected—except when they are depraved and cynical. In the latter event they do not surprise us so much.

Searching among the basic elements of fiction—story, character, idea—for the secret of O'Hara's tremendous *interest*, one may be puzzled. Often the story is not expertly dramatized, yet the reader is very curious to know what will happen next. The characters may be talented, testy, unpredictable, and only superficially known, yet the reader will be fascinated in the process of getting to know about them. The ideas are limited in range and very elusive when they pretend to depth, yet they *live* compellingly in the character-action nexus. Somewhere in this complex lies the secret of O'Hara's readability—of the fact that millions of readers find it impossible to lay a story of his aside once they have started it. Perhaps the heart of it is that the characters come alive because the reader is completely involved in the living instant when he sees them responding —often surprisingly—to the problem and the situation through which they exist and grow.

In the range and breadth of his materials, O'Hara may be compared with Trollope, Balzac, Galsworthy, and James T. Farrell. While he does not approach the quality and influence of Hemingway and Faulkner, it must be acknowledged that his talent has held up considerably better than that of John Steinbeck, whose late works demonstrate the terrible pressure and exhaustion of spirit that may be suffered by the professional writer, even after he has become rich and famous. In this respect it might be argued that O'Hara has sustained his quality better than Sherwood Anderson, John Dos Passos, or Robert Penn Warren. The modern writer of roughly comparable stature who maintained his quality through an equally large body of writing is John P. Marquand. A close comparison of these two recorders of How It Was will, I believe, bring out sharply the qualities and limitations I have found in O'Hara.

* * *

John O'Hara died, aged 65, on April 11, 1970, at his home in Princeton, New Jersey— a French manor house secluded in the woods where he had lived and worked since 1953. He had recently completed The Ewings, *which was scheduled for publication the following February (1971), and had finished seventy pages of a sequel. His funeral service was held in the Princeton University Chapel, and he was buried in Princeton Cemetery. Although some critics regretted the fact that O'Hara had not seemed to fulfill the high promise of* Appointment in Samarra, *a review of all his works suggests that he maintained a fairly constant level through his long and prolific career. The promise of his early work became more commonplace as the years passed.*

Selected Bibliography

WORKS OF JOHN O'HARA

NOVELS AND NOVELLAS

Appointment in Samarra. New York: Harcourt, Brace, 1934.

Butterfield 8. New York: Harcourt, Brace, 1935.

Hope of Heaven. New York: Harcourt, Brace, 1938.

A Rage to Live. New York: Random House, 1949.

The Farmers Hotel. New York: Random House, 1951.

Ten North Frederick. New York: Random House, 1955.

A Family Party. New York: Random House, 1956.

From the Terrace. New York: Random House, 1958.

Ourselves to Know. New York: Random House, 1960.

Sermons and Soda Water. New York: Random House, 1960.

The Big Laugh. New York: Random House, 1962.

Elizabeth Appleton. New York: Random House, 1963.

The Lockwood Concern. New York: Random House, 1965.

The Instrument. New York: Random House, 1967.

Lovely Childs': A Philadelphian's Story. New York: Random House, 1969.

The Ewings. New York: Random House, 1972.

COLLECTED STORIES

The Doctor's Son and Other Stories. New York: Harcourt, Brace, 1935.

Files on Parade. New York: Harcourt, Brace, 1939.

Pal Joey. New York: Duell, Sloan and Pearce, 1940.

Pipe Night. New York: Duell, Sloan and Pearce, 1945.

Here's O'Hara. New York: Duell, Sloan and Pearce, 1946.

Hellbox. New York: Random House, 1947.

Selected Short Stories of John O'Hara, edited by Lionel Trilling. New York: Random House (Modern Library), 1956.

Assembly. New York: Random House, 1961.

The Cape Cod Lighter. New York: Random House, 1962.

49 Stories. New York: Random House (Modern Library), 1963. (Stories from the two preceding collections.)

The Hat on the Bed. New York: Random House, 1963.

The Horse Knows the Way. New York: Random House, 1964.

Waiting for Winter. New York: Random House, 1966.

And Other Stories. New York: Random House, 1968.

PLAYS

Pal Joey: The Libretto and Lyrics. New York: Random House, 1952.

Five Plays. New York: Random House, 1961.

ESSAYS

Sweet and Sour. New York: Random House, 1954.

Three Views of the Novel (with Irving Stone and MacKinlay Kantor). Washington, D.C.: Reference Department, The Library of Congress, 1957. (Pamphlet.)

My Turn. New York: Random House, 1966.

CRITICAL AND BIOGRAPHICAL STUDIES

Aldridge, John W. "Highbrow Authors and Middlebrow Books," *Playboy*, 11:119, 166–74 (April 1964).

Auchincloss, Louis. *Reflections of a Jacobite*. Boston: Houghton Mifflin, 1961.

Bier, Jesse. "O'Hara's *Appointment in Samarra*: His First and Only Real Novel," *College English*, 25:135–41 (November 1963).

Bishop, John Peale. "The Missing All," *Virginia Quarterly Review*, 13:106–21 (January 1937).

Breit, Harvey. *The Writer Observed*. Cleveland: World, 1956.

Carson, Edward Russell. *The Fiction of John O'Hara*. Pittsburgh: University of Pittsburgh Press, 1961.

Fadiman, Clifton. *Party of One*. Cleveland: World, 1955.

Grebstein, Sheldon Norman. *John O'Hara*. New York: Twayne, 1966.

Gurko, Leo. *The Angry Decade*. New York: Dodd, Mead, 1947.

Kazin, Alfred. *On Native Grounds*. New York: Reynal and Hitchcock, 1942.

————. *Contemporaries*. Boston: Little, Brown, 1962.

Podhoretz, Norman. "Gibbsville and New Leeds: The America of John O'Hara and Mary McCarthy," *Commentary*, 21:269–73 (March 1956).

Portz, John. "John O'Hara Up to Now," *College English*, 17:493–99, 516 (May 1955).

Prescott, Orville. *In My Opinion*. Indianapolis: Bobbs-Merrill, 1952.

Schwartz, Delmore. "Smile and Grin, Relax and Collapse," *Partisan Review*, 17:292–96 (March 1950).

Shannon, William V. *The American Irish*. New York: Macmillan, 1963.

Trilling, Lionel. "John O'Hara Observes Our Mores," *New York Times Book Review*, March 18, 1945, pp. 1, 9. (Reprinted as the introduction to *Selected Short Stories of John O'Hara*. New York: Random House [Modern Library], 1956.)

Van Nostrand, Albert. *The Denatured Novel*. Indianapolis: Bobbs-Merrill, 1960.

Weaver, Robert. "Twilight Area of Fiction: The Novels of John O'Hara," *Queen's Quarterly*, 66:320–25 (Summer 1959).

—CHARLES CHILD WALCUTT

Eugene O'Neill

1888-1953

WHEN Eugene O'Neill received the Nobel Prize in 1936 he was in his forty-ninth year and appeared to have concluded his career. More than thirty-five short and long plays by him had been produced in the United States, and they had won him important awards in his own country and an international reputation. But a long period of absence from the theater followed *Days without End*, which had opened in New York on January 8, 1934, and O'Neill did not return with a new play until the Theatre Guild production of *The Iceman Cometh* in 1946. Another decade of absence from the New York stage then ensued when his next play, *A Moon for the Misbegotten*, was withdrawn from a trial tour in the Midwest by O'Neill and the Theatre Guild management. Not until 1956 did another new play by him, *Long Day's Journey into Night*, reach New York. In the meantime, O'Neill had died in Boston on November 27, 1953, so that his renewed career as a dramatist, concluded by this more or less autobiographical drama and three other new pieces (*A Touch of the Poet, More Stately Mansions*, and the one-act play *Hughie*), was mainly posthumous. It may be said that O'Neill, who performed many other feats of endurance in the theater, happened to have two careers in it rather than the customary single one.

O'Neill also attracted attention with two styles of theater rather than one, being equally adept in the styles of realism and expressionism, and with two radically disproportionate types of drama, since he was equally effective in one-act plays and in cyclopean dramas twice the normal length of modern plays. His search for expressive form, in his case a combination of private compulsions and public ambitions to incorporate modern ideas and notions about life and dramatic art, led him to undertake numerous experiments with symbolic figures, masks, interior monologues, split personalities, choruses, scenic effects, rhythms, and schematizations. In O'Neill's work there is a veritable *summa* of the modern theater's aspirations and achievements as well as its more or less inevitable limitations and failures. It is largely this multifarious engagement with the possibilities of dramatic art, combined with an endeavor to apply them to significant as well as very personally felt subject matter, that made O'Neill a playwright of international importance.

In all his major work O'Neill traced the course of a modern dramatist in search of an aesthetic and spiritual center. It is not certain that he found it often, if ever, but the labor involved in the effort was usually impressive and sometimes notably rewarding. His plays embodied the ideas and conflicts of the first half of the twentieth century, assimilated its advances in dramatic art and theatrical technique, and expressed its uneasy aspirations toward tragic insights and dramatic vision. His impressiveness as a dramatist is ultimately, in fact, the result of his determined effort to trace a thread of meaning in the universe virtually emptied of meaning by a century of scientific and sociological thought. He did not, it is true, find any comforting assurances in the world, but he had the integrity to acknowledge his failure and the persistence to dramatize it with much penetration into human nature. O'Neill's experiments were not undertaken to suit the whims of a volatile trifler or the calculations of a theatrical opportunist bent on following the latest fashion; they manifest, rather, a unity of high purpose rarely exhibited by modern playwrights.

Eugene Gladstone O'Neill was born on October 16, 1888, in a hotel room in the very heart of New York's theatrical district applauded and derided as "Broadway." He was the son of the matinee idol and successful actor-manager James O'Neill, who amassed a fortune touring in a melodrama based on Alexandre Dumas's famous romantic novel *The Count of Monte Cristo*. The playwright who took so many successful liberties with dramatic form was entirely at home in the theater, and later also acted in his father's theatrical company. But it early became distressingly evident to his parent that the young O'Neill was a rebel who would be more inclined to revolt against the romantic tradition than to preserve it. O'Neill was born into a tragically disturbed family (his mother suffered from drug addiction and his elder brother was a confirmed alcoholic) and had an unstable childhood, touring the United States with his parents and receiving an irregular education in different private boarding schools. "Usually," O'Neill declared to a reporter in 1932, "a child has a regular, fixed home, but you might say I started as a trouper. I knew only actors and the stage. My mother nursed me in the wings and in dressing rooms." Encouraged by his irresponsible actor-brother James, he was inducted into the bohemian life of the theatrical world at a tender age. After a year at Princeton University, he was suspended in 1907 for a student prank. In 1909 he entered into a secret marriage, later dissolved. That same year he went prospecting for gold in Central America with a mining engineer. Having contracted malaria in the course of this fruitless expedition, he returned to his parents and joined his father's company as an actor and assistant manager for a brief period.

Growing restless again, he shipped to Buenos Aires on a Norwegian vessel and found employment for a time with American companies located in the area—an electric company, a packing plant, the Singer Sewing Machine Company. Tiring of clerical employment, he took a job on a cattle boat, tending mules while voyaging from Buenos Aires to South Africa. On his return to Argentina, he found himself unemployed and fell into a state of destitution which came to a close when he joined a British vessel bound for New York, but he promptly relapsed into a life of dissipation on the New York waterfront, frequenting a disreputable tavern, "Jimmy-the-Priest's," which he was to re-create in the milieu of two of his best-known plays, *Anna Christie* and *The Iceman Cometh*. Still attracted to the sea, however, he became an able seaman on the American Line and made a voyage to Southampton, England, before deciding to settle down to a less adventurous mode of life.

After joining his father's company again and playing a small part in *Monte Cristo*, followed by several months of intemperate living, he went to New London in Connecticut, where the family had its summer home, and joined the staff of the local newspaper, the *New London Telegraph*, as a reporter. He had begun to publish humorous poetry in a column of that newspaper when his journalistic career was abruptly terminated by a blow O'Neill could only consider ironic fate. His health undermined by his profligate mode of life, he succumbed to tuberculosis and had to be hospitalized in 1912. A term of six months in a sanatorium, however, proved to be doubly beneficial: it arrested the disease and made an avid reader and introspective artist of O'Neill. He read widely during his convalescence, falling under the influence of the Greek tragic poets and Strindberg. He began to write plays in 1913, and in 1914 enrolled in a course in playwriting given at Harvard University by the famous Professor George Pierce Baker.

The next year he moved to Greenwich Village, then regarded as the progressive "Left Bank" of New York, and in 1916 joined an avant-garde group of writers and artists who had established an amateur theatrical company. Their first season in the summer of 1915 had been presented on an abandoned wharf in the artists' colony of Provincetown, on Cape Cod, Massachusetts, and they came to call themselves the Provincetown Players. O'Neill began to write short plays for them and soon became their foremost playwright as well as one of their directors when they moved to a small theater in Greenwich Village on Macdougal Street, where theatrical experiments continued to be unfolded long after the dissolution of this company. (The best known of these have been Samuel Beckett's *Krapp's Last Tape* and Edward Albee's *The Zoo Story*.) O'Neill and his associates, the critic Kenneth Macgowan and the great American scenic artist Robert Edmond Jones, also ran a second enterprise, the Greenwich Village Theatre, from 1923 to 1927. In these years at one or the other of the theaters were produced such varied plays as Strindberg's exotic *The Spook Sonata*, O'Neill's own expressionist race-drama *All God's Chillun Got Wings*, and his naturalistic New England variant on the Phaedra-Hippolytus theme, *Desire under the Elms*. Both the Provincetown and the Greenwich Village ventures were among the most influential of groups in the seminal "little theater" movement which gained momentum after 1912 and succeeded in modernizing the American theater in the 1920's by bringing it abreast of European developments in dramatic art and at the same time discovering American backgrounds and rhythms.

The importance of O'Neill's early association with "the Provincetown" can hardly be exaggerated. He found an acceptable channel for his dramatic talent and theatrical interest because he also had an outlet for his personal rebellion in associating himself with an enterprise created by bohemian rebels against materialistic American society and the commercialism of the professional theater. In writing for the Provincetown Players and having his early plays performed before a small public of artists and intellectuals, he escaped the necessity of conforming to the popular taste to which his father had catered all his life with old-fashioned romantic theatricality. The prodigal son could deal with the life he had come to know during his years of wandering, poverty, dissipation, and desperation among common men and fellow exiles from respectable society. As a result, O'Neill made himself, in his early short plays about the seafaring life (especially those collected under the title of *S.S. Glencairn*), the first American "naturalist" in a period when the general public in America was still expecting from its playwrights discreet pictures of reality that would give no offense. At the same time, his early plays evoked a vigorous poetry of naturalism compounded of the atmosphere of the sea and the moods of the men for whom their life on ships and on the waterfront was both an occupation and an occasion for romantic escape. For O'Neill himself the sea was a symbol of the lostness of mankind in a hostile or indifferent universe, of a conspiracy of Nature against Man. Had he started his career thirty years later—say, in 1945 rather than 1915—he might indeed have been enrolled in the ranks of Existentialist writers, and another decade later in the company of the "Theater of the Absurd" playwrights.

It would appear that O'Neill became a significant figure in America because his early work was a natural synthesis of both the naturalistic and the poetic strivings of the modern theater. He combined realism of characterization with a sensitive regard for the romantic longings of characters, a naturalist's concern for environmental detail with a metaphysical flight from the particular to the general, and plodding realistic prose with a poetic flare for imagery, atmosphere, and scenic imagination; it could be said of him that he was one of the least poetic and at the same time one of the most poetic of modern dramatists.

This synthesis was apparent virtually from the beginning of his work, in the one-act plays that first drew attention to him. The cultivation of one-act drama was characteristic of the entire avant-garde movement of the period. The Provincetown Players, along with other progressive "little theaters," favored this genre for a variety of reasons. One-act plays required less professional experience to write than full-length dramas, and these novices of the theater found one-act playwriting especially congenial because it enabled them to dispense with the complicated contrivances of plot they despised as unauthentic and artificial. One-act plays were also inexpensive to produce and

easy to perform by the amateurs of the little theater movement. (The same tendency to favor the one-act drama had been marked among avant-garde writers for Antoine's Théâtre Libre between 1887 and 1890 and for the Irish national theater, the Abbey, in Dublin, before 1914.) With his decisive success in this genre, O'Neill emerged as the foremost product of the little theater in America and its major justification.

O'Neill started with short "slice-of-life" dramas dealing with the miseries, delusions, and obsessions of men adrift in the world. With the appearance of the *S.S. Glencairn* cycle of sea-pieces, beginning with the Provincetown Players' production of his atmospheric drama of the death of a common sailor, *Bound East for Cardiff*, in the summer of 1916, he became the undisputed master of the one-act play form in America. The sharply etched playlets *In the Zone* and *The Long Voyage Home* (1917) and another atmospheric piece, *The Moon of the Caribbees* (1918), along with O'Neill's first Provincetown production, made up the remarkable quartet of one-acters subsequently produced under the collective title of *S.S. Glencairn*. A number of independent pieces such as *Ile* (1917), *The Rope* (1918), and *Where the Cross Is Made* (1918) also enhanced their young author's reputation by the end of World War I. *Ile* is especially representative of his early naturalistic-symbolic style with its mordant treatment of a New England sea captain's obsessive pride in his ability to hunt whales for their "ile" (that is, oil) which drives his lonely wife mad. This little play exemplified O'Neill's taste for tragic irony, his characteristic concern with destructive obsessiveness that resembles the *hubris* of classic tragedy, and his fascination with the sea as a mystery and a seduction, and as a symbol of the malignity of fate.

The same interests soon appeared in a richer

and more complicated context when O'Neill began to write his early full-length plays. He gave his sense of tragic irony full scope in the first of these, the saturnine drama of fate and frustration *Beyond the Horizon*, produced in New York in 1920. A country lad who longs to go to sea attracts a farm girl with his dreamy romantic personality and is condemned by an unsuitable marriage to a routine life on the farm for which he is utterly unfit, while his practical-minded brother and disappointed rival in love, who was cut out to be a farmer, departs for strange lands and leads a life of adventure for which he has no particular liking. The thwarted romantic man, Robert Mayo, is an absolute failure on the farm and his marriage is destroyed by poverty and domestic recriminations, while, ironically, his unromantic brother Andrew actually prospers for a while in his adventuring and amasses a fortune (which he later loses) in romantic surroundings from which the other brother is forever barred. Only death holds the prospect of sailing "beyond the horizon" to the dying Robert Mayo, for whom life on the farm had been ensnarement and defeat. Blinded by the sexual instinct, the characters made the wrong choices in life and destroyed their chances of happiness.

In *Anna Christie*, first produced under a different title in 1920 and successfully revived a year later, it is the attraction of the sea that is blamed for the combination of circumstances making a prostitute of the heroine. She had been neglected by her father, a sea captain incapable of resisting the seductions of seafaring life. The captain, unable to understand his own behavior and overwhelmed by his sense of failure as a father, speaks of the sea as a demon and equates it with diabolic fate. And in *Diff'rent*, also produced in 1920, fate plays an ironic trick on a New England girl who broke off her engagement because her seagoing fiancé was not chaste enough to satisfy her puritanical principles; having doomed herself to a life of lonely spinsterhood, she ultimately rebels against frustration by succumbing to a designing rascal many years younger than herself. Whereas *Diff'rent* made crude use of both the irony of fate and the theme of sexual repression attributed by O'Neill's generation to the rigors of New England puritanism, *Anna Christie* moved naturally and smoothly up to its climax, the rejection of Anna by a young Irishman on his discovering her sordid past. Only the ending of the play seemed marred by vaguely promising a reunion between the lovers. (O'Neill himself was apologetic for this concession to sentiment.) But even the concluding scene, in which Anna's lover and her father have signed up for a sea voyage after a drinking bout, possessed a raffish mordancy that suited the subject and tone of the work, and did not impair the effectiveness of this justifiably popular play. Although O'Neill's dissatisfaction with it arose from a belief that he must write unalloyed tragedies to fulfill his vision of life and his destiny as a significant tragedian, he nevertheless had no reason to be ashamed of what he had accomplished in this play. He had achieved a wry tragicomedy enriched with fully flavored naturalism in dialogue and background that proved satisfying to playgoers in America and abroad, gave the play a good run on Broadway in the theatrical season of 1921–22, and won for its author a second Pulitzer Prize. (He had first received this coveted award the year before with *Beyond the Horizon*.)

In one way or another, the characters in these and other early works were entangled with circumstances which if not tragic in any strict sense of the term were destructive of happiness, and O'Neill was by no means a poor judge of his potentialities as a dramatist in believing that his forte was tragedy. He was least successful when the quality of the characters and their conflicts fell short of tragic dimension or elevation, as was the case in several minor works that followed *Anna Christie*. The earliest of these, *The Straw*, produced in 1921, dealt with the love of two tubercular patients in a sanatorium, one of whom is cured after a few months and leaves behind him the girl, whose situation is hopeless and is alleviated only by the illusion that she will join him someday. In *The First Man* (1922) a scientist, who is deficient in tragic stature, destroys his prospects of happiness by resenting the intrusion of a child into his married life; and in *Welded* (1924), a play clearly written under the influence of Strindberg although also steeped in personal experience, husband and wife are consumed with resentment while drawn to each other so powerfully by an irrational force that they cannot live apart. But it was not long before O'Neill lifted himself out of the morass of petty and pathetic situations and attained tragic power, when he combined naturalistic drama with fateful characters and atmosphere in *Desire under the Elms*, produced in the fall of 1924.

A tragedy of passion involving the third wife of a New England farmer and his son by his deceased second wife, this work was altogether dynamic and grim. Suffering in this play was produced by strong passions and conflicts of will on the part of determined characters. And over the developing destiny of the fateful lovers, Eben and his stepmother, Abbie, drawn irresistibly toward each other despite an initial conflict of interests, brood the trees, symbolic of natural fertility and mystery, of a flourishing New England farm. O'Neill, who belonged to a generation severely critical of Victorian, especially Puritan, morality, contrasted the passions of his youthful characters with the hardness and lovelessness of a Calvinist view of life. This is represented by the old farmer who has nothing but contempt for

sensitive individuals like his son Eben—whom he takes for one of the world's weaklings— and whose first and last trust is in the Old Testament God who tests men's strength with severe trials. Eben, who betrays his tyrannical father, Ephraim Cabot, is engaged in Oedipal conflict with him; and the young stepmother, Abbie, who married Ephraim because she sought security and coveted his farm, becomes tragically involved with her stepson when her suppressed hunger for love turns into reckless passion. *Desire under the Elms* held in solution O'Neill's critical view of his milieu and his interest in Freudian psychology as well as his tragic sense of life; and in this intense play he strained the boundaries of naturalistic drama until the play verged on melodrama when Abbie strangled her child in order to convince Eben that she had given herself to him out of love rather than out of a desire to deprive him of his heritage by producing a new heir to his father's farm. And in *Desire under the Elms*, as in earlier naturalistic plays, O'Neill also strained toward the estate of poetry with his symbols of fertility and an enveloping atmosphere of longing, loneliness, and lust. An imagination strengthened by a feeling for primitive severity in tone and characterization pervades this naturalistic treatment of a classic theme in which the Theseus is a lusty elderly farmer, the Hippolytus a mother-fixated son and jealous stepson, and the Phaedra a former household drudge with an ambition to secure her future as the inheritor of a thriving farm. If *Desire under the Elms* lacks the elevation it nevertheless possesses the strength of classic tragedy. If its stream of action is muddied by Freudian details of characterization in the portrayal of Eben, it nevertheless proceeds with mounting energy toward its destination, reflecting in its course the wind-swept landscape of the human soul. In any case, nothing comparable to this work in power derived from a sense of tragic character and situation had been achieved by the American theater in the hundred and fifty years of its history.

A more complacent playwright than O'Neill would have been content with this achievement and endeavored to repeat it. Not so O'Neill, who did not give the American stage another naturalistic adaptation of classic subject matter until the Theatre Guild production of *Mourning Becomes Electra* in 1931. The plays that followed *Desire under the Elms* were *The Fountain*, unsuccessfully produced in December 1925 at the Greenwich Village Theatre, and *The Great God Brown*, presented at the same theater in January 1926. They represent O'Neill's strivings to enrich the American drama with styles radically different from the naturalistic—namely, the romantic, the symbolist, and the expressionistic.

The effort started earlier, in fact, with the production of *The Emperor Jones* in November 1920, and some seven months later with *Gold*, an expanded version of the one-acter *Where the Cross Is Made*. The first production was decidedly auspicious, the second inauspicious; the first virtually introduced expressionism into the American theater, the second inaugurated O'Neill's ventures into symbolist-romantic drama, with which he succeeded only once—and but moderately even then—when the Theatre Guild produced *Marco Millions* in 1928. In the contrived and awkwardly written melodrama *Gold*, a sea captain is driven mad by his lust for gold, contracted on a desert island when, crazed by thirst, he thought he found a treasure trove. Its successor in the romantic style, *The Fountain*, fared scarcely better, with the overextended story of the legendary search of Ponce de León for the Fountain of Youth, which becomes obsessive until he finally realizes that "there is no gold but love." Only great dramatic poetry, which O'Neill was never to write, could have fulfilled

his intentions, for it was his ambition here to attain exultation and not the "morbid realism" with which he considered himself unduly taxed. He was to return to this striving for verbal ecstasy with somewhat more success in the romantic scenes of *Marco Millions*, but with generally turgid results in *Lazarus Laughed*, a boldly and nobly conceived drama in which the resurrected Lazarus teaches man to laugh at death.

Failure in romantic and symbolist drama could not, however, deter the playwright from seeking other means than realism for giving form to his vision of life and his aspirations for significant artistry. O'Neill was determined to enlarge the techniques of his playwriting, and this determination was sustained by a genuine need in his case to find suitable methods for expressing insights and attitudes for which realistic play structure seemed to him patently inadequate. Restiveness was only a secondary motive in O'Neill's case. European example, especially that of Strindberg, was a strong influence; his associates Macgowan and Jones had written enthusiastic and provocative reports on the European avant-garde in books and articles. But it was not direct example that influenced him. (He claimed to have had no knowledge of German expressionism when he conceived his first expressionist plays.) It was not theory but a felt belief in the potentialities of nonnaturalistic drama that motivated O'Neill in the series of expressionistic experiments that started with the Provincetown Players production of *The Emperor Jones* and *The Hairy Ape* in 1920 and 1922 respectively and continued, with a variety of modifications, in *All God's Chillun Got Wings* in 1924, in *The Great God Brown* in 1926, in *Strange Interlude* and *Lazarus Laughed* in 1928, and as late as 1934 in *Days without End*, a drama of a split personality played by two different actors. It was a personal pressure that dominated these plays and the statement of principles he set down for playwriting when he drafted the program note on Strindberg for the Provincetown Players production of *Spook Sonata*, which he co-produced: ". . . it is only by means of some form of 'super-naturalism' that we may express in the theater what we comprehend intuitively of that self-defeating self-obsession which is the discount we moderns have to pay for the loan of life. The old 'naturalism'—or 'realism' if you prefer . . . — no longer applies. It represents our Fathers' daring aspirations toward self-recognition by holding the family kodak up to ill-nature. But to us their old audacity is blague; we have taken too many snapshots of each other in every graceless position; we have endured too much from the banality of surfaces."

The first product of his reaching out for expressive form was *The Emperor Jones*, in which he dealt with the flight of a Caribbean Negro dictator from his aroused victims, a subject suggested to him by Haitian history, which he transformed into a succession of scenes of panic. In these vignettes, the man fleeing through the jungle is plagued by recollected events from his private past such as his slaying of a prison guard, his meager knowledge of racial history, and his superstitious fears and savage rituals.

Impacted into this drama of a frustrated escape and the influence of atavism was a powerful sense of theatricality which expressed itself most effectively in the incessant beat of tom-toms while the rebellious natives made magic and cast a silver bullet with which to destroy him, since he had fostered the belief that no other sort of bullet could harm him. O'Neill, having read accounts of Congo ritual, was impressed by the suggestive power of relentlessly repeated rhythms of the drum, "how it starts at a normal pulse and is slowly intensified until the heartbeat of everyone present

corresponds to the frenzied beat of the drum." He asked himself, "How would this sort of thing work on an audience in a theater?" The question was quickly answered by the suspense and tension built up in the audience and the conclusive success of the play, which was also revived some years later with the celebrated Paul Robeson filling the role originally created by another gifted Negro actor, Charles Gilpin. (Later, the play was turned into an effective opera by Louis Gruenberg.) O'Neill's success with *The Emperor Jones* was dual: it was an original play—virtually a dramatic monologue without intermissions in which fantasy cut across reality and the subjectivity of the protagonist was converted into objective reality for the mesmerized audience; and it was a play in which the wordless sequences were no less expressive than spoken dialogue.

The Emperor Jones was a tour de force of imaginative theater. It was followed by an even more exciting and certainly more provocative expressionistic drama, *The Hairy Ape*, which was somewhat baffling in meaning yet also richer and more complex in action and symbolization than *The Emperor Jones*. On the surface, the play was a series of vignettes dramatizing the bewilderment of a powerful stoker, Yank, when his naive confidence in brute power is shaken, and his desperate efforts to find a place for himself in the world ("*to belong*," as he puts it); on a more sophisticated level, Yank's fate expressed man's search for the meaning of his life and his alienation in the universe. Its larger, metaphysical and not readily transparent meaning was more clearly defined by O'Neill himself in an interview published in the *New York Herald Tribune* of November 16, 1924. Yank, it was plain, was not merely a portrait based on O'Neill's memory of a rough and powerful stoker whose acquaintance he had made in Jimmy-the-Priest's New York waterfront dive, but an intellectual concept of man's alienation in an indifferent universe. He was a symbol, as O'Neill put it, of man "who has lost his old harmony with nature, the harmony which he used to have as an animal and has not yet acquired in a spiritual way." The public, O'Neill complained, saw only the baffled stoker, not the symbol; yet "the symbol makes the play either important or just another play."

As O'Neill went on to explain, Yank with his narrow spirit and limited intelligence is incapable of achieving any really developed humanity, even though no longer content with his previous animal-like status. He strikes out, but blindly and in vain, against a reality he cannot affect or even comprehend: "Yank can't go forward, and so he tries to go back," as O'Neill put it. "This is what his shaking hands with the gorilla [in the last scene, set "in the monkey house at the Zoo"] meant. But he can't go back to 'belonging' either. The gorilla kills him."

O'Neill concluded that he had dramatized a universal theme: "The subject here is the same ancient one that always was and always will be the one subject for drama, and that is man and his struggle with his own fate. The struggle used to be with the gods, but is now with himself, his own past, his attempt 'to belong.' " It was to be O'Neill's primary theme in a series of plays that either failed or missed maximum effect to the degree to which in his impatience with realism he reduced characters to abstractions or harnessed them to metaphysical conceptions irreducible to concrete reality. In *The Hairy Ape* he succeeded in producing a powerful dramatic experience through the sheer vigor of the writing and the vibrancy of the action distributed in concise and visually arresting scenes. The fact, acknowledged by the playwright himself, that the public did not grasp the larger symbolic content did not greatly militate against the fascination and di-

rect effect of the play. The ambiguities in it actually whetted the public's curiosity and, at the very least, served to differentiate *The Hairy Ape* from Zolaist "slice-of-life" naturalism.

O'Neill was less fortunate in a third expressionist experiment, *All God's Chillun Got Wings*, involving the marriage of a tarnished white girl and a devoted Negro lover. Here a metaphysical conception of fate seemed somewhat arbitrarily inserted into racial and psychological conflicts sufficiently immediate to make abstruseness a limitation rather than a valid extension of the drama. O'Neill dealt here with the subject of miscegenation and an ensuing Strindbergian duel of the sexes in the course of which the neurotically jealous Ella destroys her Negro husband's chances for a career and then, after going berserk and trying to kill him, lapses into remorseful dependency upon his forgiveness and devotion. Although O'Neill was not aroused especially by racial prejudice as a national problem and was resolutely disinclined to write problem plays, the story he had chosen in this play committed him to a non-metaphysical resolution of its tensions. Instead, he dissolved the substance of this provocative drama by placing the burden of guilt on God and fate instead of on society. "Will God forgive me, Jim?" Ella asks plaintively as she sinks into a state of childishness. Jim replies, "Maybe He can forgive what you've done to me; and maybe He can forgive what I've done to you; but I don't see how He's going to forgive—Himself." This rather irrelevant interchange was nevertheless intensely moving, as were Jim's later exclamation, even less relevant to the logic of the play, when he asks God to forgive his blasphemy: "Let this fire of burning suffering purify me of selfishness and make me worthy of the child You send me for the woman You take away!" and his response to his demented wife's plea that he play with her, when he cries out brokenheartedly: "Honey, Honey, I'll play right up to the gates of Heaven with you!" Once more O'Neill's intensity of feeling and uncanny sense of theater came to the rescue of his dramatic reasoning.

The same talents saved his next expressionistic experiment, *The Great God Brown*, from total disaster, leaving him with a flawed and overworked drama that was nevertheless impressive enough to win respect for his earnestness and his theatrical imagination while disappointing sociological critics. Here, too, O'Neill hit upon a recognizable social fact, which may be defined as the defeat of the artist in a materialistic and unsympathetic society, and here, too, he concentrated on private psychology and metaphysical intimations rather than sociology. Here, however, far from veering from the logic of his argument he pursued it so persistently that he pushed schematization to extremes of abstraction and weakened credibility and reality of character in the melodramatically snarled action of the drama. In no other play did O'Neill symbolize his theme so intensively. We must remember that his early Greenwich Village associates, especially Robert Edmond Jones, had been affected in their youth by the Symbolist school of literature, drama, and scenic design inspired by the semi-mystical aesthetic aims of Gordon Craig. With such avant-garde sanctions, O'Neill went confidently ahead in this play, splitting his characters into sharply contrasted personalities and even resorting to masks in order to represent the antinomies of the artistic and the pragmatically bourgeois temperaments. At one point the masks are interchanged for the purpose of dramatizing the seemingly placid bourgeois personality's envy and attempted incorporation of the artist. To effectuate his symbolizing intentions O'Neill virtually stopped at nothing in *The Great God Brown*, making it one of his boldest as well as most transparent theatrical experiments.

O'Neill had been driven once again to expressionist experiment and formal schematization by something deeper than a penchant for showmanship and a passion for experimentation. His generation, led by such rebels against the complacent materialism of a thriving middle-class society as Van Wyck Brooks, Sinclair Lewis, and H. L. Mencken, was keenly aware of the artist's isolation in such a milieu, which was either hostile or indifferent toward him, and American writers treated the subject variously in both realistic and fanciful novels, poems, and plays. O'Neill endeavored to treat it not farcically like George S. Kaufman and Marc Connelly in their Broadway expressionistic comedy *Beggar on Horseback*, but seriously; not urbanely and fancifully as did James Branch Cabell in *Jurgen* and other novels, but tragically; not realistically like Lewis in *Main Street* and *Babbitt*, but imaginatively. Primarily he was interested, as usual, in inner tensions and the drama of the soul, and it was to this end that he invented the use of masks to accentuate conflicts and changes in individuals and, in the last part of the play, to visualize a *transfer* of personality from one character to another. For some kinds of modern plays, O'Neill, who found it necessary to abandon the use of masks later on (notably in *Mourning Becomes Electra*), was at least temporarily convinced that the mask was the solution for expressing, as he put it in an essay on the subject, "those profound hidden conflicts of the mind which the probings of psychology continue to disclose." What, after all, were the new psychological insights of the age "but a study in masks" or "an exercise in unmasking"?

Troubled by the difficulty of communicating his meaning even with the device of the mask,

O'Neill took pains to explicate his play in a newspaper article in the February 13, 1926, issue of the *New York Evening Post*. His chief character, Dion Anthony, represented in his dividedness the conflict between "the creative pagan acceptance of life," symbolized by Dionysus, constantly at war with the "masochistic, life-denying spirit of Christianity," symbolized by St. Anthony. The struggle resulted "in mutual exhaustion—creative joy in life for life's sake frustrated, rendered abortive, distorted by morality [O'Neill had in mind chiefly the puritanical morality of American society] from Pan into Satan, into a Mephistopheles mocking himself in order to feel alive." Perhaps Faust or, rather, Faust-Mephistopheles would have been a better choice of name, because O'Neill's heroine, Margaret, Dion Anthony's long-suffering wife, was the playwright's image of the Marguerite of Goethe's *Faust*, "the eternal girl-woman with a virtuous simplicity of instinct, properly oblivious to everything but the means to her end of maintaining the race." Continuing his pattern of analogies, O'Neill made the prostitute Cybel, to whom his hero resorts for comfort and counsel, "the Earth Mother doomed to segregation as a pariah in a world of unnatural laws, but patronized by her segregators, who are thus themselves the first victims of their laws" (O'Neill's direct attack on puritanical hypocrisy); and Dion's friend, rival, and employer, Brown, stands for "the visionless demi-god of our new materialistic myth," inwardly "empty and resourceless," who builds his life with "exterior things" and moves uncreatively in "superficial preordained social grooves." The peripety at the end, which conduces to confusion in the play, consists of Brown's theft of the dying Dion's mask, which symbolizes his effort to appropriate the creativity energy he had envied in Dion. But despite believing that in stealing Dion's mask he has gained the power to create, he has actually possessed himself only of "that creative power made self-destructive by complete frustration"; and, says O'Neill, the "devil of mocking doubt makes short work of him"—a provocative idea for which O'Neill unfortunately found an incredibly melodramatic plot rather than a simple objective correlative. Despite this, the play ran nearly a year in 1926. One reason was probably the dramatic fascination of the novel and atmospherically enriched action. Another and simpler reason surely was the intensity of Dion's anguish as man and artist.

The Great God Brown, which exemplifies so much of O'Neill's striving for personal expression that it became his favorite play, was its author's most "successful" failure not merely in practical but also in dramatic and poetic terms. *Marco Millions*, which followed it some two years later, was pallid by comparison. O'Neill's animus against materialistic society led him to write a sardonic comedy on the career of Marco Polo, who turned rapidly into a philistine impervious to beauty and romance despite his travels in the wondrous East of Kublai Khan and the love of Princess Kukachin, the Khan's granddaughter. The playwright proved to be too heavy-handed and repetitive, making his point long before the conclusion and overextending the play in performance with his quasi-poetic rhetoric and requirements of spectacle. A lighter touch and a swifter pace, as well as greater verbal and situational inventiveness, were needed to realize its potentialities as satiric comedy. *Marco Millions* has its felicitous passages and telling moments. It cannot be written off as a total loss in the unfolding of its author's talent. But it cannot be considered a major or consistently absorbing work.

A return to his metaphysical vein in *Lazarus*

Laughed led him into the blind alley of reiterative pseudo-philosophy from which he emerged too rarely to make this huge and unwieldy drama much more than an enormous spectacle strung upon a slender thread of plot and, despite its abundant rhetoric, a subliterary ritualistic effusion. In any case, this work was more suitable for outdoor pageantry than for the ordinary stage. Its chief interest lies in the variety of theatrical means—masks, choruses, crowds, choreographic movement, and other visual effects—O'Neill's stage-struck imagination could muster in the service of an idea. It could be said that on the level of show business, the son of the star-actor of *Monte Cristo* never quite left the spectacular romantic theater his father had turned into a livelihood; and that on the level of "art," he remained attached at heart to "Wagnerianism" or the *mélange des genres* aesthetic of Richard Wagner that influenced the late nineteenth- and the early twentieth-century theater. Inspiring these aesthetic proclivities was an earnest effort in O'Neill to express a tension that all the bohemian sophistication of the 1920's in America had been unable to allay or repress. It derived from the loss of religious faith that was traumatic in the case of the scion of an American Irish-Catholic family, and he was inwardly compelled to dwell upon the loss very much like his great Irish contemporary James Joyce.

O'Neill was aware of the possibility of pursuing substitutes and dramatized the search for them throughout his career. In *Lazarus Laughed* he temporarily found or thought he found an ersatz religion consisting of a mystical denial of death. It provided a doctrine of salvation by affirmation that was vastly more rhetorical than substantial. In *Dynamo*, his next engagement with the problem of faith, which had an unsuccessful though (largely thanks to the scenic genius of Theatre Guild designer Lee Simonson) visually stunning production early in 1929, he dramatized the substitution of machine-worship after his hero's renunciation of the puritanical faith of his fathers. While watching a dynamo in operation turning the energy of Connecticut rivers into electricity, O'Neill had been impressed with it as a veritable image of the new god of the scientific age. In *Dynamo* it became the dominant symbol, a hydroelectric generator described as "huge and black, with something of a massive female idol about it, the exciter set on the main structure like a head with blank oblong eyes above a gross, rounded torso," and it inspired him to undertake the writing of a trilogy on faith he never completed after the failure of *Dynamo* on the professional stage.

The story of the play, more simple than credible, revolved around a Calvinistically reared young American, Reuben Light, who, upon falling in love with an atheistical neighbor's daughter Ada, becomes an atheist himself. In search of a new faith to replace the old, Reuben adopts the electric generator as the symbol of his belief in science, paralleling the "Virgin and the Dynamo" contrast aptly drawn by Henry Adams. He soon finds himself worshiping the new god with the same violence with which his forebears worshiped the Old Testament deity. "O Dynamo, who gives life to things," he cries, "hear my prayer! Grant me the miracle of your love!" Driven mad by his fanaticism, he kills Ada, who made him violate his vow of undivided loyalty to the dynamo, following which he immolates himself on the lethal machine. *Dynamo* was a greater credit to its intrepid author's ambition than to his taste and discretion, and discouraged by the poor reception of the play, O'Neill abandoned his plan to write "a trilogy that will dig at the roots of the sickness of today as I feel it—the death of an old God and the failure of science and materialism to give any satisfying new one for the surviving primitive religious instinct to find a meaning for life in, and to comfort its fears of death with."

Nevertheless he could not resist his need to return to the subject of faith and the conflict with skepticism, which he described as the "big" subject behind all the little subjects of plays and novels whenever an author is not merely "scribbling around on the surface of things." He returned to the theme but with rather dreary results in *Days without End*, which O'Neill's latter-day producing organization, the Theatre Guild, presented for a short Broadway run in 1934. This play is for the most part a lesson on the need to return to conventional religious faith, but it is doubtful that O'Neill himself ever regained such faith for more than a brief period. (It remains to be noted that in Dublin the play reaped considerably more success than in New York; the conventional religious ending, in which the divided hero, John Loving, loses his skeptical, diabolical alter ego at the foot of the cross, apparently appealed more strongly to the Irish than to Americans.)

Fortunately, O'Neill had started a return to modified realism and interest in character-drama some half a dozen years earlier with *Strange Interlude*, which became a great Theatre Guild success in the year 1928. Instead of dealing with metaphysical content and struggles over faith, O'Neill concerned himself here with character dissection and inner conflict. Whatever means he adopted in this play, his schematizations and his recourse to the Elizabethan device of the "aside" on a scale never before attempted on the stage served the author's sole objective of portraying a modern woman. O'Neill showed her being driven by the strange life-force in her bloodstream to unconventional relationships, and seeking multiple possession of men's lives before peace descends upon her at the end of the "strange interlude" of her premenopausal life-history. With many details drawn from contemporary manners (the mores of the "sophisticated" 1920's) and contemporary psychology (chiefly Freudian), *Strange Interlude* proved engrossing to its New York public throughout the greater part of the long procession of revelations and incidents. The play was in nine acts (in contrast to the usual three-act play), ran from 5:30 P.M. until past 11 save for an eighty-minute dinner interval, and traced the critical relationships of a small number of characters for nearly three decades. Above all the characters stood Nina, the attractive daughter of a possessive university professor, who lost her athlete lover in World War I, regretted not having consummated her love with him, and sought fulfillment in desperate promiscuity. Later, having married a man to whom she would not bear children after being warned by his mother that there was insanity in the family, she gave birth to a son by another man (the neurologist Darrell) but could not bring herself to leave her husband and never could reveal the boy's true parentage. It takes a husband, a lover, a family friend, and an illegitimate son to fill her womanly life while at full tide. Then, as the vital flood recedes, she loses her husband to death, her emotionally drained lover to science, and her athlete son to a girl of his own age. By then, however, a twilight calm is descending on the central figure of this novel in play form, in which a vital modern woman is observed from many angles and in many situations. The resulting portrait was drawn on the stage by the gifted and resourceful Lynn Fontanne with such conviction that no one was likely to look for hidden meanings while she held the stage, which she did most of the time.

As a matter of fact, there were no hidden meanings in the play; if anything, O'Neill was only too explicit in his spoken and especially his supposedly unspoken dialogue—that is, the asides with which the author outlined the true thoughts and sentiments of the characters at the risk of redundancy. There could well be two strongly contradictory opinions about the recourse to asides. The British theater historian Allardyce Nicoll deplored them as a "somewhat tedious and fundamentally undramatic elaboration of the quite worthy convention of the 'aside' into a pretentious artistic instrument." Others found much to approve in this type of "interior dialogue," which bore considerable resemblance to the stream-of-consciousness James Joyce employed in *Ulysses*. In the excellently paced Theatre Guild production of 1928, staged by the gifted director Philip Moeller with an incredibly apt and able cast, there was little cause for complaint except for the decline of interest in the last two acts. In a highly professional New York revival given about a third of a century later by the Actors Studio Theatre, the negative opinion was more or less vindicated. Even then, however, *Strange Interlude* impressed the majority of reviewers and playgoers as a weighty experiment and, more than that, as a wide-ranging human document. What rigorous criticism was tempted to dismiss in that document as mere cliché overinsistently communicated was redeemed by effective confrontations of the chief characters and by the substantiality of Nina Leeds as a veritable incarnation of *das Ewig-Weibliche*. Nina, whose grosser and more elemental ancestress may be said to be Wedekind's Lulu, is a sort of Social Register earth goddess who encompasses during her "strange interlude" the functions of daughter, wife, mother, mistress, and superwoman whom all men find attractive and whose needs no single man is capable of fulfilling, although it is surmised that the untimely lost lover, Gordon, might have been able to satisfy them. Both as a character study and as

a dramatic novel *Strange Interlude* commanded the interest of a large public grateful for an exacting and unconventional drama. And its augmented realism was sufficiently successful to direct its author back to the paths of realism he had followed rewardingly in the early sea and waterfront plays.

This was notably apparent in his *Morning Becomes Electra* trilogy, when he domesticated or "naturalized" Greek legend and its various treatments by the Greek tragic poets. This was truly an enormous undertaking worthy of his ambition to treat significant themes and apply to them the insights and idiom of his own age. Although he employed formal elements in this work such as a truncated chorus and masklike facial expressions, these did not undercut the fundamentally naturalistic character of the work but merely punctuated and magnified it. Turning to the Orestean theme treated by Aeschylus and his successors, O'Neill localized it in New England immediately after the conclusion of the Civil War (instead of the Trojan War) in 1865, and translated and paralleled it in terms of the American environment of that period. The scion of a wealthy mercantile family, General Ezra Mannon, the Agamemnon of *Mourning Becomes Electra*, returns from the Civil War to learn that his alienated wife, Christine (the Clytemnestra of O'Neill's treatment), has been unfaithful to him with the seafaring Adam Brant, from a rival branch of the family, and to be poisoned by her when he seeks a reconciliation. In the second part of O'Neill's trilogy, as in *The Libation Bearers* of Aeschylus and the *Electra*'s of Sophocles and Euripides, the Electra character, whom O'Neill calls Lavinia, and her brother, O'Neill's Orestes, named Orin, avenge their father's death by killing their mother's lover, Adam Brant, the Aegisthus of the modern play, whereupon the mother commits suicide. In the third of the trilogy, the burden of guilt rests heavily on the son, although unlike the Orestes of the Greek plays, he did not directly murder his mother. Orin is virtually mad, and so dependent on his sister Lavinia that he won't allow her to marry anyone. At this point O'Neill whipped up the action into a rather melodramatic frenzy, with his Electra driving his Orestes to suicide, following which she is so overwhelmed with remorse that she renounces all possibilities of happiness, shutting herself up forever with her conscience in the mansion of the ill-fated Mannons.

The power of this work communicated itself instantly on the stage in the memorable Philip Moeller production of the year 1931 for the Theatre Guild. It had a neoclassical-colonial setting by Robert Edmond Jones and featured the veteran actress Nazimova in the role of Christine and Alice Brady (succeeded by Judith Anderson) in the part of Lavinia. But there was more to the play than the transcription of Greek matter into American terms. O'Neill, it is true, did not differ from the Greek tragedians in concerning himself with Fate and the working out of the family curse, the "domestic Ate," in the story of a New England Brahmin family. But it was his intention to go much further and translate fate into modern terms, an enterprise already started before him by the late nineteenth-century naturalists who found an equivalent for the Greek idea of fate in their rudimentary scientific concepts of determinism by heredity and environment. Locating the determinism more directly in the human psyche, O'Neill adopted the Freudian emphasis upon the sexual instinct, especially the much publicized Oedipus complex. His Clytemnestra had been horrified on her wedding night by her husband's brutal sexuality (a case of the libido welling up from puritanical suppression) and subsequently felt alienated from the fruit of their union, Lavinia, thus alienating her daughter and making the girl excessively attached to her father, Mannon. She had lavished possessive affection, however, on her second child, Orin, during her husband's absence when America waged war with Mexico, thus causing the son to be pathetically fixated on her. It is chiefly Oedipal resentment that pits the Electra of O'Neill's trilogy against his Clytemnestra, and it is Oedipal attachment that makes O'Neill's Orestes the tool of his sister's animosity, which results in his seeking out and killing Captain Adam Brant on his ship. Orin's act and Lavinia's provocation lead step by step then to his mother's suicide, his disturbed state of mind, his incestuous dependency on the sister (who has begun to resemble the mother she has destroyed), and his own death.

Schematization was carried too far in the play, but the Freudian interpretation produced intensely dramatic moments, especially in the mother-daughter conflict. Still, in resorting to psychoanalytical explanations and highlighting them in each of the three plays of the trilogy, O'Neill deprived his characters of tragic stature insofar as they became clinical cases, and this invited criticism from some quarters that O'Neill had written a case history rather than a tragedy. One could offer the defense that the characters and events as observed in the Theatre Guild production certainly *felt* tragic— at least until the excrescence of melodramatic action in the last part of the work. A better case could be made against the trilogy by those who noted the poverty of O'Neill's low-grade naturalistic dialogue, so distressingly at variance with the powerful passions and mounting action of the trilogy, so downright flat precisely when the language should have been made to soar, as in the scene in which Orin tells his mother that he has killed her lover:

CHRISTINE. (*stammers*) Orin! What kept you—?

ORIN. We just met Hazel. She said you were terribly frightened at being alone here. That is strange—when you have the memory of Father for company!

CHRISTINE. You—you stayed all this time—at the Bradfords'?

ORIN. We didn't go to the Bradfords'.

CHRISTINE. (*stupidly*) You didn't go—to Blackridge?

ORIN. We took the train there but we decided to stay right on and go to Boston instead.

CHRISTINE. (*terrifiedly*) To—Boston—?

ORIN. And in Boston we waited until the evening train got in. We met that train.

CHRISTINE. Ah!

ORIN. We had an idea you would take advantage of our being in Blackridge to be on it—and you were! And we followed you when you called on your lover in his cabin!

CHRISTINE. (*with a pitiful effort at indignation*) Orin! How dare you talk—! (*Then brokenly*) Orin! Don't look at me like that! Tell me—

ORIN. Your lover! Don't lie! You've lied enough, Mother! I was on deck, listening! What would you have done if you had discovered me? Would you have gotten your lover to murder me, Mother? I heard you warning him against me! But your warning was no use!

CHRISTINE. (*chokingly*) What—? Tell me—!

ORIN. I killed him!

CHRISTINE. (*with a cry of terror*) Oh—oh! I knew! (*Then clutching at* Orin) No—Orin! You—you're just telling me that—to punish me, aren't you? You said you loved me—you'd protect me—protect your mother—you couldn't murder—!

One expects less prosaic language from a master tragedian, which O'Neill narrowly missed becoming in this play.

The language and the heavy emphasis on incestuous feelings elicited unfavorable comment at first mostly in England and later in American literary circles, the most considered being perhaps Allardyce Nicoll's conclusion that "This is rather a magnificently presented case-study than a powerful tragic drama." O'Neill resented the allegation that he had borrowed his ideas, claiming that he knew enough about human nature to have written the play without having ever heard of Freud and Jung. But O'Neill had himself imposed restraints on his endeavor to write a modern high tragedy by domesticating the Orestean legend to the point of restricting his dialogue to naturalistic commonplaceness, and by asking himself (in his preparatory notes to *Mourning Becomes Electra*) whether it was possible to "get modern psychological approximation of Greek sense of fate into such a play." His play is an affirmative answer which, nevertheless, leaves unanswered the larger question O'Neill did *not* ask himself—namely, whether modern dramatic vision needs to be limited, or is actually exhausted, by "psychological approximation."

Some necessity of art and personal expression, then, kept O'Neill moving back to realistic drama as the style of writing by which his reputation would stand or fall. This led him to yield to psychopathology and lapse into sunless Gothic melodrama in *Mourning Becomes Electra*. It also led him, two years later, to the pleasant alternative of producing the genial genre painting of *Ah, Wilderness!*, a family comedy set in a small Connecticut city at the beginning of the century. A nostalgic comedy of recollection, it revolves around a bright and spirited adolescent who has his first and luckily harmless fling at low life when jilted by the daughter of a parochial father, who disapproves of the boy's penchant for the "pagan" poet Swinburne. The boy's understanding and ever-smiling father, who is the local newspaper publisher, straightens everything out to his son's satisfaction, and to the gratification of playgoers pleased at meeting O'Neill for once without his tragic mask. The popular star George M. Cohan, playing the newspaper publisher, toured this comedy of reconciliation across the nation without adding substantially to O'Neill's reputation or altering it for admirers, who cherished their memory of him as a singularly sultry dramatist. Today, *Ah, Wilderness!* falls into proper perspective as one of the most attractive of American domestic comedies—nothing less, and nothing more. For the author himself it was only a brief holiday from his most persistent memories, which were normally bleak, and from the contemporary world, about which he never felt particularly cheerful. That it represented only a vacation from a gloomy view of *la condition humaine* was to become evident in his last plays, first brought to the stage many years later while O'Neill was leading a life of mental and physical torment and, in the case of several of his plays (*Long Day's Journey into Night*, *A Touch of the Poet*, the one-acter *Hughie*, and *More Stately Mansions*), after his death in 1953.

More than a decade—twelve years, to be exact—elapsed between the middle and last periods of O'Neill's career. These were years of isolation during which he planned and wrote plays he withheld from the stage and did not publish. Illness hampered him and depression over the state of the world, which was veering rapidly toward a global war, immobilized him and kept him virtually bedridden at times. As late as 1946, he still felt that it would require strong efforts on his part to recover enough confidence in the worth of literary labor to start writing again. In a press interview he declared that "the war has thrown me completely off base. . . . I have to get back to a sense of

writing being worthwhile." Morosely, he added, "In fact, I'd have to pretend." It was not a period to encourage optimism, and there was none forthcoming from O'Neill as he brooded on the past that prepared the way for the dreadful present while at work on a tremendous cycle of plays tracing the tragic history of an American family from colonial times to his own, destroying some of his completed drafts and leaving other planned plays unwritten or unfinished.

Shortly after the conclusion of World War II, it became possible for him to entertain prospects for new productions and to allow the publication of two new plays, *The Iceman Cometh*, written in 1939, and *A Moon for the Misbegotten*, completed in 1943. Both were to a degree memory plays, the first dealing with the period of his waterfront days at Jimmy-the-Priest's dive, the second with the broken life of his alcoholic brother, James. But the mordancy of both plays derived not from memories (the autobiographical elements were thoroughly transformed) but from a strong and vivid sense of man's private and public failure, which the recently concluded holocaust and the growing materialism of the world only served to confirm. In an interview he gave to the press in September 1946, on the occasion of the Broadway opening of *The Iceman Cometh* by the Theatre Guild, O'Neill held out little hope for man. He included in his indictment his own nation, which had but recently emerged the victor and the champion of humanity from a second world war. "I'm going on the theory," he declared, "that the United States, instead of being the most successful country in the world, is the greatest failure." His country had been given more resources than any other, but while moving ahead rapidly it had not acquired any real roots because its main idea appeared to be "that everlasting game of trying to possess your own soul by the possession of something outside it." He included the rest of the world in his indictment. If the human was so "damned stupid" that in two thousand years it had not learned to heed the Biblical admonition against gaining the whole world but losing one's own soul, then it was time humanity were "dumped down the nearest drain" and the ants were given a chance to succeed where men had failed.

The Iceman Cometh, which the Theatre Guild produced with only moderate success but which was later revived with great success, proved to be one of O'Neill's most powerful as well as most pessimistic plays. Bearing considerable resemblance to Maxim Gorki's turn-of-the-century naturalistic classic *The Lower Depths* (both plays are set in a cheap boardinghouse for the disreputable and the derelict, and both show man trying to subsist on illusory hopes), *The Iceman Cometh* nevertheless presents a radically different view from that entertained by the Russian author who had stood at the dawn of the twentieth century and shared its optimism. O'Neill expressed no hope for men at all, and therefore considered illusion to be the necessary anodyne and death a welcome release for bedeviled mankind. In Harry Hope's saloon, life's exiles and failures lead a besotted and befuddled existence and subsist on hopes of recovering their lost status. Most of them are reasonably happy until their drinking companion, the flashy traveling salesman Hickey, shows up for one of his periodic drinking bouts. Instead of joining in the expected revels, however, he is bent upon making them renounce their illusions and face the truth about themselves, which is that they no longer have anything to hope for. Accepting his challenge, at last, that they leave the saloon and proceed to accomplish the restitution of reputation and position with which they have long deluded themselves, they sally forth, but only to return, one by one, frightened and dispirited. Nothing feels right any more, and even the liquor in the saloon has lost its savor and has no effect on them. Contentment returns to them only after Hickey's revelation that he has murdered his long-suffering wife, who persisted in believing in his eventual reformation as the only way to free her from the misery of loving him, although he has also hated her for her infinite trust and forbearance. ("I couldn't forgive her for forgiving me," says Hickey. "I even caught myself hating her for making me hate myself so much.")

They derive reassurance from the conviction that Hickey, who has given himself up to the police, is stark mad, and relapse into their comforting illusions. The liquor begins to have an effect on them again, and all is well with them once more, so far as they know or care. The one exception is Larry, the disenchanted radical, who also turns out to be the only convert the miserable Hickey made, for Larry is the only one who really grasped Hickey's meaning when Hickey called for the abandonment of illusions as the only way of attaining peace. The death of illusion is the end of life, death, "the Iceman," being the sole possible release. For, as Larry has said earlier about men's dependence on false hopes, "the lie of a pipe dream is what gives life to the whole misbegotten mad lot of us, drunk or sober." Larry, in fact, performs one act of kindness at once; he persuades a miserable youth, who has betrayed his anarchist mother to the police, to put an end to his inner torment by committing suicide.

Rich in detail, complex in contrivance yet seemingly natural, naturalistic in speech and situation yet also somewhat symbolic and grotesque, *The Iceman Cometh* looms large in the O'Neill canon. Even its prolixity has redeeming qualities; Hickey's confessional speech, which lasts some fifteen minutes on the stage, constitutes gripping theater. Its defects are the corrigible one of repetitiveness, some of which can be removed without injury to the play, the slight but embarrassing one of some banality of expression (as in the overuse of outmoded slang and the jejune phrase "pipe dreams" for false hopes), and the intrinsic one of spiritual torpor that derives from its author's persistent philosophy of negation.

The failure of O'Neill's next production, *A Moon for the Misbegotten*, which was withdrawn after its out-of-town tryout in February and March 1947, marked the end of its author's active participation in the theater. *The Iceman Cometh*, which opened in New York on September 2, 1946, was the last of O'Neill's plays to be seen on Broadway in his lifetime.

During his final years O'Neill was stricken with an obscure degenerative disease which made writing and finally even locomotion extremely difficult, although his mind remained clear. His third wife, actress Carlotta Monterey, whom he married in 1929, was his nurse during these years, and for long periods they lived in virtual seclusion, in Marblehead, Massachusetts, and later in Boston. He had become wholly estranged from the children, Shane and Oona, of his second marriage to Agnes Boulton. (O'Neill had been so angered by Oona's marriage, at eighteen, to Charlie Chaplin, who was the same age as O'Neill himself, that he never again—according to his wife Carlotta—mentioned her name.) His older son, Eugene, Jr., born of his short-lived first marriage to Kathleen Jenkins, committed suicide in 1950.

Three years after O'Neill's death, and a decade after *The Iceman Cometh* opened, his posthumous career on Broadway began brilliantly, with the José Quintero production of *Long Day's Journey into Night*, which had Fredric March, Florence Eldridge, Jason Robards, Jr., and Bradford Dillman in the main parts. This opening, on November 7, 1956, repeated the earlier triumph of the play's world première in Swedish at the Royal Dramatic Theatre in Stockholm on February 10, 1956. (In 1945 O'Neill had stipulated that *Long Day's Journey into Night*, which has strong autobiographical overtones, should be sealed for twenty-five years after his death. But Carlotta O'Neill, as his literary executrix, released the play for both publication and production, saying that her husband had changed his mind after the death of Eugene, Jr., at whose request O'Neill had originally withheld the play.)

In *Long Day's Journey into Night*, in many respects a simple naturalistic family drama, there were no plot contrivances, no "well-made" play intrigues, but only uncommonly moving revelations of character and human relations. These came in the wake of closely connected tensions and conflicts shattering to the young man, actually the young O'Neill, who is patently the transcriber of the events of the play. Were it not for the prosaic quality of the dialogue and the extreme length of the work, there could be no doubt whatsoever that it is a twentieth-century dramatic masterpiece.

Long Day's Journey into Night brought O'Neill back to his real forte, and that of most American playwrights—plain, honest realism of character and situation. For all that, and despite his laboring of some points (finesse was never one of his virtues), O'Neill could not be charged fairly with commonplace obviousness. He was subtle in his own way in noting the complexity of the young hero's somewhat avaricious and penny-pinching actor-father, his mother too frightened of life to be able to give up the drug habit, and his demon-driven alcoholic brother. *Long Day's Journey into Night* is perhaps the modern theater's outstanding dramatization of the ambivalences omnipresent in the human species. This alone would have given authenticity and depth to the play, which O'Neill managed to convey with much dramatic skill in a crescendo of revelations and even with some delightful humor, as in the scene in which the father tries to contradict the charge of miserliness by turning on all the lights in the parlor and then cautiously turning them out again. A forgiving spirit hovered over O'Neill when he came to write his chef-d'oeuvre (in 1940, sixteen years before its production), and his reward was the favorable response of even those members of the new generation who had found little to praise and much to blame in the playwright's earlier plays. For them, moreover, there could be special merit in the analytical, unsentimental insight that accompanied the compassion. The young O'Neill, who manifests a poet's sensitivity and a literary bent, is shown acquiring a painful understanding of life's ironies, which in the mature O'Neill's own case is not a jaundiced view of humanity but the tragic sense of life for which he became noted.

After *Long Day's Journey into Night*, the New York production of *A Moon for the Misbegotten*, which opened about half a year later (in May 1957), was bound to seem anticlimactic despite the services of the gifted British actress Wendy Hiller in the role of an over-sized farm girl who tries to bestow her love on a guilt-laden alcoholic lacking all capacity to receive, let alone return, it. Faulty in several respects, it was nevertheless another work of considerable depth and compassion, here presented largely in terms of grotesque comedy.

Also weak in some respects, *A Touch of the Poet* (which, although written in 1936, first opened on Broadway on October 2, 1958, about six months after the world première at the Royal Dramatic Theatre) is chiefly noteworthy for giving us an inkling of what its author had in mind for the dramatic cycle he had planned under the title of *A Tale of Possessors Self-Dispossessed* and abandoned. This play, the sole finished survivor of the project, dramatized the beginnings of the American family with which the cycle was to deal. Here the daughter of an Irish pretender to aristocratic status, Con Melody, reduced to keeping a pub near Boston, resolves to marry the poetical scion of a wealthy Brahmin family despite parental interference. The full significance of the play could not be established without reference to the nonexistent cycle, but its self-sufficient qualities were considerable. They were most evident in the character studies of a man who is dignified by his sense of distinction out of all proportion to his merits (he is a liar and often an inconsiderate one), his drudge of a wife who in understanding his proud spirit forgives all hurts, and his daughter Sara who scorns his pretensions but mourns for him as one dead when he renounces them.

Another play, *More Stately Mansions*, which was apparently to be the fourth in his eleven-play cycle and was to follow *A Touch of the Poet*, was retrieved from the O'Neill papers in Yale University's O'Neill Collection and produced in considerably shortened form by Dr. Karl Ragnar Gierow, the Royal Dramatic Theatre director who had staged productions of two other posthumous O'Neill works in Stockholm, in November 1962. The manuscript was revised for publication by Dr. Gierow and Donald Gallup, the curator of the O'Neill Collection at Yale. Since this version, released by the Yale University Press in 1964, was prepared from the Swedish acting script, it cannot be judged as an original O'Neil work; the original manuscript is more than twice as long as the published play. Whatever the favorable impression of the Swedish production, the published play may well strike a reader as decidedly scattered in effect. But it is plain that O'Neill wanted to indict the growth of materialism in the modern world. Con Melody's daughter Sara of *A Touch of the Poet* is here married to the young man, Simon Harford, whom she fancied. But her possessiveness and her rivalry with his equally possessive mother prove to be his undoing; the poet in him dies as he becomes a relentless materialist before breaking down mentally. O'Neill's old feeling for compulsive conflict is once more uppermost in this salvaged but rather inchoate drama, which has yet to be tested on the American stage.

Fortunately, there was one more posthumously published work of the final period that shows no decline or dispersion of O'Neill's power, the short two-character masterpiece *Hughie*, written in 1941 and published in 1959, the first of a projected series grimly entitled *By Way of Obit*. For the most part a monologue spoken by the "Broadway sport" Erie Smith to the night clerk of a shabby New York hotel in the late 1920's, *Hughie* is a tour de force that does not flag for a moment in revealing the emotional vacuity of the narrator and a deceased night clerk, Hughie, whom he used to fill with wonder at his inflated gambling exploits. Marvelously vivid and rhythmic dialogue that seems utterly authentic in its colloquialism and slang in this play recalls O'Neill's early achievements in the best sea-pieces of the *S.S. Glencairn* series. *Hughie* is the last testament to O'Neill's prowess in naturalistic playwriting and to his lingering attachment, despite his success with oversized dramas, to the spare one-act play form with which he had first established his reputation as an authentic American playwright.

Nothing needs to be added perhaps to this critical chronicle of the efforts and achievements of the one American playwright whose place in the hierarchy of world dramatists seems as secure as any twentieth-century dramatist's can be. To his critics' justifiable impatience with his laboriousness the appropriate reply is that O'Neill is the *master* of massive dramatic assault. His power is not often separable from his repetitiveness or even verbosity.

His sense of theater was so strong that more often than not his best plays, when well structured, proved to be considerably more effective on the stage than a literary reading of them could possibly suggest. His sense of drama was so rarely "posture" despite his not always trustworthy flair for theatricality that much of his work seems wrung from him rather than contrived or calculated. In a very real sense it is a testament to a uniquely tormented spirit that subsumed much of the twentieth century's dividedness and anguish, largely existential rather than topical. And while the penalty for his metaphysical concerns and brooding inwardness was often a quasi-philosophical windiness, the reward for his refusal to settle for small temporary satisfactions is an aura of greatness in the man and his labors, or, at the very least, a dark impressiveness not easily to be dismissed by dwelling on his verbal limitations. This much can be said, without fear of contradiction, of the man who, in the words of his publisher-friend Bennett Cerf, was "the first universally recognized world dramatist America produced" in some two centuries of theater in the Western hemisphere.

Selected Bibliography

WORKS OF EUGENE O'NEILL

PLAYS

Thirst. Boston: Gorham Press, 1914. (This book contains three other one-act plays by O'Neill: *Warnings*, *Fog*, and *Recklessness*.)

Bound East for Cardiff. In *The Provincetown Plays: First Series*. New York: Frank Shay, 1916.

Before Breakfast. In *The Provincetown Plays: Third Series*. New York: Frank Shay, 1916.

The Moon of the Caribbees. New York: Boni and Liveright, 1919. (This book also contains other one-act plays: *In the Zone, Where the Cross Is Made, The Rope, The Long Voyage Home,* and *Ile.*)

Beyond the Horizon. New York: Boni and Liveright, 1920.

The Emperor Jones, Different, The Straw. New York: Boni and Liveright, 1921.

Gold. New York: Boni and Liveright, 1921.

The Hairy Ape, Anna Christie, The First Man. New York: Boni and Liveright, 1924.

Desire under the Elms. New York: Boni and Liveright, 1925.

The Great God Brown, The Fountain. New York: Boni and Liveright, 1926.

Marco Millions. New York: Boni and Liveright, 1927.

Lazarus Laughed. New York: Boni and Liveright, 1927.

Strange Interlude. New York: Boni and Liveright, 1928.

Dynamo. New York: Horace Liveright, 1929.

Mourning Becomes Electra. New York: Horace Liveright, 1931.

Ah, Wilderness! New York: Random House, 1933.

Days without End. New York: Random House, 1934.

The Iceman Cometh. New York: Random House, 1946.

The Lost Plays of Eugene O'Neill. New York: New Fathoms Publication, 1950. (Unauthorized publication of immature short plays which O'Neill did not wish to publish.)

A Moon for the Misbegotten. New York: Random House, 1952.

Long Day's Journey into Night. New Haven, Conn.: Yale University Press, 1956.

A Touch of the Poet. New Haven, Conn.: Yale University Press, 1957.

New Girl in Town. (A musical based on the play *Anna Christie,* with book by George Abbott and music and lyrics by Bob Merrill.) New York: Random House, 1958.

Hughie. New Haven, Conn.: Yale University Press, 1959.

Take Me Along. (A musical based on the play *Ah, Wilderness!*) New York: Random House, 1960.

More Stately Mansions. New Haven, Conn.: Yale University Press, 1964.

Ten Lost Plays. (Authorized Edition.) New York: Random House, 1964.

(It should be noted that several of O'Neill's plays were first published in periodicals: *The Long Voyage Home* in *Smart Set,* October 1917 issue; *Ile* in *Smart Set,* May 1918 issue; *The Moon of the Caribbees* in *Smart Set,* August 1918 issue; *The Dreamy Kid* in *Theater Arts,* January 1920 issue; *The Emperor Jones* in *Theatre Arts,* January 1921 issue; *All God's Chillun Got Wings* in the *American Mercury,* February 1924 issue.)

OTHER WRITINGS

"Strindberg and Our Theater," *Provincetown Playbill,* No. 1, Season of 1923-24. (Reprinted in *The Provincetown: A Story of the Theatre,* by Helen Deutsch and Stella Hanau. New York: Farrar and Rinehart, 1931. Pp. 191–93.)

"Are the Actors to Blame?" *Provincetown Playbill,* No. 1, Season of 1925–26. (Reprinted in Deutsch and Hanau, *The Provincetown.* Pp. 197–98.)

"Memoranda on Masks," *American Spectator,* November 1932.

COLLECTED EDITIONS

The Complete Plays of Eugene O'Neill, with brief notes by the author. Wilderness Edition, 12 volumes. New York: Scribner's, 1934–35.

The Plays of Eugene O'Neill. Lifetime Library Edition, 3 volumes. New York: Random House, 1946.

BIBLIOGRAPHIES

Bryer, Jackson R. "Forty Years of O'Neill Criticism: A Selected Bibliography," *Modern Drama,* 4:196–216 (September 1961).

Miller, Jordan Y. *Eugene O'Neill and the American Critic: A Summary and Bibliographical Checklist.* London: Archon Books, 1962.

Reaver, Joseph Russell. *An O'Neill Concordance.* 3 vols. Detroit: Gale Research Company, 1969.

Sanborn, Ralph, and Barrett H. Clark. *A Bibliography of the Works of Eugene O'Neill.* New York: Random House, 1931.

Sanborn, Ralph. "Check-List of the First Publication of the Plays of Eugene O'Neill," in

Barrett H. Clark's *Eugene O'Neill: The Man and His Plays.*

"The Theatre of O'Neill," *Greenwich Playbill* (program of O'Neill's *The Fountain*), No. 3, Season of 1925–26. (A list of plays, including manuscripts lost or destroyed by O'Neill.)

CRITICAL AND BIOGRAPHICAL STUDIES

BOOKS AND PAMPHLETS

Bentley, Eric R. *In Search of Theater.* New York: Knopf, 1953. Pp. 233–47.

―――. "Introduction to O'Neill," in *Major Writers of America,* edited by Perry Miller. New York: Harcourt, Brace & World, 1962. Vol. 2, pp. 557–75.

Block, Anita. *The Changing World in Plays and Theatre.* Boston: Little, Brown, 1939. Pp. 137–93.

Bogard, Travis. *Contour in Time: The Plays of Eugene O'Neill.* New York: Oxford University Press, 1972.

Boulton, Agnes. *Part of a Long Story.* Garden City, N.Y.: Doubleday, 1958.

Bowen, Croswell. *The Curse of the Misbegotten.* New York: McGraw-Hill, 1959.

Brown, John Mason. *Letters from Greenroom Ghosts.* New York: Viking, 1934.

―――. *Seeing More Things.* New York: Whittlesey House, 1948. Pp 257–65.

―――. *Still Seeing Things.* New York: McGraw-Hill, 1950. Pp. 185–95.

Brustein, Robert. *The Theatre of Revolt.* Boston: Little, Brown, 1964. Pp. 319–60.

Buck, Philo Melvin, Jr. *Directions in Contemporary Literature.* New York: Oxford University Press, 1942. Pp. 125–47.

Carpenter, Frederick I. *Eugene O'Neill.* New York: Twayne, 1964.

Clark, Barrett H. *Eugene O'Neill: The Man and His Plays.* Revised edition. New York: Dover, 1947.

Cargill, Oscar, N. Bryllion Fagin, William J. Fisher, editors. *O'Neill and His Plays.* New York: New York University Press, 1961.

Downer, Alan S. *Fifty Years of American Drama, 1900–1950.* Chicago: Regnery, 1951. Pp. 64–70, 92–97.

Engel, Edwin A. *The Haunted Heroes of Eugene O'Neill.* Cambridge, Mass.: Harvard University Press, 1953.

Falk, Doris V. *Eugene O'Neill and the Tragic Tension: An Interpretive Study of the Plays.* New Brunswick, N.J.: Rutgers University Press, 1958.

Gagey, Edmond M. *Revolution in American Drama.* New York: Columbia University Press, 1947. Pp. 39–70.

Gassner, John. *Masters of the Drama.* Revised edition. New York: Dover, 1954. Pp. 639–61, 735–36.

―――. *Theatre at the Crossroads.* New York: Holt, Rinehart, and Winston, 1960. Pp. 66–76.

―――. *The Theatre in Our Times.* New York: Crown, 1954. Pp. 249–66.

―――. editor. *O'Neill: A Collection of Critical Essays.* Englewood Cliffs, N.J.: Prentice-Hall, 1964.

Geddes, Virgil. *The Melodramadness of Eugene O'Neill.* Brookfield Pamphlets No. 4. Brookfield, Conn.: Brookfield Players, 1934.

Gelb, Arthur, and Barbara Gelb. *O'Neill.* New York: Harper, 1962.

Helburn, Theresa. *A Wayward Quest.* Boston: Little, Brown, 1960. Pp. 256–80.

Hicks, Granville. *The Great Tradition.* New York: Macmillan, 1933. Pp. 207–56.

Kerr, Walter. *Pieces at Eight.* New York: Simon and Schuster, 1957. Pp. 117–49.

Krutch, Joseph Wood. *The American Drama since 1918.* New York: Random House, 1939. Pp. 73–133.

Lamm, Martin. *Modern Drama,* translated by Karin Elliott. New York: Philosophical Library, 1953. Pp. 315–33.

Langner, Lawrence. *The Magic Curtain.* New York: Dutton, 1951. Pp. 228–42, 397–409.

McCarthy, Mary. *Sights and Spectacles, 1937–1956.* New York: Farrar, Straus, and Cudahy, 1956. Pp. 80–88.

Miller, Jordan Y. *Playwright's Progress: O'Neill and the Critics.* Chicago: Scott, Foresman, 1965.

Moses, Montrose J., and John Mason Brown. *The American Theatre as Seen by Its Critics, 1752–1934.* New York: Norton, 1934. Pp. 209–11, 265–72, 287–89.

Nathan, George Jean. *Passing Judgments*. New York: Knopf, 1935. Pp. 66–73, 112–26.

―――. *The Theatre of the Moment*. New York: Knopf, 1936. Pp. 196–207.

―――. *Theatre Book of the Year, 1946–47*. New York: Knopf, 1947. Pp. 93–111.

―――. *The World of George Jean Nathan*, edited by Charles Angoff. New York: Knopf, 1952. Pp. 30–43, 395–411.

Nicoll, Allardyce. *World Drama from Æschylus to Anouilh*. New York: Harcourt, Brace, n.d. [1950?] Pp. 880–931.

Raleigh, John H. *The Plays of Eugene O'Neill*. Carbondale: Southern Illinois University Press, 1965.

Sheaffer, Louis. *O'Neill: Son and Playwright*. Boston: Little, Brown, 1968.

Shipley, Joseph T. *The Art of Eugene O'Neill*. University of Washington Chapbooks No. 13. Seattle: University of Washington Book Store, 1928.

Sievers, W. David. *Freud on Broadway*. New York: Hermitage House, 1955. Pp. 97–133.

Skinner, Richard Dana. *Eugene O'Neill, A Poet's Quest*. New York: Longmans, Green, 1935.

Spiller, Robert E. *The Cycle of American Literature*. New York: Macmillan, 1955. Pp. 243–74.

Tiusanen, Timo. *O'Neill's Scenic Images*. Princeton, N.J.: Princeton University Press, 1968.

Winther, Sophus Keith. *Eugene O'Neill, A Critical Study*. New York: Random House, 1934.

Young, Stark. *Immortal Shadows*. New York: Scribners, 1948. Pp. 61–66, 91–95, 132–39, 261–64.

ARTICLES

Alexander, Doris M. *"Strange Interlude* and Schopenhauer," *American Literature,* 25:213–28 (May 1953).

―――. "Psychological Fate in *Mourning Becomes Electra,*" *PMLA,* 68:923–34 (December 1953).

Asselnian, Roger. *"Mourning Becomes Electra* as a Tragedy," *Modern Drama,* 1:143–50 (December 1958).

Conlin, Matthew T. "The Tragic Effect in *Autumn Fire* and *Desire under the Elms,*" *Modern Drama,* 1:228–35 (February 1959).

Falk, Doris V. "That Paradox, O'Neill," *Modern Drama,* 6:221–38 (December 1963).

Fergusson, Francis. "Eugene O'Neill," *Hound and Horn,* 3:145–60 (January–March 1930).

Frenz, Horst. "Eugene O'Neill's Plays Printed Abroad," *College English,* 5:340–41 (March 1944).

Herbert, Edward. "Eugene O'Neill: An Evaluation by Fellow Playwrights," *Modern Drama,* 6:239–40 (December 1963).

Isaacs, Edith J. R. "Meet Eugene O'Neill," *Theatre Arts,* 30:576–87 (October 1946).

"The Ordeal of Eugene O'Neill," *Time,* 48:71–78 (October 21, 1946).

Raleigh, John Henry. "O'Neill's Long Day's Journey into Night and New England Irish-Catholicism," *Partisan Review,* 26:573–92 (Fall 1959).

Weigand, Charmion von. "The Quest of Eugene O'Neill," *New Theatre,* 2:12–17, 30–32 (September 1935).

Weissman, Philip. "Conscious and Unconscious Autobiographical Dramas of Eugene O'Neill," *Journal of the American Psychoanalytic Association,* 5:432–60 (July 1957).

―*JOHN GASSNER*

Edgar Allan Poe

1809-1849

THE most contradictory judgments have been passed on Edgar Allan Poe's character and works. The Reverend Rufus Griswold, whom he had the unfortunate idea of appointing his literary executor, branded him a perverse neurotic, a drunkard and drug addict "who walked the streets, in madness or melancholy, with lips moving in indistinct curses." For Baudelaire, on the contrary, he was a "fallen angel who remembered heaven," a "Byron gone astray in a bad world." Whereas Emerson looked down upon that "jingle man" who shook his bells and called their sound poetry, Tennyson admired him as an equal and Yeats (on an official occasion, it is true) proclaimed that he was "so certainly the greatest of American poets, and always, and for all lands, a great lyric poet." For James Russell Lowell, he was "three-fifths . . . genius and two-fifths fudge," while Mallarmé piously raised the monument of a sonnet over his grave and Paul Valéry acclaimed the author of *Eureka* as one of the greatest thinkers who ever lived. Writers as dissimilar as Mark Twain and Henry James rejected him, the former because he found him "unreadable" and the latter because it seemed to him that "an enthusiasm for Poe [was] the mark of a decidedly primitive stage of reflection." But William Carlos Williams, for his part, praised him for giving "the sense for the

first time in America that literature is serious, not a matter of courtesy but of truth." Who was right? Whom are we to believe? T. S. Eliot, who denounced his "slipshod writing," or George Bernard Shaw, who found him "exquisitely refined"?

These divergences are indeed perfectly justified and stem to a large extent from the constant contrast between the real and the Ideal (the capital was his) in Poe's own life and from the consequent duplicity (in the etymological meaning of the word) of his personality. Thus, though he would have liked to be of aristocratic southern lineage, he was born in Boston, on January 19, 1809, of poor actor parents who happened to be playing there at the time. His father, David Poe, who came from a good Baltimore family, was a mediocre actor and a heavy drinker who was soon to desert his wife and vanish forever. On the contrary, his mother, Elizabeth Arnold Poe, seems to have been a charming and talented actress, but she died of tuberculosis in Richmond, Virginia, in December 1811 at the age of twenty-four. This sudden death probably warped Poe for the rest of his life. He was not quite three, but he always remembered—more or less unconsciously—his mother vomiting blood and being carried away from him forever by sinister men dressed in black. He was then taken into the home of John and Frances Allan—hence his middle name. John Allan was a successful and ambitious Richmond merchant. The couple were childless, so they reared the boy as if he were their only son, but they never formally adopted him. In 1815 they took him to England and sent him to private schools there, notably to Manor House School at Stoke Newington which Poe later used as a setting for the childhood of his hero in "William Wilson." The boy was athletic and brilliant. His foster parents, especially Mrs. Allan, doted on him, but as he moved through adolescence this apparently fortunate situation quickly deteriorated; he felt more and more insecure and estranged from his schoolmates because of his lowly origin and more and more antagonistic to Mr. Allan out of love for his valetudinarian foster mother—a standard Oedipal relationship. Being a precocious and passionate boy, while still at school he fell in love with the beautiful young mother of one of his friends, Mrs. Jane Stanard, whose memory inspired the first of his poems, "To Helen," and with a young neighbor, Sarah Elmira Royster, but her parents disapproved of him since he was penniless, and the courtship was soon broken off.

Although his practical-minded foster father wanted him to work as a clerk in his business, Poe managed to be sent to the University of Virginia in 1826. There he studied French, Spanish, Italian, and Latin, read Byron and Campbell, and had an excellent scholastic record. But the University of Virginia in those days was a wild, dissolute place (like Oxford in "William Wilson"). Poe got into difficulties almost at once because Mr. Allan had parsimoniously not provided him with enough money to pay for his fees and other necessities; then he took to drinking and gambling, accumulating debts in excess of $2000. His foster father refused to pay his "debts of honor," so Poe could not remain at Charlottesville. It was the end of his dream of a university education and he decided to break with Mr. Allan. He left Richmond in March 1827 for Boston, his birthplace, and enlisted in the army as a common soldier under the name of Edgar A. Perry. He was stationed for over a year on Sullivan's Island in Charleston Harbor, which he would describe in "The Gold Bug." Surprisingly enough, he adapted very well to military discipline and quickly rose to the rank of regimental sergeant major, the highest noncommissioned grade in the army. Yet he soon became tired of the routine of military life in peacetime and fretted at the thought of serving out his full five-year term of enlistment—or, rather, he now dreamed of becoming an officer like his colonel, whom he admired. He wrote repentingly to Mr. Allan and reconciled with him after the death of Mrs. Allan in February 1829. With Allan's support he got his discharge and an appointment to West Point, which he entered on July 1, 1830.

During this period of nearly perfect social adaptation he must have cherished dreams of an entirely different kind, though, for in the summer of 1827, while still at Boston he published at his own expense a thin volume, *Tamerlane and Other Poems*, "by a Bostonian," which passed unnoticed. That he did so at such an early date (he was only eighteen) in spite of his reduced circumstances shows his faith in himself and his belief that he had something original to say. Undiscouraged by the failure of this first volume, he published a second one at Baltimore in December 1829: *Al Aaraaf, Tamerlane, and Minor Poems*. As the title shows, it was a revised and enlarged edition of his first book. It received hardly more critical attention than its predecessor.

At West Point, the same thing happened as

at the University of Virginia. Mr. Allan, who had remarried in the meantime, did not provide Poe with adequate funds. In January 1831 Poe wrote to him: "You sent me to W. Point like a beggar. The same difficulties are threatening me as before at Charlottesville—and I must resign." He kept his word. Though he had been a very good student until then, he decided to have himself expelled by deliberately cutting classes and disregarding orders. He was therefore court-martialed for "gross neglect of duties" in January 1831 and left West Point the following month.

Once again, though more destitute than ever, he succeeded in 1831 in publishing a new edition of his poems, simply entitled *Poems, Second Edition*. The appearance of this new book at such a time proves his extraordinary perseverance, but he was again ignored by critics. Yet the book included "To Helen," "Israfel," "The City in the Sea," "The Sleeper," "Lenore," "The Valley of Unrest," and an interesting introductory statement of poetic principle, "Letter to Mr.—— ——."

By now Poe was in the greatest difficulties. He had settled in New York, but could find no job there. His pathetic calls for help to Mr. Allan remained unanswered. He devised all sorts of wild schemes—he thought for a time of joining the Polish army—which came to nothing. He was eventually obliged to take refuge with his aunt, Mrs. Clemm, in Baltimore. Baltimore was then an active publishing center and it was natural for him to seek employment there now that he had made up his mind to live by his pen.

Having failed to attract attention as a poet, he turned to story writing and worked frantically. In 1831 he competed for the prize offered for the best short story by the *Philadelphia Saturday Courier*. He submitted five: "Metzengerstein," "The Duke de l'Omelette,"

"A Tale of Jerusalem," "A Decided Loss," and "The Bargain Lost." He did not win the prize, which was given to a mawkish tale, but all five of his stories were later published in the *Courier* (in 1832). It must be admitted that only one of them was first-rate: "Metzengerstein." Poe had by then embarked on an ambitious project: he had planned a series of tales supposedly told by members of a rather farcical literary group, the Folio Club, in imitation of Boccaccio's *Decameron* and Chaucer's *Canterbury Tales*, a prefiguration in a way of Dickens' famous Pickwick Club. But he could find no publisher for his stories, and in an attempt to make a breakthrough he once more entered a contest in June 1833. The competition was organized by the *Baltimore Saturday Visitor* and Poe sent one poem, "The Coliseum," and six stories: "Epimanes," "MS. Found in a Bottle," "Lionizing," "The Visionary," "Siope," and "A Descent into the Maelström." This time he won the short-story award with "MS. Found in a Bottle" and his troubles were temporarily brought to an end, for one of the judges of the contest, a wealthy lawyer and amateur novelist, John P. Kennedy, befriended him.

On Kennedy's recommendation Poe became assistant editor of the *Southern Literary Messenger,* published at Richmond by T. W. White. Poe now went through a period of emotional instability during which he apparently resorted to the bottle to steady his nerves. He was no habitual drunkard and never wrote under the influence of drink, for he was very frugal and of a sober inclination, but he was extremely sensitive and given to excruciating fits of depression, so that he could not at times resist the temptation of using alcohol as a sort of moral anesthetic. Unfortunately he was inordinately affected by even one glass and then lost all sense of dignity and decency. As he put it himself: "My sensitive temperament could not stand an excitement which was an every-day matter to my companions." In any event, after a month, White discharged him but relented when Poe pleaded to be reinstated.

Poe brought Mrs. Clemm and her daughter Virginia to live with him in Richmond and in May 1836 he married his young cousin, who was boldly declared to be "of the full age of twenty-one years," while actually she was not quite fourteen and looked very immature. In all likelihood the marriage was never consummated, but Poe felt very happy with his child-wife ("Sis") and with Mrs. Clemm ("dear Muddy") as mother-in-law and devoted housekeeper.

This was a period of intense production for Poe. He wrote stories, many forceful and slashing reviews in the manner of the Edinburgh reviewers, waging war on mediocrity, trying to enforce high literary standards, attacking "the heresy of the didactic," and denouncing plagiarism even where there was none. Unfortunately his efforts were often wasted on rather trivial works. He also composed a drama in verse, *Politian*, set in Renaissance Italy in the manner of Byron and Shelley, and *The Narrative of Arthur Gordon Pym*, two installments of which appeared in the *Messenger*, and which was published in book form in 1838. This was his only attempt at a long story, but it is in fact a series of separate short stories strung together. Under his dynamic editorship, the *Southern Literary Messenger* became the leading review of the South and its subscription list rose, in a year's time, from five hundred to nearly thirty-five hundred. But White objected to Poe's continued intemperance and resented his editorial authority and even his success. He dismissed him in January 1837. Poe then went to New York in the hope of finding another editorial position there. He was unsuccessful and in the summer of 1838

moved to Philadelphia, where he lived for the next five years and became in July 1839 the editor of *Burton's Gentleman's Magazine*. Under the pressure of financial need he wrote unceasingly—in particular a piece of hackwork, *The Conchologist's First Book*, for which he was (justly) accused of plagiarism in his turn, but also "Ligeia" (for the *American Museum*), "The Man That Was Used Up," "The Fall of the House of Usher," "William Wilson," "The Conversation of Eiros and Charmion," and "Morella" (for the *Gentleman's Magazine*). Soon, however, the story of his editorship of the *Southern Literary Messenger* repeated itself. Burton and Poe quarreled over editorial policies and Poe was fired in the summer of 1840.

In that year he at last found a publisher for a collection of his stories, which appeared in two volumes in Philadelphia under the title *Tales of the Grotesque and Arabesque*. They were well received by critics, but sold rather slowly. So Poe's financial problem remained unsolved and, after he had failed to find backers for a literary journal called *The Penn Magazine,* of which only the prospectus was ever printed, he joined the staff of *Graham's Magazine* and became its editor in April 1841. This was another very productive period. It was then that he published his reviews of Longfellow's *Ballads* and Hawthorne's *Twice-Told Tales* in which he defined his conception of poetry and fiction, and such stories as "The Man of the Crowd," "The Murders in the Rue Morgue," "The Island of the Fay," "The Colloquy of Monos and Una," "Eleonora," "The Oval Portrait," and "The Masque of the Red Death." Yet for all his success and brilliance he once more lost his job, in May 1842, after only thirteen months, for the same reasons as before.

His dismissal from *Graham's Magazine* did not interrupt his creation of fiction, but he found it very difficult sometimes to place his stories. He sold "The Mystery of Marie Rogêt," "The Pit and the Pendulum," "The Tell-Tale Heart," and "The Black Cat" for paltry sums to second-rate magazines. In April 1844, realizing that he could not make a living in Philadelphia as a free-lance writer, though he had won a $100 prize for "The Gold Bug" in 1843, he moved to New York, which was to remain his home until his death five years later. But he encountered the same difficulties in earning a living as in Philadelphia, though at first he scored a few resounding successes. Thus he had hardly settled there when, on April 13, 1844, he published in the *New York Sun* what is now known as "The Balloon Hoax," a tale in the form of a news item. It appeared under the caption "Astounding News by Electric Express via Norfolk! The Atlantic Crossed in Three Days—Signal Triumph of Mr. Monck's Flying-Machine . . ." The description was so graphic that everyone was taken in. But Poe was none the richer for it and the only job he found was that of assistant editor of the *Evening Mirror*. It was in this periodical that "The Raven" first appeared on January 29, 1845. The poem immediately caught the imagination of the public and was reprinted all over the country and even abroad in all kinds of newspapers and magazines, but Poe pocketed only a few dollars for his pains. However, 1845 was on the whole a lucky year for him. In July there appeared another collection of his *Tales* (only twelve of them, though) and in November another edition of his poems under the title *The Raven and Other Poems*. Besides, he was offered a better position as assistant editor of the weekly *Broadway Journal*, of which he soon became the editor. He even obtained control of the paper and thus very nearly realized his ambition of becoming the sole proprietor of a periodical, but the *Broadway Journal* died on his hands

during the first weeks of 1846. Despite all his feverish exertions—and though he then wrote such a fine story as "The Cask of Amontillado" and such a brilliant essay as "The Philosophy of Composition"—he had been growing poorer and poorer all the time and was in such distress at the end of 1846 that the *New York Express* and the Philadelphia *Saturday Evening Post* asked his friends and admirers to come to his aid. He was then living with Virginia and Mrs. Clemm in a diminutive wooden cottage at Fordham, and Virginia, though dying of consumption, had to sleep in an unheated room. After six years of marriage she had become fatally ill, and her slowly progressing illness between 1842 and 1847 had driven Poe to distraction.

Virginia eventually died on January 30, 1847, and Poe broke down, though he felt relieved in a way from "the horrible never-ending oscillation between hope and despair." Thus, like the hero of one of his own tales, he was constantly threatened and tortured by the pendulum of fate swinging between the extremes of the human condition. All his life he craved love and tenderness, but was doomed to lose in turn all the women he loved: his mother, Mrs. Stanard, Mrs. Allan, and Virginia. He longed for wealth and luxury, and yet, for all his talent and frenzied efforts, was condemned to destitution. He dreamed of fame and never succeeded in publishing a complete edition of his works or founding a review of his own. When he reached manhood after a sheltered childhood and adolescence he encountered nothing but failures and denials. So, instead of really living, he took refuge from the physical world in the private world of his dreams—in other words, in the world of his tales—and gradually identified himself with those phantoms of himself who haunt his stories. As is frequent with artists, nature in his case imitated art. He became the spiritual brother of his doomed heroes. His life was quite literally "a descent into the Maelström," a slow, inexorable descent into the abyss which attracted him irresistibly and was to claim him at forty years of age. He remained perfectly lucid to the end, but, unlike the hero of "A Descent into the Maelström," he lost the will to extricate himself from the whirlpool which was sucking him down. His art failed to save him. His works reflect this double aspect of his personality: the abandonment of the self-destructive romantic artist and the self-control of the conscious and conscientious craftsman, the passivity of the dreamer indifferent to all that exists outside his dream world and the restless activity of a keen mind always on the alert.

Portraits of Poe always show him fullface, but the only really revelatory portrait of him would be a head with a double profile, like that of the Roman god Janus, one side turned toward reality, the other toward dreams. Poe was himself perfectly aware of this duality. When describing the detective who appears in several of his tales, C. Auguste Dupin, he pointed out: "I often dwelt meditatively upon the old philosophy of the Bi-Part Soul, and amused myself with the fancy of a double Dupin—the creative and the resolvent." He divided his tales into tales of imagination and tales of ratiocination. The former were written by a Dionysiac and inspired creator, the latter by a lucid and impassive analyst.

The tales of imagination are the undisputed domain of fear. Poe again and again tries to make us experience the same feelings as the narrator of "The Fall of the House of Usher": "a sense of insufferable gloom pervaded my spirit. . . . There was an iciness, a sinking, a sickening of the heart. . . . There can be no doubt that the consciousness of the rapid increase of my superstition . . . served mainly to accelerate the increase itself. Such, I have long known, is the paradoxical law of all sentiments having terror as a basis. . . . An irrepressible tremor gradually pervaded my frame; and, at length, there sat upon my very heart an incubus of utterly causeless alarm." This irrational fear, which rises gradually and eventually invades the whole being, soon leads Poe's heroes to insanity and death.

The world of Poe's tales is a nightmarish universe. You cross wasted lands, silent, forsaken landscapes where both life and waters stagnate. Here and there you catch sight of lugubrious feudal buildings suggestive of horrible and mysterious happenings, like the gloomy abbey in which the hero of "Ligeia" takes refuge "in one of the wildest and least frequented portions of fair England." The inside of these sinister buildings is just as disquieting as the outside. Everything is dark there, from the ebony furniture to the oaken ceiling. The walls are hung with heavy tapestries to which mysterious drafts constantly give "a hideous and uneasy animation." Even the windows are "of a leaden hue," so that the rays of either the sun or moon passing through fall "with a ghastly lustre on the objects within." To make things worse, it is usually at night in the ghastly (one of his favorite adjectives) or red-blood light of the moon that Poe's tales take place—or in the middle of terrific storms lit up by lurid flashes of lightning. In this strange world even the baptism of Morella's daughter takes place at night! His heroes are tortured solitaries, with a tainted heredity, addicted to drink or drugs. They know that they are condemned sooner or later to lose their minds or their lives and presently indeed they die or kill before our eyes under horrifying circumstances. Metzengerstein is a victim of "morbid melancholy" and "hereditary ill-health." The nervous illness of Roderick Usher passes from hypochondriacal hyperesthesia to delirious telepathy. The odious protagonists of "The Tell-Tale Heart," "The Imp of the Perverse," and "The Black Cat" suffer from irresistible homicidal manias, and in "Berenice" Egaeus is impelled by a furious "monomania" to finish off the girl he loves in order to possess himself of her teeth. In this ghoulish universe love turns to vampirism and sadistic necrophilia.

Such an accumulation of horrible details inevitably leads the reader to ask himself whether Poe was sincere when he wrote these tales, whether they were the gratuitous play of his imagination or the true expression of a terror which he really felt in his inmost heart. There is room for hesitation, for there was in Poe's time a strong taste for Gothic romances and fantastic tales which he seems to have shared and at any rate deliberately exploited. He mentions Mrs. Radcliffe at the beginning of "The Oval Portrait" and on several occasions praises William Godwin's *Caleb Williams*. Moreover he must have read the works of Charles Brockden Brown and we know that he admired Hawthorne's tales. He must also have been acquainted with E. T. A. Hoffmann's tales—with "Das Majorat" in particular, at least in the summary which Walter Scott gave in his essay on Hoffman, for there exist some striking similarities between this tale and "The Fall of the House of Usher."

Some critics have therefore claimed that Poe was a mere mystifier who wrote his stories only to please the public and follow the current fashion. Indeed, more than once he himself pretends to be joking and describes horrible events with apparent unconcern. At the beginning of his career, in 1835, he wrote to White: "The subject [of "Berenice"] is by far too horrible, and I confess that I hesitated in sending it to you especially as a specimen of my capabilities. The Tale originated in a bet that I could produce nothing effective on a subject so singular, provided I treated it seriously." The next year, referring to his early

tales, he wrote to Kennedy: "Most of them were *intended* for half banter, half satire—although I might not have fully acknowledged this to be their aim even to myself." And finally, eight years later, in "The Premature Burial," he spoke of tales of horror with surprising skepticism. After a misadventure which was in itself a parody of the tale of horror, since he merely dreamed his premature burial, the supposed narrator declares that from then on he completely changed his way of life and got rid of his morbid obsessions by ceasing to read Edward Young's *Night Thoughts*.

Thus Poe's attitude toward his own tales is much more complex than is commonly realized. He is never completely taken in by his own imagination. His apparent frenzy is always accompanied by lucidity. His fear is often tinged with skepticism—but conversely his skepticism with fear, as is shown by the concluding lines of "The Premature Burial": "Alas! the grim legion of sepulchral terrors cannot be regarded as altogether fanciful—but, like the Demons in whose company Afrasiab made his voyage down the Oxus, they must sleep, or they will devour us—they must be suffered to slumber, or we perish."

So, for all his gibes and feigned detachment, fear finally prevails, and there is no denying that his "tales of imagination" were not mere literary exercises or hoaxes. They wholly committed him. His own tragic life is the best proof of it. He has sometimes been accused of being a histrion, but if it is true that he sometimes behaved like one, he forgot he was playing a part and killed himself in the last act with a real dagger (figuratively speaking). He declared himself in 1840 in the preface to his *Tales of the Grotesque and Arabesque*: "If in many of my productions terror has been the thesis, I maintain that terror is not of Germany but of the soul."

This terror which haunted his soul, like any

form of fear, whatever its occasion or immediate cause may be, was in the last analysis a panic fear of death, as appears in particular in the vivid descriptions of the deaths of his characters—of Ligeia especially. Sometimes it takes the form of a fear of the void, an insufferable vertigo and an unspeakable horror which overwhelms the hero's soul just as he is going to be swallowed by a bottomless pit, as in "MS. Found in a Bottle." Arthur Gordon Pym disappears in the same way in an awful white chasm at the end of the narrative that recounts his adventures. Only the hero of "A Descent into the Maelström" escapes a similar fate thanks to his Dupin-like coolness and power of observation. At other times Poe imagines final annihilation in the form of an absolute silence suddenly spreading over the whole world and filling all creatures with terror, as in "Silence—A Fable" and the sonnet also entitled "Silence."

This fear of death and engulfment by nothingness (or God?) which constitutes the very matter of most of Poe's tales is not exceptional per se. All men experience it, but it reaches a rare degree of intensity in his works and often takes the form of phobias and manias of a decidedly abnormal character. He thus describes with a curious complacency, as if they were his own, cases of morbid claustrophobia in "The Premature Burial," at the beginning of "The Pit and the Pendulum," and in the first episode of "The Narrative of Arthur Gordon Pym." On other occasions Poe visibly takes pleasure in accumulating macabre and loathsome details. He seems to have a partiality for corpses in a state of advanced decay and never fails to emphasize the nauseating smell which they exhale—as in "The Facts in the Case of M. Valdemar," for instance, when M. Valdemar's body, which had been kept for seven moths in a cataleptic state, sud-

denly disintegrates. There are even times when this fascination with corpses takes the form of true necrophilia, as in "The Oblong Box;" and the case of Egaeus in "Berenice" is still clearer since he goes as far as digging up the body of his beloved.

Some of Poe's tales also contain undeniable traces of sadism. His half-mad murderers delight in torturing their victims and eventually killing them with devilish savagery. "The old man's terror *must* have been extreme," jubilantly exclaims the murderer of "The Tell-Tale Heart." We are frequently made to witness the dismemberment of corpses, horrible mutilations, or scenes of cannibalism, as in "The Narrative of Arthur Gordon Pym." Even in such a sober tale as "The Murders in the Rue Morgue," Poe cannot resist the temptation of giving all kinds of precise details about the horrible condition of the victims' corpses. In "The Pit and the Pendulum," in spite of all the pity that Poe seems to feel for the unfortunate hero, we may wonder if in his inmost heart he does not secretly admire the Inquisitors' demoniac ingenuity.

Side by side with these signs of sadism, there are also unmistakable indications of masochism, which Poe in "The Philosophy of Composition" sympathetically calls "the human thirst for self-torture." Most of his sick heroes are afflicted with it. It is this perverse instinct which impels them to sink deeper into their nightmares and eventually surrender to madness and confess their crimes publicly at the end in order to be punished and thus suffer still more. In its extreme form this neurosis completely neutralizes the instinct of self-preservation and turns into a passionate desire for self-destruction. This is precisely what happens to Metzengerstein, Roderick Usher, and all the murderers who people Poe's tales. They are all irresistibly attracted and fascinated by death.

Thus Poe constantly allows unavowable thoughts and feelings to rise from the inmost recesses of his soul and give shape in his tales to horrible imaginings. He dreams aloud, and we witness the extraordinary adventures which he took pleasure in inventing because he was not allowed to live them. His heroes are projections of his real and secret self, which, for fear of being condemned and suppressed, his social self was obliged to keep hidden. At the beginning of "The Man of the Crowd" he declares: "It was well said of a certain German book that 'er lässt sich nicht lesen'—it does not permit itself to be read. There are some secrets which do not permit themselves to be told." He was unable completely to hide his own thoughts, though. Impelled by the same desire to confess as so many of his characters, he gave free play to the obsessions which tortured him and lent them to his heroes in order to revel in them by proxy. His tales—especially those which he called "tales of imagination" —were not the result of a conscious effort, but were to a large extent dictated to him by his subconscious cravings, as Gaston Bachelard has shown in his books on the four elements. They are not gratuitous inventions or intellectual fabrications, but veiled confessions. Besides, the return of the same themes and the permanence of certain phobias or manias show that Poe was a prey to well-defined obsessions and obeyed irresistible motivations.

Hence the special quality of the fantastic element in his tales. For we must here use the word "fantastic" rather than "supernatural." Poe himself used it in "The Island of the Fay": "These fancies, and such as these, have always given to my meditations . . . a tinge of what the every-day world would not fail to term fantastic." By this word he probably meant the intrusion of mysterious elements upon the world of the senses, but this intrusion in his case always took place without the exterior intervention of specters, monsters, devils, or miracles. In his tales terror intrudes into the everyday world in a more subtle way. It is aroused by the visions and hallucinations of his characters. The fantastic element is thus here of a subjective, or more precisely, oneiric, origin. No ghosts or supernatural happenings are needed. We deal only with nightmares described as such—though sometimes an objective element is slyly added, as in "Metzengerstein" when the portion of the tapestry representing the horse of one of the Berlifitzings suddenly vanishes at the very moment when the selfsame horse appears alive in the yard of the castle. We might think that Metzengerstein is the victim of an illusion if he were the only witness to this disappearance, but since it is also observed by one of his pages, we must admit that it is an objective phenomenon and not a mere hallucination. Exceptionally in this particular example, fantasy yields to the supernatural, but everywhere else it is linked up with morbid states which become the source of frightening and phantasmagoric visions. As Baudelaire noted, the fantastic element in Poe's tales is grounded in "*exceptions* in human life and in nature . . . hallucinations . . . hysteria usurping the place of the will, contradiction set up between the nerves and the mind, and personality so out of joint that it expresses grief with a laugh. He . . . describes . . . all that imaginary world which floats around a high-strung man and leads him into evil." "Poe is a writer who is all nerves," he concluded. Indeed, in "Shadow—A Parable," Poe makes this statement which is tantamount to a confession: "There were things around us and about of which I can render no distinct account—things material and spiritual—heaviness in the atmosphere—a sense of suffocation —anxiety—and, above all, that terrible state of existence which the nervous experience when the senses are keenly living and awake, and meanwhile the powers of thought lie dormant."

If Baudelaire had written in our time, he would have spoken of neuroses rather than nerves. Poe is the writer of neuroses. "The Premature Burial" shows he was fully aware that the epileptic and cataleptic states of his heroes were the consequence rather than the cause of their morbid thoughts; he discovered before Freud that the health of the body depends on the health of the mind.

The hidden cause of his own neurotic condition—which he desperately tried to escape by drinking and even perhaps by taking drugs—has been diagnosed by one of Freud's friends and disciples, Marie Bonaparte. She has set forth her thesis in a bulky book full of insight and ingenuity whose general conclusions are irrefutable even if some of her interpretations seem too systematic. According to her, all the disorders from which Poe suffered can be explained by the Oedipus complex and the incurable trauma caused by the tragic disappearance of his mother when he was only three years old. The image of his beautiful and frail young mother sapped by consumption seems indeed to have dominated his whole life and probably explains why he could marry only a child-wife in the person of his cousin Virginia. It is obvious too that all his "ethereal" heroines (the adjective is his), Berenice, Morella, Madeline Usher, Eleonora, Ligeia, are mere reflections of that beloved mother too soon taken from him. Most of them, besides, are introduced to us as cousins of the narrator and close kin to his mother. These lucid and translucid women, lucid like himself and translucid like his mother, inspire his heroes with intellectual rather than sensual passions, with passionate friendship rather than desire. Every-

thing happens as if Poe had forever exhausted all the possibilities of love in his relation with his mother and he or his heroes could only love sick or dying women like his own mother. Love and death are indissolubly merged both in his works and in his life.

Thus Poe's fantastic tales, which on account of their very nature should be quite impersonal, in fact plunge their roots to the inmost recesses of his being. Each of them in a way masks the mouth of a cave in the darkness of which creep monstrous creatures, the author's obsessions and phobias. Or, to use another image, each of his tales is palimpsest, and we must try to read under the legible text the almost completely faded scrawl which it hides and which will clarify everything if we succeed in deciphering it. "The supposition that the book of an author is a thing apart from the author's *Self* is, I think, ill-founded," he once declared.

Like Baudelaire, his French translator and counterpart, Poe could have addressed his reader as "hypocritical reader, my brother!" Whether we like it or not, we feel secret bonds with him and his heroes—who at times look strangely Kafkaesque or Faulknerian. Indeed, they are both romantic figures and prefigurations of the twentieth-century existentialist hero. They live in an empty, dehumanized, and dechristianized world, plunged in deep melancholy, trailing clouds of glory (and European romanticism), absolutely pure and sexless, refusing to notice the turbid waters into which their dreams sink their snakelike roots. They are often shut up in a secluded place of no exit. They are dark Narcissuses involved in a desperate search for their identity and haunted by an obscure sense of guilt; they feel alienated from the world that surrounds them. They spend their time talking with their double (the narrator) or trying to guess his thoughts (Dupin whose intellect tries to identify itself with that of his opponent); or they struggle with him and finally kill him like William Wilson and, in a way, Prospero in "The Masque of the Red Death." Whether they kill their double (and consequently themselves) or some apparently alien victim, they do so in order to find and define themselves. "I kill, therefore I am." But self-knowledge thus leads to nothing but self-destruction. The application of Socrates' advice "Know thyself" here only results in the realization that the self is bound to die, will sooner or later be sucked in by nothingness. A rather despairing conclusion.

Though he was always unconsciously guided by the secret obsessions of his imagination, Poe did not follow his inspiration blindly. Another faculty constantly interfered. Even in his fantastic tales he never lets himself go. There is method in his madness. Madness, moreover, is not incompatible with reason, as he himself observed on several occasions, notably in "The System of Doctor Tarr and Professor Fether." It sometimes consists in stubbornly making right deductions from wrong premises. Poe, at any rate, knew how to impose a strict discipline on his nightmares. The data of his morbid and undoubtedly disordered imagination are always controlled by a severe method and presented in the form of a clear and logical train of events bound together by connections between causes and effects. In other words, his reason always rules his creative activity. He wanted it so.

According to him, inspiration and reason are compatible; they even combine harmoniously with each other. In his fantastic tales he has succeeded in balancing the two opposite faculties, but so great was the power of reason over him that he composed under its exclusive guidance a series of tales which he rather pedantically called "tales of ratiocination":

"The Murders in the Rue Morgue," "The Purloined Letter," "The Gold Bug," "The Mystery of Marie Rogêt," and "Maelzel's Chess-Player." In these tales he behaves as a perfect rationalist and even goes so far as to deny the existence of the supernatural. "In my own heart," he makes the narrator of "The Mystery of Marie Rogêt" declare, "there dwells no faith in praeternature. That Nature and its God are two, no man who thinks will deny. That the latter, creating the former, can, at will, control or modify it, is also unquestionable. I say 'at will'; for the question is of will, and not, as the insanity of logic has assumed, of power. It is not that the Deity *cannot* modify his laws, but that we insult him in imagining a possible necessity for modification." Poe thus fully shares the views of the scientists for whom the only existing phenomena are those of the physical world obeying a set of immutable laws which can be rationally accounted for and expressed in mathematical formulas. We are a long way from the state of mind of the narrator of "The Fall of the House of Usher," whose intelligence on the contrary capitulates before a number of strange happenings which he considers inexplicable: "I was forced to fall back upon the unsatisfactory conclusion, that while, beyond doubt, there *are* combinations of very simple natural objects which have the power of thus affecting us, still the analysis of this power lies among considerations beyond our depth."

Thus reason triumphs in the tales of ratiocination and Poe again and again sings its praises: "As the strong man exults in his physical ability," he exclaims at the beginning of "The Murders in the Rue Morgue," "delighting in such exercises as call his muscles into action, so glories the analyst in that moral activity which *disentangles*. He derives pleasure from even the most trivial occupations bringing his talent into play. He is fond of enigmas, of conundrums, hieroglyphics; exhibiting in his solutions of each a degree of *acumen* which appears to the ordinary apprehension praeternatural."

Poe here describes his own tastes and activities. He was passionately fond of riddles and puzzles. When he was editor of *Graham's Magazine* he wrote a series of articles on cryptography and claimed in one that he had defied the readers of the *Alexander's Weekly Messenger* to send him a cryptogram which he could not decipher. He had received, he said, about one hundred coded messages, all of which he had succeeded in decoding, except one which he had proved to be indecipherable. He was very proud of his ability—though professionals nowadays look down upon him as a mere amateur—and he paraded it in particular in "The Gold Bug."

He applied his ingenuity to all kinds of other problems. In "Maelzel's Chess-Player," for instance, he proved that this famous automaton, which had just been exhibited in a number of American cities, could be nothing but a machine with a man hidden inside. His demonstration in seventeen points is conducted with impeccable logic and his conclusions are incontrovertible. Poe, besides, exhibits a truly scientific spirit by fastening on a seemingly trivial detail—the fact that the automaton always used its left hand—and by basing all his reasoning upon it. For as he points out in "The Murders in the Rue Morgue," "it is by these deviations from the plane of the ordinary, that reason feels its way, if at all, in its search for the true."

Poe could take to pieces with the greatest skill any intellectual mechanism or solve any kind of problem, but he could also do the reverse and build up piece by piece the most plausible and convincing hoax in the world, as he did when he published "The Balloon Hoax" in the *New York Sun* in 1844. "The Murders in the Rue Morgue" is a feat of the same kind, since Poe had to organize and combine the details of the murders with the same regard for logic and consistency as if he were reporting them for a newspaper. It only remained for him then to tell the events in the reverse order, beginning with the still-warm bodies of the victims and working his way back from there to the murderer. Contrary to what the reader may think, the author's ingenuity here does not consist in unraveling the threads of a complex plot, but in weaving a strong web, as Poe himself pointed out in a letter to the poet and critic Philip Pendleton Cooke: "Where is the ingenuity of unravelling a web which you yourself (the author) have woven for the express purpose of unravelling? The reader is made to confound the ingenuity of the suppositious Dupin with that of the writer of the story." At any rate, whether the creative process works backwards or forwards, the interest of this kind of tale is essentially of an intellectual order. The author poses such a complex problem that the reader is unable to solve it, but the author helps him, proves in turn the absurdity of a number of hypotheses, and eventually reaches the only possible solution. What matters is the discovery of the culprit and not the analysis of his or her motives. The human or psychological interest is therefore completely lacking—especially in "The Murders in the Rue Morgue," in which the murderer is not even a man but an orangutang.

So, by applying the most rigorous logic to the writing of fiction, Poe discovered the detective story. Voltaire, it is true, had already created Zadig, but Dupin and his companion were the immediate predecessors of Sherlock Holmes and Dr. Watson and through these had a numberless posterity. However, Poe only exceptionally gave free play to his faculties of analysis and deduction. Most of the time, he preferred to combine them with his imagination and the dark forces of his subconscious. He succeeded in effecting the difficult synthesis of these antagonistic elements thanks to a deliberate strategy of applying to the data provided by his imagination a number of well-defined aesthetic principles.

It is remarkable that even in his very first tales, though he wrote them when he was hardly over twenty, Poe reached mastery of his art. He owed it not only to his full knowledge of the requirements of this difficult genre which demands both conciseness and concentration, but also to the conscious and deliberate fusion of his visionary faculties and his analytical intelligence. In "Magazine-Writing—Peter Snook," he lays it down as a principle that "There is no greater mistake than the supposition that a true originality is a mere matter of impulse or inspiration. To originate is carefully, patiently, and understandingly to combine."

Thus, for Poe—whether he wrote in prose or verse—inspiration was necessary, but not sufficient. He reached at a very early date a voluntarist conception of literary creation which he set forth in several critical essays, "The Philosophy of Composition," "The Poetic Principle," "Fancy and Imagination," and in reviews of Longfellow's poems, Dickens' *Barnaby Rudge*, and above all Hawthorne's *Twice-Told Tales*. All these essays overlap and repeat each other, which proves Poe's belief in the importance of his thesis. And that he should have felt it necessary to write all this dogmatic criticism shows how deeply convinced he was of the power of reason in this field.

To begin with, Poe asserts that inspiration is a legend and a myth and those who claim to have written under its influence are only imposters. According to him *poeta fit, non nascitur*: you are not born a man of genius, you become one, provided you are sufficiently diligent—and intelligent, for everything depends on the will and a judicious application of the intellect. To prove the truth of this paradox, Poe gives as an example his one work that had met with the greatest and most immediate success. "The Raven." He takes it to pieces in "The Philosophy of Composition" in order to show "that no one point in its composition is referable either to accident or intuition—that the work proceeded, step by step, to its completion with the precision and rigid consequence of a mathematical problem."

Yet we cannot take Poe's word for it and blindly accept his thesis that a poet is not an inspired artist but a clever technician knowing how to obtain a deliberately chosen effect by appropriate means. Baudelaire, for all his sympathy with such an aesthetics, could not help voicing some doubts when he commented on "The Philosophy of Composition": "Did he make himself, by a strange and amusing vanity, much less inspired than he naturally was? . . . I should be rather inclined to think so." Indeed, how can we put stock in Poe's so-called confession and believe that "The Raven" was the work of Poe-Dupin alone without the help of the other Poe, the inspired neurotic? It is impossible in particular to believe that his famous refrain was not given to him after long gropings (he had already used "no more" in the "Sonnet—To Zante" and "The Haunted Palace"). Besides, we do know that "The Raven" was not the result of a few hours' lucid work. Its composition was spread over several months. He let it grow organically as it were (conformably with the precepts of romantic aesthetics), and this at a time when Virginia was dying and he was reduced to nearly complete destitution. It is not surprising under such circumstances that "The Raven" should have spontaneously expressed his agony, his haunting fear of the future, his terror at the thought that his beloved wife was soon to disappear forever. It is not a feat of virtuosity, but a cry of pain—even if its form has been cleverly wrought. Poe's account of the genesis of this poem is nothing but an a posteriori analysis. In fact, "The Raven" was to a large extent the result of inspiration, imposed on the poet before being perfected by the craftsman. In a way he confessed this semi-mystification in one of his "Marginalia": "It is the curse of a certain order of mind, that it can never rest satisfied with the consciousness of its ability to do a thing. Not even is it content with doing it. It must both know and show how it is done."

Poe, however, did not underestimate the importance of intuition, as this note shows: "That the imagination has not been unjustly ranked as supreme among the mental faculties, appears from the intense consciousness, on the part of the imaginative man, that the faculty in question brings his soul often to a glimpse of things supernal and eternal—to the very verge of the great secrets. . . . Some of the most profound knowledge—perhaps all *very* profound knowledge—has originated from a highly stimulated imagination. Great intellects *guess* well." But for all the intense awareness of what he owed to inspiration, Poe nevertheless preferred to lay emphasis on analysis and conscious arrangement, all those aspects of the creative activity which can be clearly defined and, to some extent, codified, with regard to the tale as well as poetry.

Poe considered the tale a superior form of art. It is superior to the novel, according to him, and even, to some extent, to poetry: "the tale has a point of superiority even over the poem. In fact, while the *rhythm* of this latter is an essential aid in the development of the poem's highest idea—the idea of the Beautiful—the artificialities of this rhythm are an inseparable bar to the development of all points of thought or expression which have their basis in *Truth*. But Truth is often, and in very great degree, the aim of the tale."

But in order to deserve this eminent status in literature the tale must meet well-defined requirements. And at this point Poe—like Aristotle in his *Poetics*—formulates a number of rules, the first of which bears the name of "unity or totality of interest." It could more simply be called the rule of "unity of effect or impression"—and it is meant to apply to poems as well as tales. Poe defines it in his review of Longfellow's *Ballads*: "in pieces of less extent, the pleasure is *unique*, in the proper acceptation of this term—the understanding is employed, without difficulty, in the contemplation of the picture *as a whole*; and thus its effect will depend, in great measure, upon the perfection of its finish, upon the nice adaptation of its constituent parts, and, especially, upon what is rightly termed by Schlegel *the unity or totality of interest*."

Granting the principle of unity of impression, there remains the problem of determining how it can best be obtained. According to Poe, the first requirement is brevity. One can create an effect of totality or unity only in a sufficiently brief piece. And this is the reason why he thought a poem must not exceed "what can comfortably be read at one sitting, that is to say about a hundred lines, for, if two sittings be required, the affairs of the world interfere, and every thing like totality of effect is at once destroyed." As regards prose, conditions are different. The reader can endure more without having to stretch out his legs. It seemed to him therefore that the ideal length of a short prose narrative was that of a text requiring "from a half-hour to one or two hours in its perusal." In his opinion, such a narrative is superior to a novel, which "deprives itself, of course, of the immense force derivable from *totality*" simply because it cannot be read at one sitting.

The second requirement to be met in order to obtain unity of effect is of the same kind as the first one and directly derives from it. A narrative can be brief only if the action which it recounts takes place in a fairly restricted space. Poe gives this rule a rather barbarous name. He calls it "close circumscription of space." It is much the same thing as the rule of unity of place prescribed by Aristotle, but it is less rigid. The author is not required to keep the actors in one room; he is merely advised not to let them stray away too far from a central point.

As to the third requirement, it is reminiscent of Aristotle's rule of unity of action. Poe does not give it any name, but it concerns the plot and consists in asserting that all the details of a narrative must be closely subordinated to the whole. A tale must be self-sufficient and "should contain within itself all that is requisite for its own comprehension" and nothing else, a prescription which is curiously consonant with the principles of New Criticism.

In practice Poe used two main methods to obtain that impression of unity and homogeneity which he valued so much: subjective narratives and what he called "concatenation." Indeed, all his tales are told in the first person singular, the narrative being placed either in the mouth of the hero or in that of his confidant. This device enabled Poe to link up the incidents with one another by placing them inside one consciousness, and at the same time to fuse them into one by means of comments whose presence under such circumstances seems quite natural. He was aware of the advantages of this method, for in reviewing one of Captain Marryat's books he wrote: "The *commenting* force can never be safely disregarded. It is far better to have a dearth of incident, with skilful observations upon it, than the utmost variety of event, without." Authorial comment, he affirmed in the review of a novel by William Ainsworth, has "a binding power" which gives unity to the most desultory narratives. On the other hand, he always strove to relate closely to one another the various incidents of a tale by very carefully establishing connections between cause and effect—which made D. H. Lawrence protest that Poe was "rather a scientist than an artist."

Another of Poe's preoccupations was the creation of verisimilitude. In his critical essays, however, he hardly touches upon it because, in his opinion, it was the natural result of that concatenation at which he aimed all the time. Yet in one of his reviews he incidentally reveals one of the devices he used to convince the reader of the authenticity of the extraordinary episodes he related, namely the extreme precision of some details. He was not the inventor of this technique; he acknowledged it implicitly when he praised Defoe. His method, however, was somewhat different from that of Defoe in *Robinson Crusoe* or *A Journal of the Plague Year* since he had to adapt it to his own purpose. "It consists principally," he said, "in avoiding, as may easily be done, that *directness* of expression which we have noted in *Sheppard Lee* [by Robert M. Bird] and thus leaving much to the imagination—in writing as if the author were firmly impressed with the truth, yet astonished at the immensity of the wonders he relates, and for which, professedly, he neither claims nor anticipates credence—in minuteness of detail, especially upon points which have no immediate bearing upon the general story [for example, the description of the House of Usher and the apparently incidental mention of the fissure in the façade]—this minuteness not being at variance with indirectness of expression—in short, by making use of the infinity of arts which give verisimilitude to a narration."

It is thus clear that Poe deliberately applied to the fantastic tale some of the devices of the realistic novel. He loved small details and, like Dupin, had a keen sense of observation. Hence his precise descriptions of the setting in some of his tales: the old abbey bought in England by Ligeia's husband, the castle where Prospero and his court take refuge in "The Masque of the Red Death," the school attended by William Wilson in his childhood—hence also the pseudo-scientific substructure of "The Unparalleled Adventure of One Hans Pfaall." It was his way of rooting fantasy in reality, but conversely he also had to avoid precision as soon as he touched on fantasy; he then had to suggest and use, as he said, "indirect" means of expression. Passages of realistic description appear in his tales only as isles of light in a dark landscape. He recommended against accumulating details: "An outline frequently stirs the spirit more pleasantly than the most elaborate picture." Generally speaking, he had only contempt for pure realism: "That the chief merit of a picture is its *truth*, is an assertion deplorably erroneous. Even in Painting, which is, more essentially than Poesy, a mimetic art, the proposition cannot be sustained."

Poe's aim was not exclusively truth, but also what he called "passion, or the excitement of the heart," which "although attainable, to a certain extent, in poetry [is] far more readily attainable in prose." Hence his emphasis on the "tone" of the tale aside from the contents, on the impression to be produced rather than on the purely narrative element. Besides, he thought that a tale must not be a mere narrative, for then its "hardness" and "nakedness" would "repel the artistical eye." "Two things are invariably required," he claimed: "first some amount of complexity, or more properly

adaptation; and secondly, some amount of suggestiveness—some undercurrent, however indefinite, of meaning. . . . It is this latter, in especial, which imparts to a work of art so much of that *richness* (to borrow from colloquy a forcible term). . . ."

In other words, the reader must feel beyond the letter of the narrative the presence of a spirit which confers on all the details and incidents a precious but inexpressible meaning. Here Poe joins hands with Coleridge and the German romantics. He wants his tales to bring the reader into contact with what he called "the Ideal" or, as he also said, borrowing the word from Augustus Wilhelm Schlegel, he wants them to be "mystic."

Such was his ultimate aim. His tales were not ends in themselves, but a means to make us feel the mystery and horror of our condition. We must go beyond the surface of his narratives. Most of his texts are only pretexts which he uses to take us beyond appearances. His purpose was not simply to build perfect plots, but to make us share his dreams, and through the rational to reveal the irrational to us.

All these aesthetic principles often seem to verge on transcendentalism. But Poe, who felt only contempt for Emerson and his disciples, would have indignantly rejected such an insinuation. He equated transcendentalism with the surrender of intelligence and the failure of reason. For his part he was ready to accept the existence of a mystery at the center of the universe, but his intelligence, as *Eureka* shows, strove to pierce it and eventually reached, instead of Emerson's vague pantheism, what Allen Tate has called a form of panlogism. Poe's rationalism, like the hero of "A Descent into the Maelström," resisted the fascination of the abyss and refused to be engulfed by a hazy spiritualism.

However, though Poe tried hard to maintain equipoise on all levels between his reason and his imagination, it is obvious that Roderick Usher repeatedly got the better of the Dupin within him. He was closer at heart to his haunted criminals than to his impassive detective. In the last analysis, therefore, for all their rational construction and cleverly organized narrative contents, his tales are lyric outbursts in disguise, in which the "I" of the speaker corresponds less to fictitious characters than to Poe himself, had he let himself go. And this is one of the reasons why he never succeeded in creating any lifelike characters in his tales (his personal experience of life was much too limited). He gave as an excuse that the extreme brevity of the tale does not lend itself to the study in depth of characters, but the true reason was that he was himself the hero of all his tales. If Roderick Usher, Egaeus, Metzengerstein, and even Dupin are all alike, if Ligeia, Morella, and Eleonora look like sisters, it is because, whether he consciously wanted to or not, he always takes the story of his own life as a starting point, a rather empty story on the whole since he had mostly lived in his dreams, imprisoned by his neuroses and obsessed by the image of his dead mother. What he makes the narrator of "Berenice" confess is probably partly true of himself: "The realities of the world affected me as visions, and as visions only, while the wild ideas of the land of dreams became, in turn,—not the material of my every-day existence—but in very deed that existence utterly and solely in itself."

This further explains why he rebelled against the moralizing literature of the America of his time, why he protested against what he called "didacticism." His only care and preoccupation was to take himself, that is to say his dreams, as the subject of his tales under the pretext of entertaining the reader.

What Joseph Wood Krutch has said of Poe's detective stories, that he invented the genre in order not to go mad, applies to all his tales.

Describing the arabesques of his reveries in fictional narratives helped him to exorcise his inner demons. But he had still another derivative: humor. Besides his tales of imagination and ratiocination, he also wrote what he called grotesque tales: "The Devil in the Belfrey," "Lionizing," "Four Beasts in One; the Homo-Cameleopard," "Some Words with a Mummy," "The Angel of the Odd," "The System of Doctor Tarr and Professor Fether," "The Duke de l'Omelette," "Loss of Breath," "Bon-Bon," "How to Write a Blackwood Article," "Peter Pendulum," "The Spectacles," "Mystification," "Why the Little Frenchman Wears His Hand in a Sling," "Never Bet the Devil Your Head," "The Man That Was Used Up" (which was taken up by Nathanael West in *A Cool Million*), etc. All these tales, which have often been neglected by critics, are above all parodies now of himself, now of others, or, rather, of himself as well as others, since he had such deep affinities with the fantastic tales which were then so popular. The lucid reasoner in him could not but make fun of the ghosts conjured up by his neurotic self. Torn by his neuroses, tormented in all likelihood by his sexual impotence, baffled by life, Poe nevertheless refused to acknowledge his defeat and preferred to laugh at his misfortune rather than lament over it. The black humor of his tales expresses this courageously concealed despair; it is a desperate challenge to the blind forces which overcome the defenseless individual. As André Breton put it, it is "a higher revolt of the mind."

"Loss of Breath" is quite characteristic in this respect. Its subtitle, "A Tale neither in nor out of 'Blackwood,'" immediately stamps it as a parody. It is a warning that we must not take it seriously. There is little danger that we should, for the very first lines are made comic by the incongruous contrast between the epic bombast of the tone and the triviality of the subject. Poe's humor here as elsewhere is based on exaggeration and overstatement—as in Dickens. The reader suddenly finds himself in a world of hyperboles in which there is no happy mean between obesity and extreme leanness, between a vociferating voice and a whisper. These absurd contrasts are irresistibly ludicrous and one cannot help laughing, either, at the cascade of misfortunes which happen to the hero with quasi-mechanical regularity. "Mechanics stuck on life is always laughable," as Bergson noted. The reader indulges in all this merriment without any qualms, for though his tormentors break Mr. Lacko'breath's head and arms, cut his ears, disembowel him, and finally hang him, he remains as insensitive to pain as Donald Duck in a Walt Disney cartoon. He is—and so are we—anesthetized by humor. We live with him in a nonsensical world in which man is nothing but a wooden puppet and life and death have no meaning. Everything becomes relative and extremes meet and merge. It is the realm of paradox. The most commonly accepted notions are denied or reversed in the most unexpected manner and with a great show of seriousness. The logic of the tale is impeccable, but all the incidents derive from a deliberately absurd premise, namely that you can lose and find your breath, just as you can lose and find your purse—or a character in a tale of imagination can lose and find his shadow. The starting point is the literal interpretation of a common phrase, "to lose one's breath"—humorists often use this trick—and this provides the first link in a chain of irresistibly comic episodes. The underlying subject, however, is tragic despite the apparently happy ending. It is the story of a newly married man suddenly stricken with sexual impotence and excluded from life. It reveals under the disguise of a farce the secret wound from which Poe suffered all his life, the source of all his torments and terrors.

Except for a half-dozen very popular poems, Poe is chiefly known nowadays as a teller of tales. The corpus of his poems, besides, is extremely small. Yet his supreme ambition was to be a poet: "Events not to be controlled have prevented me from making, at any time, any serious effort in what, under happier circumstances, would have been the field of my choice." He ranked poetry higher than prose (when he was not pleading the cause of the tale), because it is "the desire of the moth for the star," "the rhythmical creation of Beauty," and "Beauty is the sole legitimate province of the poem"—whereas the domain of prose is merely Truth. In other words, the writing of prose is a human occupation—whereas, when a poet writes verse, he creates something in the full sense of the word; he rivals God. Before Whitman, Poe stripped poetry of all the adventitious elements which tended to hide it, whether epic, descriptive, or didactic. His aim was pure poetry, his ideal a sheer lyric outburst. Consequently, he denounced prolixity and, as we have already seen, insisted that a poem must be short: "a long poem does not exist . . . the phrase, 'a long poem,' is simply a flat contradiction in terms."

Such were the principles he laid down in "The Poetic Principle" (1850). In practice he succeeded only gradually in purging his own poems of heterogeneous elements. "Tamerlane" (1827) and "Al Aaraaf" (1829) are long poems somewhat in Shelley's manner and to some extent tell a story. Even "The Raven" (1845) is in a way a tale in verse rather than a pure poem. But his ultimate object was a self-sufficient and self-contained poem similar to the long, smooth, white vault painted by Usher, completely cut off from the everyday world of common sense and hard material objects, containing nothing but evanescent and ethereal dreaming visions. "Oh! nothing earthly save the ray/ (Thrown back from flowers) of Beauty's eye . . ." he exclaimed at the very beginning of "Al Aaraaf." He aspired after what he called "supernal Beauty" rather than plastic Beauty, "the Beauty above" rather than "the Beauty before us." The poet according to him must be "inspired by an ecstatic prescience of the glories beyond the grave." It seemed to him that such a form of poetry produced "an elevating excitement of the Soul" independent of both the "Heart" (matter, the body) and the "Intellect" (reason). He wanted the poet's imagination to reach beyond itself, so to speak, and his ideal was Israfel, the angel "whose heartstrings are a lute," singing "an unimpassioned song" to spiritual love ("the true, the divine Eros—the Uranian, as distinguished from the Dionaean Venus").

It is out of this rarefied matter that Poe wrote most of his shorter poems on the twin themes of Eros and Thanatos, love and death —"To Helen" (1831) for instance, which is addressed to an ideal rather than to any real woman, to a goddess from another world whom the poet worships for her holiness rather than her beauty. The last stanza is an apotheosis: Helen is suddenly metamorphosed into Psyche (the soul). The communion of souls replaces the union of bodies. Indefiniteness displaces sensuousness ("The naked senses sometime see too little—but then *always* they see too much") and the poem becomes something out of space and out of time, a rare aerial orchid without any roots. "For Annie" (1849) in the same way sings the Lethean peace of death:

> Thank Heaven! the crisis—
> The danger is past . . .
> And the fever called "Living"
> Is conquered at last.

"Ulalume" (1847) in the form of strange and infinitely sad images expresses indirectly all the mystery and terror of death—in application of the principle that "the death of a beautiful woman is, unquestionably, the most poetical topic in the world—and equally is it beyond doubt that the lips best suited for such a topic are those of a bereaved lover."

So, in his poetry as in his tales, Poe turns his back on the world of the senses and a poem in his hands becomes an end in itself. He believed in what he called the "poem *per se*—this poem which is a poem and nothing more—this poem written solely for the poem's sake." He would undoubtedly have subscribed to Archibald MacLeish's prescription that "A poem should not mean/But be." He was already preparing the way for some of the most extreme experiments of the French Symbolists.

He believed in the power of images (or more specifically of sad and dreamy evocations), and also, like the French Symbolists, in music. He wanted the reader "to see with his ear." He was an extraordinarily skillful metrist, passionately interested in prosody, as his essay on "The Rationale of Verse" (1848) testifies. He was not satisfied with mere harmony, which, according to him, consists of "the regular alternation of syllables differing in quantity" and is a matter of rhythm. He insisted that over and above harmony there must be "melody," which is a matter of sounds. Hence his emphasis on rhymes and refrains and his frequent use of alliterations. "The perception of pleasure in the equality of sounds is the principle of music," he maintained. In the name of this principle he multiplied rich and even opulent rhymes and combined them in ingenious stanzaic patterns in order to obtain, as he said, both "equality and unexpectedness," both anticipation and surprise. His supreme aim was incantation, what he called "the magic power of verse." All the clever prosodical devices he used and sometimes invented were intended to hypnotize the reader by appealing almost exclusively to his ear (which is the most passive of senses) and thus stir emotions and passions at a deep and almost elemental level.

Unfortunately, however, he had a tendency to overdo it. He too often and too deliberately strained after effect. At such times his poems develop mechanically instead of organically. They are the fruit of artifice rather than art. The excessive accumulation of alliterations and rich rhymes again and again betrays his desire to show off his technical virtuosity. Though he praises "the concord of sound and sense principle," he then completely sacrifices sense to sound and truly deserves the epithet of "jingle man" which Emerson applied to him. Aldous Huxley has devastatingly criticized his oversonorous rhymes: "Poe's rich rhymes . . . are seldom above suspicion. That dank tarn of Auber is only very dubiously a fit poetical companion for the tenth month. . . . On other occasions Poe's proper names rhyme not only well enough, but actually, in the particular context, much too well. Dead D'Elormie [in "The Bridal Ballad"] is first cousin to Edward Lear's aged Uncle Arly sitting on a heap of barley—ludicrous, but also (unlike dear Uncle Arly) horribly vulgar, because of the too musical lusciousness of his invented name and his display . . . of an obviously faked Norman pedigree. Dead D'Elormie is a poetical disaster." Allen Tate, for his part, objects to the insistence and monotony of Poe's rhythms, which, he says, are for the metronome, not the human ear. T. S. Eliot summed up the case by concluding that "his versification is not, like that of the greatest masters of prosody, of the kind which yields a richer melody, through study and long habituation, to the maturing sensibility of the reader returning to it at times throughout his life. Its effect is immediate and undeveloping; it is probably much the same for the sensitive schoolboy and for the ripe mind and cultivated ear."

There is thus a general agreement among writers of the English-speaking world that Poe as a poet has a very limited range and suffers from exasperating defects. Yet he has been praised to the skies by such French poets as Baudelaire, Mallarmé, and Paul Valéry. The reason for this discrepancy is that these poets because of linguistic differences have not felt the vulgarities of Poe's manner. They have been sensitive only to the high seriousness of his poetic quest and been filled with admiration for the boldness of his attempt to express the inexpressible by means of words.

Such was his ambition—or, according to some, his megalomania—that he considered no undertaking too difficult for his genius and he even attempted to solve the riddle of the universe in the middle of his distress after the death of Virginia. The result was a supreme "prose-poem," *Eureka*. The title itself is a shout of triumph: "I have found! I have found the answer!" Poe-Dupin had decoded the secret message of God thanks to his usual combination of intuition and deduction. In this brilliant essay written in lucid, unpretentious prose, Poe expounds a cosmogony, "a survey of the universe" contemplated in its oneness and diversity. It is a grandiose vision based on the findings of Newton, Laplace, Leibnitz, Alexander von Humboldt, and other cosmologists, and Poe's conclusions are quite consonant with the conclusions of contemporary physicists. He makes a distinction between the universe of stars studied by astronomers, which is limited, and the universe of space, which contains it and is infinite, its center, in Pascal's phrase, being everywhere and its circumference nowhere. An irresistible intuition, which is the sum of shadowy and elusive inductions and deductions in his inmost mind, makes him posit a God in the middle of this infinite void space, a God that is "not-Matter," therefore Spirit, who originally created matter by dint of volition out of his Spirit or from Nihility—

pure matter in a state of absolute "simplicity," i.e., of oneness, which then exploded into apparently infinite multiplicity and diversity. Thus the physical world in Poe's hands becomes essentially energy, perpetual motion, permanent tension between centrifugal and centripetal forces, between attraction which is of the body and repulsion which is of the soul, or between gravity and electricity. Because "the atoms were, at some remote epoch of time, even *more than together* . . . because originally and therefore normally they were *One* . . . now, in all circumstances, they struggle *back* to this absolutely, this irrelatively, this unconditionally *one*," as the law of gravity shows. This "awful Present" leads to a "still more awful Future," for all will eventually coalesce and return to Unity and therefore to that Nothingness which both fascinates and frightens so many of Poe's heroes: "The final globe of globes will instantaneously disappear, and . . . God will remain all in all." A tragic denouement to a perfect plot. *Eureka* in a way enlarges the dimensions of the cosmos of Poe's fantastic tales. It celebrates in metaphysical terms both the irresistible dynamism of life and the terror of death. It posits the essential unity of the cosmos toward which all his characters irresistibly gravitate.

The story of the cosmos does not stop there, however; there is a postscript to it, for Poe imagines the processes of diffusion and concentration may be reversed forever and forever, "a novel universe swelling into existence, and then subsiding into nothingness, at every throb of the Heart Divine," that is to say of his own heart, since we are part and parcel of the spiritual ether which pervades all matter, of "this Divine Being, who thus passes his Eternity in perpetual variation of Concentrated Self and almost Infinite Self-Diffusion." At the end of *Eureka*, the poet becomes God or God becomes the supreme poet.

Actually this apotheosis never took place—in this world at least. After he had written *Eureka*, Poe was torn by the two opposite forces of attraction and repulsion which he had described. He craved for death and wrote to his aunt and mother-in-law, Mrs. Clemm: "I must die. I have no desire to live since I have done 'Eureka.'" And at the same time he was frantically looking for a substitute for Virginia (and his mother) among a group of widows whom he courted all at once, rushing from one to the other, trying to make them promise to marry him. He thus went to Richmond in July 1849 to call on his former childhood sweetheart, Mrs. Sarah Elmira Royster Shelton. On the way back he stopped at Baltimore and no one knows what happened to him there. A few days later he was found unconscious in a gutter and taken to a hospital. He died there without regaining consciousness on October 7, 1849, at the age of forty.

Two days later, the Reverend Rufus Griswold, his treacherous literary executor, launched him on his checkered posthumous career by declaring that in Poe "literary art had lost one of its most brilliant but erratic stars." From then on Poe was to be reviled by some and extravagantly lauded by others. His main weakness, besides the ethereality of his matter, is indisputably his style. Although Walter de la Mare thought that his "heightened language" captures the fancy, most readers find it on the contrary irritating, pretentious, verbose, needlessly mannered and stilted. D. H. Lawrence in particular writes: "Poe has been so praised for his style. But it seems to me a meretricious affair. 'Her marble hand' [Ligeia's] and 'the elasticity of her footfall' seem more like chair-springs and mantel-pieces than a human creature." But the most savage criticism came from Aldous Huxley in "Vulgarity in Literature." According to him Poe "is, as it were, one of Nature's Gentlemen, unhappily cursed with incorrigible bad taste." He cannot resist the lure of paste jewels. He loves superlatives and, contrary to what Pudd'nhead Wilson and Ezra Pound were later to recommend, he never uses a noun without coupling it with an adjective, preferably vague and suggestive of gloom, horror, vastness, strangeness, or indefiniteness.

Despite this proliferation of adjectives, Poe's language gives an impression of poverty and monotony, at least as far as the vocabulary of sensations is concerned. His is an intellectual style. He is not really interested in the physical world. The only precise sensuous details that he mentions are visual (sight being the most intellectual of our senses) and refer to colors—especially black, gray, and white (a sinister color with him), followed far behind by red and brown, the colors of blood, but even then he will be more interested in displaying his verbal virtuosity by playing with such words as "ebony," "sable," "swarthy," "dusky," "inky" for "black" than in defining a sensuous quality.

Thus lack of sensuousness, however, was to some extent deliberate and consistent with that "ideality," as he called it, with which he wanted his tales to be permeated. "The indefinite," he claimed, "is an element in the true ποίησις (poiesis.)" He had therefore to wrench the reader from his usual surroundings by using "rare and radiant" words, and that is why to common words of Anglo-Saxon origin he systematically preferred Latin terms. In the fantastic world of his tales, grass is never green but "verdant," an illness becomes a "malady," an outline a "contour." His characters do not see the sky but "heaven" or "the firmament," and they speak an outlandish language: "The days have never been when thou couldst love me—but her whom in life thou didst abhor, in death thou shalt adore."

The reason for Poe's relative failure is the discrepancy between the irrational nature of what he wanted to convey and the imperturbably intellectual character of his means of expression. In his writings, as in life, even when raving mad, he always behaved and expressed himself like an eighteenth-century gentleman. He felt like a romantic and even like a twentieth-century neurotic, but described his disintegrating personality in the prim and elegant language of an English essayist of the age of Steele and Addison, or of a romancer of the Gothic school. Whitman realized this and appraised him with his usual uncanny insight: "I was not an admirer [of Poe's poems], tho' I always saw that beyond their limited range of melody (like perpetual chimes of music bells, ringing from lower b flat up to g) they were melodious expressions, and perhaps never excell'd ones, of certain pronounc'd phases of human morbidity."

And yet it works. The charm operates. We cannot read or reread his best tales and poems without a thrill. Though his heroes behave in a Grand Guignol manner in rather inauthentic settings and speak an unreal language, we feel a secret kinship with them. The same nightmarish monsters which haunt them roam the deeper layers of our minds. Their fears and obsessions are ours too—at least potentially. They echo in our souls and make us aware of unplumbed depths in our inmost hearts.

Selected Bibliography

WORKS OF EDGAR ALLAN POE

PRINCIPAL SEPARATE WORKS
Tamerlane and Other Poems, "by a Bostonian." Boston: Calvin F. S. Thomas, Printer, 1827.
Al Aaraaf, Tamerlane, and Minor Poems. Baltimore: Hatch and Dunning, 1829.

Poems. Second Edition. New York: Elam Bliss, 1831.

The Narrative of Arthur Gordon Pym. New York: Harper and Brother, 1838.

Tales of the Grotesque and Arabesque. 2 vols. Philadelphia: Lea and Blanchard, 1840.

Tales. New York: Wiley and Putnam, 1845.

The Raven and Other Poems. New York: Wiley and Putnam, 1845.

Eureka: A Prose Poem. New York: Geo. P. Putnam, 1848.

COLLECTED AND SELECTED EDITIONS

The Works of the Late Edgar Allan Poe, with a memoir by Rufus Wilmot Griswold and "Notices of His Life and Genius" by N. P. Willis and J. R. Lowell. 4 vols. New York: J. S. Redfield, 1850–56.

The Works of E. A. Poe, edited by John H. Ingram. 4 vols. New York: W. J. Widdleton, 1876.

The Works of Edgar Allan Poe, edited by Richard H. Stoddard. 6 vols. New York: A. C. Armstrong, 1884.

The Works of Edgar Allan Poe, edited by Edmund C. Stedman and George E. Woodberry. 10 vols. Chicago: Stone and Kimball, 1894–95.

The Complete Works of Edgar Allan Poe (Virginia Edition), edited by James A. Harrison. 17 vols. New York: George D. Sproul, 1902. (Also printed as the Monticello Edition in the same year.)

The Complete Works of E. A. Poe, with Biography and Introduction by Nathan H. Dole. 10 vols. Akron, Ohio: Werner Co., 1908.

The Complete Poems of E. A. Poe, edited by J. H. Whitty. Boston: Houghton Mifflin, 1911.

The Poems of Edgar Allan Poe, edited by Killis Campbell. Boston: Ginn, 1917.

The Works of Edgar Allan Poe, with Biographical Introduction by Hervey Allen. New York: W. J. Black, 1927.

Selected Poems of E. A. Poe, edited by Thomas O. Mabbott. New York: Macmillan, 1928.

The Complete Poems and Stories of E. A. Poe, with Selections from His Critical Writings, edited by Arthur H. Quinn. 2 vols. New York: Knopf, 1946.

The Letters of Edgar Allan Poe, edited by John

W. Ostrom. Cambridge, Mass.: Harvard University Press, 1948. Reprinted with Supplement, New York: Gordian Press, 1966.

Collected Works of Edgar Allan Poe, edited by Thomas Ollive Mabbott. Vol. I, *Poems.* Cambridge, Mass.: Harvard University Press, 1969.

BIBLIOGRAPHIES

Dameron, J. Lesley. *Edgar Allan Poe: A Checklist of Criticism, 1942–1960.* Charlottesville: Bibliographical Society of the University of Virginia, 1966.

Heartman, Charles F., and James R. Canny. *A Bibliography of First Printings of the Writings of Edgar Allan Poe.* Hattiesburg, Miss.: The Book Farm, 1943.

Hubbell, Jay B. "Poe," in *Eight American Authors: A Review of Research and Criticism,* edited by James Woodress. Revised edition, New York: Norton, 1971. (Paperback, 1972).

Robbins, J. Albert. *Checklist of E. A. Poe.* Columbus, Ohio: Merrill, 1969.

Robertson, John W. *Bibliography of the Writings of Edgar Allan Poe.* 2 vols. San Francisco: 1934.

A periodical, *Poe Studies* (formerly *Poe Newsletter*), 1968– , publishes at least twice yearly articles, notes, and exhaustive bibliographies on Poe.

CONCORDANCE

Booth, Bradford, and Claude E. Jones. *A Concordance of the Poetical Works of Edgar Allan Poe.* Baltimore: Johns Hopkins Press, 1941.

CRITICAL AND
BIOGRAPHICAL STUDIES

Alexander, Jean. *Affidavits of Genius: E. A. Poe and the French Critics, 1874–1924.* Port Washington, N.Y.: Kennicat Press, 1971.

Allen, Hervey. *Israfel: The Life and Times of Edgar Allan Poe.* 2 vols. New York: Doran, 1926.

Allen, Michael. *Poe and the British Magazine Tradition.* Cambridge, Mass.: Harvard University Press, 1969.

Bachelard, Gaston. *L'Eau et les rêves.* Paris: Corti, 1942.

————. *L'Air et les songes*. Paris: Corti, 1943.

Baudelaire, Charles. *Baudelaire on Poe: Critical Papers*, translated by Lois and Francis E. Hyslop, Jr. State College, Pa.: Bald College Press, 1952.

Benton, Richard P. *New Approaches to Poe: A Symposium*. Hartford, Conn.: Transcendental Books, 1971.

Bittner, William. *Poe, a Biography*. Boston: Little, Brown, 1962.

Bonaparte, Marie. *The Life and Works of Edgar Allan Poe*, translated by John Rodker. London: Imago, 1949.

Broussard, Louis. *The Measure of Poe*. Norman: University of Oklahoma Press, 1969.

————. *Poe's Vision of Man*. Storrs: University of Connecticut Press, 1972.

Buranelli, Vincent. *Edgar Allan Poe*. New York: Twayne, 1961.

Campbell, Killis. *The Mind of Poe and Other Studies*. Cambridge, Mass.: Harvard University Press, 1933.

Carlson, Eric W., ed. *The Recognition of Edgar Allan Poe*. Ann Arbor: University of Michigan Press, 1966. (An anthology of Poe criticism.)

Cobb, Palmer. *The Influence of E. T. A. Hoffman on the Tales of E. A. Poe*. Chapel Hill: North Carolina University Press, 1908.

Davidson, Edward H. *Poe: A Critical Study*. Cambridge, Mass.: Harvard University Press, 1957.

Eliot, T. S. "From Poe to Valéry," *Hudson Review*, 2:327–43 (August 1949).

Fagin, N. Bryllion. *The Histrionic Mr. Poe*. Baltimore: Johns Hopkins Press, 1949.

Fiedler, Leslie A. *Love and Death in the American Novel*. New York: Criterion Books, 1960.

Foerster, Norman. *American Criticism: A Study in Literary Theory from Poe to the Present Day*. New York: Houghton Mifflin, 1928.

Hoffman, Daniel. *Poe Poe Poe Poe Poe Poe Poe*. Garden City, N.Y.: Doubleday, 1972.

Huxley, Aldous. "Vulgarity in Literature," in *Music at Night*. London: Chatto and Windus, 1930.

Krutch, Joseph Wood. *Edgar Allan Poe: A Study in Genius*. New York: Knopf, 1926.

Lawrence, D. H. *Studies in Classic American Literature*. London: Thomas Seltzer, 1923.

————. *Poe and France: The Last Twenty Years*. Baltimore: E. A. Poe Society, 1970.

Moss, Sidney. *Discoveries in Poe*. Notre Dame, Ind.: University of Notre Dame Press, 1970.

————. *Poe's Major Crisis: His Libel Suit and New York's Literary World*. Durham, N.C.: Duke University Press, 1970.

Parks, Edw. *Edgar Allan Poe as Literary Critic*. Athens: University of Georgia Press, 1964.

Pollin, Burton R. *Dictionary of Names and Titles in Poe's Collected Works*. New York: Da Capo, 1968.

Quinn, Arthur Hobson. *Edgar Allan Poe: A Critical Biography*. New York: Appleton-Century, 1941.

Quinn, Patrick F. *The French Face of Edgar Poe*. Carbondale: Southern Illinois University Press, 1957.

Rans, Geoffrey. *Edgar Allan Poe*. Edinburgh and London: Oliver and Boyd, 1965.

Regan, Robert, ed. *Poe—A Collection of Critical Essays*. Englewood Cliffs, N.J.: Prentice-Hall, 1967.

Shanks, Edward. *Edgar Allan Poe*. London: Macmillan, 1937.

Stovall, Floyd. *Edgar Poe the Poet: Essays New and Old on the Man and His Work*. Charlottesville: University of Virginia Press, 1969.

Tate, Allen. "The Angelic Imagination: Poe and the Power of Words," *Kenyon Review*, 14: 455–75 (Summer 1952).

————. "Our Cousin, Mr. Poe," in *Collected Essays*. Denver: Swallow, 1959.

Wagenknecht, Edward. *Edgar Allan Poe—The Man Behind the Legend*. New York: Oxford University Press, 1963.

Winters, Yvor. "Edgar Allan Poe: A Crisis in the History of American Obscurantism," in *Maule's Curse*. New York: New Directions, 1938.

Woodberry, George E. *Edgar Allan Poe*. Boston, 1885.

————. *The Life of Edgar Allan Poe, Personal and Literary, with His Chief Correspondence with Men of Letters*. 2 vols. Boston, 1909.

Woodson, Thomas, ed. *Twentieth Century Interpretations of "The Fall of the House of Usher."* Englewood Cliffs, N.J.: Prentice-Hall, 1969.

—ROGER ASSELINEAU

Katherine Anne Porter

1890-1980

KATHERINE ANNE PORTER was born May 15, 1890, at Indian Creek, Texas. She was educated in convent schools in Louisiana and has lived in New York, Mexico, Paris, and for short periods elsewhere in the United States and in Europe. Her first published volume was a limited edition of a few stories published under the title *Flowering Judas* in 1930. In 1935 this book was expanded and republished. A second volume, *Pale Horse, Pale Rider*, containing three long stories, appeared in 1939. *The Leaning Tower and Other Stories* was published in 1944. A collection of essays and magazine articles, *The Days Before*, appeared in 1952. Ten years later, after a period of relative silence, the novel that had been announced twenty years earlier came out under the title *Ship of Fools*, and it gave Miss Porter her first big commercial and popular success.

Katherine Anne Porter's output has not been great, considering the years that she has been writing; but there is probably no other writer of fiction in America who has maintained so consistently high a level. Her subjects are drawn from her own background in the South, life in Mexico, in the urban East, in Europe, and, in one case at least, in the Rocky Mountains. Miss Porter's method, as she herself has confessed, is to write "from memory," even in certain instances to employ her past

self as principal character. When a remembered incident strikes her as having significance, she makes a note when details accumulate, she adds more notes. At some point in the process, all the details seem to merge into a pattern. With her notes about her, but seldom used, she writes the story. Most of her notes begin simply: "Remember!"

How such moments occur we can deduce from a passage in her short story "The Grave." Here the principal character is a woman named Miranda (Katherine Anne Porter's name for the character based on her own experience), who is recalling certain events from childhood. "One day she was picking her path among the puddles and crushed refuse of a market street in a strange city of a strange country, when without warning, plain and clear in its true colors as if she looked through a frame upon a scene that had not stirred nor changed since the moment it happened, the episode of that far-off day leaped from its burial place before her mind's eye." What "leaped," of course, was not merely the episode, but the total composition, as suggested by the phrase "from its burial place," for the story is about the discovery of treasure (knowledge) by two children digging about in the abandoned grave of an old burial ground.

Born and educated in the South, converted

to Catholicism, Miss Porter retains Catholic and southern habits of mind. Her awareness, as she says of Miranda, is a "powerful social sense" that detects special and subtle meanings in experience and translates them into fiction. If we think of Miranda's background as being roughly parallel to Miss Porter's, we can say that Katherine Anne Porter's family had moved, within the lifetime of her grandmother, from Kentucky into Louisiana, and from there to Texas. As with most southern families, it had retained a strong sense of family unity as well as an awareness of its place in the framework of southern history and southern society. The grandfather, although he had died before the family left Kentucky, and even though the move itself necessitated by his imprudence, moved with the family each time they were uprooted, for his grave ". . . . had been twice disturbed in his long repose by the constancy and possessiveness of his widow. She removed his bones first to Louisiana and then to Texas as if she had set out to find her own burial place, knowing well she would never return to the places she had left."

The family was Scots-Presbyterian, inheriting a rugged stubbornness as its national legacy, a determined set of moral values from its religion. When the grandmother talked about "all the important appearances of life, and especially about the rearing of the young," she "relied with perfect acquiescence on the dogma that children were conceived in sin and brought forth in iniquity." Miranda, her brother, and her sister, we are told, "loved their Grandmother; she was the only reality to them in a world that seemed otherwise without fixed authority or refuge . . . just the same they felt that Grandmother was a tyrant, and they wished to be free of her." Miranda's rebellion took the form of running away from the convent and eloping, and something of this sort occurred in the life of Katherine Anne Porter.

As a nonpracticing Catholic and a liberal southerner, Miss Porter has found the principal themes in her fiction in the tensions provided between fixed social and moral positions and the necessities of movement and alteration. Within a broad framework, she has dealt subtly with the distinctions between orthodox Christianity and revolution, between Roman and Protestant attitudes, between desire and responsibility, between reality and the dream. In brief, she has utilized the divine vision, but she has qualified it by focusing sharply upon "the human condition"; she has rejected irresponsible decision, as she has indecision. Her fiction portrays a small but inclusive, grotesque but convincing, world, rendered as at times absurd, always pathetic, but rendered, finally, with compassion.

Katherine Anne Porter's first published story was "María Concepción," completed in the summer of 1922 and published in *Century* magazine in December of that year. Her next story, "He," appeared in *New Masses* in 1927, followed by "Magic" in *transition* and "Rope" in the *Second American Caravan* in 1928. "The Jilting of Granny Weatherall" appeared in *transition* in 1929 and *"Flowering Judas"* was printed in *Hound and Horn* in the spring of 1930. These stories were collected in a volume titled *Flowering Judas and Other Stories* and printed in a limited edition of 600 copies later in 1930.

This small volume contained some of Miss Porter's best work, and the response to it was immediate. In the second, and regular, edition in 1935, four new stories were added: "Theft," "That Tree," "The Cracked Looking-Glass," and "Hacienda."

The contents of this first volume remain characteristic of Katherine Anne Porter's subject matter and themes. Her use of her Mexican experiences is obvious in such stories as "María Concepción," "Flowering Judas," "That Tree," and "Hacienda." Her southern background supplied the material for "Magic," "He," and "The Jilting of Granny Weatherall." Her Catholic upbringing is reflected in "Flowering Judas," in "The Cracked Looking-Glass," and, less obviously, in "That Tree." Her use of an urban background, less frequent than the rural, appears in "Theft."

Christian morality in a world where traditional values are threatened is at the heart of all these stories; and they are, ultimately, complex fables in which the tensions between the old order and the new provide a dramatic framework for the events. In "María Concepción," we have a story of competition between wife and mistress, set in the simple surroundings of a primitive Mexican village. Here moral choice is made, not alone by the principal characters, but by the whole community, for they condone the killing of the mistress by the wife, not because they approve of bloodshed, but because they believe that, in a contest between simple sexual pleasure and the marriage bed, marriage and the family must win out. In "Hacienda," many social levels of modern Mexico are represented, ranging from the Indians who manufacture don Genaro's pulque and the simple peasants of the village to the Russian film troupe and the American impresario from Hollywood. What is rendered, finally, is a complicated wasteland inhabited by a new order that has rejected the old values, but has discovered no common basis for the new. The result is a small comedy of no-manners, set in a land that still reflects, though dimly, its former mannered vitality.

"The Jilting of Granny Weatherall" tells the story of the death of its aged and crotchety heroine, whose passing is portrayed as a second betrayal at the altar. Granny had been betrayed by one bridegroom early in life, and the betrayal had rankled; now she is betrayed by the holy bridegroom, whose coming she had pathetically awaited on her deathbed. The other side of the coin is depicted in "The Cracked Looking-Glass," where the marriage of a young woman to an older man is revealed as the incomplete image reflected by a broken mirror, the sensibilities warped and tangled by unfulfillment. "That Tree" is the story of an American writer in Mexico whose midwestern bride destroys his integrity as a poet, deserts him, then returns only after he has succeeded as a hack. It is a study in shallow love accomplished through superficial success.

The problem of the modern wasteland, as displayed in these stories, is the pathetic inability of man to live according to his dreams. This pathos appears in its most specific and controlled form in the title story, "Flowering Judas." In this work, modern experience is presented, not so much as a fragmentation of manners and belief but rather as an ironic tension between two powerful competing forces: Christian faith and revolutionary hope. Caught between these two is the heroine, Laura, an American girl of southern Catholic background, who lends her support to the Mexican Marxist forces of revolution.

Laura's predicament is that she cannot free herself from her early religious training and beliefs, so cannot give herself wholly to the revolutionary cause. This condition places her in a kind of limbo, like the old man in T. S. Eliot's "Gerontion" (from which poem Miss Porter found her title, perhaps even her theme), who complains that he has lost his "sight, smell, hearing, taste and touch." Likewise, Laura loses the use of her senses. Although a beautiful woman, she clothes herself like a nun and can respond to none of the would-be lovers who woo her. She rejects Braggioni, the revolutionary general; she outwits the young army captain who takes her riding; she unknowingly teases a young man from the Typographers Union by throwing him a rose (the symbol of love) when she can feel nothing for him. She even fails to react to the children whom she teaches when they bring her flowers and scribble on the blackboard "We lov ar ticher." Her principal contribution to the cause is to carry narcotics to the prisoners in jail, so that they may sleep away their imprisonment.

The story is one of Laura's inability to love. She cannot love erotically as a woman, humanely as a dedicated revolutionary, or divinely as a communicant in the church. Without love, the story says, the world is a wasteland; but Miss Porter goes on to examine and develop the consequences of this condition. Her central imagery is taken from the concept of Christian atonement, but with overtones of the pagan ritual that preceded the sacrament, derived certainly from Eliot's poem that contains the title of the story:

In the juvescence of the year
Came Christ the tiger
In depraved May, dogwood and chestnut,
    flowering judas
To be eaten, to be divided, to be drunk
Among whispers.

"Christ the tiger" refers to the pagan ritual in which the blood of a slain tiger is drunk in order to engender in the participants the courage of the tiger heart. The Christian ritual is symbolic rather than direct: the symbolic blood of Christ is drunk in remembrance of atonement; that is, to recall the agony and symbolically to engender the virtues of Christ in the participants. In the Christian sacrament, faith in, and love of, Christ alters the substance of bread and wine into the spiritual flesh and blood of Christ. Without faith-love the act becomes cannibalistic, for there is no such alteration, as there was not in the pagan sacrament. By a subtle alteration (or misreading) of Eliot's line, Miss Porter has Laura eat, not the blood

of Christ the tiger, but the blossoms of the flowering Judas, the symbol of Christ's betrayer; so that Laura's betrayal of Christ, of Braggioni, and of Eugenio (the prisoner who dies of an overdose of her drugs) becomes a betrayal of man, a cannibalistic, not a saving, gesture, as Eugenio reminds her when he appears to her in her guilty dream that ends the story.

In "Flowering Judas," with all its accumulated symbols and background mythology, Katherine Anne Porter achieved more than a mere definition of modern man's condition, she embodied an attitude that demonstrated the necessity for the application of the ancient verities of faith and love as a fructifying element in any human existence, whether of the old order or the new.

Miss Porter's second volume of stories, *Pale Horse, Pale Rider: Three Short Novels,* which appeared in 1939, is composed of three long short stories (not short novels, as the title suggested): "Old Mortality," "Noon Wine," and the title story, "Pale Horse, Pale Rider." In two of these stories, "Old Mortality" and "Pale Horse, Pale Rider," the events for the first time concern the character named Miranda. In the third, "Noon Wine," the narrator appears to be Miranda (or the author herself) in a remembered incident from childhood.

These facts are of little importance as far as a reading or an evaluation of the works is concerned, but they may be of considerable interest to anyone curious about the manner in which Miss Porter composes her stories. She has called her method writing from memory. Once, in describing how she had come to write the story "Old Mortality," her tongue slipped and instead of saying "Miranda's father said . . ." she made the remark "*My father* said . . ." On the other hand, Laura of "Flowering Judas," although she appears to resemble

Miranda in the Catholic background, the experience in Mexico, the interest in social causes, the relation to Mexican children's art, was modeled on an American friend of Miss Porter's, a schoolteacher in Mexico during the author's residence there. She was not, of course, merely a portrait of that girl; she was, Miss Porter supposed, a combination of a good many people, just as was the character Braggioni in the same story. On the other hand, the events of "Pale Horse, Pale Rider" were many of them actual events that took place when Miss Porter was working as a reporter on the *Rocky Mountain News* in Denver during World War I.

One of the important things to notice about Miss Porter's characters is that the central figures all exhibit qualities that have some point of similarity with her own experience. If they are Irish or Mexican, they are also Roman Catholic, or they are political liberals. They are usually southern. This may account for the relatively small amount that Miss Porter has written, but it also could account for the consistently high level that her work represents. When necessary she displays a range of perception of ordinary manners and mannerisms that is almost uncanny; but usually such qualities as are rendered are attached to persons well within the limits of her own experience.

The long short story "Noon Wine" is a case in point. The events of this story center upon a Mr. Thompson, a West Texas farmer, and upon his guilt—the psychological effects of his unpremeditated killing of an intruder on his farm. The whole atmosphere of the Thompson place, as rendered by Miss Porter, seems to suggest that such an event must actually have occurred in the years between 1896 and 1905, even if not precisely as it is related in the story. It is clear that the author knew very well the kind of people Mr. and Mrs. Thompson were,

even if she did not know exactly these same persons. Mr. Helton, a workman in the story, who is a Swede and who came from North Dakota, is an interesting and successful character, occupying his proper place in the story, but his role is not made so prominent as that of the Thompsons, and thus does not bear so heavy a weight of probability. We can imagine that the story began from a memory either of the event or of the character of Mr. Thompson, or both, in the mind of the author, who was probably about eleven or twelve years of age at the time of the murder and suicide. It could have begun from the events alone, and the characters could have been supplied from other memories; but however it happened, the character at the center of the story is of a type that Miss Porter could have known well, while the less familiar Mr. Helton got into the story only because he was necessary to the events.

The important point here is that such memory as we are talking about in discussing Miss Porter's work is not "mere memory," not only a memory of something that occurred, but something that happened with the long history of personal, family, and regional events; finally, within an even longer history. In referring to a friendship between Miranda's grandmother and a Negro maid in a later story, Miss Porter writes: "The friendship between the two old women had begun in early childhood, and was based on what seemed even to them almost mythical events." Miss Porter treats her memories also as "mythical events."

When we speak of myth, we are, of course, referring to a form of tribal memory, a preserving of events of the past as a means of justifying and explaining the views of the present. Every society adapts "myth" to its own purposes, either myths that it has transported from elsewhere and uses as a means of organizing its memories, or myths that it has created from its own past. Herman Melville has spoken of "historic memory," implying that it is at least one quality of the artist's general "pre-science."

There can be no better phrase to describe Miss Porter's special sensibility than to call it "historic memory." Such memory, though it does, as Melville explained, "go far backward through long defiles of doom," begins with the specific present: the young girl finding a carved dove in an abandoned grave and trading it for a gold ring, another remembering the image of a dead aunt preserved in a family photograph as the family memory and contrasting it with the living present, the memory of illness and death during the influenza epidemic, the memories of Mexican revolutionaries, of moving picture companies on location, of Mexican women and West Texas farmers stirred to violence by passion. Partly these memories are controlled by a Catholic sensibility that seeks out the ceremony and order in the events, partly by a southern habit of thought that metamorphoses reality into "romance," not the romance of inferior southern authors, who see the events as picturesque and quaint manifestations of a peculiar social order, but something nearer the "romance" that Nathaniel Hawthorne sought in his New England novels, a romance that links man of the present with his ideals, the long legendary concepts of man in a continued and continuing past.

The rendering and utilization of myth is, in Katherine Anne Porter's stories, both subject matter and method. Neither as a southerner nor as a Catholic is she orthodox (that is, she does not mistake the myth for the reality); for her it becomes only another kind of reality. The important thing in a short story such as "The Jilting of Granny Weatherall" is not merely that a proud and stubborn old lady dies, unable to forget the jilting of a long-lost lover, but that the story reflects a particular, but not uncommon, attitude toward death. What is significant in a story such as "Flowering Judas" is not that Laura fails to escape the conflict between a conservative upbringing and the desire to assist in liberal political causes, but that such a conflict is at the bottom of the whole idea of man's Christian redemption; that there is something Christlike about such a dilemma.

Perhaps the most complete instance of a short story that utilizes a specifically southern background and memory for the creation of this larger, more generalized "truth" is "Old Mortality," where Miss Porter's subject matter is southern attitudes as expressed through family history, and where the theme is concerned with the nature of reality—particularly with self-definition. The story is told from the point of view of Miranda between the ages of eight and eighteen, and its details agree with all the other Miranda stories insofar as they relate events in a family that had moved from Kentucky to Louisiana and from there to Texas. At the center of the story are the memories of a girl, Amy, about whose long courtship and brief marriage to "Uncle Gabriel" the aura of romance has accumulated. We meet her first in a photograph in the family parlor, "a spirited-looking young woman, with dark curly hair cropped and parted on the side, a short oval face with straight eyebrows, and a large curved mouth." The family legend represents her as vivacious, daring, and extremely beautiful girl, against whom the beauty and grace of later members of the family are forever to be judged. It tells of her using her cruel beauty to tantalize Uncle Gabriel until he despaired of ever winning her, of her precipitating events at a ball that caused a family scandal and disgrace. It tells of her sad suffering from an incurable illness, of her sudden and romantic marriage to Gabriel, and of her early death.

But the legend, which is more than just a romantic memory of Aunt Amy, is also a reflection of the family's attitude toward all events of the past—memories which Miranda can't share and an attitude that she cannot adopt because of discrepancies that she senses between such stories as related by the family and the actual facts that she perceives in the people and events that surround her in the everyday life of the present. In the photograph of Amy, for instance, "The clothes were not even romantic looking, but merely most terribly out of fashion"; in the talk about the slimness of the women in the family, Miranda is reminded of Great-Aunt Keziah, in Kentucky, whose husband, Great-Uncle John Jacob, "had refused to allow her to ride his good horses after she had achieved two hundred and twenty pounds"; in watching her grandmother crying over her accumulation of ornaments of the past, Miranda sees only "dowdy little wreaths and necklaces, some of them made of pearly shells; such moth-eaten bunches of pink ostrich feathers for the hair; such clumsy big breast pins and bracelets of gold and colored enamel; such silly-looking combs, standing up on tall teeth capped with seed pearls and French paste." Yet despite these disappointing incongruities, the child Miranda struggled to believe there was "a life beyond a life in this world, as well as in the next"; such episodes as members of the family remembered confirmed "the nobility of human feeling, the divinity of man's vision of the unseen, the importance of life and death, the depths of the human heart, the romantic value of tragedy."

Another view is suggested in the second section of the story, when Miranda and her sister have become schoolgirls in a New Orleans convent. During vacation on their grandmother's farm, they had read books detailing accounts of how "beautiful but unlucky maidens, who for mysterious reasons had been trapped by nuns and priests in dire collusion . . . 'immured' in convents, where they were forced to take the veil—an appalling rite during which the victims shrieked dreadfully—and condemned forever after to most uncomfortable and disorderly existences. They seemed to divide their time between lying chained in dark cells and assisting other nuns to bury throttled infants under stones in moldering rat-infested dungeons." In Miranda's actual experience at the convent, no one even hinted that she should become a nun. "On the contrary Miranda felt that the discouraging attitude of Sister Claude and Sister Austin and Sister Ursula towards her expressed ambition to be a nun barely veiled a deeply critical knowledge of her spiritual deficiencies."

The most disheartening disillusion during this period came, however, when Miranda actually met the legendary Uncle Gabriel for the first time. His race horse was running in New Orleans and her father had taken her to bet a dollar on it, despite the fact that odds against the horse were a hundred to one. " 'Can that be our Uncle Gabriel?' " Miranda asked herself. " 'Is that Aunt Amy's handsome romantic beau? Is that the man who wrote the poem about our Aunt Amy?' " Uncle Gabriel, as she met him, "was a shabby fat man with blood-shot blue eyes, sad beaten eyes, and a big melancholy laugh, like a groan." His language was coarse, and he was a drunkard. Even though his horse won the race and brought Miranda a hundred unexpected dollars—an event that had the making of a legend in itself—Miranda saw that victory had been purchased, not as a result of beauty, but at the price of agony; for the mare when seen close up "was bleeding at the nose," and "Her eyes were wild and her knees were trembling."

In legend, the past was beautiful or tragic. In art, it might be horrible and dangerous. In the present of Miranda's experience, it was ugly or merely commonplace. In the first section of "Old Mortality," we get the view of the past as seen through the eyes of the elders with their memories, not as it actually was, but as they wanted it to be. In section two, we get the view of it through the eyes of Miranda herself, who judges it merely as it is reflected in her present. By section three, Miranda is eighteen. She has eloped and married, but she it still struggling to understand her own relationship to the past. To her, her elopement seemed in the romantic tradition of Aunt Amy and Uncle Gabriel, although we soon learn that the marriage is, in fact, a failure. We meet her on the train coming home for the funeral of Uncle Gabriel. His body has been returned to lie beside Amy's as though in a final attempt to justify the legend, even though he has married again, and (it is hinted) there are better and more real reasons for him to be buried beside his second wife, who had shared the greater part of his wandering, homeless, and meaningless existence. On the train, Miranda runs into Cousin Eva, also returning for the funeral, whose own life had been burdened by a constant comparison with the legend of Amy. While Amy was beautiful, thoughtless, impulsive, and daring, Cousin Eva had been homely, studious, and dedicated to high purposes. Amy had died and been preserved in the romantic legend; Eva had lived to develop a character and a reputation as a fighter for women's rights. In a sense, Cousin Eva's good works, too, were part of her own legend of homeliness and dedication. At bottom, Miranda finds her a bitter, prematurely aged woman; but it is Cousin Eva who provides her with a third view of the legend of Aunt Amy. She hints that it was nothing but sublimated sex that caused the young girls of Amy's day to behave as they did. " 'Those parties and dances were their market, a girl couldn't afford to miss out, there were always rivals waiting to cut the ground

from under her. . . . It was just sex,' she said in despair, 'their minds dwelt on nothing else. They didn't call it that, it was all smothered under pretty names, but that's all it was, sex.' "

The older generation, then, had two ways of looking at the past: the romantic way of Miranda's father and of other members of the family, and the "enlightened" way of Cousin Eva. Each way was different, and each was wrong. But the old did have something in common; they had their memories. Thus, when the train arrived at the station, it was Cousin Eva and Miranda's father who sat together in the back seat of the automobile and talked about old times; it was Miranda who was excluded from these memories, and who sat beside the driver in the front. Yet Miranda feels that she has a memory now and the beginning of her own legend—the legend of her elopement. Strangely enough, neither Cousin Eva nor her father will accept it. When reminded by Miranda of it, Cousin Eva says: "Shameful, shameful . . . If you had been my child I should have brought you home and spanked you." Her father resented it. When he met her at the train, he showed it in his coldness.

"He had not forgiven her, she knew that. When would he? She could not guess, but she felt it would come of itself, without words and without acknowledgment on either side, for by the time it arrived neither of them would need to remember what had caused their division, nor why it had seemed so important. Surely old people cannot hold their grudges forever because the young want to live, too, she thought, in her arrogance, her pride. I will make my own mistakes, not yours; I cannot depend upon you beyond a certain point, why depend at all? There was something more beyond, but this was a first step to take, and she took it, walking in silence beside her elders who were no longer Cousin Eva and Father, since they had forgotten her presence, but had become Eva and

Harry, who knew each other well, who were comfortable with each other, being contemporaries on equal terms, who occupied by right their place in this world, at the time of life to which they had arrived by paths familiar to them both. They need not play their roles of daughter, of son, to aged persons who did not understand them; nor of father and elderly female cousin to young persons whom they did not understand. They were precisely themselves; their eyes cleared, their voices relaxed into perfect naturalness, they need not weigh their words or calculate the effect of their manner. 'It is I who have no place,' thought Miranda. 'Where are my people and my own time?' "

Miranda is not merely a southern child, in southern history, reflected through the sensibility of a southern author, even though she is, partly at least, all these things. She is any child, anywhere, seeking definition of herself through her past and present. Katherine Anne Porter's southern history, whether legendary or actual, provides the concrete experience through which "historic memory" may function. Thus when she wrote the concluding sentence of "Old Mortality," she was expressing, not the dilemma of Miranda alone, but the dilemma of all who seek understanding. "At least I can know the truth about what happens to me," Miranda thinks, "making a promise to herself, in her hopefulness, her ignorance."

"Old Mortality" is an initiation story, a familiar type among the forms of fiction. Yet the initiation story itself falls into two kinds: one in which the character himself undergoes the initiation and grows into knowledge; another in which the character has only partial awareness of what his experience means, but through which the reader is brought to knowledge. "Old Mortality" is of the first kind. Miss Porter's other Miranda story in this volume, "Pale Horse, Pale Rider," is of the second.

"Pale Horse, Pale Rider" is set in the concluding days of World War I. Miranda is now twenty-four years of age and is working as a reporter on a western newspaper. She falls in love with Adam Barclay, a second lieutenant from Texas who has completed his training and is awaiting orders for shipment overseas. Events of the story concern their attempts to preserve sanity in the nightmare hysteria of war: the pressure to buy "Liberty Bonds," the enforced attentions of society ladies upon hospitalized soldiers, the confusion of identities amid the constant movement and uniformed dress, and, finally, the influenza epidemic that struck senselessly and without warning. Miranda contracts influenza. She recovers, but Adam has been infected by her, and when she wakes from delirium, she learns that he has died.

The parallel between Miss Porter's story and the Adam and Eve legend (the initial initiation) is interesting and meaningful. It recalls the author's use of Christian atonement to define and clarify the events of "Flowering Judas." As Eve was tempted to knowledge, and through her temptation brought about Adam's fall, so Miranda, who sees through the incompleteness and the pretense of the war orators, wishes to face the facts of life and death in wartime; but in so doing she brings about the death of her lover.

The use of the legend raises the story to a level above its specific time and place, so that it is really a story about how a person faces death (knowledge) anytime, anywhere. A second legend fortifies and enriches the first; it is Miranda's childhood fable of the Pale Horseman, the not wholly fearful rider who calls to escort her into the land of death, but to whom she says, "I'm not going with you this time." Death (evil) is a tempter, and one is more cleverly armed to resist him when one has knowledge (truth). Adam, who is presented as more innocent than Miranda (". . . there was no resentment or revolt in him. Pure, she thought, all the way through, flawless, complete, as the sacrificial lamb must be"), appears unaware of danger, though he is facing the most direct threat of death in war. Miranda's delirium in her illness is really a descent into a world of her own evil, a world that is represented during full consciousness by all the hypocrisies and cruelties of war and wartime. When she recovers, it is to discover that Adam, the personification of health and life, had ridden away with the pale rider. But Miranda's descent is also a descent into knowledge (one of Miss Porter's later stories is titled "The Downward Path to Wisdom"); death and evil were facts to be faced and recognized for what they were, not hidden behind war slogans or the smooth phrases of the patriotic orators. Adam was gone and he could not be summoned back, either by magic or by an act of will. All that was left was time ("the dead cold light of tomorrow"). The war, too, was a descent, and so the theme broadens and picks up all the specific ugly incidents connected with wartime hysteria. Adam's death was, of course, the final descent, and this fact suggests that love, which was the means by which Miranda is saved, was also a first step toward death.

"She said, 'I love you,' and stood up trembling, trying by the mere act of her will to bring him to sight before her. If I could call you up from the grave I would, she said, if I could see your ghost I would say, I believe. . . . 'I believe,' she said aloud. 'Oh, let me see you once more.' The room was silent, empty, the shade was gone from it, struck away by the sudden violence of her rising and speaking aloud. She came to herself as if out of sleep. Oh, no, that is not the way, I must never do that, she warned herself."

Miranda's awareness of the finality of death is heightened by the irony of the fact that Adam met death, not on the battlefield, but through her, at a training camp on the very eve of the armistice.

The three stories of *Pale Horse, Pale Rider* appeared in print originally in 1937 and 1938. "Noon Wine" was published in *Story* in June 1937; "Old Mortality" and "Pale Horse, Pale Rider" both appeared in the *Southern Review*, in the spring and summer issues of 1938.

In Katherine Anne Porter's third collection, *The Leaning Tower and Other Stories,* which came out in 1944, there are six related stories dealing with Miranda and the background of Miranda's family, two unrelated stories, and the long title story, "The Leaning Tower," recounting the experiences of a young American in Berlin in the days just preceding World War II.

During the period between the appearance of *Pale Horse, Pale Rider* and that of *The Leaning Tower,* Katherine Anne Porter's literary reputation developed slowly and in a way unusual in American letters. Little was known about her personally, and legends accumulated. It was known that she was a beautiful woman and that she had been associated in some way with the film colony in Mexico, and it was rumored that she had been one of the early silent film heroines, perhaps a Mack Sennett bathing beauty. It was said that she moved often from place to place and that she carried with her a huge trunkful of unfinished material that she would not allow to be published because she was not convinced of its value. She was said to have engaged in a love affair with a Mexican revolutionary. She was thought to be ill with some fatal disease. Word did get around that she was working on a long novel and that she had projected a biography of Cotton Mather.

Most of these rumors were at best half-truths, as we now know, but they were circulated without malice, almost with affection, by young writers in search of a public image for an author whom they admired and whom each felt he had discovered for himself. Miss Porter had first gone to Mexico, she has told us, with her father. In 1931 she sailed from Mexico to Europe as the recipient of a Guggenheim fellowship. She was married to an American government official. During the middle thirties she lived in Baton Rouge, Louisiana, where her second husband was business manager of the *Southern Review,* and in New York and Connecticut, where she experienced near-poverty. In 1937 the Book-of-the-Month Club gave her a special award of $2500, "in consideration of her previous achievement and her promise for the future." She did not become a known personality on the national literary scene until after World War II, when she emerged as a favorite lecturer at writers' conferences and a visiting lecturer at several American universities. Of her career, she once said, "I went to Europe in 1931 an unknown and returned to find myself a celebrity."

The Leaning Tower and Other Stories is a more uneven collection than the two previous books. Six of the nine stories had previous publication in magazines, beginning in 1935 with the appearance of "The Circus" in the *Southern Review* and "The Grave" in the *Virginia Quarterly Review.* In 1936, "The Old Order" appeared in the *Southern Review* and was reprinted in the *Best American Short Stories* for that year. "A Day's Work" was printed in the *Nation* in 1940. "The Leaning Tower" appeared in the *Southern Review* in 1941.

Each of the related stories in *The Leaning Tower* gains something from the others, as this group of stories shapes into a kind of mythical corpus of the family. Some are slighter than others, little more than character sketches, justifying their presence more by what they contribute to the general legend than by what they themselves represent as stories. At their best,

as in "The Grave" and "The Old Order," they rank among Miss Porter's most successful works. The two shorter stories not dealing with Miranda's background, "The Downward Path to Wisdom" and "A Day's Work," display the author at her near best; while the long story that closes the volume and supplies its title, "The Leaning Tower," comes the nearest to failure of anything that Katherine Anne Porter has published.

"The Source" is one of the slighter pieces, dealing as it does with the grandmother's annual visit to the farm in her late years, recounting little more than how she put the Negro quarters into shape again and how she took her customary ride on her old horse, the last of a long line she had owned; but it does evoke an excellent image of the willful and courageous old lady that we are to meet again in other stories of this group. The story is told from the point of view of the three grandchildren whom she had taken in after the death of their mother (Maria, Paul, and Miranda), undoubtedly with Miranda as recorder, although this is not insisted upon. We are told that "They loved their Grandmother; she was the only reality to them in a world that seemed otherwise without fixed authority or refuge, since their mother had died so early that only the eldest girl remembered her vaguely; just the same they felt that Grandmother was a tyrant, and they wished to be free of her." It is the ambivalence of the children toward the old lady that justifies calling so slight a piece a story at all. Miranda and her sister and brother come to recognize the difficulty of making a simple judgment, either of persons such as their grandmother or of the things these people do. This recognition is one stage of the complex initiation that Miranda undergoes in all of the stories in which she figures.

The second story, "The Witness," is similarly the sketch of a single character, again told from the children's point of view. It is an account of Uncle Jimbilly, the former slave, who carved miniature tombstones from blocks of wood to be placed over the graves of the children's pets. Uncle Jimbilly is firm in his simple, almost primitive, morality. From him the children hear exorbitant threats of punishment awaiting them for some accidental misdeed, listen to extravagant accounts of tortures practiced upon heathen unbelievers; but they come to know, by the very exaggeration of his accounts and threats, that Uncle Jimbilly's aim is not so much to evoke terror in them as it is to gain expression for his own subordinated emotions. Again the reader feels that he is looking in upon another colorful stage of childhood recognition.

"The Last Leaf" is the story of Aunt Nannie, wife of Uncle Jimbilly, to whom she had been married "with truly royal policy, with an eye to the blood and family stability," in the days of slavery. Aunt Nannie had been the personal servant and lifelong companion of the children's grandmother. Now having survived the grandmother and resigned to her own end, old Nannie had asked for and been granted the use of a small cottage on the family place. The story ends with an incident between Nannie and Uncle Jimbilly, when the old man, from whom she had been separated for many years, attempts to move in with her. " 'I don' aim to pass my las' days waitin on no man,' " Nannie tells him; " 'I've served my time, I've done my do, and dat's all.' "

It is in "The Old Order" that we learn about Nannie's relationship to the grandmother. Here we are given the most complete background of Miranda's family available in any of the stories. The grandmother was, we are told, the great-granddaughter of "Kentucky's most famous pioneer" (Daniel Boone). She is the daughter "of a notably heroic captain in the War of 1812." Born Sophia Jane Gay in 1827, the grandmother had been given Nannie as a companion when her father bought her and her parents at the slave market in New Orleans while the grandmother was still a child. Nannie and Sophia Jane grew up together, and both were married the same year. Each had many children. Nannie served as wet nurse for Sophia Jane's first four children; then, when Nannie fell ill at the time of the fourth, Sophia Jane nursed the Negro baby along with her own. Grandmother had married a Macdonald, a second cousin, and in him she came later to see "all the faults she had most abhorred in her elder brother: lack of aim, failure to act at crises, a philosophic detachment from practical affairs, a tendency to set projects on foot and then leave them to perish or to be finished by someone else; and a profound conviction that everyone around him should be happy to wait upon him hand and foot." He died in middle age, leaving her with a family of nine living children that she moved from Kentucky to Louisiana, then to Texas. He left her "with all the responsibilities of a man but with none of the privileges."

Sophia Jane had three married sons in Texas at the time of her death, although one of her daughters-in-law had died at the birth of her third child (Miranda), and the grandmother had taken the children in as her own. She died at the home of another daughter-in-law, "after a day spent in helping the Mexican gardener . . . put the garden to rights," just after saying to her son and daughter-in-law how well she felt "in the bracing mountain air."

The authority of this story lies in the unnamed narrator, who is, we can be sure, Miranda, speaking again for the three surviving children of Sophia Jane's son Harry. Through it the author explores the family background, centering about the lifelong relationship between Sophia Jane and Aunt Nannie, the white mistress and the black slave, servant, and companion. It is in the importance given these events by the authority of the teller that the story gains its significance. As suggested earlier, the events in Miranda's (Katherine Anne Porter's) memories take on a mythical character that is part of the emotional education of the surviving grandchildren.

Another story, "The Circus," is the first story in this volume told clearly from Miranda's point of view, and it adds details to the background of family events depicted in "The Old Order," yet has the sharp focus of a story in which events are centered about a single character. These events take place during a time of family reunion, when Miranda, still very young, is allowed to accompany the family to a circus. Her grandmother, father, brother and sister, cousins and aunts are all present when Miranda becomes frightened at the sight of a clown performing on a high wire and has to be taken home by a Negro servant. Meanwhile, she has felt intimations of evil in the eyes of the roughly dressed little boys peering up from the dust beneath the women's skirts; she has measured appearance and reality in the close-up glimpse she got of a dwarf-clown, whom she had not thought could be human, let alone adult; she experiences remorse and compassion in the realization that she has spoiled the day for Dicey, the Negro servant. She tries banishing the terror by transforming it in her mind into childhood visions of romance; but when sleep comes, the terror, the terribly "real" image, returns, and she must turn again to the sympathetic and resigned patience of Dicey.

The most successful of these stories, apart from their place in the general mythical background, is the second Miranda story, "The Grave." It rivals in its completeness such earlier stories as "Flowering Judas," "Old Mortality," and "Pale Horse, Pale Rider." As in "The Circus," Miranda is a child, several years older, and the events are portrayed from the point of view of an adult narrator who is the grown Miranda. It is a story of sexual initiation but one in which the term "sex" has the widest possible implications. In it Miranda, "with her powerful social sense, which was like a fine set of antennae radiating from every pore of her skin," discovers her own feminine nature in the unearthing of a gold ring from the abandoned grave where her grandfather had once been buried. The grave, as title and as symbol, has multiple significance. Abandoned, it recalls the movement and the fluctuating fortunes of the family. As one of the several resting places of her grandparent, it reminds her of the whole family myth. When her brother Paul shoots a rabbit, and it is discovered that the animal contained a family of unborn young buried inside its body, this discovery conveyed to Miranda the puzzling and ambiguous nature of death and birth. There are three graves in the story. First, there is the actual grave, then there is the grave of the dead mother rabbit's body, and, finally, there is the grave of the mind, the repository of knowledge and memory, "heaped over by accumulated thousands of impressions," until the moment "when without warning, plain and clear in its true colors . . . [the childhood scene] leaped from its burial place" in the knowing mind of the mature Miranda.

"The Grave," which is the last of the Miranda stories in this volume, suggests the movement from innocence to knowledge, from the innocence of the dove (which is one of the objects found in the grave), to the gold ring (which is Miranda's sign for the luxury of her own femininity), to the dead mother rabbit (the mystery of birth and death). In the awareness of decay and death comes the important knowledge of the mature self, felt but not understood, recognized in its completeness only later when recalled by a similar sensual awareness.

"The Downward Path to Wisdom" (which does not appear to be related to the Miranda series, although there is the occurrence of the name Stephen, who was one of Miranda's uncles) is a more cruel, less subtle, initiation, this time of a young boy caught in the terrifying events of family discord. The child's "wisdom" becomes finally a protective awareness that he hates everyone with whom he has come into contact: his parents, his grandmother, his uncle, the servant, and even the little girl who had aroused in him the first stirring of masculine ego.

"A Day's Work" is a story of adults, set in an Irish-Catholic background similar to that of Miss Porter's earlier "The Cracked Looking-Glass." In this story, the author displays the same aversion to Catholic puritanism that she had earlier shown to midwestern Protestant puritanism in her story "That Tree." It is a "depression story," a pathetic tale of a man's attempt to preserve his male dignity in the face of the loss of his job and all prospects for the future and in the presence of a vindictive wife who hides her moral ugliness behind a public mask of pious self-righteousness. It is a story of human failure, complex in its suggestion of causes, humorous in many of its incidents, caustic in its criticism of aspects of society and human character, tough in its denial of hope; yet compassionate in its over-all tone and aim.

In one way or another, all these short stories in *The Leaning Tower* represent Katherine Anne Porter at her usual high level of competence. However, in the title story, "The Leaning Tower," her sensitivity appears to have failed her. The story is remarkable pri-

marily for its difference from the stories that had come before. Where the central symbolism of "Flowering Judas" and "The Grave" had been functionally and unobtrusively integrated with the events, the symbol of the tawdry replica of the Leaning Tower of Pisa that appears in this work seems almost willfully applied. Where the righteous anger of Miranda against the vulgar pressures of the war had permeated the telling of "Pale Horse, Pale Rider," a similar emotion in "The Leaning Tower" is dissipated by its focus upon objects incapable of containing it. Where the characters of "Noon Wine" emerged through the rendering of specific detail into the warmth of true humanity, the characters in this story remain wooden figures, almost caricatures. Where the events of Miranda's coming of age in "Old Mortality" were suffused with the glow of girlish memory and illuminated by the background family myth, the incidents in Berlin in the early thirties that take place in "The Leaning Tower" are presented through the inadequate mind of a young American visitor whose memories, if they may be called that, come indirectly and secondhand.

There is, perhaps, an explanation for the failure of this story. It was written in the period just preceding our entry into World War II, years filled with such events as the Spanish Civil War, the German invasion of Poland, and the fall of France, yet the story is set almost ten years earlier, in the Germany barely preceding the rise of Hitler; thus, the author was writing under the impulse of emotions aroused by events at the time of composition, which must have clouded (if not falsified) memories of the original events. Even so, such intense awareness as we are accustomed to in Katherine Anne Porter might have succeeded in transcending these limitations had she not chosen to tell the story through the eyes of a young man, attributing to him insights that seem more appropriate to a Miranda than to the person he was intended to be. His character remains in doubt; therefore, he becomes a doubtful authority for the other characters and events that are rendered through him. Even the fact that he comes from western Texas, which would appear to ally him with the background myth of Miranda and her family, does little to convince us of his worthiness for the difficult role the author has assigned him.

The story itself is a simple one. Charles Upton, having heard in his childhood of the wonders of Berlin from one of his friends, has come from America to Germany in the winter of 1931 to study art. Moving from a dreary hotel into a rooming house run by a middle-aged Viennese woman, Charles becomes acquainted with the woman's three other lodgers: Hans von Gehring, a Heidelberg student who is in Berlin to have an infected dueling scar treated; Tadeusz Mey, a Polish pianist; and Otto Bussen, a peasant-born student of mathematics from the University of Berlin. A good deal of the story is made up of talk among the four roomers, much of it about various nationalities and classes in their different backgrounds. It all ends in a New Year's Eve drinking party at a small restaurant run by two friends of Otto, where the mixture of politics, sex, *Gemütlichkeit*, and mutual distrust appears intended to render the dislocated world of Germany in the 1930's and to foreshadow the violent events to come. Unlike other Katherine Anne Porter stories, "The Leaning Tower" fails to make its point through characterization and plot—the talk is not good enough, the incidents too spare to carry such implications—and so the story falls back upon its title image, the small replica of the Tower of Pisa that Charles awkwardly knocks off its pedestal on his first visit to the pension. The ornament is returned the night of the party, imperfectly mended, to serve as symbol for the futile attempts of man to hold onto memories and dreams, perhaps, in its mending, symbolic of the fate of German society between the two wars. But the symbol is imperfectly integrated with the events; it remains a symbol, shedding its own single light, taking on no added dimensions from the action or the characters in the story.

Following the publication of *The Leaning Tower* in 1944, eighteen years were to elapse before the appearance of any more fiction by Katherine Anne Porter in book form. In 1962, her long-awaited novel (excerpts from which had appeared in magazines over the years) was published under the title *Ship of Fools*. It had an immediate critical success, which was not unusual; what was unusual was its tremendous commercial success, not only gaining for its author the financial security that had eluded her for forty years, but also removing from her the onus of being known primarily as "a writer's writer."

The setting of *Ship of Fools* is a German vessel sailing from Veracruz, Mexico, to Bremerhaven, Germany, in 1931, thus paralleling the author's first voyage to Europe after winning a Guggenheim Foundation fellowship. Miss Porter's first title was to have been *The Promised Land*. It was then changed to *No Safe Harbour* and was identified as such in the excerpts that began appearing in periodicals in 1944 and continued almost to the date of publication. Its final title, Miss Porter tells us in a prefatory note, was taken from a moral allegory by Sebastian Brant, *Das Narrenschiff*, published in Latin as *Stultifera Navis* in 1494. Miss Porter's *Ship of Fools* is also an allegory. It might be called "a moral allegory for our time," or, perhaps more accurately reflecting the present concerns, "an existentialist fable." The ship is called *Vera* (truth), and the most general contrast represented in its passengers and crew (who are the characters of the novel) is a familiar one from the author's short fiction: a juxtaposition of passionate, indolent, irresponsible Latins with the cold, calculating, and self-righteous Nordics. These extremes not only represent a majority of the passengers and crew, but also suggest the beginning of the voyage in Mexico and its ending in Germany. Adding the necessary complexity are the characters that fall between these extremes: an Indian nursemaid, four Americans, a family of Swiss, a Mexican political agitator, a Basque, a Swede, and six Cuban medical students on their way to France. As a voyage, it may be likened to Dante's progress in *The Divine Comedy*, not in any specific way, but in the sense that Katherine Anne Porter, in this novel, is concerned with arriving at a sense of felicity for our time in much the way that Dante was for his. *Ship of Fools* is a comedy for today in the same high sense that Dante used the term in the fourteenth century.

The word "fool," as used by Miss Porter in her title, contains a double irony. In one sense she is using it as Brant must have used it, as "God's fool," suggesting man's foolishness as compared to God's wisdom. Similarly, the foolishness of the acts committed aboard ship resemble the absurdities of human action as portrayed by modern existentialism. Whether one takes the traditional Christian view of man as fool or the modern atheistic view of man as absurd, one comes from either with a feeling that truth is being expressed, only the framework has been altered. In each case man is viewed as a pathetic creature, struggling in one instance to overcome his limitations and approach God's province, in the other to organize the actions of his life around an impossible dream. In each case, he is more to be pitied than condemned.

Appropriate to this ideological point of view, Miss Porter has chosen in *Ship of Fools* to see the action from the position of an omniscient narrator (something unusual, and considered particularly risky, in our time). The authorial eye is located mostly away from and above the characters, effaced in the modern manner, but capable upon occasion of moving into their very minds to provide insights into their often warped, sometimes tender, occasionally right ways of thinking. Necessary to this view is a strong sense of authorial responsibility, and Miss Porter gains this, one feels, by the extreme honesty and objectivity of her vision. She has, as she has been reported to have said to a friend, not "loaded the dice" against her characters. "I would not take sides," she said. "I was on everybody's side."

It might be objected that to be "on everybody's side" is to be on no side, but the attitude behind such a statement illuminates what has been constant in Katherine Anne Porter's work: a sense of understanding based on a firm belief in the imperfectibility of man, but an understanding held with compassion. Understanding without compassion might have led to bitterness, cynicism, even arrogance; compassion without understanding could easily have led to sentimentality.

The action of *Ship of Fools* is made up of three sections: Part I, Embarkation; Part II, High Sea; Part III, The Harbors. Each is prefaced with an epigram. The first is a quotation from Baudelaire: "*Quand partons-nous vers le bonheur?*" (When do we sail for happiness?); the second is from a song by Brahms: "*Kein Haus, Keine Heimat*" (No House, No Home); the third is from Saint Paul: "For here have we no continuing city . . ." Glenway Wescott has warned the reader not to put too much emphasis upon Miss Porter's allegorical intentions. To disregard them, however, would be more serious, particularly the implications of the section headings: man persists in setting sail for happiness, only to find himself, after all, houseless and homeless, to become aware at last that his city is doomed. It is significant that Miss Porter gives only the first clause of Paul's advice to the Hebrews. The complete verse reads: "For here have we no continuing city, but we seek one to come." To have quoted the verse entire would have been to acknowledge the hopes and consolation of orthodox Christianity. Miss Porter's consolation is of another sort, not un-Christian, but certainly secular. Like Miranda in "Pale Horse, Pale Rider," she is unable to invoke the mystery: "Oh, no, that is not the way, I must never do that, she warned herself." As with Miranda, the reality lies only in "the dazed silence that follows the ceasing of the heavy guns; noiseless houses with the shades drawn, empty streets, the dead cold light of tomorrow." Yet the recurring hope ("Now there would be time for everything"), the recurring struggle.

Ship of Fools is a story of forlorn hope and recurring struggle. In Part I we become acquainted with the various characters, recognize their relations to each other, necessary or personal, as groups and nationalities; we come to sense their very real and pathetic isolation. In Part II, which has more than half the book's pages, the major events occur; and this might be called The Wasteland Section (*Kein Haus, Keine Heimat*), containing as it does the torment of the passengers in steerage, the struggle for detachment or for involvement of the passengers and ship's officers above, their regimented hates and their pathetic attempts to love. In Part III, as the ship nears its destination, the effects of the preceding events begin to tell. A bacchanalian fiesta put on by a group of Spanish dancers in honor of the captain brings out all the hidden fears, guilts, and repressions of the participants, followed by the usual remorse and readjustment in relationships.

We see the passengers of the ship *Vera* first as they assemble for boarding in the Mexican port town of Veracruz. We see them through the eyes of the townspeople, who, the author tells us, "live as initiates in local custom"; we see them from the point of view of the author, against a background of "alternate violence and lethargy"; they remain at a distance, a cosmopolitan group fleeing Mexico, or being deported, or merely departing on some private errand; we watch them undergo the many little inconveniences of leaving a foreign port, see them "emerging from the mildewed dimness of the customs sheds, blinking their eyes against the blinding sunlight," all having "the look of invalids crawling into hospital on their last legs."

The cast of characters is necessarily large. Among the passengers and crew in the upper class, the Germans appear in greatest number. They include Frau Rittersdorf, whose husband died in the war and who keeps a journal; Frau Otto Schmitt, recently widowed, accompanying her husband's remains back to the fatherland; Herr Siegfried Rieber, publisher of a ladies' garment trade magazine; Fräulein Lizzi Spöckenkieker, who is said to own three ladies' dress shops; Herr Karl Glocken, a hunchback; Herr Wilhelm Freytag, who works for an oil company, is married to a Jewess, and is returning to Germany to fetch his wife and her mother back to Mexico; Herr Julius Löwenthal, a Jewish manufacturer and salesman of Catholic religious articles; and the following groups: Herr Professor Hutten, his wife, and their bulldog Bébé; Herr Karl Baumgartner, his wife, and son Hans; Herr Wilibald Graf, a dying man in a wheelchair, who is accompanied by his nephew and attendant, Johann.

The second largest group are the Spaniards and Mexicans. The Spaniards include a singing and dancing group, made up of four men and four women, along with the two children, twins, of one of the couples; and La Condesa, who is called a "déclassée noble-woman who has lived many years in Cuba," but is now being deported as a political undesirable to Tenerife. The Mexicans include the wife of an attaché to the Mexican embassy in Paris, her infant child, and an Indian nurse; two Catholic priests; and a bride and groom going on a honeymoon to Spain.

Other nationals included are four Americans: William Denny, a young Texas engineer; Mary Treadwell, a forty-five-year-old divorcée; and an unmarried couple, David Scott and Jenny Brown, traveling together to Europe. There is a Swiss family, Herr Heinrich Lutz, his wife, and their adolescent daughter. There is a Swede, Arne Hansen. There is a group of six medical students from Cuba. The occupants of the steerage are almost nine hundred Spanish workmen being deported from Cuba after the failure of the Cuban sugar crop.

It is difficult to say who are the principal characters in the events of the novel. Obviously Miss Porter has attempted to give each his share in the action. Among the ship's personnel, the doctor and the captain appear most prominent. Captain Thiele is the embodiment of Teutonic authority, firm, unyielding, formal, and wrongheaded. Dr. Schumann represents, within the German *Kultur*, almost exactly the opposite. He is warm and compassionate, although somewhat impersonal; he is a devout Bavarian Catholic with a heart condition that might cause death at any moment, suffering, too, from guilt at his inability to do more than supply drugs for the patient for whom he would do most, La Condesa. Among the passengers, relations are established between Arne Hansen, trapped in his masculine, but sterile, lust, and Amparo, the Spanish dancer-prostitute; between Jenny Brown, the American companion of David Scott, and Wilhelm Freytag, who has a Jewish wife in Germany; between Jo-

hann, the nephew of Wilibald Graf, and Concha, another of the Spanish women, who effects Johann's sexual initiation, not without tenderness, but for a price; between William Denny, a carbuncular young American, and Pastora, a third Spanish dancer, who provide a study in awkwardness and frustration; and, finally, there is the highly comic affair between Siegfried Rieber and Lizzi Spöckenkieker that ends in estrangement after weeks of teasing and attempted conquest. The one character among the voyagers who chooses isolation, as protection against personal pain and disgust, is Julius Löwenthal, the Jew. The single relationship that is evoked but rendered with slight detail is that of the Mexican newlyweds, who appear in their momentary bliss as entirely sufficient unto themselves.

The steerage passengers are seen generally only as a group, viewed from above by the first-class passengers; but from them do emerge two figures of significance to the novel. One is a Basque, known only as Echegaray, who carves wooden figures with a penknife and who is drowned when he jumps overboard to save the Huttens' bulldog, cast into the sea by the Spanish twins. The other is an unnamed political agitator who makes fun of the religious observances among the steerage passengers and is struck over the head with a wrench by one of them after he had laughed during the services for Echegaray.

The significance of these two figures, like the significance of the Mexican honeymooners, lies in the very vagueness with which the author presents them, almost without name, with only the brief and fatal accident to define the one, with only his political position and his wound to define the other. Both are, in a sense, savior figures, reminiscent of Miss Porter's use of such figures in "Flowering Judas," but presented with less insistence in the novel than in the short story. Also, an additional level of significance is added in the case of the Basque, who, if he is a crucified Christ in his plunge into the sea and dies ironically in an attempt to save an aged and repulsive bulldog, is also a "creator," whose artistry is presented as more genuine than that of the American couple in the upper class who call themselves artists. The agitator, as modern savior, is allied to La Condesa (the political exile), who, like Eugenio of "Flowering Judas," can gain peace only in the sleepy world of drugs administered by Dr. Schumann. The ship's doctor, like Laura, serves the cause of betrayal, and so is inhibited from meaningful action.

The similarity of these themes in the novel and in the short story suggests that the themes of *Ship of Fools* may not be too different from themes present in the earlier works and that the principal differences lie in the necessary richness of the longer work and in the technical excellence that integrates and unifies so diverse a body of material. We can see in the puritanical Protestantism of the German society on the ship a resemblance to the attitude of Miriam, the midwestern schoolteacher wife of the artist-turned-journalist of "That Tree," where self-righteous self-assurance appears to triumph over the more leisurely, apparently indolent, ambitions of the poet. We can see in the cheerful amorality of the Spanish dancers a resemblance to María Rosa and Juan Villegas in "María Concepción." There is a hint of María Concepción herself in the brief appearance of the Indian nurse for Señora de Ortega's infant on board the ship. The vacillations and misunderstandings of Jenny Brown and David Scott are reminiscent of the husband-wife relationship in "Rope." Ric and Rac, the Spanish twins of the novel, have no counterparts in the short stories, but they do, nevertheless, represent what Miranda reported

as her grandmother's conviction in "The Old Order," that children were born in evil, thus were to a degree the embodiment of it in its most simple and direct form.

Incidents of special importance in the novel include the banishing of Herr Freytag from the captain's table because it is learned that he has married a Jew, the throwing overboard of Frau Hutten's bulldog (which resulted in the death and burial of Echegaray), the riot in the steerage that followed the funeral of the drowned Basque, the posting on the bulletin board of "truth notes" concerning the various passengers by the Cuban students, the meetings of Dr. Schumann and La Condesa, and, finally, the various events preceding, during, and following the fiesta put on in honor of the captain by the Spanish dancing troupe. These would include the stopover at Santa Cruz, where the Spaniards steal the tawdry prizes to be given away at the party; the fight between Herr Rieber and Arne Hansen; the recognition of special qualities of character by Frau Rittersdorf and Mary Treadwell; the quarrel and reconciliation of the Baumgartners; the rebellion of Johann against Herr Graf that leads to his going to Concha; the humiliating beating of William Denny; and the ironic confrontation between the proper Prussian captain and the easygoing members of the Spanish dancing group.

There is little "story," in the conventional sense, in *Ship of Fools*. Perhaps the nearest thing to it is the affair between Jenny Brown and David Scott, because the fluctuations of love and hate, or even like and dislike, are acted out during the voyage, and their relationship had a prior origin in Mexico and presumably will have a future in Europe. There is a sense, however, in which each character represents a little "story" of his own, and each thread of plot is intertwined with others to form the over-all pattern of the book. We come to know each character briefly at a moment that constitutes for most of them a particular crisis or alteration of attitude. But the individual stories are not resolved; rather, what serves for resolution resides in the remarkable ability of the author to make the total composition come alive, both in its rendering of the individual characters and in its evoking a kind of over-all theme, or meaning. Yet it is less a "meaning," in the sense of reducible paraphrase, than it is an attitude subtly conveyed.

Perhaps the nearest Katherine Anne Porter comes to expressing what the story is about is when she has Mary Treadwell interpret the effusive show of manners between Herr and Frau Baumgartner at the end of the voyage (significantly Miss Porter put the major portion of the passage in italics): "What they were saying to each other was only, *Love me, love me in spite of all! Whether or not I love you, whether I am fit to love, whether you are able to love, even if there is no such thing as love, love me!*" Where had the trouble come from? Mrs. Treadwell considers her own case:". . . what had it been but the childish refusal to admit and accept on some term or other the difference between what one hoped was true and what one discovers to be the mere laws of the human condition?" *The mere laws of the human condition!* This is skepticism, and if we need a name to distinguish Miss Porter's special attitude, perhaps "skepticism" will do. The only truth available to man lies in "the human condition."

It is the human condition that is represented aboard the *Vera*. But that condition varies from country to country and race to race; it differs even in individuals. The one thing we can know is that the dream, whether it be of race superiority or of the perfect relation between man and woman, will never be achieved. Man becomes "foolish," in that quasi-religious

sense, when he pursues it; but pursue it he will, because that, too, is part of "the human condition." The novel says it better than this, because the skill of the author proved equal to the larger and more complicated intentions that the book itself embodies.

The critical reception of *Ship of Fools* when it first appeared was almost unanimously enthusiastic. What dissent occurred concerned itself with three features of the novel: the rendering of the characters, the pessimism of the theme, and what some critics considered an absence of suspense. Stanley Kauffmann, a reviewer for the *New Republic*, wrote: "The characters are well perceived and described, but we know all that Miss Porter can say about them after the third or fourth of their episodes." Granville Hicks, writing for the *Saturday Review*, said: "There is in [the novel], so far as I can see, no sense of human possibility. Although we have known her people uncommonly well, we watch unconcerned as, in the curiously muted ending, they drift away from us." The *New Yorker* review by Howard Moss complained that *Ship of Fools* was "devoid of one of the excitements of realistic fiction. The reader is never given that special satisfaction of the drama of design, in which the strings having come unwound, are ultimately tied together in a knot. Miss Porter scorns patness and falseness, but by the very choice of her method, she also lets go of suspense."

It is difficult to answer the charge of dullness or of inadequate character portrayal except by counter-assertion. One can point to the novel's tremendous popular success, but Theodore Solotaroff, writing in *Commentary*, dismisses this explanation by calling the novel the long-awaited work of a beloved figure— the "Eleanor Roosevelt" of letters. In a curiously vituperative article, he characterizes *Ship of Fools* as "massive, unexciting, and saturnine." Such charges are reminiscent of the response made to another American work a century earlier, when one critic called *Moby Dick* ". . . trash, belonging to the worst school of Bedlam literature." Many considered Melville's novel dull, its action clogged by extraneous matter.

There is, however, a key to Miss Porter's method—a key that has long since opened and preserved the treasures of Herman Melville's masterpiece. This method is pointed out most clearly by Eric Auerbach in his critical volume *Mimesis*. Auerbach discusses a puzzling quality of epic narrative, what he calls the retarding principle and what Goethe characterized as "the retarding element appropriate to Homeric epic." Such retardation consisted in the breaking off of a dramatic incident in order to shift and explore the background character of the event. It was, Auerbach maintains, "In dire opposition to the element of suspense." Miss Porter utilizes this retarding principle in the construction of her comic-epic, much as it was used by Dante in *The Divine Comedy*, for the purposes of deepening and enriching her narrative; and these are the qualities that impressed most critics of the novel.

The charge that *Ship of Fools* shows little "sense of human possibility" reminds us of early charges made against another significant American work, *The Waste Land* of T. S. Eliot. As does Eliot in his poem, Miss Porter portrays much of modern life as sterile and impotent, but she also suggests, as does Eliot, the fructifying possibilities of love. She is less extreme than Jean-Paul Sartre in her rendering of what is disgusting and absurd in human life, nearer to Albert Camus in her attitude of detached observation; superior, perhaps, to either in the over-all sense of compassion that finally pervades her work.

In addition to *Ship of Fools* and her three volumes of short fiction, Katherine Anne Porter has written magazine articles, book reviews,

introductions to books by other authors, and she has engaged in various symposia on the problems of the writer and the craft of writing. A collection of such writing appeared in 1952, titled *The Days Before*. In it she lists her nonfiction under three headings: critical writings, personal and particular pieces, and articles dealing with Mexico.

As a literary critic, Miss Porter appears more allied to the European method of the personal essay than to any of the current American fashions, perhaps because of the sense of private awareness that she conveys. Yet her discussions of authors as various as Thomas Hardy, Willa Cather, and Katherine Mansfield consist of more than personal insight. Her own standards for writing come forth clearly in her reply to questions asked her in a symposium in 1939. She had been asked whether Henry James or Walt Whitman had the most relevancy "to the present and future of American writing." She replied: "Henry James and Walt Whitman are relevant to the past and present of American literature or of any other literature"; but, she went on, "For myself I choose James, holding as I do with the conscious, disciplined artist, the serious expert against the expansive, indiscriminately 'cosmic' sort."

Katherine Anne Porter is a major figure in what has become a literary revival in American letters in the twentieth century. If the first American Renaissance (so named by F. O. Matthiessen) occurred in the mid-nineteenth century with the writings of Emerson, Thoreau, Whitman, Hawthorne, Melville, James, and Twain, the second would include such contemporaries of Miss Porter as Theodore Dreiser, Ezra Pound, T. S. Eliot, Sherwood Anderson, Robert Frost, Wallace Stevens, William Carlos Williams, Hart Crane, Ernest Hemingway, F. Scott Fitzgerald, William Faulkner, and John Steinbeck.

Strictly speaking, the first "renaissance" was less a rebirth than it was a birth—a coming of age in American letters; it was not a movement in literature, but, rather, an upsurge of creative power. The same might be said of what was truly a "renaissance" in the twentieth century. In neither case did the achieving writers represent a common concept either of American attitudes or of an American craft. There is a sense in which Hawthorne and Melville may be seen as motivated, at least in part, by a spirit of rebellion against certain contemporary attitudes, notably those of the so-called transcendentalists. Similarly, there is a sense in which such authors as Thoreau and Whitman (in some respects Twain) may be seen as a literary continuation of Emersonian transcendentalism.

In Miss Porter's generation, the dichotomy remained. Sherwood Anderson, Ernest Hemingway, and John Steinbeck, among the prose writers, continue a tradition that would appear to have been first given shape in Emerson, carried on with some alteration in the writings of Mark Twain and Stephen Crane. On the other hand, F. Scott Fitzgerald and (to a lesser extent) William Faulkner and Katherine Anne Porter derive from Hawthorne, Melville, and James. What this means is that in our literary traditions a split between two somewhat contrary attitudes still prevails and that Katherine Anne Porter's preference, as she herself makes clear with the necessary qualifications, remains with what we might call the "ameliorists"—those writers who would not make so severe a break with the traditions and ideas of Europe as was implicit in the writings of Emerson, Whitman, and Twain.

Speaking generally upon what is a complex subject, we might also say that such southern contemporaries of Miss Porter as William Faulkner, Allen Tate, John Crowe Ransom, Caroline Gordon, and Robert Penn Warren fall into this classification, and Katherine Anne Porter remains one with her region. In some respects she is even more pure in her devotion to craft, more austere in her opposition to what might be called "leveling" or "popularizing" tendencies than any other American writer since Henry James.

James has obviously been Miss Porter's model as craftsman, but she speaks often of her early attraction to a very different kind of writer, Laurence Sterne, in whose eighteenth-century manner she had steeped herself. Among women writers, she admired Katherine Mansfield and disliked Gertrude Stein. What she admired in Mansfield was "a certain grim, quiet ruthlessness of judgment, an unsparing and sometimes cruel eye, a natural malicious wit, and intelligent humor"; what she disliked in Gertrude Stein was the absence of moral, intellectual, and aesthetic judgment. It is true, perhaps, that what Katherine Anne Porter liked best in others were qualities nearest to her own, but such preferences were based less on personal prejudice than they were on the same tough, intellectual honesty that governed her own writing.

Katherine Anne Porter at the age of seventy-two announced that she had three more books to write. With the completion of *Ship of Fools*, additional short stories by Miss Porter began to appear in American magazines. One of these, "St. Augustine and the Bullfights," has been called by Glenway Wescott a masterpiece; while another, "Holiday," won the O. Henry Awards' first prize for 1962. In 1965, *The Collected Stories of Katherine Anne Porter* appeared. It contained "Holiday" and three other stories previously uncollected, "The Fig Tree," "Virgin Violeta," and "The Martyr." The first of these belonged to the Miranda group of stories, the other two to the group of stories with Mexican settings. None of these, except for minor revisions, has been written recently. It has been rumored that Miss Porter is still working upon the long-promised book on Cotton Mather.

Selected Bibliography

WORKS OF
KATHERINE ANNE PORTER

Flowering Judas and Other Stories. New York: Harcourt, Brace, 1930. (Limited edition.)

Katherine Anne Porter's French Song Book. Paris: Harrison, 1933.

Hacienda. New York: Harrison, 1934.

Flowering Judas and Other Stories. New York: Harcourt, Brace, 1935.

Noon Wine. Detroit: Schuman's, 1937.

Pale Horse, Pale Rider: Three Short Novels. New York: Harcourt, Brace, 1939.

The Leaning Tower and Other Stories. New York: Harcourt, Brace, 1944.

The Days Before. New York: Harcourt, Brace, 1952.

Ship of Fools. Boston: Little, Brown, 1962.

The Collected Stories of Katherine Anne Porter. New York: Harcourt, Brace & World, 1965.

Christmas Story. New York: Dell, 1967.

BIBLIOGRAPHIES

Schwartz, Edward. *Katherine Anne Porter: A Critical Bibliography* (with an introduction by Robert Penn Warren). New York: New York Public Library, 1953.

Sylvester, William A. "Selected and Critical Bibliography of the Uncollected Works of Katherine Anne Porter," *Bulletin of Bibliography*, 19:36 (January 1947).

CRITICAL STUDIES

Allen, Charles G. "Katherine Anne Porter: Psychology as Art," *Southwest Review*, 41:223–30. (Summer 1956).

Block, Maxine, ed. *Current Biography.* New York: H. W. Wilson, 1940. (Portrait.)

Current-Garcia, E., and W. R. Patrick. "The Short Story in America," in *American Short Stories.* New York: Scott, Foresman, 1952. Pp. xliii, lxi.

Hartley, Lodowick. "Katherine Anne Porter," *Sewanee Review*, 48:206–16 (April 1940).

Herbst, Josephine. "Miss Porter and Miss Stein," *Partisan Review*, 15:568–72 (May 1948).

Johnson, J. W. "Another Look at Katherine Anne Porter," *Virginia Quarterly Review*, 36:598–613 (Fall 1960).

Kaplan, Charles. "True Witness: Katherine Anne Porter," *Colorado Quarterly*, 7:319–27 (Winter 1959).

Marshall, Margaret. "Writers in the Wilderness: Katherine Anne Porter," *Nation*, 150:473–75 (April 13, 1940).

Mooney, Harry John, Jr. *The Fiction and Criticism of Katherine Anne Porter.* Pittsburgh: University of Pittsburgh Press, 1957.

Schorer, Mark. "Biographia Literaria," *New Republic*, 127:18–19 (November 10, 1952).

Schwartz, Edward. "The Way of Dissent: Katherine Anne Porter's Critical Position," *Western Humanities Review*, 8:119–30 (Spring 1954).

Warren, Robert Penn. "Katherine Anne Porter (Irony with a Center)," *Kenyon Review*, 4:29–42 (Winter 1942).

Wescott, Glenway. "Katherine Anne Porter: The Making of a Novel," *Atlantic*, 209:43–49 (April 1962).

West, Ray B., Jr. "Katherine Anne Porter: Symbol and Theme in 'Flowering Judas,'" *Accent*, 7:182–87 (Spring 1947).

———. "Katherine Anne Porter and 'Historic Memory,'" *Hopkins Review*, 6:16–27 (Fall 1952).

———. *The Short Story in America.* Chicago: Regnery, 1952. Pp. 72–76.

Wilson, Edmund. "Katherine Anne Porter," *New Yorker*, 20:72–75 (September 30, 1944).

Young, Vernon A. "The Art of Katherine Anne Porter," *New Mexico Quarterly*, 15:326–41 (Autumn 1945).

—*RAY B. WEST, JR.*

Ezra Pound

1885-1972

O<small>N THE</small> afternoon of December 7, 1941, Ezra Pound, a famous American literary expatriate, left his home in Rapallo, Italy, took a train for Rome, and over the state radio read the following:

"Europe calling. Pound speaking. Ezra Pound speaking, and I think I am perhaps speaking a bit more to England than to the United States, but you folks may as well hear it. They say an Englishman's head is made of wood and the American head made of watermelon. Easier to get something into the American head but nigh impossible to make it stick there for ten minutes. Of course, I don't know what good I am doing. I mean what immediate good, but some things you folks on both sides of the wretched ocean will have to learn, war or no war, sooner or later. Now, what I had to say about the state of mind in England in 1919, I said in Cantos 14 and 15. Some of your philosophists and fancy thinkers would have called it the spiritual side of England. I undertook to say state of mind.

"I can't say my remarks were heeded. I thought I got 'em simple enough. In fact, some people complained that several of the words contained no more than four or five letters, some six. Now I hold that no Catholic has ever been or ever will be puzzled by what I said in those Cantos. I have, however, never asked for any sympathy when misunderstood. I go on, try to make my meaning clear and then clearer, and in the long run, people who listen to me, very few of 'em do, but the members of that small and select minority do know more in the long run than those who listen to say H. G. (Chubby) Wells and the liberal stooges. What I am getting at is, a friend said to me the other day that he was glad I had the politics I have got but that he didn't understand how I, as a North American United Stateser, could have it. Well, that looks simple to me. On the Confucian system, very few start right and then go on, start at the roots and move upwards. The pattern often is simple. Whereas, if you start constructing from the twig downwards, you get into a muddle. My politics seem to me simple. My idea of a state or empire is more like a hedgehog or porcupine—chunky and well-defended. I don't cotton to the idea o' my country bein' an octopus, weak in the tentacles and suffering from stomach ulcers and colic gastritis."

For this, one of a hundred broadcasts, he was paid about ten dollars.

Pound's sentences and paragraphs suggest the disordered mind of a cracker-barrel sage. They do not sound like the work of a man who had made a career out of refining and purifying the English language, improving it as a vehicle for civilized discourse, or of the poet whom T. S. Eliot had called *il miglior fabbro,* the better craftsman. In fact, the broadcasts were so incomprehensible that the Italian government once took Pound off the air, suspecting him of sending code messages to the United States.

Pound (born in 1885) entered the University of Pennsylvania in 1901, but took his degree at Hamilton College. He returned to Pennsylvania for an M.A. At Pennsylvania he was friendly with William Carlos Williams and Hilda Doolittle. He spent a year in Europe before doing a teaching stint at Wabash College, in Indiana. The young Pound was a curious combination of bohemian, scholar, and poet. He also saw himself as a very important teacher. In the early years of his career there were those who accepted Pound not merely as a poetic genius but as a writer who was revolutionizing English and American poetry. There is some justification for both of the latter claims.

There is also, however, a great deal of misunderstanding about Pound, and perhaps even misrepresentation. The fact is that in December 1945 Ezra Pound was declared insane. There can be no doubt that his rantings over the radio are mad. In this respect, they are not very different from some of the later *Cantos* and the later essays. The earliest prose—for example, the fine study of Henry James—is perceptive and cogent, and the poetry written during the same period, mostly before World War I, is often carefully wrought and subtle. But even then, in the poetry, one is never wholly certain which of the Pound voices is the real Pound.

Pound the lyricist is most frequently in view, and it is in his lyricism that he has had his greatest success. This is best exhibited, perhaps, in the early *Cantos.* It appears intermittently, sometimes in explosive flashes, in the later *Cantos,* but usually the lyricism is not sustained; in its place one finds anecdotes, cryptic and gnomic utterances, dirty jokes, obscenities of various sorts, and a harsh insistence on the importance to culture of certain political leaders and economists.

The majority of Pound's critics find the *Cantos* his most important literary contribution. Various efforts have been made to say what they are about. Perhaps the easiest way of getting at their subject matter is to say they are about Pound's reactions to his own reading, of Homer, Ovid, or Remy de Gourmont, of various economists and political leaders, and Pound's own literary recollections, usually memories of London or Paris. As the years went by Pound became less interested in literature than in economics, although he continued to express literary interests in the *Cantos,* and his interest in translating from Greek and Latin remained fairly constant.

After leaving London, in 1920, Pound became less and less a discoverer of true talents, and more and more the angry and, as he saw it, rejected prophet. Occasional successes in his poems and translations are reminiscent of the early genius and promise of Pound, but for the most part Pound's literary career was all downhill.

The young Pound had long wanted to meet William Butler Yeats, whom he believed to be the greatest poet of the previous one hundred years. In 1908, during his second trip abroad, they did meet. In London, Pound set up a lecture course at the Regent Street Polytechnic, and here during the winter of 1908–09, he met Dorothy Shakespear and her mother, Olivia Shakespear, friend of many literary men and in particular of Yeats. Pound and Yeats were to see a great deal of each other, drawn together by common interests and perhaps later by Pound's marriage to Dorothy Shakespear and Yeats's marriage to the daughter of Mrs. Shakespear's sister-in-law.

Personæ of Ezra Pound was published in 1909, and at least one reviewer found in it echoes of Yeats. The same year, Pound was advising Williams to read Yeats's essays, and Yeats was writing to his friend Lady Gregory that Pound's poetry is "definitely music, with strong marked time and yet it is effective speech." Sometimes their egos contended, as on the evening, according to fellow poet Ernest Rhys, a group went to the Old Cheshire Cheese, where Yeats held forth at length on the ways of bringing music and poetry together. Pound sought attention by eating two red tulips. When Yeats finished his monologue, Pound recited "Ballad of the Goodly Fere."

Pound was soon recognized as a literary figure of some eminence. In 1909 he became friendly with Ford Madox Hueffer (later Ford Madox Ford) and at one of the latter's parties met the young D. H. Lawrence. In 1910 he returned to the United States. After several months spent with his parents, Pound lived for a short time in New York. He saw quite a bit of Yeats's father, John Butler Yeats, who was living and painting in New York, and Dr. Williams. He also strengthened his position as literary foreign correspondent, and when he returned to London he was busily officious, writing advice to Harriet Monroe, editor of *Poetry*, and pontificating in literary groups. Pound's *Ripostes* was published in 1912. The widow of Ernest Fenollosa, having seen Pound's work in *Poetry*, brought him her husband's manuscripts. Fenollosa, a Bostonian, was the first Westerner to open up classical Japanese drama. Pound spent several years working on the plays. *Certain Noble Plays of Japan* was published, in 1916, by the Cuala Press, run by Yeats's sister, and Yeats wrote the introduction.

Reminiscences of the period, including those by Douglas Goldring, Richard Aldington, J. G. Fletcher, Conrad Aiken, Ernest Rhys, Wyndham Lewis, Ford Madox Ford, and many others, have amply testified to Pound's literary activities in London in the years before World War I.

William Carlos Williams, who visited London in 1910, recalled that Pound "lived the poet as few of us had the nerve to live that exalted role in our time." Having little money, he wore a fur-lined overcoat indoors and out during cold weather, and a broad-brimmed hat. Williams observed that Pound kept a candle lit before the picture of Dorothy Shakespear on his dresser. Pound as a dandified bohemian was never offstage.

In May 1911 Pound wrote his father: "Yeats I like very much. I've seen him a great deal, almost daily. . . . He is, as I have said, a very great man, and he improves on acquaintance." In London, Yeats lived at Woburn Place, off the Euston Road. Yeats believed his reputation was declining; he had digestive trouble and difficulties with his eyes. Pound attended to the older poet's needs, reading to him and instructing him in ways of being more "definite and concrete" in his poetry. Pound sometimes organized dinners for literary people, then took them to Woburn Place, where Yeats held forth.

In 1912, Pound altered, without permission, some poems Yeats had given him to send to *Poetry*. Yeats was infuriated, but then forgave the bumptious and arrogant young Pound. Pound had set out to make Yeats more modern. During the winters of 1913–14, 1914–15, and 1915–16 he acted as "Uncle William's secretary" at a small house, Stone Cottage, in Sussex. Pound wrote his mother that he regarded the job "as a duty to posterity." When Pound married, he brought his wife to live at Stone Cottage. Yeats enjoyed hearing the young couple discuss modern critical doctrines. He was not enthusiastic about *des imagistes* with whom Pound was closely associated, but admitted their "satiric intensity." In 1916 Yeats handed over his father's letters for Pound to edit for the Cuala Press, saying he represented "the most aggressive contemporary school of the young."

Pound's revisions of Yeats's poetry were in the direction of conciseness and clarity. A revision from the later years perhaps illustrates the nature of the changes. This is from a draft of "From the Antigone":

Overcome, O bitter sweetness,
The rich man and his affairs,
The fat flocks and the field's fatness,
Mariners, wild harvesters;
Overcome Gods upon Parnassus;
Overcome the Empyrean; hurl
Heaven and Earth out of their places—
Inhabitant of the soft cheek of a girl
And into the same calamity
That brother and brother, friend and friend,
Family and family,
City and city may contend
By that great glory driven wild—
Pray I will and sing I must
And yet I weep—Oedipus' child
Descends into the loveless dust.

Pound made the eighth line follow the first, substituted "That in" for "And into" in the ninth line, and dropped "that" from the tenth line. Thus the poem was made to read:

Overcome—O bitter sweetness,
Inhabitant of the soft cheek of a girl—
The fat flocks and the field's fatness . . .
          hurl
Heaven and Earth out of their places,
That in the same calamity
Brother and brother, friend and friend,
Family and family,
City and city many contend . . .

Without question, Pound's changes greatly improve the poem.

On one occasion, in the winter of 1914, Pound organized a small group of poets to honor Wilfrid Scawen Blunt, then seventy-four. The poets were Sturge Moore, Victor Plarr, Frederic Manning, F. S. Flint, Richard Aldington, and Yeats. A dinner was held at Blunt's estate. Pound presented Blunt a marble box carved by Gaudier-Brzeska, containing poems by all the poets. Pound also read an address honoring Blunt. The latter replied; then Yeats talked about the state of poetry, saying those who came to honor Blunt represented different schools. "To Sturge Moore, for instance, the world is impersonal. . . . Pound has a desire personally to insult the world. He has a volume of manuscript at present in which his insults to the world are so deadly that it is a rather complicated publishing problem." Writing Canto LXXXI, years later, Pound recalled the occasion, saying it was not vanity to have taken the pains to honor Blunt—

To have gathered from the air a live tradition
or from a fine old eye the unconquered flame.

One may say the same for Pound's relationship with Yeats. Pound took from the air a live tradition. And Yeats sloughed off more and more of the 1890's. Perhaps it was Pound's work on the Japanese Noh plays, as much as anything, that helped Yeats discover a new direction, at least gave him a new kind of symbolic action. His *The Hawk's Well*, founded on the Noh, was performed at Lady Cunard's house in Cavendish Square, April 2, 1916. Seeing the play changed Eliot's view of Yeats: "Yeats was well-known, of course; but to me, at least, Yeats did not appear, until after 1917 [he should say, 1916], to be anything but a minor survivor of the 90's. After that date, I saw him very differently. I remember clearly my impression of the first performance of *The Hawk's Well*, in a London drawing room, with a celebrated Japanese-dancer in the role of the hawk, to which Pound took me. And thereafter one saw Yeats rather as a more eminent contemporary than an elder from whom one could learn."

Conrad Aiken had introduced Eliot to Pound in 1915. Eliot was unable to find an editor willing to accept any of his poems. Pound admired Eliot's work, and sent "Prufrock" to *Poetry*. It caused at least a mild sensation, helped to get the modernist movement under way, and launched Eliot's career. Pound edited *Catholic Anthology* (1915) for the purpose, he said, of getting sixteen pages of Eliot into print at once. Also through Pound's efforts Eliot's first volume of poems was published in 1917 by the Egoist Press.

Eliot remembers Pound's quarters at 5 Holland Place, "a small dark flat in Kensington." Because of his restless energy and fidgety manner, Pound struck Eliot as ready for some new move or involvement. "In America, he would no doubt have seemed on the point of going abroad; in London, he always seemed on the point of crossing the Channel."

Pound's attitude toward the United States and, by implication, his hopes and ambitions for himself can be seen in *Patria Mia*, written in 1912 but unpublished until 1950. A publisher in Chicago, to whom it had been sent, lost the manuscript, and it was recovered, more than a generation later, when the firm moved to new quarters. Between 1913 and 1950 Pound had lived in Paris and Rapallo, witnessed two wars, published innumerable articles and books, been indicted for treason and imprisoned in an institution for the insane for several years. *Patria Mia* sheds light on Pound's career in the years following its composition. It is not as incoherent as his later books and pamphlets on politics and economics, but it rambles and is certainly not the tightly organized argument Pound believed he

was writing. It also suggests the disappointment he would suffer.

Pound, in *Patria Mia*, is giving advice to America. He says, for example, what changes should be made in American colleges and graduate schools, and how magazine editorial policies should be altered. The underlying theme of each of his suggestions is that a genuine poet—and he would not have had to go far to find one—should be hired to stimulate academic life or give the right sort of advice to editors.

Pound's essential criticism of America repeats what Henry James said in *The American Scene* (1907), that Americans were obsessed by money and material acquisitions. Pound wrote: "It is not strange, for every man, or practically every man, with enough mental energy to make him interesting to be engaged in either business or politics. And our politics are by now no more than a branch of business." A detailed comparison of *Patria Mia* and *The American Scene* might prove useful. Probably it would show that James's perceptiveness as well as his capacity for coherently ordering his impressions and arguments greatly transcended Pound's.

Curiously, Pound's affection for America comes through strongly. After his visit, James had to return to Rye in England to compose himself. Something in Pound responds to the vigor and rawness of America. One finds him, for example, saying New York City is probably the most beautiful city in the world:

"And New York is the most beautiful city in the world?

"It is not far from it. No urban nights are like the nights there. I have looked down across the city from high windows. It is then that the great buildings lose reality and take on their magical powers. They are immaterial; that is to say one sees but the lighted windows.

"Squares after squares of flame, set and cut

into the aether. Here is our poetry, for we have pulled down the stars to our will.

"As for the harbour, and the city from the harbour. A huge Irishman stood beside me the last time I went back there and he tried vainly to express himself by repeating:—

" 'It uccedes Lundun.'

" 'It uccedes Lundun.'

"I have seen Cadiz from the water. The thin, white lotus beyond a dazzle of blue. I know somewhat of cities. The Irishman thought of size alone. I thought of the beauty, and beside it Venice seems like a tawdry scene in a playhouse. New York is out of doors.

"And as for Venice; when Mr. Marinetti and his friends [a "modernist" group] shall have succeeded in destroying that ancient city, we will rebuild Venice on the Jersey mud flats and use the same for a tea-shop."

Pound has great hopes for America. The millionaires and industrialists will be obliged to subsidize the arts, just as wealthy merchants and princes had during the Renaissance. He believes they will do this. Pound also says that when an American investigating "in any art or *metier* has learned what is the best, he will never after be content with the second-rate. It is by this trait that we are a young nation and a strong one. An old nation weighs the cost of the best, and asks if the best is worth while."

Pound tries to isolate American qualities. He cites "a certain generosity," "a certain carelessness, or looseness," "a hatred of the sordid," a "desire for largeness," and "a willingness to stand exposed." He feels these qualities in Whitman—

Camerado, this is no book,
Who touches this touches a man.

Pound dismisses Whitman because he is not a craftsman, not an artist, but at the same time makes him an American symbol: "Whitman established the national *timbre*. One may not

need him at home. It is in the air, this tonic of his. But if one is abroad; if one is ever likely to forget one's birth-right, to lose faith, being surrounded by disparagers, one can find, in Whitman, the reassurance. Whitman goes bail for the nation."

Pound deplores the genteel tradition, although he does not refer to it as such. He deplores the practice of editors of the *Atlantic* and other magazines (he cites Howells by name) of running imitations from the Greek Anthology, regular in meters and optimistic in attitude. They do not ask, he says, whether a poem is the work of a serious artist, whether the form is in accordance with the subject and the author's intention, or whether the idiom is the inevitable expression of a generation's collective view. At one point he refers to Coleridge's doctrine of organic form.

America can, he adds, produce genuine art. He says James was a true novelist, in the school of Flaubert and Turgenev, and a diagnostician "of all that is fine in American life." His second example is the painter Whistler, who "proved once and for all . . . that being born an American does not eternally damn a man or prevent him from the ultimate and highest achievement in the arts."

Considering Pound's long years in Europe, and his later attacks on American society and culture, *Patria Mia* is a strange book. In one place Pound wrote: "If a man's work require him to live in exile, let him suffer, or enjoy, his exile gladly. But it would be about as easy for an American to become a Chinaman or a Hindoo as for him to acquire an Englishness, or a Frenchness, or a European-ness that is more than half a skin deep."

Eliot observed Pound's passion to teach, saying he was reminded of Irving Babbitt, who also had a passion for giving people the right doctrines to believe. Eliot adds that the two men might have appeared even more alike if Pound had stayed at home and become a professor. And since he wrote this in 1946, Eliot might be implying that if Pound had been connected with an American university his mental health might have been better and he would not have managed to get into so much trouble.

Pound, however, had an enormous talent for getting into trouble. Wyndham Lewis' theory about Pound and England is fairly simple, and may well be true. English literary life, he said, was filled with well-educated amateurs. They resisted Pound's "fierce quest for perfection," and besides they disliked Americans. By 1918 Pound had grown into a "prickly, aloof, rebel mandarin." Pound, he says, "knew his England very well," but refused to "come to terms with it." He did what he had to do—he moved across the Channel to Paris.

But first a look at some of Pound's many concerns during his English period.

Between 1908 and 1920, Pound edited anthologies and contributed to them translations from various languages, and wrote his own poetry. During this period, which probably was the high point of his career as a poet and of his influence on other poets, he published at least fourteen volumes of poetry. What sort of poet was he in those years? As usual in discussing Pound, there can be no simple answer. Wyndham Lewis tries to say why: "Ezra Pound, I feel, is probably a poet of a higher and rarer order than it is easy at all times to realise, because of much irrelevant dust picked up by his personality as it rushes, strides, or charges across the temporal scene." Also, the poetry is very uneven, and Pound writes in different voices.

Pound could be a sort of Sinclair Lewis, blasting the amenities of the genteel tradition. In "L'Homme Moyen Sensuel," for example, he wrote:

Still I'd respect you more if you could bury
Mabie, and Lyman Abbot and George
    Woodberry,
For minds so wholly founded upon quotations
Are not the best of pulse for infant nations. . . .

While he was in England, he would take similar swipes at anyone or any expression that threatened his notions of perfection in verse or any of various critical theories. In these years Pound's blasts sometimes had verve and resonance; in later years they would often be harsh and vituperative.

R. P. Blackmur has made a good point about Pound as poet. He compares "Hugh Selwyn Mauberley" with "Homage to Sextus Propertius." The former—a series of related poems about a figure much like Pound himself who is critical of his milieu and is offering advice on how poetry should be written—he finds clever, the work of an excellent craftsman. The things the poem "says" are not very original or they are the usual complaints of the exiled poet, looking out from his *tour d'ivoire.* Oddly, it is as "translator" that Pound is original. Blackmur points out that Pound does not translate Propertius; he presents an English equivalent. For example, when Propertius writes, "Let verse run smoothly, polished with fine pumice," Pound writes, "We have to keep our erasers in order." Propertius writes, "Narrow is the path that leads to the Muses"; Pound writes, "And there is no high-road to the Muses."

Pound is not especially imaginative in creating the substance of his own poems. His gift is verbal, and he is at his best when using another poet's substance for his own purposes. In the *Cantos,* as we shall see, he is not quite a translator, but he does rely on the substance of earlier poems.

F. R. Leavis has emphasized Pound's wit, especially in "Hugh Selwyn Mauberley." He finds the "verse is extraordinarily subtle," says that "critical activity accompanies feeling," and finds the poem "serious and light at the same time, sardonic and poignant, flippant and intense;" "Mauberley," he concludes, is a "great poem." John Espey in *Ezra Pound's Mauberley* has studied the poem brilliantly and with a detailed attention, especially to sources, probably never before given a poem. One's response to this sort of exegesis could be, *Now, really, ought not a poem so obviously witty, poised, critical, etc., give up its secrets more easily?* Perhaps the answer would be that the odd bits of arcana in Pound's mind are of such a nature that one must studiously search them out before being able to respond fully to his wit, grace, and critical poise. In other words, one has to decide whether the finished poem justifies a special course of study in preparation for reading it.

There is, as indicated earlier, yet another side to Pound's poetry—its lyricism. This will probably prove to be his greatest strength. In *The Translations of Ezra Pound* there are about seventy pages of poems translated from Provençal and Italian poets. All of these translations are lyrics.

During the years when Pound was leading the modernist revolt he was also writing poems from older literary conventions. A few lines from " 'Blandula, Tenulla, Vagula' " will serve as an example:

What has thou, O my soul, with paradise?
Will we not rather, when our freedom's won,
Get us to some clear place wherein the sun
Lets drift in on us through the olive leaves

This has the lyric force, though not the meditative quality and natural colors, of Wallace Stevens' "Sunday Morning," one of the great poems of our age, and a sustained performance probably beyond Pound at any stage of his career.

Another characteristic early lyric is "Erat Hora." It exhibits Pound's preoccupation with light as a symbol of love, beauty, and mutability.

> Nay, whatever comes
> One hour was sunlit and the most high gods
> May not make boast of any better thing
> Than to have watched that hour as it passed.

Pound is commonly seen as one who explained, justified, and rationalized the modernist idiom in poetry. All this is true. He has also written in that idiom. But at his best, as in occasional passages in the *Cantos*, he is a lyricist in the company of Herrick, Waller, or Ben Jonson, though certainly of a lesser order. His "translations" from Chinese poetry have a similar lyric quality. "The River Merchant's Wife: A Letter," written in a subdued tone, is as beautiful as any poem in the Pound canon.

In literary histories, however, Pound is usually treated as an Imagist or Vorticist. He was involved with both Imagism and Vorticism, but the nature of his involvement is a somewhat complicated story. In 1909, Pound had been introduced to a group led by T. E. Hulme that met regularly in a Soho restaurant to talk about poetry. He read "Sestina Altaforte" in tones that brought all eyes in the room to astonished attention. It was this group that began the Imagist movement, but within a year it broke up. There was a second group, in 1910, which also lasted about a year.

T. E. Hulme, a Cambridge man, a poet of sorts and a philosopher, was the dominating figure. He was a hard-living man, given to violence. He was killed later in the war. Hulme was skeptical, but willing to analyze as well as scoff. At the Soho meetings, on Thursdays, over spaghetti and wine, Hulme expounded his ideas. Poetry, he said, was lost in romantic smoothness, vagueness, fatuousness, and general insipidity. He wanted a period of dry, hard verse. Poetry needed a new convention. Man, he also said, was a limited creature. One need not descend a deep well to plumb his depths; a bucket would do!

In *Ripostes* Pound printed five of Hulme's poems. "In publishing his *Complete Poetical Works* at thirty," Pound wrote, "Mr. Hulme has set an enviable example to many of his contemporaries who have had less to say. They are reprinted here for good fellowship; for good custom, a custom out of Tuscany and of Provence; and thirdly, for convenience, seeing their smallness of bulk; and for good memory, seeing that they recall certain evenings and meetings of two years gone, dull enough at the time, but rather pleasant to look back upon."

F. S. Flint and others have said that Pound did not establish the Imagist movement—he promoted it. Flint said the Hulme group assumed the need for experiment and studied Japanese, Hebrew, and French Symbolists, always giving close attention to imagery. Pound, according to Flint, was studying troubadour poetry and the discussions interested him only when he could relate them to troubadour poetry. In one of his essays Pound wrote: "I think the artist should master all known forms and systems of metric, and I have with some persistence set about doing this, searching particularly into those periods wherein the systems came to birth or attained their maturity." It is true that Pound was studying troubadour poetry but he was also studying music, art (he especially promoted the sculptor Gaudier-Brzeska), the relationship of prose to poetry, and Oriental drama and poetry, among other things.

Rhythms in music and poetry were a fairly constant preoccupation with Pound. Rhythm, he said, determines pitch and melody; pitch depends on the frequency with which sounds strike the ear; variations in pitch control melody. In poetry, he continued, the frequency of vowel or consonant sounds produces a pitch; a changed frequency makes for higher or lower sound, and variation produces the melody of a line. Pound wrote articles and talked volubly about this and related observations, after he had met Arnold Dolmetsch and read his book, *The Interpretation of Music of the XVIIth and XVIIIth Centuries*. In one article he quotes from one of Dolmetsch's eighteenth-century sources, François Couperin, *L'Art de toucher le Clavecin* (1717): "I find that we confuse Time, or Measure, with what is called Cadence or Movement. Measure defines the quantity and equality of the beats; Cadence is properly the spirit, the soul that must be added." There seems to be nothing revolutionary in this, but Pound uses it to whip the vers libre movement. "It is too late to prevent *vers libre*. But, conceivably, one might improve it, and one might stop at least a little of the idiotic and narrow discussion based on an ignorance of music." He sees Couperin as justification for saying true vers libre ("You must bind perfectly what you play") was in the old music. Pound also quoted Eliot: "*Vers libre* does not exist. . . . There is no escape from metre; there is only mastery of it."

Another considerable influence on Pound was Ford Madox Ford (he was Ford Madox Hueffer until World War I), who had been a close associate of Conrad and James. In 1935, Pound wrote Dr. Williams: "I did Fordie as much justice as anyone (or almost anyone) did —but still not enough! Fordie knew more about writing than any of 'them' or 'us.'"

Ford belonged to what he called the Impressionist tradition. A scene is described and reacted to—it exists in the descriptions and in the vividness of the reaction. But the reaction is aesthetic, not didactic. He avoided a poetic stance, or being "literary." He used the "language of my own day," frequently a kind of prose, "to register my own times in terms of my own times." Especially, he said, poetry should be a response to life, not to books. (It is odd that Pound should single this out, since his own response is largely to books.)

Pound contributed a fairly long article to *Poetry*, entitled "Mr. Hueffer and the Prose Tradition," during the same year he issued *Des Imagistes*, a collection of poems by the Imagists. Pound refers to Stendhal's remark that prose was a higher form than poetry, and says Mr. Hueffer is a distinguished prose writer. He finds Hueffer a fine poet, saying "On Heaven" is "the best poem yet written in the 'twentieth-century fashion.'" Hueffer believed "poetry should be written at least as well as prose." Pound says Hueffer's poetry is "revolutionary," because of an "insistence upon clarity and precision, upon the prose tradition." The prose influence on modern poetry has been considerable, and one might reasonably infer that Pound's comments as well as his own practice were a considerable influence on other poets.

Before 1912, Pound had little to say about images, but thereafter he had much to say. Among Pound's "discoveries" were Hilda Doolittle ("H.D." and Richard Aldington. In talking to them about their poetry he called them *imagistes*. In *Ripostes* he connected *des imagistes* and the "group of 1909." (Later, in 1939, Pound minimized the Hulme influence, and emphasized Ford's.) In 1913, in *Poetry*, Pound published "A Few Don'ts" and defined the Image: "An 'Image' is that which presents an intellectual and emotional complex in an instant of time. I use the word 'complex' rather in the technical sense employed by the newer psychologists. . . . It is the presentation of such a 'complex' instantaneously which gives that

sense of sudden liberation; that sense of freedom from time limits and space limits; that sense of sudden growth, which we experience in the presence of the greatest works of art."

Other magazines followed *Poetry* in promoting Imagism. Alfred Kreymborg had asked for contributions to his magazine, the *Glebe*, and Pound sent him poems by Aldington, H.D., Flint, Hueffer, Williams, Connell, Lowell, Upward, Cournos, and James Joyce. *Des Imagistes* received a lot of attention in the United States, but in England, published by Harold Monro, it was a bust. Amy Lowell, in London, wanted to do a new anthology of Imagist poetry. Pound insisted on being editor, but she fought him and won. Thereafter the movement became what he called "Amygism."

Besides, Pound was in a new movement and associating with painters and sculptors. It was called Vorticism. Wyndham Lewis, Gaudier-Brzeska, and Pound were the guiding spirits. *Blast*, edited by Lewis, appeared in 1914. Two of the principles governing its policy were developed from earlier Pound statements: one, the necessity for a vigorous impact ("The vortex is the point of maximum energy"), and, two, recognition of the image as "the primary pigment of poetry." A long Imagist poem is not possible because the image is a vortex "from which, through which, and into which, ideas are constantly rushing." A poem has a visual basis, and makes the intangible concrete. The doctrine seems remarkably close to the one he had stated in *Poetry*.

Pound's interest in the image also derived from his deep involvement with Fenollosa's manuscripts, on Chinese as well as Japanese literature. As "Hugh Selwyn Mauberly" suggests, Pound felt a kinship with the poets of the 1890's. He was also very taken with Whistler; in fact, the first poem Pound published in *Poetry* (October 1912) was "To Whistler,

American." From Whistler he took the idea of "poetry as picture." In "Au Jardin" there are lines such as these: "she danced like a pink moth in the shrubbery" and "From amber lattices upon the cobalt night."

In his September 1914 article in the *Fortnightly Review* on Vorticism he says he wrote a haiku-like sentence:

'The apparition of these faces in a crowd; Petals on a wet, black bough.'

He quotes a well-known haiku—

The fallen blossom flies back to its branch: A butterfly.

Pound recognized in studying this that a descriptive or sometimes lyrical passage was followed by a vivid image. Earl Miner, the closest student of Japanese influences on Pound, calls this the "super pository method." Pound was to employ this technique frequently; for example, in these lines from the lovely "Liu Ch'e":

There is no sound of foot-fall, and the leaves Scurry into heaps and lie still, And she the rejoicer of the heart is beneath them:

A wet leaf that clings to the threshold.

Other notable examples are "A Song of the Degrees," "Ts'ai Chih," "Coitus," "The Encounter," "Fish and Shadow," and "Cantus Planis." One also finds the super pository method employed in the *Cantos*. In using the Chinese written characters, or ideograms, which he does in certain *Cantos*, Pound believed his method was similar to the super pository—use of a vivid image causing many of the preceding elements to cohere. However, since few of his readers understand the ideograms it is difficult to accept Pound's insistence on using them.

Miner says that Arthur Waley's *The Nō Plays of Japan* is the authoritative scholarly translation; the Pound-Fenollosa version is often unscholarly and based on misunderstanding of the historical contexts. Occasional passages, he adds, are beautifully executed. Although Pound's efforts with the Noh were not generally successful, he did learn things that contributed to his theory of the image.

In a note at the end of *Suma Genji*, Pound said the Noh has "what we may call Unity of Image . . . the red maple leaves and the snow flurry in *Nishikigi*, the pines in *Takasago*, the blue-grey waves and wave pattern in *Suma Genji*, the mantle of feathers in the play of that name, *Hagoromo*." The Noh gave Pound suggestions for organizing poems longer than the haiku, or concise imagistic poems. Frequently in the *Cantos* Pound juxtaposes legends from Greek and Japanese sources, scenes from different cultures, and various heroes or villains, all in a seemingly haphazard way. Then he employs an image, or metaphor (a term he apparently chose not to use), that discovers a theme or essence common to the hitherto disparate elements.

Thus Pound's involvement with the image is not a simple matter.

Especially through Whistler and Théophile Gautier he felt the pull of the "Art for Art's Sake" movement. Pound was an aesthete. His commitment to Imagism and Vorticism was complicated by his interest in Chinese poetry and the Japanese Noh. Pound also theorized about the relationship between music (in the British *Who's Who* he identified himself as "poet and composer") and the conversational or prose line. On one occasion he had provided his contemporaries with a little anthology of nineteenth-century French poets, Baudelaire, Verlaine, Laforgue, the Symbolists. Their influence on Eliot, however, was greater than it was on Pound. The city, the automobile, and social life did not deeply engage him. There is a sense, then, in which Pound is not a modernist poet. Or perhaps one should say he was a modernist only briefly. Pound has a pantheon of writers who helped sustain his vision of the world as it ought to be, and more and more he turned to them.

During the English period, Pound studied Propertius, Arnaut Daniel, Dante, Cavalcanti, Stendhal, Flaubert, Gautier, James, and many others. The writers who did not interest Pound reveal strange deficiencies in his views of human conduct and in his own sensibilities. Joseph Conrad does not loom very large, and "them Rooshans," as he called them, go almost unmentioned. Tolstoi, Dostoevski, and Chekhov were uninteresting to Pound.

Three writers, Remy de Gourmont, Ovid, especially in Golding's translation of the *Metamorphoses*, and Robert Browning seem to have held pre-eminence in his pantheon. One might guess that Gourmont and Ovid, more than any other writers, satisfy Pound's dream of the world, and help him create his imaginary Great Good Place. Browning he likes for other reasons: for his craftsmanship, and apparently for writing poetry so much like Pound's own. He especially likes Browning for having written *Sordello*, the poem that made possible the *Cantos*, in which one finds exquisitely beautiful lyric passages, vivid imagistic scenes, tags from many languages, and Pound's racist and economic theories.

Pound several times links the names of Ovid, Propertius, and Remy de Gourmont. He quotes Propertius as saying: *Ingenium nobis ipsa puella facit*. In "Rémy de Gourmont, A Distinction," he says: "Gourmont's wisdom is not wholly unlike the wisdom which those ignorant of Latin may, if the gods favor their understanding, derive from Golding's *Metamorphoses*."

Gourmont (1858–1915) profoundly impressed Pound. In the months before Gourmont's death, Pound was in correspondence with him about contributing to an international journal. Gourmont replied that he was exhausted, sick, and probably would not be of any great help in Pound's enterprise; he also doubted that Americans were "capable of enough mental liberty to read my books." However, he was willing to let Pound help them try to "respect French individualism," and "the sense of liberty which some of us have in so great degree."

In the essay cited above, Pound says, "Gourmont prepared our era." As in most of his other essays, Pound generalizes for a page or two, sets up a thesis, points out the writer's special contributions to civilized understanding, quotes copiously, lists bibliography, then clouts the reader on the back of the head, telling him to pay closer attention.

Gourmont does not, Pound says, "grant the duality of body and soul, or at least suggests that this medieval duality is unsatisfactory." James, whom Pound contrasts with Gourmont, intellectualized passion; emotions to him "were more or less things other people had and that one didn't go into." Sex in Gourmont's works is pervasive, like a drop of dye in a clear jar of water. Sex is related to sensibilities, and therefore to "the domain of aesthetics." This belief was back of Gourmont's concern with resonance in expressing emotion; knowing that ideas have little value apart from the modality of the mind receiving them, he differentiated characters by the modes of their sensibilities.

Gourmont's thesis is that man is a sensual creature, and should not be intimidated by the Christian teachings about modesty, chastity, and so on. Voluptuousness and sensual pleasure are their own excuse for being.

Gourmont's *Physique de l'Amour*, which Pound translated, is filled with such remarks as this: "Il y aurait peut-être une certain corrélation entre le copulation complète et profonde et le développement cérébral." A great deal of biological lore is exhibited, all of it focused on the sex habits of insects, fish, birds, and animals.

Probably Gourmont felt he was writing an amusing and mildly titillating essay on man in nature. Pound, in a postscript, is less playful, and develops a thesis that "the brain itself is, in origin and development, only a sort of great clot of genital fluid held in suspense or reserve. . . ." Pound offers no scientific information to justify his theory. He is creating a little myth. There need be no quarrel between "cerebralist and viveur," he says, "if the brain is thus conceived not as a separate and desiccated organ, but as the very fluid of life itself."

Gourmont and Pound were both interested in Provençal poetry, in late Latin poets, and in literary eroticism. John Espey says that many sections and stanzas of "Hugh Selwyn Mauberley" bear witness to Pound's reading of Gourmont. Pound's earliest pieces on Gourmont appeared in 1913. Evidences of Gourmont's influence appear, for example, in the unabashed sexuality of Canto XXXIX. Pound's admiration for Gourmont never changed. He refers admiringly to him in *Jefferson and/or Mussolini* (1935) and elsewhere. When Gourmont died, Pound wrote: "his thoughts had the property of life. They, the thoughts, were all related to life, they were immersed in the manifest universe while he thought them, they were not cut out, put on shelves and in bottles." Over the years in one form or another, Pound continued to repeat this; it is an expression of his doctrine, *make it new*.

Early and late in his career, Pound praises Ovid—"there is great wisdom in Ovid." In 1934, from Rapallo, in making up a reading list for a correspondent, he wrote: "There are a few things out of print. Golding's translation of Ovid's *Metamorphoses*, CERTAINLY . . . and being an institution of learning yr. Eng. prof. will never have heard of it; though it was good enough for Wm. Shakespear. *And* any dept. of English is a farce without it." Elsewhere he uses Golding's translation to berate Milton's Latinity, contrasting the former's natural "contemporary speech" with Milton's "vague pompous words." The quality of translations, he says, decreased as "translators ceased being interested in the subject matter of their original."

Golding's Ovid has some charm, if only because of its studied innocence and naïveté. If Golding falls short of greatness, as he does, he manages a difficult meter about as well as could be expected. For example,

The Damsels at the sight of man quite out of
    countnance dasht,
(Bicause they everichone were bare and naked
    to the quicke)
Did beate their hands against their brests,
    and cast out such a shricke,
That all the wood did ring thereof: and cling-
    ing to their dame
Did all they could to hide both hir and eke
    themselves for shame

It seems unlikely that Pound was greatly influenced by Golding's language, or his ingenuous playfulness. Pound's *Metamorphoses* is more "distanced," calmer, and seen in lights and shadows. There can be no doubt that he responds at some very deep level to the *Metamorphoses*. Gilbert Murray's account of Ovid's "vision" is a prose equivalent to what Pound tries to catch in his poetry. "What a world it is that he has created in the *Metamorphoses*! It draws its denizens from all the boundless resources of Greek mythology, a world of live forests and mountains and rivers, in which every plant and flower has a story and nearly always a love story; where the moon is indeed not a moon but an orbèd maiden, and the Sun-

rise weeps because she is still young and her
belovèd is old; and the stars are human souls;
and the Sun sees human virgins in the depths
of forests and almost swoons at their beauty
and pursues them; and other virgins, who feel
the same way about him, commit great sins
from jealousy . . . and turn into flowers; and
all the youths and maidens are indescribably
beautiful and adventurous and passionate. . . .
A world of wonderful children where nobody
is really cross or wicked except the grown-ups;
Juno, for instance . . . His criticism of life is
very slight."

Robert Browning, as was observed earlier,
was another of Pound's culture heroes. In his
usual fashion of reordering literary history in
a sentence or two, Pound has said the decline
of England began on the day Landor packed
his bags and moved to Tuscany. Thereafter
Shelley, Keats, Byron, Beddoes lived on the
Continent. Later there was "the edifying spectacle of Browning in Italy and Tennyson in
Buckingham Palace." Pound admired in
Browning many of the virtues he saw in
Crabbe—realism, precision, terseness, the
charged line, objectivity. And perhaps Pound's
affection for Italy is involved with Browning's
love for that country. On a number of occasions Pound had advised perplexed readers of
the *Cantos* to take a good look at *Sordello*.

A passage in Book Two of *Sordello* seems to
have suggested the method of the *Cantos*. The
troubador Sordello is musing on the delights of
reading:

—had he ever turned, in fact
From Elys, to sing Elys?—from each fit
Of rapture to contrive a song of it?
True, this snatch or the other seemed to wind
Into a treasure, helped himself to find
A beauty in himself; for, see, he soared
By means of that mere snatch, to many a hoard

Of fancies; as some falling cone bears soft
The eye along the fir-tree spire, aloft
To a dove's nest. . . .
Have they [men] fancies—
slow, perchance,
Not at their beck, which indistinctly glance
Until, by song, each floating part be linked
To each, and all grow palpable, distinct!
He pondered this.

Pound found in *Sordello* a method that would
allow him to muse upon and re-create his
readings.

The first three *Cantos* appeared in *Poetry*,
June, July, August 1917. In the June 1917
Canto I, subsequently dropped, Pound addresses Browning affectionately as "Bob Browning," telling him *Sordello* is an "art-form" and
adding the modern world needs such a "rag-
bag" in which to toss "all its thought." It does
not matter, he says, that the anachronisms in
Sordello are egregious—a poem should create
a sense of life. He proposes to give up the
"intaglio method," presumably the images associated with *des imagistes* and haiku, and
enter a timeless fictional world—"you mix
your eras," peopled by soldiers with robes "half
Roman, half like the Knave of Hearts." Pound
also proposes to use the "meditative, semi-
dramatic, semi-epic" form of *Sordello*.

In *Sordello*, Browning had one man, Sordello, against whom to focus his "catch," and
the Vitorians had a set of beliefs. In Pound's
"beastly and cantankerous age" doctrine is
elusive and contradictory. Who ought to be
Pound's Sordello? He cannot be sure. Pound
evokes earlier worlds—Tuscany, China, Egypt.
He does not believe that re-created history is
true—"take it all for lies." Nor are his own
imaginings "reality." There is a plurality of
worlds. What the artist creates are "worlds
enough." Artists discover new ways of seeing
as in Pound's own time. There are, for ex-

ample, the paintings of Lewis and Picasso, reflecting "the new world about us." Pound later said there are three planes in the *Cantos*, the "permanent" represented by characteristics of the gods; the "recurrent" archetypal fictional characters like Odysseus, or real, like Sir Philip Sidney; and "casual," the trivial, accidental events that form no pattern or design.

Canto I ends with "So that:" and Canto II begins with "Hang it all, there can be but one *Sordello*!" Browning takes his place with the many authors and texts Pound will cite.

Pound and Browning continue the descent into Hades introduced by Odysseus in Canto I. In *The Spirit of Romance*, Pound wrote, "Ovid, before Browning, raises the dead and dissects their mental processes; he walks with the people of myth." In *Make It New* Pound described Canto I as a close translation from the *Odyssey*.

Pound has also pointed out that the language of Canto II is, like the language of *Sordello*, highly charged. "The artist seeks out the luminous detail and presents it. He does not comment."

In the new Canto I, Odysseus symbolizes the male, active, and intelligent, and Aphrodite the female, stimulant to creative action. Canto II develops these themes. Sordello is looked upon in different ways, in Browning's mind, in Pound's, and in the finished work *Sordello*. The focus shifts to So-shu, a demiurge in Chinese mythology. The scene fades into yet another, and a seal appears: the seal is feminine, it suggests the human; and, strangely, its eyes are the eyes of Picasso. Patterns recur. Eleanor of Aquitaine is like Helen of Troy, who is like Aphrodite, who is like Atalanta. The waves cover a new scene—and other metamorphoses take place. These changes come about as Pound thinks of a passage in the *Iliad* or *Odyssey,* or a Noh drama. A new image lights up, frequently emerging from the shadows of an ancient book. One character suggests another. A Greek water-scape suggests an Irish waterscape. A tree suggests Daphne. Always there is flow. New identities emerge and fade. Pound loves to work variations on the old myths. His imagination responds to them, as it almost never does—except in anger or contempt—to the civilization around him.

In Canto III, Pound remembers his stay in Venice in 1908, in his self-imposed exile. It was there he paid to have *A Lume Spento* printed. Pound recalls (this first appeared in the June 1917 Canto I) his own visit to Venice, eyeing young Italian girls, as Browning had, and eating hard rolls for breakfast—

> So, for what it's worth,
> I have my background;
>   And you had your background . . .

The Fourth Canto was published in forty copies on Japanese vellum by John Rodker in October 1919. In America it appeared in the *Dial* for June 1920. Canto IV is interesting if only because the literary allusions show how profoundly Pound's culture is the culture of books. In this Canto there is an illusion to Pindar, another to Catullus, yet another to the swallow Itys, and this suggests a similar tale by one of the troubadors, and so on.

Culture, for Pound, is the Mediterranean basin, especially in antiquity, with brief visits to the Renaissance or times long ago in Japan or China. The scenes evoked are like the winter dreams of a literary man with special interests in the classics, Provençal poetry, the Japanese Noh, and Chinese poetry. And the metamorphoses provide a constant discovery of the vitality in the old tales and a temporary stasis in a world of flux. They also provide escape from the dismal realities of the twentieth century.

In *It Was the Nightingale*, Ford Madox Ford said Pound's move to Paris was caused by Pound's challenging Lascelles Abercrombie to a duel. Abercrombie had written a piece for the *Times Literary Supplement*, favoring Milton. Prior to this he had enraged Pound by successfully running a magazine, *New Numbers*, in which he printed Georgian poetry. After his challenge, according to Ford, Pound was visited by the police. Another version of the story is that Abercrombie suggested they bombard each other with unsold copies of their books. In either case, Pound's ire would not be easily soothed. Shortly thereafter Pound took up residence in Paris.

Paris was soon to have a great deal of literary excitement, because of the presence of Joyce, Gertrude Stein, Ford, Hemingway, F. Scott Fitzgerald, Proust, Aragon, Cocteau, and many others. Pound was involved with some of these writers. He also continued to contribute to various magazines, and did a Paris letter for the *Dial*. And in Paris he could more easily live his role as aesthete. Margaret Anderson, for whose *Little Review* Pound was foreign editor, recalls his wearing a velvet beret, a flowing tie, and an emerald on his earlobe! He seemed more at home in Paris, but he did not give up all the relationships he had established in London. For example, his relationship with Joyce entered a new and, for Joyce, a very significant phase.

Pound's "discovery" of Joyce had come about as a result of his asking Joyce—who was struggling against poverty and suffering the refusal of printers to handle *Dubliners*—for permission to reprint "I hear an army charging upon the land" in *Des Imagistes*. As advisory editor for the *Egoist*, edited by Dora Marsden and later Harriet Weaver, he had asked for work in prose. Joyce sent the opening of *A Portrait of the Artist as a Young Man*. It was accepted, and, following a generous advance to Joyce, the novel ran serially in the *Egoist*. At the end of 1913, thanks to Pound,

Joyce found himself in the very middle of a literary revolution. While the *Portrait* was still being serialized, *Dubliners* finally appeared, and Pound reviewed it, saying Joyce had earned a place for himself "among English contemporary prose writers."

From Paris, Pound advised Joyce to join him. Joyce wrote a letter (July 1, 1920) saying, "My address in Paris will be chez M. Ezra Pound, Hotel de l'Elysée, rue de Beaune 9." Temperamentally the two men were unlike and did not make easy companions—but they remained friendly. Joyce never forgot Pound's generosity. And when he was broadcasting over Rome radio during the war Pound devoted one talk to celebrating Joyce's career.

In Paris, Pound also continued his relationship with Eliot. On one, now famous, occasion, Pound blue-penciled the poem that would be published as *The Waste Land*. "It was in 1922 [1921]," Eliot has written, "that I placed before him in Paris the manuscript of a sprawling chaotic poem called The Waste Land, which left his hands about half its size, in the form in which it appears in print." With the publication of the earlier version in the facsimile edition readers can now judge the rightness or wrongness of his admiration for Pound's performance as editor.

In Paris, Pound also continued his relationship with Ford, who later recalled Pound's sponsoring the music of George Antheil, and taking up sculpture. "Mr. Pound fiercely struck blocks of granite with sledge hammers." Pound told Ford he had little time for literature, but he did help Ford to get John Quinn, a New York philanthropist, to subsidize the short-lived *Transatlantic Review* and also helped get contributions. Pound introduced Ford to Ernest Hemingway, who had submitted his stories to Pound's blue pencil. Pound was ballyhooing him as a magnificent new writer. As one might expect, Gertrude Stein, Hemingway's other mentor, and Pound were not ardent admirers of each other. Miss Stein called him a "village explainer" and he called her "a charming old fraud."

In 1923, Pound and Hemingway toured Italian battlefields. Hemingway explained the strategy of a Renaissance soldier of fortune, Sigismondo de Malatesta. The trip was the beginning of Pound's decision to live in Italy, and in Malatesta he found a new hero for glorification in the *Cantos*.

Sigismondo de Malatesta, warrior, schemer, passionate male, and lover of beauty, delighted Pound. Malatesta must have been full of guile and a violent man even to survive in the political struggles in which he contested, with Pius II and other feudal monarchs, but in honoring his powers as an opportunist Pound jauntily shapes fifteenth-century Italian history to suit his own purposes. His use of letters and documents gives his "history" (in Cantos VIII, IX, and X) an air of being a disinterested glimpse of a thoroughly great man, Sigismondo Malatesta.

Clearly what endeared Malatesta to Pound was that he left behind him, although unfinished, a beautiful building, the Tempio. Sword in hand, standing neck deep in a marsh, or despoiling a city, Malatesta carried a dream in his head.

Considering his earlier productivity, Pound published little during his Paris period. He had, however, discovered Malatesta. And a look at *A Draft of XVI Cantos*, published soon after he moved to Rapallo, shows that he had discovered another cultural hero, Kung, or in the Latinized version of his name, Confucius. (Pound had acquainted himself with James Legge's twenty-eight volumes of *Chinese Classics*, 1861–86.) Mostly he refers to *The Analects* and *The Unwobbling Pivot* and the *Great Digest*, later translated by him under these titles.

Confucius had gained a reputation as a philosopher prime minister of Lu, but he resigned in 495 B.C. when the monarch gave himself to pleasure, and he visited other states as a teacher. Confucius, in Pound's words, said such things as "If a man does not discipline himself he cannot bring discipline into his home," and "One courteous family can lift a whole state into courtesy."

A difficulty in reading Canto XIII and others like it is that one cannot understand the allusions—for example, the elliptical conversation Confucius has in one village or another—unless one knows the context from which Pound took them.

Occasionally there are lovely passages in the *Cantos*, but increasingly Ezra Pound becomes less and less the poet bent on creating new images and identities, and more and more the insistent teacher.

After some months of indecision, Pound and his wife settled in Rapallo, a seaside village on the Italian Riviera. It has been described by Yeats, who took up residence there in 1929: "Mountains that shelter the bay from all but the strongest wind, bare brown branches of low vines and of tall trees blurring their outline as though with a soft mist; houses mirrored in an almost motionless sea . . . The little town described in An Ode on a Grecian Urn." There Pound lived for twenty years, until his arrest by American troops, following his indictment for treason. Occasionally he visited Paris and London, but mostly he remained in Rapallo. The dramatist Gerhart Hauptmann lived there in the summer, and visitors included Aldington, Ford, Antheil, Max Beerbohm, and others. Pound occasionally had disciples living nearby. Knowing him to be a famous poet, the townspeople treated him deferentially.

One might expect the quiet town and the almost motionless sea to have helped Pound write more *Cantos* in which Ovidian nymphs were pursued by ardent young swains, and there are some such *Cantos*. But there are many more in which he quarrels with America, its culture and universities, but especially its economy and banking system.

Pound believed that a good government was possible only when the state controlled money. This was best done, for the good of all of the people, by a benevolent dictator, like Mussolini. Other ideal "dictators," as seen by Pound, are Jefferson, Adams, Jackson, Confucius, a Chinese ruler, Quang-Ngau-chè, and others. Another wise ruler, according to Pound, was Martin Van Buren, and he implies there has been a conspiracy, at least of stupidity, to keep his *Autobiography* untaught in American universities.

Pound's objections to American capitalism derive from his belief that a man should be rewarded according to the worth of his work. Under our "leisure class" society, one makes money by manipulating money, not by producing worthwhile products or beautiful artifacts. Thus the many references in the *Cantos* to usury.

In Rapallo, Pound appears to have read certain works in an obsessive way; for example, the works of John Adams. About eighty pages of the *Cantos* deal with Adams. As he had in the Malatesta *Cantos*, Pound quotes endlessly, transcribing phrases. Malatesta, however, was partially transformed and lives as a fictional creation. Adams is lost in the transcription from his own writings.

At one period, Pound seemed ready to give up literature. Salvation was to be found only in economics, in the writings of Douglas, Gesell, and Orage. In a letter written in 1934, Yeats reported that Pound "would talk nothing but politics. . . . He urged me to read the works of Captain Douglas who alone knew what caused our suffering. He took away my manuscript ["King of the Clock Tower"] and went away denouncing Dublin as 'a reactionary hole' because I had said that I was reading Shakespeare, would go on to Chaucer, and found all that I wanted of modern life in 'detection and the wild West.' Next day his judgment came and that in a single word 'Putrid.' "

In addition to his explaining the nature of economics and politics to the English-speaking world, Pound had been explaining the ABC's of reading and how to read. In the *New York Herald Tribune Books* he wrote: "The great writers need no debunking. The pap is not in them and doesn't need to be squeezed out. They do not lend themselves to imperial and sentimental exploitations. A civilization was founded on Homer, civilization not a mere bloated empire. The Macedonian domination rose and grew after the sophists. It also subsided." In such an article, Pound sometimes makes acute observations, but the sentences and paragraphs are often discrete, and the author seems distracted and unsure of the unifying idea of his discourse. There is also a disturbing immaturity and naïveté in Pound's pronouncements: "Really one DON'T need to know a language. One NEEDS, damn well needs, to know the few hundred words in the few really good poems that any language has in it." Or "It takes about 600 to make a civilization."

Pound's prose works during the late 1920's and the 1930's reveal that he repeated many things he had said earlier, and that he continued his engagement with America. His slangy wit gradually grows cruder, and his vulgarity coarser.

In 1930, the Black Sun Press of Caresse Crosby issued his *Imaginary Letters*. Some of these were written during his London period, and some of them were from later years. In one of the letters, he says he is told Russia is much like America. He infers that both are "barbarous" countries. In another, he says he hopes "to hear the last of these Russians," adding that the talk about the Russian soul bores him silly—"The Russian (large R, definite article, Artzibasheff, Bustikosseff, Slobingobski, Spititoutski and Co. Amalgamated, communatated, etc.). 'The Russian,' my dear Caroline, is nothing but the western European with his conning-tower or his top-layer . . . removed. . . . Civilized man, *any* civilized man who has a normal lining in his stomach, may become Russian for the price of a little mixed alcohol, or of, perhaps a good deal of mixed alcohol, but it is a matter of shillings, not a matter of dynamic attainment. Once, and perhaps only once, have I been drunk enough to feel like a Russian. Try it, my dearest young lady, try it. Try it and clear your mind, free your life from this obsession of Russians (if Lenin and Co. have not freed you.)"

In a letter on the language of Joyce and modern literature at its best, he says: "The author [of an article he is citing] says, and I think with reason, that wherever Joyce has made use of lice, or dung, or other disgusting unpleasantness he has done so with the intention, and with, as a considerable artist, the result of heightening some effect of beauty, or twisting tighter some intensity." He calls this Joyce's "metal finish." It is, he says, similar to his own "sterilized surgery." Shortly he adds, as an example of his own "vigour," a "fairly Baudelairian but . . . nowhere inevitable" sonnet of his, or, rather, the two stanzas he can recall:

One night stretched out along a hebrew
    bitch—
Like two corpses at the undertakers—
This carcass, sold alike to jews and quakers
Reminded me of beauty noble and rich.

These lines are not unlike those to be found in many of the later *Cantos*. Pound is like a small boy writing dirty verses on the lavatory wall. Pound's comments indicate he knew he had not written a successful poem, but he seems not to have recognized the shocking crassness of which he was capable.

From Rapallo, Pound sent out his advice to the world, especially to his "fellow 'Muricans." One such piece of advice is called *ABC of Reading*. It was published by an American university press, Yale. "How to Study Poetry," two prefatory paragraphs, never mentions poetry—or the study of poetry. "Warning," a kind of introduction, contains seven paragraphs, each about a different subject. In Section One, Chapter One, he says our way of looking at objects should be more scientific; we should emulate the biologist who compares one specimen with another. Then he discusses Fenollosa's *Essay on the Chinese Written Character*, adding that organized university life in America and England had made it almost impossible for him to get the essay published. Next he says medieval man wasn't as victimized by terminology as we are. He then returns to Fenollosa, and presents the Chinese picture words or images for man, tree, sun, and sun in the tree's branches, meaning the East. Fenollosa, he continues, demonstrated that the Chinese "word" or "ideogram" for red "is based on something everyone KNOWS." The implication seems to be that the English word *red* is based on knowledge no one has or experience no one has had! In Section Two we are told about Laboratory Condition—that is, that experiencing art is preferable to hearing discussions of it. To make this point, Pound lists the programs played by several "serious musicians" on one occasion in Rapallo, adding that the best volume of musical criticism he has ever encountered is Boris De Schloezer's *Stravinsky*. Lastly there is "The Ideogrammic Method or the Method of Science." In these paragraphs he mentions neither ideograms nor scientific methods. He says you cannot prevent Mr. Buggins from preferring a painting by Carlo Dolci to one by Cosimo Tura, but if you have them next to each other "you can very seriously impede his setting up a false tradition. . . ." Finally he says that a middle-aged man knows the *rightness* of what he knows. A young man may be right, but he doesn't know *how* right he may be.

The chapter says almost nothing, and is wildly incoherent. Certainly a writer lacking Pound's reputation, ironically a reputation as a great explicator, would not have stood a chance of having a publisher accept this book. If an academic adviser had received such a chapter as the opening of a candidate's M.A. thesis he would have been obligated to dismiss it as the gibberish it is. *ABC of Reading* reads like the comments of an ex-schoolmaster who has been bereft of his senses. One reading an occasional sentence might feel that the ex-schoolmaster was only mad north-northeast, but reading it entirely makes clear that this is the work of a deranged mind.

Another of these strange volumes was published in England as *Guide to Kulchur*, and in the United States as *Culture*. The same subjects recur. There are discussions of Confucius, Vorticism, tradition, textbooks, Provençal poets, the nature of first-rate novels, decline of the Adams family, etc., etc. Typically, "Tradition" examines several discrete subjects, none of them especially illuminating. It opens with a discussion of Frobenius, one of Pound's heroes. He quotes several tags from antiquity, refers to Confucian harmonies, Madame Tussaud's, an unnamed general, etc. Pound is telling the reader that he can understand his own culture only if he understands some other culture. *"I am not, in these slight memories, merely 'pickin' daisies.' A man does not know his own ADDRESS (in time) until he knows where his own time and milieu stand in relation to other times and conditions."* But the "slight

memories" Pound recounts are mostly empty prattling. For example, he mentions a book entitled *With the Empress Dowager of China* by K. A. Carl. "This book," he says, "records a high degree of civilization." Then these sentences follow, in the same paragraph. "Fenollosa is said to have been the second European to be able to take part in a Noh performance. The whole civilization reflected in Noh is a high civilization." Individually the three sentences make a kind of sense. In sequence they make no sense. Nor do they make sense in terms of the paragraphs preceding them, or the paragraphs that follow.

It needs to be said that Pound's prose in these books, as well as in his economic and political pamphlets, is quite as disordered as the phrases and sentences in the later *Cantos*. Some critics have rationalized the fragmented passages of the *Cantos* as a new "poetic strategy." The truth would seem to be that Pound was no longer capable of the kind of coherence he had sometimes achieved as a young man.

In the *Cantos*, as the years pass, there is an increasing dependence on violence and shock, on obscenities and scatological descriptions. Worse, there is an airy indifference when Pound mentions genocide or mass suffering. F. R. Leavis, an early admirer of Pound's contributions as poet, critic, and man of letters, has said, "The spectacle of Pound's degeneration is a terrible one, and no one ought to pretend that it is anything but what it is."

Pound returned to the United States in 1939; received an honorary degree from Hamilton College; and went to Washington, where he talked with Senator Borah, Secretary of Agriculture Wallace, and others, attempting to prove to them that a change in economic policies would avert war. Back in Italy when the war began, he broadcast over Rome radio, attacking Roosevelt's policies. After Pearl Harbor, when Pound and his wife tried to leave Italy, an unidentified American official refused them permission to board a diplomatic train leaving Rome. Shortly he resumed his broadcasts. As a series they are undoubtedly the most curious efforts at propaganda ever allowed over a national radio. Pound talked about London as he had known it, E. E. Cummings, Joyce, Chinese philosophy, economics, and his own *Cantos*. No wonder the Italians suspected him of being an American agent. But the United States attorney general asked for his indictment, and when the Americans reached Genoa, in northern Italy, Pound gave himself up.

Imprisoned at Pisa in the summer of 1945, under harsh circumstances, he suffered hallucinations and a collapse. After medical care, he was treated more humanely and resumed his writing. In November he was flown to Washington. Eventually he was committed to St. Elizabeth's, a federal hospital for the insane, and remained there until the United States dropped its indictment thirteen years later, when he returned to Italy.

During this period he continued to write pamphlets, contribute *Cantos* to various magazines—and generally repeat the same opinions he had expressed in his broadcasts.

Much of the writing from this period is rant, fustion, and bombast, but there are two partial exceptions, *The Pisan Cantos*, for which he received the Bollingen Award (which fluttered literary dovecotes and caused several angry editorials), and *Women of Trachis*, a translation from Sophocles. In *The Pisan Cantos* there are occasional beautiful phrases, but there is no evidence that Pound had recovered the clarity of vision and metaphorical powers of the early *Cantos*. *The Pisan Cantos* are, like his radio talks, filled with discrete observa-

tions, and non sequiturs. But there is also a new dimension.

He thinks back over his life in London, France, and Rapallo, and recalls what Ford, or Yeats, or Hemingway, or whoever, had said. Pound the aesthete has disappeared and Pound the preacher appears only intermittently. There is an awareness of human anguish, of ancient folly, and of Pound's own vanity.

If the hoar frost grip thy tent
Thou wilt give thanks when night is spent.

The Pisan Cantos are the disordered work of a man who has been through hell.

In *Women of Trachis*, Pound achieves something like the immediacy of language that he achieved in "Propertius." Where Lewis Campbell has

Dear child, dear boy! even from the lowliest
    head
Wise counsel may come forth.

(he is referring to wise advice coming from a slave), Pound says:

See here, son, this slave talks sense,
    more than some free folks.

It's the American idiom, but probably a lot closer to Sophocles' intent than is Campbell's idiom. *Women of Trachis* is a remarkable performance when set against some of Pound's ranting prose.

How should one view the life and career of Ezra Pound? Several eminent writers, including Yeats, Eliot, and Hemingway, have stated their indebtedness to him. Without doubt he was a catalytic agent in many of the movements associated with modernism. As for his place as a poet, posterity will decide. Current critical estimates are diverse and irreconcilable. What Auden had to say about Yeats applies to Pound:

Time that is intolerant
Of the brave and innocent,
And indifferent in a week
To a beautiful physique,

Worships language and forgives
Everyone by whom it lives;
Pardons cowardice, conceit,
Lays its honours at their feet.

Presumably Time will forgive or at least forget the offenses or errors of Ezra Pound. If his poetry achieves a place in the permanent canon of English and American poetry, Time, as Auden says, will lay its honors at his feet.

* * * * *

Ezra Pound died in Venice, in self-imposed exile from the United States, on November 1, 1972. He was 87 years old.

Selected Bibliography

SELECTED WORKS OF EZRA POUND

Pound has published such a large number of books and contributed to so many collections, anthologies, and magazines that a full listing of his works would fill many pages. The titles listed below are intended to suggest the variety of his writing.

A Lume Spento. Venice: A. Antonini, 1908. (Limited edition.)

Personæ of Ezra Pound. London: Elkin Mathews, 1909.

Exultations of Ezra Pound. London: Elkin Mathews, 1909.

The Spirit of Romance. London: Dent, 1910.

Provença: Poems Selected from Personæ, Exultations, and Canzoniere of Ezra Pound. Boston: Small, Maynard, 1910.

Canzoni of Ezra Pound. London: Elkin Mathews, 1911.

The Ripostes of Ezra Pound Whereunto Are Appended the Complete Poetical Works of T. E. Hulme, with Prefatory Note. London: Swift, 1912.

Des Imagistes: An Anthology of the Imagists, edited by Ezra Pound. New York: Boni, 1914; London: Poetry Book Shop, 1914.

"Homage to Wilfrid Blunt," *Poetry,* 3:220–23 (March 1914).

"Vorticism," *Fortnightly Review,* 102:461–71 (September 1914).

Review of *Ernest Dowson,* by Victor Plarr, *Poetry, 6:43–45* (April 1915).

'Noh,' or Accomplishment: A Study of the Classical Stage of Japan (with Ernest Fenollosa). London: Macmillan, 1916; New York: Knopf, 1917.

Gaudier-Brzeska: A Memoir. London: John Lane, 1916. (Reissued, New York: New Directions, 1960.) (Reissued again by New Directions, 1970. Edition includes 30 pages of illustrations and articles about Gaudier-Brzeska since 1916.)

Certain Noble Plays of Japan, from the manuscripts of Ernest Fenollosa, chosen and finished by Ezra Pound. Churchtown, Dundrum: Cuala Press, 1916.

Lustra of Ezra Pound. London: Elkin Mathews, 1916; New York: Knopf, 1917.

"T. S. Eliot," *Poetry,* 10:264–71 (August 1917). (Review of *Prufrock and Other Observations,* by T. S. Eliot.)

"Irony, Laforgue, and Some Satire," *Poetry,* 11:93–98 (November 1917).

Pavannes and Divisions. New York: Knopf, 1918.

"The Hard and the Soft in French Poetry," *Poetry,* 11:264–71 (February 1918).

The Natural Philosophy of Love, by Remy de Gourmont, translated by Ezra Pound. New York: Boni and Liveright, 1922.

A Draft of XVI Cantos of Ezra Pound. Paris: Three Mountains Press, 1924 or 1925. (Limited edition.)

Personæ: The Collected Poems of Ezra Pound. New York: Boni and Liveright, 1926. (Reprinted with additional poems, New York: New Directions, 1949.)

Imaginary Letters. Paris: Black Sun Press, 1930. (Limited edition.)

ABC of Reading. London: Routledge, 1934; New Haven: Yale University Press, 1934.

Jefferson and/or Mussolini. London: Nott, 1935; New York: Liveright, 1936.

Polite Essays. London: Faber and Faber, 1937; Norfolk, Conn.: New Directions, 1939.

Guide to Kulchur. London: Faber and Faber, 1938; (as *Culture*) Norfolk, Conn.; New Directions, 1938.

The Pisan Cantos. New York: New Directions, 1948.

The Cantos of Ezra Pound. New York: New Directions, 1948. (Cantos 1–71 and 74–84.)

Selected Poems. New York: New Directions, 1949.

Section: Rock-Drill: 85–95 de los cantares. New York: New Directions, 1949.

Money pamphlets. 6 vols. London: Peter Russell, 1950–52. (These were published earlier in Italy.)

The Letters of Ezra Pound, edited by T. D. D. Paige. New York: Harcourt, Brace, 1950.

Patria Mia. Chicago: R. F. Seymour, 1950.

The Translations of Ezra Pound, edited by Hugh Kenner. New York: New Directions, 1954.

Literary Essays, edited by T. S. Eliot. New York: New Directions, 1954.

The Classic Anthology Defined by Confucius. Cambridge, Mass.: Harvard University Press, 1954.

Women of Trachis, by Sophocles, translated by Ezra Pound. London: Neville Spearman, 1956.

Thrones: 96–109 de los cantares. New York: New Directions, 1959.

Impact. Chicago: Regnery, 1960.

Pound/Joyce: Letters of Ezra Pound to James Joyce, edited by Forrest Read. New York: New Directions, 1967.

Drafts and Fragments of Cantos CX–CXVII. New York: New Directions and The Stone Wall Press, 1968.

BIBLIOGRAPHICAL AIDS

Edwards, John, comp. *A Preliminary Checklist of the Writings of Ezra Pound.* New Haven: Kirgo-Books, 1953.

Edwards, John, and W. W. Vasse, eds. *Annotated Index to the Cantos of Ezra Pound.* Berkeley: University of California Press, 1958.

Gallup, Donald C. *A Bibliography of Ezra Pound.* London: Rupert Hart Davis, 1963.

CRITICAL AND BIOGRAPHICAL STUDIES

Baumann, Walter. *A Rose in the Steel Dust: An Examination of the Cantos of Ezra Pound.* Coral Gables, Fla.: University of Miami Press, 1970.

Blackmur, R. P. *Language as Gesture.* New York: Harcourt, Brace, 1952.

Davie, Donald. *Ezra Pound: Poet as Sculptor.* New York: Oxford University Press, 1964.

Dembo, L. S. *The Confucian Odes of Ezra Pound: A Critical Appraisal.* Berkeley: University of California Press, 1963.

Edwards, John, ed. *The Pound Newsletter.* Berkeley: University of California, 1954–56.

Eliot, T. S. *The Waste Land: A Facsimile and Transcript of the Original Drafts, including the Annotations of Ezra Pound,* edited by Valerie Eliot. New York: Harcourt Brace Jovanovich, 1971.

Elliott, George P. "On Pound—Poet of Many Voices," *Carleton Miscellany,* 2:79–103 (Summer 1961). (Published at Carleton College, Northfield, Minn.)

Emery, Clark. *Ideas into Action: A Study of Pound's Cantos.* Coral Gables, Fla.: University of Miami Press, 1958.

Espey, John. *Ezra Pound's Mauberley; A Study in Composition.* Berkeley: University of California Press, 1955.

Goodwin, K. L. *The Influence of Ezra Pound.* New York: Oxford University Press, 1967.

Hutchins, Patricia. *Ezra Pound's Kensington: An Exploration, 1885–1913.* London: Faber and Faber; Chicago: Regnery, 1965.

Kenner, Hugh. *The Poetry of Ezra Pound.* New York: New Directions, 1951.

Leary, Lewis, ed. *Motive and Method in the Cantos of Ezra Pound.* New York: Columbia University Press, 1954.

Leavis, F. R. *New Bearings in English Poetry.* London: Chatto and Windus, 1932.

Mayo, Robert, ed. *The Analyst.* Evanston, Ill.: Northwestern University (Department of English), 1953–date. (Various scholars annotate the *Cantos* in this publication, which appears at intervals.)

Miner, Earl. *The Japanese Tradition in British and American Literature*. Princeton, N.J.: Princeton University Press, 1958.

Mullins, Eustace. *This Difficult Individual, Ezra Pound*. New York: Fleet, 1961.

Norman, Charles. *Ezra Pound*. New York: Macmillan, 1960. (Revised edition, New York: Funk and Wagnalls, 1969.)

O'Connor, William Van, and Edward Stone, eds. *A Casebook on Ezra Pound*. New York: Crowell, 1959.

Pearlman, Daniel. *The Barb of Time*. New York: Oxford University Press, 1969.

Putnam, Samuel. *Paris Was Our Mistress*. New York: Viking Press, 1947.

Quarterly Review of Literature, Ezra Pound Issue, Vol. 5, No. 2 (1949). (Published at Bard College, Annandale, New York.)

Quinn, Sister M. Bernetta. *The Metamorphic Tradition in Modern Poetry*. New Brunswick, N.J.: Rutgers University Press, 1955.

Rosenthal, M. L. *A Primer of Ezra Pound*. New York: Macmillan, 1960.

Russell, Peter, ed. *An Examination of Ezra Pound*. New York: New Directions, 1950.

Stock, Noel. *Poet in Exile: Ezra Pound*. Manchester, England: Manchester University Press; New York: Barnes and Noble, 1964.

————. *Reading the Cantos: A Study of Meaning in Ezra Pound*. London: Routledge and K. Paul, 1967.

————. *The Life of Ezra Pound*. London: Routledge and K. Paul, 1970.

————, ed. *Ezra Pound Perspectives: Essays in Honor of His Eightieth Birthday*. Chicago: Regnery, 1965.

Sutton, Walter, ed. *Ezra Pound: A Collection of Critical Essays*. Englewood Cliffs, N.J.: Prentice-Hall, 1963.

Wright, George. *The Poet in the Poem*. Berkeley: University of California Press, 1960.

—WILLIAM VAN O'CONNOR

John Crowe Ransom

1888-1974

WHEN he was writing his poem "Survey of Literature" and first put down the mischievous couplet

> In all the good Greek of Plato
> I lack my roastbeef and potato,

John Crowe Ransom may have had in mind no more than the amusing incongruity of the rhyming words. He had long been a poet of unexpected and witty conjunctions, though none had brought together things further apart than the supernal philosopher and the earthy tuber. But here was more than just a funny *mot*. If he had aimed at suggesting the informing force of his poetry, criticism, and teaching, Ransom scarcely could have done so more neatly or provided a more teasing example of that force at work. For he was one who liked his ideas entangled with things, even if this meant endangering some of the lofty purity of the ideas. He objected to the good Greek of Plato because, as he said later, it "fails to coincide with the original world of perception, which is [a] world populated by . . . stubborn and contingent objects." He preferred poetry which represented that original world by including the objects, however rebellious they might seem to be.

Yet he had long been puzzled by the way the poets brought it off. For a poem managed to offer a more or less logical plan (roughly the Platonic idea) and an aggregate of substantial and sometimes even superfluous or contradictory details (the roastbeef and potato). Why, he had often wondered, did not the logic force out all but a few of the details? Why did not the details overwhelm the logic? He had proposed several explanations over the years, but none quite pleased him, and in 1955 he took up the problem once more in an essay entitled "The Concrete Universal: Observations on the Understanding of Poetry." For the occasion he went back to Kant and Hegel.

According to Kant, as Ransom read him, poetry is a representation of Natural Beauty, which appears whenever the subject of a work of art shows, with some additional material, the outline of a Moral Universal. By means of metaphor the universal finds a place among the concrete local details. But Hegel, Ransom said, was, like Plato, one of the old persuasion. (One wonders what Ransom might have done with "Hegel" and "bagel.") Hegel wanted his universals pure and would have them prevail without any interference from stubborn and contingent objects. Indeed, he wanted to reform nature so that everything fitted neatly under the patterns of the universals with nothing left over, nothing for metaphor and for poetry. Faced with this possibility, Ransom believed, "the defenders of poetry would not mind saying that they are not prepared to abandon nature, because that would be the abandonment of metaphor, which in turn would mean the abandonment of poetry; which, when they have weighed it, would be a serious abridgment of the range of the human experience."

Ransom had not really explained how a poem managed to have both its logical plan and its energetic details, but he had shown once more that he stood not far from Kant on the side of nature and poetry. Many years earlier he had affirmed his loyalty to them, in part simply because he liked them as they were, but also because he had always distrusted abstractions and particularly systems which claimed to have the ultimate Pure Idea and proposed that whatever did not fit the Idea could be ignored—if it were not to be suppressed. Ransom thought that man and his world were too complex ever to be more than partially accounted for by any one system, be it scientific, metaphysical, ethical, aesthetic, or political. To see things as they were, or to see them as well as he could, man needed a double vision capable of perceiving an idea and the food upon the table, which was lumpish and only partially conformed to the idea even though it nourished him. Man needed the binoculars of poetry fitted with the lens of metaphor. To help him look at his experience through them has been the final intention of all of Ransom's thought, writing and teaching.

His earliest intellectual recollection, he once remarked, was of a fury against abstraction, a fury aroused by his observations rather than by anything he had read. He was born on April 30, 1888, in Pulaski, Tennessee, and spent most of his boyhood in small towns in the central region of the state, where his father served as a Methodist minister. The life of a minister's son in a little community is never easy. The congregation expects him to be a model of deportment, but he is goaded by his companions into small delinquencies to prove that he is not a sissy. Often he rebels against the beliefs of his father which have helped to put him in such a difficult position. It is altogether possible that Ransom's fury began as impatience with the dogmas of the Methodist Church. Be that as it may, he was from the beginning an inveterate skeptic, and his first poem, written many years later, describes the restlessness of a young man whose sweetheart's attention has been distracted by thoughts of God from himself and the beauty of their surroundings. The poet would have subscribed without reservation to the anti-Hegelianism of the critic.

At fifteen Ransom entered Vanderbilt University, where at the time the instruction in Latin and Greek was excellent but that in English literature was feeble. He went in for the classics and philosophy and did so well that he was appointed a Rhodes scholar in literary humanities. At Oxford he met Christopher Morley, another American student who later had a modest reputation as novelist, journalist, and wit. Morley had organized a little discussion club and at its meetings Ransom heard talk of modern poetry, which he began to read with enthusiasm and some bewilderment. The classics had not prepared him for the seemingly irregular meters, the startling images, and the intensely personal tone, and he was excited by the concreteness which on comparison made classical literature and philosophy seem to him dry and abstract. He began to have misgivings about his choice of specialization; but he had to support himself, and after finishing his work at Oxford he taught Latin in a preparatory school for a year. Then he heard of an opening for an instructor in English at Vanderbilt. He applied and was accepted on the basis of his excellent record even though he had no advanced training in the subject. He remained at the university for nearly a quarter of a century during which he became one of the finest teachers of our time and a noted figure in the so-called Southern Renaissance.

The cliché "Southern Renaissance" has become such a staple of criticism that any discussion of a modern southern writer can scarcely avoid it. Actually there was no renaissance because there had been no significant body of serious writing preceding it. In all the South, which in 1920 H. L. Mencken called the Sahara of the Bozart, there had been only one or two writers of major stature and these had been ignored or repudiated by their fellow southerners. Then during the decade following World War I there suddenly appeared in the South a disproportionately large share of the important figures of contemporary American letters, among them Ransom, William Faulkner, Katherine Anne Porter, Allen Tate, Thomas Wolfe, Robert Penn Warren, and Caroline Gordon, to name but a few. How did this happen and what does it mean for their work that they were *southern* writers?

So far there has been no satisfactory explanation of the phenomenon and probably there never will be. But there have been some fruitful suggestions regarding the forces that brought it about even if the pattern of these forces cannot be wholly made out. Of twentieth-century American writers the southerners alone inherited both a conglomerate of exceedingly varied and dramatic material and the shared customs, attitudes, and beliefs which, though enfeebled and disappearing with increasing speed, might still serve to order and interpret the history of a whole region and the lives of the men who had dwelt there. The southern writers had at hand—in the very lore of their own families—the story of the conquest of a great and fertile wilderness and the

attempt to establish in a single generation a quasi-feudal society governed by a self-proclaimed aristocracy. It is easy to laugh at the pioneers' pretensions to gentility and the elaborate code of manners which had been taken, along with the names for their big new mansions, from the pages of Scott's novels; but the code worked: it gave direction and dignity to lives which might otherwise have been insufferably bleak. (This is something which the present-day humanitarian, shocked by the expense of spirit in the system, all too easily overlooks or denies. The code was outrageous; from a modern point of view it may even seem more than a little crazy; but it gave many men a sense of their own worth. Some of those to whom it gave the most were small farmers actually oppressed and deprived by the economy on which the code rested.) These writers had, too, the story of the defeat of the Old South and of the protracted agony as power passed from the "aristocrats" to profiteers who did not scruple to enrich themselves from the suffering of their oppressed region before setting up as aristocrats themselves. Finally they had the pathetic attempt of the heirs of the Confederate captains to assuage their humiliation with a legend of an Old South surpassing in baronial splendor the wildest fancies of its founders and the failure of these heirs to pass on to their own children, those of the writers' generation, a culture that would prepare the latter to cope with the modern world.

It was not a total failure. One might even argue from the example of these writers that it was the nearest thing to a success of its kind in modern America. For the code furnished them, as it had furnished the antebellum planters and their imitators, with means for defining and measuring a man and his conduct. It did not matter whether they themselves accepted or rejected the code. What mattered was that over a span of three generations enough men had accepted and attempted to live by it to fulfill a prerequisite for any significant literature using the history of the region: that the conduct of the men who had lived out that history be judged, at least within the history itself, by something more than private whims. What a southern gentleman chose to do or refrain from doing meant something to himself and his community in well-understood terms. The writers could assert that within the world represented by their works this was good, that was bad; this would cost agonies of conscience, that would diminish the burden of living; this would set a man against his neighbor, that would bring honor and power among men. The writers had, as it were, a good portion of their task already done for them. To put it all too briefly, they had inherited a mythopoeic image of man, and as a consequence their writing has a scope and intensity, a moral passion, and a pervasive awareness of the mystery and irony of man's fate not often found in the work of other Americans of their time.

The society which gave them such magnificent materials did not pass on any substantial literary standards. Before their time the South had scarcely tolerated and had almost wholly ignored any serious writing, which inevitably was critical of the *status quo*. This region, which for so long had been beleaguered from without, would not permit the slightest attack from within. Damp memorials and maudlin fiction flattering the self-images of the upper classes were all that was acceptable, and the southern writers needed contact with the outside world if they were to use their heritage. In one way or another, each of the leaders of the "renaissance" got it, Faulkner through Sherwood Anderson, for example, and Ransom, a bit earlier, through Oxford and Morley.

This and the very act of writing put them somewhat apart. Yet almost all of them had known full participation in the life of their communities, and they shared qualities with many other southerners. Two of the most striking were an affinity for unusual diction and an affinity for violence, both qualities found in political oratory, the one art encouraged in the South. As the techiness of the self-proclaimed aristocrats was often accompanied by great punctiliousness on all points of conduct, so the violence of these writers (not in their lives but in their vision of man) may seethe below the surface of an elaborate style. It often appears in narratives of the man at war with the code. Where individualism and great pressure to conform appear together as they long have in the South, intense and vivid stories are possible, and these writers, even in their poetry, have been essentially storytellers writing more of things and events than of ideas. Southern culture glorified the life of action and made a hero of the soldier and outdoorsman; serious intellectual interest was conspicuously absent and the artist or contemplative man was regarded as a dull dog indeed. These writers, though themselves somewhat beyond the pale, seem nevertheless to have accepted unconsciously attitudes of their region. Faulkner has denied that he is an artist and has attempted to define the best of manhood in terms of the ritual of the hunt. Tate uses the soldier and outmoded weapons as symbols of lost traditions that gave significance to life. But whether or not these writers accept the attitudes of their fellow southerners, they have rarely written about the alienated intellectual, great as his isolation might be in the South and near as his experience might seem to their own. This stereotype belongs to a metropolitan tradition that was not part of their formative experience. Indeed, though enormously intelligent, they are not intellectuals in the sense of this tradition, and they seem to have more than a little of the southern distrust of ideas.

Ransom is truly a southern writer. But the

regional qualities are to be found in his style and his vision rather than his subjects, for in all his career he has published only four poems treating specifically southern themes or backgrounds. The qualities, violence coupled with elegance, affinity for unusual diction, concern with the insignia of feudalism and the chevalier as the embodiment of its values, mockery of the man of ideas, and so forth, are transformed by Ransom's double vision and irony into a poetry so conspicuously his own that his individuality rather than any regionalism first impresses the reader. And quite properly, for the value of Ransom's poetry comes mostly from those aspects which make him different from all other contemporary writers, southern or not. Yet it is difficult to conceive of such poetry being written in twentieth-century America by anyone not from the South.

He began writing it abruptly and so badly that though certain individual and regional qualities are present, anyone reading his early poems without his name upon them would not take them for his or, indeed, for the work of a southerner. Characteristic features of his later style and vision were obscured by clumsy technique, and the ideas often seem naively commonplace or just plain crude. In the first years after his return to Vanderbilt he was struggling with a reading program to make up for his lack of training when on an impulse he wrote a free-verse poem, "Sunset," about the girl distracted by God. It was a late and inauspicious start, and if the friend to whom he showed it had not been encouraging, he might have stopped there. But within a year he had enough poems for a small volume which Morley arranged to have published. Its title, *Poems about God*, was misleading. Few were about Him; some were scarcely poems.

Ransom had gone for instruction, not to the classics, but to English poetry—particularly that of the nineteenth century, though he was completely untouched by Swinburne and the *fin de siècle* poetry so much admired by his generation. While reading Browning he observed that every line seemed to have a little punch, some trick of phrasing or rhythm which startled the reader into closer attention and pleased him with its unexpectedness. This became his whole poetic: he would put a little punch into each of his own lines. But the outcome gave neither pleasure nor an impression of force, for the lines tended to be spastic. Ransom has never reprinted these poems, but those who hunt them out will discover traces of the poet to come in the odd words he chose (*escheat* is one of them), in the slant rhymes, the self-depreciatory tone, the satire against romantic idealists, and the pervasive mistrust of fulsome generalizations, especially of the moral order. The characteristic pluralism is there, only it looks more like confusion and want of skill.

Shortly before he took to writing poetry, Ransom was asked to participate in arguments that swirled around Sidney Mttron-Hirsch, a self-taught mystic then in his early thirties, who delighted in debates with Vanderbilt undergraduates. This remarkable man had quit high school to travel about the world and study Oriental philosophy, Rosicrucianism, mystical numerology, astrology, and the more recondite passages of ancient Hebrew texts. No one could have been less like Ransom, but they were soon close friends, and Ransom sat in on many a discussion before the war broke up the group and left Hirsch brooding over dead languages and Kepler.

After the war, during which Ransom served overseas as an artillery officer, many young men from other parts of the country who hoped to become writers stayed in France or settled in Greenwich Village; but one by one Hirsch's friends came back to Nashville to take up the arguments where they had left off. Ransom was hard at poetry once more and one evening brought some of his work to read to the others. Before long the rest were bringing samples of their own verse and the discussions had shifted from philosophy to poetry. Hirsch amiably accepted the change and presided with imperturbable dignity over the readings, which took place almost every fortnight. The group had no theory of poetry, and no outside poets had more than a momentary influence, though most of the members had definite preferences. In the fall of 1921 Allen Tate, then an undergraduate at Vanderbilt, joined the group and soon after proclaimed that Hart Crane and Eliot were his mentors. His own poetry showed the effects of his immersion in their work and that of the modern poets they approved, and he was able to persuade some of the members who joined later of the virtues of the experimentalists. But he could not change the tastes or the styles of the original group. They had read the Symbolists and they kept up with *The Dial*, but they were too conservative to be affected by the new fashions in verse. So conservative, indeed, that Ransom, who maintained in arguments with Tate that Eliot's work was fragmentary and undisciplined, was nevertheless looked on by some of the others as a fierce modernist. Their conservatism, however, did not extend to accepting the manner and matter of earlier southern poetry. They did not regard themselves as southern writers, preferring to consider themselves members of an international community of letters. Ransom was particularly vigorous in castigating any hints of the moonlight-and-magnolias idiom. Yet despite their cosmopolitan pretensions, they were unlike most other young poets of their time, for they were essentially amateurs addressing their work to some ideal citizen of Nashville:

gentleman, classicist, and Vanderbilt man with a preference for Blake, Keats, Tennyson, Poe, and Hardy.

Early in 1922 Hirsch proposed founding a magazine of verse, and at just about the time that Ransom turned thirty-four, *The Fugitive* appeared. It ran for nineteen issues before being suspended in December 1925—an extraordinary record for a little magazine, especially as, after several years of losing money on it, the Fugitives ended with a small reserve of funds. (They had to give up publishing the magazine because none of them had time to edit it.) Anyone leafing through it today would be puzzled by its longevity, for most of the poetry apart from Ransom's is insipid. Tate's is laboriously modern, while the poems of Robert Penn Warren, who joined the group early in 1924, show only flickers of his blazing talent. Most of the Fugitives, as the group was promptly dubbed when the magazine was launched, were very minor poets, but they were acute and candid critics. The meetings and the magazine provided an invaluable stimulus and training for the three most gifted members, and it was during the Fugitive interval that Ransom mastered his craft. The poems he published in the magazine make up the bulk of his finest work; after the Fugitives abandoned the magazine he gradually ceased to write poetry. The group, too, slowly disintegrated. Several of its most vigorous and talented members left Nashville before the end of 1925; the novelty of getting together to talk about poetry had worn away, and without the magazine there was less need for them to meet. By 1928 the Fugitive interval was over. Ransom's own interests now turned toward aesthetics and public affairs. Yet, as will be seen, his commitment was still the same beneath the apparent change; he continued to love poetry and the world's body and to mistrust all "Platonic" abstractions.

The poems of the Fugitive period are so different from those in *Poems about God* that the change, which seems to have come quite suddenly, is almost miraculous. Sometime during the winter of 1921–22 Ransom, who had been trying the sonnet form with little success, wrote "Necrological," which resembled neither his earlier work nor any other poetry then being written in America. Like so many of the poems to come, it was a little fable:

The friar had said his paternosters duly
And scourged his limbs, and afterwards would
    have slept;
But with much riddling his head became
    unruly,
He arose, from the quiet monastery he crept.

Dawn lightened the place where the battle had
    been won.
The people were dead—it is easy he thought to
    die—
These dead remained, but the living all were
    gone,
Gone with the wailing trumps of victory.

The dead men wore no raiment against the air,
Bartholomew's men had spoiled them where
    they fell;
In defeat the heroes' bodies were whitely bare,
The field was white like meads of asphodel.

Not all were white; some gory and fabulous
Whom the sword had pierced and then the grey
    wolf eaten;
But the brother reasoned that heroes' flesh was
    thus.
Flesh fails, and the postured bones lie weather-
    beaten.

The lords of chivalry lay prone and shattered.
The gentle and the bodyguard of yeomen;
Bartholomew's stroke went home—but little it
    mattered,

Bartholomew went to be stricken of other
    foemen.

Beneath the blue ogive of the firmament
Was a dead warrior, clutching whose mighty
    knees
Was a leman, who with her flame had warmed
    his tent,
For him enduring all men's pleasantries.

Close by the sable stream that purged the plain
Lay the white stallion and his rider thrown,
The great beast had spilled there his little brain,
And the little groin of the knight was spilled by
    a stone.

The youth possessed him then of a crooked
    blade
Deep in the belly of a lugubrious wight;
He fingered it well, and it was cunningly made;
But strange apparatus was it for a Carmelite.

Then he sat upon a hill and bowed his head
As under a riddle, and in a deep surmise
So still that he likened himself unto those dead
Whom the kites of Heaven solicited with sweet
    cries.

(The version quoted is from *Poems and Essays*, 1955, the most readily available collection of Ransom's poetry; it has been slightly revised.)

On first reading this poem one is impressed by the knowing antiquarianism, the light, almost mincing manner, and the all-suffusing irony—qualities to be found throughout the poems Ransom wrote during the next six years on which his reputation as a poet is established. In this period he took much of his diction and imagery from the literature of an interval beginning with Caxton and Malory and extending to Milton, who was the subject of a course he taught at the time. Some words, such as *springe, thole, frore, halidom, ounce* (leopard), *bruited,* and *lordings,* suggest the chivalric romance (and the later *Faerie Queene* and *Idylls of the King),* while others, such as *perdure, concumbant, pernoctated, diurnity, ambulant, theogony,* and *saeculum,* recall the latinate language of Renaissance scholars—not so much of Milton, though the latinism of Milton's language fascinated Ransom, as of Sir Thomas Browne and Jeremy Taylor. Remembering the southern interest in knighthood and all its heraldry and ritual, in colorful language, and in the trappings (if not always the substance) of classical learning, one might suppose that such antiquarianism, certainly, is a distinctive mark of the southern poet. It is an easy and convenient supposition, but one would be wise not to go beyond saying that Ransom's southern background probably encouraged it. For one thing, there is an important difference between his use of such material and that of a county laureate losing himself in a dream of fair ladies or evoking the Golden Age before The War. Ransom's is more critical and more learned. He had gone back to the original sources. Thus when he wrote "Necrological" he had been reading medieval and Renaissance history and the poem was based on an episode in the career of Charles the Bold, Duke of Burgundy (1433–1477). The words and images that evoke the remote and glamorous age of chivalry are juxtaposed against blunt, commonplace, and notably unpoetic ones and the delicate tints and languorous lines of romance are set beside the harsh colors and angles which characterize the brute facts of man's condition. Thus we have the trumpets glittering in the distance under the bright blue sky, the curious weapons, the raptorial lords, the faithful mistress, and the monastery in the background. But the bodies are half-eaten, the sword has been thrust ungallantly through the knight's belly, the arrogant virility of the warrior is now but a little groin spilled by a stone,

and the stupidity of this whole way of life is suggested by the little brain of the great stallion (the cult of the horse being central to both the chivalric romance and the feudalism of the Old South) and by the small account taken of so much death and despoliation.

Here, too, were most of the themes Ransom engaged in his mature poetry: the mixed vitality and mortality of flesh, beauty, and love; the disparity between the ideal (the "meads of asphodel") and the actual ("the postured bones lie weather-beaten"); the inadequacy of abstractions such as the friar's dogma in accounting for the range and complexity of man's experience and feelings; and the conflict between duty and desire. Again and again these themes and others like them reappear in the poems and offer a picture resembling the spheres sometimes seen on ancient maps—one sphere representing the world of the heart's desire and the other the world as it truly is; or, to put it somewhat differently, one representing the world as the Hegelian intellect would have it—orderly, predictable, amenable to man's needs and uses—and the other the world known to the poet (if he be a realist)—disorderly, contingent, and indifferent to man. The double vision of the subjects is sustained by the pluralism of their treatment. Mention has been made of the mixing of the rare and the commonplace in diction, but this is only part of the technique which combines the contemporary with the archaic, the lay with the learned, the informal with the formal, the written with the colloquial, and the terse rooted in Anglo-Saxon with the polysyllabic rooted in Latin and Greek. So too the handling of images and tropes: the charming is poised with the disgusting, the dainty with the coarse, the novel with the banal. Even the rhymes and meters mingle extremes of regularity and irregularity, the almost predictable with the wholly unexpected. Conjunctions that would have seemed clumsy in the contexts of the earlier poems now added depth and intensity to the work.

Behind the themes and style was a conception of the mind of as much importance to Ransom's writing as the attitude toward abstractions with which it was closely associated. Ransom believed that man had once been nearly whole and his apprehension and response, though incomplete, had been integrated and effective; but now man was riven into reason and sensibility, which had small communion, with the result that his apprehension was confused and fragmented and his response crippled or even paralyzed. Freud, Eliot, and the bewildering tempo and variety of modern life have helped to make the dissociation of the intellect one of the most pervasive and familiar themes in contemporary literature. But Ransom's conception, though it resembles the binary image of the mind put forward in Freud's early speculations, was essentially his own and derived with his fury against abstractions from his observations. He modified it in small ways after reading Kant, Coleridge, Bergson, and Freud, but the strongest outside influence on it was the traditional Hebraic-Christian belief in the conflict of the body and soul, with which, if one allows for a radical shift in attitude, it has close affinity. It underlay his poems of the Fugitive period and all of his thought and writing thereafter down to the latest effort to account for the mingled medium of verse.

As Ransom saw it, the reason delighted in universal patterns in the world's body which it wrenched forth for inspection and possible use. The sensibility delighted in all the sensuous qualities of particulars including the overplus which by its superfluity, uniqueness, or plain contrariness could not be brought under the patterns beloved by the reason. When the reason and sensibility worked together, man was stable and healthy. The reason managed his practical affairs and the sensibility enabled him to enjoy the color and variety of his experience. Moreover, the reason brought a degree of order and meaning to his life, while the sensibility reminded him of the ultimate insufficiency of his universals and kept him from expecting more order and meaning than was possible. But since the beginning of modern science the reason had scored such spectacular successes in dealing with material things that it had become arrogant and tyrannical. It boldly denied the validity of any truth or the value of an experience which did not accord precisely with its abstractions. Taking into account only its own version of the world it formulated misleading or impossibly stern concepts of Duty, Honor, Work, and Self-Denial which denied the sensibility its harmless pleasures. It suspected beauty, art, manners, and love of being subversive. Except in such places as the easygoing South, where a conservative people clung to a way of life under which the sensibility could still prevail, contemporary life had become dismal and man quite misunderstood his own nature. With each day he became more conceited and more miserable.

"Necrological" is certainly much more than a parable upon this conflict. The convolutions of its irony turn back upon themselves so often that it is difficult to say just what it is. Yet in the friar one has a rough equivalent of modern man made indecisive by the conflict within. The friar finds that his little formulas ("it is easy he thought to die," "heroes' flesh was thus./Flesh fails") are not enough to explain away the fascination of the warriors' life, grisly as it may be. He is another victim left upon the battlefield. He is also the man who lives outside the code.

It would have been easy, particularly for a

southerner, to have written a poem comparing a drab friar with a gay and lusty knight, an inhibited man of ideas with an ebullient man of feeling and action. In the struggle between the reason and the sensibility, Ransom was all for the latter, and one knowing this but unfamiliar with his inveterate skepticism and his habit of looking at all things from several angles might expect him to extoll the gallant cavaliers of Milady Sensibility. But Ransom understood well enough that beneath their gorgeous panoply all knights were simply men. Glorifying action and feeling at the expense of ideas was as much a falsification as the excessive abstraction of the rationalists. He had a certain wry sympathy with the romantic temperament, but he thought the tendency to exalt emotion and sensuous experience to be potentially misleading and dogmatic in its own way. He took sides with the sensibility because he thought it was oppressed under the present regime, not because he wanted to see it dominate human behavior and values.

As a matter of fact, however, his poem "Armageddon" did use the drab ecclesiastic and the colorful cavalier to dramatize the conflict and, indirectly but unmistakably, to satirize the puritanical North and the indulgent South. The stereotypes were employed deliberately to tease and startle the reader, for the "parfit gentil knight" is Satan and the cleric Christ Himself.

Antichrist, playing his lissome flute and merry
As was his wont, debouched upon the plain;
Then came a swirl of dust, and Christ drew
    rein,
Brooding upon his frugal breviary.

Now which shall die, the roundel, rose, and
    hall,
Or else the tonsured beadsman's monkery?
For Christ and Antichrist arm cap-a-pie,
The prospect charms the soul of the lean jackal.

They do not fight. After an exchange of courtesies, they retire to the nearby hall of Antichrist, where Christ gives up his cassock for a more fashionable garb and even allows his hair and beard to be dressed and scented.

And so the Wolf said Brother to the Lamb,
The True Heir keeping with the poor Impostor,
The rubric and the holy paternoster
Were jangled strangely with the dithyramb.

But one of Christ's followers, outraged at the spectacle of the two princes banqueting and peacefully conversing on theology and the arts, reminds Christ of his duty and the ancient struggle is taken up once more:

Christ and his myrmidons, Christ at the head,
Chanted of death and glory and no
    complaisance;
Antichrist and the armies of malfeasance
Made songs of innocence and no bloodshed.

The immortal Adversary shook his head:
If now they fought too long, then he would
    famish;
And if much blood was shed, why, he was
    squeamish:
"These Armageddons weary me much," he
    said.

Despite the feebleness of the last foot, the poem is pleasantly clever and deftly mantained throughout most of its eighty lines, but when the reader has gotten over his surprise at seeing Christ depicted as the bloodthirsty Wolf and Satan as the gentle Lamb, he may find it less interesting and meaningful than "Necrological" —more a series of witticisms, all of about the same sort, than an ironic and penetrating study of the confusion of values. The joke is exceedingly well told, but it lacks the force of Ransom's best work.

To dramatize the conflict of honor and desire, Ransom again deployed the imagery of medieval warfare in "April Lovers," which belongs to the period of "Necrological," and in "The Equilibrists," one of his latest and best poems. Such imagery helped to bring into the poems faint but appropriate echoes of the metrical romances about Tristram and Iseult and other figures in whom the same conflict raged. In "The Equilibrists," the man, remembering his beloved's "Long white arms and milky skin," thinks of her body as "a white field ready for love." But down from the gaunt fortress of her mind grey doves come flying to warn him away.

Predicament indeed, which thus discovers
Honor among thieves, Honor between lovers.
O such a little word is Honor, they feel!
But the grey word is between them cold as
    steel.

Eventually

. . . these lovers fully were come
Into their torture of equilibrium;
Dreadfully had forsworn each other, and yet
They were bound each to each, and they did
    not forget.

Death brings no surcease. They can neither ascend bodiless to Heaven nor descend honorless to Hell. But the vibrance of their suffering sends forth an immortal radiance, and any stranger wandering by is warned by their epitaph to let them lie *perilous and beautiful.* Ransom, who would rarely settle for one view, discovered incandescence in an analogue of the very division he deplored, but only because the desire was as powerful as the dogma. The fearful opposition keeps them delicately and beautifully poised above the abyss instead of exploding and hurling them into confusion and darkness. One might add that such exquisite balancing of powerful opposing forces in the organization of his poems was a particular characteristic of Ransom's style. He liked to work on a narrow line where one false move would plunge him into the ludicrous and sentimental or worse still into archness. He did not often slip.

These lovers cannot seize the day because like those in "Vaunting Oak" they are "instructed of much mortality" and for them the act of love is destructive; in "April Lovers," for example, it would reduce the beloved to "an unutterable cinder." Ransom himself was so instructed, and this may help to explain his insistence on permitting the sensibility to enjoy the ephemeral pleasures of the natural world. With his double vision he saw death precisely where the greatest energy and beauty seemed triumphant, and evil and suffering patiently waiting where innocence and joyousness seemed most secure. Often he chose children or adults having a childlike simplicity to show the abrupt and unwarranted invasions of death and misery. "Bells for John Whiteside's Daughter," his best-known poem, stresses the unexpectedness and shock of death by focusing on a little girl's seemingly boundless energy. "First Travels of Max" (which is not in *Selected Poems* or *Poems and Essays* but may be found in *Chills and Fever*) and "Janet Waking" treat the effect of the invasion on the child itself, a favorite subject of Ransom's friend, Robert Penn Warren.

In the first poem, which is Ransom's equivalent of Warren's "Revelation," little Max, who has slapped his nurse and quarreled with his sisters, goes to Fool's Forest, armed with a stick, which he pretends is St. Michael's sword, a stone, which he has commanded to become a "brandnew revolver," and innocence, which he has impaired by squabbling and neglecting his prayers. He meets the Devil and a Red Witch "with a wide bosom yellow as butter." After promising to return and cut off her head, he flees to his sunny lawn. But the witch's laugh goes with him. Things, he has discovered on his first travels, are not as Nurse and the storybooks said. In "Janet Waking," we are shown a little girl exactly as she might appear on the pages of, say, the *Ladies' Home Journal*:

Beautifully Janet slept
Till it was deeply morning. She woke then
And thought about her dainty-feathered hen,
To see how it had kept.

One kiss she gave her mother.
Only a small one gave she to her daddy
Who would have kissed each curl of his shining
   baby;
No kiss at all for her brother.

"Old Chucky, old Chucky!" she cried,
Running across the world upon the grass
To Chucky's house, and listening. But alas,
Her Chucky had died.

A "transmogrifying bee" had killed him, and Janet, "weeping fast as she had breath,"

. . . would not be instructed in how deep
Was the forgetful kingdom of death.

Nowhere does Ransom mix his modes with more steely control. He tricks the reader into a mawkish stock response, then with the absurd bee (the noun staggering under the weight of the Johnsonian adjective) and the old barn yard fowl jerks us back into the real world, where we are shown Janet waking to a new and dreadful knowledge. We, too, waken to an understanding of how inadequate is our idealized and sentimental conception of childhood and the feelings of children.

Yet, though he ridicules sentimentality and regards romanticism with distrust, he shows a grudging admiration for those ingenuous ones who manage, against all contrary experience, to preserve their innocence and their aspirations. To describe them he turned to *märchen* and the world of Mother Goose and Grimms' fairy tales, a world of cottages, burghers, buxom housewives, and aged eccentrics such as Tom, the piper's son who was "privy to great dreams, and secret in vainglory" but proved in the end not to be a changeling prince. In "Captain Carpenter" he brought together the conventions of both *märchen* and chivalric romances to describe a not quite indestructible Don Quixote. The good captain is little Max gone back to Fool's Forest, which is simply the world. Or, rather, he isn't Max, for the child learned that evil was too much for him, but the captain never does, and the poem is really about the terrible cost of such innocence: its failure in the practical realm, its triumph in the realm of the spirit. Like Conrad, Ransom had a certain tenderness for those so sure of the rightness of their transparently simple code of behavior that they never think of giving up. Captain Carpenter is his version of Captain MacWhirr. He himself is Marlow, without Marlow's nihilistic despair. Ransom has seen how badly men can behave, but he has never conceded that Man is absurd.

If we follow his lead and omit *Poems about God*, we may think of Ransom's career in poetry as overlapping the span of *The Fugitive*, from April 1922 until December 1925, by a little at each end. When it was suspended he published some poems elsewhere, but after 1927 there were only four more: "Prelude to an Evening" (1934), "Of Margaret" (1934), "Painted Head" (1934), and "Address to the Scholars of New England" (1939). Throughout the interval of the magazine he had brought one or two poems in virtually their final form to the fortnightly meetings of the group. From these and a few others he took seventy-nine poems and a sequence of twenty-one sonnets for his two volumes, *Chills and*

Fever (1924) and *Two Gentlemen in Bonds* (1927). When preparing his *Selected Poems* for publication in 1945, he dropped the sonnet sequence altogether and kept only forty-two poems, five of which had not been published in the earlier volumes. For his *Poems and Essays* (1955) two poems were recovered from *Two Gentlemen in Bonds*, bringing the total to forty-four. In his opinion, therefore, fewer than half of his mature poems deserved reprinting. One might wish to see some of the omitted poems included, but it cannot be denied that Ransom chose his best pieces. There is scarcely a weak poem and but a few weak lines in the lot, and from it one may fairly determine the definitive qualities of his verse and decide for oneself its ultimate value.

The qualities are striking, for Ransom is one of the great stylists of modern American poetry. Here is poetry of unabashed elegance and artifice, both carried at times to the edge of affectation and preciousness. This poetry is *made* and proudly exhibits its technical ingenuity. It is not smooth but angular and diffracting, and the lights that flash upon its surfaces come from many directions—from architecture, anatomy, and theology, to cite only a few. The allusiveness and the contrivance with clichés bring the poetry perilously near the pedant's tedious whimsy, but so tight is Ransom's control that where he incurs this danger, it is precisely the pedantry and whimsy that are mocked. Yet if learning is treated lightly, this is nonetheless poetry of the library and study. Probably only a literary scholar could have written it, and it demands some scholarship on the reader's part for its fullest appreciation.

All poetry stands at no less than one remove from the experience it treats. It is not a chunk of life but an aggregate of words which have their own forms that do not correspond exactly to the shape of the subject. Much of Ransom's poetry stands at two removes from the experience, for instead of looking directly at life he has, in many instances, looked into other works, into other aggregates of words such as the Bible, Shakespeare, sermons, bestiaries, seventeenth-century lyrics, nineteenth-century novels, and the chivalric romances and children's stories already mentioned. Yet in all the poems one finds few specific references and direct quotations. The opening lines of "Somewhere Is Such a Kingdom" typify his method, so different from elaborate mosaics of allusion and quotation in Pound's *Cantos* and Eliot's *The Waste Land*:

> The famous kingdom of the birds
> Has a sweet tongue and liquid words,
> The red-birds polish their notes
> In their easy practised throats.
> Smooth as orators are the thrushes
> Of the airy city of the bushes,
> And God reward the fierce cock wrens
> Who have such suavity with their hens.

Though there is not a single direct allusion, the poem points straight back to *The Parliament of Fowls* and the conventions of medieval beast tales and less directly to Chaucer's "Nun's Priest's Tale." The last lines refer to wrens, but one who does not know Chaucer's Chanticleer misses half their meaning.

Nowhere in the *Selected Poems* does one see a naturalistic setting and scarcely a single action or person is directly glimpsed. The landscapes of "Necrological" and "Armageddon" come from old tapestries and illuminated manuscripts. That haughty beauty, Emily Hardcastle, is observed through a bifocal lens which seems made up of Meredith and the Grimms with a faint tint from Young Lochinvar. The poet is present in his own person in only two poems, the very early "Winter Remembered" and the late "Prelude to an Evening." (Ransom is quite insistent that "Agitato ma non troppo" in *Chills and Fever* is not about himself, though the Fugitives who first heard it thought it was.) Elsewhere he assumes the persona of a sympathetic but somewhat obtuse observer. This, then, is poetry at once personal in style and impersonal in statement. Yet for all its artifice and reserve it is neither unrealistic nor unemotional. The style is deliberately offered as a thing of delight in itself, which it is. But it is also a means of looking at man from unique angles and communicating subtle and complex feelings about what has been observed.

The scholarship, eccentric conjunctions, irregularities, and latent violence have suggested to many readers a similarity with the poetry of John Donne. Ransom is after Edward Taylor, Emily Dickinson, and Wallace Stevens the most metaphysical of American poets if one does not count Eliot. But Ransom did not read Donne with much attention until after his style was formed and does not consider Donne to have had any influence on his poetry. Still, the resemblance goes beyond similarity of the styles and has some significance. Both poets wrote in periods of experiment and tumult following the collapse of feudalistic societies; both are poignantly aware of death in the midst of life; and both would have men live fully yet with knowledge of their true condition, and they mock the conformists for their timidity and the sentimentalists for nostalgic longings after a world that never was. Violence in Ransom's poetry is only apparently abrupt and disruptive; its effects are carefully balanced and distributed throughout the whole organization of the poem. One has the sense of powerful internal forces precisely poised and counterpoised within the hard, crystalline style and structure. The violence in Donne is frequently erratic. It gives an impression of

tremendous energy but it may work against the poem instead of accumulating intensity and meaning. Nevertheless, his poetry has more range and penetration: it dares to do more, and does.

But a serious comparison with Donne implies considerable praise, and to say that Ransom's poetry is for the most part more orderly but of smaller scope is not to suggest that it is foppish or trifling for all its studied manner. It has, at the last, a supremely important point to make: the world man has is far from being the world man wants and all too easily deludes himself into thinking he possesses. In support of this Ransom illustrates a few simple situations in a variety of ways with considerable resourcefulness. Man and all his works, he keeps showing us, fade and disappear; his delusions make him at once foolish and sublime; love frequently destroys what it most prizes; innocence can be preserved only by ignorance; small triumphs may be possible, but ultimate defeat is certain; and man has always been the same and has endured the same fate. That is not the whole story. The dimensions of the little fables and of the style itself restrict the vision and there are things beyond its compass to be observed and thought upon. But Ransom has looked long and hard at what falls within his scope and written well and truly of what he has seen. Now we too can see it.

In 1926 Ransom took a leave from teaching to write a book on aesthetics which was never published. In a letter to Allen Tate he observed that in poetry one found "Opposition and at the same time Reconciliation between the Conceptual or Formal and the Individual or Concrete. . . . They coexist." Beside this he added, "This obvious fact was what started me off years ago into this whole way of reasoning." His book was going to explain how this and other such coexistences were possible in the fine arts. But his explanation did not quite satisfy him and, as may be seen from the material cited at the beginning of this study, he was still looking for one some three decades later. Throughout his search he has clung to a distinction which he made in 1924 when he compared the monism of scientific exposition with the pluralism of poetry and added that "the excellence of art is in its superfluities, since it accompanies these abstracts [such as those in the statements of science] with much of that tissue of the concrete in which they were discovered," thereby "managing also to suggest the infinity of [the] original context." Here, in little, is the argument for the ontological significance of poetry which has been the central thesis of all his speculation on poetics and literary criticism.

Beginning with his assumptions about the divided mind, Ransom inferred that where science appeals to the reason, poetry and the other fine arts satisfy the whole man. The argument and phonetic design of a poem give pleasure to the reason; the variants on the design and the particulars through which the argument is developed delight the sensibility. "The purest aesthetic experience" is simply contemplation of "those infinities of particularity which are the objects of our world: the landscapes, the people, the flora, the merest things," and the aesthetic attitude "is definable with fair accuracy in the simple and almost sentimental terms: the love of nature."

Sometime after he had begun to elaborate this thesis Ransom used it in "Painted Head," one of his most ingenious poems. A portrait showing only the head of its subject reminds the speaker that such separation of the head and body

Stirs up an old illusion of grandeur

By tickling the instinct of heads to be
Absolute and to try decapitation
And to play truant from the body bush;

. . . .

And an image thus. The body bears the head
(So hardly one they terribly are two)
Feeds and obeys and unto please what end?
Not to the glory of tyrant head but to

The increase of body. Beauty is of body.
The flesh contouring shallowly on a head
Is a rock-garden needing body's love
And best bodiness to colorify

The big blue birds sitting and sea-shell flats
And caves, and on the iron acropolis
To spread the hyacinthine hair and rear
The olive garden for the nightingales.

In the "iron acropolis" and "rock-garden" are echoes of the "grey tower" among the lilies of "The Equilibrists." As metaphors representing the effects of contrary forces in man these do well enough. But insofar as they propose an actual and prevailing condition of the mind (for the mind-body division is really psychical) they represent an outmoded psychology which imposed considerable limitations on Ransom's speculation. It was one thing to use cleavage as a figure of speech: it was quite another to found a theory of science and poetry on it. But that is what Ransom was about.

Science, he wrote in 1929, is "simply the strict intellectual technique by which we pursue any of our practical objectives. . . . Science is pragmatic, and bent only on using nature." Science "cannot afford to see in nature any content further than what the scientific terms permit. As a way of knowledge it is possible to us only on condition that we anesthetize ourselves and become comparatively insensible." Having benumbed part of himself, the scientist is free to use "a superior cunning that enables him to get the objects of appetite out of nature faster, in greater purity, and in more abundance." Hence the scientific processes "crucify our organic sensibility while they drive furiously toward their abstracts," until science finally becomes "an order of experience in which we mutilate and prey upon nature; we seek our practical objectives at any cost, and always at the cost of not appreciating the setting from which we have taken them."

No one who has seen for himself what man has done to forests and rivers will deny that we do indeed mutilate and prey upon nature. But this is not science, no matter how much technology is present in the rape. Ransom simply did not know how utterly devoid of self-interest free scientific thinking is, how affectionately the scientist regards the natural material with which he works, how happy—even how gay—he feels when he plays freely with many kinds and combinations of vivid images and stumbles upon a hypothesis in virtually the same way that a poet comes to a brilliant and unforeseen phrase. It is true that the statement of his hypothesis may be exceedingly abstract and may appear wholly devoid of feeling to those who know nothing of the experience behind it. But one cannot reason back from the statement to the motives and the state of mind that produced it. This is what Ransom tried to do, and the consequence was a misconception of science and scientists which in turn led to the formulation of an oversimplified theory of the nature, content, and appeal of poetry and of the aims and procedures of criticism. The conception of the mind and the fury against abstraction which had served his poetry well when qualified by narrative and image now served his poetics ill. To the poems they gave a unique vision; to the critical essays they brought myopia. They also helped to involve Ransom in a curious excursion into public affairs.

In the summer of 1925 John Scopes was convicted at Dayton, Tennessee, of violating the state's new laws forbidding the teaching in public schools of any theory that man had evolved from lower forms. Actually, there had been two trials, one at Dayton and one in the northern press, which ridiculed the entire South as slothful, superstitious, backward, and depraved. At first the Fugitives regarded the courtroom trial as just a bit of midsummer madness, but as the attack in the press grew more outrageous, they became aware of loyalties to which they had never given any thought. Ransom, Tate, and Donald Davidson (who had been Ransom's first friend in what became the Fugitive group and who later brought Tate into it) wanted to answer the North, but they did not know where to begin. They believed that the old-fashioned, leisurely South had a more satisfying way of life than the progressive North, but literature, to which they naturally turned for confirmation, offered little support and virtually none was to be found among the other fine arts. Meanwhile, Ransom had been pursuing his speculations on science and poetry, and the more he thought about them, the more it seemed that poetry was but one of a number of analogous means of representing man's sense of the character and value of his experience. Among these were the other arts, religious rituals, public ceremonies, traditional codes of conduct, and, supremely, myth. All of these brought order and meaning into the flux of life without denying the presence and even the charm of contingency and particularity in the local scene—and without denying the mysteriousness and uncontrollableness of the universe. They had the pluralism he missed in science and the monistic philosophies. Suddenly he saw that he had an answer to the North, and in nine furious weeks of the summer of 1929 he wrote *God without Thunder*, a defense of southern fundamentalists for clinging to their myths as more sufficient and satisfying representations of life than the new rationalism.

Science and the modern liberal sects which tried to adapt themselves to it had made a benign scientist of God and failed to instruct man in the true nature of the universe and to prepare him for his often baffling fate. Above all, they made no allowance for evil. The fundamentalists, whatever their errors of fact, never forgot the wrathful God *with* thunder who created evil as well as good and whose ways were inscrutable. They had a myth which, by Ransom's definition, resorted "to the supernatural in order to represent the fullness of the natural" and was realistic in the same sense that literature may be. Trouble arose when man supposed that the representations of science, which lacked the "fullness of the natural," were the only valid ones.

In the course of this extraordinary book Ransom suggested that poetry, the arts, ritual, tradition, and the mythic way of looking at nature thrive best in an agrarian culture based on an economy dominated by small subsistence farms. Working directly and closely with nature man finds aesthetic satisfaction and is kept from conceitedness and greed by the many reminders of the limits of his power and understanding. But in an industrial culture he is cut off from nature. He gets into the way of thinking that machinery can give him limitless control over it, and he is denied the little indulgences of the sensibility. His arts and religions wither and he lives miserably in a rectilinear jungle of factories and efficiency apartments.

Tate and Davidson had long held the same view of agrarian and industrial cultures, and with Ransom they set about preparing a symposium, *I'll Take My Stand*, by "Twelve Southerners," which argued the superiority of the southern over the northern way of life. (Of the "Twelve" only Robert Penn Warren, along with Ransom, Tate, and Davidson, had been a Fugitive. Other Fugitives were either indifferent or opposed to the symposium.) Ransom contributed a "Statement of Principles" and an essay entitled "Reconstructed but Unregenerate," in which he rehearsed the arguments of *God without Thunder* and urged the South to remain essentially agrarian. But neither he nor any other contributor proposed a program of social action to preserve the southern way of life, for the Agrarians, as they were promptly called even though they were never a group in the sense that the Fugitives had been, were trying to define and defend values, not lead a movement. However, between the inception and the publication of the book the Great Depression began and the South was especially stricken. Critics of the book took the contributors to task for proclaiming the virtues of life on a southern farm when farmers of that region were bankrupt and many were being dispossessed. Agreeing that the agrarian culture was in mortal danger, Ransom and his friends did turn now to social action. Ransom himself wrote a book on economics (which was never published) and with the others joined associations, appeared in public debates, and wrote many essays, but except for stimulating discussion of regional problems they accomplished nothing. For one thing, they had overlooked the boredom and drudgery on a real subsistence farm. The nature they said man loved was not the nature most southern farmers worked with. They had attributed aesthetic richness and satisfaction to conditions which all too frequently permitted no development of taste and understanding and bred hostility toward ideas and the arts. Ransom was a bit like Captain Carpenter where agrarianism was concerned. His odd ideas of science and the human psyche had misled him into precisely the kind of innocent idealism he had so often satirized.

Throughout the hubbub over Agrarianism Ransom continued to ponder the nature of poetry, and in 1938 he gathered his deliberations in a collection of miscellaneous essays entitled *The World's Body*. Though he had emphasized the aesthetic satisfaction of the arts when defending an agrarian culture, his main concern in this book was ontological. All art, he had come to believe, originates in a sentimental attachment for beloved objects which the artist wishes to honor through his labor. It is essentially imitative; selection and arrangement of material are governed first by the need for verisimilitude, and the test of success is the accuracy with which it suggests the whole substance of the precious object. As a source of knowledge about the qualities of that object, a work of art is superior to any scientific account. Indeed, it is even better than the object itself because it cannot be used, it can only be contemplated. As ritual in human relations checks the appetites and enables men to savor occasions and persons, so the form of the work restrains thoughts of the biotic usefulness of the object and enables man to perceive qualities which he fails to take in while in the presence of the object itself. In poetry, the meter is especially effective in compelling a leisurely, undemanding study of the subject. Thus *cognition* is "the essential element in poetic experience"; aesthetic satisfaction amounts simply to enjoyment of the sensuous qualities and the rich particularity of both the subject and the poem, held together but not entirely contained within its argument.

His ideas were now in much the form they were to keep over the next twenty years, but they were not yet widely known when in the fall of 1937 he left Vanderbilt for Kenyon College in Gambier, Ohio. For some time his interest in Agrarianism had been waning, but his interest in criticism was greater than ever. As he told Tate soon after settling into his new position, there seemed to be a huge future for criticism and he hoped they might work to establish its foundations. An opportunity was not long in coming.

He was nearly fifty years old when the president of Kenyon asked him to serve as the editor of a new quarterly and thereby opened up to him a field which made him a famous and controversial figure throughout American letters. The original proposal was for a magazine devoted to the fine arts, philosophy, and public affairs, and a measure of Ransom's disenchantment with Agrarianism was his insistence that the magazine should concentrate on arts and letters and leave public affairs alone. He had his way and the *Kenyon Review* began publication in January 1939. The war nearly put an end to it, but Ransom and the college managed to keep it going, and over the next two decades, during which he served as its chief editor, Ransom made it one of the most influential journals in the nation. It showed its editor's predilections. Though it published some excellent stories and poems, particularly by new young writers to whom Ransom generously gave precious space (and helpful comments on manuscripts he could not take), the magazine's character and importance derived mainly from the essays on literature and criticism by Ransom, Tate, Warren, R. P. Blackmur, Kenneth Burke, and William Empson.

Most of these emphasized the distinctively poetic meanings of poems and the cognitive function of literature, which were the chief concern of Ransom's next book, *The New Criticism* (1941). For some time literary studies in America had concentrated upon the antecedents and social contexts of literature and upon furnishing reliable texts. Criticism that was more than simple impressionism tended to evaluate works in terms of their ethical, psychological, and political interest and efficacy. Scholarship had accomplished prodigious feats in gathering data for re-creating vanished cultures and facilitating understanding of works from the past. Criticism had sometimes unreasonably demanded that works prove their usefulness in bringing about nonliterary ends, but it had affirmed that literature was, among other things, the words of a man speaking of men to men and that these words had consequences which might be of human significance. Though he wished they would pay more attention to the poem as poem, Ransom had no quarrel with the literary historians; he did, however, feel strongly that much of the criticism was at fault for demanding that a poem be something other than it was and then scolding the poet because it was an inferior example of, say, an argument in favor of a more equitable distribution of the world's goods. Looking about he had found some "new" critics (most of whom had been in business for twenty years) who seemed to think, as he did, that poetry was a unique form of discourse and that the first business of the critic was to find out exactly what, in its own terms and its own way, a poem was saying that had not and could not be said elsewhere. Yet even these critics—Ivor Richards, Empson, Eliot, and Yvor Winters were the ones he singled out for discussion—did not go far enough to suit him, and he ended the book with a chapter entitled "Wanted: An Ontological Critic" which set forth his latest ideas about the special knowledge of the subject a poem might offer, how that knowledge got into the poem, and what the critic might be expected to do about it.

It is necessary to say something concerning the peculiar reputation of this book before going on to discuss Ransom's ideas, for its title was borrowed and bestowed upon a supposedly new movement over which much ink has been spilled, most of it wastefully. In the colleges and universities throughout the land were young men and women who had become impatient with traditional studies of literature. It seemed to them that whenever they wanted to talk about a poem, they were asked to talk instead about the life and times of the poet. If they got to the poem at all it was to consider it as an example of the poet's "thought" or to discuss problems relating to such matters as the date and accuracy of the text. The essayists writing for the *Kenyon Review* and other quarterlies seemed to them to be nearer the mark, and, taking Ransom's title for their own uses, they began to talk about the New Criticism in a way that alarmed and scandalized some of their elders. After the war they were joined by many veterans who were not inclined to give to academic authorities much more respect than they had accorded their officers. When told about the heroic labors of some literary historian or editor, they often responded with a blank stare or even a snort of impatience. They were interested in poetry and they were in a hurry: now how about getting to the point?

There may have been a subtler factor at work, too. In those first years of the Atomic Age when science was making such bewildering and terrifying advances and scientists, whether they wanted to or not, were making decisions on which the fate of mankind might hang, students of literature often had moments of panic in which it seemed that their subject was either obsolete or irrelevant and that no responsible adult should give to it the time and energy demanded by graduate study. At such times it was comforting to read what Ransom said about poetry as an act of "total cerebration" and a source of unique and indispensable knowledge, especially as his argument always included some genial and ironic patronizing of science for pretending that *its* knowledge was so grand.

Be that as it may, Ransom's name and his book's title became battle cries through which many troubled and rebellious young people worked off some of their hostility and frustration. This probably did a lot of good, but it did some harm as well. Many conventional scholars who had not bothered to read the "new" critics got the impression that there really was some sort of movement under way led by unschooled ruffians bent on setting fire to the groves of Academe. Rude things were said and terms such as *poet, critic*, and *historian* became positively insulting when used in certain companies.

As the supposed leaders repeatedly pointed out, there never was any New Criticism in the sense of a movement having headquarters, official publications, and a body of shared assumptions, though some of the more excitable defenders of traditional scholarship were sure there was and talked and wrote in such a way as to suggest that they looked under the bed every night lest Mr. Ransom be hiding there preparing to do some deadly mischief with a bound volume of his infamous review. What was new was exactly what Ransom had said it was: an attention to those details of the medium and content which differentiated the poetic statement from all others. One real gain that came of the hubbub was that despite all the confusion a generation of students, many of whom are now among our most perceptive teachers and critics, were convinced that their first responsibility is to find out what a poem is and what it means and that all the resources they can bring to bear upon this problem, including the historical, are valuable. For this Ransom deserves as much credit as any man, not simply as theorist and editor but as the friend and mentor of some of the finest and most influential minds in contemporary American letters and as the founder in 1948 of the Kenyon School of English (since 1951 the School of Letters at Indiana University), where graduate students wishing to supplement the conventional courses of the universities have been able to study with men such as Tate, Empson, and Kenneth Burke. If Ransom had done no more than help to bring about the new respect for poetry as a medium and the new devotion to its texts as well as to its textual problems, he would be a figure of lasting importance.

In view of the uproar it is surprising to find that in *The New Criticism* Ransom merely elaborates the assumptions already set down in *God without Thunder* and *The World's Body*. Poetry, he now said, was made up of a *structure*, consisting of the argument and the phonetic and grammatical forms (meter, stanza, sentence, and so forth), and *texture*, consisting of the independent qualities of the details of diction, imagery, sound, and the subject itself, which are luxuriant, unpredictable, and at times even irrelevant to the business of the structure. The texture tends to make the structure indeterminate; yet the process cannot be carried too far, for there must be a recognizable support for the texture. However, the structure can be "comfortably general" and only "weakly regulatory" and still discharge its function. The distribution of forces is a delicate problem which must be solved anew with each poem. In fact, "an almost quantitative rule might be formulated, as one that is suggestive if not binding: the more difficult the final structure, the less rich should be the distraction of the texture; and the richer the texture as we proceed towards the structure, the more generalized and simple may be the structure in the end."

Together the structure and texture present the most thoroughgoing account of the thingness of the subject that may be had, for the abstract universals explicit or latent in the determinate structure have been loosened and qualified by the texture and the final poem has the ambiguity and fullness of the actual world and experience of man. "To define the structure-texture procedure of poets," Ransom said a little grandly, "is to define poetic strategy." And "I cannot but think that the distinction of these elements, and especially of D M [the determinate meaning before the requirements of meter and other aspects of the determinate form have helped to loosen it up] and I M [the indeterminate final meaning of the poem resulting from the interaction of structure and texture], is the vocation *par excellence* of criticism."

In that last phrase one confronts some major limitations of Ransom's thinking. The "vocation *par excellence* of criticism" has always been and always will be determining the value of a work. Understanding obviously has to precede judgment, and Ransom has been right to insist all along that the only way to understand a poem is to read it as a poem and not something else. Moreover, he himself had suggested criteria of value before this when he called for verisimilitude and referred to the aesthetic satisfaction furnished by the details (or, to use his later term, the texture). But he neglected judgment while insisting upon cognition, and it was his dominating interest in the latter which led him into this extraordinary statement. Even when speaking of aesthetic value, he largely ignored the appeal of form. In 1936 he wrote to Tate, "You are looking, I believe, for something special in the aesthetic experience, whereas I can see only an ordinary sci-

entific or animal core plus glittering contingency." This is even more remarkable than it seems. Among the Fugitives Ransom had defended traditional forms and deplored the supposed formlessness of the modernists for whom Tate ardently campaigned. In his first poems he had tried to put a little punch into every line and in his later work he had mixed his modes and varied his forms to the very edge of disintegration; yet much of the distinction of his poetry was due to the superlative harmony, proportion, balance, and ultimate appropriateness and consistency he managed to impose upon widely varied and rebellious elements. Still, from what he has said about the nature of poetry and criticism it almost seems that Ransom, a poet of superb formal order, enjoys most what gets into the poem in defiance of such order.

And when discussing the content it is always the fidelity of the unique representation that he stresses. Nothing is said of the interpretation that inevitably comes as a consequence of the selection and arrangement of the materials even when interpretation is not at all an intention of the poet. Such interpretations, deliberate or not, ultimately derive from assumptions about the nature and value of the subject, though the assumptions may be quite unconscious. The "truth" of these assumptions is something the critic must take into account along with the precision with which the subject has been represented. Reading Ransom one gets the impression that ontological value is, like aesthetic interest, a quantitative function of the texture and the more of the latter, the merrier all around. As for the significance of the poem—how much its representation and interpretation matter—no mention is made of this. The nearest Ransom comes to engaging it is in his assumption that the subject is beloved (hence of importance at least to the creator) and in his strictures against the critics who judge poetry for its efficacy in practical affairs. These critics at least see that the human significance of a poem may be more than how accurately it limns its subject and how much glittering contingency it manages to carry along.

Even the claims for the ontological status of poetry are strangely confused. Ransom seems to make no adequate distinction between a statement that is *about* something and a statement that is supposed to be *like* something. A poem is a statement about something, but Ransom argues that a poem is a statement that is like its subject: their organisms closely resemble each other. "The confusion of our language," he wrote in *The New Criticism*, "is a testimony to the confusion of the world. The density or connotativeness of poetic language reflects the world's density." This seems innocent enough until one gets down to asking what he means by *testimony* and *reflects* and finds that he apparently believes the relation of the argument to the contingent details (or, later, of structure to texture) is essentially the same as the relation of the scientist's or philosopher's universals to the concrete body of the world. A poem has its own kind of being, which may be confused and dense, and the world's body has another kind, or rather, many another kind. Any knowledge we may acquire of the world's kind comes from what the poem states *about* it and not from any organic parallel between the poem and its subject. Ransom is probably right in claiming that the structure-texture combination has a unique ontological significance, but for all its sophistication and charm, his argument is an odd one for a theorist with so much experience as a poet.

It is so odd, indeed, that one wonders how Ransom came to have so much apparent influence. Standing at a distance, one sees that he has contributed little to a theory of poetry and criticism, and what he has rests on some shaky grounds—his conception of a compartmentalized mind, his idea of science, his views regarding the artist's love of nature (he himself wrote scarcely a single line describing nature), his unsatisfactory argument on the ontology of poetry. The climate of the times helped to make him, whether he would or no, the patron of the young Turks of American letters, but that alone could scarcely have given such weight to his views. Then one goes back to his books and all at once the suspect or eccentric assumptions seem far less important and his influence is much easier to understand. There is crankiness in them, but there is also much plain good sense. He may fool himself a bit about poetry, but he almost never fools himself or the reader about a poem. He wants to know what the lines before him mean and how they convey that meaning, and he keeps after them until he finds out. He respects the poem, and as teacher, editor, theorist, and critic, he has helped to make us respect it, too.

He will be one of the gainers from this. Inevitably his reputation in criticism will decline. The theories are too insubstantial and the criticism itself (of which there is surprisingly little, considering how much he wrote about it) is too occasional. But his reputation as a poet, which is high, will continue to rise. The more we follow his example and read poetry closely, the more we will prize his own, which is the best evidence he has given for the aesthetic interest and the ontological importance of the medium. It is exquisitely balanced and articulated; its texture is as rich and brilliant as Ransom himself could desire; and from it we learn things about the world's body we did not know before. What we learn is significant. Reading him we are at once delighted and made profoundly aware of what it is to be men with all the burden and glory of our contradictions.

This, I believe, is how Ransom, that genial pluralist, would like to have it.

Selected Bibliography

WORKS OF
JOHN CROWE RANSOM

SEPARATE WORKS

Poems about God. New York: Henry Holt, 1919.

Chills and Fever. New York: Knopf, 1924.

Two Gentlemen in Bonds. New York: Knopf, 1927.

God without Thunder: An Unorthodox Defense of Orthodoxy. New York: Harcourt, Brace, 1930.

The World's Body. New York: Scribners, 1938.

The New Criticism. Norfolk, Conn.: New Directions, 1941.

SELECTED POEMS

Grace after Meat. London: L. and V. Woolf, 1924.

Selected Poems. New York: Knopf, 1969.

OTHER WORKS

"Reconstructed but Unregenerate," in *I'll Take My Stand,* by Twelve Southerners. New York: Harper, 1930. (Ransom was principally responsible for the "Statement of Principles" in this book.)

"Criticism as Pure Speculation," in *The Intent of the Critic,* edited by Donald A. Stauffer. Princeton, N.J.: Princeton University Press, 1941.

The Kenyon Critics: Studies in Modern Literature from the Kenyon Review, edited by John Crowe Ransom. Cleveland: World, 1951.

Hardy, Thomas. *Selected Poems,* edited with an introduction by John Crowe Ransom. New York: Macmillan, 1961.

CRITICAL AND
BIOGRAPHICAL STUDIES

Special "Homage to John Crowe Ransom" Issue, *Sewanee Review,* 56:365–476 (Summer 1948).

Bradbury, John M. *The Fugitives: A Critical Account.* Chapel Hill: University of North Carolina Press, 1958.

Buffington, Robert. *The Equilibrist: A Study of John Crowe Ransom's Poems.* Nashville, Tenn.: Vanderbilt University Press, 1967.

Cowan, Louise. *The Fugitive Group: A Literary History.* Baton Rouge: Louisiana State University Press, 1959.

Knight, Karl F. *The Poetry of John Crowe Ransom: A Study of Diction, Metaphor and Symbol.* London: Mouton and Company, 1964.

Schwartz, Delmore. "Instructed of Much Mortality," *Sewanee Review,* 54:439–48 (Summer 1946).

Stewart, John L. *The Burden of Time: The Fugitives and Agrarians.* Princeton, N.J.: Princeton University Press, 1965. Pp. 1–306.

Warren, Robert Penn. "John Crowe Ransom: A Study in Irony," *Virginia Quarterly Review,* 2:93–112 (January 1935).

Williams, Miller. *The Poetry of John Crowe Ransom.* New Brunswick, N.J.: Rutgers University Press, 1972.

Winters, Yvor. *In Defense of Reason.* New York: Swallow Press and Morrow, 1947. Pp. 502–55.

Young, Thomas Daniel, ed. *John Crowe Ransom: Critical Essays and a Bibliography.* Baton Rouge: Louisiana State University Press, 1968.

—*JOHN L. STEWART*

Edwin Arlington Robinson
1869-1935

GRANTED a real talent and an access to experience, a poet deserves the name and earns it chiefly by his honesty. It is never enough that he be up with or beyond the times; who knows what those are? Technical feats rise, shine, evaporate, and fall, and there are unread poets who could have taught Shakespeare lessons in prosody. The sources from which poets "steal" metaphors and ideas often show the difference between knowing all about poetry and being a poet: it is not a matter of know how, for if it were, Abraham Cowley would be greater than John Milton and Edward Young than Samuel Johnson. What is necessary is to see and to say with that direct honesty of vision that is apparently accessible only to genius and is therefore to the ordinary critic the least readily detectable of poetic qualities. A passion torn to tatters, a fit of the vapors, or a commitment to slogans of whatever degree of sophistication does not argue a true poetic vision; what counts supremely is the double commitment to the Muse and to the view of things the Muse inspires. In many cases, poets take years to find the vision, to see it for what it is, and that seeing may be only momentary and fleeting, but we know ultimately whether the poet has seen indeed or whether he has merely faked and trumped up. Larger or smaller, deeper or shallower, vision truly seen

and honestly shown marks the poet, and it may be said fairly enough that in few instances have the contemporary critics shared enough of the visionary power or the honesty to see the poet's for what they are.

Edwin Arlington Robinson is a poet of true vision and unimpeachable honesty. Lest that sound forbidding—suggestive of something crabbed, angular, and inept—one should add that he had a consummate mastery of versification and rhetoric, that he could pile on the colors with the best of them, and that he had the inventiveness to tease the mind with symbol and intellectual puzzle. He indulged these capacities from time to time, the latter most frequently, but not until his later years did he allow them to assume the upper hand. All of Robinson's best work is the product of a sensibility that was on guard against fraud, that concerned itself with making into form what vision had discovered. The word "seeing" occurs frequently in Robinson, on various levels of seriousness and relevance; for this poet honesty is not so much what one has as what one tries to achieve after however much time spent among deceptions, lies, illusions. He knew a great many people, including members of his own family, who perished by such chimeras. He was born into, and grew to full maturity in, a time that is a kind of *locus classicus* for all lies on whatever scale. See Henry Adams, the later works of Mark Twain, and any history of the years just before the Great War and of that war itself. The era marked Robinson, for good and for ill. It disillusioned him with democracy and with the classic New England liberalism, and it "dated" him hopelessly in the eyes of the later generation of poets and literary folk.

To an older friend he wrote from his death-bed in the New York Hospital: "I doubt if you would care much for Auden and Spender. They are for the youngsters." It is not un-typical of the man that he should have read these poets and be in a position to speak of them, yet give the impression of being the old fogy; ironically he puts himself in the position of his correspondent, who was twenty years his senior, and sees perfectly the faults of that rigidity of taste and habit likely to come with age. The diffidence, the hesitancy, with which he always expressed and qualified opinions stayed with him all his life, even in the era of his apparent preeminence after achieving both fame and something like fortune. His fine poem "Hillcrest," written at the artists' summer colony in Peterborough, New Hampshire, which was founded and maintained by the widow of the musician Edward MacDowell, expresses his acute sense of the insignificance of human achievement and the ephemeral na-ture of any one man's claim to rightness. He was a considerable "lion" at the MacDowell Colony during his latter years and he enjoyed being lionized, yet he never forgot that ". . . great oaks return/To acorns out of which they grew." In 1925, with a Pulitzer prize and other awards to his credit (if that is the phrase!), he wrote thus to a friend asking for a *Blue Guide* to London: "I'm not going to London, but sometimes I like to take up that book. It is al-most as exciting as an illustrated seed cat-alogue, and far more reliable."

Small wonder that the generation of Pound and Eliot did not find Robinson's work and aesthetic congenial, chiefly because they never took the trouble to read him, but also, and understandably, because the era of which Rob-inson was inevitably part had finally ended in the hitherto unknown destructiveness of World War I. The period between the American Civil War and the War to End War may seem to us in retrospect not to lack appeal; to those who lived in it, like Henry Adams and Mark Twain, it seemed the shabbiest, most degrading of times. We can read their separate records of it: *The Education of Henry Adams* and *The Gilded Age*; in the latter. Twain created the most memorable of all fictional persons repre-sentative of the promoter in that raucous era, Colonel Beriah Sellers, the immortal specula-tor and harebrained proponent of get-rich-quick. He might well have been the spiritual godfather of Robinson and of his entire gen-eration.

Robinson's youth and young manhood, the years leading up to *The Torrent and the Night Before* (1896), seem to have been lived in a barren time indeed. He was born in the tiny village of Head Tide, Maine, in 1869, at the very dawn of the Gilded Age, and though the family moved very shortly thereafter to the larger town of Gardiner, Maine, on the Ken-nebec River, we today can see both the provin-ciality on the one hand and the national craze for speculation and wealth on the other which equally marked the Robinson family and many others of the period. Despite all that might be said of Maine's natural beauty, its classical New England heritage, its abiding interest in learning and literature, and its tough moral legacy of Puritanism (rather less severe in Maine than elsewhere in New England), the fact remains that the Gardiner of 1870–1900 was a typical American boom town with its trade in lumber, ice, and shipping as well as certain manufactures. The more substantial capitalists of the town had interests in western properties and speculative enterprises: lumber, land, railroads, mines. And just as the depredation of the land of Maine and other parts of the country typified the attitude of the exploiters, so did their driving, piratical Philistinism in the arts and culture generally set the tone of public and private taste. Poetry, real poetry, had to go underground. From the death of Emily Dickinson (and who had ever heard of her?) in 1886, and of Whitman in 1892, until the renascence at the time of World War I, there is almost literally nothing in the poetry of America. Stephen Crane died young and inchoate; all the early promise of Vachel Lindsay and Edgar Lee Masters turned to little or nothing much, and the one truly impressive, salient figure of this lonely time is that of the lonely, dedicated, self-deprecating man for whom, if ever for any poet, the time was out of joint.

Robinson's father had moved to Gardiner in anticipation of a boom in his business; he was concerned in the lumber trade and had ventured into speculation in western property. He was a man of a not insensitive nature and in different circumstances might have shown his oldest and youngest boys more sympathy. The poet's mother was a woman of some literary taste, though perhaps we may feel free to be skeptical of the quality of such taste as it impinged upon the sensibility of her son. It should be said that in Robinson's early years he read as poets usually do: widely, omnivorously, wholly without discrimination, and it may be that much that was bad had as strong an effect upon him as the good. Be that as it may, the good was not entirely lacking, in literature, education, and recreation. There was a literary set in Gardiner and notable among its members was Dr. Alanson Tucker Schumann, a physician and poet whose infatuation with poetry led him to Robinson when the latter was a boy in high school. Perhaps Robinson may have had him partly in mind when he spoke in "The Wandering Jew" of a "fealty that presents/The tribute of a tempered ear/To an untempered eloquence." But the boy learned a great deal from Schumann, particularly verse forms and a respect for them. Under that kindly tutelage Robinson wrote ballades, villanelles, rondeaus, and other forms so dear to the post-Pre-Raphaelite heart. Nor was the regimen anything but beneficial: Schumann was a taskmaster and Robinson learned a respect for scrupulous workmanship the results of which may be seen not only all through his work, but more directly in such early poems as the villanelle "The House on the Hill," which exhibits the typically Robinsonian merging of the old, traditional form with the laconic, sinewy plain diction that was both new and typical of the region, and "The Ballade of Broken Flutes," Robinson's statement of his mission as the bringer of a new kind of poetry. Is it mere coincidence that the poet's mother was descended from the family of America's first poet, Anne Bradstreet?

And of course Gardiner was the home of Laura E. Richards, the daughter of Julia Ward Howe who wrote "The Battle Hymn of the Republic." Mrs. Richards was an author and the friend of authors; whatever one may think of her taste and her own literary work, one must acknowledge both her great humanity and her insight. She practically dragged the young, shy poet out of hiding and into her ebullient, charming family, where Robinson found another home after his own had disintegrated. Here he found stimulation of various kinds: the companionship of Mrs. Richards, her architect husband, and their sons and daughters, and simple recognition as a poet. True, we may see in the influence of the family certain limiting factors, of taste and of ideas, but Mrs. Richards was certainly on sure ground in preferring and encouraging the lyrical rather than the philosophical Robinson. It would seem that Robinson himself took little advice from anyone throughout his career, but he took from the Richardses affection and a sense of identity as poet. Perhaps Miss Rosalind Richards is the woman of Hagedorn's hints (in his biography) and perhaps we shall know one day when the documents pertaining to the poet deposited in the Houghton Library at Harvard are made available.

Love and marriage were not to be for Robinson. Gardiner, the Tilbury Town of the poems, left a mark on him, in part because of its very nature as a town of its time and place and in part because of the personal tragedies and wounds he knew there. So many of the portraits of his early volumes seem drawn from life, his own or another's, that the reader never forgets what Gardiner meant to him always. For years the young man was to all intents and purposes an idler and a failure; the consciousness that he was so considered embittered him far beyond anything the actual opinion of his fellow townsmen seems to have warranted. Many admired and liked him, but it was not a merely parochial matter with Robinson: his response to the realization that he was indeed a poet is characteristically American. If art is considered trivial and idle in America, he might have said, then I can justify my life and work only by success. And success means publication and profits, money and position. After all, Gardiner, along with all America, strove mightily with Roscoe Conkling, the Stalwart Republican from New York, and President U. S. Grant for the power and the money that are success, and when in their turn Robinson's father and both brothers failed in the scramble, the young man might well have felt in his heart that he was doomed with the rest of his kin. He saw, in any event, a vision of American life that marked him permanently. The moral collapse of his brothers, on top of the horrible death by diphtheria of his mother and the disintegration of his father, could scarcely be accounted for by the philosophies and theologies of a century of New England storekeepers. After all, Puritanism no longer worked as a creed; Unitarianism had given way to Mrs. Eddy's gospel of Christian Science, and the sages of Concord provided pretty thin gruel to the hungry poet of the Grant-McKinley dispensation.

The young Robinson, classically, was a sensitive youth—he was born with his skin inside out, as he said himself—and though he had friends (friends were his passion) and loved his years at the Gardiner High School, he was always an enigma to his associates and to his family, who let him go his dreamy way, but scarcely thought that he would ever outshine the brilliant, handsome Dean, the oldest, or the driving, vital Herman, next in order. To a Freudian, all things are Oedipal and there is indeed a case for seeing in Robinson's life the familiar pattern of the unwanted third son, rejected, kindly enough, by the father and kept at a distance by a too-beloved mother. In his later years, Robinson seems to have gained help from a psychiatrist who was also a poet, Dr. Merrill Moore. Gardiner in the eighties and nineties knew no such amenities, and one may perhaps be permitted to feel a callous relief since if Robinson had the anguish, we have the poetry. Yet we must feel pity as well, for the years following Robinson's graduation from high school, with the exception of two at Harvard, must have been an almost unrelieved agony of soul. Dean, the star of the family, was breaking up under the influence of drugs; he contracted the habit while trying to force himself into the exhausting routine of a country doctor. The father, Edward Robinson, decayed physically while his investments vanished; Herman, now married and with two small daughters, somehow seemed to have lost his way. Colonel Beriah Sellers like a proper godfather had vowed things in Herman's name. Yet before the smash became total, E.A.R. had his two years as a special student at Harvard. Following a period of isolation and near-despair after his graduation from high school, Cambridge, Boston, and Harvard came as deliverers and saviors. The young poet learned something of languages and literatures, of taverns and aesthetics, of the theater and above all of opera, particularly Wagner. When the money gave out and he had to leave, he even then knew he had been saved, though Barrett Wendell, the critic and Harvard professor, years later, when Robinson told him he had to leave Harvard after two years, growled, "You were damn lucky." Perhaps he was.

Try as one will, one cannot help the conviction that throughout his life Robinson was the victim of the classic strategy of America with its artists, poets in particular, perhaps. It would seem that the formative years provide a diet too thin, too miserly and deficient in nutriment, the last years a regimen of indigestible fats: success, when and if it comes, comes with a vengeance, frequently confirming the artist in his worst faults and conferring on him both an authority of opinion beyond his competence and opportunities to sell not just his work but himself to commercial interests. But before Robinson could have reached any such position, he knew fully what neglect and unsuccess could be. His was for a time the world of the down-and-out, the panhandlers and outcasts. Abject poverty and slavery to alcohol went hand in hand. In later years he himself said that the only thing that saved him was that he never took a drink before six in the evening.

Yet the worst was isolation, isolation from the best minds of his time and from those whose work and thought might have been useful and encouraging to him. Kind, understanding, and helpful as Robinson's friends were (and indeed they kept him alive and in health for years with simple charity), they do not seem to us today men and women who could have helped him in his struggle to learn and to grow as a poet; in all humility, we must call them second-rate. Of the poets with whom he was well acquainted, three names stand out: William Vaughn Moody, Josephine Preston Peabody, and Ridgely Torrence, of whom the first two were far better known in their time than Robinson. There were literary figures of various shades of distinction among his friends and associates, notably Mrs. Richards, yet again there was none who seemed to have the insight into the true quality of his best work that would have helped the poet to grow. For all the voluminous correspondence with the literary and near literary which carried Robinson on through many years, there can be no escaping the conclusion that time, place, and circumstance conspired to deprive him of incentives toward development, growth, and change. His first book sets a pattern which will not be broken, and in his beginning is his end.

Robinson is a nineteenth-century product, a Romantic, and a scion of the New England stock. Did he not say himself that had he lived in the time of Brook Farm he would have been strongly tempted to go along? One can see in him the qualities that made a Jones Very, and although he repudiated both Thoreau and Emerson, as philosophers or thinkers, he admired Emerson's poetry, saturated himself in nineteenth-century prose and poetry, and generally conformed to the canons of taste of the sensitive, provincial, cultivated New Englander. It was some old atavistic urge that led him to Poe and to Hawthorne, to the darker side. He seems to have known nothing of Melville, though he liked Whitman and Twain, particularly the former, but it should be said that like most New Englanders of the age, his eyes were on England rather than his own country—for literature at least—and surely his love of Cowper and Crabbe shows how much more comfortable he was with traditional English verse than with that of the Decadents. He dismissed the *Yellow Book* as mere sensation. He seemed to feel kinship among poets of the nineties only with Kipling and Hardy. And all his tastes, like his ideas and convictions, came early and came to stay. In this as in so much else he is typical of his race and milieu, the New England eccentric with the eccentricity raised to genius and the right to his crotchets confirmed and made great by virtue of his earning and living that right to the end and with the utmost rigor. It is not too much to say that Robinson worked out to its conclusion and at large what Emily Dickinson, tentatively, found and named in the decay of the New England sensibility. The tradition still lives, and strongly, in the work of Robert Lowell, in whose dramatic soliloquies or monologues one may find the plain, vital influence of Robinson and his peculiar, involute syntax. *The Mills of the Kavanaughs* is Lowell's obeisance—and perhaps farewell—to his master.

After the destruction of family ties, for the most part, with Gardiner, Robinson went to live in New York, where he stayed almost without intermission, except for long summers at the MacDowell Colony, until his death in 1935. He knew poverty so great that he was often without proper food and clothing and lived on the charity of his friends. His first books made no impression on the "little sonnet men" who reviewed for magazines, nor did any periodicals think it worthwhile to publish this unknown when after all Clinton Scollard and George Edward Woodberry and many another sweetsinger were the acknowledged masters. Robinson's first two books were published at

his own expense and that of friends, and the manuscript of *Captain Craig* (1902) languished in a brothel until the editor who had left it there came back, not presumably for the manuscript. He turned it down in any case. In 1905, President Theodore Roosevelt, who had heard of Robinson's work through his son Kermit, found a place, a sinecure, in the New York Custom House for the poet, and for four years Robinson knew financial independence. He also knew bondage to drink. At any rate, he did not write much in these years at the Custom House; it was an extended period of frustration which finally disappeared, and in 1910 he published *The Town Down the River*.

In this volume we may see the typically Robinsonian themes and approaches, but with possibly three exceptions, none of the poems represents the finest he could do. "For a Dead Lady" surely shows him at his best in one of his veins, and to a lesser extent and in a less formidable vein, "Two Gardens in Linndale." And "Momus" has a terse, bitter strength that characterizes the epigrammatic strain that is one of his most pungent. It would appear that in these years Robinson was looking for a stance, a position from which to view his own experience and his ideas. As he grew older and took to writing the long narrative poems, his tendency to become oracular, cryptic, and philosophical by turns overcame the achieved starkness of his view; moreover in his letters one may find evidence that Robinson, when he was at his best as poet, had no thoroughgoing idea of his own best qualities. At one time a young lady who was writing a graduate thesis on the philosophy in his work wrote to ask him certain questions. In his reply he told her that he wished she could concern herself less with the philosophy and more with the poetry, a recommendation we may properly wish the poet himself had adopted. For the fatal New England fascination with cloudy abstractions miscalled thought or profundity overcame Robinson and he never broke the spell, except as it would seem almost inadvertently. Even in as interesting a long narrative as *Amaranth* (1934) the nightmare atmosphere, the very real subject, the grim humor, and the subdued lyricism frequently get lost in the interminable rehashing of Favorite Transcendentalisms: what is Truth? or Reality? In the Arthurian trilogy of a few years before we can see much the same tendency.

Robinson is a late Romantic, a Victorian, a transcendentalist whose lust after the abstract was inveterate and nearly always, when indulged, destructive. The moment of stasis, of balance, when he treats the Vast with steady eye and nerve, is to be found in "The Man against the Sky" in the volume of that title (1916); he met the subject with all its imponderables and impalpables head on in that poem, and never fully recovered. Although "The Man against the Sky" solves nothing—and it is of course unfashionable to do other than dismiss it—it nonetheless seems to be almost the last time in literature (Western) when a poet singlehanded calls down the Eternal Verities and Cosmic Powers and asks them to declare themselves. It is an altogether remarkable performance and would have been wholly impossible for a more "sophisticated" poet; one knows why Mr. Eliot characterized Robinson as "negligible"; the direct attack is hardly the Eliot strategy.

Yet there are times and poems that put real questions and often imply real answers. Essentially, like any good poet, Robinson is less the philosopher than the metaphysician, and the question for him is the old ontological one. "The Man against the Sky" sums up the essence of Robinson's thought and feeling on the subject, thought and feeling which when they are working poetically prompt most of his best work, in both shorter lyrics and the poems of middle length. How does a man reconcile the idea of a beneficent, omnipotent God with the naked and frightening facts of existence? "What inexorable cause/ Makes time so vicious in his reaping"? God or no God, for Robinson the true question is this: Is there a life after this one? If so, then it is all worth it, the suffering and the terror. If not, then why live? Yet in fact men do not often commit suicide, a phenomenon which Robinson seizes upon as a kind of proof that man does not end with the grave. Again and again, he will assert his belief in immortality and the ultimate importance of this life, while he utterly rejects materialism. Everywhere, in the poems, letters, and reported comment, such a deliberate choice of belief crops up, implied or stated. For all their polarities of style and rhetoric, "The Man against the Sky" and Wallace Stevens' "Sunday Morning" are complementary and classical views of the single question, and clearly emerge less from differing philosophies than from opposed temperaments. There is a will to doubt as well as to belief, and the existentialists' answer is not the only possible one. If truly philosophical influence on Robinson's views can be found, it seems clear, from Mr. Stevick's essay mentioned in the bibliography at the end of this essay, that William James played the leading part in such influence. Yet even here it should be noted that James himself emphasizes that in dealing with such matters, he has entered the realm of metaphysics, and Robinson's discomfort under the rubric "philosopher" ought to be taken at least as seriously as any quasi-philosophical propositions he may seem to enunciate.

Robinson was a poet and poems are made with words, yet as a man so conspicuously of his century and heritage he was often at war with mere language and all unknowingly. By his own testimony it was words that fascinated him, that made and kept him a poet and a fine one, though the New Englander and the Victorian in him insisted that he must be the Seer, the Prophet, the Unacknowledged Legislator. Small wonder that in the direct conflict of these tendencies poetry is sometimes annihilated, and grist to the Ph.D. mill accumulates. This is not to say that Robinson had no mind and no ideas; it is simply that he mistook speculation in verse for poetic thought, as did unnumbered nineteenth-century writers before him. Still, each time he got a long poem out of his system and had as it were satisfied the Transcendental Philosopher in him, he could turn to real poetry again, and in *The Three Taverns* (1920) and *Avon's Harvest* (1921) he published some half-dozen of his best poems; even in the volume *Dionysius in Doubt* (1925), the last of his books containing short lyrics, there are two of his best sonnets, "New England" and "The Sheaves," and one or two others of real quality. But after that, there are only the long narratives, for the most part one each year up to his death. Of these, only *Amaranth* would seem to bear repeated reading, and that in part for reasons not wholly artistic.

He had in a sense become a Man of Letters in the solid nineteenth-century sense of the term and the punctual appearance of a new volume seemed necessary to him—not, one supposes, because he needed the money as he himself claimed, but because publication, so long denied him, was both compensatory and reassuring. It made him as poet real to himself; when there was no book, there was no poet and no man, for rarely has an American poet lived in and for his work as did Robinson. One might say that apart from it, he had no life at all, at least after he went to New York to live. "If only they had said something about me! It would not have mattered what. They could have called me stupid or crazy if they liked. But they said nothing. Nobody devoted as much as an inch to me. I did not exist." If this,

Robinson's own statement, is not absolutely true, it is near enough to full accuracy to convey the near-despair the poet must have felt during the years of total neglect. Friends helped, as did alcohol until it interfered with the poetry and then it was alcohol that had to go. But the lean years made a permanent and damaging mark on Robinson as poet, though they seem to have deepened his capacity as a man for the understanding of suffering, loneliness, and despair, as many of his letters testify. Deliberately reticent for fear of damaging self-exposure, he seems to have become more and more committed to one of his less attractive poetic characteristics, that of overqualification. Even in his letters, as apparently in conversation, his statements are frequently qualified by a deprecatory admission that the exact opposite may well be the case. Eventually this not unattractive personal quality is to become a stylistic tic and finally almost a major poetic device. In "Eros Turannos" we can note the modifying, qualifying lines and phrases. By the time of the long narratives, the tendency has solidified and we observe the not uncommon phenomenon of a poet's self-parody: his complication of the simple and his propensity for giving to us for complex what is merely complicated and obscured, in other words, overqualified. These lines for *Cavender's House* (1929) illustrate the point:

He knew there was a woman with two hands
Watching him, but he saw no more of her
Than would assure him she was there. He feared
To see her face, and he feared not to see it;
And then he found it as it was before,
Languid and unrevealing. Her eyes closed,
And her lips moved as if repeating words
That had no meaning. . . .

Robinson tried, over a period of years, to write drama and fiction that would make some money—to no avail—and one suspects that in this case failure derived from a shortcoming he himself pointed out: he had no real subject. He later destroyed all his manuscripts of fiction, but two Ibsenite plays were published which leave no doubt that what is a bore in the poems is equally so in the plays. The truth is that the lack of a real subject in his later years, coupled with a growing inaptitude for straightforward storytelling, finally rendered narrative for the most part unavailable to him. The lines just quoted show how far he has come from the concrete and the sensuous and he will go even farther. Yet up until the last ten years of his life he was capable of first-rate work in various stanza forms, notably the sonnet.

Neglect, near-despair, and poverty had formed him and they worked themselves out to the bitter end even in the days of success. "Why don't they *read* me?" he would ask in mock despair. It was, and is, a good question and one surely that many a poet would like a fit answer to. They didn't read him because they did not like his tone of voice. For all that has been written of Robinson's originality, one is hard put to it to say precisely where the innovations lie. He is simple. Yet his vocabulary is frequently polysyllabic and his metric jingly and derived. He seems rarely to be aware of the natural world or of the city, or if he does use the city as locale it is only in the vaguest, most perfunctory way as a stylized background. None of the qualities we associate with the Imagists, with Pound or Eliot, or with the ferment of the period is here, nor is there a trace of Frost's feeling for and against nature and rural New England. Even as serenely autumnal and lovely a poem as "Isaac and Archibald" lacks the specific and the minutely noted detail we think of as central to "nature poetry," whatever that may be. It is far closer to Wordsworth than to Frost and perhaps to Cowper than to either of the others in feeling. But one cannot read Robinson expecting certain things and

find what he has to tell. If in his own time editors and others dismissed him because they thought his work grim and "pessimistic" they were at least nearer the right track than those who, enamored of the Great Rebellion, thought of him as a stuffy, mindless Yankee who had failed to get the word. The fact is, of course, that Robinson, between two movements and two worlds, could not be accepted by either. When triumph and commercial success came, they came late and for the most part in response to relatively inferior work.

Robinson loved words. Shy and almost wholly inarticulate in company, he wrote with great labor and with total absorption; not unexpectedly, therefore, he frequently confused best and worst in his work and failed to see where the logic of his own poetic intelligence took him. In his love of the involute and the tangential, he is kin to Henry James; in his fascination with language and metric, to Tennyson. But in his penetrating, naked vision of the reality that underlies human predicaments he seems close to the French novelists of the late nineteenth century and to Ibsen. He professed dislike of Flaubert and he sometimes inveighed against the sexual concern of many of the naturalists, yet Zola and Whitman cast a spell on him, however briefly. Kipling's capacity to make poetry out of the commonplace interested and excited him, but more than all of these there was a Yankee eclecticism of language that made him go anywhere for words that would when pressed together make something hard, curious, and impenetrable. Milton, Shakespeare, Browning, Crabbe, Tennyson, Cowper, and a host of Romantics supply part of the vocabulary and the subject matter a vocabulary discovers for itself.

And what is the subject? the temper of it and the tone in which it comes to us? "When the stars are shining blue/ There will yet be left a few/ Themes availing—/ And these failing,/ Momus, there'll be you." Here is one of the faces of his Muse, and another was Pity; not tenderness or really what we would call sympathy, but pity for poor souls caught in the trap that their own weakness and fate have combined to spring. Viewed from the modern point of view, many of the best poems lack what is called compassion, as witness the destruction of Pink, Miss Watchman, and Atlas in *Amaranth*. We somehow demand that the poet express a feeling for the fates of his doomed victims. Robinson will not gratify the common expectations, for he is concerned to show the plight and to imply the terror and the rigor of the doom—a doom, one sees, both merited and gratuitous. When this fate is a secretion from the poem and not its nominal subject, the poem is likely to be terse, packed, and utterly objective: the poet presents certain people in certain predicaments and tells what happened. In nearly every case we can see that the issue is one of illusion overcoming the sense of reality. At times illusion is shown as something a character wills and achieves; a state which the person deliberately chooses as preferable to actuality or as providing the only alternative to suicide. Job's wife, Robinson implies, is the stern realist and recommends to Job that he "curse God and die." She has seized "the swift logic of a woman." But though many of Robinson's fated creatures do indeed doom themselves by failing to "see," as he puts it, there are occasionally those who, staking their lives and honors on "illusions," come through triumphantly.

Conrad might have understood these poems had he known them. For Robinson as for Conrad, illusion is the very stuff of living and the naked realist is either the complete and successful Romantic, or a suicide. Illusion is willed and forced into some kind of reality, or it is escape. And in the latter case, it will eventually destroy its slave. The mother in "The Gift of God" forces her wholly inaccurate dream of her son's worth into what is for her the realm of fact which nothing can violate because it rests on limitless unselfish love. The wife in "Eros Turannos" has chosen to deceive herself but has reached a point at which the extent of the deception and its origins are about to reveal themselves—with destruction inevitable. In "Veteran Sirens" the women who "cry out for time to end his levity" have discovered that the joke is on them and not on anyone else; the wife of "The Mill" needs only to know what she knows and to have heard her husband say "There are no millers any more." After that, what else can happen than does?

In creating his effects of fate and of "levity," Robinson relies heavily on a hard surface of objective statement, an intermittent current of humor—from gentle to sardonic—and a metric that seems frequently at odds with the subject matter, as though a pastoral elegy should be set to the tune of "Jingle Bells." The tripping, sometimes metronomic, measure alternates with sonorities, as the language alternates between the homely phrase and the "grand manner." In "Mr. Flood's Party" we see a similar technique in imagery: the juxtaposition of the grand and the ordinary, Eben Flood with his jug of hard cider to his lips "like Roland's ghost, winding a silent horn." The image and the language are at once evocative, original, and straight out of the tradition. And they are meant to be, for the "larger humor of the thing," as Robinson says in another place. The very objectivity with which Robinson views his destroyed and self-destroying characters allows him to forgo compassion and to present their plights with humor while he never shirks the rigor and the pity of the particular destiny. It is an appeal to us, as readers, to apply the same technique to our own capacities for self-deception, to see ourselves as "the clerks of time" or to watch "great oaks return/ To acorns out of which they grew." The humor and levity arise from Robinson's refusal, when he is at his best, to consider human error as necessarily cosmically tragic. His Captain Craig, indomitable in defeat and death, is in fact a failure not only in the world's eyes, but in the eyes of the perceptive beholder and perhaps in his own too. And of course Robinson implies that all men are failures in this sense; "poets and kings are but the clerks of time." Hence "the larger humor," the levity, can be felt only by sensibilities realistic enough to understand their own plights and to relate those plights to the whole human condition.

Of course, there are occasions and poems when this sort of humor will not do, will not answer the call of a spirit too appalled at the workings of fate to achieve the right tone. In much of Robinson's work there is another face to the god of reality and understanding. Some facts are too horrible to face and too gratuitously violent for understanding. Poems like "For a Dead Lady" and "The Mill" belong to this category. In the former there is no attempt whatever at mitigating the horror or at achieving acceptance or understanding. Such things are simply *there*. To understand would be to play God; to accept would be demonic. On the whole, this side of the Robinsonian subject is less common than the former; it is not, for example, commonly to be seen at all in the longer poems, where frequently violent acts, often perverted acts, create denouement or tragic conflict almost as though violence has for Robinson taken the place of what might be termed the irrational principle in life. In *Lancelot* and *Amaranth*, to cite two of Robinson's best long narratives, understanding, acceptance, and the promise of a new life form the very basis of the subject and the theme, but it must be confessed that some of Robinson's finest work moves in the direction of stating or implying that at the center of our existence is something implacable, irrational, and not to be propitiated. The old cliché often used of Robinson that he celebrated the success of failure and the failure of success has only a limited application, notable in such a poem as "Old Trails"; actually, he found little reward in failure as such, nor do his failures like Captain Craig and Eben Flood in any sense "triumph"; they are as deluded as the man who congratulates himself on his success. Men fall short of essential humanity and it is here that Robinson's irony usually comes into play, in poems which treat of people in particular situations which show them as inadequate to the human demands made upon them. These poems have plot, action, place, and time; they nearly always involve a man or a woman who is confronted with a situation, involving others, which demands a radical reappraisal of the self and one's conduct. The character is called upon to discard a cherished image of himself, and nearly always, in refusing or failing to do so, the character suffers disaster.

In order to see how Robinson works out the fates of such people in such poems, it might be well to look closely at two or three of the best examples and try to see what goes on. The best poems of the sort described have a dense, deceptive surface, organized in a seemingly careful, orderly way and proceeding quietly, baldly almost, while the narrator subtly assumes the point of view of the reader and imperceptibly helps him to assess and understand, finally leaving with him the realization that the ending is both inevitable and wholly human. The following analyses, then, attempt to show how certain of Robinson's best poems, each representative of a different aspect of the Robinsonian subject, achieve the desired effect.

"Eros Turannos" unfolds as narrative, compressed and suggestive yet without the trickery that occasionally irritates us, as in the case of "The Whip" or "How Annandale Went Out."

Most noticeably, the language is general, the tone expository, the purpose of the poem communication rather than expression. Adumbrated in the first stanza, certain images, whose latent power and meanings are reserved until the final lines, have the function of motifs, repeated constantly and expanded as the poem opens out into suggestion. There are three such images or symbols: waves, tree, stairs leading down. Throughout, these symbols control and provide a center for the meanings possible to the poem, and from the mention of "downward years" and "foamless weirs" in the first stanza to the triple vision of the last four lines these elements recur, the same but altered. As is the case with so many Robinson poems, the reader must supply, from the general materials provided, his own construction, yet the poet has seen to it that there can be only one possible final product. The poem contains two complementary parts: the abstract, generalized statement and the symbolic counterpart of that statement, each constituting a kind of gloss upon the other; each moves through the poem parallel to the other, until at the end they become fused in the concrete images. In addition to the three symbols mentioned, we find also that of blindness and dimness, summed up in the single word "veil" yet continually present in the words "mask," "blurred," "dimmed," "fades," "illusion." All this culminates in the sweeping final image: "Or like a stairway to the sea/ Where down the blind are driven." Yet such inner order, such tight articulation as these examples may indicate, derives no more from the concrete than from the generalized; contrary to Marianne Moore's professed belief, not all imaginary gardens need have actual toads in them, nor, conversely, do we have to bother with the toad at all if our garden is imagined truly enough. What we must have is room—for toads or non-toads, but room anyhow, and Robinson seems to say that there will be more room if we don't clutter the garden with too many particular sorts of fauna and flora. For in "Eros Turannos" we are not told the where or the wherefore; only, and it is everything, the how and the just so. In the hinted-at complexity of the woman's emotion, in the suggested vagueness of the man's worthlessness, lies the whole history of human trust and self-deception: none shall see this incident for what it really is, and the woman who hides her trouble has as much of the truth as "we" who guess and guess yet, the poem implies, without coming nearer to the truth than men usually do.

"Eros Turannos" is the Robinsonian archetype, for in it we can find the basic elements, the structural pattern, that he was to use frequently and with large success. The most cursory reading affords a glimpse into the potential power as well as the dangers of such a form; Robinson's use of it provides examples of both. In the poem in question he reaches an ultimate kind of equipoise of statement and suggestion, generalization and concretion. The first three words of the poem set the tone, provide the key to a "plot" which the rest will set before us. "She fears him": simple statement; what follows will explore the statement, and we shall try to observe the method and evaluate its effect.

> She fears him, and will always ask
>   What fated her to choose him;
> She meets in his engaging mask
>   All reasons to refuse him;
> But what she meets and what she fears
> Are less than are the downward years,
> Drawn slowly to the foamless weirs
>   Of age, were she to lose him.

The epigrammatic tone of the verse strikes one immediately; we are aware that here is a kind of expository writing, capable in its generality of evoking a good deal more than the words state. Important though unobtrusive imagery not only reinforces and enriches the exposition but by calculated ambiguity as well sets a tone of suspense and fatality. The man wears a mask: he conceals something that at once repels and attracts her; notice the play on "engaging" and the implications that involves. The motif is an important one for the poem, as is that contained in the metaphor of "weirs," since these two suggestions of deception, distrust, entrapment, blindness, and decline will be continually alluded to throughout the poem, to find an ultimate range of meaning in the final lines.

The second stanza will in such expressions as "blurred" and "to sound" keep us in mind of the motifs mentioned, without actually requiring new imagistic material or forcing us to re-imagine the earlier metaphors. The intent here is not to be vague but to retain in the reader's consciousness what has gone before as that consciousness acquires new impressions. Hence, in stanza three, Robinson can now introduce a suggestive sketch of the man's nature while he reminds of the woman's and continues to explore it:

> A sense of ocean and old trees
> Envelops and allures him;
> Tradition, touching all he sees,
> Beguiles and reassures him;

That engaging mask of his becomes apparent to us here in this man who finds a solace and security in the love of his wife and in her solid place in the community, and yet the sinister note first sounded in the image of "weirs" is lightly alluded to in the phrase "a sense of ocean." Moreover, that he too is "beguiled" presents a possibility of irony beyond what has yet been exploited.

> And all her doubts of what he says
> Are dimmed with what she knows of days—

Till even prejudice delays
And fades, and she secures him.

The possibilities are many. We grasp readily enough the pathos of her situation: a woman with a worthless husband, proud and sensitive to what the town is whispering yet ready to submit to any indignity, to close her eyes and ears, rather than live alone. Surely a common enough theme in American writing and one that allows the poet to suggest rather than dramatize. Again, in "dimmed" we catch an echo of what has gone before, and in the last two lines the abstract noun "prejudice" with its deliberately general verbs "delays" and "fades" presents no image but rather provokes the imagination to a vision of domestic unhappiness familiar to us all, either in fiction or empirically. And of course the finality of "secures," ironic neither in itself nor in its position in the stanza, takes on irony when we see what such security must be: the woman finds peace only by blinding herself and by seeing the man as she wishes to see him.

Stanza four once again recapitulates and explores. Statement alternates with image, the inner suffering with the world's vision of it:

> And home, where passion lived and died,
> Becomes a place where she can hide,
> While all the town and harbor side
> Vibrate with her seclusion.

If this stanza forms the climax of the plot, so to speak, the next comes to a kind of stasis, the complication of events and motives and themes we see so often in Henry James. The outside world of critical townspeople, hinted at before, now comes to the foreground, and we get a complication of attitudes and views—the world's, the woman's, the man's, our own—and the poet's is ours too. Yet even in a passage as seemingly prosaic and bare as this, Robinson keeps us mindful of what has gone before. In stanza four such words as "falling," "wave," "illusion," "hide," and "harbor" have served to keep us in mind of the various themes as well as to advance the plot, and in the fifth stanza Robinson presents us with a series of possible views of the matter, tells us twice that this is a "story," reiterates that deception and hiding are the main themes, as in the metaphorical expression "veil" and in the simple statement "As if the story of a house/ Were told, or ever could be." And at last, in the final lines, thematic, narrative, and symbolic materials merge in the three images that accumulate power as they move from the simple to the complex, from the active to the passive, from the less to the more terrible:

> Though like waves breaking it may be,
> Or like a changed familiar tree,
> Or like a stairway to the sea
>   Where down the blind are driven.

For the attentive reader the narrative cannot fail; Robinson has given us the suggestive outline we need and told us how, in general, to think about this story. He has kept us constantly aware of place, time, actors, and action even though such awareness is only lightly provoked and not insisted on. In the last stanza the curious downward flow of the poem, the flow of the speculation, reaches an ultimate debouchment—"where down the blind are driven." Apart from the metrical power, the movement of the poem is significant; Robinson has packed it with words that suggest descent, depth, and removal from sight, so that the terrible acceptance of the notion that we must "take what the god has given" becomes more terrible, more final as it issues out in the logic of statement and imagery and in the logic of the plot.

If much of the poem's power depends upon the interaction of statement and suggestion, still another source of energy is the metric. Robinson here uses a favorite device of his, feminine rhymes, in alternating tetrameter and trimeter lines, and gives to soft-sounding, polysyllabic words important metrical functions; as a result, when he does invert a foot or wrench the rhythm or use a monosyllable, the effect is striking out of all proportion to its apparent surface value. Surely the plucking, sounding quality of the word "vibrate" in the last line of the fourth stanza is proof of this, though equally effective is the position of "down" and "blind" in the final line of the poem.

Contemporary verse has experimented with meters, rhyme, and rhythm to such an extent that one has to attune the ear to Robinson's verse; at first it sounds jingly and mechanical, perhaps inept, but after we make a trial of them, the skill, the calculation, have their way and the occasional deviations from the set pattern take on the greater power because they are deviations:

> Pity, I learned, was not the least
> Of time's offending benefits
> That had now for so long impugned
> The conservation of his wits:
> Rather it was that I should yield,
> Alone, the fealty that presents
> The tribute of a tempered ear
> To an untempered eloquence.

This stanza from "The Wandering Jew" shows the style. This is mastery of prosody—old-fashioned command of the medium. The reversing of feet, use of alternately polysyllabic and monosyllabic words of syncopation ("To an untempered eloquence") are devices subtly and sparingly used. The last stanza of the same poem gives another instance, and here the running on of the sense through three and a half lines adds to the effect:

Whether he still defies or not
The failure of an angry task
That relegates him out of time
To chaos, I can only ask.
But as I knew him, so he was;
And somewhere among men to-day
Those old, unyielding eyes may flash,
And flinch—and look the other way.

Deviation implies a basic pattern, and although in many cases, particularly in the blank-verse narratives, syllable counting mars the prosody, nonetheless the best poems subtly attune themselves to the "tempered ear," syncopate on occasion, and jingle to good effect.

This analysis is technical and only partial; it seems to presuppose that we must lapse into Cleanth Brooks's "heresy of paraphrase." Granted. Yet this but begs a question, inasmuch as all of Robinson's poetry assumes that one will want to find the paraphrasable element the poet has carefully provided. These are poems *about* something, and what the something is we must discover. That is why we should consider Robinson as a poet with a prose in view; to read "Eros Turannos" or "For a Dead Lady" or "The Gift of God" is to feel that the scope of a long naturalistic novel has emerged from a few stanzas. Yet Allen Tate, in a brief essay, says that Robinson's lyrics are "dramatic" and that T. S. Eliot observes this to be a characteristic of the best modern verse. One is really at a loss to know what the word "dramatic" means in this regard; Robinson's poetry is not dramatic in any sense of the word commonly accepted, unless it be that Robinson, like Henry James, frequently unfolds a scene. To look for anything like drama in the poems is idle, in that the excitement they convey is of a muted sort, akin to that which James himself generates. This poet wears no masks; he is simply at a distance from his poem, un-

folding the "plot," letting us see and letting us make what applications we will. This directness, this prose element, in Robinson's verse is easy enough to find, less so to define or characterize. One can say this, however: just as Pope was at his best in a poetry that had morality and man in society as its subject matter and its criterion, so Robinson is happiest as a poet when he starts with a specific human situation or relationship, with a "story." "Eros Turannos" is *about* the marriage of untrue minds, but specifically it is not about just untrueness and minds; it is about untrue man A and suffering, self-deluding woman B, as well as about those worldly wisemen who conjecture and have all the "dope." Usually unsuccessful in speculative verse, Robinson excels in just this naturalistic case history, this story of a Maine Emma Bovary. If the theme is still failure, Robinson rings a peculiar change upon it, since at last the poem forces us to accept the implication that there *is* and must be a "kindly veil between/ Her visions and those we have seen"; that all of us must "take what the god has given," for failure is, in Robinson's world, the condition of man and human life. We do the best we can. In "Old Trails," the best one can is not often good, and what is indeed success in the world's eyes has a very shoddy look to those who recognize the success as merely "a safer way/ Than growing old alone among the ghosts." It is the success of Chad in James's *The Ambassadors*, who will go home to the prosperous mills and Mamie and Mom, not that of Strether, who could have had the money and the ease but took the way of "growing old among the ghosts."

A briefer, more compact poem than "Old Trails," one that deals with another aspect of the theme, is the sonnet "The Clerks," which for all its seeming spareness is a very rich, very deft performance. The octave opens colloquially, gives us a general location and an unspecified number of clerks; the speaker is the poet, as poet and as man. Robinson draws an evocative, generalized sketch of the clerks' past, of their prime as well as of the slow attrition of time and labor, and affirms that despite the wear they have sustained these men are still good and human. It is in the sestet that the poem moves out into suggestion, that it implies a conceit by which we can see how all men are clerks, time-servers, who are subject to fears and visions, who are high and low, and who as they tier up also cut down and trim away. To call the poem a conceit is no mere exercise of wit, for Robinson has clearly punned on many unobtrusive words in the sonnet. What is the clerks' "ancient air"? Does it mean simply that the men are old and tired? or that their manner is one of recalling grand old times of companionship that never really existed? or that one must take "air" literally to mean their musty smell of the store? These possibilities are rendered the more complex by the phrase "shopworn brotherhood" immediately following, for then the visual element is reinforced, the atmosphere of shoddiness and shabbiness, of Rotary club good-fellowship, and the simple language has invested itself with imagistic material that is both olfactory and visual. And of course, one may well suspect sarcasm in the assertion that "the men were just as good,/ And just as human as they ever were." How good were they? Yet lest anyone feel this is too cynical, Robinson carefully equates the clerks with "poets and kings."

As is the case with "Eros Turannos," this poem proceeds from the general to the specific and back to the general again, a generality now enlarged to include comment on and a kind of definition of the human condition. Throughout there have been ironic overtones, ironic according to the irony we have seen as peculiarly Robinsonian in that it forms one quadrant of the total view. It has to do here with the discrepancy between the vision men have of their lives and the actuality they have lived. The poet here implies that such discrepancy, such imperfection of vision is immutably "human" and perhaps therefore, and ironically, "good." That the clerks (and we are all clerks) see themselves as at once changed and the same, "fair" yet only called so, serves as the kind of lie men exist by, a lie that becomes an "ache" on the one hand and the very nutriment that supports life on the other. You, all you who secretly cherish some irrational hope or comfort, merely "feed yourselves with your descent," your ancestry, your career, your abject position miscalled a progress. For all of us there can be only the wastage, the building up to the point of dissatisfaction, the clipping away to the point of despair.

Despite the almost insupportable rigor of Robinson's attitude, we can hardly accuse him of cynicism or of hopelessness. In every instance his view of people is warm and understanding, not as the patronizing seer but as the fellow sufferer. Such feeling informs the poems we have discussed and fills "The Gift of God" with humanity no cynic could imagine, no despair encompass. For in this poem the theme of failure turns once more, this time in an unexpected way so that we see Robinson affirming self-deception of this specific kind as more human, more the gauge of true love than all the snide fact-finding the rest of the world would recommend. The poem is about a mother's stubborn, blind love for a worthless (or perhaps merely ordinary) son, and this in the teeth of all the evidence her neighbors would be delighted to retail. Again, the poem is a compact narrative; again the irony exists outside the poem, not in its expression. As in so many of the best poems, Robinson says in effect: here is the reality, here is the illusion. *You* compare them and say which is which and if possible which is the correct moral choice.

The metaphorical material we can roughly classify as made up of imagery relating to royalty, apotheosis, sacrifice, and love. From the first few lines we are aware of a quality which, by allusion to the Annunciation and the anointing of kings, establishes the mother's cherished illusion and thereby makes acceptance of the emergent irony inescapably the reader's duty; he must compare the fact and the fiction for and by himself; Robinson will not say anything in such a way as to make the responsibility for choice his own rather than the reader's. He will simply render the situation and leave us to judge it, for all of Robinson's poems presuppose an outside world of critics and judges, of ourselves, people who see and observe more or less clearly. His irony is external; it lies in the always hinted-at conflict between the public life and the private, between the thing seen from the inside and from the outside, with the poet, the speaker, presenting a third vision, not one that reconciles or cancels the other two, but one which simply adds a dimension and shows us that "everything is true in a different sense."

If the dominant motifs in "The Gift of God" are as indicated above, the progression of the poem follows undeviatingly the pattern suggested. In the first stanza Annunciation; the second, Nativity; the third, vision; the fourth, a stasis in which the mother seems to accept her son's unusual merit and her own vision of him as real; the fifth, a further extension of vision beyond anything actual; the sixth, the culmination of this calculated vision in the apotheosis. More than a schematized structure, the poem depends not only on the articulation of motifs and a plot, but equally on symbolic material that interacts with the stated or implied events in the "plot." Thus, from the outset the poet has juxtaposed the illusory vision and the "firmness" of the mother's faith in it; the language has a flavor of vague association with kingship, biblical story, and legend, notably conveyed by such words as "shining," "degree," "anointed," "sacrilege," "transmutes," and "crowns." Yet in the careful arrangement of his poem Robinson has not oversimplified the mother's attitude. She maintains her "innocence unwrung" (and the irony of the allusion is not insisted on) despite the common knowledge of people who know, of course, better, and Robinson more than implies the innocence of her love in the elevated yet unmetaphorical diction he uses. Not until the final stanza does he open the poem out, and suddenly show the apotheosis in the image of "roses thrown on marble stairs," subtly compressing into the last three lines the total pathos of the poem, for the son ascending in the mother's dream is "clouded" by a "fall": the greatness his mother envisions is belied by what we see. And who is in the right? For in the final turn of the "plot," is it not the mother who gives the roses of love and the marble of enduring faith? Is the dream not as solid and as real as human love can make it? If we doubt this notion, we need only observe the value Robinson places on the verb "transmutes" in stanza five: "*Transmutes* him with her faith and praise." She has, by an absolute miracle of alchemy, transmuted base material into precious; by an act of faith, however misplaced, found the philosopher's stone, which is love wholly purged of self.

What we have come to realize is that in these poems we have been considering we are concerned with narrative—narrative of a peculiar kind in which the story is not just about the events, people, and relationships but about the very poetic devices which are the vehicle of the narration and its insights. In "The Gift of God" symbol and theme have a narrative function; they must do in brief and without obtrusiveness what long passages of dialogue, exposition, and description would effect in a novel. As a result, the reader is compelled to take the entire poem in at once; he either "understands" it or he does not. Naturally there are subtleties which emerge only after many readings; yet because these poems are narratives, Robinson must concentrate upon communication, upon giving us a surface that is at once dense yet readily available to the understanding.

> As one apart, immune, alone,
> Or featured for the shining ones,
> And like to none that she has known
> Of other women's other sons,—
> The firm fruition of her need,
> He shines anointed; and he blurs
> Her vision, till it seems indeed
> A sacrilege to call him hers.

This is on one hand simple telling of plot: the mother sees her son as unique and feels unworthy to be his mother. Simple enough. But the story is more than this, more than a cold telling of the facts about the mother's vision of her son. We see on the other hand that it is her need of the son, and of the vision of him, which complicates the story, while the suggestion of kingship, ritual, and sacrifice in the diction, with the implication of self-immolation and deception, further extends the possibilities of meaning.

All this we grasp more readily than we may realize, for Robinson prepares for his effects very early and while he extends meaning is careful to recapitulate, to restate and reemphasize the while he varies and complicates:

> She sees him rather at the goal,
> Still shining; and her dream foretells

The proper shining of a soul
Where nothing ordinary dwells.

In these lines Robinson affirms the mother's illusion—it is a "dream" that "foretells"—and recapitulates the theme of kingship, of near-divinity, in the repetition of "shining." The stanza that follows gives the poem its turn, states specifically that the son is merely ordinary, that the mother deludes herself, that her motive in so doing is "innocent," and in stanza five the poem, as we have seen, turns once more, pivots on the verb "transmute," turns away from the simple ironical comparison we have been experiencing and reveals a transmuted relationship: son to mother, vision to fact, and an ultimate apotheosis of the mother under the guise of a mistaken view of the son. The poem is about all these things and is equally about the means of their accomplishment within the poem. This is a poetry of surfaces, dense and deceptive surfaces to be sure but still a poetry that insists on the communication of a whole meaning, totally and at once:

> She crowns him with her gratefulness,
> And says again that life is good;
> And should the gift of God be less
> In him than in her motherhood,
> His fame, though vague, will not be small,
> As upward through her dream he fares,
> Half clouded with a crimson fall
> Of roses thrown on marble stairs.

The recapitulation, the tying together, of the symbolic and thematic materials serves in this, the last stanza, a narrative as well as an expressive purpose. The tone is epigrammatic rather than prosaic and must shift delicately, come to the edge of banality, then turn off and finally achieve a muted sublimity that runs every risk of sentimentality and rhetoric yet never falters. The verse requires of us what it requires of itself: a toughness that can encompass the trite and mawkish without on the one hand turning sentimental itself or on the other resorting to an easy irony. The technique is the opposite of dramatic in that Robinson leaves as much to the reader as he possibly can; he uses no persona; the conflict-in-action before our eyes, as it unfolds itself at once, passes through complications, and returns to the starting point, the same yet altered and, to some degree, understood. To this extent Robinson is ratiocinative rather than dramatic; what we and the characters themselves think about the "plot" is as important as the plot, becomes indeed the full meaning of the plot.

Here, again, Robinson is likely to seem behind the times to certain readers. The narrative mode is unpopular in contemporary verse, and even poems about people who are not legendary or at least historical seem to be out of fashion. But the form is an old and honorable one with practitioners as variously gifted as Crabbe, Chaucer, Skelton, Prior, Tennyson, Browning, Kipling, certain Pre-Raphaelites and Decadents, a not inconsiderable company. And Wordsworth made a form of his own of it. Nearly always, the temptation is to move to the long narrative, the viability of which in recent decades is a vexed question. Nonetheless, however strongly dramatic monologue persists in our own era, the narrative lyric has largely disappeared, largely because of the tendency of most modern poetry to be, on the one hand, abstract, philosophical, didactic, or, on the other, rhapsodic, quasi-mystical, symbolist. Certain of the best practitioners in each mode transcend boundaries and mingle the two; one thinks of Stevens and Yeats here. But a Hart Crane, a Dylan Thomas, a Pound: these poets have a particular country from which they rarely stray with success. Robinson had, of course, a historical and local advantage: the nineteenth century was still available to him as an influence and a source, and his upbring-

ing served to keep him isolated, during his formative years, from a too-doctrinaire rejection of his heritage. There is a disadvantage in rebellion and experiment, as there is in indiscriminate acceptance. Robinson took over much Romantic feeling and practice because it suited him. What did not suit him in it was its diction, it remoteness from real experience, and its mere rhetoric. For him, the narrative lyric represented an eclectic form combining many sorts of Romantic poetry, but with the superaddition of a new vocabulary, a sense of real life in a particular time and place, and a zeal for solid truth. Hence his deliberate omission from *Tristram* of the love potion. That was too much to swallow!

For all that has been said of the shorter poems, we are still left with the vexed question of the blank-verse narratives, the longer and the shorter. Clearly, any attentive reader will single out for first place among the latter such poems as "Isaac and Archibald," "Aunt Imogen," "Rembrandt to Rembrandt," and "The Three Taverns." All are notable for the absence of that garrulity which grew on Robinson, particularly in the last decade of his life, as well as for their structure and genuine intellectual content: in them Robinson thinks as a poet doing a job of work should think. The first is a New England pastoral, muted yet rich in tone, gently ironic yet lyrical, and marked by the poet's characteristic humorous self-deprecation as well as his insight into both youth and age. The second poem, less ambitious perhaps, is a marvel of escape from a trap that seems to promise certain capture in sentimentality; it is the story of an old maid who finds her annual emotional release in a month's stay with her sister and her children. What saves the poem is its utter honesty of feeling and language; the poem is not about pathos—pathos simply leaks out of the plain account the poet gives. But "Rembrandt to

Rembrandt," a more ambitious piece, addresses itself to the problem of the solitary artist and in so doing is even more intimately autobiographical in feeling than the others. Again, the poem never makes the mistake of being about its own emotions; Robinson here concentrates on the artist's agonized yet sardonic assessment of his own plight. There is no solution, no dedication to the higher aims; only the realization that he moves among demons of self-doubt, self-delusion, and self-pity. Something of the same kind appears in "The Three Taverns," in which St. Paul seems to be analyzing for us the relative importance of faith and the Law. And here Robinson, abandoning a heritage of Calvinism and a more recent tradition of Puritan fideism, comes out strongly, in the persona of Paul, for a faith at once personal and based on authority, ruled finally by wisdom slowly and painstakingly acquired. There are to be few sudden visions and visitations and those only for the elect.

If the foregoing remarks indicate, as they should, that in these shorter narratives Robinson is doing the poet's work with economy, high intelligence, and skill, what is to follow must of necessity show the other side of the coin. One must say candidly that with the exception of parts of the Arthurian cycle and of *Amaranth*, all the later long narratives are arid, badly thought out, and, as it were, tired. The reasons for this decay appear earlier and there is no need to rehearse them. Briefly, however, here are some of the qualities which these long poems show.

Merlin (1917), *Lancelot* (1920), and *Tristram* (1927) make up the Arthurian cycle and for all their failings surely treat the epic Arthurian theme with greater meaning and importance than do any other works of modern times, T. H. White's possibly excepted. The poems are of course allegorical in conception, at least in the case of the first two, and *Lancelot* really comes close to maintaining a successful interplay of the actual and the symbolic on an extended scale. Yet we have to admit that Robinson's besetting sins, the overelaboration of the obvious and whimsical garrulity, always potential in his work, here begin to exert their fatal influence. Everything Robinson wrote in blank verse in the last fifteen or twenty years of his life is too long, too diffuse, too manneristic. One feels that, like James, Robinson began to enjoy his own work too much, the sound of his own voice tended to intoxicate him. But enough—there are superb passages in *Merlin* and the characters of Vivian and Merlin are real and believable; Lancelot, Arthur, and Guinevere are also powerfully imagined, particularly Lancelot in the poem of that name. If Gawain is hopelessly tedious with the tedious whimsy that grew on Robinson, the figure of Lancelot emerges as heroic, human yet larger than life, a great soldier and a man of noble nature.

Fundamentally, the weakness of the whole cycle derives from Robinson's uneasy poetic and structural compromise: here is myth, symbol, allegory, yet here equally are men and women of the twentieth century. Reconciliation of these disparate parts is, if not impossible, at least an immensely formidable task. Robinson comes close to success in *Lancelot* only because myth, symbol, and allegory disappear when the poem is at its best and we have the powerfully conveyed triangular affair of Arthur, Guinevere, and Lancelot. In *Tristram*—Robinson's great popular success— there is much lyric beauty but the poem is fatally flawed by a love affair at once sticky and verbose and by characters more reminiscent of routine historical novels than of men and women out of myth and legend. And the later narratives, though perhaps less embarrassing in their portrayals of love and lovers, do fatally remind one of *Redbook*, if only in the names of heroines: Laramie, Gabrielle, Natalie, Karen. Only *Amaranth*, in returning to the old subject of failure and self-delusion in artists, touches reality and by fits and starts finds life and meaning. Robinson's last poem, *King Jasper* (1935), is another raid on the abstract by way of allegory and shows the poet's exhaustion—he was on his deathbed when it was completed—as do perhaps to some extent all these late narratives. "A series of conversations terminated by an accident." This dismissal of Ibsen's *A Doll's House* quoted by Yeats might serve to characterize the general effect of these poems on the modern reader, and if it seems sweeping and harsh, any qualifications can serve only to mitigate the judgment, not revoke it.

Yet Robinson stands alone among American poets in his devotion to the long poem. *Captain Craig* remains unique in our annals, rivaled in England by one or two of John Masefield's. In the narrative poem of moderate length, like "Isaac and Archibald," there is no one to touch him; Wordsworth's "Michael" and Keats's "Lamia" would seem the sole competitors in the genre throughout modern times. Robinson of course precedes Frost, in both time and originality, as a writer of short narratives. Frost's "The Death of the Hired Man," for example, lacks both the verbal complexity and the metrical subtlety of Robinson; when Frost turns to such a poem as "Out, Out," however, he is on firm ground indeed where none can outdo him. Both poets clearly find the compressed, elliptically told story their "supreme fiction." It is entirely possible that certain readers can never bring themselves to enjoy verse of this sort—muted, ironic, understated. For some, Robinson is less exciting than, say, Wallace Stevens, born only ten years after Robinson, just as Coleridge seems to many readers more exciting than Wordsworth, Hopkins more daring and absorbing than Tennyson. One might put it this way: Robinson in his best work has no specific religious or philosophical position to recommend, as neither Keats nor Wordsworth has; Hopkins, Stevens, Pound—these are poets who want to sell us something, a theory, a set of ideas or principles. If we like the principles we will love the poetry. For some, Robinson has a defect which goes far, in their view, to cancel out most if not all of his great merit; there is a certain dryness and mechanicalness of tone and feeling which for certain readers will always be an insuperable obstacle, as the "egotistical-sublime" of Wordsworth will always limit his audience. The reader who likes "Michael" will probably like "Isaac and Archibald." Robinson writes about himself in a guise some of us can recognize and enjoy; he does not pose, he does not try to give opinions. Personality in a poet is of the essence. We must like him as he speaks to us or we had better not read him.

That his poetic personality included a strong lyrical element cannot be denied, though it is frequently overlooked, largely because the poet rarely indulged it. We have seen that it was at least once overindulged in *Tristram* and we know that Robinson often kept it in reserve that its appearance might have the greater effect. The language, the imagery, of this lyricism derive largely from nineteenth-century sources, as in the opening lines of "The Man against the Sky," in which poem, as in "The Dark Hills," a deliberate use of highly colored rhetoric is central to the purpose. Unlike many poets of recent years, Robinson was not afraid of lyricism, nor, unlike still others, did he try to overwhelm the reader with "original" and striking imagery. The image of Eben Flood like "Roland's ghost winding a silent horn" is a typical example of one kind of Robinsonian lyricism in that it is euphonious, nostalgic, traditional—and wittily ironic.

But not all Robinson's lyrical flights are of these two sorts, the rhetorical or the ironic. Many occur as climaxes to poems which have begun in a muted, somber tone, rise gradually, and reach a peak of grandeur and eloquence in the final lines. We can observe the technique in such poems as "The White Lights," "On the Night of a Friend's Wedding," "The Sheaves," and of course, "The Gift of God." But there are still those poems which are primarily, almost purely, lyrical, and though few critics think of Robinson as a lyricist, or even as a poet of great versatility, a thorough reading of his work discloses a number of fine poems of quiet but powerful lyric intensity. "Luke Havergal" is one, a poem of almost macabre symbolism. Others, like "Pasa Thalassa Thalassa" and "The Wilderness," with their overtones of Kipling and Swinburne, seem Pre-Raphaelite in quality, as does the "Villanelle of Change." There remains nonetheless the conviction that Robinson's greatest triumphs and happiest effects derive from the "mixed" lyric, the poem rooted in situation which combines narrative, lyrical and ironic, often humorous, qualities with the intent of creating a more complex emotional state in the reader than that effected by the "pure" lyric. "The House on the Hill," "Veteran Sirens," "John Evereldown," and "New England," all display in their differing accents and rhythms the possibilities of this "mixed" form. Wit, pathos, lyrical power, and understatement combine in varied ways to produce complex states of feeling. It is one of the truly Robinsonian characteristics which can be called both modern and highly personal, characteristic of the man and the manner.

Finally, it must be avowed that any writer with a marked manner—and Robinson's manner is strongly marked—offends certain sensibilities, and those often the most acute. The defects and virtues of a poet are so closely allied that frequently they go hand in hand and it takes many bad poems to generate one good one. Robinson's fault was of course to mistake the attempt for the achieved thing. Can anyone say Robinson is alone in such misapprehension? We have seen the damaging effects on Robinson of exile from the kind of give-and-take the knowledge of the better contemporary minds can provide. He had protected his one talent so long and under such stress that we cannot wonder that he took little advice and criticism when it came to him. He was not a Browning; his latter days were divided between the MacDowell Colony in the summers, New York, and visits to friends and to "Tilbury Town," whither he now came as her most famous son—and can we imagine what that must have done to his long-battered pride? But he was not spoiled. He did not surround himself with doting women, or go to tea-fights and give readings—he shrank from these with horror, and a touch of cynicism. He kept on writing, as we have seen, and writing increasingly to satisfy, perhaps to justify, a conception of himself as poet and as man. The great fault of the nineteenth-century men of letters was to publish everything, and Robinson was of his time in this as in so much else. But his successes are many and large—in the narrative poem, the sonnet, the reflective lyric, the narrative lyric, and the dramatic monologue. Limited by environment, tradition, and circumstance, he yet managed to write the finest poems written in America between 1900 and 1920. In England and Ireland were Hardy, Yeats, and Wilfrid Owen and there were Pound and Eliot to be heard. Yet if we consider calmly, apart from notions of "influence" and contemporaneity, we will be forced to admit that the latter two men's work had not by this time achieved the self-contained excellence here under discussion. For all the obvious repetitiousness and aridity of Robinson's later work, twenty years of productiveness, and productiveness of excellence, is an unusually long period for an American writer. Robinson is not Great as Dante and Shakespeare and Milton and Sophocles are Great, but he is in the very front rank of American writers.

Selected Bibliography

WORKS OF
EDWARD ARLINGTON ROBINSON

The Torrent and the Night Before. Cambridge, Mass.: Privately printed, 1896.

The Children of the Night. Boston: Badger, 1897.

Captain Craig. Boston and New York: Houghton Mifflin, 1902.

The Town Down the River. New York: Scribners, 1910.

Van Zorn. New York: Macmillan, 1914. (Play.)

The Porcupine. New York: Macmillan, 1915. (Play.)

The Man against the Sky. New York: Macmillan, 1916.

Merlin. New York: Macmillan, 1917.

Lancelot. New York: Seltzer, 1920.

The Three Taverns. New York: Macmillan, 1920.

Avon's Harvest. New York: Macmillan, 1921.

Collected Poems. New York: Macmillan, 1921.

Roman Bartholow. New York: Macmillan, 1923.

The Man Who Died Twice. New York: Macmillan, 1924.

Dionysius in Doubt. New York: Macmillan, 1925.

Tristram. New York: Macmillan, 1927.

Sonnets 1889–1927. New York: Gaige, 1928.

Cavender's House. New York: Macmillan, 1929.

Collected Poems. New York: Macmillan, 1929.

The Glory of the Nightingales. New York: Macmillan, 1930.

Selected Poems. New York: Macmillan, 1931.

Matthias at the Door. New York: Macmillan, 1931.

Nicodemus. New York: Macmillan, 1932.

Talifer. New York: Macmillan, 1933.

Amaranth. New York: Macmillan, 1934.

King Jasper. New York: Macmillan, 1935.

Collected Poems. New York: Macmillan, 1937.

Selected Early Poems and Letters of E. A. Robinson, edited by Charles T. Davis. New York: Holt, 1960.

Selected Poems, edited by Morton Dauwen Zabel, with an Introduction by James Dickey. New York: Macmillan, 1965.

LETTERS

Letters of Edwin Arlington Robinson to Howard George Schmitt, edited by Carl J. Weber. Waterville, Maine: Colby College Library, 1943.

Selected Letters of Edwin Arlington Robinson, with an Introduction by Ridgely Torrence. New York: Macmillan, 1940.

Untriangulated Stars: Letters of Edwin Arlington Robinson to Harry de Forest Smith, edited by Denham Sutcliffe. Cambridge, Mass.: Harvard University Press, 1947.

BIBLIOGRAPHIES

Hogan, Charles Beecher. *A Bibliography of Edwin Arlington Robinson.* New Haven, Conn.: Yale University Press, 1936.

Lippincott, Lillian. *A Bibliography of the Writings and Criticism of Edwin Arlington Robinson.* Boston: Faxton, 1937.

CRITICAL AND
BIOGRAPHICAL STUDIES

Barnard, Ellsworth. *Edwin Arlington Robinson: A Critical Study.* New York: Macmillan, 1952.

————. *Edwin Arlington Robinson: Centenary Essays.* Athens: University of Georgia Press, 1969.

Coffin, R. P. T. *New Poetry of New England: Frost and Robinson.* Baltimore, Md.: Johns Hopkins Press, 1938.

Coxe, Louis. *Edwin Arlington Robinson: The Life of Poetry.* New York: Pegasus, 1969.

Fussell, Edwin S. *Edwin Arlington Robinson: The Literary Background of a Traditional Poet.* Berkeley: University of California Press, 1954.

Hagedorn, Hermann. *Edwin Arlington Robinson.* New York: Macmillan, 1938.

Neff, Emery. *Edwin Arlington Robinson.* American Men of Letters Series. New York: Sloane, 1948.

Robinson, W. R. *Edwin Arlington Robinson: A Poetry of the Act.* Cleveland: Press of Case Western Reserve University, 1967.

Smith, Chard Powers. *Where the Light Falls: A Portrait of Edwin Arlington Robinson.* New York: Macmillan, 1965.

Stevick, Robert D. "Robinson and William James." *University of Kansas City Review,* 25:293–301 (June 1959).

Winters, Yvor. *Edwin Arlington Robinson.* The Makers of Modern Literature Series. Norfolk, Conn.: New Directions, 1946.

—LOUIS COXE

Theodore Roethke

1908-1963

*I*T IS sometimes said of modern poetry that its day is over, that the revolution which swept through all the arts from about 1910 until a decade after World War I died out in the political anxiety and commitment of the 1930's, and that while the great poets who created the modern idiom—Yeats, Eliot, and Pound, for example—pursued their own ways to artistic maturity, writers growing up after them could no longer find the stimulating atmosphere of participation in what Randall Jarrell so aptly called "an individual but irregularly cooperative experimentalism." To a certain extent that view is correct: there has been no concerted poetic movement of real consequence here or in England since the work of Auden, Spender, Day Lewis, and MacNeice in the thirties. Yet even if the excited collective activity inspired by radical and widespread creative ferment gradually dissipated in those years, there was no lack of purpose and talent among the American poets who began to publish notable work near the outset of World War II or the others who appeared soon afterwards.

In his essay "The End of the Line," from which I quoted above, Randall Jarrell acted as a brilliant self-appointed spokesman for his contemporaries, for Robert Lowell, John Frederick Nims, Karl Shapiro, Richard Eberhart, Richard Wilbur, and Theodore Roethke, as well as for himself, when he defined the situation of the younger poet in 1942. "Today, for the poet," he said, "there is an embarrassment of choices: young poets can choose—do choose—to write anything from surrealism to imitations of Robert Bridges; the only thing they have no choice about is making their own choice. The Muse, forsaking her sterner laws, says to everyone: 'Do what you will.' "

The American poets of that generation did exactly what they willed and have produced, without the impetus of any common enterprise other than devotion to their art, a remarkable body of poetry. Ironically enough, they are poets on whom the label of academicism has been fastened occasionally; yet outside of the fact that many of them like Roethke have taught for a living that word, with its pejorative overtones, would seem to have little application. We have academic verse when a poet, instead of learning from the poetic tradition by remaining alive and open to its possibilities in relation to his own gifts and aspirations, submits himself to it automatically or, to change the metaphor, polishes the surface of old conventions. The weakness of the academic writer lies in an acceptance of literature before personal experience and imagination as the source of his art. But the poets I have named, and some not mentioned, showed originality, concern for language, and an abiding honesty toward the facts of their experience. If comparisons with the pioneer writers of twentieth-century modernism do not offer these successors the historical advantage, there is still no doubt in my mind that two or three of the latter can already hold their own surprisingly well in such formidable company.

Of all these later poets Theodore Roethke appears the most considerable, in terms of imaginative daring, stylistic achievement, richness of diction, variety and fullness of music, and unity of vision. From his first book, published in 1941, to the posthumous volume *The Far Field* (1964) he consistently proved himself a poet discontented with the restrictions of a settled manner of composition. This is not to say, of course, that Roethke lacked steadiness or certitude, that he was frivolous or insubstantial; quite the reverse. His poetry grew in distinct stages, each one with its own peculiar qualities and aims, each one expanding and developing from its predecessor, each providing its own special means of furthering the poet's central themes and subjecting them to different modes of apprehension. We should not be surprised then in reading through Roethke's books to discover a wide range of moods and styles: tightly controlled formal lyrics, dramatic monologues and something like an interior monologue, nonsense verse, love lyrics, and meditative poems composed in a very free fashion. His experience reaches from the most extraordinary intuition of the life of nature to lightning flashes of mystical illumination.

To fit Roethke definitely within a given tradition or to link him finally with other poets, past or present, who share certain of his predilections is tempting but too easy. He expressed an affection for John Clare and borrowed the title for his third book from Wordsworth's *The Prelude*, yet he was not drawn to the natural world in quite the same way as either of them, though he maintained affinities with both. Again one might like to proclaim him an investigator of the irrational, a poet obsessed with the pure flow of inner experience, with the preconscious and the unconscious: a poet similar to the young Dylan Thomas or Paul Eluard. Or perhaps he should be classed with the visionary poets he so admired: Blake, Whitman, and Yeats. No doubt every one of these attempts at classification would tell us a partial truth about Roethke, but none would give us the whole of it. He was, in fact, equally at home with any of these other poets, though we will be defeated in the endeavor to read his poetry honestly if we settle for a particular category in which to lodge him and so avoid further thought. Roethke needs first to be seen through his own work.

Behind the profusion of experience we have noted in Roethke's writing one comes upon a preoccupation with the poet's own self as the primary matter of artistic exploration and knowledge, an interest which endows the poems with a sense of personal urgency, even necessity. What do we mean by this self? I think the self, as we shall want to use the word here, can best be called the main principle of the poet's individual life—or for that matter, of any human life—a principle of identity and of being which is generally spiritual in character but also reaches into the realm of the physical. It partakes of what Martin Buber includes in his definition of the "primary word *I-Thou*," which is the speech of a person's entire being in relationship with the other creatures and things of the world, for Roethke viewed the self as continually seeking a harmonious dialogue with all that is. The bulk of Roethke's poetry derives its imaginative strength from the author's restless quest for that communion in which self and creation are joined. Though they take the self as theme we cannot look in these poems for the sort of personal element we associate with the later work of Robert Lowell. Yet they are in their way just as intimate, maybe even more intimate, since some penetrate the protective screen of conscious thought. Lowell focuses often on other personalities, the family, the world of historical time, while Roethke's concentration either is inward, almost untouched by public happenings or by history, or turns outward to the existence of things in nature. But in order to understand his fundamental attachment to this theme of the self we must now look closely at its development within a growing body of poetry.

By any standards *Open House* (1941) is a remarkable first collection of poetry. Roethke's sensitive use of language and his craftsmanship stand out on every page; and if one returns to this book after reading his other work it becomes plain that the author's main interests were already present here. The title poem is a frank announcement of his intention to use himself in some way as the material of his art, but we are not told how. The poem is sharp in its personal disclosure and might justifiably serve as a motto for all of Roethke's subsequent verse:

> My secrets cry aloud.
> I have no need for tongue.
> My heart keeps open house,
> My doors are widely swung.
> An epic of the eyes
> My love, with no disguise.
>
> My truths are all foreknown,
> This anguish self-revealed.
> I'm naked to the bone,
> With nakedness my shield.
> Myself is what I wear:
> I keep the spirit spare.

These sparse, carefully rhymed stanzas characterize Roethke's earlier poetic technique, and their kind is visible everywhere in *Open House*. A certain economy and simplicity of diction, as well as insistent, forceful rhythms, more freely employed as he matured, are in fact lasting trademarks of his style, even though he abandoned some of them almost entirely on occasion in favor of experiments with considerably looser forms. Such departures are especially evident in the long sequence of interior monologues from *The Lost Son* and *Praise to the End*, in the "Meditations of an Old Woman" from *Words for the Wind*, and in the "North American Sequence" from *The Far Field*. But the experiments are always interspersed, even in later work, with returns to the simple lyric. Here, as an illustration, is a stanza from "Once More, the Round," which Roethke wrote for his 1962 New Year's greeting:

> Now I adore my life,
> With the Bird, the abiding Leaf,
> With the Fish, the questing Snail,
> And the Eye altering All;
> And I dance with William Blake
> For love, for Love's sake.

The two subjects on which Roethke's imagination most often fastens in *Open House* are the correspondence between the poet's inner life and the life of nature, and the strengths or weaknesses of the individual psyche. Frequently he tries to demonstrate hidden relationships in the processes of both, as in "The Light Comes Brighter," a poem which begins with a very direct account of winter's end and the arrival of spring to a particular landscape:

> The light comes brighter from the east; the caw
> Of restive crows is sharper on the ear.
> A walker at the river's edge may hear
> A cannon crack announce an early thaw.

The sun cuts deep into the heavy drift,
Though still the guarded snow is winter-sealed,
At bridgeheads buckled ice begins to shift,
The river overflows the level field.

The observation and description are quite accurate and undoubtedly derive from the poet's childhood experience of the Michigan countryside. But as in the poetry of Léonie Adams, which Roethke always admired, nature yields a secret analogy with human existence, though it does not appear until the closing lines:

And soon a branch, part of a hidden scene,
The leafy mind, that long was furled,
Will turn its private substance into green,
And young shoots spread upon our inner world.

Mind and nature are bound in these lines by certain laws and enjoy a common awakening. Still we are left to tease out most of the implications for ourselves because the poet merely hints at the possibilities of this comparison in the present poem. In many of the other poems in this volume Roethke offers further seasonal descriptions but never makes the implied correspondences with human life any more definite than what we have already seen in the lines quoted.

Elsewhere in the book he takes the durability of the mind by itself as artistic material; and in a few poems which show an indebtedness to W. H. Auden he portrays the opposition to this mental stability through the figures of those victimized by unconscious forces, inherited sicknesses that threaten to destroy psychic balance:

Exhausted fathers thinned the blood,
You curse the legacy of pain;
Darling of an infected brood,
You feel disaster climb the vein.

These last poems, though they are of little aesthetic interest so far as the bulk of Roethke's writing is concerned, possess some value in foreshadowing the motives behind the tremendous imaginative leap he took in the seven years between *Open House* and *The Lost Son*. For the powers of the unconscious had at last to be dealt with, and are dealt with in the astonishing sequence of interior monologues which record the poet's odyssey through subterranean regions of the psyche, a spiritual journey that remains one of the boldest experiments in modern American poetry. Taken altogether the poems in *Open House* are indicative of Roethke's major themes, but they hardly prepare the reader for the change to an intensely subjective vision in the next book or for the readjustment of his perceptions demanded by this shift. With *The Lost Son* (1948) he emerges as a poet of undeniable originality and stature, whose writing bears its own stylistic signature.

The section of poems with which *The Lost Son* opens may catch by complete surprise the reader who has seen nothing but Roethke's previous work. While emphasis on nature is still maintained, attention has now moved away from the earlier images of natural and seasonal activity in the larger sense to a reduced, microscopic scrutiny of plant life that seems almost scientific in its precision but is obviously prompted by the poet's intuition, passion, and sympathy. What in preceding poems would most likely have been a careful description of the outer appearance of a plant or flower becomes an attempt to seize imaginatively the essential life of the flower, as in the haunting "Orchids," where it overlaps ours:

They lean over the path,
Adder-mouthed,
Swaying close to the face,
Coming out, soft and deceptive,

Limp and damp, delicate as a young bird's
    tongue;
Their fluttery fledgling lips
Move slowly,
Drawing in the warm air.

The basis for this sudden alteration in distance and perspective must have been the poet's decision to utilize his close experience in childhood with plants and flowers as substantial matter for his art. However it came about the choice was fortunate because it marked out the route his poetic imagination was to take and, one likes to think, even urged him on his way by revealing the similarities existing between his human life and that of the inhabitants of the plant kingdom which had played so important a part in his youth. Through this new personal vision of the vegetable and mineral, insect and animal, knowledge of which he owed to his boyhood, Roethke found before him the difficult problems of spiritual evolution and the search for psychic identity.

The poet was born in Saginaw, Michigan, in 1908, received his education at the University of Michigan and Harvard, and subsequently taught at Lafayette College, Pennsylvania State University, Bennington College, and for some time at the University of Washington in Seattle, where he was professor of English and poet in residence at the time of his death on August 1, 1963. As a boy he grew up in and around the greenhouses that were the center of the Roethke family's floral establishment, one of the largest and most famous of its time. The business was both retail and wholesale; it was operated by Roethke's father and his Uncle Charlie, aided by a staff of trained florists and also by a working crew of eccentric figures which included the three marvelous old ladies Frau Bauman, Frau Schmidt, and Frau

Schwartze, about whom the poet wrote a wonderful and moving elegy that captures the beauty and pleasure of these women at their task. I quote here only a few lines from the first stanza:

Gone the three ancient ladies
Who creaked on the greenhouse ladders,
Reaching up white strings
To wind, to wind
The sweet-pea tendrils, the smilax,
Nasturtiums, the climbing
Roses, to straighten
Carnations, red
Chrysanthemums; the stiff
Stems, jointed like corn,
They tied and tucked,—
These nurses of nobody else.

As a boy Roethke played and worked around these greenhouses. Many of his experiences he transformed elegantly, and often humorously, into poems: we need only look at "Big Wind," "Old Florist," "Child on Top of a Greenhouse," and the poem above to be conscious of that. But from the same intimate knowledge of his father's greenhouses he began those poetic ventures into the scarcely visible except to the eye of a determined and fascinated observer—motions of plant life that we noticed in "Orchids." In another poem, appropriately entitled "The Minimal," Roethke renders himself in the act of watching:

I study the lives on a leaf: the little
Sleepers, numb nudgers in cold dimensions,
Beetles in caves, newts, stone-deaf fishes,
Lice tethered to long limp subterranean weeds,
Squirmers in bogs,
And bacterial creepers
Wriggling through wounds
Like elvers in ponds,
Their wan mouths kissing the warm sutures,

Cleaning and caressing,
Creeping and healing.

In the poet's attentive gaze this tiny world increases its size and comes curiously near in its procedures to the one we would like to believe is exclusively man's. Something in the human psyche responds to these minute activities, discovers a mysterious, even terrifying, attraction to levels of existence to which reason or intelligence would quickly assign an inferior value. But an indispensable part of the imaginative breakthrough Roethke achieves in his second book is just this exposure of himself to subrational elements. Thus the disturbing quality in these poems results from the dramatic re-creation of affinities with the lower orders of life, parallels we have banished from thought. And how startling it is for the scientific, technological mind of contemporary man to countenance such images of his origins, of archaic sources of life he shares with lesser forms than himself. If Roethke's endeavors start with a return to his own past experience, the poems surpass the barriers of privacy to delineate hidden patterns in creation; and they accomplish this with a freshness of language and imaginative energy unmatched by any other poet since Dylan Thomas. A poem like "Cuttings, later" brings poet—and thus reader—and the newly born plants into a correspondence so delicate and yet profound that there can be only one true conclusion: a kind of psychic rebirth for the poet through his sympathetic contemplation of propagating plants:

This urge, wrestle, resurrection of dry sticks,
Cut stems struggling to put down feet,
What saint strained so much,
Rose on such lopped limbs to a new life?

I can hear, underground, that sucking and
    sobbing,

In my veins, in my bones I feel it,—
The small waters seeping upward,
The tight grains parting at last.
When sprouts break out,
Slippery as fish,
I quail, lean to beginnings, sheath-wet.

Roethke's inclination in these poems to reveal a deep and permanent tie between the "minimal" world of flowers, plants, and small creatures he so benevolently scrutinizes and the inner world of man prepares for the sequence of experimental monologues, the first of which appear in the last section of *The Lost Son* and which are continued in *Praise to the End* (1951). The sequence poems are, so far as I know, unique in modern literature. Undoubtedly they owe their inspiration to the poet's pursuit of the correspondences just mentioned and to the fact that his previous work keeps insisting on such an immersion in the prerational and unconscious areas of experience in the hope of bringing unity to the self and gaining a new harmony with creation.

The poems are grouped around an associational scheme, as Roethke once suggested, and seem closer perhaps to certain experimental tendencies in the modern novel, such as stream of consciousness, than they do to the efforts of most contemporary poets. "Each poem"—there are fourteen in all—"is complete in itself," Roethke says in his "Open Letter" from *Mid-Century American Poets*, "yet each in a sense is a stage in a kind of struggle out of the slime; part of a slow spiritual progress; an effort to be born, and later, to become something more." The poems treat portions of a spiritual journey undertaken by a child-protagonist, a journey the narrative of which does not develop in a direct, logical manner because it is viewed internally through the fluid movements and reactions of the protagonist's mind.

This protagonist, through whom we comprehend whatever happens in the poems, plays a double role: he is both a mask for the poet and a universal type, any man, for Roethke is at pains to avoid the limitations of a totally personal significance in the experience created by this poetic sequence. The journey, while it is basically psychic and spiritual, also has similarities with quest myths: the hero's descent into the underworld of the self; a series of ordeals he must pass or an enemy to be vanquished; his victorious return to familiar reality, which is now changed by his efforts. This sort of parallel will make it clear at once that while Roethke's primary intention is the "struggle for spiritual identity" (his phrase) in the individual protagonist, that struggle symbolizes a more general body of human experience. This last dimension is, however, implied rather than heavily outlined through a detailed system of allusion.

In several of the poems we have seen from *The Lost Son*, as well as in a number of others that cannot be discussed here, Roethke presses back toward the very beginnings of existence in his concentration on the life process of plants. This practice by itself is sufficient to separate his interests from his contemporaries' and to display his genuine innovation. Roethke wishes in these poems to uncover through his imagination the laws of growth in a flower and relate them to the development of the human self, though it is done metaphorically rather than scientifically. But short lyric poems are ultimately unsatisfactory as vehicles for such ambitions because they are not flexible enough and do not readily permit the singular approach to experience the poet now envisages. What he is aiming at is a poetic "history of the psyche" (his phrase) which opens with the earliest stages of life and traces the evolution of the spirit in its ordeal of inner and outer conflicts, its desire for "unity of being," to borrow a term from Dante by way of Yeats, that final condition of grace which is a harmony of the self with all things. In Roethke's later work the love of man and woman is involved in this idea of unity and so is an awareness of the Divine. Yet the protagonist's route in the poems is anything but easy, for regressive instincts, desires to remain on the lowest plane of existence or to become a lump of inanimate matter, war upon the natural impulse to growth. The spirit tries to release the self from these destructive attractions and to rise toward the full embrace of life. Nature is the context in which the individual assumes at last his rightful identity, finds love, and engages the spirit in further encounters. Roethke depicted some of the terrors and humiliations attending this venture into buried regions in a poem entitled "The Return":

A cold key let me in
That self-infected lair;
And I lay down with my life,
With the rags and rotting clothes,
With a stump of scraggy fang
Bared for a hunter's boot.

The self-imposed, and no doubt personally necessary, journey on which the poet sets forth with the first poem of the sequence (as rearranged by Roethke in the order he wishes in *Words for the Wind*), "Where Knock Is Open Wide," immediately alters ordinary spatial and temporal dimensions. Spatial because the poems view a secret landscape of the inner self that resembles the external world only in fragmentary details supplied by memory or momentary perceptions, and these are heightened, distorted, or transfigured, as in a dream, by the various struggles of the spirit in its search for freedom and unity. Temporal because the poet, or the projection of himself which is the protagonist, needs to go back to his childhood experience so that he can relive this evolutionary process in writing about it. Thus we witness the activity of the poems from the standpoint of the poet-protagonist himself.

It has already been suggested that these poems carry echoes of archetypal patterns from other modes of experience, particularly mythical and religious. Because the protagonist travels into the regions of memory, the preconscious and the unconscious, he shows distinct similarity to the heroes of myth whom Jung saw as representative of the quest for psychic wholeness. Like those fabulous heroes or the lesser ones of fairy tales Roethke's lone protagonist must endure the trials and dangers of a mission into the darkness of personal history. The prize to be won is rebirth and illumination, what is called in one of the poems "a condition of joy."

The title of "Where Knock Is Open Wide" is taken from Christopher Smart's poem of praise and celebration, "Song to David," LXXVII, but Roethke's piece, which presents the sensations and thoughts of earliest childhood, seems to use the line from Smart to imply birth and entry into the world. From this aspect Roethke's poem somewhat resembles Dylan Thomas' "Before I Knocked," which describes experiences of a child (in this case, Jesus) in the womb. Indeed, Thomas is probably the only one of Roethke's immediate contemporaries who also investigates successfully the fluid exchange of past and present within the self. Roethke establishes his atmosphere with childish perceptions:

> A kitten can
> Bite with his feet;
> Papa and Mamma
> Have more teeth.

He goes on in a few lines to what appears to be an image of birth:

> Once upon a tree
> I came across a time . . .

The tree is a species of the common symbol of the Tree of Life, and the next line recalls the protagonist's introduction to time. A stanza further on we learn the nature of the journey and something of its method:

> What's the time, papa-seed?
> Everything has been twice.
> My father is a fish.

This brief passage draws the protagonist back toward the instant of his conception and fixes our attention on the movement into his personal past, which is a reversal of the temporal order. The middle line makes plain the fact that the poet is not simply rendering the original stages of development in a fictional individual but reliving them in himself to interpret their meaning. We seem to hear the voices of the protagonist and the poet blending in this line. The identification of the father with a fish has again a double reference: first, in allusion to a fishing trip of the father and son, bits of which are given later; second, in hinting at the evolutionary scheme emphasized previously. This process of evolution we witness in the protagonist is universal and leads away, as Roethke writes in his "Open Letter," from "the mire," where "man is no more than a shape writhing from the old rock." In the third section of the poem he sounds the same theme by employing the word "fish" once again, but now as a verb instead of a substantive. This change marks a step forward from domination by an image of ancestry among the lower forms of life to an active desire on the protagonist's part for self-completion:

> A worm has a mouth.
> Who keeps me last?
> Fish me out.
> Please.

Since our point of observation is located within the protagonist's mind, though not at the level of reason or calculation, certain external facts such as his changing age are not always easily determined. We gather, however, that the poems extend over a period from early childhood into late adolescence. Roethke's associative technique allows him to shift back and forth freely in the history of his protagonist, and so he can bring his artistic weight to bear on the themes which matter to him without particular regard for the consistency of linear time. The present poem ranges from the first years of life with their scraps of nonsense verse and nursery songs, through a brief section touching on the small boy's religious emotions, then his fishing trip, and ending with the initial signs of anxiety and guilt which accompany the feeling of desolation caused by the father's death. The narrative progression of the poems, if we may thus speak of it, depends upon Roethke's concern for the advances and setbacks of the evolving spirit.

The loss of his father empties the protagonist's world of its paternal image of God as well:

> Kisses come back,
> I said to Papa;
> He was all whitey bones
> And skin like paper.
>
> God's somewhere else,
> I said to Mamma.
> The evening came
> A long long time.

The last two lines predict a period of deprivation and loneliness to come. And in the next poem, "I Need, I Need," with its title so sharply indicative of the child's terrible hunger for affection and stability, he alternates between a search for the mother:

> A deep dish. Lumps in it.
> I can't taste my mother.

solitude and melancholy:

> Went down cellar,
> Talked to a faucet;
> The drippy water
> Had nothing to say.

and a final resort to the diversion of children's habits, rhymes, and games:

> A one is a two is
> I know what you is:
> You're not very nice,—
> So touch my toes twice.

But, clearly enough, these diversions exhibit the inner divisions and turmoil of the protagonist, too. In later sections of the poem a gradual easing of tensions occurs, succeeded by intimations of human possibility and of an abiding kinship with physical creation: "Hear me, soft ears and roundy stones! / It's a dear life I can touch." The poem finally closes by emphasizing two of the traditional four elements thought to compose the universe, water and fire:

> I said to the gate,
> Who else knows
> What water does?
> Dew ate the fire.

Here the gate symbolizes all that prevents the protagonist from rebirth into the world, from the potential of his existence. Like beings, objects, and places in fairy tale and folklore, creatures and things in Roethke's poetic cosmos are invested with magical properties, can hinder or help the spirit in its growth. Thus the protagonist seeks the true way by asking questions in this subterranean and animistic kingdom from which he must obtain new life or sink back into the "dark pond"—as Roethke calls the deep unconscious—where oblivion awaits him. The water mentioned in the passage above should not, however, be identified with that sinister place; rather it signifies a continuation of the journey into daylight, the constant will of the self to accomplish, in Robert Frost's words, this "serial ordeal."

Dew consumes one fire in this same stanza only to disclose another kind in the next. The first should probably be understood as the fever of discord in the protagonist, while the second, which appears momentarily in the poem's final lines—"I know another fire. / Has roots."—surely is meant to remind us of fire's ancient use as a symbol of spirit. So we realize that the entire movement of the first two poems in the sequence constitutes an ascent from origins, from the introduction to death, the experience of fear and isolation, to the recognition of freedom and possibility beyond present conditions, though such prospects are never mistaken for a guarantee of security. Life, as it is seen in Roethke's poetry, can best be defined as always becoming.

"Bring the Day!" fulfills the promise of spiritual progress implied before. It is a celebration of self and nature together in a newly won relation, and as such it marks the conversion of the haunted landscape of unknown terrors and hidden demons projected by the self into the radiant external world of insects and birds, grass and flowers. The poem begins with an exuberant burst of song which sounds as if Roethke might have had both John Lyly and Edward Lear in mind when he wrote it:

> Bees and lilies there were,
> Bees and lilies there were,
> Either to other,—
> Which would you rather?
> Bees and lilies were there.

This mood of celebration, of self-possession and joy, prevails throughout the poem. Nature guides the protagonist further along the path he must travel and hints in symbols which recall those of "I Need, I Need" at the pattern of his journey from confinement to fluidity: "The grass says what the wind says: / Begin with the rock; / End with water."

The third and concluding section shows the emergent self in the image of a tiny bird waking to existence, feeling a little its own possibilities, and facing a life that has cast off its ties with the past and only looks forward. The gentle lyricism of the stanza again points up Roethke's uncanny sensitiveness to the subtlest details of nature and their covert human meanings:

> O small bird wakening,
> Light as a hand among blossoms,
> Hardly any old angels are around any more.
> The air's quiet under the small leaves.
> The dust, the long dust, stays.
> The spiders sail into summer.
> It's time to begin!
> To begin!

Following this poem three others, "Give Way, Ye Gates," "Sensibility! O La!" and "O Lull Me, Lull Me," lead up to "The Lost Son," which is the key poem of the sequence and, as Roethke said himself, the one with the most obvious narrative construction. The poems preceding "The Lost Son" continue to test various lines of inner tension we have already noted in the protagonist. Sexual agony, lack of identity, and solitude are cast as barriers against the vital energy of the spirit in its evolution but with no lasting success. The closing portion of "O Lull Me, Lull Me" measures the spirit's achievement and attests once more to the protagonist's intuition of harmony with creation:

> I'm more than when I was born;
> I could say hello to things;
> I could talk to a snail;

I see what sings!
What sings!

Light, movements of air, flowing water, and the music of song supply Roethke with some favorite metaphors for these sudden revelations of increase and communion. And they are peculiarly appropriate and effective metaphors because their source is the great world of nature, which stands, as we have seen, as the foundation and setting for the poet's investigation of human reality. In Roethke's writing man is always viewed in the framework of nature, or at least is never far distant from it. Whether the immediate subject is the individual self, love between man and woman, or some kind of visionary experience, it partakes of that natural world in evident or indirect relationships, in the physical details of imagery. Finally, in some of his last poems such as "The Far Field," "Meditation at Oyster River," and "The Rose" Roethke sees the realm of the spiritual beginning in nature; yet he never denies the validity of the natural in favor of the transcendental. He tends rather to hold them in his vision simultaneously, for to his imagination they blend and interchange endlessly.

"The Lost Son," as Hilton Kramer wrote in his fine essay on Roethke, summarizes the main theme and the developments which appear loosely in the sequence as a whole. The first of the poems from this group we examined took the early phases of life as their point of departure, but here the reference to a cemetery in the opening line and the attraction to death which it signifies states at once the conflict with the evolving self whose pull is toward fulfillment and maturity. The remainder of this initial section, which is entitled "The Flight," treats the confused and often tormented condition of the child-protagonist as he tries to learn the direction he must take to escape those forces working solely for his anguish or destruction. In keeping with Roethke's preoccupation with the irrational and subliminal side of his protagonist's experience the poem assumes the strange aura of dream and fairy tale we have come to expect of the entire sequence. The protagonist undertakes his journey without certainty of his bearings or his goal. All he can do, it seems, is ask questions and go where chance or the guidance of the spirit may lead him. The environment through which he travels (again we should stress the subjective character of his perceptions) displays hostility, though he has obvious feelings of sympathy for the smallest creatures, whose size and innocence resemble his own:

> At Woodlawn I heard the dead cry:
> I was lulled by the slamming of iron,
> A slow drip over stones,
> Toads brooding in wells.
> All the leaves stuck out their tongues;
> I shook the softening chalk of my bones,
> Saying,
> Snail, snail, glister me forward,
> Bird, soft-sigh me home.

As in previous poems from the sequence Roethke juxtaposes fragments of children's songs, nursery rhymes, and riddles with apparently factual descriptions; thus he keeps a balance between external and subjective reality. But even the fairly straightforward passages distillate a symbolic meaning in terms of the quest on which the protagonist is bound:

> Hunting along the river,
> Down among the rubbish, the bug-riddled
>   foliage,
> By the muddy pond-edge, by the bog-holes,
> By the shrunken lake, hunting, in the heat
>   of summer.

The river with its steady flow, suggesting progress, intensifies by contrast the image of frustrated and unrewarded searching by the protagonist near those places, holes and slippery mud patches, that spell out the dangers of regression and defeat to his odyssey.

In "The Pit," the second part of the poem which is only one stanza long, the seductiveness of a descent into the earth, a relinquishing of self to the dark body of the mother, becomes an active threat to the protagonist. But an inner warning, perhaps by the spirit, prevents him from succumbing to what I think we must call a strong death-wish or a refusal of any further hardships in the search for human completion:

> Where do the roots go?
>   Look down under the leaves.
> Who put the moss there?
>   These stones have been here too long.
> Who stunned the dirt into noise?
>   Ask the mole, he knows.
> I feel the slime of a wet nest.
>   Beware Mother Mildew.
> Nibble again, fish nerves.

The section following treats sexual agonies and alienation. Roethke builds up to a terrifying climax the tension between the protagonist and his surroundings. The short, terse lines which he handles so deftly are essential to the poet's creation of this climactic atmosphere:

> The weeds whined,
> The snakes cried,
> The cows and briars
> Said to me: Die.

But the full weight of the poem up to this point, which is brought to bear on the word "Die," is released in the next stanzas, and we suddenly realize that the protagonist has survived the worst of his trials. He finds himself at the calm center of a storm and recognizes that he is poised on the threshold of a new spiritual phase, of transformation and rebirth: "Do the bones cast out their fire? / Is the seed leaving the old bed? These buds are live as birds." Still more lines of conflict succeed these indications of change, but they terminate at last in a gentle apprehension of natural things, which is, in its turn, broken by an unexpected, violent flash of interior illumination and a period of turbulence ending in the restoration of the protagonist to the familiar climate of daily life.

The two concluding portions of the poem bring the protagonist home to his father's greenhouse and to an interval of waiting. The boy's sensitive awareness of the existence of the roses he tends and watches there ("The roses kept breathing in the dark. / They had many mouths to breathe with.") should also be understood to connote the self-recognition earned through his troublesome journey. Like these flowers he enjoys a precarious and fragile state of being; his scrutiny of their gradual response to the coming light of day duplicates a perception of his own slow ascent from the abyss of inner tensions:

A fine haze moved off the leaves;
Frost melted on far panes;
The rose, the chrysanthemum turned toward
    the light.
Even the hushed forms, the bent yellowy weeds
Moved in a slow up-sway.

The stately, graceful quality of this stanza, contrasting sharply with the clipped style of previous parts, leads us without disruption into the meditative attitude of the final section, in which the winter landscape, bare yet enduring, mirrors in its stark forms and objects the present condition of the protagonist. From this symbolic notation with its imagery of the "bones of weeds" and of "light" moving "slowly over the frozen field, / Over the dry seedcrowns, / The beautiful surviving bones /

Swinging in the wind" there comes a shift to the mind of the protagonist deeply immersed in what has been happening to him. His mind also moves, but "not alone, / Through the clear air, in the silence." The poem closes with two stanzas reflecting the spiritual questions raised by the boy's experience as recounted in the first three sections of the poem and, presumably, in the other poems of the sequence placed before "The Lost Son":

> Was it light?
> Was it light within?
> Was it light within light?
> Stillness becoming alive,
> Yet still?

> A lively understandable spirit
> Once entertained you.
> It will come again.
> Be still.
> Wait.

We can hardly fail to notice here a recollection of T. S. Eliot's *Four Quartets*, a series of poems which parallel Roethke's in some respects. Both works are explorations of the self, its past history and its developments, though Eliot has no intention of representing those prerational areas of the mind into which Roethke so daringly plunges. Both works seek realization in a spiritual order, but Roethke declines to step into religious orthodoxy and relies upon his own intuition, while Eliot integrates his mystical perceptions with the traditions and beliefs of Catholic Christianity. Yet Roethke's reference to the senior poet is too obvious to be merely an unconscious allusion. I think we should see it as a deliberate echo of *Four Quartets* but also as a statement of difference. The illumination which occurs in "The Lost Son" may be a divine visitation or a gift of grace; however, it lacks any explicit theological structure of the kind embodied in

so many of the details in Eliot's poems. For Roethke this moment of light appears to be given as a matter of course and is accepted as completely natural. Certainly it is merited to a degree by the ordeal through which the protagonist has passed, but it surely is not achieved in the sense in which Eliot achieves those mystical experiences at the heart of *Four Quartets*, that is, by prayer, selflessness, and meditation. Roethke's is the more Protestant approach, one that bases itself firmly on personal knowledge and evidence, on the lone individual's apprehension of the transcendent. And such a description applies to mystical poems like "In a Dark Time," included in *The Far Field*.

The purpose of this visitation at the close of "The Lost Son" is clear all the same, for it displays the progress of the spirit over the longest and most difficult stage of evolution. In the seven remaining poems of the sequence Roethke continues to record the advances and lapses of his protagonist, though we are by now conscious of the latter's increasing maturity. But he has not yet escaped the pains of sexuality and of alienation: they have become the problems of a person who has left childhood behind and arrived at a more comprehensive vision of himself and of the world around him. The poet even tells us the protagonist's age in the third part of "Praise to the End!":

> The sun came out;
> The lake turned green;
> Romped upon the goldy grass,
> Aged thirteen.

In spite of persistent obstacles passages of lyrical exaltation occur with greater frequency than they do in the poems preceding "The Lost Son." Such superior moments, with their pleasure in the beauty and variety of nature, look forward to some of Roethke's last poetry. Stanzas like the following from "I Cry, Love!

Love!" (which takes its title from William Blake's "Visions of the Daughters of Albion") prepare the way for the vision of life we find in "The Far Field" or "Meditations of an Old Woman":

I hear the owls, the soft callers, coming down
    from the hemlocks.
The bats weave in and out of the willows,
Wing-crooked and sure,
Downward and upward,
Dipping and veering close to the motionless
    water.

A fish jumps, shaking out flakes of moonlight.
A single wave starts lightly and easily
    shoreward,
Wrinkling between reeds in shallower water,
Lifting a few twigs and floating leaves,
Then washing up over small stones.

The shine on the face of the lake
Tilts, backward and forward.
The water recedes slowly,
Gently rocking.

After the unusual and striking techniques which he introduces for his special purposes in the sequence poems, Roethke turns back again to a more formal manner in the early 1950's. In some of this work, most notably in "Four for Sir John Davies" and later in "The Dying Man," he makes use of cadences somewhat reminiscent of those in the poetry of Yeats, but these are intentional effects on Roethke's part and not, as some critics would have us believe, signs of weakness and of an unassimilated influence. Roethke ably defended himself against such charges in his essay "How to Write Like Somebody Else," pointing out that the poet needs to work forward consciously from his predecessors, that "the language itself is a compound . . ." And finally, he adds, "the very fact" that the poet "has the support of a tradition, or an older writer, will enable him to be more himself—or more than himself."

What Roethke says on this subject is profoundly true and is peculiarly applicable to himself. With his sequence finished he could no longer exercise the devices employed there: that vein was thoroughly mined and could only be kept open at the risk of repetition, boredom, and stultification. But he had learned a good deal from the sequence, and the themes which engaged his imagination were far from exhausted; in fact, one might venture to say that the exploration of the past, of personal history, served to make the present very available to him. The evolution of the self was not done, and the love poems begun during this period show that this evolution was entering a new, more expansive phase which related the self to the other, or the beloved. Technically speaking, Roethke tested the possibilities of a formal style, but with a daring, a liberty and passion that go beyond the urgencies of amorous feeling. His experiments in the sequence poems freed him to attempt an altered diction and looser syntax, more exclamatory, interrogative, and aphoristic lines:

I'd say it to my horse: we live beyond
Our outer skin. Who's whistling up my sleeve?
I see a heron prancing in his pond;
I know a dance the elephants believe.
The living all assemble! What's the cue?—
Do what the clumsy partner wants to do!

To get a better impression of the distance Roethke has traveled thus far in his poetic style, let us set next to those lines above from "Four for Sir John Davies" a stanza from "The Heron" in *Open House* which will call to mind the more restricted, tense character of the poet's first work:

The heron stands in water where the swamp
Has deepened to the blackness of a pool,

Or balances with one leg on a hump
Of marsh grass heaped above a musk-rat hole.

The piece which best prepares us for the considerable group of love poems now gathered into their own section of *Words for the Wind* is "Four for Sir John Davies," an ambitious poetic cycle that appeared among the last pages of Roethke's Pulitzer Prize volume of selected poems, *The Waking* (1953). As the title implies a little covertly, the basic metaphor of the poem is dancing. Roethke draws openly on two other poets to enlarge the dimensions of his poems: they are the sixteenth-century English poet to whom these four pieces are dedicated and William Butler Yeats. From Davies' *Orchestra* (1594), a long philosophical poem on the harmonious relations of the various spheres of being in the universe, Roethke gains support for the cosmic scheme he includes in the first poem, "The Dance." But since *Orchestra* is constructed about a supposed dispute between Penelope and her suitor Antinous, who tries to persuade her to dance, the sexual theme has also already been evoked, though as yet only indirectly. And it is to Yeats that Roethke looks for precedence in the treatment of sexual love through the figure of the dance, as well as for certain rhythms and qualities of tone and diction.

"The Dance" begins with the poet recalling the universal system to be found in Davies' poem, then questioning whether man any longer conceives of the world in terms of the dance within his own mind. Whatever the answer to that question may be, he affirms his own participation in such a cosmic dance and even humorously identifies himself with the shambling but pleasurable gait of bears:

The great wheel turns its axle when it can;
I need a place to sing, and dancing-room,
And I have made a promise to my ears
I'll sing and whistle romping with the bears.

But Roethke intends something more than mild self-mockery here, for the bears in their dance throw into relief the sheer physical aspect of existence—in the poet as well as in themselves: "O watch his body sway!— / This animal remembering to be gay." The poem carries this note into the third stanza with emphasis now placed on the poet's own isolated dancing. In spite of the elation accompanying this joyous, willed activity there is an incompleteness in what he does that can only be corrected by the appearance of the beloved. This beginning poem of the four closes with a stanza expressing Roethke's debt to Yeats:

I take this cadence from a man named Yeats;
I take it, and I give it back again:
For other tunes and other wanton beats
Have tossed my heart and fiddled through my
    brain.
Yes, I was dancing-mad, and how
That came to be the bears and Yeats would
    know.

The next poem, "The Partner," brings together the poet and his beloved in the dance. It becomes clear immediately that their relationship is more than sensual, more even than love between two persons, for overtly sexual gestures generate metaphysical overtones until we sense that Roethke attains a kind of visionary intuition of human possibility through his dancing lovers:

Things loll and loiter. Who condones the lost?
This joy outleaps the dog. Who cares? Who
    cares?
I gave her kisses back, and woke a ghost.
O what lewd music crept into our ears!
The body and the soul know how to play
In that dark world where gods have lost their
    way.

The "dark world" of which the poet speaks is undoubtedly the maze of love and bodily attraction. It may further imply the realm of the human, fully realized in the sexual and spiritual bond of the pair, as opposed to a supernatural plane of being altogether removed from life. We enter that world more completely in "The Wraith," where lover and beloved apparently exchange identities through their union. Though this poem aims specifically in its imagery and reference at the intense moment of completion in the sexual act, it extends past that in Roethke's speculations on the meaning of the act. Certainly we do not exaggerate in saying that he wishes to reveal the spiritual transcendence emerging from carnal love in the poem:

> There was a body, and it cast a spell,—
> God pity those but wanton to the knees,—
> The flesh can make the spirit visible . . .

The wraith, "a shape alone, / Impaled on light, and whirling slowly down," who is the poet's image of his beloved, is briefly associated with Dante's Beatrice in the first stanza of "The Vigil." In those lines Roethke asserts the purity of the lover's vision of the beloved. Created from his "longing" it may be contradicted but not destroyed by the reality of the loved one as a person. But the allusion to Dante and Beatrice goes further because it supports the transcendental experience recorded in the poem's last stanza, an experience which never denies the physical nature of the love relationship and yet presents it as the cause of a breakthrough in the spiritual order:

The world is for the living. Who are they?
We dared the dark to reach the white and
    warm.
She was the wind when wind was in my way;
Alive at noon, I perished in her form.
Who rise from flesh to spirit know the fall:
The word outleaps the world, and light is all.

Such a visionary climax is predicted by the similar but less comprehensive bursts of illumination in "The Lost Son" and other poems of that sequence. Even more important is the fact that moments of this kind recur throughout the love poems and again, of course, in the unmistakably visionary and meditative work that follows. It is necessary to understand first of all that Roethke's love poems are not just evocations of the beloved or descriptions of his aroused emotions with regard to her; these play their part in what he writes, but it is only one part. As I hinted earlier, this group of poems brings to a certain measure of fulfillment the evolution of the self begun with the childhood and adolescence poems. So Roethke tends to locate the loved woman at the center of the physical universe: through her he communes with that world and its elements, and has his vision transformed. Once more we think of the reference to Dante, of Beatrice's guidance which brings that poet to a revelation of the Divine. Surely the beloved in Roethke's poems, though she can change swiftly from a wraithlike to an earthy creature, functions in a manner closely resembling her predecessor.

A poem that is one of the most fully achieved as well as one of the most representative of the considerations discussed here is "Words for the Wind," which gives its title to Roethke's collected verse. Other of the love poems do take up various strands of the themes of death, spirit versus flesh, ultimate belief, and so forth, but they gain much more prominence in "The Dying Man," an elegy to Yeats, and "Meditations of an Old Woman." In a recent anthology, *Poet's Choice*, edited by Paul Engle and Joseph Langland, Roethke says that "Words for the Wind" was written as an epithalamion to his bride during their honeymoon visit at W. H. Auden's villa in Ischia, but these are merely the external circumstances of composition. The poem itself is literally a song of joy, a mood in the poet which arises from delight in his companion but overflows into the world outside. Perhaps it would be even more accurate to say that his love for this woman awakens and refines in him a knowledge of a participation in the life of creation, in the being of all things. His beloved merges with flowers, the wind, a stone, the moon, and so she appears to be present in almost every living thing, in objects or the elements. As the last line of the opening stanza intimates, he has the sensitive reverence for them we think of in a St. Francis of Assisi, who would make a particularly appropriate patron saint for Roethke's poetry:

> Love, love, a lily's my care,
> She's sweeter than a tree.
> Loving, I use the air
> Most lovingly: I breathe;
> Mad in the wind I wear
> Myself as I should be,
> All's even with the odd,
> My brother the vine is glad.

Not only does this love result in a harmony with the cosmos but it accomplishes an internal balance too. The self that was, so to speak, divided against itself in many previous poems arrives at unity through another person, a woman who is frankly physical and sexual but is furthermore a creature of spiritual and mythological proportions. In the intensified perception of the poem we see her continual metamorphosis, her changing roles, but at the same time she remains a constant image within the poet himself, the archetypal female principle dwelling in man which Jung called the *Anima*:

> The shallow stream runs slack;
> The wind creaks slowly by;
> Out of a nestling's beak

> Comes a tremulous cry
> I cannot answer back;
> A shape from deep in the eye—
> That woman I saw in a stone—
> Keeps pace when I walk alone.

In spite of this disclosure of a psychic image Roethke concentrates most of his imaginative powers on the external world and the forms of nature. The second section of the poem is devoted almost totally to natural imagery through which the course of love and the person of the beloved are traced. Here we find creation transfigured by the lovers who move within it and color it with their complex of emotions, "the burden of this joy":

> The sun declares the earth;
> The stones leap in the stream;
> On a wide plain, beyond
> The far stretch of a dream,
> A field breaks like the sea;
> The wind's white with her name,
> And I walk with the wind.

Love in the figure of this woman "wakes the ends of life," Roethke tells us, and I do not believe it is misleading to say that she and the poems about her suggested to the poet some of the approaches and devices of his later writing. "The Dying Man" and "Meditations of an Old Woman," the two poetic cycles which conclude *Words for the Wind*, are meditative and both employ the persona or mask to obtain a more objective dramatization of viewpoint.

At the start of "The Dying Man" the imagined voice of Yeats alternates and blends with Roethke's through the five lyrics composing it, and the style is itself a combination of the poetic speech of the two men. This adaptation of the Yeatsian manner and mood is not merely casual but quite intentional. In his late poems Yeats was, of course, paradoxical, outrageous, and extremely powerful, with a seemingly boundless reserve of energy to dispose to these ends. He brought together spiritual and sensual modes of experience in unexpected, even sensational, ways and under the harsh light of his irony. Roethke wished at times to use his poetry as Yeats did, to probe the extremes of perception and knowledge which the self may attain. "The Dying Man" is just such an imaginative effort; and the fact that it is both an elegy for Yeats and a utilization of some of his language and techniques should not prevent us from seeing how Roethke is really examining himself and his own situation.

The opening poem, "His Words," records the message of "a dying man / . . . to his gathered kin." This man is presumably Yeats, and what he says seems an amalgam of the thought of Blake and Yeats. Here the last stanza proves most influential in stirring the mind of the poem's narrator (Roethke himself) to his own observations:

> "A man sees, as he dies,
>   Death's possibilities;
>   My heart sways with the world.
> I am that final thing,
> A man learning to sing."

The second poem begins with the revaluation of his life and work which these last words and the death following them force upon the poet-narrator. In addition, he feels the potentialities of existence revived: "I thought myself reborn." The subsequent stanzas range back over past experience, the poet's love and its opposite, the darkest moments of the spirit when he "dared to question all." A knocking "at the gate" announces most probably the presence of death, but the poet puts that off in the concluding line.

Three other poems, "The Wall," "The Exulting," and "They Sing, They Sing," make up the rest of the cycle. All of them reach beyond the bounds of a reasoned arrangement of ideas and perceptions in favor of a terse but ecstatic and visionary utterance. Themes are intermingled, but they include the poet's psychic burdens:

> A ghost comes out of the unconscious mind
> To grope my sill: It moans to be reborn!
> The figure at my back is not my friend;
> The hand upon my shoulder turns to horn.

and the fusion of natural and transcendental knowledge:

> Though it reject dry borders of the seen,
> What sensual eye can keep an image pure,
> Leaning across a sill to greet the dawn?

These passages, taken from "The Wall," both use the image of the sill as the apparent threshold separating the conscious self from the unconscious and from external reality. The wall turns up in the third stanza as the limit of what can be known, and thus the poet can recognize his dilemma as that of "a spirit raging at the visible."

"The Exulting" begins with a statement of the childlike innocence and freedom which once satisfied the poet but which now have aroused further yearnings:

> I love the world; I want more than the world,
> Or after-image of the inner eye.

Yet the most explicit account of the object of his desires, if it can be so described, is withheld until the final stanzas of the last poem. There nature asserts itself as a means of revelation for Roethke, and he has a vision of reality corresponding to the words of the dying man in the initial section of the poem—"Eternity is Now"—a vision that calls to mind Blake's famous passage from "The Marriage of Heaven and Hell": "If the doors of perception were cleansed every thing would appear to man as it is, infinite." The world gives the poet intuitions of the eternal and the infinite through its temporal, finite creatures and things—if he has learned how to see or has been granted this frightening clairvoyance:

I've the lark's word for it, who sings alone:
What's seen recedes; Forever's what we
  know!—
Eternity defined, and strewn with straw,
The fury of the slug beneath the stone.
The vision moves, and yet remains the same.
In heaven's praise, I dread the thing I am.

The poem's ending lines, of great strength and beauty, set forth the loneliness and uncertainty but also the singular determination of the poet in his confrontation of the unknowable or the void where the Divine may be sought. Roethke furnishes no answers and, as he does elsewhere, keeps within the strict confines of his personal perceivings:

Nor can imagination do it all
In this last place of light: he dares to live
Who stops being a bird, yet beats his wings
Against the immense immeasurable emptiness
  of things.

"Meditations of an Old Woman," a longer and superior group of poems, consists of several dramatic monologues spoken by an aging lady, modeled on the poet's mother, who muses on her past, on the meanings of an individual's existence, as she faces the prospect of death. Over and above those poems included in *Words for the Wind* and in the volume of light verse (which also reprints the so-called greenhouse poems) *I Am! Says the Lamb* (1961) there are a considerable number of later poems. Roethke planned a book for them, completing it shortly before his death; it appeared as *The Far Field* the following year. It ought to be said that the "North American Sequence" poems take the

manner and technique of the "Meditations" as their starting place; some of them become even looser in form; other poems are fragmentary, explosive, and epigrammatic; some turn to a taut lyricism. Many are shaped by that mixture of description and reflection so prominent in the "Meditations." Through these poems runs a continued fascination with ultimate questions of mortality, God, the final significance of human life. Of course these are questions about the self too, and they constantly bring Roethke's evolutionary theme to its highest level, that is, to occasions of visionary knowledge. But we should look at "Meditations of an Old Woman" both as the foundation of later work and as the last part of *Words for the Wind*.

The "First Meditation," which inaugurates the series of five poems, offers the reader opening stanzas that create a harsh mood of old age, winter, frailty, and severely restricted expectations. We can capture something of the ominous quality of this section from the initial lines:

On love's worst ugly day,
The weeds hiss at the edge of the field,
The small winds make their chilly indictments.

Thus the title and the beginning provide us with the personal situation from which the speaker's memories and thoughts are set in motion. As Roethke so frequently does, he expresses the condition of a person's life through happenings or objects in nature. The old woman's recognition of death is conveyed vividly by external events: "stones loosen on the obscure hillside, / And a tree tilts from its roots, / Toppling down an embankment." And here we must remember that it is *her mind* which entertains these images of sliding stones and falling trees.

In spite of the temporal erosion that has worn away the speaker as though she were a thing exposed to wind and dust and rain there is an essential life of the spirit preserved in her described by Roethke as "light as a seed." Small that life may be, but it has a toughness and resiliency which enables it to burst forth with a vigorous assertion of its own being. The effort of the spirit to be renewed is characteristically reflected in careful details of the actions of nonhuman creatures, a fish, for example:

So the spirit tries for another life,
Another way and place in which to continue;
Or a salmon, tired, moving up a shallow stream,
Nudges into a back-eddy, a sandy inlet,
Bumping against sticks and bottom-stones,
      then swinging
Around, back into the tiny maincurrent, the
      rush of brownish-white water,
Still swimming forward—
So, I suppose, the spirit journeys.

This passage could be seen as a paradigm of the five poems, for the old woman's meditation, which spans the period of time in the poetic cycle, is analogous to the rest enjoyed by the salmon before he renews his journey against the stream. For precisely this brief duration we are allowed to enter the speaker's mind and witness her thoughts.

Within her consciousness, as might be expected, there are alternating currents of imagery and ideas. Her attention may shift rather abruptly from past to present, from the actual to the speculative, from knowledge to dream, as we would naturally imagine it to do readily in a person of advanced age who has a lifetime to think upon and its termination to face. Yet whatever these fluctuations of consciousness might be and however random they might seem at first glance, all of them contribute to a pattern of repeated affirmations of life which reach a peak of lyrical strength at the end of "What Can I Tell My Bones?"

In contrast to this pattern the poems also contain the elements of despair, evil, and nothingness: all that thwarts the steady forward movement of the spirit. One could, in a more comprehensive study of Roethke's poetry, draw up two lists, of his positive and negative imagery, and not simply for the poems under discussion but for his work in general. We have already noticed some of the recurring metaphors and symbols in passing. Most of them will be familiar to the reader who has watched the texts with care. On the positive side we find spring and summer; the sun and moon; small creatures of the bird, insect, and fish variety; wind and flowing water; flowers, plants, and grass. On the negative side would appear winter; aridity; still and muddy waters; holes, pits, or caves; dust; desolate landscapes. The old lady in her reflections also must countenance the memory of negative experience, if only to defeat it. In the following lines we can see how she conceives the life-denying by bringing it together in her mind with the life-giving and the sacramental:

I have gone into the waste lonely places
Behind the eye; the lost acres at the edge of
      smoky cities.
What's beyond never crumbles like an
      embankment,
Explodes like a rose, or thrusts wings over the
      Caribbean.
There are no pursuing forms, faces on walls:
Only the motes of dust in the immaculate
      hallways,
The darkness of falling hair, the warnings from
      lint and spiders,
The vines graying to a fine powder.
There is no riven tree, or lamb dropped by an
      eagle.

Like D. H. Lawrence, with whom the critic Kenneth Burke once very interestingly compared him, Roethke locates a substantial moral vocabulary in the natural order. Perhaps these uses are not intentional in every case of such imagery, but certainly his images very often serve a purpose of the kind I have named.

The moments of ecstasy in these poems, as elsewhere in Roethke's previous work, tend to occur through the life of nature or within its boundaries. "I'm Here," the second of the "Meditations," is largely devoted to memories of the old woman's girlhood years: from them arise scenes of an innocence, an awakening of flesh and spirit in concord with the surrounding world:

> I was queen of the vale—
> For a short while,
> Living all my heart's summer alone,
> Ward of my spirit,
> Running through high grasses,
> My thighs brushing against flower crowns;
> Leaning, out of all breath,
> Bracing my back against a sapling,
> Making it quiver with my body . . .

And again:

> The body, delighting in thresholds,
> Rocks in and out of itself.
> A bird, small as a leaf,
> Sings in the first
> Sunlight.

The closing poem compels the speaker once more to encounter the forbidding prospect of a slow crumbling away to death; yet it is at last her love for all things, especially the commonplace or simple things of which our everyday world is made, that urges her back from somber meditation to the flow of existence. The tired, aging lady with whom the cycle of poems began emerges from shelter as if life had just been given her by an "agency outside . . . Unprayed-for, / And final." But Roethke is not explicit about this agency as yet. Later poems such as "In a Dark Time" recount the poet's

experience of God in trancelike visions. The emphasis in the "Meditations" falls upon earthly possibility, the self's embrace of the entire horizon of existence open to it:

> The sun! The sun! And all we can become!
> And the time ripe for running to the moon!
> In the long fields, I leave my father's eye;
> And shake the secrets from my deepest bones;
> My spirit rises with the rising wind;
> I'm thick with leaves and tender as a dove,
> I take the liberties a short life permits—
> I seek my own meekness;
> I recover my tenderness by long looking.
> By midnight I love everything alive.
> Who took the darkness from the air?
> I'm wet with another life.
> Yea, I have gone and stayed.

Though cut tragically short by his premature death, Roethke's career is brought to a magnificent conclusion in the poems of *The Far Field*. Here we find an extension of his amazing, always increasing versatility in formal arrangement and experiment, his ability to explore several avenues of poetic endeavor simultaneously without sacrificing the value of one to the interests of another. In these poems various thematic preoccupations—the identity of the self, its relation to the beloved, to nature, and to God—also achieve rewarding fulfillment.

The book is organized in four sections. The first and last, "North American Sequence" and "Sequence, Sometimes Metaphysical," though contrasting in manner, are concerned with a search for the Divine and with spiritual illumination. In between there is a sizable group of love poems and a section of miscellaneous pieces aptly called "Mixed Sequence." The love poems, written for his wife, Beatrice, even include, with humor and understanding, the moments of their discord; but these are far outnumbered by celebrations of the ecstasy and joy of their relationship. At the end of the section we discover the incredibly moving and prophetic "Wish for a Young Wife":

> My lizard, my lovely writher,
> May your limbs never wither,
> May the eyes in your face
> Survive the green ice
> Of envy's mean gaze;
> May you live out your life
> Without hate, without grief,
> And your hair ever blaze,
> In the sun, in the sun,
> When I am undone,
> When I am no one.

Of this kind of short lyric Roethke is a master, as we have seen in his work from the beginning. Over the years he had tested its possibilities as thought and experience deepened, and in "Sequence, Sometimes Metaphysical" he brings this taut, economical form to a peak of accomplishment in the treatment of difficult material. The twelve-poem sequence starts with "In a Dark Time," which is a statement of harrowing mystical union, and continues with poems reflecting on this encounter, as well as with other instances of spiritual revelation. While these experiences are, in one sense, extremely personal, Roethke uses recurrent images and metaphors, frequently drawn from the natural world, to objectify his inner life. Many of the pieces appeared singly in journals and made impressive reading by themselves; but now, taken altogether, they compose a cycle of visionary lyrics which must surely count among the finest in our literature. Let me quote, as an example, the first stanza of "The Tree, the Bird":

Uprose, uprose, the stony fields uprose,
And every snail dipped toward me its pure
    horn.

The sweet light met me as I walked toward
A small voice calling from a drifting cloud.
I was a finger pointing at the moon,
At ease with joy, a self-enchanted man.
Yet when I sighed, I stood outside my life,
A leaf unaltered by the midnight scene,
Part of a tree still dark, still, deathly still,
Riding the air, a willow with its kind,
Bearing its life and more, a double sound,
Kin to the wind, and the bleak whistling rain.

And, as one further instance of Roethke's power and clairvoyance in these poems, here are some lines from "Infirmity":

Things without hands take hands: there is no
    choice,—
Eternity's not easily come by.
When opposites come suddenly in place,
I teach my eyes to hear, my ears to see
How body from spirit slowly does unwind
Until we are pure spirit at the end.

The poems of "North American Sequence" stand in marked formal contrast to such lyrics and indicate a continuation of the reflective monologue of "Meditations of an Old Woman." Now, however, the poet dispenses with the dramatic mask, speaks in his own person, and records the movements of his spiritual consciousness, his quest for a final unity. Roethke wrote in his essay "Some Remarks on Rhythm" of the need for the catalogue poem, for the careful and prolonged descriptive passage; and in these pieces with their lengthy, irregular lines, deliberately placed in the Whitman tradition, he has answered his own requirements. Disclosing the progressions and setbacks of his inward states, the desire to escape from the self and its attachments, the sequence also renders in stunning detail the life of nature in profound correspondence with the poet's inward being. It is difficult to quote without taking very long sections, so I will make do with a few lines from "Meditation at Oyster River":

The self persists like a dying star,
In sleep, afraid. Death's face rises afresh,
Among the shy beasts, the deer at the salt-lick,
The doe with its sloped shoulders loping across
    the highway,
The young snake, poised in green leaves,
    waiting for its fly,
The hummingbird, whirring from quince-
    blossom to morning-glory—
With these I would be.

Roethke once said to me, a year before his death, that this might well be his last book, a judgment I found both depressing and hard to believe. It was painfully accurate though, and these late poems, preoccupied with death and the ultimate phases of spiritual quest, beautifully complete his life's work as if by intuition. Few contemporary poets can match the daring, the richness, and the freedom—which is really to say, in summary, the beauty—of the totality of his writing. Surely the intensity and clarity of Roethke's vision, in addition to his tremendous lyrical force and technical facility, place him, as John Crowe Ransom has said, in company with some of the finest modern American poets. His art shows the poet's will to extend himself, to try his skill and imagination at every turn, and his growth was organic and true. Roethke's sense of direction was bold and challenging yet unfailingly precise. The metamorphoses or transformations through which he and his poems passed are caught in the old lady's words near the end of "What Can I Tell My Bones?" What they reveal of that speaker, her aspirations and strength, they also disclose about Roethke and the magnitude of his poetic achievement:

The wind rocks with my wish; the rain shields
    me;
I live in light's extreme; I stretch in all
    directions;
Sometimes I think I'm several.

Selected Bibliography

WORKS OF THEODORE ROETHKE

POETRY

Open House. New York: Knopf, 1941.

The Lost Son and Other Poems. Garden City, N.Y.: Doubleday, 1948.

Praise to the End. Garden City, N.Y.: Doubleday, 1951.

The Waking: Poems 1933–1953. Garden City, N.Y.: Doubleday, 1953.

Words for the Wind: The Collected Verse of Theodore Roethke. Garden City, N.Y.: Doubleday, 1958.

I Am! Says the Lamb. Garden City, N.Y.: Doubleday, 1961.

Sequence, Sometimes Metaphysical. Iowa City: Stonewall Press, 1963.

The Far Field. Garden City, N.Y.: Doubleday, 1964.

The Collected Poems of Theodore Roethke. Garden City, N.Y.: Doubleday, 1966.

PROSE

On the Poet and His Craft: Selected Prose of Theodore Roethke, edited by Ralph J. Mills, Jr. Seattle: University of Washington Press, 1965.

Selected Letters of Theodore Roethke, edited by Ralph J. Mills, Jr. Seattle: University of Washington Press, 1968.

MISCELLANEOUS

Straw for the Fire: Selections from Theodore Roethke's Notebooks 1943–1963, edited by David Wagoner. Garden City, N.Y.: Doubleday, 1972.

BIBLIOGRAPHY

Matheson, John William. *Theodore Roethke: A Bibliography*. University of Washington, Master of Librarianship thesis, 1958.

McLeod, James R. *Theodore Roethke: A Manuscript Checklist*. Kent, Ohio: Kent State University Press, 1971.

———. *Theodore Roethke: A Bibliography*. Kent, Ohio: Kent State University Press, 1972.

BIOGRAPHY

Seager, Allan. *The Glass House: The Life of Theodore Roethke*. New York: McGraw-Hill, 1968.

CRITICAL STUDIES

Arnett, Carroll. "Minimal to Maximal: Theodore Roethke's Dialectic," *College English*, 18:414–16 (May 1957).

Bogan, Louise. "Stitched in Bone," in *Trial Balances*, edited by Ann Winslow. New York: Macmillan, 1935. Pp. 138–39.

Burke, Kenneth. "The Vegetal Radicalism of Theodore Roethke," *Sewanee Review*, 58:68–108 (Winter 1950).

Dickey, James. "Theodore Roethke," in *Babel to Byzantium: Poets and Poetry Now*. New York: Noonday Press, 1968. Pp. 147–52.

Gross, Harvey. *Sound and Form in Modern Poetry*. Ann Arbor: University of Michigan Press, 1964.

Kramer, Hilton. "The Poetry of Theodore Roethke," *Western Review*, 18:131–46 (Winter 1954).

Kunitz, Stanley. "News of the Root," *Poetry*, 73:222–25 (January 1949).

———. "Theodore Roethke," *New York Review of Books*, 1:22 (October 17, 1963).

———. "Roethke: Poet of Transformations," *New Republic*, 152: 23–29 (January 23, 1965).

Lee, Charlotte I. "The Line as a Rhythmic Unit in the Poetry of Theodore Roethke," *Speech Monographs*, 30:15–22 (March 1963).

Malkoff, Karl. *Theodore Roethke: An Introduction to the Poetry*. New York: Columbia University Press, 1966.

Martz, William J. *The Achievement of Theodore Roethke*. Glenview, Ill.: Scott, Foresman, 1966.

Mills, Ralph J., Jr. "Roethke's Garden," *Poetry*, 100: 54–59 (April 1962).

———. "Theodore Roethke," in *Contemporary American Poetry*. New York: Random House, 1965. Pp. 48–71.

———. *Creation's Very Self: On the Personal Element in Recent American Poetry*. Fort Worth: Texas Christian University Press, 1969.

Northwest Review, 11 (Summer 1971). Special issue on Theodore Roethke.

Ostroff, Anthony, ed. *The Contemporary Poet as Artist and Critic*. Boston: Little, Brown, 1964. (This includes essays on Roethke's "In a Dark Time" by John Crowe Ransom, Babette Deutsch, and Stanley Kunitz, with a reply by the poet.)

Rosenthal, M. L. *The Modern Poets*. New York: Oxford University Press, 1960. Pp. 240–44.

Scott, Nathan A., Jr. *The Wild Prayer of Longing*. New Haven, Conn.: Yale University Press, 1971.

Schwartz, Delmore. "The Cunning and Craft of the Unconscious and the Preconscious," *Poetry*, 94:203–05 (June 1959).

Southworth, James G. "The Poetry of Theodore Roethke," *College English*, 21:326–38 (March 1960).

Spender, Stephen. "Words for the Wind," *New Republic*, 141:21–22 (August 10, 1959).

Staples, Hugh B. "The Rose in the Sea-Wind: A Reading of Theodore Roethke's 'North American Sequence,'" *American Literature*, 6:189–203 (May 1964).

Stein, Arnold, ed. *Theodore Roethke: Essays on the Poetry*. Seattle: University of Washington Press, 1965.

Tate, Allen. "In Memoriam—Theodore Roethke, 1908–1963," *Encounter*, 21:68 (October 1963).

Vernon, John. "Theodore Roethke's *Praise to the End!* Poems," *Iowa Review*, 2:60–79 (Fall 1971).

Waggoner, Hyatt H. *American Poets from the Puritans to the Present*. Boston: Houghton Mifflin, 1968.

Winters, Yvor. "The Poems of Theodore Roethke," *Kenyon Review*, 3:514–16 (Autumn 1941).

—*RALPH J. MILLS, JR.*

J. D. Salinger

1919-

HOLDEN CAULFIELD, the fumbling adolescent nauseated by the grossness of the world's body, may be the characteristic hero of contemporary fiction and the modern world. There can be no doubt that for modern American youth, Holden is an embodiment of their secret terrors and their accumulated hostilities, their slender joys and their magnified agonies. In his persistent innocence and his blundering virtue, he may represent to the rest of the world an adolescent America uncertainly searching for the lost garden, suspicious of alien or intimate entanglements, reluctant to encounter the horrors of reality.

No other writer since World War II has achieved the heights of popularity of J. D. (for Jerome David) Salinger. And his popularity has rested primarily on one hero, Holden Caulfield, and on one book, *The Catcher in the Rye.* Something of the intensity of the public adulation of the novelist was suggested by the appearance of his picture on the cover of *Time* magazine on September 15, 1961, together with an accompanying story that perpetuated at the same time that it extended the myth of the man and writer. Something of the depth of Salinger's academic reputation may be gauged by the publication in 1962 and 1963 of five casebooks containing source materials for use in the classroom study of Salinger. For an author born in 1919 (January 1), Salinger has excited an astonishing amount and variety of commentary by any standard of measurement. Those who have felt unmoved to appreciate have felt compelled to dissent. No writer since the 1920's—the era of Fitzgerald and Hemingway—has aroused so much public and critical interest.

But unlike Fitzgerald and Hemingway, Salinger has refused to live in public the role of American Author. The known facts of Salinger's life are sparse and undramatic. He was born in New York City the son of a Jewish father and an Irish mother, the second of two children, the first being his sister Doris. He graduated from Valley Forge Military Academy in 1936, where his I.Q. was recorded as 115. In the next few years he attended sporadically a number of colleges, including New York University, without completing a program for a degree. In 1937–38 he made a brief visit to Austria and Poland in the service of his father's meat-import business. Shortly after, he found his way into a short-story writing class taught by Whit Burnett at Columbia. In 1940, at the age of 21, he published his first story, "The Young Folks," in *Story*.

Like other young men of his generation, Salinger's perspective on life was molded by his experience in World War II. The spiritual crisis in which every Salinger hero finds himself was probably shaped, at least embryonically, in the boredom, frustrations, agonies, and horrors of the world at righteous war with itself. Salinger was drafted in 1942, was stationed for a time in Tennessee, then England (Tiverton, Devonshire), and, in 1944, landed on Utah Beach on D Day. His subsequent participation in five campaigns was surely sufficient to confirm his distaste for military experience. And if we are allowed to read any autobiography at all in his work, we may readily guess that the war was responsible for, or at least brought to the surface, an alienation from modern existence so profound as to manifest itself at times in an overpowering spiritual nausea.

Salinger began to publish stories widely during the war. He gradually moved from the little magazines to the popular mass-circulation magazines, such as *Collier's* and *Saturday Evening Post*, and finally, during the latter forties, began to publish almost exclusively in the *New Yorker*. In 1951 *The Catcher in the Rye* was published and distributed as a Book-of-the-Month Club selection; it was followed in 1953 by *Nine Stories*. Salinger married Claire Douglas, a Radcliffe graduate born in England, in 1955, and settled in Cornish, New Hampshire; two children were born, a daughter in 1955 and a son in 1960. After 1953, Salinger's productivity markedly declined. He published two slender books which brought together pairs of stories published previously in the *New Yorker*: *Franny and Zooey* (1961), containing stories first published in 1955 and 1957; and *Raise High the Roof Beam, Carpenters; and Seymour: An Introduction* (1963), with stories first published in 1955 and 1959. A prolonged silence was broken in 1965 with the publication of "Hapworth 16, 1924" in the *New Yorker*.

From 1940 to 1953, Salinger published a total of thirty stories. The rigorous selection for *Nine Stories* left twenty-one stories buried in the magazines. Although some of these stories are embarrassingly immature, others are accomplished and impressive and show an astonishingly rapid advance in craft and deepening of thematic complexity (see the bibliography for a chronological listing of the stories). The young heroines of some of these stories clearly link with the empty-headed flappers of the early F. Scott Fitzgerald, and also are forerunners of Salinger's own later and much more complex young heroines, Muriel, Esmé, Phoebe, and Franny. Some of the stories focus on young men who, however adolescent and callow and painfully innocent, are usually redeemed by the achievement of some kind of moral awareness that is both sobering and maturing; these young men are forerunners of such later characters as Holden Caulfield, Seymour Glass, and Seymour's brother Buddy. One story, a novella, worth singling out from the rest—"The Inverted Forest"—tells the tragic tale of a brilliant poet whose talent is ultimately destroyed by himself and those about him. The poet (Raymond Ford) is clearly an early version of Seymour Glass, and it is worthy of note in passing that among his favorite poets are Walt Whitman and Rainer Maria Rilke.

Some six of these early stories deal directly with materials that would turn up again in *The Catcher in the Rye*. Four of these ("Last Day of the Last Furlough," "A Boy in France," "This Sandwich Has No Mayonnaise," and "The Stranger") present two soldiers, Babe Gladwaller and Vincent Caulfield, who are buddies and who share one characteristic— each is deeply concerned, almost to the point of obsession, about a younger member of his family, Babe with his sister Mattie, who foreshadows Esmé and Phoebe, and Vincent with his kid brother Holden, who is missing in action. Two other stories ("I'm Crazy" and "Slight Rebellion off Madison") are in fact early versions of some of the episodes in *Catcher*, and reveal Salinger in process of discovering his major themes and experimenting with what were to develop into his most effective techniques.

The Catcher in the Rye is a deceptively simple, enormously rich book whose sources of appeal run in deep and complexly varied veins. The very young are likely to identify with Holden and to see the adult world in which he sojourns as completely phony and worthless; the book thus becomes a handbook for rebels and a guide to the failures of the establishment. The older generation is likely to identify with some part of the society that is satirized, and to see Holden as a bright but sick boy whose psyche needs adjustment before he can, as he will, find his niche and settle down. Holden as ideal rebel or Holden as neurotic misfit—the evidence for either interpretation lies loosely on the surface of the novel. Beneath the surface lies the evilence for a more complicated as well as more convincing Holden than some of his admirers are willing to recognize.

A brief summary of *Catcher* suggests the episodic nature of its structure. Holden Caulfield flunks out of Pencey Prep in Pennsylvania and starts out on the terrible journey to his home in New York, where he must face his parents after this latest in a series of expulsions. The journey becomes a combination nightmare and burlesque where horror and comedy mix in inexplicable fashion. Holden has a series of encounters with people, but never a genuine engagement (as he observes, "People never give your message to anybody"). His roommate at Pencey, Stradlater, is a clean-cut youth but a "secret slob." The boy next door, Ackley, is a slob in public—but still can provide occasional company for a lonely Holden. On the train to New York, Holden meets the mother of one of his classmates—and lies "like a madman" to reassure her of her illusions about her "sensitive" son ("That guy . . . was about as sensitive as a goddam toilet seat"). In the big city he calls a faded name he pulls out of his wallet—a former burlesque stripper, Faith Cavendish—and has a talk but does not connect. He drifts into the company of three female tourists, all naïve greenhorns, in a nightclub—and gets stuck for the entire evening's bill. At another nightclub he runs into a "boring" friend of his older brother, D. B. (now "prostituting" himself by writing for the movies), and escapes ("People are always ruining things for you"). Back at his hotel, he acquiesces in a suggestion from the elevator "guy" and is visited in his room by Sunny; but feeling "more depressed than sexy," he tells her he isn't in the mood and attempts to pay her off with the agreed-on price of five dollars—when she demands ten, a demand backed up by the fists of the brutish elevator boy, Maurice. So ends the first day of Holden's odyssey.

On the next day, Sunday, the journey begins again, but with a new cast of characters. Holden's first encounter at breakfast is a pleasant one, with two nuns to whom he insists on giving ten of his few remaining dollars. Holden then begins to drift with the day. He passes a poor, Sunday-dressed family, whose little boy is singing "If a body catch a body coming through the rye"; he walks over to his beloved Museum of Natural History ("everything always stayed right where it was"), but decides not to go in. In the afternoon, he takes his old girl friend, Sally Hayes, to see the Lunts in a play (both turn out to be phony), quarrels with her over his proposal to run away, and is left alone. Next he goes to Radio City Music Hall and sees a phony movie, after which he meets Carl Luce, an old schoolmate now at Columbia, who is a specialist on "flits" (Holden asks him, "What're you majoring in? . . . Perverts?"). Left alone again (Holden seems always to be left alone when he is most lonesome), Holden gets drunk, calls Sally, is rebuffed, and finally goes home to his sister Phoebe, alone in the family apartment. After a challenge from Phoebe to name something he likes, and after he finally settles on being a catcher in the rye, keeping the little kids from falling over "some crazy cliff," Holden goes over to stay the night with his former English teacher, Mr. Antolini, arriving in the Antolini apartment just after the end of a drinking party. Mr. Antolini talks like a father to Holden, quoting Wilhelm Stekel on the meaning of genuine maturity, "The mark of the immature man is that he wants to die nobly for a cause, while the mark of the mature man is that he wants to live humbly for one." After drifting off to sleep on the Antolini couch, Holden awakens in fright to find Mr. Antolini patting him on the head. He quickly concocts some clumsy excuse about getting his bags, and runs from this threatening show of affection—that may be "something perverty."

As Holden leaves the Antolini apartment, the light of Monday morning is brightening the sky. But his only thought is to execute immediately his plan to run off to the West. He writes Phoebe a note at school to meet him at noon near the Metropolitan Museum, and, as he is waiting for her, he visits the depths of the Egyptian tomb. He feels sick, passes out briefly, and then recovers, to go out to meet Phoebe. She has come to run away with him, but he tells her that she must stay at home, that he isn't going anywhere anyway. They visit the zoo, watch the bears briefly, and then go to the carrousel. As she rides round and round on the carrousel, Holden makes up his mind to stay, to quit running; and, in the middle of a drenching rain, as he watches Phoebe go around in her endless circle on the carrousel, he begins

to feel "so damn happy" that he ends up "damn near bawling."

This skeleton of events in *Catcher* distorts the book considerably, and demonstrates how dependent it is on incidental detail, what might even be called plot irrelevancies, for its most moving and profound meanings. Such detail and such crucially relevant irrelevancies are woven into the book's very texture. Salinger is able to achieve this loose-seeming yet tightly woven structure through ingenious exploitation of his chosen point of view. Like Mark Twain in *Huckleberry Finn*, Salinger appears to have hit upon the perfect way of telling the tale— or of letting the tale tell itself. Holden speaks out in his own idiom, and although his clichés belong to us all, the intonation and gesture are his own—and they strike home. Moreover, Salinger carefully places Holden on the psychiatrist's couch in California, apparently on the way to some kind of recovery from his spiritual collapse (we learn on the opening page of the novel that D. B. may be driving him home the next month). This allows Holden a free play of mind around the events he recounts, enabling him to see them from a more objective perspective than he could possibly have had during their actual happening, and enabling him also to move back beyond those three critical days into his past in recollection of more distant excursions, encounters, and collisions that seem somehow to have a bearing on his predicament. This point of view results in the novel's marvelous richness of texture.

As the Holden on his journey is re-created for us by the Holden on the psychiatrist's couch, we recognize that the journey is more than movement through space—it is a movement, also, from innocence to knowledge, from self-ignorance to self-awareness, from isolation to involvement. For example, in the episode in which Holden urges Sally Hayes to run off with him, and she balks, he tells her, "You give me a royal pain in the ass, if you want to know the truth." In the midst of his "madman" apologies, Sally's somewhat pompous indignation undermines his serious intention, and he laughs. The narrator Holden comments: "I have one of these very loud, stupid laughs. I mean if I ever sat behind myself in a movie or something, I'd probably lean over and tell myself to please shut up. It made old Sally madder than ever." In retrospect Holden is able to see what he only half comprehended when he was with Sally—that he shares the responsibility for this one more failure in his frantic attempt to communicate with people and break out of his isolation. In his retrospective examination of the episode, Holden says: "If you want to know the truth, I don't even know why I started all that stuff with her. . . . I probably wouldn't've taken her even if she'd wanted to go with me." Holden thus penetrates to his own deception and his own phoniness, and is one more step on the way to the kind of involved awareness that will enable him at the end, after he has finished reconstructing his tale, to say: "About all I know is, I sort of *miss* everybody I told about." This knowledge, though it is casually presented in the closing lines of the book, is a difficult, profound, and mature knowledge that lies at the novel's center of gravity. It involves both a recognition that there can be no self-monopoly of innocence and a discovery that there can be no shield from complicity.

Holden's quest, then, may be stated in a number of ways. In one sense, his quest is a quest to preserve an innocence that is in peril of vanishing—the innocence of childhood, the spotless innocence of a self horrified at contamination in the ordinary and inevitable involvements of life. In another sense, the quest is a quest for an ideal but un-human love that will meet all demands but make none; a relationship so sensitively attuned that all means of communication, however subtle, will remain alertly open, and all the messages, in whatever language, will get through. Perhaps in its profoundest sense Holden's quest is a quest for identity, a search for the self—he does, for example, go through a number of guises, such as Rudolf Schmidt when he talks with his classmate's mother or Jim Steele when he is visited by the prostitute Sunny. But he remains, however he might wish to the contrary, Holden Caulfield, and the self he is led to discover is Holden's and none other. And that self he discovers is a human self and an involved self that cannot, finally, break what Hawthorne once called the "magnetic chain of humanity"; he cannot deny the love within him when he begins to miss all the people, "bastards" included, he has told about.

Holden vacillates throughout *Catcher* between the imperative of involvement and revulsion at involvement, and the result is a dual series of compelling images that act as magnets that both attract and repel. He is driven first to make some connection; like Whitman's "Noiseless Patient Spider," Holden launches forth filament after filament, but his "gossamer thread" never catches anywhere—until at the end it catches Phoebe in an entangled web from which Holden is obligated to release her. At the same time that he is casting forth, out of the agony of his loneliness, the filaments spun from his soul, Holden is repelled to the point of nausea (he is frequently about to puke or vomit) by the fundamental physicality of the human predicament. This inescapable physicality is a phenomenon of all human relationships, all human situations, by their very nature of being human. It is this terrible knowledge to which Holden must reconcile himself. Even a casual relationship with a schoolmate is heavily colored and shaped by the individual's imprisonment in his physical identity. For instance, Ackley's teeth are mossy-looking, his face is pimpled, and his room is filled with a "funny stink"—all matters of acute painfulness for Holden to adjust to when in the desperation of his isolation he seeks out Ackley for companionship (launching forth a filament). It is in a context of this kind that Holden's attitude toward sex, that most intense form of all human involvement, must be placed in order to comprehend both the fascination and the fear that he feels at its invocation. This ambivalence is portrayed vividly in the episode in which Holden looks out of his New York hotel window and is confronted by a series of scenes of sexual tragicomedy (an episode functionally reminiscent of the humanity-embroiled prison episode in Graham Greene's *The Power and the Glory*), and comments: "The trouble was, that kind of junk is sort of fascinating to watch, even if you don't want it to be. . . . Sometimes I can think of *very* crumby stuff I wouldn't mind doing if the opportunity came up." The insight is penetrating, and the understanding is a step beyond wisdom.

Just as one part of Holden drives him forward in his painful quest for some responsive relationship with people, in spite of the terror of the physical, another and deeper part urges his withdrawal and flight, and even the ultimate disengagement of death—the utter abandonment of physicality. A controlling image in this sequence is that of the abandoned ducks on the frozen lagoon in Central Park. Obviously Holden repeatedly sees his own plight symbolized by the forlorn and freezing ducks. Another image that recurs is Holden's dead brother Allie's baseball mitt, in which are inscribed the poems of Emily Dickinson (a poet whose dominant subject was death). Again and again, Holden (like Emily Dickinson) imagines his own death, as, for example, after the de-

grading incident with the hotel pimp and the prostitute: "What I really felt like, though, was committing suicide. I felt like jumping out the window. I probably would've done it, too, if I'd been sure somebody'd cover me up as soon as I landed." The tone of levity betrays just how deep the suicidal impulse is lodged—to surge again on later occasions dangerously near to the surface. Holden's fascinated interest in the Museum of Natural History, particularly in those human scenes (a squaw, an Eskimo) statically preserved behind glass, where nobody moves and nothing changes, no matter how many times you come back—this intense interest is clearly related in some subterranean way to his deepest instincts. And when Phoebe challenges Holden to name something he really likes, the only response he at first can make is to name the dead—his brother Allie; or James Castle, the boy who was teased by his schoolmates into committing suicide by jumping out the dormitory window.

On one level, *The Catcher in the Rye* may be read as a story of death and rebirth. It is symbolically relevant that the time of year is deep winter: it is the time of Christmas, a season of expiration and parturition. Holden is fated, at the critical age of sixteen years, to fall from innocence, to experience the death of the old self and to arise a new Holden to confront the world afresh—much like Ishmael and his symbolic immersion and resurrection at the end of *Moby Dick*. The metaphor of the fall is sounded again and again in the closing pages of the novel. Holden himself introduces it, when talking with Phoebe, in his vision of himself as the catcher in the rye. His own stance at the edge of the cliff, is, in fact, precarious; ironically he is unable to prevent his own imminent fall. Mr. Antolini sounds the warning for Holden, directly and fervently, when he tells him that he is heading for "a terrible, terrible fall," and adds: "This fall I think you're riding for—it's a special kind of fall, a horrible kind. The man falling isn't permitted to feel or hear himself hit bottom. He just keeps falling and falling." It is only a short while after this warning that Holden awakens to find Mr. Antolini patting him on the head, abandons in panic this last refuge open to him, and starts to run—or fall—again. The precise motives behind Mr. Antolini's odd, but very human, gesture are obscure, as Holden himself comes shortly to realize: his patting Holden's head is, in its context, certainly a suggestive physical act; but it is also, surely, an act of profound, human, nonsexual affection, a gesture of the spirit as much as of the hand. Mr. Antolini's motives (he has been drinking) are no doubt muddled in his own mind. But Holden's shrinking back in horror from this physical touch, his immediate assumption that Mr. Antolini is a "flit" on the make, betrays his revulsion at the inevitable mixture of the dark and the light in any human act—a mixture inevitable because of the inescapable *physicality* of the human condition. It is from this level of lofty innocence that Holden is doomed to fall.

Holden's running from the Antolini apartment takes him some distance, indeed, on the way in his fall from innocence. He begins to realize that he has made a mistake, that he has misjudged Mr. Antolini, or has been too cold and severe in his behavior; and he becomes depressed and "screwed up" as he recalls that it was Mr. Antolini who had picked up the dead boy, James Castle, after he committed suicide. As Holden walks along the street in a critical state, something "spooky" begins to happen. He recalls: "Every time I came to the end of a block and stepped off the goddam curb, I had this feeling that I'd never get to the other side of the street. I thought I'd just go down, down, down, and nobody'd ever see me again." His sensation of

falling is counterbalanced by his fantasy of flight to the Far West where he will become a deaf-mute, cut off from the world in a kind of living death, his innocence desperately preserved. But the real world, the terribly physical world, continues to press in—and down—on him. At Phoebe's school, he rubs out one obscenity only to be confronted with another, scratched deeply into the wall. He decides, "If you had a million years to do it in, you couldn't rub out even *half* the 'Fuck You' signs in the world. It's impossible." Holden is thus close to realizing the futility of any attempt to be a catcher in the rye: the kids cannot, in the world as it is, be shielded from the crazy cliff. While waiting at the Metropolitan Museum for Phoebe, Holden descends into the Egyptian tomb, where he finds it "nice and peaceful"—until he notices the obscenity once more, scrawled in red crayon, "under the glass part of the wall." He then imagines his own tombstone, displaying under his own name the revolting words of the obscenity.

At this point, Holden's horror and his dream, his revulsion at the world and his fantasy of death, come together in the image of his tombstone and he finds himself confronting the critical moment of decision—life or death; the world with all its obscenities or suicide with all its denials. The image of the tombstone bearing the obscenity suggests that suicide itself would be a kind of ultimate capitulation to the terrible physicality of life, an ironic involvement of the flesh at the very moment of abdication of the flesh. Death thus becomes not a gesture of defiance but of surrender. Holden feels both nausea and faintness, and he actually passes out momentarily, and falls to the floor, a final fall that marks the end of the descent. When he arises, he feels better; the crisis is past, the choice for life symbolically made, the slow ascent begun. Phoebe's spontaneous generosity expressed in her willingness to run away with him confirms his decision to stay, to become involved, and to rejoin the human race. In the closing pages of the novel, as he watches Phoebe, in her blue coat, go around and around on the carousel, Holden becomes afraid that as she grabs for the gold ring, she will fall, but he restrains himself: "The thing with kids is, if they want to grab for the gold ring, you have to let them do it, and not say anything. If they fall off, they fall off, but it's bad if you say anything to them." Gone now is the dream of being the catcher in the rye. Whether in the fields of rye, or on the circular carrousel, children must eventually fall, as Holden has fallen. Holden can be happy—"so damn happy"—now in the knowledge that Phoebe is held by the magic and endless circle of the carrousel in a suspended state of perfect and impenetrable innocence, and his happiness can be intensified and rendered poignant in the mature awareness that the state is momentary, that the music will stop and the magic circle break, that the fall, finally, cannot be stayed. (It may be worth noting, parenthetically, that one of Salinger's favorite poets, Rilke, has a poem entitled "The Carrousel," in which there is a "little blue girl," and in which the carrousel "circles and turns and has no goal.")

For all its seriousness, *Catcher in the Rye* is one of the funniest books in American literature, and much has been said relating its humor to the native American tradition, and particularly to Mark Twain's *Huckleberry Finn*. Perhaps of equal importance with its connections to the past is the role of *Catcher* in the development of the post-World War II "black" humor, the humor that has occasional elements of irresponsibility, cruelty, despair, and insanity. Examples are Wright Morris' *Ceremony in Lone Tree* (1960), Joseph Heller's *Catch*-22 (1961), and Ken Kesey's *One Flew over the Cuckoo's Nest* (1962). One

small episode in *Catcher* will suggest its place in this new direction of contemporary American humor. After leaving the Antolini apartment, as Holden is wandering in a daze about the streets, he comes upon a small vignette that seems to sum up the weird incongruities of modern life as he has encountered it: ". . . I passed these two guys that were unloading this big Christmas tree off a truck. One guy kept saying to the other guy, 'Hold the sonuvabitch *up*! Hold it *up*, for Chrissake!' It certainly was a gorgeous way to talk about a Christmas tree. It was sort of funny, though, in an awful way, and I started to sort of laugh. It was about the *worst* thing I could've done, because the minute I started to laugh I thought I was going to vomit. I really did, I even started to, but it went away. I don't know why." It is, of course, *for the sake of Christ* that the tree has been reaped and hauled and now put into place. But the mover's remark, "Hold it *up*, for Chrissake," is only ironically and absurdly an invocation of this now lost original meaning, embedded like a fossil in language—the language not of a blessing but of a curse.

Absurdity, nausea—these terms seem recurrently relevant to Holden's predicament as he hangs suspended between laughter and sickness. And is not Holden's predicament in some sense the modern predicament? At one point he remarks: ". . . I'm sort of glad they've got the atomic bomb invented. If there's ever another war, I'm going to sit right the hell on top of it. I'll volunteer for it, I swear to God I will." Perhaps the post-World War II comedy of blackness points the way of endurance in an insanely reeling world: if we do not at times feel nausea at contemporary horrors, we are, in a way, already dead; if we cannot occasionally laugh at contemporary absurdities, we shall in the darkness of our despair soon die.

The chasteness of the title *Nine Stories* (1953) is in line with the severity of the selection. The stories Salinger chose are late stories, published between 1948 and 1953—all, with two exceptions, in the *New Yorker*. Although the tales in *Nine Stories* are arranged in the order of their publication (see the bibliography), it is illuminating to look at them in a series of thematic groupings. Before rearranging the order, however, it is useful to note that the opening and closing stories of the volume portray violent deaths, the first (Seymour Glass's) a certain suicide, the second (Teddy's) a foreseen "accident." It is possible that the nature of the one death may help in understanding the other. Indeed, there are thematic echoes and reverberations throughout *Nine Stories* which give the volume a singleness of impact which belies its multiplicity.

The dominant theme which recurs, in richly varied thematic contexts, is alienation, an alienation which may conclude in some kind of reconciliation or accommodation, but which may also result in distortion of the soul, bitterness, nausea, and the ultimate withdrawal into death. The causes of the alienation are frequently obscure but always complex. Sometimes society seems at fault, in the horrors of racial prejudice or the horrors of war. But sometimes the fault seems to lie in a failure of personal relationships—the filament (of Whitman's spider) is launched, but does not catch; or caught, does not hold. Sometimes, however, the cause of alienation lies deeply within, in a turbulence of the spirit—plunging the individual into a dark night of the soul, or dazzling him in the ecstasy of a vision of mystical union —two radically different states that mystics have always found in close conjunction.

"Down at the Dinghy" (which holds the center position in *Nine Stories*) is the single story in the volume dealing directly with a social issue—racial prejudice; a young boy, four-year-old Lionel Tannenbaum, has heard a housekeeper call his father a "kike," and has run away to the family dinghy, from which his mother (who is, incidentally, Boo Boo Glass) finally coaxes him—discovering, ironically, that he thought a kike "one of those things that go up in the *air*" (a kite).

Several stories are tales of estrangement in love, both premarital and marital. Perhaps the most optimistic of these is "Just before the War with the Eskimos": a sensitive, perceptive young man (Franklin Graff) who has been kept out of the war—and somewhat out of life— because of a bad "ticker," has drifted into an unwholesome relationship with what appears to be a homosexual; when Ginnie Mannox comes home with his sister one day, the young man launches forth a filament that appears to catch (he had written eight letters to Ginnie's sister that went unanswered), and she accepts his zany offer of a leftover chicken sandwich and leaves determined to come back. "The Laughing Man" describes the sad end rather than the happy beginning of a relationship: John Gedsudski, a young law student, is in charge of a group of young boys (the Comanches), and keeps them entertained between ballgames by narrating an endless tale about a kind of deformed Robin Hood (with a "hairless, pecan-shaped head and a face that featured . . . an enormous oval cavity below the nose"); when the young man's relationship with Mary Hudson blossoms, and she even participates in the ballgames, the plot of his tale proliferates with great energy and gusto, but when they quarrel and part (no cause is given), he bitterly describes the brutal captivity and death of his "laughing man," unforgettably shocking his young Comanches.

Two stories describe marital estrangement and betrayal. "Uncle Wiggily in Connecticut" portrays a conformist world in which a suburban housewife, Eloise, drinking with an old school chum, gradually reveals the hidden source of her antagonism toward her daughter (who has a naughty imaginary playmate) and her indifference toward her husband: she recalls with alcoholic vividness her old love (his name is Walt Glass) killed during World War II by the absurd explosion of a toy Japanese stove. "Pretty Mouth and Green My Eyes" is an urbanized tale of the managerial set and consists of two telephone conversations that take place after a cocktail party, initiated each time by a junior executive to a superior in the same firm, the first to inquire whether the older man saw the younger's wife leave the party, the second to explain that the wife has just come home; but the irony is that the wife is in bed with the older man even as he takes the two calls.

But Salinger's best stories portray an alienation more profound and more unsettling than that produced by the shock of racial prejudice or the shock of the failure of love. The most celebrated example of this more ambiguous alienation is found in "For Esmé—with Love and Squalor," a tale of war and spiritual crisis told by the protagonist some six healing years after the searing events. But the events remain so vividly painful that the narrator must envelop them in anonymity and must remove them from himself by placing them in the third person. In England during the war, in training for duty in Europe, the narrator meets and has tea with thirteen-year-old Esmé and her five-year-old brother Charles, and discovers a moment of human warmth and sanity to relieve the dreariness and insanity of camp life in wartime. Esmé is all the more endearing for the mature role she has bravely assumed in her family after the death of her father, slain in North Africa. The scene shifts to occupied Bavaria after five campaigns (and V-E Day), and the narration suddenly shifts into the third person. Sergeant X, feeling "his mind dislodge itself and teeter, like insecure luggage on an overhead rack," picks up from the table a book

by Goebbels entitled *Die Zeit Ohne Beispiel* ("The Unprecedented Era"), once owned by a low-ranking Nazi that X himself had arrested, and finds written in it, "Dear God, life is hell." Sergeant X writes under this inscription a quotation from Dostoevski: "Fathers and teachers, I ponder 'What is hell?' I maintain that it is the suffering of being unable to love."

It is precisely this hell that Sergeant X is experiencing, as is immediately demonstrated by the intrusion of his companion on the five campaigns, Corporal Z, an insensitive, vacuous individual whose very physical presence—belches, brick-red slicked-down hair, overdecorated uniform, and all—is overwhelming. Corporal Z's brutalized, dehumanized conversation at this moment of spiritual crisis, especially his casual recollection of the cat he cruelly and meaninglessly shot while with his buddy during a moment of battle tension, triggers the revulsion in Sergeant X that causes him immediately to vomit. But a sickness of the soul—the sickness of being unable to love —cannot be regurgitated. Left alone, Sergeant X aimlessly looks through his mail and finds a package that turns out to contain a letter from Esmé together with her father's watch which she had been wearing on their first and only encounter. The letter and watch are like a fresh breeze that blows through and cleanses the sickroom of the soul. They provide an illumination that renews and refreshes Sergeant X's darkened spirit, as he once again—in the presence, however remote, of such innocent affection—feels himself able to love. In his nausea at humanity, he had, perhaps, been near suicide; the watch that Esmé sent him restored to him a reservoir of time that he had been on the verge of losing forever.

"De Daumier-Smith's Blue Period" tells the story of a young man, at loose ends with life, who obtains a job as an instructor at a Canadian correspondence art school, run by a Japanese man and his wife; among his mediocre students is a talented nun who attracts his attention and to whom he writes a long, almost intimate letter, which precipitates the nun's withdrawal from the course; shortly after, the school is closed down for being improperly licensed and De Daumier-Smith returns to his former life to pick up the threads he had cut. Of course, the story is much more than this bare outline shows. The episode is the crucial, formative experience in the protagonist's life, but it is, fundamentally, an experience of the spirit. The young man, who narrates his own story, is a kind of Ishmael at the beginning, his mother dead, his stepfather providing a tenuous hotel existence in New York; he is sickened by the multitudes of people in the city, prays to be alone, and suddenly discovers that everything he touches turns to "solid loneliness." It is out of a mixture of frustration and desperation that he applies for the art school job in Canada under the fantastic name of De Daumier-Smith—in search of a new identity.

The thematic focal point of the story is an orthopedic appliances shop underneath the second-floor art school. There two incidents occur, one "hideous" (a dark night), the other "transcendent" (an illumination), that determine the fate of the narrator. After he has mailed his long, adulatory letter to the nun about her work, even suggesting that he visit her, and is living in a kind of exalted anticipation of her reply, he pauses one evening before the window of the shop and is inexplicably plunged into gloom: "The thought was forced on me that no matter how coolly or sensibly or gracefully I might one day learn to live my life, I would always at best be a visitor in a garden of enamel urinals and bedpans, with a sightless, wooden dummy-deity standing by in a marked-down rupture truss." The thought is unendurable, and De Daumier-Smith rushes off to bed and forces his mind to envision a

visit with the nun at her convent, in a relationship "without sin" but in a purity of image "too ecstatic to hold in place."

After receiving word that the nun has been withdrawn from the art course, De Daumier-Smith is depressed, angrily writes letters dismissing his other students, and goes out for a walk—only to pause once again before the terrible window. This time there is a girl in a "green, yellow and lavender" dress in the window changing the truss on the wooden dummy; when she sees the narrator, she becomes flustered, starts to exit, and falls on her bottom (recalling the "buttocks to buttocks" bus scene in New York earlier in the story). As De Daumier-Smith reaches out to help her, his fingers are stopped by the glass of the window —and the "Experience" occurs: "Suddenly . . . the sun came up and sped toward the bridge of my nose at the rate of ninety-three million miles a second. Blinded and very frightened— I had to put my hand on the glass to keep my balance. The thing lasted for no more than a few seconds. When I got my sight back, the girl had gone from the window, leaving behind her a shimmering field of exquisite, twice-blessed, enamel flowers." In spite of the narrator's protests, the incident has all the elements of some kind of "genuine mysticism." De Daumier-Smith's mystic response to the girl in the window is reminiscent of Stephen Dedalus' reaction to his glimpse of the wading girl in *A Portrait of the Artist as a Young Man*—a glimpse that deflected him from priesthood and sent him out to encounter the world. The narrator, in returning to his former life, is symbolically rejoining the human race; he has made the decision to become more than just a "visitor" in the physical universe.

In "Teddy," Salinger carries experimentation in mystical fiction about as far as it can be carried without entering the realm of fantasy, and even in "Teddy" there are elements of the fantastic. Ten-year-old Theodore McArdle, on an ocean voyage with his irritable, quarreling parents and his six-year-old sister (who, he says, doesn't like him), is gradually revealed to us as the most remarkable child in Salinger's large gallery of remarkable children. He holds the Vedantic theory of reincarnation, and believes that in his last incarnation he was "making very nice spiritual advancement." He had his first mystical experience at an early age: "I was six when I saw that everything was God, and my hair stood up. . . . It was on a Sunday, I remember. My sister was only a very tiny child then, and she was drinking her milk, and all of a sudden I saw that *she* was God and the *milk* was God. I mean, all she was doing was pouring God into God, if you know what I mean." But perhaps Teddy's most marvelous gift is his intuitive grasp of the future—not clairvoyance, but a sense of the need for increased awareness or concern at certain potentially hazardous times. He writes in his diary: "It will either happen today or February 14, 1958 when I am sixteen. It is ridiculous to mention even." The reference, we find out later, is to his own death. In his final conversation with a fellow passenger, the teacher Bob Nicholson, he says that death is a minor matter, really ("All you do is get the heck out of your body when you die"), and that it could happen to him that very day—say, for example, if he went down to the swimming pool, found it empty, and was pushed in by his small sister (who, after all, "hasn't been a human being for very many lives"). As events turn out, this is precisely what happens, as Nicholson realizes on his way following Teddy down to the pool—when he suddenly hears the piercing scream of Teddy's sister, no doubt hysterical in fear and horror at what she has done.

If we accept the world created by Salinger in this story, we do not mourn for Teddy, but recognize that he is on his way to another in-carnation, and closer in the cycle that will bring him to the final and permanent meditation with God. In the story, Salinger was probably experimenting with rather than expressing belief, and the tale should be accepted in that spirit. More important, however, than Teddy's gift of intuitive foresight are his desire for meditation, his dislike of sentimentality, and his distaste for logic. It is through periodical retreat and meditation that he is able to achieve his remarkable knowledge—or make "spiritual advancement." Poetry and love are too frequently destroyed by sentimentality; thus Teddy prefers Japanese poetry (" 'Nothing in the voice of the cicada intimates how soon it will die' "), and thus he loves God ("If *I* were God, I certainly wouldn't want people to love me sentimentally"). Adam brought logic into the world by his eating of the apple, and man has been an apple-eater ever since; man must "vomit" up this "logic and intellectual stuff" if he ever wants "to see things as they really are" (the language here—especially the image of vomiting—is revealing as it relates to the re-curring nausea in Salinger's heroes). After man has emptied himself of the "intellectual stuff," he might, through meditation, be able to get back the conscious knowledge that he has somehow lost. ("I grew my own body. . . . Nobody else did it for me. So if I grew it, I must have known *how* to grow it. Unconsciously, at least. I may have lost the *conscious* knowledge of how to grow it sometime in the last few hundred thousand years, but the knowledge is still *there* . . .") Whatever we may think of Teddy—and I think that we must accept him (if necessary through willing suspension of disbelief) as a genuine mystic, spiritually advanced far beyond the general level of this world, operating on the very highest levels of cosmic consciousness—it is clear that he is too much for this world to contain. Like Melville's Billy Budd with his colossal innocence, Teddy with his staggering spirituality must die, as he himself seems to understand, before he unsettles society from its foundations.

The opening tale of *Nine Stories*, "A Perfect Day for Bananafish," gains in meaning in the light of all the stories that follow it. Moreover, as it presents a crucial episode in the saga of Seymour Glass, discussion of it may well stand as a prologue to treatment of Salinger's longer and later stories devoted to the Glass family. Of the seven children of Bessie and Les Glass, three appear in *Nine Stories*—Boo Boo, the third of the children, is the mother in "Down at the Dinghy," Walt, one of the twins who came next, is the remembered dead soldier and lover in "Uncle Wiggily in Connecticut," and Seymour, the first of them all and the family guru, is the central character of "A Perfect Day for Bananafish." There are two major scenes in the story, the first in which Muriel Glass talks long distance from Florida with her mother in New York about the peculiar behavior of Muriel's husband Seymour, and the second in which Seymour out on the beach takes little Sybil Carpenter on her float into the water and talks with her about any number of things—including bananafish. At the end of the story, Seymour walks into the hotel room where Muriel lies sleeping and puts a bullet in his temple.

To assume that Seymour is simply a psychotic is to render the story meaningless. To interpret his suicide as his simple and direct device to sever his marriage to a vacuous, spiritually shallow girl is to reduce the story to the dimensions of the daily tabloid. Although Seymour's suicide is explored in some detail in the later Glass stories, it is possible, as it should be, to read the story without the later amplifications and discover a Seymour who is not inconsistent with the Seymour of the later books. In the conversation between Muriel and her mother, along with its expression of a fad-dish and naive faith in psychoanalysis, several hints about Seymour's behavior are dropped but left unexplained. For example, Seymour has apparently had some kind of obsession about trees, repeatedly stares at them, and has apparently run his father-in-law's car into one. A Freudian critic might well see phallic significance in this obsession, and it would be hard to deny that the tree has some such suggestion. But the obsession is surely more complex than such an interpretation allows. Seymour's fascination for trees may well be born of his intuitive grasp of the tree's deep and enduring natural knowledge of its place and its role (as Teddy would say, it knows unconsciously how to grow and how to be).

Although Seymour shares with Holden Caulfield and Sergeant X an acute sensitivity, ranging from revulsion to ecstasy, to the physicality of the world, his Sybil does not serve (as Phoebe and Esmé serve their young men) to deflect him from self-destruction (although she does, as a kind of inverted sibyl, young rather than ancient, confirm his deepest intuitions). Nor does Seymour seem to have the agitation of Holden or the nausea of Sergeant X. Seymour displays, rather, a tragic resignation. His story of the bananafish that swims into the hole and consumes bananas until he is too fat to come out, and therefore must die, is a paradigm of his own situation. He is a bananafish, not because he has indulged his senses to the point of grossness, but rather because of his keen sensitivity to the overwhelming physicality of existence—his senses have been ravaged by the physical world, and he has found himself entrapped and must die. His figurative fatness might well be another man's real leanness. When we observe Muriel, at the opening of the story, reading an article called "Sex Is Fun—or Hell" (rather than the poetry of Rilke, for example, which Seymour has recommended), we come to sense that for the

Glasses sex must be hell: Seymour's surfeit would be for Muriel a kind of abstention.

When Seymour leaves Sybil, he kisses the arch of her foot; immediately after, on the elevator, he angrily accuses a woman of sneaking a look at his feet. This keen sensitivity about the feet epitomizes Seymour's attitude toward the physical. The kiss for him represents symbolically the glut of any number of bananas; a glance (or apparent glance) from a stranger at this intimate and sensitive physical embodiment of the self becomes extremely painful, so painful that continued physical existence is unendurable. When he walks into the bedroom, the only sense operative is the sense of smell: he is overwhelmed by the odor of the "new calfskin luggage and nail-lacquer remover." Even at the end, his senses remain glutted. Seymour Glass can *see more* (in trees, for instance) because he has begun to vomit up the apple of logic, and possess, like Teddy, a magnified spiritual consciousness. Every physical fact has become a virtual spiritual maze. But sadly, those about him can think only of his "maladjustment" and his possible "cure" through psychoanalysis (precisely the thing, according to Zooey later, that precipitated the suicide). As it is painful for Seymour to see anyone mean to a dog, he would not kill himself to hurt Muriel. On the contrary, his suicide is a release for her to engage life again at a level she can apprehend, and a release for himself from a physicality that has simply ceased to be endurable. It is the only escape from his bananahole.

After *Nine Stories*, Salinger's imagination appears to have been completely absorbed by the Glass family; and in spite of Seymour's suicide, he remains a dominant presence throughout. Although "Franny" and "Zooey" were published as two seperate stories in the *New Yorker*, they make a remarkably unified novel. Franny, youngest of the Glasses' seven children, goes to visit her college boyfriend, Lane Coutell, at his Ivy League school, where the plans call for lunch at the posh local restaurant, attendance at the football game, and a general good time (there are several hints that they are sleeping together). But over martinis, as Lane talks about the success of one of his papers on Flaubert's testicularity (a Freudian analysis which he might try to publish), and as Franny talks about her disillusionment with all her professors, who are pedants and phonies, she suddenly excuses herself, goes to the ladies' room, and gives way to a violent fit of trembling and tears. When she returns, Lane notices the little pea-green book in her purse, and she begins to talk about it—The Way of a Pilgrim—and a form of prayer recommended in it, involving an endless repetition of the Jesus prayer—"Lord Jesus Christ, have mercy on me." As Franny tries to explain how the prayer is supposed to work, Lane expresses his skepticism (". . . all those religious experiences have a very obvious psychological background"), and Franny is swept up again in a wave of nausea, this time passing out in the restaurant. She comes to in the manager's office, she concurs in Lane's plans for a quiet afternoon of rest, and as she is left alone at the end her lips are moving with a repetition of the Jesus prayer.

The narration shifts from third to first person in "Zooey," but the narrator, Buddy Glass, introduces himself only to fade behind the third person again soon after. The scene shifts to the Glass family apartment in New York, where the mother Bessie and the sixth of the seven Glass children, a television actor, Zooey, are ministering to the needs of Franny, now home and languishing on the living room couch. There are three major scenes, all domestic, in "Zooey." The first takes place in the family bathroom, where Zooey is first discovered in the tub rereading a four-year-old letter from his older brother Buddy; the room is invaded by Bessie, bent on enlisting Zooey's help in succoring the sick child Franny. In the bantering conversation that ensues, surely the longest bathroom scene in all literature, Bessie's general density and particularly her reliance on psychoanalysis indicates that she is making the usual mistake in analyzing the soul-sickness of her children. In the next scene, Zooey goes to the living room where he gradually and gently lures Franny out of her shell and then tries to shock her out of her sickness by describing to her her "little stink of piousness" and the "little snotty crusade" she is "leading against everybody." The shock merely intensifies Franny's anguish, and Zooey retreats, this time to the sacrosanct room once occupied by Seymour and Buddy Glass and which still has the phone listed in Seymour's name. There, after a period of communion with Seymour's spirit, Zooey, a handkerchief over his mouth to disguise his voice, calls Franny over the sacred phone, and she takes the call in her parents' bedroom. On Seymour's phone pretending to be Buddy, Zooey finally wins his way to Franny's understanding; she discovers that she is speaking with Zooey, but she continues to listen, and is at last persuaded to eat Bessie's "consecrated chicken soup," and to return to her theater activities—in short, to rejoin the human race. At the end, Franny is suffused with an inexplicable joy that causes her to smile just before falling into a "deep, dreamless sleep"—clearly the sleep of renewal and resuscitation.

The pattern that Franny follows, from nausea to joy, from withdrawal to return, is the familiar one in Salinger, as witness Holden Caulfield or Sergeant X. This is the first time, however, that Salinger has created a female

for tracing out the pattern. Perhaps it was inevitable that first readers of "Franny" would assume that she was pregnant, thus neatly explaining for themselves her nausea and fainting. It is, however, quite clear that her sickness is of the spirit. But, one might well ask, if Franny has had the kind of religious and spiritual education which Salinger depicts as inevitable for one growing up in the Glass household, why should she encounter a spiritual crisis with which she cannot cope at this time in her life? The answer seems to be, as suggested by Zooey, that it is precisely this early religious initiation that has somehow brought on the crisis. Franny is suffering from an excess of piety—an excess which is dehumanizing her and cutting her off from (in Hawthorne's words again) the "magnetic chain of humanity." When speaking of the phony poets at her school, whose poems are just some kind of "terribly fascinating, syntaxy *droppings*," she exclaims: "I'm sick of just liking people." And she later cries out, "I'm just sick of ego, ego, ego. My own and everybody else's." Through Zooey, she learns that her use of the Jesus prayer has handicapped rather than helped her spiritually, because of her distorted notions of Jesus. In saying the Jesus prayer, she has been trying to lay up spiritual treasures for herself much like the people she criticizes are trying, in one way or another, to lay up material or intellectual treasures for themselves. "This is God's universe," Zooey tells Franny, "not yours." And he asks: ". . . who in the Bible besides Jesus knew —*knew*—that we're carrying the Kingdom of Heaven around with us, *inside*, where we're all too goddam stupid and sentimental and unimaginative to look?" The only reason to say the Jesus prayer is to develop "Christ-Consciousness"—"*Not* to set up some little cozy, holier-than-thou trysting place with some sticky, adorable divine personage."

Shocked—or blasted—out of her alienating, self-righteous piety, Franny is prepared for the final insight that Zooey has to give her, an insight that Seymour passed along to Zooey, in preparing for one of the radio shows (all the Glass children have appeared on a radio program entitled "It's a Wise Child"). Seymour told the reluctant Zooey that he should shine his shoes for "the Fat Lady." Over the years, the image of the Fat Lady—sitting on a porch, swatting flies, with a case of cancer, her radio going full blast—has grown in Zooey's mind into an image of suffering humanity, an embodiment, ultimately, of Christ. Zooey tells Franny: "There isn't anyone *any*where that isn't Seymour's Fat Lady. Don't you know that? . . . And don't you know—*listen* to me, now—*don't you know who that Fat Lady really is?* . . . Ah, buddy, Ah, buddy. It's Christ Himself. Christ Himself, buddy." This is the intuitive knowledge that at last replaces Franny's revulsion with joy, and brings a smile to her lips—the smile of return.

Though "Zooey" is the story of Franny's road back, it is also in some sense the story of Zooey's supreme effort. For in truth, Zooey understands Franny so well because he has "been there" himself; indeed, he makes the journey frequently, but is always able to return—on his own power. Both he and Franny have, he says, been made into freaks by their older brothers, Seymour and Buddy. The moment that Zooey gets into a room with somebody, he tells Franny, "I either turn into a goddam *seer* or a human hatpin. The Prince of Bores." He sees the phoniness of his television associates—but he has learned to like them, and even the things about them that at first repel. But he exclaims to Franny, "I'm sick to death of being the heavy in everybody's life." The act of spiritual resurrection that he performs for Franny is frighteningly exhaust-ing—his fresh shirt is drenched with sweat and he himself profoundly exhausted. The effort takes toll because he is renewing himself at the same time he is saving Franny.

When Zooey is introduced, we are told (by Buddy, the self-suppressed narrator) that there is superimposed on his face an "undiminish-able . . . joy." As Zooey sits in the bathtub in the opening scene, he is returning to the source of both his spiritual tension and his intuitive wisdom, Seymour and Buddy, via Buddy's four-year-old letter. In the letter Buddy describes a recent experience at the supermarket: when he asked a little girl the names of her two boyfriends, the little girl replied, "Bobby and Dorothy." The little girl, Buddy saw, instinctively realized what Seymour once told him, ". . . that all legitimate religious study *must* lead to unlearning the differences, the illusory differences, between boys and girls, animals and stones, day and night, heat and cold." Later, while talking in the living room with Franny, Zooey himself glances out the drapeless windows and sees a little drama in progress: a small girl in a red tam is hiding behind a tree from her dog wearing a green collar; the "anguish of separation" is followed by the "joy of reunion." From this sharply etched and intensely suggestive vignette Zooey draws the inspiration to force Franny to see the anguish of her own separation and the need for a reunion of joy. In the final scene of the story, when Zooey goes into Seymour's old room, he glances over the items tacked on an expanse of beaver board—quotations culled from everywhere, from the *Bhagavad Gita* to Ring Lardner, from Epictetus and Marcus Aurelius to Kafka and Anna Karenina. From a brief communion with these and with Seymour's diary cards, Zooey gathers the strength to make the final and supreme effort to rescue Franny from her isolation.

The techniques introduced in *Franny and Zooey* are characteristic of Salinger's later work. The humor of *Catcher* has almost disappeared, and replacing the fast-moving and richly varied narrative sequence of the earlier novel is an almost static narrative pattern moving from one long conversation to another, interspersed with occasional monologues or individual readings of letters, diaries, or journals. This change no doubt accounts in part for the lack of popularity of these later works. But compensating somewhat for the loss of humor and variety are gains, perhaps, in particularity and profundity. The accretion of physical detail in these stories is sometimes astonishing—as, for example, when we are introduced to the contents of the Glass medicine cabinet. And the physical details are not excess baggage but functional, each object pulling its own weight. A major example is Zooey's cigar, which serves as material and substantial ballast both to his slight build and to his mystic tendencies of thought: his cigar keeps Zooey grounded. As for the profundity, these later stories explore not so much the phoniness of the world and the self (as *Catcher* did) but the other side of the coin, the sources of insight and stability that enable an individual to come to terms with himself and the world. Although whatever wisdom the books have must be, ultimately, attributed to Salinger, as he has dramatized it through the Glasses, there is great use made throughout of what might be called secondary sources; sometimes these books look like reading lists for courses in comparative religion, or indexes for religious encyclopedias. The narrator Buddy is a college teacher who lectures to the faculty once a week on Zen and Mahayana Buddhism. He and Seymour, Buddy's letter to Zooey reveals, wanted Franny and Zooey "to know who and what Jesus and Gautama and Lao-tse and Shankaracharya and Hui-neng and Sri Ramakrishna" were before finding out "too much" about Homer, Shakespeare, Blake, or Whitman. Of course this technique is not new to Salinger, but never before did it seem to threaten narrative or displace theme. Still, at his best Salinger renders this material functional, subordinate to the human drama he is portraying. Buddy says in his prologue to "Zooey": "I say that my current offering isn't a mystical story, or a religiously mystifying story, at all. *I* say it's a compound, or multiple, love story, pure and complicated." Salinger's later works must not be read as religious tracts, no matter how tempting the reading lists make such an interpretation. Zooey himself demonstrates the vast distance separating the cold printed words of the sages, however wise, and the warm human act of actual, breathing involvement with people when he turns from Seymour's bulletin board of miscellaneous wisdom to tell Franny about the Fat Lady and the flies.

In the two stories of *Raise High the Roof Beam, Carpenters; and Seymour: An Introduction*, Buddy Glass remains the narrator throughout, and rather than suppressing himself, as in "Zooey," tends constantly to become his own main character. In "Raise High" Buddy is a soldier on leave to attend his brother's wedding in New York in 1942, but Seymour does not appear. The bride, Muriel, is left waiting at the church, to everybody's horror, but everything is made right when Seymour later elopes with her. The story itself is concerned, therefore, not so much with the wedding as with the reaction of a number of people, including Buddy, to Seymour's strange behavior. After a long wait at the church, and after the bride has left with her parents, Buddy gets caught in a taxicab with the bride's matron of honor and her lieutenant husband, with an aunt of the bride, and with a tiny deaf-mute who turns out to be the bride's father's uncle. The taxicab gets trapped by a parade and the conversation about Seymour lurches and languishes, taking on new life when the understandably upset matron of honor finds out that Buddy is a brother of the groom. The matron of honor divulges the information that she has previously garnered from the bride's mother (who has consulted her psychiatrist) that Seymour is schizoid and, probably, a latent homosexual. When he was a boy, the matron of honor relates with some relish, he struck one of the girls on the Glass children's radio program, "It's a Wise Child"—the blow necessitating nine stitches in the face of the girl, now a famous actress. When the occupants of the taxi finally get out to find a cold drink, the place they try is closed and Buddy brings them all up to his and Seymour's nearby apartment, where they marvel over the pictures of the Glass prodigies, drink some hastily concocted Tom Collinses, and prod Buddy with slightly hostile questions about his brother and himself. When they discover by phone that the elopement has set things right, the hostility somewhat abates and the unwanted guests depart.

"Raise High" is ingeniously constructed to focus on a series of superficially "normal" and negative attitudes toward Seymour by trapping them in a frame—the narrator's commentary —of sympathetic and understanding exploration of Seymour's real character. By this running contrast, the views tossed out by the matron of honor and assented to generally by her listeners are shown to be banal, inane, and embarrassingly gross. Buddy prefaces his story with the Taoist tale of the horse judge who picked a superlative horse but did not know its color or sex, illustrating the difference in perceiving essentials and externals. Buddy's story of the wedding is, in a sense, an elaboration of this tale—the wedding guests never arrive beyond the externals in judging Seymour; Buddy sees into the essentials—the "spiritual mechanism" itself. He has, of course, certain advantages. He has known Seymour a long time; he has at hand Seymour's diary that can bring him up to date on Seymour's feelings about Muriel; and he has an unexpected ally—the tiny deaf-mute, who seems in some mysterious, mystic way to be a judge of superlative horses himself. This little man functions as some kind of saint or guru who remains throughout sublimely, blissfully disengaged. The one verbal response he makes (in writing) in reply to the invitation to get out of the taxi with the others for a drink, is—characteristically— "Delighted." He is life's delighted man, bestowing his blessing with his smile and his cigar on all the anguished people around him. He is the one guest that remains as the others leave, to lend his understanding but unhearing ear to Buddy's explanation of Seymour's behavior. The boy Seymour struck Charlotte Mayhew with a rock, Buddy tells the tiny man, "because she looked so beautiful sitting there in the middle of the driveway with Boo Boo's cat." The deaf-mute grins and agrees. He is the one guest who can grasp this paradox of the "spiritual mechanism."

Seymour's diary, which Buddy reads in the bathroom, reveals with some fullness the relationship between Seymour and Muriel. It is clear that he sees her as a steadying force in his own highly strung, keyed-up existence. He loves her, therefore, for those qualities he himself does not possess—her somewhat simple tastes and broad, low-keyed emotional responses. "How I love and need her undiscriminating heart," he writes; and "How I worship her simplicity, her terrible honesty. How I rely on it." In short, Seymour sees beyond the vulgar externals of Muriel to her potential "spiritual mechanism." Although he senses that he does not make her "really happy," his consolation is that she has a "basically undeviating love for the institution of marriage itself." Muriel's mother, however, is a different matter. Muriel has told her how Seymour got the scars on his wrist (this is the only reference to a previous attempt at suicide in the Glass stories), and Mrs. Fedder is disturbed because Seymour has said once at dinner that he would like to be a dead cat (he explains later to Muriel that "in Zen Buddhism a master was once asked what was the most valuable thing in the world, and the master answered that a dead cat was, because no one could put a price on it"). Although Mrs. Fedder possesses no "understanding or taste for the main current of poetry that flows through things, all things," Seymour still asserts "I love her. I find her unimaginably brave."

At one of the Fedder dinner parties, Seymour repeats a remark he'd made as a youngster on the radio, that Lincoln at Gettysburg should have remained silent and shaken his fist at the audience. Mrs. Fedder's psychiatrist tells Seymour he is a perfectionist and explains to him the "virtues of living the imperfect life, of accepting one's own and others' weaknesses." Seymour writes in his diary: "I agree with him, but only in theory. I'll champion indiscrimination till doomsday, on the ground that it leads to health and a kind of very real, enviable happiness. *Followed purely*, it's the way of the Tao, and undoubtedly the highest way. But for a discriminating man to achieve this, it would mean that he would have to disposses himself of poetry, go *beyond* poetry." *Followed purely*—there is the rub, and the irony. Seymour is the purest of its actual followers in the story (compare, for example, the matron of honor and other wedding guests),

and yet he recognizes himself that he falls short. Seymour's "fault" is his keen attunement to the "current of poetry that flows through things." "I have scars on my hands from touching certain people," he writes, in a bizarre confession of intimate sensitivity. "I'm a kind of paranoic in reverse. I suspect people of plotting to make me happy." They are plotting, of course, with their psychiatrists, to adjust Seymour to *their* imperfections, their hypocrisies and phoniness, as they cannot adjust to his shortcomings, his revulsions and ecstasies. The result, ultimately, will be his suicide—not a gesture of defiance and contempt, but a gesture of sad capitulation.

"Seymour: An Introduction" continues the exploration of the saint of the Glass family, but for the first time Salinger frees himself from the restrictive demands of dramatizing in detail a small segment in time (the day of the wedding, or the day of the suicide) and ranges freely over the whole of Seymour's biography. Or rather, Buddy Glass, novelist and teacher, so ranges, as he is the narrator. When Buddy surfaces briefly in that prologue to "Zooey," he says that what he is about to relate is less like a short story than a "prose home movie." This metaphor seems apt for "Seymour: An Introduction." Buddy presents a series of miscellaneous portraits of Seymour without bothering to provide a narrative thread on which to hang them. The structure that he does provide has more to do with Buddy than with Seymour. In the opening pages of the story, Buddy presents to the reader an "unpretentious bouquet of very early-blooming parentheses: (((()))) ." The story that follows is full of parenthetical comments, in the form of intimate asides to the reader, about Buddy himself and about the agony of composition. Indeed, Buddy seems to be writing the story while he is in process of having some kind of nervous or spiritual breakdown (at one point he specifies acute hepatitis), and as his collapse becomes more evident, the story of Seymour becomes less coherent and at times fades to the background. But nevertheless, reconstruction of Seymour's story is excellent therapy, self-administered, for Buddy's ailing spirit; and he comes through, if not healed, at least reconciled to—even happy in—his fate. Buddy thus joins the gallery of Salinger characters—Holden, Sergeant X, Franny, and even Zooey—who suffer a sickness of the soul, but, through some marvelous renewal, survive. They all withdraw, but they also all return.

Seymour alone, among Salinger's suffering heroes, makes the ultimate withdrawal, and Buddy seems driven to explain why. After a long, rambling prologue, a kind of "thesaurus of undetached prefatory remarks" about himself, his reader, and his brother Seymour, Buddy begins a semi-systematic treatment of his subject. He presents Seymour the poet, Seymour the critic, and, finally, Seymour as a physical entity. Serving somewhat in the capacity of his brother's literary executor, Buddy has in his possession 184 of Seymour's short poems: they look "substantially like an English translation of a sort of double haiku." Seymour, Buddy assures us, will eventually stand with the three or four "*very* nearly nonexpendable" American poets. But since he is forbidden to present here the poems directly (by Seymour's wife, we are told in a footnote), Buddy paraphrases the two he considers best. A young married woman and mother who is having an affair returns home one night from a "tryst" and finds an inflated balloon on her bed. A young suburban widower sits on his lawn at night looking at the moon while a "bored white cat" comes up, rolls over, and bites his left hand. Buddy would be the first to admit that the poems lose something—a great deal—in "translation by paraphrase."

But the pattern is clear: ordinary minor moments of extraordinary illumination or epiphany; finely etched vignettes which reveal the "spiritual mechanism" beneath the externals.

As a critic, Seymour is represented through his commentary on a number of Buddy's stories, and the essence of his advice is summed up in two questions he tells Buddy he will be asked as a writer when he dies: "*Were most of your stars out? Were you busy writing your heart out?*" Although Seymour's questions, like his poems, cannot really be paraphrased, he seems to suggest that *insight* and *feeling*—in their deepest senses—must be involved in great writing; and for the reader they become those elusive, indefinable qualities that are profoundly moving and illuminating. A description of Seymour as a physical entity almost proves Buddy's undoing. As he moves through a catalogue of Seymour's physical characteristics—hair, ears, eyes, nose, voice, skin, clothes—he becomes progressively more intrusive and less coherent, at times, apparently, painfully near disintegration (for example, he announces after a brief passage on Seymour's ears, "I'm going to bed. . . . The hands are sweating, the bowels churning. The Integrated Man is simply not at home").

"Seymour: An Introduction" seems not so much a story as an assemblage of notes, observations, anecdotes, and irrelevancies ("blooming parentheses"), much like Buddy's (or Salinger's) journal, from which a story might one day be made. The Seymour that emerges is generally consistent with the Seymour we have come to know already; new material is presented, new complexities revealed, but no genuinely new dimensions are added to his portrait. In a way, then, the story is Buddy's, as we see him for the first time in all his agony of spirit attempting to retain and strengthen his grasp on the elusive truths lurking in Seymour's life. He seems in desperate need of them. He introduces himself at the beginning, with some irony, as an "ecstatically happy man"; and at the end, as he prepares to go to class, he realizes that "no single thing" he does is "more important than going into that awful Room 307." As Seymour once said, "all we do our whole lives is go from one little piece of Holy Ground to the next."

"Seymour: An Introduction" may be said to have the form that conceals form, with all the seeming irrelevancies deliberately designed to create an even greater than usual illusion of reality—the real reality (a technique, incidentally, not uncommon, as witness Dostoevski's *Notes from the Underground* or Rilke's *The Notebook of Malte Laurids Brigge*). But, still, there is a lingering doubt about the author's control, a doubt that is somewhat reinforced by Buddy's recurrent resemblance to Salinger. Throughout the story, references are made, particularly to the works that Buddy has written, that force this identification. One of Buddy's works is clearly *The Catcher in the Rye*, two others are "Raise High the Roof Beam, Carpenters" (in which Buddy was narrator) and "A Perfect Day for Bananafish" (in which he was not), and still another is "Teddy" (Buddy even quotes from it). Such details as these and others do not, of course, prove anything, but they do suggest—and *just* suggest—that Salinger is revealing, however obliquely, his own loss of control and diffusion of talent.

Salinger's long silence after the appearance of "Seymour: An Introduction" in 1959 was ended in 1965 with the publication of another chapter in the Glass saga, "Hapworth 16, 1924." This story did nothing to reassure those who hoped for a return to the earlier brilliance of *Catcher in the Rye*. Indeed, it tended to accentuate those characteristics of the later work which most readers found disturbing—a tedious length, a humor often self-consciously cute, a muting of narrative in favor of philosophical asides. But in spite of its apparent defects, the story was an important addition to the life of the Glasses, particularly as it shed new light on the remarkable character of Seymour.

"Hapworth 16, 1924" opens with a brief note by Buddy Glass introducing a long, long letter—the entire body of the story—from seven-year-old Seymour at summer camp to his vaudeville-touring family. The letter is startling not only for its length (around 30,000 words) but also for its casually revealed assumptions. Seymour (as well as his five-year-old brother Buddy, with him at camp) is now in one of a sequence of appearances or incarnations about which he seems to have transcendent or superhuman knowledge. He confesses that a "vein of instability" runs through him "like some turbulent river"—a "troublesome instability" that remained uncorrected in his "previous two appearances." This revelation, together with his foreknowledge of his death at age 31, is surely meant to shed light on his suicide in 1948, some twenty-four years after this letter was written. He says at one point: "I for one do not look forward to being distracted by charming lusts of the body, quite day in and day out, for the few, blissful, remaining years allotted to me in this appearance."

Seymour's unusual knowledge of the past and insight into the future derive from "two, tantalizing, tiny portals" in his mind which have opened involuntarily and which give him foresight not only of his own life but also of the lives of others. At one point he has a "stunning glimpse" of Buddy, "quite bereft" of Seymour's "dubious, loving company," busily at work writing stories on his "very large, jet-black, very moving, gorgeous typewriter." The effect of such passages is difficult to describe or assess. They seem both preposterous and ironic.

Is Salinger pulling our leg? Or is he drawing a portrait of the seer and saint as a young man? Or is he seriously presenting his genuine belief alongside Seymour's? "Hapworth 16, 1924" ends with a long list of books that Seymour requests be sent to him at summer camp. The list ranges from the complete works of Dickens and Tolstoi to *The Gayatri Prayer* and Porter Smith's *Chinese Materia Medica*. Few men could get through this interminable reading list in a lifetime, let alone in a summer. And most readers are likely to be disturbed by the diffuseness and miscellaneousness of all the materials in this story, elements which seem to confirm the deterioration of talent (and mind) detected in "Seymour: An Introduction."

Like Eliot or Melville, Salinger is full enough of quotations from literature and references to writers to suggest his own literary context and tradition. References range astonishingly through the poetry and religious literature of India, China, Japan, and throughout Western literature from Blake, Dostoevski, and Rilke to Kierkegaard and Kafka. But in spite of this wide scattering of interests and attractions, Salinger is not a Zen Buddhist or a philosopher or a poet. He is an American novelist writing in the American tradition. At one point in "Zooey," Buddy Glass says, significantly, that *The Great Gatsby* was his *Tom Sawyer* when he was twelve. The confession reveals a fundamental affinity for the native tradition.

Salinger is allied, in a basic way, to the joyful mysticism of Whitman, but he responds, too, to the mystical anguish of Emily Dickinson as well as to the macabre humor of Mark Twain. He no doubt finds much for himself in the idiom and prose rhythms of Ring Lardner, and he is attracted by F. Scott Fitzgerald's poetic style as well as his explorations of idealism and reality. From his own era, we might guess that his sympathies would be attracted to Wright Morris' probing of time, and John Updike's examination of the relation of spirit and matter. But the basic patterns of his novels, the patterns of withdrawal and return, of the search for the ideal and the discovery of self, of the fall from innocence and the acknowledgment of complicity, are also the basic patterns of Hawthorne and Melville, though these are two writers that he does not mention. He does refer to Eliot, but never with enthusiasm; and though he did not entirely escape the wasteland vision, it is clear that his tastes (and his themes) are more closely akin to affirmative poetry of the mystical tradition.

Something of a paradox emerges from this alignment of American writers with Salinger —and this paradox brings us close to the heart of Salinger's achievement. Salinger's work may be described, metaphorically, as a cry of mystical joy transcendent over the modern wasteland and its agony. Two lines from Whitman's "Song of Myself" may suggest the thematic center of Salinger's work. The first (which he quotes in "The Inverted Forest"): "I am the man, I suffer'd, I was there." The second: "It is not chaos or death—it is form, union, plan—it is eternal life—it is Happiness." Translated into the modern idiom of Salinger, these basic feelings might be reconstructed: although modern man feels "his mind dislodge itself and teeter, like insecure luggage on an overhead rack," he must, to maintain his sanity, develop his understanding "for the main current of poetry that flows through things, all things." Like Seymour, he must go his appointed rounds, realizing that "all we do our whole lives is go from one little piece of Holy Ground to the next."

Although Salinger's total creative production, to date, has been relatively small, his impact and influence—and his artistic achievement—have been enormous. No serious history of post-World War II American fiction can be written without awarding him a place in the first rank, and even, perhaps, the pre-eminent position.

Selected Bibliography

WORKS OF J. D. SALINGER

UNCOLLECTED SHORT STORIES

"The Young Folks," *Story*, 16:26–30 (March–April 1940).

"Go See Eddie," *University of Kansas City Review*, 7:121–24 (December 1940).

"The Hang of It," *Collier's*, 108:22 (July 12, 1941).

"The Heart of a Broken Story," *Esquire*, 16:32, 131–33 (September 1941).

"The Long Debut of Lois Taggett," *Story*, 21:28–34 (September–October 1942). Reprinted in *Story: The Fiction of the Forties*, edited by Whit and Hallie S. Burnett. New York: Dutton, 1949. Pp. 153–62.

"Personal Notes on an Infantryman," *Collier's*, 110:96 (December 12, 1942).

"The Varioni Brothers," *Saturday Evening Post*, 216:12–13, 76–77 (July 17, 1943).

"Both Parties Concerned," *Saturday Evening Post*, 216:14, 47–48 (February 26, 1944).

"Soft-Boiled Sergeant," *Saturday Evening Post*, 216:18, 82, 84–85 (April 15, 1944).

"Last Day of the Last Furlough," *Saturday Evening Post*, 217:26–27, 61–62, 64 (July 15, 1944).

"Once a Week Won't Kill You," *Story*, 25:23–27 (November–December 1944).

"Elaine," *Story*, 26:38–47 (March–April 1945).

"A Boy in France," *Saturday Evening Post*, 217:21, 92 (March 31, 1945).

"This Sandwich Has No Mayonnaise," *Esquire*, 25:54–56, 147–49 (October 1945). Reprinted in *The Armchair Esquire*, edited by Arnold Gingrich and L. Rush Hills. New York: Putnam, 1958. Pp. 187–97.

"The Stranger," *Collier's*, 116:18, 77 (December 1, 1945).

"I'm Crazy," *Collier's*, 116:36, 48, 51 (December 22, 1945).

"Slight Rebellion off Madison," *New Yorker*, 22:76–79 (December 21, 1946).

"A Young Girl in 1941 with No Waist at All," *Mademoiselle*, 25:222–23, 292–302 (May 1947).

"The Inverted Forest," *Cosmopolitan*, 123:73–80, 85–86, 88, 90, 92, 95–96, 98, 100, 102, 107, 109 (December 1947). Reprinted in *Cosmopolitan*, 150:111–32 (March 1961).

"A Girl I Knew," *Good Housekeeping*, 126:37, 186, 188, 191–96 (February 1948). Reprinted in *Best American Short Stories of 1949; and the Yearbook of the American Short Story*, edited by Martha J. Foley. Boston: Houghton Mifflin, 1949. Pp. 248–60.

"Blue Melody," *Cosmopolitan*, 125:51, 112–19 (September 1948).

"Hapworth 16, 1924," *New Yorker*, 41:32–113 (June 19, 1965).

NOVELS AND COLLECTIONS OF SHORT STORIES

The Catcher in the Rye. Boston: Little, Brown, 1951.

Nine Stories. Boston: Little, Brown, 1953. (Contains the following stories which first appeared as indicated: "A Perfect Day for Bananafish," *New Yorker*, 23:21–25 (January 31, 1948); "Uncle Wiggily in Connecticut," *New Yorker*, 24:30–36 (March 20, 1948); "Just before the War with the Eskimos," *New Yorker*, 24:37–40, 42, 44, 46 (June 5, 1948); "The Laughing Man," *New Yorker*, 25:27–32 (March 19, 1949); "Down at the Dinghy," *Harper's*, 198:87–91 (April 1949); "For Esmé—with Love and Squalor," *New Yorker*, 26:28–36 (April 8, 1950); "Pretty Mouth and Green My Eyes," *New Yorker*, 27:20–24 (July 14, 1951); "De Daumier-Smith's Blue Period," *World Review* (London), May 1952, pp. 33–48; "Teddy," *New Yorker*, 28:26–36, 38 (January 31, 1953).)

Franny and Zooey. Boston: Little, Brown, 1961. (Contains the following stories which first appeared as indicated: "Franny," *New Yorker*, 30:24–32, 35–43 (January 29, 1955);

"Zooey," *New Yorker,* 33:32–42, 44–139 May 4, 1957).)

Raise High the Roof Beam, Carpenters; and Seymour: An Introduction. Boston: Little, Brown, 1963. (Contains the following stories which first appeared as indicated: "Raise High the Roof Beam, Carpenters," *New Yorker,* 31:51–58, 60–116 (November 19, 1955); "Seymour: An Introduction," *New Yorker,* 35:42–52, 54–111 (June 6, 1959).)

BIBLIOGRAPHY

Fiene, Donald F. "J. D. Salinger: A Bibliography," *Wisconsin Studies in Contemporary Literature,* 4:109–49 (Winter 1963).

CRITICAL AND BIOGRAPHICAL STUDIES

Belcher, William F., and James W. Lee, eds. *J. D. Salinger and the Critics.* Belmont, Calif.: Wadsworth Publishing Company, 1962. (Contains 24 essays by a variety of critics.)

French, Warren. *J. D. Salinger.* New York: Twayne, 1963.

Grunwald, Henry Anatole, ed. *Salinger: A Critical and Personal Portrait.* New York: Harper, 1962. (A large selection of articles by various critics.)

Gwynne, Frederick L., and Joseph L. Blotner. *The Fiction of J. D. Salinger.* Pittsburgh: University of Pittsburgh Press, 1958.

Hamilton, Kenneth. *J. D. Salinger.* Grand Rapids, Mich.: William B. Eerdmans, 1967.

Laser, Marvin, and Norman Fruman, eds. *Studies in J. D. Salinger: Reviews, Essays, and Critiques of The Catcher in the Rye and Other Fiction.* New York: Odyssey Press, 1963.

Marsden, Malcolm M., ed. *If You Really Want to Know: A Catcher Casebook.* Chicago: Scott, Foresman, 1963.

Modern Fiction Studies, XII, 299–390 (Special Salinger Number).

Simonson, Harold P., and Philip E. Hager, eds. *Salinger's "Catcher in the Rye": Clamor vs. Criticism.* Boston: D. C. Heath and Company, 1963.

Wisconsin Studies in Contemporary Literature. Special Number: Salinger. 4:1–160 (Winter 1963).

—*JAMES E. MILLER, JR.*

Carl Sandburg

1878-1967

CARL SANDBURG never won the Nobel Prize, but some Americans thought that he should have, and when Hemingway received it in 1954 he told reporters that it should have gone to Sandburg. Later in the year at the National Book Awards program in New York when Harvey Breit, of the *New York Times Book Review* staff, asked Sandburg how he felt about Hemingway's friendly gesture, he replied: "Harvey Breit, I want to tell you that sometime thirty years from now when the Breit boys are sitting around, one boy will say, 'Did Carl Sandburg ever win the Nobel Prize?' and one Breit boy will say, 'Ernest Hemingway gave it to him in 1954.' "

Whether or not Sandburg deserved the Nobel Prize, he was at least as well known and widely read in his own country as Hemingway, though perhaps not as famous abroad, for he had not outrun General Patton's tanks in the World War II invasion of Germany or led the vanguard in "liberating" Paris, to mention only two of Hemingway's fabulous adventures. Yet in his own way Sandburg was also newsworthy. No other American writer was at the same time so widely read and heard: hundreds of audiences had been entertained by his baritone voice, reading his poems, singing American folk ballads which he had collected, accompanying himself on his ubiquitous guitar, the familiar lock of unruly hair drooping over one eye. Innumerable photographs in newspapers and magazines and animated images on television and motion picture screens had made his face as much of a popular icon as Mark Twain's a generation earlier.

Of course these comparisons only establish the fact that Carl Sandburg was a great celebrity and a superb professional entertainer. Was he a great poet? At the peak of his productivity—say from 1930 to the entry of the United States in World War II—there seemed little doubt that he was, though even then some dissenting critical voices could be heard. By the time of his death in the late 1960's his reputation seemed less secure, though as a biographer of Lincoln he had no contemporary rival, and as a symbolical "voice of America" he was rivaled only by the New England poet Robert Frost, who bitterly resented any comparison. Actually, the competition of poets is always a mitigating factor in their reputations, especially contemporary. Friends of Frost tended to downgrade the prosodically free-wheeling Sandburg. Admirers of T. S. Eliot were not inclined to hold a high opinion of the folksy author of *The People, Yes*. Though Ezra Pound had some appreciation of the revolutionary modernity of Sandburg, he "put him down," as Ben Jonson did Shakespeare, for his "small Latin and less Greek," or in Pound's own words, as "a lumberjack who has taught himself all that he knows." Lumberjacking happened to be one of the few occupations Sandburg had never tried, but he was unquestionably self-taught.

Whatever Carl Sandburg's future rank in literature may be—and posthumous reputations are impossible to predict (witness Melville, Whitman, and Emily Dickinson)—he was, as Thomas Lask declared in the *New York Times* at the time of Sandburg's death on July 23, 1967, "the American bard. The sense of being American informed everything he wrote." Sandburg's success as the voice and conscience of his time and generation, to a degree Whitman would have envied, is sufficient justification for a critical study of his life and career. This is the most rewarding approach to this enormously productive writer. The question of his "minor" or "major" status can wait for time to answer.

The America Sandburg knew and wrote about—at least until after World War II—was "mid-America," life on the prairies of Illinois and the shores of Lake Michigan from Milwaukee to Chicago and Harbert, Michigan. His mind was still lively and his typewriter busy during most of his final twenty-two years at Flat Rock, North Carolina, but his formative years were spent in the Midwest of his contemporaries Theodore Dreiser, Sherwood Anderson, Sinclair Lewis, Edgar Lee Masters, and Ernest Hemingway—the Hemingway of the Nick Adams stories, which some critics think his best. It can hardly be accidental that these men who were some of the most innovative and influential authors in America from World War I to the beginning of World War II all had a similar background. By the end of World War II the spurt of midwestern literary energy had nearly spent itself and passed to the South. But the two decades between the wars were dominated by these mid-American poets and novelists.

In changing the course of American literature Sandburg and his western contemporaries were, to be sure, assisted by their equally western predecessors Mark Twain, Hamlin Garland, and William Dean Howells. All of these writers were largely self-taught, like Abraham Lincoln, who grew up in Indiana and Illinois. The first white settlers to arrive in this region in their covered wagons, like the later impoverished emigrants from northern Europe, had had little formal education, and the traditions they brought with them were severely tested and modified by the harsh life of the frontier and the crude towns built in reckless haste. Experience was their school. The world that Dreiser, Anderson, Sandburg, and Hemingway knew bore little resemblance to the cultured society of Henry James, Edith Wharton, and Edwin Arlington Robinson. Empiricism shaped both their ethics and their aesthetics. In this sense they were all "from Missouri," skeptical of authority, disdainful of conventions, and personally independent to the point of eccentricity. Consequently their attitude toward human experience was realistic, the subject of their fiction and verse the life of ordinary people, and their style shaped by the idiom and rhythms of mid-American speech.

These midwestern writers were acutely conscious of social inequalities and injustices, and several were professed Socialists, including Sandburg. In religion they were mainly agnostic, though tolerant of the religious experience of others, and they had a somewhat Emersonian attitude toward nature (Emerson was always one of Sandburg's favorite authors). Their life-style was stubbornly individualistic, in speech, manners, opinions, and artistic self-expression. Sandburg's clothes never seemed to fit properly, and his indifference to his appearance was so pronounced as finally to suggest a theatrical pose; but it was entirely in character with the role he played in lecturing and singing ballads, and in harmony, too, with his own personality, for clothes were never more than a practical necessity to him.

Sandburg's indifference to fashion began with his early life in Galesburg, Illinois, where he was born January 6, 1878, near the tracks of the Chicago, Burlington, and Quincy Railroad, for which his father worked as a blacksmith. Both parents were Swedish immigrants who had come to the United States separately. Clara Anderson was working as a hotel chambermaid in another small Illinois town when she met August Sandburg, member of a railroad gang passing through. They were married in 1874 and settled in Galesburg after August was transferred to the C.B.&Q. repair shop. He could read his Swedish Bible but never learned to write, having to sign his name with an X. Mrs. Sandburg could write personal letters in colloquial Swedish and phonetically spelled English. Neither was the least interested in books, except for the Bible, and Carl had to discover the world of literature without any encouragement at home.

In primary school Carl learned the alphabet and began reading in a "primer" which had puzzling sentences about a ladies' tea party. He had never tasted tea (the Swedes preferred coffee) and he thought the ladies' conversation very silly. But he soon became fascinated by words, spoken or written. Several years later he received a card from the public library and became an avid reader, especially of history and biographies of American Revolution heroes. He was disappointed to find the biographies of Civil War generals dull and unconvincing; strange, he thought, because he had talked with men who had fought in this more recent war and he found their stories absorbingly interesting. Many of the older people in

Galesburg remembered Lincoln's debate with Judge Douglas at Knox College. A plaque on one of the buildings commemorated the historic spot, and Sandburg many times stopped to read it.

One of the subjects young Sandburg enjoyed most in school was geography; both the places and the people in other parts of the world stirred his imagination. Literature did not yet arouse much enthusiasm in him, especially the poetry of Longfellow and the novels of Dickens, his teachers' favorites. He read *Tom Sawyer* and *Huckleberry Finn*, but at the time preferred James Otis' *Toby Tyler: or, Ten Weeks with a Circus*, and Charles Coffin's *The Boys of '76*. He read detective stories, too, of course out of school, but found them less absorbing than Champlin's *Young Folks' Cyclopaedia of Persons and Places*. He was not bored by school, however, and liked most of his teachers, but after he finished the eighth grade he had to go to work to help his father support the family of five children (not counting two boys who died of diphtheria at an early age). But for a bright, observant, and gregarious boy with endless curiosity and a sympathetic nature, education really began after he quit school. In his own revealing account of his boyhood in *Always the Young Strangers* (1953) he could say, looking back from maturity:

"In those years as a boy in that prairie town I got education in scraps and pieces of many kinds, not knowing that they were part of my education. I met people in Galesburg who were puzzling to me, and later when I read Shakespeare I found those same people were puzzling him. I met little wonders of many kinds among animals and plants that never lost their wonder for me, and I found later that these same wonders had a deep interest for Emerson, Thoreau, and Walt Whitman. I met superstitions, folk tales, and folklore while I was a young spalpeen, 'a broth of a boy,' long before I read books about them. All had their part, small or large, in the education I got outside of books and schools."

Not surprisingly, it was also outside school that the "young spalpeen" learned "that crime and politics are tangled with each other, that law and justice sometimes can be a monkey business with a bad smell." He made this declaration in *Always the Young Strangers* regarding a particularly revolting murder in Chicago of a Dr. Cronin, "leader in a camp of the Clanna-Gael fighters for the freedom of Ireland." One of the accused was "handy at passing money to jurymen" and went free. Another man allegedly connected with the murder "went free in a hurry on 'habeas corpus,' later was put on trial for jury bribing, and wriggled out free."

"Of course," Sandburg continues, "we got education out of the Cronin murder and the first and second trials. We learned that in time of peace, and no war on, men can kill a man not for money but because the man stands for something they hate and they want him out of the way. We learned that juries can be fixed, that if a convicted man waits a few years and gets a second trial there may be important witnesses who have died or moved away or somehow can't be found. . . . We learned things we didn't hear about in the Seventh Ward school and we never read about them in the detective stories of those days. . . ."

After a great variety of short-term jobs, delivering milk, cutting ice on the lake, assisting carpenters, painters, plumbers, barbers, druggists, etc., Sandburg decided at eighteen to see the country by traveling as a hobo to the wheat fields of Kansas. He rode freight trains, stopping at towns along the way to earn a little money at dishwashing or other temporary employment. He met other hoboes and shared food with them in their "jungles" near the rail-road tracks. After working with a threshing crew he "bummed" his way to the Rocky Mountains and back home.

Sandburg was trying to learn the house-painting trade when the American battleship *Maine* was sunk in Havana harbor on February 15, 1898. Believing with most other Americans that Spain was responsible (exactly who or what caused the explosion has never been definitely known), he enlisted in the Sixth Infantry Regiment of the Illinois Volunteers. With this regiment he drilled for two months in Virginia, saw the national capitol while on leave, was transported to Guantánamo Bay in Cuba, then hastily shipped to Guánica, Puerto Rico, because of an epidemic of yellow fever in Cuba. The short war was nearly over before the Illinois soldiers arrived, and they saw no fighting, though they suffered in the tropical heat from wearing heavy wool Civil War uniforms, from thousands of insect bites, from dysentery and spoiled food which war profiteers had sold to the United States government.

As a "war veteran" Sandburg was admitted to Lombard College—the "other" college in Galesburg—without a high school diploma or an entrance examination. He supported himself by serving with the local fire department, studying and sleeping at night in the firehouse. The most remarkable teacher at Lombard, a man who won distinction later as an economist in Washington, D.C., was Professor Philip Green Wright. He taught English, mathematics, astronomy, and economics—some indication of the kind of college Lombard was. He took a special interest in Carl and gave him his first competent instruction in writing.

In college Sandburg played basketball and baseball, acted in a musical comedy, contributed to a literary magazine, and edited the college yearbook, but left in the spring of his senior year without a degree—probably because he had failed to take some courses required for graduation. These courses may have been in mathematics, because this was one of the subjects which later prevented his passing the entrance examination to West Point after he had been nominated by his congressman. His other failure was in English grammar.

Though Sandburg left college without a definite goal in life, he had experienced the satisfaction of writing down his own thoughts and seeing them in print in the college publications. But he was restless and began wandering again, this time in the East. He spent ten days in a Pittsburgh jail (for "deadbeating" his way on a freight train) before returning to Galesburg. Home again and without employment, he completed a batch of poems. Professor Wright had a small printing press in his basement, and there Sandburg's first three slender volumes were set up and privately printed: *In Reckless Ecstasy* in 1904 and *The Plaint of a Rose* and *Incidentals* in 1905.

It might surprise readers of Sandburg's *Chicago Poems* to find that he derived the title of his first book from the popular, romantic, and third-rate contemporary Marie Corelli, who praised the "reckless ecstasies of language." At this stage in his development as a poet Sandburg believed simply that "there are depths of life that logic cannot sound. It takes feeling." To produce this *feeling* he used the galloping meter of a Kipling, or almost any other popular poet of the period, as in the embarrassingly trite "Pulse-Beats and Pen-Strokes":

> For the hovels shall pass and the shackles
>   drop,
> The gods shall tumble and the systems fall;
> And the things they will make, with their
>   loves at stake,
> Shall be the gladness of each and all.

However, *Incidentals*, a collection of aphorisms, was in a prose-poetry form suggestive of Sandburg's maturer style:

What is shame?
Shame is the feeling you have when you agree
  with the woman who loves you that you are
    the
man she thinks you are . . .

Truth consists of paradoxes and a paradox
is two facts that stand on opposite hilltops
and across the intervening valley call
each other liars.

These juvenilia Sandburg was glad to forget, and they have never been reprinted, except for brief quotations in Harry Golden's *Carl Sandburg* and in an article I wrote for an academic magazine.

Chicago was the place that Sandburg later made famous in his poems, but he could have written a book on Galesburg, Illinois, similar to Sherwood Anderson's psychological study of people in *Winesburg, Ohio*, or epitaphs of tragic failure like those in Edgar Lee Masters' *Spoon River Anthology*. In fact, sketches of such stories and biographies Sandburg did publish in *Always the Young Strangers*, with the difference that the outright failures he mentions were few. Collectively the subjects of his sketches were a cross section of the nation, or in Sandburg's own words: "This small town of Galesburg, as I look back on it, was a piece of the American Republic. Breeds and blood strains that figure in history were there for me, as a boy to see and hear in their faces and their ways of talking and acting."

From 1902 to 1906 Sandburg wandered away and returned to Galesburg, supporting himself mainly by peddling stereoptican pictures, but he also contributed to a Chicago magazine called *Tomorrow*. In 1906 he became associate editor of another magazine in Chicago called *Lyceumite*, and began giving lectures on Walt Whitman. It was in Chicago that he met Winfield R. Gaylord, an organizer of the Social Democratic party in Wisconsin.

The doctrines of the party strongly appealed to him and he accepted an offer to join Mr. Gaylord in his work.

Sandburg continued to lecture on Whitman, but gave most of his time to traveling and addressing workingmen in Wisconsin. "Labor is beginning to realize its power," he told them. "We no longer beg, we demand old-age pensions; we demand a minimum wage; we demand industrial accident insurance; we demand unemployment insurance; and we demand the eight-hour day, which must become the basic law of the land." These demands which seemed so radical in 1907–9 would become "the basic law of the land," not under a Socialist president but under the administration of Franklin D. Roosevelt and be extended in subsequent Democratic and Republican administrations. Yet the pioneers for these laws were those Wisconsin Socialists La Follette and Gaylord, and party recruiters like Carl Sandburg.

One day in 1908 at the Milwaukee Socialist headquarters Sandburg met Lilian Steichen, a schoolteacher from Illinois, who was there because she had been employed by the party to translate Socialist classics from French and German into English. She and Sandburg were immediately attracted to each other and were married several months later, a happy marriage that lasted until Sandburg's death. Mrs. Sandburg was the sister of Edward Steichen, who became a world-famous photographer and one of the poet's staunchest friends.

From recruiting members for the Socialist party Sandburg made an easy transition to Milwaukee journalism. He did reporting and wrote feature articles and some editorials for the *News*, the *Sentinel*, and the *Journal*. Milwaukee elected a Socialist mayor, Emil Seidel, and he employed Sandburg as a private secretary. But newspaper work remained his chief vocation. In 1912 he joined the liberal *Milwaukee Leader*, then went to the *Chicago Daily World* and, several newspaper jobs later, to the *Chicago Daily News*, with which he remained until the success of his biography of Lincoln, *The Prairie Years*, made it possible for him to resign and buy a farm in Harbert, Michigan, where his wife raised goats and he could give his full time to poetry and biography, with intervals of lecturing.

Sandburg's fierce sympathy with poor people, the oppressed and the exploited, which was to find expression in all his writing—in fact, was often the main reason for his writing at all—became permanently imbedded in his conscience and consciousness during his few years of propagating socialism in Wisconsin. However, he was never a Marxist, though he had read *Das Kapital* at Lombard with Professor Wright. He was more of a Populist and social reformer, perhaps influenced somewhat by "Teddy" Roosevelt in the early years of the twentieth century, and certainly by the muckraking journalists: Ida Tarbell, who wrote about the greed of John D. Rockefeller; Lincoln Steffens, who uncovered political corruption in the cities; and Upton Sinclair, the Socialist novelist, who shocked the nation into beginning pure-food legislation after *The Jungle* (1906) revealed the incredibly unsanitary conditions of the packing industry in Chicago. (Sinclair's equally strong indictment of the exploitation of laboring men, especially the nearly illiterate newcomers from Europe, by factory employers, real-estate dealers, and merchants did not produce such prompt results.) Sandburg, like Sinclair, was more concerned with the actual condition of the workingmen's lives than with ideology.

In 1908 Sandburg campaigned for Eugene V. Debs for the presidency, and in 1915 he and Jack London often wrote the entire contents of the *International Socialist Review*, using a variety of pseudonyms. At the outbreak of World War I he shared the pacifist views of other Socialists (Social Democrats in Wisconsin, trade-union Socialists in New York City, Fabians in England, and Christian Socialists in Germany, France, and Italy). He expressed his horror of killing in a group of "War Poems" (1914–15), and in the *International Socialist Review* he argued that soldiers were actually exploited laborers:

"It's a workingman's world. Shovels and shovelling take more time of soldiers than guns and shooting. Twenty-one million men on the battlefields of Europe are shovelling more than shooting. Not only have they dug hundreds of miles of trenches, but around and under the trenches are tunnels and labyrinthian catacombs. All dug by shovels. Technically, in social science and economics, the soldier is a parasite and a curious louse of the masterclass imposed on the working class. Yet strictly now the soldier is a worker, a toiler on and under the land. He's a sucker, a shovelman who gets board and clothes from the government that called him to the colors. A mucker-gunman—that's what a soldier is."

Yet when the United States finally entered World War I, Sandburg broke with the Social Democrats and supported President Wilson. As Harry Golden recalls, "Outside Milwaukee the Wisconsin Socialists never made great headway until 1918, when they got the votes of many people of German descent who opposed America's entry into World War I. It was the kind of success that helped kill [the party]."

Sandburg never returned to the Socialist party, but he remained personally loyal to Debs and invited him to his home in suburban Chicago after Debs was released from prison. In 1933 Sandburg lost the friendship of Robert Frost by supporting Roosevelt and the New Deal. Six years later President Roosevelt warmly thanked him for a radio broadcast endorsing his policies and candidacy for a second term. Sandburg also did some campaigning

for John F. Kennedy in 1960. He could count Justice William O. Douglas and Adlai Stevenson as personal friends, but at the same time he admired Republican Earl Warren. Thus the Social Democrat of the early twentieth century was, by mid-century, securely in the mainstream of American politics.

While still extremely busy in newspaper work and writing articles and editorials for Socialist magazines, Sandburg somehow found time to compose the poems which began to create a literary reputation for him when *Chicago Poems* was published in 1916. Some of these poems had attracted attention when first published by Harriet Monroe in *Poetry*, a magazine she started in Chicago in 1912. In fact, his poetic fame might be said to have begun with the publication of "Chicago" in *Poetry* in 1914. This was the key poem in the collection Henry Holt and Company published, a volume declared by Amy Lowell in the *New York Times Book Review*, to be "one of the most original books this age has produced."

In "Chicago" Sandburg admits all the faults of the city familiar to the world as the "stormy, husky, brawling . . . crooked . . . brutal" place where painted women lure farm boys under the gas lamps, gunmen kill and go free to kill again, and factory workers and their families starve because of low wages or unemployment. But this is not a social-protest poem. It is a lyric tribute to the vibrant, proud, happy, and laughing "City of the Big Shoulders . . . a tall bold slugger set vivid against the little soft cities . . ." If Chicago lacks the culture and beauty of the older cities, its inhabitants can take pride in its youth, vitality, and joy in being alive. This is the Chicago myth created by Sandburg, and it gave a great stimulation to midwestern literature.

In "Skyscraper" the poet strives to give the building a "soul." The skyscraper, he says, acquired its soul from the men who built it, those who dug the foundation, erected the girders, carried the mortar, laid the brick and fitted the stone, strung miles of wires and pipes; and later the stenographers, scrubbing women, and watchmen who worked in it. He ignores the business executives, but perhaps they have no soul-power to spare. Anyway, this is the manner in which the poet humanizes inanimate steel and stone.

In his newspaper prose Sandburg continued to fight for the causes he had espoused since his first affiliation with the Social Democratic party, but in most of his poems he attacked social evils obliquely. One exception was "To a Contemporary Bunk Shooter" (previously printed in *New Masses* undisguised as "Billy Sunday"):

> You come along . . . tearing your shirt. . . . yelling about Jesus.
>
> · · · · · · · · · · · · · · ·
>
> He never came near clean people or dirty people but they felt cleaner because he came along. It was your crowd of bankers and business men and lawyers hired the sluggers and murderers who put Jesus out of the running.

He calls Billy Sunday "a bug-house peddler of second-hand gospel," telling "people living in shanties" that they can live in "mansions in the skies after they're dead and the worms have eaten 'em." Doubtless Billy Sunday deserved this cuffing, but the poem was indeed propaganda for the *New Masses*.

A prominent theme in *Chicago Poems* is the longing of ordinary people for the beauty and happiness they have never known. This clutching at dreams was not a creation of Sandburg's fantasy, but a social phenomenon which he accurately observed. The fact is confirmed by the contemporary midwestern novelists, Dreiser especially, whose early novels are repositories of social history. For example, in *Sister Carrie* (1900) the heroine is an unsophisticated girl who leaves a small town in Wisconsin to go to Chicago in search of pleasure and excitement. She finds only poverty, drudgery, and monotony until, by instinctive self-preservation from cold and hunger, she becomes a "kept woman." Yet in spite of subsequent fame and wealth in the theater, she never finds self-fulfillment, and continues dreaming of the happiness she has somehow missed. Many of the people in Sandburg's poems are brothers and sisters of Sister Carrie, such as "Mamie":

> Mamie beat her head against the bars of a little Indiana town and dreamed of romance and big things off somewhere the way the railroad trains all ran.

She thought of suicide and then decided that, "if she was going to die she might as well die struggling for a clutch of romance among the streets of Chicago."

> She has a job now at six dollars a week in the basement of the Boston store
> And even now she beats her head against the bars in the same old way and wonders if there is a bigger place the railroads run to from Chicago where maybe there is
>> romance
>> and big things
>> and real dreams
>> that never go smash.

A more cheerful theme in *Chicago Poems* is the laughter and joy workmen manage to find in spite of their toil and poverty. The face of the Jewish fish crier on Maxwell Street is the face "of a man terribly glad to be selling fish, terribly glad that God made fish, and customers to whom he may call his wares from a push-cart." The poet searches for "Happiness" and finds it one Sunday afternoon on the banks of the Desplaines River in "a crowd of Hungarians under the trees with their women and children and a keg of beer and an accordion." In "Fellow Citizens" the poet is told by a millionaire, an advertising executive named Jim Kirch, and the mayor that they are happy, but he discovers a man on Gilpin Place, near Hull House, making accordions and guitars which he plays himself after he has finished them, and "he had it all over the butter millionaire, Jim Kirch and the mayor when it came to happiness."

In the use of slang and undignified language Sandburg achieved in actuality the theory which Wordsworth set forth in his Preface to *Lyrical Ballads*: to "present incidents and situations from common life . . . in a selection of language really used by men . . ." Sandburg's poems are also more realistic than Wordsworth's, or even naturalistic (in the Zola sense), as in "The Walking Man of Rodin," with "The skull found always crumbling neighbor of the ankles." Yet Sandburg is also just as definitely romantic in his ability to see beauty in the commonplace. "The Shovel Man," for example, is

> A dago working for a dollar six bits a day
> And a dark-eyed woman in the old coun-
> try dreams of him for one of the world's
> ready men with a pair of fresh lips and
> a kiss better than all the wild grapes
> that ever grew in Tuscany.

Perhaps it is not surprising that Sandburg most often found this beauty in the lives of foreign-born workmen, people like his own Swedish parents; but these recent Americans also constituted a large segment of the Chicago population. Sandburg was indeed at this period the Chicago poet.

In his second volume of poetry, *Cornhuskers* (1918), Sandburg played less the role of the urban poet and wrote more about rural sights and sounds and his wider experiences during World War I. He was now traveling more, lecturing, reading his poems, collecting and singing the folk ballads which he published later in *The American Songbag* (1927). His three daughters (Margaret, born in 1911, Janet in 1914, and Helga in 1918) also began to have an emotional effect on his literary imagination as he entertained them with the kind of child-fantasy stories he published in 1922 in *Rootabaga Stories*.

Cornhuskers opens with "Prairie," a poem partly autobiographical, partly cosmic, partly prophetic:

> I was born on the prairie and the milk of
> its wheat, the red of its clover, the eyes
> of its women, gave me a song and a
> slogan.
>
> Here the water went down, the icebergs
> slid with gravel, the gaps and the val-
> leys hissed, and the black loam came,
> and the yellow sandy loam.
>
> . . . .
>
> O prairie mother, I am one of your boys.
>
> . . . .
>
> I speak of new cities and new people.
> I tell you the past is a bucket of ashes.
> I tell you yesterday is a wind gone down,
> a sun dropped in the west.
> I tell you there is nothing in the world,
> only an ocean of tomorrows,
> a sky of tomorrows.
>
> I am a brother of the cornhuskers who say
> at sundown:
> Tomorrow is a day.

In these poems Sandburg shows his fondness for elemental things: sky, moon, stars, wind, birds, and animals. He celebrates nature in all seasons, but especially late summer and autumn: the ripening corn, the yellow cornflower in autumn wind, the blue of larkspur and Canadian thistle, and red-ripe tomatoes. In "Wilderness" he feels kinship with a wolf, a fox, a hog, a fish, a baboon, an eagle, and a mockingbird, and exclaims, "O, I got a zoo, I got a menagerie, inside my ribs." But he is over-fond of baby metaphors. In "Baby Face" the "white moon comes in on a baby face." In "The Year" buds "open baby fists/ Into hands of broad flowers," while the winds sing "lullabies." "Handfuls" narrowly escapes sentimentality:

> Blossoms of babies
> Blinking their stories
> Come soft
> On the dusk and the babble;
> Little red gamblers,
> Handfuls that slept in the dust.

This book is dedicated to Janet and Margaret, each of whom gets a poem. In "Sixteen Months" the adoring father sees on Janet's lips the blue mist of dreams, smoke, and haze on "ten miles of corn" in morning sunlight. This is stretching metaphors to their limit. As "Child Margaret" writes the Arabic symbols, 1 and 7 have a military stance, 6 and 9 dance, 2 is a trapeze actor, 3 is humpbacked, and 8 knock-kneed. "Each number is a bran-new rag doll." This whimsical side of the poet may have surprised some readers who had Sandburg tagged as "the Chicago poet."

But Sandburg was a poet of many moods. In "Sunset from Omaha Hotel Window" he finds "The gloaming is bitter/ As in Chicago/ or Kenosha." From the observation car of a train he enjoys the "Still Life" pictures of the rolling prairie, new-mown hay, Holstein cows, a signalman in a Kansas City tower. Sitting by a stream radiator on a winter day he thinks about "Horses and Men in Rain," delivering milk or coal, grocery boys, mail carriers. His memory and sympathy are panoramic, like Whitman's in "Song of Myself"; but also nostalgic; and his empathy is selective, not the all-embracing compassion of the Messianic Whitman. He empathizes with the Greeks he saw in Keokuk working on a railroad; a pawnshop operator on a back street; lonely men in oyster boats in the Chesapeake Bay. He writes elegies for Adelaide Crapsey, the Brooklyn girl who composed poems in Japanese forms while dying of an incurable illness; for Don Magregor, the Colorado miner accused of murder, who died with Pancho Villa in Mexico; Buffalo Bill, hero of prairie boys; and "Old Osawatomie," now "six feet of dust under the morning stars."

Sandburg has often been compared to Whitman, and he frequently wrote on the same themes, but always with his own handling of them. The long verses of "Prairie" look superficially like Whitman's form, but the music is different. A major distinction is in their treatment of the theme of death. To Whitman death was always beautiful, an old mother crooning a lullaby from the ocean of immortality, but to Sandburg death is the final irony of life—stillness, nothingness. In "Cool Tombs" Abraham Lincoln and his assassin, Ulysses Grant and the "con men" who brought shame to his administration, lovely Pocahontas and "a streetful of people" are all equalized "in the dust . . . in the cool tombs." This is one of Sandburg's most beautiful lyrics, and most devastatingly ironic. In "Grass" the scars of World War I will be covered by the perennial grass, not in a Pantheistic transmutation of men into vegetation, but as nature erases the scars of human violation of life. Instead of Whitman's consolation, one is reminded of Hemingway's *nada*—"it was all nada." In Shenandoah Valley lie "The blue nobody remembers, the gray nobody remembers . . ." But generalizing about the brevity of life and the sureness of death in "Loam" the poet does seem to find some consolation in the eternal cycle:

In the loam we sleep,

. . . .

We rise;
To shape of rose leaf,
Of face and shoulder.

We stand, then,
To a whiff of life,
Lifted to the silver of the sun
Over and out of the loam
A day.

And "In Tall Grass," seeing a honeycomb and bees buzzing "in the dried head of a horse in a pasture corner," he would "ask no better a winding sheet . . ."

Sandburg's first reaction to World War I was that of most Socialists throughout the world. In "A Million Young Workmen, 1915" he exclaims with the bitterness of Stephen Crane in *War Is Kind*:

And oh, it would have been a great job of killing and a new and beautiful thing under the sun if the million knew why they hacked and tore each other to death.

. . . .

I dreamed a million ghosts of the young workmen rose in their shirts all soaked in crimson . . . and yelled:
God damn the grinning kings, God damn the kaiser and the czar.

However, in "The Four Brothers," subtitled "Notes for War Songs (November, 1917)," Sandburg's mood is that of Whitman in his recruiting "Beat! Beat! Drums!":

I say now, by God, only fighters today will save the world, nothing but fighters will keep alive the names of those who left red prints of bleeding feet at Valley Forge in Christmas snow.

In fact, this is Sandburg's "Battle Hymn of the Republic," in which he has an apocalyptic vision that

Out of it all a God who knows is sweeping clean,
Out of it all a God who sees and pierces through,
is breaking and cleaning out an old thousand years,
is making ready for a new thousand years.

In spite of its unevenness *Cornhuskers* is one of his finest volumes of poems. The unevenness probably reflects the turbulence of the period in which these poems were written, 1915–18.

Smoke and Steel (1920) also shows the excitement of the war period, and some of the disillusionment of the aftermath, but especially the former in the jazzy rhythms of "Honky Tonk in Cleveland, Ohio" and "Jazz Fantasia." The title of the book is misleading, for most of the poems are neither social protest nor depiction of industrial life. In the title poem the poet sees "smoke" not as pollution or factory ugliness but as a parallel to human blood:

And always dark in the heart and through it,
Smoke and the blood of a man.
Pittsburgh, Youngstown, Gary—they make their steel with men.

The last clause is not uttered in sarcasm, for the poet who had prayed in *Cornhuskers* to be beaten on an anvil into a crowbar or a rivet for a skyscraper saw inspiring strength and beauty in steel. In the blast furnaces he now sees "women dancing,/ Dancing out of the flues and smokestacks . . ."

"The Sins of Kalamazoo," says Sandburg, are "neither scarlet nor crimson" but "a convict gray, a dishwater drab," and so is the place itself. Yet he has "loved the white dawn frost of early winter silver/ And purple over your railroad tracks and lumber yards." Sandburg, one should remember, was a contemporary of the Ash Can School of painters, whom he had almost parodied in "Nocturne in a Deserted Brickyard" in *Chicago Poems*.

There are intimations, almost premonitions, of Eliot's *Waste Land* and *Hollow Men* in some passages in *Smoke and Steel*. In "Four Preludes on Playthings of the Wind" the cedar doors are broken and the golden girls vanished from the city which thought itself "the greatest city,/ the greatest nation:/ nothing like us ever was." Now the black crows caw and the rats scribble their hieroglyphic footprints on dusty doorsills. The squabbling of European nations at the peace table had disillusioned Sandburg as early as March 1919, the date he gave for "The Liars":

Across their tables they fixed it up,
Behind their doors away from the mob.
And the guns did a job that nicked off millions.

. . . .

    And now
    Out of the butcher's job
    And the boneyard junk the maggots have
        cleaned,
    Where the jaws of skulls tell the jokes of war
        ghosts,
    Out of this they are calling now: Let's go back
        where we were.

. . . .

So I hear The People tell each other:

. . . .

To hell with 'em all,
The liars who lie to nations,
The liars who lie to The People.

The closest Sandburg himself got to the war was as a Scripps newspaper correspondent in Stockholm from October 1918 to May 1919. His assignment was not the war itself but interviews with people who had been in or near the war zone, or had escaped the turmoil in Russia. His dispatches were little more than human-interest stories for newspaper readers. But crossing the North Atlantic in late autumn provoked atavistic sensations in the descendant of that ancient seafaring nation. However, seeing the many statues of kings on the streets of Stockholm aroused his democratic antipathy. He admired the Riksdag bridge held up by massive stones, and took special interest, as he would have in Chicago, in the old women selling apples or cleaning windows, and fishermen casting their nets beneath the bridge. So he decided that he would rather have young men read "five lines of one of my poems" then have a bronze statue on the "king's street."

An important influence unconnected with the war which became obvious in *Smoke and Steel* was the Japanese haiku. Sandburg had already become more aware of images because of the Imagistic movement discussed and practiced by Ezra Pound and Amy Lowell in Harriet Monroe's *Poetry*. However, though his "Fog" in *Chicago Poems* has often been cited as an Imagistic poem, it seems to have been written without any influence from Pound or Lowell. But the haiku taught him to insinuate cryptic wisdom in an image. In the folksy "Put Off the Wedding Five Times and Nobody Comes to It" he throws off the remark, "It will always come back to me in the blur of that hokku: The heart of a woman of thirty is like the red ball of the sun seen through a mist."

("Blur" seems inaccurate here; perhaps he means ambiguity.) A final section of short poems in *Smoke and Steel* contains several excellent adaptations of the Japanese haiku. For example, "Thin Strips":

Under a peach tree I saw petals scattered
. . . torn strips of a bride's dress, I heard
a woman laugh many years ago.

Or "Wistful":

Wishes left on your lips
The mark of their wings.
Regrets fly kites in your eyes.

Sandburg's third volume of poetry was followed not by another book of poems but by *Rootabaga Stories* (1922), stories he had made up to amuse his three little daughters. These stories have a fairy-tale sense of unreality, with transformations, actions that defy gravity, and the reduction of winds, moons, landscapes, and human actions to child-fantasy dimensions. But much of the fun is in the names and places, with their absurd sounds, outrageous puns, and comic imagery. There is the family that named its first boy Gimme the Ax and its first girl Ax Me No Questions. Jason Squiff wears a popcorn hat, popcorn mittens, and popcorn shoes. Henry Hagglyhoagly plays the guitar with his mittens on. Another story tells how "The animals lost their tails and got them back again traveling from Philadelphia to Medicine Hat." These are not Aesop fables or miraculous stories with a moral. The "morals" are themselves jokes, like "Never Kick a Slipper at the Moon" when the moon looks like the toe and heel of a dancer's foot, for the shoe will go on to the moon. The verbal humor is the strongest indication that these tales were written by a poet.

The year following the publication of *Rootabaga Stories* Sandburg discussed with Alfred Harcourt, a New York publisher then working

for Henry Holt, what book to write next. He had been interested in Abraham Lincoln since his boyhood, and for some years had been collecting Lincoln material: books, newspaper clippings, anecdotes told by people he met, and subjective impressions. Mindful of the success of Sandburg's book of stories for children, Harcourt suggested a life of Lincoln for teenagers, and this was the book Sandburg intended to write when he began his first Lincoln biography. But the work grew in the writing until it became two hefty volumes, written in simple language, imaginative detail, and a fictional style acceptable in a juvenile book, but much too long and detailed for this genre. It was published as *Abraham Lincoln: The Prairie Years* (1926) for general readers.

The narrative of *Prairie Years* rests on the known facts of Lincoln's early life, but many basic facts were unknown, or had been blurred in oral transmission, or had become displaced by folklore. Thus Sandburg attempts to fill in missing information or to elaborate meager facts. Regarding Lincoln's legitimacy, he tells the rumors and mentions the ambiguities. He has no doubt that Lincoln himself was legitimate, but his grandmother, Lucy Hanks, was as a girl "too free and easy in her behavior," and had borne a child, Nancy, while living with a man she had not legally married. "What was clear in the years that had passed was that Lucy . . . had married a man she wanted, Henry Sparrow, and nine children had come and they were all learning to read and write under her teaching. Since she had married the talk about her running wild had let down."

Sandburg gives Nancy Hanks a husband, Thomas Lincoln, and imagines her home in May 1808, the year preceding Abraham Lincoln's birth:

"The Lincolns had a cabin of their own to live in. It stood among wild crab-apple trees.

"And the smell of wild crab-apple blossoms, and the low crying of all wild things, came keen that summer to the nostrils of Nancy Hanks.

"The summer stars that year shook out pain and warning, strange laughters, for Nancy Hanks."

The crabapple blossoms may well have been real, but how did the biographer know that "summer stars that year shook out pain and warning" to Nancy Hanks, as an annunciation of her future son of historic destiny? At the age of seven this son, himself, experiences spells of deep wonder, loneliness, and mysterious premonitions in the Indiana wilderness. His heroic qualities also soon begin to manifest themselves. At eighteen he can "take an ax at the end of the handle and hold it out in a straight horiontal line, easy and steady . . ." One day he walks thirty-four miles just to hear a lawyer make a speech. He becomes a famous wrestler, seemingly invincible. But he never misuses his fabulous strength, and of course his mind and character acquire the toughness and resilience, as if by supernatural design, which he will later need as president of a nation divided by a tragic war. He is the Cinderella hero of folklore, epic, and romance. And yet, in view of the incredible courage, strength, and endurance which Lincoln, as historical fact, did exhibit in the presidency, these symbolical details do not seem exaggerated, but possible and convincing.

Edmund Wilson has bitterly denounced Sandburg's biography of Lincoln (without distinguishing the *Prairie Years* from the *War Years*) as "romantic and sentimental rubbish." In *Patriotic Gore* he says, "there are moments when one is tempted to feel that the cruellest thing that has happened to Lincoln since he was shot by Booth has been to fall into the hands of Carl Sandburg." As an example,

Wilson cites Sandburg's handling of the Ann Rutledge "love story":

"After the first evening in which Lincoln had sat next to her and found that bashful words tumbling from his tongue's end really spelled themselves out into sensible talk, her face, as he went away, kept coming back. So often all else would fade out of his mind and there would be only this riddle of a pink-fair face, a mouth and eyes in a frame of light corn-silk hair. He could ask himself what it meant and search his heart for an answer and no answer would come. A trembling took his body and dark waves ran through him sometimes when she spoke so simple a thing as, 'The corn is getting high, isn't it?' "

"The corn is getting high, indeed!" says Wilson. But he fails to give Sandburg credit for honestly admitting later that he had been "taken in" by this legend. When he condensed *The Prairie Years* for his one-volume *Abraham Lincoln* (1954) he changed the famous love affair to hypothesis and left out the "corny" description of Lincoln's emotions: "She was 21 and Lincoln 25 and in the few visits he had time for in this year when surveying and politics pressed him hard, he may have gone no further than to be a comforter. He may have touched and stroked her auburn hair once or more as he looked deep into her blue eyes and said no slightest word as to what hopes lay deep in his heart. . . . They were both young, with hope endless, and it could have been he had moments when the sky was to him a sheaf of blue dreams . . ."

As Lincoln grows up in *The Prairie Years* Sandburg has more historical documents to draw upon, and the Lincoln in the state legislature, in Congress, and in the Chicago convention which nominated him for the presidency is almost wholly believable. Of course for the Lincoln-Douglas debates there were the printed speeches themselves, and newspaper accounts of the campaign for the presidency. Though Sandburg consistently keeps his hero a man basically honest in spite of his driving ambition, he is shown making deals (or consenting to them after they are made by his supporters), compromising as any politician must, and following expediency rather than conscience when that is advantageous. Sandburg is especially effective in showing how circumstances often guided Lincoln's conduct. As the president-elect sets out for Washington to be inaugurated, he is still growing in stature, and in tragic foreboding, a hero in an epic which will end, as he himself half-suspects, in his own physical destruction.

The enormous financial success of *The Prairie Years* encouraged Sandburg to continue his biography through Lincoln's presidency. He now felt a heavy responsibility to tell the story completely and accurately, and he sought professional help from librarians, historians, and book dealers in assembling source material. For the first time in his life he had financial security, and he could concentrate on his one consuming ambition, a complete and reliable biography of Abraham Lincoln.

The great economic depression which began with the stock-market crash in 1929 did not seriously affect Sandburg's personal life or literary plans. Of course a man with the social conscience which all his works display could not be indifferent to the suffering and discouragement of the millions of unemployed or underemployed Americans. Though as a Socialist he had criticized the established economic system, he still believed in the soundness of American society and the ability of its people to make needed changes. To reassert his faith in the common people and to help them regain confidence in themselves, he wrote and

published *The People, Yes* (1936). An amalgam of folk wisdom and wit, verbal clichés, tall tales, preaching, slangy conversation, "cracker-barrel" philosophy, and Carl Sandburg cheerfulness, the book served its purpose, as Steinbeck's *Grapes of Wrath* did in another manner. It was wildly praised by people who liked Sandburg, and mostly ignored by those who did not. Mark Van Doren in a lecture on Sandburg at the Library of Congress in 1969 said, "*The People, Yes* is talk, nothing but talk." Van Doren did not mean this in a derogatory sense, and he was right. In this long talky poem we hear the voices of hundreds of Americans, and by listening we learn what kind of people they are, their ambitions, prejudices, superstitions, sense of humor, optimism, generosity, and sense of identity. But *The People, Yes* now seems repetitious and tedious— at least to this reader.

Three years later Sandburg published his truly monumental *Abraham Lincoln: The War Years* in four thick volumes, nearly 2500 pages. The critics were enthusiastic, the sales excellent, and it was awarded a Pulitzer Prize in 1940. Sandburg's six volumes of Lincoln biography were a culmination of thirty years of collecting, pondering, and writing about Lincoln. *The War Years* remains his most ambitious work, and it may be his most lasting. In spite of some lapses which scholars have pointed out, it is well documented—factual, solid, meticulously detailed. At times it seems too detailed, as if the author had emptied his filing drawers, but as a consequence Lincoln's life can be seen, felt, and heard from day to day, often in a chaos of conflicting advice, contradictory responsibilities, and demands for decisions which cannot wait for needed information. Under these pressures Lincoln is seen manfully struggling to make the right decisions, and Sandburg does not blink his misjudgments, or sometimes failure to act at all. He is not seen as an idealist, a man of conscience, but always as a shrewd pragmatist, who will save the Union any way he can, with or without slavery. Sandburg also quotes contemporary criticism of Lincoln's failures and imagined failures, so that he may be seen from within and from without. His notorious fondness for stories is copiously illustrated, as might be expected of the author of *The People, Yes*.

Lincoln believed slavery wrong, and he would abolish it if he could, and finally did— or thought he had—but the time must be right. Considering the circumstances so fully presented in *The War Years*, it seems almost miraculous that any man could have held the Union together and won the war in spite of the profusion of graft, incompetent generals and other officials, "Copperhead" subversion, and personal antagonisms within the government, even in the president's Cabinet. That Lincoln did hold on and win makes him seem like a superman, but Sandburg does not load the dice in his favor, as he had at times in *The Prairie Years*. This biography is not only an honest and revealing account of Lincoln's "war years," but also one of the most revealing books ever written on how the American government works—how it looks from the inside in time of great crisis, tragic failures, and creeping success.

Sandburg's enjoyment of his literary triumph was severely tempered by a new, stupendous national crisis which affected him deeply. His total commitment to America's entrance into World War II caused him to undertake the boldest literary experiment of his career, a "novel" covering the whole span of American experience, from the coming of the Pilgrims to the horrors of World War II and the possible consequences of dropping the atom bomb on Japanese cities. This long, complicated work he called *Remembrance Rock* (1948), not from Plymouth Rock, but a rock-shrine in the garden of a fictional Supreme Court justice who slightly resembles Justice Oliver Wendell Holmes. Under the rock the justice had deposited soil from all the places most crucial in American history, and at the end of the novel his grandchildren and their wives and wives-to-be bring the symbolical collection up to date:

"At Remembrance Rock at high noon they laid in metal-bottomed crevices the little prepared copper boxes—gravel from Sicily, sand from Utah Beach on the Normandy coast, rainbow-tinted sand from a coral atoll in the South Pacific, harsh black volcanic ash from Okinawa. They packed in soil at the base of the boulder, leaving no sign of the sacred receptacle underneath."

The whole structure of this novel, if it may be so classified, is as obviously symbolical (its chief fault) as the many kinds of sand under the rock. Some of the characters are historical and some are fictional, representing the earliest white settlers of America, the period of the American Revolution, the migrations into and across the Great Plains, the Civil War, and World War II.

As in all of his writings, Sandburg is facile with conversation in *Remembrance Rock*, but the reader is made too aware of what each speaker "stands for." The story has heroic people and epic action, yet the total effect is that of a patriotic pageant rather than a novel. One can applaud the author's lofty intentions and his great effort without enjoying his art. This literary experiment was a labor of love, and Sandburg was hurt by the failure of the critics to warm up to it. It is not likely to remain as permanently valuable as his one-volume *Abraham Lincoln* (1954), his "distillation" of *The Prairie Years* and *The War Years*, or his big *Complete Poems*.

When the *Complete Poems* appeared in

1950, it was widely reviewed, yet did not receive the high praise of Sandburg's Lincoln biographies. This may have been partly because the fashions in poetry had changed since the years of the depression when *The People, Yes* was so well received. Poetry was now cerebral, dense, and intricately allusive under the influence of Pound and Eliot. The objections to Sandburg's poems were not so much their sententiousness, for Pound and Eliot were as sententious in their own ways as any poet could be, but to his irreverent attitude toward the art of poetry. One of the reviewers of *Complete Poems* was William Carlos Williams, whose poems might appear to be as spontaneously improvised as Sandburg's, but Williams had taken to brooding on his art and concocting theories about how an American poet ought to write, and he thought Sandburg had not given enough thought to these matters. Of course the "New Critics" frowned upon all tendentious poetry, and regarded structure, imagery, tension, and irony as more important than message. They did not so much condemn Sandburg as ignore him, because, they thought, he structured his poems by intuition or whim, and gave these critics few subtleties or ambiguities to challenge their ingenuity. In brief, Sandburg did not need to be explicated.

Complete Poems contains in chronological order the six books of poems (not counting the three privately printed booklets) Sandburg had published before 1950. Its appearance should have given critics an excellent opportunity to evaluate Sandburg's whole career as a poet. But actually none of the reviewers for major publications undertook this task. In fact, their reviews gave the impression that Sandburg was still the "Chicago poet" of 1916, that he had not grown or changed significantly. Evidently it was easier to fall back on the old clichés and stereotypes than to read (or reread) these more than seven hundred poems—seventy-two in a "New Section," some published for the first time anywhere.

Sandburg *had* grown, *had* changed, and several of his finest poems were to be found in the "New Section." Probably the critics had not read the best of these new poems, though they had been published before, but in magazines regarded as nonliterary: "The Fireborn Are at Home in Fire" and "Mr. Longfellow and His Boy" in *Collier's Magazine*; "The Long Shadow of Lincoln: A Litany," in the *Saturday Evening Post*; and the elegy on President Roosevelt, "When Death Came April Twelve 1945," in *Woman's Home Companion*. Of course it is true that one would not expect poems of such high literary quality (or even poems at all) in these mass publications, but a work of art should not be judged by the place of its unveiling.

By 1950 Sandburg had, in the eyes of some critics, two counts against him: he was so famous that he could sell his poems at high prices, and his poems were read and enjoyed by a large public. Even Frost was beginning to suffer from his popularity, but he had several critics of considerable prestige to defend him. Also his life-style protected him to some extent from the curse of success. But Sandburg's folksy manners and his love affair with "the people" were a constant affront and irritant to academic minds, and most literary critics were, and are, either in or close to the academic world. This is not special pleading for Sandburg; it is one observer's explanation of the manner in which *Complete Poems* was reviewed. The fact that the book won the Pulitzer Prize in poetry for that year does not contradict this explanation, nor do the honorary degrees showered upon Sandburg by universities.

In a preface called modestly "Notes for a Preface" Sandburg quotes with approval theories of poetry from Yeats, Synge, Macaulay, and Oliver Wendell Holmes. For example, from Synge: "When men lose their poetic feeling for ordinary life, and cannot write poetry of ordinary things, their exalted poetry is likely to lose its strength of exaltation, in the way men cease to build beautiful churches when they have lost happiness in building shops. Many of the older poets, such as Villon and Herrick and Burns, used the whole of their personal life as their material, and the verse written in this way was read by strong men, and thieves, and deacons, not by little cliques only." It is hardly necessary to add that Sandburg tried to be just such a poet.

In defense of his abandoning rhyme and meter Sandburg quotes a famous rhymester, Dr. Oliver Wendell Holmes: "Rhythm alone is a tether, and not a very long one. But rhymes are iron fetters . . ." Tethers and fetters had always been intolerable to Sandburg, as he discovered as early as 1905. Also as a reader and contributor to *Poetry* in its early years, he was aware of the arguments for and against "free verse," a form (or, as its opponents said, lack of form) in which the phrase is the prosodic unit and the words themselves create their own rhythms. More important than where Sandburg learned free-verse techniques is the fact that he had an excellent ear for the musical sequence of sounds, the balancing and counterpointing of phrase against phrase. Sandburg wrote for both the ear and the eye. His famous "Chicago" poem has an almost architectural structure, beginning with the short, pithy salutation epithets:

> Hog Butcher for the World,
> Tool Maker, Stacker of Wheat . . .

Then come the twelve factual statements modified by the poet's own affirmation blocked out in parallel form:

> They tell me you are wicked and I believe

them, for I have seen your painted women under the gas lamps luring the farm boys. . . .

The seventh statement emphasizes the series of participles by spacing them as single lines, or verses:

> Fierce as a dog with tongue lapping for
>   action, cunning as a savage pitted against
>   the wilderness,
>   Bareheaded,
>   Shoveling,
>   Wrecking,
>   Planning,
>   Building, breaking, rebuilding . . .

Both the line breaks and the accents in the phrases play variations on the tempo, slowing or speeding up the sounds to add emphasis. The difference between these long lines and ordinary prose is in the skillful paralleling and accumulating of grammatical units (phrases and clauses). The resulting rhythm is grammatical, or rhetorical, rather than metrical.

Though scarcely any two of Sandburg's poems look alike on the page, or sound alike when read aloud, his sense of form seldom faltered. Notice the pattern of the opening lines of "Pencils" (*Smoke and Steel*):

> Pencils
> telling where the wind comes from
>   open a story.
>
> Pencils
> telling where the wind goes
>   end a story.
>
>   These eager pencils
>   come to a stop
>   . . . only . . . when the stars high over
>   come to a stop.

"Canadians and Pottawatomies" (*Good Morning, America*) is almost as syllabic (i.e., equal number of syllables in each line) as a poem by Marianne Moore:

> I have seen a loneliness sit
> in the dark and nothing lit up.
> I have seen a loneliness sit
> in the dark lit up like a Christ-
> mas tree, a Hallowe'en pumpkin.

One of the many ways in which Sandburg's sense of rhythm became more subtle and sensitive was in his handling of syllabic weight, timbre, and vowel tone. This development culminated in the marvelous tone poem "When Death Came April Twelve 1945," which opens:

> Can a bell ring in the heart
> telling the time, telling a moment,
> telling off a stillness come,
> in the afternoon a stillness come
> and now never come morning?

The bell intones throughout the elegy, not mechanically as in Poe's "The Bells," but resonating the deep feelings of the nation grieving for its lost commander, and the sons lost in the South Pacific or on European soil, all now sleeping after toil and battle. The tones of the poem, reinforcing the images of stillness and silence, have the empathy of cleansing and calming the emotions of the readers (hearers). In every technical detail the elegy is almost perfectly ordered, timed, and developed from the opening "Can a bell ring in the heart" to

> the somber consoles rolling sorrow,
> the choirs in ancient laments—chanting:
> "Dreamer, sleep deep,
> Toiler, sleep long,
> Fighter, be rested now,
> Commander, sweet good night."

Though Sandburg's patriotism had never been aroused before as it was during World War II, when he was willing to use his talents in any way possible to aid the preservation of a "free world," he was no blind patriot or jingoist. For the poem he read at William and Mary College in 1944, "The Long Shadow of Lincoln: A Litany," he used for an epigraph a quotation from Lincoln's 1862 message to Congress: "We can succeed only by concert. . . . The dogmas of the quiet past are inadequate to the stormy present. The occasion is piled high with difficulty, and we must rise with the occasion. As our case is new so we must think anew and act anew. We must disenthrall ourselves. . . ."

Sandburg knew the importance of *disenthralling ourselves* in the aftermath of World War II. His "Litany" begins:

> Be sad, be cool, be kind,
> remembering those now dreamdust
> hallowed in the ruts and gullics,
> solemn bones under the smooth blue sea,
> faces warblown in a falling rain.

Remember and weep, he says, but "Make your wit a guard and cover." Looking toward peace and the difficulties of maintaining it, " 'We must disenthrall ourselves.' "

> There is dust alive
> with dreams of The Republic,
> with dreams of the Family of Man
> flung wide on a shrinking globe
>
> . . . .
>
> The earth laughs, the sun laughs
> over every wise harvest of man,
> over man looking toward peace
> by the light of the hard old teaching:
> "We must disenthrall ourselves."

Few men were less warped by the war, better kept their wit, or remained as sane as Carl Sandburg. In a group of poems for the "Present Hour" there is "Jan, the Son of Thomas," who asks:

Was I not always a laughing man?
Did I ever fail of ready jests?
Have I added a final supreme jest?
They may write where my ashes quiver:
    "He loved mankind for its very faults.
    He knew how to forget all wars past.
      He so acted
      as to forget the next war."

Sandburg did not believe with a certain "handsome mournful galoot" (T. S. Eliot?) that "The human race is its own Enemy Number One."

For him the Family of Man stinks now
    and if you look back
    for him it always has stunk.

In "Many Handles" Sandburg warns against "abstractions" and rigid classifications:

In the Dark Ages many there and then
had fun and took love and made visions
and listened when Voices came.
Then as now were the Unafraid.
Then as now, "What if I am dropped into levels
    of ambiguous dust and covered
    over and forgotten? Have I in my
    time taken worse?"

. . . .

Should it be the Dark Ages recur, will there be again the Immeasurable Men, the Incalculable Women?

Though the poem ends with a question, the implication is plain that there will be great men and women for a new Dark Age, if it comes. In spite of a terrible premonition of a future atomic war, Sandburg counsels in "The Unknown War,"

Be calm, collected, easy.
In the face of the next war to come, be calm.
In the faint light and smoke of the flash and the mushroom of the first bomb blast of the Third World War, keep your wits collected.

. . . .

We shall do the necessary.
We shall meet the inevitable.

Thirteen years after the appearance of *Complete Poems*, Sandburg published still another volume of poetry called *Honey and Salt*. The title poem is skeptical, witty, and philosophical on the permanence of love.

Is there any way of measuring love?
Yes but not till long afterward
when the beat of your heart has gone
many miles, far into the big numbers.
Is the key to love in passion, knowledge,
    affection?
All three—along with moonlight, roses,
    groceries,
givings and forgivings, gettings and forgettings,
    keepsakes and room rent,
    pearls of memory along with ham and
    eggs.

If love is "locked away and kept," it "gathers dust and mildew." How long does it last? "As long as glass bubbles handled with care / or two hot-house orchids in a blizzard / or one solid immovable steel anvil . . ." But

There are sanctuaries
    holding honey and salt.
There are those who
    spill and spend.

Many of the poems in this volume are about love, which was never sweeter or more savory than now for this eighty-five-year-old lover. Several poems are affectionate devotions to his one and only wife, and "Out of the Rainbow End" is a fond compliment to his brother-in-law Edward Steichen, whose hobby was growing delphiniums. But Sandburg knows also that "Love Is a Deep and a Dark and a Lonely":

> and you take it deep take it dark
> and take it with a lonely winding
> and when the winding gets too lonely
> then may come the windflowers
>
> . . . .
>
> like leaves of windflowers bending low
> and bending to be never broken.

The longest and most ambitious poem in *Honey and Salt* is "Timesweep." The theme might be said to be the same as "Wilderness" (1918), in which the poet lyrically boasted of his kinship with foxes, wolves, and other wild animals. But "Timesweep" is both more genuinely lyrical and more philosophical, lyrical in the poet's empathy with the natural forces and creatures with which he feels a sympathetic kinship, and philosophical in his knowledge of his place in the cosmic scheme. Since Sandburg has so often been compared with Whitman by many critics, it is interesting to place this poem beside passages treating the same theme in "Song of Myself." In section 31 Whitman declares:

> I find I incorporate gneiss, coal, long-threaded
>   moss, fruits, grains, esculent roots,
> And am stucco'd with quadrupeds and birds
>   all over,
> And have distanced what is behind me for
>   good reasons,
> But call any thing back again when I desire it.

Then in section 44 Whitman returns to his evolutionary transmigration:

> I am an acme of things accomplish'd, and I an
>   encloser of things to be.
> My feet strike an apex of the apices of the
>   stairs,

> On every step bunches of ages, and larger
>   bunches between the steps,
> All below duly travel'd, and still I mount and
>   mount.
>
> . . . .
>
> Before I was born out of my mother genera-
>   tions guided me,
> My embryo has never been torpid, nothing
>   could overlay it.
>
> For it the nebula cohered to an orb,
> The long slow strata piled to rest it on,
> Vast vegetables gave it sustenance,
> Monstrous sauroids transported it in their
>   mouths and deposited it with care.

Sandburg's poem is more personal, less "prophetic" in tone, more aware of human limitations, but the lyrical utterance of a sensitive man who enjoys the sights and sounds of his physical existence:

> The pink nipples of the earth in springtime,
> The long black eyelashes of summer's look,
> The harvest laughter of tawny autumn,
> The winter silence of land in snow covers,
> Each speaks its own oaths of the cool and the
>   flame of naked possessions clothed and
>   come naked again:
>   The sea knows it all.
>   They crept out of the sea.

The poet wonders where he came from, and whether there is any going back:

> Is it told in my dreams and hankerings, looking
>   back at what I was, seeing what I am?
>   Like so a man talking to himself
>   of the bitter, the sweet, the bittersweet:
>   he had heard likenings of himself:
> Cock of the walk, brave as a lion, fierce as a
>   tiger,
> Stubborn as a mule, mean as a louse, crazy as
>   a bedbug,

Soft as a kitten, slimy as an octopus, one poor
fish.

Yes, man, "proud man, with a peacock
strut" is "a beast out of the jungle," an animal
related to all the other animals. Frank Norris
and other American naturalists of the late
nineteenth century had used this thought to
demolish man's pretensions to a special creation in the image of God and his delusions of
free will. Sandburg has no such intentions:

What is this load I carry out of yesterday?
What are these bygones of dreams, moans,
    shadows?
What jargons, what gibberish, must I yet
    unlearn?

He knows that his origins are in a "dim
plasm in the sea . . . a drop of jelly," and the
countless swimmers and crawlers who preceded the creature called man:

I have had a thousand fish faces, sea faces,
sliding off into land faces, monkey faces—
    I began in a dim green mist
                        of floating faces.

He acknowledges his kindred and feels a degree of identity with them, and wonders what
right he has to feel wiser than they. To the
elephant he says the "Ignorance we share and
share alike is immeasurable."

I have been woven among meshes of long ropes
and fine filaments: older than the rocks and
fresh as the dawn of this morning today are
the everliving roots who begot me,
who poured me as one more seeker
one more swimmer in the gold and gray
    procession
of phantoms laughing, fighting, singing, moan-
ing toward the great cool calm of the fixed
return to the filaments of dust.

But he also knows that he is "more than a
traveler out of Nowhere":

Sea and land, sky and air, begot me Somewhere.
Where I go from here and now, or if I go at all
    again, the
Maker of sea and land, of sky and air, can
    tell.

Knowledge that some almost infinite (or
perhaps infinite) chain of life begot him out of
Nowhere to Somewhere gives Sandburg sufficient assurance of a *purpose* at work, however
humanly unknowable. He will not worry about
theology, or teleology. Yet "Timesweep"
throws more light on Sandburg's philosophy
than any other literary work of his. At the end
of this last poem we find a summation of his
humanism, rooted in his early socialism, and
consolidated by a lifetime of effort to pro-
pagate the idea that the Family of Man is One
Man:

There is only one man in the world
and his name is All men.

. . . .

There is only one Maker in the world
and His children cover the earth
and they are named All God's Children.

The poet who wrote this poem had come a
long way on the road of art since writing
"Chicago." No one knows the range of Sandburg who has not read the "new" poems in his
collected *Complete Poems* and observed the
further enrichment of his canon in *Honey and
Salt*. In his "Notes for a Preface" to *Complete
Poems* he remarked: "I have written by different methods and in a wide miscellany of moods
and have seldom been afraid to travel in lands
and seas where I met fresh scenes and new
songs. All my life I have been trying to learn
to read, to see and hear, and to write. At sixty-

five I began my first novel, and the five years lacking a month I took to finish it, I was still traveling, still a seeker. I should like to think that as I go on writing there will be sentences truly alive, with verbs quivering, with nouns giving color and echoes. It could be, in the grace of God, I shall live to be eighty-nine, as did Hokusai, and speaking my farewell to earthly scenes, I might paraphrase: 'If God had let me live five years longer I should have been a writer.' "

Carl Sandburg did live to be eighty-nine, and he did not need five additional years to become a writer; he had been a writer, a prolific one, and at times a masterful one, for many years. When he became a poet is a subject on which critics have disagreed, and will doubtless continue to do so, but we might paraphrase his quotation from the Japanese painter and say that God created Sandburg a writer, but by his own efforts he became a poet.

Selected Bibliography

WORKS OF CARL SANDBURG

The titles listed below include the published writings of Carl Sandburg with the exception of limited editions, prefaces and introductions to works by other authors, addresses, and recorded readings and talks.

ANTHOLOGIES

Walt Whitman's *Leaves of Grass,* with an introduction by Carl Sandburg. New York: Boni and Liveright, 1921.

The American Songbag. New York: Broadcast Music, 1927.

New American Songbag. New York: Broadcast Music [1950].

BIOGRAPHY AND AUTOBIOGRAPHY

Abraham Lincoln: The Prairie Years. 2 vols. New York: Harcourt, Brace, 1926.

Abe Lincoln Grows Up, with illustrations by James Daugherty. New York: Harcourt, Brace [1928]. (From *Abraham Lincoln: The Prairie Years.*)

Steichen the Photographer. New York: Harcourt, Brace, 1929.

Mary Lincoln: Wife and Widow (with Paul M. Angle). New York: Harcourt, Brace, 1932.

Abraham Lincoln: The War Years. 4 vols. New York: Harcourt, Brace, 1939.

Storm over the Land. New York: Harcourt, Brace, 1942. (From *Abraham Lincoln: The War Years.*)

Always the Young Strangers. New York: Harcourt, Brace, 1953.

Abraham Lincoln: The Prairie Years and the War Years. New York: Harcourt, Brace, 1954. ("A distillation.")

FOR YOUNG READERS

Rootabaga Stories. New York: Harcourt, Brace, 1922.

Rootabaga Pigeons. New York: Harcourt, Brace, 1923.

Abe Lincoln Grows Up. New York: Harcourt, Brace, 1928.

Early Moon. New York: Harcourt, Brace, 1930.

Prairie-Town Boy. New York: Harcourt, Brace, 1955. (From *Always the Young Strangers.*)

Wind Song. New York: Harcourt, Brace, 1960.

The Wedding Procession of the Rag Doll and the Broom Handle and Who Was in It. New York: Harcourt, Brace, 1967.

NOVEL AND STORIES

Potato Face. New York: Harcourt, Brace, 1930. ("Rootabaga stories for adults.")

Remembrance Rock. New York: Harcourt, Brace, 1948.

POETRY

In Reckless Ecstasy. Galesburg: Asgard Press, 1904. (Private press.)

The Plaint of a Rose. Galesburg: Asgard Press [1905?].

Incidentals. Galesburg: Asgard Press [1905].

Chicago Poems. New York: Henry Holt, 1916.

Cornhuskers. New York: Henry Holt, 1918.

Smoke and Steel. New York: Harcourt, Brace, 1920.

Slabs of the Sunburnt West. New York: Harcourt, Brace, 1922.

Good Morning, America. New York: Harcourt, Brace, 1928.

The People, Yes. New York: Harcourt, Brace, 1936.

Complete Poems. New York: Harcourt, Brace, 1950.

Honey and Salt. New York: Harcourt, Brace, 1963.

SELECTED EDITIONS OF POETRY

Selected Poems of Carl Sandburg, edited by Rebecca West. New York: Harcourt, Brace, 1926.

Poems of the Midwest. Cleveland and New York: World Publishing Company, 1946. (*Chicago Poems* and *Cornhuskers.*)

The Sandburg Range. New York: Harcourt, Brace, 1957. (Selection of poetry and prose.)

Harvest Poems: 1910–1960. New York: Harcourt, Brace, 1960.

PROSE MISCELLANY

The Chicago Race Riots (July 1919), with an introduction by Walter Lippmann. New York: Harcourt, Brace and Howe, 1919. (Reprinted from the *Chicago Daily News.*)

Home Front Memo. New York: Harcourt, Brace, 1943.

The Photographs of Abraham Lincoln (with Frederick H. Meserve). New York: Harcourt, Brace, 1944.

Lincoln Collector: The Story of Oliver R. Barrett's Great Private Collection. New York: Harcourt, Brace, 1949.

Address before a Joint Session of Congress, February 12, 1959. New York: Harcourt, Brace [1959]. (Published also in Washington, D.C., Worcester, Mass., and Cedar Rapids, Iowa.)

LETTERS

The Letters of Carl Sandburg, edited by Herbert Mitgang. New York: Harcourt, Brace and World, 1968. (Contains a useful chronological table.)

BIBLIOGRAPHIES

Harry Golden's *Carl Sandburg* (see Biographies below) has a checklist of Sandburg's works and *Honey and Salt* (see Poetry above) has a classified checklist.

The Sandburg Range: An Exhibit of Materials from Carl Sandburg's Library Placed on Display in the University of Illinois Library on January 6, 1958, with an introduction by John T. Flanagan; bibliographical descriptions and notes by Leslie W. Dunlap. University of Illinois Library, Adah Patton Memorial Fund, Publication Number Six. [Urbana, 1958.]

Van Doren, Mark. *Carl Sandburg,* with a bibliography of Sandburg materials in the collections of the Library of Congress. Washington, D.C.: Library of Congress, 1969. (This is the most extensive bibliography of Sandburg, including translations, addresses, introductions and prefaces, articles, interviews and conversations, manuscripts, musical settings, phonograph records, motion pictures.)

BIOGRAPHIES

Callahan, North. *Carl Sandburg: Lincoln of Our Time.* New York: New York University Press, 1970.

Golden, Harry. *Carl Sandburg.* Cleveland and New York: World Publishing Company, 1961.

CRITICAL STUDIES

Allen, Gay Wilson. "Carl Sandburg: Fire and Smoke," *South Atlantic Quarterly,* 59:315–31 (Summer 1960).

Basler, Roy P. "Your Friend the Poet—Carl Sandburg," *Midway,* 10:3–15 (Autumn 1969).

Cargill, Oscar. "Carl Sandburg: Crusader and Mystic," *College English,* 11:365–72 (April 1950).

Van Doren, Mark. *Carl Sandburg.* Washington, D.C.: Library of Congress, 1969.

Williams, William Carlos. Review of Carl Sandburg's *Complete Poems,* in *Poetry,* 7–8:345ff (September 1951).

—GAY WILSON ALLEN

George Santayana

1863-1952

DESPITE his firm and well-deserved reputation as a man of letters, George Santayana will be remembered, as he himself would have wished, primarily as a philosopher. This is not because his more strictly theoretical studies overshadow his other writings. It is rather that his memorable achievements as a poet and as a novelist, as a literary critic and as an observer of modern life, are throughout philosophical in spirit. Indeed everything that he touched seemed to turn to philosophy; and it is for his comprehension, his patient and persistent thoughtfulness, usually unmoved by the pressure of contemporary opinion, that we most admire his work.

To be sure, such thoughtfulness can constitute a limitation as well as a virtue. Ideas may solidify into preconceptions and impose a burden on the imagination. Thus Santayana's poetry and his fiction, however charming or enlightening, sometimes lack that adventurous immediacy of encounter that distinguishes the cry of a living occasion from a more deliberate meditation. His poems and the incidents and characters of his novel may at times appear as aptly chosen and elegantly executed supplements to philosophical reflection, in which understanding takes dominion over imagination. On the other hand, in his theoretical works, imagination, serving as a handmaiden to un-

derstanding, often clarifies and enlivens the progress of Santayana's argument. His choice of words is happy and invigorating even when his style is most literal. His more figurative language is often brilliant. Lucid metaphor lends his utterance a power of communication that the clichés of professional philosophy often lack, while marginal example and analogy indicate the direction of this thought and give it a concrete reference so that, as the argument unfolds, the reader feels its continued pertinence to the world of his experience.

One must admit that Santayana's work as a philosopher is not distinguished by any radical originality of doctrine. In the academic histories of American philosophy he will receive briefer notice and occupy a more modest position than his contemporaries William James, C. S. Peirce, and John Dewey. But Santayana's work taken as a whole, if we consider the scope of his thought and the variety of literary form in which it is expressed, seems as rich an offering as that made by any thinker of our century. In his work, religion, arts and letters, science, and social policy receive generous consideration and the common sense of the layman is treated with respect. All these are seen as contributing to the conscious self-interpretation of the individual in whose life civilization is realized. Although he hesitated to use the word—since its use might seem to ignore, at once, the values of religion and our sense of dependence upon nature—we may do well to think of him as a humanist, perhaps the greatest humanist of his period. Santayana's work as a whole may be characterized as a voluminous essay on man and on man's interpretation of his own situation. This essay, a long-sustained meditation, offers us, on the one hand, a perspective of human nature and, on the other, a striking portrait of Santayana himself. In more ways than one, Santayana reminds us of Montaigne. The circumstances of his life bred an independence of thought even surpassing that of the French philosopher. Indeed, Santayana may be said to have had freedom—at least an intellectual freedom—thrust upon him.

Jorge Agustín Nicolás Ruiz de Santayana y Borrás was born in 1863 in Madrid of Spanish parents. He remained a Spanish citizen throughout his life. But after his early childhood he saw little of Spain. He was brought to America at the age of nine, to be educated in Boston with the children of his mother's first marriage. Señora Santayana had been married to George Sturgis, a member of a prominent Boston family of international merchants. Before his death, she had promised Sturgis to educate their children in Boston, and she kept her word, although in the end it involved a separation from Colonel Santayana, who found New England and its climate less than congenial. Thus George Santayana's boyhood was spent as a poor relation in the heart of the well-to-do Boston that he was to describe with brilliant irony in the most telling passages of *The Last Puritan*. He studied at the Boston Latin School, acquiring English as a second language which came to replace his mother tongue. Despite the anticlericalism of his parents, Santayana was as a boy attracted by Roman Catholicism.

In this he was influenced by his half sister Susana. But almost from the first he maintained an independence of judgment that led him at an early age to the study of philosophy; and his early reading included Lucretius and Spinoza.

At the age of nineteen, Santayana entered Harvard College where he took advantage of the elective system then coming into force to devote himself primarily to philosophy. He wrote poetry from time to time and contributed a number of humorous drawings to the *Lampoon*. Both as an undergraduate and as a graduate, he studied philosophy and psychology under William James and, like T. S. Eliot after him, he completed his studies by writing a doctoral dissertation under Josiah Royce. Royce persuaded him to write on the philosophy of Hermann Lotze, a German professor who enjoyed a considerable reputation at the time. Santayana would have preferred to work on Schopenhauer as a more congenial and interesting subject.

After completing his graduate studies, which included a period in Berlin, where he heard Friedrich Paulsen's lectures, Santayana taught at Harvard. He became a very successful teacher, especially of undergraduates, an ornament even to the Harvard department of philosophy, then at the height of its reputation. Among his students may be counted Gertrude Stein, T. S. Eliot, Walter Lippmann, and Bronson Cutting, while Wallace Stevens, as an undergraduate, submitted poetry to him. Santayana lectured with an apparently extemporaneous lucidity—which, however, Eliot occasionally found soporific—on Plato and other figures in the history of philosophy and on the philosophy of art, which led to the publication in 1896 of *The Sense of Beauty*, the first important systematic treatment of the subject in America and one that remains a classic in its field. During these years he visited Oxford, where he continued his study of Greek thought, and lectured for a brief period in Paris. From his school days on, Santayana was a prolific and persistent writer and by the early years of this century he had won recognition as a poet, a critic, a philosopher, and a consummate master of English prose.

Never entirely content as a college teacher, required as he said to lecture "under forced draught," and often ill at ease in the cultural climate of New England, Santayana resigned from the Harvard faculty as soon as his circumstances permitted, and from 1912 until his death in 1952, he lived quietly in Europe, at first briefly in Spain, during World War I in England, later in France, and finally in Rome, for some years at a hotel on the Piazza Barberini. Santayana's later life was one of "studious ease," devoted to philosophical and literary pursuits. He lived simply in retirement but not in isolation, a bachelor who "like the Pope" did not return visits. During World War II and thereafter until his death, Santayana was cared for—with affectionate concern as his health failed—at the nursing home of the "Blue Sisters" in Rome.

For Santayana philosophy, disciplined by a wholesome respect for the work of the natural scientist, participates with religion and the arts in what he described as the "life of reason." Reason, in this interpretation, is not limited to discursive argument but pursues by any means available an envisagement or adumbration of the values open to human realization. These values are conceived as satisfying the instinctive motivations of human nature, and reason is interpreted as "instinct enlightened by reflection." Thus, throughout his work, Santayana thought of himself as a student of morals concerned with the attitudes and ideals that contribute to the quality of our life.

As a sympathetic critic of religion, Santayana insisted that the vitality of the religious life may spring from the recognition and enjoyment of ideals to which we find ourselves committed quite aside from any belief in their supernatural origin or miraculous revelation. These ideals are entertained in imaginative and symbolic form before they appear as discursive concepts. They may seem to be products of human imagination and Santayana sometimes, especially in his earlier writings, calls them fictions. Yet they are not arbitrary imperatives. Their importance, one might say their authority, springs from their relevance to our experience as they take their place in the life of reason. Thus religion requires no assertion of historical fact and no appeal to the supernatural. For Santayana, reason may clarify but cannot overreach experience. Thus the idea of the supernatural is dismissed along with the central doctrines of traditional religion, the immortality of the soul and the existence of God. Through all his work, Santayana offers a recurrent reminder that our life cannot be divorced from its natural environment within which it must seek its fulfillment. The ways of nature, as open to our observation, remind us to expect no miracles in our favor and to recognize the extent of our ignorance. The very sight of the sea, the mountains, and the stars should teach us humility and warn us, as it did the first philosophers of Greece, not to consider human life or any idealism, however humane, as the "center and pivot of the universe." The heavens themselves declare the "indifferent, non-censorious infinity of nature." There follows a firm refusal to think of our world as motivated by supernatural forces or called into being as the realization of a divine purpose. We have no evidence to support the belief that mind can exist apart from a material milieu from which it draws its vitality; and the unspeakable variety of possible life, whose emerging species are often in conflict, suggests no providential responsibility. Nature, it is true, makes possible our human existence and the occasional emergence of human idealism, but it is not itself subject to the power or the authority of these ideals. As Santayana saw it, the refusal to accept the self-sufficiency of nature impeded modern thought, often making human self-knowledge impossible and clouding the vision even of the great philosophers.

Some students of the history of ideas may choose to classify Santayana's philosophy as post-Nietzschean in character. Like Zarathustra, Santayana faced his world well aware that "God is dead" and that man must take responsibility for the ideals to which he finds himself committed unsupported by a belief in divine revelation. Yet, unlike Nietzsche, Santayana did not enjoy the role of iconoclast, nor on the other hand did he find freedom from supernatural authority an oppressive burden. The resultant responsibility did not breed a malignant anxiety or a sense of bewilderment. The practical wisdom of the Greeks and the insight into human nature offered by Christian thinkers remain sources of enlightenment, if considered critically. One may profit by the great traditions without attaching an arbitrary authority to them. It is true that in his earlier years Santayana sometimes felt a sense of loss and thought of himself as an exile from a traditional faith. This attitude is often reflected in his poetry. As he grew older, however, he took increasing satisfaction in his ability to see things clearly and to speak his mind with a quiet assurance. His intent lay in freeing religion from the embarrassment of untenable doctrine and including it as an effective element within the life of reason. He was not eager to break with religion, but drastically to purify it. In the America of the early twentieth century, such an attitude aroused far greater resistance than it would have a generation later and called for a greater firmness of character. Thus Santayana mentions the relief that he felt while lecturing at the Sorbonne, where he no longer had to remind himself that his ideas might be considered unwholesome.

As he surveyed the American scene, Santayana found the polite culture of the educated classes less than congenial. He noted, now with ironic detachment, now with something like compassion, the agonized conscience or sense of sinfulness that still lingered in Calvinist New England and elsewhere. This he contrasted with the self-confident and superficial mysticism of the Transcendentalists who had reacted against their Puritan background; also with the romantic doctrine that the highest achievement of the artist stands above moral considerations. He found all these attitudes sadly wanting, while at the same time he viewed with equal suspicion the secular faith in the importance of material progress that sometimes took the place of these more genteel ways of thought.

Nor was Santayana ready to accept democratic ideas of government as standing beyond any serious criticism, successful democracy being possible, on his view, only under unusual conditions. Nonetheless, as a student of social relations and social values, he recognized clearly that the whole exists for the parts. It is only in the lives of individuals, in their health and happiness, that social well-being can be achieved. Such an achievement is by no means assured. Santayana never argued that history is moving automatically toward a social or political millennium. Thus he held aloof from the several forms of dogmatic optimism that had tempted nineteenth-century philosophers. The historical extrapolations of both liberals and Marxians seemed to him naive, if not dishonest.

Committed, as he was, to the "life of reason," Santayana found himself, in the first decades of the century, ill at ease as he considered the intellectual temper of the age both in Europe and America. In the early years, there were moments when he spoke out in a harsh spirit of denunciation which in later life he would have considered a rather futile gesture. But he was never reconciled to what seemed to him the shallowness, the confused and aggressive sentimentality, and the self-deceit of the time. Competitive nationalism and the dream of unlimited material progress, even if dignified by the myths of creative evolution and human perfectibility, offered no vision of enduring value. The only institutions, religious or academic, capable of resisting the attraction of these brash ideals or idols of the tribe were themselves often too demoralized and disoriented to be effective. As a result the life of reason was impoverished and civilization seemed to be stumbling in a state of aggressive confusion toward a new barbarism or cultural bankruptcy.

To be sure, this attitude of Santayana's was by no means unique. It reminds us, for instance, of the more scornful moments of E. A. Robinson as expressed in his poem "Cassandra":

> Your Dollar is your only Word,
> The wrath of it your only fear.
>
> . . . .
>
> You have the ages for your guide,
> But not the wisdom to be led.
>
> . . . .
>
> Are you to pay for what you have
> With all you are?

In these famous lines, Robinson spoke with greater power but with no greater bitterness than the young Santayana. Neither writer had to wait for the catastrophe of World War I to free him from the presiding illusions of his generation. In later life, Santayana was able to survey the current scene more patiently, accepting human blindness and perversity without indignation. In his early writing he met with scorn the hypocrisy "That talks of freedom and is slave to riches," a hypocrisy that breeds only conflict and confusion.

> What would you gain, ye seekers, with your
>   striving,
> Or what vast Babel raise you on your
>   shoulders?
> You multiply distresses, and your children
>   Surely will curse you.

These forebodings may have been premature but, a full lifetime after their expression, they carry a warning not to be lightly brushed aside.

Santayana's naturalism and his repudiation of the moral outlook of his contemporaries constitute the more negative aspect of his philosophy. This stands as a background for his more positive intention as a moralist to put first things first in the consideration of human affairs. This enterprise was essentially a critique of Western civilization and was directed toward a reconciliation of Greek and Christian ethics. He willingly endorsed the ideal of self-realization and the harmonious development of the capacities and talents of the individual, although he saw clearly that its pursuit should not tolerate a ruthless self-assertion but should rather be guided by disciplined self-knowledge and tempered by human sympathies and a sense of social responsibility.

On the other hand, he spoke with persuasive eloquence of moments when the sense of selfhood is overcome as the life of the spirit culminates in disinterested intelligence and disinterested admiration, virtues which, he believed, carry with them their own rewards. Santayana describes this maturity or freedom of the spirit as an activity of contemplation. Yet it may achieve not only an intellectual satisfaction but also the enjoyment of things beautiful and the admiration of the many forms of human excellence. The spirit is set free by the happy recognition of things worthwhile in themselves. Such freedom may culminate in a religious affirmation of a way of life. Yet the spirit cannot dominate its world, and its vision is often distracted by hardships and temptations, while its cherished ideals are thwarted by circumstance. The spirit cannot escape disappointment, even disillusion. Still the recognition and enjoyment of ideal possibilities, even though but partially realized, can transform our existence and, as Santayana once put it, help to make a long life worth more than a short one. The spirit need not in the freedom of its transcendence ignore or repudiate its world. Thus Santayana recognized the virtue of Christian charity as a practical expression of spiritual maturity. "Charity will always judge a soul not by what it has succeeded in fashioning externally, not by the body or the words, or the works that are the wreckage of its voyage, but by the elements of light and love that the soul infused into that inevitable tragedy." It is only after we have come fully to recognize the insecurity of our existence and to admit that the human enterprise can achieve no more than a passing shadow, even a caricature, of perfection that we are ready to share fully in such insight.

Here Santayana's philosophy appears as profoundly Christian in moral orientation. Nonetheless there are many readers inclined to interpret the final achievement of the spirit as a subordination of human attitudes and evaluations to the supremacy of aesthetic enjoyment. According to such a reading, imagination may be said to offer us a purely aesthetic perfection that lures our attention away from the shabby incompleteness of our world and reconciles us, at least momentarily, to existence. Such a philosophy, recalling passages from Schopenhauer and Pater, may have briefly appealed to Santayana in his younger days, as some of the sonnets suggest. But in his mature thought

Santayana is more inclined to subordinate the aesthetic to the moral. He dismisses the notion of art for art's sake: "Beauty, being a good is a moral good; and the practice and enjoyment of art, like all practice and enjoyment, fall within the sphere of morals."

This philosophy not only appears in Santayana's more systematic and theoretical writings but is reflected in his poems, his occasional essays, and his novel, *The Last Puritan.* Santayana's attitude reflects the influence of Platonism, of Christian ethics, and of ancient and modern naturalism; and yet, perhaps because of his profound sincerity, it does not seem to be an eclectic compromise but a reconciliation of ideas that we cannot honestly overlook once they are freed from their supernatural entanglements. Santayana was well aware that these ideas belong to our civilization, and he never insisted upon the novelty of his thought. He took pleasure in declaring his debt to his great predecessors and he looked back upon the European tradition in a spirit of gratitude, almost of piety.

His relation to his contemporaries and immediate predecessors, however, was another matter. He was little inclined to commit himself to the narrowing influence of a school or a program, and he preferred to stand alone. It is not, to be sure, difficult to recognize certain affinities: with Matthew Arnold, for example, and with Ritschlian theology. But despite these echoes, Santayana first appeared upon the American scene as an independent, even an isolated, thinker. As a result he has been sometimes misunderstood and the reception of his work has been varied. Its tone has vacillated from an almost reverent admiration to an unqualified hostility. He has been warmly accepted as a champion of sanity, an archenemy of intellectual dishonesty; and he has been condemned now as an aesthete, now as a sentimentalist. To many he has appeared as the prototype of the philosopher for whom contemplation, humane and yet personally disinterested, is a natural and spontaneous attitude, and whose quiet voice clarifies, even epitomizes, our civilization. This estimate has found its most memorable expression in Wallace Stevens' beautiful poem, "To an Old Philosopher in Rome," written at the time of Santayana's death in that city. Stevens, who had since his student days at Harvard followed Santayana's work, saluted him as "The one invulnerable man among / Crude captains," yet added the moving lines "each of us / Beholds himself in you, and hears his voice / In yours, master and commiserable man." Stevens saw clearly that for Santayana the life of the spirit springs from an awareness of things human and mortal: "The life of the city never lets go, nor do you / Ever want it to." Stevens found in Santayana's philosophy a few congenial ideas that are reflected in his own concept of poetry as the matrix and vehicle of a "supreme fiction" that gives meaning to our lives. He praised Santayana as an intellectual and spiritual leader and spoke warmly of the charm of his poetry. This Stevens admired despite the great difference between his own restless and independent style and the more traditional tone of Santayana's verse.

As a philosopher, Santayana has enjoyed a wider influence among laymen than in strictly professional and academic circles. Unlike the work of James, Dewey, or Whitehead his writings have not encouraged the formation of a school of professional thought, although a few distinguished followers have interpreted and developed his argument with sympathy. Of these Irwin Edman is perhaps the best known, but one should add the names of B. A. G. Fuller, the brilliant historian of philosophy, and John Herman Randall whose widely read *Making of the Modern Mind* contains numerous references to Santayana as representing the

attitudes of our century. Santayana's obvious sincerity and his modesty have won the hearts of many. His witty refusal to pose as a polymath, a temptation all too common among professional writers on philosophy, has at once amused and impressed readers. His remark, "I am an ignorant man, almost a poet," has disarmed many critics, both literary and philosophical—as also his admission that his own arguments might well have been more cogently stated had he mastered the techniques of mathematical logic. Here Santayana accepted a criticism of his work offered by Bertrand Russell. Russell, however, was generous enough to point out that Santayana's contribution contains more than a little truth despite its literary and therefore, for Russell, primitive style of presentation. Santayana took this criticism in good part. After all, he was addressing a public of thoughtful laymen, not a profession of technically trained specialists; and he preferred to do so.

In America, Santayana's reputation as a critic has in part centered upon the fact that in 1911 he coined a phrase that has been used again and again by other writers. He spoke of the "genteel tradition" in American philosophy and letters, suggesting that polite literature had remained too long under the influence of a Puritan heritage, only to some extent softened by the influence of the Transcendentalists. American, or at least New England, culture can hardly be said to have had a genuine youth or springtime of its own. It acquired at birth the mature, even sophisticated, attitudes of an older tradition. This conservatism, at once timid and haughty, was symbolized by the colonial mansion and its suburban facsimile. It tended to ignore the issues emerging from the new regime of factory and skyscraper and thus to divorce "culture" from "life" to the detriment of both. Santayana's phrase, "the genteel tradition," became a cliché repeated with slight changes of meaning in many noteworthy contexts, among them Sinclair Lewis' speech in acceptance of the Nobel Prize. Such writers as Vernon Parrington and Malcolm Cowley found the phrase a useful one, and for some years it was a commonplace of literary conversation.

Despite widespread recognition, Santayana did not always win the sympathy of his readers. Many who admired his prose found his attitude one of condescending disapproval and, despite his censure of the genteel tradition, of withdrawal from the modern scene. This impression is the partial outcome of Santayana's more than academic readiness to interpret and evaluate the present in terms of the past and his cautious reserve before new ideas and modes of expression. Santayana was, to be sure, no mere antiquarian; and yet after turning the pages of his witty *Dialogues in Limbo*, where he converses with Democritus and Socrates, one might picture him as hesitating upon the threshold of our century and accepting its invitation with courteous, if slightly ironical, reservations, insisting upon bringing with him his own philosophy and his own sense of value.

Even Santayana's kindly teacher William James, who recognized his great talents, praised his work with reservations. Displeased by his rather callow distaste for Browning and Whitman, James spoke of the "moribund latinity" of Santayana's criticism and the fastidious detachment of his "white marble mind." For James, these remarks were little more than friendly banter but they are nevertheless characteristic of a considerable body of adverse opinion. Somewhat sharper is the acid reference by Paul Shorey, the Plato scholar, to Santayana as "that dainty unassimilated man." But perhaps the most trenchant repudiation of Santayana's criticism came from Van Wyck Brooks who found his attitude toward his American predecessors narrowly prejudiced. Brooks's judgment is not without foundation. Santayana's treatment of the Transcendentalists was often high-handed. Certainly Emerson had no intention of fostering a genteel tradition and was more hospitable toward new movements than the young Santayana, especially in the case of Whitman.

Some critics have condemned Santayana as a sentimental champion of the attitudes of Roman Catholicism, accepted without its underlying theology. Such comment is less perverse than that interpreting Santayana as an aesthete committed to the dogma of art for art's sake, but it is still wide of the mark. This misconception has been perpetuated by the witticism that for Santayana "there is no God and Mary is his mother." This remark, perhaps initiated in a playful moment by Bertrand Russell, has been repeated so often that it has acquired a spurious authority. Its last prominent appearance is in a poem by Robert Lowell. Yet it remains a travesty. Santayana's respect for the Christian tradition was by no means a sentimental affectation. It sprang from the fact that he shared with another atheist, the poet A. E. Housman, the firm conviction that Luke 17:33 expresses the most important truth that ever was uttered. "Whosoever shall seek to save his life shall lose it, and whosoever shall lose his life shall preserve it."

Santayana was Catholic in his sympathies only in the sense that he found Catholicism more congenial than its Protestant opponent. But he belonged to neither group intellectually or emotionally. It is true that he found in Roman worship a greater warmth of feeling than was apparent in Boston Unitarianism, and certainly he was dismayed by the aggressive aspects of a Protestantism that thinks "optimism akin to piety" and "poverty a sort of dishonorable punishment." But the Roman attitude toward religion, centering upon the unqualified acceptance of an institutional authority, was not acceptable to him. His was not the contrite or guilty consciousness that Hegel attributed to the Middle Ages. Surely no one can follow Santayana's reflections on Dante, whose poetry he recognized as the magnificent culmination of medieval Christianity, without noticing important reservations. He could not, for instance, sympathize with Dante's moments of uneasy fearfulness that seem at times to mar, if not to distort, the virtue of humility; and he did not hesitate to contrast the courage of Goethe's Faust with what he took to be Dante's timidity.

It is true that Santayana's air of detachment and cosmopolitan independence has alienated some readers; and one can understand that the famous words in which he made a virtue of this detachment may seem to many little more than an eloquent exaggeration that, strangely enough, echoes Martin Luther. "In the past or in the future, my language and my borrowed knowledge would have been different, but under whatever sky I had been born, since it is the same sky, I should have had the same philosophy." So bold an assumption should hardly be expressed with such an air of confidence. Nor is this self-interpretation quite consistent with Santayana's profound respect for the moral values inherited from the Greek and Christian traditions, under whose influence he lived and thought. However this may be, one might fairly call him a man without a country. After his childhood he was never at home in his native land to which he paid only occasional visits and whose language he found, as a man of letters, not fully at his command; and both in England and in America his attitude was that of a visitor well acquainted with the life and language of the country but still essentially that of a spectator. His habitual attitude was, as he would say, "under whatever sky"—that of the wandering scholar. This suited him well and was profoundly characteristic of his philosophy.

Yet Santayana's contribution as a philosopher and a man of letters has a proper place in the history of American culture. After all, although during the last forty years of his life he lived solely in Europe, he was throughout his career influential on the American scene rather more than elsewhere; and his thinking, despite its independence, may, as he himself admitted, often be interpreted as a response to his encounter with American life and thought, certainly more so than to that of any other country. *The Last Puritan* is as much a comment upon American life, viewed from within, as any work of Henry James or William Dean Howells. Again, some of Santayana's most cogent writing occurs in essays in which he deliberately undertook to influence American opinion. Nonetheless, despite his genuine interest in things American, Santayana felt little attachment and no real loyalty to the United States. This is clearly apparent to the reader. If we are to profit fully from his criticism of American life, we must accept his occasional outbursts of irritation. In the long run, his prejudices were superficial and his more deliberate judgments intended to be fair. In this connection, one should not overlook that exuberant piece of satirical doggerel entitled "Young Sammy's First Wild Oats," a sprightly comment upon the American imperialism of the Spanish War. One could wish that all criticism of American policy were as generous, as thoughtful, and as witty.

There remains an important ground of difference between Santayana's philosophy of life and American thought whether popular or academic. Santayana did not find in democracy any obvious superiority over other modes of government. He considered Thomas Jefferson a fanatic and he viewed the ideal of popular sovereignty with frank suspicion. Certainly it was not to be saluted as time's noblest offspring whose vices are to be discounted as superficial blemishes. Nor are we to suppose that a universal franchise and a bill of rights can guarantee a sense of fellowship and community or a concern for one's neighbor's happiness. They may, indeed, awaken in some a ruthless competitiveness and in others an aggressive conformity. Santayana's political theory is essentially Platonic. Authority should reside in the decisions of carefully trained and personally disinterested administrators who are dedicated to their vocation. To be sure, Santayana admired some features of the fascist corporate state, but he considered Mussolini an unscrupulous, even a wicked, man. He had no more sympathy for the charismatic adventurer or self-appointed dictator than had Plato.

Santayana's political theory is, philosophically speaking, a restatement of an ancient tradition. If anywhere, it is in his philosophy of art that his thinking approaches genuine originality. Even here his ideas are not revolutionary but his argument frees itself from standardized interpretations and displays a freshness of its own. For Santayana value enters the universe with the emergence of conscious awareness. "The good when actually realized is a joy taken in the immediate." There is no such thing as a value that cannot be enjoyed. This seems most obviously true when we consider the status of the beautiful. Beauty must be defined in terms of pleasure or satisfied taste. It is, indeed, nothing more than pleasure taken directly in the contemplation of an object. "The test is always the same. Does the thing actually please?" To delight in jewels because they are expensive is vulgar and "self-excommunication" from intrinsic enjoyment. To love glass beads for their own sake may be barbarous but, for all that, a genuine appreciation. We do not enjoy the beauty of an object because it reminds us of something else or because it serves as a means to an end. In our enjoyment of the beautiful, our pleasure is inseparable from the presence of an object before our perception. Yet we do not feel that the beautiful object produces our pleasure or comfort as, let us say, a blanket or a bed warmer might do. On the contrary, we take a direct pleasure in the thing itself. This statement might seem a commonplace in the philosophy of art. But Santayana goes further and offers a challenging observation. We are, he insists, moved to recognize our delight as an actual quality of the object, a quality as proper to its existence as its shape or color. The sense of beauty objectifies our pleasure. Our delight is transmuted in a moment of self-forgetfulness into a sense of the object's value. In reality, this value lies in the object's fitness or adaptation to our powers of perception and enjoyment. The sense of beauty carries with it a fleeting intimation that we need not always be at odds with our world. It offers a fulfillment that at times recompenses us for the anxieties and frustrations of our existence.

There are many kinds of beauty since there are many kinds of objects that offer us such direct enjoyment. Thus we can find beauty in the charm of a flower, the harmony of line and color in a landscape or a picture, the "glorious monotony of the stars," the expressive power of a poem or a painting. If we define the sense of beauty as a feeling of objectified pleasure, we must admit that beauty does not arise in isolation from other values, since the enjoyment that we take in a beautiful object always has a character of its own distinct from its purely aesthetic aspect as an objectification of pleasure. There are many kinds of pleasure that can be objectified. Indeed such enjoyment may be directed toward objects of moral significance. Poetry can pass into religion as it celebrates attitudes and ideals whose presence in symbolic form claims our full attention and our spontaneous admiration.

Santayana's best criticism is philosophical in spirit; and his critical essays offer an attractive and informal introduction to his thought as a whole. His studies of individual authors include patient attempts to perceive their characteristic attitudes and to undersand the view of things that each has come to accept. His evaluations are presented in terms of his own philosophy. He may, to be sure, speak occasionally of more strictly literary matters. He praises both Shakespeare's exuberance of language, which grants the verbal medium a spectacular prominence of its own and the apparently effortless transparency of Dante's verse. But he does not analyze such features at length, and he does not offer close readings of chosen passages. In his thinking the literary critic is never isolated from the moralist. Thus Santayana's first adventures in criticism contributed as much to a philosophy of civilization as to an appreciation of literature. In his earlier essays, he recognized the cultural importance of imagination, especially the imagination of the poet, as it furthers the life of reason. Poetry may be described as "rational," not because it follows a pattern of discursive argument but because, as in a Sophoclean chorus, it brings a presiding order into our life of thought and feeling, helping us, in the words of Plato's *Timaeus*, "to cope with what is unmeasured and chaotic in our minds." Devotion to this ideal of rational poetry led Santayana at one time to view with condescension the work of those authors who seek something less comprehensive. "To dwell, as irrational poets do, on some private experience, on some emotion without representative or ulterior value, then, seems a waste of time. Fiction becomes less interesting than affairs, and poetry turns into a sort of incom-

petent whimper, a childish foreshortening of the outspread world."

When such "short-winded" poetry becomes self-confident and assertive, valuing intensity of experience for its own sake, it may be described as barbarous. Poetry of this sort, headstrong and irrational, is to be contrasted with the "victorious" imagination that, overcoming the confusion and vacillations of our daily lives, places us within a "cosmos" or scheme of ideal order and value. Here we may be reminded of Paul Valéry's "hero" who in "Ode secrète" singles out the constellations and identifies each in an act of pictorial imagination, thus translating mere experience into orientation and taking possession of his world. A victorious imagination takes dominion over our consciousness, synthesizing rather than interrupting experience. As the centuries pass, such dominion may take many forms. Each one of these deserves sympathetic participation, but it was in the poetry of the Greeks that Santayana first discovered the moral power of the imagination. In 1900, he praised ancient literature as happily embodying the life of reason: "The ancients found poetry not so much in sensible accidents as in essential forms and noble associations; and this fact marks very clearly their superior education. They dominated the world as we no longer dominate it, and lived, as we are too distracted to live in the presence of the rational and the important."

Santayana's uncompromising devotion to the ideal of rational poetry led him to condemn Browning and Whitman as gifted barbarians and to regret the absence of a presiding religious or moral commitment in Shakespeare. Santayana sharply rebuked Browning for his failure to grasp the religious spirit that had inspired the Italy to which he seemed so devoted. Browning "saw, he studied, and he painted a decapitated Italy. His vision could not mount so high as her head." It was clear to Santayana that widespread sympathies and alert sensibility even when combined with rare powers of description and expression cannot bring literature to its highest stage of development, since they cannot by themselves or in union bring order and direction into our lives. Thus, in Santayana's early thinking Shakespeare stands below Dante and Lucretius. Furthermore, all theory that supports the maxim "art for art's sake" is grossly inadequate since it praises a moment of aesthetic enjoyment isolated from a more comprehensive sense of value. This conviction led Santayana to write two adversely critical reviews of Croce's *Aesthetic*. In these essays, Santayana is virtually defining his own position by repudiating the thought of the Italian philosopher. Santayana could not tolerate Croce's doctrine that intuitive expression, the act of imaginative synthesis whereby feeling (i.e., any feeling) is embodied in imagery, constitutes in itself the intrinsic value of the arts. For Santayana, at this period, aesthetic experience enjoys no isolated autonomy. It cannot retain its value if separated from the complex of interests and ideals over which the rational imagination seeks to preside. This attitude was cogently expressed in 1910 in the opening lines of *Three Philosophical Poets*. "The sole advantage in possessing great works of literature lies in what they can help us to become." The function of the critic is that of a cicerone whose interpretation opens the masterpieces of the past to a reading public, keeping "their perennial humanity living and capable of assimilation."

For the poetry of classical polytheism Santayana felt a lively sympathy which he shared with many of the romantic poets, but for reasons of his own. In a few notable passages, he presents us with a charming, if somewhat idealized, picture of ancient poetry. "All that we may fairly imagine to have been in the mind of the pious singer is the sense that something divine comes down among us in the crises of our existence . . . The gods sometimes appear, and when they do they bring us a foretaste of that sublime victory of mind over matter which we may never gain in experience but which may constantly be gained in thought . . . A god is a conceived victory of mind over Nature. A visible god is the consciousness of such a victory momentarily attained. The vision soon vanishes, the sense of omnipotence is soon dispelled by recurring conflicts with hostile forces; but the momentary illusion of that realized good has left us with the perennial knowledge of good as an ideal. Therein lies the essence and the function of religion."

Great poetry need not, however, confine itself to the celebration of human life in mythic fashion. It may concern itself more directly with our place in nature and remind us that we cannot in all honesty hope to escape from our world. This sense of reality is an indispensable element of the life of reason, which owes as much to Lucretius as to Pindar. The materialism as well as the mythology of the ancients deserves respect, not that it presents an accurate account of the origin of things but rather that it is a reminder of our dependence upon them.

The philosophy of Lucretius is one of thoughtful resignation, springing from a wholesome sense of human limitations, human life being but a part of nature. "All things are dust, and to dust they return; a dust, however, eternally fertile, and destined to fall perpetually into new, and doubtless beautiful, forms. . . . To perceive universal mutation, to feel the vanity of life, has always been the beginning of seriousness. It is the condition for any beautiful, measured, or tender philosophy. Prior to that, everything is barbarous, both in morals and in poetry; for until then mankind has not learned to renounce anything, has not outgrown the instinctive egotism and optimism of the young animal, and has not removed the centre of its being, or of its faith, from the will to the imagination."

Santayana interprets the wisdom of Lucretius as centering upon a recognition that "nothing arises save by the death of something else." This fact must be recognized not only by the materialist but by any poet or philosopher who squarely faces the human situation. Death, including the death of each of us, is a moment of nature, in a sense a part of life. We must accept it, as we accept our presence in the world, in a spirit of natural piety. Santayana reminds us, however, that Lucretius' practical psychology is at times faulty. Thus his advocacy of the Epicurean doctrine, that there is nothing to feel in death so that "where we are, death is not; where death is we are not," is hardly a firm bulwark against the dread of mortality. We can take shelter behind it only by ignoring or trying to ignore the fact that the fear of death is often for many of us a love of life. But this love may be more than a mere clinging to existence. It may carry us beyond ourselves in a flood of self-forgetfulness as we discover the ideal perfections that our own existence all too meagerly reflects. The Platonist and the Christian praise this attitude of love and admiration as in itself an approach to an ideal. Such thought reaches its poetic culmination in the myths of Plato and in Dante's great poem on Heaven and Hell. Dante's vision includes a brilliant hierarchy of possible achievements open to those in whose lives love has healed the moral and spiritual blindness by which human nature is constantly threatened. This is a blindness capable of terminating the growth of the spirit and reducing it to a state of permanent and hopeless frustration, where the love of life has yielded to despair.

But Santayana remains a naturalist. For him, love, humility, self-forgetfulness, and self-transcendence may free the human spirit without the benefit of supernatural interference; nor need we think of salvation as a metaphysical escape from our world. Yet we may willingly forgive Dante his supernaturalism and cherish his ideal of salvation which may help us to accept our destiny in peace of mind, a peace not purchased, as that of the Stoics and Epicureans so often has been, at the expense of human sympathies. For all his supernatural trappings, Dante may help us to recognize that love may be its own reward. We may even profit by the celestial cadre of Dante's poetry. It offers more than fanciful embellishment or marginal illumination. It contains a symbolic language which, when properly read, clarifies our sense of value. All told, Dante stands as the type of a consummate poet. Despite his medieval contrition and his exaggerated fearfulness, his moral vision is clear and confident and his sense of value deeply significant even for those who cannot accept the literal truth of his world drama. When discussing Dante, Santayana brought to full and detailed exemplification the ideal of poetry that was first sketched in 1900 in the opening pages of *Interpretations of Poetry and Religion,* where he had written: "Poetry is called religion when it intervenes in life; and religion, when it merely supervenes upon life, is seen to be nothing but poetry . . . For the dignity of religion, like that of poetry and of every moral ideal, lies precisely in its ideal adequacy, in its fit rendering of the meanings and values of life, in its anticipation of perfection."

These words apply happily to Dante's achievement as Santayana conceives of it. But this attitude is a transitional one, and the argument of *Three Philosophical Poets* carries us beyond any unqualified approbation of Dante. Dante, although a consummate poet and unrivaled as a master of supernatural symbolism, lacks Lucretius' concern for the goings-on of nature considered without reference to any possible anthropocentric interpretation. What is more, Dante lacks Goethe's Faust-like eagerness, characteristic of many romantic artists, to participate imaginatively in the manifold possibilities of human experience, each to be enjoyed for its own sake, without references to the values established by a comprehensive philosophy of life. Thus Santayana's treatment of Dante in *Three Philosophical Poets* marks a significant departure from his earlier position.

Santayana had learned from William James rather more than the latter recognized when he censured his pupil's "moribund latinity." Under James's tutelage, Santayana came to give full attention to the rich detail of immediate awareness taken *in concreto*, the "unadulterated, unexplained, instant fact of experience," accepted with a minimum of intellectual assumptions. The character of such experience may be slurred over by a mind unable or unwilling to free itself from the pressures of tradition or prejudice. Such an attitude can undermine the life of reason, and isolate from reality the cultural life of a whole nation. On the other hand, sheer sensation is just as barren as any dogma arbitrarily taken to be self-evident. The poet who merely swims "out into the sea of sensibility . . . to picture all possible things, real or unreal, human or inhuman, would bring materials only to the workshop of art; he would not be an artist." For Santayana a mind may be free, sincere, and articulate, and yet remain bewildered. Experience accepted as an end and a justification of life is a self-defeating ideal that can result in the restlessness and recurring ennui, the sense of frustration, with which the enthusiasm of the romantic so often ends. It can also invite a self-centered irresponsibility, which Santayana found in Goethe and so sharply condemned, perhaps caricatured, in the witty dialogue of *The Last Puritan*. At no time could Santayana abide the romantic theology that justifies Faust's ultimate salvation.

The Santayana of *Three Philosophical Poets* tries deliberately to avoid extremes. Although himself no Kantian, his literary theory echoes the seminal insight of Immanuel Kant upon which so much of modern philosophy is founded. "Concepts without perceptions are empty, perceptions without concepts are blind," or, as Santayana would prefer to say, bewildered. Experience must seek understanding or wander in confusion; yet understanding must be continually refreshed by experience or it will wither into a narrow and brittle ideology, a genteel tradition, remote from life and increasingly irrelevant to our experience. Thus the supreme poet will not be one to confine himself to the imaginative envisagement of a comprehensive ideal. Whatever his sense of value, he will recognize our place in the world, accepting our physical predicament and repudiating too eager an anthropomorphic interpretation or evaluation of nature. At least, he will always recognize that our ideals do not shape or control our world. Nor will his idealism constitute a barrier between his thinking and that of other men. He will be able to comprehend with sympathy the experience of life open to those who do not share his vision. He will be at home, like Shakespeare, in the pluriverse of human affairs, ambitions, and ideals as they appear among men of varied and contrasting temperament and background. Yet he will hold firmly to the idealism that has taken shape within his own experience.

Santayana hastens to remind us that this "supreme poet is in limbo still." For all his virtues he does not exist. The supreme poet is himself an ideal. Once we are willing to admit that, although reflecting a genuine possibility, the supreme poet has not existed and may never exist, we find ourselves inclined toward a far more tolerant consideration and grateful acceptance of those poets who do. Santayana was no longer eager to condemn irrational poetry, and he ceased to use such terms as "barbarous" or "childish" when writing of famous men. In fact, his thinking seemed in later years to be moved by his growing disapproval of a certain narrowness which he felt to be present in the criticism of the neohumanists, like Irving Babbitt, and more especially in that of T. S. Eliot. As the years pass, we find Santayana defending Shakespeare against Dante in reply to Eliot. The fact that Shakespeare, unlike Sophocles or Dante, does not offer us a vision of the best to be enjoyed, so to speak, in its own right need not keep us from recognizing the moral significance of many passages and incidents in his plays. The nihilism of Macbeth's "Tomorrow and tomorrow and tomorrow" is not to be condemned, as T. S. Eliot once supposed, as a statement of an inferior or truncated philosophy. Taken in context, this passage may be seen magnificently to epitomize the state of mind and the view of life that Macbeth at the end of his career cannot escape, a fact which he, being still something of a hero and thus unable wholly to deceive himself, remains capable of grasping. Read in this way, the speech is a noble one and its connotations within the structure of the play are by no means nihilistic. Macbeth's cry of despair tells us more of "moral evil and of good" than most poets—and most philosophers —ever succeed in doing. As a moralist, Santayana cannot help but admire, and even participate in, the many human perspectives that Shakespeare sets before us. To be sure, his many insights are not subordinated to any central or overarching ideal, expressed either as concept or symbol. Nor is any supernatural support recognized or invoked. Again and again, Shakespeare penetrates and evaluates the manifold complexities of human motivation, of human actions, their character and

consequences, without trying to reduce his concrete pluriverse to an ordered cosmos. Tragedy and comedy may be found on every hand but there is no inclusive world drama or divine comedy. Santayana was well aware that our modern world is not a cosmos and that the poet must be, in Stevens' phrase, a "connoisseur of chaos." Although he is privileged in his own life and work to resist the pressure of what he may call "absolute" fact, he must not overlook its presence or seek wholly to triumph over it.

Perhaps this later attitude of Santayana's is expressed most happily in his warm appreciation of Charles Dickens, whose novels he praises in the same spirit that led him to revise his opinion of Shakespeare. Dickens, far more than Shakespeare, is "disinherited" in that his thinking is not organized about ideas. He derives, in fact, little or nothing from the great traditions of thought. Yet Dickens' sympathetic participation in life is complete and genuine, for he feels the presence of good and evil intensely and finds people more important than institutions. But, despite his humanity, Dickens is a master of "pure" or "merciless" comedy. In a few exuberant sentences, perhaps the finest that he ever wrote although he once called them sophomoric, Santayana paid his respects to comedy of this sort and to the naive but uncompromising wisdom that lies behind it. "The most grotesque creatures of Dickens are not exaggerations or mockeries of something other than themselves; they arise because nature generates them, like toadstools; they exist because they can't help it, as we all do. The fact that these perfectly self-justified beings are absurd appears only by comparison, and from outside; circumstances, or the expectations of other people, make them ridiculous and force them to contradict themselves; but in nature it is no crime to be exceptional. . . . If Oedipus and Lear and Cleopatra do not seem ridiculous, it is only because tragic reflection has taken them out of the context in which, in real life, they would have figured. If we saw them as facts, and not as emanations of a poet's dream, we should laugh at them till doomsday; what grotesque presumption, what silly whims, what mad contradiction of the simplest realities! Yet we should not laugh at them without feeling how real their griefs were; as real and terrible as the griefs of children and of dreams. But facts, however serious inwardly, are always absurd outwardly; and the just critic of life sees both truths at once, as Cervantes did in *Don Quixote*. A pompous idealist who does not see the ridiculous in *all* things is the dupe of his sympathy and abstraction; and a clown, who does not see that these ridiculous creatures are living quite in earnest, is the dupe of his egotism. Dickens saw the absurdity, and understood the life; I think he was a good philosopher."

As we have seen, Santayana's criticism grew more generous and more tolerant with the years, and he came gradually to recognize many achievements that he had once been inclined to overlook. He admitted that successful poetry need not be rich in wisdom or perceive the moral burden of life. It may, in a spirit of sheer lyricism, confine itself to a moment of awareness if only "it utters the vital impulses of that moment with enough completeness." By 1922 he had outgrown his outright condemnation of "shortwinded" verse and anticipated Wallace Stevens' belief that the poem may be the cry of an occasion. This late attitude remained, however, one of toleration. Santayana never retreated from the position that great literature must clarify our sense of ultimate values.

Santayana has spoken of Emerson as one "whose religion was all poetry, a poet whose only pleasure was thought." These words we might well apply to their author, at least while we consider his achievement as a poet. In a remarkably honest and astute passage of self-criticism, Santayana has characterized his own verse in almost similar terms. Santayana's poetry reflects for the most part his earlier conception of literary value, and of this he was clearly aware. His poems do not, as a rule, spring from the "chance experience of a stray individual." They contain, on the contrary, passages of sustained meditation, in fact, his philosophy in the making. His poetry lacks, as he himself readily admitted, that "magic and pregnancy of phrase" that constitutes the "creation of a fresh idiom" and marks the highest achievement of the poet. But readers generally respect the thoughtfulness of his verse and enjoy the "aura of literary and religious associations" that surrounds it. In his poetry, Santayana's acceptance of tradition both of theme and of style may amount to submissiveness that welcomes and celebrates a rich heritage of idea and feeling. His poems transpose ideas into a pictorial imagery traditionally appropriate and realized in an elegant, although rarely a very powerful, diction.

Much of Santayana's poetry seems today flaccid and without energy. In his prose, he aimed at clarity of thought and invited the sympathy of the reader, subordinating all matters of style to these intentions. In his verse, form and manner often seem to have been ends in themselves and thus to resist the full realization of meaning. And yet at least once or twice Santayana completely escaped these limitations. The lines on Cape Cod are translucent and flawless and quite without any distracting artificiality. In this poem, language, rhythm, and imagery yield fully to the sense of forlorn exile that is sustained throughout. The scene becomes a haunting symbol of loneliness, an end of the world, whose beauty lives in its very desolation. In his early life, Santayana sometimes thought of himself as an exile, and these lines spring from an experience as deeply felt as that in any of the sonnets, less doctrinaire in concept, and more spontaneous in expression.

The low sandy beach and the thin scrub pine,
The wide reach of bay and the long sky line,—
   O, I am far from home!

· · · · · · · · · · · · · · ·

The wretched stumps all charred and burned,
And the deep soft rut where the cartwheel
    turned,—
   Why is the world so old?

We may compare the sad monotone of the Cape Cod shoreline with the rich and sensuous charm of the Mediterranean, celebrated in the sapphic stanzas of Santayana's fifth ode. This poem is less haunting and more contrived than the lines on Cape Cod and not as obviously a personal confession. Yet the Northman's longing for the southern sea and the sense of fulfillment with which he returns to it reveal the nostalgia of the author. This nostalgia, or sense of alienation, inspired much of Santayana's poetry. As he outgrew it, his need to express himself in verse seems almost to have evaporated.

One should not overlook Santayana's occasional success as an author of light verse. His parody, or rather his translation into modern dress, of Shakespeare's "When in disgrace with fortune and men's eyes" is brilliant, a very acceptable poem in its own right, free of the archaic artificiality of his own earlier sonnets. I have already mentioned "Young Sammy's First Wild Oats" which may today remind us of some of Auden's more whimsical work. It is a masterpiece of its kind. Its wit is penetrating and the apparently careless verse suits the convivial occasion on which the poem was read. The author of such spirited yet good-natured polemic could have made of himself, had he wished to do so, a very formidable pamphle-

teer. One might add that the poetic dialogue in Santayana's closet drama, when satirical in spirit, comes at times suddenly to life and deserves consideration apart from its otherwise rather undistinguished context.

In his novel, *The Last Puritan*, Santayana presented a brilliant picture, now ironical, now sympathetic, of the America that he had known and known well before he retired to Europe. His attention is turned for the most part to the manners, attitudes, and beliefs of well-to-do and cultivated people in New England and New York. There are memorable glimpses of life at Harvard as well as pictures of Eton and scenes from British clerical and scholastic life, some sympathetic and some downright hilarious in their irony. These, along with many scenes from his memoirs, *Persons and Places*, establish their author's reputation as an acute and witty observer of life and manners. Beneath these superficial adornments, *The Last Puritan* develops a somber theme that is central to Santayana's philosophy. Santayana describes in the person of Oliver Alden a human life distorted and frustrated by an unrelenting obsession, an "absolutist conscience," perhaps more Stoic than Puritan, that suspects all motives not presented as obligations. A sense of duty, often a rationalized acceptance of convention, overwhelms all other springs of action, darkens the vision, and thwarts the achievement of a generous and gifted youth, who is alienated from his world and deprived of the ability to enjoy things freely and for their own sake. As Santayana points out in the Prologue, Oliver felt it necessary always to be master of himself. For Santayana this insistence indicates a spiritual immaturity, although it may well appear as an infirmity of noble minds; and in Oliver's case it was indeed just this. In his life, the spirit wished always to govern and was never content merely to understand or to enjoy. A strict moral judgment too often took the place of spontaneous admiration and a watchful self-scrutiny made self-forgetfulness and self-surrender almost impossible. Thus the spirit deprived itself of its richest fulfillment.

It is owing to Santayana's skill as a literary portraitist that young Alden appears throughout as a sympathetic figure. He might so easily have seemed a stuffy and conceited prig. But his instinctive kindliness, his modesty, his sincerity, and perhaps a certain naiveté protect him from such awkwardness. After all, his conscience is not aggressive. He tolerates other attitudes with patient generosity as he considers his family and his friends, treating even his tyrannical mother, a truly decadent Puritan, with courtesy while learning to ignore her inept sarcasm. He is kindly and tolerant and profoundly honest, but, as he grows to maturity, less and less capable of carefree enjoyment.

Even as a schoolboy, Oliver came to interpret all his relationships as obligations and to see his life as a network of minor commitments extending from athletic competition, which came to bore him, to all sorts of family duties including eventual matrimony. He is at last freed from this self-imprisonment by the frankness of the young lady whom for some years he had intended to marry and whom he had treated with an exemplary chivalry. Love, she tells him, must be happy, natural, and unreasoning and she makes it clear that she would have preferred the attentions of his debonair cousin. Oliver accepts this rebuff with outward calm, but he is profoundly shaken by the picture of himself that has been set before him. He feels that he has in a sense lived the life of a conscript and in profound relief, almost enthusiasm, he promises himself a new freedom. Yet only in the vaguest terms can he tell himself what this freedom will be like—a freedom that he is never to experience since a few months after his change of heart he is killed in a motor accident.

Santayana surrounds Oliver Alden with a number of fascinating characters. His cousin Mario Van de Weyer, kindhearted and often irresponsible, with a bubbling sense of humor, finds something enjoyable in almost any situation, if only its incongruity; and he seems disposed by nature to a happy acceptance of his lot. He is sometimes baffled, but not repelled by Oliver's unrelenting self-criticism; while the wealthy Oliver often feels himself responsible for his cousin's well-being. Neither character is morally complete. Mario makes himself too easily at home in his world, while Oliver is never sure of himself and there is always something clumsy about his earnestness. Oliver's uncle Nathaniel, whose conscience stands beyond self-criticism, presents in his humorless self-assurance and intolerance an inversion of Puritan integrity. The fact that we find Nathaniel credible and enjoy his outrageous, even heartless, eccentricities reminds us of Santayana's debt to Dickens. There are also Oliver's father, Peter Alden, the restless dilettante whose life is one long fruitless escape from Nathaniel and from Oliver's mother; the saintly and poverty-stricken Vicar who understands Oliver without being able to help him; the Vicar's son, captain of Peter Alden's magnificent yacht, a cheerful and plausible rascal whom the young Oliver at first mistakes for a hero; Oliver's young German governess in whose kindly soul the wisdom of Goethe and the philosophy of the romantics have inspired a muddled sentimentalism; and Oliver's cousin, the sharp-tongued cripple Caleb Wetherbee, a Catholic convert who spends his wealth trying to introduce into New England a truly medieval monasticism. Each of these finds a place in Santayana's philosophy and there are times when this is perhaps a shade too obvious especially in the case of cousin Caleb. Still, it is quite possible to enjoy Santayana's book for just what he tells us it pretends to be—a memoir written by a retired professor of philosophy concerning one of his favorite students whose short life has reflected the virtues and the grave limitations of a dying tradition. The reader makes the acquaintance not only of the student and his friends and relatives, but also briefly of the professor himself; and they are all very interesting people. They are perhaps rather larger than life in that they are remarkably articulate and their attitudes very well defined. But in most cases we may welcome them for that very reason. Even so, our enjoyment of *The Last Puritan* is not purely intellectual. To the humane reader, Oliver is more than an example or a period piece. He appears as a very decent and gifted young man who deserves a happier life than he has been able to find for himself. After all, there are still many people who can draw from their own experience a ready sympathy for his predicament.

The Last Puritan was not published until 1936, although Santayana had returned to the manuscript off and on over many years. The story, however, is brought to a close with Oliver's sudden death shortly after the Armistice of 1918. The American reader of the mid-thirties might perhaps have wondered—as might the reader of today—what sort of a person Oliver would have become had he lived through the moral confusion of the twenties and faced the social challenge of the great depression. Santayana seems also to have asked himself this question. There is a brief suggestion in the Prologue that we might have found Oliver active in left-wing, perhaps revolutionary, circles, accepting the need of radical reform as a compelling source of obligation. He might even have been capable of "imposing no matter what regimen on us by force." This

dismal picture seems hardly consistent with Oliver's state of mind before his death. At that time, he was more ready than ever before to accept the "miscellaneous madness" of the world, to "practise charity," and to keep himself "as much as possible from complicity in wrong." One would hardly expect a new authoritarianism to follow upon so sober a moment of open-mindedness. Strangely enough, it may well be that the reader's—the American reader's—confidence in Oliver Alden surpasses Santayana's. The air of futility that surrounds the last events of the story may not seem inevitable to everyone. Then for the first time Oliver was ready to face his world, free of the narrow preconceptions of his upbringing, ready to understand attitudes that had been beyond his scope—perhaps even to understand, or to begin to understand, the wisdom of his friend and teacher, the retired professor of philosophy.

Over the years, Santayana's orientation as a philosopher changed but little. In his later writings, however, the skeptical caution, always latent in his thought, received a greater emphasis. As always, he accepted the results of scientific inquiry as constituting our most trustworthy knowledge of the world. Yet, he insisted, we must recognize that our knowledge, however well founded in observation and however consistently formulated, remains the product of human thinking subject to the limitations of our situation and to assumptions that this situation forces upon us. Knowledge is interpreted as springing from belief and belief from something very like instinct. In the 1920's, Santayana argued that in a viable philosophy of life insistence upon intellectual certainty surpassing that of practical belief is out of place. He undertook to support this observation by considering, or reconsidering in the spirit of the early modern philosophers, just how far we may go toward claiming certain or irrefutable knowledge of any kind. This led him to an exercise, somewhat in the manner of Descartes' *Meditations*, concerning "those things of which we may doubt." He carried these skeptical reflections well beyond the limits reached by Descartes and came to rest in a position remarkably similar to that from which David Hume had challenged the philosophers of the eighteenth century. Like Hume, he turned away from the pursuit of certainty toward an examination of the effective beliefs that are taken for granted in our overt behavior.

No statements concerning the existence of things in a world around us or concerning our own existence as thinking beings can escape all possibility of doubt, that is, if we think of doubt as a purely intellectual exercise. Descartes cannot help us here. The famous *cogito ergo sum*—"I think, therefore I am"—does not carry the mathematical certainty that Descartes attributed to it. The skeptical exercises by which he challenged our commonplace perceptions and the familiar propositions of our common sense cannot be brought to a halt so easily. If we follow in Descartes' footsteps, rigorously demanding an absolute certainty, we will end with accepting the reality, not of an enduring thinking subject, but of something far "thinner" and much less satisfying—a moment of isolated sentience, of truncated consciousness. Such a position may be described as a "solipsism of the present moment." This radical skepticism, although, as Santayana believed, internally consistent, springs from a narrow and academic interpretation of the life of reason. The reasoning by which we live is not to be divorced from the common sense that presides over our daily behavior. As Santayana had insisted in his earlier writings, reason is to be defined as "instinct enlightened by reflection," and the primitive beliefs that guide our

conduct are instinctive in nature. These beliefs are as indispensable to our conscious life as breathing is to our bodily existence. Without them, we would be overwhelmed by the restless multiplicity of sensation and feeling that constitutes the raw material of our stream of consciousness. This flux of sheer sensibility does not yield us a picture of things and events until we subject many of its fleeting elements to a scheme of interpretation, until we recognize them as symbols indicating the presence of enduring objects in a world of objects spatially related to our own bodies. We do not derive this interpretation from experience, since without such interpretation we have no experience worth the name, only a whirl of sensation and feeling. Without the initial aid of instinctive interpretation our awareness would lack the continuity even of a dream and conscious selfhood, as we come to know it, would be impossible.

These primordial beliefs are practical in function rather than strictly representative. Their value lies in their contributing toward our survival, not in their grasping the nature or penetrating the structure of things. They support certain attitudes of alertness that further our safety and well-being, and in doing so they give us our first dim sense of ourselves and of our world, compromising what Santayana has called the "original articles of the animal creed." Here we find such effective, although inarticulate, beliefs as that things seen may be edible—or dangerous; things lost or sought may be found. These beliefs or attitudes involve others more fundamental: that there is a world or arena of possible action spread out in space wherein we as moving organisms may operate, that there is a future relevant to these operations that may offer us threats or attractive incentives, and that seeming accidents may have concealed causes. Such assumptions, made without deliberation, constitute what

Santayana calls "animal faith," about which our perception of things and our knowledge of the world has gradually taken shape. These assumptions are supported, even encouraged and reinforced, by experience, but they are by no means self-evident propositions in their own right or what Descartes would call "clear and distinct ideas." They are taken for granted in action rather than established by argument or intuitive insight. Nature, or the "realm of matter," in which as living organisms we find a place, enters our thinking as the realm of possible action. The patterns of time and space, enduring substance and causal efficacy, about which our idea of nature is built may well be no more than useful rules of thumb, in themselves gross oversimplifications of reality. Yet these schemes of interpretation, however imperfect, bring our thinking into a rough and ready contact with the world around us, and they contribute to our sense of our own existence. We think of ourselves as caught up in the goings-on of nature to which we must adapt our behavior if we are to survive. Animal faith carries with it a sense of our dependence upon things that we can only partially control, that at once support and threaten our existence.

Such being its origin, our knowledge, even when refined by the mathematics of science, must remain tentative. One of the chief functions of philosophy is to remind us of the shallowness of our understanding of things and the massive background of our ignorance. We can readily tease ourselves out of thought by asking ourselves, for instance, whether our physical world has had a beginning in time, whether it is infinite or finite in extent, whether time is unreturning or circular, discrete or continuous. Absolute truth lies quite beyond our reach and the very idea of truth brings upon us a sense of humility.

There is a difference, however, between humility and frustration. The natural sciences are self-correcting modes of inquiry and we may hope to render the view of things that animal faith has opened to us more extensive and more consistent even if it can never approach completeness. And, after all, human well-being does not require omniscience. It is far more important that we know what we want than what we are made of. A sense of direction is more satisfying than a knowledge of our origins. To achieve it, we must ask ourselves what possibilities of life we find most worth pursuing. In answering this question in patience and honesty we complete the living pattern that nature has, so to speak, offered us. In doing so, we are not, as Bergson, Sartre, or Whitehead would insist, fashioning our lives or creating ourselves. We are discovering a path upon which we have already unknowingly set foot, or, to put it in another way, in our discovery, one of nature's uncertain and vacillating variations shapes into something approaching completion. In these moments, we do not seek to initiate, to control, or to create. Our attitude is one of grateful acceptance, a serendipity, even though the ideal that we contemplate has come to our attention in the restless activity of our own imagination. For us, the worth of the ideal lies in its drawing us out of our self-centered anxieties into a moment of disinterested admiration. Such admiration, if it resists inevitable distractions and disappointment, adds a new quality to our existence.

These ideals, whose presence before our imagination can transfigure our lives, receive a new interpretation in Santayana's later philosophy. Ideals are not facts of nature or of history since neither nature nor human nature attains perfection. Nature and history afford only the occasions upon which our imagination grasps the ideal, be it of animal adaptation to circumstance, of social justice, or of individual integrity. Here we may follow Plato. Strictly speaking, ideals do not exist. They are not features of the concrete world. In Santayana's later vocabulary, they are called "essences" rather than existing things. They belong, not to the "realm of matter," the world of interacting concretions that come to be and pass away, each in its time, but to an order or realm of timeless, or unchanging, entities. This approaches orthodox Platonism, but Santayana finds it necessary to add a reservation. Ideals as timeless entities do not exercise an influence upon the goings-on of nature. Here, despite the skeptical caution of his later thinking, Santayana remains fully convinced that the origin and development of life are subject to a contingent interplay of forces and conditions in no way directed toward or controlled by an ideal perfection. Ideals do not exist in nature nor are they supernatural powers influencing the course of nature or of history. They need not, however, be described as fictitious products of hypocrisy or of wishful sentimentality. In the life of the individual they may play a very different role. Here they may stand as genuine objects of prolonged and discriminating reflection. The universe of discourse to which ideals belong is part of a wider "realm of essence." For Santayana, as for Whitehead, this realm or order includes many items besides the ideals of human life. It includes all objects directly open to our attention rather than those merely postulated as objects of belief, actually enduring for a time as features of the concrete world. Thus I believe in the enduring existence of my watch while at a given moment I may glimpse patches of color that support this belief. A shade of color is an essence as is also a spatial pattern like that of the circle. But my watch, unlike an essence, is a concrete existent and as such, unlike an essence, has a history of its own. It was manufactured at a certain time and place under certain specific, even unique, conditions. It has been subject to many influences of wear and tear and of climate. It has been repaired just so often and in just so many ways. No such history belongs to or characterizes an essence. The color yellow and the pattern circle are exempt from such conditioning, although they may serve as indications of the watch's presence and may be mentioned in our description of the watch. We may, on the other hand, contemplate essences that do not indicate existent things as well as those that qualify our belief in them. Consider the structures of certain non-Euclidean geometries.

Ideals occupy a position of their own within the realm of essence. They are not like colors or familiar shapes. They do not indicate actual conditions in the concrete world, past, present, or future. Yet their presence before our attention may manifest a sense of direction on our part, even though they are, so to speak, beyond our reach and will never be completely realized. In this respect, ideals are like targets on which we cannot hope to hit the center, but whose presence brings order out of random play and makes evaluation possible. Perhaps they should be compared to targets seen through shifting mists so that their very discernment calls for concerted effort. Here our analogy breaks down, since the ideal, unlike the marksman's paper target, may appear as an object beautiful in itself. Any essence that as an ideal offers a disinterested self-transcendence to human beings, if only perhaps to a few, belongs to the "realm of the spirit" and commands the respect of any student of human nature. The essences that constitute the realm of the spirit may appear as surpassingly beautiful as we center upon them—or objectify in them—our most sincere and enduring admiration.

The ultimate justification of philosophy and the arts lies in the fact that they may help the individual toward a spiritual affirmation according to his own vocation. Their function is to enlighten, not to command. This does not mean that the arts serve only as handmaidens of religion. They may enrich our lives as well as offering them an ultimate significance. In the enjoyment of the arts, we may take delight in essence for its own sake. We may welcome the sheer structure or character of any object, if we can wholly surrender our attention to it without being concerned with its importance in the world of our immediate practical interests. There is a freedom born of detachment. This freedom accompanies the sense of beauty and reaches its fullest manifestation in the enduring self-transcendence of a religious commitment. Even momentary contemplation brings with it a new attitude that carries us beyond the concerns that first awakened our animal faith or belief in nature. This contrast between animal faith and spiritual contemplation constitutes the central theme of Santayana's later philosophy. Without the first man cannot live; without the second he cannot hope to live well. Thus the life of reason must include a defense of the life of the spirit. From its first awakening the spirit may be distracted by practical anxieties, and its contribution may be undermined by intellectual dishonesty or distorted, even annulled, by an insistence upon the exclusive authority of a single insight. Santayana's career as a philosopher and a man of letters was devoted to protecting the life of the spirit from these indignities.

Selected Bibliography

PRINCIPAL WORKS
OF GEORGE SANTAYANA

Lotze's System of Philosophy (Harvard University doctoral dissertation, 1889), edited with an introduction by Paul Grimley Kuntz. Bloomington: Indiana University Press, 1971.

The Sense of Beauty: Being the Outlines of Aesthetic Theory. New York: Scribners, 1896.

Interpretations of Poetry and Religion. New York: Scribners, 1900.

The Life of Reason, or the Phases of Human Progress: Vol. I, *Reason in Common Sense;* Vol. II, *Reason in Society;* Vol. III, *Reason in Religion;* Vol. IV, *Reason in Art;* Vol. V, *Reason in Science.* New York: Scribners, 1905–6. One-volume edition revised and abridged by Santayana and Daniel Cory, 1954.

Three Philosophical Poets: Lucretius, Dante, and Goethe. Cambridge, Mass.: Harvard University Press, 1910.

Character and Opinion in the United States, with Reminiscences of William James and Josiah Royce and Academic Life in America. New York: Scribners, 1920.

Soliloquies in England and Later Soliloquies. New York: Scribners, 1922.

Scepticism and Animal Faith: Introduction to a System of Philosophy. New York: Scribners, 1923.

Poems, selected by the author and revised. New York: Scribners, 1923. (Contains a remarkable preface by Santayana.)

Dialogues in Limbo. New York: Scribners, 1926. New and enlarged edition, 1948.

The Realms of Being: Book First, *The Realm of Essence,* 1927; Book Second, *The Realm of Matter,* 1930; Book Third, *The Realm of Truth,* 1938; Book Fourth, *The Realm of Spirit,* 1940. New York: Scribners. One-volume edition, 1942.

The Last Puritan: A Memoir in the Form of a Novel. New York: Scribners, 1936.

The Philosophy of Santayana, selections edited, with an introductory essay, by Irwin Edman. New York: Modern Library, 1936. Enlarged edition, Scribners, 1953. (Contains an autobiographical essay, selected sonnets, book reviews, and occasional pieces, besides selections from the philosophical works.)

The Idea of Christ in the Gospels: Or God in Man, A Critical Essay. New York: Scribners, 1946.

Dominations and Powers: Reflections on Liberty,

Society and Government. New York: Scribners, 1951.

Essays in Literary Criticism of George Santayana, selections edited with an introduction by Irving Singer. New York: Scribners, 1956.

The Genteel Tradition: Nine Essays by George Santayana, edited with an introduction by Douglas L. Wilson, Cambridge, Mass.: Harvard University Press, 1967. (Contains "The Genteel Tradition in American Philosophy," "The Genteel Tradition at Bay," and the poem "Young Sammy's First Wild Oats.")

Selected Critical Writings of George Santayana, edited by Norman Henfrey. 2 vols. New York: Cambridge University Press, 1968.

AUTOBIOGRAPHY AND LETTERS

Persons and Places: Vol. I, *The Background of My Life,* 1944; Vol. II, *The Middle Span,* 1945; Vol. III, *My Host the World,* 1953. New York: Scribners.

The Letters of George Santayana, edited with introduction and commentary by Daniel Cory. New York: Scribners, 1955.

CRITICAL AND BIOGRAPHICAL STUDIES

Arnett, Willard E. *George Santayana.* Great American Thinkers Series. New York: Washington Square Press, 1968.

Ashmore, Jerome. *Santayana, Art, and Aesthetics.* Cleveland, Ohio: The Press of Western Reserve University, 1966.

Cory, Daniel. *Santayana the Late Years: A Portrait with Letters.* New York: Braziller, 1963.

Howgate, George W. *George Santayana.* Philadelphia: University of Pennsylvania Press, 1938.

Schilpp, Paul A., ed. *The Philosophy of George Santayana.* 2nd edition. La Salle, Ill.: Open Court, 1951. (Essays by a number of critics including Bertrand Russell and John Dewey, with an introduction and replies by Santayana; bibliography.)

—*NEWTON P. STALLKNECHT*